A
COMMENTARY
on the
NEW TESTAMENT

by Robert Hawker

Volume Three
Philippians - Revelation

Solid Ground Christian Books
Birmingham, Alabama USA

Solid Ground Christian Books

2090 Columbiana Rd. Suite 2000
Birmingham AL 35216
205-443-0311
sgcb@charter.net
http://solid-ground-books.com

The Poor Man's New Testament Commentary: Volume Three
by Robert Hawker (1753-1827)

Taken from the 1815 edition by Sherwood, Neely and Jones of London

ISBN – 1-932474-38-2

Acknowledgements

This reprint of Robert Hawker's *Poor Man's Commentary* has been accomplished, in God's good providence, by the assistance of many in the United States and England, who desire to see this excellent work made available to the public again. We wish to acknowledge and express thanks to them for their work and generosity. Mr. Jeremy Roe, Ossett, West Yorkshire, England, allowed us to use his set of Hawker's commentary for the reprint. And the following churches provided funds for the layout and printing costs.

Bethel Baptist Church
Spring Lake, North Carolina
Rupert Rivenbark, Pastor

Sovereign Grace Baptist Church
The Dalles, Oregon
Norm Wells, Pastor

Grace Baptist Church of Danville
Danville, Kentucky
Don Fortner, Pastor

The Poor Man's Commentary may be obtained in Great Britain through

CBO Publications
21 Queen Street
Ossett
West Yorkshire
WF5 8AS
www.christianbookshopossett.co.uk

Manufactured in the United States of America

A COMMENTARY ON THE NEW TESTAMENT.

THE EPISTLE OF PAUL THE APOSTLE TO THE PHILIPPIANS.

GENERAL OBSERVATIONS.

PHILIPPI was the chief city of *Macedon*. It took its name from *Philip*, the father of *Alexander* the *Great*, so called by a misnomer. For characters of his description must be *little indeed*, according to the testimony of scripture: *for that which is highly esteemed among men is abomination in the sight of God!* It was near this city (as Profane Writers tell us) was fought the battle between *Antony* and *Brutus*. Names, which but for their connexion with the history of the Church of CHRIST, like those of more ancient date, the *Sennacheribs*, and *Nebuchadnezzars* of old, would have been but little known, but *their memorial have perished with them*. And however mortifying to the pride of human nature it may be, to the ungodly of every age, whether antient or modern, certain it is, that the whole memoirs of such characters, with their rise and fall, in all the revolutions of kingdoms and and empires, are intended no further than as they minister to the Church of CHRIST. Although *they think not so, neither do they intend it;* yet to this one purpose the whole of their labors tend; and which, when accomplished, like the scaffolding to a building no longer useful, will be taken down and destroyed.

It was in this city the LORD erected a Church to his dear SON. And *Paul* was the highly honored instrument to the establishment of it. By a vision of the night the LORD directed him to go to *Macedon*. And GOD the HOLY GHOST, in the persons of *Lydia* and the *Jailor*, formed the Church, in these humble beginnings. See Acts xvi. Afterwards, we find the Apostle made a second visit to the Church at *Philippi*, in his way to *Jerusalem*. Acts xx. 6.

The Epistle is but short, though sweet. *Paul* wrote it while he was a Prisoner at *Rome*. It hath been observed, and well observed, that those scriptures have more than an ordinary savor of JESUS in them, which have been penned while the Writers of them were in tribulation. *David* was in the wilderness when he wrote those golden psalms lxiii. and cxlii. *John* was in *Patmos* when he sent to the Church the book of the Revelations. And *Paul* in prison at the time he wrote this Epistle to the *Philippians*, and his second Epistle to *Timothy*. If men shut the LORD's faithful ones *in*, they cannot keep JESUS *out*. Sweet, and sure, is that promise, *I will be with thee in trouble!* Psm. xci. 15.

The date of *Paul's* Epistle to the *Philippians* is differently marked by Ecclesiastical Writers. It could not be earlier, and perhaps not much later, than in the year of our LORD GOD 60: about the *fifth* year of the reign of *Nero*.

I have only here again, as in all former instances, when entering upon the perusal of those inspired writings, to call the Reader to join my spirit in prayer, at the mercy-seat of GOD in CHRIST, for divine light, to guide both Writer and Reader of this *Poor Man's Commentary* through the several pages, that that gracious promise may be ours. *All thy Children shall be taught of the* LORD, *and great shall be the peace of thy children.* Isaiah liv. 13.

CHAPTER I.

CONTENTS.

The Apostle, under GOD *the* HOLY GHOST, *opens his Epistle to the Church with his usual Salutation. He praiseth the* LORD *for his Mercies towards them. In Allusion to his Prison State, he tells them of his Readiness to suffer in the Cause of* CHRIST.

PAUL and Timotheus, the servants of Jesus Christ, to all the saints in Christ Jesus which are at Philippi, with the bishops and deacons:

2 Grace *be* unto you, and peace, from God our Father, and *from* the Lord Jesus Christ:

The first object which engageth our attention, in the opening of this Epistle, is of the persons to whom it is addressed; namely, *to all the saints in* CHRIST JESUS, *which were at Philippi, with the bishops and deacons.* Saints, in scripture language, means regenerated sinners. *Called to be saints,* as the Apostle elsewhere terms it. 1 Cor. i. 2. Similar to the Apostle Jude's expression; *sanctified by* GOD *the* FATHER, *and preserved in* JESUS CHRIST, *and called,* Jude 1. Reader! it is most essentially necessary to have this always in view, through the whole of this Epistle; yea, in all the inspired writings of the Apostles. For there are some things said in them which cannot have reference to the world at large; but are belonging to the Church of GOD only. And it is the grossest of all mistakes to make application to mankind in general of what belongs only to the saints of GOD. The Apostle's salutations is to the Church. *Grace be unto you, and peace, from* GOD *our* FATHER, *and from the* LORD JESUS CHRIST.

The *bishops,* and *deacons,* are taken from those saints. What those offices of the Church were, in those early days, is not so easy to be determined. Perhaps the same, as in other Epistles, are called *Elders.* 1 Pet. v. 1. But one thing is certain, that as *Paul* addressed this Epistle to the Church at *Philippi,* and calls them *bishops,* and *deacons,* in the plural, there were more than *one,* if not *many,* of that order, in this Church. Of consequence, the primitive Church, under the Apostles, differed from modern Episcopacy, where there is but one bishop in a Diocese. And one thing more is as certain, namely, that as the *Saints* are mentioned, prior to the *bishops* and *deacons,* the office of the *latter,* of what kind soever it might be, must have been intended by way of ministry to the *former.* Peter, who stiles himself an *Elder,* seems to intimate, by what he recommended to the Elders, that they should consider themselves servants, and not *lords over* GOD's *heritage :* even as CHRIST himself, who though LORD *of all, became servant of all.* And that their services should be *not by constraint but willingly ; not for filthy lucre, but of a ready mind.* 1 Pet. v. 2, 3. And what is still more important to observe, from this address of *Paul,* it is very evident, that as those *bishops,* and *deacons,* are included with the *saints in* CHRIST JESUS; the whole were considered by him, as forming the body of the Church of CHRIST; and consequently all had experienced the regenerating power of the HOLY GHOST. And, to be sure, the very idea of servants in the ministry of GOD's holy word and ordinances, carries with it an assurance of having an eminency in the knowledge of divine things, from divine teachings, and from the quickening influences of GOD the SPIRIT. For to suppose Elders, Bishops, and Deacons, engaged as instruments under the HOLY GHOST, for the conversion of others, while unconverted themselves, would be the most preposterous of all imaginations! Such could not have been the case in the Church, of *Philippi.* The Apostle directs his Epistle to this Church, as *saints in* CHRIST JESUS, with the *bishops* and *deacons,* how many soever of each order there might be. And to such he sends his Apostolic benediction of Grace. Reader! let You and I behold this Church of the *Philippians,* in this most endearing view, and now *hear what the* SPIRIT *saith unto the Churches!*

3 I thank my God upon every remembrance of you,

4 Always in every prayer of mine for you all making request with joy.

5 For your fellowship in the gospel from the first day until now:

6 Being confident of this very thing, that he which hath begun a good work in you will perform *it* until the day of Jesus Christ:

7 Even as it is meet for me to think this of you all, because I have you in my heart; inasmuch as both in my bonds, and in the defence and confirmation of the gospel, ye all are partakers of my grace.

8 For God is my record, how greatly I long after you all in the bowels of Jesus Christ.

9 And this I pray, that your love may abound yet more and more in knowledge and *in* all judgement;

10 That ye may approve things that are excellent; that ye may be sincere and without offence till the day of Christ;

11 Being filled with the fruits of righteousness, which are by Jesus Christ, unto the glory and praise of God.

I admire the Apostle's entrance into the subject of his Epistle. He first blesseth GOD, and then blesseth the Church in the LORD's name. And he blessed GOD as his GOD in CHRIST. *I thank my* GOD, he saith. Right and property in GOD, as a Covenant GOD in CHRIST, is the only solid foundation for the assurance of faith. And the cause for which *Paul* found his heart led out into prayer to GOD, in the consciousness that the Church at *Philippi* was established in grace, would have had no such effect upon the Apostle's mind, had not *Paul* himself felt and enjoyed his own establishment in the faith. The Reader will readily enter into an apprehension of these things. He, and he only, that knows the blessedness of the fellowship of the Gospel himself, can describe what joy of the heart that is, which takes part in the felicity of others on the same account.

I beg the Reader not to overlook the confidence with which the Apostle tells the Church of their safety in grace. He that begun the good work is a wise Master-builder, who never entered upon so grand a concern, as the salvation of the soul, to leave it unfinished. And the reason is evident. Because the beginning of the good work in *regeneration*, is, in fact, but the finishing the first and original purposes of GOD in *election*, the confirming it in *redemption*, and now by quickening the soul, which was before *dead in trespasses and sins*, to the knowledge and enjoyment of it in *regeneration*, becomes an earnest and pledge of an interest in it to all eternity. This work of regeneration by the HOLY GHOST, though, in fact, the *last* in point of order among the Persons of the GODHEAD, is the *first* in point of our apprehension to the knowledge of the love of GOD. By this gracious act, GOD's children are brought into spiritual life, to discover their having been *chosen* of GOD the FATHER before the world, and *redeemed* by GOD the SON in the time-state of the Church, and now, by *regeneration*, made *partakers of an inheritance with the saints in light*. Hence, this *good work*, as *Paul* calls it, (and beyond all conception both of goodness and of greatness it is,) becomes the earnest of our adoption-character, and our union with CHRIST JESUS. It is impossible, therefore, but that it must be compleated, being secured by such principles, and not founded in human worth, but divine grace. *Because I live*, (saith JESUS,) *ye shall live also*. John xiv. 19.

12 But I would ye should understand, brethren, that the things *which happened* unto me have fallen out rather unto the furtherance of the gospel;

13 So that my bonds in Christ are manifest in all the palace, and in all other *places;*

14 And many of the brethren in the Lord, waxing confident by my bonds, are much more bold to speak the word without fear.

It should seem, by what the Apostle here saith, that the Church at *Philippi* had so much affection for *Paul*, (as they well might,) that on account of his imprisonment, they were anxious to know the event. And *Paul's* regard for them was not behind. But how graciously the LORD overruled the malice of his enemies, in causing even the imprisonment of his servant to minister to his glory. He tells them, that as his bonds in CHRIST was known in the palace of the emperor, it had occasioned some enquiry concerning the faith in CHRIST. And we know, that it was made instrumental in the hand of the LORD, for the conversion of some of *Nero's* houshold. For, in the close of this Epistle, he tells the Church of *Philippi*, that amidst the salutations of the brethren which were with him at that time in *Rome*, they chiefly desired to salute the Church which were of *Cæsar's* houshold. And *Paul* further adds, that his chains had made many bold to preach CHRIST. Reader! do not overlook these things. They are not uncommon now. How many have I known who have felt confidence from the exercise of the LORD's tried ones? Yea, what instances have I not observed, where the LORD hath raised up glory to himself, and comfort to his people, from the malice of his enemies?

15 Some indeed preach Christ even of envy and strife; and some also of good will:

16 The one preach Christ of contention, not sincerely, supposing to add affliction to my bonds.

17 But the other of love, knowing that I am set for the defence of the gospel.

18 What then? notwithstanding every way, whether in pretence, or in truth, Christ is preached; and I therein do rejoice, yea, and will rejoice.

19 For I know that this shall turn to my salvation through your prayer, and the supply of the Spirit of Jesus Christ.

20 According to my earnest expectation, and *my* hope, that in nothing I shall be ashamed, but *that* with all boldness as always, *so* now also Christ shall be magnified in my body, whether *it be* by life or by death.

21 For to me to live *is* Christ, and to die *is* gain.

22 But if I live in the flesh, this *is* the fruit of my labour: yet wot I shall choose I wot not.

23 For I am in a strait betwixt two, having a desire to depart, and to be with Christ; which is far better:

24 Nevertheless to abide in the flesh *is* more needful for you.

25 And having this confidence, I know that I shall abide and continue with you all for your furtherance and joy of faith;

26 That your rejoicing may be more abundant in Jesus Christ for me by my coming to you again.

There is somewhat very striking in the Apostle's account of these different preachers. Who could they be that preached CHRIST, even of envy and strife? Not, surely, regenerated men! And yet, is it not possible, even for GOD's own children, in preaching, to do so? May not as well as in all the other circumstances of life, men feel the breakings out of corruption, so as to mingle in holy seasons, as well as upon all other occasions? Is it not possible for jealousy to appear in the ministry, as well as in other parts of life? Alas! where, or in what part of his time-state upon earth, is a child of GOD exempt from corruption, in all that pertains to the flesh? As to those who preached Christ out of good will; there is somewhat very blessed in this relation, however weakly and imperfect it was done. But what we have most to admire on this occasion is, that the great soul of the Apostle rejoiced at every thing, and in every thing, provided Christ was the one glorious subject of all preaching. Let the interest of my Lord and Master be forwarded, (said *Paul*,) and I care not about the instrument, or the motive by which he is guided. Oh! the triumphs of grace through Christ.

I very earnestly entreat the Reader, particularly to remark what *Paul* saith of himself, and, of consequence, all the Lord's people like himself, who are conscious of being in a justified state before God in Christ. He had no choice whether to live or die. And, if the Lord had referred it to the Apostle to have made his own choice, very sure I am that *Paul* would have referred it back again. And what I observe of this great Apostle, may be said of much humbler saints. When *Paul* looked forward, and beheld that eternal weight of glory which awaited him, his holy soul could not but long for the body to be dissolved, that in spirit he might be with the Lord. But when he looked around and beheld Christ's Church comforted and refreshed by his personal ministry, *Paul* felt a willingness to postpone his own everlasting happiness, for the promotion of the everlasting happiness of the Lord's people. Hence, the Apostle was suspended in his desires. He paused over the prospect; and, therefore, left it with the Lord. And so, I am fully convinced, is it with many of the faithful of the Lord, in every age of the Church. They long for Christ. They long to be with Christ. And nothing here below, as it concerns themselves, could make them for a moment wish to remain in the prison of a sinful body, no, not an hour. But, if Jesus employs them in his service, and condescends to make them useful to his Church and people, willingly will they delay their own personal felicity, in the presence of God and the Lamb, to forward the everlasting happiness of their brethren upon earth.

Reader! what saith your personal apprehension of these things? It would sound somewhat strange, to say to a child of God, and especially to a minister of Christ, I do not wish your departure for a long time from the Church upon earth, though very sure I am, whenever the Lord shall call you out of life, it will be but to exchange the Church below for the Church above. But out of love to the Lord's little ones, in this sorrowful world, I earnestly hope your personal enjoyment of Christ in heaven will be many years postponed. This would be an extraordinary thing to say. But yet, such are the motives to wish, that Jesus will not take home his chosen ones, in compassion to his Church in the wilderness, that godly souls cannot but mourn and cry out, Help, Lord! when *the faithful are diminished from among the children of men*.

Zealous, faithful servants of the Lord are but few here below. And, while they shine as lights in the world, in the midst of a crooked and perverse generation, we cannot but regret when any of them cease to lighten around, for we too sensibly feel the darkness their absence makes. It is a sad sign of approaching night, when the Lord extinguishes his brightest luminaries! And, in relation to themselves, though the change in every sense makes for their good, yet they need not depart to enjoy Christ. For they do enjoy by faith, a real personal communion and fellowship with the Father, and with his Son Jesus Christ, by God the Spirit. And, moreover, in one way they can and do, promote the Lord's glory upon earth, which they cannot in heaven. There are no sinners there ignorant of Christ's Person, and of his Godhead and salvation. But there are thousands here of the Lord's own redeemed ones, while in the unrecovered state of our Adam-nature, to whom the Lord can make them useful, in speaking of his princely royalties, and his loving kindness and mercy.

27 Only let your conversation be as it becometh the gospel of Christ: that whether I come and see you, or else be absent, I may hear of your affairs, that ye stand fast in one spirit, with one mind striving together for the faith of the gospel;

28 And in nothing terrified by your adversaries: which is to them an evident token of perdition, but to you of salvation, and that of God.

29 For unto you it is given in the behalf of Christ, not only to believe on him, but also to suffer for his sake;

30 Having the same conflict which ye saw in me, *and* now hear *to be* in me.

By the conversation, which the Apostle recommends as becoming the Gospel of Christ, must be meant the general frame and deportment of the whole life, such as is suited to a child of God, savingly called by grace, and regenerated by the Holy Spirit. The Apostle is writing to the Church it should be remembered. And the Church forms one body in Christ. The common interest and happiness of the whole, in the glory of their Lord, is the one uniform conversation, which should mark every member. They all speak the same language, even the language of Canaan. They all wear the same garments, even Christ's robe of righteousness. They all eat the same spiritual meat, even the bread of life. And they all drink the same spiritual drink. For Christ is both the bread of life, and the water of life to all. Hence, a uniformity of conversation, pursuits, and desires, form the distinguishing feature of this royal family, whom Christ *hath made Kings and Priests, to* God *and the* Father. Reader! is it so in your instance? Do men of the world look at you as men wondered at? Do they think it strange, that ye run not with them to the same excess of riot, speaking evil of you? And are these among the marks by which the carnal take knowledge of you, that ye have been with Jesus? There is not, perhaps, a more alarming thing to the enemies of Christ, and his people, than when they see the firmness with which the Lord's tried ones are borne up, under the cruel pressure of their persecution. It is, as the Apostle saith to them, *an evident token of perdition.* They see, they feel, their nothingness, and forebode their misery, when their threats, and menaces, and punishments which they inflict, are lost upon the objects of their bitterness. What a beautiful example of this the HOLY GHOST hath recorded of the three children in the Court of *Babylon*. *We will not* (said they) *serve thy gods.* The King's visage changed with rage, but inward horror was felt at the same time in his soul. Dan. iii. 17, 18. It is so. It must be so. Such things are for signs, yea evident tokens of perdition to the enemies of our GOD, and of his CHRIST. But they afford at the same time to the LORD's people, sweet manifestations of salvation, and that of GOD!

Reader! do not overlook that precious verse, and the doctrine contained in it, that it is *given* to the Church, in *behalf* of CHRIST, not only to believe on him, but also, if needful, to suffer for his sake. Yes! faith and fortitude are the LORD's gifts, and not our graces. When a child of GOD believes to the salvation of his soul, the strength of that faith, and all the parts of that faith, are from the LORD. It is blessed to believe, blessed to be firm in that belief: blessed to believe always. But the largest portions of faith are all the LORD's gifts. And wherein no man's faith differs from another, the different measures of grace are His, who is both the Author, and Finisher of faith. So that the strong in faith, when taught of GOD, in the exercise of it, will always rejoice in the great *object* of faith, the LORD JESUS; and not in themselves, from the *fruits* and *effects* of it. Oh! for grace both to believe in CHRIST; and, if needs be, to suffer for his sake.

REFLECTIONS.

BLESSED be GOD the HOLY GHOST for his servant's gracious instruction in this chapter. How truly delightful is it to trace the ministry of *Paul* from such slender beginnings, in raising a Church to the LORD at *Philippi*, and then furnishing the Church, both at *Philippi*, and throughout the world, with this divine portion of the LORD's holy word, and his pleasure in the government of it. Surely, O LORD, the whole Church, in every age, both then and now, and during all the time-state of its continuance upon earth, must find cause to bless thee for such tokens of thy love over it.

Reader! let us both seek grace from the LORD, to improve what the HOLY GHOST hath here taught by *Paul*, of the confidence every child of GOD derives in regeneration, for the sure consummation of grace in glory. All that are new born in CHRIST, as well as *Paul*, may be confident *of this very thing, that He which hath begun the good work, will perform it until the day of* JESUS CHRIST. *For whom the* LORD *called, them he also justified; and whom he justified, them he also glorified.*

My soul! listen to what *Paul* saith. See that your whole conversation is corresponding to the whole character of a child of GOD. Prove thy right and freedom to the city, which hath foundation, whose builder, and Maker, is GOD, by the marks of citizenship. Let thy conversation be in heaven, from whence thou art looking for thy SAVIOR, the LORD JESUS CHRIST. And oh! for the constraining love of JESUS, to rejoice as saints of old did, when suffering shame and reproach for JESUS.

CHAP. II.

CONTENTS.

We have here one of the most precious Views of JESUS. *Paul exhorts the Church by* CHRIST's *Example. He shews the Blessedness of a Life of Faith and Humility.*

IF *there be* therefore any consolation in Christ, if any comfort of love, if any fellowship of the Spirit, if any bowels and mercies,

2 Fulfil ye my joy, that ye be like-minded, having the same love, *being* of one accord, of one mind.

3 *Let* nothing *be done* through strife or vainglory; but in lowliness of mind let each esteem other better than themselves.

4 Look not every man on his own things, but every man also on the things of others.

5 Let this mind be in you, which was also in Christ Jesus:

6 Who, being in the form of God, thought it not robbery to be equal with God:

7 But made himself of no reputation, and took upon him the form of a servant, and was made in the likeness of men:

8 And being found in fashion as a man, he humbled himself, and became obedient unto death, even the death of the cross.

9 Wherefore God also hath highly exalted him, and given him a name which is above every name:

10 That at the name of Jesus every knee should bow, of *things* in heaven, and *things* in earth, and *things* under the earth;

11 And *that* every tongue should confess that Jesus Christ *is* Lord, to the glory of God the Father.

The opening of this Chapter, in several of the first verses of it, is abundantly sweet and interesting; and I could find subject matter to say much, yea, to fill many pages, in dwelling on those great and unanswerable arguments for following up what the Apostle so affectionately recommends. Who indeed can need more than the consolation of CHRIST, the fellowship of the SPIRIT, and the bowels and mercies of GOD, to endear, and enforce every thing that he enjoins. But while I hope the Reader will feel grace to all that *Paul* hath said on this ground; (as I pray for grace to feel the same motives myself) I must beg to pass over all these things, as the *fruits* and *effects* in the divine life, to attend to the grand *cause* of the whole, in the Person and work of JESUS, as here set forth by the Apostle. Never surely was there exhibited, before the world, such a representation as *Paul* hath here drawn of his LORD and Master. All subjects in comparison of it are light and uninteresting. Cold and insensible indeed must be that man's soul that can hear, or read, what *Paul* hath here said of the LORD JESUS CHRIST, and hear, or read it, unmoved. I lament the shortness I am constrained to prescribe to myself, in a work of this kind, when the subject itself is endless. But the Reader will I hope indulge me, while glancing at some of the great points of it.

The Apostle begins the relation he hath here set forth of his divine Master, in marking down the *first*, and *leading* feature of all in his essential nature and GODHEAD. *Who being in the form of* GOD, *and with whom it was no robbery to be equal with* GOD. If there were no other portions in the Scriptures, which openly and fully declare the essential divinity of CHRIST, this one most plainly reveals it. This glory of the GODHEAD of CHRIST, as the SON of GOD, is spoken of, substantially, and essentially, as his nature, his own; underived, equal with GOD. Reader! observe this; for it is most blessed.

The *second* volume *Paul* marks, in this world of mystery, CHRIST's Person, is, *his making himself of no reputation*. This is the great point in the beginning of CHRIST's humiliation. The SON of GOD vacating his glory; emptying himself of it, as the word in the original means. And here begins also, as standing towards the Church, the wonders of his Person. For when the SON of GOD condescended, for the vast purposes contained in the design, to take into union with himself that holy portion of our nature, which might form and constitute with the GODHEAD one CHRIST: there was still such glory attached to his Person, as GOD and man united, as demanded the universal adoration, love, and obedience of all creatures. Hence we read, that when GOD the FATHER *bringeth in the first begotten into the world, he saith: And let all the Angels of* GOD *worship him.* Heb. i. 6. So that, before a single act had been wrought by CHRIST for the redemption of the Church only, the SON of GOD had betrothed our nature to himself: he had a Personal glory, as GOD-man, which called for all the praise of creation. Let the Reader mark this also!

But *Paul* goes on to the *third* volume, in this mysterious work, when he saith: He not only made himself of no reputation, *but took on him the form of a servant, and was made in the likeness of men, and being found in fashion as a man, he humbled himself, and became obedient unto death, even the death of the cross.* Language fails to describe, what the utmost stretch of the human mind cannot adequately conceive, the vastness of this work. But the great stress of this immense design, as recorded in this Scripture, lies in CHRIST's unparalleled humility, in this self-debasement, and in this state submitting to the death of the cross; and this, not passively, but actively, and voluntarily; and all this, sustaining personal dishonor, shame, and pain, for those great purposes, for which the whole was intended.

Now, then, the Apostle introduceth the subject, of the grand, and pre-disposing cause of all, namely, *to the glory of* GOD *the* FATHER. This was the first, and ultimate object. The SON of GOD divests himself of his glory, for the FATHER's glory. He emptieth himself of his personal honor, for the FATHER's honor. And, by this process, he brings in a greater revenue, both of glory, and honor, than sin in man had tarnished, or could have tarnished, by millions of beings, and in millions of years. And thus we see, (though all we now see, is but as through a glass darkly,) how deep, and sure, the infinite designs of GOD have been laid, for revealing the LORD's glory, and making known to the Church, what *Paul* calls *the manifold wisdom of* GOD. Ephes. iii. 10.

Well might the Apostle make that blessed conclusion which he hath made, to this mysterious subject, concerning the exaltation of the LORD JESUS; and the universal bending of every knee, and the confession of every tongue, to his glory. For if the whole creation of GOD could be convened into one congregation, and proclamation was made, for sin and Satan, every man's own guilty conscience, and all the arrests of GOD's law and justice, to give in their claims, on the sinner, for his dishonoring GOD by sin; it must be found, that CHRIST, as the sinner's representative, (and made a surety by GOD himself, Heb. vii. 21, 22.) hath done more, to honor GOD, than all the sins of men hath done, to dishonor him. Yea, so infinitely precious, so incalculably great, hath been, and is, the vast merits, and blood-shedding of CHRIST, in doing away sin by the sacrifice of himself; that over and above the honor restored to GOD by the LORD JESUS, there is a redundancy of merit, that millions of ages can never so fully recompense, so as to say, the whole is paid, and nothing more is due.

Now, Reader, pause over the vast subject, and ponder it well. And although, what I have brought before you, is but the merest outlines of the mystery, of GOD *manifest in the flesh,* (for the dimensions of the whole is infinite,) yet, as a man who hath ascended an high hill, and looketh round to the utmost horizon, can only take into his view a small part of what is before him, though he is ravished with the boundless prospect: so the heart, can only contemplate in part, the vast subject. Oh! what praise must be suited for Him, whom GOD, in his mediator-character, *hath highly exalted, and given a Name above every name?* It is blessed to behold CHRIST, in all his *personal*-glories, and in all his *relative*-glories, and in all his *office*-glories, as GOD-Man Mediator. When *John* saw him by vision in heaven, he beheld, that on *his head were many crowns.* Rev. xix. 12. And, beyond all doubt, the SON of GOD in our nature, hath acquired glory like so many rays of brightness, by every personal act of his, which belong to him as GOD-Man Mediator. Reader! it will be your happiness, and mine, to see him as *John* saw him, with the many crowns, if we can behold the very crown of our own personal redemption, among them upon his sacred head. For as JESUS, when *ascending* from earth to heaven, was crowned with glory and honor, for his triumphs in redemption: Heb. ii. 9 so is He crowned by every single redeemed sinner, when he *descends* in the power of his SPIRIT, upon that sinner's heart, to give him *the light of the knowledge of the glory of* GOD *in the face of* JESUS CHRIST! Then it is, the heart is regenerated, and made joyful in the LORD: the knee of faith and love bends before Him; and the tongue bursts forth, in praises to his name, and in the loudest acclamations confesseth, that JESUS CHRIST *is* LORD *to the glory of* GOD *the* FATHER.

12 Wherefore, my beloved, as ye have always obeyed, not as in my presence only, but now much more in my absence, work out your own salvation with fear and trembling.

13 For it is God which worketh in you both to will and to do of *his* good pleasure.

I pause over these verses, to consider them by themselves, as they ought to be considered. For, notwithstanding they begin with a *Wherefore*, yet they do not seem to have any immediate connection, with what was said before, or what follows. And I pause over them the rather, because, perhaps few verses in the word of GOD, have been more insisted upon, by a certain persuasion of men, in bringing them forward to support their different opinions, by way of strengthening, as they would fain suppose, their favorite doctrines. Reader! it would be always well, if we were to come to the Scriptures with a teachable mind to *learn*, and not with a view to *teach*, or to take portions of them here and there, to give a supposed strength to our own opinion, already formed. If, like children, and with the simplicity of little children, (for the highest taught child of GOD in this life is no more,) we were all to sit at the feet of JESUS for instruction; party spirit, would not then be carried to the extent, to which it sometimes most unhappily is.

In relation to this well-known passage, in which we are commanded *to work out our own salvation with fear and trembling;* the words which immediately follow, (and which from the word *for,* seems very plainly to intimate, that they are to be joined to what went before,) gives the reason for this great attention: because, *it is* GOD *which worketh in you, both to will, and to do, of his good pleasure.* In humbly offering my judgment upon the passage, I shall rather do it by enquiry, than by decision; rather in proposing to the Reader, what appears to me to be the genuine sense of it, than in positively saying, what it is. I would, therefore, very meekly ask, whether it can be supposed, that the HOLY GHOST, when commanding the Church to work out their own salvation with fear and trembling, meant to intimate, that salvation was in any part procurable by man's work, instead of CHRIST's blood, and righteousness? Doth not GOD the HOLY GHOST, in every part of his Scriptures, ascribe the whole of salvation to the LORD JESUS? Are we not told, again and again, that there is salvation in no other? Nay, is not every part, and portion of salvation, from beginning to end, in awakening, regenerating, redeeming, justifying, sanctifying grace; all expressly said, to be God's gift, and not man's deservings? And, is not Christ himself declared to be, both the Alpha, and Omega; the Author, and the Finisher, of our faith? When the Reader hath duly pondered these things, I would beg his attention to the further view of the subject.

Upon the supposition, that any part of salvation depended upon our working it out, while, by so much, the infinitely precious value of Christ's blood and righteousness is thereby lessened, as not being the *whole* cause of acceptance before God, but depending at the same time, upon our working out our own salvation, to co-operate with it; it becomes a question of vast moment, to ascertain, in what way, and by what means, this working out is to be accomplished; since the word of God uniformly in every part, most decidedly declares, and every child of God, savingly called by grace, daily knows the same, that *we are not sufficient of ourselves to think* (much less to do,) *any thing as of ourselves, but our sufficiency is of* God. 2 Cor. iii. 5. If the working out our own salvation, here spoken of, with fear and trembling, be meant to imply, an atom, by way of assisting in the cause, or of obtaining acceptance with God, would it not have been said: what work of this meritorious kind became necessary; and what things are essential, to the accomplishment of this purpose? If *working*, according to our general idea of working in labors after holiness, and the like, be here meant; would the Holy Ghost have left the subject in so undetermined a manner, without particularly specifying, what works those were, which in fear and trembling, we were to secure our own salvation by; and which, if this be supposed the sense of the expression to work, lessens, if not totally throws to the ground, the merits of Christ's death; and raiseth up causes for our taking confidence before God, for our good works, which all the other parts of Scripture unceasingly labor to destroy.

If it be asked, in what sense I accept this Scripture? I humbly answer; I accept it simply as the whole passage stands altogether, one complete whole. *Work out your own salvation with fear and trembling: for it is* God *which worketh in you, both to will and to do, of his good pleasure.* If it be God, which worketh in me to *will;* so that I cannot will a good thought, or intention, without the Lord willeth it in me, neither when the Lord hath worked in me that will; I cannot *do* that good purpose, without he that first moved it, gives energy to the performance of it, well doth it become me to be always alive and active in the important work, which this Almighty mover is working in me, both to *will* and to *do of his good pleasure.* The work I am thus working out, is not the work of labor, or of merit, or of justification, or of recommendation to God, but simply an employment, in a constant attendance upon it, and that of such earnestness and anxiety, as men of the world, when engaged in an arduous concern, are fearful and trembling in, lest they should fail of success. Not a bondage fear, but an holy, child-like fear. Not a fear of the loss of divine love for the adoption of children prevents such apprehensions, and the faithful Covenant promises of God in Christ, render it impossible. But the fear of an holy weariness in the path of grace, as those who rejoice in full assurance of faith, but *rejoice with trembling.* Beholding the wreck of our fallen nature, in the instance of the floating carcases all around, we bless the

God of our salvation, that he hath brought us by his grace safe on shore, while we tremble to look back and see the tremendous storm from whence we have escaped. If this be the meaning of the passage, it is truly blessed, and in exact conformity to the whole tenor of Scripture. I find, through grace, the Lord working in me, both to will and to do of his good pleasure. He worketh in me, to shew me my total helplessness in myself, and my compleat all-sufficiency in Christ. Conscious of the infinite importance of salvation, I feel the Lord's grace, prompting me to an unceasing desire after the Lord, so that I am working *from* life, not *for* life; *from* grace, not *for* grace. And thus I am going humbly and softly all my days, as one, who hath an object of such infinite moment before him, that while rejoicing in Christ, I am trembling in myself. These are my views of the scripture, and which I now leave with the Reader to his own judgment, under the Lord's blessing.

14 Do all things without murmurings and disputings:

15 That ye may be blameless and harmless, the sons of God, without rebuke, in the midst of a crooked and perverse nation, among whom ye shine as lights in the world;

16 Holding forth the word of life: that I may rejoice in the day of Christ, that I have not run in vain, neither laboured in vain.

17 Yea, and if I be offered upon the sacrifice and service of your faith, I joy, and rejoice with you all.

18 For the same cause also do ye joy, and rejoice with me.

19 But I trust in the Lord Jesus to send Timotheus shortly unto you, that I also may be of good comfort, when I know your state.

20 For I have no man like-minded, who will naturally care for your state.

21 For all seek their own, not the things which are Jesus Christ's.

22 But ye know the proof of him, that, as a son with the Father, he hath served with me in the gospel.

23 Him therefore I hope to send presently, so soon as I shall see how it will go with me.

24 But I trust in the Lord that I also myself shall come shortly.

25 Yet I supposed it necessary to send to you Epaphroditus, my brother, and companion in labour, and fellow-soldier, but your messenger, and he that ministered to my wants.

26 For he longed after you all, and was full of heaviness, because that ye had heard that he had been sick.

27 For indeed he was sick nigh unto death; but God had mercy on him; and not on him only, but on me also, lest I should have sorrow upon sorrow.

28 I sent him therefore the more carefully, that, when ye see him again, ye may rejoice, and that I may be the less sorrowful.

29 Receive him therefore in the Lord with all gladness; and hold such in reputation:

30 Because for the work of Christ he was nigh unto death, not regarding his life, to supply your lack of service toward me.

All that is contained within these verses, is so plain, as to need no Comment. They beautifully set forth the state of the Church in *Paul's* days, and shew, what mutual affection subsisted, between the several members of CHRIST's mystical body. They manifest the Apostle's anxiety, for the spiritual, and temporal welfare, of the Church; the affection of *Timothy*, and *Epaphroditus*, for the people; and their regard for the Apostle, and them. Nothing can give a more interesting testimony, with what love they took part in each other's concern, than what is said in the close of this Chapter. We shall do well, to keep it in remembrance as a lovely model of the primitive Church. And let us beg of the Great Head of the Church, to cement all his members at the present hour in himself, and to one another, by the same sweet spirit of union, that all the world may know, whose we are, and to whom we belong, by that oneness of soul, which distinguish all the regenerated disciples of JESUS CHRIST.

REFLECTIONS.

READER! do not fail to remark, both the nature of the arguments, and the affectionate claims of them, by which the Apostle aims to allure the Church to a oneness of mind and heart, to CHRIST and his people. What could he say more persuasively in those high claims, than when recommending them by the consolations of CHRIST, the fellowship of the HOLY GHOST; and the bowels, and mercies, of GOD the FATHER? But, while I earnestly desire the Reader to remark this, as he goes, I beg him yet more particularly to attend to what GOD the HOLY GHOST hath recorded, in this most blessed Chapter, concerning the Person, GODHEAD, manhood, grace, and glory, of the LORD JESUS CHRIST; and the FATHER's glory in Him. Reader! was there ever a more precious form of words, brought together within the compass of a few verses, than what is here done, to exalt, and extol, to the Church's view, the personal dignity, and the personal humbleness, of CHRIST, in the accomplishment of the great purposes of revelation? Who that reads it, and reads it with an enlightened eye, but must feel his whole soul going forth in desires after CHRIST, to be able to comprehend with all saints, what is *the breadth, and length, and depth, and height, of the love of* CHRIST, *which passeth knowledge!* Oh! for grace, that the same mind may be in us, which was in CHRIST JESUS!

Reader! let us seek strength from the LORD, for every act of faith upon the LORD, that while both the LORD's word and our daily experience teach us, that it *is* GOD *which worketh in us, both to will and to do of his good pleasure;* that *will* may be discovered by us, in leading us wholly to CHRIST; and that *doing,* may be made known to us, to be the LORD's *work* in us: *for we are his workmanship, created in* CHRIST JESUS *unto good works, which* GOD *hath before ordained that we should walk in them.* LORD! I would beg for myself, and for all thy redeemed ones, to be so found, in the daily exercise of thy *willing,* and *doing,* in me, with an holy fear, and trembling, as those who had always before their eyes the infinite importance of their own salvation; while confident of safety, in the Covenant-promises of GOD my FATHER, and the compleat, and finished redemption, of the LORD JESUS CHRIST. LORD! grant, that I may have my whole conversation here below, while continuing in the present time-state of the Church, as the *blameless, and harmless sons of* GOD, *without rebuke; holding forth the word of life, and in the midst of a crooked, and perverse nation, shining as lights in the world!*

CHAP. III.

CONTENTS.

In this Chapter, the Apostle warns the Church against false Teachers. He as strongly points out, and that in his own Example, what are the infallible Marks of Grace in the Heart; namely, to win CHRIST, and be found in Him. *He closeth the Chapter with the solemn Account of the End of the Carnal, and the blessed Termination of the Life of the Godly.*

FINALLY, my brethren, rejoice in the Lord. To write the same things to you, to me indeed *is* not grievous, but for you *it is* safe.

2 Beware of dogs, beware of evil-workers, beware of the concision.

3 For we are the circumcision, which worship God in the spirit, and rejoice in Christ Jesus, and have no confidence in the flesh.

4 Though I might also have confidence in the flesh. If any other man thinketh that he hath whereof he might trust in the flesh, I more;

5 Circumcised the eighth day of the stock of Israel, *of* the tribe of Benjamin, an Hebrew of the Hebrews; as touching the law, a Pharisee;

6 Concerning zeal: persecuting the church; touching the righteousness which is in the law, blameless.

7 But what things were gain to me, those I counted loss for Christ.

8 Yea, doubtless, and I count all things *but* loss for the excellency of the knowledge of Christ Jesus my Lord: for whom I have suffered the loss of all things, and do count them *but* dung, that I may win Christ.

9 And be found in him, not having mine own righteousness, which is of the law, but that which is through the faith of Christ, the righteousness which is of God by faith:

10 That I may know him, and the power of his resurrection, and the fellowship of his sufferings, being made conformable unto his death;

11 If by any means I might attain unto the resurrection of the dead.

12 Not as though I had already attained, either were already perfect: but I follow after, if that I may apprehend that for which also I am apprehended of Christ Jesus.

13 Brethren, I count not myself to have apprehended: but *this* one thing *I do*, forgetting those things which are behind, and reaching forth unto these things which are before.

14 I press toward the mark for the prize of the high calling of God in Christ Jesus.

15 Let us therefore, as many as be perfect, be thus minded: and if in any thing ye be otherwise minded, God shall reveal even this unto you.

16 Nevertheless, whereto we have already attained, let us walk by the same rule, let us mind the same thing.

By the opening of this Chapter, one might have been led to conceive, that the Apostle was drawing to a conclusion. And, it is probable, that when he began it, with the word *finally*, such was his intention. But, whatever was *Paul's* intention herein, GOD the HOLY GHOST it appears, had more for him to say to his Church. And, we have reason to bless that gracious, and Almighty LORD of the ministry, that he had; and for leading out the mind of the Apostle, as he hath here done, in so many sweet and precious truths. And, we have reason to bless the LORD yet further, for causing the same to be recorded, and handed down to the Church, through all the intermediate ages, to the present hour. Oh! LORD the SPIRIT! add a blessing more: and cause the blessed doctrines to be written in the hearts of thy people!

How delightfully the Church is commanded to rejoice in the LORD, while cautioned to beware of the malice, and subtilty of their enemies. And, beyond all doubt, in every heart of GOD's children, which is savingly regenerated by the HOLY GHOST, there is an everlasting cause, for unceasingly rejoicing in CHRIST; notwithstanding the holy caution, with which every justified believer is called upon, to walk through the whole of his pilgrimage state. Reader! do not fail to remark the vast difference, between rejoicing in the LORD, and taking confidence in the flesh.

The different characters here spoken of by the Apostle, of *dogs*, and *evil workers*, and *the concision*, contrasted to the *true circumcision*, which worship GOD *in the spirit*, very clearly define, the seed of the Serpent, from the seed of the Woman. One line in the Book of the Revelations, is enough, in explaining the whole. *Without are dogs.* Rev. xxii. 15. And everlastingly must be so. An eternal line of distinction marks the goats from the sheep: the tares, from the wheat: and the children of the wicked one, from the children of the Kingdom. Various have been the opinions, and many the enquiries, of learned men, in endeavouring to ascertain the Apostle's meaning, of *Concision*. But, while men of natural learning, untaught of GOD, have amused themselves with different conjectures, which *minister questions more than godly edifying;* the HOLY GHOST hath made it plain to the humblest capacities of GOD's children. The fleshly concision, be it what it may, is opposed to the spiritual circumcision of the heart: similar to what *the children of the bond-woman are to the children of the free.* If the Reader would see our LORD's own Comment on this subject, he will find it beautifully set forth; Matt.

xiii. 30. And, if he desires a further illustration of the same, his servant the Apostle hath given it; Gal. iv. 22—31.

But the Apostle, in what is here before us, hath plainly shewn, what is the true circumcision of the heart in regeneration, when he saith: *for we are the circumcision, which worship* GOD *in the spirit, and rejoice in* CHRIST JESUS, *and have no confidence in the flesh.* Surely the features of character, which define the LORD's people from the carnal world, are as brightly drawn in those words, as if written with a sun-beam. And, to heighten them the more, *Paul* contrasts them, to what his own portrait was, before that sovereign grace had made the change. If good works, or zeal for GOD's honor, or birthright by nature from *Abraham*, could have justified before GOD; who stood so high in these things, as *Paul?* But, what saith this great Apostle, after the LORD had called him by his grace, to reveal his SON in him? *I count all things but loss* (saith he) *for the excellency of the knowledge of* CHRIST JESUS *my* LORD, *for whom I have suffered the loss of all things, and do count them but dung, that I may win* CHRIST, *and be found in him.*

Reader! I pray you to pause over the Apostle's account of himself. Observe, with what abhorrence he speaks of his own righteousness, and all his former privileges, before he was brought into a state of conversion. He calls the whole *dung*; and, like the Prophet, considered all, as *filthy rags*. Isaiah lxiv. 6. And, observe how he sums up the whole of his wishes and desires, under those two grand branches of all happiness, namely, *to win* CHRIST, *and to be found in him*.

Not that the Apostle had any question, or doubt, upon his mind, as to his own personal knowledge *of* CHRIST, and his interest *in* CHRIST. For he had before told the Church, in the former part of this same Epistle, that *he was confident of this very thing, that He which had begun the good work in them, would perform it unto the day of* JESUS CHRIST. Chap. i. 6. And, long before this, he had blessed GOD, when writing to the Church at *Ephesus*, in that, GOD had chosen, and predestinated the Church, to the adoption of children; and that it should be holy, and without blame before him in love; and both accepted the Church in CHRIST, and the Church had found redemption in CHRIST's blood. Ephes. i. 3—10. So that *Paul*, by his expressions in this place, of winning CHRIST, and being found in him, did not mean as though the blessings had not been obtained, or were in the least doubtful. But, his evident design, in thus writing to the Church was, to express his holy joy at the happy change, in throwing away all his former righteousness, which was of the law, as so much dung, and dross; and to be wholly found in CHRIST, and the righteousness which is of GOD by faith.

And, if we take into the account, the whole of *Paul's* ministry, on this important point, as may be gathered from his preaching, and Epistles; the subject will appear exceedingly plain, that the Apostle, from first to last, after his conversion, made CHRIST the whole of his salvation. If there be a single point upon earth, more clearly ascertained, one, than another, concerning the Apostle's judgment upon this great doctrine; no man of candor can hesitate to say, that the uniform plan of this inspired Apostle, in all his ministry, and in all his labors, was, to exalt CHRIST, and to humble the sinner. His whole preaching was, to hold up the Lord Jesus Christ, as Jehovah's One (and only One) Ordinance, for salvation to every one that believes. In conformity to the whole College of Apostles, in their plan of preaching, after being sent forth by the Holy Ghost, Paul preached as they did, that *salvation was in no other; neither is there any other name under heaven given among men whereby we must be saved.* Acts iv. 12. And, like them, Paul had but one text, one sermon, one subject; whether in the temple, or from house to house, as they did, so did he, *cease not to teach, and to preach* Jesus Christ. Acts v. 42. Neither do we ever find him mingling the Law with the Gospel! So far from it, that he expressly taught the *Galatian* Church, that *if righteousness come by the law, then* Christ *is dead in vain.* Gal. ii. 21. Christ (said he) *is become of no effect unto you: whosoever of you are justified by the law, ye are fallen from grace.* Gal. v. 4. Do we ever find him preaching any other doctrine, but salvation *wholly* by the blood of the Lamb; and justification *solely* in the righteousness of Jesus Christ? So far from it, that he speaks with an holy indignation, and abhorrence, at the bare idea: God *forbid* (said he) *that I should glory save in the cross of our* Lord Jesus Christ; *by whom the world is crucified unto me, and I unto the world.* Gal. vi. 14. And, as he said this to the Church of the *Galatians;* so, in like manner, he entered his protest against all other doctrines, but Christ and his cross, when writing to the Church of the *Corinthians: I determined* (said he) *not to know any thing among you, save* Jesus Christ, *and him crucified.* 1 Cor. ii. 2. And in the preceding Chapter he had assigned a most satisfying reason for it. *For the preaching of the cross* (said he) *is to them that perish foolishness; but unto us which are saved,* (Reader! mark, which *are* saved, not, *to be* saved;) *it is the power of* God. 1 Cor. i. 18.

Now, again, I beg the Reader to pause over this statement; and let him remark, that it is wholly scriptural. And, when the Reader hath duly pondered it, let him ask his own heart; (for to the heart of the Reader I appeal, if so be the Holy Ghost hath regenerated him); for an unregenerated Reader can be no judge in the matter, no more than a blind man is of colors, or a deaf man of sound:) was *Paul* a preacher of free grace, or was he not? Did he, or did he not, hold up Christ, and him crucified, as the whole of salvation? Did he, or did he not, wholly throw aside the law, in a way of justification before God; and declare, that Christ *was the end of the law for righteousness to every one that believeth?* Rom. x. 4. And, did he, or did he not, in relation to his own personal salvation, while preaching the same to all the Church, as in this Chapter is declared, that *he counted all things but dung, that he might win* Christ, *and be found in him?* And if these, and the like questions, are answered, as they must be answered by every man of candor, and as *Paul* himself, if alive, would answer them; wherefore should not all that are truly regenerated, and taught of God the Holy Ghost, as he was, join issue with him, and make the same conclusion as he did? *For by grace are ye saved through faith; and that not of yourselves, it is the gift of* God, *not of works, lest any man should boast.* Ephes. ii. 8, 9.

I have dwelt longer upon this subject, than I otherwise should have done, not because of its importance only, but because some modern Writers, in the awful day in which the Church of GOD now is, have ventured, in contradiction to those most plain truths of Scripture, to insinuate, as if the inculcation of such doctrines as salvation by CHRIST alone, were dangerous. They have, indeed, made a violent blow, at all the great articles by which the faith once delivered unto the saints are distinguished. And were those blessed foundation truths within the reach of their arm, they would wish to dig them up, and reduce the whole Gospel to a mere system of morality, and the miserable piety of fallen, sinful creatures. But this is as futile, as throwing snow-balls at the sun. The sovereignty of GOD the FATHER, in his electing love of the Church; the redemption of the Church, by the sole labors, righteousness, and death, of the SON of GOD; and the final perseverance of the saints, by the graces, influences, and renewing strength, of GOD the HOLY GHOST: these soul-supporting doctrines, are not in danger of suffering harm, much less of annihilation, by an arm of flesh, or all the powers of darkness. They have stood all the ravages of time, and all the revolutions of empires; and must stand, through all the time-state of the Church, like the divine Author of our holy faith, *the same yesterday, and to-day, and for ever.* See Commentary on 1 Thessalonians xi. 4—10.

But, is the Reader astonished at the attack made on those fundamental articles of *the faith which was once delivered unto the saints?* So am not I. We are taught to expect it, and especially in the last times. 1 Tim. iv. 1. *Paul* told the Church at *Ephesus,* that after his departure, not only from without, grievous wolves would enter in among them, not sparing the flock: but, what was more distressing to hear; *I know,* (said he,) *that also of your ownselves shall men arise, speaking perverse things, to draw away disciples after them.* Acts xx. 29, 30. And the word of GOD traceth the evil to its source. For, as long as men are unacquainted *with the plague of their own heart,* their employment in sacred things will give them but a very superficial knowledge, either of their own corruptions before GOD, or of the infinite extent of malignity in sin, which can yield to nothing to do away, but the blood, and righteousness of the LORD JESUS CHRIST. There is in every man by nature, a free-will righteousness, in his very heart. We are all born with it. And so closely is it woven into the very texture of the old *Adam-*nature of the body, that even after a work of grace hath passed upon the soul of the child of GOD; it lurks still in the flesh, and some taints of it he carries with him, even to his grave. And, in instances where the mere form of godliness appears, in much seeming zeal, without the power by regeneration; there the utmost bitterness will manifest itself, in opposing the doctrines of free grace. *Paul* felt this to the full, in the days of his unregeneracy; and made a very honest confession of it, when by conversion the LORD led him to see it. *I verily thought* (said he) *with myself, that I ought to do many things contrary to the name of* JESUS *of Nazareth.* Acts xxvi. 9.

And if, after mentioning the name, and testimony, of so great an Apostle, the humble writer of this *Poor Man's Commentary,* may venture to speak of himself, he would, with the deepest self-abasement of spirit say, that many a year did he conceive the same. Indeed, there is scarce a spot of ground, marked by the feet of daring unbelief, and disputation, against GOD's sovereignty in his election of grace, with the many sweet, and precious blessings, which take their rise from that fountain of everlasting love, and make glad the Church of GOD, but I have trodden. I have gone over the whole of the field of controversy, on these grand points; and, inch by inch, contended on the awful side of unbelief, until driven out by the overwhelming testimony of divine truth, brought home to my heart, by the arrows of conviction, from the hand of GOD the HOLY GHOST. I can, therefore, readily enter into a full apprehension of those men's feelings, who contend on that ground, by what my own once were. And under the hope, that He who hath taught me, will teach them; I can, and do, truly pity, and compassionate their ignorance, in the recollection of my own. When GOD the HOLY GHOST shall have brought them into a clearer view of things, on those glorious truths, (as I bless his Majesty, he hath me,) they will look back, as I now do, and stand astonished, which to admire most; the LORD's forbearance, or man's presumption.

But, in the mean time, as an old man going out of life, it behoves me, *having received his testimony, to set to his seal, that* GOD *is true.* John iii. 33. I hesitate not to say, therefore, that all such writers, or preachers, if a work of grace from GOD the SPIRIT, is happily begun in their heart, (and with all others I have nothing at present to do,) the LORD, for wise and gracious purposes, hath not as yet brought them into a full acquaintance, (as he will at length do,) *with the plague of their own heart.* They have been convinced of sin, no doubt; for this is among the first works of GOD the SPIRIT, after regeneration. But they have not fully learnt, as hereafter they will learn, what *Paul* calls, the *old man of sin;* and that *sin by the commandment, might become exceeding sinful.* Rom. vii. 13. GOD the HOLY GHOST doth by his children, as we for the most part do by our's. In our system of education, we instruct them, as their tender capacities will bear. *Here a little, and there a little.* When the LORD brought his Israel out of Egypt, he would not lead them through the way of the land of the *Philistines,* although that was near; for GOD said, lest peradventure the people repent, when they see war, and return to Egypt. Exodus xiii. 17. So is it now, in the LORD's deliverance of his Israel, from spiritual Egypt. He doth not bring his people all at once acquainted with the depth of sin in their fallen nature, lest they should despond, at the prospect of such a war. But the LORD leads them into this knowledge, as they are enabled to bear it. Hence, those persons to whom I am now alluding, are not, while they so write, or preach, brought into a thorough acquaintance with *the plague of their own heart.* They have not descended, like the Prophet, into the chambers of imagery, from one degree of information to another, to discover the greater abominations of themselves, and their own corruptions. Ezek. viii. 8—13. They see only, as the poor man did in part, when JESUS first touched his eyes, and *beheld men, as trees walking.* But, if they are the LORD's, and He hath begun the good work in their souls; they will have their spiritual apprehensions exercised, into larger discoveries, both of their own totally helpless, lost estate, and of the ability in CHRIST alone for salvation. And then, like *Paul,* they will *preach the faith which once they labored to destroy.* Some such, I myself have known.

And, as it was with the Church in his instance, so hath it been upon those occasions, with me, in their's: I have *glorified* God *in them.* Gal. i. 23, 24. See Chap. iv. 8. and Commentary.

I must not dismiss the view of this blessed Scripture, in the Apostle's longings *to win* Christ, *and be found in him;* without offering a short observation on that part also, connected with *Paul's* desire, when he saith, that *he followeth after it that he might apprehend that, for which also* (saith *Paul*) *I am apprehended of* Christ Jesus. There is somewhat well worthy our attention in this. There is a vast difference between Christ's apprehending of his people, and their apprehending him. Christ's apprehending us is the *cause,* and our apprehending him, but the *effect.* It is by this, as it is by love. His love of us is the *cause* of our love of him. *We love him because he first loved us.* This is the *effect.* John iv. 19. In like manner, had not Christ first apprehended us, we never should have apprehended him. Nay, more than this. Besides the Lord's apprehending all the members of his mystical body, in that one vast comprehensive union, by which he holds the whole; had he not taken the gracious method he hath done, by his Spirit, in drawing out our hearts to the love of him, and inclining our souls by his grace, to lay hold of him in faith; never should we have done it, or even desired it, but have remained for ever, in the natural enmity of our own hearts against him. When, therefore, the Apostle expresseth his desire to apprehend Christ, as Christ apprehended him; he meant it not for any further security (for Christ's holding him makes this effectual,) but for delight. Not, as if he needed greater safety, for that was impossible; but for the greater triumph of faith. The child, held in the bosom of a tender mother, owes its safety, not from throwing its little playful arms round the mother's neck, but wholly from her support, beneath the infant's body. Perhaps the unconscious babe may, in the moment of forgetfulness, forego its holding; but not so the mother. In like manner, it is pleasant to faith, and *Paul* wished it, to apprehend Christ, as Christ apprehends us; but the security of *Paul,* and all the children of God like *Paul,* is founded alone in Christ. *Hold thou me up,* (said one of old,) *and I shall be safe.* Psm. cxix. 117. And *Moses* was directed by the Holy Ghost, to assure this to the Church, when he said: *the eternal* God *is thy refuge; and underneath are the everlasting arms.* Deut. xxxiii. 27.

17 Brethren, be followers together of me, and mark them which walk so as ye have us for an ensample.

18 (For many walk, of whom I have told you often, and now tell you even weeping, *that they are* the enemies of the cross of Christ:

19 Whose end *is* destruction, whose God *is their* belly, and *whose* glory *is* in their shame, who mind earthly things.)

20 For our conversation is in heaven; from

whence also we look for the Saviour, the Lord Jesus Christ.

21 Who shall change our vile body, that it may be fashioned like unto his glorious body, according to the working whereby he is able even to subdue all things unto himself.

We have a very awful account of the *many*, whom the Apostle here describes, as enemies to the cross of CHRIST. He could not mean the openly profane, neither the openly despisers of CHRIST; for in the case of either, distressing as the view is, *Paul* needed not to have cautioned the Church against them. It appears very plainly, that as their sin is marked by the Apostle as against the cross of CHRIST; it was the doctrine of redemption solely by CHRIST's blood and righteousness, against which their enmity was shewn. And well might *Paul* weep, in beholding such characters. *Their end*, he said, *was destruction.* Carnal confidence, naturally producing such an end. And what possible hope can there be of salvation, where the only means of obtaining it is rejected?

Reader! observe, how sweetly the Apostle relieves the minds of the Church, in reminding them of their confidence in JESUS. *Our conversation* (saith he) *is in heaven.* Not only a citizenship there; but their affections already gone before, to take possession, and to carry on correspondence with the inhabitants. We live below. But we breathe the atmosphere above. And He, who is the LORD of the country, even our dear LORD JESUS CHRIST, we are always on the look-out for, who is shortly expected to come, to take us to himself, that where he is, there we may be also.

And, what I yet more particularly beg the Reader to observe, *Paul saith*, that when he comes, he will change the vile bodies of his people, that they may be fashioned like unto his glorious body. By which, it should seem, the Apostle meant, that the saints of GOD, which are alive in the body, at CHRIST's coming, shall be instantly changed, without passing by death through the grave. While those that are asleep in JESUS, shall be also raised by the same Almighty power, from the dust, with glorified bodies. And this vast change, in both instances, is the special, and personal privilege, of CHRIST's redeemed ones, from their union with him. Not so the Christless dead. JESUS solemnly declares, how they are to be risen: John v. 28, 29. And the HOLY GHOST as sweetly speaks, how the dead in CHRIST shall arise, by the SPIRIT dwelling in them. Rom. viii. 11. Rev. xiv. 13.

And Reader, suffer me, on this most interesting subject to add one word more. When GOD the HOLY GHOST, in this scripture, by his servant the Apostle, saith, that CHRIST shall change our *vile* bodies; and this is said of the saints of GOD; nothing can be more evident, than that the *bodies* of regenerated believers, notwithstanding the holiness of the spirit, in being born again, whether in the grave, or alive, at the coming of CHRIST, are not changed by grace. If they were changed, they could not be said to be *vile.* If a perfection in part, even in the smallest part on the body, had taken place, at the regeneration of the spirit; that part, even in the thousandth degree, could no longer be said to be *vile*: neither could it be capable, as we see, and know it is, in every instance of corruption. Acts xiii. 36, 37. I conceive this to be so important a point of doctrine, and involves in it so many interesting consequences, that I pray the Reader not to pass away from it too hastily. It certainly is not very generally, if at all, attended to, or considered. The commonly received opinion, even by the godly, on this point is, that at regeneration, we are sanctified in part, both in body, and spirit. Whereas, if, as *Paul* saith here, CHRIST at his coming, will change our *vile* bodies; most certain it is, that no change whatever is made on the body at the new-birth, but the vast work is on the spirit *only*. And this is most plainly the case. The spirit at regeneration, is made as holy as it ever will be, being made a *partaker of the divine nature;* and having had given unto it, *all things that pertain to life and godliness.* 2 Pet. i. 3, 4. And the body remains the same, unchanged by grace, but vile, and full of sin. And hence, when it drops to its original dust, it is expressly said to be sown in *corruption,* to be sown in *weakness,* to be sown a *natural* body. And hence, as CHRIST will change the vile bodies of his saints, which are alive at his coming: so, by his resurrection, he will raise up the bodies of his saints, which sleep in the dust, and which were sown in corruption. JESUS will raise them in *incorruption,* that they may be all fashioned like to his *glorious* body, whereby he is able, even to subdue all things unto himself. Oh! precious JESUS! thou who art the resurrection and the life! May my flesh rest in hope of this assured blessedness!

REFLECTIONS.

READER! is it your happiness, as I trust it is mine, to do as the Apostle commands, to rejoice in the LORD. And are we both the true circumcision, which worship GOD in the spirit, rejoice in CHRIST JESUS, and have no confidence in the flesh! Oh! what dung, and dross, is all creature-righteousness. LORD JESUS! let it never be mine. May I be enabled, like *Paul,* to count all things but loss for the excellency of the knowledge of CHRIST JESUS my LORD. Oh! to win CHRIST, and to be found in him!

Do thou, Almighty GOD the SPIRIT, be unceasingly holding up to my view, the preciousness of JESUS; and warming my heart with his love. And cause me, like the Prophet, to be always on the watchtower, for my LORD's return: that whether at midnight, or cockcrowing, or in the morning; I may be waiting his chariot wheels, that when he cometh, I may instantly arise to receive him. Oh! LORD! I shall see thy face in glory. I shall be satisfied, when I awake with thy likeness.

CHAP. IV.

CONTENTS.

In this Chapter, Paul *closeth his Epistle. It consists chiefly of Exhortations. The Apostle's great Joy at the Prosperity of the Church.*

THEREFORE, my brethren, dearly beloved and longed for, my joy and crown, so stand fast in the Lord, *my* dearly beloved.

2 I beseech Euodias, and beseech Syntyche, that they be of the same mind in the Lord.

3 And I intreat thee also, true yoke-fellow, help those women which laboured with me in the gospel, with Clement also, and *with* other my fellow-labourers, whose names *are* in the book of life.

What a lovely frame of mind *Paul* enjoyed? And how continually we find proofs of it, in his writings. He hardly knows how to express himself, in shutting up his Epistle to the Church, in terms sufficiently strong, to shew his affection. *Brethren, dearly beloved, and longed for; my joy, and crown.* And again he repeats, *dearly beloved.* Reader! do not overlook in it, the change grace wrought: neither in the *effect*, on Paul's mind, forget the source, in God's grace. He that was once breathing out nothing but threatenings, and slaughters, against the disciples of the Lord; now unable to find words of sufficient tenderness. Acts ix. 1. And, Reader! while not overlooking the cause; connect with it, for every other occasion, of the Lord's people, how easily the same grace which converted *Paul* from a Lion to a Lamb, can convert the souls of his redeemed, from *darkness to light, and from the power of sin and Satan, to the living* God.

We have no account in any other part of Scripture, concerning those Persons *Paul* speaks of: *Euodias, Syntyche, and Clement.* No doubt, members of the Church at *Philippi*; and of the body of Christ. But let not the Reader overlook, how sweetly the Apostle intimates their union, and interest in Christ, in having their names in the book of life. This is the first, and predisposing cause, of all the blessedness of the Church. The names, by which is meant, the Persons of Christ's mystical body, are all given by the Father to the Son; are all known by him, and loved by him, from all eternity. And Christ's love of them, in redeeming them, washing them in his blood, watching over them, and carrying them, through all the time-state of their being here below, until he brings them all home to glory: all, and every Covenant mercy in Christ, ariseth from the first, and original source; they were *chosen in* Christ *before the foundation of the world.* Ephes. i. 4. And hence, from the same everlasting love, and on the same account, all the blessings they receive, from the quickening, and regenerating grace of GOD the HOLY GHOST, with all his gifts, and graces, from the first moment of GOD's electing love, until grace is summed up in glory: the whole, and every one, springs from hence, *their names are written in the book of life.*

Not that GOD needs such records, as we do, in our transactions in life; but it is spoken in accommodation to our apprehension of things. It is expressive, both of GOD's purposes, and decrees; and of the personal choice the LORD hath made, of every one. Sweet, and precious truth! And, so infinitely important is it, in the view of CHRIST, that he bid his disciples rejoice more in the assurance of it, than even the devils being made subject to them through his name. And, beyond all doubt, it is an infinitely greater motive for joy: just as much as a *cause* is beyond an *effect.* See Luke x. 20. Heb. xii. 23.

4 Rejoice in the Lord alway: *and* again I say, Rejoice.

5 Let your moderation be known unto all men. The Lord *is* at hand.

6 Be careful for nothing; but in every thing by prayer and supplication with thanksgiving let your requests be made known unto God.

7 And the peace of God, which passeth all understanding, shall keep your hearts and minds through Christ Jesus.

These Apostolic exhortations, very sweetly, and seasonably follow what *Paul* had before said, of the names of the Church being written in the book of life. For who but must rejoice, yea, and rejoice alway, when conscious of such an eternal sonship in CHRIST? Reader! the people of GOD have reason to blush, when any thing for a moment damps their joy, from the trifling events of this dying world. Children, of the King eternal, immortal, invisible, going home to their Father's house; can there be a single affliction, or sorrow, sufficient to induce distress, while these vast thoughts are cherished in the mind? Every moment lessens our abode here, and brings us nearer to our everlasting inheritance. So fast are we hastening on, that even since I began the first line, in this observation, I am by so much further on, towards the glorious open view of GOD in CHRIST. Is not this enough to make every regenerated child of GOD rejoice, and to rejoice alway? Is GOD my FATHER, who hath chosen me in CHRIST that I should be holy, and without blame before him in love? Hath he from everlasting predestinated me with the Church to the adoption of children by JESUS CHRIST to himself? Am I accepted in the Beloved, have redemption in CHRIST's blood; the forgiveness of all my sins, according to the riches of his grace; regenerated by GOD the SPIRIT, and sealed, unto the day of redemption: and shall I cease to rejoice alway; and when GOD the HOLY GHOST by his servant saith also, *again I say rejoice?* Reader! do you not behold in these things, what an everlasting source, of the most heart-felt rejoicing there is, when the Lord the Spirit hath brought all these things home to the believer's conscience, and formed Christ in the heart the hope of glory? Do you earnestly desire to participate in this joy unspeakable and full of glory? Do then, as the Apostle saith, and look up to God the Holy Ghost to enable you so to do. Be not poring over difficulties, in flesh and blood; but *give all diligence to make your calling and election sure.* So the Apostle taught the brethren. And, if a brother, so he speaks to you. *For if ye do these things,* that is, make your calling and election sure, *ye shall never fall: for so an entrance shall be ministered unto you abundantly into the everlasting kingdom of our* Lord *and* Savior Jesus Christ. See 2 Pet. i. 10, 11. and Commentary.

How very blessedly the Apostle speaks, of the nearness of the Lord, of the believer's casting all his care upon Jesus, of bringing all before him, of leaving all with him, of besieging the throne and mercy-seat of Jesus unceasingly, both with supplication, and thanksgiving. And, with what a blessed promise, the passage closeth: the peace of God *shall* keep your hearts and minds in Christ Jesus. Reader! bear with me, while I remind you again and again, (for I need to be continually reminded myself,) that these blessed Scriptures are not *Paul's,* but the words of God the Holy Ghost. *Paul is* but the penman of them. It is God the Spirit which endited them; for *all scripture is given by inspiration of* God. 2 Tim. iii. 16. We are too apt to lose sight of this. And when we do, we forget with it, that the promises in Christ Jesus, are not yea, and nay; but yea, and Amen. 2 Corinthians i. 19, 20. The one before us, is on this account sweet. The peace of God *shall* keep your hearts and minds in Christ Jesus.

8 Finally brethren, whatsoever things are true, whatsoever things *are* honest, whatsoever things *are* just, whatsoever things *are* pure, whatsoever things *are* lovely, whatsoever things *are* of good report, if *there be* any virtue, and if *there be* any praise, think on these things.

9 Those things, which ye have both learned, and received, and heard, and seen in me, do: and the God of peace shall be with you.

What a beautiful train of exhortation is here given to the Church, as the blessed, and sure consequences to all that went before. And what a train of the most gracious effects flow from the doctrines of grace, when received into the soul, and acted upon, by the blessed influences of God the Holy Ghost? Who will venture to charge the doctrines of grace, as leading to licentiousness? when, in fact, they are the only real check to the corrupt passions of men, to keep from it. When a child of God is truly, and savingly called by grace, and regenerated by the Holy Ghost; then, and not before, is he brought into a capability of shewing the faith of the Gospel, by his life and conversation. *Make the tree good* (said Jesus) *and his fruit good.* Matt. xii. 33. And it is one of the first, and leading principles of the Gospel, that a change of heart must take place, before the child of God can bring forth fruit unto God. Reader! if you know any thing of a work of grace having passed upon your own soul, you cannot but know this. And that scripture is fully confirmed in your own experience. *If ye by the* Spirit *do mortify the deeds of the body, ye shall live.* No man can mortify the deeds of the body any other way. Rom. viii. 13. Psm. xxii. 29.

Hence it should be observed, that these exhortations from the Holy Ghost, are given to the Church, and to the Church only. To exhort the unregenerated to things that are true, things honest, or just, or pure; would be like bidding the Æthiopian to change his skin, or the leopard his spots. Some there are, indeed, that are mightily fond of this general address, of *exhortations* to good, and *invitations* to come to Christ, and *offers* to take Christ, being made to the carnal world, to allure them, as they call it, to faith, and repentance. But this they do, because *they know not the Scriptures, neither the power of* God. They are ignorant of the plague of their own heart, or they would not so reason. They place more stress upon the power, and ability of the creature, to turn himself to God, than either the word of God, (or their own experience, if they attended to it more,) warrants. Hence, they call upon the world at large, and exhort them to good works. They make offers of Christ to such, in direct contradiction to Scripture: and, instead of inviting, as Jesus did, *the weary and heavy laden* only; and as his servants were commanded to do, the *thirsty;* they invite all. Reader! I beseech you for a moment to consider this subject, and, if the Lord be your teacher, you will soon discover the fallacy of it; and learn, that such men are guided by the pride and vanity of their own heart, (as if they possessed the power of persuasion,) and are not taught of God.

And, *first.* Let the Reader look over the whole volume of Scripture, in both Testaments, and he will discover, that all the exhortations, like those of *Paul* to the Church of the *Philippians,* are confined to the people of God. There is not a word of exhortation given to the nations among whom *Israel* sojourned, in the *Egyptians, Amalekites, Moabites, Babylonians,* or in short, any of the people of the earth. On the contrary, the Lord declared, that his people were a special people, to be everlastingly separated from them. And, as it was in the Old Testament dispensation; so is it under the New. *Invitations* to come to Christ, and *exhortations* to follow Christ, are addressed only to the Church. *Paul's* exhortation in this place begins, finally *brethren.* And all his Epistles, are to *the faithful in* Christ Jesus, *and the called to be saints.* See Chap. i. 1, 2. and Commentary. And to such, in whose minds God the Spirit hath wrought a saving conversion; those exhortations sent by the Spirit, are made blessed by the Spirit, and his grace enables them to obey them.

Secondly. As *exhortations* for adorning the doctrines of God our Savior in all things, are addressed but to the called in Christ Jesus: so, the *promises of grace* for power to perform them, are given to no other. *All the promises of* God *in* Christ Jesus, *are yea, and*

Amen. All is your's, saith the Apostle, *if ye be* Christ's. But upon no other terms, is there a promise given. *Cast out the bondwoman and her son,* is the language of the Holy Ghost: *for the son of the bond-woman shall not be heir with the son of the freewoman.* 2 Cor. i. 29. 1 Cor. iii. 21—23. Gal. iv. 22. to the end. Upon what grounds can men make *offers of* Christ to the world at large, in the face of these scriptures? It is like holding money to the view of a prisoner looking through his iron window on those passing by; but holding it out beyond all possibility of his reaching it.

Thirdly. As *exhortations* to follow Christ, and *invitations* to come to Christ, are wholly confined to the people of God: so *offers of grace,* are never found in the word of God as given to any other. When the Apostles, after the descent of the Holy Ghost, were ordained to the ministry; their first sermon was wholly to this amount. There were multitudes of Jerusalem-sinners, which heard their preaching; but, while they *preached* as the Lord Jesus had commanded them, Christ to all the world; *offers* of Christ were made only to his people. The discriminating feature is strongly marked in their sermons. *The promise is to you, and to your children, and to all that are afar off; even as many as the* Lord *our* God *shall call.* Acts ii. 39. And when *Paul,* under the same ordination, preached at *Antioch,* his words were these: *Men and Brethren, children of the stock of Abraham, and whosoever among ye feareth* God: *to you is the word of this salvation sent.* And what was the result of this preaching? This scripture records. *As many as were ordained to eternal life believed.* As many as were ordained to it; whether of the stock of *Abraham,* or of the *Gentile* Church, in whose hearts God had put his fear, believed. While the multitude of unbelieving Jews, contradicted, and blasphemed. Acts xiii. throughout. Gal. iii. 14 to the end.

I expect that great opposition will be made to this statement, if it so happens, that my *Poor Man's Commentary* should fall under the eye of any of the Pharisaical characters I have been alluding to. But these things affect me not. Those evidences I have brought, are sound, and scriptural. To shew such men, that the powers of persuasion they think they possess, are mere sound without meaning, is to do by them, as by the idols of *Micah : taking away their gods, and what have they more?* Judges xviii. 24.

But, say they, did not Christ give command, that *the Gospel should be preached to every creature?* To which I answer, with holy joy and thankfulness: Yes! praises to his name, he hath. And, by the preaching of his everlasting Gospel, he hath in numberless instances, gathered to himself, as he said he would, *his sheep which are scattered abroad.* And here is the blessedness of it. Wherever his sheep are, to whom he sends his Gospel; he gives a blessing to the Gospel sent, in causing his sheep to hear his voice. John x. 27. And we know, and from Scripture authority, that the same Gospel preached by the same Preacher hath the different effect according to our Lord's statement. *Paul,* when making *manifest the knowledge of* Christ *in every place,* was *a sweet savor of* Christ *in them that were saved:* and *a sweet savor in them that perished.* 2 Cor. ii. 14, to the end. Yea, when Christ himself was the Preacher, there were multitudes whom the LORD said, *could not hear his word.* John viii. 42, 43. Were offers of grace made to such? Can any man seriously believe, that JESUS invited *them?*

If men would, or could, read their Bibles under GOD the SPIRIT's teaching, they would soon discover, the mighty difference, between *preaching* the Gospel, and *inviting* men to CHRIST, or making *offers* of CHRIST, whom GOD invites not, and to whom no offers are made. Preaching the Gospel, or preaching CHRIST, which is one and the same, is to be done to the mixed multitude, as the Apostles did. And the reason is given in the divine word. Because the children of GOD are scattered abroad. And, where the LORD sends his word, we may safely conclude, the LORD hath children to gather from among them, by his word; and he will own, and bless it to them. But we no where read, that the Apostles made offers of CHRIST, but where, as discerners of spirits, 1 Cor. xii. 10. they saw, that those before whom they preached, had faith to be healed. See a beautiful instance: Acts xiv. 8—10. It is indeed, the province of men, when ordained by the HOLY GHOST, to lift up CHRIST, as *Moses lifted up the Serpent in the Wilderness.* And men, truly ordained by the HOLY GHOST, will do so. But they will go no further. *Moses* himself went no further. He lifted up the serpent, as a type of CHRIST: but we read of no offers, no invitations, no persuasions. These are the special gifts of GOD, and not man. Hence, *Paul,* after strongly reprobating false preachers, cried out: *for do I now persuade men, or GOD: or do I seek to please men? for if I yet pleased men, I should not be the servant of* CHRIST. Gal. i. 9, 10.

Reader! ponder well the subject; for it is highly important. If men would, or could discern, between *preaching* CHRIST, which, as I said before, if truly ordained by the HOLY GHOST, they are directed to do; and *offering* CHRIST, which is little short of blasphemy to attempt: they would shudder at the *latter,* and go forth with the deepest humility, and not fleshly pride, to the *former.* And yet, so little apprehensive are some of these self-taught men, of the vast difference, in the work; that they not only offer CHRIST without reserve, to all they meet, both in their preachings, and writings; but they urge their hearers, or readers, to an instant accepting, and to lay hold of the present opportunity, lest another should not be afforded them. If the subject was not so truly solemn as it is, one might be tempted to smile, at such ignorance, and presumption. As if *their persuasion,* and not GOD's *grace,* was the cause of acceptance. And as if that grace depended upon the will of man, to improve it, in the moment of man's offer, or it would be lost for ever. Oh! what a different statement the LORD the SPIRIT gives, of those, who received CHRIST: *which were born, not of blood, nor of the will of the flesh, nor of the will of man, but of* GOD. John i. 12, 13. See Coloss. iii. 12. and Commentary.

10 But I rejoiced in the Lord greatly, that now at the last your care of me hath flourished again : wherein ye were also careful, but ye lacked opportunity.

CH. IV.] PHILIPPIANS. 33

11 Not that I speak in respect of want: for I have learned, in whatsoever state I am, *therewith* to be content.

12 I know both how to be abased, and I know how to abound: every where and in all things I am instructed both to be full, and to be hungry, both to abound, and to suffer need.

13 I can do all things through Christ, which strengtheneth me.

14 Notwithstanding ye have well done, that ye did communicate with my affliction.

15 Now, ye Philippians, know also, that in the beginning of the gospel, when I departed from Macedonia, no church communicated with me as concerning giving and receiving, but ye only.

16 For even in Thessalonica ye sent once and again unto my necessity.

17 Not because I desire a gift: but I desire fruit that may abound to your account.

18 But I have all, and abound: I am full, having received of Epaphroditus the things *which were sent* from you, an odour of a sweet smell, a sacrifice acceptable, well-pleasing to God.

19 But my God shall supply all your need according to his riches in glory by Christ Jesus.

20 Now unto God and our Father *be* glory for ever and ever. Amen.

21 Salute every saint in Christ Jesus. The brethren which are with me greet you.

22 All the saints salute you, chiefly they that are of Cesar's household.

23 The grace of our Lord Jesus Christ *be* with you all. Amen.

It was written to the Philippians from Rome by Epaphroditus.

We have much to enlarge upon in those verses, if the limits of this *Poor Man's Commentary* would admit. But I must study shortness. It is blessed to observe the affection subsisting between the

Apostle, and the Church. What their liberal hearts sent him, in his imprisonment, is not said. But *Paul's* heart seems to have been full of it. He calls it, *an odour of a sweet smell; a sacrifice acceptable, and well pleasing to the* LORD. And there can be no question, but that JESUS looks on, knows all, and regards all: Matt. xxv. 40. I admire the confidence with which *Paul* speaks, that their wants should be all supplied. *My* GOD, saith he, *shall supply.* Observe the ground; *My* GOD. When a child of GOD can truly call GOD, his GOD, in Covenant; he brings in all Covenant-engagements as security, on which he bottoms all, for time, and for eternity. GOD hath engaged to be his people's GOD in CHRIST. And, therefore, they do but give him the credit of a faithful Covenant GOD, when they lay hold of him by faith, and depend upon him for the accomplishment. GOD's promises, are not as some mens' faith is, a yea, and nay gospel; but *all his promises are yea, and Amen, in* CHRIST JESUS. 2 Cor. i. 20. Let not the Reader overlook this for himself, if so be, his faith is grounded on the same security as the Apostle's. When a child of GOD can say, my GOD! like *Paul*, a fulness of earthly accommodations, or a scantiness, will both be sanctified. CHRIST, in a providence of good things below, will then bring no danger. And, if JESUS comes to any of his redeemed ones with a cross with him, the child of GOD will find a blessedness, in lodging both: *Paul* could do all things through CHRIST. And blessed be GOD, from the same cause, so can you, and I!

One more word on this Chapter. Though *Nero*, (who is here called *Cæsar*, as those emperors all were in those days,) was a most bitter enemy to CHRIST's people; yet, in his very household, JESUS had his chosen. Oh! what wonders are in discriminating grace! And, so dear to the heart of the Apostle was each saint of GOD, that he salutes every one personally. Yes! JESUS *calls each of his sheep by name:* and so will *Paul* honor them. John x. 3. *Salute* (saith he) *every saint in* CHRIST JESUS. No doubt, there were many poor ones in the Church at *Philippi*, as there were at *Jerusalem*: Rom. xv. 26. and as there are, in every Church of CHRIST to this day. But in CHRIST, their One glorious Head, they are all equally dear, and equally beloved. Let every one, saith *Paul*, be saluted, as the jewels of CHRIST. Oh! the loving, and tender heart of our great Apostle!

Let not the Reader overlook, neither fail, if so be he can, from the same cause, to join in the thanksgiving, and praise, of the Apostle, with which he folds up his letter to the Church. It is blessed, always to close all we say, or write, or do, with praise to GOD, and our FATHER, including the whole Persons of the GODHEAD, through *the grace of our* LORD JESUS CHRIST. *Amen.*

REFLECTIONS.

READER! before we close our attention to this precious Book of GOD, let us bend the knee together, and unitedly look up to the FATHER, SON, and HOLY GHOST, for all our mercies in CHRIST. What an invaluable treasure, the HOLY SPIRIT hath here given to the Church, in this blessed portion of his holy word! Oh! what precious views of CHRIST! Oh! what encouragement, and comfort, in him, to all his people. LORD the SPIRIT, do thou, in rich, free, and sovereign mercy, make the whole savor of CHRIST, which is in it, an engrafted word which is able to save the soul.

Faithful *Paul!* thou hast faithfully recorded, under the LORD's enditing, this sweet Scripture. The LORD counted thee faithful, putting thee into the ministry. And the Church finds cause to bless a faithful GOD for thy faithfulness, in thy preaching, and writing. Thou hast found the blessedness long since, of the two great points, which in the days of thy pilgrimage thou didst pant after: to win CHRIST, and to be found in Him. And all the faithful in CHRIST JESUS seek the same for their portion. Blessed Master of *Paul!* give each of thine grace, so to win thee, and so to be found in thee here by faith, that, ere long, all thy Church together, may live on thee in glory for evermore. Amen.

THE

EPISTLE OF PAUL THE APOSTLE

TO THE

COLOSSIANS.

GENERAL OBSERVATIONS.

SOME have thought, that *Colosse* was a city near to the island of *Rhodes;* where was placed a large statue called *Colossus,* and from whence this city took its name. But, it should rather seem, that *Colosse* was in *Phrygia,* the lesser Asia, near to the city of *Laodicea.* And this is certainly more probable, since *Paul* desires in this Epistle, that it should be read to the *Laodiceans.* Chap. iv. 16.

It appears, from one or two passages in this Epistle, that *Paul* had never been at *Colosse* in person, for he saith, that he had not seen their face in the flesh: chap. ii. 1. and had only heard of their faith in CHRIST JESUS, and love to the saints. Chap. i. 4. But we have reason to bless GOD the HOLY GHOST, for directing the mind of the Apostle, to commit to writing, and cause to be handed to us, so precious a portion of the word of GOD.

Concerning the date of this Epistle, it is generally supposed to have been written about the year 60; nearly at the same time as the Epistle to the *Philippians;* and to have been written at *Rome,* when *Paul* was a prisoner there.

The leading object of it, as most plainly appears, was, and is, to exalt the LORD JESUS CHRIST. *Paul* was highly taught concerning his LORD. And he well knew, that the most effectual way, under GOD the SPIRIT's teaching, to establish the Church in *the faith once delivered unto the saints*, must be, in holding up to their view, the Person and glories of JESUS. And, it must be confessed, that he hath done it in this Epistle, most blessedly. Reader! let you and I, as we enter upon the perusal of it, and as we pass through the several chapters of it, beg of GOD the SPIRIT, who directed the Apostle's pen, to lead and direct our hearts; that, as he saith in one of the chapters, we may find CHRIST in all; and *our hearts may be comforted, being knit together in love, and unto all riches of the full assurance of understanding, to the acknowledgment of the mystery of* GOD, *and of the* FATHER, *and of* CHRIST: *in whom are hid all the treasures of wisdom and knowledge!* Amen.

CHAPTER I.

CONTENTS.

The Apostle, after his usual Salutation, opens his Epistle, with giving Praises to GOD, *for the Account he had heard of the Church, concerning their Faith in* CHRIST. *He prays for Grace for them, that they might know* CHRIST, *in the Glories of his Person. And he describes the* LORD *most blessedly, in his Person, Offices, and Character.*

PAUL, an apostle of Jesus Christ by the will of God, and Timotheus *our* brother,

2 To the saints and faithful brethren in Christ which are at Colosse: Grace *be* unto you, and peace, from God our Father and the Lord Jesus Christ.

3 We give thanks to God and the Father of our Lord Jesus Christ, praying always for you.

4 Since we heard of your faith in Christ Jesus, and of the love *which ye have* to all the saints.

5 For the hope which is laid up for you in heaven, whereof ye heard before in the word of the truth of the gospel;

6 Which is come unto you, as *it is* in all the world, and bringeth forth fruit, as *it doth* also in you, since the day ye heard *of it*, and knew the grace of God in truth:

7 As ye also learned of Epaphras our dear fellow-servant, who is for you a faithful minister of Christ;

8 Who also declared unto us your love in the Spirit.

I do not think it necessary to dwell particularly on the several things contained in these verses, very blessed as they are, and full of instruction; having noticed much to the same purpose, in the Apostle's former Epistles, at their opening. I would only once again beg the Reader not to overlook, that here, as in all others of *Paul's* inspired writings, they are directed to the Church of GOD, and to that Church only. Had this grand point been all along attended to, in all ages of the Church, we should not have heard so many arguments brought forward of exhortations from those writings, to the ungodly, and carnal world. Offers of CHRIST, and invitations to come to CHRIST, instead of simply preaching CHRIST, and leaving GOD the SPIRIT to persuade sinners to accept CHRIST, would not have been so common as they are. Paul's Epistles on this point, are plain enough. They are sent *to the saints, and faithful brethren;* as this Epistle to the *Colossians* is. Paul knew, how high they stand in the value of CHRIST He calls them *the excellent of the earth, in whom is all his delight.* Psm. xvi. 3. And it is of such only it is said, that *the* LORD *hath pleasure in his people: and that he will beautify the meek with salvation.* Psm. cxlix. 4. And the thanks which *Paul* gives to GOD on their account, of this Church of the *Colossians,* is on the same ground; for their *faith in* CHRIST JESUS, and *the love to all the saints.*

9 For this cause we also, since the day we heard *it,* do not cease to pray for you, and to desire that ye might be filled with the knowledge of his will in all wisdom and spiritual understanding;

10 That ye might walk worthy of the LORD unto all pleasing, being fruitful in every good work, and increasing in the knowledge of God;

11 Strengthened with all might, according to his glorious power, unto all patience and long-suffering with joyfulness;

12 Giving thanks unto the Father, which hath made us meet to be partakers of the inheritance of the saints in light:

13 Who hath delivered us from the power of darkness, and hath translated *us* into the kingdom of his dear Son:

It is blessed to observe, how uniformly the Apostle joins prayer with all his spiritual employments. And, as it relates to the Church, it is blessed to observe also what are the chief objects of his prayers for the people, namely, that they might be filled with the knowledge of GOD's will in CHRIST; and strengthened with all might in the apprehension of it. Reader! it is a most important discovery, for our direction in going to the throne, to have it always in remembrance, what to pray for; and never to lose sight, at the same time, that it is GOD the SPIRIT, who alone can shew, what we should desire; and help us in our infirmities, how to plead for the supply. Rom. viii. 26, 27. The great evil of the present day is, that few, comparatively speaking, of GOD's people, have their spirits suitably exercised to apprehend, what will make most for their happiness. The great mass, even of those whom the LORD hath regenerated, and in some measure brought acquainted with the plague of their own heart, are for ever looking for a work, supposed to be wrought *in them;* and are not simply looking to, and depending upon, a work wrought *for them.* And, though every day's disappointment, shews them the error; yet, it is a long time before that they are fully weaned from it. Reader! mark *Paul's* prayer for the Church. *Strengthened with all might according to his glorious power:* not according to our supposed attainments; but the glorious power of CHRIST, in his finished work, and glory. It is blessed to be thus living upon him, in whom all salvation is found; and in whose Person, the whole Church is beheld compleat.

I admire what the Apostle saith, of giving thanks to the FATHER, both for his original choice of the Church to an inheritance in, and with CHRIST; and for the translation of the Church as children of his adoption, from the power of darkness, into the kingdom of his dear SON. Depend upon it, the beginnings of the triumphs of faith are found in these things. For, though by regeneration our eyes are opened, to see, and feel sin; and the first joy of the newly awakened soul, is the consciousness, when we are delivered, from darkness to light by CHRIST; yet, when GOD the SPIRIT hath brought us on to see further, and that it was GOD the FATHER who by his original choice of the Church in CHRIST, made us meet to be partakers of an inheritance of the saints in light; here we trace our mercies to the fountain-head, and we cry out with the Apostle: *Thanks be unto GOD, who always causeth us to triumph in* CHRIST. 2 Cor. ii. 19.

14 In whom we have redemption through his blood, *even* the forgiveness of sins:

15 Who is the image of the invisible God, the first-born of every creature:

16 For by him were all things created, that are in heaven, and that are in earth, visible and invisible, whether *they be* thrones, or dominions, or principalities, or powers: all things were created by him, and for him:

17 And he is before all things, and by him all things consist.

18 And he is the head of the body the church: who is the beginning, the first-born from the dead; that in all *things* he might have the pre-eminence.

19 For it pleased *the Father* that in him should all fulness dwell;

20 And, having made peace through the blood of his cross, by him to reconcile all things unto himself; by him, I *say,* whether *they be* things in earth, or things in heaven.

At this verse we enter upon one of the most sublime subjects which GOD the HOLY GHOST hath thought proper to bring before the Church, in his whole inspired writings. And I pray for grace to enter upon it with the most humble and profound reverence. The Apostle saith, that it refers to the *mystery which hath been hid from ages and from generations, but now is made manifest to his saints.* Reader! pause at the very entrance on it; and contemplate the distinguishing grace of GOD the HOLY GHOST, in this infinite condescension. Think of his vast grace, in the revelation. And then ponder his distinguishing love, in making this revelation known to his saints! And, if you and I can personally add, in our own instance! oh! the grace of GOD!

When we consider how infinitely glorious the self-existing, and incomprehensible JEHOVAH is, in his threefold character of Person, dwelling eternally in his own glory; and, that that glory could receive no addition from the praises of his creatures, for all his divine perfections must have been the same; though man, or angel, never had been; but yet, for their happiness, in the contemplation of his glory, he was pleased to go forth, in the manifestation of himself, in those various acts, whereby the LORD might be known, in the several departments of nature, providence, grace, and glory : I say, when we consider JEHOVAH in this view, and stand impressed with this conviction no less on our minds, that the making some manifestation of this his glory to his Church, which he chose in CHRIST before the world began, is the sole cause, for which that Church is called into being, and all the after acts of creation took place; what an holy awe, and profound reverence, do such thoughts beget in the soul? From hence, it plainly appears, that this Great, and Almighty LORD, being infinitely blessed in himself, and in the Personalities of his own nature and essence, raised up the magnificent structure of creation, in all its departments, to make the Church in CHRIST blessed in the knowledge of Himself. John xvii. 3. So that, in the Person of GOD's dear SON, he might unbosom himself, and come forth, as it were, from the invisibility of his Being: not to add to his glory, for that can receive no accession; but to make the Church happy in the suitable apprehension of Him! John i. 18. What a subject is here opened to the contemplation? A child of GOD, when regenerated in spirit, and raised from the *Adam*-fall of spiritual death, may, and can, in some measure, begin in this life the contemplation; but a whole eternity will not be enough to fill in the infinite boundless subject!

The wonders of creation, in all its vast extent, led to the view; and the infinite holiness of the divine nature, in the forming our first Parents in a state of innocency, and holiness, opened the first volume in the wonderful decree. But, when the Church of GOD had read somewhat of the gracious pages herein, the LORD turned over to the vast mystery, which He, who alone was found worthy to open the book and loose the seals, came to disclose; Rev. v. 1—10. Psm. ii. 7. and the Church began to learn, what angels had never been taught, of the mysterious union, of GOD and man in one Person, with all the vast concerns involved therein, in *the unsearchable riches of* CHRIST!

In this Chapter, and at the opening of those verses, GOD the SPIRIT graciously directed the mind of his servant the Apostle, to give the Church some of the great outlines of this subject. Not to gratify curiosity, but to awaken the most humble and godly reverence; not to pry into mysteries which are unfathomable, but to beget holy faith, and love. And, under the LORD the HOLY GHOST, the Apostle hath given to the Church, some of the several parts of this deep, and mysterious subject, one by one, as are enough, when GOD the SPIRIT gives his enlightening blessing with them, to raise up in the soul of the faithful, *a joy unspeakable, and full of glory.* The best service I can propose in this *Poor Man's Commentary*, will be to follow the footsteps of the Apostle, in the several features which he hath here marked, in those verses, of the Person of CHRIST, and of the office-characters in which he hath drawn him; from whence, if the LORD be graciously pleased to bless the review, both Writer, and Reader, may be benefited together.

And *first.* He describes his Person. He stiles him *the Image of the invisible* GOD. Not as GOD *only;* for there can be nothing visible in GOD. And his express character is, *the King eternal, immortal, invisible.* 1 Tim. i. 17. And He is said, to *dwell in the light which no man can approach unto; whom no man hath seen, or can see.* 1 Tim. vi. 16. So that, when the Holy Scriptures at any time speak of GOD in his threefold character of Person, they invariably speak of Him in this invisibility of essence. The mode of their existence is perfectly inconceivable. It never can be attained by any created faculties. The very nature of GOD would cease to be incomprehensible (which is his distinguishing property,) if brought any way down to the comprehension of any thing finite. When, therefore, CHRIST is said, as in this blessed Scripture, to be *the image of the invisible* GOD; it is not spoken of him, as GOD only: for GOD cannot be visible. In all his substance as GOD, he is invisible. Neither can it be said of CHRIST as man *only.* For the human nature alone, could never represent the GODHEAD. But, if the SON of GOD will condescend to take into union with himself an holy portion of human nature, (which to his eternal praise, and his Church's everlasting happiness, he hath done,) then in both he becomes *the image of the invisible* GOD, subsisting in this twofold nature, as that blessed Scripture expresses it: *For in him dwelleth all the fulness of the* GODHEAD *bodily.* Coloss. ii. 9. The Apostle goes on, and calls him *the first born of every creature.* And this throws a light upon what went before. *The first born,* that is, in this vast plan of JEHOVAH's mind. Indeed, both the first, and last, in all GOD's thoughts; and hence called the *Alpha,* and *Omega.* So JESUS called himself; Rev. i. 8. xi. 17. compared with Rev. xxii. 13. Not in the open manifestation of himself, when he tabernacled in substance of our flesh, in what is called *the fulness of time;* Gal. iv. 4. but as subsisting in Covenant engagements, he became the first born to represent the invisible GOD; and the model, or pattern, of all to be represented, in the after circumstances of the creation of man. Hence, at the creation of *Adam,* in the Council of JEHOVAH, it was said; *Let us make man in our image after our likeness:* Gen. i. 26. that is, after the likeness of Him who is *the image of the invisible* GOD; namely, Man subsisting in covenant-characters in the SON of GOD. And thus, GOD and man, in one Mediator, possessed of JEHOVAH *in the beginning of his ways, set up from everlasting.* Prov. viii. 22, 23.

Thirdly. From hence, the Apostle proceeds to enumerate some of the actions of CHRIST, in this GOD-man representation, as the image of the invisible GOD. *By him were all things created that are in heaven, and that are in earth: visible, and invisible; whether they be thrones, or dominions, or principalities, or powers: all things were created by him.* Pause!—What a manifest display here is, of every thing which can demonstrate supreme power? As GOD, He in whom this Image of the invisible GOD subsisted, was, and is, one in the essence of the GODHEAD, with the FATHER and the HOLY GHOST; and, therefore, in common with the FATHER and the HOLY GHOST, is the Creator of all things. And as *Man,* taken into Covenant engagements, became the Image, or Pattern, of whom the creation in human nature, was to be made like. This secret One was thus, in representation, *the Image of the invisible* GOD, and subsisting secretly in Covenant engagements for this express purpose. Hence it is said, that GOD *created all things by* JESUS CHRIST. Ephesians iii. 9.

Fourthly. The Apostle adds, that not only all things were created by him, but *for him.* Here opens another striking particularity of the greatness of CHRIST's Person. And, this is not spoken of him as GOD only; for in that case, the observation would have been unnecessary. Neither can it be in allusion to his manhood only. For in this sense, it would not have been correct. But, if we view it in reference to both natures, GOD and man, Mediator; it is both scriptural, and truly blessed. For JEHOVAH hath given him all things as GOD-Man-Mediator; John iii. 35. and given him to be *the head over all things to the Church, which is his body, the fulness of him that filleth all in all.* Ephes. i. 22, 23.

Fifthly. He is said to be *before all things, and by him all things consist.* The observations going before, plainly prove his priority to all things as Creator. So that, on this we need not enlarge. But, when it is also said, that *by him all things consist;* there is a beauty, and a blessedness in this expression, which demands somewhat more particularly to be remarked. *By him all things consist:* that is, as GOD-Man-Mediator. A somewhat to mediate, to come between the Creator, and the created. For the union of those natures rendered it necessary, in order for the works of creation to hang upon, or to consist in. Very certain it must be, to common sense, that nothing which is of creature-being, and no more, can have union with the GODHEAD. It cannot stand in connexion with the GODHEAD. And very certain it is, that nothing of mere creature-being, and no more, can stand in being alone, independent of GOD. Hence, in the Person of the GOD-Man CHRIST JESUS, in this twofold nature, there is found in him, and in him only, an adequate foundation to rest upon, and to have union with. And hence it is most blessedly said, that CHRIST is not only before all things, but *by him all things consist.*

Reader! I detain you for one short moment over this view of CHRIST, by whom all things consist, to consider, how eternally safe and secure, and how eternally blessed, and happy, must every individual member of his mystical body be, while all hang upon him, and all consist by him. Precious JESUS! how can the body perish, while the Head lives? How can JESUS's members be otherwise than blessed, while living *in,* and living *upon* JESUS?

Sixthly. Paul cannot give over. He speaks again of CHRIST; and now in his headship. *He is the Head of the body the Church.* He hath married our nature, our persons, hath come into the tenderest alliances with us, made us *members of his body, of his flesh, and of his bones.* All communications from him, are in, and from, the human nature of our LORD: so that, while his GODHEAD gives a fulness and a blessedness, to every token shewn; his manhood gives it an human sweetness, to make all the blessings also of the man, the GOD-man CHRIST JESUS.

And *lastly:* (for I must not trespass to add more,) *Paul* puts a blessed emphasis on the whole, in declaring, that he is *the first born from the dead also,* as well as *the first born of every creature:* that is, in his Mediator-character, he is the *first,* in all JEHOVAH's designs; so he must be the *last* in all his appointments. None shall come before. None shall remain after. As JESUS saith himself: *I am Alpha, and Omega; the beginning, and the ending, saith the* LORD *which is, which was, and which is to come.* Rev. i. 8. Reader! contemplate the glories of his Person, of whom such glorious things are said! JESUS! to thee, shall every knee bow, and every tongue confess, that *thou art* LORD, *to the glory of* GOD *the* FATHER! Philip. ii. 10, 11.

Having now, in as expeditious a manner as possible, followed the footsteps of the Apostle, in his description of CHRIST's Person; I would next, as I proposed, prosecute what he hath marked of those office-characters, in which he hath drawn him.

And *first.* Let us take notice of CHRIST's fulness. *For it pleased the* FATHER *that in him should all fulness dwell.* The Reader will observe, that the words *the Father,* are in Italicks. By which is meant, that they are not in the original. But our Translators have very properly introduced them; because, though all the Persons of the GODHEAD are engaged in Covenant purposes, in all things relating to CHRIST, and his Church; yet, it is among the special and personal offices of the FATHER, as appears from other parts of Scripture, the giving all things into the hands of CHRIST. His is to give both the Church and all spiritual blessings for the Church to CHRIST. John iii. 35, and xvii. 2, 4, 6.

In regard to the fulness here spoken of, as dwelling in CHRIST; care must always be had, to consider it in relation wholly to his Person, and office-character, as *Mediator.* For, as GOD, in his divine nature, and essence; all fulness, yea, all divine perfections, are his, in common with the FATHER, and the HOLY GHOST. Nothing can be said to be *given* to him in this sense, for they are his own eternally. But the Mediator-fulness, is given to him for the Church, which is his body; and in this character of headship, his is *the fulness, that filleth all in all.* Ephes. i. 17, to the end. Reader! pause over the contemplation, for it is most blessed. A fulness in himself, as GOD-Man-Mediator. A fulness of temporal, spiritual, and eternal blessings, to impart to his body the Church. A mediator-fulness, as the everlasting LORD of all creation, to rule over, and direct, in all the departments of nature, providence, grace, and glory. So that, while the LORD JESUS is in a special, and personal manner, the Head of his body the Church, for grace here, and glory for ever; he is the head of all principality, and power: Ephes. i. 22. and, as the Prophet described him, *his dominion is an everlasting dominion, and his kingdom, that which shall be for ever.* Dan. ii. 44. and iv. 34, 35. Rev. v. 13.

The Reader will not expect me to enter into a description of this *all fulness,* which it hath pleased the FATHER, to invest his dear SON as Mediator with. This exceeds all the powers of the imagination, to conceive. And no pen, or tongue, or angel, could describe, or make up the vast arithmetic, in calculation. But every child of GOD, in the circumstances of his own life, should be for ever, like the Prophet on his watch-tower, observing the unceasing tendencies of the LORD's manifestation to himself. And if he were, what an huge volume might a short life record, of the continual love-tokens, which JESUS sends his redeemed, when receiving *out of his fulness, and grace for grace.* Habak. ii. 1. John i. 16.

Secondly. Paul speaks of another office of CHRIST, namely, redemption; the great purpose which brought him from heaven. The Apostle, indeed, began his account of CHRIST's Person with this, in the opening of this paragraph, when he said: *In whom we have redemption through his blood, even the forgiveness of sins.* And here again, in the close of the sentence, he dwells upon the same soul-reviving subject most blessedly, when saying: *And having made peace through the blood of his cross, by him to reconcile all things unto himself: by him, I say, whether they be things on earth, or things in heaven.* I must entreat the Reader to observe with me, with what emphasis the HOLY GHOST holds forth to the Church, this vast work of the LORD JESUS. Redemption is CHRIST's own personal labors, and sufferings. It is to his own personal glory, and honor. The work is all his own. The glory his. And GOD the HOLY GHOST is unceasingly impressing the sense of it upon the Church. It was taught the Prophet in a vision, ages before CHRIST became incarnate, when he saw him coming up as a mighty conqueror from the war; and yet, as a servant, treading the wine-press. It was CHRIST alone, which trod the wine-press of the wrath of GOD. And of the people there was none with him. Isaiah lxiii. 1—6. Rev. xix. 15, 16.

And, I beg the Reader to observe yet further, how strong an emphasis is laid on the word *him. By him I say,* saith the Apostle. We have a similar expression, Ephes. i. 10. And the design is to shew, the special, peculiar, and personal fitness of CHRIST, as GOD-Man Mediator, to this work of redemption. For, if it could be supposed possible, that any other but the SON of GOD in our nature, could have accomplished redemption; by so much would it have lessened the greatness of his love, and ability, in doing that, which another could do. So that, it forms a special feature in the Person of our adorable *Emanuel*, that in Him alone, we find One *mighty to save*. Acts iv. 12. Heb. vii. 26. If the Reader will turn to Heb. i. 3, he will find a similar precious testimony, to this most blessed truth, that CHRIST, by *himself*, purged our sins. And, as in the redemption of his people; so in the destruction of his, and their enemies, it is his triumphs over them in it, or as it should have been rendered, (and is indeed, in the margin of the Bible,) *in himself*; meaning, his own personal triumphs over them. Coloss. ii. 13. Oh! what wonders are found, in the *Person* of the LORD JESUS CHRIST! Oh! the triumphs of his offices, and grace!

21 And you, that were some time alienated and enemies in *your* mind by wicked works, yet now hath he reconciled.

22 In the body of his flesh through death, to present you holy and unblameable and unreproveable in his sight:

23 If ye continue in the faith grounded and settled, and *be* not moved away from the hope of the gospel, which ye have heard, *and* which was preached to every creature which is under heaven; whereof I Paul am made a minister;

The Apostle, under GOD the SPIRIT, having so blessedly held forth CHRIST, in his Person, and offices; now proceeds to shew, the gracious effects of the whole, on the persons of his members. The Church of GOD, being born in the common nature of the Adam-fall, and involved in the same ruin by sin, as the world at large; the first blessed consequences of the FATHER's electing love, and the SON's redeeming grace, which the Church, in every individual member is made sensible of, is, when by the regenerating work of GOD the SPIRIT, *they that were some time alienated, and enemies in their mind, by wicked works, are now reconciled in the body of* CHRIST's *flesh; and brought from darkness to light, and from the power of sin, and Satan, to the living* GOD. I pray the Reader to observe, the beautiful harmony observed in those Covenant transactions, between the Persons of the GODHEAD. Each glorious Person concurs, and co-operates in the great design. GOD the FATHER chose the Church in CHRIST, that *it should be holy, and without blame before him in love; before the foundation of the world*. Ephes. i. 4. GOD the SON, having betrothed his Church to himself for ever, undertook, and hath accomplished his merciful purpose in the same, to redeem her from the ruins of the fall, and preserve her in himself for ever. 1 Gal. i. 4. And GOD the HOLY GHOST, by regeneration, quickens the Church, when *dead in trespasses and sins*, to a new, and spiritual life, in CHRIST JESUS; whereby she is presented, *holy, and unblameable, and unreprovable in his sight.* And thus the purposes of JEHOVAH, FATHER, SON, and SPIRIT, are accomplished, to the Redeemer's glory, and the Church's happiness; and all terminates as GOD's first, and original design, had all along in view, that the whole shall be, *to the praise of the glory of his grace, wherein he hath made us accepted in the Beloved.* See Ephesians i. 3—10. and Commentary.

Having fully established this blessed truth, we come next to observe, what the Apostle hath said of the child of GOD, *continuing in the faith, and being grounded, and settled, and not moved away from the hope of the Gospel.* The Apostle begins the verse with an *If*. If (saith he) ye continue in the faith. I beg the Reader to observe with me, that this *if*, is not in a way of condition; as if GOD's grace depended upon the will of man. This would be, if true, a sad concern; and make the promises of GOD, which are now in CHRIST JESUS, all yea, and Amen, a doubtful thing; and reduce the whole of the believer's hope, to a mere yea and nay gospel. Blessed be GOD! this is not the case. *If we believe not, yet he abideth faithful; he cannot deny himself.* 2 Tim. ii. 13. If the Reader will attend to one or two considerations on this subject, it will not only serve to put what the Apostle hath here said in a clear point of view; but explain similar passages, which we meet with in the word of GOD, of a like nature.

And *first*. The *if* here introduced, cannot be intended as any thing of condition, for obtaining those rich blessings just before spoken of; because the whole, and every part of them, are the result of GOD's original purposes, which he purposed in himself, before the world began. They were not proposed, as depending for any thing upon human merit, or human improvement; but wholly the consequence of divine will, and pleasure. GOD's Covenant love in CHRIST, and not the Church's stedfastness of faith in CHRIST, being the bottom, and foundation of security. Deut. vii. 9. Jerem. xxxii. 40.

Secondly. The blessings which the Church is here said to be brought into, in being presented *holy, and unblameable, and unreproachable, in the* LORD's *sight;* have been produced by the joint pleasure, and operations of the whole Persons of the GODHEAD. GOD the FATHER's choice, GOD the SON's redemption-work, GOD the SPIRIT's regenerating grace, have taken place. And the whole hath been unaccompanied by any act of faith, or love, or works, or obedience, on the part of the highly favored objects of the LORD's bounty. The *if*, therefore, of the Apostle, in this verse, could have no reference to the blessed things spoken of; but must have another, and a very different meaning.

Thirdly. Let the Reader yet further observe, that what the Apostle had just before taught the Church, of their being presented holy, and unblameable, and unreprovable, he speaks as of a thing done and accomplished, and not now to be done. By virtue of GOD the FATHER's love, in having chosen the Church, and CHRIST having redeemed it, and the HOLY GHOST having quickened it, the vast mercy was now bestowed. Therefore, as the Church is brought into a blessed participation of those things, from her interest in CHRIST, and union with CHRIST, in his justifying righteousness, and all the glorious consequences arising out of his redemption; her continuing stedfast in the faith cannot be made a party *cause*, but is simply an *effect*. Hence, therefore, it must immediately follow, that what is here said of continuing in the faith, hath not the smallest reference to any thing like a *condition*, either for the first appointment of GOD's original and eternal purposes, or in the accomplishment of those purposes in time by the high contracting powers; neither in the Church's being brought into the actual possession of this unspeakable mercy, in being presented holy, and unblameable, and unreprovable in GOD's sight.

It is time now to enquire what may be supposed, according to the general analogy of Scripture, to have been the Apostle's meaning, by the expression, *if ye continue in the faith, grounded and settled*. Scripture is best explained by Scripture. In the third chapter of the Epistle to the Hebrews, verses 6, and 14, the same Apostle useth similar words. He had been speaking on much the same subject, of our oneness with CHRIST. And he saith, *Whose house are we, if we hold fast the confidence, and the rejoicing of the hope, firm unto the end*. So again. *We are made partakers of* CHRIST, *if we hold the beginning of the confidence stedfast unto the end*. Now here, in both these instances, as in the former, the things proposed are not for future possession, for they are actually obtained. Hence, there is nothing of a *condition* here, no more than in the former. Very plainly, therefore, the *continuing* in the one instance, and the *holding fast* in the other, are meant but as *evidences* and *effects*, that those whose faith is so blessed, do truly live in the enjoyment of the mercies. And the child of GOD who is a partaker of CHRIST, and presented holy and unblameable as such in GOD's sight, will feel all the blessedness of this adoption-character, if, through grace, he continues firm in the faith and persuasion of his interest therein, and is not *moved away from the hope of the Gospel*.

24 Who now rejoice in my sufferings for you, and fill up that which is behind of the afflictions of Christ in my flesh, for his body's sake, which is the church:

I beg the Reader to consider this verse by itself. It is, in my esteem, a very sweet one. And the question arising out of it immediately strikes the mind, what afflictions of CHRIST were behind, in which JESUS became concerned for his body's sake, which is the Church? It is impossible *Paul* could mean that any afflictions remained for the SON of GOD to sustain, in a way of finishing redemption. All had been fully accomplished, when with a loud voice on the cross, JESUS said, *It is finished*. John xix. 30. The HOLY GHOST is express to the same, in his blessed testimony of CHRIST, that *when he had by himself purged our sins, sat down on the right hand of the Majesty on high*. Heb. i. 3. Never would the grave have delivered up such a prisoner as CHRIST by his death was, had sin not been done away. Neither heaven have admitted CHRIST to the right hand of the Majesty on high, had redemption-work not been finished! See Rom. vi. 9, 10. Heb. x. 11—25.

Neither could *Paul* have any one meaning whatever in relation to any sufferings of his. One of the great features of CHRIST's redemption-work is, that in the accomplishment of it, *His own arm brought salvation,* and *of the people there was none with him.* Isaiah lxiii. 3—5. *Paul* himself is out of the question. So that on neither of those accounts can we accept the words of this verse. There is, however, a sense, and a very sweet one, according to my view it is, in which the Apostle's words may be accepted in relation to the afflictions of CHRIST, which *Paul* calls behind. I mean in what hath respect wholly to his body the Church. And which, even now in heaven, JESUS, in his human nature, may be said to enter into a certain concern for. And in a way, though without the smallest decrease of his glory, but rather to his praise, he may be said to take part in the afflictions of his people. If the Reader will bear with me, I will endeavor to explain myself.

And, *first.* The SON of GOD, in our nature, having finished redemption-work, and returned to heaven, he wears that nature in an everlasting union with his GODHEAD. So that as GOD and man in one Person, he hath a perfect sense and apprehension of what constitutes the nature of both. He knows as GOD. He feels as man. Hence, it follows, that his consciousness of what our nature is by his own, cannot but make him enter into an intimate concern and fellow feeling, in all that belongs to his Church. He knows all, enters into the concerns of all, and feels for all. So that the foot of any of his redeemed ones upon earth cannot be crushed, but the head knows it, and feels it in heaven. In proof of this, JESUS preached it to *Paul* at the time he was persecuting his little ones. He called to him from heaven. Acts ix. 5.

Secondly. The very reason for which CHRIST took upon him our nature was, for the express purpose, that *he might be a merciful and faithful High Priest;* the HOLY GHOST gives this as the motive. *In all things it behoved him to be made like unto his brethren.* And the reason is added, *For in that he himself hath suffered being tempted: he is able to succour them that are tempted.* Heb. ii. 17, 18. What a sweet relief it is, to every tempted child of GOD, in his seasons of trial, to call this to mind. And as this high priestly office of the LORD JESUS, is the peculiar and special employment of CHRIST now in heaven; must it not form the very quality of his office, be a part to feel for those he pleads; and to sympathize in those exercises of theirs, as though they were his own? And is it not in this sense *Paul* meant the afflictions of CHRIST, which are behind, for his body's sake, which is the Church?

If it be demanded, how these feelings operate on his holy nature, and how the heart of JESUS is affected with pity, in participating with his suffering members upon earth? I presume not to answer. These subjects are not the province of man. It is the fact itself, and not the mode of operation, that the Church is concerned to know. Every attempt to investigate these mysteries is presumptuous. From all unsuitable, and unbecoming enquiries, I would wish to retire with the most profound humility. But to know, that JESUS is, from his own feelings, intimately acquainted with ours; not only knows them, as GOD, but feels for them as man; and takes part with all that concerns his redeemed: surely these are among the highest consolations of faith! Reader! I pray GOD to make the review profitable. And may GOD the HOLY GHOST, as the remembrancer of CHRIST JESUS, bring the thought continually home to the affections of the LORD's people: that in all their afflictions he is afflicted, and takes part for his body's sake, which is the Church.

25 Whereof I am made a minister, according to the dispensation of God, which is given to me for you, to fulfil the word of God;

26 *Even* the mystery which hath been hid from ages and from generations, but now is made manifest to his saints:

27 To whom God would make known what *is* the riches of the glory of this mystery among the Gentiles; which is Christ in you, the hope of glory.

28 Whom we preach, warning every man, and teaching every man in all wisdom; that we may present every man perfect in Christ Jesus:

29 Whereunto I also labour, striving according to his working, which worketh in me mightily.

I do not think it necessary to swell the pages of the *Poor Man's Commentary* on those things which are too plain to need observation. Neither in a work of this kind to lead the Reader into the investigation of what is here said, concerning the length of time in which the mystery of the Gospel was hidden from ages, and from generations. I stop the Reader only to observe, that when *Paul* speaks, as he doth here, of CHRIST in his people, *the hope of glory*, the expression means, such a revelation of the LORD, in the glories of his Person, and the compleatness of his salvation, as make him indeed, to every regenerated believer, known, and enjoyed, as *the hope of Israel, and the* SAVIOR *thereof*. *Paul* very properly here, and elsewhere, calls it, CHRIST *revealed in me*, Gal. i. 16. For it becomes an *inward* manifestation of an *outward* work. Not a work *in* me, but *for* me. Not *inherent* holiness in the sinner; but *derived* holiness from the SAVIOR. Not a supposed improvement in ourselves by the whole procuring benefit from CHRIST: yea CHRIST altogether, the LORD *our righteousness!* The blessedness of a life of faith lies in this. Yea, the blessedness of a life of glory can only be in the same. And while men, who are unacquainted with *the plague of their own heart*, are looking for holiness within, and taking comfort from their supposed progressive sanctification; looking to CHRIST to make up, if any, their deficiency: *Paul* calls off the Church from every thing of self, and self-attainments, to fix the soul wholly upon CHRIST. *Paul* himself trusted no more upon inward sanctification, as some men call it, but none ever knew, than he would upon a law righteousness in himself, to recommend him to GOD. To CHRIST he looked wholly, desiring *to win* CHRIST, *and to be found in him.* And the first, and last, consolation of this great Apostle was, that CHRIST *was made of* GOD, *unto all his Church, wisdom, and righteousness, sanctification, and redemption, that he which gloried might glory in the* LORD. 1 Cor. i. 30.

I admire the very sweet way, and manner, in which *Paul* closeth up this chapter, in addressing the Church. It is to the Church *Paul* is preaching: and to that Church he preacheth CHRIST. *Warning every man, and teaching every man in all wisdom* (saith the Apostle) *that we may present every man perfect in* CHRIST JESUS. What every man was it *Paul* warned and taught? Surely the Church. For who but the Church could be presented perfect in CHRIST JESUS? None but the members of CHRIST can be perfect in CHRIST. And what wisdom, yea, all wisdom was it, that he warned every man in? Surely CHRIST himself, who, in his comprehensive name, includes every thing contained in *that wisdom which maketh wise unto salvation.* Who therefore doth not see, that all this refers to the Church, not to the world; to CHRIST's members, and not to those who have no interest in him. But how did *Paul* know how to warn every man, and teach every man of the LORD's people, and not they that are without? Simply by preaching CHRIST, and CHRIST only. For CHRIST *is the power of* GOD, *and the wisdom of* GOD, *for salvation to every one that believeth.* Therefore, as *faith cometh by hearing, and hearing by the word of* GOD, whenever the LORD opened the eyes of any, *Paul* warned every one, and taught every one only of CHRIST. And he found, that *as many as were ordained to eternal life believed.* Acts xiii. 48. And here exhortation becomes most blessed, because they are warned and taught, and GOD the SPIRIT is their teacher, that they can be presented perfect *only in* CHRIST JESUS!

REFLECTIONS.

EVERLASTING praise to GOD the FATHER, SON, and HOLY GHOST, for the gracious discoveries made to the Church in this blessed chapter of divine love, and for all the manifestations of Covenant grace and mercy, in the Person, work, and offices of the LORD JESUS CHRIST, as the Head and Husband of his Church from one eternity to another. Oh! what a glorious view is here given of CHRIST in this Chapter! LORD! be it my study, night and day, under divine teaching, to learn and *know the only true* GOD, *and* JESUS CHRIST *whom he hath sent!*

And, oh! thou blessed *Emmanuel,* GOD and Man in One Person! Oh! may I unceasingly meditate on the glories of thy nature and essence, One with the FATHER, and the HOLY GHOST, GOD *over all, blessed for ever. Amen.* May I behold thee in thy Mediator glory, the image of the invisible GOD, the first born of every creature! And, oh! what glories do I here behold and contemplate in thy Person, before that a single act of redemption-work was wrought out by my LORD for his Church, in the time-state of her fallen nature; when as I here read, by thee all things are created that are in heaven and earth; all things were created not only by thee, but for thee, and thou art before all things, and by thee all things consist! Oh! the glories of my LORD, in creation, providence, grace, and glory! And when I call to mind thy wonders of love to the Church in time, thine incarnation, baptisms, temptations, sorrows, miracles, life, death, resurrection, ascension, return to glory, and the wonders of thine unchanging priesthood! When I behold thee now still carrying on the same design, wearing our nature, appearing in our stead, taking up the Persons and causes of all thy people, feeling *with* them, and feeling *for* them, and wilt never cease, until thou hast brought thy blood-bought sons and daughters, with all thy royal family round thy throne, to be with thee for ever? Oh! for grace, until this great day of my GOD shall come, to love thee, and to live to thee, and to hail thy wonderous name! LORD! be thou my portion day by day, that by faith in this blessed hope, I may now live, and at length, in the full assurance of glory, die, and be one with thee for ever!

CHAP. II.

CONTENTS.

Paul *is speaking very blessedly of* CHRIST. *He warns the Church against Philosophy and vain Deceit.*

FOR I would that ye knew what great conflict I have for you, and *for* them at Laodicea, and *for* as many as have not seen my face in the flesh:

2 That their hearts might be comforted, being knit together in love, and unto all riches of the full assurance of understanding, to the acknowledgement of the mystery of God, and of the Father, and of Christ;

3 In whom are hid all the treasures of wisdom and knowledge.

The opening of this Chapter gives a very lovely representation of *Paul's* mind. He had never seen the Church of the *Colossians.* But what of that? They were CHRIST's flock, and *Paul* loved them for it. Reader! is it not so to us with CHRIST himself? You and I have never seen CHRIST in the flesh. But can we not say with one of old concerning him, *whom having not seen we love; in whom though now we see him not, yet believing, we rejoice with joy unspeakable, and full of glory.* 1 Pet. i. 8.

Observe how gloriously the mystery of the HOLY THREE in One, is spoken of, and known, and enjoyed, when the souls of GOD's people are knit together in love. And observe, how blessedly CHRIST in his fulness is described: *In whom are hid all the treasures of wisdom and knowledge.* Then, Reader! if it be so, (as that it most assuredly is,) it is of no use to seek either for wisdom or knowledge elsewhere. But for the encouragement of all that seek after CHRIST, be their circumstances ever so poor or wretched, they are sure to find. Yea, JESUS, under his well-known character of Wisdom, is represented as not waiting to be sought for, but himself coming to invite every wretchedly, ignorant sinner, whom GOD the SPIRIT hath caused to see his want and misery, to come and buy wisdom of him, *without money, and without price.* Isaiah lv. 1. And those treasures being said to be hidden, doth not mean hidden by way of concealment, but by way of safety and security. They are, indeed, hidden from the wise and prudent; that is, the wise in their own eyes, and the prudent in their own conceit; but they are revealed unto babes. For so JESUS thanked his FATHER; Matt. xi. 25. And if the Reader will turn to the book of the *Proverbs,* he will find CHRIST, as Wisdom, crying aloud, and calling upon his people to come and find a fulness of wisdom and knowledge. *I love them* (saith he) *that love me, and them that seek me early shall find me. I will cause them that love me to inherit substance, and I will fill their treasures.* See Prov. viii. throughout.

4 And this I say, lest any man should beguile you with enticing words,

5 For though I be absent in the flesh, yet am I with you in the spirit, joying and beholding your order, and the stedfastness of your faith in Christ.

6 As ye have therefore received Christ Jesus the Lord, *so* walk ye in him:

7 Rooted and built up in him, and stablished in the faith, as ye have been taught, abounding therein with thanksgiving.

8 Beware lest any man spoil you through philosophy and vain deceit, after the tradition of men, after the rudiments of the world, and not after Christ.

9 For in him dwelleth all the fulness of the godhead bodily.

10 And ye are complete in him, which is the head of all principality and power:

Within the compass of these few verses, we have several very interesting subjects. I must be brief. It appears, that in the Apostle's days, as well as in ours, the Church of CHRIST had to contend with what *Paul* calls *enticing words of man's wisdom.* It was made up of *philosophy,* falsely so called, and *vain deceit.* But here was the line of distinction, *it was not after* CHRIST. Then was it *against*

CHRIST, for so CHRIST saith, *he that is not with me is against me.* Matt. xii. 30. There is nothing neutral in this war. And I beg the Reader yet further to observe, this malice to the Church of JESUS came not from the openly profane. It was not the opposition of the licentious, or the daring ungodly, but professors of religion. Yea, it should seem, from what *Paul* saith of their beguiling and enticing words, that they were very zealous for an holy life and conversation. Such were the Pharisees of our LORD's days. Such it should appear were those of *Paul's* days. Such there hath been in all days. And such, I am sure, are in ours. But the HOLY GHOST hath marked their real character by his servant, when he saith, *they are not after* CHRIST!

But, Reader! we are much more concerned to know what remedy GOD the HOLY GHOST, by his servant *Paul*, hath here pointed out to counteract their fallacy, than to go in any further search after their character. And, sure I am, that what the blessed SPIRIT hath in those few verses commanded, if attended to, and accompanied with his blessing, must prove the most effectual preservative against an whole host of Pharisees, men of false philosophy, and the rudiments of the world. It cannot possibly fail, but must for ever silence all opposition, both of the leaven of the Pharisee, and of hypocrisy, because it is wholly *of* CHRIST, it comes *from* CHRIST, it leads *to* CHRIST, and rests all *upon* CHRIST. LORD! I would say for myself, and all his people, give us to hear in this sweet scripture *what the* SPIRIT *saith unto the Churches!* And thus the LORD speaks. *As ye have therefore received* CHRIST JESUS *the* LORD, *so walk ye in him, rooted and built up in him, and stablished in the faith as ye have been taught, abounding therein with thanksgiving.* Let us examine these great points one by one.

And *first. As ye have received* CHRIST JESUS *the* LORD. The question is how have you received him? There can be but one proper way, and that is when a man receives CHRIST as a poor, needy, ruined, and undone sinner is supposed to receive him. Reader! if so be *you* have received CHRIST, it is easy for you to describe *how* you received him. You came, if you came right, under the fullest sense, that you had nothing but sin, you were nothing but a sinner, and you needed CHRIST as a whole and compleat SAVIOR. Now then it is GOD the HOLY GHOST, which in this scripture positively commands, that as you *first* received him, so are you to receive him *now*. For you have no more to bring him the *last* day of your abode on earth, in a way of recommendation, than you had the *first* day you heard of his blessed name. And as you did not halve it with CHRIST when you fled to him for salvation, so have you nothing to divide with him now. And I will be bold to say, that if this blessed precept of GOD the HOLY GHOST was closely followed, and such views of JESUS, as are here held up by the HOLY GHOST, were kept alive in all hearts, preached by all ministers in all Churches of the LORD's people, and by grace pursued by every one professing the eternal truths of the Gospel, it would tend, under the divine blessing, more effectually to silence the unhumbled pride of the Pharisee, who hath never been brought acquainted with the plague of his own heart, than all the exhortations to the carnal, and to the followers of false philosophy and the rudiments of the world.

Secondly. The very reception of CHRIST in this manner, both first and last, will cause the poor, sensible sinner to accept him under all his offices and characters. I shall receive him as CHRIST, that is, GOD and man in one Person, GOD's CHRIST, GOD's anointed, GOD's chosen, GOD's sent, GOD's sealed. Hence, I shall receive him in GOD's name and authority. I shall receive him as JESUS, a SAVIOR, for such was, and is, and will be, his name, *to save his people from their sins.* Matt. i. 21. And I shall receive him as my LORD, for the whole affections of my soul will bow before him, when the LORD hath made me *willing in the day of his power.* Psm. cx. 3. And, oh! what a blessed security shall I find against sin, and all the tremendous consequences of it, when receiving CHRIST JESUS the LORD in all the compleatness of his finished salvation; and as GOD the FATHER's remedy, of his own providing, in delivering from the wrath to come.

Thirdly. And when, under divine teaching, the soul is daily led to see and feel her daily need of CHRIST, so as to receive him *every day*, as he was received the *first day*, and to be made sensible that equally will he be needed to the very *last day*, a soul so taught of GOD, will be in no danger of philosophy or vain deceit. To walk *in* CHRIST, and to act faith *upon* CHRIST, will be the leading principle of the soul. Every duty will be undertaken only in his strength, and every desire of the soul will be but for his glory. Reader! pause over this view of the subject! Can a child of GOD do otherwise than walk *in* CHRIST, as long as he makes CHRIST the whole of salvation? Is not that man rooted and built up in CHRIST, whose springs of spiritual life are all in him? Is he not established in the faith who makes CHRIST both the Alpha and Omega, the first and the last in his salvation? But if a man comes to CHRIST at the first as a poor, self-condemned sinner, and in the after stages of life fancieth he hath now somewhat to bring to the LORD, and, therefore, brings of his own, as a procuring cause, or, as some men call it, the evidences of his calling, what is this but a departure from the original plan of coming? It cannot be said that he is now walking in CHRIST JESUS the LORD as he first received him. And, hence, this command of the HOLY GHOST is not obeyed.

Reader! bear with me while I say, that, according to my view of things, to this one cause is to be ascribed the leanness of the Church in the present day, and even some, which have, in times past, learned *the truth as it is in* JESUS. Many there are, who, when the LORD first called them from darkness to light, set out upon the sweet plan of receiving CHRIST, as GOD the HOLY GHOST hath here set him forth. But it may be said of them, as the LORD JESUS himself said to the Church at *Ephesus, I have somewhat against thee, because thou hast left thy first love.* Rev. ii. 4. It is a melancholy consideration that our affections to CHRIST should lessen, and that we should fancy we need him not as much in the after parts of life, as when first we came to him, self-condemned, and self-loathing; when it is notorious to every man who is no stranger to the plague of his own heart, that we multiply transgressions as we multiply days!

Lastly, to add no more. This sweet command of GOD the SPIRIT which bids us walk in CHRIST, under the same needy circumstances as we first received CHRIST, bids us also to *abound in* CHRIST *with thanksgiving.* Precious consideration to a child of GOD, that is daily receiving out of CHRIST'S fulness, and grace for grace. There will be cause for unceasing praise, and abounding thanksgiving, as long as we are drawing out of the wells of salvation. While I am living upon the daily alms of my LORD, every visit to his mercy-seat will be opening new cause for joy, for I shall go out empty and return full. I shall lose sight of my nothingness in my LORD's all-sufficiency. And from receiving CHRIST JESUS the LORD as I received him the first day, I shall be rooted and built up in him the last day. JESUS will be unceasingly precious, when I find my soul established in him. And while he leads me in the paths of righteousness for his Name's sake, He will be my strength and song, and I shall abound in him with thanksgiving.

I now beg the Reader's attention to what is contained in the latter part of this paragraph. *Paul* having, in what went before, stated the necessity of always receiving CHRIST the same, here gives the reason of it: *For in him dwelleth all the fulness of the* GODHEAD *bodily.* And, as if fearing such a stupendous contemplation might overwhelm the mind, (as it might well be supposed to do,) he adds, *ye are complete in him who is the head of all principality and power.* Reader! do not expect an explanation of this wonderful mystery, GOD manifest in the flesh, GOD dwelling in flesh, yea, all the fulness of the GODHEAD dwelling in him bodily! This is not the province either of men or angels to unfold. Neither is it revealed for the object of our discovery, but for our faith. One point only I beg particularly to notice in it, by way of recommending it more affectionately, as an article of faith, to the Reader's heart, and to my own: namely, that what is here said of the fulness of the GODHEAD dwelling in CHRIST bodily, most evidently and plainly means in CHRIST personal. Not as GOD is said in scripture to dwell with his people, and walk in them, which means nothing more than in a way of grace. But by the indwelling of the GODHEAD bodily in CHRIST, means a oneness and union of GOD and man in one Person; so that the human nature of CHRIST is filled with the divine nature, and both are so inseparably united, as to form but One and the same Person. Oh! the glorious truth! Oh! the vast dignity bestowed on the Church!

But how is this immense blessing enhanced to our view, when the Apostle adds, *and ye are complete in Him.* Complete, not only in all blessedness which arise out of CHRIST's offices in redemption, justification, sanctification, and the like, but compleat by means of the Church's union with CHRIST, and her oneness with him. For as CHRIST Personal, GOD and Man in One, forms his glorious name, CHRIST; so the Church's union with CHRIST, brings with it an interest in all that belongs to him as CHRIST. It is a personal union of the Church with him, as her Head and Husband. And it thereby becomes a vital, spiritual union, living in him, and living by him: *For he that is joined to the* LORD *is One Spirit.* 1 Cor. vi. 17. Ephes. v. 32.

I must not trespass in calling the Reader to the contemplation of the thousandth part of the blessings which arise out of this union. But a doctrine full of such stores of comfort, must not pass wholly unnoticed. I will beg to notice a few.

And, *first*. As the source and fountain of all, let the Reader pause over this precious view of One in his own nature, in whom the fulness of the GODHEAD dwelleth bodily. Though we can form no one idea that can bear the least proportion to what it really is, in the infinite dimensions of GODHEAD filling CHRIST's manhood; yet we may suppose that the SON of GOD, in this beauty and glory of Being, must be an object of unequalled excellency and greatness, since GOD the FATHER when contemplating him, and bringing him forth to the Church was thus heard to speak of him; *Mine Elect*, saith GOD, *in whom my soul delighteth!* Isaiah xlii. 1. Such is the glory of his Person as GOD-man, that independent of all acts or works to be afterwards wrought by him, CHRIST himself is infinitely more lovely and more beloved in GOD's esteem, than any object beside. Millions of worlds, including all their inhabitants, sink to nothing in comparison. Matt. iii. 17. Luke ix. 35. John xii. 28.

Secondly. What a view doth the contemplation of such a Being afford to the soul of a regenerated believer, when he adds to the thought of what a Person so full of glory is in himself, is also in the infinite perfections of dispensing to others! I fear that this view of our adorable CHRIST is not considered, even by the Church of GOD, as it ought in the full extent of the subject. We are apt to confine our views of CHRIST as GOD-man Mediator, as if his office was limited to his body the Church. My Brother! beg of GOD the HOLY GHOST to remove this narrow notion, and glorify the LORD JESUS CHRIST more to your view, and you will behold CHRIST as GOD-man Mediator, carrying on all the executive part of JEHOVAH's administration, in all the departments of nature, providence, grace, and glory. Our LORD JESUS CHRIST formed worlds, and both upholds all things, and governs all things. And this he doth as Mediator. Without this union of GOD and man, creation itself would have wanted a foundation. *By him all things consist.* Hence the sweetness and preciousness of this scripture, as well as the glory of it. *In him dwelleth all the fulness of the* GODHEAD *bodily.* Oh! what a glorious object of everlasting love, adoration, and delight, is our LORD JESUS! Well might the Psalmist call him, *the praise of all his saints.* Psm. cxlviii. 14.

Thirdly. But what endears the whole to the view of every truly regenerated child of GOD, and makes our meditation of JESUS so sweet, is, that while we are taught to know him as the GOD-man, in whom *dwelleth all the fulness of the* GODHEAD *bodily;* we are no less taught to behold him as *the head of his body the Church, the fulness that filleth all in all.* Hence, all he is in this relationship, he is for his people. And *they are compleat in him.* Not only compleat in being accepted in him, as the LORD their righteousness, holy in his holiness, and made perfect in his perfection, but considered as one with him, they become his mystical body. And as the Head gives life and perfection to the body; so CHRIST, as CHRIST, gives life and perfection to his. And, hence, as they are compleat in him as their head, so CHRIST is compleat in them as his members. The head of any thing could not be compleat without a body, neither can JESUS, as the head of his body the Church, be compleat without the Church his body! Reader! ponder well the unspeakable mercy! You are groaning daily, under a conscious sense of a body of sin and death you carry about with you. Look to Him, in whom alone all your perfection is. Behold him as he is in himself. *In him dwelleth all the fulness of the* GODHEAD *bodily.* Behold him as he is to his Church, *ye are compleat in him.* Behold him as he is in his relationship to that Church, *he is the Head of all principality and power.* How much more to his own body? Think, my brother, what will that great day of GOD unfold, when the perfection of this Almighty Head of ours will manifest his perfection, not only in the glories of his own body *personal,* but in the perfection of his own body *mystical,* made comely in his comeliness, and perfect in his perfection! Oh! the joy of the vast multitude of all his innumerable members, when all shall see him as he is, and know even as they are known! Oh! the rapture of the whole ransomed of the LORD, which will then return to Zion with songs of everlasting joy upon their head, when CHRIST is beheld in all the fulness of the GODHEAD bodily! And, oh! my poor soul, what will be thy joy in that great day of GOD, when after all the breaking out of thy corruptions here below, the heart-aches and head aches, by reason of sin, the fiery darts of Satan, and the scorns of the world, when thou shalt not only behold thy JESUS in all that is blessed and glorious in himself, but shalt find thyself to be a member of his mystical body, a part of JESUS himself, as one among the members of his body the Church! LORD! I bow down under the overwhelming contemplation! When will *the day break, and the shadows flee away? Haste, haste my beloved, and be thou as the hart upon the mountains of spices!*

11 In whom also ye are circumcised with the circumcision made without hands, in putting off the body of the sins of the flesh by the circumcision of Christ:

12 Buried with him in baptism, wherein also ye are risen with *him* through the faith of the operation of God, who hath raised him from the dead.

13 And you, being dead in your sins and the uncircumcision of your flesh, hath he quickened together with him, having forgiven you all trespasses;

14 Blotting out the hand-writing of ordinances that was against us, which was contrary to us, and took it out of the way, nailing it to his cross;

15 *And* having spoiled principalities and powers, he made a shew of them openly, triumphing over them in it.

On the subject of circumcision, to which these verses refer, I do not think it necessary to enlarge, having already dwelt upon it on

Romans ii. and vi. chapters. I would only in addition, take occasion from what is here said, to observe, how needful it is to eye CHRIST in all. The circumcision made with hands, and the uncircumcision made without hands, had CHRIST for their sole object. The circumcision of the Jew, and the baptism of the Gentile, both looked to Him, centered in Him, and in Him had their accomplishment. All but CHRIST is shadow. He alone is the substance.

I detain the Reader at the expression in the close of this paragraph, to remark, that when it is said of CHRIST having spoiled principalities and powers, and made a shew of them openly, triumphing over them in it; the original is much stronger, for it saith, triumphing over them *in himself* meaning, that his triumphs were personal. JESUS took the glory to himself. And the margin of the Bible very properly hath so retained it. It is always blessed to eye CHRIST's Person in all, for his Person, in all the work of redemption, is the glorious object of our faith and hope. See chap. i. 20. and Commentary.

16 Let no man therefore judge you in meat, or in drink, or in respect of an holiday, or of the new moon, or of the sabbath *days:*

17 Which are a shadow of things to come; but the body *is* of Christ.

18 Let no man beguile you of your reward in a voluntary humility and worshipping of angels, intruding into those things which he hath not seen, vainly puffed up by his fleshly mind;

19 And not holding the Head, from which all the body by joints and bands having nourishment ministered, and knit together, increaseth with the increase of God.

20 Wherefore if ye be dead with Christ from the rudiments of the world, why, as though living in the world, are ye subject to ordinances,

21 (Touch not; taste not; handle not;

22 Which all are to perish with the using;) after the commandments and doctrines of men?

23 Which things have indeed a shew of wisdom in will worship, and humility, and neglecting of the body; not in any honour to the satisfying of the flesh.

It should be observed by the Reader, for the right apprehension of what is here said on the subject of dispute about ordinances, that they related to the Jewish and Gentile Church. The *Jews* converted to the Gospel, brought with them many of their Jewish prejudices. And the *Gentiles* having no attachment to those things, were not unfrequently reproved, it should seem, by their brethren the *Jews*, for not observing them. *Paul* desires that these things may die away, and that no unkind censure may any more be heard about the new moon feasts, or the alteration of the *Jewish* sabbath day to the first day of the week, in honor of the LORD's rising. He aims to call the attention of both from the shadow to the substance, from ordinances to CHRIST.

But though in these disputes the Church of GOD hath now no concern, yet much improvement may be made from what *Paul* hath here said on the subject of ordinances. It hath been in all ages, and still is too much the propensity in the human mind, to lay more stress upon the *means* of grace, than to regard the *end*. We are more concerned to observe the *shadow*, than look after the *substance*. The *carcase* is substituted for the *life*. Men feed, as the Prophet speaks, upon ashes. Isaiah xliv. 20. Hence, any thing, and every thing but CHRIST make up a *form*, where there is no *power* of *godliness*. The Apostle sums up the whole of this lure of religion, in a full comprehension, when he calls it, *vainly puffed up by his fleshly mind.* Alas! what pure form of worship is to be found in the present day wholly free from this leaven? What Church of CHRIST upon earth is there, that is *so holding the Head*, as to receive all nourishment alone from him, and to *increase with the increase of* GOD?

Reader! let You and I learn from this striking passage, the necessity of being dead with CHRIST from the rudiments of the world, that we may so use ordinances, as not being subject to them. A soul dead with CHRIST to those things, hath life with CHRIST in spiritual things. The life of CHRIST in the soul, hath fellowship and communion with CHRIST in all that belongs to him, his life, his obedience, his death, his resurrection, ascension, glory. The soul is justified freely, fully, everlastingly. He is one with Him, and accepted in Him. Hence, though he useth ordinances, yet but as mediums only to lead to CHRIST, as chariots to carry him to CHRIST. He is not subject to them, much less to substitute them in the place of CHRIST, or make them part SAVIORS. All are subordinate, and as *things which perish with using.* CHRIST is the one, and only one object in every desire, in all pursuits, and all attainments. What one of old said, all find, and all blessedness follows in this enjoyment. *Whom have I in heaven but thee? and there is none upon earth that I desire beside thee. My flesh and my heart faileth: thou art the strength of my heart, and my portion for ever.* Psm. lxxiii. 25, 26.

REFLECTIONS.

WHAT a lovely view doth this Chapter open with of *Paul's* love for the Church, in his soul exercises for their spiritual welfare. And what a contradiction of sinners did CHRIST endure against himself for his Church and people, lest his exercised ones should grow faint, and be weary in their minds. Oh! thou unequalled pattern of every thing that is fair, and good, and lovely!

Oh! Lord the Holy Ghost! let thy Church praise thee for the gracious remedy thou hast taught in this chapter against philosophy and vain deceit, the tradition of men, and the rudiments of the world. It is, indeed, a sure relief, when a poor sinner is enabled, through all the time-state of the Church, to receive Christ as he first received him, when called out of darkness to light, and both to receive Christ, and to come to Christ, and to live upon Christ, from first to last, the same needy, helpless, self-condemned, self-loathing sinner still. Lord! be it my portion thus to receive Christ, and thus to walk in Christ, and to be rooted and built up in him, to the Lord's glory, and my joy.

Lord! keep thy Church from being beguiled with enticing words. Keep all thy redeemed from being vainly puffed up with a fleshly mind. Ye Ministers of my God, hold up the glorious Head, from which all the body having nourishment ministered, and knit together, may increase with the increase of God. Ye fathers, to the children make known his name!

CHAP. III.

CONTENTS.

This Chapter opens with very glorious and precious Views of the Church's Safety in Christ. *And it is closed with suitable Exhortations arising therefrom.*

IF ye then be risen with Christ, seek those things which are above, where Christ sitteth on the right hand of God.

2 Set your affection on things above, not on things on the earth.

3 For ye are dead, and your life is hid with Christ in God.

4 When Christ, *who* is our life, shall appear, then shall ye also appear with him in glory.

The Apostle begins with calling upon the Church, as the risen members of Christ's mystical body, to a suitable and corresponding frame. The Reader will do well to connect what *Paul* hath here said of being risen with Christ, with what he had before said of the Church being *complete in* Christ, being *quickened together with* Christ, and having had *forgiven to them all trespasses.* See chap. ii. 10, 13. As such he now calls upon the members of Christ's body, who were once dead in their sins, but now brought forth into a new and spiritual life in Christ, their glorious Head, to manifest the reality of this new life, by living *to* Christ, and *upon* Christ, and causing their whole affections to center *in* Christ, as the members of the body live by the head. Let the Reader mark this; and he will then learn here, as in the other Epistles, that it is the Church to whom *Paul* writes, and not to the unawakened, ungodly, and carnal world. All exhortations of this kind are addressed to the *living Church* in CHRIST. And, indeed, common sense might plainly shew it, if men did but attend properly to the subject. For, until CHRIST be received, how can he be lived upon? What communion can an unawakened, unregenerated sinner, dead in trespasses and sins, have with a living SAVIOR? The object must be known before we can set our affections upon him. And, hence, when GOD quickens the sinner, then, and not before, those effects follow. 2 Cor. iv. 6. Ephes. ii. 1. and v. 14.

I hardly know where to begin in my observations on what the Apostle hath said of a life *hid with* CHRIST *in* GOD. Such deep mysteries are contained in the subject. And as to ending a Commentary upon the doctrine, this is impossible. I can only allow myself to glance at some few of the more prominent features, which appear here and there, in the contemplation of those deep things of GOD, and beg of the Almighty Author of his holy word, to guide both my heart and pen to offer no observations but what are in perfect conformity to his divine truth.

The Apostle begins with stating the situation of the Church, recovered from the *Adam-*fall of nature. *For ye are dead.* Not dead *in* sin, but dead *to* sin. Neither dead in body. For, as *Adam* in his transgression died, not in body, but in spirit, when he fell under the sentence of death, at the original transgression; so all his seed, while dead in trespasses and sins, are not dead in body, but in spirit. In neither sense, therefore, did *Paul*, in this place, mean the Church was dead. But the death here intended to be understood, is what *Paul* had before shewn. Dead with CHRIST in his death, having been crucified with him as the members of his body; buried with him by baptism into death; risen with him through the faith of the operation of GOD; and by means of which, *having redemption in his blood, the forgiveness of all their sins, according to the riches of his grace.*

And your life is hid with CHRIST *in* GOD. Here is a depth of subject which angels cannot explore. The life that is here said to be hid, cannot mean a *natural* life, for this, though derived at first *from* CHRIST, kept up and maintained in CHRIST, is not hidden. And the *carnal* and *sinful* life is too visible, from day to day, in the workings and breakings out of it, to be called hidden. But the life hid with CHRIST is *spiritual*. And blessedly so it is. For all, and every part of it is in, and from, CHRIST. From the first moment of regeneration, when a soul is quickened in CHRIST, until brought home to glory, all the communications are from JESUS. He is the life and breath, and food, and sustenance, and strength, and support; yea, the fountain of all life: *All my springs*, said one of old, *are in thee.* Psm. lxxxvii. 7. These things are plain to be understood, though not describable in all their operations. But when the Apostle adds, that this life is not only hid with CHRIST, but *with* CHRIST *in* GOD; here we have a bottom of mystery unfathomable! Our LORD hath said the same in those memorable words of his prayer: *That they all may be one; as thou,* FATHER, *art in me, and I in thee, that they also may be one with us.* John xvii. 21. But this, though confirming the precious truth, doth not further explain it. Indeed to faculties merely created, it should seem it is impossible to convey adequate apprehension. All we can do, in subjects of this mysterious nature, (which are given to us for the acceptation of our faith, and not for our investigation,) is to follow the command, *compare spiritual things with spiritual.* 1 Cor. ii. 13. In this before us, where our life is said to be in CHRIST, we are told that this life is hid with CHRIST *in* GOD. In that, by the same writer, where our reconciliation is made with GOD by CHRIST, the words are, GOD *was in* CHRIST. 2 Cor. v. 19. And what do we learn from both viewed together, but that every blessing relating to the Church, is in CHRIST, and from our union with him, we are interested in all, and that CHRIST, as CHRIST, gives an everlasting security to all our blessings, because CHRIST is in GOD, and GOD in CHRIST. Here, if we rest, is enough to form the firmest assurance of faith. And what can any child of GOD want more, when he calls to remembrance, that all the three heavenly witnesses join in testimony to this precious record; that GOD *hath given to us eternal life, and this life is in his* SON. 1 John v. 7—11.

When CHRIST, *who is our life, shall appear, then shall ye appear with him in glory.* Here we come in to open day-light. And this sums up all we need to know. One with CHRIST, and a life hid with CHRIST, and with CHRIST in GOD; assured of these great and glorious truths, we ground all that is blessed in the exercise of hope, for all we need in a life of faith, and grace, here below. But, when the testimony of these divine things closeth with an assurance, that *when He who is now our life shall appear, we shall appear with him in glory;* what can the utmost desire of the redeemed child of GOD figure to himself more blessed, to keep his expectation alive, and to have his affection always above, in the assured hope, *of a joy unspeakable and full of glory.*

I pray the Reader not to dismiss this precious portion of GOD's word, before that he hath taken with him some of the many very blessed things contained in it.

First. Let him pause, and consider the blessedness of a life in CHRIST. It is, to all intents, and purposes, being made a partaker of the divine nature. So the HOLY GHOST, by his servant the Apostle, declares it. *According* (saith he) *as his divine power hath given unto us all things that pertain to life and godliness.* And he adds, being made *partakers of the divine nature.* 2 Pet. i. 3, 4. Yea, the LORD JESUS, calls it eternal life. *That I should give eternal life, to as many as thou hast given me.* John xvii. 2. And how should it be otherwise, when CHRIST declares, that there is an union between himself and people. *I in them, and thou in me.* John xvii. 23. Reader! ponder the thought well, for it is most blessed.

Secondly. Consider the security of this life. It is in CHRIST, and with CHRIST, in GOD. And what then shall ever arise, to make it liable to loss, or interruption? *Paul* saith it is hidden. Hence, it is not discoverable by any enemies; and if it be not within their knowledge to discover, how shall it be within their reach to take away? How sweetly JESUS speaks to this point. *My sheep hear my voice: and I know them: and they follow me. And I give unto them eternal life; and they shall never perish, neither shall any pluck them out of my hand. My* FATHER *which gave them me is greater than all, and none is able to pluck them out of my* FATHER'S *hand. I and my* FATHER *are One.* John x. 27—30. And elsewhere JESUS saith: *because I live, ye shall live also.* John xiv. 19.

Thirdly. Its being hidden with CHRIST, which secures it from the ravages of the world; secures it no less, from their notice, and observation. It is blessed, yea, very blessed, to eat of that bread in secret, which JESUS himself hands to his people; and which none knoweth, saving him that receiveth it. And who shall number up the many visits, and love-tokens of JESUS, to his people? See some of his promises. John xiv. 23. Rev. iii. 20, 21. And even when at any time we lose sight of him, JESUS never loseth sight of us. Hidden as our spiritual life in CHRIST may be, to our view; there is no remission or interruption with him. The Church thought her LORD had withdrawn, when she said: *the* LORD *hath forsaken me, and my* LORD *hath forgotten me!* But was it so? Read, and behold the reverse: Isaiah xlix. 14—17. Reader! if the LORD hath in mercy awakened you from the death of sin, to a life hidden with CHRIST in GOD; ponder over these unspeakable mercies. Life, and union with CHRIST; hidden, and secure; eternal, and everlasting. Neither is it a small sweetener of those mercies which are unspeakable and full of glory, that *the world knoweth us not, because it knew him not.* 1 John iii. 1.

5 Mortify therefore your members which are upon the earth; fornication, uncleanness, inordinate affection, evil concupiscence, and covetousness, which is idolatry;

6 For which things' sake the wrath of God cometh on the children of disobedience:

7 In the which ye also walked some time, when ye lived in them.

8 But now ye also put off all these; anger, wrath, malice, blasphemy, filthy communication out of your mouth.

9 Lie not one to another, seeing that ye have put off the old man with his deeds.

10 And have put on the new *man*, which is renewed in knowledge after the image of him that created him:

11 Where there is neither Greek nor Jew; circumcision nor uncircumcision, Barbarian, Scythian, bond *nor* free: but Christ *is* all, and in all.

I pray the Reader to observe with me, the particular expression of the Apostle, when he saith: *mortify, therefore, your members which are upon earth.* The word *therefore* is an inference from what went before, of a life hidden with CHRIST in GOD: meaning, as plain as words can render it, that from CHRIST, grace must be obtained, to subdue all the corrupt affections of our members, which are earthly; and which he enumerates. And this corresponds to what the HOLY GHOST by *Paul* taught elsewhere. It is *by the* SPIRIT, believers *mortify the deeds of the body, and live.* Rom. viii. 13. And here, as in all other parts of the sacred writings, the HOLY GHOST teacheth the Church, to consider the spirit, when quickened from the death of trespasses and sins, to be brought forth into a new, and spiritual life; and as such, to be perfectly holy in CHRIST, being made *a partaker of the divine nature, having escaped the corruption that is in the world through lust.* 2 Pet. i. 4. Whereas, the body remains the same, unregenerated, unrenewed, and as *Paul* himself found it to the last, and groaned under it accordingly; *a body of sin and death.* Rom. vii. 24. To mortify, therefore, this body by the spirit; is what is here commanded, and enjoined. These members are properly said to be upon the earth, meaning wholly earthly. And for the sins of which, in the unregenerate, or as is called here *the children of disobedience,* GOD's judgment follows them. And these different characters are strikingly set forth, under the similitudes *of the old man, and the new.* But these things, are so plain, and self-evident, that I think it unnecessary to enlarge on them in this place.

12 Put on therefore, as the elect of God, holy and beloved, bowels of mercies, kindness, humbleness of mind, meekness, long-suffering;

13 Forbearing one another, and forgiving one another, if any man have a quarrel against any: even as Christ forgave you, so also *do* ye.

14 And above all these things *put on* charity, which is the bond of perfectness.

15 And let the peace of God rule in your hearts, to the which also ye are called in one body; and be ye thankful.

16 Let the word of Christ dwell in you richly in all wisdom; teaching and admonishing one another in psalms and hymns and spiritual songs, singing with grace in your hearts to the Lord.

17 And whatsoever ye do in word or deed, *do* all in the name of the Lord Jesus, giving thanks to God and the Father by him.

I beg the Reader, at the entrance on this paragraph, as at the former, particularly to notice, to whom God the Holy Ghost is speaking. It is to the *elect of* God. And that elect, the regenerated. Let the Reader never lose sight of these things, while going over those blessed Epistles and he will then discover, that these exhortations are to the Church, when brought into a state of grace. *Paul* considers the Church, to whom he is writing, as savingly, and effectually called. They are said to be *circumcised with the circumcision made without hands, in putting off the body of the sins of the flesh by the circumcision of* Christ: *having all their trespasses forgiven them, buried with* Christ *in baptism, and risen with him through the faith of the operation of* God. Chap. ii. 10—15. It is to such, as elect of God, the Holy Ghost, by his servant the Apostle, calls, to put on, as *the elect of* God, *holy and beloved bowels of mercies,* and the like. But how shall any but of this description, put on such things? And, if they are to put these things on, *as* the elect of God; how absurd must it be in others to call on men that are *not* elect to put them on?

The Reader might be at a loss to conceive, what would appear to him in theory to be impossible, that there were persons who could be found, to call upon any but the elect of God, to put them on. But the fact is, that there are not only such who do; but who are angry with those who do not. Men, unacquainted with the plague of their own hearts, and who fancy, that every man is possessed of free will to do all that is right, continually complain, that the ungodly are not called upon to faith, and repentance, which they conceive to be in every man's power to exercise. But such men woefully err, because *they know not the Scripture, neither the power of* God. The Holy Ghost hath uniformly set forth in the Scriptures, the total inability of man, to *think*, much less to *do*, any thing as of himself; and it is fully shewn, that all his sufficiency is of God. 2 Cor. iii. 5. Nothing, indeed, can be more decisive in point, than the striking passage before us: *Put on as the elect of* God. None but the elect of God can put on these things. Neither can the peace of God rule in any other hearts, or the word of Christ dwell in them richly in all wisdom.

18 Wives, submit yourselves unto your own husbands, as it is fit in the Lord:

19 Husbands, love *your* wives, and be not bitter against them.

20 Children, obey *your* parents in all things; for this is well pleasing unto the Lord.

21 Fathers, provoke not your children *to anger,* lest they be discouraged.

22 Servants, obey in all things *your* masters according to the flesh; not with eye-service, as men-pleasers; but in singleness of heart, fearing God:

23 And whatsoever ye do, do *it* heartily, as to the Lord, and not unto men:

24 Knowing that of the Lord ye shall receive the reward of the inheritance: for ye serve the Lord Christ.

25 But he that doeth wrong shall receive for the wrong which he hath done: and there is no respect of persons.

I do not think it necessary to swell our pages, with enlarging on what is so evidently plain in these verses. *Paul* having spoken to the Church in a general way; now addresseth himself personally to the individual members, in their relative situations. Wives, and Husbands, and Children, and Fathers, and Servants; are each called upon, to adorn the doctrine of GOD our SAVIOR, in all things. And the elect of GOD, who are truly, and savingly called, are, and must be, living instances of such things, wherever they are found. Look round every neighborhood, in every house, and family, and see if there be any, who are regenerated by the HOLY GHOST; (and it is *of such* only Paul speaks, and *to such* as elect of GOD, he enjoins those things;) and sure I am, they are, and must be, eminent examples of *believers, in word, in conversation, in charity, in spirit, in faith, in purity.* 1 Tim. iv. 12. And the Apostle in the close of this Chapter, gives the reason, or foundation of it: because *whatsoever is done, in word, or deed, is done heartily as to the* LORD, *and not unto men.* It is done, not from labors without, but grace within. Not in man's strength, but the LORD's. Oh! the blessedness of that sure, unerring principle, when GOD worketh in his elect, to whom he enjoins bowels of mercies, and in whom he new creates them; both *to will, and to do, of his good pleasure.* Then the child of GOD can say, and none but the child of GOD can ever say, I can do nothing by myself, but *I can do all things through* CHRIST, *which strengtheneth me.* Philippians iv. 13.

REFLECTIONS.

OH! thou risen, and exalted LORD JESUS! send down thine ascension-gifts, and raise all my spiritual affections after thee, that I may no longer grovel here below, but seek thee, who art above! Didst thou not promise this, thou dear LORD, before thy departure; that when thou wert lifted up, thou wouldest draw all thy people unto thee? Oh! then, *draw me, that I may run after thee, for thou art the* LORD *my* GOD! Precious, yea, exceedingly precious, is that assurance to my soul, that the life of all thy Church, is hid with CHRIST in GOD. And sure I am, that when JESUS shall appear, then will all thy redeemed appear with thee in glory.

And, oh! thou Almighty LORD the SPIRIT! do thou, by thy sweet influences, enable me to mortify all my earthly part. Grant, gracious GOD, that the flesh may be subdued by the spirit; and that by thy strength, I may mortify the deeds of the body and live. And, as the elect of GOD, may I find grace, to put on bowels of mercy, to the whole houshold of faith, while doing good to all men; yea, may the peace of G od rule in my heart, always having in remembrance, how C hrist hath forgiven me; may my compassions go forth, to all around, Oh! what are all the little quarrels of this dying world, to those who are conscious, of that deadly breach being made up, in the blood of C hrist, which sin, and Satan, had made, between G od and his people. May all the relations of life, in Wives, and Husbands, and Children, and Parents, and Servants, and Masters, be everlastingly looking to J esus ; that, while beholding him, all their minds may be influenced into love and tenderness: and all their conduct regulated by his example. Precious L ord J esus ! be thou my G od , my guide, and my portion for ever!

CHAP. IV.

CONTENTS.

The Apostle prosecutes the same Subject of Exhortation, in the opening of this Chapter. He enjoins a Continuance in Prayer, with Watchfulness, and Thanksgiving. He concludes the Epistle with Salutations.

MASTERS, give unto *your* servants that which is just and equal; knowing that ye also have a Master in heaven.

2 Continue in prayer, and watch in the same with thanksgiving;

3 Withal praying also for us, that God would open unto us a door of utterance, to speak the mystery of Christ, for which I am also in bonds:

4 That I may make it manifest, as I ought to speak.

5 Walk in wisdom toward them that are without, redeeming the time.

6 Let your speech *be* alway with grace, seasoned with salt, that ye may know how ye ought to answer every man.

I do not think it needful to dwell upon what is here said; the subjects contained in these verses, and the manner in which the Apostle hath recommended the things contained in them, being so very plain, and self-evident. Just only would I observe, with what earnestness *Paul*, though so great an Apostle, desired to be remembered in their prayers. It hath been an anxious desire of the Church in all ages, in the several members of C hrist 's mystical body, to be mentioned by one another at the Court, when seeing the King in his beauty. And G od 's faithful ministers have been very earnest, in this particular, with their people. Some that I have read of, have gone so far as to say, that they have known, when their people have been fervent in prayer for them in their labors of love, by the blessings which have followed in their ministry. Surely such a thought, if duly considered, would, in the LORD's hand, make a Church, sound in the faith, be very desirous to go often to court, and ask the LORD to bless his servants!

How sweet, and edifying, would be the conversation of the LORD's people, if always framed upon the Apostle's plan. The name of JESUS, and the sweet savor of his love, if continually made the subject of discourse, would have similar effect, to give a relish to the conversation of GOD's people, as salt hath, to make our ordinary food savory. CHRIST is indeed the salt of the Covenant. Levit. ii. 13. Mark ix. 50. But alas! how little is it made the general matter of discourse! See Malachi iii. 16—18.

7 All my state shall Tychicus declare unto you, *who is* a beloved brother, and a faithful minister and fellow-servant in the Lord:

8 Whom I have sent unto you for the same purpose, that he might know your estate, and comfort your hearts;

9 With Onesimus, a faithful and beloved brother, who is *one* of you. They shall make known unto you all things which *are done* here.

10 Aristarchus my fellow-prisoner saluteth you, and Marcus, sister's son to Barnabas, (touching whom ye received commandments; if he come unto you receive him ;

11 And Jesus, which is called Justus, who are of the circumcision. These only *are my* fellow-workers unto the kingdom of God, which have been a comfort unto me.

12 Epaphras, who is *one* of you, a servant of Christ, saluteth you, always labouring fervently for you in prayers, that ye may stand perfect and complete in all the will of God.

13 For I bear him record, that he hath a great zeal for you, and them *that are* in Laodicea, and them in Hierapolis.

14 Luke, the beloved physician, and Demas, greet you.

15 Salute the brethren which are in Laodicea, and Nymphas, and the church which is in his house.

16 And when this epistle is read among you, cause that it be read also in the church of the Laodiceans; and that ye likewise read the *epistle* from Laodicea.

17 And say to Archippus, Take heed to the ministry which thou has received in the Lord, that thou fulfil it.

18 The salutation by the hand of me Paul. Remember my bonds. Grace *be* with you. Amen.

¶ Written from Rome to the Colossians by Tychicus and Onesimus.

I have not interrupted the whole of these verses, as it did not appear necessary to make any break in them; being chiefly speaking of persons, and the Apostle's affectionate remembrance of them. A short observation is all that will be needful upon the whole.

Tychichus we have an account of, in other parts of *Paul's* writings. 1 Cor. xvi. 17. Ephes. vi. 21. 2 Tim. iv. 12. And, it appears from Acts xx. 4. that he was a companion of the Apostle's. The honorable testimony given of him, though short, is beyond all magnificent titles of the great in this world. *A beloved brother, a faithful minister, and fellow servant in the* LORD! *Onesimus,* whom *Paul* also calls a faithful, and beloved brother, *Paul* felt so much interest for, that he wrote that very sweet, and interesting Epistle to *Philemon,* wholly on his account. *Aristarchus,* it should seem, was a man of *Macedon,* as the history of *Paul's* travels in the book of the Acts relates. Acts xix. 29. and xx. 4. *Marcus,* is probably the same as we read of, Acts xv. 37, &c. *Peter* also mentions this man. 1 Pet. v. 13. And *Paul,* in 2 Tim. iv. 11. and in his Epistle to *Philemon,* 24. *Jesus,* called *Justus,* is probably the same, as the one mentioned of *Corinth.* Acts xviii. 7. *Jesus* is the same name as *Joshua,* in the Hebrew; and his other name *Justus,* was given him, it hath been thought by some, on account of his worthy character. *Epaphras* was noticed in the opening of this Epistle: Chap. i. 7. And, from the manner in which the Apostle hath spoken of him again, in the close of his letter, it shews him to have been a zealous, and an affectionate servant of the Church. Oh! that the LORD would send many an *Epaphras* to his Churches! *Luke,* the beloved Physician, not beloved so much as a physician for the body, but as beloved of the LORD, and as one of his members; and we have reason to bless GOD for his services, the Gospel which bears his name, and the Acts of the Apostles, being both from his penmanship. *Demas,* if the same as mentioned, 2 Tim. iv. 10. affords an awful instance, how far profession may go, without a work of real conversion of the heart to GOD. The brethren at *Laodicea,* and

Nymphas, we have no further account of, neither of the epistle from *Laodicea*. It should seem, that some one had sent an epistle to *Paul*, from *Laodicea*; and not, that it was an Epistle, as some have thought, from *Paul* to that Church. Had it been his, no doubt it would have been written, as all his Epistles were, under inspiration, and consequently have been preserved, and handed down to the Church. What the Apostle directed to be said to *Archippus*, hath been supposed as implying negligence in his ministry. But had this been the case, surely *Paul* would not have spared him. And, in his Epistle to *Philemon*, written much about the same time, he calls him his beloved *Archippus*. Be this, however, the case, or not, it serves to teach all who minister in holy things, how earnest they ought to be:—*first*, to know, that like *Archippus*, they have received the ministry in, and from the LORD: and, *secondly*, that they fulfil it. Heb. xiii. 17, 18. It should seem, that after *Tychicus*, or *Onesimus*, or perhaps both together, had written down (as *Baruch* did from the Prophet *Jeremiah's* mouth, Jerem. xxxvi. 18.) the Epistle; *Paul* put his name to it, by way of confirmation. But let the Reader observe, how the beginning, and ending, are the same: *Grace be unto you*, or *with you*. Amen. So should all Epistles be. And so all are, which GOD the SPIRIT indites.

REFLECTIONS.

BLESSING, and honor, and glory, and power, be unto him that sitteth upon the throne; and unto the Lamb, for ever and ever! What praise sufficient, or what glory equal, can the Church upon earth, and the redeemed in heaven, render, to the One glorious JEHOVAH, FATHER, SON, and HOLY GHOST, for the unequalled love manifested to the Church, in JESUS CHRIST! And what everlasting thanksgiving, doth the reading of those holy Scriptures call forth, in the daily use of them, from beholding, with what a world of grace, the precious records have been preserved, and handed down, from age to age, to the joy of the Church, and the glory of the Almighty Head of it. Oh! LORD the SPIRIT! do thou, in thine Almighty ministry, bless thine holy word to all thy sent servants, and the people among whom thou shalt send them, to minister, that both him that labors in the word and doctrine, and those among whom the ministry is exercised, may be blessed together.

We bless our GOD for the service of his Apostle, in this instance of his labors of love, in this Epistle to the Church; by which, *he being dead yet speaketh*. And our GOD will continue to bless its use to the Church to the latest posterity. May the LORD accompany the present perusal of it to the divine honor, and our furtherance in grace, through JESUS CHRIST. Amen.

THE FIRST EPISTLE OF PAUL THE APOSTLE TO THE THESSALONIANS.

GENERAL OBSERVATIONS.

THESSALONICA, the chief city of *Macedonia*, is said to have derived its name from *Philip*, king of *Macedon*, in consequence of a victory which he obtained in *Thessalia*. From such corrupt and sinful causes, do sometimes, and not unfrequently, spring, the memorable records of men. It is indeed in correspondence with our fallen nature. Sin hath introduced all the baleful effects, which that nature, unregenerated by grace, is subject to, in the multiform fruits of it, from the womb to the grave. And names of places, and monuments, to perpetuate what is called the splendid victories of heroes, both ancient and modern, perpetuate more generally their sin, and shame.

The city of *Thessalonica*, at the time when the Apostle wrote this blessed Epistle, was a large, flourishing, and much peopled place. Now, for many centuries past, it hath been overrun with the impostures of the false prophet; and is in the possession of the Turks. Here once, the LORD had a portion of his Church. But, as he himself said of other places, so here, he hath removed the Candlestick, Rev. ii. 5. We have great cause to bless God for our mercies, in this review of the divine judgments. While we contemplate our high privileges as a nation, in this particular: we may hear, and ought to feel, the strong expostulating words of the Apostle: *Are we better than they?* And, with the immediate answer: *No, in no wise! All are under sin.* Rom. iii. 9.

The date of this Epistle is generally marked as early as the year 52; and as such, must have been the *first*, in point of time, of all *Paul's* writings.

The distinguishing feature which marks every Chapter, like all the Apostle's Epistles, and preachings, is CHRIST. And, oh! how sweetly, and blessedly, hath he held him forth to the Church, through the whole of it. Reader! what a mercy was it to you, to me, to the whole Church of the LORD, that the HOLY GHOST called *Paul* by a vision to visit *Macedonia?*

Acts xvi. 9 to the end, and Acts xvii. And, what a mercy was it, for all the Church of GOD, that the HOLY GHOST prompted the Apostle to write this Epistle, and endited the blessed contents of it? And what a mercy, to preserve the precious records safe to this present hour, and cause them to be handed down to us? And, (shall I add,) what a mercy of mercies, in all these things, if the LORD hath given us the enlightened understanding, in the apprehension of them; so that, as *Paul* said to this very church, in the opening of this Epistle, our election of GOD is known, because *the Gospel is come unto us, not in word only, but also in power, and in the* HOLY GHOST, *and in much assurance!* Chap. i. 4, 5. Oh! LORD the SPIRIT! direct, and guide the heart and pen, in this feeble work, of the *Poor Man's Commentary*, and cause it to minister *to the glory of* GOD, *in the face of* JESUS CHRIST.

CHAPTER I.

CONTENTS.

The Apostle opens his Epistle with his usual Salutations. He tells the Thessalonians, *how earnest his Prayers were for the Church. And he teacheth them to observe the Marks of their Election, by the blessed Effects of it.*

PAUL, and Silvanus, and Timotheus, unto the church of the Thessalonians, *which is* in God the Father, and *in* the Lord Jesus Christ: Grace *be* unto you, and peace, from God our Father, and the Lord Jesus Christ.

2 We give thanks to God always for you all, making mention of you in our prayers;

3 Remembering without ceasing your work of faith, and labour of love, and patience of hope in our Lord Jesus Christ, in the sight of God and our Father:

It is worthy observation, the great humbleness of *Paul's* mind. Though so eminently distinguished by the LORD, as an Apostle; he fails not to take into union with himself, the faithful brethren. Oh! how sweet is it to behold the testimonies of grace manifested in the affections of the LORD's people!

4 Knowing, brethren beloved, your election of God.

5 For our gospel came not unto you in word only, but also in power, and in the Holy Ghost, and in much assurance; as ye know what manner of men we were among you for your sake.

6 And ye became followers of us, and of the Lord, having received the word in much affliction, with joy of the Holy Ghost:

7 So that ye were ensamples to all that believe in Macedonia and Achaia.

8 For from you sounded out the word of the Lord not only in Macedonia and Achaia, but also in every place your faith to God-ward is spread abroad; so that we need not speak any thing.

9 For they themselves shew of us what manner of entering in we had unto you, and how ye turned to God from idols to serve the living and true God;

10 And to wait for his son from heaven, whom he raised from the dead, *even* Jesus, which delivered us from the wrath to come.

When the Reader hath duly pondered the marks, and characters, by which the election, according to grace, is known in the soul, as the Apostle hath here noted them; I shall request his attention to the subject itself. It is a most decided testimony, which GOD the HOLY GHOST hath elsewhere given, by which the elect of GOD are known. *For whom he did foreknow, he also did predestinate, to be conformed to the image of his* SON, *that he might be the first-born, among many brethren. Moreover, whom he did predestinate, them he also called: and whom he called, them he also justified: and whom he justified, them he also glorified.* Rom. viii. 29, 30.

First.—I beg the Reader to notice, one by one, the marks and characters of election, which GOD the HOLY GHOST, hath here shewn to be the true standard, by which the Church of GOD, as well as the Church of the *Thessalonians*, might know the blessed truth. The Apostle begins with that decided testimony, in that the Gospel came not in word only, but in power, and in the HOLY GHOST, and much assurance! Reader! do not fail to note this down in the deepest memorandums of your heart. Yea, beg of GOD the SPIRIT to do it for you. Oh! how unanswerably conclusive is it, when a child of GOD is quickened under the word of GOD, which is the sword of the SPIRIT. When, like *Lydia*, the LORD opens the heart, and gives the hearing ear, and the seeing eye; so that he finds the word, *quick, and powerful, and sharper than any two edged sword.* All before this, made no impression upon his mind. But, when the

LORD came in the word, and by the word; he finds the powerful, quickening, illuminating, sanctifying, and renewing teachings; and cries out with *David: I shall never forget thy precepts, for with them thou hast quickened me.* Psalm cxix. 93. 2 Cor. x. 4, 5. Hebrews iv. 12. 1 Cor. xiv. 23—25.

Secondly. Another evidence, which follows the former, the Apostle hath here noted, as the way, whereby the child of GOD shall know his election; namely, when the regenerated heart is enabled to discern GOD's faithful servants coming to them in the LORD's name. *Ye know* (saith *Paul*) *what manner of men we were among you.* Souls truly awakened, know *the joyful sound; and walk in the light of* GOD's *countenance. My sheep hear my voice,* saith JESUS, *and they follow me. A stranger they will not follow, for they know not the voice of strangers.* John x. 3—5. It is a most decided mark, whereby we know our election of GOD, when we cannot receive false doctrines, nor follow teachers, unsent of the LORD. The glorious, and discriminating truths of grace, the elect of GOD delight in. They are regenerated, and therefore they know, from their own souls' experience, what manner of men those among them are, who hold up CHRIST, as the One only Ordinance of Heaven: Who inculcate among their people, salvation in his blood and righteousness, without works: Who exclude all other topics, as CHRIST and his Apostle excluded them; determining to know nothing among men, but JESUS CHRIST, and him crucified. And from the same reasons as *Paul* did; because they know CHRIST, and CHRIST alone, to be *the wisdom of* GOD, *and the power of* GOD, *for salvation to every one that believeth.* Men, unacquainted with the plague of their own heart, and being vainly puffed up with their fleshly mind, will attempt in themselves, and recommend to others, to compliment GOD, with talking of the remains of somewhat within, that is good. But the truly regenerated, have learnt, and are daily learning, both in themselves, and all others, that *the heart is deceitful above all things, and desperately wicked;* yea, so wicked, that *none can know it;* in the depths of wickedness, in their unrenewed body of flesh, but *He who searcheth the heart, and trieth the reins.* Jerem. xvii. 9, 10. Rev. ii. 18, 23. Reader! do not overlook this *second* mark, whereby the brethren beloved know their election of GOD, they follow that pure preaching, which is *the truth as it is in* JESUS; and they follow such only under the LORD the SPIRIT's teaching, who preach CHRIST, and CHRIST only, the One Ordinance of GOD's own providing, for the elect of GOD.

Thirdly. The elect of GOD, are said to know of this distinguishing mercy over them, in *having received the word in much affliction, with joy of the* HOLY GHOST. This is a very precious, and most decisive testimony. And the more so, because it is personal, and peculiar to GOD's elect. They who are for throwing into the back ground, as much as possible, those glorious proofs of GOD's sovereignty, in electing grace, and predestinating his chosen, to the adoption of children by JESUS CHRIST to himself; Ephes. i. 4, 5. know nothing of what the Apostle hath here said, of *receiving, the word in much affliction, and yet* in *joy of the* HOLY GHOST. These are contradictions in such men's view. For they know nothing more of receiving either the written word, or the uncreated WORD, but in a whole unbroken heart, unconscious of the depth of the plague of it; and unconscious that CHRIST is the sole healer. Exod. xv. 26. And, where there are slight views of sin, there will be but small affliction in the remembrance of it. Such never can receive the word *which is quick, and powerful, and sharper than any two edged sword*, Heb. iv. 12. in much affliction. And, as they that are soul-whole, cannot receive the word in much affliction; so the joy of the HOLY GHOST is unfelt, and unknown, by all such characters; for they have never learnt, from that Almighty SPIRIT, that salvation is in no other but JESUS CHRIST. Reader! it will be your mercy, if you have not so learned CHRIST. If you know your election of GOD, in having *received the word in much affliction;* you can tell me, or rather your own soul, how deeply you lay under the convictions of sin, and your own conscience, when you saw sin in all its tremendous consequences, as you stood in yourself, before GOD. And you also can tell, what kind of joy of the soul that was, when first the Day-spring from on high visited you. Joy, indeed, of the HOLY GHOST, when the LORD shews a poor sinner, that there is more in CHRIST to justify before GOD, than there is sin in the soul to condemn. Such will know their election, *having received the word in much affliction, and with joy of the* HOLY GHOST. But a heart unbroke by sin, can neither know CHRIST's redemption from it, nor the electing love of GOD in it.

Fourthly. A child of GOD knows his election of GOD, in being led by the SPIRIT, so as to become an *ensample to all that believe*. This is a very blessed testimony to the adoption-character of the LORD's people. For the HOLY GHOST laid it down, as a most decided proof of sonship; that *as many as are led by the* SPIRIT *of* GOD, *they are the sons of* GOD. Rom. viii. 14. And this, and this only, becomes the security of a child of GOD, to be *an example of the believers in word, in conversation, in charity, in faith, in purity,* 1 Tim. iv. 12. There can be no dependance, for the exercise of any single grace, but in the SPIRIT. *If we live in the* SPIRIT, *we shall also walk in the* SPIRIT. But without the SPIRIT, not a single affection of our fallen sinful nature, can we either mortify, or subdue. Rom. viii. 13. They who talk otherwise, are unacquainted with the plague of their own heart. To address the ungodly with exhortation to good works, manifests the blindness of their own minds. The Apostle's testimony in this scripture, of a state of election, and the proof of it, in being *ensamples,* is ensamples *to all that believe.* What hath this to do with the unregenerate? Reader! note these things, and consider their importance.

Fifthly. The Apostle adds another very delightful testimony, whereby the beloved brethren know their election of GOD, when he saith, that *from them sounded out the word of the* LORD *in every place, so that their faith to* GOD-*ward was spread abroad.* This is not simply confined to preachers of the word, when sent by the HOLY GHOST; but means the conversation of the godly in every place, when, from the abundance of the heart, the mouth speaketh. Every child of GOD, when regenerated himself, will delight to converse with all that are regenerated. And the language of his heart is expressed in the words of the HOLY GHOST: *Come and hear, all ye that fear* GOD; *and I will declare what he hath done for my soul.*

Psm. lxvi. 16. This is to sound out the word of the LORD, and to give testimony of our election of GOD. And, while this marks the features of character, in all that are regenerated: all that are sent out to preach the Gospel by the HOLY GHOST, (and it is awful in any to preach it unsent by him,) hold forth the word of life, by *preaching, not offering* CHRIST. It is their province to preach CHRIST. It belongs only to the HOLY GHOST to *offer*, and *give* power to accept CHRIST, to his people. Hence, *Paul's* sermon was preached to all that heard it; but it was *sent* to *the children of the stock of Abraham, and whosoever among them feared* GOD. Acts xiii. 26. Gal. iii. 29.

I hope by this time the Reader is led to see, how very blessedly the HOLY GHOST, by his servant the Apostle, hath given the marks, and evidences, in this Chapter, by which the Church *then*, and by the same tokens *now*, may *know their election of* GOD. But, while we find cause to bless GOD, both for the revelation of the doctrine itself, and the way by which all his children in grace may discover their personal interest in it; I would take occasion, from the very plain, and decided manner, in which the HOLY GHOST hath here marked it down, to offer an observation or two upon it. And I confess, that I am the more prompted to this service, from the consideration of the awful day in which the Church of GOD now dwells; when the glorious truths of our holy faith, in which consists the whole life, and spirit of the Gospel of CHRIST, are so lightly esteemed and regarded.

First. I beg the Reader to remark with me, that the election, and choice of the Church in CHRIST, is revealed in, and through, the whole word of GOD, as the distinguished act of GOD the FATHER; and as the result of his own sovereignty, will, and pleasure. The Bible is full of proofs to testify, that *the manifold wisdom of* GOD, should be made known to the Church in this way, *according to the eternal purpose which he purposed in* CHRIST JESUS *our* LORD. Ephes. iii. 10, 11. So that, each glorious Person, in these high and solemn transactions, as they relate to the Church, might be known, in their several acts of grace, towards the LORD's people. GOD the FATHER in election, GOD the SON in redemption, and GOD the HOLY GHOST in regeneration, according to the good pleasure of his will. I stay not to make quotations in proof, for this would be little otherwise than bringing forth the whole Bible. Let the Reader consult a few. Deut. x. 14, 15. Isaiah xliii. 21. Malachi i. 2, 3. Ephes. i. 4—10.

Secondly. It is very blessed to observe, how CHRIST spake of election, preached it, and delighted in it. Speaking of his people, he calls them GOD's *own elect*. Luke xviii. 7. Speaking of them as precious in his sight, JESUS doth this in a peculiar sweet, and gracious manner, as being his FATHER's gift. *Thine they were, and thou gavest them me*. John xvii. 6. *I pray for them. I pray not for the world, but for them which thou hast given me, for they are thine; and all mine are thine, and thine are mine, and I am glorified in them*. John xvii. 9, 10. Speaking to them, JESUS said: *Ye have not chosen me, but I have chosen you. If the world hate you, ye know that it hated me, before it hated you. If ye were of the world, the world would love his own; but because ye are not of the world, but I have chosen you out of the world, therefore the world hateth you.* John xv. 16, 18, 19.

So in like manner in his preaching. The very first sermon CHRIST preached in the Jewish Synagogue, after taking his text from the prophecy of Isaiah, and applying the words of the Prophet to himself; he immediately opened his discourse with the doctrine of election. *Many widows* (said JESUS) *were in Israel in the days of Elias, but unto none of them was Elias sent, save unto Sarepta, a city of Sidon, to a woman that was a widow. And many lepers were in Israel in the time of Eliseus the Prophet, and none of them was cleansed, saving Naaman the Syrian.* And what I beg the Reader to observe with me concerning this preaching of election by CHRIST, is this, that it brought upon him the same condemnation as it doth invariably upon all his sent servants, both then and now. As long as the SON of GOD held forth the words of the Prophet concerning salvation, and made application of it to himself, it is said, that *all bare him witness, and wondered at the gracious words which proceeded out of his mouth.* But no sooner did CHRIST preach the doctrine of election, in shewing that GOD sent his servant but to one poor widow, and one poor leper in Israel; they understood what CHRIST meant, and we read, that *all they in the synagogue were filled with wrath, and rose up and thrust him out of the city, and led him to the brow of the hill, intending to cast him down headlong.* Luke iv. 16—30. Such is the bitterness in every man's heart by nature against the precious doctrine of election, though CHRIST himself be the preacher. Reader! do you know of the like bitterness against it *now* in you? Certainly it was so *once?*

And if it be not so *now,* it is sovereign grace alone that hath rooted it out. Well do I remember, and in the remembrance bless GOD for the change, when my proud, unhumbled heart, rose up in daring rebellion against it! And well, therefore, may I now forbear anger against those who oppose it, when I call to mind how very long the graciousness of my GOD forbore with me. I do lament, however, when, at any time, I hear of young, presumptuous men, who are just come forth of the shell of human education, daringly preach against a doctrine they know nothing of, though many of them have subscribed to support it. It is awful to hear such setting up their bold opinion against the sovereignty of GOD, and presuming to charge those whom GOD hath taught and sent to preach the everlasting, unchanging love of GOD to his Church, as shewing too much regard to the doctrines of election, predestination, and the decrees of GOD. Upon all those occasions, I would pray for grace to follow the HOLY GHOST's directions concerning the ministry. *The servant of the* LORD *must not strive; but be gentle unto all men, apt to teach, patient, in meekness, instructing those that oppose themselves; if* GOD *peradventure will give them repentance* (as I bless his holy name he hath me,) *to the acknowledging of the truth; and that they may recover themselves out of the snare of the devil, who are taken captive by him at his will.* 2 Tim. ii. 24, 25, 26.

Once more. I observed that our dear LORD not only spake of election, and preached it, but that he *delighted* in it. And what an higher proof can we have of his great pleasure therein, than in the instance we have upon record, when he expressed himself to his divine FATHER, for the manifestation of his electing love to his disciples, in those memorable words: *At that time* JESUS *answered and said, I thank thee, O* FATHER, LORD *of heaven and earth, because thou hast hid these things from the wise and prudent, and hast revealed them unto babes. Even so,* FATHER, *for so it seemed good in thy sight.* Matt. xi. 25, 26. Reader! pause, I beseech you, over the solemn subject, for it is most solemn! Did it seem good in GOD the FATHER's sight, to make such distinguishing proofs of his electing and predestinating will and pleasure, as to hide it from the wise in their own eyes, and the prudent in their own conceit, and reveal his precious truths to babes in CHRIST? Did JESUS delight so much in this electing love, as to thank the FATHER for such displays of it? Doth the HOLY GHOST abound towards the elect Church of GOD in CHRIST, as to have made *known unto us the mystery of his will, according to his good pleasure, which he hath purposed in himself?* Ephes. i. 8, 9. And shall not the Church of GOD, to whom these precious truths are made known, while hidden from the world, take delight in them, and thank GOD for them also? Shall there be any, to whom, by regenerating grace, the LORD hath made known this mystery of his will, be silent and regardless of such unspeakable mercy? Shall we not, on the contrary, while overwhelmed with the contemplation, cry out with the astonished Apostle: LORD! *how is it that thou hast manifested thyself unto me, and not unto the world?* John xiv. 22.

May I be permitted upon so interesting a subject to trespass a little longer, I would add to all that hath been said, that the doctrine of GOD's election, so truly scriptural, so truly blessed, and so very full, in confirmation of GOD's sovereignty, carries with it a certain degree of evidence, independent of every other, from the universal hatred, which all men in a state of unrenewed nature uniformly bear against it. Since the LORD in mercy brought me to the knowledge of himself, and into an acquaintance with the plague of my own heart, I have been led into this discovery also. It appears most decidedly, that the former hatred I had to this sovereignty of JEHOVAH in election, and the universal hatred of all unregenerate minds to the same divine truth, is an additional testimony in its favor. Oh! how blessed it is, when to all the other glorious assurances of our most holy faith, the LORD gives us to see, that by grace we not only differ from ourselves in what we were before, but from the world. How blessedly to this point is that prayer of JESUS. *I have given them thy word, and the world hath hated them because they are not of the world, even as I am not of the world!* John xvii. 14.

Reader! perhaps I shall surprize you by what I am going to observe, but the fact is most certain and sure. Amidst all the hatred of mankind, in every instance of the unawakened and unregenerate, throughout the whole earth, to the doctrine of GOD's sovereignty in election, GOD hath so constructed the human mind in such a way and manner, that he absolutely overrules every son and daughter of *Adam,* from the first dawn of reason to the close of life, in acting or thinking, to practise election in all they say or do; and this every day, and hour of the day, during the whole of their existence upon earth. There is not an action or design; there is not a motive of conduct in thought, word, or deed, more or less, but what manifests in the whole race of men, their election to one way rather than to another; whether they walk or talk, go hither or thither, associate with this rather than that, eat of one food rather than another, and, in short, in the whole tenor of their daily pursuits, habits, dress, and all the circumstances of life; choice, and election guides them in all. So, then, while every man, yea, every child is guided by the capricious whim and purpose of his own heart, to make his daily election, as his wayward humor guides him; the LORD, who is the only Being that, from his unerring wisdom, cannot make a wrong choice, shall be the only One, according to man's daring presumption, which shall be restrained from making his election. Is not this the real state of the case? And can any thing more fully demonstrate the awfulness of man's fall by sin, which hath induced such tremendous effects in his very nature? And doth not this wonderful display of divine wisdom, by overruling the human mind to do *that* which he denies his Creator *to do*, seem to say, as if the LORD would convict such daring sinners to their face, by making them continually practise themselves, what they call in question and arraign in their Maker. And when we consider, that it is in election only the LORD thus compels the whole earth to the practice, in whatever country or clime, whatever form or constitution of religion, or none; wherever a human being is found, the very nature of man is such, that he shall practise election; doth it not, I say, seem to intimate the LORD's overruling such a wonderful event to his own glory; that while all the race of men by nature hate GOD's election, they shall condemn themselves by their own daily practice of it, and thus, however unconscious, bear their unwilling testimony to the great truth. Reader! see to it once more, whether the Apostle's marks are in your own testimony, and that you can say to yourself, as he did to the Church; *Knowing, brethren beloved, your election of* GOD!

REFLECTIONS.

READER! is it our privilege, like this Church, to give thanks to GOD always for the divine grace, and mercy, and love, bestowed upon us? Can it be said to you, and to me, as the Apostle did to the *Thessalonians*, in the remembrance of our work of faith, and labor of love, and patience of hope in our LORD JESUS CHRIST, in the sight of GOD our FATHER? Can we with full assurance of faith, and in the enjoyment of the same testimonies as *Paul* here marked down, take up the well-grounded confidence of our election of GOD? Oh! then, let us see to it, that our faith in JESUS is a working faith, working by love. That our hope is that hope founded in CHRIST, and his blood and righteousness, which maketh not ashamed. That our patience is that which the Apostle elsewhere describes, and which worketh experience. And in the exercise of which, we wait for the return of the SON of GOD from heaven, who hath delivered us from the wrath to come. This will be an honorable testimony to the SPIRIT's work in our heart, and will most plainly shew, in the midst of the awful day in which we live, what manner of entering in the word of grace hath had in our souls; and how, through the regenerating power of the Spirit, the Lord hath turned our hearts from idols to serve the living and true God. Blessed be the electing love of God the Father, the redemption by Christ, and the quickening of God the Holy Ghost!

CHAP. II.

CONTENTS.

In this Chapter the Apostle dwells chiefly upon his Labors among them as a Minister of Christ. *He strongly expresseth his Affection for the People.*

FOR yourselves, brethren, know our entrance in unto you, that it was not in vain:

2 But even after that we had suffered before, and were shamefully entreated, as ye know, at Philippi, we were bold in our God to speak unto you the gospel of God with much contention.

3 For our exhortation *was* not of deceit, nor of uncleanness, nor in guile:

4 But as we were allowed of God to be put in trust with the gospel, even so we speak; not as pleasing men, but God, which trieth our hearts.

5 For neither at any time used we flattering words, as ye know, nor a cloke of covetousness; God *is* witness:

6 Nor of men sought we glory, neither of you, nor *yet* of others, when we might have been burdensome, as the apostles of Christ.

7 But we were gentle among you, even as a nurse cherisheth her children:

8 So being affectionately desirous of you, we were willing to have imparted unto you, not the gospel of God only, but also our own souls, because ye were dear unto us.

9 For ye remember, brethren, our labour and travail: for labouring night and day, because we would not be chargeable unto any of you, we preached unto you the gospel of God.

10 Ye *are* witnesses, and God *also*, how holily and justly and unblameably we behaved ourselves among you that believe.

11 As you know how we exhorted and comforted and charged every one of you, as a father *doth* his children,

12 That ye would walk worthy of God, who hath called you unto his kingdom and glory.

I have always considered this Chapter, since I knew any thing of the Lord, with peculiar pleasure, as opening the very heart of a faithful minister of Christ. And if the Reader be taught of God the Spirit, how rightly to appreciate divine things, I venture to believe that he will think with me, that the whole Chapter from beginning to end, furnisheth one of the most finished portraits of a truly ordained minister of the Lord Jesus. Oh! that it pleased the Almighty Lord of the harvest, to send such laborers into his harvest! Oh! that we could look round, and behold many such coming forth in this awful day, that we might be led to hope the Lord would not then remove our Candlestick out of its place! Rev. ii. 5.

I cannot propose, in a *Poor Man's Commentary*, to follow the Apostle through all the parts of the ministerial labors which he hath enumerated in this Chapter. But I shall select a few of the most striking, and such as were not confined to the days of the Apostles, but more or less, correspond to the general state of the Church in all ages.

And I shall begin with the one which *Paul* himself hath begun with, namely, the decided testimony that the Lord the Holy Ghost sent him and his few faithful companions to labor in the word and doctrine, from the evident blessings which attended their ministry. *You yourselves know, brethren, that our entrance in unto you was not in vain.* Reader! it were to be most earnestly sought for from the Lord, that the Churches of the living God, both the people and the minister have the Lord's testimony that his presence is among them, by his blessings which go before and follow the word. There is somewhat tremendously awful, when men run unsent into the ministry, to whom it might be said, *who hath required this at your hand when ye tread my courts?* Isaiah i. 12. And to behold multitudes expressing seeming anxiety for the conversion of others, which never were converted themselves, is among the awful signs of the present times!

The next beautiful feature of character in *Paul's* ministry is, what he hath marked of opposition. Never was there a faithful servant of Christ as yet unopposed. And very certain it is, that there never will be, for then would *the offence of the cross be ceased.* The Apostle appears to have marked it down, as a never failing token, upon every occasion, that wherever *the* Lord *opened a great and effectual door* to preach his Gospel, there would be sure to be found many adversaries. 1 Cor. xvi. 9. Hence the shameful treatment *Paul* met at *Philippi*, is blessedly explained, by the success *Paul* found there in the Lord's blessing upon it. *Lydia* and the *Jailor* are upon everlasting record, wherefore the devil roared, and stirred up his agents to oppose and scourge the Apostles; and how many more the Lord might have called there, we are left to form hopes. See Acts xvi. And such is the case in all ages. Wherever the Lord sends his faithful servants to gather his redeemed from among the world, the Gospel of God must be delivered *with much contention.* To preach Christ, and Christ only, to insist upon the everlasting love of God the Father, as *Paul* did, in choosing the Church in Christ before the foundation of the world, predestinating that Church to the adoption of children by Jesus Christ to himself, according to the good pleasure of his will, to preach wholly and solely, as *Paul* did, redemption through the blood of Christ, and to insist, moreover, that without the regeneration of the heart by God the Spirit, as Christ himself did, there can be no entrance into his kingdom to preach these glorious truths, as the whole of salvation will be, indeed, with much contention. All modern Pharisees of the world will take offence at such preaching, and such preachers, as the antient ones did at Christ himself, and will not barely oppose, but raise an hue and cry against both. And it is a blessed testimony to the truth when such men oppose it. For, as they know not the plague of their own heart, and never entered by the door of regeneration into the sheepfold, how shall they know the glorious, distinguishing truths of the Gospel? Ephes. i. 4—10. John iii. 3. and x. 1.

The Apostle hath given another most striking character of his faithfulness in the ministry, when he said, *For our exhortation was not of deceit, nor of uncleanness, nor in guile. But, as we were allowed to be put in trust with the Gospel, even so we speak; not as pleasing men, but God which trieth our hearts.* What a lovely account is here of a faithful minister of Jesus Christ! But it is a solemn question to ask, whether such are not of deceit, and uncleanness, and guile, who call themselves ministers of Christ, and yet are men pleasers. To bolster up Pharisees in compliments of their goodness, to suppress the grand and distinguishing doctrines of election, Christ's atonement, and the final perseverance of the saints in submission to such men's false opinions, to suffer the Lord's people to go lean, in keeping back the precious consolations of the Gospel, that the proud may be gratified in having smooth things preached before them; these are awful signs of unfaithfulness in the ministry, wherever they are found! And what a striking appeal the Apostle makes, in confirmation of his faithfulness, when he doth it both before God and man. *For neither* (saith he) *at any time used we flattering words,* ye know. *Nor a cloke of covetousness,* God is witness. How very blessed it must be thus to act in the ministry! The real Church of Christ knows no distinction of persons. All are equally dear to Jesus. And equally dear they must be to his faithful ministers. That servant of the Lord, that is himself conscious of the plague of his own heart, will exercise the greater jealousy over his people. And, as more danger is to be dreaded from the leaven of the Pharisee, than from all the other causes of evil whatever; he that knows his own heart will spare not others. He will never fawn nor flatter, but rather, as *Paul* commanded *Timothy, reprove, rebuke, exhort, with all long-suffering and doctrine.* And, if ever there was a day in which this faithfulness was more imperiously necessary than another, the present is so. *Paul* said *the time would come when they would not endure sound doctrine; but after their own lusts would heap to themselves teachers having itching ears; turning away their ears from the truth, and being turned unto fables.* 2 Tim. iv. 2—4. And had the Apostle pointed to this very age, as the day he alluded to, it could not have been more correct in description. Instead of making CHRIST the all in all, as *Paul* did, human perfection is cried up, and men are complimented with their zeal and liberality, and almsdeeds, in promoting, as it is called, the spread of the Gospel. Where is the model of CHRIST's preaching discoverable in such Essays? Who that reads CHRIST's first Sermon in the Jewish Synagogue, can find any traces of it in the discourses of modern times? His was *to preach the Gospel to the poor, to heal the broken-hearted, to preach deliverance to the captives, and recovering of sight to the blind.* Luke iv. 18. Happy the people who sit under preaching formed on this plan?

One word more. We never can too much admire the affection with which *Paul* describes his labors, and those of his companions in the ministry, as he hath here represented it. *We were gentle among you,* (saith he,) *even as a nurse cherisheth her children.* The image is most tender, and is designed to represent how very watchful the faithful servants of the LORD are of his fold, and how affectionately they bear with all the weaknesses and wants, and even waywardness of the babes and the young of CHRIST's family. But, while I admire *Paul's* figure of the nurse, I cannot but remark his modesty also, in taking that of the nurse, and not of the mother. The nurse, yea, the tenderest nurse is not the real, but only the foster mother. JESUS hath taken this image of the mother to himself, and to himself alone it belongs; and, therefore, *Paul* doth not presume to use it. *As one whom his mother comforteth, so will I comfort you.* Isaiah lxvi. 13. But I pray the Reader to observe what a fulness of love the Apostle hath summed up in his expressions, when he saith, that *being so affectionately desirous of the* LORD's *people, they were willing to have imparted to them, not the Gospel of* GOD *only, but also their own souls, because they were dear to them.* It is hardly possible, in the cold and selfish times in which we live, to enter into an apprehension of the warmth of *Paul's* heart. All he had, and all he knew; his gifts, and graces, and enjoyments were all for the people, among whom he labored in word and doctrine; yea, his very soul was theirs, because CHRIST and his members are all one. Oh! what a lovely view of the affectionate minister of CHRIST! If the Reader would wish to see the several features more largely drawn, I refer him to Acts xx. 17, &c.

We must not overlook the disinterested conduct of *Paul* and his companions in their ministerial services, that it was all free, and without cost or charges. He labored night and day at his trade of tent-making, that the Gospel might bring no expence to his hearers. See Acts xviii. 3. Not, as he elsewhere said, because that he had no right of eating of their bread, while he fed them with the bread of life; see 1 Cor. ix. 14. and Commentary; but because it was delightful to his generous mind to be not burdensome to the people. He knew the blessedness and truth, in his own experience of his LORD's words, and acted upon them. Acts xx. 33—35. Reader! do not overlook this part also of *Paul's* character!

Allow me to add one word more on this beautiful passage, in which the outlines of a faithful minister of CHRIST is so correctly drawn. I beg the Reader to observe how the Apostle tells the Church that they were witnesses, and GOD also, how holily and justly, and unblameably, they had behaved themselves among them, and also had exhorted and charged them as a father doth his children, that they would also walk worthy of GOD, who had called them unto his kingdom and glory.

I entreat the Reader to be the more attentive to this feature of the ministerial character, as drawn by GOD the HOLY GHOST with the pen of *Paul*, because many, either from ignorance or perversity, are perpetually mistaking the subject, as though they who preach the great truths of the Gospel in GOD's electing love, CHRIST's redeeming blood and righteousness, and GOD the SPIRIT's regenerating grace, do not inculcate obedience, neither exhort to godliness and an holy life. Whereas the fact is the very reverse. Preachers sent by GOD the HOLY GHOST, (and none unsent by him are sent at all,) being themselves regenerated, (and an unregenerate man was never ordained by the HOLY GHOST,) begin the subject where CHRIST begins it. *Make the tree good,* (saith JESUS,) *and his fruit good.* Matt. xii. 33. Until the sinner is born again, he is dead in trespasses and sins. Ephesians ii. 1. Hence, when a soul is himself renewed and ordained by the HOLY GHOST, and sent forth to preach CHRIST, he simply preacheth CHRIST, and nothing beside. He doth, as *Moses* did in the wilderness, *lift up the* SON *of man, that whosoever believeth in him may not perish, but have eternal life.* John iii. 14, 15. And when GOD the SPIRIT, who sends the word, gives power to the word, and by his regenerating grace quickens the sinner to a new and spiritual life, then all the blessed effects are the consequence, which the Apostle here describes. Holiness of life and conversation will always follow the renewed life. But to do as some modern teachers would prescribe, namely, to address the ungodly, and call them to faith and repentance, is like bidding the *Æthiopian* to change his skin, and the leopard his spots. Reader! do pause over the beautiful portrait which the HOLY GHOST himself hath drawn by *Paul*, of a faithful minister of CHRIST, and admire the loveliness of his character!

13 For this cause also thank we God without ceasing, because, when ye received the word of God which ye heard of us, ye received *it* not *as* the word of men, but as it is in truth, the word of God which effectually worketh also in you that believe.

14 For ye, brethren, became followers of the churches of God which in Judea are in Christ

Jesus: for ye also have suffered like things of your own countrymen, even as they *have* of the Jews:

15 Who both killed the Lord Jesus and their own prophets, and have persecuted us; and they please not God, and are contrary to all men;

16 Forbidding us to speak to the Gentiles that they might be saved, to fill up their sin alway: for the wrath is come upon them to the uttermost:

17 But we, brethren, being taken from you for a short time in presence, not in heart, endeavoured the more abundantly to see your face with great desire.

18 Wherefore we would have come unto you, even I Paul, once and again; but Satan hindered us.

19 For what *is* our hope, or joy, or crown of rejoicing? *Are* not even ye in the presence of our Lord Jesus Christ at his coming?

20 For ye are our glory and joy.

How very lovely it is to observe the Apostle following up the account he gave the Church, of his going in and out before them with thanksgivings to the Lord for the success of his ministry! And I beg the Reader to observe no less, how blessedly he traceth all the success of his labors to this one source, in the Lord's disposing them to receive the word of God, not as the word of men, but as it is in truth, *the word of* God. It is always blessed to behold Christ's' servants referring all the glory where alone it is due. We have a beautiful instance, Acts iii. 12.

We can easily conceive what the Apostle alludes to, when he saith, that he was taken away from them, meaning, as his history informs us, when he was hurried away at the time the uproar was made against *Paul* and his companions; Acts xvii. 5. And the hindrance of *Satan*, meaning his agents, was what *Paul* more than once noticed. See Rom. i. 13.

I admire the expression of the Apostle, when he calls the Church their hope and joy. Not that he meant that he was their hope, or they his, for both rested wholly upon Christ, and Christ is all the joy of the Church, both in heaven and earth. But *Paul* beheld the Church of the *Thessalonians* as a beautiful building, founded with himself wholly in Christ; and in the labor of the work, the wise Master-builder had condescended to employ *Paul* and his companions. As such, their furtherance in the knowledge and love of Christ, became a subject of great joy to the Apostle. And he was looking forward to the day of Christ's coming, with holy rapture and delight, as the blessed period, when he should see them and the whole Church arrived to that perfection *in* Christ, and *of*, and *from* Christ, as he hath described to the Church of the *Ephesians.* Chap. iv. 13.

Reader! pause, and contemplate the holy view, for it is both holy and blessed. This perfection in Christ, is Christ himself made perfect in his Church. We are said to come *in the unity of the faith, and of the knowledge of the* Son *of* God *to a perfect man;* namely, Christ in his fulness, having all his mystical body, his saints, then fully and perfectly prepared in body, soul, and spirit, for the everlasting enjoyment of their Lord to all eternity. Every member brought home. Every faculty most compleatly blessed. All deriving their beauty *from* Christ, and all made holy *in* Christ. This will be the wonder of heaven, when Christ's glory and beauty will communicate and reflect both glory and beauty to all his members, and all the vast ends of the Son of God, in marrying human nature, will be consummated, and seen by worlds of admiring spectators, and Christ will be beheld everlastingly blessed and glorious in Himself and in them, and they in Him, and shine as the stars around his Person for evermore. Reader! well might *Paul* express himself as he did, in the contemplation of this glory, which shall be revealed! And well may you and I look forward to this great day of God, if we now know him here in grace, for we shall then assuredly know him in glory. *He shall come* (saith the Apostle) *to be glorified in his saints, and to be admired in all them that believe.* 2 Thes. i. 10.

REFLECTIONS.

Let as many ministers of the Lord Jesus Christ as read this precious chapter, beg for grace, to be enabled to follow the Apostle's example in their ministry, and humbly pray for the same success. Oh! what an arduous undertaking, what a solemn trust, what distinguished honor, and what vast responsibility. Who that considered it as he ought, but would rather shrink from the high calling, than run unsent! But let every faithful servant of Jesus not despond. Jesus is the all-sufficiency both of his ministers and people. And he that looks wholly to Jesus, and draws all his resources from Jesus, whether minister or people, will never fail of finding an all-sufficiency for his own soul, and for his labor among others. Where God the Spirit ordains, he will give the suited supply. And those words of the Lord are sufficient to carry the servant through the whole of his labor. *Lo! I am with you alway, even unto the end of the world!*

And no less, ye people of God! do you hold up the hands of the Lord's servant, who goeth in and out before you by the Lord's appointment, by prayer and supplication, for a blessing on his labors. It is a sweet encouragement to the faithful laborer in the Lord's vineyard, when he knows that his people go before with their prayers to the Lord for his blessing, and follow him for supplications for pardon to all his imperfections. And where the Lord hath blessed a Church with a faithful servant, who taketh the oversight of the Church of Christ, *not by constraint, but willingly; not for filthy lucre, but of a ready mind:* what may not be hoped for from the divine blessing on such a congregation, both of minister and people! LORD, the SPIRIT! send *Pastors after thine own heart, which shall feed thy people with knowledge and understanding!*

CHAP. III.

CONTENTS.

This is a short but interesting Chapter. Every Verse is expressive of the Apostle's Love for the Church. Amidst his Sufferings, he finds Comforts in their Soul-prosperity.

WHEREFORE when we could no longer forbear, we thought it good to be left at Athens alone;

2 And sent Timotheus, our brother, and minister of God, and our fellow-labourer in the Gospel of Christ, to establish you, and to comfort you concerning your faith:

By *Paul's* sending *Timothy* to the Church of the *Thessalonians,* while he himself stood much in need of this young man's services, we plainly discover how little he regarded himself when the welfare of the Church was before him. I have often thought, and prayed for grace to follow it, that the whole life of CHRIST's ministers ought to be directed in no one pursuit but the LORD's glory, in waiting upon and enquiring into the wants of the LORD's people. If there was less selfishness about my poor heart, I should consider it no interruption, but rather rejoice in the occasion which called me from (otherwise the pleasing employment of) study, to listen to the complaints and enquiries of the humble, and the weak of the LORD's family. And, I believe, that among those faithful ones in CHRIST's service, who have sought out, without waiting to be sent for, the sorrowful and tempted in the houshold of faith; they have found their own souls often refreshed, when the LORD hath caused them to minister to the refreshment of others. *Paul* himself found this to be the case, for he told the Church, that he *longed to see them, that he might impart unto them some spiritual gift, to the end they might be established, and himself comforted by the mutual faith both in them and him.* Rom. i. 11, 12. And very sure I am, that next to the word of GOD, in the LORD's teaching, sick rooms and dying chambers are the best books, under the SPIRIT's explaining them, from whence a minister, ordained of GOD the HOLY GHOST, may learn subjects for preaching.

3 That no man should be moved by these afflictions: for yourselves know that we are appointed thereunto.

4 For verily, when we were with you, we told you before that we should suffer tribulation; even as it came to pass, and ye know.

It should seem, that part of the sorrows of the *Thessalonians* was on the Apostle's account. They knew that he had been driven from them by the storm raised round the house of *Jason*, from whence the brethren had sent away *Paul* by night. See Acts xvii. 1—15. And as he had been obliged to flee to *Athens* from *Berea*, their fears on his account were increased. How sweetly *Paul* reminds them of what he had continually preached as the true marks of the Apostolic character. *No man should be moved by afflictions.* It is JESUS which appoints, watches over, regulates, and sanctifies them. How little understood are those things in the present hour? If a faithful minister of CHRIST was to be sought for, in the present day by this mark of persecution, to what congregation would the enquiry be made? The general feature of the times is, to soften as much as may be, doctrines which are not palatable, for others of a more accommodating spirit. The primitive days of our fathers, after the LORD in his mercy had caused this land to emerge from popery, were remarkable for holding forth the word of life. The great truths of our holy faith, such as the election of GOD, redemption wholly by CHRIST, the regeneration by the HOLY GHOST, and the everlasting safety of the Church, in the final perseverance of the LORD's redeemed ones, were never lost sight of in their ministry. But how are these esteemed in the present hour, when, under the delusive pretence of spreading the truths of GOD, men of the most opposite principles in religion mingle together, concealing their different views of faith, that they may give no offence to each other. What would *Paul* have said to this smothering spirit, had he lived in these days? His affectionate Epistle to the *Thessalonians*, in charging them not to be moved by the afflictions of persecution, would have been totally unnecessary.

5 For this cause, when I could no longer forbear, I sent to know your faith, lest by some means the tempter have tempted you, and our labour be in vain.

6 But now when Timotheus came from you unto us, and brought us good tidings of your faith and charity, and that ye have good remembrance of us always, desiring greatly to see us, as we also *to see* you:

7 Therefore, brethren, we were comforted over you all in our affliction and distress by your faith.

8 For now we live, if ye stand fast in the Lord.

9 For what thanks can we render to God again

for you, for all the joy wherewith we joy for your sakes before our God:

10 Night and day praying exceedingly that we might see your face, and might perfect that which is lacking in your faith?

In the present day of the Gospel, when the spirit of persecution is known only in name, it is hardly possible to conceive, how the minds of the faithful were exercised, when, as *Paul* here saith, he could no longer forbear to know how they stood in the faith; and how the heart of the Apostle rejoiced, in the tidings he received, of the Church's welfare. It is blessed when the Church centers all in Christ. The least departure from this, is going off the foundation. But when all rests on Christ, and all is built up in Christ; perfect peace, and happiness, will mark the order, and joy of the people. Blessedly *Paul* calls this life. *For now we live* (saith he) *if ye stand fast in the* Lord.

11 Now God himself and our Father, and our Lord Jesus Christ, direct our way unto you.

12 And the Lord make you to increase and abound in love one toward another, and toward all *men*, even as we *do* toward you:

13 To the end he may establish your hearts unblameable in holiness before God, even our Father, at the coming of our Lord Jesus Christ with all his saints.

Some have thought, that the whole Persons of the Godhead are included in this prayer of the Apostle. God himself the Holy Ghost the great Author of his holy word; and our Father; and our Lord Jesus Christ. But whether so, or not, certainly the whole Godhead is engaged, in those Covenant-acts, as relating to the Church. And in all our removals, from place to place, the Lord's people are under the special, and personal presence, and blessing, of the whole Godhead. See John xiv. 23, 26. Rev. i. 4, 5. And, it is very precious to a child of God, when he finds a corresponding effect in his own soul, that his access *to* God, and communion *with* God, as well as the gracious visits *from* God; are all bringing testimony with them of those blessings. For this becomes a practical evidence, of living under the constant influence of the love of God, the grace of the Lord Jesus Christ, and the communion of the Holy Ghost. 2 Cor. xiii. 14.

REFLECTIONS.

Who can behold the affection, manifested by the Apostle to the Church, as set forth in this Chapter, without being struck with the conviction, that there is, there must be, in every faithful minister of

CHRIST ordained, and sent forth, as *Paul* was, by the HOLY GHOST, somewhat of the same love and affection. How is it possible for that man to be earnest in the service of souls, whose own soul is not melted by grace, into an ardent desire, for their everlasting welfare? Coldness, deadness, and an indifferency, argue, yea, prove, an unsuitableness for the ministry. And, whatever gifts and talents of the head a man may possess, in the mere letter-knowledge of the truths of GOD; he will never enter into the ministry with an earnestness to win souls, except a sense of his own salvation, makes him feel for others. Blessed *Paul* counts it *his* life, while the Church lived. The salvation of the people, was his hope, and crown of rejoicing. And hence, he could, and did say: *as you have acknowledged, so we trust you shall acknowledge even to the end, that we are your rejoicing, as ye also are ours, in the day of the* LORD JESUS. Reader! it will be your happiness, and mine, to discover our hearts brought into the same oneness of spirit, in CHRIST. His is the glory, and ours is the happiness. And, while both minister and people, are established by his grace, in him; we shall then be accepted, *unblameable in holiness in him, before* GOD, *even our* FATHER, *at the coming of our* LORD JESUS CHRIST *with all his saints.*

CHAP. IV.

CONTENTS.

The Apostle is here exhorting the Church, to the blessed Fruits, and Effects, of Regeneration. He sweetly comforts the LORD's *People, on the Subject of the Body sleeping in* JESUS.

FURTHERMORE then we beseech you, brethren, and exhort *you* by the Lord Jesus, that as ye have received of us how ye ought to walk and to please God, *so* ye would abound more and more.

2 For ye know what commandments we gave you by the Lord Jesus.

3 For this is the will of God, *even* your sanctification, that ye should abstain from fornication:

4 That every one of you should know how to possess his vessel in sanctification and honour;

5 Not in the lust of concupiscense, even as the Gentiles which know not God.

6 That no *man* go beyond and defraud his brother in *any* matter: because that the Lord *is* the

avenger of all such, as we also have forewarned you and testified.

7 For God hath not called us unto uncleanness, but unto holiness.

8 He therefore that despiseth, despiseth not man, but God, who hath also given unto us his holy Spirit.

In the opening of this Chapter, we find the Apostle, calling upon the Church, to exercise those distinguishing features of character, which are the immediate fruits of regeneration. *If we live in the spirit, let us also walk in the spirit.* Now, for the better apprehension of the subject itself, as well as the special arguments, by which alone the Apostle calls upon believers to the practice of holiness; I very earnestly beg the Reader to attend to what the Apostle hath said, in these verses. *First.* It is to the Church *Paul* here speaks; and not unto the unawakened, carnal, and ungodly world. He considers them as in a state of regeneration; for he saith: *as ye have received of us how ye ought to walk and please* God. A plain proof that he considered them as such, who from being called out of the Adam-nature of sin, had received Christ Jesus as the whole of salvation; and were looking to him for grace in the exercise of all gospel sanctification. *Secondly.* As the principle of the new life by regeneration, was wrought in the heart; so the effect of it would manifest itself in the life, in all holy conversation, and godliness. Nothing can be more manifest, that this is the whole drift of the Apostle's precept. *As ye have received of us how ye ought to walk.* There can be no walk, for there is no life, in one, *dead in trespasses and sins.* But, as the Church was no longer dead in trespasses and sins; so, from the new life imparted, it was expected, suitable actions of life would appear. Ye have received of us the knowledge of these things; look to it then, that there be a suitable correspondence.

And this appears with yet further evidence, from what follows. For *this is the will of* God *even your sanctification.* God's will is, that Christ is made of God unto his people, *wisdom, righteousness, sanctification, and redemption.* 1 Cor. i. 30. Then, as this is God's will, and Christ is the sanctification of his people; this life of Christ in the soul, will manifest itself, in all corresponding conduct. Christ reigns, and rules within; and is the source of every thing blessed to his people. Hence, therefore, it is known from the actions without, that Christ reigns within. *For they that are* Christ's *have crucified the flesh with the affections and lusts.* Gal. v. 24.

And, it should be observed yet further, that the sins of our corrupt nature, which the *Gentiles* were much addicted to, were not considered by them, in the light which the Gospel regarded. Hence *Paul*, writing to a Church chiefly gathered from *Gentiles*, found occasion, more particularly to advert to this subject. And where the Holy Spirit was given, which a state of regeneration implies, it became an interesting part of the Apostle's exhortations, to shew the Church, how effectually his Almighty power was manifested, in the lives of GOD's people, in that work of the new-birth, wrought upon the heart. Agreeably to what *John,* the beloved Apostle, taught, *Whoever is born of* GOD, *doth not commit sin; for his seed remaineth in him; and he cannot sin because he is born of* GOD. 1 John iii. 9. Reader! it is very blessed to see, where the security of GOD's people is found; that all strength in a life of grace, and righteousness, may be sought for only from the LORD! For further views on sanctification see 2 Thess. ii. 13.

9 But as touching brotherly love, ye need not that I write unto you: for ye yourselves are taught of God to love one another.

10 And indeed ye do it toward all the brethren which are in all Macedonia: but we beseech you brethren, that ye increase more and more.

11 And that ye study to be quiet, and to do your own business, and to work with your own hands, as we commanded you;

12 That ye may walk honestly toward them that are without, and *that* ye may have lack of nothing.

I do not think it necessary to offer a single observation upon these verses. Brotherly love towards one another in those who are members of CHRIST's body, is not only a principle which carries with it its own conviction, but is so strongly enforced, from the very relationship in which those members are knit to each other; that, as the Apostle saith, it is not needful to write upon it. Truly regenerated souls, are one in CHRIST. And where they are so, there can be no schism. The sorrow, or joy, which one hath, all must partake in; if this membership be truly a living principle. 1 Cor. xii. 25, 26. And, in relation to Church members, *walking honestly toward them that are without;* it were a reproach to the name of CHRIST, if the ungodly had any charge to bring against them. Very sweet to this purpose, is that comprehensive exhortation, by the HOLY GHOST to the Church: that *whatsoever things are true, honest, just, pure, lovely, and of good report; believers in* CHRIST *are expected above all men, to be eminent in the practice of these things.* Philip. iv. 8.

13 But I would not have you to be ignorant, brethren, concerning them which are asleep, that ye sorrow not, even as others which have no hope.

14 For if we believe that Jesus died and rose again, even so them also which sleep in Jesus will God bring with him.

15 For this we say unto you by the word of the

Lord, that we which are alive and remain unto the coming of the Lord shall not prevent them which are asleep.

16 For the Lord himself shall descend from heaven with a shout, with the voice of the archangel, and with the trump of God: and the dead in Christ shall rise first:

17 Then we which are alive *and* remain shall be caught up together with them in the clouds, to meet the Lord in the air: and so shall we ever be with the Lord.

18 Wherefore comfort one another with these words.

Perhaps there is not a more affectionate passage in the word of GOD, to soothe the sorrows of our nature, under the humbling prospect of the grave, in the death of our friends, and the sure departure of ourselves, than what GOD the HOLY GHOST hath here given to the Church, by his servant the Apostle. I have often read it, with, I hope, profit and delight. And I do not conceive, that a child of GOD, under divine teaching, can ever read it, but at every renewed perusal, with increasing comfort.

It appears, that the Church of the *Thessalonians* had very imperfect apprehensions, on the interesting subject of the dead in CHRIST. And it was our mercy, that their ignorance gave occasion to GOD the SPIRIT, to teach the Church, what is here so blessedly explained, concerning it. The *first* thing I beg the Reader to remark with me, in the passage, is, the expression, of being *asleep in* JESUS. He doth not call it death, but *sleep*. It is remarkable, that in relation to the death of *Lazarus*, JESUS called it *sleep*. *Our friend Lazarus sleepeth; but I go that I may awake him out of sleep!* See John xi. 11. and Commentary. The blessed dead, which die in CHRIST, die in union with his Person. As such, they are part of CHRIST. The voice *John* heard from heaven, declared this, and bid the beloved Apostle write it down. Rev. xiv. 13. Hence, this is more properly called sleep, than death; for by virtue of this union, there is a principle, by which they are still part of CHRIST, and by which the LORD becomes to them at the last day, *the resurrection and the life.* John xi. 25. So that, in death, or life, CHRIST is the believer's portion; and the believer is a member of CHRIST's mystical body. And this oneness, union, and interest in CHRIST, so totally differs from the Christless dead, that the HOLY GHOST is pleased to call it sleep, rather than death. *They sleep in* JESUS.

Secondly. The HOLY GHOST by *Paul*, commands the Church concerning all such, that the sorrow which surviving believers feel, in their departure, is not to be as the grief of those who mourn over the hopeless dead. The LORD doth not forbid all sorrow; for the LORD allows nature's feelings to have vent. And JESUS himself wept at the grave of *Lazarus.* John xi. 25. But the tears of GOD's people, shed over the remains of the dead which die in the LORD, are like the spiced wine of the Pomegranate. The tears of nature, are sweetened in CHRIST. There is a blessed hope, yea, an assured hope, they shall again live. See a beautiful account by Job, xiv. 13—15.

Thirdly. The belief in CHRIST's resurrection, brings up after it, a full assurance, of the resurrection of all his members. They who sleep in JESUS, must arise with JESUS. For CHRIST died, and arose, as the common head of his body the Church. Not as a private person; but in a public capacity. Hence, in his resurrection, the Church, in every individual member, is included; for CHRIST was declared to be the first fruits of them that sleep. *For to this end,* (saith the HOLY GHOST by *Paul,*) CHRIST *both died, and rose, and revived, that he might be* LORD *both of the dead and living.* Rom. xiv. 9. See 1 Cor. xv. and Commentary.

Fourthly. There is somewhat particularly striking, in the Apostle's manner of expression on this subject, when he saith: *For this we say unto you by the word of the* LORD. It is not said when *Paul* received this message to deliver to the Church. Neither doth he make any other preface, by way of introduction. But, it should seem, from the words themselves, that though all the Apostle delivered to the Church, was in the LORD's name, and by the LORD's authority; yet he had now somewhat to deliver on this subject, of the resurrection of the bodies of saints sleeping in JESUS: and of the change to be wrought on the bodies of saints, which would be found alive at the last day; which he had not had either the knowledge of himself before, or direction to communicate to the Church. Hence, like the Prophets of old, who frequently, in the midst of their preaching, called up the attention of the Church yet more strikingly, with breaking off, and saying; *Thus saith the* LORD: so *Paul* here adopts a similar manner of expression, and saith: *For this we say unto you by the word of the* LORD. Reader! we have great cause to bless GOD the SPIRIT, for this special revelation, on a subject so very interesting, both to ourselves, and to all the members of CHRIST's mystical body, whereby we learn, under divine teaching, wherefore *we ought not to sorrow,* concerning the departed in CHRIST, *as others that have no hope.* And I pray the Reader, to be particularly attentive, to the very blessed manner, in which GOD the HOLY GHOST hath taught the Church, on those most momentous points.

The Apostle begins with the state of those saints of GOD, which are found in the body at CHRIST's coming. *We* (saith he) *which are alive and remain unto the coming of the* LORD *shall not prevent them which are asleep.* Now, let the Reader observe, that by the *we, which are alive; Paul* did not mean himself, or any of the Church of GOD then living. For, in his second Epistle to this same Church, he positively declared to them, that *the day of* CHRIST *was not at hand.* For (saith he) *that day shall not come except there come a falling away first, and that man of sin be revealed, the son of perdition.* 1 Thess. ii. 1—3. But *Paul* speaks in the name of the Church, in that part of CHRIST's members which shall be alive, when CHRIST comes *to be glorified in his saints, and to be admired in all them that believe.* 2 Thess. i. 10. Hence, by the way, we are taught, that there shall be a portion of CHRIST's mystical body alive, at his second coming.

The Apostle next proceeds, in the name of the LORD, to shew the Church, how they are to be disposed of, who pass not through the territories of death, and the grave, to the embraces of CHRIST. *We shall not prevent them* (saith *Paul*) *which are asleep.* The word *prevent* is an old English word, and means, *to go before:* we shall not be first changed, before the dead which sleep in JESUS shall be awakened to CHRIST's arms. This is a sweet thought, on every account. For it shews the watchful care of JESUS, over his sleeping members; and becomes a blessed comment of the LORD's own, on that sweet Scripture: *Precious in the sight of the* LORD *is the death of his saints.* Psm. cxvi. 15. And it is blessed on another account. The living members of CHRIST's mystical body, will find their spirits abundantly strengthened, in beholding the dead in CHRIST arise to the wonders of eternity. And what joy will burst forth, at the second voice of the Archangel, and the trump of GOD! Yea, what inexpressible emotions will be felt by all the living in CHRIST, at that time, when they shall see JESUS personally descending from heaven, in all the splendor, as here described, of glory?

Next, *Paul* describes the wonderful change, after the dead in CHRIST have first risen, which will instantly follow, on the bodies of the saints then living. *Then we* (saith he) *which are alive and remain, shall be caught up together with them in the clouds, to meet the* LORD *in the air. And so shall we ever be with the* LORD! The Apostle doth not say *how* the change of our vile bodies, which have not gone down to the grave, shall be accomplished. It is sufficient for the Church to know, that it shall be done: though the process we are not made acquainted with. But, as those bodies of the saints, which are sown in corruption, are promised to be raised in incorruption; and their natural bodies, raised spiritual bodies: 1 Cor. xv. 44. we are led to conclude, the same change will be accomplished, though not in the same way: So that all the members of CHRIST's mystical body, shall be alike prepared, and qualified, for the everlasting enjoyment of GOD in glory. Oh! what unknown felicity will the saints of GOD be brought into, when those bodies, which now interrupt the spiritual pleasures of the renewed soul, will interrupt them no more; yea, then will join in all their enjoyments. Well might the Apostle add: *wherefore comfort,* or exhort *one another with these words.* Let GOD's people, under all bereaving providences, when at any time the LORD takes home any of his redeemed ones; let them call to remembrance, what GOD the HOLY GHOST hath here so sweetly, and fully unfolded: they that live in CHRIST by regeneration, sleep in JESUS at death till the resurrection. They are part of CHRIST; and whether living or dying, in life or death, they are the LORD's. And they whom the LORD appoints to be alive in the body, at his coming, shall be instantly changed into a glorified body in CHRIST, as those of CHRIST's which arise at the voice of the Archangel, and the trump of GOD. Both shall be equally blessed in CHRIST; and be everlastingly happy with him, in glory. See Jude 9.

REFLECTIONS.

READER! what a blessed consideration is it, to the renewed soul in CHRIST, that He who is made of GOD to us wisdom, and righteousness; is no less our sanctification, and redemption? And, it is among the most blessed of all thoughts, and which GOD the HOLY GHOST is for ever impressing on the minds of his people, that our oneness and union with the LORD JESUS, brings up after it, an interest, in all that belongs to him as CHRIST. Our union with his Person, gives a security to our life *in* him, our graces *from* him, and our everlasting happiness *with* him; for assuredly, where He is, there must his members be. Precious JESUS may I never lose sight of those gracious assurances of thine. *Because I live ye shall live also.*

Blessed LORD the SPIRIT! thanks to thee, for sending thy servant to teach the Church, how to regulate our sorrows, when under bereaving providences. Never let my soul mourn any more, when any die in the LORD. Tears may fall. Yea, JESUS will not be displeased when they fall. It is the funeral of nature. And JESUS, who wept himself at *Lazarus's* tomb, will not be angry if any weep at mine. But grace triumphs. It is not death, but sleep, yea, a sweet refreshing sleep, when JESUS calls home his members. But while we hear the voice which *John* heard, we may write it as the inscription on the graves of the saints. *Blessed are the dead which die in the* LORD! And, as sure as they sleep in JESUS; so sure GOD will bring them with JESUS in that day when he comes. And ye members of CHRIST, who are yet unborn, whom JESUS shall appoint to be alive at his coming; ye also shall partake in the triumphs of his coming. Though ye go not down to the grave, yet will the LORD change your vile bodies, under which ye groan, and fashion them like unto his glorious body; according to the power whereby he is able to subdue all things to himself. LORD! give grace to thy Church, that amidst all the dying circumstances of thy people here below, we may be able *to comfort*, and to exhort *one another with these words!*

CHAP. V.

CONTENTS.

The Apostle closeth his Epistle in this Chapter. He describes the striking Difference of the LORD's *coming, as he will appear to his Church, and to the Ungodly. He again exhorts the Church to be comforted: and closeth the Epistle with his Apostolic Blessing.*

BUT of the times and the seasons, brethren, ye have no need that I write unto you.

2 For yourselves know perfectly that the day of the Lord so cometh as a thief in the night.

3 For when they shall say, Peace and safety; then sudden destruction cometh upon them, as travail upon a woman with child; and they shall not escape.

The Apostle in the close of the former Chapter, having so blessedly spoken to the Church, concerning the great day of God; begins this, with shewing the dreadful effects, the Lord's coming would have on the minds of the ungodly. He makes use of two very striking similitudes, to represent the horrible distress, with which the graceless, and unawakened, will be overtaken in that day. *First,* that of a thief, coming at the dark hour of midnight into a man's house, when all are asleep, in apparent quiet, and safety; to surprize, and murder the unconscious inhabitants. And, *secondly,* that of a woman in travail, whose agonies, for the time, are supposed to be the sharpest our nature is capable of feeling; and are therefore called (*dolores tergiversantes*) thundering pains. And this latter is rendered still more striking in resemblance, because the pains of child-bearing, are the fruits of our first mother's transgression, and entailed upon all her daughters, passing through the hour of nature's extremity. Gen. iii. 16. And the sinner's day of wrath, is the fruit also, of our own transgression. Oh! who shall conceive, or imagine, the horrors of that day, to every Christless son, and daughter of *Adam?* *Where shall the ungodly and the sinner appear?* What paleness, and convulsion of soul, will that sentence induce; *depart ye cursed!* Matt. xxv. 41.

4 But ye, brethren, are not in darkness, that that day should overtake you as a thief.

5 Ye are all children of light, and the children of the day: we are not of the night, nor of darkness.

6 Therefore let us not sleep, as *do* others; but let us watch and be sober.

7 For they that sleep sleep in the night, and they that be drunken are drunken in the night.

8 But let us, who are of the day, be sober, putting on the breast-plate of faith and love: and for an helmet, the hope of salvation.

9 For God hath not appointed us to wrath, but to obtain salvation by our Lord Jesus Christ,

10 Who died for us, that, whether we wake or sleep, we should live together with him.

11 Wherefore comfort yourselves together, and edify one another, even as also ye do.

How very gracious was it in the Lord the Spirit, while describing the awful events of this great day of God, as they will overtake the wicked; to comfort the Lord's people, with the assurance of their safety, when surrounded with such tremendous judgments, in their view, before them? And, I beg the Reader to be careful with me to observe, from whence, and in what, their safety is found. Not in themselves, or their own attainments. For wherein do they differ from others? and what have they which they did not receive? Not from birth, or descendants in nature. For all are alike born in the same *Adam*-stock, of whom Scripture bears testimony, *there is none good, no not one.* Rom. iii. 12. Not in works of righteousness which they have done; for they were by nature children of wrath, even as others. Ephes. ii. 3. But *Paul* blessedly shews the cause; because by the water of regeneration, and a renewing of the HOLY GHOST, shed upon them abundantly, through JESUS CHRIST our LORD. Titus iii. 3—7. And here again, the Apostle sums up all in one, the sole cause, of their safety, and their everlasting blessedness in CHRIST JESUS; because GOD (saith he) *hath not appointed them to wrath, but to obtain salvation by our* LORD JESUS CHRIST. And hence, the Apostle adds, *He died for us, that whether we wake or sleep, we should live together with him.* Song v. 2. Matt. xxv. 5. Here is the sole cause of mercy. This the glorious security of the Church. Hence no day can overtake them, no surprize of the midnight hour alarm. Sleeping, or waking, they are the LORD's.

I cannot suffer myself, neither the Reader, to pass away from these most blessed, and precious assurances, of GOD the SPIRIT, without first desiring to pause over them, and ponder well their deep importance, on that great subject contained in them. And I desire to do this the rather, because they come in with a strength of argument, at once perfectly irresistible, and unanswerable, to silence the presumptuous reasoning of men untaught by the HOLY GHOST, who venture, in direct defiance to all the glorious promises of GOD, to call the doctrine of the final perseverance of the saints, unscriptural, and highly dangerous. These men are so full in their apprehensions, of human worth, and human works, that they cannot ascribe the whole salvation to the finished redemption by the LORD JESUS CHRIST; but will make the purposes of GOD's grace, still to be depending upon the will of man. Alas! what is not the unhumbled pride of our fallen nature capable of bringing forth, where men are not taught of GOD, and remain unacquainted with the plague of their own heart? I very earnestly beg the Reader, to ponder well this precious scripture, looking up to GOD the HOLY GHOST to be his Teacher; and then, to his cool, and serious judgment, under the LORD I will leave the subject.

If, as GOD the HOLY GHOST by *Paul*, here taught the Church, that GOD hath *not* appointed the Church to wrath, but *hath* appointed them to obtain salvation, by our LORD JESUS CHRIST; can GOD's appointments be frustrated of their end? And if not, can that be unscriptural, or dangerous which inculcates, under divine teaching, such blessed truths? If GOD, who appoints these blessed things, to save from wrath, and to obtain salvation, hath in confirmation also, secured the means for the accomplishment of his purposes; is it possible to suppose, that any peradventure shall arise, which GOD did not foresee; and for which GOD made no provision? If, as a blessed security to the Church, GOD the FATHER, who hath not appointed to wrath, but hath appointed unto salvation; hath made the whole everlastingly secure; having chosen the Church in CHRIST, before the foundation of the world, that it should be holy, and without blame before him in love; and hath predestinated the Church unto the adoption of children by JESUS CHRIST unto himself; accepting the Church in the Beloved: if, on the part of GOD the FATHER, in the high Covenant offices of his everlasting love, he hath mercifully made such ample provisions of security, for the sure accomplishment of his purposes; can either men, or devils, frustrate his designs? Moreover, the HOLY GHOST hath added in this very scripture, another blessed cause of assurance. He that appointed us to obtain salvation by our LORD JESUS CHRIST, hath confirmed it in CHRIST; for, we are here told, CHRIST *died for us, that whether we wake, or sleep, we should live together with him.* Hence, here is also, *the Pillar, and ground of the truth.* Neither doth the subject stop here. For GOD the SPIRIT hath engaged, to *regenerate* those, whom GOD hath *chosen,* and for whom CHRIST *died;* and, in confirmation that he hath done it, in this very chapter, the LORD declares, that they are not in darkness, as are the ungodly, whom the day of GOD will overtake as a *thief in the night; but that they are children of the light, and the children of the day.* Now then, in the face of these, and numberless other scriptures to the same purport, shall we be told, that GOD'S purposes are doubtful? That the final perseverance of the elect, is unscriptural, and dangerous? Are such men indeed so desperately blind, as to suppose, GOD hath appointed the means, but is uncertain of the end? Oh! what a leanness, and poverty of soul, must there be in congregations under such teaching? Surely it may be said of all such men, as *Job* did to his Pharisaical instructors: *miserable comforters are ye all, physicians of no value?*

Reader! I pray you for the LORD'S glory, and your own personal happiness, look up to GOD for his instruction on this momentous point. Hear what the LORD saith to confirm his word unto his people. *Wherein* GOD *willing more abundantly to shew unto the heirs of promise the immutability of his counsel, confirmed it by an oath: That by two immutable things, in which it was impossible for* GOD *to lie, we might have a strong consolation, who have fled for refuge, to lay hold upon the hope set before us.* Heb. vi. 17, 18. Here observe the several gracious expressions. GOD'S immutable purpose, formed wholly in himself, without any regard to the mutability of his chosen people. That purpose confirmed by two immutable things, GOD'S word, and GOD'S oath. And confirmed with this express design, that *the heirs of promise,* (mark the expression, *heirs of promise,* not workers of the law, see Gal. iii. 15 to the end,) might have a strong consolation. And all this because GOD was willing that those heirs of promise should have his gracious purpose more abundantly shewn unto them, to confirm all his promises; yea, and Amen in CHRIST JESUS. Now then put the whole together. Here is the immutable purpose, will, and pleasure of Him, *with whom is no variableness, neither shadow of turning. Of his own will begat he us with the word of truth, that we should be a kind of first-fruits of his creatures.* James i. 17, 18. And, hence, CHRIST in allusion to it, saith, that in order for the sure accomplishment of it, the LORD will cut short the times of persecution in his Church. For speaking of those exercises, JESUS saith, that *except the* LORD *had shortened those days, no flesh should be saved. But for the elect's sake, whom he hath chosen, he hath shortened the days.* And the LORD further confirms the everlasting safety of his people, in that he shews the impossibility of deceiving the elect, Mark xiii. 19—22. So that GOD's purpose is founded in himself, and established in *the covenant, ordered in all things and sure.* 2 Sam. xxiii. 5. It is confirmed in the blood and righteousness of CHRIST. Ephes. i. 7. And the people which are *the heirs of promise,* are made willing, by the regenerating work of GOD the SPIRIT, according to covenant engagements *in the day of his power.* Psm. cx. 3. And what crowns the whole, as this immutability of GOD's will was not founded in any expectation from man, or liable to change from the mutability of man, neither depended upon any thing good or bad in the objects of this distinguishing mercy; so the ultimate blessings given to those heirs of promise, were not given them for their merit, or to be kept back for their undeservings. Among the very first clauses in the charter of grace, we find the merciful design expressed in these words: *For the children being not yet born, neither having done any good or evil, that the purpose of* GOD *according to election might stand, not of works, but of him that calleth; it was said the elder shall serve the younger.* Rom. ix. 11. And, hence, the Almighty Founder, which in his own immutability formed the counsel of his will, formed, no less, all suitable provision to make the heirs of promise everlastingly blessed, and happy in their heritage. *For whom he did foreknow, he also did predestinate to be conformed to the image of his* SON, *that he might be the first-born among many brethren. Moreover, whom he did predestinate, them he also called: and whom he called, them he also justified: and whom he justified, them he also glorified.* Rom. viii. 29, 30. And what shall we then say to these things? Not, surely, as those say who call the consolations arising from those doctrines wrong, yea, and the doctrines themselves unscriptural and dangerous, but rather to hear what the LORD JESUS himself saith in comforting his people, with the full assurance of faith. *Fear not little flock; for it is your* FATHER's *good pleasure to give you the kingdom!* Luke xii. 32.

12 And we beseech you, brethren, to know them which labour among you, and are over you in the Lord, and admonish you;

13 And to esteem them very highly in love for their work's sake. *And* be at peace among yourselves.

14 Now we exhort you brethren, warn them that are unruly, comfort the feeble-minded, support the weak, be patient toward all *men.*

15 See that none render evil for evil unto any *man;* but ever follow that which is good, both among yourselves, and to all *men.*

16 Rejoice evermore.

17 Pray without ceasing.

18 In every thing give thanks: for this is the will of God in Christ Jesus concerning you.

19 Quench not the Spirit.

20 Despise not prophesyings.

21 Prove all things; hold fast that which is good.

22 Abstain from all appearance of evil.

23 And the very God of peace sanctify you wholly; and *I pray God* your whole spirit and soul and body be preserved blameless unto the coming of our Lord Jesus Christ.

We have much subject for the most interesting meditation and improvement, contained within these verses. But the several heads of discourse dwelt upon, are too plain to need a Comment. The love and affection to be shewn to faithful ministers, in an esteem for their persons, and yet more for their doctrines; the rebuke to be manifested to the unruly; the forbearance of returning evil for evil; and the earnestness of following every thing that is in conformity to the Gospel of CHRIST: these are so blessedly set forth by the Apostle, as to supersede the necessity of adding any further observations in this *Poor Man's Commentary.* Unless, indeed, it be, to beg of GOD for grace, both to the Writer and Reader, that we may be eminent in the exercise of such things.

And I beg the Reader to notice with me, how earnestly the Apostle follows up his several exhortations, in recommending that holy joy of the Spirit, which a truly regenerated child, conscious of his personal interest in the Covenant of grace is justly entitled to. And those who feel the sweet teachings of GOD the HOLY GHOST, will most earnestly desire both to rejoice and to pray, and never quench those motions of GOD the SPIRIT, but to abound in hope, and joy, and peace, in believing, that both his prophecies, and his blessings may have an abiding influence in their hearts.

I detain the Reader over that verse in which *Paul* considers our nature as compounded of *spirit, soul, and body.* It is well known, that we are generally supposed to be composed but of *two* principles, namely, *soul* and *body.* But, certainly, the Apostle is correct, for there are *three.* By the *spirit* is meant that immortal part, which, in consequence of the *Adam*-nature fall, is dead in trespasses and sins, but by the HOLY GHOST, in every child of GOD, is quickened to a new and spiritual life. And being part of CHRIST, can die no more, but is holy and without blame in CHRIST for ever. The *soul,* as it is called here by the Apostle, is that thinking faculty which man hath in common with some other animals of the inferior creation, concerning which the Psalmist speaks, that *in that very day when the breath of man goeth forth, he returneth to his earth, and his thoughts perish.* Psm. cxlvi. 4. And the *body,* it is hardly necessary to observe, is the mere mass of flesh and bones. Hence, by this view of our nature, the great doctrines of grace are seen in the clearest manner. The *spirit*, which in a state of unrenewed nature, like all the mass of *Adam's* race, is dead in trespasses and sins; when, (as in the instance of every child of GOD,) it is regenerated and born again, is made a partaker of the divine nature; the HOLY GHOST, by that sovereign act, hath, *according to his divine power, given unto us all things that pertain to life and godliness.* 2 Pet. i. 3, 4. So that this new-born babe in CHRIST is born perfect in all his parts; and in respect to the spiritual life imparted, is as holy as it ever can be in heaven. Grow it will in grace, as a new-born child grows in nature. But like a child in nature, it will have no other nature, but the same for ever in which it is new-born. It is *born again*, (saith an Apostle,) *not of corruptible seed, but of incorruptible, by the word of* GOD, *which liveth and abideth for ever.* 1 Pet. i. 23. But the thinking faculty, which *Paul* here calls the *soul*, and the *body* which is nothing but flesh and bones, these are never renewed during the whole time-state of the Church below; but, as *Paul* himself found in his own experience, and groaned under the daily burden thereof, they form *a body of sin and death*. Rom. vii. 18 to the end. Yet, notwithstanding the unrenewed state of the thinking faculty and the body, the whole man being in the Covenant of grace, spirit, soul, and body are included in the great purposes of redemption. And, hence, *Paul* prays that *the whole spirit, soul, and body* of GOD's children, *be preserved blameless, unto the coming of our* LORD JESUS CHRIST.

24 Faithful *is* he that calleth you, who also will do *it*.

25 Brethren, pray for us.

26 Greet all the brethren with an holy kiss.

27 I charge you by the Lord that this epistle be read unto all the holy brethren.

28 The grace of our Lord Jesus Christ *be* with you. Amen.

The first *epistle* unto the Thessalonians was written from Athens.

It is hardly necessary to make any observations upon those sweet verses, they are in themselves so plain, but they are also so beautiful and affectionate, that I hardly know how to pass them by unnoticed. I shall only, however, just remark how blessedly the Apostle assures the Church of GOD's faithfulness. GOD's call is a most decided proof of his faithfulness. *For whom he did predestinate, them he also called.* And his call looks as sure forward to justify and glorify, as it looks back to his eternal purpose, will, and pleasure in predestinating. Hence, *Peter* admonisheth the Church to prove their *election* by their *call*. Compare Rom. viii. 29, 30. with 2 Pet. i. 10.

I pray the Reader not to overlook the Apostle's desiring an interest in the prayers of the faithful. It is a sweet thought when the whole Church of God be considered as mutually helping each other in prayer. *There should be no schism in the body, but the members should have the same care one for another.* 1 Cor. xii. 25. And if so great an Apostle thus sought a remembrance by the people before the Lord, how earnest may it be supposed ought all who now minister in holy things, to say continually to the Church, *Brethren, pray for us!*

And let not the Reader overlook the Apostle's command, that *all* the brethren should be greeted, the humblest, the poorest, the least. For, as in the human body there is not a part so inconsiderable but what the whole is concerned for, and cannot but take interest in, both in its pain or pleasure; so, in the mystical body of Christ, all are equally concerned in what belongs to each member, and all, yea, the glorious Head himself Christ Jesus, *cannot*, (indeed, He would not,) *say to the feet, I have no need of you.* 1 Cor. xii. 21. Oh! what an argument ariseth therefrom, to all that christian love and affection, which ought to distinguish the members of Christ's body! 1 Cor. xii. 27.

One word more. An holy kiss for holy brethren, is a sacred and sanctified description of character for distinguishing the Lord's brethren. Heb. iii. 1. 1 Pet. ii. 9. *Holiness unto the* Lord, was to be upon the bells of the horses in the Gospel day. Zech. xiv. 20. Jesus wills this holiness in and from himself to his people. Compare Levit. xi. 44. with 1 Pet. i. 15, 16. And how needful must it be, that all the holy family should have the Scriptures of our God, which are not of any private interpretation, read to them for their instruction, exhortation, and comfort. 2 Pet. i. 20, 21. And how blessedly *Paul* closeth all with his Apostolical benediction, and which is his mark of their being his. 2 Thess. iii. 17.

REFLECTIONS.

Reader! here is a Chapter highly calculated, under God, to put to silence the ignorance of foolish men: While the ungodly are scoffing at the threatened judgment of the Lord's coming, behold with what awful and alarming account it is said that day will be known. As a thief in the night, so sudden, so unexpected. And, while the graceless will be thus surprized, both with the greatness and unlooked for horrors of that day; the prospect, like the Cloud in the camp of Israel, while dark with the blackness of despair to the enemies of our God and his Christ, will be bright and shining to all the Lord's people, who are the children of the light, and of the day. Oh! the blessedness of that assurance, God *hath not appointed us unto wrath, but unto salvation, through* Jesus Christ *our* Lord!

Blessed be God the Holy Ghost for commanding his Scriptures to be read unto all the holy brethren. A plain proof of the sin and folly of that class of men, who would shut up the word of God from the common people. God be blessed for his mercy to this land, in that we have the Scriptures open to us, *which are able to make us wise unto salvation, through* Jesus Christ *our* Lord. And blessed be the Lord for the ministry of his faithful servant *Paul*, in this very sweet Epistle, and for all the inspired writings which GOD the SPIRIT taught him to send to the Churches! Ere long, the Church will meet with him, and all the faithful servants of the LORD, in every age of the Church, which have ministered in the name of the LORD. In the mean time, may GOD the SPIRIT cause his unction to enlighten all his people in the reading of them. And while the grace of GOD is directing the Church upon earth, may both the Church in earth and heaven be continually ascribing glory to the united source of all mercy, FATHER, SON, and HOLY GHOST, now, and for evermore. Amen.

THE SECOND EPISTLE OF PAUL THE APOSTLE TO THE THESSALONIANS.

GENERAL OBSERVATIONS.

IT is more than probable, that this *second* Epistle to the Church of the *Thessalonians* was written not a longer space after the first, than *two years*. The chief scope of it seems to have been by way of fortifying their minds against the assaults of persecution, which ran very high at that time. It should seem also, that the Church of GOD in *Thessalonica* had conceived the day of judgment to be at hand. And, if one may conjecture from what the Apostle hath said in various parts of this Epistle, many of the people were tempted therefrom to neglect the honest attention to their calling, and the care of their families. But while *Paul* sets himself in this Epistle to correct these things, he doth not lose sight of making JESUS the grand feature of this, as well as his other writings and preachings.

I do not think it necessary to make any further detention by way of Preface, to the immediately entering upon the Epistle itself, only first to beg the Reader to bend the knee in prayer with me before the Almighty Author of it, the HOLY GHOST, to bless it to the Church in every age, till time shall be no more.

CHAPTER I.

CONTENTS.

The Apostle opens his Epistle with his usual Benediction. He desires to bless GOD *for the Prosperity of the Church at Thessalonica. He comforts the People under all their Trials, with the assured Prospect of* CHRIST's *coming.*

PAUL, and Silvanus, and Timotheus, unto the church of the Thessalonians in God our Father and the Lord Jesus Christ:

2 Grace unto you, and peace, from God our Father and the Lord Jesus Christ.

It is really delightful to observe how uniformly the Apostle keeps in view the grace of GOD, when writing to the Churches. And as GOD's grace, in the everlasting love of his purpose, counsel, will, and pleasure, is the source and spring of all the blessings which follow in the Church of peace, and mercy in redemption, with all their blissful consequences, we may well account for the Apostle's beginning all he had to offer the Church in this manner.

I would beg the Reader to pause over it a moment, and consider some few of the wonderful properties of grace. The first, and best, and highest sense of it, as it relates to JEHOVAH's exercise of it towards the Church from all eternity, is, in itself, one of the most blessed subjects which can call up the exercise of our awakened faculties, either in time, or in eternity. Grace, in its original source and spring, hath no one motive but as it arose in the divine mind. No predisposing cause, but GOD's pleasure. Neither worthiness, nor unworthiness, in the persons on whom he causeth his grace to shine, being in the least concerned. It would cease to be grace, if the LORD had been moved to exercise it from the foreview of merit, in any of those on whom he bestowed it, or if he withheld it from the knowledge of undeservings among any of his creatures. Paul elsewhere defines grace with this divine property. *If by grace,* (saith he,) *then is it no more works: otherwise grace is no more grace.* Rom. xi. 6. Nay, in numberless instances it should seem, as if the LORD would shew, that *where sin abounded, grace should much more abound;* and, like the high water of the tide, arise over every thing of our undeservings which seemed to oppose it. *Paul* calls his own conversion a proof. *The grace of our* LORD (saith he) *was exceeding abundant.* 1 Tim. i. 14, 15. Reader! do not overlook this scriptural account of grace, from the exercise of which all our mercies flow. Redemption by CHRIST, regeneration by the HOLY GHOST, justification before GOD in CHRIST without works; yea, against all undeservings, sanctification in CHRIST, the forming the spirit anew in CHRIST JESUS, together with all those gracious dispositions formed in the new nature by the HOLY GHOST, all, all flow as so many streams from this one fountain. And the whole sum and substance of the Bible, in the ultimate design of JEHOVAH going forth in acts of creation, redemption, providence, grace, and everlasting happiness to the Church, is to this one point, and no other; to *the praise of the glory of his grace, wherein he hath made us accepted in the Beloved.* Ephes. i. 6.

3 We are bound to thank God always for you, brethren, as it is meet, because that your faith groweth exceedingly, and the charity of every one of you all toward each other aboundeth.

4 So that we ourselves glory in you in the churches of God for your patience and faith in all your persecutions and tribulations that ye endure:

5 *Which is* a manifest token of the righteous judgment of God, that ye may be counted worthy of the kingdom of God, for which ye also suffer:

6 Seeing *it is* a righteous thing with God to recompense tribulation to them that trouble you:

We have several very beautiful and blessed consequences arising out of these verses, which the Reader will do well to notice one by one. *First.* Observe how blessedly *Paul* ascends to the fountain head, in ascribing all glory to the great Head of the Church, for their prosperity. He takes no notice of men or things, ordinances or ministers; these in *Paul's* view were secondary and subordinate. *Who then is Paul, and who is Apollos, but ministers by whom ye believed, even as the* LORD *gave to every man?* 1 Cor. iii. 5. How delightful is it to refer all the glory where alone it is due, and to bless GOD, as it is meet, when faith towards GOD, and charity towards men, grow under the LORD's favor!

Secondly. Let the Reader observe the growth of faith and brotherly love, as twin graces coming from the LORD. They grow and increase under divine cultivation, and they are very blessed evidences of GOD's elect children. *Paul* elsewhere distinguisheth it from the mere professional belief, so common among the carnal world, by calling it, *the faith of* GOD's *elect, and the acknowledging of the truth, which is after godliness.* Titus i. 1. Let the Reader, therefore, carefully mark the vast difference. When a child of GOD is new born, and that immense work of GOD the SPIRIT by regeneration, is wrought in quickening the sinner, which was before dead in trespasses and sins, the spiritual life is given, which can die no more. Being made a partaker of the divine nature, this principle is as holy as it ever can be. But, like a new-born child in nature, so the child in grace groweth and *increaseth with all the increase of* GOD. Coloss. ii. 19. 2 Pet. iii. 18. And let the Reader remark yet further, that these graces of faith and charity, with all others that are thereby induced from the spiritual life, given by the HOLY GHOST to the child of GOD, are the *fruits* and *effects* resulting from the love of the HOLY THREE in One, in their covenant-offices and characters. Faith and love, however exceedingly they grow and abound, form no *cause* in the great work of salvation. CHRIST's Person, in his blood and righteousness, is the sole *cause*. Our faith in him, and love to all saints, are *effects*.

Thirdly. When the Apostle saith, that he, and his faithful companion in the ministry, gloried in the Churches of GOD, let the Reader recollect, that no more can be meant, but that of holy joy, that the LORD blessed them with his grace. It was a constant maxim of *Paul*, that *no man should glory in men.* 1 Cor. iii. 21. And, therefore, he did not tell the Church, in this place, that their good deeds, or their zeal, no, nor their faith and charity, as their acts, were subjects of his glory. He only meant to say, that the LORD's blessing upon them, opened a source of giving glory to GOD, and he rejoiced in their progress in grace.

Fourthly. I beg the Reader to remark with me, how *Paul* interprets the LORD's blessing upon his Church, a sure token of the LORD's displeasure to their enemies. And I beg the Reader to remark it the rather, because the same holds good in all ages of the Church. Depend upon it, in whatever congregation of the LORD's faithful people, the LORD's cause prospers, while the LORD manifests his favor thereby to them; this becomes his frown upon those who oppose them. *David* was so convinced of this, that he made it a subject of prayer, that by the LORD's countenancing him, his enemies might behold it, and hang their heads. *Shew me* (said he) *a token for good: that they which hate me, may see it, and be ashamed: because thou,* LORD, *hath holpen me, and comforted me.* Psm. lxxxvi. 17. Reader! do bring this decision, (for it is the LORD's own decision, and upon scriptural grounds,) into practice, for forming righteous judgment in the present awful day. While the great and glorious truths of the Gospel are frittering away through the land, and flimsy subjects supply the place of preaching GOD's electing love, CHRIST's redeeming grace, and the SPIRIT's regenerating mercy; while places which our forefathers, of blessed memory, occupied, and where those precious truths, whereon was founded all the hope, and joy, and comfort of their truly regenerated souls, once were continually heard, now resound with daring denials of CHRIST's finished salvation, and the final perseverance of thy saints; look and see where GOD owns and blesseth his word, and where congregations are, among whom conversion work, and confirming work are going on. This will be the way to discover, what the Apostle here calls, *the manifest token of the righteous judgment of* GOD. The LORD hath engaged *to honor them who honor him.* 1 Sam. ii. 30. And we may reasonably expect to behold GOD's electing love manifested in the assemblies where GOD's electing love is faithfully preached, and CHRIST's redeeming mercy felt and enjoyed, where redemption by his blood is insisted on as the sole cause of salvation. And GOD the SPIRIT doth, and will, awaken sinners, dead in trespasses and sins, where he sends his faithful servants to preach to the congregation, as the Prophet sent by him did to the dry bones in the valley, whose whole movement, breath, and life, can only come from his sovereign power. Ezek. xxxvii. 4, 5. This will be the way to decide where righteous judgment is formed, not from conclusions drawn from *numbers*, but from conclusions drawn from *the real work of* GOD *upon the heart.* Oh!

the high favor the GOD of all grace manifesteth to that real congregation of *Zion,* called by what name soever it may be among men, whom *the* LORD *shall count when he writeth up the people, that this and that man was born there.* Psm. lxxxvii. 5, 6.

7 And to you who are troubled rest with us, when the Lord Jesus shall be revealed from heaven with his mighty angels,

8 In flaming fire, taking vengeance on them that know not God, and that obey not the gospel of our Lord Jesus Christ:

9 Who shall be punished with everlasting destruction from the presence of the Lord, and from the glory of his power:

10 When he shall come to be glorified in his saints, and to be admired in all them that believe (because our testimony among you was believed) in that day.

There is somewhat very interesting and affectionate in what is said in the opening of this paragraph. To such troubles as are sharp and severe, arising from persecution, and under which the spirit faints; there is nothing can bring relief equal to the prospect of the great day of GOD. *Paul,* therefore, bids the Church to rest with him and his exercised companions in this blessed hope. I know not which to contemplate most, in respect to the awful solemnity with which the Apostle hath here represented the coming of CHRIST, whether the destruction of his foes, or the salvation of his people. The imagination can form nothing to itself, which can either give an idea of the alarming nature of the one, or the unspeakable joy of the other. But the admiration of CHRIST's Person, is said to form the whole of the felicity of his saints. And, most certainly, the union of GOD and man in one Person, must of itself become such an object of glory, as cannot fail to arrest, and to fix the whole attention of every beholder. But who shall describe it? Who shall form conception of the divine features of Him, *in whom dwelleth all the fulness of the* GODHEAD *bodily?*

11 Wherefore also we pray always for you, that our God would count you worthy of *this* calling, and fulfil all the good pleasure of *his* goodness, and the work of faith with power:

12 That the name of our Lord Jesus Christ may be glorified in you, and ye in him, according to the grace of our God, and the Lord Jesus Christ.

I pray the Reader to observe how sweetly *Paul* closeth the Chapter, as he had begun, with prayer. What can be more proper for ministers, than to open and close all their ministerial services in the same manner. By the LORD's counting the people worthy of this calling, cannot be supposed to mean any worthiness in them, for he had before ascribed all to the grace of GOD. But the counting worthy of this calling, means the LORD's counting them one with JESUS; so that now, when the Church comes to be glorified in JESUS, the blessed testimonies of all that is past may appear in their first call by grace, and their being justified, adopted, sanctified, and the whole events they had past through, from grace to glory, might shew their union and oneness with CHRIST from everlasting; so, that as all along their lives had been hid with CHRIST in GOD; now, when CHRIST, who is their life, appears, *they appear with him in glory*. Coloss. iii. 3, 4.

REFLECTIONS.

READER! it were well, if truly regenerated souls would frequently, and with a suitable solemnity of holy joy, contemplate the great day of CHRIST's coming, which the Apostle here proposeth to the Church, as the sure support to all the exercises and trials of life. For what damps the highest prosperity of sinners, becomes the richest encouragement to comfort, under all the pressure of evil, to the saints. And, if the people of GOD would learn, under grace, to connect with their prospect of CHRIST's coming, their union and interest in that glory in which he comes, what a joy unspeakable and full of glory would this bring with it to their souls. And, as the human nature of CHRIST united to his divine, gives a right and interest in all that is divine, and the glory of the GODHEAD is communicated to the human nature, and dwells in it; so our union with CHRIST gives a right and interest in all that belongs to CHRIST, as CHRIST, for communication in all that is communicable, and we derive out of his fulness, grace here, and glory hereafter. This was the very end for which the Church was predestinated, that we might be conformed to his image. May the LORD give to all his redeemed ones, grace, so to contemplate CHRIST, and so to wait for his coming, that his precious name may be glorified in his people, and they in him, *according to the grace of* GOD, *and our* LORD JESUS CHRIST.

CHAP. II.

CONTENTS.

The Apostle forewarns the Church in this Chapter, of a falling away of Professors. He very awfully describes the coming of Antichrist, before CHRIST's *appearing. And takes occasion therefrom to bless* GOD, *for the Church having been chosen to Sanctification from the Beginning.*

NOW we beseech you, brethren, by the coming of our Lord Jesus Christ, and *by* our gathering together unto him,

2 That ye be not soon shaken in mind, or be troubled, neither by spirit, nor by word, nor by letter as from us, as that the day of Christ is at hand.

3 Let no man deceive you by any means: for *that day shall not come*, except there come a falling away first, and that man of sin be revealed, the son of perdition;

It should seem, from the opening of this Chapter, that the Church had at this time, strong apprehensions in their mind, that the day of the LORD was at hand. And it is probable, from what the Apostle saith in those verses, that the Church of the *Thessalonians* had been strengthened in this opinion, by their misconstruction of the Apostle's former letter. 1 Thess. iv. 15. *Paul*, therefore, in this Chapter corrects this error; and, under the Spirit of prophecy, relates to the Church, an awful event, which must first take place in the earth, which should be the most distressing in its consequences, to the Church of the LORD, that could be. The great day of GOD, saith he, shall not come, except there come a falling away first, and that Man of Sin be revealed, the Son of Perdition. Reader! pause over this account, before you go further. *A falling away.* Not from grace. Not the people of GOD. *Paul* had before told the Church, in his former Epistle to the *Thessalonians*, that *their election of* GOD *was known.* 1 Thess. i. 4. And in the same Epistle, he had fully declared, that GOD *had not appointed* his people *unto wrath, but to obtain salvation.* 1 Thess. v. 9. The falling away, therefore, hath no respect whatever, to the real Church of CHRIST; but wholly to the mere nominal Professors of Christianity, and which were numerous as soon as the Empire became Christian, and nations possessed belief in CHRIST, merely as a religion of state policy, without one act of grace in CHRIST. A falling away from this profession became, and hath continued common, ever since. But what hath this to do with CHRIST? Men cannot fall away from what they never had! A man cannot lose grace, who never had grace. There is but one real, and decisive mark of the true faith in CHRIST; namely, the being regenerated, and born again of the HOLY GHOST. All the profession in the world, of believing in CHRIST, is no profession at all, as to its vital principles, before this act is wrought in the soul. And, therefore, men falling away from a mere profession, is all that *Paul* meant, by the expression. But, there never was, neither is it possible it should be, a falling away, in a single instance, of a child of GOD, whom GOD the SPIRIT hath regenerated: for that happy soul is thereby made *partaker of the divine nature, having escaped the corruption that is in the world through lust.* 2 Pet. i. 3, 4. The *man of sin*, and the *son of perdition*, come next to be considered. The account the Apostle gives is very alarming.

4 Who opposeth and exalteth himself above all that is called God, or that is worshipped; so that he as God sitteth in the temple of God, shewing himself that he is God.

5 Remember ye not, that, when I was yet with you, I told you these things?

6 And now ye know what withholdeth that he might be revealed in his time.

7 For the mystery of iniquity doth already work: only he who now letteth *will let* until he be taken out of the way.

8 And then shall that wicked be revealed, whom the Lord shall consume with the spirit of his mouth, and shall destroy with the brightness of his coming:

9 *Even him*, whose coming is after the working of Satan with all power and signs and lying wonders,

10 And with all deceivableness of unrighteousness in them that perish; because they received not the love of the truth, that they might be saved.

11 And for this cause God shall send them strong delusion, that they should believe a lie:

12 That they all might be damned who believed not the truth, but had pleasure in unrighteousness.

We have here a very awful prophecy, and most awfully hath it been fulfilled, and still is now fulfilling, in the earth. And what makes it still, if possible, more awful is, that though the Apostle, by the expressions *man of sin*, and *the son of perdition*, might seem at first view, to allude to somewhat *personal*; yet it is not so. It is national: yea, general. It was long since said, by the beloved Apostle *John*, that as Antichrist should come: so, *there were in his days* (and how increased in our's) *many Antichrists.* 1 John ii. 18. The best service which I can render, under the Lord, to the Reader of this *Poor Man's Commentary*, in helping to the proper apprehension of the solemn subject contained within these verses, will be, to gather out the several parts of the passage, one by one, and then consider them, as they appear before us.

And *first*. Let the Reader remark with me, the *names*, by which the Apostle hath distinguished this heresy. He calls it *the man of sin; the son of perdition: the mystery of iniquity; that wicked, which shall be revealed: him whose coming is after the working of Satan:*

and who comes *with all power, and signs, and lying wonders; and with all deceivableness of unrighteousness.* These are the awful names, by which the HOLY GHOST hath made known to the Church through *Paul,* in this scripture, the alarming heresy, which was to appear.

Secondly. The *acts,* and *deeds,* by which the character of this delusion should be discovered. He is said *to oppose and exalt himself, above all that is called* GOD, *or that is worshipped. That he as God, sitteth in the temple of* GOD, *shewing himself that he is God.* And he is known by the power he is said to assume, and *the signs, and lying wonders he comes with, after the working of Satan; and with all deceivableness of unrighteousness.*

Thirdly. The awful consequences which shall follow, in *them that perish,* which are his followers. GOD *shall send them strong delusions, that they should believe a lie; that all might be damned who believed not the truth, but had pleasure in unrighteousness.*

Fourthly. The sure destruction of this Wicked himself, whom the LORD *shall consume with the spirit of his mouth, and destroy with the brightness of his coming.* So much for the Apostle's description of this awful heresy; which, under the LORD the SPIRIT, he told the Church, would be revealed in the after times, when the LORD, who then withheld it, would remove the cause of obstruction out of the way. Now let us, under the LORD's teaching, look at those characters, one by one; and examine, by scripture testimony, and the facts which have since appeared, to what age of the Church they particularly refer. And, *first,* respecting the names. The *man of sin,* and the *son of perdition;* the *mystery of iniquity,* and *the wicked.* It is plain that these all refer to one and the same. And not simply to one person; but rather the name of one, and the same heresy. Not *Satan,* who is emphatically called the Wicked One; for this heresy is said to be *after the working of Satan;* consequently could not be *Satan* himself. Neither any new revelation of the traitor *Judas,* whom our LORD calls *the son of perdition.* John xvii. 12. For JESUS did not so name him, as though he, and he only, should be known by that name. All are sons of perdition, which are lost. Neither did the Apostle mean any individual person, among the enemies of CHRIST, which in after ages shall arise to oppose CHRIST's Gospel, however desperately wicked, and bitter they might be. It is not a person, but a body; an apostacy from the Church, a falling away; still professing CHRIST, but in works denying him. For the character is further defined, of *sitting in* GOD's *temple, and calling himself god; yea, exalting himself above all that is called* GOD.

And where are we to look for the fulfilment of this prophecy? If a Church professing Christianity can be found, to whom those titles clearly belong; there will remain no shadow of doubt, but that this is the very one the Apostle had in view, in this scripture prophecy. And all that have written upon the subject, from the first moment the scriptures have been commented upon, to the present hour, have uniformly, and with one voice, declared it to be the Church of *Rome.* The selling of indulgencies, pardons, grants, and the like, are too nearly allied to *the man of sin;* and where practised, too strikingly represent him, whom *Paul* describes as *sitting in the temple of* GOD, *shewing himself that he is* GOD. And it is to oppose Christ in all his offices, as the Prophet, Priest, and King of his Church; when teaching the worship of saints; when setting up merit, and joining intercessors with Christ; and when taking up the title of supremacy, as head of the Church. And, it is certainly not a little remarkable in confirmation, that what *Paul* calls in this place, *the mystery of iniquity*, in allusion to the heresy he had been describing; *John*, in the book of the Revelations, calls *Mystery, Babylon the Great, the Mother of harlots, and abominations of the earth*. Rev. xvii. 5. From these, and numberless other testimonies, which, if necessary, might be brought forward, there cannot be the shadow of a doubt, but that the Apostacy the Apostle had in view in this scripture the See of *Rome* was all along designed.

But it would have been a blessing to the true Church of Christ, if apostasy had marked only the character of the See of *Rome*. Alas! what errors have sprung up, in this our own land, in what is called the Reformed Church. Who that reads the beloved Apostle's account of his days, and takes the same mirror to look in for ours; but must be struck with the resemblance. *Little children* (said he) *it is the last time, and as ye have heard that antichrist shall come, even now are there many antichrists: whereby we know that it is the last time.* 1 John ii. 18. Let any man read this blessed Epistle of *John*, and then look to the professions of men around him! Let him behold how the Godhead of Christ is denied: the Person, Godhead, and Ministry of God the Holy Ghost is questioned; and then say, are there not many Antichrists?

And, let my Reader bear with me, to make one observation more. What did the Apostle mean, in this scripture, by *deceivableness of unrighteousness?* Mark the expression. *With all deceivableness of unrighteousness in them that perish.* Did there need, the Church should be told, that unrighteousness would end in destruction? Certainly this could not be *Paul's* meaning. Neither in the common sense, and acceptation of the word, unrighteousness could never deceive a man with hopes of being saved by it. But, if a self-righteous *Pharisee*, fancying himself righteous before God; makes his own good deeds, and prayers, and alms, and ordinances, a part Savior; all of which are unrighteous before God: here is a fallacy indeed, deep, and wretched. And this will well suit the name of *all deceivableness of unrighteousness*. Reader! it is right to exercise a jealousy over our own hearts. The day is awful. In contending earnestly for the faith once delivered unto the saints, we not only labor to preserve God's truth, but our own happiness. And it is a truth well worth laboring for. *For if righteousness come by the law, then* Christ *is dead in vain*. Gal. ii. 21.

13 But we are bound to give thanks alway to God for you, brethren beloved of the Lord, because God hath from the beginning chosen you to salvation through sanctification of the Spirit and belief of the truth:

14 Whereunto he called you by our gospel, to

the obtaining of the glory of our Lord Jesus Christ.

15 Therefore, brethren, stand fast, and hold the traditions which ye have been taught, whether by word, or our epistle.

16 Now our Lord Jesus Christ himself, and God, even our Father, which hath loved us, and hath given *us* everlasting consolation and good hope through grace,

17 Comfort your hearts, and establish you in every good word and work.

What a sweet scripture is here! And how blessedly it comes in, to relieve the mind, after looking at the sad account of the heresy described in the foregoing verses? *Paul* found a constant cause, and so may we also, *to give thanks to* GOD *always for the* Church *being chosen from the beginning to salvation through the sanctification of the* SPIRIT, *and belief of the truth.* There is an uncommon degree of beauty, in the strength of expression made use of, in what the Apostle here saith, on sanctification; in the cause, and antiquity of it. It would form more the subject of a treatise, than to offer a few passing observations, on these verses; but I beg the Reader's indulgence, to detain him a moment or two, upon the passage.

Sanctification, or to sanctify, hath a different meaning in the different scriptures. But the most general sense is, either to set apart, consecrate, or dedicate, to a sacred service: or to purify, cleanse, and make holy, what was before unholy in our nature. In the *former*, CHRIST is said to have *sanctified himself.* John xvii. 19. In the *latter*, the Church, when regenerated, is said *to be washed, to be sanctified, to be justified, in the name of the* LORD JESUS, *and by the* SPIRIT *of our* GOD. 1 Cor. vi. 11. These distinctions, if attended to, through the whole of the Old Testament and the New, would, under GOD the SPIRIT, open a clearer apprehension than is generally received, upon the subject of sanctification.

It is very blessed to observe, what a beautiful order there is adopted, and carried on, through all the departments of divine love to the Church, in the several acts of the Persons of the GODHEAD. Hence, each glorious Person hath taken part, in all the acts of grace, manifested towards every individual of CHRIST's mystical body. Thus in sanctification, the Church is said *to be sanctified by* GOD *the* FATHER, in his choosing, electing, separating love, when he chose the whole body in CHRIST, before the foundation of the world, to be *holy and without blame before him in love.* Ephes. i. 4. But this sanctification is as expressly ascribed to the LORD JESUS CHRIST, in that it is said, *we are sanctified through the offering of the body of* JESUS CHRIST *once for all. For by one offering he hath perfected for ever them that are sanctified.* Heb. x. 10, 14. But here again, these gracious personal acts in the FATHER and the SON, do not supersede, or render unnecessary, the same personal tendencies of love, in the HOLY GHOST: for the LORD the SPIRIT is not only said to sanctify the brethren beloved, in this verse of the Apostle's; but *Peter*, in opening his Epistle to the Church, expressly addresseth it to *the Elect according to the foreknowledge of* GOD *the* FATHER, *through sanctification of the* SPIRIT, *unto obedience and sprinkling of the blood of* JESUS CHRIST. 1 Pet. i. 2. And what can more plainly, and decidedly prove, the personal election, redemption, and sanctification, of the whole Church of GOD in JESUS CHRIST our LORD.

But, while these grand, and indeed (as they may well be called) fundamental truths of the Gospel, are generally received, and admitted in the Church of the faithful, as so many standards of decision, against which there is no appeal; the glorious doctrine of sanctification, doth not seem to be as clearly understood, as those of election, and redemption. The more generally received opinion is, that at regeneration, we are regenerated but in part; and that as well in body as spirit. There is a perfection (say they) of parts of the new man, in both of the LORD's people, but only in degrees. Though there be a compleat perfection in CHRIST, in which they are interested; yet their sanctification is imperfect. They are in a progressive state of holiness, and progressive sanctification; but not compleat in either. This I apprehend, is the general received opinion.

I am well aware, that the whole tide of Commentators are against me, while I would desire, with all humility of soul, instead of swimming with them down the stream, to bear up my feeble bark to the torrent of this opinion. I beg, as I have before done, my Reader's indulgence, to state the reasons for which I differ. If I err, I pray the LORD to pardon me, and preserve his people from adopting my errors.

In the *first* place. I humbly conceive, that as all our blessings of the Church of GOD in CHRIST, result from the joint love, and grace, of the whole Persons of the GODHEAD, in their covenant characters; so have they been pleased to manifest those acts of favor in such a way, as do endear the Almighty Authors of our blessings to our affections, with equal adoration, love, and praise, as the united source in CHRIST. It was but one act of GOD the FATHER, when in his infinite mind, he chose the Church in CHRIST; and which, when chosen, became a compleat, perfect, and immutable purpose, remaining for ever. In like manner, it was but one act in the purpose of GOD the SON, in relation to all the concerns in redemption; for by *the one offering of himself once offered, he hath perfected for ever them that are sanctified.* And the act of regeneration, or new birth, by GOD the HOLY GHOST, when considered as quickening the sinner dead in trespasses and sins, could be but one act; by which, as the Apostle saith, *being born again, not of corruptible seed but of incorruptible, liveth, and abideth for ever.* 1 Pet. i. 23. Beheld, in this point of view, there is a beautiful order, and analogy, in those several acts of divine agency, which not only manifest equal acts of the GODHEAD, towards the objects of their love; but also demonstrate, each act, to be equally essential, to all the great purposes of their spiritual being, and well-being, in CHRIST.

But on the supposition, that this act of GOD the SPIRIT, in regeneration, is but in part; not only this beautiful order and equality in those acts of grace is destroyed, but a train of the most painful consequences arise, which involve the mind in endless apprehensions, concerning the eventual perfection. And wherefore should the work of regeneration and the sanctification included in it, be an imperfect act of GOD the SPIRIT, more than the act of election in GOD the FATHER, or redemption by GOD the SON? If it be only for one moment admitted, that regeneration doth not renew the body, neither was ever intended, during the time state of the Church, to renew the body; every difficulty vanisheth. And what can more plainly declare this, than our LORD's own words, in his blessed discourse on regeneration? *That* (said JESUS) *which is born of the flesh, is flesh: and that which is born of the* SPIRIT *is spirit.* John iii. 6. If at our regeneration, the work was wrought *by* flesh, or *on* flesh; the thing would be just the reverse of what it is. But CHRIST saith: that which is born of the SPIRIT, is spirit. Words, in my view as plain as words can express, that the blessed act of regeneration, is by the SPIRIT; and that it is *on* the spirit; and that that which is born of the SPIRIT, is *only* spirit. The LORD draws a line of distinction, between the flesh, and the spirit, as if in confirmation of the subject. If this be the sense of our LORD's words, (and I think it will be difficult to prove the contrary,) it will follow, that no alteration whatever, is made on the body at regeneration. No part of it is sanctified. The work is on the spirit; and which wholly regenerated, is justified, and sanctified, by the HOLY GHOST in CHRIST JESUS.

Secondly. Upon the presumption of correctness in the foregoing statement, it will then follow, that the new born child of GOD, though sanctified in CHRIST, and to whom CHRIST is made of GOD, both *wisdom, righteousness, sanctification, and redemption;* hath no inherent holiness in himself, for his body is still the creature of sin; and so far is it from being in a progressive state of holiness, that it is daily the subject of sin, and tending to corruption. Let those who are advocates for the progressive sanctification, and holiness of the creature, state to us the causes, how it is, on the supposition the *body,* as well as the *spirit* of a regenerated child, is made perfect in part; that such opposition should take place, as continually doth take place, between the flesh and the spirit, when the spirit is regenerated? Gal. v. 17. According to *Paul's* statement of himself, this conflict never began with him, until he was regenerated. Before the killing power of the law came on his conscience at his conversion, he tells us, that he was alive in all the self-confidence of his own holiness. *But,* (saith he,) *when the commandment came, sin revived and I died.* Rom. vii. 9. And hence, at a period of nearly *three-and-twenty years* after his conversion, he groaned under the conscious sense, that in him, that is, saith he, *in my flesh dwelleth no good thing.* Rom. vii. 18. Can the advocates for progressive sanctification, explain these things, upon any principles whatever, if the body was in part sanctified? And will they at the same time, on the presumption of a body in part sanctified shew, how it was, that holy men of old, when conscious of a work of grace upon their souls, still groaned in the consciousness at the same time, of their being *vile;* Job xl. 4. of having *their sin always before them;* Psm. li. 3. of being of *unclean lips:* Isaiah vi. 5. and of their *comeliness turned into corruption?* Dan. x. 8. Nay, will those advocates for progressive sanctification, kindly say, whether while insisting upon inherent holiness, and the whole man becoming more perfect in others, they truly experience such things in themselves? Are they more holy, more heavenly minded, more weaned from the world, than they were in times past? If they say yes, to such heart-searching questions; they will but afford stronger testimony of their ignorance of the plague of their own heart, and prove the LORD's assertion, when he saith, *the heart is deceitful above all things, and desperately wicked; who can know it?* Jerem. xvii. 9.

Thirdly. The very tendency of the body to corruption, and the daily removing of the pins of our earthly tabernacle, loudly proclaim, that in order to its being raised a *spiritual* body, it must first be a *natural* body. Whereas, if it were now a spiritual body, or in part spiritual; that part, even to the ten thousandth part could not corrupt. But it is wholly corruption. And, when the spirit leaves the body, the earthly part (as one said to me when calling me to bury the dead) cries for its original earth. And here indeed comes in, to our delight, and joy, the LORD JESUS in the power of his resurrection, as a quickening SPIRIT. Of none but JEHOVAH's HOLY ONE, could it ever be said, he was not liable to corruption. It was impossible in this account, that *the pains of death could hold him!* Psalm. xvi. 10. Acts ii. 24.

I am well aware, (as I said before,) that the great tide of Commentators are against me. And I am also well aware, that to men unacquainted with the plague of their own heart, I shall expose myself to their displeasure, by the view I have given of the subject. But these things do not move me. If one only of the LORD's humbled ones, shall herefrom, through grace, be led to be more out of love with themselves, and more in love with CHRIST JESUS; I shall find cause to bless GOD for his teachings. This will be to grow in grace; not in sanctification. Growth in grace leads to the greater knowledge of the LORD, as the Apostle states it. 2 Pet. iii. 18. Grace is an humbling principle. He that groweth in grace, layeth lower, and lower, in the dust before GOD. And, from being humbled more and more, every day, in himself; JESUS, and his great salvation, will be increasingly precious. This is to grow in grace; and not in sanctification.

But still, it will be yet further contended, that on the supposition, there is no change wrought on the body, when the spirit is regenerated; how doth this correspond to what the scriptures declare, that *our bodies are the temple of the* HOLY GHOST, *which dwelleth in us?* 1 Cor. vi. 19. (See Commentary there). Can it be supposed, that GOD the SPIRIT will dwell in a nature unregenerated, and unsanctified? To which I answer. Every act of grace, in the Persons of the GODHEAD, toward our nature, continually opens subjects of unceasing wonder, adoration, and the lowliest prostration of soul and body. But the indwelling residence of GOD the SPIRIT, is not more the subject of astonishment than that of GOD the FATHER's making his abode with the redeemed; John xiv. 23. or GOD the SON, for the purpose of redemption, being *made in the likeness of sinful flesh.* Rom. viii. 3. We are taught to consider all and every part of the LORD's tendencies to his Church as full of mystery. 1 Tim. iii. 16.

And, it should be continually remembered by us, that great as our wonder is, in the mystery of godliness, we are not called upon to explain the *causes;* but believe only, and bless GOD for the *effects.* And the very manner, in which the Apostle hath informed the Church of this astonishing condescension in GOD the HOLY GHOST, in making the body of his people his temple, implies the sense he wished the people to have of it. *What!* (saith he,) *know ye not, that your body is the temple of the* HOLY GHOST *which is in you?* Great would have been the mercy either way, and every way, in this act of grace, when we consider the infinite distance between GOD and his creatures; had the LORD made those bodies compleatly holy, and then have dwelt in them. But it is very plain, from *Paul's* manner of speaking, that he would have the Church consider the wonders, in the HOLY GHOST dwelling in them, because they were, in their unregenerated bodies, so altogether corrupt, and unholy. *What!* saith he, *know ye not?* As if he had said, what think ye of the unequalled grace, that the HOLY ONE who inhabiteth eternity, and who is himself holiness, in himself should dwell in the bodies of nothing but filth and defilement! Oh! the grace of GOD.

I must not enlarge: though the subject itself affords occasion. I shall leave the Reader to his own conclusions, under the LORD. For my own part, I desire to bless GOD for those humbling views, the consciousness of a body virtually all sin, and hastening daily to corruption, keeps alive, through grace in my soul. The daily workings of corruption in my heart (I know not what other men's hearts feel) sheweth me, that the carnal mind is still carnal. Psm. xxxvi. 1. Rom. vii. 14. I feel a daily warfare. I groan, being burdened. I not only feel these workings when unoccupied with divine things, but often in the house of GOD. Like *Paul,* I know what it is, that *when I would do good evil is present with me.* Rom. vii. 21. In the pulpit, at the table of the LORD, at the mercy-seat, often when in a moment of sweet communion with my GOD and SAVIOR; a train of thoughts rush through me like unbidden guests, and rob GOD at his face of his glory, and my soul for the time, of comfort! Can a body, where such things are, be in part renewed? Am I in a progressive state of holiness, in a body where I find such cause of humblings; and which I loath? Sweet scripture! which explains all, and leads me to CHRIST for all. GOD *hath from the beginning chosen you to salvation, through sanctification of the* SPIRIT, *and belief of the truth, whereunto he hath called you by the Gospel; and to the obtaining of the glory of our* LORD JESUS CHRIST! See 1 Cor. v. and vi. Chapters, and Commentary.

REFLECTIONS.

WHO that reads the solemn account of the great day of CHRIST's appearing, but must stand with astonishment, in beholding the awful end of the ungodly, and the everlasting happiness of GOD's people!

Reader! think what an awful account is here given, of *the man of sin,* and the *son of perdition!* Oh! what deplorable consequences would follow, if ever again the *mystery of iniquity,* and that *Wicked,* should be revealed in this our land. And yet is there not, in the present hour, him, whose coming is after *Satan*, in what the Apostle calls, *the deceivableness of unrighteousness!*

Blessed be God for his Church! It is still as the remnant of *Jacob*, in the midst of many people, a dew from the Lord. And God hath from the beginning chosen it. And God to the present hour doth choose it, and so He will to the latest posterity, *to salvation, through sanctification of the* Spirit, *and belief of the truth.* May the Lord be the strength of his people, to help them to stand fast in his name. And may our Lord Jesus Christ, and God, even our Father, comfort and stablish all his redeemed to the end. Amen.

CHAP. III.

CONTENTS.

The Apostle closeth his Epistle with this Chapter. He takes an affectionate Leave of the Church, begs an Interest in the Prayers of the People, and prays the Lord *to bless them.*

FINALLY, brethren, pray for us, that the word of the Lord may have *free* course, and be glorified, even as *it is* with you.

2 And that we may be delivered from unreasonable and wicked men: for all *men* have not faith.

3 But the Lord is faithful, who shall stablish you, and keep *you* from evil.

4 And we have confidence in the Lord touching you, that ye both do and will do the things which we command you.

5 And the Lord direct your hearts into the love of God, and into the patient waiting for Christ.

In folding up this beautiful Epistle, the Apostle makes an earnest, and an affectionate request, to be remembered by the Church at the throne in prayer, together with *Silvanus*, and *Timotheus*, whom he joined with himself in this letter. And I beg the Reader to remark with me, the great burden of his request, namely, that the word of the Lord might be blessed among the Lord's people. *Paul* makes use of the figure of a free course, which like an unobstructed river, runs on, and washes, and makes fruitful every place where the Lord sends it. And, observe, it is God's glory, when his people are made blessed by the free course of his word. Every child of God should remember this. It becomes a great strengthener to faith, when the Lord enables any of his to consider, that when our souls being made blessed in Christ, Christ is glorified in us. We not only bless him with our hearts, when we give him praise for his mercies, but we glorify him also when our wants give him occasion to fill into our emptiness.

And let the Reader further observe the drift of *Paul's* prayer, that he, and his faithful companions, who preached the truth as it is in JESUS, might be delivered from the opposers of those precious doctrines, *Paul*, and his brethren in the ministry, taught. Not the openly profane, but false teachers. *Paul* could not mean the openly profane, when he said, for all men have not faith. This was too notorious a truth to need the remark. But the all men the Apostle here alluded to, which had not faith, were plainly those who preached unsent. Men who had not *the faith of* GOD's *elect*. Titus i. 1. May the LORD deliver all his faithful, both ministers and congregations, from such men, in all ages of his Church!

The Reader will not overlook, I hope, the very blessed prayer *Paul* closed up this paragraph with. He opened the first part of it with calling upon the Church to pray for him and his companions. And here, in the close of it, after assuring the Church of GOD's faithfulness, to stablish and keep them from evil, he recompenseth their kindness in praying for them. And what a sweet and comprehensive prayer it is? Surely none but GOD the SPIRIT could have taught it. *And the* LORD (said he) *direct your hearts into the love of* GOD, *and into the patient waiting for*, (or, as the margin renders it, the patience of,) CHRIST. Reader! do observe how all the Persons of the GODHEAD are here included in this short, but blessed prayer. The LORD the SPIRIT *direct your hearts.* And where directed? *Into the love of* GOD. And how is this to be attained? *In a patient waiting on, and through* CHRIST. And short as this direction is, if the Reader be taught of the same GOD who directs the heart to mark the LORD's leadings, he will discover that this is the direct way, and the only way to comfort. The child of GOD that goes to the throne in any thing of his own, such as his experiences, or his enlargements, as men call them, or the exercises of his own graces, is going a round-about way, and wearying himself for very vanity. Whereas direct acts of faith upon CHRIST's Person, and the pleadings of CHRIST's blood and righteousness, and GOD's faithful covenant promises in CHRIST; the precious soul that doth so, is truly directed by the LORD the HOLY GHOST, and led by the hand to the mercy-seat of GOD in CHRIST. Such a soul must speed well, thus led, thus fed, thus taught, and thus enabled to plead. I warrant ye, on the authority of GOD's yea and Amen-promises, he shall prove a wrestling seed of the stock of *Jacob*, and come off a prevailing descendant of the true *Israel*. To all such, whom I met at any time going to the pardon office of JESUS CHRIST, I would say, oh! remember me when you see the King, for sure I am you will get near to him. Yea, I would beg of GOD the HOLY GHOST to direct my heart to go with them. And what might not a company of CHRIST's redeemed ones expect, when going together to the Heavenly Court, whose hearts were all directed by the same Almighty LORD, *into the love of* GOD, *and into the patient waiting for* JESUS CHRIST?

6 Now we command you, brethren, in the name of our Lord Jesus Christ, that ye withdraw yourselves from every brother that walketh disor-

derly, and not after the tradition which ye received of us.

7 For yourselves know how ye ought to follow us: for we behaved not ourselves disorderly among you.

8 Neither did we eat any man's bread for nought: but wrought with labour and travail night and day, that we might not be chargeable to any of you:

9 Not because we have not power, but to make ourselves an ensample unto you to follow us.

10 For even when we were with you, this we commanded you, that if any would not work, neither should he eat.

11 For we hear that there are some which walk among you disorderly, working not at all, but are busy bodies.

12 Now them that are such we command and exhort by our Lord Jesus Christ, that with quietness they work, and eat their own bread.

In order for the better apprehension of this part of the Epistle, we must consider CHRIST's Church as one family. And a family wisely regulated and ordered, must be guided by one uniform plan, for the comfort of the whole body, as well as spiritual. It appears from what the Apostle saith here, that there were some which had joined the Church, who had not first joined the LORD. And it is worthy our observation, that notwithstanding the Apostle possessed a divine gift of discerning spirits in matters of moment; yet, even in the Churches under his own direction, some men crept in who had no part in the matter. In the Church of the *Romans,* we find the Apostle reproving such who served not the LORD JESUS CHRIST, but their own belly. Rom. xvi. 18. see also Philip. iii. 18, 19. There have been such in all professing Churches of the saints in all ages. Nay, *Paul* himself saith, *there must be also, even heresies among them, that they which are approved may be made manifest among them.* 1 Cor. xi. 19. Reader! do not overlook these things. In the present day the view is highly profitable. It is a great point to make a right distinction between real and nominal Christians, as well as between the professor and the profane. When idle and disorderly persons creep into a Church, and cover themselves over with a name to live, while virtually dead before GOD; we may expect all such consequences will follow, as *Paul* hath here described. And it is a melancholy consideration when this conduct is found among the humbler walks of life, who follow the ordinances, as those of old did the LORD himself, *not because they saw the miracles, but because they did eat of the loaves and were filled.* John vi. 26.

But the Apostle, not only speaks in this scripture, of the idle among the poor, but the disorderly also. And, it is more than probable, that these were chiefly among the rich; as riches, and what is called the good things of this life, are more likely to open temptations to indulgence, in things disorderly. It is a sad, sad thing, when wealth, and worldly rank, tempt churches to admit into their community, any whom GOD hath not admitted. Such men may fill the coffer, but they themselves add nothing to the real number of CHRIST's Church. How blessedly our great Apostle speaks of his fears on this ground. *I am jealous over you,* said he to the *Corinthian* Church, *with a godly jealousy, that I may present you as a chaste virgin to* CHRIST. 2 Cor. xi. 2. It is one thing to entertain suspicious opinions, ungrounded, and ill-formed, of any professor, and another, to be jealous over one another, with a godly jealousy. But if Churches professing the eternal, and unalterable truths of GOD, were to admit none into Church fellowship, but such as had fellowship with the FATHER, and with his SON JESUS CHRIST there would be no idle among the poor, neither disorderly among the rich. And very blessedly then, would the whole body, *holding the Head and being knit together, increase, with all the increase of* GOD. Coloss. ii. 19.

13 But ye, brethren, be not weary in welldoing.

14 And if any man obey not our word by this epistle, note that man, and have no company with him, that he may be ashamed.

15 Yet count *him* not as an enemy, but admonish *him* as a brother.

16 Now the Lord of peace himself give you peace always by all means. The Lord *be* with you all.

17 The salutation of Paul with mine own hand, which is the token in every epistle: so I write.

18 The grace of our Lord Jesus Christ *be* with you all. Amen.

The second *epistle* to the Thessalonians was written from Athens.

The Apostle, having pointed out the errors, and infirmities, which creep into the Church, closeth his Epistle with his usual kindness, in recommending tenderness, and affection, one towards another, among the people. I admire *Paul's* charge, that brethren should not *be weary in well doing.* By which, if I apprehend him right, he doth not refer to acts of grace, and faith, in the exercises of their high calling, towards GOD; for that is always understood: but rather, after what he had been speaking, of the idle and disorderly, not to be discouraged, if any acts of kindness the Church had shewn such persons, were abused, and unthankfully treated. It is a melancholy thing, to be sure, to behold at any time, the bounties of gracious souls, misapplied by the ungracious. But, it is much more to be deplored, that such misapplications, should ever operate, to check the liberal hand, and heart, and make them follow the reverse of *Paul's* precept; *and be weary in well doing.* Not so the Lord. And not so his command. *That ye may be* (said that unequalled Example, of requiting blessing for cursing,) *the children of your* Father *which is in heaven: for he maketh his sun to rise on the evil, and on the good; and sendeth rain on the just, and on the unjust.* Matthew v. 45.

I do not think it necessary, to swell the pages of this *Poor Man's Commentary,* with any further observations, on the close of the Apostle's Epistle. His method is, for the most part, the same in all his writings. They are full of zeal to the Lord's cause, and love to his Church; and very plainly read to us, the heart of the Apostle. Let us rather join in the benediction, for it is truly blessed; and say to the whole Church, as he did: *the grace of our* Lord Jesus Christ *be with you all. Amen.*

REFLECTIONS.

Blessed be the Lord Jehovah in his threefold character of Persons, for all the mercies, grace, and love, manifested to the Church of God, in Jesus Christ. And blessed be the Lord the Spirit, for this precious portion of his holy word, from the ministry of his servant the Apostle. Add to it, Lord, the blessing of making it life, and spirit, to the souls of all thy redeemed: and do thou, blessed God, for it is thine own sweet office-work alone to accomplish it, *direct our hearts into the love of* God, *and into the patient waiting for* Christ.

And, oh! thou Almighty Minister, under whose government the entire welfare, and prosperity of the Church depends; do thou watch over all the congregations of the faithful, that idleness, and disorderly conduct, may find no shelter; neither the poor of thy people be neglected, in the daily ministration. Lord, the work is thine, and thine alone the glory. Make thy ministers faithful: and let the Church be blessed. Farewell Paul! the Church of the *Thessalonians* have praised God for thy labors of love: and all the Churches, to whom thy writings have been sent by the Holy Ghost, have blessed, and do bless God, for calling thee to the ministry. But oh! thou glorious Head, and praise of all thy saints, be thou eternally loved, and adored, for all the *Pauls*, and the Pastors, of thy Church! All is thine, Almighty Jesus! And for all we praise thee! Amen.

THE FIRST EPISTLE OF PAUL THE APOSTLE TO TIMOTHY.

GENERAL OBSERVATIONS.

WE here enter upon the further labors of the Apostle Paul. The foregoing Epistles were all directed to the Churches. This, and the second Epistle, together with the two following, to *Titus* and *Philemon*, are to persons. But the subject manner of the whole is the same. All *Paul's* preachings, writings, and ministry, treat of nothing but CHRIST. CHRIST is *Paul's* text, sermon, and application.

Timothy, to whom *Paul* here writes, was of jewish descent by the mother's side, but his father was a *Greek*. It was *Timothy's* mercy, that he had been early taught the Scriptures. And the LORD, in his providence, brought him under the Gospel while a youth. In the Acts of the Apostles we meet with the first account of him at *Lystra*. After which we read frequently of him as *Paul's* companion.

The subject of this Epistle need not further be noticed in this place. We shall discover the Apostle's design, under GOD the HOLY GHOST, as we prosecute the several chapters. It is said to have been written by the Apostle at *Laodicea*, and, probably, about the year 55, though some place it later. However, it carries with it marks of divine inspiration. I only detain the Reader in begging of him to enter upon the perusal with me in prayer, that the same Almighty LORD, which hath graciously given us this sweet Scripture, will as graciously give us the understanding heart to apprehend his merciful instructions in it, that it may be *profitable for doctrine, for reproof, for correction, for instruction in righteousness*, that as the children of GOD, *we may be perfect, thoroughly furnished unto all good works*.

CHAPTER I.

CONTENTS.

The Apostle opens his Epistle with the usual Salutation. He reminds Timothy *of the Truth. He speaks very blessedly of the* LORD's *Grace, and the exceeding Abundance of it in his Conversion.*

PAUL, an apostle of Jesus Christ by the commandment of God our Saviour, and Lord Jesus Christ, *which is* our hope.

2 Unto Timothy, *my* own son in the faith: Grace, mercy, *and* peace, from God our Father, and Jesus Christ our Lord.

I think it not improper to observe to the Reader, that, notwithstanding *Paul* was well known to *Timothy*, yet he reminds this youth of his Apostolic authority. His first miraculous call by CHRIST; Acts ix. 3, &c. his after ordination by the HOLY GHOST; Acts xiii. 1—5. and the revelation GOD the FATHER made of his dear SON in *Paul*, that he might preach CHRIST, these things he would not lose sight of. Gal. i. 15, 16. And I beg to observe in *Paul's* address to *Timothy* in these verses, another thing, which I also think not improper to remark, namely, in calling *Timothy his own son in the faith*. From whence some have concluded, *Paul* meant to say, that he was his *spiritual father*. But, notwithstanding the very great fondness which some have to this title, certain it is, *Paul* never used it himself. It is well known that *Timothy* was no relation to *Paul* after the *flesh*, his father being a Greek, and his mother a Jewess. Acts xvi. 1. And it is as certain, that *Timothy* was not *spiritually* related, if there be such a thing, (which I much doubt,) to the Apostle by conversion, for he was well reported of by the brethren that were at *Lystra* and *Iconium*, before *Paul* had ever seen him. Acts xvi. 2. So that *Paul* calling him his own son after the faith, certainly had no allusion to this subject, for he was not, in this sense, his *spiritual father*. This title hath given great occasion to indulge spiritual pride with many in the Church of GOD, and the enemy of souls, who well knows the weak and vulnerable parts of our nature, hath, in numberless instances, made an handle of it, to induce very unbecoming things being said in the Church. What the Apostle meant by naming those he called *children*, and of having begotten them to the Gospel by his instrumentality, I would not presume to speak decidedly upon. But one thing I do venture to believe, the Apostle never meant from it, that in the succeeding ages of the Church, any should arrogate to themselves, under cover of his example, such titles. The places in Scripture where this subject is in the least hinted at are but few, and those, if examined closely, may, perhaps, without violence, be construed to a different meaning. 1 Cor. iv. 14, 15. 2 Cor. xii. 14. Gal. iv. 19. 1 Thess. ii. 11. Titus i. 4. Philem. 10. But it shocks the mind, when we hear from pulpits, and read in sermons, and behold in inscriptions on tombstones of ministers, those sacred words of the Prophet, in allusion to CHRIST, and which, as the HOLY GHOST hath himself explained, can belong to no other, as if to be spoken by such worms of the earth at the last day; *Behold, I and the children whom the* LORD *hath given me.* Isaiah viii. 18. Heb. ii. 13. Supposing every thing that can be supposed in favor of this spiritual name, as relating to *Paul* and his ministry, would any man that considers his miraculous conversion, ordination, and the visions of GOD given him, take from such an instance confidence to call their ministry in the word by such a term? And is it not to be apprehended, by the very common use made of it in these modern times, that many have called themselves spiritual fathers, in the supposed conversion of others, concerning whom great doubts may be entertained whether they were ever converted themselves? But here I leave the subject.

3 As I besought thee to abide still at Ephesus, when I went into Macedonia, that thou mightest charge some that they teach no other doctrine.

4 Neither give heed to fables and endless genealogies, which minister questions, rather than godly edifying, which is in faith: *so do.*

5 Now the end of the commandment is charity out of a pure heart, and *of* a good conscience, and *of* faith unfeigned:

6 From which some having swerved have turned aside unto vain jangling;

7 Desiring to be teachers of the law; understanding neither what they say, nor whereof they affirm.

8 But we know that the law is good, *if* a man use it lawfully.

9 Knowing this, that the law is not made for a righteous man, but for the lawless and disobedient, for the ungodly and for sinners, for unholy and profane, for murderers of fathers and murderers of mothers, for manslayers;

10 For whoremongers, for them that defile themselves with mankind, for men-stealers, for liars, for perjured persons, and if there be any other thing that is contrary to sound doctrine.

11 According to the glorious gospel of the blessed God, which was committed to my trust.

I consider what the Apostle hath here said on the subject of the law, to be one of the most decisive and unanswerable determinations, (and from inspiration itself,) which ever hath been, or can be given, to quiet the minds of the faithful respecting it. And sure I am, if it were attended to, under the divine teaching, it would put an end to all the disputes with which the people of God have been disturbed on the point, by the vain arguments and reasonings of men. A moment's attention will place the Apostle's statement of the subject, concerning the law, in a clear light.

First. The Apostle sets down the great excellency of the law, as it is in itself. *We know,* (saith he,) *that the law is good.* And the holiness, perfection, and everlasting blessedness of all that is good, confirms every tittle of the law. *Sooner,* saith CHRIST, *shall heaven and earth pass, than one tittle of it to fail.* Luke xvi. 17. The law is the very transcript of the mind of GOD. And, therefore, when CHRIST came in the purity of his nature to fulfil the law, he sums up the infinite blessedness of it in these words: *I delight to do thy will, O my* GOD; *yea, thy law is within my heart;* or, as the margin of the Bible renders it, *in the midst of my bowels;* meaning, that his whole human nature was formed in the perfect holiness of it, and wrapped up in it. Psm. xl. 8. Seen in this point of view, how truly blessed is it! Well might *Paul* say, *we know that the law is good!*

Secondly. *Paul* qualifies the character of the law, as it relates to a poor sinner who hath broken the whole of it, by adding, that *it is good, if a man use it lawfully.* That is, if in a conscious sense of the infinite purity of the law itself, and its demands of unsinning obedience, with condemnation to every son and daughter of *Adam* who breaks it, we so use it, as those who are conscious of having sinned, and come short of GOD's glory, we lay hold of CHRIST, as *the end of the law for righteousness to every one that believeth.* In this sense the law is good indeed, and this is to use it lawfully. For by CHRIST's perfect obedience to the whole law, in our room and stead, and as the Head of his body the Church, we are accepted as holy in him. And this comes up to what the LORD said by the Prophet; *Surely shall one say, in the* LORD *have I righteousness and strength. In the* LORD *shall all the seed of Israel be justified, and shall glory.* Isaiah xlv. 24, 25.

Thirdly. The Apostle next proceeds to define the purposes of the law. *Knowing this, that the law is not made for a righteous man.* The law, which was delivered on Mount Sinai, the HOLY GHOST informs the Church, *was added because of transgressions.* Gal. iii. 19. And *Paul,* in his own experience, declares, that *he should not have known sin but by the law; for he should not have known lust, except the law had said, Thou shalt not covet.* Rom. vii. 7. Hence we learn, that as from the fall of the first man, none was righteous before GOD, the law was designed to teach sinners GOD's holiness, and their total depravity. And this became a blessed way to set forth the holiness of the GOD-man CHRIST JESUS, who only could, and did, obey the whole law of GOD. And how blessedly in him is seen, that all his seed are considered righteous and holy before GOD.

Fourthly. The Apostle closeth this part of the subject, with shewing for whom the law was made, and whom it universally condemns, being out of CHRIST. And a melancholy catalogue it forms! The law against all such stands unrepealed, unalterable, and everlastingly fixed. And in confirmation, *Paul* adds, *according to the glorious Gospel of the blessed* GOD! Reader! ponder the vast subject. Behold! how universally condemning the law is against all unrighteousness and ungodliness of men! See, the only possible safety from its condemnation is in CHRIST! Call to mind that every man by nature is in this state of condemnation, until called by sovereign grace! And when you have duly pondered the subject, and heard the unalterable sentence of all that live and die in the unregenerated state of the unrenewed mind, then ask your heart whether you yourself, personally considered, are interested in the blessed deliverance from it, which *Paul* describes: *And such were some of you: but ye are washed, but ye are sanctified, but ye are justified in the name of the* LORD JESUS, *and by the* SPIRIT *of our* GOD. 1 Cor. vi. 11.

12 And I thank Christ Jesus our Lord, who hath enabled me, for that he counted me faithful, putting me into the ministry;

13 Who was before a blasphemer, and a persecutor, and injurious: but I obtained mercy, because I did *it* ignorantly in unbelief.

14 And the grace of our Lord was exceeding abundant with faith and love which is in Christ Jesus.

15 This *is* a faithful saying, and worthy of all acceptation, that Christ Jesus came into the world to save sinners; of whom I am chief.

16 Howbeit for this cause I obtained mercy, that in me first Jesus Christ might shew forth all long-suffering, for a pattern to them which should hereafter believe on him to life everlasting.

17 Now unto the King eternal, immortal, invisible, the only wise God, *be* honour and glory for ever and ever. Amen.

Every word, more or less, in this account, *Paul* gives of his conversion, and the LORD's abundant grace, yea, exceeding abundant grace, as *Paul* calls it, in this sovereign display of love, is so full of instruction, that I do hope my Reader will not be offended if I call his attention to some of the leading particulars *Paul* dwells upon, as they affected his own mind. It is evident GOD the HOLY GHOST was pleased, that again and again the Church should be refreshed with the history. And sure I am no child of GOD can attend to it too often. I refer the Reader of this *Poor Man's Commentary* to what hath been already offered to his meditation, on the LORD's compelling Kings, and the Gentile Court, in the case of *Agrippa*, to hear *Paul* rehearse it; see Acts xxvi. 23. and Commentary; and also before the Sanhedrim and the court of the Jews. Acts xxii. 21. When the Reader hath turned to those Scriptures, and pondered that part of the subject, I beg his attention to some other observations which arise from the Scripture before us, in *Paul's* relation of the same wonderful work of his conversion to his beloved *Timothy*.

And, *first*. Let the Reader remark the view *Paul* had of the divine mercy shewn him, in putting him into the ministry, who was before a blasphemer, a persecutor, and injurious. He evidently alludes here to the awful conduct he was pursuing at the time of his conversion. *Paul* seems to intimate, that as there is a fulness of the iniquity of the *Amorite*, before which measure is filled, there is no ripeness for destruction, Gen. xv. 16. so there is a fulness of transgression, which the LORD's chosen ones heap up, in the *Adam*-nature of their fallen-state, before the time of their conversion arrives; the recovery from which tends to heighten to their astonished view, as they look back upon the past, the LORD's long-suffering, and their heights of daring rebellion. In the instance of *Paul*, he called to mind how he had, by his cruelties, compelled the saints of GOD to blaspheme; and which seemed to have wrought upon his mind, in the recollection, the bitterest part of his desperately wicked provocations. Reader! observe to what length, GOD's chosen ones run in offences! And observe in the midst of all, when sinning with an high hand, how the LORD still is watching over them, and, in spite of all hell's temptations, keeping them from the unpardonable sin! Oh! the wonders of grace! What a subject of this nature will be to be opened, in every child of GOD's life, when we come into eternity?

Secondly. Let the Reader observe, what the Apostle saith of his obtaining mercy, *because he did it ignorantly in unbelief*. *Paul* did not mean that this was the cause for which the LORD called him; or for which the LORD pardoned him. His call was, as the LORD told *Ananias*: because he was a *chosen vessel;* and from everlasting had been appointed to bear testimony for CHRIST, before Jew and Gentile. Acts ix. 15. Neither was his ignorance the least excuse for his blasphemy, or for the persecution he manifested, to the poor saints of CHRIST. And *Paul* plainly testifieth, that he did not conceive his ignorance pleaded excuse; for, in this very account, he declares himself to be the chief of sinners. And how could he be supposed obtaining mercy for ignorance which was *determined* ignorance? It is plain, that he heard the wisdom of *Stephen*, and could not resist the spirit by which he spake; though he was among the first of them that stoned him. Acts vi. 10. But the whole is designed to shew, in *Paul's* instance, the desperately wicked state of the unregenerate while in nature; to enhance the sovereignty of Almighty grace in the recovery. From both which, it is plain, that the chosen vessels of GOD are, by nature, and by practice, in the same awful circumstances, as the whole *Adam*-race, all alike *dead in trespasses and sins*.

Thirdly, The time of *Paul's* conversion was a circumstance which in his view tended to heighten still more the unspeakable mercy; and made it, what *Paul* called it, *the exceeding abundant grace of the* Lord. It was in the very moment when he was hot in the pursuit of the blood of the saints. Like a savage beast of prey, he was breathing out nothing but threatenings and slaughter against the saints of the Lord. Acts ix. 1. The Lord met him, as in the field of battle, and unhorsed him in a moment. And, no doubt, many a time after this, as often as *Paul* thought of it, his only astonishment was, that the Lord, who struck him to the ground, had not struck him at once into hell. If it be asked, wherefore such forbearance? The Lord himself answered *Ananias,* when he expressed the same wonder. *He is a chosen vessel* (said the Lord) *unto me.* Reader! do you know any thing of sovereign grace? If so: say, how was you employed when the Lord called *you?* If not persecuting as *Paul* was, the Church of God; yet prosecuting at least the lusts of the flesh, and the desires of an unawakened mind. Oh! what a source of soul-feeling doth the recollection of our ill, and hell-deservings, when the Lord first manifested his grace in conversion, open to all the after reviews of life? And what a spring of true repentance, causing the tears to fall, when we look back, and behold ourselves cast out like the infant to perish, and Jesus *passing by, and bidding us in our blood, live?* Ezek. xvi. 6.

Fourthly. What a blessed conclusion the Holy Ghost taught *Paul* to make, from his conversion, for the instruction of others; when, under the full impression, in the review he cried out: *This is a faithful saying, and worthy of all acceptation, that* Christ Jesus *came into the world to save sinners, of whom I am chief.* Worthy indeed, in every point of view! Worthy, as the gift of God; the price of Christ's blood; the effectual application of it by the Spirit. And it becomes the highest testimony of divine faithfulness; because in it God proves himself the faithful God, being faithful to his Covenant promises in Christ, to a thousand generations. And let not the Reader overlook what a stress *Paul* lays upon that proof of divine faithfulness, for all acceptation in that, even to him, the chief of sinners, that faithfulness had been shewn. There is somewhat very sweet in this. *Paul* saith, that he is chief of sinners; by which he meant, in greatness; and in the aggravated circumstances of his sins, against the Person of Christ. I beg the Reader to mark this with peculiar notice. *Paul* takes no count of his morality, and the strict observance of the *Pharisee.* All these sunk to nothing in his view. But his daring opposition to the Person and Gospel of Christ, made him so odious to himself, that he beheld himself as the chief of sinners. And, in consequence, he always considered himself as such to the close of life. He wrote this Epistle to *Timothy* towards the end of his ministry; and we see he still retained this view of himself. He doth not say, I *was,* but I *am,* the chief of sinners.

One word more. Let not the Reader overlook the cause *Paul* assigns, for this abundant mercy, shewn him: that in me, said *Paul, first,* Jesus Christ *might shew forth all long suffering, for a pattern to them which should hereafter believe on him to life everlasting.* As if the Apostle had said, who shall ever despond, or despair of obtaining pardon, and peace in the blood of the cross, whose heart is broken for sin, while beholding *Paul* the persecutor, the blasphemer, and injurious; brought into the grace of JESUS? In this first, and greatest of all examples, what GOD can, and will do; and what, through the gracious work of GOD the SPIRIT on the heart, CHRIST's blood and righteousness can, and doth accomplish; the vilest of the vile may be encouraged! Blessed be GOD the HOLY GHOST, for causing so illustrious an instance of the sovereignty of Almighty grace, to be recorded, and handed down, through all ages, to the present time, in the Church of GOD!

Largely as I have trespassed, the case is too interesting to be dismissed, without closing it with an observation or two more. *Paul* could not fold it up, without ascribing honor and glory, for ever and ever, to *the King eternal, immortal, invisible, the only wise* GOD: that is, to the FATHER, SON, and HOLY GHOST, whom all along, in all *Paul's* writings and preachings, he considered, as the united source of all his mercy, in CHRIST. And such must every child of GOD, who can, and doth discover, tokens of regenerating, and converting grace, in his own history. And there is somewhat striking in the circumstances of every man's conversion, when duly considered, which comes home in characters special, and peculiar, to endear, and recommend it personally to every heart. And though it may not, for it is not necessary it should, be attended with similar circumstances, like those of *Paul;* yet, in all instances, the LORD's distinguishing love-tokens may be seen in every particular.

Reader! let it be supposed an *early conversion* of the heart to GOD, while in youth. Oh! what a mercy is it, when, like this *Timothy,* it may be said, that from a child, the regenerated soul hath known the holy scriptures. And to whom the LORD saith, as to Israel of old: *I remember thee, the kindness of thy youth, the love of thine espousals; when thou wentest after me in a wilderness, in a land that was not sown.* Jerem. ii. 2. And suppose a *later conversion* is appointed, which, like *Paul,* or like the thief on the cross at the eleventh hour, think what abounding mercy, where there had been long abounding sin!

There are also special manifestations, which the LORD sheweth in seasons of conversion, not only in making known the grace itself, but in the manner of its work. *Some,* like *Paul,* lay days in the pangs of the new-birth; while *others,* like *Lydia,* the LORD at once opens the heart, to attend to the truths of salvation. GOD is a sovereign, and Almighty Agent, and worketh after the counsel of his own will. Some precious souls, have had so easy a transition, from the death of sin, to the new life in righteousness; that when comparing their call of GOD with that of others, they have been tempted at times to question the reality of it. But the HOLY GHOST hath given the Church by *Paul,* an infallible testimony, to ascertain every man's election, and call, by the effects which follow. See 1 Thess. i. 4. and Commentary. And so far is an early, and an effectual call, from becoming questionable, when the blessed consequences of the new-birth appear, by the actions of the new-life; that it carries with it, sweet testimonies of divine love. The call of *Matthew,* was of this kind; and the LORD JESUS had so marked it: Matt. ix. 9—13.

Such *Zaccheus*; Luke xix 1—10. Such the *Philippians*; Philip. i. 5. And such is the blessed variety by which the Lord calls his own, that perhaps, there are scarcely two cases exactly alike. Oh! what a subject of divine love would it open, if all the courtings, and wooings of Jesus, by his Holy Spirit, were made known, by which he wins over the affections to himself, when God the Spirit hath quickened the sinner which was before *dead in trespasses and sins!* Say, dear Lord! how didst thou work upon my stony heart, the hardest sure, ever wrought upon, when thou didst make me *willing, in the day of thy power?*

18 This charge I commit unto thee son Timothy, according to the prophecies which went before on thee, that thou by them mightest war a good warfare;

19 Holding faith, and a good conscience; which some having put away concerning faith have made shipwreck.

20 Of whom is Hymeneus and Alexander; whom I have delivered unto Satan, that they may learn not to blaspheme.

Paul having, in the recollection of his wonderful conversion, in some measure departed from the subject he was before speaking of, concerning the law, and the Gospel, (verses 8—11.) now returns to it, and gives charge to his beloved *Timothy*, how he should preach Christ, and Christ only, agreeably to the prophecies, which *Timothy*, who had been taught in them, well understood, as referring to Christ. And he points to the strong assurances of faith, and a good conscience, both God the Spirit's gift; which some who have made a profession, but who never felt the power, had relinquished. Reader! what a beautiful distinction this forms, (and I take occasion by the way to remark it,) between the blessed work of God the Spirit in regeneration, from whence come faith and a good conscience; and the mere profession of Christ, taken up for the moment, from hearsay, not heart-felt knowledge, and put down again from the same cause!

This *Hymeneus* is the same as spoken of 2 Tim. ii. 17, 18. And *Alexander* is most likely to be the Copper-smith. 2 Tim. iv. 14. *Paul's* delivery of them to *Satan*, seems to have been for correction. We have a similar passage, 1 Cor. v. 5. to the notes on which I refer.

REFLECTIONS.

Reader! the more we traverse the inspired writings of this great Apostle, the more we find cause to bless God for his ministry. What affection he here manifests, to the Church of Christ! What love to *Timothy*, as a minister in the Church! What earnestness he expresseth, that he should be found faithful! And what delight he takes, to go over again and again, the wonderful story of his conversion! No expressions can he find, sufficiently humbling, to set forth his own worthlessness: neither any sufficiently exalted, to praise the riches of GOD's grace. Surely the HOLY GHOST intended, from the frequency of this record to be brought before the Church, to shew poor sinners, that no state is too polluted, no life of sin too abandoned, to be out of the reach of CHRIST's blood. Yes! *Paul!* thou art indeed a pattern of the exceeding riches of grace; yea, and abundant grace, to all that hereafter believe on the LORD JESUS to everlasting life. Oh! blessed JESUS! enable me in thy strength to hold faith, and a good conscience, in thee; and daily to cry out with *Paul:* Now to the King eternal, immortal, invisible, the only wise GOD, be honor and glory, for ever, and ever. Amen.

CHAP. II.

CONTENTS.

The Apostle is prosecuting the Subject of his Advice to Timothy, *in this Chapter. He exhorts, that Prayers be made, that Women be adorned with plain Apparel. He closeth with a sweet Promise.*

I Exhort, therefore, that first of all, supplications, prayers, intercessions, *and* giving of thanks, be made for all men;

2 For kings, and *for* all that are in authority; that we may lead a quiet and peaceable life in all godliness and honesty.

3 For this *is* good and acceptable in the sight of God our Saviour;

4 Who will have all men to be saved, and to come unto the knowledge of the truth.

We shall do well to observe, what the HOLY GHOST hath here commanded by *Paul,* on the subject of prayer. It is for *all men.* By which we learn, what is here meant, by praying for all, in this indiscriminate manner. The passage indeed explains itself: *that we may lead a quiet, and peaceable life, in all godliness and honesty.* It is simply for *temporal* things; similar to what GOD commanded the Prophet on the subject of prayer, when the Church was going into captivity. *Seek the peace of the city,* (saith the LORD,) *whither I have caused you to be carried away captive, and pray unto the* LORD *for it: for in the peace thereof shall ye have peace.* Jerem. xxix. 7. And the close of this paragraph, becomes a further confirmation. *For this is good, and acceptable, in the sight of* GOD *our* SAVIOR; *who will have all men to be saved, and to come unto the knowledge of the truth.* What saving is this, which GOD our SAVIOR is said, that he would have all men to have? Not salvation surely. For if so, how comes it to pass, that all are not saved; or that any is lost. The loss of a single soul, if this were the sense of the passage, would prove, that what GOD willed, came not to pass. And this would throw down all GOD's divine attributes. But, if the words be interpreted by what went before, in allusion to *temporal* safety; then it follows, that our prayers for *all men*, while having an eye only to their *temporal* prosperity, are in perfect agreement, with all men having *temporal* safety in CHRIST: and which CHRIST, as the Maker, and Upholder of all things, is the sole cause of. See Chap. iv. 10. and Commentary.

Reader! I take occasion from this passage, to offer a short observation on prayer, which I conceive to be of no small importance, to regard, in our spiritual life. I mean, in always confining our petitions in prayer for spiritual blessings, to the Church; in conformity to the pattern of CHRIST. *I pray not for the world,* (said JESUS,) *but for them which thou hast given me.* John xvii. 9. It is certainly most suitable, and becoming in the Church, and every individual of the Church, to follow CHRIST's example in this, as well as upon every other occasion which is imitable. As we know not who are, or who are not, the members of CHRIST's body, in numberless cases, we cannot often speak of persons as JESUS did; yet, we shall still follow the LORD's steps in this particular in prayer, if we always qualify our petitions for spiritual blessings for any, with subjoining: If it be the LORD's holy will and pleasure. A child of GOD, when seeking grace for his family, for his little ones, and bringing them to ordinances with this view, to present them before the LORD, for his blessing; will not err, as long as he asketh, all he asketh for them, with this gratifying clause: *If it be thy holy will.* It was thus the people brought their sick and diseased to the LORD JESUS, in the days of his flesh; beseeching him that they might only *touch the hem of his garment.* Mark vi. 55, 56. And if we do the same now, in the day of CHRIST's power; here we ought to rest. And, if the LORD gives a spirit of prayer for them; it is a blessed hope, that the LORD will answer it in mercy. Further we cannot presume, neither to be wise above what is written, or to dictate to the LORD of his doings.

5 For *there is* one God, and one mediator between God and men, the man Christ Jesus.

6 Who gave himself a ransom for all, to be testified in due time.

7 Whereunto I am ordained a preacher, and an apostle, (I speak the truth in Christ, *and* lie not;) a teacher of the Gentiles in faith and verity.

Every portion in these verses is important, and merits our special attention. When *Paul* here speaks of One GOD, in allusion to the unity of his divine nature, and essence, he evidently is speaking of that unity, as manifested to the Church, in the Covenant transactions of the FATHER, SON, and HOLY GHOST; by way of shewing the unity of design, in all the grace shewn the Church, from the HOLY THREE IN ONE. And hence, having declared this oneness in GOD, both in his nature, and purposes; the Apostle immediately adds: *and one Mediator between* GOD *and men; the Man* CHRIST JESUS. I admire the Apostle's manner of expression, on this subject. He first sets down the unity, both of the essence, and of the grace, in relation to Covenant-settlements in the divine nature, as existing in a plurality of Persons: One in nature, and one in design. He then introduceth Him, by whose mediation alone, (for he expressly calls him One Mediator, because, in fact, there could be no other:) the purposes of this Covenant, could only be transacted. And, while the very nature of his Office implied his GODHEAD; the Apostle no less took care to express his manhood; and therefore, calls him *the Man* CHRIST JESUS. As both the Person of CHRIST, and the office of CHRIST, as Mediator, are points of infinite consequence, for the Reader to have a clear apprehension concerning, he will not be displeased, if I consider the subject somewhat more particularly.

The very idea of mediation, carries with it the conviction, that some breach must have existed, between two, or more parties, which, before this quarrel, had been in amity with each other. Such was the case between GOD and man, when CHRIST came forth, under this character, of Mediator. When at creation, *Adam* was first formed, we are told, that GOD *saw every thing which he had made, and behold it was very good.* Gen. i. 31. Consequently, there was perfect harmony at that time, between GOD and man. But, when *Adam* fell by transgression, a deadly breach took place. And CHRIST, as GOD and man in one Person, could be the only Mediator, to make it up. How CHRIST accomplished it, is not in this place so much dwelt upon, for this is fully set forth in other parts of scripture. But the Apostle is here chiefly adverting to his Person, and his office, as Mediator. A few words on each, will serve, under the LORD's teaching, to set the matter in a clear light. The LORD graciously instruct both Writer and Reader.

A Mediator, to bring about a reconciliation between parties so dissimilar, as an holy GOD, and unholy man; must be supposed, in the very nature of things, to possess abilities of a very peculiar kind, and such as but for the wonderful, and mysterious union, of GOD and man in one Person, never could have been found. He, that undertook to make up the awful breach, which sin had made, between GOD and man; must know, what was suitable to the dignity of GOD to receive; and what corresponded to the nature of man to offer. And, as in the *latter* instance, it was evident in the first face of things, that man had nothing in himself to offer, but by a substitute, which CHRIST in his human nature could only accomplish: so in the *former*, none but GOD, who knew what sin is, and what became suitable for GOD to receive, could form any one conception whatever, of the plan, by which peace might be obtained; and, therefore, CHRIST in his divine nature, could only be competent, both to the knowledge, and to the accomplishment. And such, therefore, is CHRIST: GOD and Man in one Person. And, of all subjects upon earth, as connected with our redemption, this is the most blessed, and consolatory. He, that undertook to mediate peace by the blood of his cross: and He alone, by partaking of both natures, GOD and man, became, what *Job* so ardently longed to behold, a proper *Days-man*, as the Patriarch called him, that could *lay his hand upon both parties.* Job ix. 33. He, and He alone, *the man* God's *fellow,* as God himself called him, became the only One, competent to the arduous work. Zech. xiii. 7. And oh! what grace, love, mercy, tenderness, wisdom, and compassion, are all manifested, in the high undertaking?

In this office of mediation, it behoveth him, who acted in this high character of Mediator, to do justice to God; and yet, to do it in such a way, and manner, as should be not ruinous to man. And this, the Lord Jesus accomplished, in becoming the sinner's Surety; whereby, in his obedience and death, he did more to glorify God, than could have been done by the punishment of man, to all eternity. Hence, his Godhead not only furnished ability, for the performance of both, but stamped upon both an infinite value, which more than recompensed the injury done by man; and procured a redundancy of merit, for the everlasting happiness of man in the favor of God, which an whole eternity can never fully repay. And herein lay the blessedness of Christ, as God-Man-Mediator, the only possible One suited to the office. For had Christ not been God, the merit of his obedience could not have satisfied. In this case, there would not have been an Almightiness of power in him, to raise our nature from the ruins of the fall; neither, to have conquered sin and Satan, death and hell, by his personal victories; in the triumphs over which, our salvation was everlastingly concerned. And had Christ not been man, his obedience would not have been the obedience the law required; neither could he have made his soul an offering for sin. But now, by the union of both, in one Person, he hath manifested himself to have been the *One,* and the only One, all-sufficient, and all-glorious *Mediator, between* God *and man; the man* Christ Jesus. Heb. ii. 14.

Let the Reader next attend to what is said, of his *giving himself a ransom for all to be testified in due time.* A wonderful expression! *Gave himself.* Not any costly offering; not gifts of gold, nor all the spices of the East: Not thousands of rams, nor ten thousands of rivers of oil. But himself. The Holy Ghost lays great stress upon this precious word, *him* and *himself.* See Ephes. i. 10. Coloss. i. 20. Heb. i. 3. See Commentary. *A ransom for all.* Who are meant by all? Not surely all mankind. For in that case, all that is said of his elect Church, would be an unnecessary distinction. Besides, if all mankind are included in this ransom; then all must be everlastingly saved: and the final destruction of the ungodly, which scripture asserts, cannot take place. But the *all* for whom Christ gave himself a ransom, is explained in the latter part of the verse; those *who are testified of in due time:* that is, in whom God the Spirit regenerates, and witnesseth to their spirits, that *they are the sons of* God. Rom. viii. 14—16. Our Lord himself, when speaking of the subject of his giving himself a ransom, declares that it is for *many;* which is to the same purport. See Matt. xx. 28. And *Paul* takes up the same subject as his divine Master, through the whole of his preaching, when declaring himself an Apostle for this purpose, to be a *teacher of the Gentiles,* on those great points *in faith and verity.*

8 I will therefore that men pray every where, lifting up holy hands, without wrath and doubting.

9 In like manner also, that women adorn themselves in modest apparel, with shamefacedness and sobriety; not with broidered hair, or gold, or pearls, or costly array;

10 But (which becometh women professing godliness) with good works.

11 Let the woman learn in silence with all subjection.

12 But I suffer not a woman to teach, nor to usurp authority over the man, but to be in silence.

13 For Adam was first formed, then Eve.

14 And Adam was not deceived, but the woman being deceived was in the transgression.

15 Notwithstanding she shall be saved in childbearing, if they continue in faith and charity, and holiness with sobriety.

I do not think it necessary to swell our pages by a Comment on what is so plain as to need none. I will only, therefore, detain the Reader to observe, on the latter part of this paragraph, a word or two, in relation to what is said of our first Parents. The question is, did the HOLY GHOST, by *Paul*, mean to throw the whole blame upon the Woman, being deceived; when it is said, *Adam* was not deceived? I confess I dare not speak decidedly upon it. But yet, I rather think, the man was the greater transgressor of the two. The Woman was deceived by the subtlety of the Serpent. But *Adam* was *not* deceived, the HOLY GHOST saith. And, as he sinned against light and knowledge; and chose to be involved with his wife in the ruin, rather than obey GOD; it should seem, that he was the most daring sinner. But, be this as it may, the sweet conclusion of promise, with which the Chapter ends, comes in to the relief of both, in a very gracious manner. *She shall be saved in child-bearing;* that is, not an absolute promise, that women of *faith*, and in the *love of* GOD, shall all be carried through the hour of nature's extremity, in the bearing of children; notwithstanding the sentence on the first woman, in the garden, for her transgression, that *in sorrow she should bring forth children:* Gen. iii. 16. for well we know, many a gracious woman hath died in that season. But the promise seems to be of a *spiritual* nature. And the child-bearing here spoken of, is of *Eve's* seed, even CHRIST. In the child-bearing of Him, shall she (and all of faith in CHRIST like her) be saved, notwithstanding the original, and actual transgressions, of herself, and all her children. This appears to me to. be the meaning of the passage. *Eve* herself, personally considered, could have no other interest in the promise, than in this, or somewhat a similar spiritual sense, since she herself had been dead for ages before this promise was given.

REFLECTIONS.

IN the opening of this Chapter, we derive authority for the use of prayer, not only for the Church, but for the world: while the precept, which enjoins prayers for all men, plainly directs, to what the subject of those prayers should lead. And, while the Church becomes a blessing, as a dew from the LORD, in the midst of many people, to keep the whole community from consuming drought; the Church derives protection, in temporal quietness, from the prosperity of the nation where it dwells.

Blessed Mediator of thy people! Every renewed view of thee, is refreshing to the soul! LORD! let it be testified in due time, to all thy blood-bought children, the infinitely precious ransom, which thou hast given of thyself, to redeem them from all iniquity. And oh! let the sweet assurance of salvation, in the child-bearing, when our great *Emmanuel* was born of a woman, open an everlasting source of consolation, to all his faithful seed. And if it please our GOD, let all the faithful daughters of thy chosen generation, while partaking in the *Eve*-fruit of transgression, in passing through the hour of sorrow, partake also in this sweet promise in thee; and cause them by thy HOLY SPIRIT, *to continue in faith, and charity, and holiness, with sobriety.*

CHAP. III.

CONTENTS.

The Apostle here enters upon the Subject of the Ministry. He shews how the Office should be sacredly observed: with their Connections. The Chapter closeth most blessedly, concerning the great Mystery of Godliness.

THIS *is* a true saying, If a man desire the office of a bishop, he desireth a good work.

2 A bishop then must be blameless, the husband of one wife, vigilant, sober, of good behaviour, given to hospitality, apt to teach;

3 Not given to wine, no striker, not greedy of filthy lucre; but patient, not a brawler, not covetous.

4 One that ruleth well his own house, having his children in subjection with all gravity;

5 (For if a man know not how to rule his own house, how shall he take care of the church of God?)

6 Not a novice, lest being lifted up with pride he fall into the condemnation of the devil.

7 Moreover he must have a good report of them which are without; lest he fall into reproach and the snare of the devil.

8 Likewise *must* the deacons *be* grave, not double-tongued, not given to much wine, not greedy of filthy lucre;

9 Holding the mystery of the faith in a pure conscience.

10 And let these also first be proved; then let them use the office of a deacon, being *found* blameless.

11 Even so *must their* wives *be* grave, not slanderers, sober, faithful in all things.

12 Let the deacons be the husbands of one wife, ruling their children and their own houses well.

13 For they that have used the office of a deacon well purchase to themselves a good degree, and great boldness in the faith which is in Christ Jesus.

14 These things write I unto thee, hoping to come unto thee shortly:

15 But if I tarry long, that thou mayest know how thou oughtest to behave thyself in the house of God, which is the church of the living God, the pillar and ground of the truth.

I do not think it necessary, in a work of this kind, intended for *the poor in spirit*, and the humble in Christ's flock; and not likely to fall under the notice of the high in rank, and dignity; the bishops, and shepherds of the fold; to enter into an account of their offices. Indeed, the Apostle hath said all that can be necessary, on the subject. One point only I venture to remark, in what *Paul* hath here said; namely, he calls the office of a bishop a *good work*. And a good work, or labor, it most assuredly is, if well followed. The close of the service will shew, that the highest, and the lowest office of the ministry of souls, is alike an accountable trust, where men will be answerable as servants, not as lords. Among men, it may be proper, to preserve distinctions of rank, and honor. But in the sight of God, these things lose their very name. Usefulness, deligence, faithfulness, and honesty, are the qualifications then to be accounted for; and none else will stand the examination. It were well, if all who minister in holy things, of whatever rank they move up and down in, among men, were every day, before they enter upon their sacred function, or mingle in family duties, of reading the scriptures, and prayer; to read over in private, what *Paul* hath here marked down, from the inspiration of GOD the HOLY GHOST. This would serve, under the same Almighty Teacher's influence, to shew, how all ought to behave themselves in the house of GOD. That as CHRIST himself, is both the foundation, and pillar of his Church; so, his servants, which minister faithfully in his name, may be found as monumental pillars, bearing inscriptions, to his truth and glory.

16 And without controversy great is the mystery of godliness: God was manifest in the flesh, justified in the Spirit, seen of angels, preached unto the Gentiles, believed on in the world, received up into glory.

What a rich cluster of mysteries is here! All blessedly hanging together, like some large bunch of the richest grapes, on the most luxuriant Vine! The mystery begins with, GOD *manifest in the flesh:* and the verse ends with, CHRIST *received up into glory.* GOD the SON, tabernacling in a body of flesh! *Justified in the* SPIRIT; both in the formation of that pure portion of human nature, wrought by his miraculous impregnation, in the womb of the Virgin, in testifying at CHRIST's baptism, in all his miracles; when he offered himself through the eternal SPIRIT on the cross; when risen from the dead, when returned to glory; and when, in exact conformity to the LORD's most sure promise, GOD the HOLY GHOST came down at *Pentecost,* in an open display of his Person, and Offices; and now in a private manifestation in the hearts of all CHRIST's seed, from the first moment of regeneration, until grace is finished in glory. In all these, and numberless other instances, CHRIST is justified in the SPIRIT, when *he takes of* CHRIST, *and shews to the people.* And *seen of angels,* who saw him at his birth, attended him in his temptations in the wilderness, in his agonies in the garden, at his resurrection, ascension, and return to glory. *Preached to the Gentiles.* And this became a mystery to the Jewish Church, that GOD *should also to the Gentiles, grant repentance unto life.* Acts xi. 18. And what was yet, and is now, and ever must be, a greater mystery still, that CHRIST should be *believed on in the world.* For such is the natural enmity of every man's mind by the fall; that nothing short of sovereign grace can gain acceptance for CHRIST, in a single heart. And there must be the concurring operation of all the Persons of the GODHEAD, in the drawings of the FATHER, John vi. 44. the manifestations of the SON, 1 John v. 20. and the quickenings of the HOLY GHOST, to induce belief in the soul. Ephes. ii. 1. And the LORD's being *received up into glory,* closeth the wonderful account, in this precious mystery of godliness, which, without controversy, must be acknowledged great! Reader! what a mercy is your's, and mine, if through grace, we can both subscribe to the blessed contents? Great as the mystery of godliness is, God hath revealed the truth of the whole to our spirit. 1 Cor. ii. 10.

REFLECTIONS.

Oh! Lord the Spirit! do thou in mercy to the Church, ordain Pastors after thine own heart: and make all such, as thou hast called to the ministry, however known, or distinguished among men, more anxious to win souls, than to gain kingdoms.

Precious Jesus! let the mystery of thine incarnation be the constant, unceasing subject of my meditation! Oh! the love of Christ which passeth knowledge! Didst thou, dear Lord, who when rich beyond all the calculation of riches, condescend for our sakes to be made poor, that we through thy poverty might be made rich! And, oh! the sweet testimony of God the Spirit, in justifying all the works of Christ, both to the Person of Christ, and in the heart of his people, in his finished salvation. Angels, behold; Gentiles, believe; yea, my poor blind and stony heart is made *willing in the day of* God's *power*. And God the Father hath given assurance unto all men of the mystery of godliness, in having raised Christ from the dead, and received him up into glory. Blessed, blessed for ever, be God for Jesus Christ!

CHAP. IV.

CONTENTS.

God *the* Holy Ghost *is here introduced as speaking expressly of the Latter-day Heresies.* Paul *cautions* Timothy *to be on the look-out with the Church against the Times of such Peril.*

NOW the Spirit speaketh expressly, that in the latter times some shall depart from the faith, giving heed to seducing spirits, and doctrines of devils;

2 Speaking lies in hypocrisy; having their consciences seared with a hot iron;

3 Forbidding to marry, *and commanding* to abstain from meats, which God hath created to be received with thanksgiving of them which believe and know the truth.

4 For every creature of God *is* good, and nothing to be refused, if it be received with thanksgiving:

5 For it is sanctified by the word of God and prayer.

The opening of this chapter is uncommonly interesting. When God the Spirit speaks, well may man hear. But beside this attention in a general way, there is somewhat here, which from the manner of expression made use of, calls up that attention with more awakened earnestness. God the Spirit *speaketh expressly.* We do not find a similar phrase in all the Bible. We very frequently hear of the Lord speaking by his servants the Prophets, in the Old Testament Scripture, saying, *Thus saith the* Lord; and, *The* Lord *hath spoken.* But here the Spirit, in his Person, is described as speaking, and speaking *expressly.* Was it not as if to silence the awful blasphemy of the latter day times, which we now live to see, when his Almighty Person, and ministry, and glory, in the œconomy of grace, are so openly denied? If the Spirit speaketh expressly, can He be otherwise than a Person who thus performs the action of a Person? And if the Spirit at such a distance as *Paul* wrote, spoke expressly in declaring the heresies which should come in the last days, could He be less than God who thus exercised the perfection and attribute of foreknowledge? And if the Holy Ghost thus spake in the Church at that period, did He not thereby exercise his ministry in the Church when he thus presided over? Reader! if this verse alone be fully considered, what an unanswerable decision doth it give to the blasphemies of some, and the disregard of others, in this God-dishonoring, Christ-despising, Holy Ghost disowning generation?

I do not think it necessary in this place, to go over again the many precious testimonies with which the word of God abounds, to the Person and ministry of God the Holy Ghost, having already, in many parts of this *Poor Man's Commentary,* somewhat largely considered the subject. I would particularly refer the Reader on this account to Acts chapters ii. and xiii. and Heb. ix.

But we must not stop here. If the Spirit speaketh expressly, and speaketh of the latter-day heresies, which so plainly refer to our own times, we have yet a more abundant reason to attend, and *to hear what the* Spirit *saith unto the Churches.* Rev. ii. 29. The relation of them is truly awful. *Some shall depart from the faith, giving heed to seducing spirits, and doctrines of devils; speaking lies in hypocrisy, having their conscience seared with a hot iron.* Oh! what a trembling account! But, blessed be God, though *some* shall be thus found, yet not *all.* And the *faith,* though *some* depart from, is not *the faith of* God's *elect;* for God hath said of all such, that in *the everlasting covenant he hath made with them, he will put his fear in their hearts, that they shall not depart from him.* Titus i. 1. Jerem. xxxii. 40. A departure from the mere faith of a profession, may be, and indeed must be, for it holds by nothing which can keep it. It was taken up by hearsay, or head-knowledge, and will be put down again when these fail. But where God the Spirit regenerates, there the faith of God's elect is given, and, through grace, the soul then chooses *that good part, which shall not be taken away.* Luke x. 42.

I cannot, in a work of this kind, enter into a long discourse concerning the heresies here spoken of expressly by the Holy Ghost. Very sure I am, that the same Almighty Lord who foretold the people of their coming, will keep his people from finally falling by them. But it is impossible to say to what lengths they may be permitted to proceed. It is the happiness of the Church, however, that their security is in CHRIST, And though the LORD JESUS hath admonished his people, that there will be awful judgments, and delusions so great, that, *if it were possible, they would deceive even the very elect;* yet the LORD's most gracious words, while he speaks of those things, decidedly prove, at the same time, that to deceive them is impossible. Mark xiii. 22.

What greater apostacy, among Professors of Christianity, than the present days manifest, may be yet for to come, I know not, and what *seducing spirits, and doctrines of devils,* as we approach nearer the end of the world will appear, is not for me to conceive. Very much more than even the crying sins which now come with uncovered front before us, may, according to Scripture, be looked for. Mark xiii. 20. Rev. xii. 12. But, in my apprehension, there never was a period, since the Reformation of less vital godliness, and more of the form and carcase of religion, than the present. It is too notorious to be unknown, and too awful to be known without trembling for the eventual consequences. But, when we find a liberty assumed, under the cover of religious freedom, of denying all the glorious and distinguishing truths of our most holy faith, and both the press and pulpit, in every direction, teem with discourses which set at nought that *faith which was once delivered unto the saints,* we may reasonably conclude that impending judgments are not far remote. Jude 3—7.

And what appears to me among the most alarming signs of the present times is, that many who profess themselves the glorious truths, which distinguish our holy faith, manifest a total indifferency as to the conviction of them by others. There is a spirit of accommodation crept in among us, under the specious covering of universal love, which makes a sacrifice of divine truths. We conceal our belief in what is dearer to us than life, in order that those with whom we mingle for general purposes of charity, may not take offence. And we fondly persuade ourselves that all descriptions of religion may meet together, and join to promote the divine glory, when those blessed truths which bring the greatest glory to the LORD, are cautiously kept out of view. Surely, that faith can be but little valued by us, if fearful to be owned. And if the GODHEAD of CHRIST, redemption by his blood, justification by his righteousness, be dearer to me, (as that they are,) than my necessary food, I cannot, I dare not, conceal those sentiments, nor knowingly join with those who deny them, under the mistaken idea of promoting the divine glory, while restraining the open confession of my faith to the divine praise. The LORD pardon me if I err. But according to my view of things, this accommodating spirit is among the most awful signs of the present day. I know that I am singular. But it appears a time to be singular. GOD the SPIRIT hath spoken expressly of those latter ages of the Church. Consistent with my apprehension of the LORD's speaking, let others think as they may, I cannot think otherwise than I have said. Though concealing our attachment to the great truths of GOD, may not amount to a *denial,* yet is it not a tacit *departure* from the faith? Though not *giving heed to seducing spirits,* yet is it not giving in to a *Laodicean* spirit, which the Son of God so highly condemns? Rev. iii. 15, 16.

6 If thou put the brethren in remembrance of these things, thou shalt be a good minister of Jesus Christ, nourished up in the words of faith and of good doctrine, whereunto thou hast attained.

7 But refuse profane and old wives' fables, and exercise thyself *rather unto* godliness.

8 For bodily exercise profiteth little: but godliness *is* profitable unto all things, having promise of the life that now is, and of that which is to come.

9 This *is* a faithful saying, and worthy of all acceptation.

The Apostle's advice to *Timothy*, is in no small degree of correspondence to what I have on the preceding verses remarked. If it behoved this young man to put the brethren in mind of those great truths *Paul* had before been delivering to him, and if by doing so he would shew himself to be a good minister of Jesus Christ, the same holds good of all the Lord's people, whether ministers or saints, in all ages of the Church. And if the Spirit hath spoken expressly of the latter-day heresies, it must be an awful thing in them who profess faith in the momentous truths of the Gospel, to be silent about them, when heresies appear!

10 For therefore we both labour and suffer reproach, because we trust in the living God, who is the Saviour of all men, specially of those that believe.

11 These things command and teach.

12 Let no man despise thy youth; but be thou an example of the believers, in word, in conversation, in charity, in spirit, in faith, in purity.

13 Till I come, give attendance to reading, to exhortation, to doctrine.

14 Neglect not the gift that is in thee, which was given thee by prophecy, with the laying on of the hands of the presbytery.

15 Meditate upon these things; give thyself wholly to them; that thy profiting may appear to all.

16 Take heed unto thyself, and unto the doctrine; continue in them: for in doing this thou shalt both save thyself, and them that hear thee.

If in connection with what the Apostle here saith of the living GOD being *the* SAVIOR *of all men, specially of those that believe,* the Reader will consult what was offered in this *Commentary* on chap. ii. 4. he will, under divine teaching, discover in what sense both those Scriptures are intended. GOD our SAVIOR is, in truth, the SAVIOR of all men, in nature, and providence. For He is both the Maker and Upholder of all things. The very enemies of CHRIST, are upheld by CHRIST; for all power is his, in heaven, and in earth. In his mysterious union of Person, and his government; every thing is ruled by his controul. *The deceived and the deceiver are his.* Job xii. 16. See those scriptures, Coloss. i. 16, 17. Heb. i. 2, 3. Matt. xxviii. 18. Ephes. i. 10. Hence it is most truly and blessedly said, that CHRIST is *the* SAVIOR *of all men.* For *he killeth, and he maketh alive; he wounds and he heals.* Deut. xxxii. 39. But while those things are strictly true, in relation to the departments, both of nature and providence; in the departments of grace and glory, as this scripture most blessedly adds, he is specially *the* SAVIOR *of those that believe.* In no sense but the *former,* as relating to *temporal* things, can JESUS be said to be the SAVIOR of all men. And in none but the *latter,* in things both temporal, spiritual, and eternal; can any but his body the Church have claim? Ephes. i. 22, 23. Oh! if the world did but consider how much they owe their preservation, and the enjoyment of the most common blessings of nature and providence, to the LORD JESUS, how would they stand amazed at his goodness, and be shocked at their own undeservings! And if the LORD's people had but a more lively sense of their special mercies, in all the departments of life, nature, providence, grace, and glory: how would their souls be often melted in them, in the contemplation of that *love of* CHRIST, *which passeth knowledge.* Ephes. iii. 19.

I detain the Reader no longer, than just to observe, what a lovely representation is given, in the different parts of this Chapter, of what constitutes a faithful Minister of CHRIST! And what a life, if closely followed up, in the various departments of it, must be such a service? Happy the LORD's people who have such a servant! And *happy the people who have the* LORD *for their* GOD!

REFLECTIONS.

O LORD the SPIRIT! let thy Church have grace to praise thee, for the love manifested towards it, and thy watchful care over it, through all generations. Yea, blessed LORD, we have to thank thee, for the gracious warnings, which thou hast expressly spoken of, concerning the awful heresies which will beset the Church from the world. Truly, LORD, there are already many Antichrists, by which we know *it is the last time.* O do thou help thy truly regenerated ones to resist all and every one of them, whether seducing spirits, or doctrines of devils, and be stedfast in the faith: and when at any time *the Enemy cometh in like a flood,* do thou, Almighty SPIRIT, *lift up a standard against him!*

Be gracious also to the Ministers, and Stewards, of thy mysteries. Cause them to put the brethren in remembrance of all the great and glorious truths of our most holy faith; that they may prove themselves good ministers of JESUS CHRIST, nourished up in the words of faith, and of good doctrine; refusing profane and old wives' fables, and exercising themselves unto godliness.

And, dearest LORD JESUS! we praise thee for thy upholding, and preserving providence, over all men; and specially for thy saving health unto thy people. Here we learn, O LORD, how it is for thy sake the world standeth; and while thou art carrying on thy salvation, the ungodly remain. And until thou hast brought home thy redeemed to glory, the seed time and harvest, the tares and the wheat, shall not cease. Oh! let thy children learn to whom the whole difference is owing. And while they enjoy thy distinguishing grace, often may they hear the voice: *Destroy it not: for a blessing is in it!*

CHAP. V.

CONTENTS.

The Apostle is here instructing Timothy, *as a Minister of* CHRIST, *how to conduct himself in the Church of* GOD : *and especially towards Elders, aged Women, and younger Persons.*

REBUKE not an elder, but intreat *him* as a father; *and* the younger men as brethren;

2 The elder women as mothers; the younger as sisters, with all purity.

3 Honour widows that are widows indeed.

4 But if any widow have children or nephews, let them learn first to shew piety at home, and to requite their parents: for that is good and acceptable before God.

5 Now she that is a widow indeed, and desolate, trusteth in God, and continueth in supplications and prayers night and day.

6 But she that liveth in pleasure is dead while she liveth.

7 And these things give in charge, that they may be blameless.

8 But if any provide not for his own, and specially for those of his own house, he hath denied the faith, and is worse than an infidel.

I forbear to comment on those directions. They are too plain to need any. I only pause over the last of those verses, to observe the very strong language *Paul* useth, when speaking of a man's not providing for his own, in calling him worse than an Infidel. And it is the highest reproach to a member of Christ's body, when he passeth by the ties of grace; while we find carnal men are sometimes so eminent for observance of them in the ties of nature. And the argument runs thus: a carnal man, when entering into the concerns of his natural alliances, proves thereby the common nature he feels for those with whom he is interested. If therefore a man professeth to be a partaker of grace, and consequently supposed to be a member of Christ's mystical body; and yet can behold another member suffer want in any sense, either spiritual or temporal, and doth not relieve him, he denies the very principle which he professeth; and is worse than the Infidel, who knows nothing of gracious feelings, and makes no profession of them. Reader! if this maxim of the Apostle was made the standard on those occasions, to ascertain a man's faith, is it not to be feared, that very frequently many would be found that do not come up to it? And yet *John*, the beloved Apostle, gives it to the Church, for a general rule, to ascertain character. *We know* (saith he) *that we have passed from death unto life, because we love the brethren.* 1 John iii. 14.

9 Let not a widow be taken into the number under threescore years old, having been the wife of one man.

10 Well reported of for good works; if she have brought up children, if she have lodged strangers, if she have washed the saints' feet, if she have relieved the afflicted, if she have diligently followed every good work.

11 But the younger widows refuse: for when they have begun to wax wanton against Christ, they will marry;

12 Having damnation, because they have cast off their first faith.

13 And withal they learn *to be* idle, wandering about from house to house; and not only idle, but tatlers also and busy-bodies, speaking things which they ought not.

14 I will therefore that the younger women marry, bear children, guide the house, give none occasion to the adversary to speak reproachfully.

15 For some are already turned aside after Satan.

16 If any man or woman that believeth have widows, let them relieve them, and let not the church be charged; that it may relieve them that are widows indeed.

It is worthy remark, what attention the HOLY GHOST hath shewn to the honorable women, in every age of the Church, whom He had graciously regenerated, and made eminent for services to his household. What blessed characters are given to the *Sarahs*, and *Rebekahs*, and *Rachels*, and *Deborahs*, and *Jaels*, and *Hannahs* of the Old Testament Scripture: and how interesting the *Maries*, and *Elizabeths*, and *Joannas*, and *Dorcases*; and other holy women of the New? Mothers in Israel are among the excellent in the earth; and are handed down to us with such marks of blessed testimony as shew, that their names are *written in the book of life*, and are enrolled among those *of whom the world is not worthy*. Heb. xi. 35 to the end.

17 Let the elders that rule well be counted worthy of double honour, especially they who labour in the word and doctrine.

18 For the scripture saith, Thou shalt not muzzle the ox that treadeth out the corn, and the labourer *is* worthy of his reward.

19 Against an elder receive not an accusation, but before two or three witnesses.

20 Them that sin rebuke before all, that others also may fear.

It is very blessed to observe how attentive the HOLY GHOST is, that none of his household shall be overlooked, or forgotten, in the provision he here makes for his Ministers, to watch over, in their daily ministration. The Elders are here introduced, as being worthy of double honor. Age is honorable. And if they are among the Ministers of CHRIST; their long services are considered as yet the more entitled to this attention. 1 Cor. ix. 11. The Apostle useth a striking figure to illustrate the precept. He quotes a passage in the Old Testament scripture, of the tenderness shewn the ox, when treading out the corn, that he did it unmuzzled: purposely, that as he trod out food from the ears of corn for others, he might himself partake. And the sense is, if a minister of CHRIST, while laboring like the ox to give food of a spiritual nature to the people, is himself sustained with portions of the same; this is but a just privilege. And who would begrudge him his moiety? And to be ready to receive an accusation against such, must argue a sad mind.

21 I charge *thee* before God, and the Lord Jesus Christ, and the elect angels, that thou observe

these things without preferring one before another, doing nothing by partiality.

22 Lay hands suddenly on no man, neither be partaker of other men's sins; keep thyself pure.

23 Drink no longer water, but use a little wine for thy stomach's sake and thine often infirmities.

24 Some men's sins are open before hand, going before to judgment; and some men they follow after.

25 Likewise also the good works *of some* are manifest before hand: and they that are otherwise cannot be hid.

I admire the Apostle's solemn charge to *Timothy*. Let the Reader figure to himself the venerable Apostle, standing to admonish the young Bishop, (as he is supposed to have been,) on those grand points, which he here enjoins. Modern times can furnish no idea of what this must have been. But if all charges were directed to such a purpose, and delivered as before GOD, and under his authority, as this of *Paul's* was, we should form very different judgment to what we are now accustomed to form on this subject. By *the elect Angels*, we are to understand those chosen to be kept by CHRIST. Not in union with CHRIST. *For verily he took not on him the nature of angels.* Heb. ii. 16. But elect Angels preserved in their integrity by him: and different from those which fell, not being elect. Jude 6. Elect Angels therefore preserved *by* CHRIST; but not as the church is elect and preserved *in* CHRIST. And let the Reader here learn, by the way, this precious truth. Election is not confined to men but reacheth to Angels. And all from Him and his pleasure *who worketh after the counsel of his own will.* But let the Reader no less keep in remembrance this precious truth also. Though there are elect Angels, which are kept by CHRIST, perfect, and secure from the possibility of falling, yet they have no union with CHRIST as we have. He is their LORD and Preserver by *dominion.* But He is our LORD, Head, and Husband by *union.* Oh! the preciousness of that Scripture, he *passed by the nature of angels, and took on him the seed of Abraham.* Heb. ii. 16.

Now *Paul* chargeth *Timothy* before GOD, and the LORD JESUS CHRIST, and the elect angels, to observe these things, meaning the duties of his function. It is a sweet thought! Angels we know are ministering spirits. They attend the LORD's people, watch over them for good, encamp about them, and minister to their comfort. And, as they attended CHRIST when he returned to glory, so will they grace his triumph when *he shall come to be glorified in his saints, and to be admired in all that believe.* 2 Thess. i. 10. See Heb. ii. 16. and Commentary. I do not think it necessary to offer any observations on what follows in this chapter, as they chiefly relate to the persons of the Apostle and *Timothy.* And I am unwilling to swell our Commentary beyond the limits of what may be proper.

REFLECTIONS.

READER! behold how venerable, in the sight of GOD the SPIRIT, are the hoary saints considered, when we see such a charge given concerning them. Blessedly GOD hath said, *even to your old age, I am he, and even to hoar hairs will I carry you!* And, therefore, the LORD, who watches over them himself, will have no rebuke given them from others. Our fathers in the Church, and our mothers in Israel, are counted worthy of double honor, when the hoary head is found in the righteousness of CHRIST.

And blessed are those Ministers and Stewards of GOD's mysteries which labor in the word and doctrine, who do nothing by partiality, but view all the members of CHRIST's mystical body, equally entitled to their good offices, and to their affection, without preferring one before another. LORD make all thy servants faithful, and let thy people praise thee, that GOD in all things may be glorified in, and through JESUS CHRIST.

CHAP. VI.

CONTENTS.

The Apostle is prosecuting, in this Chapter, his Exhortation to Timothy *concerning Church government. And having noticed several wise Regulations on this Subject with others, closeth his Epistle with praying for Grace to be with him.*

LET as many servants as are under the yoke count their own masters worthy of all honour, that the name of God and *his* doctrine be not blasphemed.

2 And they that have believing masters, let them not despise *them*, because they are brethren; but rather do *them* service, because they are faithful and beloved, partakers of the benefit. These things teach and exhort.

3 If any man teach otherwise, and consent not to wholesome words, *even* the words of our Lord Jesus Christ, and to the doctrine which is according to godliness;

4 He is proud, knowing nothing, but doting about questions and strifes of words, whereof cometh envy, strife, railings, evil surmisings,

5 Perverse disputings of men of corrupt minds, and destitute of the truth, supposing that gain is godliness: from such withdraw thyself.

6 But godliness with contentment is great gain.

7 For we brought nothing into *this* world, *and it is* certain we can carry nothing out.

8 And having food and raiment, let us be therewith content.

9 But they that will be rich fall into temptation and a snare, and *into many* foolish and hurtful lusts, which drown men in destruction and perdition.

10 For the love of money is the root of all evil: which while some coveted after, they have erred from the faith, and pierced themselves through with many sorrows.

The corruption of human nature which hath produced all the evils of life, very early in the world, among other deadly fruits, produced that abominable traffic the Slave trade, and which, awful to relate, hath continued from one generation to another, even to the present hour.

This chapter opens with directions to both servants and masters concerning their mutual behavior to each other, in those instances where sovereign grace hath called a child of GOD from either department. It is hardly possible to conceive what effects have followed the conversion of the heart to GOD, in cases where masters have been called by grace, who were before concerned in this nefarious practice. Oh! the change when GOD changeth the heart!

The Apostle hath beautifully closed this paragraph, in shewing the folly, as well as wickedness of coveting more than the common necessaries of life; and by that humbling truth, of bringing nothing into the world, and the consciousness of carrying nothing out. It is a similar expression to that of *Job. Naked* (said he) *came I out of my mother's womb, and naked shall I return thither.* Job i. 21. Oh! who that considers his original nakedness and helplessness, when coming first from the womb of the earth, or from the womb of his mother, and the humbling state to which he will shortly return, to the same poverty and insensibility again, would be anxious to load himself with golden clay, or croud between those periods of entering and returning from the world, anxieties for any thing, but *the one thing needful.* Precious JESUS! be thou my portion, for durable riches and righteousness are only with thee. Having thee, thou dear LORD! thou wilt cause me, indeed, *to inherit substance, and thou wilt fill, and be thyself all my treasure.* Prov. viii. 18—21.

11 But thou, O man of God, flee these things; and follow after righteousness, godliness, faith, love, patience, meekness.

12 Fight the good fight of faith, lay hold on

eternal life, whereunto thou art also called, and hast professed a good profession before many witnesses.

13 I give thee charge in the sight of God, who quickeneth all things, and *before* Christ Jesus, who before Pontius Pilate witnessed a good confession.

14 That thou keep *this* commandment without spot, unrebukeable, until the appearing of our Lord Jesus Christ:

15 Which in his times he shall shew, *who is* the blessed and only Potentate; the King of kings, and Lord of lords;

16 Who only hath immortality, dwelling in the light which no man can approach unto; whom no man hath seen, nor can see: to whom *be* honour and power everlasting. Amen.

There is somewhat particularly striking in the name which Paul here gives to *Timothy*, as a minister of Christ, *Man of* God. Man of God, by virtue of right, in electing, redeeming, regenerating grace; and, specially, as ministering in holy things. So the Prophets of old were distinguished. 2 Kings iv. throughout. And the direction to flee from the corrupt affections of the heart, and the pursuits of the world, and follow Christ and his righteousness, with all the sweet and blessed connections in Christ, is very beautiful.

What a very sublime description is here given of the divine essence? God, in his threefold character of Persons, is undoubtedly invisible, and incomprehensible, and never to be known, or seen, or apprehended, but in the Person of the God-man Mediator. It is the Son of God who hath come forth from the invisibility of Jehovah, to make known all that can be made known of the essence and nature of God. John i. 18. See Coloss. i. 20. and Commentary.

17 Charge them that are rich in this world, that they be not high-minded, nor trust in uncertain riches, but in the living God, who giveth us richly all things to enjoy;

18 That they do good, that they be rich in good works, ready to distribute, willing to communicate.

19 Laying up in store for themselves a good foundation against the time to come, that they may lay hold on eternal life.

20 O Timothy, keep that which is committed to thy trust, avoiding profane *and* vain babblings, and oppositions of science falsely so called:

21 Which some professing have erred concerning the faith. Grace *be* with thee. Amen.

The first to Timothy was written from Laodicea, which is the chiefest city of Phrygia Pacatiana.

These are all most beautiful, and highly interesting recommendations, to the faithful discharge of the several relative obligations, which arise out of the diversities of life. But they are too plain to need a Comment. And where grace is begun in the heart, divine teaching both dictates and gives ability to the performance. Here, indeed, lies the great beauty of all Gospel truths, that in all cases where God the Spirit hath quickened to a new and spiritual life, there will be a quickening also, and a strength imparted to the performance. Blessedly the Apostle hath shewn this, when drawing the carnal state of an unawakened nature, and the blessed effects which follow being taken out of it. *If so be,* (saith *Paul,*) *ye have heard* Christ, *and have been taught by him, as the truth is in* Jesus: *that ye put off concerning the former conversation the old man, which is corrupt according to the deceitful lusts; and be renewed in the spirit of your mind; and that ye put on the new man, which after* God, *is created in righteousness and true holiness.* Ephes. iv. 21—24. It were unnecessary to offer any observations upon the Apostle's conclusion of grace. Every thing that is truly blessed is contained in it, as it relates to all the Persons of the Godhead, in their joint love and favor to the Church. So *Paul* prays, and then closeth his Epistle with Amen.

REFLECTIONS.

Reader! think what a lovely family that is of the all lovely, and all loving Jesus, which considers all the members as mutually engaged, and everlastingly supposed to be actuated by one spirit, for the general and compleat happiness of the whole. Oh! if masters would thus consider servants, and servants masters, there could be no schism of the body, but all would study each other's happiness, and have the same care one for another. And, surely, if any thing under grace can tend to the promotion of this great end, the consciousness of a dying, sinful, sorrowful world, from which we are hourly departing, and from which as we brought nothing in, we can carry nothing out, would be enough to induce these blessed effects.

But, oh! precious Jesus! It is thou Lord who must both go before, and guide in this, and every path, which thy redeemed have to follow. Blessed and glorious Potentate! Oh! what a good confession didst thou witness before many witnesses! Lord! grant to all thy servants to keep the commandment of the same confession, without spot, and unrebukable, until thy appearing. Jesus will shortly come. He, and He alone, will shew, as the only visible Jehovah, who is the blessed and only Potentate, *King of kings, and* Lord *of lords!* Till then may every knee bow, and every tongue con-

THE
SECOND EPISTLE OF PAUL THE APOSTLE
TO
TIMOTHY.

GENERAL OBSERVATIONS.

IT hath been the generally received opinion in the Church, in all ages, that this *second* Epistle to *Timothy* was the last the Apostle ever wrote. And, from that memorable expression, in the last Chapter of it, where he speaks of the time of his departure being at hand; Chap. iv. 6. it certainly becomes highly probable. It is supposed to have been written after an interval of full nine years, from the former: and bears date, Anno 64.

We are more interested to ascertain the characters of inspiration in it, than to be particularly anxious in ascertaining the date. And this divine mark is in every Chapter and verse, more or less. Very plain and positive proofs we have, that He who guided *Paul*'s tongue to preach CHRIST, here guided his pen to record him. I do not think it necessary, in these general observations, to go over the outlines of the Epistle, being in itself so short. But I cannot enter upon it, without first begging the LORD the SPIRIT, to open and explain all the blessed contents of it to our hearts, that our faith in Him may not be founded *in the wisdom of men, but in the power of* GOD.

CHAPTER I.
CONTENTS.

Paul *opens his Epistle in his usual Manner: professeth his great Love to* Timothy: *admonisheth him on the great Offices of the Ministry; and treats of many blessed Truths of the Gospel.*

PAUL, an apostle of Jesus Christ by the will of God, according to the promise of life which is in Christ Jesus,

2 To Timothy, *my* dearly beloved son: Grace, mercy, *and* peace, from God the Father, and Christ Jesus our Lord.

3 I thank God, whom I serve from *my* forefathers with pure conscience, that without ceasing I have remembrance of thee in my prayers night and day;

4 Greatly desiring to see thee, being mindful of thy tears, that I may be filled with joy:

5 When I call to remembrance the unfeigned faith that is in thee, which dwelt first in thy grandmother Lois, and thy mother Eunice; and I am persuaded that in thee also.

6 Wherefore I put thee in remembrance that thou stir up the gift of God, which is in thee by the putting on of my hands.

7 For God hath not given us the spirit of fear; but of power, and of love, and of a sound mind.

8 Be not thou therefore ashamed of the testimony of our Lord, nor of me his prisoner: but be thou partaker of the afflictions of the gospel according to the power of God;

There is somewhat very striking, in what the Apostle here saith, *of the promise of life which is in* CHRIST JESUS. Let the Reader notice it, for it is well worthy his notice. Here is life, that is, eternal life. And this is promised: not to be attained. It is of grace, a free gift, an unconditional gift, wholly of grace, and in distinction to works; in distinction to the law, and in opposition to it. And it is in CHRIST JESUS. CHRIST himself is life, and life eternal; and He himself is the promise. Hence, his seed, his children, are called *heirs of promise, and heirs of eternal life in* CHRIST JESUS. Heb. vi. 17. Rom. viii. 17. These are precious things. And *Paul* puts *Timothy* in remembrance of them, by way of stirring up this gift of GOD, which was in him. I do not in this *Poor Man's Commentary* wish to dwell upon things of lesser moment, having objects of an higher nature to regard. *Paul's* desiring to see *Timothy*, and his remembrance of *Timothy's* relations, with an account of their characters; these are things which have long since passed away, and with which we have nothing to do. Being limited, therefore, to compress what I have to offer on these holy scriptures, into as narrow a space as possible; I wholly wish to confine my humble observations, to the more important points of doctrine, which the HOLY GHOST hath graciously recorded, in these inspired writings.

9 Who hath saved us, and called *us* with an holy calling, not according to our works, but according to his own purpose and grace, which was given us in Christ Jesus before the world began;

10 But is now made manifest by the appearing of our Saviour Jesus Christ, who hath abolished death, and hath brought light and immortality to light through the gospel:

11 Whereunto I am appointed a preacher, and an apostle, and a teacher of the Gentiles.

12 For the which cause I also suffer these things: nevertheless I am not ashamed: for I know whom I have believed, and am persuaded that he is able to keep that which I have committed unto him against that day.

13 Hold fast the form of sound words, which thou hast heard of me, in faith and love which is in Christ Jesus.

I pray the Reader to mark, one by one, the blessedness of this most precious portion of scripture, with which the Apostle begins this paragraph; and then, under divine teaching, he will discover, in the blessed fruits which follow from what the Apostle hath said, how causes produce effects; and not effects give birth to causes.

And, first. *Who hath saved us.* Here is the divine glory, as set forth, independent of any motive, or cause whatever, but his own sovereign will and pleasure. God saving his people, with an everlasting salvation. No moving cause, no procuring cause, no assisting cause. Here is not a word said of either. *Who hath saved us.* It is spoken of, as a thing already done. And this, as we shall perceive, when we analyze the verse, as a given principle, given us in CHRIST JESUS, *before the world began.* Compare what is here said, with those scriptures. Ephes. i. 4, 5. Rom. ix. 11. John xvii. 6. Titus i. 1, 2.

Secondly. Now comes the effectual calling of the saved. For thus it is written. Who hath saved us, and *called us.* So then, salvation, or the predestinated purpose of GOD, of the Church to salvation in CHRIST, is *before* calling. A most plain, palpable, and decided proof, that nothing of creature-worth, or creature-ability, are taken into the account. But *calling* is the *effect,* and not the *cause* of salvation. For so the charter of grace runs. *For whom he did foreknow, he also did predestinate, to be conformed to the image of his* SON, *that he might be the first-born among many brethren. Moreover, whom he did predestinate, them he also called; and whom he called, them he also justified; and whom he justified, them he also glorified.* Rom. viii. 29, 30.

Thirdly. The Church is said to be saved, and called, *with an holy calling.* Not any holiness in the Church, or from foreseeing holiness in the Church; for it is immediately added, *not according to our works.* It could not be according to our works, for the saving is said to have been *before* the world began. Neither could it be from any works *after,* for when the Church is quickened, in every individual member of CHRIST's mystical body; the sinner is said to be quickened, that was before *dead in trespasses and sins.* Ephes. ii. 1. Neither could it be from the prospect of any thing to be wrought of holiness in us, *after* grace is received; for this scripture saith, that it was GOD's purpose, and grace given us in CHRIST JESUS, and that *before the world began.* Hence, every testimony bears a beautiful correspondence to all the other parts of scripture, that grace, and salvation, are all of GOD, not of man. *We are saved by grace through faith; and that not of ourselves, it is the gift of* GOD, *not of works, lest any man should boast.* Ephes. ii. 8, 9. Hence, the Apostle, in another place observes, that *it is not by works of righteousness which we have done, but according to his mercy he saved us by the washing of regeneration, and renewing of the* HOLY GHOST *shed on us abundantly through* JESUS CHRIST *our* SAVIOR. Titus iii. 5, 6.

Fourthly. The Apostle, having thus laid down all the grand particulars, of being *first* saved, *then* called; and called with an *holy* calling, even his holiness which called; and in his holiness, in whom we are called; next runs up the whole of the blessedness of the Church, to Him in whom the Church is holy, and in whom made blessed; by declaring, that all this was done by GOD's purpose, and grace, in giving the Church *to* JESUS, and giving all our holiness, and blessedness, *in* JESUS, and to be received by us *from* JESUS; *before the world began.* And thus manifesting the several express, and distinct personal acts, of the FATHER's purpose, grace, and gifts; the SON's holiness, in which the Church is saved, and made holy; and the SPIRIT's calling, and regenerating mercy, in rendering the whole effectual, for grace here, and glory for ever. Reader! pause, and contemplate the preciousness of this scripture, and see, whether the sense of it doth not bring the soul upon the knees, to cry out, with the Apostle: *thanks be unto* GOD *for his unspeakable gift!* 2 Cor. ix. 15. And while the impression is warm upon your mind, then observe what *Paul* hath said in the following verses, and enquire, whether his conclusion, must not be the natural, and unavoidable conclusion, of every regenerated child of GOD? Hath not CHRIST brought life and immortality to light, by his Gospel, which teacheth such precious things? Must not *Paul,* nay, must not every man, taught as *Paul* was, and through grace brought into the same views, and confirmed in the same truths; declare, that he knows whom he hath believed? Can there be any thing like a yea and nay Gospel, in these solemn assurances of JEHOVAH? And can an assurance that He, who hath saved, and called from the first, without works, will cause his grace to be doubtful as to the end? Will any man dare to reprove, for comforting GOD's elect with such assurances; and call it unscriptural, and highly dangerous, to teach them, what GOD hath in his holy scriptures taught them, that they shall never perish, whom he hath so saved, and so called? Oh! the preciousness of those sweet scriptures! *Yea, let* GOD *be true, but every man liar.* Rom. iii. 4. And may that GOD, that hath commanded his servants saying, *Comfort ye, comfort ye, my people, saith your* GOD, Isaiah xl. 1. comfort them himself, against all those, who would make the hearts of the LORD's people sad, whom the LORD hath not made sad; and confirm his word unto his servants, wherein he hath caused us to hope. May his *saving,* and *calling* purposes, given to them in CHRIST JESUS, before the world began, be followed up, by establishing them, as the Apostle was, *in the truth, as it is in* JESUS! And may every truly regenerated child of GOD shout aloud, with the same holy triumph as *Paul* did, for his confidence in CHRIST is the same: *I know whom I have believed; and am persuaded, that he is able to keep that which I have committed unto him, against that day.*

14 That good thing which was committed unto thee keep by the Holy Ghost which dwelleth in us.

15 This thou knowest, that all they which are in Asia be turned away from me; of whom are Phygellus and Hermogenes.

16 The Lord give mercy unto the house of Onesiphorus; for he oft refreshed me, and was not ashamed of my chain:

17 But, when he was in Rome, he sought me out very diligently, and found *me.*

18 The Lord grant unto him that he may find mercy of the Lord in that day; and in how many things he ministered unto me at Ephesus, thou knowest very well.

The principal thing to be noticed by us in this paragraph, is in the first verse. And it is indeed, so highly principal and important, that I must beg the Reader's closest attention to it, as among one of the grand and momentous truths of our most holy faith. May the LORD be my Teacher, while I humbly attempt to speak of it! *That good thing which was committed unto thee, keep by the* HOLY GHOST *which dwelleth in us.* The first question, which strikes the mind on reading this blessed scripture, (for it is a very blessed scripture,) is, to enquire, what good thing the Apostle means? It cannot be the gift of the HOLY GHOST himself, for the Apostle immediately connects with it, that GOD the HOLY GHOST dwelleth in us. Then it will follow, that it is not GOD the HOLY GHOST's Person; but his graces, his gifts, his works, in shedding abroad the love of GOD the FATHER in our hearts, as his regenerated creatures; and directing our whole spirits, into the patient waiting upon, and enjoyment of, the LORD JESUS CHRIST. Reader! do observe the preciousness of this expression, which *Paul* makes use of, concerning that good thing. It is indeed, the *one thing,* and the only one *needful.* It includes GOD the FATHER, in our knowledge of his love, and favor, manifested in all his purposes, counsel, will, and pleasure, of his Covenant grace in CHRIST. And it includes no less, all that belongs to CHRIST and his Person, CHRIST and his relations, CHRIST and his offices, CHRIST and his salvation. The good thing, committed to the Church in CHRIST, by the gifts, and workings of the SPIRIT, includes the whole of this blessedness; for it is CHRIST *in you the hope of glory.* So that, GOD the SPIRIT first comes to renew the soul, and then fills the soul with his graces. He first inhabits our souls and bodies as his temple, and then gives grace to his inhabitation. He first enters our spirit, for his indwelling residence; and then gives that good thing for the spirit to keep, by his Almighty Power, being himself *that holiness which becometh his house for ever.* Oh! what a wonder of grace, in a wonder-working GOD! See 1 Cor. vi. 18, 19. and Commentary.

Reader! are you amazed at the grace of GOD the SPIRIT? So am I. But our amazement at the greatness of the mercy, doth not render it less true, and sure. According to human reasoning, we should be ready to say: Surely the HOLY GHOST, whose name is emphatically HOLY, will first cleanse the soul and body; and then inhabit them. How can it be possible to suppose, that a Being, *who is of purer eyes, than to behold iniquity,* will dwell in a body of pollution? But here, as in numberless other instances, GOD's *thoughts are not our thoughts; neither his ways our ways.* Most certain it is, that GOD the HOLY GHOST doth dwell in his people. So JESUS promised he should; yea, He himself so said: and the fact is unquestionable. John xiv. 17. Ezek. xxxvi. 25—27. And equally certain it is, that our bodies are still bodies of sin, and uncleanness; yea, and continue so, during the whole time-state of the Church upon earth. For though the spirit is quickened, and regenerated; *the flesh profiteth nothing.* Paul felt, and acknowledged to the last, and every man like *Paul*, whom GOD the HOLY GHOST hath brought acquainted with the plague of his own heart, will acknowledge the same; that in a man's own flesh, *dwelleth no good thing.* Rom. vii. 1. But is it not, by this very process, of GOD the SPIRIT's indwelling residence, we are sanctified? Doth not the LORD say: *I will sprinkle clean water upon you, and ye shall be clean; from all your filthiness, and from all your idols, will I cleanse you.* Ezek. xxxvi. 25. And do we not, in the circumstances of common life, take pure water, to cleanse filthy vessels? Is not the HOLY GHOST *a Spirit of judgment, and a Spirit of burning?* Isaiah iv. 4. And will he not, as fire, purely purge our dross, consume all our lusts, and *take away all our tin?* Isaiah i. 25. Reader! it is very blessed, thus to know GOD the HOLY GHOST, both in his Person, and GODHEAD, and ministry; and also, in the exercise of his graces, by his indwelling power in our hearts. *That good thing,* which is thereby *committed unto us; we then keep, by the* HOLY GHOST *which dwelleth in us.* See Jude 20, 21.

I do not think it necessary to detain the Reader, with any long observations on the latter part of this paragraph. The departure of the mere professors, which the Apostle speaks of, in *Asia*, is similar to the departure of all such, in every age of the Church. Nothing short of regeneration, constitutes a child of GOD. Where this blessed work is wrought, there can be no possibility of departure, so as to fall away finally. Chap. ii. 19. And where this is not, there must be an everlasting falling away, and a final separation from GOD for ever. If the Reader will read Heb. vi. 1—8. with Commentary, he will soon discover, under the LORD's teaching, the striking difference, between Professor, and Possessor; between the LORD's people, and the profane. It is very possible, that these men, *Phygellus*, and *Hermogenes*, were persons who had made more noise than others, in talking about religion. False meteors of the night, shine for a moment, with more glare than the stated planets. But soon go out, in obscure darkness. Oh! what numbers have there been, of such as *Phygellus*, and *Hermogenes*, in all ages of the Church! *Paul's* testimony of *Onesiphorus*, is short, but sweet. I admire the suitableness of his name which signifies, to bring *usefulness*. And the LORD made him very useful, to his servant the Apostle. But I add no more.

REFLECTIONS.

WHAT a lovely representation *Paul* hath given in this Chapter, of the Covenant love, and faithfulness, of GOD the FATHER, in the promise of life which is in CHRIST JESUS! And how sure is it made, in having saved his people before calling them, and then calling them with an holy calling; not of their holiness, or of their works, but his own purpose, and grace. Oh! the faithfulness, and love, of a faithful Covenant GOD and FATHER, in CHRIST JESUS!

And no less blessedly doth *Paul* speak, of his adorable LORD and SAVIOR. He it is, saith *Paul*, which hath abolished death, and brought life and immortality to light, through his Gospel. Who then, with such views, can doubt salvation, while knowing whom he hath believed? Who can fear, but in the end, to be everlastingly happy in CHRIST; while living *to* CHRIST, and having communion *with* CHRIST; being persuaded, that He is able to keep that which the soul hath committed unto him against that day!

And, with equal joy we behold, how *Paul* triumphs, in the love, and favor of GOD the HOLY GHOST; (and so may all truly regenerated believers in CHRIST,) conscious of that good thing, committed to them by his Almighty Power! Blessed be the FATHER, SON, and SPIRIT, for these unspeakable mercies! LORD! let my poor soul, never be ashamed of the LORD's testimony; nor of the golden chain, of being CHRIST's prisoner!

CHAP. II.

CONTENTS.

The Apostle is exhorting Timothy *in this Chapter, to Firmness, Constancy, and Perseverance. He useth several very beautiful Figures, in the Recommendation of those Graces.*

THOU therefore, my son, be strong in the grace that is in Christ Jesus.

2 And the things that thou hast heard of me among many witnesses, the same commit thou to

faithful men, who shall be able to teach others also.

3 Thou therefore endure hardness, as a good soldier of Jesus Christ.

4 No man that warreth entangleth himself with the affairs of *this* life; that he may please him who hath chosen him to be a soldier.

5 And if a man also strive for masteries, *yet* is he not crowned, except he strive lawfully.

6 The husbandman that laboureth must be first partaker of the fruits.

7 Consider what I say; and the Lord give thee understanding in all things.

I beg the Reader, at the entrance on this Chapter, to observe, the manner of expression made use of, concerning grace. *Paul* calls upon *Timothy* to be strong in grace. What grace? Not the grace in him, and which by regeneration he had received. But the grace that is *in* CHRIST JESUS. A very precious distinction. The grace that is in me, given by the LORD, is *from* the LORD, and depends, both for continuance, and to be kept alive, wholly upon the unceasing supplies issuing *from* JESUS; similar to those streams which are only kept running, as long as the fountain sends forth, to their continuance. If this was well observed, and well understood, we should learn a most important truth, for daily use. There is no living upon past attainments. The grace I had from CHRIST the first day, I need every day, and to the last day. My spiritual strength, is in CHRIST: not in what I feel, nor in what I have; but wholly in Him. And this life is kept up, in the constant receiving of fresh communications *from* Him, and living *to* Him, and living *upon* Him. This is to be *strong in the grace that is in* CHRIST JESUS. There is no other strength. No inherent, no progressive holiness!

And the conflicts to which *Paul* tells *Timothy* he will be called, while committing the glorious truths of the Gospel to faithful men; plainly shew the necessity of the measure, to bear him up, in a suited strength, which cannot be derived from himself, but from the LORD. The hardness of the soldier, and the enterprize of those, who contend in races; and the unwearied labor of the husbandmen: all imply the earnestness, which attend a life of faith in CHRIST. But these descriptions are very sweetly accompanied, with assurances, that the LORD will give his servants to be first partakers of the grace which they bring to his people. They shall eat of the bread they minister in his name to others. They shall drink of the river, whose streams make glad the city of GOD. 1 John i. 1. 2. Psm. xlvi. 4. I hope the Reader will not pass away from this view of the subject, before that he hath duly pondered it, and considered the vast importance of it. All grace is from CHRIST. And all the grace we receive from CHRIST, is fed and maintained by continued supplies in CHRIST. And faith is but one, and the same unceasing act, in receiving of his fulness, and *grace for grace.* John i. 16. None but those who perform every act of faith upon CHRIST, and his grace, know the blessedness of it.

8 Remember that Jesus Christ of the seed of David was raised from the dead according to my gospel.

9 Wherein I suffer trouble, as an evil doer, *even* unto bonds; but the word of God is not bound.

10 Therefore I endure all things for the elect's sakes, that they may also obtain the salvation which is in Christ Jesus with eternal glory.

It is delightful to behold, how the LORD calls his people to exercises. *Paul* had eminently asserted the resurrection of the dead in all his preaching, as the foundation stone of a believer's hope. And this above every other point of the Gospel, brought upon him the indignation of the carnal world. *Paul* therefore bids *Timothy* remember, that his persecutions were on this account. And he insinuates thereby that *Timothy* must not be surprized if he meets with similar treatment. And he chargeth him not to shrink from it. But what I chiefly beg the Reader to keep in view in this passage is, what *Paul* observes, that it is for the elect's sake, he endured all things, Yes! *Paul's* whole labors, services, preachings, writings, are all directed to this one end. As his divine LORD and Master had all along in view his Church, and both laboured and suffered for them only; so *Paul* expressly declares that his sufferings were all to the same end. John xvii. 9. 1 Thess. v. 9.

11 *It is* a faithful saying: For if we be dead with *him,* we shall also live with *him:*

12 If we suffer, we shall also reign with *him:* if we deny *him* he also will deny us:

13 If we believe not, *yet* he abideth faithful: he cannot deny himself.

Let the Reader particularly attend to the statement here made, for it is most blessed. Here is a presupposed case, the child of GOD is dead with CHRIST. And so he is. For by regeneration he is brought forth into spiritual life, proving thereby his being *chosen* in CHRIST, before the foundation of the world. Ephes. i. 4, 5. And *redeemed* by CHRIST, as a member of his mystical body. Ephes. i. 7. And, regenerated by the HOLY GHOST, he is quickened to a new and spiritual life in CHRIST. Hence he is dead with CHRIST. For when CHRIST was crucified, all his members were crucified with him. Gal. ii. 20. When CHRIST died; he died, not in a private capacity, but publicly, as the head of his body the Church whom he represented as their Surety; and consequently each member in the eye of the law, died with him. Coloss. iii. 3. So that from that moment the whole body of Christ is dead, in a legal sense to a covenant of works. And therefore it must follow, that as in him they were all crucified, and died; so they are equally from their oneness with him, interested in his life. And, oh! what a faithful saying this is?

Some of God's children have been not a little alarmed, at what is said of the Lord's denying them if they deny him. As if Christ's love of his people depended upon their love of him. But blessed be God! our love of Christ forms no standard for his love of us. 1 John iv. 19. It is not the weakness and infirmity of Christ's dear children, in their daily frail and imperfect walk of faith that is here alluded to, which may truly be said to be a denial of Christ. For when I doubt his word, or call his providences or his promises in question, no doubt that these things proceed from unbelief. Such was the case of the Church. Isaiah, xlix. 14. Lament. iii. 18. But this is not the denial the Apostle had in contemplation. The apostacy of hypocrites, and the false profession of those who call themselves christians, which are so only in name, who deny Christ's Godhead, redemption by his blood, and the works of the Spirit; these, with others of a like nature, are the points *Paul* had in view, when speaking of the denial of Christ, which calls for his denial of us. And beyond all question, such denials must be followed with destruction. For so Christ hath said. Matt. x. 32. 33. Mark viii. 38.

But what a sweet relief is the following verse, to comfort the feeble minded who would rather die than intentionally deny Christ: *If we believe not yet he abideth faithful, he cannot deny himself.* Reader! cherish the blessed assurance, for it is most blessed. God's faithfulness doth not depend upon man's belief. His yea, and Amen, are founded in himself, and not in our improvement. It is indeed blessed and refreshing to the soul, when a regenerated child of God enjoys those love-tokens of God in Christ, by the lively actings of faith upon him. But the Lord's grace is not founded in human merit; and therefore depends not upon human improvement. Oh! the preciousness of an unchangeable God's purposes in Christ. Jer. xxxii. 40. Heb. vi. 16, to the end.

14 Of these things put *them* in remembrance, charging *them* before the Lord that they strive not about words to no profit, *but* to the subverting of the hearers.

15 Study to shew thyself approved unto God, a workman that needeth not to be ashamed, rightly dividing the word of truth.

16 But shun profane *and* vain babblings; for they will increase unto more ungodliness.

17 And their word will eat as doth a canker: of whom is Hymeneus and Philetus;

18 Who concerning the truth have erred, say-

ing that the resurrection is past already; and overthrow the faith of some.

We cannot sufficiently admire the very great attention of the Apostle in following up his advice to his beloved *Timothy*, how to conduct himself in the *Church of God*, as a minister of CHRIST. In these verses, he calls off his attention from using words to no profit, but to the subverting of the hearers; and directs him to study how to approve himself to GOD: becoming a workman that needeth not to be ashamed: rightly dividing the word of truth. The dividing rightly the word of truth, seems to be a figure borrowed from the custom in the Jewish Church, when dividing the sacrifice; wherein care was had, that the part consecrated as holy to the LORD might not be kept back; and that which was the portion of the Offerer might be preserved. So that a workman in the ministry which rightly divideth the word of truth, hath an eye to the whole family of CHRIST. He comforts mourners, supports the weak, rouseth the careless, allures wanderers, and holds up CHRIST for distressed weary souls, as a rest and consolation. And while speaking to men, hath chiefly his eye unto GOD: that his blessing may go before, accompany, and follow his labors. That man can never shew himself approved unto GOD, that doth not make CHRIST what GOD hath made him, the whole of salvation. Now if CHRIST be the Alpha, and Omega, in JEHOVAH's view, in his concerns of the Church: he must be so in the ministry of his servants. And by thus holding up CHRIST as *Moses* lifted up the serpent in the wilderness; he follows the footsteps of the HOLY GHOST, and makes JESUS the whole of salvation, to every one that believeth, of the Jew first and also of the Gentile.

19 Nevertheless the foundation of God standeth sure, having this seal, The Lord knoweth them that are his. And, Let every one that nameth the name of Christ depart from iniquity.

20 But in a great house there are not only vessels of gold and of silver, but also of wood and of earth; and some to honour and some to dishonour.

21 If a man therefore purge himself from these, he shall be a vessel unto honour, sanctified, and meet for the master's use, *and* prepared unto every good work.

Reader! what a glorious truth is here! How are all the persons of the GODHEAD brought into one view, in their Covenant offices and characters to confirm the everlasting purposes toward the Church in CHRIST. The foundation is in GOD's eternal decree, and therefore most sure. Ephes. i. 4. It is founded also in CHRIST the rock of ages. Deut. xxxii. 4, 18, 31. 1 Cor. iii. 11. And it is sealed by the HOLY GHOST. Ephes. i. 13. And the sure consequence resulting from this everlasting security, is that the LORD willeth them by hi grace, while enjoining them by his precept, to depart from errors both in faith and practice. God's biddings are enablings where the work of regeneration hath passed on the heart.

The similitude which *Paul* adopts to illustrate the doctrine he is upon, is very beautiful. He considers the Church of Christ, as a great house, where many enter: for it is an open house. And both Professor and Profane, as well as the children of the household will come. But the difference is at once marked. The vessels of mercy are called *gold* and *silver*. Such are Christ's Jewels. Malachi iii. 17. The vessels of *wood* and *earth* are to dishonor. There needs no further comment. The figure explains itself. But how doth the subject strike the mind of the child of God, when he calls to remembrance from what source alone, the one is chosen to honor, and the other to dishonor! And how doth that question involuntarily arise in the mind, on such a review; Lord, *how is it that thou dost manifest thyself unto us, and not unto the world?* John xiv. 22.

22 Flee also youthful lusts: but follow righteousness, faith, charity, peace, with them that call on the Lord out of a pure heart.

23 But foolish and unlearned questions avoid, knowing that they do gender strifes.

24 And the servant of the Lord must not strive; but be gentle unto all *men*, apt to teach, patient.

25 In meekness instructing those that oppose themselves; if God peradventure will give them repentance to the acknowledging of the truth.

26 And *that* they may recover themselves out of the snare of the devil, who are taken captive by him at his will.

Paul is here again harping on his favorite string. His zeal for Christ's cause in the Church, is always uppermost in his heart. And therefore he can never say enough to *Timothy* to prompt him to watch over the flock. Oh! what anxiety he expresseth, that the youthful lusts of pride, and vain glory, which young men and young ministers too often feel in their preaching, should give way wholly to the preaching Christ. The fear of man, and the desire of praise in man, bring a snare. It is blessed, where grace abounds, to be kept low, and like *Paul*, to be content to be nothing, so that Christ be glorified.

REFLECTIONS.

Blessed Lord Jesus! how sweetly hath thy servant taught the Church, and every humble member of it like myself, to seek strength only in thee, and the grace in my Lord; and not from any thing in our own attainments. Oh! for grace in a daily, hourly communication from Christ, to be strong in the grace that is in Christ Jesus: that I may abide in thee, as thou hast said, convinced that without thee, I can do nothing. And may GOD the SPIRIT continually teach me my need, then lead to thee for a supply; then open a communication between my full LORD and my empty soul; and then keep it everlastingly open, to my joy, and my LORD's glory.

Glory to a faithful Covenant GOD and FATHER in CHRIST JESUS! may my soul never for a moment lose sight of thy faithfulness, amidst all my unbelievings. Oh! the preciousness of that scripture. *If we believe not, yet he abideth faithful: he cannot deny himself:* LORD! I see nothing but evil, unbelief, and emptiness in all I do or say. I am content that it should be so. I am nothing, yea worse than nothing: that my poverty may make me hunger more for the riches of thy grace. Oh! to be a vessel unto honor, sanctified, and meat for the master's use, and prepared by grace for every good work.

LORD the SPIRIT! do thou seal my soul, unto the day of eternal redemption. This will form a blessed *nevertheless* to all my unworthiness. *The foundation of* GOD *standeth sure.* And in proclaiming this foundation, and this assurance, let all thy sent servants shew themselves approved unto GOD; and workmen which need not to be ashamed; and let all thy people *follow righteousness, faith, charity, peace, with them that call on the* LORD, *out of a pure heart.*

CHAP. III.

CONTENTS.

The Apostle in this Chapter, foretells of perilous Times. He speaks of certain Enemies of the Truth: and closeth with a warm Recommendation of the Holy Scriptures, as making wise unto Salvation.

THIS know also, that in the last days perilous times shall come.

2 For men shall be lovers of their ownselves, covetous, boasters, proud, blasphemers, disobedient to parents, unthankful, unholy,

3 Without natural affection, truce-breakers, false accusers, incontinent, fierce, despisers of those that are good,

4 Traitors, heady, high-minded, lovers of pleasures more than lovers of God;

5 Having a form of godliness, but denying the power thereof; from such turn away.

6 For of this sort are they which creep into houses, and lead captive silly women laden with sins, led away with divers lusts.

7 Ever learning, and never able to come to the knowledge of the truth.

8 Now as Jannes and Jambres withstood Moses, so do these also resist the truth: men of corrupt minds, reprobate concerning the faith.

9 But they shall proceed no further: for their folly shall be manifest unto all *men*, as their's also was.

We have here, an awful prophecy of awful times. And as it bears no date, we have authority to make application of it to any period, yea, and to every period of the Church, where is discoverable a correspondence, between the prediction and what appears to be the accomplishment. It hath been pretty much the custom with Commentators, to make a very general application of what is here said to the Church of *Rome*. And no doubt very many of the characters belong to that See. The merits of works, and supererogation; the pride and blasphemy, the form without the power of godliness; the creeping into houses, and leading captive silly women; with confessions, purgatory, penance, and the like which distinguish that creed; are high demonstrations, that the Apostle had in view, such a profession of religion, when he wrote these words in this Chapter. But had this heresy been the only one, here spoken of in relation to the perilous times of the last days; I should not have thought it necessary, to have dwelt upon it, with any observations in this *Poor Man's Commentary*. But convinced as I am, that the true Church of Christ hath as much to apprehend of danger from other quarters in the apostacies around; and which, unless I greatly err indeed, the Holy Ghost in this scripture more immediately had in view; I cannot consider myself justified in passing over the passage now before us, as if the See of *Rome* was only meant, when I verily believe our dangers are greater from other sources, in and among ourselves, and that the spirit of prophecy in this scripture, had them in contemplation.

I have in the former Epistle of *Paul* to *Timothy*, (Chapter iv. and the first and following verses,) already stated my thoughts on some of the latter day heresies. It will not be necessary therefore in this place to enlarge. I shall dismiss the subject with only observing; that what God the Spirit, by his servant the Apostle, hath here said, is enough, surely, to keep every child of God upon the look-out, for those perilous times here predicted; which if not already come, (as it should plainly seem they are,) cannot be very far remote, and may be near indeed. One grand consolation to the true Church of Christ remains, to comfort her members during the most awful times; namely, her everlasting safety is in no hazard. *If it were possible,* Jesus saith, *they would deceive the very elect*. Mark xiii. 22. But our Lord's manner of expression proves, that it is impossible. And yet, though assured, that not one of Christ's little ones shall perish; it is enough to make the people of God to be deeply affected, with the prospect of those awful times, which threaten the Lord's indignation on a sinful land. Isaiah, i. 4. The righteous soul of *Lot* was vexed with the filthy conversation of the wicked in his day,' 2 Pet. ii. 7. *Moses* had his *Jannes* and his *Jambres* to oppose him with their enchantments. Exod. vii. 11. And *David* speaks of rivers of tears running down at beholding the breaches made by the wicked on God's holy law. Psm. cxix. 136. And if the Lord should remove the golden candlestick of Ordinances from us; or give up Professors to their *form*, as *Paul* here speaks, wholly void of all the *power of Godliness:* very awful will be the consequence, though the eternal safety of Christ's Church cannot be affected! But I forbear to dwell upon the subject. Precious Jesus! do as thou hast said. *Watch over thy Church, and water her every moment. Keep her night and day, lest any hurt her?* Isaiah xxvii. 2, 3. If the Reader wishes a sweet Chapter of consolation on this subject, I refer him to Zephaniah iii.

10 But thou hast fully known my doctrine, manner of life, purpose, faith, long-suffering, charity, patience,

11 Persecutions, afflictions, which came unto me at Antioch, at Iconium, at Lystra; what persecutions I endured; but out of *them* all the Lord delivered me.

12 Yea, and all that will live godly in Christ Jesus shall suffer persecution.

13 But evil men and seducers shall wax worse and worse, deceiving, and being deceived.

I beg the Reader to notice, what a blessed relief the Holy Ghost here proposeth to *Timothy*, from the melancholy statement, the preceding verses had given, in the example of his faithful servant the Apostle. The single character of *Paul*, was enough to bear down an whole host of heretics, and to remove from *Timothy's* mind, all concern for the apostacy of such characters. And the same holds equally good now. For what in fact are all the heresies of the present generation, but all springing out of one and the same deadly stock, in the fall of man. They vary in their branches, in shape and form; but their bearings are all one and the same. They appear differently to our dimsighted view, in order to deceive more artfully; but they all arise from that original apostacy. The glorious truths, on which the very being of the gospel depends, are so little regarded by the generality of Professors, that they are seldom heard; and when heard, for the most part, by the great mass of the people, disbelieved and called in question. Men shrink from insisting upon the distinguishing features of our holy faith. The people love to have their wine mingled with water. And too often in compliment to the itching ears of such men, the blessed doctrines, which are the life of the soul, are kept in the back ground.

That such is the case, is evident from the stillness and quiet, into which the bulk is fallen. *Paul* saith in this account of himself to *Timothy*, that *he had fully known his doctrine, manner of life, long sufferings, persecutions, afflictions, and the like.* And all these he opposeth, to the character of those who had a *form*, but not the *power* of godliness. The Apostle would have escaped these persecutions, had he temporized with such men. But because he simply preached CHRIST in the electing love of GOD the FATHER, the betrothing and redeeming love of GOD the SON, and the regenerating love of GOD the SPIRIT, *what persecutions*, saith the Apostle, *I endured.* But Reader, was it ever known, in any age of the Church, that a preacher was persecuted for complimenting mens goodness at the expence of GOD's truth? Did ever the *Pharisee* take offence at exhortations delivered to the people, while he thought, however needful to others, he wanted them not himself. All that know not the plague of their own heart, will relish no doctrines, which tend to bring upon a level, the whole Adam-race, in the present fallen state; and bitterness enough will manifest itself from all of that complexion, to the Preacher that cries down the perfection of the creature, and exalts only the SAVIOUR. So equally sure is it now, in the present day, as it was in *Paul's* day, that *all who will live godly in* CHRIST JESUS, *shall suffer persecution.*

14 But continue thou in the things which thou hast learned and hast been assured of, knowing of whom thou hast learned *them;*

15 And that from a child thou hast known the holy scriptures, which are able to make thee wise unto salvation through faith which is in Christ Jesus.

16 All scripture *is* given by inspiration of God, and *is* profitable for doctrine, for reproof, for correction, for instruction in righteousness:

17 That the man of God may be perfect, throughly furnished unto all good works.

What a beautiful close the Apostle makes, in his advice to *Timothy*, as a security through grace from the general apostacy of the then times. And the same holds equally good now. A continuance in the delight and enjoyment of all the great truths of GOD, must follow divine teaching. And *Paul* doth not speak of it, as though the thing was doubtful. Here, indeed, lies the distinguishing glory of a regenerated state, as marked from all the flaming professions, void of it in the world. The child of GOD knows the inspiration of scripture to be such, from the correspondence of what is said in it bears to his own heart. And the threefold witness, the Apostle elsewhere describes, of the HOLY GHOST; the sacred word, and his own heart, confirms all he learns from GOD. 2 Cor. xiii. 1. But where there is no divine teaching; no work of GOD the SPIRIT, in regenerating the fallen nature; there the blindness of heart remains, untaken away, and bitterness breaks out in a variety of directions against that preaching, which *contends for the faith once delivered to the saints;* and leaves no room for the *Pharisee's* righteousness to be puffed up. Reader! beg of God the Holy Ghost, to be always under the Lord's teaching, that in his blessed scriptures, you may be *made wise unto salvation, through faith which is in* Christ Jesus.

REFLECTIONS.

Reader! while the Apostle is thus speaking to the Church, of the perilous times that should come, may we not say with *John: Little Children, it is the last time. And as we have heard that Antichrist shall come, even now are there many Antichrists; whereby we know that it is the last time.* But, Reader! who can hear what the beloved Apostle hath added to this solemn scripture, without the most painful concern? *They went out from us, but they were not of us!* It is distressing enough to be told by the Spirit in prophecy, that the Church shall be assaulted by heresies, in the latter day dispensation; and that we are of those latter ages in which those heresies appear, but to be told, that even in the Churches, where the truth as it is in Jesus is professed, men shall arise *speaking perverse things to draw away disciples after them;* these are trembling dispensations indeed. But, Reader! do not overlook the security of the faithful. That unction from the Holy One, which all truly regenerated children of God in Christ possess, teacheth all things, and will keep the Lord's people; and the wicked one shall touch them not. This is our promise. And a blessed promise it is, in this present evil day.

And shall not you and I bless God the Spirit both for the information, and the means of security? Do we not behold in this chapter, sufficient marks of character, for discerning the signs of the times, to judge faithful servants of the Lord, from time-pleasers? Where we behold men lovers of their ownselves, proud, boasters, and the like; and a leanness of soul among the people, who are content with the form of godliness, but deny, and are ignorant of the power thereof: and when we contrast such a state, with that which *Paul* describes of himself, (and which more or less must distinguish all like *Paul*), whose doctrine and manner of life cannot but beget hatred, evil speaking and persecution; from all Pharisees, and mere nominal Professors of religion; are not the different characters as clearly defined, as if drawn by a sun-beam? Blessed be God the Holy Ghost, for his gracious foretelling of those perilous times; and for his divine teaching of his people to try the spirits, and to discern them. Reader! let us be waiting at wisdom's gate, in these awful days of heresy. And let us behold and see, how *evil men, and seducers,* among Pharisees, and mere Professors, *wax worse and worse;* more wretched, more lean of soul, deceiving men like themselves, not God's people, and being themselves deceived. And let those holy scriptures of our God, which are profitable for all things to the man of God, be daily in our hand, while God the Spirit is instructing our heart; that we may be found of that happy number, made strong by grace, in *the faith which is in* Christ Jesus.

CHAP. IV.

CONTENTS.

The Apostle is here closing his Epistle, and, therefore, impresseth his Exhortations on Timothy, with the tenderest Affection. He speaks of several who were Enemies to the Cross; and sends his Salutations to several, who were Friends: and concludes with his usual Apostolic Blessing, in praying for Grace.

I Charge *thee* therefore before God, and the Lord Jesus Christ, who shall judge the quick and the dead at his appearing and his kingdom;

2 Preach the word; be instant in season, out of season; reprove, rebuke, exhort with all long-suffering and doctrine.

3 For the time will come when they will not endure sound doctrine; but after their own lusts shall they heap to themselves teachers; having itching ears;

4 And they shall turn away *their* ears from the truth, and shall be turned unto fables.

5 But watch thou in all things, endure afflictions, do the work of an evangelist, make full proof of thy ministry.

I pray the Reader to remark, the earnestness, with which *Paul* chargeth *Timothy*, on this momentous ground, to be faithful, and diligent in his ministry. Though *Timothy* was very dear to *Paul;* yet the LORD JESUS CHRIST, and his cause, was infinitely dearer. And, let the Reader yet further remark, in what a solemn manner the Apostle introduceth the LORD, both FATHER and SON, including the HOLY GHOST, who is the Almighty Speaker by *Paul,* as looking on, while he thus chargeth *Timothy* to faithfulness. Yea, he seems by his expression, as if he had brought this young man before the presence of the LORD, and then bids him behold, who were witnesses to this renewed Ordination! Oh! that GOD the HOLY GHOST would carry the conviction of this solemn scripture, to the consciences of those, who run unsent of GOD; that the awful prospect of His coming to judge the quick and dead at his appearing, might stop the mouths of them, *who serve not our* LORD JESUS CHRIST, *but their own bellies!* Rom. xvi. 18.

And, while the Reader particularly noticeth the Apostle's charge to the faithful Preacher; let him no less observe, the special cause, for giving a command so earnest, in relation to the people. *The time will come,* (saith Paul,) *when they will not endure sound doctrine.* What an awful account. We read in the Old Testament scripture of some, *who said to the Prophets: prophecy not unto us right things, speak unto us smooth things, prophecy deceits.* Isaiah xxx. 10. But here seems, if possible, a more awful delusion, when the sound doctrines of the Gospel, men will not hear, nor endure. It is worthy the Reader's observation, that the LORD JESUS himself, in allusion to the latter-day dispensation, declared, the delusion should be so great, that had not the LORD shortened it, no flesh could be saved. But, saith JESUS, (and a sweet saying it is, to the LORD's people,) *for the elect's sake, whom he hath chosen, he hath shortened the days.* Mark xiii. 20. *Paul,* in taking leave of the Church at *Ephesus,* beheld, with great concern, the alarming times of the latter-day heresies. Acts xx. 25, to the end.

Let the Reader observe further on this subject, that when the Apostle spake of a time that would come, when men would not endure sound doctrine, he then spake of a distant day. But if we consider the signs of the present time, that day is actually come. Surely it is impossible for any child in grace, to contemplate the circumstances going on in the Churches professing godliness, and where the Gospel is repeatedly said to be preached; without being struck with the most palpable conviction, that men *do not endure sound doctrine, but, after their own lusts, are heaping to themselves teachers having itching ears.*

If there be a doctrine of the Gospel of CHRIST, more eminently to be insisted upon, one than another, in being the bottom, and foundation of every other; surely, the everlasting love of GOD in the choice of his Church in CHRIST, is that doctrine. For from hence ariseth the redemption of the Church by CHRIST, from the *Adam*-fall of sin: and the regeneration of the Spirit, by GOD the HOLY GHOST. In short, all, and every one of the momentous doctrines of grace, are the result of this first, pre-disposing, and eternal love of GOD to the Church in CHRIST, before all worlds. Ephes. iii. 9, 10, 11. As such, can it be otherwise supposed, than that this glorious, fundamental article of our most holy faith, should be the constant, unwearied subject of every Preacher's discourse; and the joy of every hearer's heart, in all Churches of the Saints? From hence, as from a foundation, all the after-building in grace, must arise. And to this, every wise master builder, (as *Paul* calls preachers,) hath respect, as forming the basis of the whole superstructure. Could it ever have been supposed then, that any age of the Church, would be found, that would go off this foundation? Yes! saith the HOLY GHOST, the time will come, when they will not endure sound doctrine. That time is indeed now come; and come with such awful forerunners of evil, that the grand truths of our holy faith, are frittering away, so as by many to be nearly given up. The glorious doctrines of election; redemption solely by CHRIST, as a finished salvation; and the Person, GODHEAD, and Ministry of the HOLY GHOST: these truths are seldom spoken of by some, and relinquished by others. Nay, the departure from sound doctrine, hath been so great, that in the self-importance of vain minds, some have gone so far, as to form comparative statements, between the doctrines of election, predestination, the atonement, and the like; and what they call other topics, and in their view, of a supposed equally important nature, that in the presumption of their minds they have turned the attention of the faithful to the former, as disproportioned.

Alas! what blind leaders of the blind, must such men be! And what a leanness of soul must be found, in the congregations, where such men minister? For what proportion (to use their own words) can there be, between the drops of the bucket, and the ocean; or the small dust of the balance, and the whole earth? And yet, far less must there be, between the glorious purposes of JEHOVAH, in his electing love of his Church in CHRIST; than all the counsels, wills, and works of men, and angels, to all eternity. But such men see it not. And hence neither they, nor their congregations, can endure sound doctrine. The itching ears of the one, and the unhumbled pride of the other, are in quest of somewhat, which shall gratify the lusts of both. The lust of the *Pharisee*, is satiated, in the compliment paid to his self-righteousness; and the lust of the *Professor* is not less indulged, in the having a name to live, while virtually dead before GOD. And both Preacher, and Hearer, sit down in the complacency of their own self-importance.

Reader! I pray you to pause over the awful prospect Persons of the complexion I am adverting to, with confidence tell us, that the piety of our days is reviving. Whereas, GOD the HOLY GHOST speaketh expressly, that in the last days perilous times shall come. And the SON of GOD hath left upon record, that so general will be the apostacy of the last days, that *if it were possible, they should deceive even the very elect.* Mark xiii. 22. If these men were taught of GOD, and acquainted with the plague of their own heart these things alone would be enough to convince them of their error. But, alas! they are too full of self-importance. *Paul's* charge to *Timothy*, before GOD, and the LORD JESUS CHRIST, to be instant *in season, and out of season, and to reprove, rebuke, and exhort with all long suffering and doctrine,* (which implies much opposition to a faithful ministry,) they know not. The fashionable congregations they address, according to their system, require neither reproof nor rebuke. And thus for the most part such men live, and, it is to be feared, too often die, full of their own good deeds, and literally strangers to their own corruptions before GOD.

But, what a blessed relief hath GOD the HOLY GHOST given, to the alarming view of such men, in the short, but sweet portrait he hath drawn, by the Apostle, of what form the outlines of a faithful servant of CHRIST. *But watch thou in all things; endure afflictions; do the work of an Evangelist: make full proof of thy ministry.* Without entering into all the parts of the ministerial character, which would form a volume, rather than to be comprized within the limits of a short observation, which this work can only allow; suffer me to ask, what afflictions from men, would the work of an Evangelist bring upon a preacher, whose chief bent is to compliment his hearers? And what watchings do those men go through, for the souls of the people, who know nothing of the doubts, and fears, and spiritual distresses, of exercised believers? What full proof can they give of their ministry, whose services are confined to the pulpit? *Paul,* who recommends this conduct to *Timothy*, and who preached the sound doctrines of election, redemption, and regeneration, continually; was himself a living example of what he enjoined. He entered into the spiritual concerns of all the LORD's people, and made their case his own. *Who is weak* (saith he) *and I am not weak? Who is offended and I burn not?* 2 Cor. xi. 29. Faithful servant of Jesus! Hadst thou lived in these days, what burning of soul wouldest thou have felt, at the conduct of those, who, though professing Christ, cannot endure sound doctrine!

6 For I am now ready to be offered, and the time of my departure is at hand.

7 I have fought a good fight, I have finished *my* course, I have kept the faith.

8 Henceforth there is laid up for me a crown of righteousness, which the Lord, the righteous judge, shall give me at that day: and not to me only, but unto all them also that love his appearing.

It appears very plain, that *Paul* knew his departure was near. And it is also very plain, he knew that he should finish his course by martyrdom. But what a firmness of mind he manifested in the prospect. He had before said, Christ *should be magnified in his body, whether by life, or death.* Philip. i. 20. And now the hour is arrived. He reviews the past, and contemplates what is to come. And, under the conscious assurance of an oneness and interest in Christ, he triumphs, in having fought *the good fight of faith.* I pray the Reader to notice this. The fight of faith, and the victory of faith, are both in, and from Christ. *Paul* utters not a word of his services, or labors, or sufferings. He well knew, that these added not an atom, to his acceptance before God. Christ, and Christ alone, was *Paul's* triumphs. Sweet, and precious consideration, to the child of God.

In like manner, the crown of righteousness laid up for him, was not for services, or sufferings, but wholly the respect of the free gift of God in Christ; and Christ's right, and the believer's right, from his union, and interest in Christ. And I pray the Reader particularly to notice the Apostle's expressions. He doth not merely call it a crown, neither a crown of glory, but *a crown of righteousness.* And, no doubt, eminently on this account; because it is Christ's due for his people, though not their's. Christ had purchased it for them, though to them it comes free. And it is but just in God, the righteous God, to give it to them as Christ's right; though on their part, they have no pretensions to it from their own merit. Reader! there is a great sweetness in this view. As sinners, all we have given to us, is God's free grace. But, as members of Christ, we have a claim to what is Christ's right. And it is, therefore, a crown of righteousness, to which all his redeemed family are justly entitled, by the blood-shedding, obedience, and death, of the Lord Jesus Christ.

And, there is one point more, which must not be overlooked, in this sweet scripture. *Paul* saith, that this crown of righteousness, is not laid up only for him; but for all them that love the Lord's appearing. Oh! how very blessed is this assurance. And who is there among the truly regenerated in the Lord's family, but what doth love his appearing? True, the moment is solemn. The first view of Jesus, on the spirit departing from the body, must be indeed overwhelming. But yet, there is glory in it. We then see him face to face, whom by faith we have often looked at, and loved with a joy unspeakable, and full of glory. Still, the sight will be more rapturous, than confounding. We shall see him, as he is. And that is, all lovely. And, if we love his appearing now, we shall love his appearing then. If CHRIST in his ordinances, CHRIST in his visits, CHRIST in his work on poor sinners, and manifestations to his saints; if these are appearings, in which our souls rejoice; this is to love his appearing in grace, and very sure, all such must love his appearing in glory. Precious JESUS! keep my soul alive, in the daily expectation of thy coming!

9 Do thy diligence to come shortly unto me.

10 For Demas hath forsaken me, having loved this present world, and is departed unto Thessalonica; Crescens to Galatia, Titus unto Dalmatia.

11 Only Luke is with me. Take Mark, and bring him with thee: for he is profitable to me for the ministry.

12 And Tychicus have I sent to Ephesus.

13 The cloke that I left at Troas with Carpus, when thou comest, bring *with thee*, and the books, *but* especially the parchments.

14 Alexander the coppersmith did me much evil: the Lord reward him according to his works:

15 Of whom be thou ware also; for he hath greatly withstood our words.

16 At my first answer no man stood with me, but all *men* forsook me; *I pray God* that it may not be laid to their charge.

17 Notwithstanding the Lord stood with me, and strengthened me; that by me the preaching might be fully known, and *that* all the Gentiles might hear: and I was delivered out of the mouth of the lion.

18 And the Lord shall deliver me from every evil work, and will preserve *me* unto his heavenly kingdom: to whom *be* glory for ever and ever. Amen.

19 Salute Prisca and Aquila, and the household of Onesiphorus.

20 Erastus abode at Corinth: but Trophimus have I left at Miletum sick.

21 Do thy diligence to come before winter. Eubulus greeteth thee, and Pudens, and Linus, and Claudia, and all the brethren.

22 The Lord Jesus Christ *be* with thy spirit. Grace *be* with you. Amen.

The second *epistle* unto Timotheus, ordained the first bishop of the church of the Ephesians, was written from Rome, when Paul was brought before Nero the second time.

What is here said of *Demas*, may be said, and must be said, of all mere nominal professors, who follow CHRIST only for a name, and were never regenerated, and called by GOD. If the Reader would learn, under the LORD, to form this one estimate, for ascertaining real, from mere formal godliness; it would enable him, both for himself, and for all around him, to discern *him that serveth* GOD, *from him that serveth him not:* I mean, by the regeneration of the heart. Where the HOLY GHOST hath wrought this saving work upon the spirit; there the LORD dwells for ever. And none of this description, shall ever, *Demas*-like, forsake the LORD finally. Sweetly the scriptures bear testimony to this safety, when saying: *Though he fall, he shall not utterly be cast down; for the* LORD *upholdeth him with his hand.* Psm xxxvii. 24. Jerem. xxxii. 40.

What a blessed improvement the Apostle makes, from the defection of men, to remark the faithfulness of the LORD. It is sweet, yea, very sweet, from creature unkindness, to learn to value more Creator, and Redeemer love. *Paul*, no doubt, felt the wound at such a season, when he stood to answer for his life. But it afforded only greater blessedness, from the LORD's personal grace, and mercy. I hardly think it necessary to remind the Reader, of an infinitely greater than *Paul*, who at the hall of *Pilate* was treated thus by his disciples, when all forsook him and fled. Precious JESUS! preeminent in all things: sufferings, as well as glory. Reader! there is a time coming, when all friends, however reluctantly on all sides, must leave both you, and me, and we must stand alone before GOD. I mean, when the LORD shall undress our earthly tabernacle at death. Oh! for grace now, to say then: Notwithstanding, the LORD will stand by me, and strengthen me; notwithstanding all my unworthiness, and undeservings; JESUS's Person, blood and righteousness, will be *my strength and my song, for he is my salvation.* Isaiah xii.

I do not think it necessary, to dwell with enquiries about any of those persons the Apostle noticeth in the close of this Epistle. They are all passed away in the flood of time, and their dwelling place, like the flower of the field, knoweth them no more. Sweetly the Apostle folds up his Epistle, as I pray GOD, may be my portion, in the close of life: *The* LORD JESUS CHRIST *be with thy spirit: Grace be with thee. Amen.*

REFLECTIONS.

Almighty God and Father! may all, whom the Holy Ghost hath made ministers in the service of the Church of Jesus, hear the solemn charge of *Paul* to *Timothy*, to prompt to faithfulness in their high calling. And, no less, Almighty Jesus! may the sure expectation of thy appearing, and thy kingdom, to judge the quick and dead, awaken such, to be diligent in thy service to thy coming. Lord! give them grace to preach the word, and to be constant, in season, out of season; and especially in these awful times, when the way of truth is evil spoken of, and men will not endure sound doctrine. And, oh! thou blessed, and Almighty Spirit of all truth, do thou guard, and guide, lead, and instruct all thy family; that the hearts of thy people, may not be turned unto fables.

Blessed be a faithful Covenant-God in Christ, for the fulfilment of his faithful promise, in the instance of *Paul,* in giving such a Pastor, after his own heart. The Church of God bless the Lord for this man's services, in all his past labors; and in all his future usefulness. Oh! grant, Lord, that all thy faithful, whether ministers, or people, may like *Paul,* and from the same cause, live and die, in the full assurance of faith, in expectation of the crown of righteousness, which the Lord the righteous Judge, will give at that day to all them that love our Lord's appearing!

Praises to the Father, Son, and Spirit, for this, and all the other precious portions of God's word; to make the Church, under divine teaching, more and more acquainted with the Person, and glory of Jesus, *for* the happiness *of the life that now is, and that which is to come.* Amen.

THE
EPISTLE OF PAUL THE APOSTLE
TO
TITUS.

GENERAL OBSERVATIONS.

THIS Epistle of *Paul* to *Titus* is but short, though highly interesting, and we have much cause to bless God the Holy Ghost for it. Very clear marks of the Lord's inspiration are discoverable in it.

It is supposed by some to have been written from *Rome;* and others have thought that *Paul* wrote it from *Ephesus.* In either case the time must differ, though it generally bears the date of our Lord God 55.

The Person to whom *Paul* wrote it, is in several parts of the Apostle's other writings spoken of in very high terms of affection. *Paul* calls him *Titus* his own son, and his brother and partner and fellow helper; and as one who walked in the same spirit; and in the same steps. 2 Cor. xii. 18. see also Gal. ii. 1—3. 2 Cor. viii. 23. So that he was evidently very dear to *Paul*.

The subject of the Epistle is generally concerning the blessed doctrines of the Gospel; and directions to *Titus* concerning the ministry. I beg the Reader to enter upon the perusal of it, on the knee of prayer, that the Almighty Author of his written Word, may lead the souls of his people by it, to the uncreated WORD, and bless it in JESUS CHRIST.

CHAPTER I.

CONTENTS.

The Apostle opens his Epistle, with his usual Benediction. He points out to Titus *the Qualifications for the Ministry. He gives a sad Account of the* Grecians, *among whom Titus dwelt; and concludes the Chapter with the same.*

PAUL, a servant of God, and an apostle of Jesus Christ, according to the faith of God's elect, and the acknowledging of the truth which is after godliness;

2 In hope of eternal life, which God, that cannot lie, promised before the world began;

3 But hath in due times manifested his word through preaching, which is committed unto me, according to the commandment of God our Saviour;

I detain the Reader at the very entrance on this Epistle, to observe to him, the striking expression of the Apostle on the subject of faith. He calls it *the faith of* GOD's *elect.* I would not speak decidedly on the occasion, because I would rather that the godly Reader should, under grace, decide for himself. But I would humbly ask, doth not the Apostle, by the very phrase, evidently imply, that amidst all the professions of faith, to be met with in the world, there is but one, which is true and genuine, namely, the faith of GOD's elect? And what that is, the scriptures, in every part shew. The faith of GOD's elect, looks at the special act of JEHOVAH, in the purposes, will, decrees, and pleasure, of his infinite and eternal mind, as manifested in his threefold Personality of character, toward the Church of GOD, in CHRIST JESUS. And this faith of GOD's elect, is the special gift of GOD to the elect; distinguished from all other, and is the *fruit* and *effect*, of the first, original, and eternal *cause,* in GOD's election; whereby, without any regard to any one motive whatever, but GOD's own free will and pleasure, he hath *chosen the Church in* CHRIST, *to be holy and without blame before him in love.* Ephes. i. 4. And hence, in the riches of his grace, hath made all suitable provision, for the accomplishment of all the purposes, connected with this act of sovereign love, during the whole time-state of the Church, until the LORD hath brought her home to eternal glory. The faith of GOD's elect, includes, therefore, in its view, all the blessed acts, and works of grace to render the whole effectual, for the accomplishment of that *hope of eternal life, which* GOD *that cannot lie, promised before the world began.* This is the faith of GOD's elect.

And what tends to make it special, and endear it yet more, is, that it is only in the privilege of the elect themselves to exercise; and they only by GOD's gift. For so the charter of grace runs. *Unto you it is given in the behalf of* CHRIST, *to believe on him.* Philip. i. 29. Sweetly therefore the same Apostle, when writing to the *Thessalonians,* dwells upon the subject, when he saith; *But we are bound to give thanks alway to* GOD, *for you brethren, beloved of the* LORD, *because* GOD *hath, from the beginning, chosen you to salvation, through sanctification of the* SPIRIT, *and belief of the truth.* 2 Thess. ii. 13. Reader! do not hastily turn away from the view of this most precious scripture, of the faith of GOD's elect. Look at the distinguishing properties of it, again and again, with thanksgiving and praise. Observe, it is not the common faith of men, or devils. It is not historical faith, hearsay faith, head knowledge faith. But it is the special, personal faith, of GOD's elect. It is a given faith, the fruit and effect of the same source and cause; from whence all the blessings connected with it spring; namely, the electing love of GOD. It cannot be possessed by any, but the elect. And by them only, as the gift of GOD. Oh! the preciousness of the faith of GOD's elect! LORD give it me to possess, in all its blessed, distinguishing properties! May my spirit live, in the daily, hourly enjoyment of it; having it kept always alive in my soul, in living upon CHRIST, and CHRIST in GOD; as manifested in the electing, predestinating love of GOD my FATHER; the blessed betrothing, redeeming, justifying, sanctifying love of GOD my SAVIOUR; and the regenerating soul-quickening, spiritual-life-preserving grace of GOD the HOLY GHOST. Oh! the unspeakable mercies, which give birth to the faith of GOD's elect!

But it would be wrong to pass over unnoticed what the Apostle saith in connection with the faith of GOD's elect, namely, *and the acknowledging of the truth, which is after godliness.* This was blessedly added by the Apostle, as if to put a stop to the charge against the faith of GOD's elect, as though it were a doctrine contrary to godliness. Whereas the fact is, there can be no real godliness without it. All the labored attempts of carnal men, to make a shew of outside godliness, having no spring within, can be but a shew; for it hath no resource, to give life to it at first, or keep it alive after. But the faith of GOD's elect being founded in the love of GOD, hath, for its spring, the grace of GOD, which bringeth salvation: and this both teacheth and enableth to *the denying ungod-*

liness and worldly lusts, and to the living soberly, righteously, and godly, in this present world; looking for that blessed hope, and the glorious appearing of the great GOD *and our* SAVIOR JESUS CHRIST. Chap. ii. 11—13. The faith of GOD's elect, can never fail of producing those effects, in every instance. And no faith, but the faith of GOD's elect can produce them. The faith of devils, the faith of mere Professors, and Pharisees, the lip confession, learnt from the creeds of men, and all the other trumpery of human invention, have no belief, but that which produceth fear and trembling. James ii. 19. It is only the faith of GOD's elect, which connects with it the acknowledging of the truth, and the practical effects of truth, *which is after godliness.*

One word more on this paragraph. What is this faith of GOD's elect exercised upon? Paul saith; *in hope of eternal life, which* GOD, *that cannot lie, promised before the world began.* Reader! I beseech you look at the bottom, and foundation of this hope. Paul calls it *a blessed hope.* Chap. ii. 13. And a blessed hope indeed it is, in all the properties of it. For *first.* It originated in GOD's own purpose, and that from all eternity. Nothing moving the LORD to it, but his own infinite mind; and his holy will and pleasure. Not our misery or need; for it was before the world began; and, consequently, neither our misery, nor his mercy to that misery, gave rise to it, for it was before both. The Apostle saith, that it was *according to the eternal purpose, which he purposed in* CHRIST JESUS *our* LORD. Ephes. iii. 9—11. What a bottom is here to found the sure mercies of *David* upon; when beheld as *in* GOD, and *from* GOD, and *by* GOD; and that from all eternity?

Secondly. Consider the sweet properties of it, and it will appear indeed *a blessed hope.* All are founded in Covenant securities, in which every thing is provided for, to make it permanent, sure, and everlasting. The antient settlements of eternity, in the council of peace, between the Persons of the GODHEAD, all are so formed, as to guard against the possibility of failure. GOD the FATHER, who cannot lie, hath sworn to it. CHRIST, who is our Righteousness, hath fulfilled all the purposes concerning it. GOD the SPIRIT, who is all holy; confirms it in the hearts of the people. And, as all the individual members, for whom this eternal life is designed, and to whom it is given, are all chosen and numbered, in the decrees of GOD; nothing can arise, to prevent the accomplishment of it, from any causes whatever, during the time-state of the Church, but what hath been foreseen and provided for from all eternity.

And, *lastly,* to mention no more. What endears it, and recommends it to every heart, of the highly favored objects of this divine promise is, that it is altogether free, unsought for, yea, unthought of; and neither bestowed for deservings, or restrained by undeservings; but freely given without regard to either, as if to magnify the riches of divine grace, and to display divine sovereignty according to that unalterable scripture: *I will have mercy on whom I will have mercy; and I will have compassion on whom I will have compassion.* Exod. xxxiii. 19. with Romans ix. 15. Oh! the riches of GOD's eternal purposes in CHRIST! Oh! the sweet, and precious faith of GOD's elect!

4 To Titus, *mine* own son after the common faith: Grace, mercy, *and* peace, from God the Father and the Lord Jesus Christ our Saviour.

5 For this cause left I thee in Crete, that thou shouldst set in order the things that are wanting, and ordain elders in every city, as I had appointed thee:

6 If any be blameless, the husband of one wife, having faithful children, not accused of riot, or unruly.

7 For a bishop must be blameless, as the steward of God; not self-willed, not soon angry, not given to wine, no striker, not given to filthy lucre;

8 But a lover of hospitality, a lover of good men, sober, just, holy, temperate;

9 Holding fast the faithful word as he hath been taught, that he may be able by sound doctrine both to exhort and to convince the gainsayers.

10 For there are many unruly and vain talkers and deceivers, specially they of the circumcision:

11 Whose mouths must be stopped, who subvert whole houses, teaching things which they ought not, for filthy lucre's sake.

I have, in the opening of the first Epistle of *Paul* to *Timothy*, given my views of what the Apostle meant, in calling those companions of his *sons*. On this point I need not enlarge. Neither shall I detain the Reader, with any unnecessary observations, on the history of *Crete*, where *Paul* saith he left *Titus*, to arrange the government of the Church in that place. We know but little of this place from scripture. It was one of those islands, in the *Mediterranean* Sea, where *Paul*, in his voyage, passed. Acts xxvii. 7. But it could not have been at that time, the Apostle left *Titus* there. It might have been more likely, when he went over various parts of *Greece*. Acts xx. 2. But this is not so material, to our present purpose, to enquire. I would rather call upon the Reader, to remark, with me, *Paul's* anxiety as is here, and elsewhere expressed, respecting the ordination for the ministry. Let any person bring into one view, all that the aged Apostle, hath said on this subject, in his Epistles to the Churches, and to Persons; and it will strike him, I think, as it doth me, with full conviction, that nothing lay nearer the heart of *Paul*, than the caution, which ought to be observed, in sending men to labor in the word and doctrine. If the Reader will indulge me, I will take advantage from what the Apostle hath here charged upon *Titus*, on the subject, to offer a short observation.

The work of the ministry, is in itself so arduous, its duties so various, and its eventful consequences so infinitely important; that no man of the least seriousness, if he thought at all, would run unsent. *Paul*, when speaking of himself on this occasion, seems to express the greatness of his surprize, that one, less than the least of all saints, should have the grace given to him for such a purpose; *that I* (said he) *should preach among the Gentiles the unsearchable riches of* CHRIST. Ephes. iii. 8. Had the Apostle considered the gifts of nature, or of art, as qualifying for the ministry; certainly his liberal education, and his powers of eloquence, might have been thought very suitable requisites. But in *Paul's* view, these things rather hindered, than forwarded the LORD's service. *What things were gain to me; those* (said he) *I counted loss for* CHRIST. Philip. iii. 7. And certain it is, the Apostle had in view at all times, his wonderful conversion; and his call of JESUS to be his Apostle; as well as the ordination of the HOLY GHOST to the ministry; as the great authority, by which he acted, in the service of the LORD. How would *Paul* have shuddered, had he been told of men, rushing into the ministry, unsent of GOD, and unanointed by the HOLY GHOST? What a contradiction in terms, would it have appeared to the Apostle's mind, had he heard of Preachers going forth to the conversion of others, when unconverted themselves? The characters *Paul* here speaks of, whom *Titus* was to ordain, were such as not only lived in the Spirit, and walked in the Spirit, in the exercise of the graces of the HOLY GHOST, he hath here enumerated; but *holding fast the faithful word, which he himself had been taught;* that *he might be able, by sound doctrine, both to exhort and convince gainsayers.* But how awfully doth the Apostle speak of *many unruly and vain talkers; whose mouths* (he saith) *must be stopped: and who teach things, which they ought not, for filthy lucre's sake.*

Reader! let us turn from the view, for it is most awful. Let us seek relief to our mind, from the painful contemplation in beholding, if but a moment, the beautiful account of *Paul's* own ministry. *Paul* stood amazed, at the grace shewn him, that the LORD should count him faithful, putting him into the ministry. And the constant sense he had of his own vileness; and the discoveries made to him, of the Person, glory, excellency, and riches of CHRIST and his grace tended to keep the Apostle always at the feet of JESUS, humbled, and self abased before him. And it was thus *Paul* went forth to the ministry, preaching CHRIST. It was CHRIST that *Paul* preached. CHRIST, as he is in himself; and CHRIST, as he is to his people. The plainest, the simplest language, and not excellency of human gifts, and human attainments, marked all his discourses. *Seeing then* (said he) *that we have such hope, we use great plainness of speech.* 2 Cor. iii. 12. Blessed be GOD for putting him into the ministry! Blessed be GOD for all the grace given to him, in this service. And blessed be GOD, for every instance both then, and now, and in all ages of the Church, where JESUS his Almighty Master, hath blessed his ministry, to the souls of his people!

12 One of themselves, *even* a prophet of their own, said, The Cretians *are* always liars, evil beasts, slow bellies.

13 This witness is true. Wherefore rebuke them sharply, that they may be sound in the faith.

14 Not giving heed to Jewish fables and commandments of men, that turn from the truth.

15 Unto the pure all things *are* pure: but unto them that are defiled and unbelieving *is* nothing pure; but even their mind and conscience is defiled.

16 They profess that they know God; but in works they deny *him*, being abominable and disobedient, and unto every good work reprobate.

The words of this first verse are a quotation from one of their Profane Writers; and the Apostle declares, that what is here said was correct. Lying is the common crime of all human nature. The scripture saith, *the wicked are estranged from the womb; they go astray, as soon as they be born, speaking lies.* Psm. lviii. 3. Reader! it is our mercy to know it: and in that knowledge, to be looking to JESUS, for deliverance from this, and every other evil of our fallen nature, in his righteousness; *who is the way, and the truth, and the life.* John xiv. 6. And while *Cretians,* or *Jews,* or all other carnal, and unregenerated men, are giving heed, to mere fables and commandments of men: seeking in outward things, acceptance with GOD; how blessed is it, to mark the vast difference, arising from inward and renewing grace, in the soul, making all things pure, where GOD hath purified the heart, through faith. Oh! the blessedness of being born again. It is this which makes the whole state blessed. A child of GOD, renewed of GOD, from the *Adam*-nature of the fall, is brought at once into a state of justification before GOD, and this regeneration makes the new creature alive, in the spiritual enjoyment of union with CHRIST. All things, pertaining to life, and godliness, are pure to him, in CHRIST. Whereas to the unregenerate, defiled as they are in the old nature of sin; there can be nothing pure. Their persons, and their prayers, their sacraments, and their offerings are all alike offensive; and can never find acceptance with GOD. For all are offered without an eye to CHRIST, and consequently sin. They may, and perhaps do, profess, as the Jews of old did, to know GOD. Yea, they may acknowledge, as many nominal Christians do, in creeds and prayer books, their belief in the Persons of the GODHEAD. But all this, is but a profession, void of saving knowledge. Where no work of grace hath passed upon the soul; there no real knowledge of GOD in CHRIST is found. And the close of this Chapter awfully states the case of some, wherefore they are in this unbelieving condition; *being,* saith the Apostle *abominable and disobedient, and unto every good work reprobate*; or void of judgment, (as the margin of the Bible renders it;) that is, without understanding. See Job xxviii. 28. compared with Isaiah xxvii. 11. and Jude 4. Reader! do not pass away from this scripture, without pondering over the distinguishing mercy. Oh! what a work of GOD is that, which by quickening from a death in trespasses and sins, brings the child of GOD into a new and spiritual life, to the knowledge of GOD the FATHER's love, the SAVIOUR's grace, and the SPIRIT's fellowship? What a work is wrought, when the child of GOD is new born? Reader! hath the LORD wrought it in your instance? Can you say with Paul: GOD *who is rich in mercy, for his great love, wherewith he loved us; even when we were dead in sins, hath quickened us together with* CHRIST? Ephes. ii. 4, 5.

REFLECTIONS.

I desire to bless GOD the HOLY GHOST, for all his abundant mercies in his divine teachings, and his holy scriptures of truth. And beg his grace, to give me a right understanding in all things, that my faith, may be the faith of GOD's elect. None but this, I am well assured, can come up to the standard of *the truth which is after godliness.* And whatsoever is not of this faith, is sin. Precious LORD JESUS! thou great Author, and finisher of faith, increase my faith!

And do thou, Almighty FATHER of mercies; confirm, and establish my soul, in this blessed hope of eternal life, founded in thine everlasting love; and secured in thine unchangeable promise, given in CHRIST JESUS before the world began. Oh! the preciousness of this life, which is eternal; confirmed by covenant engagements; revealed in the holy scriptures; and resulting from free, unmerited, unsought for, yea, unthought of grace!

Oh! LORD the SPIRIT! distinguish thine ordained servants in the ministry, by the special marks of thine own ordination. They, whom thou hast sent forth, will, through thy grace, be found blameless in CHRIST, as the stewards of GOD. But, LORD! stop the mouths of those, who run unsent of thee. The pure in spirit, by regenerating grace, will be pure. But to the unregenerate, who are still in the old unrenewed nature, nothing is pure. Praises to our GOD in CHRIST, for discriminating grace!

CHAP. II.

CONTENTS.

The Apostle is following up the same Directions to Titus, *in this Chapter, as the former. His Doctrine, and Commands to the Aged, and Youthful, and Servants, are dwelt upon. The Apostle, blessedly speaks, of the Grace of* GOD *in* CHRIST, *and the Design of its appearing.*

BUT speak thou the things which become sound doctrine:

2 That the aged men be sober, grave, temperate, sound in faith, in charity, in patience.

3 The aged women likewise, that *they be* in behaviour as becometh holiness, not false accusers, not given to much wine, teachers of good things;

4 That they may teach the young women to be sober, to love their husbands, to love their children,

5 *To be* discreet, chaste, keepers at home, good, obedient to their own husbands, that the word of God be not blasphemed.

6 Young men likewise exhort to be sober minded.

7 In all things shewing thyself a pattern of good works: in doctrine *shewing* uncorruptness, gravity, sincerity,

8 Sound speech, that cannot be condemned, that he that is of the contrary part may be ashamed, having no evil thing to say of you.

9 *Exhort* servants to be obedient unto their own masters, *and* to please *them* well in all *things;* not answering again;

10 Not purloining, but shewing all good fidelity: that they may adorn the doctrine of God our Saviour in all things.

I admire the Apostle's expression, when he calls the great, and distinguishing truths of the gospel, *sound:* meaning, what is firm to depend upon, in opposition to what is rotten, and deceitful. The doctrines of grace, by which *Paul* means, the electing love of God to his Church; redemption by CHRIST; justification by his blood, and righteousness; the regeneration of the HOLY GHOST; and the final perseverance of the saints. These are sound, solid, substantial truths; founded in the promise of GOD, who cannot lie; and such as GOD will have his people taught, and established in. For to this purpose, the LORD himself hath confirmed the whole, by word and oath. And at the time the LORD did it, he expressly said, that it was on this very account, because, *he was willing more abundantly to shew unto the heirs of promise, the immutability of his counsel.* Heb. vi. 17, 18. And can any man be so presumptuous as to suppose, that GOD hath appointed the means, and will not bless the end. Will any man daringly put forth his hand to touch the ark, as if GOD cannot without him, preserve it from falling? It is astonishing, what the proud presumptuous reasoning of the human heart is capable of producing on subjects of this nature. And hence, while the LORD declares, that he will have the heirs of promise comforted with the assurance of his unalterable purpose, and counsel; such men wish to guard, as they term it, the Gospel, lest the grace of God, which bringeth salvation, should lead to licentiousness. If those men would, or could, but attend to one single point of the Gospel, and make this the standard by which to ascertain their opinions, they might be modest enough to learn, that Christ himself hath formed the fence, which none can go over. Those five words of our Lord, puts an everlasting silence to all their presumptuous reasoning: *Ye must be born again.* John iii. 7. Every one that is born again (and it is to such only that *assurance is given*) hath in him the testimony of God the Father's electing love; Christ's redeeming grace, and the Holy Ghost's sovereign work upon their souls. And all that are thus born again, are infallibly secured from finally falling. And it is awful, in any one, to call it unscriptural, and highly dangerous, to question concerning such, their final perseverance, or to withold from them the Lord's assurance, when the Lord himself hath commanded concerning them saying; *Comfort ye, Comfort ye my people, saith your* God. *Speak ye comfortably to Jerusalem, and cry unto her: that her warfare is accomplished: that her iniquity is pardoned: for she hath received of the* Lord's *hand;* (and so she hath, in the Personal sufferings, and death of her Head, and Husband, and Surety,) *double for all her sins.* Isaiah xl. 1, 2. Reader! do you look to God the Spirit, for the testimonies and evidences, of the new-birth. And if through grace, you discern the precious marks, of the Lord the Spirit's regenerating work, upon your soul; listen to the same Almighty Teacher's own witness, to your sonship in God, and your redemption by Christ, against an host of self-righteous, and self-taught men! Rom. viii. 16, 17. 2 Cor. v. 5.

Let not the Reader overlook the very beautiful, and striking inferences which the Apostle raiseth, from the subject of *sound doctrine.* The aged men and women: the younger women, in their married state; and the young men; and servants also in families; all orders in social life, which are here commanded to be spoken to, by *Titus,* are *the sound in faith.* Let not the Reader overlook this: for this is the foundation, on which the Apostle grounds his exhortation. They are therefore the members of the Church; truly regenerated believers. It is to them, the precept is given, that they may all act, under the influence of the Spirit, which they have received, as becometh sound doctrine. *Paul* is not teaching *Titus* to expect those things from the unconverted. *Make the tree good,* (saith the Lord Jesus himself,) *and his fruit good.* Matt. xii. 33. But without the change of heart by the regenerating work of God the Holy Ghost: neither the aged, nor the young, can be sound in good works, not being sound in the faith. *Men do not gather grapes from thorns, nor figs from thistles.* And that *Paul* so meant, and so said, is evident, from what he observes will follow, lives of grace, manifested in lives of practice; that *the word of* God, (saith he,) *be not blasphemed;* and *that they of a contrary part,* (mark the expression,) *may be ashamed, having no evil thing to say of you.* By which, as plain as words can make it, the Apostle draws the line of distinction, between the Church of regenerated believers, and the contrary part of the ungodly and unawakened. All which plainly prove, that those scriptures are all along as *Paul* intended them designed for, *the saints of* God *and the faithful in* Christ Jesus. Ephes. i. 1. Chap. i. 4.

11 For the grace of God that bringeth salvation hath appeared to all men,

12 Teaching us that, denying ungodliness and worldly lusts, we should live soberly, righteously, and godly, in this present world;

13 Looking for that blessed hope, and the glorious appearing of the great God and our Saviour Jesus Christ;

14 Who gave himself for us, that he might redeem us from all iniquity, and purify unto himself a peculiar people, zealous of good works.

15 These things speak, and exhort, and rebuke with all authority. Let no man despise thee.

I beg the Reader's close attention to the whole paragraph. And I pray God the Spirit to be my Teacher. By *the grace of* God *which bringeth salvation*, is evidently meant the Gospel, which makes it known. And by its having appeared unto all men; can mean no more, than that now it is no longer hid as it was before the revelation by Jesus Christ. Ephes. iii. 5—11. But being now preached openly to both Jew and Gentile, the obvious tendency of it is, to make known salvation by Jesus Christ. And in this sense, it hath appeared unto all men, wheresoever the Gospel is preached; though the effects of it will be different, as the Gospel itself declares. But in no other sense, can it be said, to have appeared unto all men; for thousands, and tens of thousands, have never heard of the Gospel, nor ever will. Millions have died without the knowledge of it; as was designed they should. And multitudes, to whom the outward ministry of the word hath been delivered, have never felt or known, the inward saving power. Hence, when the Lord Jesus Christ himself was the Preacher, what troops of hearers turned from him, with the most fastidious indifferency, and even contempt. *Chorazin*, and *Bethsaida* and *Capernaum* in this sense, were exalted to heaven, it might be said, by reason of their gospel privileges. But they were cast down to hell, by reason of their despising them. Matt. xi. 20—24.

It is curious to behold, in the present day, the great concern which some men seemingly profess, for the salvation of others; who never felt any real concern for their own. And it is among the signs of the times, that multitudes are engaged in societies as all eager to send the Bible abroad, to be read by all the world, who never, in numberless instances, read it themselves. But where is the path of duty, and the consolation by grace to the truly regenerated child of God? Surely it is written, as with a sun-beam. To wait like the Prophet, on his watch-tower, the leadings of the Lord. Habak. ii. 1, 4. Where Jesus leads, there follow. Where the Lord, and not man, opens the door, there enter. In the mean time, *to stand still, and see the salvation of the* Lord. Exod. xiv. 13. Isaiah xxx. 7. The cause of Christ is of no doubtful issue. His Church must stand. His cause must prosper, Not one of his little ones hath perished in all the dark ages which are past. Not one shall perish in all that is to come. This sweet and consoling promise of the Lord, brings up after it, all that is necessary: *All that the* Father *giveth me, shall come to me. And of all which he hath given me, I should lose nothing, but should raise it up at the last day.* John vi. 37—40.

But while these grand events are made everlastingly sure, and certain, by Covenant-settlements; (2 Sam. i. 2, 3, 5. and the grace of God, which bringeth salvation, hath appeared for the accomplishment of them; the Holy Ghost hath very blessedly added in this sweet scripture, *that it teacheth us,* (that is, the regenerated Church,) *that denying ungodliness, and worldly lusts, we should live soberly, righteously, and godly, in this present world.* Reader! do mark the loveliness and force of the words here used. That it is *the us,* who are truly, and savingly called by grace, which are thus expected to live, is obvious to the plainest sense. For we know, by woeful experience, in the awful crimes going on daily in this nation of professing christianity, and the sad instances of capital punishments which continually follow; that no teaching of the Gospel, no, nor all the threatened punishment to disobedience, can give the least bias to the carnal, and ungodly, to restrain from evil, and to compel to good. Grace only can accomplish this purpose. Some that have the privilege of hearing of this grace of God, which bringeth salvation, and hath appeared to them in the outward ministry of the word; only manifest a greater bitterness of heart against it, by awakening, and calling forth their greater enmity against God and his Christ. And *others,* when they hear of the restraints of the Gospel, to deny ungodliness, and worldly lusts, only feel their corrupt passions the stronger, as dropsical persons thirst the more, because the very nature of their disorder is to drink. And, it is among the plainest truths of our most holy faith, that as without the new birth in regeneration, not one of the fallen race of *Adam,* hath the least tendency to any real act of good; so, by this quickening principle from the Spirit of holiness alone, is imparted the desire, both of *denying ungodliness, and worldly lusts; and of living soberly, righteously, and godly, in this present world.* And, as this is a point of such immense consequence; and the Apostle hath also in this same sweet scripture, added to what is here said, a further testimony concerning it, in that he tells us, Christ *gave himself for us, that he might redeem us from all iniquity; and purify to himself a peculiar people zealous of good works* I would crave my Reader's indulgence, to dwell a little longer on the interesting subject.

I stay not to remark, the nature of that claim, which Christ hath upon his redeemed, by virtue of his having bought them out of the hands of justice, by his blood. This, though a most blessed consideration, would lead rather to another subject. Here it might be shewn, that, according to all the principles of law and equity, what a man redeems is his own; and what he buys, is his property. And CHRIST, having bought his Church with his blood, might justly make her his servant for ever. But I am not now taking up the subject in that point of view. I am simply considering, how the blessed consequences are induced, whereby the redeemed, and regenerated Church, is both *taught*, and by grace is *made*, this peculiar people, CHRIST, and not they, hath *purified* unto himself; whereby they do become *zealous of good works, and deny all ungodliness and worldly lusts, and live soberly, righteously, and godly, in this present world.*

In confirmation of these precious things, I beg the Reader to observe, *first;* that by the original, and eternal purposes of GOD in election, this was one great point, when GOD chose the Church in CHRIST, that the whole body should *be holy and without blame before him in love.* Ephes. i. 4. And hence, by this will and act of GOD, the Church, when *quickened,* which was before in the Adam-nature of the fall, *dead in trespasses and sins,* is said *to be created in* CHRIST JESUS *unto good works, which* GOD *had before ordained that the Church should walk in them.* Ephes. ii. 1—10. I beg that this may be marked down, in the memorandum of the Reader's mind, in characters strongly impressed, suited to its importance. Oh! LORD the SPIRIT! well knowing the treachery of my poor, forgetful heart; do thou write the blessed truth therein with thine own living principles of grace.

Secondly. It is said among the Covenant-promises of the FATHER to the SON: *Thy people shall be willing in the day of thy power.* Psm. cx. 3. Hence, in that blessed day, when the LORD calls the poor sinner from darkness to light, and from the power of *Satan* to the living GOD; there is a willingness imparted, to follow the Lamb, whithersoever he goeth. They are then made volunteers, in the service of GOD; and, amidst all the corruption of the flesh, with their spirit they serve the law of GOD. Hence *David* cried out, under the feeling sense he had of quickening mercies: *I will run the way of thy commandments, when thou hast enlarged my heart.* Psm. cxix. 32.

Thirdly. A willingness, without ability, would not be sufficient; and the LORD doth not leave his purposes to a peradventure. And, moreover, his people are here said to be a peculiar people, not merely *willing,* but *zealous* of good works. Here, therefore, comes in, to our joy and comfort, what this scripture so blessedly adds; that when CHRIST redeemed his Church from all iniquity, it was to *purify* her unto himself. Hence, therefore, it will follow, that while the LORD wills his people to this zeal for good works, he imparts also an ability at the same time, to perform them. It were much to be wished, that those who are so fond of exhorting the world, to what the world hath no power to do; would turn their attention, to what the scripture declares, of the LORD's people, they are enabled through grace to do. Such derive from CHRIST all the power they have, and by which they are enabled to perform what is enjoined them. Hence that beautiful scripture: *Work out your own salvation with fear and trembling. For it is* GOD *which worketh in you, both to will, and to do, of his good pleasure.* Philip. ii. 12, 13. Reader! ponder well these things. Behold how the LORD hath made provision, that the good works he hath created his people *to*, he hath ordained and given ability to walk *in*. His willings, are enablings. With the precept, there is accompanied the promise; and with the teaching to deny ungodliness, and to walk godly, there is a power imparted, to the restraining from the *one*, and to the performance of the *other*.

One word more on this very blessed paragraph. The Apostle saith, that the Church, in the daily exercise of godliness, is to be *looking for that blessed hope, and the glorious appearing of the great* GOD *and our* SAVIOR JESUS CHRIST: or, as it might have been rendered, the great GOD, *even* our SAVIOR JESUS CHRIST. For I must take the freedom to say, that it is the LORD JESUS CHRIST, and He only, who is here spoken of. And this appears very evident for several reasons. *First.* The Greek article, which is placed before the words *great* GOD, is not used again before the words our SAVIOR JESUS CHRIST, as is usually done, except when meaning one and the same Person; and therefore, the omission in the latter part, implies, that it is exegetical of the first. *Secondly.* The Greek article here rendered *and*, before our SAVIOR, is, in many places in the New Testament, translated *even*. See Rom. xv. 6. 2 Cor. i. 3. 2 Cor. xi. 31. Philip. iv. 20. 2 Thess. ii. 16. 1 Pet. i. 3, &c. *Thirdly.* The *appearing* which is here spoken of, uniformly means CHRIST, through all the scripture. We are taught to expect CHRIST to appear, but never is it said of the FATHER. Coloss. i. 27. 1 Thess. v. 16. 2 Thess. i. 10. *Fourthly.* It is one of the peculiar characters of CHRIST our SAVIOR. But never under the article of redemption, do we find the Person of the FATHER, or of the HOLY GHOST, so spoken of. From all these causes there cannot be a doubt, but that it is the Person of CHRIST for whom the Church is said to look. Reader! ask your own heart then, who less than GOD can be so described?

Concerning this appearing of CHRIST, and the hope and expectation of his coming, which the Church is said to be looking for, I beg the Reader to remark with me, one or two striking particularities. *First.* It is spoken of, as a *blessed hope*, and a *glorious appearing* to the Church, who are described, as looking for it with delight, in a life of faith and holy conversation. A plain proof, that the Church is considered, as in a justified state before GOD. For it could never be called a *blessed* hope, if there were any doubts remaining, in what state the child of GOD would be then found. If any sin should then remain on the conscience, unwashed by the blood of CHRIST, the hope, and expectation of CHRIST's coming, could not be called *blessed*. Many there are, that under the garb of a supposed humility, suppose it somewhat presumptuous to talk with certainty, on this infinitely momentous point. But this is more an affected humility, than real. It is no more than faith warrants to every child of GOD, *to believe the record which* GOD *hath given of his dear* SON. And *he that hath the* SON, it is said, *hath life.* 1 John v. 10, 11. He hath it now, by faith, as much in reality, as the Church in heaven, hath by sight. And, therefore, to a child of GOD, regenerated by the HOLY GHOST, and justified by the blood, and righteousness of CHRIST; he is as really, and truly saved now by CHRIST, as the Church is in heaven.

Secondly. The Church is said to be looking for Christ's appearing, with a blessed hope of expectation, as if bringing into present enjoyment by faith, that glory which will then be realized to their possession; and thus embracing by anticipation, their inheritance, which nothing but their minority of being, now prevents them from entering upon. And this becomes an absolute confirmation, of the final perseverance of the saints. It was this assurance made *Paul* call it blessed. And *Peter* no less speaks as of not only looking for it, but *hasting unto the coming of it.* 2 Pet. iii. 12. Both which were impossible, if the shadow of a doubt remained on the mind, as to the final issue of the great event.

I only detain the Reader just to remark, how the Apostle enforceth on the mind of *Titus,* in the close of this Chapter, his dwelling on these things, in his preaching among the people. These sound doctrines of grace and salvation, founded, and secured in the everlasting love of God, and the redemption by the Lord Jesus Christ, confirming the faith of the saints, and their eternal safety in Christ: these, (saith he,) boldly, firmly, and faithfully, do thou speak, and exhort. And, if any dare oppose, rebuke all such with all authority, that none may despise thee, as if ignorant of these great truths; or for thy keeping them back. Reader! who can disprove what God the Spirit teacheth! Who shall presume to question the hope of the faithful in Christ Jesus, which God the Holy Ghost calleth blessed?

REFLECTIONS.

Reader! is there not renewed occasion, at the close of this, and every Chapter, for all the marked attention, God the Holy Ghost hath shewn the Church, in watching over the interests, and happiness of his people, that both *young men and maidens, old men and children, may praise the name of the* Lord: *for his name only is excellent, and his praise above heaven and earth?* And what a lovely family of the Lord's would it be, if all were sound in doctrine, sound in faith; and *all adorning the doctrine of* God *our* Savior *in all things!*

Blessed be the Father, Son, and Spirit, that the grace of God that bringeth salvation, hath appeared. And blessed be the Lord, that He hath both taught his Church, and given her members ability, by a life of faith, upon the Son of God, to deny all ungodliness, and worldly lusts; to put off the old man, which is corrupt; and to put on the new man, which, after God, is created in righteousness, and true holiness. Oh! for grace, to be always on the look out, for that blessed hope, and the glorious appearing of Jesus. Lord! we groan being burthened, under the weaknesses, and unworthinesses of our vile body. Haste, haste my Beloved, and bring on that blessed day, when *thou wilt change our vile bodies, and fashion them like unto thy glorious body, according to the mighty working, whereby thou art able even to subdue all things unto thyself.*

CHAP. III.

CONTENTS.

The Chapter opens with a Continuation of Exhortations. The Apostle blessedly speaks of the Doctrine of Regeneration. He closeth the Epistle with Directions, and his Apostolical Benediction.

PUT them in mind to be subject to principalities and powers, to obey magistrates, to be ready to every good work.

2 To speak evil of no man, to be no brawlers, *but* gentle, shewing all meekness unto all men.

3 For we ourselves also were sometimes foolish, disobedient, deceived, serving divers lusts and pleasures, living in malice and envy, hateful, *and* hating one another.

We cannot sufficiently admire, the very happy method the Apostle adopted, to conciliate the minds of the people to the observance of those civil obligations he here recommended, in shewing, in his own instance, as well as in all others, how unavoidably disposed a state of unrenewed nature is, to every thing that is evil. What an humble representation *Paul* hath here made of himself, and all mankind, considered only in the state of original corruption. Reader! it is always blessed, to have it in remembrance. Nothing, under the teachings of GOD the SPIRIT, can be more profitable. It tends to lower all pharisaical pride, which might creep into the heart. It tends, through grace, to keep the soul humble in the dust before GOD. It keeps open a stream of true godly sorrow, in the consciousness of our first nothingness, and continued undeservings. And, what is preferable to all, it doth endear the Person, and work, and relations, and offices of CHRIST, to the soul; and thereby sweetly enforceth our need of JESUS, and our everlasting dependance upon him, and his blood and righteousness, more and more. Oh! thou dear LORD! how very precious, yea, increasingly precious, art thou to my soul, when I look back, and contemplate the awful state of that foolish, disobedient, unrenewed nature, in which I was born; the many years I continued in it, serving divers lusts and pleasures, living in malice and envy, hateful and hating; and the remains of indwelling corruption, even to this hour, which marks the body of sin, I carry about with me! Oh! the blessedness of knowing it; and the distinguishing mercy of so knowing it, as to loath myself for my own deformity, that I may be looking only to JESUS for holiness and salvation.

4 But after that the kindness and love of God our Saviour toward man appeared,

5 Not by works of righteousness which we have

done, but according to his mercy he saved us, by the washing of regeneration, and renewing of the Holy Ghost;

6 Which he shed on us abundantly through Jesus Christ our Saviour;

7 That being justified by his grace, we should be made heirs according to the hope of eternal life

8 *This is* a faithful saying, and these things will that thou affirm constantly, that they which have believed in God might be careful to maintain good works. These things are good and profitable unto men.

I beg the Reader to make a full pause over the wonderful relation given of the divine mercy, in the sovereign act of grace, here ascribed to the personal agency of GOD the HOLY GHOST. And I beg of him to ponder it yet more, as being the first act which is wrought openly upon the child of GOD in a life of grace, which calls him forth into a spiritual apprehension of things, to know his election, and adoption character; his being in CHRIST, and his interest from CHRIST, to all the privileges of a child of GOD, and an heir of the kingdom. Before this act of regeneration is wrought, though chosen in CHRIST and being one with CHRIST, in an everlasting Covenant, *ordered in all things and sure;* the child of GOD, like the child in nature, born to a great inheritance, hath no consciousness of it. But when the hour is come, and the washing of regeneration takes place; the new born heir of the inheritance, which is incorruptible, undefiled, and that fadeth not away, is brought forth, to a spiritual, and eternal life in CHRIST, which can die no more. I must compress a great deal within a small compass, and, therefore, shall only mark down, one by one, a few of the more prominent features, of those acts of mercy.

And, *first:* let the Reader notice with me, what the Apostle saith in the introduction of the subject. It was *after, that the kindness and love of* GOD our SAVIOR *toward man appeared*. By which, perhaps, is meant, that not only after GOD the FATHER's everlasting love, in the original choice of the Church in CHRIST, had taken place; but also, after the love of GOD our SAVIOR, in coming, during the time-state of the Church, to redeem his Church from the ruin of the fall, had been accomplished, GOD the SPIRIT came to accomplish his Almighty purpose of grace no less; and by that act of regeneration, brought the child of GOD into an ability of enjoying the vast privileges of GOD the FATHER's electing love, and GOD the SON's redeeming mercy.

Secondly. Let the Reader also observe, how the Apostle traceth the mercy to its own original source. *Not by works of righteousness which we have done*. No! it would cease to have been grace, had any merit, on the part of the creature, been taken into the account

But so far is this from being the case, that the scripture uniformly, in every part, makes it appear, that, *as it was when we were without strength, in due time* CHRIST *died for the ungodly:* Rom. v. 6. so it was when *we were dead in trespasses and sins;* the HOLY GHOST quickened the Church, into a new and spiritual life. Ephes. ii. 1.

Thirdly. Let the Reader duly consider no less, the cause for which GOD the HOLY GHOST accomplisheth this sovereign act of his, in every instance; namely, as He saith himself, by the Apostle: *Because ye are sons,* GOD *hath sent forth the* SPIRIT *of his* SON *into your hearts, crying Abba* FATHER! Gal. iv. 6. Because ye are sons. It is not that this act of GOD the HOLY GHOST, may make them so; for sons they were before, though sinful sons. But because *ye are sons,* GOD the HOLY GHOST stands engaged, in Covenant engagements, to recover every individual child of GOD, whom GOD the FATHER hath given to his SON, and whom he hath predestinated to the adoption of children by JESUS CHRIST to himself; and whose redemption, GOD the SON hath purchased by his blood; GOD the HOLY GHOST hath undertaken, and will perform it in every instance, to quicken into spiritual life, from the death of sin, in the Adam-nature fall, and make *willing in the day of his power.* See those scriptures Ephes. i. 4, 5. Coloss. i. 14—22. Isaiah xliv. 3, 4, 5. Ezek. xxxvii. 11—14. I have dwelt the more particularly on this sweet feature of our holy faith, (for it is both sweet, and precious,) that the Reader may be in no danger, (if it so pleaseth the LORD,) of being led away by the ill-judged, and mistaken expressions of some, who, from being ignorant of the electing, and predestinating love of GOD's adoption of his children by CHRIST before all worlds, have called them heirs of hell, and children of the devil, when before conversion. But, blessed be GOD! they never were in the least related to such a stock, even in their worst days, when doing the work of Satan, and wearing his livery. They were always, and from everlasting, GOD's children; though long rebellious children. See Gal. iv. 6. and Ephes. ii. 3. with Commentary, both places. Isaiah xxx. 1.

Fourthly. The regeneration of the child of GOD, is of such vast importance, in the principles of our holy faith, that before it is wrought, we have no proper apprehension of any one saving mercy. So that, it is this immense act of grace, (than which an equally great one can never more, even in heaven itself, be done,) which brings the soul into life and light, *and joy and peace in believing, abounding in hope through the power of the* HOLY GHOST. Rom. xv. 13. From this blessed day, the spirit hath witnessing from the SPIRIT, of our adoption character. Rom. viii. 16. Justification also, which is an act of GOD, conceived in the eternal purpose of GOD from all eternity, and by which the persons of his elect are accepted in CHRIST, as justified freely by his blood and righteousness; this immense mercy also is in the right of enjoyment at regeneration. And, as the Apostle here speaks, being justified by his grace, they are made heirs according to the hope of eternal life; all these blessings begin to open upon the soul: neither can they ever after close, but extend more and more to the view, under divine teaching, by the HOLY GHOST. Well, therefore, might the Apostle run up all these things, to the fountain head in regeneration; and seeing such blessedness pours in therefrom upon the human state, charge *Titus* to affirm these things constantly, as a faithful saying; and enjoin all that believe in God, from a work of regeneration having passed upon their spirit, to be careful to maintain good works, which are the gracious fruits, and effects, through divine influences, which must result therefrom. Reader! what saith the experience of your heart, in correspondence to these precious things?

9 But avoid foolish questions, and genealogies, and contentions, and strivings about the law; for they are unprofitable and vain.

10 A man that is an heretick after the first and second admonition reject;

11 Knowing that he that is such is subverted, and sinneth, being condemned of himself.

Among the antient Philosophers there were many foolish questions continually discussed in the schools; and the Jews were not a little addicted to the same. 2 Timothy ii. 23. And what *Paul* saith of heresies, holds good in all ages. It may be proper for a child of God, in the presence of heretics, to give his testimony *to the truth as it is in* Jesus. But the Holy Ghost hath here decidedly said, that after the first, and second admonition, he is no longer to talk with him, but reject him. And the Lord hath in many other parts of his sacred word, commanded the faithful to separate themselves from such communion, and to have no fellowship with them. 2 Cor. vi. 14 to the end. Ephes. v. ix. Rev. xviii. 4. I may be singular for aught I know; but in the present awful day, marked as it specially is by the Holy Ghost, as a day of rebuke, and blasphemy; (1 Tim. iv. 1, 2. 2 Pet. ii. 1, 2, 3, &c.) I cannot see upon what plausible pretences, true believers in Christ can mingle up in society with unbelievers, who scorn the principal doctrines of our holy faith. It was never known in the history of mankind, that while one nation is at war with another nation, the subjects of each met in friendship together; or their garrisons, and harbors, were open to one another. And wherefore should it be less high treason to the Majesty of Heaven, or one that professeth himself to be a faithful subject of Christ's kingdom, and believeth in all the glorious doctrines of grace, to sit down, and join hand in hand, under the idea of extending Christian knowledge, with those who deny the Godhead of Christ; the doctrine of the Three Holy Persons in the Godhead, and all the precious truths, which are the alone glory of the Christian faith?

12 When I shall send Artemas unto thee, or Tychicus, be diligent to come unto me to Nicopolis: for I have determined there to winter.

13 Bring Zenas the lawyer and Apollos on their journey diligently, that nothing be wanting unto them.

14 And let our's also learn to maintain good works for necessary uses, that they be not unfruitful.

15 All that are with me salute thee. Greet them that love us in the faith. Grace *be* with you all. Amen.

It was written to Titus, ordained the first bishop of the church of the Cretians, from Nicopolis of Macedonia.

I have nothing to offer on what is here said of those Persons. All of them, have passed away long since, in their generation. And both the Writer and Reader of this *Poor Man's Commentary* are hastening fast after them. *Greet them*, saith *Paul, that love us in the faith.* So say I. *Grace be with them all, Amen!*

REFLECTIONS.

READER! I would pass by all observations on men and things, while reading this sweet scripture, and beg for grace to have all my thoughts directed to that one, glorious contemplation, brought before the Church in this Chapter, namely, the kindness and love of GOD the FATHER toward man, in his original, and eternal purpose, concerning the Church in CHRIST; JESUS's mercy, in betrothing, and redeeming his Church; and GOD the SPIRIT, pouring out his regenerating, and renewing grace, which he hath shed abundantly on the Church, and is for ever shedding, on all the members of the body, through JESUS CHRIST our SAVIOR. Oh! the unspeakable felicity of being justified by the LORD's grace, and made heirs according to the hope of eternal life!

Blessed SPIRIT of all Truth! praises to thine Almighty name, for this precious portion of thine inspired scripture, through the ministry of thy servant *Paul*. The memory of all the *Paul's*, and *Titus's*, which GOD the HOLY GHOST hath raised up as servants in his Church, is precious; and thy faithful, desire grace to bless the LORD for their labors of love. But, oh! thou HOLY LORD the Comforter! what praise shall we offer thee, for thine Almighty Ministry, in the glorifying our dear Redeemer, the LORD JESUS CHRIST? Glory, praise, and power, be unto our Covenant GOD in CHRIST, FATHER, SON, and HOLY GHOST, now, and ever. Amen.

THE EPISTLE OF PAUL THE APOSTLE TO PHILEMON.

GENERAL OBSERVATIONS.

THIS short, but lovely Epistle, must have been written while *Paul* was a prisoner at *Rome:* and at that time when he had liberty to receive in his own hired house, all that came to him. Acts xxviii. 30. This seems evident, because *Onesimus*, on whose account the Apostle wrote to *Philemon*, then attended *Paul's* preaching, and the LORD blessed the word to him. Hence the probable date, was Anno 60; though some place it later.

The design of this letter seems to have been, to reconcile *Philemon* to his runaway servant, *Onesimus.* The outlines of the subject is in the Epistle. It will not be necessary, therefore, in this place to enlarge upon it. As the HOLY GHOST hath classed it among the writings of his inspiration, it will be proper to enter upon the perusal of it in prayer. May the LORD bless it to the glory of GOD, in our edification, through JESUS CHRIST.

THE EPISTLE TO PHILEMON.

CONTENTS.

The Apostle very affectionately addresseth Philemon, *on the Subject of his receiving back his Servant* Onesimus, *and forgiving him all Wrongs. He opens his Epistle, with his usual Salutation, of Grace, and Peace; and closeth with the same.*

PAUL, a prisoner of Jesus Christ, and Timothy *our* brother, unto Philemon our dearly beloved, and fellow labourer.

2 And to *our* beloved Apphia, and Archippus our fellow-soldier, and to the church in thy house:

3 Grace to you, and peace, from God our Father and the Lord Jesus Christ.

We never can sufficiently admire the uniformity in *Paul's* writings, in his entrance on all, how grace was always uppermost in his heart. It is a blessed testimony our LORD himself hath laid down, of what is the ruling principle within: *when out of the abundance of the heart the mouth speaketh.* Luke vi. 45. And the Apostle appears to be speaking forth his very soul, whenever the Name of his LORD is in his discourse. And it is worth noticing, though of very inferior consideration to what hath been just said, that as *Paul* was attempting by this letter, to conciliate the affections of *Philemon*, towards *Onesimus*, he joins in his address his beloved *Timothy*, as probably well known to *Philemon*; and includes the beloved *Apphia*, and *Archippus*, among the addressed: the *former* it should seem to have been the wife, or sister of *Philemon*, and the *latter* the minister of the Church to which *Philemon* belonged. See Coloss. iv. 17. and the two lines after the 18th verse. I have just glanced at these things, before we enter upon the subject of *Paul's* letter, as proper not to be overlooked. And would now beg the Reader's attention to the Epistle itself, than which, in whatever way or manner it be considered, nothing can be found, among all the records of antiquity, of a more beautiful, and highly finished composition. If it were not where it is, folded up in the sacred pages of divine truths, it would be classed among the first productions of mankind, be carefully deposited in every museum of literature, and recommended by all the admirers of the fine arts, as the most correct standard of letter writing. But while this view of the Epistle, upon these grounds, becomes matter of reproach to those who despise, or overlook its beauties, merely because it is scripture; this is not the cause for which the child of GOD chiefly prizeth it. The best recommendation in it is, that it is the word of GOD. And the beautiful feature which endears it to the affection, is the grace it holds forth to the Church, as exemplified in the LORD's mercy to *Onesimus*. We shall form discoveries of this, as we prosecute the Epistle.

4 I thank my God, making mention of thee always in my prayers.

5 Hearing of thy love and faith, which thou hast toward the Lord Jesus, and toward all saints;

6 That the communication of thy faith may become effectual by the acknowledging of every good thing, which is in you in Christ Jesus.

7 For we have great joy and consolation in thy love, because the bowels of the saints are refreshed by thee, brother.

It is a blessed thing, when we find errands to the mercy-seat in blessing GOD, for grace shewn to his people and it should seem, that *Paul* found frequent cause to go there, for the LORD's blessing on his ministry. The Apostle hath given a very honorable testimony to the character of *Philemon*. But let the Reader observe, to whom *Paul* gives all the glory. Every good thing in *Philemon* is ascribed wholly to the Lord Jesus. And though *Paul* was now writing to this man on a subject of favor, he would not compliment him at the expence of truth, and in the fashion of modern times, extol the creature, and bolster him up in fancied worth, when both his ability to refresh the bowels of the saints, and an heart to do it, were from the Lord. Oh! how much to be wished it were, that such faithfulness was in all ministers, and people, professing godliness. What volumes, on the contrary, have been printed and published, of thanks to men, where no mention hath been made of God!

8 Wherefore, though I might be much bold in Christ, to enjoin thee that which is convenient.

9 Yet for love's sake I rather beseech *thee*, being such an one as Paul the aged, and now also a prisoner of Jesus Christ.

10 I beseech thee for my son Onesimus, whom I have begotten in my bonds:

11 Which in time past was to thee unprofitable, but now profitable to thee and to me:

12 Whom I have sent again: thou therefore receive him, that is, mine own bowels:

13 Whom I would have retained with me, that in thy stead he might have ministered unto me in the bonds of the gospel:

14 But without thy mind would I do nothing; that thy benefit should not be as it were of necessity, but willingly.

15 For perhaps he therefore departed for a season, that thou shouldest receive him for ever.

16 Not now as a servant, but above a servant, a brother beloved, specially to me, but how much more unto thee, both in the flesh, and in the Lord?

17 If thou count me therefore a partner, receive him as myself.

18 If he hath wronged thee, or oweth *thee* ought, put that on mine account;

19 I Paul have written *it* with mine own hand, I will repay *it:* albeit I do not say to thee how thou owest unto me even thine own self besides.

PHILEMON. 199

20 Yea, brother, let me have joy of thee in the Lord; refresh my bowels in the Lord.

The Apostle now enters upon the principal subject of his Epistle, and for which he wrote. And, if we gather into one point of view, the several parts of his letter, it should seem, (though we have no certain history to determine it by,) that this *Onesimus* had ran away from his master; and, it is probable, had robbed him. Fleeing to *Rome*, he had there been brought under the ministry of the Apostle. And it should seem likely also, that the LORD had done by him as the LORD did by *Lydia*, *had opened his heart to attend to the things which were spoken of Paul.* Acts xvi. 14. After the LORD had wrought this work of grace upon the mind of *Onesimus*, Paul sent him back to his master, with this letter of recommendation; and in this most engaging manner, sought to influence the mind of *Philemon*, not barely to forgive him, but to rejoice over his conversion, and receive him as a brother in CHRIST. And, it is well worthy the Reader's observation, how striking the arguments, *Paul* adopted, to prevail upon the affections of *Philemon*.

First. He observes, that if the Apostle rejoiced in his recovery by grace, to whom *Onesimus* was a stranger, *how much more* (saith he) *unto thee, both in the flesh, and in the* LORD. Masters are secondary parents, a kind of foster-fathers. And believing masters exercise a spiritual guardianship over their household. And to have servants who are brethren in the LORD, not only secures their fidelity, but their affection; and opens to a better alliance of nearness, and dearness, which is to last for ever.

Secondly. Paul toucheth another string of melody, when he saith: *if thou count me a partner, receive him as myself.* This riseth yet higher, though on the same scale. For this considers CHRIST and his members as one. And, therefore, *Paul*, and *Philemon*, and *Onesimus*, being in grace, are all partners in all that belongs to CHRIST JESUS.

Thirdly. The Apostle adds another very forcible argument namely, that if *Onesimus* had wronged *Philemon*, or owed him aught, he would be answerable for it. Though in saying this *Paul* insinuated, that so much on spiritual considerations *Philemon* was indebted to him, that even himself he owed to him. Hence, *Paul* assumed for granted, that *Philemon* would refresh his bowels, in complying with his wishes, and even doing more than he asked. Who, but must admire the affection and wisdom of the Apostle, in this beautiful Epistle, endited as it evidently was, by the HOLY GHOST.

But when the Reader hath paid all due attention to the subject, as it relates to those several parties; I would ask, is there not an instruction arising out of it, which opens to a subject yet more profitable, both to the Writer, and the Reader of this *Poor Man's Commentary?* When a poor long lost sinner is recovered by sovereign grace, from all his departures from the LORD, in the Adam-nature of sin, by which from the first in original apostacy, we have all run away from GOD; how blessed, when brought back, and discovered to be a brother beloved, especially to all his spiritual relations, who then find their double relation to him both in the flesh by nature, and in the LORD by spirit? Surely, whoever by his own regeneration, knows his partnership in CHRIST's mystical body, must receive such an one, as one in the Lord. And whatever wrongs may have been done, before the work of grace was wrought; conscious of mutual corruption by nature, and by practice; how unanswerable the argument, to mutual forgiveness? Yea, as we have all sinned, and have all wronged, and come short of the glory of God; oh! how sweet, that all is put to Jesus's account, and who hath been, and is, the Surety, and Sponsor of all his people. Precious Jesus! who, that in this view of thy paying our debt of ten thousand talents; can go forth against a brother for his hundred pence. Here, dearest Lord, as in all things, thou shalt have the pre-eminency!

21 Having confidence in thy obedience I wrote unto thee, knowing that thou wilt also do more then I say.

22 But withal prepare me also a lodging: for I trust that through your prayers I shall be given unto you.

23 There salute thee Epaphras, my fellow-prisoner in Christ Jesus;

24 Marcus, Aristarchus, Demas, Lucas, my fellow-labourers.

25 The grace of our Lord Jesus Christ *be* with your spirit. Amen.

Written from Rome to Philemon, by Onesimus a servant.

I do not think it needful to detain the Reader, on what is contained in these verses. They serve to express the love, and attachment of the saints, to each other, in the first ages of the Gospel. The Lord grant, if it be his blessed will, that the latter day dispensation, may be so distinguished!

REFLECTIONS.

Reader! do not fail to observe in this short Epistle, short as it is, the wonderful ways and works of God. In the family of *Philemon*, under all the means of grace, the heart of *Onesimus* remains hardened! But after his departure and unfaithfulness to his Master, the grace of God meets him elsewhere, and the Lord changeth the heart of stone into an heart of flesh. And who of God's redeemed Ones, but can say the same? Blessed Jesus, thou art the Brother born for adversity. Do, thou, Lord receive all thine as those for whom thou hast answered! Praised be a Covenant God in Christ for all his mercies. Amen.

THE EPISTLE OF PAUL THE APOSTLE

TO THE

HEBREWS.

GENERAL OBSERVATIONS.

I WOULD seek grace from God the Holy Ghost, the Almighty Author of this blessed portion of his holy word, to enter upon the perusal of it, with the most earnest prayer, and praise; and with the most profound humility and joy. No part of the word of God hath in it more blessed views of the glory of Christ's Person, and Godhead, and Offices, and Character. And none, which more blessedly brings him home to the affections of his people, under all the endearments of union and interest, as the Lord our Righteousness. Oh! that God the Holy Ghost may glorify Him, to his Church's apprehension, under all; and form him, in every heart of his redeemed, *the hope of glory.*

There have been doubts, in the minds of some, whether the Apostle *Paul* was, or was not, the Pen-man, God the Spirit made use of, for writing this Epistle. But none of the faithful taught of God, ever doubted, that the Epistle itself, was the immediate work of divine inspiration. Indeed every age of the Church, hath furnished witnesses for God, in confirmation of its divine authority. The seal of the Spirit, in the heart, to the truths of God, written there, becomes an infallible testimony. Hence the royal Psalmist exclaimed; *I shall never forget thy word, for by it thou hast quickened me.* Psm. cxix. 93. And whoever reads the book of the Hebrews, with an enlightened eye, under the leadings of God the Holy Ghost, the Almighty Author of it, will not fail to discover, that the Apostle *Paul*, is evidently the inspired Pen-man of it. What he saith of *Timothy*, in the last Chapter, verse 23, when it be considered, that *Paul* wrote it from *Rome*, and the probable date of it also, Anno 63 or 64; form a correspondence, to the Apostle's then imprisonment. And yet more decisive is *Peter's* testimony. For *Peter's* Epistle was written to the strangers, (that is, the ten tribes of the *Jews* or *Hebrews*,) scattered at that time, throughout the lower *Asia.* 1 Pet. i. 1. In this Epistle *Peter* refers to this book of the *Hebrews*, when he saith to them, *our beloved brother Paul also, according to the wisdom given unto him, hath written unto you.* 2 Pet. iii. 15. Now no part of *Paul's* writings but this Epistle, was written to the *Jews.* All his other Epistles were to the *Gentile* Churches, and to particular persons, as *Timothy, Titus,* and *Philemon.* And this also explains the cause, wherefore the Apostle did not begin this Epistle to the Hebrews with his usual salutation.

I do not think it necessary in this place, to enter into a large, and circumstantial account, of the Contents of this blessed Epistle. All the interesting particulars, will meet us in their proper place. It will be sufficient here to observe, that the one, great, and leading design, of the whole is, to exalt the LORD JESUS CHRIST. Hence his Person, as GOD, and as GOD-Man; his offices, characters, relations; his royal, prophetical, and priestly offices; are most blessedly set forth. And what is worthy of most especial notice is, that the human nature of CHRIST, is displayed in so dear, and interesting a light; and the precious consequences resulting from it to his people, so enlarged upon, and recommended to their tenderest regard; as is not perhaps so fully inculcated in any other of the Apostle's writings. So that upon the whole, the Epistle to the *Hebrews* is a most blessed part of the divine word: and for which the Church of the faithful, can never be sufficiently thankful to GOD the HOLY GHOST. I will no longer detain the Reader, from entering upon its perusal, than only first to look up with prayer, to the Almighty Author of it, that while passing over it, he will be pleased, mercifully to shine on the heart, of both the Writer, and the Reader, (if it be his holy will,) of this *Poor Man's Commentary.* And from hence, that the LORD JESUS, who is the whole sum and substance of its contents, may be made manifest in every part of it; so blessedly seen by faith, and enjoyed in hope, as to be glorified in the heart; and GOD *the* FATHER *glorified in his dear* SON. Amen.

CHAPTER I.

CONTENTS.

GOD *is declared in the opening of this Chapter, as speaking to the Church, by his* SON. *Then follows a short, but exalted Description, of the Glories of* CHRIST'S *Person and Character.*

GOD, who at sundry times and in divers manners spake in time past unto the fathers by the prophets,

2 Hath in these last days spoken unto us by *his* Son, whom he hath appointed heir of all things, by whom also he made the worlds;

From the opening of the Epistle, in the solemn and striking manner, in which we have the SON of GOD introduced; I humbly conceive, that GOD the SPIRIT, intended thereby that the Church, should have proper conceptions of the dignity of his Person, before we are brought acquainted with the nature of his offices. Hence a line of everlasting distinction, is at once drawn, between him, and the highest order, of all his servants, whether angels, or men. And whereas in all former revelations, GOD spake in time past, through the ministry of the Prophets; now in this last and final dispensation, he speaks openly to the Church by his SON.

Now before the Reader goes a step further, I pray him to pause and consider, in what a glorious display of dignity and power, the SON of GOD is here introduced. In no method, but the Gospel method, could this manifestation be made. When GOD went forth in acts of *creation*, there was nothing of a *personal* nature in relation to the manner of existence, in the divine essence made known. The HOLY THREE in ONE, are represented indeed, as confering on the subject of forming man's creation, different from what is said at the creation of other inferior creatures: but nothing more, by which the personal manifestations of each might be known. Gen. i. 26. It is in *redemption*, the several distinct acts of each glorious Person, in the GODHEAD, become manifest: so that we may truly say, the first footsteps of the HOLY Persons of the GODHEAD are first traced in CHRIST; and the love of GOD in CHRIST to his Church here first broke forth, in open revelation to the Church. The SON of GOD comes forth from the invisibility, in which GOD in his threefold character of Persons by his very nature, and essence dwells; and makes known the sacred purposes of his will. GOD *hath spoken to us by his* SON. To this agrees in beautiful correspondence, what another inspired Apostle hath recorded: *No man hath seen* GOD *at any time. The only begotten* SON, *which is in the bosom of the* FATHER, *he hath declared him.* John i. 18. How the SON of GOD comes, and through what medium, his communications are made; is spoken of elsewhere. We are informed of his incarnation, and all the blessed events connected with that mysterious act, in those scriptures, which sum up the account of his wonderful Person, and character, by saying, that *in Him dwelleth all the fulness of the* GODHEAD *bodily.* Coloss. ii. 9. But in this place, no more is said, in relation to the difference between him, and his servants, than that the last days revelation, are not as were the former. This glorious truth, marks the striking distinction; and here it stands, as the title page, and contents of this whole book of GOD; GOD *hath spoken to us by his* SON. I pray the Reader, to note this, in the deepest memorandums of his heart, in proof of the GODHEAD of CHRIST and then prosecute what next follows, concerning his Person and Offices.

He is said, to be *appointed heir of all things.* This cannot be said of him as GOD; for his heirship, if it were supposed taken in this sense, could not be an *appointed* heirship: for by birth-right it is his. But in the mystery of his Person, it is spoken of him as God-Man. And in this sense, he is truly, and properly *appointed heir of all things*. And the Church, are made heirs in him. *Heirs of* God, *and joint heirs with* Christ. Rom. viii. 17. Oh! the privilege of God's children!

By whom also he made the worlds. Yes! this is a most clear, and decided doctrine, of scripture. God created *all things by* Jesus Christ. Ephes. iii. 9. And according to the Holy Ghost's account, by *Paul*, to the Church of the *Colossians*: not only all things were created by Him, but *for* Him; and by Him, *all things consist.* Indeed from that most blessed scripture, as well as some others, we are led to conclude, that without this mysterious Person, in his double nature, God and Man, in One; there could have been nothing, for creation to have rested upon. Nothing could have stood, or subsisted, but by dependence upon God. And yet nothing could have stood, in any way of subsistence *with* God. In the person therefore of God-Man alone, we find an adequate foundation to rest upon. And of Him, and Him only, as is soon after said, in this chapter, and confirmed by other scriptures, we find One competent to the Almighty work, of *upholding all things by the word of his power*. John i. 3, 4. I pray the Reader not to pass away before that he hath looked for further confirmation, to Colossians i. 15—17, with Commentary.

3 Who being the brightness of *his* glory, and the express image of his person, and upholding all things by the word of his power, when he had by himself purged our sins, sat down on the right hand of the Majesty on high;

The Holy Ghost by his servant hath here given a further description of the infinite dignity of Christ's Person. *Who being the brightness of his glory, and the express image of his Person; and upholding all things by the word of his power.* I pray the Reader to mark, with due attention, those glorious distinctions of character, by which the Person of Christ is here revealed. He is said, to be *the brightness of his* Father's *glory*. Not *made* so, but *being* so. Consequently the same oneness of nature, and essence with the Father. And when it is added, *the express image of his Person*; meaning, that by virtue of the Son of God, assuming manhood, he becomes the visible representation, of what without this medium, was, and is, and cannot but be invisible; agreeably to that blessed scripture, that *in Him dwelleth all the fulness of the* Godhead *bodily.* Coloss. ii. 9. And in relation to his *upholding all things by the word of his power,* nothing can be more plain, than that, as God-Man Mediator, he hath *power given him over all flesh, that he should give eternal life to as many as the* Father *hath given him*. John xvii. 2. And no less, doth he uphold, the whole of Creation, which he hath made; being the natural, and immediate result, for which God in his threefold character of Persons, went forth in acts of creation, by Jesus Christ, that he, as the visible Jehovah, in all Covenant transactions, should reign, and controul all things, in all the departments of nature, providence, grace, and glory. Dan. iv, 34, 35. Ephes. i. 10. Reader! pause, before you proceed further; and contemplate the glories of his Person, as here drawn, by the HOLY GHOST. Well might *Paul* desire, to relinquish all other knowledge, for the knowledge of CHRIST. Philip. iii. 8, 9. And well might he pray, for the Church, that this, above all other blessings, might be their portion. Ephes. i. 15, to the end. And yet, Reader! this is He *whom man despiseth!* This is He *whom the nation abhorreth.* Isaiah xlix. 7. What man? What nation? Yea, every man, and every nation, unacquainted with his mysterious Person, GOD-Man! And is not the present, as well as the nation of the Jews of old, a CHRIST-despising generation? But concerning those, to whom GOD the HOLY GHOST hath revealed him, JESUS thus speaks; FATHER! *I will, that they also whom thou hast given me, be with me where I am, that they may behold my glory, which thou hast given me.* John xvii. 24.

But the scripture proceeds, *When he had by himself, purged our sins, sat down on the right hand of the Majesty on high.* Reader! pray observe, what an emphasis, GOD the HOLY GHOST, lays on this account, of CHRIST. The purging our sins, is made to appear, a greater work in *the Heir of all things;* than even *the creation of the worlds* by him. For the *one* was simply the act of his Almighty power: But the *other*, is not only the act of his Almighty power, and his Almighty love; but the giving of himself in the purging our sins by himself. Not merely, an exertion of power: not the gift of his property, his works, or actions, or will, or design: not giving his creation, and all the creatures he had given life unto, in calling them into being; not these; but *himself*, his Person, his whole human nature; as he himself calleth it, *my flesh which I will give for the life of the world!* John vi. 51. The preciousness of the work; the love of Him that performed it; and the extensiveness of the efficacy of it; none but GOD himself, can form any idea thereof. It is said, that his very name is such, that *no man knew but he himself.* Rev. xix. 12. And if so, what must be his work: and such a work, as that of purging our sins by himself? Reader! I know not how to leave the sweet meditation. JESUS *by himself*, purged our sins! It was *himself*, his own proper Person; himself, both Altar, Priest, and Sacrifice. He made himself an offering for sins; yea, to sum up all, as this sweet scripture hath it, for none can be more full, or more expressive: *by himself purged our sins!* Oh! the love of GOD which passeth knowledge! The FATHER gave his SON, *his elect in whom his soul delighteth.* The SON gave himself, and by himself purged our sins. And GOD the HOLY GHOST confirms the whole by regeneration, to his redeemed; for in the whole manifestations of grace, *he was justified in the* SPIRIT. 1 Tim. iii. 16.

But we must not stop here. When he had by himself purged our sins, *sat down on the right hand of the Majesty on high.* There is a vast deal of importance in those scriptures, connected together: and it is plain, that they are joined here by the HOLY GHOST, purposely for the comfort and joy of the Church, on this account. It is, as if the LORD had said, by way of confirmation, that JESUS by himself hath purged and done away all your sins; and he is returned to heaven, and is sat down on the right hand of the Majesty on high, having finished the work the FATHER gave him to do. Paul in one scripture, and Peter in another, make this return of CHRIST to heaven, as the most complete answer, to all the accusations of hell, and the sinner's conscience; yea, to all the demands of GOD's law, and justice on account of sin. *Who* (saith *Paul*) *shall lay any thing to the charge of* GOD's *elect? It is* GOD *that justifieth. Who is he that condemneth? It is* CHRIST *that died; yea, rather that is risen again, who is even at the right hand of* GOD. Rom. viii. 33, 39. As much as to say; what fears can now arise, to distress the LORD's redeemed ones? GOD the FATHER hath received him, at the heavenly Court, and said unto him; *sit thou at my right hand, until I make thine enemies thy footstool*. Psm. cx. 1. And *Peter* following up the same blessed truth, with a rapture of holy joy and triumph, tells the Church, that CHRIST is *gone into heaven, and is on the right hand of* GOD: *angels, and authorities, being made subject unto him.* 1 Pet. iii. 22. Reader! do not lose sight of these blessed things, for they are most blessed. Your JESUS would never have returned to his FATHER, had his work been unfinished. He hereby proved, that he had by himself purged our sins. Hence this act, most fully certified, that not only sin, with all its tremendous consequences, was for ever done away: but that justification to life, was also secured, by his entrance into heaven. Hence that sweet scripture; *he was delivered for our offences, and raised again for our justification.* Rom. iv. 25. Neither is this all. For CHRIST's *sitting down*, at the right hand of the Majesty on high, is spoken of, in another scripture, as contrasted to the actions of those Priests who daily *stand* to minister in sacrifices. *For every priest, standeth daily ministering and offering oftentimes the same sacrifices, which can never take away sin. But this man after he had offered one sacrifice for sins, for ever sat down on the right hand of* GOD: *from henceforth expecting, till his enemies be made his footstool*: (according to GOD's word and oath. Psm. cx.) *for by one offering, he hath perfected, for ever, them that are sanctified.* Heb. x. 11—14. Nothing can be more beautiful and decisive, on this ground than those different actions of standing and sitting. The priests of old *stood*, while in their ministry, in proof that they had no power to finish it: and their daily labors, as daily carried conviction with them, that they were only, *the shadow of good things to come.* Heb. x. 1. But JESUS when he had by himself purged our sins, returned to glory, and sat down, in proof, that he had entered into his rest *once for all*, having *obtained eternal redemption for us.* Heb. ix. 11, 12. Once more. The HOLY GHOST is express also to teach the Church, that in this entrance of CHRIST into heaven, it is as our fore-runner; Heb. vi. 20. And where his redeemed must follow. Nay, we are said already by faith *to sit together with* CHRIST *in heavenly places.* Ephes. ii. 6. So that the justified believer in CHRIST, is now by faith, already in heaven, with his glorious Head: and shortly will be there in person. For so the promise runs. *Where I am; there shall ye be also.* John xiv. 1—3. *To him that overcometh, will I grant to sit with me in my throne; even as I also overcame, and am sat down with my* FATHER *in his throne.* Rev. iii. 20. Reader! think what precious things, are contained in the bosom of this short, but comprehensive scripture, concerning our glorious

LORD: *when he had by himself purged our sins, sat down on the right hand of the Majesty on high.*

4 Being made so much better than the angels, as he hath by inheritance obtained a more excellent name than they.

5 For unto which of the angels said he at any time, Thou art my Son, this day have I begotten thee? And again, I will be to him a Father, and he shall be to me a Son?

6 And again, when he bringeth in the first-begotten into the world, he saith, And let all the angels of God worship him.

7 And of the angels he saith, Who maketh his angels spirits, and his ministers a flame of fire.

We shall have occasion in the next Chapter, somewhat more particularly to treat of the nature of Angels, when we come to speak of the SON of GOD, passing by the nature of Angels, to take upon him the seed of *Abraham.* I therefore for the present pass it by, with only just observing, that the superiority of the SON of GOD in our Nature, GOD and Man, to that of Angels is evident, from every part of scripture, and with the most decided testimony. A few of the prominent points, in this Chapter, explained by other portions in the word of GOD, will set this matter in a clear light.

First. It is here said, that *he hath by inheritance obtained a more excellent name than they:* that is, than Angels. Now by inheritance, it should be observed, that as SON of GOD, one with the FATHER *over all* GOD *blessed for ever;* his inheritance is his, by right, and not acquired, or given. But as *heir of all things* to which he is *appointed* as GOD-Man-Mediator, here in this sense, he hath obtained this dignity, and which is infinitely above all Angels. His GOD-HEAD confers to his human nature a dignity, infinitely superior to Angels. For such things can never be spoken of them; neither can any of them be called *heir of all things.*

Secondly. We not only hear GOD's command issuing from the throne, when he bringeth in the first begotten into the world, or Angels to worship him; but we have on scripture record, an account of their adoration of CHRIST, as GOD-Man-Mediator. *Isaiah* the Prophet hath given the relation of a vision, which he saw of the kind. And that there might be no misapprehension concerning whose glory it was: *John* the Apostle declared the glory the prophet saw, was *the glory of* CHRIST. Compare Isaiah vi. 1. with John xii. 41. And we have another account to the same purport, Rev. v. 11—13.

Thirdly. CHRIST is expressly declared to be, not only the Creator of all things, visible, and invisible; whether thrones, or dominions, or principalities, or powers; but he is said to be the head of them, and they are all subject unto him. Compare Coloss. i. 16. with 1

Pet. iii. 22. So that they are his ministering servants; and, as the several principles of fire and lightening, and winds, and tempests, are directed by Him, in their agency: so it is said, that *he maketh his angels spirits, and his ministers a flame of fire.*

And all these things are said in a way, so immediately directed for the exaltation of CHRIST, in opposition to Angels; that it is demanded by way of question, When, or where, are Angels so distinguished? To which of the Angels, (said the LORD,) at any time; *Thou art my* SON: *this day have I begotten thee?* To which the answer must be, Yea, and is implied in the very question; to none of them! Of whom among them did ever GOD say, *I will be to him a* FATHER, *and he shall be to me a* SON? To not a single creature of them. So that while GOD is the head of dominion to Angels; in CHRIST alone, is he united by nature. And therefore CHRIST is by so much better than the Angels, in that he hath, as GOD an inheritance of his own, underived; and as GOD-Man, an obtained inheritance, as being *appointed heir of all things.* See Chap. ii. throughout.

8 But unto the Son *he saith*, Thy throne, O God, *is* for ever and ever: a sceptre of righteousness *is* the sceptre of thy kingdom.

9 Thou hast loved righteousness, and hated iniquity; therefore God, *even* thy God, hath anointed thee with the oil of gladness above thy fellows.

What a glorious testimony is here given, to the Person of CHRIST, as CHRIST; that is, as GOD-Man-Mediator. True indeed, as GOD, one with the FATHER, and the HOLY GHOST, his throne of GODHEAD is for ever and ever. And under this view, such things as ascribe eternity, glory, and all other divine attributes, are all his. But very evidently, from the quotation of this passage from the Prophet, when celebrating the glories of the Messiah, Psm. xlv. 6, 7. As well as what follows, in what is said of his fellows; the words both in the Prophet, and in this quotation by the Apostle, are spoken of CHRIST, as GOD-Man-Mediator. And most blessed they are indeed. CHRIST is all this, and every thing, that is great, and glorious, as the Head, and Husband of his Church, and people. But I need not, in this place, dwell upon the subject. All the Bible is full of CHRIST, and his royalty. I will rather beg, to direct the attention of the Reader to what is here said of CHRIST's fellows: for some very sweet, and precious views, according to my apprehension, arise herefrom.

The name of *fellows*, according to the original, carries with it somewhat very near, and intimate. Partners, Consorts, companions; meaning a right in all that CHRIST hath, in his headship; which is communicable both here in grace, and hereafter in glory. He, the Sun to fill them with light. He the fountain from which the streams which flow, *make glad the city of* GOD. Hence, as One, and the same anointing, which was poured by the HOLY GHOST on CHRIST, descended to all the members of his body; they are called by the same names, as their glorious LORD. He is king in Sion. And they are *made kings and priests by him unto* God *and the* Father. Rev. i. 6. He is said to have the Spirit given unto him, *without measure.* John iii. 35. And to every one of them is given grace, *according to the measure of the gift of* Christ. Ephes. iv. 7. And hence, the words in this verse, which are rendered *above* thy fellows; may be read also *for* thy fellows: and both are equally beautiful, and correct.

But under this view of the subject, what I would more immediately call upon the Reader to remark with me, on this fellowship, this partnership, of Christ, and his Church; Christ and his members, his body is this; that the anointing, our glorious Head; *this man of unction,* as he is called, or *this holy thing:* Luke i. 35. Was, and is, with an express eye to his body the Church. Christ, as God is called Jehovah's fellow. Zech. xiii. 6. And Christ, as man, in this place, as well as elsewhere, hath his fellows, in his members. Psm. xlv. 7. Zech. iii. 8. It forms one of the sweetest of all subjects, the contemplation of Christ, and his Church, in this oneness, and fellowship. The whole Church in every individual member, of his mystical body, were from all eternity chosen in Christ, and set up with Christ: And the whole body, in the purpose of Jehovah, were chosen in him, and for him, as fellows, and partners, and companions; to receive *from* him, and to enjoy *with* him, all that is communicable, in name, and honor, and happiness, and affection; during the time-state of grace upon earth: and glory in heaven.

Reader! beg for grace from the Lord the Spirit, to meditate upon the blissful subject; for indeed, and in truth, it is most blissful. Very certain it is, that God our Father's choosing the Church in Christ; and adopting the Church as Sons by Christ, was for this express purpose, for the glorifying of his dear Son, in his fellows, and members. It is God's choosing us in Christ; giving us this relationship in Christ; making us one with Christ; fellows with Christ; as Christ is fellow to God; which forms the foundation of all the blessedness which follows. There cannot be the shadow of a doubt, but in the very will, and purpose of Jehovah, that his dear Son should take upon him human nature; the first, the great, the ultimate end, and design of all, connected with the vast scheme, was to manifest the glory of the Son of God. Every thing therefore in all the subsequent events, was so ordered and arranged, as should minister best to this one purpose. The glory of Christ's Person shall be advanced in every thing. Will fellows, partners, companions, to whom Christ, by communicating of himself, contribute to this end? Jesus shall have a Church. Will the fall of this Church afford occasion to the glories of redemption? The whole events included in this high dispensation shall also follow, that Jesus shall get glory in our redemption. In short, whatever hath a tendency to magnify the personal glory of the Son of God, shall take place, for God's design all along, and from beginning to end, is to glorify the Lord Jesus. And most blessed as it is, to know, that from everlasting, God our Father hath loved the Church, with an everlasting love; and in proof hath chosen, predestinated, adopted, and accepted the Church in the Beloved, as children by Jesus Christ to himself: yet all, and every part, of this vast dispensation, in this manifold wisdom of God, is, with an eye, to the Person of JESUS. *You have not chosen me* (saith CHRIST) *but I have chosen you.* John xv. 16. GOD's choice of the Church, is for CHRIST, and his glory. And even the recovery of our nature from the *Adam*-fall of sin: though it hath our salvation in view, by the wonderful means adopted; yet this, is but the secondary consideration in GOD's design; the first, and grand object, is, to exalt the Personal glory of his dear SON. So sweetly speaks the LORD, by the Prophet: *Behold! my servant shall deal prudently; he shall be exalted, and extolled, and be very high. As many were astonished at thee, his visage was so marred more than any man; and his form more than the sons of men. So shall he sprinkle many nations; the kings shall shut their mouths at him; for that which had not been told them, shall they see; and that which they had not heard, shall they consider.* Isaiah lii. 13—15.

10 And, Thou, Lord, in the beginning hast laid the foundation of the earth; and the heavens are the works of thine hands.

11 They shall perish; but thou remainest; and they all shall wax old, as doth a garment;

12 And as a vesture shalt thou fold them up, and they shall be changed: but thou art the same, and thy years shall not fail.

13 But to which of the angels said he, at any time, Sit on my right hand, until I make thine enemies thy footstool?

14 Are they not all ministering spirits, sent forth to minister for them who shall be heirs of salvation?

I will not, (for I must not,) tresspass any further in this Chapter. But oh! what a subject is here again opened to our meditation, on the eternal nature of CHRIST's Person; and of the everlasting duration of his kingdom! How endeared to CHRIST's Church, is the consideration of the unchangeable, unfading, and eternal nature of CHRIST's love to his people. Amidst all changes, there is none can be here. JESUS lives, and loves, and reigns for ever. He is the Rock of Ages. LORD! (said one of old, under the fixed conviction by grace of these things,) *thou hast been our dwelling place in all generations!* Psm. xc. 1. And here the redeemed soul finds a safe, and sure hiding place, from every storm, and evil. What though friends die, JESUS liveth. What, though the earth be removed, or we are removed from it; this sweet view of JESUS, and an assured oneness in JESUS, brings up all. The heavens may perish, and all things below change like a vesture. Here is the believer's confidence: *But thou art the same!* The same in thy Person. The same in thy love. And the same, in all the Covenant-securities for ever. Hallelu-JAH! The LORD GOD Omnipotent reigneth! Amen.

REFLECTIONS.

Praises to the Lord Jehovah, Father, Son, and Holy Ghost, for the eternal purpose, which he purposed in Christ Jesus our Lord! And praises to his holy name, that he hath been pleased to make known the fellowship of the mystery, hid in God from the beginning of the world, which in times past was opened in divers manners to the fathers by the prophets; but now, in these last days, fully, and completely made known to the Church, in the Person of his dear Son! Lord Jesus! we hail thy glorious appearing, in all the revelations thou hast made! We adore thee for thy *natural*, and *essential* glories, as One with the Father. We adore thee in all thy *mediatorial* characters, as God-Man, *heir of all things!* And we would desire grace to praise thee, love thee, delight in thee, for all thy finished redemption-work, and grace, manifested to thy Church, and People; that when by thyself thou hadst purged our sins, thou didst take thy seat at the right hand of the Majesty on high. Oh! the rapture and the joy, that Jesus, by inheritance hath obtained a more excellent name than angels; and that his people, his fellows, by their union with him, and their right in him, are begotten to the same heritage, and will enter into the joy of their Lord. Oh! that God the Spirit, who in grace and love, hath brought the Church acquainted with these precious things, may daily, by his quickening, and renewing influences, anoint all the fellows of Christ, with the same oil of gladness, as their glorious Head. And while our God and Father saith unto his dear Son, *Thy throne, O God, is for ever and ever;* all his adopted children may know their oneness and interest in Christ, and in that kingdom, which cannot fail!

CHAP. II.

CONTENTS.

The Apostle is prosecuting the same blissful Subject in this Chapter as in the former, in speaking of the Glories of Christ. *His Love to the Church, in taking our Nature: and the Blessedness it brings to all his People.*

THEREFORE we ought to give the more earnest heed to the things which we have heard, lest at any time we should let *them* slip.

2 For if the word spoken by angels was stedfast, and every transgression and disobedience received a just recompence of reward;

3 How shall we escape, if we neglect so great salvation; which at the first began to be spoken by the Lord, and was confirmed unto us by them that heard *him;*

4 God also bearing *them* witness, both with signs and wonders, and with divers miracles, and gifts of the Holy Ghost, according to his own will?

The opening of this Chapter, is an inference from the close of the former. The Apostle having said such blessed things, in shewing the vast superiority of the Gospel dispensation, to all revelations which went before; reminds the Church, how important it must be, to have these things always in remembrance. And, as our memories are so treacherous, to be the more earnest to seek for grace, that we might not forget them. Reader! here is one of the sweet offices of God the Holy Ghost, particularly endeared to us. You, and I, are forgetful of divine things. Jesus saith, that the Holy Ghost *shall bring all things to our remembrance, whatsoever he himself hath said unto us.* John xiv. 26. And shall not you and I look up to that gracious, and loving Teacher, and say, Lord! be thou the Remembrancer of Christ Jesus; that none of his precious words, and the glorious things belonging to his Almighty Person, and offices, may at any time slip from our minds?

Paul adds a striking argument for this attention. If the law given by the ministry of angels, formed a subject of such high concern, that the least breach of it, produced punishment; what must the neglect of such great salvation bring forth, which the Son of God himself hath brought? The manner in which the question is here put, proves that it is impossible to escape. And indeed, when we consider, not only the greatness of the salvation itself, but the Almightiness of Him by whom it is wrought; every one who hears of it, must stand convicted, in his own conscience, that the neglect of it, cannot fail to produce the inevitable consequences, of everlasting condemnation. It is impossible to escape. Reader! pause one moment over the solemn consideration. The love, wisdom, and power, of all the Persons of the Godhead, have been manifested, in the contrivance of this salvation. The mysterious nature of that Almighty Being, who hath brought it; the greatness of his labor, sufferings, agonies, blood-shedding, and death, by means of which alone it could be accomplished: the infinite preciousness of the thing itself, and the everlasting consequences involved in it; all carry the fullest conviction with them, how impossible it must be, in any to escape, who slight, or despise such great salvation!

5 For unto the angels hath he not put in subjection the world to come, whereof we speak.

6 But one in a certain place testified, saying, What is man, that thou art mindful of him? or the son of man, that thou visitest him?

7 Thou madest him a little lower than the angels; thou crownest him with glory and honour, and didst set him over the works of thy hands:

8 Thou hast put all things in subjection under his feet. For in that he put all in subjection under him, he left nothing *that* is not put under him. But now we see not yet all things put under him.

9 But we see Jesus, who was made a little lower than the angels for the suffering of death, crowned with glory and honour; that he by the grace of God should taste death for every man.

10 For it became him, for whom *are* all things, and by whom *are* all things, in bringing many sons unto glory, to make the captain of their salvation perfect through sufferings.

11 For both he that sanctifieth and they who are sanctified *are* all of one: for which cause he is not ashamed to call them brethren.

12 Saying, I will declare thy name unto my brethren, in the midst of the church will I sing praise unto thee.

13 And again, I will put my trust in him. And again, Behold I and the children which God hath given me.

I will not detain the Reader with all the observations that might be made on these verses; for this would lead too far, in a work of this kind. A few of the more prominent points, are all I shall here offer. And *first*. What the Apostle saith, of One in a certain place testifying of man; doth not refer to the first man *Adam*, or to mankind in general; but specially, and personally, to some identical one, and which is evidently CHRIST. It is a quotation from the viiith Psalm. JESUS himself hath very plainly made application of it to himself: Matt. xxi. 16. And the words are expressive of the astonishment the child of GOD finds, when truly regenerated by the HOLY GHOST, of the infinite condescension of JEHOVAH, by a means so wonderful as the incarnation of the SON of GOD, accomplishing redemption.

Secondly. The making him a little lower than the angels, for the suffering of death; and yet, at the same time, putting all things, both men, and angels, and devils; yea, the whole creation, both visible, and invisible, under his feet; so that there is nothing left, but what is under the subjection of CHRIST: these are points, which arrest the mind, and call forth both the astonishment, love, and praise, of all the Church of GOD!

Thirdly. CHRIST is said to have *tasted death for every man.* The phrase is an expression to intimate knowledge of death. It is a figure borrowed from the common circumstances of mankind, such as when, in order to ascertain what a thing is, and to have a personal knowledge of it, we taste it. Such was the case here, in allusion to CHRIST's death. *By the grace of* GOD *he tasted it;* that is, he endured it. When it is added, *for every man,* it is not to be supposed, that his death was intended a ransom for every individual of the human race; but for every one of his brethren, *the heirs of salvation,* as they are called: Chap. i. 14. And the following verses, of *the many sons* he is to bring to glory; the persons whom *he is not ashamed to call brethren;* and the *children whom* GOD *hath given him:* these terms very plainly define, and mark the characters of those, for whom CHRIST tasted death.

Fourthly. The necessity of CHRIST's death, in being made perfect through sufferings, is also very blessedly expressed. *It became him for whom are all things, and by whom are all things,* so to be perfected. And this sweet Scripture, is in exact correspondence to the whole testimony of the written word. For He that is heir of all things, is heir also of death. He is *the first born from the dead; that in all things he might have the pre-eminence.* Colossians i. 18. Rev. i. 5.

Fifthly. The oneness of nature, between CHRIST and his people, is also most blessedly marked, in these verses. *Both he that sanctified, and they who are sanctified are all of one.* Yes! CHRIST is himself the whole, and sole sanctification of his people. They have no holiness, but what is derived from him. They were first chosen to be holy, and without blame in CHRIST, before the foundation of the world. Ephes. i. 4. They are redeemed from all iniquity by Him, during the time-state of the Church. Ephes. i. 7. They are regenerated by the HOLY GHOST, and made new creatures in CHRIST JESUS, when born again. 2 Cor. v. 17. And CHRIST is made of GOD to them, during the whole of their time-state upon earth, until grace is finished in glory, and for ever; *wisdom, righteousness, sanctification, and redemption.* 1 Cor. i. 30. Hence those sweet scriptures which follow, in those verses, and are confirmed throughout the whole word of GOD. Psm. xxii. 22. Psm. xviii. 2. Isaiah viii. 18. 2 Thess. ii. 13, 14.

14 Forasmuch then as the children are partakers of flesh and blood, he also himself likewise took part of the same; that through death he might destroy him that had the power of death, that is, the devil.

15 And deliver them who through fear of death were all their life-time subject to bondage.

I beg the Reader's attention to this scripture, with that earnestness its great importance demands; for it is most blessed. *First:* let it be well noticed, the reason here assigned, for the SON of GOD taking upon him the nature of man; namely, because the children whom the FATHER had given him, were partakers of flesh and blood. To be sure, JESUS would take part of the same; for how else could he be married to his Church? Had he taken any other nature but the nature of man, what union could there have been between them? And I beg the Reader to notice also, how decided a proof those expressions, of CHRIST's children being partakers of flesh and blood, on whose account he took the same, is hereby given, both of CHRIST's pre-existence as Head, and Husband of his Church, set up from everlasting; and his own eternal power and GODHEAD, in that it is said, he himself likewise took part of the same. This action of CHRIST, and this cause, in the SON of GOD taking flesh and blood, are unanswerable evidences, in proof of his GODHEAD. And the Reader may do well, in the present sinful, CHRIST-despising generation, to remark them as he goes. See Luke i. 38. and Commentary.

Secondly. Let it be observed also, another motive here spoken of, for which the SON of GOD took part of the same flesh and blood as his children; namely, that *through death he might destroy him which had the power of death, that is, the devil; and deliver them, who through fear of death, are all their life-time subject to bondage.* What a glorious account is here? But how came the devil to have the power of death? And by what means were the children of GOD, his captives, to be in such bondage? The scriptures give most satisfactory answers to these questions: and which serve, at the same time, to prove the liberty, whereby the LORD JESUS hath made his children free; and to enhance the preciousness of the LORD JESUS himself for his grace.

The Devil, by seducing our nature, in the *Adam*-fall transgression, not only brought in death; but universal captivity. *Sin entered into the world, and death by sin: and so death passed upon all men, for that all have sinned.* Rom. v. 12. And hence, the devil may be truly said, in this sense to have the power of death: yea, and lawfully too. For, so the scripture confirms it. *For of whom a man is overcome: of the same is he brought into bondage.* 2 Pet. ii. 19. And hence, though CHRIST by his death, hath overcome death; and destroyed him that had the power of death; yet we find many of GOD's dear children are still subject to bondage, in the fear of death; yea, many of them also, who are convinced of their redemption by CHRIST, and their interest in CHRIST. This *fruit* of *Adam's* sin, they taste in bondage fears; though they triumph in CHRIST, by his great deliverance from the *curse* of it. Reader! pause over the subject. What hath thy GOD, thy SAVIOR, by JESUS wrought! Oh! see to it, if thou knowest the blessedness of this sweet scripture, and believeth the record that GOD hath given of his dear SON; that no unsuitable, unbecoming fears of death arise in the mind, when CHRIST hath taken flesh and blood, on purpose to destroy both him that had the power of death, and death itself; and which he hath most effectually done; and to deliver his redeemed, from being all their life time, through fear of a shadow, subject to bondage. Psm. xxiii. 4.

One word more on this precious scripture. There can be no doubt, but that as by sin we were all *lawful* captives to *Satan*; it must be a *lawful* act alone, that can make us free, from that captivity. This the SON of GOD accomplished, by destroying Satan, and delivering his people. And so GOD the FATHER engaged for, in Covenant promises. *Shall the prey be taken from the mighty, or the lawful* (mark the word *lawful*) *captive delivered? But thus saith the* LORD: *Even the captives of the mighty shall be taken away, and the prey of the ter-*

rible delivered; for I will contend with him, that contendeth with thee; and I will save thy children. Isaiah xlix. 24, 25. Oh! what a scripture is here! How full in point! How unanswerable in Covenant promises! Oh! the love of GOD our FATHER to our glorious Head, and to the Church in him!

Reader! again I say, do not turn away from the precious view, (for it is most precious,) which ariseth out of this blessed scripture, of the SON of GOD taking flesh and blood for such gracious purposes, because his children were partakers of the same. JESUS hath, in our nature, conquered him which first conquered us. And JESUS hath conquered both death and him, that had the power of death, by his own death; and by his rising to life again, hath opened to us everlasting life. Yea JESUS hath done more. He hath conquered the devil *in us*, by regeneration; and hath taken the strong man armed which kept us in bondage, and spoiled his armor. And JESUS hath overcome the devil *by us*, in every act of grace, by which, through the HOLY SPIRIT, we are enabled *to mortify the deeds of the body;* and when our Spirit *lusteth against the flesh.* Rom. viii. 13. Gal. v. 17. And that sweet promise, carries us on, with sure victory: *the* GOD *of peace will bruise Satan under our feet shortly.* Rom. xvi. 20. Precious GOD and SAVIOR! adored be thy name for taking our nature upon thee! In due time thou wilt come to cast the devil, and all his hellish crew into the bottomless pit. And then thy Church shall see his fall, and rejoice over him for ever. Rev. 20 throughout.

16 For verily he took not on *him the nature of* angels; but he took on *him* the seed of Abraham.

17 Wherefore in all things it behoved him to be made like unto *his* brethren, that he might be a merciful and faithful high priest in things *pertaining* to God, to make reconciliation for the sins of the people.

18 For in that he himself hath suffered being tempted, he is able to succour them that are tempted.

There is somewhat so very gracious in what is here said, of the SON of GOD, passing by the nature of Angels, and taking on him the seed of Abraham; that I would beg my Reader's indulgence to be somewhat more particular, in marking the distinguishing mercy. And in order that we may have the clearest apprehension of the subject, according to what is stated of it in scripture, it will not be amiss; first to make enquiry into the circumstances of that class of Beings, whose nature the SON of GOD passed by, when he took upon him the nature of man: before that we consider that class of Beings to whom JESUS manifested such distinguishing love in taking their nature. We have a large account of Angels, if taken altogether, in the word of GOD, to shew their high rank and dignity in the scale of being. They are evidently of the same family as man, considered as in CHRIST their head. Ephes. iii. 15. The elect Angels, so called,

1 Tim. v. 21, are spoken of, as deriving both their being, and well being from, and in, CHRIST. Coloss. i. 18. And as their Creator, they are commanded to worship him. Heb. i. 6. They ministered to his Person, upon earth, at his incarnation. Luke ii. 13. at his temptation, Matt. iv. 11. his agony in the garden, Luke xxii. 43. at the tomb, on his resurrection, Matt. xxviii. 2, 7. his ascension, Acts i. 10, 11. and when the LORD shall come again to judge the world, they will attend him. Matt. xvi. 27. and the Church of his redeemed shall see the heavens open, and they shall behold them *ascending, and descending, upon the* SON *of Man,* John i. 51. Gen. xxviii. 12. But while these very blessed things are spoken of Angels, in proof of their high dignity and character, we are taught in this precious scripture; that the SON of GOD, *verily took not on him the nature of Angels; but he took on him the seed of Abraham.* Let us humbly look into some of the causes, as far as holy scripture hath explained the subject, by way of marking the distinguishing mercy.

And *first,* to begin our enquiry of the scripture account of Angels. It appears, from several parts of the word of GOD, that there are Angels, which stand in a somewhat nearer relation to CHRIST, than that of being created by Him; for they are called, *Elect Angels,* 1 Tim. v. 21. by which it may reasonably be supposed, that some influence, or power, is manifested by CHRIST towards them, which differs wholly from what simply belongs to Creating, and Preserving them in Being with the whole Creation of GOD. For in this sense, Hell itself is preserved, and the fallen Angels, *which are reserved in everlasting chains under darkness, to the judgment of the great day.* Jude 6. But then, this influence, or power, of special grace and favor differs totally from that, which is shewn the elect of CHRIST among men. With those, there is an *union* with CHRIST and they form CHRIST's mystical body. He is the *head of his body the Church.* And they are *members of his body, of his flesh, and of his bones.* Coloss. i. 18. Ephes. v. 30. Such things are never said of Angels. Moreover, CHRIST is the Redeemer of his elect men, which by nature in the *Adam*-fall, are all involved in ruin. But CHRIST is never said to be the Redeemer of Angels, in any part of the word of GOD. Indeed the Elect Angels needed not redemption, CHRIST hath kept them from falling. And for the fallen Angels, cast out of heaven, no Redeemer was ever to be provided, according to the Covenant of eternity. Hence we discover, the striking difference, respecting Angels and Men.

Secondly. It appears, however, from scripture, that as the Elect Angels, not only owe their Being, and their well Being to CHRIST; so are they in some special way, or manner, in the same family with Elect Men; and with them are Worshippers of CHRIST. When JEHOVAH bringeth in the first begotten into the world, he saith; *And let all the Angels of* GOD *worship him.* Heb. i. 6. And agreeably to this command, when *John* saw heaven open, and the Church praising CHRIST; he saith, that he heard also *the voice of many Angels round about the throne,* joining in the song. Rev. v. 11, 12. From hence we must infer, that the kingdom of CHRIST, is composed of Angels and Men; and that they are Worshippers together of CHRIST as GOD-Man Mediator. I might enlarge much on this point. But I dare not: The limits of a *Poor Man's Commentary* will not admit. But when we consider, what the word of God relates on this subject; that *the Angels are ministering spirits sent forth to minister to them that are heirs of salvation*; Heb. i. 14. that they evidently attend the assemblies of God's people; for women professing godliness are commanded to cover their heads in worship, *because of the Angels;* 1 Cor. xi. 10. and that they rejoice over the conversion of the Lord's people, when brought out of the *Adam*-darkness; these things seem somewhat to imply, that Elect Angels are of the same family, in point of service and worship, as Elect Men; only they are not united to Christ, and have not that relationship with Jesus, which we have, by his taking our nature upon him.

Thirdly. It should seem moreover probable, by what *John* saw in his vision, that though in point of intellect, Elect Angels being wholly spiritual, are higher than men; on which account perhaps it is said, that when at the resurrection the Church shall arise, a *spiritual* body, of that which was sown *natural;* we shall be like the Angels; Matt. xxii. 30. Yet, their knowledge of Christ, and his redemption-work, is not derived from the heavenly Court, but from the earthly Courts of our worship. It is said by the Holy Ghost, in the Epistle to the Church at *Ephesus*, that it is *to the intent that now unto the principalities and powers* (meaning Angels) *might be known by the Church, the manifold wisdom of* God. Ephes. iii. 10. From hence it should seem, that as the Elect Angels, which are ministering servants, and attend the assemblies of God's people; where Christ is proclaimed in his fulness and glory; they hear and learn: and hence they rejoice in beholding the conversion of sinners, which brings such glory to the Lord.

But I pause. I shall pursue this part of the subject no further. It is no doubt, a pleasing consideration to regard, what the scripture hath said, concerning the Elect Angels. And it is pleasing also, to consider them, as in this way connected into one family of worship, in the adoration of Christ with ourselves. And I can conceive, that the consciousness of their presence, in our assemblies of worship, though invisible to us, would occasion, if properly considered, no small solemnity, and not unfrequently holy joy. Yea, such a thought, under grace, might be productive of much good, if we sometimes considered, with what compassion they must behold heirs of God, and joint heirs with Christ, when they observe us cold, and too often inattentive in the great concerns of salvation! But I add no more.

It is time to attend to the account of Christ's regard to us before Angels. Though so much may be said of Angels; and is said of them; yet we are here told, concerning Jesus, that *verily he took not on him the nature of Angels: but he took on him the seed of Abraham.* This is our mercy. This, our highest dignity, and honor. And the Holy Ghost blessedly assigns the causes.

And, *first.* It is the human nature, not the angelic, Christ betrothed to himself. Before the foundation of the world, the Church was chosen in him. Jesus was set up from everlasting, as the Head and Husband of his people: and then he himself saith, *his delights were with the sons of men.* Ephes. i. 4. Psm. viii. 25—31.

Secondly. It was the Elect Church, and not the Elect Angels, which became ruined by the fall. Consequently the nature he had to redeem, that nature he took. To have taken the nature of Angels to redeem the nature of Man, would have been unsuitable and improper. Hence, as by one *man sin entered into the world, and death by sin:* by one man, came also *justification to life.* Rom. v. throughout. An Angel's nature could not have corresponded to purposes of this kind.

Thirdly. A deliverance from the condemnation of the broken law of God, required a sacrifice. *For without shedding of blood, there is no remission.* Heb. ix. 22. But had Christ taken an Angel's nature, he could have made no offering for sin. Redemption could only be effected, by *the offering of the body of* Jesus Christ *once for all;* whereby *he hath perfected for ever them that are sanctified.* Heb. x. 1—14.

Fourthly. It was a law in *Israel,* that no man, who was a stranger in the land, should be king over the people. *Thou shalt in any wise set him to be king over thee, who is one of thy kindred.* Deut. xvii. 15. To whom then, did the right of government belong, but to Jesus? Here was indeed One born for it; to whom all his Mother's children might bend before. Gen. xlix. 8. Philip. ii. 9, 10, 11.

And, *lastly*, to mention no more. The Holy Ghost here saith, that *in all things,* it behoved Christ to be made like unto his brethren; that he might be a merciful, and faithful High Priest, in things pertaining to God. So then, this union of nature, this blessed compound of God and Man in one Person, was that only, which could answer the vast purposes of Jehovah, in the work of redemption. It may be said, indeed, that as God, he could not acquire either a greater knowledge of our wants, in taking upon him our nature; or a greater disposition to mercy towards us, by this union. But it must be said also, at the same time, that if it added not to his knowledge, or his disposition to mercy; yet it gave him a more perfect personal apprehension of them, in a knowledge by fellow feeling, how they acted upon our nature; and how the relief from them might best affect us. Besides, by taking the nature of man, he taught man how to come to him, under exercises. *Ye know the heart of a stranger,* (said the Lord,) *for ye were strangers.* So I can tell Jesus. He knoweth *our* frame by his *own.* Had he taken the nature of Angels, of what use would it have been, to have said to Jesus, he knoweth the nature of Angels, what consolation would this have been to flesh and blood? Oh! precious Jesus! never, never, let me lose sight of this sweet scripture, with all the blessed encouragements arising out of it: my God, my Jesus, took not on him the nature of Angels, but he took on him, the seed of Abraham, that he might be a merciful, and faithful high Priest to God!

REFLECTIONS.

Oh! for grace to take heed to those things, which I have heard of God's covenant love and salvation; that, through the sweet office of God the Holy Ghost, as the Remembrancer of Christ Jesus, I may never let them slip. And do thou blessed Lord, put such an holy jealousy and fear in my heart, that I may never depart from thee, nor neglect so great salvation.

Praises to my gracious God and Savior! who in his great condescension for the sufferings of death, was made a little lower than the Angels; and yet was then, and is now, and eternally must be, the Lord both of Angels and Men. And oh! what a thought! He who is the High and Lofty One, which inhabiteth eternity, is also in the same moment, in his human nature, one with his people. *For both he that sanctifieth, and they who are sanctified, are all of one.* And is it so, (oh! thou blessed Lord,) that thou art not ashamed to call thy people brethren? Lord! grant that I may never feel that false pride, and be ashamed to call thee so! Surely I will tell all the world, whose I am, and whom I serve; and say to all I meet, Jesus is not ashamed to call me brother. And shall I not say to thee with delight, and joy, in the language of thy Church of old: *Oh! that thou wert as my brother that sucked the breasts of my mother: when I should find thee without, I would kiss thee; yea, I should not be despised.*

Reader! do you know the Lord? If so, think of your mercies, and rightly make use of them; amidst the present sinful and adulterous Christ-despising generation! Will you be cast down, because of the temptation, and have your soul discouraged by reason of the way? Oh! blessed be the way, however tempted it may be, if it thereby leads the soul, more frequently, more closely, to Jesus. Darkness is a mercy, if it drives me to Jesus the light. Poverty of soul is true riches, if my pinchings endear his enlargements! It is blessed to know, and blessed to feel, all spiritual wants; to make the soul more sensible, that there is no fulness but in Jesus. Lord the Spirit! cause my soul then to live upon Christ!

CHAP. III.

CONTENTS.

The Holy Ghost *is here still preaching* Christ. *The* Lord, *the* Spirit, *calls upon the Church, to pause, and contemplate, the Person of* Jesus. *He draws a Comparison between* Christ *and* Moses. *He shews the awful State of Unbelief!*

WHEREFORE, holy brethren, partakers of the heavenly calling, consider the Apostle and high Priest of our profession, Christ Jesus;

2 Who was faithful to him that appointed him, as also Moses *was faithful* in all his house.

3 For this man was counted worthy of more glory than Moses, inasmuch as he who hath builded the house hath more honour than the house.

4 For every house is builded by some *man*; but he that built all things *is* God.

5 And Moses verily *was* faithful in all his house, as a servant, for a testimony of those things which were to be spoken after;

6 But Christ as a son over his own house; whose house are we, if we hold fast the confidence and the rejoicing of the hope firm unto the end.

Who, but must admire, the very beautiful method, in which the Apostle opens this Chapter! Having in those two which are preceding, drawn out, in the most animated manner, to view, the Person of the Son of God; both in his divine nature, and in his human; and in the mysterious union of both; he now stands and calls upon the Church to behold and consider him! And what a glorious sight would it be, had we our spiritual senses, and the organs of vision so quickened and enlarged, as to form suitable apprehensions, of his infinite dignity and greatness? I would beg the Reader's attention, to the very great beauty, contained in these few verses on this subject, both as it relates to the persons called upon to behold Christ; and Christ himself.

And first, let him remark of the *persons* called upon. They are said to be, *holy brethren, partakers of the heavenly calling.* By which, as I have uniformly all the way along observed, in all the Apostle's writings, is meant, the *Church*, as distinguished from the carnal world. *Holy brethren:* by virtue of their oneness with Christ, being holy in Christ. Originally, and eternally, chosen by God the Father in Christ, to be *holy, and without blame before him in love.* And predestinated, to the *adoption of children* for this purpose. And willed by the same Lord, to this holiness, as the final end of their creation in Christ. *Be ye holy, for I am holy.* And hence, by regeneration, made so, in Christ. And *brethren;* not only of each other, but of Christ their elder brother; being chosen in the same eternal purpose of God; and formed in the same Womb of eternity. Hence, Jesus is not ashamed to call them brethren.

And they are all *partakers of the heavenly calling.* For they are alike said to be *a chosen generation, a royal priesthood, an holy nation, a peculiar people.* 1 Pet. ii. 9. Hence, from everlasting having been set apart in the grace union, with their glorious Head and Husband, they partake, in all the communicable grace, which flows from Jesus, to his members here; and in all that is communicable of glory from him, in the life to come. Now, it is to such, Paul calls to the contemplation of their adorable Lord Jesus Christ. And indeed it is such, and such only, that can take pleasure and find interest in the view. For to a carnal mind, there is no beauty to desire him: while to the faithful, and believing, regenerated by grace, he is *the altogether lovely, and the fairest among ten thousand!*

Let the Reader next look to Christ, and consider, while obeying the Apostle's call to behold Christ, the very gracious characters which *Paul* here particularly holds forth for the contemplation of his redeemed to view him under. *First*, the *Apostle;* and next with it, *the high Priest of our profession.* These he singles out, amongst numberless other most lovely, and engaging characters, as being more immediately suited to the subject, he had them before him. Reader! do not fail to mark them. If JESUS be dear to you, as your high Priest: (and how would a throne of grace be accessible or blessed without him,) surely to behold CHRIST in this office, as sent and authorised, as the Almighty Apostle from GOD, must endear him, and make him so. Here indeed lies the vast stress, of the whole blessedness of the gospel. CHRIST is the great high Priest, Altar, and Sacrifice; in whom alone, and by whom alone, all our approaches to the throne are made. But it is JEHOVAH's authority, which gives efficacy to all. CHRIST is the great Apostle come *from* GOD; and faith's great warrant to come *to* GOD by him. And the child of GOD, taught of GOD the SPIRIT, these precious, distinct, and at the same time, united views; finds all the encouragement to give him an holy boldness. For the poor sinner, that thus comes to GOD, in, and by CHRIST; comes to GOD, in GOD's own way. This is the remedy of GOD's own providing. And therefore it can never fail. It is, as if a child of GOD should say; how can I fear, how can I doubt of acceptance with GOD, as long as I come to GOD, in this new and living way of GOD's Apostle, and high Priest? CHRIST's blood and righteousness my offering; and GOD's own appointment for my pleading? Oh! that all the holy brethren, partakers of the heavenly calling, may daily hear, the command of GOD the HOLY GHOST, by his servant the Apostle, in this sweet scripture; and feel the blessed influence of the SPIRIT, at the same time in their hearts; and *consider the Apostle and High Priest of our profession* CHRIST JESUS!

I beg the Reader next to notice, the beautiful method, which GOD the HOLY GHOST adopts, in order to glorify the LORD JESUS. Indeed, it is a grand feature this, in the SPIRIT's teaching. He began this Epistle, with shewing the vast superiority of the LORD JESUS CHRIST to Angels; declaring that he was not only Him, by whom JEHOVAH made the worlds; but that when JEHOVAH brought him in, as the first begotten into the world, he commanded *all the Angels of* GOD *to worship him.* Chap. i. 2—6. And here, while writing again to the *Hebrews,* and knowing their attachment to their great minister *Moses,* the Apostle introduceth *Moses* to their view, by way of manifesting, that *Moses,* though such a Prophet as never before arose in Israel, *whom the* LORD *knew face to face, in all the signs and wonders,* which the LORD sent him to do; yet, compared to CHRIST, was no more than a servant to a Son. Deut. xxxiv. 10, 11. And to confirm it, if possible, yet more, under the similitude of an house, and builder, the Apostle states that *Moses,* as a creature, or as an house which could not make or build itself, was but as both in the LORD's hand. Now he that built all things *(and all things were made by* CHRIST, *and without Him, was not any thing made, that was made:* John i. 3.) is, and must be, GOD: and consequently CHRIST is GOD. Reader! what can be more decisive, in confirmation of the true, and proper GODHEAD of our LORD JESUS CHRIST.

Neither, according to my apprehension of things, was it without an eye to the firm establishment of this glorious truth, of the GOD-HEAD of CHRIST, in the mind of the Church at this place; that the HOLY GHOST, thus guided *Paul* to write, because the LORD was about to speak so much, as he hath done, of the true, and proper manhood of CHRIST also. For the LORD the SPIRIT is here opening to the Church's view, CHRIST's faithfulness in his office, of the priesthood. *For this man,* (saith the LORD,) *was faithful to him that appointed him,* and consequently *counted worthy of more glory than Moses.* Certainly, when the SON of GOD stood up at the call of his FATHER, as the Head and Husband, and Sponsor, and Surety of his Church; he became in her law-room, and stead, the servant of JEHOVAH; and as such, faithfulness became him and his house for ever! And what can be more blessed to the Church, than the consciousness and assurance of CHRIST, as GOD-Man Mediator, being a faithful High Priest to GOD and Man; and acting in that high capacity, in all he did for his Church, his house, *whose house are we?*

I detain the Reader, over what is here said, (and repeated with some little variation in verse 14,) to observe, that when it is added, *whose house are we, if we hold fast the confidence and the rejoicing of the hope, firm unto the end:* this is not said, as if our being CHRIST's house, was made, in the least, conditional, or in any way depended upon somewhat to be done, or held fast by us. If it were, indeed, it would reduce the house of CHRIST itself to a peradventure; and make the whole of GOD's grace to rest upon the will of man. If the Reader will notice the words, a little more closely, he will discover, through divine teaching, that it is our *confidence,* and our *rejoicing* which we are said to hold fast, and not our interest in CHRIST, if we would know for our joy, that we are CHRIST's house. My happiness, and my enjoyment of my interest in CHRIST, will indeed be more or less, as, through grace, I find strength, to hold fast my confidence in CHRIST. But my safety in CHRIST, is in the LORD's holding *me* fast; and not *I* him. Men, who read their Bibles, untaught of GOD the SPIRIT, may fancy that such *ifs* and *buts* as they meet with here and there, are put for conditions and causes. But certainly not so. Here are no such things. CHRIST's house, is of GOD the FATHER's laying in CHRIST himself, the sure foundation in Zion. And all his members are living stones, built up by GOD himself in this house, for *an holy temple to the* LORD, *and an habitation of* GOD *through the* SPIRIT. Isaiah xxviii. 16. 1 Pet. ii. 5. Ephes. ii. 20—22.

Reader! I beseech you, as you value your privileges, and high calling in CHRIST; learn of GOD the SPIRIT how to estimate your safety in CHRIST. So wretchedly low at present is the tide of things, in the spiritual life of GOD in the soul, according to modern profession, of what some men call the Gospel; that in this land, where once it stood at high water mark, it is now nearly gone out, and left our shore at the lowest ebb. They do not live upon CHRIST, but upon their own self attainments. And while any thing in self, can be found to satisfy their minds, they are at ease; though they have no communication, from the ocean of CHRIST, in those streams, which alone can truly *make glad the city of* GOD. Psm. xlvi. 4.

7 Wherefore (as the Holy Ghost saith, To-day if ye will hear his voice,

8 Harden not your hearts, as in the provocation, in the day of temptation in the wilderness.

9 When your fathers tempted me, proved me, and saw my works forty years.

10 Wherefore I was grieved with that generation, and said, They do alway err in *their* heart; and they have not known my ways.

11 So I sware in my wrath, They shall not enter into my rest.)

12 Take heed, brethren, lest there be in any of you an evil heart of unbelief, in departing from the living God.

13 But exhort one another daily, while it is called To-day; lest any of you be hardened through the deceitfulness of sin.

14 For we are made partakers of Christ, if we hold the beginning of our confidence stedfast unto the end:

15 While it is said, To day if ye will hear his voice, harden not your hearts as in the provocation.

16 For some, when they had heard, did provoke: howbeit not all that came out of Egypt by Moses.

17 But with whom was he grieved forty years? *was it* not with them that had sinned, whose carcases fell in the wilderness?

18 And to whom sware he that they should not enter into his rest, but to them that believed not?

19 So we see that they could not enter in because of unbelief.

I pause the more frequent over those verses, where God the Holy Ghost is spoken of, in any of his more express *personal* acts, in order to direct the Reader's attention to the subject. Among the latter-day heresies, the denial of his Person and Godhead, is specially marked. And the Reader will do well to consider, how very often the Lord hath ascribed to himself personal exercises; such as *speaking* and *commanding*, and the like, as if to guard the Church against this deadly sin. Surely the thing itself, being so plain, as all the ministry of the HOLY GHOST must imply; it need not have been said as here; *Wherefore as the* HOLY GHOST *saith;* unless it had been intended in a more palpable way, and manner, to keep the minds of the faithful always alive, in their attention, both to his Person, and GODHEAD. See Chap. ix. 8. and Commentary.

Concerning what is here said, by GOD the HOLY GHOST, in charging the people, to be on the watch, lest an evil heart of unbelief should creep in among them; (and he holds up before them the history of those whose carcases fell in the wilderness, by way of remark, I shall beg to offer a few brief observations.

And, first. Let the Reader take notice, to whom these words are spoken, namely, to the *brethren*. Not to the carnal and unregenerate; but to those of whom is is said, verse 14, for *we are made partakers of* CHRIST; or, as it might have been rendered, for *we have been made* partakers of CHRIST; for it refers to an act past: and an act made on GOD's part; not on ours: having been so made, *before the foundation of the world*. Ephes. i. 4, 5. Let the Reader make this his first observation on the passage. It is to the Church, the brethren, to whom the HOLY GHOST speaks.

Secondly. They are admonished to take heed against an hardness of heart, and an evil heart of unbelief. Now this is not the original stony heart, which the Church, as well as the whole *Adam*-race, have by nature. For the LORD promised to take this away: and in regeneration it is actually taken away. Ezek. xxxvi. 26. with John iii. 3—8. But it is that hardness of heart, which even the LORD's people, in the unrenewed part of their nature, their body of sin which they carry about with them, are too apt to imbibe, from mingling with carnal company, and an absence from ordinances, neglect in reading the word of GOD: and a shyness, or little frequency at the mercy seat. These things bring on coldness, and distance, between CHRIST and the soul: and like the Church, a sleepy, slothful frame, is felt. Song v. 2. and Commentary.

Thirdly. The LORD plainly shews in what follows, by calling upon the Church *to exhort one another*, that it is the Church, and not the carnal which is here admonished; and by the remedy proposed by exhortation, it is as plain, that absence from the LORD, and his courts, and inattention to the several means of grace, were referred to, as the causes of inducing this hardness, and insensibility of heart, and unbelief.

Fourthly. The carcases of those which fell in the wilderness, plainly shew, that they differed wholly from the LORD's people, here admonished. They are so spoken of elsewhere, as those *with whom* GOD *was not well pleased*. 1 Cor. x. 5. And who were they? Not the LORD's people in CHRIST, who from everlasting *are chosen in him;* predestinated to *the adoption of children* by JESUS CHRIST to himself; and *accepted in the beloved*. Ephes. i. 4, 5, 6. Who are they then. I answer, the children of Israel, *after the flesh:* or perhaps also partly that mixed multitude, which went up out of Egypt with *Moses*. See Exod. xii. 37, 38. and Numb. xiv. 26—37. Those men, while the miracles of the LORD's servant in *Egypt*, were warm in their remembrance, followed *Israel*, but they knew not the LORD; neither followed the LORD. Hence the expressions. *For some, howbeit not all.* See Reader! distinguishing grace! And do not forget, what GOD the SPIRIT hath also said, on the same subject. *For they are not all Israel which are of Israel. Neither because they are the seed of Abraham are they all children: but in Isaac, shall thy seed be called.* Rom. ix. 6, 7. The nation of Israel, as a nation, like any other nation where there is a professing Church, as a professing Church, did all enjoy the outward privileges. They had all the *Manna*, and all drank of the *Rock;* the *Cloud* to screen by day, and the *pillar of fire* by night. But these were only common things to them like Ordinances. Unbelief *then*, and unregeneration *now*, produce the same effect. The five words of CHRIST, *Ye must be born again:* John iii. 7. becomes the sole qualification to an entrance into CHRIST's kingdom.

REFLECTIONS.

PAUSE, my soul, and chearfully obey, the LORD the SPIRIT, and consider, as thou art commanded and hast such abundant reason to do; consider, the Apostle and High Priest of thy profession CHRIST JESUS! Yes! thou glorious GOD and SAVIOR! I would desire to contemplate thy Person, character, offices, and relations! I would desire grace, and a spirit of wisdom and revelation in the knowledge of thee, to behold thee in all that concerns thy Mediatorial glory, in thy faithfulness to thy FATHER, and to thy people. I would gaze on thee, until my whole soul was swallowed up in the contemplation; and until that I found myself one with my LORD in that house, over which, as his own, CHRIST is the rightful owner; and which house, is CHRIST's body the Church, and He *the fulness which filleth all in all.*

And do thou, Almighty GOD the HOLY GHOST, give me continual grace, to keep in remembrance thy precious exhortation to thy people. LORD! let nothing of sin cleave to my poor fallen nature; neither suffer me to be at any time hardened with the deceitfulness of it. Oh! the long suffering of my GOD, to the forty years provocation of the people in the wilderness! Oh! the numberless years of the LORD's long suffering now! Cause me, O LORD, to mark that grace which kept back thy people from murmuring *then,* when the LORD brought *Israel* out of *Egypt* by *Moses;* that though *some*, (even the *Israel* after the flesh,) when they had heard, did provoke; yet not *all*, (even those whom grace restrained.) They fell not after the same example of unbelief. And cause me, O LORD, to know *now*, that it is grace, and grace alone, by which any are kept *by the power of* GOD *through faith unto salvation.* Do thou, O LORD the HOLY GHOST! who here so sweetly holds forth our great and glorious Apostle, and High Priest, JESUS CHRIST, to thy Church's view, give grace to the apprehension and knowledge of Him; that through thy blessed influences thy people may all rejoice in him, to the praise of the glory of His grace, *who hath made us accepted in the Beloved.*

CHAP. IV.

CONTENTS.

The same precious Subject is continued through this whole Chapter. The LORD's *People are here shewn, that* CHRIST *is their Rest.* CHRIST *having passed into the Heavens, is made an unanswerable Argument, to come unto him boldly.*

LET us therefore fear, lest, a promise being left *us* of entering into his rest, any of you should seem to come short of it.

2 For unto us was the gospel preached, as well as unto them: but the word preached did not profit them, not being mixed with faith in them that heard *it*.

3 For we which have believed do enter into rest, as he said, As I have sworn in my wrath, If they shall enter into my rest: although the works were finished from the foundation of the world.

4 For he spake in a certain place of the seventh *day* on this wise, And God did rest the seventh day from all his works.

5 And in this *place* again, If they shall enter into my rest.

6 Seeing therefore it remaineth that some must enter therein, and they to whom it was first preached entered not in because of unbelief.

7 (Again, he limiteth a certain day, saying in David, To-day, after so long a time; as it is said, To day if ye will hear his voice, harden not your hearts.

8 For if Jesus had given them rest, then would he not afterward have spoken of another day.

9 There remaineth therefore a rest to the people of God.

10 For he that is entered into his rest, he also hath ceased from his own works, as God *did* from his.)

11 Let us labour therefore to enter into that

rest, lest any man fall after the same example of unbelief.

The opening of this Chapter is so immediately connected with the close of the former, that it becomes the very inference of it. *Let us therefore fear,* saith the Apostle, while beholding the awful carcases of unbelievers, as from such distinguishing grace as we have received, in being given to believe in GOD for salvation, we have abundant reason to *rejoice with trembling.* Psm. ii. 11. The fear here spoken of, cannot mean a fear of coming short of CHRIST; for the Apostle had before said, *we are made partakers of* CHRIST; and *we are his house.* Neither are we called upon to the exercise of *bondage* fear, while conscious of having received *a spirit of adoption, whereby we cry Abba* FATHER. Rom. viii. 15. Neither can the *seeming* to come short of it, mean the seeming so to a believer's *own soul;* for it is expressly added, (ver. 3.) *For we which have believed do enter into rest.* A plain proof, that the child of GOD, resting on CHRIST, could not doubt his interest *in* CHRIST. But what then is to be supposed the fear here recommended, and to be sought after? Certainly that holy, jealous, child-like fear, which an obedient son wishes to have always before him, not to do or say any thing towards a kind father, which might grieve him. Such as is inculcated towards the HOLY SPIRIT. Ephes. iv. 30. And the Apostle beautifully illustrates the subject, by a case in point. The Gospel was preached in the old Church, in type, and figure, as it is now in substance, and reality, in the New. But there were then hearers who never felt the power of it, as there are now; and, consequently, to both alike, it is unprofitable. But the mark is decisive, where *faith cometh by hearing.* A child of GOD regenerated, heareth to the salvation of the soul. The unawakened doth not. And the LORD JESUS himself sets this down, as the sure, unerring testimony, in his account, to the carnal Jews. *He that is of* GOD, (saith CHRIST,) *heareth* GOD's *words. Ye therefore hear them not, because ye are not of* GOD. John viii. 47.

I admire the very beautiful manner of expression, made use of in these verses, in allusion to the LORD's resting, after the works of creation. *And* GOD *did rest the seventh day from all his works.* What rest? Not in a way of taking repose, as (speaking after the manner of men) we are said to do, when tired, and our work is over. But the calling into being of creatures, then ceased; and GOD rested from it, in a way of creation, when the whole which the LORD ordained to bring forth into life, was made. It is in this sense, the expression plainly means. And the same is meant of the personal work of CHRIST, as CHRIST. *For he that is entered into his rest, he also hath ceased from his own works as* GOD *did from his.* Yes! For when JESUS had *by himself purged our sins, he sat down on the right hand of the Majesty on high.* Chap. i. 3. Herein CHRIST, as our High Priest, differed from all other priests, who always *stood* ministering. And so far from ceasing, their offerings were daily. CHRIST's but once, and that in effect for ever. Oh! the preciousness of CHRIST! And true believers also, when ceasing from seeking justification, either in whole, or in part, from any, or all the works of their own; but count themselves, and every thing in themselves, filthy, and unclean; hanging upon CHRIST only, as the vessel upon the nail in a sure place: such may be said, as indeed was said before, (verse 3.) to rest on CHRIST, and enter by faith upon the enjoyment of it.

It may not be improper to observe, on what is said of JESUS, not having given the people rest, that it doth not mean the LORD JESUS CHRIST, but *Joshua*, the son of *Nun*, who succeeded *Moses* in the ministry of the Church. See Joshua i. 1. The name *Joshua*, is the same in the Hebrew language, as JESUS; and signifies SAVIOR. But though *Joshua* did bring the people into *Canaan*, yet this was only typical of a better rest, *which remaineth for the people of* GOD. Hence it is plain, by the LORD's speaking of another rest, this of *Joshua's* was not the one intended. CHRIST himself is indeed *the rest wherewith the* LORD *causeth the weary to rest, and this is the refreshing.* Isaiah xxviii. 12. Reader! it will be your happiness, and mine, if, under divine teaching, we are come to CHRIST, as our rest; and from a knowledge of Him, are made sensible of his bountiful dealing with us, in the rest of salvation. Matt. xi. 28, &c. Psm. cxvi. 7.

12 For the word of God *is* quick, and powerful, and sharper than any two edged sword, piercing even to the dividing asunder of soul and spirit, and of the joints and marrow, and *is* a discerner of the thoughts and intents of the heart.

13 Neither is there any creature that is not manifest in his sight: but all things *are* naked and open unto the eyes of him with whom we have to do.

The WORD of GOD is here evidently intended to mean, the uncreated WORD, of which *John* speaks in his Gospel. John i. 1. And let the Reader pause, and observe, what is here said of CHRIST's glory on this ground. His eyes, like a flame of fire, penetrates through all coverings. He is the Almighty *Zephnath-paaneah*, the great Revealer of secrets. What a folly to think that any thing can escape his observation? What an unanswerable proof of his GODHEAD?

14 Seeing then that we have a great high priest, that is passed into the heavens, Jesus the Son of God, let us hold fast *our* profession.

15 For we have not an high priest which cannot be touched with the feeling of our infirmities; but was in all points tempted like as *we are, yet* without sin.

16 Let us therefore come boldly unto the throne

of grace, that we may obtain mercy, and find grace to help in time of need.

I include these verses within one reading, because they are so interwoven, that it were a pity to consider them distinctly, for they form one beautiful whole. And yet, they open to so many volumes of subject, that a whole life of grace can never go over the several parts of them, so as to say, there is no more to be said upon them. In a *Poor Man's Commentary* I must study shortness, and therefore can only glance at the outlines.

And, *first.* We are called upon to follow the LAMB whithersoever he goeth; and here we are said to behold, with full confidence, our great High Priest, as passed into the heavens, JESUS the SON of GOD. I admire the manner in which this blessed truth is spoken. *Seeing then,* saith the Apostle; as if (and which is in reality the case,) all dispute about it was done away. There is a special emphasis on the words, *seeing then. He is gone into heaven,* (saith Peter). There CHRIST our forerunner, is entered. *And is on the right hand of* GOD: *angels, and authorities, and powers, being made subject unto him.* 1 Pet. iii. 22. And I admire the Apostle's joining to this account of CHRIST'S return to heaven, both the office of CHRIST, and the name of CHRIST. He had before in the second Chapter, spoken somewhat largely of CHRIST, as a Priest, and an High Priest; and here he calls him a *great* High Priest. And, as the Apostle delighted upon all occasions, to introduce the name of his LORD, whenever an opportunity offered, he adds to the account of our great High Priest having passed into the heavens; his name, JESUS *the* SON *of* GOD! Reader! note this down first, in your looking to Him, who is thus passed into the heavens. It is JESUS, GOD'S dear SON, and your dear High Priest; yea, your great High Priest!

Secondly, Paul herefrom, draws the strongest of all arguments, that we should *hold fast our profession.* Not as if this depended upon any strength in ourselves to hold it; but, that in CHRIST'S strength we should grasp it, and carry it about with us as the credentials of our faith, rather parting with life than with a belief in CHRIST. Isa. xxvii. 5. And this holding fast, implies making use of CHRIST upon all occasions; continually acting faith upon him; depending in him; and in spite of all temptations, resolutely holding on, and holding out, as those, who in a consciousness that He who is our great High Priest is passed into the heavens, hath obtained eternal redemption for us, by his blood and righteousness, and is now returned to heaven, to see the merit of it recompensed in some measure and degree, (though fully it never can be through all eternity,) to all his people. This is our profession. And the consciousness of CHRIST being passed into the heavens, is enough in itself to make all his people, in spite of hell and sin, to hold it fast.

Thirdly. But the next persuasion from these precious words, riseth still higher. *For we have not an High Priest which cannot be touched with the feeling of our infirmities, but was in all points tempted like as we are, yet without sin.* Of all the consolations and encouragements, under the trials of the faithful, these views of JESUS, are certainly the greatest, and the best. *First,* as they relate to CHRIST'S Person. And, *Secondly,* as they relate to his High Priestly Office.

Reader! what a thought is it, to lead the child of GOD to the mercy-seat of GOD in CHRIST, with every comfortable assurance of success, when we consider who it is we go to, what a knowledge he hath of our persons, wants, circumstances, trials, and difficulties; what a personal experience he himself hath had of the same things, being when upon earth *in all points tempted like as we are, yet without sin.* In all things else the same.

It is possible I may be singular. But, if I am, I can truly say I find the blessedness of it; and would not think otherwise than I do, on those sweet points, for a thousand worlds. I frequently say to myself, when my necessities compel me to go to the throne, (and, Reader, I fear, notwithstanding the frank and tender reception I always meet with there, when I go to my GOD and SAVIOR, I should seldom go there, did not my wants make me;) but I frequently say, was not JESUS made an High Priest purposely that He might be merciful? Was it not his deep love, and his deep affection to sinners, which made Him, of all others, the most fitted to be our High Priest? And will he not exercise it towards me? Doth not the very nature of an High Priest call for mercy? Would the office itself be needed, if there were not poor sinners to receive from it? It is most true, and it is most blessed in the truth, that JESUS is a great High Priest, and is passed into the heavens, in proof of his Almighty greatness, and his Almighty power; but what endears JESUS to my heart still more, is, that he is a merciful and faithful High Priest, in things pertaining to GOD; and can have compassion on the ignorant, and on them that are out of the way; in that, he himself was once encompassed with our infirmity, and was *in all points tempted like as we are, yet without sin.* Reader! is it not this which gives a lift to poor, tried, buffeted, tempted souls, and enables them to come *boldly to the throne of grace, to obtain mercy, and find grace to help in time of need?*

One word more. It is an additional argument, and the Apostle most blessedly blends it with the former; that not only CHRIST's greatness, and CHRIST's fellow-feeling and compassion, make him a suited High Priest for his people, and such as none other, but GOD and Man in one Person, can be; but also, that the exercises he himself hath gone through, and the sorrows in those exercises he hath borne, give him such a personal knowledge of all the cases and circumstances of his people, as nothing but the having trod the path himself could have brought him acquainted with. And, although it is most true, that as GOD he could have no additional knowledge, neither be more merciful, in taking upon him our nature, yet, had JESUS the SON of GOD not been man, as well as GOD, he could not have had human affections, and human feelings, in a personal experience of what human sorrows are. So that it doth tend to give yet further encouragement to go to JESUS, when we keep in remembrance, that he not only knows as GOD, but that he feels as man. And in his own breast, we have this sweet and affectionate advocate, in that *he knoweth our frame by his own, and how to administer the suited relief.*

Precious LORD JESUS! do thou, by the sweet influences of thy blessed SPIRIT, keep those views everlastingly alive in my heart; that my soul may have the most lively actings of faith, upon thy

Person, as GOD-Man, and thy knowledge, as having gone before in the tabulated path in my nature; so that I may not only come, but come boldly to thy mercy-seat, and always *obtain mercy, and find grace to help in time of need!*

REFLECTIONS.

How shall I properly prize my mercies, in the grace the LORD gives me, to receive and believe in JESUS; when I am told, as in this Chapter, that the *professing Israel* of old, to whom the Gospel was preached, found no profit, *not being mixed with faith in them that heard it.* Oh! how plain and evident it is, from the experience of mankind in all ages, that grace makes all the difference between *him who serveth* GOD, *and him who serveth him not.* LORD! cause thy Church, thy people, thy redeemed, to rest in CHRIST and his finished work, as GOD in creation, and CHRIST in redemption, rested from theirs. Oh! the sweet thought! There is a rest, and CHRIST is that rest, *which remaineth for the people of* GOD.

Oh! thou uncreated WORD! let my soul be always under thy soul-warning, and spirit-comforting power. And, as all things are naked, and open to thine all-piercing sight, do thou, LORD, impart the very grace thou seest to be needful for me. Oh! thou risen and exalted SAVIOR! Thou art indeed passed into the heavens. Thither would my soul by faith and love follow thee. JESUS knoweth me, feeleth for me, is sensibly touched with the circumstances of my infirmities. Surely, JESUS can, and JESUS will, impart all necessary strength, and my GOD and SAVIOR, will make me more than conqueror, through his grace helping me!

CHAP. V.

CONTENTS.

The same most precious Subject, as in the former Chapter, is carried on in this. Melchizedec *is spoken of. Precious Views of* CHRIST.

FOR every high priest taken from among men is ordained for men in things *pertaining* to God, that he may offer both gifts and sacrifices for sins:

2 Who can have compassion on the ignorant, and on them that are out of the way; for that he himself also is compassed with infirmity.

3 And by reason hereof he ought, as for the people, so also for himself, to offer for sins.

4 And no man taketh this honour unto himself, but he that is called of God, as *was* Aaron.

5 So also Christ glorified not himself to be made an high priest; but he that said unto him, Thou art my Son, to day have I begotten thee.

This is a very blessed Chapter. Every verse, more or less, is big with importance. It opens with shewing the nature and office of an High Priest. The very name implies somewhat of mediation. And, when considered with an eye to solemn transactions between GOD and Man, it is eminently so. The *first* feature described of his Person, who is an High Priest, is, that *he must be taken from among men.* He, that hath to mediate between GOD and men, must himself be a man, and not an angel; for an angel could not enter into the feelings of men; and therefore, could not be properly interested for those, in whose name he acted. *Secondly,* Not only must he be a man, who can, from his own feelings, judge how to act for man, and one of a nature like himself, but he must be able *to offer both gifts and sacrifices for sins. Gifts,* if needful, to obtain favor; and *sacrifices,* to do away the guilt of sin, in the way of GOD's appointment. I need not tell the Reader, that in all this, there is an allusion to the law. Indeed, all this is beautifully represented, as what the law required, and which was typical of CHRIST; in order to shew, how GOD the HOLY GHOST, under the gifts and sacrifices under the law, shadowed forth CHRIST; and how CHRIST, in the Gospel, hath fully become himself the whole substance of the law. If the Reader will turn to the law concerning gifts and sacrifices, he will discover how graciously the LORD the HOLY GHOST appointed those things in his Church, by way of preaching CHRIST in figure; until He, to whom the whole refered, came in Person, *to do away sin, by the sacrifice of himself.* Heb. ix. 26.

The priest, that was anointed to minister in holy things, was to form his judgment concerning sins done through ignorance by any of the people, and appoint a suitable sacrifice accordingly. The Reader will find a large account of this, Levit. iv. throughout, for both priest and people. And again, Numb. xv. 24—29. And, in like manner, concerning presumptuous sins. Levit. vi. and Numb. xv. 30. Now, upon all those occasions, the High Priest was supposed to enter into the feelings of the people, and to make, in some measure, their interest his own. So that none could be fit for an High Priest, but one taken from among men; and even among men, none but he who had a feeling heart, and who, from a consciousness that he himself was compassed with infirmities, *could have compassion on the ignorant, and on them that are out of the way.* And, after all these qualifications, still no man had an authority to take the office of High Priest upon him, uncalled of GOD. *Aaron* was specially called of GOD. And so much so, that the daring presumption of *Korah,* and his company, who sought the priesthood, uncalled, was punished with an awful death. See Numb. xvi. 1—35. Reader! if such a tremendous judgment, under the law, followed the unhallowed attempt of men to minister in holy things before the LORD, what may be ultimately expected to follow those, who, under the Gospel, run unsent, uncalled, and not only rush, like the unthinking horse to the battle, into the sacred department of the ministry, but profess to be moved by the HOLY GHOST, albeit every thing seems to speak concerning them, as in that Scripture : *I have not sent these prophets, yet they ran: I have not spoken to them, yet they prophesied.* Jer. xxiii. 21.

Reader! I need not, I should hope, call upon you to observe, what is in itself so very plain; that all that is here said, in these verses, concerning the High Priest, taken from among men, with those qualifications, and appointed of GOD, is here said, expressly to shew how CHRIST was taken from among men; how suited he was to such an office of mercy, and how fully authorized, and called of GOD to the appointment? But, Reader! though this was the evident intention of GOD the HOLY GHOST in this Scripture; and though, at first view, in reading what is here said of the great Jewish High Priest, *Aaron;* every child of GOD, who is taught of GOD, cannot but be immediately led, to contemplate the unequalled suitableness of our Almighty *Aaron,* the LORD JESUS CHRIST; as the One, and the only One, capable in all its departments to the performance of this high office: yet, I should be unpardonably remiss, in a work of this kind, to pass away from so interesting a subject, without first offering an observation or two upon it. The thoughts which arise out of it, are indeed very plain and striking; but they are not on that account the less beautiful and important. Let us look at a few of them.

And, *first.* As every High Priest was taken from among men, so the SON of GOD took upon him our nature for this express purpose, so that he also was taken from among men. For we are told, that *in all things it behoved him to be made like unto his brethren, that he might be a merciful and faithful High Priest, in things pertaining unto* GOD. Heb. ii. 17. And hence, when, in the counsel of peace, between the Persons of the GODHEAD, the LORD JEHOVAH is represented in Scripture as speaking in vision to his HOLY ONE, these are the words which were spoken, *I have laid help upon* ONE *that is mighty; I have exalted One chosen out of the people.* Psm. lxxxix. 19. And as JESUS, our great High Priest, was taken from among men, so was he ordained for men. For there would have needed no High Priest, nor sacrifice, had there been no sinners. But, as CHRIST's Church, CHRIST's people, his spouse, whom he betrothed to himself before all worlds, had fallen into sin; the SON of GOD came to redeem her from all sin, by the sacrifice of himself. And, as GOD the FATHER, first gave her to his dear SON, so GOD the FATHER ordained CHRIST from among men, to be an High Priest, to act the part of an High Priest, to redeem her to himself, and *to present her to himself a glorious Church; not having spot, or wrinkle, or any such thing, but to be without blame before him in love.* Eph. v. 26, 27.

Secondly. As no man, among men, would have suited the office of an High Priest, according to what this blessed Chapter saith, but such as could have compassion on the ignorant, and on them that are out of the way; so the great feature of character, in our dear LORD, to constitute him High Priest, was eminently his great meekness and tenderness of heart. GOD the FATHER's account of him was this by the Prophet. Meek and lowly: Isa. xlii. 1—4. compared with Matt. ii. 28, 29. and Matt. xii. 17—21. And, although in point of holiness, CHRIST was *holy, harmless, and undefiled:* and, in point of power, *made higher than the heavens:* and, in point of understanding, *in him were hid all the treasures of wisdom and knowledge;* yet, though all these were indeed requisites for the high office of the Priesthood, it was the infinite compassions of his heart, which made him so peculiarly suited for our High Priest, and more immediately hath endeared him to the affections of his people. Heb. vii. 26. Coloss. ii. 3. Heb. iv. 14, 15, 16.

Thirdly. Our great High Priest, as in Person and qualifications, so in gifts and sacrifices, hath infinitely transcended all the offerings made by mere men. The priest taken from among men, who had a tender heart, and who, upon due consideration of the sinner's offence, when he came to him, knew how to distinguish, and to make an offering accordingly, between sins of ignorance, and sins of presumption, acted in a very suitable manner, as the law appointed, (see Levit. iv. and Numb. xvi.) but the gifts and offerings of JESUS, were *himself,* which not only included an all-sufficient ransom for all sins, both of omission and commission, but carried with it such an over-value, resulting from the dignity of his Person, and the preciousness of the offering, as can never be fully recompensed to the Church of GOD, to all eternity. Reader! think of this! Such is the efficacy of CHRIST's merits and sacrifice, that the remuneration to the LORD's body the Church, can never be made, so as to say, there is nothing more to be received, in a way of acknowledgment, to all eternity!

Fourthly. One very blessed view meets us in this subject, of a similarity in the cases of the Jewish High Priest, to that of our Almighty LORD, only here also, as in all other comparisons with an infinite suriority on the part of JESUS; I mean, in that it is said, the High Priest taken from among men, must have been one that could have compassion on the ignorant, and on them that were out of the way, in that *he himself also was compassed with infirmity.* Here opens a most precious view of JESUS. Though in himself he knew no sin, yet he personally knew all the sinless infirmities of our nature. Though none of our sins was put *in* him, yet the LORD laid *on* him the iniquities of all his people. Isa. liii. 6. Though, in himself, temptations had no power, yet, temptations, in all the varieties of being tempted, he knew; and was in all points tempted as we are. And, though *no guile was found in his mouth,* yet, surely, in the years he lived in our world, all the sin he beheld in his people, became so many wounds to his heart. If *the filthy conversation of the wicked vexed the soul of Lot day by day*; what must the holy JESUS have felt, when he *endured such a contradiction of sinners against himself?* 2 Pet. ii. 8. Heb. xii. 3. Reader! here again contemplate the suitableness of the LORD JESUS, in his High Priestly Office, for the boundless compassion of his heart, and for the compassion he must still feel for the ignorant of his people, and all their infirmities, seeing he himself was compassed with all of them; though in himself without sin, and liable to none of them in the possibility of error.

Fifthly. We must not overlook one feature more belonging to our LORD, as our great High Priest, to which the Jewish high priest could bear no comparison. I mean, that the interests of CHRIST are blended with the interests of the people. He that acted as an high priest in the Jewish church for men, and was taken from among men, might have had, and no doubt he had being from the Lord's appointment, a feeling heart. But he could go no further. If he succeeded not when he had made his offering, he might indeed lament in secret, as holy men of old did, over the sins of the people. But, with our High Priest, there can be no failure. His Church is his body. Her concerns are his. The glory of Christ, is more than all the events to his people. That glory ensures his Church's interest. Hence, she must succeed in all her members. Jesus must see *of the travail of his soul, and be satisfied.* Isa. liii. 11. And, hence that blessed intercession of Christ, as our High Priest: Father! I will! *that they also whom thou hast given me, be with me where I am, that they may behold my glory.* John xvii. 24.

Lastly: and as the crown of all. As no man presumed to act as an High Priest, in the Church of God, uncalled of God, so sweetly are we told, in this blessed Scripture, that Christ, though Son of God, and equal with the Father and the Holy Ghost, in his divine nature, yet, when taking upon him our nature, glorified not himself to be made an High Priest, but was called to it; yea, and sworn into it, (different from all other priests, Heb. vii. 21.) and consecrated in it, an High Priest for ever, in an unchangeable priesthood, after the order of *Melchizedec!* This is a grand point ever to be kept in view, in our remembrance of the priesthood of Christ. This gives validity and efficacy to all. Here is the warrant to faith to believe *the record which* God *gives of his dear* Son. Hence, every child of God, coming to the mercy-seat of God in Christ, finds confidence and boldness in the double view, that Jehovah's authority, and his name, is in Christ; and, therefore, in the efficacy of Christ's blood and righteousness, he cannot but meet with a most gracious reception. Heb. x. 19—23. Reader! I must not trespass any longer. The subject, indeed, is in itself endless. Oh! for grace to have it always in view! Jesus is my High Priest. He was, and is, and ever must be, One with the Father over all God blessed for ever, Amen. He was also, in his human nature, taken from among men. He can have compassion, yea, boundless compassion. Not simply by taking our nature only, but by having known that nature compassed with infirmities. And now in heaven he wears that nature still. And he cannot but recollect his former exercises, when on earth, and which hath everlastingly suited him, by past experiences, for sympathy, and fellow-feeling for his people here below. Precious High Priest of thy people! surely, all thy redeemed upon earth are as dear to thee, and as much watched over by thee, and loved and regarded by thee, as thy redeemed in heaven. Isaiah xxvii. 3.

6 As he saith also in another *place,* Thou *art* a priest for ever after the order of Melchisedec.

I will not detain the Reader with a long observation on what the Holy Ghost hath here said, concerning the same authority which made Christ High Priest, which said also unto him, *Thou art my* Son, *to-day have I begotten thee.* To enter into the whole of this passage to the full, and follow it up with the remarks which arise out of the Scripture, would fill many pages. Let it in this place be sufficient to observe, that, in whatever sense the words be taken, they are most highly expressive of the eternal nature and glory of the SON of GOD. They are a quotation from the second Psalm; where CHRIST, being set by JEHOVAH as King on his holy hill of Zion the Church; and having, as is represented by vision in the Revelations, been alone found *worthy to open the book, and loose the seals thereof,* (Rev. v. 1—10.) now, as King in Zion, declares the decree. And the first Chapter in this mysterious volume, which none but CHRIST could open, is the sovereign purpose of JEHOVAH, and addressed to CHRIST, as CHRIST, *Thou art my* SON, *this day have I begotten thee.* Reader! pause one moment, and remark the superior blessedness of all that GOD the FATHER saith to his dear SON, to every other declaration whatever. Very blessed it is to hear the LORD speaking in a way of grace to the Church. And very blessed, when all that the LORD saith to the Church, the LORD gives grace to hear and obey. But, oh! how sweet beyond the expression of all language is it, when we hear the LORD the FATHER speaking to his dear SON, concerning his blessing the Church in Him? Here GOD the FATHER is the Almighty Speaker; CHRIST is the sum and substance of all his proclamations to the Church; and GOD the HOLY GHOST gives the hearing ear, and the seeing eye, *to believe the record* GOD *hath given of his* SON. 1 John v. 10, 11.

The blessedness of the words themselves, in confirmation, that He who called CHRIST to be an High Priest, said also unto him, *Thou art my* SON, *to-day have I begotten thee;* very plainly were designed to shew, that in no office of Sonship, or Priesthood, did CHRIST, as CHRIST, enter uncalled of GOD. So that the words are very important, in proof of CHRIST's authority. But, it should be observed also, that they are no less very precious, in confirmation of CHRIST's being set up from everlasting, in his high Mediator-character. *To-day* cannot refer to the nature and essence of the SON of GOD, as GOD; for eternity is never called, in Scripture language, *to-day.* And although CHRIST, as CHRIST, could not have been set up in his Mediator-character from everlasting, had he not in his divine nature and essence as GOD, been one with the FATHER and the HOLY GHOST from all eternity; yet, here the HOLY GHOST is evidently speaking of CHRIST, as CHRIST, in his character of Mediator. This is the decree which the Book, when unsealed and opened, was found to contain; and the SON of GOD, who came forth from the bosom of the FATHER, came forth to declare. John i. But it was no decree, nor the result of any covenant-settlement, between the persons of the GODHEAD, concerning man's redemption, to declare the SON of GOD, as SON of GOD in his essence of GODHEAD; for this he was, and is, and will be, in the eternity of his nature, for ever. In relation to CHRIST being said to be a Priest, after the order of *Melchizedec,* we shall have occasion to speak of it more fully, Chap. vii. to which therefore I refer.

7 Who in the days of his flesh, when he had offered up prayers and supplications with strong crying and tears unto him that was able to save him from death, and was heard in that he feared;

8 Though he were a Son, yet learned he obedience by the things which he suffered;

In these verses we have a most interesting account of our Lord. It will be our mercy to consider what the Holy Ghost hath here said of Jesus. By *the days of his flesh*, must be understood, the different state to that of his glory. The expression is strong to this purpose. The *days* of his flesh; not the flesh that is his human nature itself, for that he hath the same still, but the time of his abode in our world, accomplishing the redemption of his people. During this period of the Son of God's humiliation on earth, he was subject to all the feelings and infirmities of that nature, which he had assumed, and was *in all points tempted like as we are, yet without sin.* Heb. iv. 15. And it is our mercy that he was so; because it proves the certainty of his having been made like to his brethren, that he might be a merciful and faithful High Priest, in things pertaining to God. Hence, under this consciousness, I can, and do, go to Jesus, because he knows what my nature is by his own. He not only knows it, as God, but he feels it as man. He, who in the days of his flesh offered up prayers and supplications with strong crying and tears, will assuredly now, in the day of his power, take part in his High Priestly Office with his people, when in their depth of sorrow they cry to the depth of divine mercy. Psm. cxxx. 1—3.

I beg the Reader not to overlook what is said of Christ being heard, in that he feared. It is not said that Christ was *fearful*, but that he *feared*. There is a *natural* fear, which, no doubt, the Lord Jesus, by taking our nature, felt; for, without it, he could not be said to be in *all things made like unto his brethren.* Heb. ii. 17. And, in confirmation, we read, that in his agony in the garden, *he was sore amazed.* Mark xiv. 33. And beside this *natural* fear, there is a *godly* fear, which marks the Lord's people, and is the gift of the Holy Spirit. The Lord promiseth this as a covenant blessing: Jerem. xxxii. 40. This the Lord Jesus himself possessed, when the Spirit of Jehovah rested upon him. Isaiah xi. 2. Such views will help us to understand, concerning those cries of Jesus which he offered up, in the days of his flesh, when it is said, *he was heard in that he feared.*

One word more on this interesting passage. The Son of God it is said, *learned obedience by the things which he suffered.* By which I presume is meant, that he learned, not as Son of God, but in his human nature, by personal feeling, in human sufferings, and human exercises. He acquired in that school, the full apprehension of suffering obedience, in suffering distresses; and, in a personal sense, of what we feel, he knew, what our exercises are. Sweet thought! *In that he himself, hath suffered, being tempted; he knoweth how to succour them that are tempted!*

9 And being made perfect, he became the author of eternal salvation unto all them that obey him;

10 Called of God an high priest after the order of Melchisedec.

11 Of whom we have many things to say, and hard to be uttered, seeing ye are dull of hearing.

12 For when for the time ye ought to be teachers, ye have need that one teach you again, which *be* the first principles of the oracles of God; and are become such as have need of milk, and not of strong meat.

13 For every one that useth milk *is* unskilful in the word of righteousness: for he is a babe.

14 But strong meat belongeth to them that are of full age, *even* those who by reason of use have their senses exercised to discern both good and evil.

There is somewhat particularly striking, in these words, concerning CHRIST, *being made perfect.* By which, we must of course accept the terms, as referring wholly to his character of Mediator. The perfection of the GODHEAD, can never be said to be *made.* And it is most evident, and plain, from all the concurrent testimony of scripture, that every act of perfection, revealed or made manifest; and all the revelations made of JEHOVAH, are in the Person of the GOD-Man CHRIST JESUS. As in *creation*, it is most decidedly said, that *all things were made by him, and that without him was not any thing made that was made;* so in all the after acts of *grace;* every communication of JEHOVAH, in redemption, providence, grace, glory: all are wholly in, and by CHRIST. It is the SON of GOD, which in our nature came forth, from the invisibility of GOD, to make known GOD, and the purposes of his will, to his creatures. And in a more especial manner, the whole work of redemption is said to be his. He became the Author of it; and that eternal. A plain proof of the eternity of *his* nature by whom it is wrought.

Whether CHRIST, or *Melchizedec*, be meant, by what is here said, of having much to relate, and yet hard to be uttered, is not so clearly shewn. The person of CHRIST and his priesthood: or in relation to *Melchizedec*, and his priesthood; vast things are folded up in mystery, which the LORD only can unfold to his people. *Paul* speaking of his LORD, calls his Gospel *the unsearchable, riches of* CHRIST. Ephes. iii. 8. And what is unsearchable cannot be fully revealed. But from the figures, or similitudes, of babes in CHRIST, unskilful in the word of righteousness, we learn, how deep the science is; and how much like children, yea, and little children too, the LORD's people are, during their minority in this world. Very blessed it is, when the LORD the SPIRIT, leads on the people of GOD, to acquire fuller views of the Person, and work, and glory of CHRIST; and when the actings of their faith are going forth, in continual exercise upon Him, as *the* LORD *our righteousness.* Oh! for grace, to be always sending in, before the LORD, the cry of the soul: LORD! *increase our faith!*

REFLECTIONS.

Precious great High Priest of thy people! Lord! I would hail thee as both my Priest, Altar, and Sacrifice. Thou wert indeed taken from among men: for in thy human nature, thou wert alone suited for the high office. Who, like Jesus, could have compassion on the ignorant, and on them that are out of the way: from a knowledge, like Jesus, of the infirmities of our nature, tempted in all points like as we are, yet without sin? And who like Jesus, could be begotten to the Sonship of his holy nature, and be sworn into the office of an high priest for ever, after the order of *Melchizedec?* Surely Lord, none but Jesus could offer up gifts and sacrifices for sins. Neither could there be any thing short of thy divine nature, to offer gifts and sacrifices *upon*, and to give acceptance and efficacy *to*, all offerings, but the Person, blood, and righteousness of God's dear Son? And oh! what everlasting efficacy, hath the one offering of my God and Savior wrought; and his everlasting unchanging priesthood, made secure, to render both his priesthood and his sacrifice of eternal duration, confirmed also by the oath of Him, who hath sworn, and will not repent; *Thou art a Priest for ever after the order of Melchizedec!*

Oh! for grace from God the Spirit, never to lose sight of the mercy-seat itself, that the whole purpose, for which it is erected is for mercy. There would have needed no mercy-seat, had not Christ's children been sinners. Neither would God the Father have constituted his dear Son, as high Priest, and formed him in our nature in this office, but that he might have compassion on the ignorant, and on them that are out of the way. The very office itself, and the conscious sense of Him who sits there, are full to this purpose, that God hath chosen Jesus expressly with this view; and Jesus hath infinite dimensions of love, that he might be a merciful and faithful high Priest, in things pertaining to God, to make reconciliation for the sins of his people. Lord! may I never lose sight of these things! may I always have in contemplation thy Person, and thy high priestly office; and by faith, behold my Lord, still clothed in a vesture, dipped in blood, as if to tell me, Jesus wears these robes, in proof of his unceasing office. Let me day by day, come boldly to thy throne, and *find grace to help, in all time of need.*

CHAP. VI.

CONTENTS.

The Hebrews are exhorted to Perseverance in the Faith. The Case of the Unregenerate is considered. The Chapter ends, in a very blessed Manner, in relating the Will of Jehovah, *that the Heirs of Promise, should be shewn his unchangeable Counsel concerning them!*

THEREFORE leaving the principles of the doctrine of Christ, let us go on unto perfection; not laying again the foundation of repentance from dead works, and of faith toward God.

2 Of the doctrine of baptisms, and of laying on of hands, and of resurrection of the dead, and of eternal judgment.

3 And this will we do, if God permit.

This Chapter opens in a very beautiful and striking manner. CHRIST is considered as the whole sum and substance of the Gospel; and as such, the Gospel is here called *the doctrine* of CHRIST. And the reason is plain. Because all the purpose, will, and decree, of JEHOVAH; in his threefold character of Person, are made known, and revealed in, and by CHRIST. CHRIST himself is JEHOVAH's salvation. Hence, CHRIST is called the CHRIST of GOD; the sent of GOD, the sealed of GOD, the lamb of GOD, and the like; in all the parts of the divine word. And what is everlastingly to be kept in view, in these our contemplations of CHRIST is, that it is the Person of CHRIST, which is all along spoken of, as the great object of faith. JESUS himself, in a very blessed and comprehensive manner, sums up the whole of the principles of everlasting life, when he saith it is *seeing the* SON, *and believing on him.* John vi. 40. So that it is not simply the doctrines of CHRIST, but CHRIST himself, which faith hath for its object, of hope and trust, and confidence, and joy; and which of necessity include, the doctrines of CHRIST as the greater include the less. And hence, this blessed Chapter opens with observing that the Church, when brought into a state of regeneration, should leave, (that is, should pass on,) from what we have been taught, of the first rudiments of the word, in repentance, and the like; to study CHRIST. Like those, who from the first hearing of the LORD, are going on to a greater knowledge of him; who passing through the outer courts, are now introduced into the inner apartments of the king's presence, and becoming daily more and more acquainted, with the LORD, in having *fellowship with the* FATHER, *and with his* SON JESUS CHRIST. 1 John i. 3. *Paul* hath another beautiful train of ideas, to the same effect, when he saith; that the measure of grace, given to the several orders in the Church, is *for the perfecting of the saints, for the work of the ministry; for the edifying of the body of* CHRIST; *till we all come, in the unity of the faith, and of the knowledge of the* SON *of* GOD, *unto a perfect man, unto the measure of the stature, of the fulness of* CHRIST. Ephes. iv. 12, 13.

I know not, whether I explain myself to the Reader's apprehension. But according to my view of what the HOLY GHOST here saith, it should seem, that the LORD is drawing a line of distinction, between CHRIST, as he is in himself; and the fullness of all things, as he stands to his people, and all ordinances whatever. Repentance, faith, doctrine of baptisms, laying on of hands and the like, are all in their respective places to be suitably regarded, as means of grace; but all, and every one of them, are but *effects*, and not, in the smallest degree, as any procuring *cause* of our salvation. CHRIST himself is the sole *cause;* and consequently ought to be the sole *object,* of a believer's hope and trust. And therefore to seek comfort from any thing beside, or to rest in any thing short of centering all in CHRIST, is to seek the living among the dead. Let us (saith the Apostle) leave these, as the principles we began with, when first we heard of the LORD JESUS, and every other ordinance, to live upon the GOD of Ordinances; and be more earnest to be satisfied, with the substance, than the being amused with the shadow.

Reader! pause over this view of the subject. There is nothing more highly important, to the comfort and peace of a child of GOD, than a clear apprehension of having CHRIST, our one only portion, and living upon him. Many of CHRIST's little ones, are unconscious of this; and therefore live below their privileges. They know the LORD, and love the LORD, and professedly are looking for salvation only in the LORD. But notwithstanding these things, they are more occupied with what are called the doctrines of CHRIST than CHRIST himself. They enjoy CHRIST at second hand. They look at him through ordinances, and through the exercise of their graces. Surely there is an error here. It is CHRIST himself, which ought to be the first object in our view, and every other concern, but as mediums, and channels, to pass through to him. It is true, indeed, that the doctrines of CHRIST, and the ordinances of CHRIST, are all valuable, as connected with him; and in having him, we have all. But for a child of GOD, to be more intent upon them, than upon him; to be more pleased, with some supposed gracious disposition wrought *in us,* than in the glorious, and complete work, CHRIST hath wrought *for us;* this is putting the *effect,* for the *cause;* and the *servant* in the place of his *master.* This is not making CHRIST in our view, what CHRIST is, in GOD's view; the Alpha, and Omega the first, and the last: the author and finisher of salvation. CHRIST is the first in all GOD's thoughts, and the last, and ultimate object of all GOD's designs. I know, that there are many of GOD's dear children, who would tremble if they were found, having any other views; and who would not intentially for the world, place any object before CHRIST, or in the room of CHRIST; but certainly, this is the case, when we take comfort in any grace, without eyeing CHRIST in the grace; and are found magnifying the *effects* of CHRIST's love, more than CHRIST himself. It is a sad consequence of our fallen state, and the imperfection of our faith, when the Person of CHRIST is hidden from our dim-sighted view, in a cloud of his own gifts.

4 For *it is* impossible for those who were once enlightened, and have tasted of the heavenly gift, and were made partakers of the Holy Ghost.

5 And have tasted the good word of God, and the powers of the world to come.

6 If they shall fall away, to renew them again unto repentance; seeing they crucify to themselves the Son of God afresh, and put *him* to an open shame.

7 For the earth which drinketh in the rain that cometh oft upon it, and bringeth forth herbs meet for them by whom it is dressed, receiveth blessing from God.

8 But that which beareth thorns and briers *is* rejected, and *is* nigh unto cursing; whose end *is* to be burned.

9 But, beloved, we are persuaded better things of you, and things that accompany salvation, though we thus speak.

10 For God *is* not unrighteous to forget your work and labour of love, which ye have shewed toward his name, in that ye have ministered to the saints, and do minister.

11 And we desire that every one of you do shew the same diligence to the full assurance of hope unto the end.

12 That ye be not slothful, but followers of them who through faith and patience inherit the promises.

In the opening of this paragraph, we have those memorable verses of scripture, which, for want of due attention, to divine teaching, by the perversion of *some*, and the mistaken apprehension of *others*, have given rise, to much anxiety, in weak minds, through the slenderness of their faith. There can be no doubt, but that God the Holy Ghost is drawing the portrait of finished hypocrites; for there is not a single feature, in the whole of what is represented, of those falling away, which belongs to a child of God. The persons here described, under such a flaming profession, never were *in* grace; and therefore impossible to have fallen *from* grace. They fell from a profession only, and as such, it became impossible to renew them again to repentance. As the subject in itself is so highly important, and as a right apprehension of the Lord's words, is so truly interesting to every regenerated child of God, and, especially, the weak in faith, I shall hope the Reader's indulgence, if I enter upon the whole of it, very particularly. For my own part, I am very fully convinced, that the passage, hath no one reference whatever to the Church of God: that the Lord the Holy Ghost is speaking of hypocrites, and the unregenerate *only*; and that the whole subject, if duly considered, is calculated more to comfort, than to distress the Lord's people. May God the Spirit, the blessed Author of his holy word, be our Teacher in it, and guide both Writer and Reader of this *Poor Man's Commentary*, into all truth.

And here I beg the Reader, again to remark, what I have so often observed to him, in the course of this little work; that GOD the HOLY GHOST, is writing this whole Epistle to the *Church;* to them *who are the heirs of salvation.* This is a great point always to have in view, and to keep in remembrance, as we prosecute every part of this Epistle. See Chap. i. 2, 3, 9, 14.

Let me next desire the Reader, to look back to the concluding verses of the preceding Chapter, where he expressly speaketh to the Church, as being in grace, though weak in the faith. The LORD tells them, that when for a time they ought to have been teachers, they were so weak in faith, and their progress in the divine life, had been so inconsiderable, that they need, like little children, to go over their first lessons again. See Chap. v. 12. to the end. And hence, the LORD opens this Chapter, with bidding them to leave the first principles of doctrine, and go on to perfection, namely, to CHRIST himself, Chap. vi. 1. Now let the Reader pause, and ask himself, whether the very expressions, which the LORD the HOLY GHOST here useth, towards the Church, do not very fully prove, that they were in grace, though in a low and languishing condition? How could they be said, that for the time they ought to have been teachers, if they themselves had never learnt? How could even milk suit them, if they were dead in trespasses and sins? Mark these things as proofs, from the LORD the SPIRIT himself, that the Persons to whom he wrote were considered by him as regenerate.

Thirdly. Let the Reader further observe in this paragraph that while the LORD is speaking of the impossibility to renew hypocrites, who made a flaming profession of godliness, but never had felt the power of it; the LORD at the same time is speaking to the Church, and calling them *beloved,* concerning whom he was *persuaded better things, and things which accompany salvation;* that they had *ministered to the saints their labor of love,* and that they were *still ministering;* and that GOD *would not forget it!* And hence, having before called upon them, to forget first principles, and go on to CHRIST; they would now *shew the same diligence to the full assurance of hope, unto the end:* and no longer *be slothful, but followers of them, who through faith and patience inherit the promises.* And in a following chapter, the LORD bids them, *to call their former days to remembrance, in which, after they were illuminated, they endured a great fight of affliction.* And therefore, as *they knew in themselves, that they had in heaven a better, and an enduring substance, they should not cast away the confidence, which hath great recompence of reward.* Chap. x. 32—35.

Let the Reader ponder well, these features of character in the Church, to whom GOD the HOLY GHOST sends this Epistle; and mark in them, the clear testimonies which they carry with them, of being in a state of regeneration. And when he hath duly considered this point, I will next request him to attend to the several outlines, which the same Almighty LORD hath drawn of those unregenerate, concerning whom he speaks in those verses. Let us look at them one by one.

And *first.* They are said to have been *once enlightened.* By which I apprehend is meant, an enlightening in headknowledge. And it is astonishing to conceive, to what lengths men, who have been agcustomed to sit under the sound of the Gospel may go, in this way, without possessing an atom of saving grace. But the doctrine of CHRIST, in insisting on the new birth, throws to the ground all, and every pretension short of this. John iii. 7. It is *with the heart, man believeth unto righteousness.* Rom. x. 10. If head-knowledge, would make wise unto salvation, the devil himself, would be in a salvable state; for he told CHRIST, he knew him. Mark i. 24. I presume no one will venture to call this enlightening, a mark of regeneration.

Secondly. They are said to have *tasted of the heavenly gift.* Yes, CHRIST is the heavenly gift, in the Gospel sent down from heaven. And these hypocrites had so far tasted it, as to dislike it. Redemption by CHRIST'S blood, and righteousness alone: no *Pharisee* will relish, but, like children, which nauseate medicine, though it tendeth to heal, yet spit it out of their mouth. Here again, we find no mark of real grace.

Thirdly. They are said to be made *partakers of the* HOLY GHOST. This, in the first view, carries with it somewhat more plausible; but when looked into, is but seemingly so, for it hath no more of real saving grace, than the former. Every one may, in one sense, be said, to be made partakers of the HOLY GHOST, who is brought under the preaching of the Gospel, and partakes in the ordinances and means of grace. They whose carcases fell in the wilderness, as well as the faithful, whom the LORD brought into *Canaan* were all alike partakers of the Manna, and drank of the Rock, and had the carnal ordinances of the worldly sanctuary. Heb. ix 1. But, none except the chosen seed, eyed CHRIST in all. Nay, further, some there have been in all ages of the Church, which may be said to have been made partakers of the HOLY GHOST, in his *outward* gifts of working miracles; and who yet, were never partakers of the HOLY GHOST, in his *inward* regenerating grace. The magicians in the court of *Pharaoh,* to a certain degree, were permitted to exercise power; and *Judas* in the college of Apostles, without all doubt, had the same faculty, in *outward* acts with them. Luke ix. 1. But in the midst of these, there was no inward work of GOD the SPIRIT on either; and the new-birth is the only infallible character.

Fourthly. Those persons are said, to have tasted *the good word of* GOD and the *powers of the world to come.* Not drank into the spirit of those precious things; not relished them. The HOLY GHOST dwells particularly on *tasting,* as if to shew their aversion. They tasted of the good word of GOD, so as to manifest their more deadly hatred to it; and they heard enough of the powers of the world to come, as in their consciences to believe there is an hereafter, in which it will be well with the righteous, and ill with the wicked; but, like *Balaam,* though sufficiently convinced of those solemn truths, as now and then to send forth the wish *to die the death of the righteous,* yet never awakened by grace to live their life. Numb. xxiii. 10.

Reader! pause over those portraits of character, for they are truly awful, and perhaps much more general than is imagined. But what hath the child of GOD to do with such things, in whose spirit the HOLY SPIRIT beareth witness that he *is* born of GOD? They are indeed very awful monuments for the children of GOD to contemplate, as they pass on their pilgrimage state. We behold in them to what an height of elevation nature may go in a way of resembling grace.

And they ought to serve, as no doubt God the Holy Ghost intended them to serve, to make the regenerated the more awakened, to leave the first principles of the doctrines, and press on after Christ. But while such clear marks are discoverable between nature and grace, surely the children of God ought not to confound one with the other. To be led into the conclusion, that there may be a falling from grace, because men who never were in grace, have for a while taken up with a profession, and then dropped it, is forming conclusions from false premises. Nature, in her highest attainments, is but nature. Nothing can rise above its level. It is very possible, that by hearing sermons, attending the means of grace, and the like, the understanding may be much enlightened. The young man in the Gospel, who came to Christ, at first seemed to look fair for heaven. *Paul*, the Apostle, while a Pharisee, thought himself not far from glory. But in both, at the time, there was not a single act of renewing grace wrought in their heart. The unregenerate mind is still carnal, and enmity against God. The tiger, though chained, is the tiger still. Nothing short of the new-birth is grace. Where this is, it is impossible to fall away, for the Scripture saith, that the highly beloved objects *are made partakers of the divine nature, having escaped the corruption that is in the world through lust.* 2 Pet. i. 3, 4. Where this is not, the most flaming profession will go out in obscure darkness. *They have the form, but not the power of godliness.* 2 Tim. iii. 5.

Before I dismiss this view of the subject, I would add one observation more, by way of confirming what hath been said, namely, that in all that is said of those hypocrites, there is not a single circumstance, even hinted at, of those precious fruits and effects being found in them, which arise from grace in the heart, and where a saving act of regeneration hath passed upon the soul. In this whole account of being enlightened, and having tasted of the heavenly gift, we read nothing of faith, or love, an adherence to Jesus, or affection to his people; not a word of an holy life and conversation, all which are the sure consequences of the new-birth. But, all that is said from beginning to end, is no more than what may be said of mere professors only, who are like *clouds without water*, carried about with mere wind of doctrine; who, though they have a name to live, are virtually dead before God.

Hence, as is here said, if they fall away from this profession, and openly deny it, and (as hath been seen in many instances,) after having put on a sanctity of appearance, and by restraints induced by the fear or praise of men, have for a while seemingly escaped the pollution which is in the world through lust, at length return, like a dog to his vomit, and as the sow that was washed, to her wallowing in the mire; they only manifest that all that was before seen of them, was but the efforts of nature, not grace. And how shall they be rendered again to the same profession? The thing is impossible. They may indeed, like *Judas, repent themselves,* and do as he did, hang themselves; but the Lord will not grant to them his grace of repentance, in the regeneration of the heart. And for this plain reason. They do in effect, by their denial of that faith they once owned in head, though felt it not in heart, *crucify to themselves the Son of God afresh, and put him to an open shame.* For, as, when the

Gospel of CHRIST was preached, and made known to them, that is, when they were once enlightened with the head knowledge, that the SON of GOD had been crucified for his people; and their sense and understanding, though not their affections, were gained to the acknowledgment of those glorious truths, connected with CHRIST and his great salvation; they professed to receive them, and believe them; but now by their apostacy from the truth, as it is in JESUS, they crucify to themselves the SON of GOD afresh, either by denying his GODHEAD as the SON of GOD, or that his offering on the cross was not a sufficient sacrifice for the redemption of his people; that he hath not risen from the dead; salvation is not finished, and somewhat more is needed for justification before GOD; in either, or all of these, or the like objections, this is to crucify the SON of GOD afresh, and put him to an open shame. And utterly impossible is it, in such cases, to renew such men to repentance. I beg the Reader to mark the expression, they crucify to themselves. Yes! in their apostacy and denial they fully prove CHRIST was never crucified *for* them; for they have no part, nor lot in the one all-sufficient sacrifice of CHRIST upon the cross; and therefore they insult the soul-travail and agonies which CHRIST sustained by their despising the efficacy of his blood. Such become hardened in iniquity, and their *last end is worse than the first.*

The figure of the earth drinking in the rain, is a beautiful similitude in a way of further illustration. For, as the rain falls alike on the earth, both where the pure herbs are, and where the thorns are; so the dew of the Gospel descends upon the whole visible Church, both real and nominal. But while the regenerated, under the genial influence, bring forth to the glory of GOD; the mere professor only sends forth nothing but the rank weeds and briars of the state of nature, unredeemed from the curse, and whose end is to be burned.

And the next verse, wherein the Apostle calls the Church *beloved*, and declares his persuasion of better things concerning the members of it, is so utterly opposed to what went before, as can hardly be reconciled, upon any other idea, than that the HOLY GHOST intended the whole representation he hath here made of such flaming profession void of all vital godliness, but as a matter of comfort to the LORD's people under all their short comings and attainments. For, slender as their growth had been, yet they had truly been regenerated. Babes as they still were, yet this argued the new-birth. So that there is, and ever must be, an everlasting *difference* between the falling away of professors, who never were in grace, and those whom the LORD hath quickened. For while the child of GOD, when born of that *incorruptible seed which liveth and abideth for ever*, (and must so live and abide for ever, however dormant to our view, the spiritual seed sometimes appears, because *it remaineth in him*, 1 Pet. i. 23. 1 John iii. 9.) hath a renewed nature, the Scriptures no where speak of mere professors, amidst all the high elevations of nature, as *being born again.* The stony ground hearers, receive the word with great joy, but no fruit followed, because they had no root. And when those flashes of joy subsided, they soon died away. Hence the Prophet speaks, *There shall be no more thence an infant of days, nor an old man that hath not filled his days, for the child* (regenerated) *shall die an hundred years old; but the sinner, being an hundred years old* (yet unregenerated) *shall be accursed.* Isa. lxv. 20.

Such, then, according to my view of this blessed Scripture, appears to be the doctrine contained in it. The HOLY GHOST is writing to the Church, considered in a state of regeneration; not unsimilar to the same purport as when writing to the *Corinthians;* babes in CHRIST, but yet too much occupied in worldly things, and of consequence, making slow progress in spiritual attainments, 1 Cor. iii. 1, 2. He tells them, in opening his Epistle, in confirmation of their new-birth, and justification in CHRIST, that CHRIST *had by himself purged their sins;* and that they were heirs of salvation, Chap. i. 3, 14. that CHRIST had not taken *the nature of angels,* but *the seed of Abraham,* on their account; and that, *having himself suffered, being tempted;* he knew how *to succor them that were tempted.* Chap. ii. 14, 18. that they were *partakers of* CHRIST, as a rich blessing not to be lost, and therefore were *to hold fast their confidence of hope firm to the end.* Chap. iii. 14. And that having such *an High Priest as the* SON *of* GOD, *passed into the heavens, they were to come boldly to the throne of grace, and obtain mercy and find grace to help in time of need.* Chap. iv. 14, 15, 16. These, and the like things, they had been assured of in the preceding chapters; and in this the LORD tells them, that now they ought to go on to perfection, because they might, according to the time they had been in grace, have been teachers; which is a plain proof that they had not only been taught of GOD, and consequently regenerated; but that they had been a long time in a state of conversion. So that as the HOLY GHOST, by the Apostle, in the close of this account blessedly saith, when he calls them also beloved, *we are persuaded better things of you,* (than of those Apostates,) *and things that accompany salvation, though we thus speak:* that is though we thus speak of your slow progress in the divine life. And the LORD adds, that GOD's faithfulness and love are engaged to them, *for they had ministered and still did minister to the saints of* GOD, *as saints of* GOD. An account of which we have, Chap. x. 32. to end, and which is spoken as the effect of their early days conversion. I beg the Reader to turn to that Chapter, in proof. So that upon the whole, however low the waters of the sanctuary then ran to their view, for their comfort, yet they were in grace, and the LORD considered them as such, and charged them to be no longer slothful, but *followers of them, who through faith and patience inherit the promises.*

And now, my brother, in summing up the whole, I commend you to the grace of GOD, wherein (if in regeneration) you stand, that *you may rejoice in hope of the glory of* GOD. Painful and humbling as it is to a child of GOD, to feel such continual deadness of soul, such coldness of affection, the little growth in grace, yea, as it sometimes appears to you, rather growing imperfections, and under which you groan continually; nevertheless, these all differ from professing hypocrites. Such never groan, for they never felt the plague of their own heart, neither entered in by the door into the sheepfold. John x. 1. And, therefore, when at any time you behold such meteors in the professing Church, and see the blaze of their supposed gifts and talents, either as preachers or hearers, and then are tempted to draw conclusions unfavorable to yourself, from your long knowledge of the LORD, and your short comings; call to remembrance what GOD the HOLY GHOST hath here taught, and wait and see the end of those men. *Oh! how suddenly do they consume, perish, and come to a fearful end! But the salvation of the righteous is of the* Lord; *he is their strength in time of trouble. And the* Lord *shall help them and deliver them: he shall deliver them from the wicked, and save them, because they trust in him.* Psm. xxxvii. 39, 40.

13 For when God made promise to Abraham, because he could sware by no greater, he sware by himself,

14 Saying, surely blessing I will bless thee, and multiplying I will multiply thee.

15 And so, after he had patiently endured, he obtained the promise.

16 For men verily sware by the greater: and an oath for confirmation *is* to them an end of all strife.

17 Wherein God, willing more abundantly to shew unto the heirs of promise the immutability of his counsel, confirmed *it* by an oath.

18 That by two immutable things, in which *it was* impossible for God to lie, we might have a strong consolation, who have fled for refuge to lay hold upon the hope set before us:

19 Which *hope* we have as an anchor of the soul, both sure and stedfast, and which entereth into that within the vail;

20 Whither the forerunner is for us entered, *even* Jesus, made an high priest for ever, after the order of Melchisedec.

In this most blessed portion, we have the same glorious truths confirmed to us, as in the former. Indeed, as I before observed, it should seem, that God the Holy Ghost intended this precious chapter to answer the double purpose, that while dashing to the ground all the presumptuous hopes of mere professors and hypocrites; he might teach the Church to rest their confidence, not in their attainments, but in the divine faithfulness. It is blessed to observe, how the Lord delights in reminding his people of his word and his oath to *Abraham.* For as Christ was sworn into his office by oath, before the world began; so Christ, when beginning to manifest himself in his priestly office, did it with an oath. Compare Psm. cx. 4. with Gen. xxii. 16, 17. That this was Christ, who made oath to *Abraham,* is unquestionable, for he is called the Angel of the Lord, or the Messenger of the Covenant, as Malachi iii. 1. And it is further blessed to observe the sweetness of expression, *because he could swear by no greater.* Reader! what a proof is this, by the way, of the Godhead of Christ? So the Lord again speaks by his servant the Prophet: Isa. xlv. 23. compared with Philip. ii. 10, 11. As Jehovah, in his threefold character of Person, can find no object of complacency and delight but in himself, in the image of the invisible God Christ Jesus: so none to swear by, to confirm his purposes and decrees concerning the Church, but the same. Compare Matt. xvii. 3. with 2 Pet. i. 16—18.

But we must not stop here. The fatherly love of God, in his most gracious designs towards his Church in Christ, is yet to be considered from this blessed Scripture. And, perhaps, there is not a portion in the word of God more in point, to assure to us this first, and eternal, and unchangeable purpose, will, and pleasure of Jehovah, in his love to the Church, than in what is here said. It is blessed, yea, very blessed, to ponder over it; and I pray the Reader to do it most attentively, looking for divine teaching to make it profitable.

First. Let us observe what is first said: *Wherein* God *willing more abundantly to shew unto the heirs of promise the immutability of his counsels, confirmed it by an oath.* Pause, Reader! Think of God the Father's love, in this gracious, wonderful condescension. Was it not enough, in our God and Father, to choose the Church in Christ before the foundation of the world, to be holy, and without blame before him in love; to adopt the several members of Christ's body to himself, as children in Christ Jesus: Ephes. i. 4, 5, 6. to present them to Christ: John vii. 2. to accept them in Christ: to redeem them by Christ: to regenerate them by his Holy Spirit; and to give them the assurance of eternal life: I say, Was it not enough, for that God who cannot lie, to manifest, by such rich, free, and unmerited promises, his love of the Church in Christ; but as if consulting the weakness, and infirmity of our faith, hath confirmed the whole by an oath? Well may we exclaim with the Apostle: *Behold! what manner of love the* Father *hath bestowed upon us?* 1 John iii. 1. Reader! do not overlook this fatherly love of God. Here it is, at this great bottom, on which the whole superstructure of the Church in Christ rests; faith begins her triumphs!

Secondly. In this precious view of the subject, observe the reason God the Father hath assigned, for this special act of grace, both in promising, and confirming that promise with an oath, namely, that the heirs of promise might see, and depend upon the immutability of his counsel; that there is nothing fickle, or inconstant, in the mind of God, towards his people; but that he is of one mind, and none can change him: and, therefore, they might have a strong consolation, who have taken refuge in a Covenant God in Christ. Now, Reader! beg of God the Almighty Promiser of such precious things, that you may have always grace, to believe in Him also, as an Almighty Performer of such unspeakable mercy: and, as it is a mercy which is wholly founded in God, and hath nothing to make it sure, in the will or performance of man; you may give God the credit of God, and never for a moment disbelieve *the record which he hath given of his Son.* 1 John v. 10—12. And, if these things are true, (as who will dare to question,) what must those men be about, or how do they give us any testimonies of their being taught of God, who would insinuate that the everlasting safety of the Church in Christ is doubtful, and that the final perseverance of the saints is unscriptural, and highly dangerous? So then it appears, that GOD himself is willing, more abundantly, that the heirs of promise should be firmly established, in the blessed consolation of His sovereign, and unchangeable will, and which he hath for that purpose made sure by oath, for their eternal safety and happiness: and poor blind man is unwilling GOD's people, the heirs of promise, should depend upon a refuge so sure, and certain! How truly awful such a conduct.

Thirdly. One precious point more remains to be noticed in this very sweet portion, namely, the title by which the LORD our GOD and FATHER here calls his chosen *the heirs of promise.* The very thought of this peculiar mark of GOD's love, filled the heart of *Paul* with holy joy. Hence, when to the Church he was drawing the everlasting line of distinction between the children of the bond-woman, and the children of the free, he cried out, *now we brethren,* (said he,) *as Isaac was, are the children of promise.* Gal. iv. 28. And children of promise indeed they are. GOD himself is the FATHER, and the Almighty Promiser of all their being, and well being in CHRIST. This is their charter: *I will be to them a* GOD, *and they shall be my people.* Jer. xxxi. 33. GOD the SON, is himself, in his Mediator-character, the first promise in the Bible, and all the promises are in Him, *yea, and Amen.* Gen. iii. 15. 2 Cor. i. 20. And as CHRIST is the heir of all things, so they are heirs of GOD, by reason of their being chosen in Him, and having union with Him, and joint heirs with him. Heb. i. 2. Gal. iv. 7. Rom. viii. 17. GOD the HOLY GHOST, is himself the Almighty SPIRIT of promise, whereby *believers are sealed unto the day of redemption.* Ephes. i. 13, 14. Hence, the children of CHRIST, whom GOD hath chosen in Him, and given to Him, are heirs of promise, being conceived in the womb of promise, before they were born of flesh. John i. 13. Psm. cx. 3. 2 Tim. i. 1. Titus i. 1. James i. 18. And, as to eternal life, they are all the sure heirs of this promise also, as in grace they are the sure possessors, when born again of the HOLY GHOST, from the *Adam*-nature of sin and corruption. See a string of the richest promises to this amount. Isa. lxvi. 8—14.

I must not enlarge. But, did I dare to swell the pages of this *Poor Man's Commentary,* what an endless subject is here proposed in GOD the FATHER's purposes; CHRIST, our refuge, anchor, and sure abiding place; and GOD the SPIRIT opening to our faith a view of Him, our forerunner, even JESUS, entered within the vail, having taken possession of the promised inheritance, in the name, and for the persons of all the heirs of promise. But I must shut up this Chapter. Views of *Melchizedec* will meet us in the next. And the LORD pardon the defects in the Commentary on this; and bless what is offered, as far as is agreeable to his truths, and the Reader's profit, in JESUS CHRIST. Amen.

REFLECTIONS.

CALLED upon as the Church is, in this Chapter, to leave behind first principles in the awakening of the soul to the convictions of sin, and having then but slight views of CHRIST, let us seek from GOD the SPIRIT, that growth in grace which marks those who have long known the LORD, and long found our own nothingness in every thing out of Christ; that we may discover that life, and light, and joy, are only in Christ; while deadness, darkness, and sorrow, are in all we say or do.

But, Reader! while divine teaching infallibly leads every child of God into this conclusion, sooner or later, let no child of God be led away, from the features of character God the Holy Ghost hath here drawn of hypocrites, to fancy that such distinguish him also. They differ as wide as the east from the west. God's children are indeed full of defects and unworthiness, and undeservings; nevertheless, they are still children. The new spiritual life imparted to them in regeneration, however, to their view, at times appears hardly discernible, is in them *a well of water, springing up to everlasting life*. But, the unawakened nature of the hypocrite, amidst all appearance of plentiful showers, is all outward and forming pools only, like *Job's* friends, prove deceitful, as the brook which in summer seasons dry away.

Reader! if so be the Lord hath caused you to know his grace, and by regeneration you are led to the precious discovery of being an heir of promise, see here the unspeakable love of God, and his willingness more abundantly, that his children shall live upon, and rejoice in, the immutability of his counsel. Oh! the strength of that consolation, founded in God the Father's will! Jesus's person, blood, and righteousness, and the Holy Ghost's regenerating, sanctifying, and renewing mercy. Jesus! be thou the anchor of my soul, both sure and stedfast! Not like the mariner's anchor beneath, but above; not founded on any thing breakable, but in things which are eternal. Not formed by the wisdom of men; but in the power of God. Precious, precious Jesus! thou art the Rock of ages! Thy work is perfect. Blessed, for ever blessed, be God, for Jesus Christ.

CHAP. VII.

CONTENTS.

Some Account of Melchizedec. Christ *blessedly spoken of, under his High Priestly Character, and the Excellency of his Person and Office.*

FOR this Melchisedec, king of Salem, priest of the most high God, who met Abraham returning from the slaughter of the kings, and blessed him;

2 To whom also Abraham gave a tenth part of all; first being by interpretation King of righteousness, and after that also King of Salem, which is, King of peace;

3 Without father, without mother, without de-

scent, having neither beginning of days, nor end of life; but made like unto the Son of God; abideth a priest continually.

4 Now consider how great this man *was*, unto whom even the patriarch Abraham gave the tenth of the spoils.

5 And verily they that are of the sons of Levi, who receive the office of the priesthood, have a commandment to take tithes of the people according to the law, that is, of their brethren, though they come out of the loins of Abraham:

6 But he whose descent is not counted from them received tithes of Abraham, and blessed him that had the promises.

7 And without all contradiction the less is blessed of the better.

8 And here men that die receive tithes; but there he *receiveth them*, of whom it is witnessed that he liveth.

9 And as I may so say, Levi also, who receiveth tithes, payed tithes in Abraham.

10 For he was yet in the loins of his father, when Melchisedec met him.

The HOLY GHOST, by the Apostle, had more than once mentioned this extraordinary person *Melchizedec*; but now he enters into a more particular account of him in this Chapter. He hath given us several very leading characters in relation to his office, by way of illustrating the glorious Person, of whom he was a type, which are truly interesting. And, although the LORD hath been pleased to leave some obscurity in the subject who *Melchizedec* was, yet, there is enough to call forth the warmest praises of the Church to GOD the HOLY GHOST, for an information which tends to raise our views of the LORD JESUS CHRIST, in the most exalted and blessed manner.

The LORD opens the Chapter with his name, *Melchizedec*, which is a compound word from *Melek*, King, and *Tzedek*, Justice; and, as the blessed SPIRIT himself hath rendered it, *King of righteousness*. If the Reader hath my *Poor Man's Concordance* by him, which was lately published in Penny Numbers, he will find a particular account of this name, *Melchizedec*.

The LORD the SPIRIT next proceeds to state the scriptural history, which He had before given of *Melchizedec*, as in Gen. xiv. 18, &c. in which we behold him in his High Priestly office. See Gen. xiv. and Commentary. And having thus introduced him to the Church, both by name and office, and described him as *King of righteousness*, and *King of peace*; the LORD adds one feature more concerning the wonders of his Person, which had not been before mentioned, and which raiseth the greatness of his character, beyond any being merely human, for he saith, *without father, without mother, without descent, having neither beginning of days, nor end of life; but made like unto the* SON *of* GOD, *abideth a Priest continually.* And now the HOLY GHOST bids the Church consider how great this man was.

It hath pleased the LORD to throw a veil over the person of this most extraordinary man, which must for ever preclude an absolute decision concerning him, while the Church is in her present time state. But, as a type of JESUS, what is here said is abundant to give the most satifying conviction, how infinitely great the LORD JESUS must be, to whom a man, without father or mother, or beginning of days, or end of life, only ministered but as a shadow. I will beg the Reader's consideration of the subject in this point of view, as of all others the most profitable.

Amidst all the obscurity we meet in this account of *Melchizedec,* if he be considered as a type of CHRIST, nothing could have been so happily chosen for that representation. He is declared to be greater than *Abraham,* with whom the promises of the Covenant were deposited. He is said to be greater than *Aaron :* for he was not only priest of the most High GOD, before *Aaron* was born, but before the Church of *Israel* was formed. And as typical of CHRIST, *Melchizedec* is set forth as no other type, in all the word of GOD is done, I mean for the eternity of CHRIST's nature; for this could never have been shadowed by any expressions like those which conceal *Melchizedec's* origin, in having neither *father, nor mother, beginning of days or end of life.* I wish the Reader to pay a more than ordinary attention to this great point.

Upon a subject of such vast moment, I desire never to speak decidedly; but rather propose, what I have to offer, in a way of question, to the Reader's own judgment. And hence I would ask, on the supposition, GOD the HOLY GHOST really intended, that *Melchizedec* should be a type of the LORD JESUS CHRIST; how could he represent the eternity of CHRIST, in any form of words than in the very words he hath chosen? *Without father, without mother, without descent, having* neither *beginning of days, or end of life.* In all the types of CHRIST, which have relation to his *offices,* there is no obscurity whatever. The *Brazen Serpent,* the *Rock,* the *Manna,* the *Passover:* the morning and evening *Lamb:* the day of *atonement;* all these are types and shadows, which have their accomplishment in CHRIST's *offices:* and these, when explained by divine teaching, open very clear, and decided demonstrations, to the several parts of CHRIST's *offices,* unto which they ministered. But here, where GOD the HOLY GHOST, would set forth to the Church, the eternity of CHRIST's *Person;* there was no being, either man, or angel, which could in any way, or form whatever, prefigure CHRIST's eternal nature; and therefore *Melchizedec,* shall typify the greatness and superiority of his *priesthood,* beyond every other; but of his *Person,* the eternity of his Being shall be shewn by a total silence, from whence he sprung; and declaring him to have been *without father, without mother, without descent, having neither beginning of days, nor end of life.* I beg once more the Reader to study the subject a little closely. I do not (as I said before) wish to speak decidedly. But on the presumption, GOD the HOLY GHOST did intend, to bring forward this man *Melchizedec,* as a type of JESUS; let any one say, how could the LORD more fully imply by figure, the eternity of the SON of GOD, acting as our High Priest? In all the records of men we meet in scripture history, it is the invariable custom, to introduce Persons, who are more eminently distinguished than others, with their genealogy, from father to son: and sometimes, this is carried on through a long pedigree. But here, where the greatest man among the Patriarchs which ever lived; greater than *Abraham,* greater than *Aaron,* and the Priest of the most high GOD is introduced, we are told that he is *without father, without mother, without descent, having neither beginning of days, nor end of life.* And wherefore this obscurity? Is it not (I ask the question) because, in this very instance, this greater than *Abraham,* and all the Patriarchs, was hereby to typify His Person, in the eternity of his nature, concerning whom the Prophet, in after ages demanded; *And who shall declare his generation?* Isaiah liii. 8.

I pass by making any observations, on the several things spoken of, concerning the inferiority, implied in the Levitical priesthood. For if the eternity of CHRIST, as here shadowed forth, be admitted, all beside follow of course. *Levi,* receiving tythes, who paid tythes in *Abraham,* is a beautiful thought, to represent the oneness of CHRIST, and his people. For all the seed of CHRIST, are in CHRIST virtually, and truly so, before they are brought to the knowledge of CHRIST, as *Abraham* did to *Melchizedec.* It is a blessed point to have always in view, that by the antient and eternal settlements among the Persons of the GODHEAD; CHRIST and his seed, were from everlasting One. That holy portion of human nature, which was to form one with the divine nature of the SON of GOD, and thereby constitute one Person, CHRIST, contained in it, the millions of the persons of CHRIST's seed, which were to arise out of it, to form CHRIST's mystical body, to all eternity. Hence it is said, that both *He that sanctifieth, and they that are sanctified are all of one.* Heb. ii. 11. So that the seed of CHRIST, before they are brought to lay hold of CHRIST, are, (as *Levi* was, in the loins of *Abraham,*) one with CHRIST, from all eternity. JESUS could not have been the Head of his body the Church, as Head, one moment before the body, as the body: neither the everlasting FATHER before he had children; neither Husband before the Church was his Wife. So very blessed is the consideration of the eternity of CHRIST's Person; and his character, and relation, as the Head of his body the Church ; *the fulness of him, which filleth all in all.* Ephes. xxii. 23.

11 If therefore perfection were by the Levitical priesthood, (for under it the people received the law,) what further need *was there* that another priest should rise after the order of Melchisedec, and not be called after the order of Aaron?

12 For the priesthood being changed, there is made of necessity a change also of the law.

13 For he of whom these things are spoken pertaineth to another tribe, of which no man gave attendance at the altar.

14 For *it is* evident that our Lord sprang out of Juda; of which tribe Moses spake nothing concerning priesthood.

15 And it is yet far more evident: for that after the similitude of Melchisedec, there ariseth another priest.

16 Who is made, not after the law of a carnal commandment, but after the power of an endless life.

17 For he testifieth, Thou *art* a priest for ever after the order of Melchisedec.

18 For there is verily a disannulling of the commandment going before for the weakness and unprofitableness thereof.

19 For the law made nothing perfect, but the bringing in of a better hope *did;* by the which we draw nigh unto God.

20 And inasmuch as not without an oath *he was made priest:*

21 (For those priests were made without an oath; but this with an oath by him that said unto him, The Lord sware and will not repent, Thou *art* a priest for ever after the order of Melchisedec:)

22 By so much was Jesus made a surety of a better testament.

23 And they truly were many priests, because they were not suffered to continue by reason of death.

24 But this *man,* because he continueth ever, hath an unchangeable priesthood,

So much having been said of *Melchizedec,* and his ministry, as typical of CHRIST, by way of shewing the infinite greatness of CHRIST's Person; and the infinite superiority of CHRIST's office of

CH. VII.]   HEBREWS.   257

Priesthood to all other; the Chapter now takes up the subject, in shewing, the imperfection of the law, and the Priesthood, under that dispensation, to answer the purpose of salvation; and which become, as it was designed, to enhance the dignity of CHRIST, and to shew the vast importance of his office of Priesthood. Perfection was never intended by the Levitical Priesthood. It was designed, but as *a shadow of good things to come.* The very nature of its service, carried with it the fullest conviction, that it never could, as *pertaining to the conscience, make the comers thereunto perfect.* The daily use of it, manifested its weakness. And void of an eye to some substance, which it was supposed to prefigure, there could be no one affinity whatever, between the sin of a man, and the blood of a beast. Hence the Apostle saith; *the law made nothing perfect.* The Sinner, the Levite, the Priest, and the whole service, could none of them derive sanctity, nor communicate sanctity by it. But the whole, being simply an outward sign, or symbol, of some more important effect, shadowed forth its own imperfection; the more fully to introduce the substance, to which it referred. And thus, as a preliminary to the Gospel of CHRIST, became very useful in its way; for while it made nothing perfect, *the bringing in of a better hope did, by the which we draw nigh unto* GOD.

And not only the law, but the priests of the law, manifested their insufficiency. No oath either introduced them at the first, or afterwards confirmed them, in their office. But JESUS's consecration had both. Moreover, the multitude of the daily Priests; and the necessity of their succession, by reason of death, carried together with both, the imperfection of their order. Whereas CHRIST, in the eternity of his nature; and the perpetual, and unchanging quality of his office; demonstrated the truth of his having been called to it by Him, who sware, and could not repent, when he said to him, *Thou art a Priest for ever after the order of Melchizedec.* Psm. cx. 4.

I must not trespass. But what a multitude of sweet thoughts, arise out of this one view of JESUS and the perfection of his Priesthood, as contrasted to the imperfection of the law, and the poverty, and helplessness of the Levitical priesthood? And again, how is the whole heightened in the recollection, that the very appointment of all before CHRIST was only shadowy representations; but his the substance, to which they all ministered? And still more as all were but mere shadows, and CHRIST the one only matter of the whole, his very Priesthood must be engaged to render the whole effectual. CHRIST had never been made an High Priest, nor introduced with such a world of solemnity, and importance into it, but with the fullest assurance, that all the purposes of his high administration, must be accomplished. So infinitely precious, and so everlastingly made sure, are the ends, for which CHRIST was made an High Priest; and that *not after the law of a carnal commandment, but after the power of an endless life.*

25 Wherefore he is able also to save them to the uttermost that come unto God by him, seeing he ever liveth to make intercession for them.

26 For such an high priest became us, *who is* holy, harmless, undefiled, separate from sinners, and made higher than the heavens;

27 Who needeth not daily, as those high priests, to offer up sacrifice, first for his own sins, and then for the people's: for this he did once, when he offered up himself.

28 For the law maketh men high priests which have infirmity; but the word of the oath, which was since the law, *maketh* the Son, who is consecrated for evermore.

The opening of this paragraph, in what is said of CHRIST's ability to save; and which carries with it also his disposition to save, which is the very nature of his office, and for which he was made High Priest, is, without exception, one of the sweetest and most persuasive of all possible arguments, to come to the pardon-office of JESUS CHRIST: The Almightiness of his Person; the efficacy of his sacrifice; the unceasing, and everlasting nature of his office, as High Priest: and the consciousness of his ever living, to see the whole rendered effectual, in the offering he once made, for his people on the cross; what a strength of argument the whole brings with it, to lead the LORD's people to his throne? And when it is said, that this salvation of the LORD JESUS, is to the uttermost; what is the uttermost? Take in the greatest extent the imagination can conceive, to the utmost horizon of thought, yet this ceaseth to be the uttermost, if there be aught beyond it? And what a lift up this is to all the discouragements of temptation; all heart-straitenings in prayer; all coldness, deadness, wanderings, fears, unbelief, and the like. For it is not, what the uttermost of our imagination makes it, but what that uttermost in GOD's view is. Not what we conceive of divine mercy; but what that divine mercy can, and will shew, in displaying the riches of grace?

And if the first verse in this paragraph is so full of sweetness and persuasion, in the contemplation of CHRIST's office to encourage poor sensible sinners to come to GOD by CHRIST, how exceedingly the argument is heightened, when to this is added, as the next verse speaks, CHRIST's personal glory and greatness. *For such an High Priest became us, who is holy, harmless, undefiled, separate from sinners, and made higher than the heavens.* Was there ever any form of words like these, brought together into one view to set up and exalt, the glory of the LORD JESUS, and to establish all the divine qualities of his essential, and mediatorial perfections? Surely the man must be hoodwinked, and blind, to all the possibilities of blindness, who can read this account of the SON of GOD in our nature, and yet pause a moment, from concluding the Almightiness of his character. So perfectly *holy*, in the underived nature of that holiness, as to be holiness itself, in the abstract. So *harmless*, that no guile was found in his mouth. So *undefiled* that no taint of evil could affect him: being in himself altogether pure. And so *separate from sinners,* that though taking the nature of those he came to redeem, he had none of their defilement; underived from the *Adam* corrupt stock, but formed holy, and pure, by miraculous impregnation, without the intervention of an human father; And *made higher than the heavens:* that is higher than all the Angels, having, by inheritance, obtained a more excellent name than they. And here I beg the Reader to pause, and mark, the striking distinction in the Mediator-character from that of Angels. The elect Angels are indeed sinless. But they are in themselves capable of sinning. And that they are preserved from sinning, is because they are elect. For as Angels which were not elect have fallen! so their nature is thereby proved capable of falling. Hence we read, *that* GOD *puts no trust in his servants; and his Angels he charged with folly;* Job. iv. 18. by which is meant, a capability of sinning. So that the personal glory of CHRIST, as CHRIST, is infinitely beyond all creation; yea, CHRIST is the source, and cause, of the Angels being kept from sin; as elect Angels in him. He himself is *made higher than the heavens.* Reader! do not overlook, or ever lose sight of CHRIST, in this most blessed view of his personal holiness and glory.

And what follows, in the succeeding verses of the Chapter, have yet 'a further tendency to illustrate, and confirm the same most precious, soul-reviving truth. *Who needeth not daily, as those high priests did, to offer up sacrifice, first for his own sins, and then for the peoples'.* If men would, or could read their Bibles with an enlightened eye, here they would behold that everlasting line of distinction, drawn between CHRIST and every other high Priest, as would silence in endless darkness, the daring presumption of those wretched, and deluded men, who presume to question the GODHEAD of CHRIST. If CHRIST was so holy, harmless, and undefiled, that he needed no offering, no sacrifice, no mediation for himself; can any thing more fully express the divinity of his nature, than such an account by the HOLY GHOST? Surely he would have needed to have made an offering for himself, as well as for others, had he not as GODMan, been all this as here described; for it was this personal holiness of nature, which made all offerings for himself useless, and gave such everlasting merit and efficacy to the offering he once offered for others. Heb. x. 14.

One word more. The close of this Chapter, is as interesting in proof to this doctrine, as either of the precious verses which went before, and forms a delightful finish to the whole subject. *For the law maketh men high priests, which have infirmity.* Yes! indeed, for the law is obliged to make such men priests, if the law will have high priests at all. They must offer blood for themselves first, and then for the errors of the people. Heb. ix. 7. And such high priests had all infirmity, yea sins. And they were many, not one; for they were not able to continue, by reason of death. So then, they were sinners themselves, and they offered for sinners. Alas! what sins of themselves, or of others, could their offerings take away? Now look to JESUS. *The word of the oath* made CHRIST the SON an High Priest, and that for ever; yea, *consecrated for evermore,* an eternal, unchangeable, unsinning priesthood. Psm. cx. 4. It is said to have been since the law. Yes! the Levitical priesthood was formed to shadow forth CHRIST's priesthood. But CHRIST was a Priest in the day he was begotten. Psm. ii. 7. Heb. v. 5, 6. And also, *the Lamb slain from the foundation of the world.* Rev. xiii. 8. Nevertheless, the public ministry of CHRIST's priesthood, and sacrifice, was since the law, when *by the one offering of himself once offered, he perfected for ever them that are sanctified.* Heb. x. 14. But his SONSHIP, hath been from everlasting. And this was prior to his Priesthood; and both gave dignity, and efficacy to it. Reader! what a cloud of witnesses have we to the Personal glory, and essential Divinity, of the SON of GOD! And what then must be the eternal worth, and efficacy of all his Offices?

REFLECTIONS.

EVERLASTING thanks be given to GOD the HOLY GHOST, for this most sweet and precious Chapter. Never, surely, but for the LORD himself explaining to us in this portion of his holy word, what he had before related concerning *Melchizedec*, in other parts of his revelation; should we have conceived suitable apprehensions on the subject. But now, by his gracious condescension, in saying so much as is here related, of that Priest of the Most High GOD, do we behold the wonders of his Person, and Office, and the still greater Personage, to whom all that went before ministered. Hail! thou great, thou Almighty *Melchizedec* of thy People? Truly, LORD JESUS! thou hast been sworn into thine office by JEHOVAH's Oath; and well therefrom do I feel confidence to come unto thee, as the LORD's High Priest, and my High Priest for ever. LORD! I desire grace, and power, to do what is here commanded the Church, namely, to consider, how great the *Melchizedec* was, whom *Abraham* saw; and therefrom to consider, how much greater my LORD JESUS is, to whom even *Melchizedec* acted but as a type and shadow!

Precious LORD JESUS! thou art a Priest upon thy throne! Thou hast an unchangeable priesthood! And indeed, and in truth, such an High Priest as thou art, my poor soul needed: One that can, and will save to the uttermost, all that come to GOD by thee; and One who is holy, harmless, undefiled, separate from sinners, and made higher than the heavens. And, very sure I am, that though, in thy personal glory, all this, and more, is thine; yet, amidst all the exaltation of thy state, no change hath taken place in thy nature; JESUS, is JESUS still. The same lovely, and all-loving JESUS. Here below, men that have infirmities are made priests; but our JESUS that is above, though touched with the feelings of our infirmities, yet, in himself, he is separate from sinners, and made higher than the heavens. He knows our frame by his own, though without sin; and his priesthood is for ever. LORD! take up my cause, for sure I am, I shall not then fail; thou art consecrated for evermore!

CHAP. VIII.

CONTENTS.

We have more, and more precious Views of the LORD JESUS *in this Chapter.* CHRIST *the true tabernacle.* GOD'S *Covenant Love, secured in* CHRIST, *by Word and Oath.*

NOW of the things which we have spoken *this is* the sum: We have such an high priest, who is set on the right hand of the throne of the majesty in the heavens;

2 A minister of the sanctuary, and of the true tabernacle, which the Lord pitched, and not man.

I would not for the world knowingly strain a single word in scripture, by way of making it speak more, or less, than is intended; but I would pause over these verses, and humbly ask, whether GOD the HOLY GHOST, in the opening of this Chapter, did not mean to call the Church to behold CHRIST as the sum and substance of all revelation? Let the Reader recollect, how blessedly the HOLY GHOST had been speaking, in the *seven* preceding Chapters, concerning CHRIST. Beginning in the first Chapter with proclamations of his eternal Power and GODHEAD, then of his Mediator glories; and in the second Chapter, of his human nature; and in the following, largely dwelling upon the many sweet, and endearing features of his offices, and particularly of his Priesthood: and, having followed him from the time of having purged our sins by himself, until he held him forth as seated as *a Priest upon his throne,* in glory.; the LORD the SPIRIT begins this Chapter in a form of words, such as can hardly be found in the whole book of GOD. *Now of the things* (saith the LORD) *which we have spoken this is the sum.* As if the whole of revelation was here brought into one view, in the Person of CHRIST. And no doubt it is. For CHRIST, as CHRIST, is the visible JEHOVAH. There could have been no revelation of JEHOVAH in his threefold character of Person, but in, and by Him. He is come forth from the bosom of the FATHER to declare him. John i. 18. And, let the Reader further observe, how blessedly the HOLY GHOST represents him, as having passed into the heavens, and there *sat down*, contrary to the priests on earth, who always *stood* ministering. Chap. x. 11. Numberless beauties are contained in this short verse. *First.* JESUS being seated as the High Priest of his people, on the right hand of the Majesty in the heavens, carries with it the most palpable conviction, that he hath by himself purged our sins; and in proof, is set down on the right hand of GOD. *Secondly.* It becomes no less a proof, that CHRIST hath been accepted as our Surety in redemption, or he never would have been received there. CHRIST'S sitting down on the right hand of the Majesty in heaven, is in perfect conformity to GOD'S word, and oath. *Sit thou on my right hand until I make thine enemies thy footstool.* Psm. cx. 1. John xvii. 4. *Thirdly.* Having such an High Priest there, our Advocate, whom GOD the FATHER heareth alway; the same becomes an everlasting assurance, that all the concerns of his people, JESUS undertakes, and accomplisheth. No prayers can go unheard. No petitions remain unanswered. And all the ascension-gifts he is purposely exalted to bestow, are as certain, and sure, as if they were already in hand. GOD the HOLY GHOST is come down, in confirmation, that CHRIST is gone up. *He hath led captivity captive, and received gifts for men, yea, for the rebellious, that the* LORD GOD *might dwell among them.* Psm. lxviii. 18. And, *lastly,* to add no more; the sum and substance of the whole scripture being to tell the Church, that He who was dead, and is alive, and now liveth for evermore, and is on the throne of the Majesty on high, is purposely there for his people, waiting to be gracious, and delighted to be by them employed. So he appeared to *John,* in his priestly vesture, dipped in blood, as if to say: See! I wear the vestments of office. Bring all your causes to me, and leave all with confidence in my hand.

But we must not stop here. He that is our High Priest, the HOLY GHOST adds, is also *a Minister of the Sanctuary, and of the true tabernacle which the* LORD *pitched, and not man.* These offices also, are special, personal offices, peculiarly belonging to our LORD JESUS CHRIST, and to no other, and in which his people have everlasting concern. This sanctuary is not a *worldly sanctuary of carnal ordinances;* such as we read of Chap. ix. 1, 10. Neither is it an *earthly* sanctuary; neither is it an *heavenly* one; for then, it needed not to have been said, which *the* LORD pitched and not *man.* For it is well known, none but the LORD is the maker of heaven. But by the sanctuary, I should apprehend, is meant, the whole body of the Church, whom CHRIST, by the one offering of himself, once offered, hath perfected for ever, as sanctified in himself. Psm. cxiv. 2. Isaiah lxiii. 18. And by the true tabernacle, which the LORD pitched, and not man, can be meant no other, according to my view, than the human nature of CHRIST, *in whom dwelleth all the fulness of the* GODHEAD *bodily.* And I am the more inclined to this opinion, because, all that is here said, is with the intention to magnify and exalt the LORD JESUS, by shewing, that all that was in the wilderness Church, was designed, but as the shadows of good things to come, and that all pointed to, and centered in CHRIST. Now, as the tabernacle in the wilderness, had frequently the *Shechinah,* or manifestation of the divine presence in it; here, was a lively representation of the SON of GOD, tabernacling in our nature, when *he became flesh, and dwelt among us.* And as the tabernacle was but a poor building, and to outward appearance, looking very wretched and mean; so the human nature, in which the SON of GOD tabernacled, was poor indeed, and had nothing of beauty, that we should desire him.

But the greatest point in this description remains to be considered. It is said, that the LORD pitched this true tabernacle, and not man. Yes! The whole Persons of the GODHEAD co-operated in the work. GOD the FATHER, prepared the body. So spake CHRIST by the SPIRIT of prophecy. Compare Psm. xl. 6, 7. with Heb. x. 5. GOD the SON took the nature of man upon him. Heb. ii. 14, 16. And GOD the HOLY GHOST, formed that holy thing, so called. Luke i. 35. Reader! do not hastily pass away, from the view of a subject so truly blessed. This true tabernacle which the LORD pitched, and not man, is the only real temple, either in heaven, or on earth, for the divine residence. The divine essence, may, in one sense, be said to dwell every where; for, in the perfection of his Omnipresence, he fills heaven and earth. And GOD dwells by the influences of his SPIRIT in the hearts of his people. But it is not in either sense of this meaning, the tabernacle of the human nature of the SON of GOD, is inhabited by the indwelling residence of JEHOVAH. It is bodily in CHRIST, as fire in iron; essentially, personally, and eternally. Moreover, this is the only temple, CHRIST's body, for meeting with his people. Here, the LORD comes to meet and bless them. In him, the LORD speaks to his people; and they to him. Oh! the blessedness of this true tabernacle, which the LORD pitched, and not man. How ought the redeemed to delight in CHRIST, and to be always going to CHRIST. It was the consciousness of this made *David* cry out; *One thing have I desired of the* LORD *that I will seek after; that I may dwell in the house of the* LORD *all the days of my life, to behold the beauty of the* LORD, *and to enquire in his temple.* Psm. xxvii. 4. Oh! for grace, to be often eyeing CHRIST, as the sum of the things the HOLY GHOST hath here spoken. Such an High Priest, set on the right hand of the throne of the Majesty in the heavens. A minister of the sanctuary, and of the true tabernacle which the LORD pitched, and not man!

3 For every high priest is ordained to offer gifts and sacrifices; wherefore *it is* of necessity that this man have somewhat also to offer.

4 For if he were on earth, he should not be a priest, seeing that there are priests that offer gifts according to the law:

In the close of the first of these verses, I beg to observe, that there is no word in the original for what our translators have rendered *man*. And as the pronoun *this* might have been more properly connected with the word *person*, being more agreeable to the analogy of faith, I confess that I prefer it. The reading then will be, wherefore it is of necessity, that this *person* have somewhat also to offer. And this is true. As *man*, considered without an eye to the GODHEAD, he had nothing equivalent to offer. And, as GOD, without respect to his manhood, he could not offer. But in the union of both, as one *person*, GOD and Man, oh! what an offering did he make, whereby *he hath perfected for ever them that are sanctified!* Heb. x. 10—14.

I have so largely dwelt on the blessed features of the LORD JESUS in his priestly office, in the preceding Chapters of this Epistle, that it will be the less necessary to enlarge on them here. It is very true, indeed, GOD the HOLY GHOST evidently takes pleasure in bringing them continually forward. And what that matchless Teacher delights in, we may well follow. And so I would indeed, if the limits of a *Poor Man's Commentary* admitted it. But as this is not the case, I rather refer the Reader to what hath been offered upon CHRIST's priesthood, and particularly in the fifth Chapter, than swell the present pages.

But one point must be noticed here, as not being noticed before, in relation to Christ's priesthood, namely, when it is said, *for if he were on earth, he should not be a priest.* This is a subject very highly interesting to be considered, and which ought to be well understood. In the explaining of which, it will serve to throw no small light on it, if we look back and observe, how the Holy Ghost hath throughout scripture, shadowed forth Christ in the law. When the High Priest, on the day of atonement, had made the sacrifice for the sins of the people, he entered with the blood into the holy place. Levit. xvi. 2—15—34. And this is explained to the Church, of what God the Holy Ghost intended by it. Heb. ix. 6—12. and Commentary. Now, then, had the High Priest, when making the sacrifice, not gone into the holy place, the service would have been incomplete. Hence, in like manner, if Christ, to whom this whole service referred, remained on earth, after that he had made his soul an offering for sin, the presentation of it before God on the mercy-seat would not have been compleat! It was one great part of his office to carry up his blood to the throne, (the propitiatory,) as a full and compleat propitiation. Having paid the ransom of his Church by his blood, he virtually takes the price, the current coin of the merchant with him to heaven, and puts it down upon the mercy-seat. Here was, in the fullest sense of the words, offering both gifts and the sacrifice for sin. And hence it is said, that the priests on earth serve unto the example and shadow of heavenly things.

And, moreover, it must be further added, that Christ's priesthood, which, after the order of *Melchizedec,* was an everlasting priesthood, could not have been accomplished had he remained on earth. For, in this case, how would he have entered into heaven as the forerunner of his people? How would he have gone as a public head, and been placed above all principality and power? How would he have taken possession of heaven in our name; and we, by faith, beholding ourselves *now raised up together, and made to sit together with him in heavenly places,* in Christ Jesus? Ephes. ii. 6. Reader! do you not know what it is now, by faith, thus to realize and substantiate things that are far off, and bring them nigh? If your faith be the faith of God's elect, the faith once delivered to the saints, you cannot but know it by this divine property, which the Holy Ghost hath marked it by; it is *the substance of things hoped for, the evidence of things not seen. For by it the Elders obtained a good report.* Heb. xi. 1, 2. True, indeed, you are not yet entered upon the heavenly country. But, like them, you have seen it afar off, and are persuaded of it, and have by faith embraced it. *We see not yet* (saith the Apostle,) *all things put under* Jesus. No! For he hath *not yet made all his enemies his footstool.* This will take place at the final retribution of all things, *when he shall see the travail of his soul, and be satisfied.* Isa. liii. 10. But, in the mean time, we see him *crowned with glory and honor;* and ourselves, by faith, crowned with him, in the sure and certain expectation of it, when he will come to take us home to himself, that *where he is, there we may be also.* John xiv. 3.

5 Who serve unto the example and shadow of heavenly things, as Moses was admonished of God

when he was about to make the tabernacle: for, See, saith he, *that* thou make all things according to the pattern shewed to thee in the mount.

6 But now hath he obtained a more excellent ministry, by how much also he is the mediator of a better covenant, which was established upon better promises.

It is very blessed to behold how attentive the HOLY GHOST was, in all his appointments relating to the Church in the wilderness, that every thing should be the express pattern of CHRIST, and his Gospel Church. And, while it serves to teach us how infinitely important the things themselves must be to which those shadows ministered; how sure is it also, that GOD the SPIRIT was the Almighty Minister then, as He is now.

In relation to the better ministry of CHRIST, and the order of the New Testament dispensation being established upon better promises, every part and portion of the word of GOD most fully shews. But what I beg the Reader more immediately to keep in view, and never lose sight of, is this, that JESUS himself is the whole of the covenant. So JEHOVAH declared him to be, Isa. xlix. 8. and so his people, when regenerated of the HOLY GHOST, prove him to their soul's comfort. It was formed with JESUS in the eternal counsels, before the world. It was confirmed by JESUS, during the time-state of his abode on earth. To Him the whole was entrusted. *By* Him the whole hath been fulfilled. All the blessings of it are *in* his Almighty hands; and *from* Him, all must flow of grace here, and glory hereafter. So that the LORD JESUS comprehends in his own Person, as GOD-MAN Mediator, the one, full, and compleat covenant. He is the Messenger, the Administrator, the Head, the Sum, the Substance of the whole. Precious LORD JESUS! blessed be GOD, who hath given thee for a covenant of the people!

7 For if that first *covenant* had been faultless, then should no place have been sought for the second.

8 For finding fault with them, he saith, Behold, the days come, saith the Lord, when I will make a new covenant with the house of Israel, and with the house of Judah:

9 Not according to the covenant that I made with their fathers in the day when I took them by the hand to lead them out of the land of Egypt; because they continued not in my covenant, and I regarded them not, saith the Lord.

10 For this *is* the covenant that I will make with

the house of Israel after those days, saith the Lord; I will put my laws into their mind, and write them in their hearts: and I will be to them a God, and they shall be to me a people:

11 And they shall not teach every man his neighbour, and every man his brother, saying, Know the Lord: for all shall know me from the least to the greatest.

12 For I will be merciful to their unrighteousness, and their sins and their iniquities will I remember no more.

13 In that he saith, A new *covenant*, he hath made the first old. Now that which decayeth and waxeth old *is* ready to vanish away.

In order to have a clear apprehension of what is here said, it will be necessary to attend to the words of scripture, simply as they are. When the HOLY GHOST speaks, as in this place, of a *first* covenant, and a *second;* and of a *new* covenant, and an *old;* the Reader must not suppose is meant, that the one differed from the other in substance, or that any change had taken place in the mind of GOD. Not so. There hath been from everlasting in reality but one and the same covenant, namely, the LORD JESUS CHRIST. He is the sole covenant of the people. Neither can his Gospel be called a new revelation, differing from the Old Testament in sum and substance, for the Gospel was preached to *Abraham.* Gal. iii. 8. I have shewn this, I hope, very clearly, in the Preface to this *Poor Man's Commentary.* But the meaning of this most beautiful passage (which is taken from the prophecy of Jeremiah xxxi. 31—34.) is the spiritual illustration of GOD's covenant in CHRIST, in which the several agencies of each glorious person of the GODHEAD, are blessedly shewn in the FATHER's electing, pardoning, justifying, accepting love; GOD the SON's betrothing, redeeming grace; and GOD the SPIRIT's quickening, sanctifying, sealing mercy. And the blessed effects arising from the whole are also here displayed, in the spiritual knowledge which the whole Church of GOD in CHRIST shall derive from the latter-day dispensation. So much of divine light, and divine knowledge, shall be diffused by the openly tabernacling of the SON of GOD in our nature, that from the highest to the lowest, and from the least to the greatest, all the children shall know the LORD; and that not in an hearsay or speculative apprehension of GOD, but a personal, spiritual, soul-enjoyment of Him. GOD shall be known in his threefold character of Person, in the FATHER's love, the SON's grace, and the SPIRIT's fellowship, and in such a blessed way and manner, as shall refresh the whole Church, and raise up a revenue of glory to the LORD. Isa. liv. 13. John xiv. 23—27.

REFLECTIONS.

Reader! is this indeed the sum and substance of what God the Holy Ghost hath been blessing the Church with, in such gracious teachings concerning 'the Lord Jesus; that He is gone into heaven, and is set down on the right hand of the throne of Majesty: oh! then, for grace to follow him thither by faith! For, as sure as Jesus the Son of God is gone there, so sure is He gone as the Head and Husband, the Surety and Representative of his body the Church, *the fulness that filleth all in all.* Yes! He hath taken possession of heaven itself in their name. And all his redeemed ones may already, by virtue of their union with Him, behold themselves by faith, as *raised up together with* Christ, *and made to sit together in heavenly places in* Christ Jesus. Oh! glorious Jesus! *Minister of the Sanctuary,* and of the true tabernacle, which the Lord hath pitched, and not man!

And blessed be God the Holy Ghost for this precious scripture! We now see, through thy divine teaching, how needful it was for our Lord to go away. Had he remained on earth, though he had made his soul an offering for sin, yet could he not have been a priest. Yes! thou dear Lord, it was necessary that thou shouldest priest it also for thy redeemed in heaven. Oh! Lord the Spirit! give us grace to be always following our Jesus by faith, and employing our great High Priest with our daily prayers and praises, until we come to see him, as He is, and dwell with him for ever.

Praises to our God and Father for his covenant Christ. Oh! may God the Father be to me a God in Christ, and make me his among his people. Oh! that Jesus, my Husband, may be to me my unceasing High Priest, Advocate, and Intercessor. And God the Holy Ghost, my Teacher, and the Glorifier of Jesus unto the day of his coming!

CHAP. IX.

CONTENTS.

We have in this Chapter some Account of the Furniture of the Old Tabernacle in the Wilderness. To this succeeds a most blessed Account of Christ, *whom the* Holy Ghost *meant to prefigure by this worldly Sanctuary.*

THEN verily the first *covenant* had also ordinances of divine service, and a worldly sanctuary.

2 For there was a tabernacle made; the first, wherein *was* the candlestick, and the table, and the shewbread; which is called the sanctuary.

3 And after the second veil, the tabernacle which is called the Holiest of all;

4 Which had the golden censer, and the ark of

the covenant overlaid round about with gold, wherein *was* the golden pot that had manna, and Aaron's rod that budded, and the tables of the covenant;

5 And over the cherubims of glory shadowing the mercy-seat; of which we cannot now speak particularly.

How gracious was it in GOD the HOLY GHOST, to give the Church an account, as he hath here done, of the furniture of the tabernacle; and so blessedly explained the subject, as he hath hereafter done in this chapter, in relation to CHRIST. Oh! the goodness and condescension of GOD the SPIRIT! Truly was it said, by our dear LORD, concerning him, when teaching his disciples to be on the look out for his coming after CHRIST's departure, *he shall not speak of himself.* And where do we find the blessed SPIRIT speaking of himself? *But he shall glorify me,* said JESUS. And, oh! Reader, how doth the HOLY GHOST indeed glorify my LORD to my poor soul, when He shews me more and more the plague of my own heart; and that there is none in heaven or earth that can bring a remedy for it, but the LORD JESUS CHRIST? John xvi. 13, 14. I do hope, before we close this Chapter, both, the Writer and Reader (if it be the LORD's holy will) may find cause to raise a renewed monument of praise to the HOLY SPIRIT, for what He hath here revealed of all-precious JESUS!

I desire the Reader, one by one, to observe the several articles here enumerated, in what belonged to what is called the first covenant. All were costly. And as all was of GOD's own appointment in divine service, and yet were but typical and preparatory to the Gospel Church of CHRIST, they serve the more to shew of what vast importance in GOD's sight must have been, and still is, that glorious dispensation by CHRIST, which was thus set forth with such a world of attention? The first court, which was called *the holy place,* and used in daily service, contained the *candlestic,* to intimate, perhaps, that as the light there shining communicates brightness around, so CHRIST, in his Church, is the sole light of his Church. The *table,* which is said to have been made of *Shittim-wood,* Exod. xxv. 10, and which was not liable to be worm-eaten, was perhaps typical of the incorruptible nature of CHRIST's humanity, which, though subject to death, as the sacrifice for sin, yet not to corruption. Psm. xvi. And as a table is a place of fellowship in families, where the several members partake of the same viands, it is probable that the HOLY GHOST might intend to convey, by this representation, the communion and fellowship CHRIST and his members have with each other. All these were, in what was called the *sanctuary,* or holy place, to distinguish it both from the world without, and the holy of holies within. Here was performed all the ordinary service of the priests, in their daily ministration. CHRIST must be the daily light, and life, and food, and communion of his people. To Him do all his redeemed, whom he hath made kings and priests to the FATHER, daily come, and *by him offer the sacrifice of praise to* GOD *continually, that is the fruit of our lips, giving thanks to his name.* Heb. xiii. 15.

By the second vail is meant *within* the vail, for there was but one vail in the sanctuary. Exod. xxvi. 33. and which was rent in the moment of CHRIST's death, to imply that all intervening obstructions, which kept the people of GOD from the LORD, was now done away by that death. JESUS had then removed for ever the vail spread over all nations. Isa. xxv. 6—8. Coloss. ii. 14. Hence the call to draw nigh, Heb. x. 19—23. The furniture within this vail, which was called *the holy of holies,* was, no doubt, highly significant also; but, as the Apostle's speaking of those things in full declared that he could not now speak particularly, so may we. That they were all typical, seems to be without all doubt, for *the law itself was a shadow of good things to come.* But there is a certain obscurity thrown over such things as are not immediately necessary to be known, for wise and good purposes. We can, and do, through divine teaching, behold the figure of CHRIST, in the golden *Censer:* see Rev. viii. 3, 4. and in the Ark also, there could be no other than CHRIST intended, who is to all his elect as the Ark was to *Noah,* into which the Patriarch entered by faith. Hebrews xi. 7. The *Pot* that had *manna,* which in its nature is so perishing, and yet so wonderfully preserved by this means, very strongly, and aptly represented CHRIST, preserving our nature. And the *Rod* that budded, pointed to Him, who is JEHOVAH's rod of strength, and the everlasting bud, blossom, and fruit of JEHOVAH's eternal love, to all his people for ever. Psm. cx. 2. The *tables of the Covenant,* perhaps had an allusion to GOD's New Testament dispensation, when GOD promised to write them in the living tables of the heart of his people. Heb. viii. 10. 2 Cor. iii. 3. And the *Cherubim of glory,* could mean no other than what from the first, at the gate of *Eden,* represented the glorious Persons in JEHOVAH. Through all the word of GOD it is plain, the *Cherubim* could have allusion to none but the LORD. Reader! think with what a vast preparation the Gospel of CHRIST hath been ushered in; and how infinitely important, therefore, it must be? Oh! for grace, to contemplate more and more, the Person of the LORD JESUS, in whom all centre, and who is the sum and substance of all!

6 Now when these things were thus ordained, the priests went always into the first tabernacle, accomplishing the service *of* God.

7 But into the second *went* the high priest alone once every year, not without blood, which he offered for himself, and *for* the errors of the people:

8 The Holy Ghost this signifying, that the way into the holiest of all was not yet made manifest, while as the first tabernacle was yet standing.

9 Which *was* a figure for the time then present,

in which were offered both gifts and sacrifices, that could not make him that did the service perfect, as pertaining to the conscience;

10 *Which stood* only in meats and drinks and divers washings, and carnal ordinances, imposed *on them* until the time of reformation.

I very earnestly beg the Reader to indulge me, with calling his attention to what is here said of GOD the HOLY GHOST, which, in my view, most decidedly shews, and to a demonstration, both the Person, GODHEAD, and Ministry of the HOLY GHOST; and that it is He, who all along, from the beginning, had been the Almighty Minister in the Church of GOD; and now is the whole, and every part, both in the ordination, and the efficiency of it, being from, and by Him. And, as nothing can be equally important to the child of GOD, to be always waiting on the LORD the SPIRIT's ministry, in an age when He is so little known, and regarded, I crave permission to state what is here said, with all that attention it so loudly demands. The LORD make the statement profitable, if it be strictly consistent with his truth, to his people.

And, *first.* I desire the Reader to remark with me, the name by which the LORD the SPIRIT is here mentioned, namely, the HOLY GHOST. And let it be shewn, if it can, by any common sense argument whatever, wherefore a name, so defining personality, should be given to any one, but under the idea of a Person? The HOLY GHOST is here said to have a meaning in a certain appointment, and that appointment is fully confirming a will, design, and pleasure. The HOLY GHOST *this signifying.*

Secondly. The signification here spoken of, being in allusion to the ordinances in the sanctuary service, could have been in the appointment of none but GOD. The services must imply, that they were GOD's services. The priests and servants ministering in them, GOD's priests and servants; and consequently, the LORD the SPIRIT, here called by his special personal name, the HOLY GHOST, could be no other than GOD.

Thirdly. The HOLY GHOST thus manifesting both his Person and GODHEAD; the *former* by actions which could belong only to personality, and the *latter* in appointments of holy services, which belonged to none but GOD to appoint: so by those actions and appointments during the Old Testament dispensation, which began with the Church, and shadowing events, which reached to the New Testament dispensation in the days of the Gospel, and to extend to the latest Period of time most plainly, and decidedly proved, that the personal ministry; of GOD the HOLY GHOST, hath been all along exercised, and that he hath uniformly presided over the Church, in all ages. So that here is, in this blessed Scripture, the most full, and ample testimony, to the Person, GODHEAD, and Ministry, of the LORD the SPIRIT.

I stay not in this place to enquire into what is here said of the HOLY GHOST's signifying by those services his divine intention. This meets us in all the shadows of his appointment, under the law, when we discover them ministering to CHRIST, who is the substance of all.

But I will in this place, with the Reader's indulgence, take one moment longer, just to add to what has been said a short observation, and which I hope will not be unsuited to the former, on the particular name, and title of God the Holy Ghost.

Wherefore is God the Spirit specially, and personally, called the Holy Ghost? I have often pondered the expression. It cannot be, with the most distant intention, of implying, any thing more holy in his nature, and essence than in the other Persons of the Godhead. The whole three Persons are One, in nature, essence, and perfections. And hence it hath been supposed, and with good reason, that the ascription of Holy, is trebled, in the hymns of Angels, and the spirits of just men made perfect, on this account, when they cry out *Holy, Holy, Holy, is the* Lord *of hosts!* Isaiah, vi. 3. Rev. iv. 8. But it should seem, that this name is specially, and personally given to the Holy Ghost, in reference to his office-character, in the special work of redemption. His office by regeneration is to quicken the redeemed, and chosen, of the Lord, from the death of sin, to a life of holiness in Christ. And if so, what an endearedness of character, doth it give to the souls of God's people, concerning God the Holy Ghost? How precious doth the Lord the Spirit appear on this account? And what a sanctity of conduct, ought it to induce in our spirits, when we call to mind, *that our bodies are the temple of the* Holy Ghost *which is in us?* 1 Cor. vi. 19.

11 But Christ being come an high priest of good things to come, by a greater and more perfect tabernacle, not made with hands, that is to say, not of this building;

12 Neither by the blood of goats and calves, but by his own blood, he entered in once into the holy place, having obtained eternal redemption *for us*.

13 For if the blood of bulls and of goats, and the ashes of an heifer sprinkling the unclean, sanctifieth to the purifying of the flesh:

14 How much more shall the blood of Christ, who through the eternal Spirit offered himself without spot to God, purge your conscience from dead works to serve the living God?

I did not detain the Reader, under the view of the foregoing verses to remark, how blessedly the Holy Ghost, by those shadowing representations, taught the Church, that all pointed to Christ, and in him had their accomplishment; because I knew, that under this paragraph we should be led to the consideration of the subject again, and might therefore enter into it, somewhat more fully. The daily entrance of the Priests into the first tabernacle, and the yearly entrance of the High Priest into the second; were all typical of Christ.

Indeed without an eye to Him, the whole had no meaning. For what could those Priests accomplish, or what virtue, or efficacy, could there be in the blood of goats, or calves, to take away sin? But what grace is shewn, in the HOLY GHOST to the Church of JESUS to keep up such an unceasing remembrance of sin, and to hold forth, such wonders as were to be manifested, in the Person and work of CHRIST, by the sacrifice of himself.

Reader! ponder well the subject, for it is for your life. Observe, CHRIST hath obtained *eternal redemption.* And he hath entered with it, by his own blood into heaven. He hath carried it up with him there, and on the mercy-seat, the propitiatory, paid it down in the full current coin of heaven. Yea! He offered it, through the eternal SPIRIT. And he was *justified by the* SPIRIT, in the deed, by his resurrection from the dead. 1 Tim. iii. 16. And GOD our FATHER hath confirmed it still more, as *the* GOD *of peace,* which brought again from the dead our LORD JESUS CHRIST, that *great Shepherd of the sheep, by the blood of the everlasting Covenant.* Heb. xiii. 20. Oh! what strength, and energy, do those united views give, to the faith of the redeemed, when pleading these precious things, before the throne!

15 And for this cause he is the mediator of the new testament, that by means of death, for the redemption of the transgressions *that were* under the first testament, they which are called might receive the promise of eternal inheritance.

16 For where a testament *is,* there must also of necessity be the death of the testator.

17 For a testament *is* of force after men are dead: otherwise it is of no strength at all while the testator liveth.

18 Whereupon neither the first *testament* was dedicated without blood.

19 For when Moses had spoken every precept to all the people according to the law, he took the blood of calves and of goats, with water, and scarlet wool, and hyssop, and sprinkled both the book, and all the people,

20 Saying, This *is* the blood of the testament which God hath injoined unto you.

21 Moreover he sprinkled likewise with blood both the tabernacle, and all the vessels of the ministry.

22 And almost all things are by the law purged with blood; and without shedding of blood is no remission.

23 *It was* therefore necessary that the patterns of things in the heavens should be purified with these; but the heavenly things themselves with better sacrifices than these.

We enter at the first of these verses, on a most interesting subject, in which CHRIST is considered, as the Testator of all the blessings, purchased by him in the Covenant, for his people; and the Testament he hath made, in the blessings Covenanted for, of grace here, and glory for ever. I beg the Reader to attend to the subject, with that attention its importance demands. CHRIST hath made his Testament or Will, in which all the several legacies are mentioned, in relation to temporal, spiritual, and eternal blessings; the things themselves are registered in the word of GOD; the blood of CHRIST is said to be the purchase; GOD the FATHER is pledged for the performance by word and oath; and is a party witness to the great transaction; and GOD the SPIRIT hath sealed the writings with his broad seal of heaven, in the charter of grace. So that it hath every confirmation to make it sure and binding.

But as all testamentary writings become of force after men are dead, and are of no value before, CHRIST the Testator to his Will, dies also, to give efficacy to his. And as CHRIST is both the Testator, Administrator, and Executor of his own Will; it became necessary that he should arise from the dead, and enter into glory, that he might pay all the legacies himself, with his own hand. This was strikingly set forth, under the law, by the shedding of blood; to intimate the Covenant or Testament being confirmed; and by the sprinkling the blood, to intimate the application. Indeed here were *four* distinct services, in the Old Testament dispensation of shedding of blood, as one alone could not have set forth in shadowy representations, those several grand and momentous truths, in the death of CHRIST. The *first* was that of the Passover. Exod. xii. teaching, that CHRIST, *our Passover is sacrificed for us, to deliver from the wrath to come.* 1 Thess. i. 10. But the Church of CHRIST, when in the *Adam*-state of a fallen nature, needed somewhat more than a deliverance from wrath; and therefore the atonement of sin, became the *second,* and which was also shadowed out, in the great day of the sin-offering. Levit. xvi. Here was shewn, how the Church being delivered from wrath, was also brought into a state of reconciliation, and favor, by the offering of the body of CHRIST. 2 Cor. v. 21. But we must not stop here. For even a deliverance from wrath, and an atonement for sin, to bring into reconciliation and favor, need also, a qualification in the LORD's people, to partake of those rich mercies. Our souls, while unregenerated by the HOLY SPIRIT, and unsanctified in the *Adam*-nature, are not made meet partakers, of the saints in light. Hence, a *third* service, in the *Jewish* Church, typified the great blessings, to be enjoyed from the LORD JESUS in the *Chris-*

tian; and by the service of the slaying of one bird, and the flying away of another in the air, was set forth, CHRIST giving himself for his Church, that he might sanctify and cleanse it, with the washing of water, by the word, and to present it to himself a glorious Church, not having spot or wrinkle, or any such thing. And thus CHRIST was set forth, by the sacrifice of the one bird, that was killed over the running water; and the LORD's entrance into heaven, in his own blood was also represented by the other bird being sprinkled with blood, and being let loose in the open field. Compare Levit. xiv. 6, 7. with Ephes. v. 26, 27. And, *lastly,* as a ratification of the whole, this of the Testament, as here set forth, is in conformity to the LORD's appointment under the law. Exod. xxiv. 8.

I will only detain the Reader, with a short observation on this whole passage, just to remark, that if the LORD JESUS CHRIST, thus died, to confirm and make sure, all his testamentary gifts to his Church and people, how necessary it must be, for every one of his redeemed ones, to prove their relationship to CHRIST, by which alone they can lay claim to all the blessings of the Covenant. When CHRIST was in the full prospect of death, he instituted the Holy Supper, as a memorial to be observed by his people for ever. And as he delivered them the sacred Cup, he said; *This cup is the new testament in my blood. Take this, and divide it among yourselves.* Luke xxii. 17, 19. Nothing could more strikingly illustrate, than the original institution of *Moses* sprinkling the book, and the people, in the Old Testament dispensation, was, in direct allusion, to this of CHRIST in the New, for JESUS hath nearly made use of the same words, verse 20. It will be our mercy, if we can prove our heirship *in* CHRIST, and our relationship *to* CHRIST, for then, all the legacies JESUS hath left his Church are our own. Reader! see to it, that as the Apostle saith, you make *your calling and election sure;* for so all temporal, spiritual, and eternal blessings, are in CHRIST, and from CHRIST; and an entrance, shall be ministered unto us abundantly, into the everlasting kingdom of our LORD and SAVIOR JESUS CHRIST. 2 Pet. i. 10, 11.

24 For Christ is not entered into the holy places made with hands, *which are* the figures of the true; but into heaven itself, now to appear in the presence of God for us:

25 Nor yet that he should offer himself often, as the high priest entereth into the holy place every year with blood of others;

26 For then must he often have suffered since the foundation of the world; but now once in the end of the world hath he appeared to put away sin by the sacrifice of himself.

27 And as it is appointed unto men once to die, but after this the judgment:

28 So Christ was once offered to bear the sins of many; and unto them that look for him shall he appear the second time without sin unto salvation.

Nothing can be more satisfactory than the conviction, that CHRIST, as our great Covenant Head and Surety, hath passed into heaven itself, and is there as our Representative. So that in fact, we are there with him. So saith the HOLY GHOST by *Paul.* Ephes. ii. 5, 6. And this entrance into heaven, and sitting down on the right hand of the Majesty on High, not only manifests the everlasting safety of his people, but also proves the perfection of his obedience and sacrifice. He needed not as those high priests, a remembrance again of sin every year. CHRIST's one offering of himself once offered, hath *perfected for ever them that are sanctified.* And it is this which every regenerated child of GOD is to plead before the throne continually; for it answers the whole demand of the law, silenceth all the accusations of Satan; is a satisfying reply to the alarms of conscience; and forms a full receipt to all the claims of justice. And what a blessed conclusion is made of the whole chapter. As death is the just sentence pronounced by the LORD on sin; and all men must partake of it naturally; so CHRIST by his death, took away the penal effects of death, in the spiritual and everlasting dominion of it, for all his people, and to them that look for him by faith in the full assurance of his salvation; he will assuredly appear again to call home his redeemed to himself, when he will personally come *to be glorified in his saints, and to be admired in all that believe!*

REFLECTIONS.

OH! the distinguishing mercy, to which, by the coming of our LORD JESUS CHRIST, the Church is brought, in exchanging a worldly sanctuary, and carnal ordinances; for the open displays of grace, in the Person, work, blood-shedding, and righteousness of our adorable High Priest, who is the whole sum and substance of every thing blessed; and having, by his own blood, obtained eternal redemption for us, is set down on the right hand of the Majesty on High. Precious LORD JESUS! thou art indeed the Testator of the New Testament in thy blood. Thou hast ensured all the blessings of the New Covenant to thy people. And blessed be the HOLY GHOST, in his Person, GODHEAD, and Ministry, for all his divine teaching, both of the old Church, in type, and figure; and the new dispensation, in sum and substance; and all of CHRIST JESUS.

LORD JESUS! let thy sweet supper for ever refresh the souls of thy redeemed, in the celebration of the New Testament in thy blood. Let it be a continual feast upon that one all-sufficient sacrifice, whereby thou hast perfected for ever them that are sanctified. Oh! let the consciousness of thy continually appearing for us, in the presence of GOD, keep our souls alive, in the expectation of thy coming, that we may look for thee the second time, without sin unto salvation.

CHAP. X.

CONTENTS.

In this Chapter the Inefficacy of the Law, and the Sufficiency of the Gospel are stated. The Lord Jesus, *is most blessedly represented, under the Spirit of Prophecy, as coming for the Salvation of his People. The gracious Encouragement, of drawing nigh by his Blood.*

FOR the law having a shadow of good things to come, *and* not the very image of the things, can never with those sacrifices which they offered year by year continually make the comers thereunto perfect.

2 For then would they not have ceased to be offered? because that the worshippers once purged should have had no more conscience of sins.

3 But in those *sacrifices there is* a remembrance again *made* of sins every year.

4 For *it is* not possible that the blood of bulls and of goats should take away sins.

I detain the Reader, at his entry on this most precious Chapter, to beg of him to remark, with me, the striking expression, which the Holy Ghost is pleased to make use of, when he calls the Law a *shadow.* For what is a shadow? It cannot be formed, but from some substance. And the substance must be *before* the shadow. My hand, or my body, placed between the light, and the earth, forms a shadow. But on the supposition, that either be removed, no shadow remains. Now then, to apply this to the subject of these verses. The Law is said to have been a shadow of good things to come. But the very existence of the shadow, implied the pre-existence of the substance. And accordingly we find, Christ is said to be *the Lamb slain from the foundation of the world.* Rev. xiii. 8. Hence, therefore, the Law acted as a shadow of this substance. And very evident it is, that Christ was set up from everlasting, and in all things he hath the pre-eminence. But, Reader! think, if it be possible, how infinitely great must be his Person; and how infinitely momentous his redemption, introduced as both have been, in a way so wonderful, and with such vast preparation?

5 Wherefore when he cometh into the world, he saith, Sacrifice and offering thou wouldest not, but a body hast thou prepared me:

6 In burnt offerings and *sacrifices* for sin thou hast had no pleasure.

7 Then said I, Lo, I come (in the volume of

the book it is written of me,) to do thy will, O God.

8 Above when he said, Sacrifice and offering, and burnt-offerings and *offering* for sin thou wouldest not, neither hadst pleasure *therein;* which are offered by the law;

9 Then said he, Lo, I come to do thy will, O God. He taketh away the first, that he may establish the second.

10 By the which will we are sanctified through the offering of the body of Jesus Christ once *for all.*

11 And every priest standeth daily ministering and offering oftentimes the same sacrifices, which can never take away sins:

12 But this man, after he had offered one sacrifice for sins, for ever sat down on the right hand of God;

13 From henceforth expecting till his enemies be made his footstool.

14 For by one offering he hath perfected for ever them that are sanctified.

It is hardly necessary for me to inform the Reader, that these words were spoken before, under the spirit of prophecy, by the LORD JESUS CHRIST, in the 40th Psalm, and at least a thousand years before CHRIST's incarnation. So infinitely interested GOD the HOLY GHOST was, that the Church should always be on the look out for the LORD JESUS CHRIST, that from the moment of the Fall, when it was promised, that the seed of the woman should bruise the serpent's Head, and he the Heel; every part of scripture, more or less, is engaged to celebrate the great event, and to admonish the Church with the expectation of his coming. Hence, we find the Prophets with one voice, and in the most lofty strain, speaking in raptures of the LORD's coming. The Patriarch *Abraham* saw the day of CHRIST afar off, rejoiced, and was glad. *Jacob* spake of the *Shiloh. David* lived, and died in the full assurance, that of his loins CHRIST should arise after the flesh. *Isaiah,* under the same divine teaching, cried out to the Church: *Behold, your* GOD *will come and save you. Jeremiah, Micah, Zechariah, Malachi,* yea, and all the Prophets. I stay not to quote passages from their inspired writings in proof, this would be almost endless.

But it is blessed to find the same preached in type and figure, as well as proclaimed in prophecy. CHRIST saith, *a body hast thou prepared me;* or, as the other scripture hath rendered the phrase, *mine ears hast thou opened,* or digged; Psm. xl. 6. alluding to the servant in *Israel,* who, when offering to serve his master for ever, had his ear bored at the door post; and for the love he bore his master, and his wife and children, thereby declared himself to be his servant for ever. Exod. xxi. 5, 6. What a sweet thought the whole furnisheth! CHRIST, as GOD-Man-Mediator, having betrothed himself to our nature, becomes the Surety, and Sponsor to JEHOVAH, for the redemption of his Wife and Children, the Church. Hence he cries, *Lo! I come to do thy will, O* GOD! *Mine ears hast thou opened!* Isaiah l. 5.

I beg the Reader to pause over this blessed view, for it is blessed. Through all the Old Testament Scripture, we find the proclamation, Lo! I come. And we find the Church on the constant look out for CHRIST's coming. The Church is introduced as saying: *It is the voice of my Beloved! behold he cometh, leaping upon the mountains, skipping upon the hills.* Song ii. 8. Zech. ii. 10, 11. Hence, as the time drew nearer, we are told, that there were some who departed not from the temple night, nor day, *waiting for the consolation of Israel:* Luke ii. 25, 37. Yea, after CHRIST actually came, the message of *John* the *Baptist* is in proof, how universal the expectation of the LORD's people was, when the question of enquiry was worded so expressly to this individual Person: *art thou he that should come, or look we for another?* Matt. xi. 3.

But, Reader! in contemplating the LORD's coming, in the days of his flesh, for the accomplishment of redemption, let us not overlook the LORD's coming now, by the sweet influences of his SPIRIT, to make that redemption personally blessed to each soul. JESUS comes now in his word, and by his ordinances, providences, promises, manifestations; and in the many, numberless, nameless ways, by which he maketh himself known to his people, otherwise than he doth to the world. And, oh! what grace in *him,* what joy to *them?* And it must be so. For there is a mutual connection between JESUS and his people. His glory is their joy; their happiness, his pleasure. While he gives out grace, their souls are made blessed in him. And when they are everlastingly housed in his embraces in heaven; he sees the travail of his soul, and is satisfied. It would be always well for every regenerated child of GOD to have this in view, for it would give strength to his faith. When an exercised soul can say, My GOD, my SAVIOR will be glorified, when I am blessed in his salvation!

For the very delightful expressions, of the one offering of the body of JESUS CHRIST once for all, and for the vast difference between the priests under the Law, *standing* daily to minister, and CHRIST for ever *sitting down* on the right hand of GOD, having obtained eternal redemption for us; I refer to Chapter i. 3. where the subject is already considered.

15 *Whereof* the Holy Ghost also is a witness to us; for after that he had said before,

16 This *is* the covenant that I will make with them after those days, saith the Lord, I will put

my laws into their hearts, and in their minds will I write them;

17 And their sins and iniquities will I remember no more.

18 Now where remission of these *is*, *there is* no more offering for sin.

Let the Reader particularly notice, how blessedly God the HOLY GHOST is introduced in this passage, as a witness to the truth of it. What a proof to his Being, Person, GODHEAD, and Ministry? Who but a Person can be a witness? And who less than GOD can witness to his own Covenant? Oh! the folly, as well as ingratitude of such men, who reject the counsel of GOD against their own souls! And let not the Reader, at the same time, overlook the blessed truth, to which GOD the HOLY GHOST bears witness. The Covenant of grace, in the pardoning of sins, is made everlastingly secure in the blood of CHRIST. CHRIST hath redeemed his Church from the curse of the law, being made a curse for her. Gal. iii. 13. And, where that redemption is, it is full, finished, and compleat. There is no more offering for sin. The sin of the Church is done away by CHRIST. How then shall there be any more offering for what doth not exist? And to this the HOLY GHOST himself is the witness. Precious truth, and precious witness, to the regenerated child of GOD! Jeremiah l. 20. Rom. viii. 1.

19 Having therefore, brethren, boldness to enter into the holiest by the blood of Jesus,

20 By a new and living way, which he hath consecrated for us, through the veil, that is to say, his flesh;

21 And *having* an high priest over the house of God;

22 Let us draw near with a true heart in full assurance of faith, having our hearts sprinkled from an evil conscience, and our bodies washed with pure water.

23 Let us hold fast the profession of *our* faith without wavering; (for he *is* faithful that promised;)

24 And let us consider one another to provoke unto love and to good works:

25 Not forsaking the assembling of ourselves together, as the manner of some *is;* but exhorting *one another;* and so much the more, as ye see the day approaching.

These words are the conclusion to the blessed doctrine going before. And they are so sweet, so gracious, so consolatory, and encouraging to every child of God, in whose spirit the SPIRIT witnesseth, by his regenerating, soul-renewing grace, that he hath interest in the full remission of sins just before spoken of; that I cannot but beg the Reader to pause over what is said, and ponder them, one by one.

First. The persons spoken to are brethren, yea, *holy brethren*, as they are called. Chap. iii. 1. And, being one with CHRIST, and interested in all belonging to CHRIST, in his communicable grace, and glory; they are indeed holy in him. 1 Cor. i. 30.

Secondly. They are said to have *boldness*, to enter in. And this ariseth from many causes. CHRIST's oneness with the FATHER, his Suretyship-engagements also being fulfilled. His own personal entrance there, and also as our representative and forerunner, the compleatness of his obedience and sacrifice, the ample reparation he hath made both to law and justice, and the reward which his Church is entitled to, by, and in him; all these, give a boldness to the whole brotherhood of CHRIST.

Thirdly. The place of entrance, namely, *into the holiest*. The Holy of Holies, in the Tabernacle, was a type of this. CHRIST is gone into heaven, which this represented. And there, by faith, we are not only commanded to follow him, but to come with boldness. For, by virtue of their oneness with him, and redemption by him, this is their final home, and their rest. JESUS declared before his return thither, that he only went before to prepare a place for them, and that he would come and receive them to himself, that where he was, there they might be also. John xiv. 3. Hence, in the lively exercises of faith upon his Person, and their interest in him, and union with him, they are expected to come with continued boldness. 1 Pet. i. 5.

Fourthly. And the way is most blessedly spoken of, in which they are to come, namely, by the blood of JESUS. Reader! do mark, how blessedly the subject riseth by gradation, higher and higher. *The blood of* JESUS! This is the sole means, by which real soul-felt communion with GOD in CHRIST, through the SPIRIT, can be carried on, and enjoyed. It is, or ought to be, the soul's daily, hourly act of faith, upon the Person, and blood of CHRIST. There can be no access, either here, or hereafter, but in, and by Him. He hath opened this way to GOD and the FATHER, by his blood. And he ever liveth to keep it open, by his intercession. Oh! it is blessed, most blessed, thus to approach. The Church in heaven, are represented as proclaiming aloud, in their hymns of praise, that this was the way they found, of access to the throne. *Thou wast slain, and hast redeemed us to* GOD *by thy blood.* Rev. v. 9.

Fifthly. The new and living way. Not *new*, as if the Old Testament saints had not the same *good old way*. For CHRIST was set up from everlasting. And He is *the Lamb slain from the foundation of the world.* But perhaps so called, because CHRIST had, in fact, been newly slain; and his vesture, which *John* saw, dipped in blood, as if flowing then fresh from his wounds. Rev. v. 6. xix. 13. And, it is probable, moreover, it may be here called a *new* way, in distinction to the old Covenant of Works under the Law, which this

Epistle throughout had been all along shewing the incompetency of, to bring sinners to GOD. Now here is a *new,* and it is a *living* way; for the Law killeth, but the SPIRIT giveth life. And JESUS himself is *the way, the truth, and the life.* Oh! what sweetness, what blessedness, what soul-encouraging strength, are in these words, to a poor sinner, condemned in his own heart of sin?

Sixthly. It is also a *consecrated* way. Yes! *For Him hath* GOD *the* FATHER *sealed.* John vi. 27. Pause, Reader, over this additional argument of the most unanswerable persuasion, to come with boldness to the mercy-seat. Here is not only the blood of JESUS, to give confidence to his redeemed, in that it *cleanseth from all sin:* 1 John i. 7. but here is JEHOVAH'S consecration of CHRIST; his own appointment, and authority. It is the very remedy of GOD'S own providing. GOD himself is the Author, the Contriver of it. He it is, that hath sworn CHRIST into his Office of High Priest, and Mediator. So that, when a poor sinner is led this way to GOD, by the sweet guidings of the HOLY GHOST, he may well find boldness; because the way he comes to GOD in CHRIST, is not only a righteousness, and a sacrifice compleat and full, and answering to all the demands of GOD'S righteous law; but because the remedy is GOD'S own. How can I possibly fail, (the poor sinner may say as he comes to the throne with boldness,) when my GOD, and FATHER, hath himself appointed it, accepted it, and commanded me, and every poor awakened sinner, so to come?

Lastly, to add no more. What a thought is that, to every child of GOD, to come, in addition to all that hath been said before, when his drawing nigh is in, and through the *vail of* CHRIST'S *flesh.* Oh! who shall speak the blessedness, or what heart here below shall conceive, the thousandth part of that endless felicity, when we consider that all our approaches to GOD is in, and through the human nature of CHRIST; and all his manifestations to us, are through the same medium? Even in glory, the felicity of the Church must be heightened by this cause. The brightness of celestial objects, and especially the revelations of GOD, in his threefold character of Person, will be softened, and tempered to our apprehensions; ripened, and made perfect, as they then will be, through the vail of CHRIST'S flesh. And both here and there, in grace, and glory, all that our JESUS makes known to us, while they are the result of his infinite power and GODHEAD, will be naturally unfolded to us, to suit our capacities. Infinite, large, eternal, they will be, because CHRIST'S GODHEAD gives these properties to them, and such they will continue for ever. But coming to us through the manhood of JESUS; this will so assimilate, and humanize them to our apprehension, and enjoyment, as to give a double blessedness to every manifestation, of grace here, and glory hereafter. Reader! behold then, with what strength of persuasion it is, that we are here commanded by the HOLY GHOST, when in a justified state in CHRIST, to come boldly to the throne, in the blood and righteousness of CHRIST, to grasp, and lay hold fast of our profession, and to exhort one another in it!

26 For if we sin wilfully after that we have received the knowledge of the truth, there remaineth no more sacrifice for sins,

27 But a certain fearful looking for of judgment and fiery indignation, which shall devour the adversaries.

I beg the Reader's close regard to these verses, because, for want of due attention, God's dear children have sometimes, through the weakness of their faith, and Satan's temptations, been apt to mistake the Lord's meaning. The Apostle by *wilful sin*, could not be supposed to imply, the common sins, and infirmities of the brethren. *For in many things we offend all.* James iii. 2. *The just man* (that is, the justified believer in Christ,) *falleth seven times, and riseth up again.* Prov. xxiv. 16. Yea, *wilful* sins against light and knowledge, are not the sin which the Apostle alluded to in this scripture. Such there are in the best of men. Paul himself confessed, that *in his flesh dwelt no good thing.* Rom. vii. throughout. And *David* hath left it upon record, that the *transgression of the wicked said within his heart,* that there was *no fear of* God *before his eyes.* Psm. xxxvi. 1. Nay, the Lord's own testimony to the same solemn truth, is, that *every imagination of the thoughts of man's heart is only evil continually.* Gen. vi. 5. And the *carnal mind,* is not only *enmity against* God; but *it is not subject to the law of* God: *neither indeed can be.* Let the Reader remark the strong emphasis of this latter clause: *neither indeed can be.* Rom. viii. 7. Many read this scripture as though it referred to the child of God before his regeneration. And there was a time, I confess, that I read it so too. But I bless God, since he mercifully brought me more into an acquaintance with the plague of my own heart, and his grace, that I have been taught better. I now see, that as the regeneration of the spirit doth not regenerate the flesh, the body of sin and death remains the same. *That which is born of the flesh, is flesh.* So Christ hath said. And so I know. It is only that which is *born of the* Spirit *is spirit.* John iii. 6. Hence, the carnal mind is carnal; neither can it be subject to the law of God, as the Holy Ghost hath declared. And it is only by the Spirit, that the deeds of the body are mortified, and the soul lives. Rom. viii. 13. Hence, neither from the testimony of scripture, neither *Paul's* own personal experience, neither the experience of the Lord's people, in all ages of the Church, could *Paul* mean by this expression to allude to, in the common sins and infirmities of the brethren, whether involuntary errors, or those of a more deliberate nature.

But, it is evident by the expression itself, there is intended some one more special act of offence, in a *wilful* transgression. Let the Reader observe, it is spoken of some *one* sin, not sins. For, if we *sin* wilfully, after that we have received the knowledge of the truth, there remaineth no more sacrifice for sins. Hence it is plain, that it was one special, particular sin, against the commission of which the Lord the Holy Ghost warned the Church. And when we consider to whom this Epistle was especially written, and the circumstances of that people, we shall soon discover, under the Lord's teaching, what this wilful sin was to which the Lord alluded. But, before we do this, let it be observed, that the expression itself, doth not speak as of a sin *done,* but if it *were* done. The *Hebrews* are not charged with doing it, only cautioned against it. I beg that this also may be properly and fully attended to, in order that no false inference may be made from it, and to which the scripture itself gives not the least countenance, as if there was a possibility implied in it of finally falling away from grace.

In order to a right apprehension of this passage, let it be *first* considered, that the Apostle is here writing to the Church of the *Hebrews;* that is, to persons who were brought up in all the prejudices of Jewish ideas, and of consequence had been in the habit of observing all the sacrifices of the law. When, therefore, by regeneration, they were gathered to the Lord, and had learnt the blessed truth, that Christ, by the *one offering of himself, once offered, had for ever perfected them that are sanctified;* a firmness of faith in this one all-sufficient offering, ought to have kept them from having the least disposition to return to any of the sacrifices of the law. Nevertheless, as in this Church of Christ, made up of true believers, there were with them, as there is with *us* now, a visible professing Church also, of men unregenerated; the weak and fearful of God's people among them were tempted by such characters to suppose, that there could be no harm in observing the sacrifices of the law, and still to look to Christ. To prevent this, and to shew the danger of such conduct, the Apostle solemnly points out that such a wilful perversion of the truth, in looking to the shadow, now the substance was come, became virtually a denial of the full and compleat sacrifice of Christ for sin; and therefore *there remaineth no more sacrifice for sins.* I am inclined to think that this was the case in this church of the *Hebrews;* and that this was the object had in view in this Scripture. We know that it was so with the Church of *Galatia*, which was composed of a mixture of Jews and Gentiles. See Gal. ii. iii. and iv. Chapters. And we know that in our own day, too many there are, who mingle law and Gospel; and but few, comparatively speaking, who live wholly upon Christ, as the sole cause of justification before God,

Secondly. Let it be further considered, that, in this Church of the *Hebrews,* there must have been, as there always is in the purest congregations upon earth, a number of mere nominal professors, who had no part nor lot in the matter. The real Church of Christ therefore, was hereby taught how to discriminate *the precious from the vile.* And this became the more necessary, because, when the after-visitation came, in the destruction of *Jerusalem,* the people of God might discover that a mere profession would not screen from the just judgment of God. This *certain fearful looking for of judgment and fiery indignation,* actually took place at the memorable siege made upon *Jerusalem*, agreeably to Christ's prediction, when the Roman soldiers, under *Titus Vespasian's* army, burnt the City and the Temple, and destroyed the people with the sword. It should seem therefore very plainly to be meant, that the *wilful sin* here spoken of, was that special act of considering the sacrifice of Christ, either not in itself sufficient for salvation, or that it might receive benefit by the addition of joining with it an attention to the sacrifices under the law. And this transgression is here pointed at, as wilfully departing from the faith, and this is done by way of preserving the real child of God from being led away by the temptation, and calling upon the Church to mark the sure destruction of mere *nominal* professors, in whose hearts no saving act of grace had been wrought by the Holy Ghost.

28 He that despiseth Moses' law died without mercy under two or three witnesses:

29 Of how much sorer punishment, suppose ye, shall he be thought worthy, who hath trodden under foot the Son of God, and hath counted the blood of the covenant, wherewith he was sanctified, an unholy thing, and hath done despite unto the Spirit of grace?

30 For we know him that hath said, Vengeance *belongeth* unto me, I will recompense, saith the Lord. And again, The Lord shall judge his people.

31 *It is* a fearful thing to fall into the hands of the living God.

In following up the same subject, *Paul* here very strikingly reminds the *Hebrews* of the strictness of the law by *Moses.* And from thence calls upon them to consider, how much more solemn, in the final administration, must be that Gospel of Christ to which the law ministered but as a shadow? And I beg the Reader to observe the strong expression here used, of *treading under foot the* Son *of* God, *and counting the blood of the covenant, wherewith* Christ *was sanctified, an unholy thing, and doing despite to the* Spirit *of grace!* I would not presume to speak decidedly, but, upon the clearest testimonies of Scripture, concerning any portion of the Word of God; but I would humbly ask, is there not in these solemn words, a plain charge brought against all who are guilty of this crime, to the Person and Offices of the Father, Son, and Holy Ghost? To God the Father, in treading under foot God's dear Son, in denying his authority, whom God hath appointed, and sworn with an oath into his office. Psm. cx. To God the Son also, in denying his Godhead, and counting the blood of the Covenant, wherewith Christ was sanctified by all the Persons of the Godhead, an unholy thing! John x. 36. John xvii. 19. Isa. xi. 2. Isa. lxi. 1. Matt. iv. 1. And to God the Holy Ghost, by whom Christ wrought his miracles, and through whom he offered himself without spot to God, when he made his soul an offering for sin. Chap. ix. 14. And what a trembling scripture follows! *Vengeance belongeth unto me!* Here needs no comment. It is indeed *a fearful thing to fall into the hands of the living* God!

32 But call to remembrance the former days, in which, after ye were illuminated, ye endured a great sight of afflictions;

33 Partly, whilst ye were made a gazing stock

both by reproaches and afflictions; and partly, whilst ye became companions of them that were so used.

34 For ye had compassion of me in my bonds, and took joyfully the spoiling of your goods, knowing in yourselves that ye have in heaven a better and an enduring substance.

35 Cast not away therefore your confidence, which hath great recompence of reward.

36 For ye have need of patience, that, after ye have done the will of God, ye might receive the promise.

37 For yet a little while, and he that shall come will come, and will not tarry.

38 Now the just shall live by faith: but if *any man* draw back, my soul shall have no pleasure in him.

39 But we are not of them who draw back unto perdition; but of them that believe to the saving of the soul.

I beg the Reader with all possible attention to observe, in confirmation of all that I have been saying, that the HOLY GHOST is all along in this Epistle comforting the Church, when drawing the line of distinction between the *real regenerated* believers in CHRIST, and mere *nominal professors.* An high flaming profession men may make, as is stated Chapter the Sixth, where there is not an atom of grace. But GOD the SPIRIT graciously teacheth his people how to estimate their different characters, by the testimonies the LORD hath given them. And I pray the Reader to observe how sweetly he comforts them, by bidding them to mark the ground, which by grace they had trodden.

But call to remembrance (saith the kind Remembrancer of JESUS) *the former days, in which, after ye were illuminated, ye endured a great sight of afflictions.* As if the LORD had said, do ye not see, and know, the certainty of your high calling in CHRIST JESUS? Have ye not got the richest testimonies of your new-birth character? When ye were once illuminated, did ye not *desire, as babes in* CHRIST, to be fed with *the sincere milk of the word, that ye might grow thereby?* And though things are low with you, in the present leanness of soul, so that when *ye ought to be teachers, ye have need to go over again the first principles of the Oracles of* GOD; yet, *call to remembrance the former days.* There was a time, when *your zeal provoked very many.* Ye were made *a gazing stock* yourselves; and ye were *companions of them that were so used.* Yea, ye took joyfully the *spoiling of your goods;* from the well-grounded confidence that ye then had, that if the LORD permitted the enemy to turn ye out of house and home, he would the sooner take you to himself in heaven. *Cast not away therefore your confidence which hath great recompense of reward.* Look forward! JESUS will soon come! And in the mean time *the just shall live by faith.* As to those who draw back from a mere profession, this is, as was before known. They draw back from lip-confession only, for they never had more. Head-knowledge is no heart-renewing. Not falling from grace, for they never were in grace, but falling from natural attainments, for they never rose higher. In such, the LORD JESUS hath no pleasure. But his children, his redeemed, the gift of his FATHER, the purchase of his blood, and the conquests of his SPIRIT; *though they fall, yet not fall away, for the LORD upholds them with his hand:* Psm. xxxvii. 24. Though they faint and draw back in the day of adversity, yet *draw not back unto perdition*, for they are still of them that *believe to the saving of the soul!* Reader! what saith your personal experience to these things? Hath the LORD the HOLY GHOST regenerated you from the *Adam*-fall of a nature once dead in trespasses and sins? Can you look back to the wormwood and the gall of that fallen state? Can you call to remembrance, as the LORD here bids his people, the former days, after ye were illuminated? No man that hath passed from death to life, can be at a loss to know the saving change. True! you have cause to lament great leanness of soul. There is indeed in the best of men, but too much reason to be humbled to the dust before GOD, for the small attainments and little progress made in divine life. But the salvation of the Church doth not spring from any holiness wrought *in us*, but from the work of CHRIST wrought *for us.* Not in *our* brokenness of heart, but in CHRIST'S *bruised and broken body on the tree.* It is indeed blessed, yea, very blessed, to feel and enjoy all the gracious effects of the precious finished salvation of CHRIST; but all we feel in the lively actings of faith, are but *effects*, and not the *cause.* He is the sole Author and Finisher of salvation. It is a sad consideration, that so many of GOD'S dear children, in the present day, live below their privileges, by living upon what passeth from the work of GOD the SPIRIT *within them*, instead of living wholly upon what CHRIST is *to them;* and that their sanctification is *in* Him. John xvii. 19. 1 Cor. i. 30.

REFLECTIONS.

PRECIOUS LORD JESUS! how blessedly hast thou manifested in thy Person, blood-shedding, and righteousness, that thou art the end of the Law for righteousness, to every one that believeth; and that the law was but a shadow of good things to come, which never could, neither ever was designed to make the comers thereunto perfect. Oh! for that sweet voice, *Lo! I come!* to be heard daily, hourly, in my soul, by the ear of faith, until I see thee as thou art, and dwell with thee for ever. Come, LORD, in thy SPIRIT, in thine ordinances, thy means of grace, and open my soul to receive thee. Come, LORD, continually in the love-visits of thy mercy, until thou shalt come in the glory of thy Majesty, to take me home to thyself, that I may dwell with thee for ever!

Praised be GOD the HOLY GHOST for the many blessed things contained in this delightful Chapter. Yes! LORD! through thy grace enabling us, we have boldness to enter into the holiest, by the blood of JESUS. And under thy leadings and influences, thy people, are hereby distinguished, from those awful characters, in this CHRIST-despising generation, who tread under-foot the SON of GOD, by denying his GODHEAD, the efficacy of his atoning blood, the blood of the Covenant; and do despite unto the SPIRIT of grace. LORD! comfort thy poor little ones, in the faith, in giving them to see, their adoption-character, and that they are not of them *that draw back unto perdition, but of them that believe to the saving of the soul!*

CHAP. XI.

CONTENTS.

Here is the Record of Old Testament Saints, who lived and died, triumphant in Faith. The sweet Assurance to New Testament Believers, that they, and all the Faithful, will together be made perfect in JESUS.

NOW faith is the substance of things hoped for, the evidence of things not seen.

2 For by it the elders obtained a good report.

3 Through faith we understand that the worlds were framed by the word of God, so that things which are seen were not made of things which do appear.

The Church of GOD can never be sufficiently thankful to the HOLY GHOST, for this most precious Chapter. It forms a compendium of the most blessed things, all leading to JESUS. The antient fathers of the Church, were accustomed to call it, the book of GOD's Martyrs. And to be sure, it doth contain, some of the most precious things, by which we are led to see, how it was they lived so strong in faith, and died so triumphant in hope, by the grace of GOD, being made perfect in their weakness. In order to enter into a proper apprehension of the blessedness of that principle of faith, in which they were made so strong by the LORD; before that we look at the effects of it in their lives, and deaths, as here recorded, it may not be amiss to attend a little more closely to the LORD's own account of faith, as stated in those words.

Now faith is the *substance* of things hoped for, the *evidence* of things not seen. There is somewhat very striking in this account of faith, as given by the HOLY GHOST himself. It is called by him a *substance,* meaning; that the object the soul resteth on being substantially formed in the mind; and which, so realizeth that object to view, as for the mind to become as perfectly assured of its existence and reality, as though seen. This is faith. And in this sense, it is the *substance* of things which are at a distance; but as perfectly alive to the soul, as though present to bodily sense. To explain great things by small. I have a child, a friend, a relation, whom I have never seen, and living at a distance from me. But I am continually receiving tokens from him by message, or by letter, both of his existence, and his affection towards me. Now, though I have never seen him, yet I no more doubt of his being and existence, than my own. I therefore substantiate, and realize in my mind, this certainty; and I am actuated by it accordingly. Such, but in an infinitely higher degree, are the great objects of faith, in relation to things supernatural, and unseen. I have received evidences upon evidences; and love tokens multiplied with love tokens from JESUS my LORD. By faith, therefore, I substantiate, and realize all those blessed things concerning JESUS. And it is to me substance. JESUS saith, *I will cause them that love me to inherit substance, and I will fill their treasures.* Prov. viii. 21. Hence, therefore, as the Apostle saith, in relation to JESUS; *Whom having not seen we love; in whom though now we see him not, yet believing, we rejoice with joy unspeakable, and full of glory; receiving the end of our faith, even the salvation of our souls.* 1 Pet. i. 8, 9. It was thus with the Patriarch and holy men of old. Their faith needed not the presence of what they believed in. GOD's testimony concerning it was enough. It became therefore the substance of things hoped for; the evidence of things not seen.

One word more concerning faith before we enter upon the blessed history, contained in this glorious Chapter, of the fruits and effects of it. Faith is the gift of GOD. Philip. i. 29. CHRIST is the Author and finisher of faith. Heb. xii. 2. Hence it must follow, that what is GOD's gift is not man's merit; and therefore the glory of faith, in the exercise of his people, is wholly the LORD's. It may perhaps appear strange to some, when I say, that I consider faith as the act of CHRIST upon my soul, more than my act of dependance upon him. Paul saith, and saith with truth, that his life of faith was not his, but the LORD's. Hear his own words. *The life* (saith he) *which I now live in the flesh, I live by the faith of the* SON *of* GOD. Mark the expression. Not *Paul's* life of faith *in* the SON of GOD, but the faith *of* the SON of GOD. Gal. ii. 20. It is not *Paul's* act upon CHRIST, but CHRIST's act upon him. And how is this proved? The life of faith, like any other life, is a life of receiving, not giving. Similar to animal life, which is wholly kept up and preserved, by receiving food, air, strength. These things are received to live upon. They are incomings, not out-goings. The incomings are first received, as the *cause.* The out-goings are exercised as the *effect.* Reader! if these things are so, how doth it reduce, and bring low the pride of all our attainments? How forcibly come home the words of the Apostle, *For who maketh thee to differ from another? And what hast thou that thou didst not receive?* 1 Cor. iv. 7.

4 By faith Abel offered unto God a more excellent sacrifice than Cain, by which he obtained witness that he was righteous, God testifying of his gifts: and by it he being dead yet speaketh.

The HOLY GHOST having first established the truth of the principle of faith itself, and having shewn both the nature of it, and the operation of it, in the properties induced by it, in the lives of the faithful; now proceeds to exemplify its gracious actings, in the lives of those holy men of old, who *by it obtained a good report.* And the LORD begins with the history of the faith of *Abel.* And nothing surely can be more strong and decisive, on the subject. The faith of *Abel* is contrasted to the unbelief of *Cain.* Both brought their offerings to the LORD. But the HOLY GHOST hath marked the vast difference. *Cain* brought of the fruits of the earth, as one that considered himself a Tenant to the LORD; and no more. He thought the LORD was, as he undoubtedly is, both LORD and Proprietor of all things. And *Cain* acknowledged him as such, and brought his rent. *Abel* brought of the firstlings of his flock, and offered in sacrifice as a sinner. And the LORD had respect unto *Abel,* and his offering: but unto *Cain,* and to his offering he had not respect. Gen. iv. 3, 5. Now we should not have known, with that clearness we now do, through divine teaching, what made the vast difference, in those men, and the LORD's different acceptance of their Persons and offerings; but from GOD the SPIRIT's teaching, in this holy scripture. But when the LORD saith, that it was *by faith Abel* offered a more excellent sacrifice than *Cain,* we discover the reason. *Abel* had an eye, by faith, to CHRIST the Promised Seed. *Abel* knew himself to be a sinner, sprung from the fallen race of *Adam,* and therefore came with the firstlings of his flock, in token of his conscious sin, and that he looked wholly for acceptance in the blood of CHRIST. *Cain* in his offering, had respect only to GOD as a Creator, neither confessing himself as a sinner, or as one needing a Redeemer; and, therefore, was the first Deist the world ever knew. Hence the LORD had respect to *Abel* and his offering; but to *Cain,* he had not respect. Hence also, the blessed testimony here given, by the HOLY GHOST to *Abel,* and the rejection of *Cain.* And though so many ages have passed since those events took place, yet are they still in relation before us. Abel, though dead, yet speaketh.

5 By faith Enoch was translated that he should not see death; and was not found, because God had translated him: for before his translation he had this testimony, that he pleased God.

6 But without faith *it is* impossible to please *him:* for he that cometh to God must believe that he is, and *that* he is a rewarder of them that diligently seek him.

To the account of the illustrious faith of *Abel,* the HOLY GHOST next brings forward his testimony to that of *Enoch,* the seventh from *Adam,* as *Jude* calls him. Jude 14. By which he meant not the seventh *Person,* or the seventh *Man,* but the seventh *generation* from *Adam,* in the line of the Promised Seed. *Adam, Sheth, Enosh, Kenan, Mahalaleel, Jered, Enoch.* See 1 Chron. 1—3. It could not be otherwise meant, for *Cain* had a son called Enoch. Gen. iv. 17—25. Respecting the translation of *Enoch*, from the account here given of it by the HOLY GHOST, it is evident, that his entrance into the World of Spirits, was not by death in the ordinary way, but as *Elijah*, by translation. The LORD simply relates the fact, and bears honorable testimony to his faith. But the LORD enlargeth on what is more important for the Church to know, that such is the importance of faith, that without it, there can be no real approach to GOD, either in prayer, or praise, or delight, or confidence, or joy. Reader! how blessed are those who know the LORD, and *walk in the light of his countenance.* Psm. lxxxix. 15.

7 By faith Noah, being warned of God of things not seen as yet, moved with fear, prepared an ark to the saving of his house; by the which he condemned the world, and became heir of the righteousness which is by faith.

Going on progressively, and according to due order, in a regular succession of those holy men of old, the HOLY GHOST here introduceth to the Church the account of *Noah's* faith. I beg the Reader to attend to some of the leading features of this great Patriarch's character. He is the first concerning whom grace is recorded. The first time we meet with that blessed word in the Bible, is in the instance of Noah. And this at a time of universal corruption, when GOD *saw that the wickedness of man was great in the earth, and that every imagination of the thoughts of his heart was only evil continually.* Gen. vi. 5. I desire the Reader to observe this. And I beg of him to observe no less, that *Noah* was included in the same common corruption. For, when it is added, *But Noah found grace in the eyes of the* LORD, (verse 8.) had that grace been the result of *Noah's* worth and excellency, grace would have lost its name, and *grace*, as the Apostle saith, *would have been no more grace.* Rom. xi. 6. This is a great point to know. And the faith of *Noah* is a confirmation of it. And if the Reader will trace the subject down from *Noah*, to the latest account of the Church, he will find one uniform history on this subject running through all. Observe the expression. *Noah* found grace. Gen. vi. 8. Where? In his own heart? No? *In the eyes of the* LORD. And hence we read what GOD said to *Noah*, *But with thee will I establish my covenant.* Gen. vi. 18. So that the very first mention made of *grace*, or covenant grace as the *cause*, and the covenant as the *effect*, are in the instance of *Noah*. And what is it but the same through all the Bible? *Thou hast found grace* (said the LORD to *Moses* in after ages,) *in my sight, and I know thee by name.* Exod. xxxiii. 17. *Fear not, Mary*, (said the Angel to her,) *for thou hast found favor with* GOD. Luke i. 30. *Go thy way*, (said the LORD to *Ananias* concerning *Paul*,) *for he is a chosen vessel unto me*. Acts ix. 15. The whole subject of every thing that is blessed turns on this hinge. Well, but say you, was not *Noah a preacher of righteousness*, (2 Pet. ii. 5.) and eminent by his faith, and by which he condemned the world, and became *heir of the righteousness which is by faith?* Yes! all these things are true; and the whole are so many blessed testimonies to the character of *Noah.* But then these are all no more than the *effects* of the first predisposing *cause.* They are all to be traced to their fountain head and source, the grace *Noah* found in the *eyes of the* Lord. This gave the bias to all that followed in the life of the Patriarch. This was the first moving and predisposing spring to all the machine. And which brings forward the Apostle's question, and carries with it, in the very bosom of the question, its own answer, *Who hath first given to the* Lord, *and it shall be recompensed again?* Rom. xi. 35. So universally and individually true is it said, and by the Lord himself, of every child of God, *I am found of them that sought me not.* Isaiah lxv. 1. Reader! what is the sweet application of those precious scriptures, as the subject concerns you and me, but that *we come boldly,* in the name of Jesus, *to his mercy-seat,* and *obtain mercy, and find grace to help in time of need.* Heb. iv. 16.

8 By faith Abraham, when he was called to go out into a place which he should after receive for an inheritance, obeyed; and he went out, not not knowing whither he went.

9 By faith he sojourned in the land of promise, as *in* a strange country, dwelling in tabernacles with Isaac and Jacob, the heirs with him of the same promise:

10 For he looked for a city which hath foundations, whose builder and maker *is* God.

11 Through faith also Sara herself received strength to conceive seed, and was delivered of a child when she was past age, because she judged him faithful who had promised.

12 Therefore sprang there even of one, and him as good as dead, *so many* as the stars of the sky in multitude, and as the sand which is by the sea shore innumerable.

How equally plain and blessed is the same doctrine concerning the sovereignty of grace, in the instance of the great father of the faithful, *Abraham?* For what was *Abraham,* when the Lord first called him? Surely, an idolater. And what prompted the Lord to call *Abraham,* but his own free, sovereign, and unmerited grace. Is not every thing the Lord said to this man to the same amount as to *Noah?* He found grace in the eyes of the Lord. *Fear not, Abram; I am thy shield, and thy exceeding great reward.* Gen. xv. 1. So everlastingly true is that blessed scripture by John. *If we love him, it is because he first loved us.* 1 John iv. 19. And all the blessed consequences resulting, in the lives and conduct of *Sarah, Isaac,* and *Jacob,* were the *fruits* and *effects;* and not in the smallest degree *causes,* or ministering to the first great and only disposing *cause,* God's purpose, grace, and favor, leading on to the accomplishment of the end intended. Reader! it is blsssed to behold the lives of the faithful, bearing testimony to God's covenant truth and faithfulness. But it is doubly blessed, to keep always in view the Lord disposing all. While the eye of the Prophet was fixed in contemplation at beholding the whirlwind from the north, and the complicated machine, wheel within wheel, moving on in endless revolvings; the whole was too deep, and too much encompassed in perplexity for his mind to understand. But, when the Lord opened to his astonished view, One, like the Son of Man above, guiding all, the Lord's glory became manifested. Ezek. i. 4—26.

It is blessed, yea, very blessed, to behold the children of God, in every age of the Church, all marked with one and the same family feature. They may be said, all of them, *to sojourn by faith in the land of promise;* for *all the promises are theirs in* Christ, by right of inheritance; 2 Cor. i. 20. and yet, every country here below is to them a strange country. Micah ii. 10. They *dwell in the midst of many people, as a dew from the* Lord, Micah v. 7. and yet *they dwell alone, and are not reckoned among the nations.* Numb. xxiii. 9. They *sojourn in tabernacles* which are moveable, liable, and expecting every moment to be taken down, Heb. xiii. 14. and yet *the eternal* God *is their refuge, and underneath are the everlasting arms.* Deut. xxxiii. 27.

13 These all died in faith, not having received the promises, but having seen them afar off, and were persuaded of *them,* and embraced *them,* and confessed that they were strangers and pilgrims on the earth.

14 For they that say such things declare plainly that they seek a country.

15 And truly, if they had been mindful of that *country* from whence they came out, they might have had opportunity to have returned.

16 But now they desire a better *country,* that is, an heavenly: wherefore God is not ashamed to be called their God: for he hath prepared for them a city.

I pray the Reader to pause over these precious things contained within the bosom of these verses. *These all died in faith.* After what I have offered on the subject of faith, in the opening of this Chapter, (to which I refer the Reader,) it will be unnecessary to dwell on that feature of faith, which respects the death of the Lord's people. They died, as they had lived, in the act of believing. They substantiated things of faith. They understood the things of Christ, as much as though they had lived in the days of Christ. The work of God the Spirit, in convincing them of their need of Christ, was as fully felt, and known, in the conscious plague of their own heart, as those on whom the Holy Ghost descended, after the Lord's ascension, and return to glory. Hence, what Christ said of One suited and belonged to all, *Abraham saw my day afar off, rejoiced, and was glad.* John viii. 56.

And I admire the very sweet, and gracious manner of expression, the Holy Ghost hath made use of, in proclaiming his honorable approbation of their exercise of faith. Though they all died in faith, yet, *not having received the promises, but having seen them afar off, and were persuaded of them, and embraced them.* Hence, in after ages, the Lord gave them this escutcheon to become their coat of arms, as in life, so in death. *They all died in faith.* This motto, marked their princely royalty. And all the faithful in Christ Jesus prove their relationship to the same noble family, in wearing the same crest and arms, from the herald's office of heaven.

Reader! let us not dismiss the view of those holy men of old, before that we have examined our state by their's, in the standard of faith. They all lived, and died, before Christ came. We all now live, since Christ came, finished redemption-work, and returned to glory. They saw not Christ in the flesh, but his day afar off. Our sight of Christ is the same. *Whom having not seen we love.* There is this difference, indeed, which makes their faith so illustrious, in comparison of ours: Christ's day to them was afar off, and many hundred years were to pass, before the fulness of time was to come, when Christ should appear. Had they, therefore, reasoned with flesh and blood, they might have staggered, as those now are so apt to do, which consult it, and, through unbelief, live below their privileges. But it is said of *Abraham,* in testimony of his reliance on the promise, that *he was strong in faith, giving glory to* God, *and being fully persuaded, that what the* Lord *had promised, he was able to perform.* Rom. iv. 20, 21. We have seen the Son of God in our nature, accomplishing redemption by his blood; and, by the regenerating work of God the Holy Ghost on the heart, every child of God hath, in his own person, a clear, and indisputable testimony, that Christ is returned to glory, and hath sent down the Holy Spirit upon his redeemed, in proof thereof. Hence, Old Testament saints, and New Testament believers, are supposed to stand upon the same level, in being *persuaded* of the assurance of the promises; and having *embraced them,* and *confessed* that they are *strangers and pilgrims* on the earth. They desire a *better country,* that is, an *heavenly:* wherefore, God *is not ashamed to be called their* God, *for he hath prepared for them a city.*

Two or three points, will square this account, and enable the Church of God in the present hour, to form judgment of the standard of their faith, by the lives of those holy men of old.

First. The Lord's bringing them into an acquaintance with the plague of their own heart, paved the way for the hearty and cordial reception of Christ, as the remedy of God's own providing, for the recovery of his Church from her fallen state in *Adam.* And here every child of God, when taught of God, and regenerated by the Holy Spirit, knows and feels the same. The corruption of nature, and the want of grace; the workings of sin, and the powers of divine love; a perfect conviction of a total ruin in the first *Adam*, that is, of the earth, earthy; and as perfect an assurance of a compleat recovery by the Almighty salvation of the second *Adam*, even the LORD from heaven; these momentous truths, by sovereign grace, are so powerfully brought home to the heart, and so in-wrought by the LORD's divine teaching, that every child of GOD, both in the ages before CHRIST's incarnation, and since, have one and the same feature of character to be known by, whose they are, and whom they serve, in the Gospel of GOD.

Secondly. The personal enjoyment each child of GOD hath, of his union in CHRIST, and interest with CHRIST, becomes another testimony, in the experience of the faithful. For amidst all the coldness and weakness of the LORD's people, in the present low estate of the Church; still the LORD hath not left himself without witness, that he hath *a seed that serve him*, and which *are counted to the* LORD *for a generation*. There are seasons, in which JESUS doth manifest himself to his people otherwise than he doth to the world. They see him in his suitableness, in his all-sufficiency. They have bread to eat, which the world knoweth not of. And the LORD sometimes comes so near in the manifestations of his love and favor, that they smell the sweet savor of his name, and feel *a joy unspeakable, and full of glory, receiving the end of their faith, even the salvation of their souls*.

And, *lastly*, to mention no more. The consciousness of the love of JESUS, and, as *Paul* saith, the assurance, that JESUS loved me, and gave himself for me, even when matters in ourselves are most dark, and discouraging; these lift up the souls of the faithful above all the things of time and sense, and induce a wise indifference to the mere dying circumstances around, in the blessed prospect of that city *which hath foundations, whose builder and maker is* GOD. Reader! Is this the faith of GOD's people? And is it *your* faith also?

17 By faith Abraham, when he was tried, offered up Isaac: and he that had received the promises offered up his only begotten *son*,

18 Of whom it was said, That in Isaac shall thy seed be called:

19 Accounting that God *was* able to raise *him* up, even from the dead; from whence also he received him in a figure.

Most illustrious as this instance of the Patriarch's faith is, and highly to *Abraham's* honor, as GOD the HOLY GHOST hath recorded it; I feel constrained to pass this view of it by, in order to attend to what is infinitely more to be regarded in it; I mean, in the typical representation it was evidently intended to set forth, of the offering of the LORD JESUS CHRIST. It appears from the whole history, that CHRIST, as the Mediator represented, was the visible JEHOVAH here appointing *Abraham* to this service. And in proof, let the Reader remark, that in the original history of this solemn transaction, while it is said in one verse, that GOD did tempt *Abraham* to the offering of his son: Gen. xxii. 1. in another it is said, that the

Angel, as GOD, calleth to him from heaven, and said: *By myself have I sworn, saith the* LORD. Gen. xxii. 15, 16. A plain proof, that it was the SON of GOD in the representation of his mediator-character, in the whole of this transaction. And indeed it could be no other, for CHRIST is the visible JEHOVAH all along spoken of in the scripture. John i. 18. And the whole may serve to teach us, of what infinite importance in the sight of JEHOVAH, is that one offering of the body of JESUS CHRIST once for all, which GOD the HOLY GHOST was pleased to shadow forth, from the very institution of sacrifices in the garden of *Eden*, to the coming of CHRIST, by type and figure through all the different periods of the world from age to age, in order to teach the Church, that *without shedding of blood, there was no remission;* and that *the blood of* CHRIST *alone cleanseth from all sin.*

20 By faith Isaac blessed Jacob and Esau concerning things to come.

21 By faith Jacob, when he was a dying, blessed both the sons of Joseph, and worshipped, *leaning* upon the top of his staff.

22 By faith Joseph, when he died, made mention of the departing of the children of Israel: and gave commandment concerning his bones.

23 By faith Moses, when he was born, was hid three months of his parents, because they saw *he was* a proper child; and they were not afraid of the king's commandment.

24 By faith Moses, when he was come to years, refused to be called the son of Pharaoh's daughter,

25 Choosing rather to suffer affliction with the people of God, then to enjoy the pleasures of sin for a season;

26 Esteeming the reproach of Christ greater riches than the treasures in Egypt: for he had respect unto the recompence of the reward.

27 By faith he forsook Egypt, not fearing the wrath of the king: for he endured, as seeing him who is invisible.

28 Through faith he kept the passover, and the sprinkling of blood, lest he that destroyed the first-born should touch them.

29 By faith they passed through the Red-sea as by dry *land:* which the Egyptians assaying to do were drowned.

30 By faith the walls of Jericho fell down, after they were compassed about seven days.

31 By faith the harlot Rahab perished not with them that believed not, when she had received the spies with peace.

I must call to remembrance the limited design of this humble work, and not indulge myself in entering upon every separate particular in relation to the actions of those illustrious champions of the faith here recorded. But otherwise I might easily shew, how strongly entrenched the LORD had made those ancient followers of the faith, in this leading, and distinguishing article, of living upon CHRIST. Surely, as *Peter* said of them, the SPIRIT *of* CHRIST *was in them*, and in all their acts, both in their public ministry, and private conversation; the two grand features of our LORD's life, and offices, they embraced with an ardor the most animated, namely, of *the sufferings of* CHRIST, *and the glory which should follow.* 1 Pet. i. 11. And, both CHRIST in his Person, and CHRIST in his ministry, those holy men, by the most lively actings of faith, were living upon, and enjoying familiar communion with. All the Patriarchs, from *Abraham* to *Moses*, lived in the daily exercise of faith upon CHRIST, and his blood-shedding and righteousness. If *Moses* was hidden by his parents, it was by faith. If, conscious of his Hebrew birth by circumcision, which he could not but know, he refused to be called the Son of *Pharaoh's* daughter; it was by faith. If he esteemed CHRIST, despised Egypt, kept the passover, and the sprinkling of blood; the whole was by faith. All, and every act, became an act of faith, by which the lives and deaths of those blood-bought, royal sons of GOD, were so distinguished; and for which, the HOLY GHOST hath handed down their names with such honorable testimony, in the word of GOD. Hence *Jacob*, when a-dying, exulted in the Covenant love, and grace of GOD in CHRIST, and cried out: *I have waited for thy salvation, O* LORD. Hence, *Joseph*, in the hour of death, looked to *Canaan*, as the sure spot, where CHRIST in after ages should come; and said, there let my bones be carried. And *Moses*, in his last farewell to *Israel*, sung his song concerning Him, *my dweller in the bush.* Deut. xxiii. 16.

32 And what shall I more say? for the time would fail me to tell of Gedeon, and *of* Barak, and *of* Samson, and *of* Jephthae; *of* David also, and Samuel, and *of* the prophets:

33 Who through faith subdued kingdoms, wrought righteousness, obtained promises, stopped the mouths of lions.

34 Quenched the violence of fire, escaped the edge of the sword, out of weakness were made strong, waxed valiant in fight, turned to flight the armies of the aliens.

35 Women received their dead raised to life again: and others were tortured, not accepting deliverance; that they might obtain a better resurrection.

36 And others had trial of *cruel* mockings and scourgings, yea, moreover of bonds and imprisonment:

37 They were stoned, they were sawn asunder, were tempted, were slain with the sword; they wandered about in sheepskins and goatskins; being destitute, afflicted, tormented;

38 (Of whom the world was not worthy: they wandered in deserts, and *in* mountains, and *in* dens and caves of the earth.

39 And these all, having obtained a good report through faith, received not the promise.

40 God having provided some better thing for us, that they without us should not be made perfect.

It were to hold the small taper of the night to the sun, to offer any observations upon what is included within these verses. Indeed, any Comment would do injury to the beautiful simplicity which runs through the whole of what the HOLY GHOST hath said. Every verse, yea, every line, manifests what an energy the whole must have acted under, when their faith induced such wonders, and by which such an holy perseverance was kept alive, under CHRIST, the great Author and Finisher of faith, in such soul-living expectations. *They received not the promises.* No! They needed them not in hand. They lived on them by faith. They had the same thing, namely, the assurance of them. And, Reader! this is the most blessed, and distinguishing feature of faith, when, in the absence of the promise, the faithful can, and do live upon the promising GOD. Oh! it is blessed, when at any time matters are dark, and discouraging, still to hang upon GOD the Almighty Promiser; when it is too dark even to see the promise itself, or to see how the LORD will accomplish it. The faithful follower of the LORD hath nothing to do with either. It is enough that the LORD hath said it. And the child of GOD will say, it is the LORD's concern, and not mine, how he will bring it to pass. In short, the blessedness of the promise itself, and the assured faithfulness of the Promiser; these are all in which the faithful are concerned. And, in every trying moment of the faithful, he hears the same Almighty Speaker calling upon him, to the same effect as the LORD did to the Patriarch of old: *Fear not, Abram, I am thy shield, and thine exceeding great reward.* Gen. xv. 1. Reader! can you set your Amen to these truths?

REFLECTIONS.

Blessed be God the Holy Ghost, the Almighty Author of his sacred Word, for this precious Chapter, which he hath so graciously given to the Church of God. Oh! for the Lord the Spirit, who hath so freely caused such illustrious acts of his people to be recorded for the consolation of the faithful, to bless it to the faithful, whenever, and wheresoever the Lord causeth it to be heard, or read, in all the Churches of the saints. And oh! that amidst all the awful circumstances of the present awful day, when, if the Son of God should come, the question of our Lord might be put forth, with trembling apprehensions for the answer; *will He find faith in the earth?* oh! grant that there may be known by our Lord, though hidden from our imperfect view, *a remnant according to the election of grace, both sons and daughters, who do not bow the knee to the image of Baal!*

Lord Jesus! thou Almighty Author and Finisher of faith! do thou increase our faith! Surely, Lord! the gift is thine; faith is thine. As none can first quicken, so none can keep alive his own soul. And, as none can first create faith; so none can exercise it, but by thee. *All our fresh springs are in thee.* Yea, Lord! Is not faith itself thine act in the soul, and the whole result of thy grace upon the heart? Precious Jesus! make thy redeemed now strong in the grace that is in thyself; that we may be *the followers of them, who inherit the promises.*

Almighty Father! All the triumphs of faith begin in thy fatherly love. Thy choice of the Church *in* Christ, and thy gift of the Church *to* Christ, become the surest testimony of thine everlasting love, which time, or eternity can shew. Oh! then, let a sense of it silence for ever all the natural Atheism, and unbelief, thy children bring with them into the world, from the *Adam*-nature, in which we are all born. Oh! gracious God and Father! let thy children stand impressed with an unshaken, and steady assurance, that thou hast not called thyself I AM, for nothing; but that the very name, by which thou hast been pleased to be made known to them, becomes a confirmation of all thy promises. I AM will give both a being, and an accomplishment, to all he hath said. Amen. Oh! then, like those holy men in Christ gone before, grant that thy people may all live, and when called upon, all die, in the faith of God's elect. And both in life and death, in time, and to all eternity, bless the united Source of all their mercies, Father, Son, and Holy Ghost, now, and ever! Amen.

CHAP. XII.

CONTENTS.

The opening of this Chapter contains an earnest and an affectionate Exhortation to the Church, from the View of the Faithful, which had been given in the preceding Chapter, to be stedfastly looking unto Jesus. *To this succeeds a striking Account of the Difference between Mount Sinai and Mount* Zion.

WHEREFORE, seeing we also are compassed about with so great a cloud of witnesses, let *us* lay aside every weight, and the sin which doth so easily beset us, and let us run with patience the race that is set before us,

2 Looking unto Jesus the author and finisher of *our* faith; who, for the joy that was set before him, endured the cross, despising the shame, and is set down at the right hand of the throne of God.

Surely, there never was a more persuasive *wherefore*, neither a more powerful motive to what the HOLY GHOST hath here recommended, by his servant the Apostle to the Church, than in following up the history given before of the faithful Patriarchs in the preceding Chapter, with holding forth the glorious Person of CHRIST in this; and making JESUS what He really is, the whole of all arguments, and the sum and substance of every persuasion to a faithful life. Precious LORD JESUS, I would say, be it my portion so to look to thee, so to behold thee, so to hang upon thee with my whole heart, and soul, and affections, as the *Alpha* and *Omega*, the *first* and the *last*, and not only the Author and Finisher of faith, but the Author and Finisher of salvation; yea, salvation itself, in all its blessedness, for time, and for eternity!

And, Reader, I pray you to pause with me over these words, and consider their beauty. A *cloud of witnesses* we are said to be encompassed with. And let it be remembered, that they are GOD's witnesses, which are the most honorable of all witnesses. They witness to GOD the FATHER's faithfulness, in his everlasting love to the Church. They witness to the Person, GODHEAD, Offices, characters, relations, redemption-work, and finished salvation of the LORD JESUS CHRIST. And they witness to the Person, GODHEAD, and Ministry, in the regenerating, soul-quickening, soul-sustaining, and soul-comforting influences of GOD the HOLY GHOST. Surrounded, therefore, with the testimony of others, and enabled by grace to give in our own, to those grand and momentous truths; the LORD is looked unto to strengthen them in their Christian warfare, and to lay aside the besetting sin of unbelief, which cleaves to all men by nature, until grace gives them new minds, and new hearts, to receive GOD's testimony of himself, and to run with patience the race that is before us; eyeing JESUS in every step of the way. And, oh! the blessedness of thus *seeing the* SON *by* faith, *and believing on him!* John vi. 40. Seeing him, as *One with the* FATHER *over all*, GOD *blessed for ever*, Seeing him as the CHRIST of GOD, the Sent of GOD, the Sealed of GOD, *full of grace and truth*. And, in this blessed view of beholding JESUS, when He, who is the Author and Finisher of faith, gives faith, to believe *the record* GOD *hath given of his dear* SON. The regenerated child of GOD beholds him, and accepts him on his bended knees, in holy joy and rapture, as JEHOVAH's one, and only one appointment and ordinance of salvation, on whom the soul may rest secure, for all the peace and happiness of the life that now is, and that which is to come. Reader! just pause to ask your own heart, are you so looking to JESUS? Is He, in your view, both the Author and Finisher of faith? Many there are, who seem very willing to make him the *Author*, but feel somewhat reluctant to accept him as the *Finisher*. And what is this but pharisaical pride? I humbly conceive, such men, if under divine teaching, might soon learn the danger of this error. Let them ask themselves this one simple question, How did I first look to Jesus? Was it not as a poor, helpless, friendless, needy, self-condemned sinner? And have I any thing of my own now, to recommend me any otherwise? Let this question be fairly applied to the heart, under divine teaching, and sure I am there will not be a child of God upon earth, if truly taught of God, but what will be then as ready to make Jesus as much the *Finisher* as the *Author* both of his faith and salvation.

3 For consider him that endured such contradiction of sinners against himself, lest ye be wearied and faint in your minds.

4 Ye have not yet resisted unto blood, striving against sin.

5 And ye have forgotten the exhortation which speaketh unto you as unto children, My son, despise not thou the chastening of the Lord, nor faint when thou art rebuked of him:

6 For whom the Lord loveth he chasteneth, and scourgeth every son whom he receiveth.

7 If ye endure chastening, God dealeth with you as with sons: for what son is he whom the father chasteneth not?

8 But if ye be without chastisement whereof all are partakers, then are ye bastards, and not sons.

9 Furthermore, we have had fathers of our flesh, which corrected *us*, and we give *them* reverence: shall we not much rather be in subjection unto the Father of spirits, and live?

10 For they verily for a few days chastened *us* after their own pleasure: but he for *our* profit, that *we* might be partakers of his holiness.

11 Now no chastening for the present seemeth to be joyous, but grievous: nevertheless, afterward it yielded the peaceable fruit of righteousness unto them which are exercised thereby.

12 Wherefore lift up the hands which hang down, and the feeble knees:

13 And make straight paths for your feet, lest that which is lame be turned out of the way, but let it rather be healed.

There is somewhat truly blessed in what is here said of the LORD JESUS. What joy could be set before him which could increase his own joy, in the glories of his own essential power and GODHEAD? And if it be meant, the joy of giving everlasting happiness to millions, in giving them a Being in himself, and a blessedness of being in himself abstracted from all personal interest, what a view doth it give of the love of CHRIST? Moreover, when we are enjoined by the HOLY GHOST to consider *Him*, in order to prevent our becoming faint under exercises, what an argument ariseth herefrom, to give confidence to the soul, in the consideration, that as *He was, so are we in this world*. And the argument runs thus: If JESUS, for our sakes, endured such things against himself, what ought we to endure, if needful, for ourselves. Oh! who shall count the contumacy, reproach, and scorn, which the SON of GOD sustained, in his Person, Offices, and characters, when he became man for our salvation? How sweetly the Apostle argues from it in the next Chapter, *to go forth without the camp, bearing his reproach?* Chap. xiii. 13. And how sweetly he adds to this argument another; in that, though some of them might, and would be called to suffering, yet hitherto they had not. Reader! there is nothing so truly accommodating, to bring a child of GOD into a blessed frame of mind, when at any time exercised with sufferings, as the consciousness of CHRIST's sorrows. The path is made sacred, which we are called upon to walk in, when we behold the footsteps in it of the LORD JESUS, and those footsteps marked with blood.

There is somewhat very affectionate and endearing in the application of that passage from Prov. iii. 11. to the cases of the LORD's suffering family. The character of a father, in the tenderness of one, is happily chosen, to represent *the* FATHER *of mercies, and the* GOD *of all comfort*. And the contrast, to the case of bastards, who are disregarded by their father, as being ashamed to own children unlawfully begotten, is as striking, to set forth the vast difference, between the children of the bond-woman, and the children of the free. Reader! it is astonishing to observe, what a decided, and marked attention, is uniformly observed through all the Bible, by way of shewing the Church, the delight the LORD takes, to mark the precious from the vile; and to instruct the Church, how to know *him that serveth* GOD, *from him that serveth him not*.

14 Follow peace with all *men*, **and holiness, without which no man shall see the Lord;**

I wish the Reader to look at this verse by itself, as so much perversion hath been made of it, that it demands this attention. *Follow peace with all men*. What peace? If it be supposed to mean the peace of GOD in CHRIST, or CHRIST himself, who is our Peace; this cannot be a mere precept directed to all men; for all men have not faith; neither do all men follow peace, or CHRIST: neither is this scripture addressed to all men; but to the Church, who are supposed to be following Christ, in the regeneration. *And holiness.* What holiness? Not, as some have supposed, holiness in the creature, for there is none holy, no, not one. And moreover, it would be in this sense, a precept to *follow it,* and not as if possessing it. The latter part of the verse, in my view, explains the whole, when it is said, *without which, no man shall see the* Lord. Now, the uniform language of scripture is, that without Christ, there can be no peace with God; neither any approach to God, but in the holiness of Jesus. *No man,* saith Christ, *cometh to the* Father *but by me.* John xiv. 6. And our entrance into the holiest, is by the blood of Jesus; and in him we have boldness to enter. Heb. x. 19, &c. Christ, therefore, is our peace, by the blood of his cross; and *through him we have access by one* Spirit *unto the* Father. Coloss. i. 20. Ephes. ii. 18. Hence, the Church, (and it is the Church all along in this Epistle which is spoken to,) is called in one whole body to follow Christ, who is both the peace, and the holiness of his people; and *without which, no man shall see the* Lord. 1 Cor. i. 30. Heb. vii. 26.

15 Looking diligently, lest any man fail of the grace of God; lest any root of bitterness springing up, trouble *you,* and thereby many be defiled;

16 Lest there *be* any fornicator, or profane person, as Esau, who for one morsel of meat sold his birthright.

17 For ye know how that afterward, when he would have inherited the blessing, he was rejected: for he found no place of repentance, though he sought it carefully with tears.

In these verses we have the Church called upon, to behold the safety of the Lord's people, by looking at the contrary character, in such as have not, neither ever had, the grace of God. Here is an earnestness recommended to the faithful, to look diligently in their assemblies among the mere professors, which form, to public view, part of the visible Church, but in reality do not, neither ever did belong to it. Such are of the bitter root, which, by springing up, and mingling with the true seed, like weeds in a garden, defile what is pure. And the case is instanced, in the history of *Esau,* who is here called a profane Person, that is a reprobate. Malachi i. 3. And this reprobation is accounted for, in despising his birth-right, which included Christ. Hence his rejection by the Lord. And what was it he sought carefully with tears? Not Christ, and the promised blessing in him, but the *earthly* blessing, which his father had settled upon his younger brother, in making him his lord. This was what he sought carefully with tears, hoping, by his exceeding bitter cries, to prevail upon his father to revoke this gift given to *Jacob.* And which, indeed, though not revoked, he obtained, when *Jacob* soon after, was obliged to flee for his life, from his fury; not returning again for many years. But the blessing of spiritual mercies in Christ, even the promised seed, *Esau* neither sought for, nor regarded. Hence, it is said, *he found no place of repentance;* or, as the margin of the Bible more strongly expresses it, *no way to change his mind;* though he sought it carefully with tears. Let the Reader turn to the history, Gen. xxvii. throughout. Gen. xxvii. 5. Reader! behold the repentance of *Esau, the worldly sorrow,* as an Apostle calls it, which *worketh death;* and learn to distinguish it from that sorrow, which is after *a godly sort,* and which worketh life. The *one,* the effects of nature; the *other* the fruits of grace; the one man's labours the *other* GOD's gift. *Esau's* and all like *Esau's,* ending in despair; *Jacob's,* and all the spiritual seed of *Jacob's,* leading to CHRIST, and life in him eternal. 2 Cor. vii. 10. 11.

18 For ye are not come unto the mount that might be touched, and that burned with fire, nor unto blackness, and darkness, and tempest,

19 And the sound of the trumpet, and the voice of words; which *voice* they that heard intreated that the word should not be spoken to them any more:

20 For they could not endure that which was commanded, and if so much as a beast touch the mountain, it shall be stoned, or thrust through with a dart.

21 And so terrible was the sight, *that* Moses said, I exceedingly fear and quake:

22 But ye are come unto mount Sion, and unto the city of the living God, the heavenly Jerusalem, and to an innumerable company of angels,

23 To the general assembly and church of the first-born which are written in heaven, and to God the judge of all, and to the spirits of just men made perfect,

24 And to Jesus the mediator of the new covenant, and to the blood of sprinkling that speaketh better things than *that of* Abel.

Within the compass of these verses, we have the most striking description drawn, and by the pencil of the HOLY GHOST himself, of the vast difference, between Mount *Sinai,* and Mount *Zion;* that is, the law, and the Gospel; a Covenant of Works; and a Covenant of Grace. And it is such a description, as is enough under divine teaching, to arrest the heart, with the most sensible apprehension, of the awfulness of the *one,* and the blessedness of the *other;* in the soul's approaches unto GOD.

The first account is of Mount *Sinai*. And the very solemn and awful demonstrations, of the LORD's presence, in giving the law; are described in characters so terrible, as even in the recital, makes the flesh to tremble. *Moses* himself, was so overwhelmed, that he said, *I exceedingly fear and quake.* And all *Israel cried out, and said unto Moses, speak thou with us, and we will hear; but let not* GOD *speak with us, lest we die.* Exod. xx. 18, 19. Nothing can be more plain, than that the leading design of the LORD, in those manifestations, of thunderings, and lightnings, and the like, were to impress the Church of GOD, with an holy awe and reverence, in the consciousness of the divine presence. And also to shew them, the blackness, darkness, dread, and horror, which every soul must feel, through divine teaching, when brought under the conviction of having broken the LORD's precepts.

And, on the other hand, in the most blessed and gracious description, given of Mount *Zion*, the Church is taught the high privilege of the LORD's redeemed ones, who now may come, and who indeed do come, to the assembly of the first-born; yea, to GOD himself *the Judge of all*, when coming in the name of JESUS, *the Mediator of the new Covenant, and to the blood of sprinkling.* And here is implied, in being come, that there is an holy familiarity, and acquaintance, in this approach; a birth-right, by the new-birth; a redemption, an adopted-character, by JESUS's blood, and righteousness; and the Covenant faithfulness of GOD the Judge of all. So that this is the Gospel privilege of GOD's redeemed ones: their stated daily, hourly, minutely mercy; to which they are supposed to come boldly, and find *mercy, and grace to help in all time of need.* Heb. iv. 16.

One point I would beg however to remark, on this different description of those Mounts, in the dispensation of the Law and the Gospel. The HOLY GHOST hath most graciously and blessedly taught the Church, in this divine scripture, from the different manifestations in which the LORD was pleased to make himself known to Old Testament saints, and New Testament believers; how blessed an alteration is made, in the mode of worship, by the open revelation of CHRIST; but it must not be understood from thence, that the way of acceptance with GOD in CHRIST, differed in the Old Testament Church from the New. Both were one, and the same. The former, was *a shadow of good things to come;* but then, as now, *the body was* CHRIST. And blessed be GOD, our fathers, both under the Law, and before the Law, as well as their children under the Gospel, in every ministration, and in every service, had an eye to *the Lamb slain from the foundation of the world.* Their services, and all the vessels of the sanctuary, yea, the Book of the Law, and all the people, were sprinkled with blood. Exod. xxiv. 6, 7, 8. Heb. ix. 19—22. And hence we find Old Testament saints chaunting their hymns of salvation to GOD, and the LAMB. *Job* knew, that his kinsman Redeemer lived. Job. xix. 25. *David* sung his dying love song, in the believing views he had, of a Covenant *ordered in all things and sure;* and which was *all his salvation, and all his desire.* 2 Sam. xxiii. 5. And indeed, all the faithful, in every age of the Church, from the first dawn of revelation, in *Abel's* faith offering, down to *Zachariah's* day at the Altar of Incense, in the moment of CHRIST's coming, blessed GOD, in the soul-living expectation of *the mercy promised.* Luke i. 72. Reader! learn to estimate, the high privileges of redemption in Jesus; and be it your daily song of thanksgiving, and praise, that you are not come to the Mount that might be touched, (that is, on which the Lord by his descent might be said to touch, though not touched by man,) and that burned with fire; but you are come to Jesus *the Mediator;* and to the *blood of sprinkling!* Oh! the blessedness, the preciousness, the unspeakable greatness of the mercy! To Jesus, your Jesus, if so be *you have tasted that the* Lord *is gracious; to whom coming.* 1 Pet. ii. 3, 4. And in, and through, and by Jesus, to God the Judge of all.

25 See that ye refuse not him that speaketh: for if they escaped not who refused him that spake on earth; much more *shall not* we *escape* if we turn away from him that *speaketh* from heaven.

26 Whose voice then shook the earth: but now he hath promised, saying, Yet once more I shake not the earth only, but also heaven.

27 And this *word,* Yet once more, signifieth the removing of those things that are shaken, as of things that are made, that those things which cannot be shaken may remain.

What solemn, but yet soul comforting views, are here given of Christ? In order to impress upon the Church, the vast, and infinite importance of hearing Christ, (which God the Father more than once gave such testimony concerning, accompanied with this express command; *hear* ye him. Matt. xvii. 5.) the Holy Ghost, hath in these verses, first drawn a line of eternal distinction, between Christ and *Moses;* and then shewn, somewhat of the outlines of the Son of God, in our nature, in testimony both of his eternal Power and Godhead; and of his office-character, as God-Man-Mediator. I beg the Reader's close attention for a few moments to this subject.

First. The line of eternal distinction between Christ and *Moses.* The Lord the Spirit calls *Moses* the man *on earth.* They escaped not, who refused him that spake *on earth.* Christ, as is elsewhere declared, is *the* Lord *from heaven.* 1 Cor. xv. 47. And *John the Baptist* hath given a blessed testimony to the same, when speaking of himself, in comparison of his Lord. *He that cometh from above saith John, is above all. He that is of the earth is earthly, and speaketh of the earth. He that cometh from heaven is above all. Ye yourselves bear me witness that I said I am not the* Christ, *but that I am sent before him.* John iii. 28, 31.

Secondly. Look at the outlines, drawn of the Son of God in this scripture; and may the Almighty Author of such a delightful scripture, make it blessed to our view, *whose voice then shook the earth.* When was this? In order to answer the question, when was this, that his voice shook the earth; we must read *Haggai's* prophecy, in the *second* Chapter, from verse the *fifth* to the *seventh;* from whence this quotation by the Apostle is made. *According to the word that I covenanted with you, when ye came out of Egypt so my* SPIRIT *remaineth with you; fear not. For thus, saith the* LORD *of hosts, yet once it is a little while, and I will shake the heavens, and the earth, and the sea, and the dry land. And I will shake all nations, and the desire of all nations shall come.* Reader! pause. Here is the LORD of hosts, the same LORD, which covenanted with his people when they came out of *Egypt*, declaring that his love, was still with his people, and his SPIRIT remaining with them. He then declares, that when *the desire of all nations* should come; which is a well-known name, and character of himself, he would shake the heavens and the earth; meaning the hearts and minds of his people, by the sovereignty of his grace. And here in this scripture, the HOLY GHOST by the Apostle refers this sovereign act of grace, to the same Person as shook the earth, when he came down on Mount *Sinai*. *Whose voice then shook the earth; but now he hath promised, saying, yet once more I shake not the earth only, but also heaven.* Hence it must be inferred, by the plainest, and most palpable evidence, that it was the SON of GOD, in his representative character of Mediator, which then shook the earth, who in the prophecy of *Haggai* declares he will again shake, not only the earth, but the heavens. The phrase *Once more* and *again,* hath a most decided reference to the same, or similar act, having been done *before.* And nothing can be more evident, than that both were the deeds of one, and the same Person. In the relation of that solemn scene at Mount *Sinai,* we are told, that *the* LORD *descended upon it in fire;* that the *whole Mount quaked greatly;* that when *Moses* spake; GOD answered him, *by a voice* Exod. xix. 18, 19. And the LORD bid the children of *Israel* by *Moses,* to observe those tokens of his presence. *Ye have seen that I have talked with you from heaven.* Exod. xx. 22. How very clear then is this blessed portion of the HOLY GHOST by *Paul;* that the LORD JESUS CHRIST, is the Almighty LORD, which is spoken of in both scriptures. Indeed, who should it be, but Him? He, and He only, is the visible JEHOVAH, in all revelations made to man.

No man hath seen GOD *at any time; but the only begotten* SON *which is in the bosom of the* FATHER *he hath declared him.* John i. 18. Oh! ye deluded miserable men, who deny the GODHEAD of CHRIST! What can possibly prevent the awful consequences prophesied of an heresy so awful, living and dying, in the hardened state of unbelief. Some of GOD's children indeed have been found, led away by the temptations of Satan and long in this state, whom sovereign grace hath recovered. Should the LORD, in his mercy, direct the eyes of such an one, to this blessed scripture; and carry conviction from it to his heart, to the acknowledging of the LORD that bought him; Oh! the greatness of the blessing, in *recovering all such from the snare of the Devil, who are taken captive by him at his will. Kiss the* SON! *lest he be angry and ye perish from the way, when his wrath is kindled but a little. Blessed are all they that put their trust in him.* Psm. ii. 12.

28 Wherefore we receiving a kingdom which cannot be moved, let us have grace, whereby we

may serve God acceptably with reverence and godly fear;
29 For our God *is* a consuming fire.

In relation to the first of these verses, let the child of God take to himself all the comfort the HOLY GHOST designed the Church, from the assurance of belonging to an immoveable kingdom, amidst all the moveable and dying circumstances of every thing here below. And let him take to himself the further comfort, that this kingdom, and the interest in it, he hath *received*, not for merit, neither working, but from the free gift of GOD. This sweet scripture saith to the Church, that it is *receiving* a kingdom, which cannot be moved. All the blessings connected with the subject confirm it. *Fear not,* (saith JESUS to his people,) *little flock, it is your heavenly* FATHER's *good pleasure to give you the kingdom.* Luke xii. 32. And how fully all the scriptures of our GOD, bear testimony to the same. The kingdom of grace, and the kingdom of glory, are both originating in the FATHER's love by gift; in receiving all the blessings for time and eternity, from the fulness that is in CHRIST JESUS; being brought into an happy, and blessed participation, by the HOLY GHOST. Well therefore might the Apostle add; *let us have grace, whereby we may serve* GOD *acceptably, with reverence and godly fear.* Let us have it? But how? By receiving it, as we receive the kingdom, which is immoveable. The citizenship to this kingdom, ensures all the privileges of it. We already have it in CHRIST our head; and from him, we are brought into the enjoyment of it, from day to day.

The last of these verses, and with which the Chapter ends; is a striking one indeed. None more so in the Bible. It hath been commonly paraphrased by saying, GOD *out of* CHRIST is a consuming fire. But this according to my apprehension, is an unwarrantable alteration of the word; and not strictly true. It is very certain, that without an eye to CHRIST, we could have no more to do with GOD in the essence of his divine nature alone, than with a devouring fire, Exod. iii. 6. But we have no authority, from all eternity, to consider JEHOVAH, but in CHRIST. 2 Cor. v. 19. And all the Persons of the GODHEAD are included, in this mysterious union. The figure therefore of fire, is here evidently meant to express GOD's nature, and essence, as He is in himself; and in his threefold character of Person; in which GOD the SON, as GOD, is as inaccessible without a Mediator, as either the Person of the FATHER, or of the HOLY GHOST. Upon so solemn a subject, I presume not to speak, but with the greatest humility and reverence; but I venture to conceive, that the HOLY GHOST was pleased by this expression, after the many blessed and gracious things which he had been bringing before the Church, in the former part of this Chapter, to shew the vast privileges in CHRIST. And as such, nothing could impress the mind of the LORD's people so solemnly, as the sacred truth with which the Apostle hath closed; *For our* GOD *is a consuming fire.*

REFLECTIONS.

READER! hear what GOD the SPIRIT saith to the Churches! Behold what animating prospects are opened to New Testament saints, in the contemplation of Old Testament believers. And while we are encompassed with such a cloud of witnessess, O LORD the SPIRIT! do thou give thy people grace, to pass on through all besetting difficulties, looking unto JESUS, the Author and Finisher of our faith. And oh! thou precious LORD JESUS! give thy people grace, to consider, and very blessedly to improve, under the sweet influences of thy SPIRIT, in marking what a contradiction of sinners, thou didst endure against thyself. LORD! who can faint when beholding the SON of GOD, in his unequalled conflicts? Surely, if JESUS learned obedience, by the things which he suffered, well may his brethren desire to be trained in the same school. Then will they know their sonship, and be sanctified under the hand of a tender FATHER. Let the *Esaus*, and the profane persons of every age, relinquish, as they always do, the blessing; but, LORD, let no root of bitterness, spring up to trouble thy *Jacobs*, and the *Israels* thy people.

Blessed be GOD, that Mount *Sinai* is no more; but the Church is come to Mount *Zion*. There may thy people, O LORD, daily come. There are the first born. There the assembly of the faithful. There JESUS, the Mediator of the New Covenant, and the blood of sprinkling. And there GOD the Judge of all. And, LORD, while through thy grace, thy people come to thee in faith; do thou help them to look forward to thy coming to them in glory. JESUS will shake both heaven and earth. But JESUS's redeemed belong to Him and in Him they receive a kingdom, which cannot be moved. Precious LORD! grant all thy grace, to serve GOD acceptably, *with reverence and godly fear.*

CHAP. XIII.

CONTENTS.

The Epistle is here closed; and a Blessed Conclusion is made. CHRIST *in his Person, Relations, and Character, the same for ever. Several weighty Exhortations are used; and the whole is summed up in praying for grace to the whole Church.*

LET brotherly love continue.

2 Be not forgetful to entertain strangers: for thereby some have entertained angels unawares.

3 Remember them that are in bonds, as bound with them; *and* them which suffer adversity, as being ourselves also in the body.

4 Marriage *is* honorable in all, and the bed undefiled; but whoremongers and adulterers God will judge.

5 *Let your* conversationt *be* without coveteousness; *and be* content with such things as ye have, for he hath said, I will never leave thee, nor forsake thee.

6 So that we may boldly say, The Lord *is* my helper, aud I will not fear what man shall do unto me.

This Chapter opens with some very engaging exhortations, arising out of the foregoing doctrines. And, first, of the brotherly love, a members of CHRIST's body, and brethren in the faith. For as the Church, in heaven and earth, is but one, so CHRIST's love to each and they to one another, should be formed upon his standard From the love of the brethren, the Church is next directed to regard strangers; simply as strangers, and from the case of *Abraham's* en tertaining the heavenly Guests he did, an inducement is made tha the Church should give kind reception to strangers, under the hop that there may be some of GOD's dear children among them, and a such, well known to Him, though unknown to them. Gen. xviii. 2 and 19. 1—3. To this precept succeeds another, namely, of ten derness to those in bonds; not merely prisoners in the body, bu bondage frames of soul. And indeed in the times in which the Apostle lived, there were opportunities for the exercise of compas sion to both. Then follows a very delightful observation on the mar riage-state. And as all marriages of honor, and undefilement are evi dently typical of CHRIST's marriage with his Church; it is ver blessed, to hear the HOLY GHOST, thus continually approving of i And this paragraph closeth with arguing the weakness of an ove anxiety for the things of the body, when GOD by his Covenar promise, hath made such ample provision, for his redeemed, in tha engagement first given to *Joshua*, and in him to all the LORD's people Joshua i. 5. I do not enlarge on these different subjects, being i themselves so plain, as to need no comment.

7 Remember them which have the rule ove you, who have spoken unto you the word o God: whose faith follow, considering the end o *their* conversation:

8 Jesus Christ the same yesterday, and to-day and for ever.

9 Be not carried about with divers and strang doctrines, for *it is* a good thing that the heart b established with grace, not with meats, whicl have not profited them that have been occupie therein.

It is truly interesting to behold, more or less, in every Epistle, wh affectionate recommendations, are given to the Church, to be attentiv in all the tokens of love and regard, to the Pastors, whom the LOR had set over them; and on the other hand, how much the trul ordained Servants in the ministry are called upon to distingui themselves, from mere hirelings, by a careful watching over, ar tenderly feeding the flock. And do observe, Reader, in this i stance now before us, how much stress is laid upon the Church's following the faith of their Pastors. A thing taken for granted, that they are not only *speaking* to their people, the word of GOD, but eminently *living* in the practice of it. And what a lovely sight, when the Pastor and People are striving together for the faith of the Gospel. But I beg the Reader also, in this account to observe, what is said, concerning the end of the Pastor's conversation, namely, JESUS CHRIST. If the Reader be particular to notice, he will see, that the words of one verse run into the other. The end of their conversation is, JESUS CHRIST. A plain proof, that the HOLY GHOST will have no other subject in his Church. Every thing centers itself in JESUS CHRIST. He that is the first and last in JEHOVAH's thoughts, is, or ought to be, the beginning and end of every faithful minister's conversation. See a beautiful picture of this, in the early Church, Acts v. 42. and Acts viii. 5.

Pause over the short, but comprehensive statement, which GOD the HOLY GHOST, hath in this verse given of the LORD our RIGHTEOUSNESS, JESUS CHRIST, *the same yesterday, and to day, and for ever!* Every word is big with importance; and to dwell upon each might fill volumes. *First.* His name, JESUS. A SAVIOR! for so the name imports. And whether considered in the GODHEAD of his nature and essence, as *one with the* FATHER, *over all,* GOD *blessed for ever;* or whether, in his twofold nature, as GOD and Man, Mediator; every way, and in all things, he is a SAVIOR, and expressly called JESUS, on that account; *for he shall save his people from their sins.* Matt. i. 21. Reader! beg for grace to be continually meditating on the sweet savor of his name, JESUS; that a name, which perfumes all heaven, may give continually fragrancy to the Church upon earth; and be in every believing heart, as the savor of the richest *ointment poured forth.* Song i. 3.

Secondly. He is not only JESUS, but JESUS CHRIST; that is, the anointed, sent, and sealed, of the FATHER, *full of grace and truth.* Reader! this is a most blessed, and interesting part of his name. JEHOVAH's name, and JEHOVAH's authority is in him, and with him. CHRIST glorified not himself, to be made an High Priest, but *was called of* GOD, *as was Aaron.* Heb. v. 4, 5. And what a warrant such a view of the LORD JESUS gives, to the fullest exercise of every believer's faith and hope; when he not only goes to the throne of grace here below, but will hereafter stand before the throne of judgment above, in the blood and righteousness of the LORD JESUS CHRIST, and also in the way of GOD's own appointing, the salvation he himself hath sent is his dear SON. Oh! the blessedness of that scripture, which Old Testament saints used; and which is the same strength to the faith of New Testament believers; *Behold! O* GOD *our shield, and look upon the face of thine Anointed.* Psm. lxxxiv. 9.

Thirdly. JESUS CHRIST *the same.* Yes! Every circumstance belonging to his Person, Offices, Characters, Relations, Royalties, faithfulness to GOD, to man, love to his Church, and people; all partake of this everlasting sameness. He is the same *yesterday.* What yesterday? In all the eternity past. Set up from everlasting in his Mediator character. Prov. viii. 23. The *Lamb slain from the foundation of the world.* Rev. xiii. 8. *To-day.* What day? Nay, the whole day of the World's continuance in the time-state of the Church. *And for ever?* That for ever, which GOD the FATHER hath marked, when he said to him: *Thy throne, O GOD, is for ever and ever!* Psm. xlv. 6. Heb. i. 8. Reader! pause over the wonderful account, and ponder well the sameness of his Person, his love, his grace, and all the unchangeableness of his GODHEAD, Mediator-character, and offices; *the same yesterday, and to-day, and for ever.* Never will a child of GOD be in danger of being carried away with divers, and strange doctrines, whose heart is established in the grace of the HOLY GHOST, having been regenerated, and taught by Him, who CHRIST is, and the everlasting unchangeableness in all that relates to his Person, and Character. LORD JESUS! thou Great Author, and Finisher of faith! do thou, in the present awful day of a CHRIST-despising generation, take to thyself thy great Name. Establish, confirm, and strengthen all thine own, in this most glorious truth; that no change of time, nor change of men, nor change of worlds, may shake them from this faith! LORD! be thou to them in time, what thou art, and will be, to all eternity; JESUS CHRIST, *the same yesterday, and to-day, and for ever.*

10 We have an altar whereof they have no right to eat which serve the tabernacle.

11 For the bodies of those beasts whose blood is brought into the sanctuary by the high priest for sin, are burned without the camp.

12 Wherefore Jesus, also that he might sanctify the people with his own blood, suffered without the gate.

13 Let us go forth therefore unto him without the camp, bearing his reproach.

14 For here have we no continuing city, but we seek one to come.

15 By him therefore let us offer the sacrifice of praise to God continually, that is, the fruit of *our* lips, giving thanks to his name.

16 But to do good, and to communicate forget not; for with such sacrifices God is well pleased.

There is but one Altar which the Church of CHRIST knoweth, and that is a precious Altar indeed; namely, CHRIST himself. It was on this Altar even his divine nature, the LORD JESUS offered himself to GOD, through the Eternal SPIRIT. Heb. ix. 14. CHRIST is our New Testament Altar, and our Sacrifice, and our High Priest, and the Sacrificer. Now they can have no right, neither benefit, in this Altar, or Sacrifice, and Sacrificer, who are looking to any sacrifice beside. And not only are they prohibited from any right to this our Altar, who serve the *Jewish* Tabernacle; but any *Christian* Tabernacle, falsely so called, that is, they who *sacrifice to their own net, and burn incense to their own drag:* Heb. i. 16. and, according to the Prophet, are building themselves up in their own fancied righteousness, and making CHRIST only a part SAVIOR with themselves.

This is a beautiful illustration of the Old Testament service, and which at once proves, that the whole of the ministry, on the great day of atonement, related but to CHRIST. Let the Reader first read the account of the appointment, as minutely related; Levit. xvi. and he will be struck with the type, in its close resemblance to CHRIST. JESUS did all this in substance, as the High Priest then did in the shadow, in the day when he suffered without the gate, that is, without *Jerusalem,* on the Mount *Calvary.* And, as the bodies of those beasts, whose blood was brought into the Sanctuary by the High Priest, for sin, were burnt without the Camp: Levit. xvi. 27. so CHRIST, in his own Person, endured the fiery indignation of sin, as the Church's representative; and then went by his own blood into heaven itself, *there to appear in the presence of* GOD *for us.* Heb. ix. 11, 12. And what a most affectionate exhortation the HOLY GHOST adds to this beautiful illustration, when he invites the Church, to go forth, from the observance of all self-offerings whatever; from the camp of the world, and from all vain things, of any fancied attainments of our own; seeking acceptance wholly in the Person, and finished salvation of our LORD JESUS CHRIST? This will indeed bring reproach; but it is CHRIST's reproach, being for his sake, and on his account. This would be doing good in the only way, in which the child of GOD, regenerated by grace, can do good; namely, communicating to others, by our word, and by our example, that CHRIST is our all, and in whom we depend for all. *With such sacrifices* GOD *is well pleased.* Yes! For the child of GOD, who dares in such a day as the present, amidst a CHRIST-despising generation, openly to avow, that he is looking wholly to CHRIST, and that he makes CHRIST his all, for life and salvation; must sacrifice both name and reputation, and sometimes many earthly comforts besides, in the connections, and relationships of natural life. And from no class whatever will he find greater bitterness manifested, than from modern Pharisees, who profess to honor CHRIST as well as he, in giving him the glory of the *procuring cause* of salvation; but contend, that what CHRIST hath done, and suffered, is not a finished salvation, but that our sincere repentance, and obedience, and faith, may on CHRIST's account be accepted of GOD. Alas! did those men but seriously consider, how wretched at the best, are all the performances of creatures such as we are, they would discover what a flimsy thing the sincerity, and obedience, and repentance, yea, faith itself, considered as an act of ours, must be to trust in, when going in before GOD. Wretched indeed would be my guilty soul, if an atom of mine became necessary for acceptance in that solemn hour!

17 Obey them that have the rule over you, and submit yourselves; for they watch for your souls as they that must give account: that they may do

it with joy, and not with grief: for that *is* unprofitable for you.

18 Pray for us: for we trust we have a good conscience, in all things willing to live honestly.

19 But I beseech *you* the rather to do this, that I may be restored to you the sooner.

Still harping upon the pleasant string of brotherly love, we have here the same sweet notes sung over again, of the people's duty to their ministers, and the affectionate request of the ministers to their people, to be by them remembered in their prayers. And what a lovely sight, to behold the aged Apostle *Paul*, seeking from the Church as a boon, what, from his voluntary, and unrecompensed labors, he might have justly demanded as a tribute. Oh! the happiness of that Church, where minister, and people, are wrestling together in prayer, before the LORD, for each other? What spiritual blessings may not be expected from such an harmony of souls, knit together as one in CHRIST?

20 Now the God of peace, that brought again from the dead our Lord Jesus that great shepherd of the sheep, through the blood of the everlasting covenant.

21 Make you perfect in every good work to do his will, working in you that which is well pleasing in his sight, through Jesus Christ: to whom *be* glory for ever and ever. Amen.

As the Apostle had begged an interest in the prayers of the people; so here, in concluding his Epistle, he looks up in prayer for the Church, and pours forth his earnest supplications for the people. But I beg the Reader to observe some of the several weighty things by which he mentions his desires, for a blessing on the Church. He calls GOD *the* GOD *of peace*. This is a blessed title, and comes with peculiar energy, after the many precious proofs the HOLY GHOST had given the Church, in this Epistle, of GOD's being at peace with his redeemed, in the blood of the cross. And the bringing CHRIST again from the dead, as *the Great Shepherd of the sheep, through the blood, of the everlasting Covenant;* is specially mentioned, I should humbly conceive, on purpose to shew, that CHRIST had made our peace by that blood; and GOD's Covenant promises of peace, were all included in that high administration. Reader! pray mark this in the deepest memorandums of your life. Beg of GOD the HOLY GHOST to mark it, with his deep impressions, on your heart; for the testimony of it is sweet. Never would the LORD have taken to himself so precious, and blessed a name, as it concerns his Church; had not CHRIST fully made that peace, and paid down on the mercy-seat the full price of his Church's redemption, in bags richer than gold, even in blood. Oh! the blessedness of it. GOD saith, *in confirmation,*

I have found a ransom. Job xxxiii. 24. 1 Pet. i. 18, 19. Gen. xxiii. 16.

I admire the preciousness, as well as the strength of the argument the Apostle useth, from this view of the GOD of peace raising CHRIST from the dead, in confirmation of the Covenant in his blood; when he makes this the bottom, and foundation, for the LORD's making the Church perfect. For, in fact, this is the same principle which now worketh in them, which then worked in CHRIST. And not only so, but from the same cause. It is covenant-work from covenant-engagements. Reader! do you understand this? If so, the LORD give you also to see, that it is a firm, and sure principle, a certain principle, a covenant principle, and never can fail. It is a part of the same first cause, which began in the free, unpurchased, unmerited, unlookedfor, unheard-of grace, till revealed, at regeneration, by the HOLY GHOST. When GOD first chose the Church in CHRIST, and to be *without blame before him in love*, all the blessed things included in this choice, were folded up, as the seed to all future generations of that fruit, is in the first acorn. The same grace which chose, the same grace compleats. So that, the resurrection of CHRIST, gave a confirmation to all included in CHRIST. And in like manner, the same power which was exerted, by virtue of CHRIST's resurrection, to raise the sinner, then *dead in trespasses and sins*, is engaged, and will assuredly go forth, in every subsequent act, to *make perfect every good work, to do his will, working in his redeemed that which is well pleasing in his sight, through* JESUS CHRIST.

I detain the Reader, just to observe the sweetness with which the Apostle closeth his prayer. *To whom be glory for ever and ever. Amen.* Surely there was somewhat more than merely a form of words in the minds of the Apostles, when we find all of them uniformly, with one heart, and one voice, thus closed up their writings. You will say, they were inspired. To which I answer: Yes! they were. And these things are no small proof of it. But while we see, that their hearts were so filled with divine love, their tongues, and pens, could not fail to give testimony to the same, when out of the abundance of the heart the mouth speaketh; I would ask, how is it that the consciousness of their inspired frame of mind, doth not affect us more? We read those blessed words but as ordinary things. We are accustomed to find the holy Apostles *beginning* their Epistles with the gracious salutations, such as *Grace, mercy, and peace be with you;* and ending them, with giving *glory, and praise, and power, unto him that sitteth upon the throne, and to the* LAMB: and we accept both but as words of course. Reader! Is it so with you? I acknowledge with shame, and sorrow, it is but too often so with me. Oh! for grace to both Writer and Reader, to be more alive to those precious things; and never more read those divine words, but with the most awakened affection!

22 And I beseech you, brethren, suffer the word of exhortation: for I have written a letter unto you in few words.

23 Know ye that *our* brother Timothy is set at

liberty; with whom, if he come shortly, I will see you.

24 Salute all them that have the rule over you, and all the saints. They of Italy salute you.

25 Grace *be* with you all. Amen.

¶ Written to the Hebrews from Italy by Timothy.

The salutations to the brethren I pass over to observe the blessed conclusion at the end. *Grace be with you all. Amen.* What could *Paul* say beyond this? And with what form of prayer could he as well close his Epistle? The close of all the dispensations among men, is to be thus, when GOD shall bring home the last stone of the spiritual building, it will be with shoutings, of *grace, grace unto it.* Zech. iv. 7. And both the Old Testament building, and the New, are but one and the same. CHRIST is the foundation-stone GOD hath laid in *Zion*, for the whole Church. And therefore, *Paul*, and every faithful Minister of the Sanctuary, like *Paul*, can say no more; neither close their ministry, or their life, in any manner more suitable, or proper for the Church of JESUS, than in the same sweet prayer: *Grace be with you all. Amen.* And may the faithful, and true Witness, CHRIST JESUS, who is the Amen, put his precious name to it Amen; and then grace will indeed be with all his people. Amen.

REFLECTIONS.

HERE let us pause, while reading the closing words of this most precious Epistle: and, as a man who hath been ascending an high hill, and is arrived at the summit of it, looks round, and takes a leisurely survey of the many beautiful prospects which come up to his view, from the rising ground he hath trodden; so may the Writer, and Reader of this *Poor Man's Commentary*, contemplate the unspeakable glories which GOD the SPIRIT hath presented before both, in this his Holy Scripture. Gracious LORD! I would say for myself, what praises do I owe thee, for the divine revelation herein contained? From the first opening of the subject, in the first Chapter, through all the portions of the sacred contents; what beauties, and glories, hast thou unveiled, of his Person, and Character, who is the LORD OUR RIGHTEOUSNESS! Beginning with the proofs of his GODHEAD, then of his Manhood, then of His glorious Person in union with *both*, as the GOD-Man-Mediator; how sweetly and blessedly hath my LORD the HOLY GHOST held him up to my view, and (shall I not hope) brought him home to my heart, in all his offices, characters, and relations, as the Prophet, Priest, and King of his people! Hail! thou Great, and glorious LORD JESUS CHRIST! thou *High Priest of thy people for ever, after the order of Melchizedec!*

Here then, let both Writer and Reader fall down on the knee of prayer and praise, before the throne; and *in* Him, and *through* Him, and *by* Him, through whom alone we can *offer the sacrifice of praise to* GOD *continually;* bless the united Source of all our mercies,

Father, Son, and Holy Ghost, the One Glorious, and Eternal Jehovah, for the Lord Jesus Christ himself, and all the fulness of grace and glory; in Him, for his Church, in time, and to all eternity.

And, as an instrument in the Lord's hand, let neither Writer, nor Reader of this little Work, overlook the faithful Apostle, whom God the Spirit was graciously pleased to appoint to this ministry, in handing down to the Church, from age to age, those sacred records, we have here gone over in the perusal. Truly, Lord, we cannot but see God the Holy Ghost's distinguishing grace to this man, in this most honorable appointment. Well is it recorded, of the Lord's personal ordination of him to the ministry, when in the Church the voice was heard: *Separate me Barnabas and Saul, for the work whereunto I have called them!* And oh! what a work indeed, not only in the then living ministry in person, to the Churches; but by his writings, in this, and the other blessed Epistles left on record for the everlasting instruction and comfort of the saints of God; whereby *he being dead, yet speaketh.* Farewell Paul! farewell, until the whole Church shall meet thee in glory, there together to praise God and the Lamb, for electing, redeeming, regenerating love, and favor, both to Pastor and People, all in One and the same glorious Head, to all eternity. Blessed be the Lord Jesus! for making thee his chosen vessel to bear his name as thou hast in those sacred writings done before Gentiles and Kings in every age of the Church.

Lord! add one blessing more. Pardon every thing of error in this humble work: and bless all that is offered upon it, as far as is agreeable to thy truth, and to thy mind, and will; that God *in all things may be glorified in* Jesus Christ. Amen.

THE GENERAL EPISTLE

OF

JAMES.

GENERAL OBSERVATIONS.

IT should seem that the term *General Epistle*, is given to this part of the Holy Scriptures, in that, it is not addressed either to any particular Church or Person; but intended for the whole of Christ's Church and People. And though it appears to have been directed to the *twelve tribes of Israel*, scattered abroad, yet not *Israel* after the flesh, but the Lord's *Israel* after the Spirit, even the children of God, wheresoever scattered.

The writer of this Epistle, under GOD the HOLY GHOST, was *James*. It is not said, whether *James*, the son of *Zebedee*, and brother of *John;* or *James*, the son of *Alpheus*. But, indeed, there needed not this distinction. For *James* the son of *Zebedee*, was murdered by *Herod*, about the year of our LORD GOD 44; whereas this Epistle could not have been of an earlier date than 60. Hence *James*, the son of *Alpheus*, must have been the penman of it.

The great and leading design of this Epistle need not be entered upon in this Preface; it will meet us in due season, in its proper place. But the objection, which *Eusebius* saith, some of the antient writers had to this Epistle, from an idea, that it was contradictory, on the subject of faith, to that of the Scriptures in general, and particularly to *Paul's* statements of it, under the HOLY GHOST, is wholly void. The supposed contradiction is merely ideal; for there never did exist the least difference between *Paul* and *James*, on this subject. Both perfectly agree; and both evidently prove, that one and the same Almighty SPIRIT, even GOD the HOLY GHOST, guided the pens of both.

I have only here, as on the entrance in every former Book, to ask that *wisdom, which is from above,* (and which this Apostle so blessedly speaks of,) to be with me in going over this part of the LORD'S sacred word, as before; and to ask it *in faith, nothing wavering.* And may the LORD, if it be his blessed will, give it in large portions, both to the Writer and Reader of this *Poor Man's Commentary; who giveth to all men liberally, and upbraideth not.*

CHAPTER I.

CONTENTS.

The Epistle opens with a general Salutation. Various Directions are given to the Church. GOD's *Grace and Love to the Church are very blessedly set forth.*

JAMES, a servant of God and of the Lord Jesus Christ, to the twelve tribes which are scattered abroad, greeting.

I detain the Reader, at the entrance, on this blessed portion of the word of GOD, to observe to him, how different from others, the Apostle enters on this service, to which the LORD the HOLY GHOST called him. He salutes the Church with *greeting,* but not as the other Apostles, in the sweet words of grace, mercy, and peace. And it is further remarkable, that *James* neither begins nor ends his Epistle in the usual terms of benediction. But it should be noticed at the same time, that *greeting* is a comprehensive word, to the same amount; and fully expressive, in whose holy and blessed Name, all the greetings of the Lord's people are made. And I beg the Reader not to overlook, that it is to the Church, and not to the world, the Epistle is sent. The *twelve tribes* can mean no other, than the Church, though scattered. Christ's people, are in all nations. Jerem. xxxii. 37 to 41. And hence, Christ is the *desire of all nations;* that is, the desire of his people in all nations. Haggai ii. 7. And I beg the Reader to observe with me, from this diversity of writing in *James*, from that of the other Apostles, what a beautiful variety, is given thereby, in setting forth the word of God. All the inspired Penmen, set forth one and the same truth; and all their labors are directed to one and the same object, in the divine glory; and all are under the guidance, and teaching of one and the same Lord the Holy Ghost; but while different gifts and talents, mark the different servants of our God; all these are gifted by *one and the self same* Spirit, *dividing to every man severally as he will.* 1 Cor. xii. 11. If the Reader will indulge me, to offer a short observation more, upon this verse, it shall be to remark, that the salutation of *James* to the Church, scattered abroad with *greeting;* teacheth the Lord's people, how best to follow up Christ's precept, to the same amount, either in person, or when writing by letter. Ignorant at times, as we are, who are, or who are not of the household of faith, we salute in general terms with mercy, grace, and peace, the faithful, as *Paul* did, *Aquila* and *Priscilla,* with *the Church that is in their house.* 1 Cor. xvi. 19. And saith our dear Lord; *if the* Son *of peace be there,* that is a child of God in Christ, *your peace shall rest upon it; if not, it shall turn to you again.* Your salutation is in Christ; and this sanctifies it to you, though not to *them.* Luke x. 5, 6.

2 My brethren, count it all joy when ye fall into divers temptations;

3 Knowing *this*, that the trying of your faith worketh patience.

4 But let patience have *her* perfect work, that ye may be perfect and entire, wanting nothing.

Observe, that it is the brethren to whom the Apostle speaks. That is, brethren in Christ, *partakers of the heavenly calling.* Carnal men can never rejoice in temptations, or trials; for *the sorrow of the world, worketh death.* But there is great cause for joy, when the faithful child of God, is called to the fellowship of God's dear Son. The Apostle *Paul* declares, that this is a testimony of God's faithfulness, 1 Cor. i. 9. See Rom. v. 1 to 5. and Commentary. Rom. viii. 29, 30. So that when a child of God falls *into* temptations, observe, the Apostle doth not say, falls *by* the temptations, but falls *into* divers temptations, there is cause of joy. For it becomes an honor, to be conformed to Christ's image. It is a mark of sonship. And it is intended, for the believer's good, and the Lord's glory. *Paul,* called a messenger of *Satan,* a *gift.* There was *given to me,* (saith he,) a thorn in the flesh, the messenger of *Satan* to buffet me. And by the sequel it proved so. *Paul's* triumph over Satan in Christ; and the Lord's glory were the more manifested in *Paul's* creature-weakness. 2 Cor. xii. 7 to 10. And the same must be the issue, in all the exercises of the faithful. For there is nothing doubtful in this war. God's promises in Covenant with Christ, the intercession of Jesus, as in the instance of *Peter;* and the ultimate ruin of *Satan,* are all in the appointment. Hence, these are sufficient motives for joy; since however painful to flesh and blood, grace is sure to triumph. See verse 12, and Commentary.

5 If any of you lack wisdom, let him ask of God, that giveth to all *men* liberally, and upbraideth not; and it shall be given him.

6 But let him ask in faith, nothing wavering. For he that wavereth is like a wave of the sea driven with the wind and tossed,

7 For let not that man think that he shall receive any thing of the Lord.

8 A double minded man *is* unstable in all his ways.

9 Let the brother of low degree rejoice in that he is exalted:

10 But the rich, in that he is made low: because as the flower of the grass he shall pass away.

11 For the sun is no sooner risen with a burning heat, but it withereth the grass, and the flower thereof falleth, and the grace of the fashion of it perisheth: so also shall the rich man fade away in his ways.

I humbly conceive, that the wisdom here spoken of, means Christ, and his graces. For Christ is *the wisdom of* God, as well as *the power of* God, *for salvation to every one that believeth.* 1 Cor. i. 24. And Christ is made of God to all his people, wisdom as well as righteousness; and sanctification as well as redemption. 1 Cor. i. 30. And as this verse follows immediately after what the Apostle had said, of taking joy in the exercises of temptation, the direction here of asking God for Christ and his strength seems to be with an express eye, to those seasons of temptation. And in this sense, this precept, blended as it is, with so sweet and sure a promise, is uncommonly beautiful and striking. Let him ask Christ, for Christ is God's gift; and God is both engaged by his Covenant promises, and Christ by his oneness and interest with his people, to be the strength of his people, and their portion for ever. Reader! pause a moment over this view, for it is blessed; yea, very blessed. God's faithfulness, in his Covenant promises, is engaged to all this. We are commanded, to count it all joy, when we fall into divers temptations. A plain, and positive assurance therefore, that the end of all trials must be blessed. Well, then, it follows, that if a child of God is to rejoice in the trial, it must be from the love of God that he is brought into it. God manifests his love, in bringing his dear ones *to* the trial. God manifests his love, in carrying them *through* it. Christ, the wisdom of God, is sure to be with them, *in* every part of it. And God's glory and his child's happiness must be the final result to bring *out* of it. So that God is glorified; Christ is honored; Satan subdued; and the child of God brought into a conformity to Christ's image; and made more than conqueror through Him, whose strength is perfected, in his people's weakness. Reader! behold, where wisdom and strength is, and conscious of a daily need of Christ, as we need our daily bread; let us seek grace to seek Christ, and we shall then be able, with the Apostle, upon every occasion of trial, to sing the same song; *Now thanks be unto* God, *who always causeth us to triumph in* Christ! 2 Cor. ii. 14.

But let him ask in faith. Yes! it is a blessed thing, when from the grace of faith *from* the Lord, we are enabled to go boldly *to* the Lord. And surely, every regenerated child of God may find confidence in that grace, to seek grace. Could we always keep in remembrance *past* mercies, they would never fail to beget the desire for *new* ones. Even among men, old friends, and long-proved friends, furnish confidence. And shall a child of God go to Jesus in bondage-frames, doubting, fearing, and questioning, whether he shall succeed? *A double minded man!* what a foolish character, to say no worse of it. Not so the Patriarchs, and holy men of old. *They staggered not at the promise of* God *through unbelief, but were strong in faith. giving glory to* God. And there have been champions of faith in later times, in this our own nation. One of them used to say, that "God's *Amen*, and Christ's *verily*, with God the Spirit's *seal*, were more sure, than all the oaths of all the great men of the earth." Reader! do not forget, however, faith is God's gift, not man's merit. Philip. i. 29.

I do not think it necessary to dwell on these verses, concerning the brother, either of high, or low degree. The doctrine is too plain to need a comment. Whether considered in a temporal, or spiritual sense, the Lord's appointments to the Lord's people, both in providence, and grace, are all blessed, when the renewed heart is enabled to discern things spiritually. The humble circumstances of the poor, gracious man, in the common wants of *nature*, are all sweetened, when the Lord's hand is seen in the appointment. The Lord cannot err, cannot be mistaken, in his ordinations. And there are numberless promises in the word of God, which would have no scope for exercise, if the Lord's people were not sometimes shut up, and straitened, in poverty of pocket, as well as mind. See a few: Job v. 19. Psalm cvii. 19. Isaiah xxxiii. 16. Rom. viii. 28. And, in relation to *spiritual* concerns; if there were no dark and cloudy days, but a perpetual sunshine, all those rich clusters of promises, in which the Lord engageth to be with his people in darkness, would be done away; neither would the child of God be able to gather them, if seasons peculiarly suited to times of gathering never came. Yea, a child of God hath found, to his great joy, when the afflicting dispensation hath passed, the blessedness even of the LORD's withdrawing, in the after returns of increased manifestations, that, as the LORD hath said himself: *For a small moment have I forsaken thee; but with great mercies will I gather thee. In a little wrath I hid my face from thee for a moment: but with everlasting kindness will I have mercy on thee, saith the* LORD *thy Redeemer.* Let the Reader turn to the sweet portion, and read it himself. Isaiah liv. 4 to the end.

12 Blessed *is* the man that endureth temptation: for when he is tried, he shall receive the crown of life, which the Lord hath promised to them that love him.

13 Let no man say when he is tempted, I am tempted of God: for God cannot be tempted with evil, neither tempteth he any man:

14 But every man is tempted, when he is drawn away of his own lust, and enticed.

15 Then when lust hath conceived, it bringeth forth sin; and sin, when it is finished, bringeth forth death.

The case of a single person is here stated, but all are included, of such as endure temptation; that is, so endure all the fiery darts of Satan and his emissaries, that, like a Target shot at, he doth not give way; but his bow remaineth in full strength, and the arms of his hands are made strong, by the hands *of the mighty* GOD *of Jacob.* Gen. xlix. 24. And we shall see the blessedness of this enduring, and rising above all Satan's devices, through CHRIST, if we consider a few particulars of this holy war, and the interest all the faithful in CHRIST have in it. The Apostle, a few verses before, called upon the brethren, to count it all joy, when they fall into divers temptations. And here he declares the blessedness of enduring temptation, and the sure crown of victory, in spiritual, and eternal life in CHRIST. Reader! let you and I attend to the subject a little. There can be no crown of victory without a battle. And the very enduring of temptation, which is this battle, is declared to be blessed.

And *first.* It is so, because *Satan* makes this furious attack upon the child of GOD, because he is the child of GOD. His bitterness is against CHRIST and his seed, CHRIST and his Church. Hence, blessed is the man that endureth temptation on this account. The LORD said at first to the serpent, *I will put enmity between thee and the woman: and between thy seed, and her seed.* Gen. iii. 15. And here it is seen, to our joy, in the Devil's malice to CHRIST's seed, and on CHRIST's account.

Secondly. The issue of these temptations, is never doubtful, as to the final termination of the contest. For though *Satan* may, and sometimes doth indeed, get a point upon the child of GOD, yea, to the extent of deep wounds, as in the instances of *David,* and of *Peter,* and multitudes of GOD's dear children beside; yet it is the end, which crowns the action. Soldiers in battle, may be hardly put to it at times, and sometimes taken prisoners, and sometimes receive dreadful wounds; yet, if victory at length is obtained by them, they lose sight of former skirmishes, prisons, or wounds, in the joy of a compleat conquest at last. Such is the sure termination of all conflicts to the faithful. During the hour of temptation by the powers of darkness, it is deeply distressing: as our LORD found it, so do we. Luke xxii. 53. Some of the LORD's best soldiers may be thrown into prison, some in tribulation ten days; Rev. ii. 10. but the time is limited, and neither his prison, or his devilish malice, shall go further. *The* GOD *of peace will bruise Satan under our feet shortly.* Rom. xvi. 20. Hence, the sweet scripture still holds good: *Blessed is the man that endureth temptation; for when he is tried, he shall receive the crown of life.*

Thirdly. The consciousness that victory is sure, and that every temptation, when sanctified of the LORD, leads to good, and not to evil, makes this enduring of it, be it what it may, blessed. The foe of GOD and man, is dreadfully angry, and ashamed to be baffled, and put to flight, by poor human nature, and especially in its present humbled state, to which, by his cursed wiles in the fall, it is brought. To be conquered by CHRIST, to be subdued by legions of angels, as we read *Michael* and his angels did vanquish *Satan;* this is nothing so humiliating as when the Worm *Jacob* is made to thresh the mountains; and a sinner saved by grace, is enabled through grace, to resist the devil, and to bruise his head, who in the members of CHRIST, may be said to bruise his heel. That temptation ministers to make a child of GOD blessed, when such ends are induced by it.

Fourthly. One of the sweet offices of CHRIST, the believer finds the blessedness of in seasons of temptation, while enabled by grace, to look up to JESUS, under them. Like the Prophet's servant in the mount, when the LORD opens the eyes to see, we discover *more to be with us, than all that are against us.* 2 Kings vi. 16. To behold JESUS, our Almighty High Priest, looking on, watching the enemy, keeping the feet of his saints, and causing the wicked to be silent in darkness before him, watering his tried ones every moment, to quench the fiery darts of the enemy; and, while Satan accuseth, CHRIST becomes our Advocate, and Propitiation: Oh! it is blessed to endure such temptations, when by such temptations we see CHRIST more immediately coming forth for us; and while Satan storms, JESUS sooths, while the Tempter fawns, the LORD rebukes him, surely all temptations cannot but be blessed which are productive of such gracious effects; and, seeing JESUS for us, with us, and putting the foe to flight, we disregard the whole, conscious that the LORD's strength is made perfect in our weakness; and even in the hottest part of the battle, we cry out with the Prophet: *rejoice not against me, O mine enemy; when I fall, I shall arise; when I sit in darkness, the* LORD *shall be a light unto me.* Micah vii. 8.

Lastly. To mention no more. The blessedness which ariseth out of the enduring temptation, and even in those instances, where for a time, the enemy gains advantage; yet, if thereby, the child of GOD learns more to discover his own nothingness, and the LORD's all sufficiency; the trial is very blessed, and very profitable. So that every recovery induceth less confidence in self, and more in CHRIST. And very sure I am, that when the LORD raiseth up his fallen ones, as in the case of *David* and *Peter*, and every renewed wound, induceth more wariness and caution, and makes CHRIST more precious and endeared; so nothing tends to confound the Devil more, than when the LORD pulls the lamb out of this Lion's mouth; makes him drop his prey, and skulk away as an enemy defeated. Reader! do you know any thing of such transactions? If so, you will know also, how to join in the Apostle's words, of *the blessedness of that man, that endureth temptation.*

But while the Apostle pronounceth a blessedness to the man that endureth temptation; (and very blessed, beyond a doubt, all such must be, where the child of GOD *endureth,* that is, sustaineth the attack of *Satan,* through grace, and ultimately is the better for it;) the temptations to evil, and which terminate in shame and disgrace, have a very different beginning and end; and, of consequence, are without blessedness. Let no man among the carnal, dare to charge this upon GOD. GOD is not the Author of such; neither can be. But the whole begins in the corrupt affections of a man's own fallen sinful nature. And the Apostle represents the progress of those affections by a climax, which riseth one upon the other, from the first seed of sin, until ripened into death. This is nature unrenewed. The other is grace contending with it. The Apostle bids the Church to notice this, and not err. And where these different causes and effects are considered, under divine teaching, no error in the apprehension will follow. See Chapter iv. 7, and Commentary.

16 Do not err, my beloved brethren.

17 Every good gift and every perfect gift is from above, and cometh down from the Father of lights, with whom is no variableness, neither shadow of turning.

18 Of his own will begat he us with the word of truth, that we should be a kind of first fruits of his creatures.

19 ¶ Wherefore, my beloved brethren, let every man be swift to hear, slow to speak, slow to wrath:

20 For the wrath of man worketh not the righteousness of God.

21 Wherefore lay apart all filthiness and superfluity of naughtiness, and receive with meekness the engrafted word, which is able to save your souls.

That Christ is the good and perfect gift here spoken of, that cometh from above, and from the Father of lights, is evident; because He is himself, all that is good and perfect, and comprehends in his Person as God-Man, every other. Having Christ, we have with him, his gifts and graces. Nevertheless, it is not the gifts and graces, but Christ, which is the one good and perfect gift; yea, every one included in Him, which cometh from above. And how sweet and precious is the thought, that He is in himself, *without variableness or shadow of turning.* Both the Giver, and the Gift, and He who gives the people grace, richly to enjoy all. Reader! pause at this place. I ask the question, but do not decide. Is not Christ, as Christ the Father's gift? John iii. 16. And hath he not given this gift to the Church, to have, and to hold for ever? Isaiah liv. 10. Is not Jesus Christ *the same yesterday, and to day, and for ever?* Heb. xiii. 8. And who is it, that by His own will, begat the Church to be a kind of first-fruits of his creatures, but God the Holy Ghost, when by regeneration the Lord first brings the child of God, by the new birth, to the knowledge of his high privilege of this good and perfect gift, Christ? 2 Pet. i. 3, 4. Ephes. i. 9. What can more blessedly manifest, the love and grace, of the Holy Three in One, towards the highly favoured objects of the chosen in Christ, than such demonstrations, of the personal and distinct acts towards them? If it be the Spirit's own will, in begetting the Church from the *Adam-*nature of the fall; is not the Lord the Spirit, the first predisposing cause, in bringing from death to life, the *chosen,* and the *redeemed* of the Lord, to the knowledge and enjoyment of their privileges? Surely He is the efficient *cause,* and his *will* his good pleasure. And the very object intended from it, namely, that we should be a kind of first fruits of his creatures; the sweet and blessed design, of the new birth in regeneration.

I see no reason to dwell in the use of arguments, to enforce the blessed consequences, which the Apostle hath so persuasively added; as the immediate result of having been so begotten. Where the Spirit dwells, and the work of regeneration is wrought; divine teaching, and divine influences, will be sure to accompany that teaching. Swiftness to hear the Lord's words; slowness to speak our own; receiving with meekness the engrafted word, with all the gracious accompaniments, will follow. It may be said of the Lord's redeemed ones now, as it was taught the Baptist of old, the way by which he should know Christ; in humble comparison to the same standard, upon whom the Spirit descends and remains; *the same is he that is born of* God. John i. 33. God's work, is a sure work. And God, in the new birth, forms the new creature, *after the image of him that created him.* Coloss. iii. 10.

22 But be ye doers of the word, and not hearers only, deceiving your own selves.

23 For if any be a hearer of the word, and not a doer, he is like unto a man beholding his natural face in a glass:

24 For he beholdeth himself, and goeth his way, and straightway forgetteth what manner of man he was.

25 But whoso looketh into the perfect law of liberty, and continueth *therein,* he being not a forgetful hearer, but a doer of the work, this man shall be blessed in his deed.

26 ¶ If any man among you seem to be religious, and bridleth not his tongue, but deceiveth his own heart, this man's religion *is* vain.

27 Pure religion and undefiled before God and the Father is this, To visit the fatherless and widows in their affliction, *and* to keep himself unspotted from the world.

Nothing can be more evident, from the whole scope of *James's* Epistle, taken in one mass of particulars, than that he is admonishing the *real* Church of GOD, made up of true, regenerated believers, against the *nominal* Church of Professors, in whose hearts, no saving change had been wrought. There were in this Apostle's days, as there have been in all ages of the Church, as well as in our days, vain talkers, whose religion consisted only in name. Such we read of. Heb. vi. 4, 5, 6. Titus 1—16. And *James,* through the whole of this Epistle, is continually speaking of these nominal christians, by way of instructing the LORD's people. I beg the Reader, to pause over the Apostle's expression, of the *perfect law of liberty.* What can be meant by it, but the Person and work of CHRIST? The engrafted word, and the uncreated word, are those mirrors here referred to, into which by looking, we behold the LORD's perfections for his people. *Paul* hath a similar figure. *But we all* (saith the Apostle) *with open face, beholding as in a glass, the glory of the* LORD *are changed into the same image, from glory to glory, even as by the* SPIRIT *of the* LORD. 2 Cor. iii. 18. Here, as in *James,* the Church of true children regenerated, and made new creatures in CHRIST JESUS, are considered, as looking wholly to JESUS. And thus looking under the SPIRIT's influence, *(for where the* SPIRIT *of the* LORD *is, there is liberty,)* to JESUS, they imbibe his graces, are made to imitate his example, and delight in all that belongs to JESUS, and the holy principles of his Gospel. This is the life of GOD's children, *a doer of the word, and not a hearer only.* Whereas the nominal professor, knoweth these things only by name. And although he may observe the greatest punctuality, in attending ordinances; yet, where the heart is not regenerated, head-knowledge is but vain. The love of CHRIST is only known, and felt, and enjoyed in the renewed man. Where this is wanting, all is wanting. Where GOD the SPIRIT hath wrought the saving change, all acts of grace, more or less, will follow; and not only the purity of those principles, begotten by regeneration, will shew themselves in the life and conversation, in visiting the fatherless and widows, in their affliction, but through the SPIRIT, the child of GOD will be enabled *to mortify the deeds of the body;* and be kept from *mingling with the heathen, and learning their works.* Psm. cvi. 35. Rom. viii. 13.

REFLECTIONS.

READER! observe the Apostle's salutation, addressed to the brethren, and see whether you have a personal interest in it. Can you count it all joy, when you fall into divers temptations? Yet! If so be, by regeneration you know the LORD, and therefrom can discover GOD's love and favor, in the appointment of exercises. To every child of GOD, renewed by grace trials, whose issue can never be finally doubtful, will always bring joy, when patience hath her perfect work, in the perfection of JESUS. In Him, and Him only, can the Church find themselves perfect and entire, and lacking nothing. And when taught these precious things, every child of GOD, will daily find his lack of wisdom, and as daily be led, to seek his supplies from Him, and in Him; *in whom are hid all the treasures of wisdom and knowledge.* Yea, and in faith, and without doubt and wavering, will the child of GOD seek it in JESUS, and from JESUS. And oh! how truly blessed is that child of GOD, who when tried, takes all his confidence in CHRIST.

Great FATHER of light! blessed for ever be thy glorious Name, for that good and perfect gift, which comprehends every other, thy dear SON! And blessed be thou, O LORD, that thy gifts and callings are without repentance. Thy will, and not our purpose; thy grace, and not our deservings, are the alone standards of thy love and favor. Oh! the blessedness of that one scripture, which hath more in it of value, than a million worlds; *Of his own will, begat he us with the word of truth!* LORD! write it in the living tablet of my heart, for daily use, and every moment's joy.

Precious JESUS! be thou the perfect law of liberty to my poor soul, to look into, as in a glass, from day to day. Oh! for a blessed conformity to my LORD's image, in all things! May GOD the HOLY GHOST, so take of the things of JESUS, and shew to me, that now by faith, I may daily behold thy face in righteousness; and ere long be satisfied in full sight, *when I awake with thy likeness.*

CHAP. II.

CONTENTS.

We have in this Chapter, an interesting Statement, of the Conduct to be observed by the LORD's *People, towards the* LORD's *Poor. And also, a blessed Account of the Works of Faith, as distinguished from a dead Faith, of a mere hearsay Knowledge!*

MY brethren, have not the faith of our Lord Jesus Christ, *the Lord* of glory, with respect of persons.

2 For if there come unto your assembly a man with a gold ring, in goodly apparel, and there come in also a poor man in vile raiment;

3 And ye have respect to him that weareth the gay cloathing, and say unto him, Sit thou here in a good place; and say to the poor, Stand thou there, or sit here under my footstool:

4 Are ye not then partial in yourselves, and are become judges of evil thoughts?

5 Hearken, my beloved brethren, Hath not God chosen the poor of this world rich in faith, and heirs of the kingdom which he hath promised to them that love him?

6 But ye have despised the poor. Do not rich men oppress you, and draw you before the judgement seats?

7 Do not they blaspheme that worthy name by the which ye are called?

8 If ye fulfil the royal law according to the scripture, Thou shalt love thy neighbour as thyself, ye do well:

9 But if ye have respect to persons, ye commit sin, and are convinced of the law as transgressors.

10 For whosoever shall keep the whole law, and yet offend in one *point*, he is guilty of all.

11 For he that said, Do not commit adultery, said also, Do not kill. Now, if thou commit no adultery, yet, if thou kill, thou art become a transgressor of the law.

12 So speak ye, and so do, as they that shall be judged by the law of liberty.

13 For he shall have judgment without mercy, that hath shewed no mercy; and mercy rejoiceth against judgment.

I have brought all these verses into one view, not for that they all refer to one, and the same subject; but to compress as much as possible, into a little compass. Very beautifully, as well as graciously, the Chapter opens, with calling upon the whole Church, of regenerated believers, as brethren of one family, to consider of relationship, and to have the same love, one for another. And to be sure, there cannot be an argument upon earth, more persuasive. And equally sure I am, that while a child of GOD, keeps in remembrance that tie, and feels the common equality, both in nature and grace; there will be no respect of Persons, more than the LORD himself hath in his providences appointed. In our Churches, however, made up as they are of nominal and real christians; distinctions will be preserved by the former; and what the Apostle here saith of partiality to the person in gay clothing, and neglect of the man in poor apparel, are but too visible. Indeed, had *James* been supposed to have been present, in our modern Churches, he could not have drawn the characters more truly. But I beg it may be observed, that this is chiefly, if not altogether, applicable to *carnal* worshippers. I should blush to have it said, if it could be said with truth, of any real and regenerated child of GOD, that he said to a brother in CHRIST, stand thou there, or sit here under my footstool.

Reader! do not hastily pass away from this very lovely description, which, by the pen of the Apostle, the HOLY GHOST hath given of the LORD's people. The words are put, in a way of question; but they decide the thing while asking of it. GOD hath chosen *the poor of this world rich in faith, and heirs of the kingdom*. Not simply poor, in outward things; though for the most part, the LORD's people are, every way poor, in body and in spirit; but spiritually poor in their own attainments; for the riches of faith, find larger scope for exercise, where the soul is always laying humble before GOD! Sweet is that scripture of the LORD, by the Prophet to this amount. Zephan. iii. 12.

I do not think it necessary to swell these pages of the *Poor Man's Commentary*, with observations, on what is so plain as to need none. And every thing, within the limits of those verses, is like the Prophet's vision, he that runs may read it. One point just let me remark on what the Apostle hath said, of a single offence committed against the law, becoming a breach of all. The fact is undeniable. And it were much to be wished, that the world at large, would consider the justice, and equity of it; for it would tend, under the grace of GOD, to carry conviction, to every man's heart, that all have sinned, and come short of the glory of the LORD; and, consequently, no flesh can be justified in the sight of GOD.

Whosoever shall keep the whole law, and yet offend in one point, is guilty of all. And for this plain reason. Because *that one* breach, as fully shews the contempt for the law giver, as the breach of all. The man could not have committed this one breach, before that he had first lost all reverence to the divine sanction. And, therefore, it is not on account of his obedience to GOD, that he doth not break all; but because the temptation to other breaches are wanting. If causes operated, with equal strength to break many, there would be no restraint in the fear of GOD, to keep back. And, therefore, all the world are found alike guilty before GOD; though all mankind, do not alike commit the same offences. The child of GOD, knows this, after regeneration hath passed upon him, in the workings and plague of his own heart. And it is to such only, CHRIST becomes exceedingly precious, who though they are kept by grace through faith, unto salvation; know, like *Paul*, that *in them, that is in their flesh, dwelleth no good thing*. Romans vii.

14 ¶ What *doth it* profit, my brethren, though a man say he hath faith, and have not works, can faith save him?

15 If a brother or sister be naked, and destitute of daily food,

16 And one of you say unto them, Depart in peace, be *ye* warmed and filled; notwithstanding ye give them not those things which are needful to the body, what *doth it* profit?

17 ¶ Even so faith, if it hath not works, is dead, being alone.

18 Yea, a man may say, Thou hast faith, and I have works: shew me thy faith without thy works, and I will shew thee my faith by my works.

19 Thou believest that there is one God; thou doest well: the devils also believe, and tremble.

20 But wilt thou know, O vain man, that faith without works is dead?

21 Was not Abraham our father justified by works, when he had offered Isaac his son upon the altar?

22 Seest thou how faith wrought with his works, and by works was faith made perfect?

23 And the scripture was fulfilled, which saith, Abraham believed God, and it was imputed unto him for righteousness: and he was called the Friend of God.

24 Ye see then how that by works a man is justified, and not by faith only.

25 Likewise also was not Rahab the harlot justified by works when she had received the messengers, and had sent *them* out another way?

26 For as the body without the spirit is dead, so faith without works is dead also.

I include all these verses, under one reading, as willing to bring the doctrine contained in them, into one view. Perhaps, no part of the word of God, hath been so little attended to, with an eye to the divine teaching, as this short but interesting passage of the Apostle; and conclusions have been drawn from it by the carnal; yea, and (for want of asking wisdom from God upon the occasion) by not a few of the Lord's people also, who have been much exercised in mind, unable to enter into a clear apprehension of the meaning. I beg the Reader to grant me a few moments indulgence. And I venture to hope, under the Lord the Spirit's enlightening grace, we shall find that nothing can be more clear than the Apostle's intention, in what is here said.

And, *first*, in order to give the fullest scope to the supposed misunderstanding, between *Paul* and *James*, on the subject of faith, I shall beg to bring before the Reader the words of each. The *first* of these great Apostles speaks so decidedly of justification only by faith, and without the deeds of the law; that no form of language can possibly be stronger, in confirmation of the doctrine. *By the deeds of the law, there shall no flesh be justified in his sight. Being justified freely by his grace, through the redemption that is in* Christ Jesus. Rom. iii. 20, 24. *But to him that worketh not, but believeth on him that justifieth the ungodly, his faith is counted for righteousness. For the promise that he should be the heir of the world, was not to Abraham, or to his seed through the law; but through the righteousness of faith. For if they which are of the law be heirs, faith is made void, and the promise made of none effect.* Rom. iv. 5, 13, 14. Christ *is become of no effect to you, whosoever of you are justified by the law; ye are fallen from grace.* Gal. v. 4. *Not of works, lest any man should boast.* Ephes. ii. 9. *Nor if righteousness come by the law, then* Christ *is dead in vain.* Gal. ii. 21. So much for *Paul* on the subject of faith.

I need not go over what the *second* of those great Apostles *James*, hath said on the subject: it is now before us. And nothing can be more plain, or express, in his statement on the subject of works. His concluding sentence, sums up all he had said before. *For as the body without the spirit is dead; so faith without works is dead also.* Now on the supposition, that both those holy men, taught, and inspired, as both were by the Holy Ghost, were speaking of one and the same thing; there would be indeed much cause for suspension, which to regard. Sentiments in that case, so very opposite, would raise fears and doubts, and distresses in the awakened and regenerated mind. But blessed be God, there is not the smallest cause for exciting any apprehension. The Apostles are in perfect harmony with each other. And *James*, so far from militating against what *Paul* hath said on the subject, doth very blessedly confirm the whole, and his observations, when rightly considered, strengthen the precious arguments of *Paul*, on the great subject of justification alone by faith. And this under the Lord's grace, will fully appear by the few following considerations.

First. Let us enquire what works those were, which *James* so much dwells upon? We may safely answer at once; not works of godliness or morality. For the two persons *James* brings forward in proof, when speaking of their being justified by works, very plainly manifests to the contrary. *Was not Abraham our father justified by works?* Abraham, when called of God, was an idolater. And *Paul*, speaking of *Abraham's* good works, declared that he had not whereof to glory before God. Rom. iv. 2. An idolater indeed, could have nothing to glory of before God. The Lord had declared before, concerning man, that *all flesh had corrupted itself,* and that *every imagination of the thoughts of his heart, was only evil continually.* Gen. vi. 5. And was *Abraham* an exception? And with respect to *Rahab* the harlot, could she be justified by the works of religion, or by works of virtue or morality; who, though faithful to God, was certainly unfaithful to man? Can any thing upon earth be more plain and self-evident, from the history of these very persons, the Apostle brings forward in proof, that whatever works *James* had in view when he declared faith without works was dead being alone, it was impossible he could mean works of godliness, or virtue, or morality.

Secondly. Upon the supposition, that the good works *James* insisted upon, as evidences of faith, and without which he saith faith itself is dead, being alone, had respect to the holiness and purity of a man's own heart; this would be directly contrary to the whole system of the Gospel; which, through all the word of God, is declared to be a faithful saying, and worthy of all acceptation, that Christ came into the world to save sinners. 1 Tim. i. 15. And in this sense, neither *Abraham* nor *Rahab,* nor all the Patriarchs, Apostles, or Prophets, could find justification in themselves before God. The doctrine of grace, is wholly founded in the reverse of good works. *For if it be of works, then is it no more of grace; otherwise grace is no more grace.* And the first and last, and ultimate design of the Gospel is, that in *the* Lord, *shall all the seed of Israel be justified, and shall glory.* Isaiah xlv. 25.

Thirdly. There is a striking difference in the manner of expression, between those great Apostles. In all the writings of *Paul,* in relation to justification, he is uniformly speaking of the method of a sinner's justification *before* God. *James,* on the contrary, is solely considering the subject, in respect to our being justified in *the sight of men.* Paul, never loseth sight of the *cause* of justification, which is Christ. *James* is speaking of the *effect.* Hence we hear the former, observing, concerning *Abraham,* that if he had been justified by works, whereby he had to glory! yet still *not before* God. Rom. iv. 2. Whereas *James* puts the case of a brother or sister, being destitute of food; and one say, depart in peace, be ye warmed or filled; notwithstanding ye gave them not those things that are needful; what doth it profit? Even so saith he, faith is dead, being alone, that is alone in justification before men. The world can form no judgment whatever, by what a man professeth; but by what he practiseth. And therefore (saith *James)* what doth it profit the world, that a man have faith, if that faith be unaccompanied with deeds?

Hence then it appears, that on the supposition of this last statement, *Paul* is speaking of the method of a sinner's justification *before* God; and James of our being justified in the *view of men;* those great Apostles differ altogether in the subject they are upon, and not in sentiment, upon the one momentous doctrine, of the method of salvation by Jesus Christ.

Fourthly, and lastly, therefore, I venture from all that hath been before offered, to observe, that God the Holy Ghost the Almighty Author, by inspiration, of all *Paul's* writings, and those of *James* no less, hath himself explained the whole, and settled the point, by placing the great doctrine of faith on its own proper basis; and in so clear, and circumstantial a manner, as, under his divine instruction, cannot be mistaken.

In proof of this, I beg the Reader once more, and somewhat more particularly to notice *James's* words. *Was not Abraham our father justified by works, when he had offered Isaac his son upon the Altar? Seest thou how faith wrought with his works, and by works was made perfect.* Now, not to notice again what hath been before observed, that the works which made perfect *Abraham's* faith, hath no respect whatever to works of morality, or virtue; it must strike every man's mind with full conviction, that *James* hath no other meaning whatever, by what is here said of works, than works of faith. The faith of *Abraham* was proved to be real, by his proceeding to act upon it. And God the Holy Ghost explains this in another part of his sacred writings, when he saith : *by faith Abraham when he was tried offered up Isaac. And he that had received the promises offered up his only begotten son. Of whom it was said, that in Isaac shall thy seed be called. Accounting that God was able to raise him even from the dead, from whence also he received him in a figure.* Heb. xi. 17, 18, 19. Now let the Reader pause over this statement, which, let him remember, is God the Holy Ghost's own. And then let him say, is not this whole transaction of the Patriarch's faith, and faith only, in the deeds of faith acting upon faith? What is the plain sense of it but this? God promised *Abraham* a son. God declared with this son, that the promised seed, meaning Christ after the flesh, should, in process of time, come from him. *Abraham* believed what God had said; and took God at his word. Soon after, *Abraham* receives a command to offer up this son, as a burnt-offering. Being strong in faith and concluding that God was able to raise his son again from the dead, he proceeded to obey God. Here then was faith carried into practice. Now, saith *James*, was not Abraham our father justified by works? Yes! most assuredly : for his faith was hereby proved, not to be a dead faith, but a living faith, and acted upon by the works of faith. But what hath this to do with works of morality, or good deeds among men? This was a transaction wholly between God and the Patriarch, in the concern of his own soul, and had no reference whatever to the transactions of common life between man and man It must be prejudice indeed, and of no ordinary kind, that would herefrom draw conclusions, that morality, and good deeds, among men, were the works *James* had in view when he said, *and by works was Abraham's faith made perfect;* when it is plain, the Apostle is wholly discoursing upon this subject, in reference to the solemn transaction between God and the Patriarch.

In like manner, as a further proof, in the instance of *Rahab*. No one for a moment can suppose, that the Apostle, when speaking of this woman being justified by works, alluded to works of goodness or morality. A woman of ill-fame could not be thought exemplary for any of these. And, with respect to her conduct towards her country, blessed as her faith, and works on that faith, were in the sight of God; yet, in the world's dictionary, she was treacherous towards man. When, therefore, we hear the Apostle demanding, was

Yes! Her receiving the spies in peace, was a work of faith indeed, which proved how true, and genuine her faith was; and became the precious *effect* of that sure *cause*. And God the Holy Ghost elsewhere bears testimony to this act of her's, upon the faith the Lord had given her, when he saith: *by faith the harlot Rahab perished not, with them that believed not.* Heb. xi. 31. But how totally foreign are both these instances to the doctrine some have raised from this Chapter; which, while the Apostle is directly producing instances to shew, that a lively faith (as in those cases) must, and will everlastingly be acted upon, in proof that it is not a dead, unprofitable faith; they draw conclusions, as if faith without morality was dead, being alone, and cannot justify before God.

From the whole, therefore, I cannot hesitate to conclude, that the Apostles *Paul* and *James*, were both taught of God; both inspired by the Holy Ghost, when writing their Epistles; both had the same views of that faith, which is of the operation of God; and both knew, that the Church hath justification before God in Christ alone, without the deeds of the law, and solely in the blood and righteousness of our Lord Jesus Christ. *James*, therefore, is only strengthening his brother *Paul's* statement of faith, in shewing, and in two such memorable instances as he produceth, how real living faith is always acted upon by real living principles; and thereby becoming subject of joy in the faithful soul, when such blessed *effects* spring out of so blessed a *cause*.

I must not suffer the Reader to pass on from this Chapter before that he hath first paused, and considered with me, the blessedness of what is here said concerning the Patriarch *Abraham*, in that *he was called the friend of* God. What title among all the sons of men can come up to this? *James*, no doubt, gathered it from these passages, 2 Chron. xx. 7. and Isaiah xli. 8. for otherwise, we do not find the very phrase, as *James* hath here worded it, in all the Bible. Every thing proves it, indeed, in the whole of *Abraham's* history; and that's enough. And Jesus so called his disciples, John xv. 15. But what I particularly beg the Reader to remark in it, is the foundation of this friendship. It is all in God. Abraham's friendship to God, which God condescends to accept, is the *effect* of God's friendship to *him*. But it is God's friendship which is the sole *cause*. And let the Reader further remark, how sweetly the Lord proved *Abraham's* faith, by the trial of demanding his son. True faith hath true properties.

Reader! do not overlook the design of the Holy Ghost, in this precious record of the Patriarch. *These things are our examples.* Every son and daughter of faith is, in like manner, the friend of God; and proved to be so by the same effects. Am I speaking to a truly regenerated child of God, who, like *Abraham*, hath been brought to believe the record God hath given of his dear Son? Then doth he know, as *Abraham* knew, God's friendship to him. My Brother! What was it but the antient, everlasting, unchanging love and friendship of God in Christ, which gave his Son to you, and for you, and chose you in him, before the foundation of the world? And what was it but from the everflowing streams of the same unalterable friendship, which gave Christ to the cross, and the Holy Spirit to the regeneration of your soul, when you neither knew that friendship, or your need of it, and was altogether unconscious of either, and was *living without* GOD, *and without* CHRIST *in the world?* Do you not thereby prove GOD's friendship to *you?*

Now, then, see for the *effects* arising from such a *cause*, which, like *Abraham*, may testify, that you are also *the friend of* GOD. Nay, start not back, nor shrink at the comparison, though your faith is not so illustrious as this great father of the faithful. Have you made no sacrifice to the LORD? Have you no *Isaacs*, no offerings to give up, on which nature would wish to lean? Doth not every regenerated child of GOD, in deed, and in truth, sacrifice his *Isaacs*, and all that nature would fain cherish, when laying low in the dust before GOD, desiring to be stripped of every thing, so that CHRIST be glorified in his salvation? Surely, however small the grace of faith, though but like a grain of mustard-seed it be, in the heart of every child of GOD; yet is it of the same source, which the LORD gave to *Abraham*, when, in the exercise of it, he manifested himself as *the friend of* GOD. It is not the greatness of our attainments; but the LORD's love, in taking it so kindly of his redeemed ones, when at any time they are enabled to bear testimony to the word of his grace. And, what the LORD said to *David*, he in effect saith to all the seed of our Almighty Spiritual David; *whereas it was in thine heart to build an house to my name; thou didst well, that it was in thine heart.* 1 Kings viii. 18. It were well if GOD's children would live more upon the LORD's love *to them*, than form conclusions of their interest in the LORD's friendship from their love *to him*. The faithful in CHRIST JESUS, will at length sit down with *Abraham*, and *Isaac*, and *Jacob*, in the Kingdom. And it will then be discovered, that the LORD's friendship, and not our deservings, hath been, and everlastingly must be, the source of all our blessedness. If *we love him, it is because he first loved us.* 1 John iv. 19.

REFLECTIONS.

OH! for grace, while reading what GOD the HOLY GHOST hath said in this Chapter, in reproving any respect of persons, in his house of prayer; that I may everlastingly keep in view the LORD's pleasure, and so have not the faith of our LORD JESUS CHRIST, as to regard the rich more than the poor; but to love the LORD's poor with peculiar delight for JESUS's sake; and GOD's chosen may be my chosen; and the poor of this world, if rich in faith, and heirs of the kingdom, may be *the excellent in whom is all my delight.*

Blessed and Eternal SPIRIT! keep my soul from all error, in the right apprehension of all thy gracious truths. Teach me, LORD, that if it were possible for a man to keep the whole law, and yet offend in one point, he is guilty of all. And, as we have all sinned, and come short of thy glory, never may my soul seek the smallest justification by the deeds of the law.

And I do beseech thee, O LORD, who leadeth thy people unto all truth, that I may so fully learn, from what thou hast here taught the Church, how unprofitable the dead faith of merely acknowledging divine truths, while not living under the influence of them, is before GOD; that my faith, like the faith of *Abraham* and *Rahab*, may be works of faith; in proof, that my profession and practice are in perfect correspondence to each other. Let my soul abhor the thought, and much more the conduct, of professing love to a poor brother or sister, while withholding from them the tokens of that love. And in the higher concerns with my GOD and SAVIOR, far be it from me, O LORD, to profess, that I know GOD, but in works deny him! Oh! for grace, while seeking justification before GOD, upon the sole footing of the Person, blood-shedding, and righteousness of the LORD JESUS CHRIST, to be found an eminent *example of the believers, in word, in conversation, in charity, in spirit, in faith, in purity!*

CHAP. III.

CONTENTS.

This Chapter contains much wholesome Exhortation to the People of GOD, *on the several Parts of Conduct. The close of it hath a beautiful Description of the Wisdom which is from above, in Opposition to that which is earthly.*

MY brethren be not many masters, knowing that we shall receive the greater condemnation.

2 For in many things we offend all. If any man offend not in word, the same *is* a perfect man, *and* able also to bridle the whole body.

3 Behold, we put bits in the horses' mouths, that they may obey us; and we turn about their whole body.

4 Behold also the ships, which though *they be* so great, and *are* driven of fierce winds, yet are they turned about with a very small helm, whithersoever the governor listeth.

5 Even so the tongue is a little member, and boasteth great things. Behold how great a matter a little fire kindleth!

6 And the tongue *is* a fire, a world of iniquity; so is the tongue among our members, that it defileth the whole body, and setteth on fire the course of nature; and it is set on fire of hell.

7 For every kind of beasts, and of birds, and of serpents, and of things in the sea, is tamed, and hath been tamed of mankind:

8 But the tongue can no man tame: *it is* an unruly evil, full of deadly poison.

9 Therewith bless we God, even the Father; and therewith curse we men, which are made after the similitude of God.

10 Out of the same mouth proceedeth blessing and cursing. My brethren these things ought not so to be.

11 Doth a fountain send forth at the same place sweet *water* and bitter.

12 Can the fig tree, my brethren, bear olive berries? either a vine, figs? so *can* no fountain both yield salt water and fresh.

13 Who is a wise man, and endued with knowledge among you? let him shew out of a good conversation his works with meekness of wisdom.

14 But if ye have bitter envying and strife in your hearts, glory not, and lie not against the truth.

We shall enter into a more perfect apprehension of the several directions we meet with in the whole of this Chapter, and indeed, it might be added, the whole of this Epistle, if we consider the general scope of the Apostle's directions, in relation to those to whom he wrote. The Church then, as the Church now, had a nominal congregation, which mingled with the people of GOD. The HOLY GHOST, therefore, by his servant the Apostle, instructs the true Church, from being led away by the practice of such men. Hence, we find in the two preceding chapters, expressions, of *double-minded men; mere hearers of the word;* men *seeming to be religious.* So again, of certain persons, who were partial observers of the law: unconscious that one offence constituted a transgressor, as truly so, as a man guilty of all. And in this Chapter, he describes the bitter envying, and strife in the heart, and of lying against the truth. The Reader will do well to consider these things. It is not the Church, to whom *James* is writing, that he chargeth with this inconsistency; for the Church is considered in a regenerate state. But it is the mere Professor, who mingled with GOD's people, though in reality, had no part, nor lot in the matter. By an attention to these different characters, what the Apostle here sets forth will be found under divine teaching, very instructive.

I would pause over the Apostle's words, of the wonderful circumstance which he takes notice of, and which, more or less, the people of GOD too fully know, and feel; that those members of ours, which under grace, are used for glorifying the LORD, in praising him, are also made the instruments of sin. With the tongue bless we GOD even the F<small>ATHER</small>. And, though a truly regenerated child of G<small>OD</small> is restrained from using the tongue to curse; yet, too often, perhaps, the tongue is used in angry words. Hence, Reader! every child of G<small>OD</small> hath an evidence in himself, when regenerated by the H<small>OLY</small> G<small>HOST</small>, of a double principle within him; grace, and corruption. Indeed, what higher proof can a child of G<small>OD</small> need, than his own heart? I have so largely considered this subject in this *Poor Man's Commentary*, upon several occasions before, and particularly in the Canticles, Chap. v. 2. and Romans vii. 7. that I rather would refer to those scriptures, than enlarge. But, as the Apostle saith, and very blessedly saith it, the *wise man*, (that is, the truly regenerated believer, made wise unto salvation, through the grace that is in C<small>HRIST</small> J<small>ESUS</small>, and who is endued with divine knowledge,) *will shew out of a good conversation his works of grace with meekness and wisdom.*

15 This wisdom descendeth not from above, but *is* earthly, sensual, devilish.

16 For where envying and strife *is*, there *is* confusion and every evil work.

17 But the wisdom that is from above is first pure, then peaceable, gentle, *and* easy to be intreated, full of mercy and good fruits, without partiality, and without hypocrisy.

18 And the fruit of righteousness is sown in peace of them that make peace.

Nothing could be more happily chosen, for the Church of G<small>OD</small> to ascertain the real character of G<small>OD</small>'s children from mere formal professors, than in the striking description here given, between the wisdom that is earthly, and the wisdom which is heavenly.

Let the Reader look into the circumstances of common life, and behold the multitude of instances which every where abound, in what may truly, and properly be called, *worldly wisdom*. See how the followers of it *rise early, late take rest, and eat the bread of carefulness*. Destitute of the S<small>PIRIT</small> of G<small>OD</small>, there is but one object such characters are everlastingly in pursuit of, however diversified by the variety of their affections; namely, to *make provision for the flesh, to fulfil the lusts thereof*. On the other hand, behold the child of G<small>OD</small>! Awakened by the descent of the H<small>OLY</small> G<small>HOST</small> in regeneration, the heart becomes interested, to seek the glorious objects which are heavenly; and to be more intent on things which are not seen, than on those which are. And, where grace hath wrought this saving change upon the heart towards G<small>OD</small>; all the blessed fruits, and effects of it will follow, in the believer's conversation with men. For the wisdom which is from above is first pure, the heart and conscience being purified by the blood of C<small>HRIST</small>. And where grace reigns, to lead the heart to G<small>OD</small>; there grace will then shew itself, in all the blessed consequences of peace on earth, and good will towards men. And all the graces of the S<small>PIRIT</small> will manifest themselves by their fruits, in the general tenor of the life and conversation. So certain and sure must be, in every instance, the blessed result of the renewed life, differing from the wisdom that is earthly, and sensual, and even devilish; because, an unawakened, unregenerate heart, is still in the *Adam*-nature of sin, and is in the snare of the devil, and led captive by him at his will.

REFLECTIONS.

PRECIOUS LORD JESUS! how sweetly doth this Chapter bring to my recollection thy tender, and endearing precept, to call no man master upon earth! for One is our Master, even CHRIST! Yes! truly, LORD, thou art, both by right and by purchase, by conquest, and by the voluntary surrender of my soul, in the day which made me willing, the day of thy power; thou art my lawful right, and highly honored Master, Sovereign, and LORD! And oh! for grace, everlastingly in willing homage, to bow my knee to the sceptre of thy grace. And as all creatures in nature have been, and are tamed and governed, let it never be said, that any of thy redeemed ones arose at any time in disobedience against thee!

And do thou, blessed and Wonderful Counsellor! in whom are hid all the treasures of wisdom and knowledge, grant me daily portions, from thyself, in that wisdom which is from above. LORD! be it my happiness to be distinguished, in all my dealings with men, from that worldly wisdom which begets envying, and strife, and every evil work; but out of a good conversation, by the in-dwelling power of GOD the HOLY GHOST, may I be enabled to show forth all the practical fruits of godliness, *with meekness of wisdom.*

CHAP. IV.

CONTENTS.

The same Subject of Exhortation is continued in this Chapter as in the former. Several striking Expressions are made use of, to enforce what the Apostle is recommending.

FROM whence *come* wars and fightings among you? *come they* not hence, *even* of your lusts that war in your members.

2 Ye lust, and have not: ye kill, and desire to have, but cannot obtain: ye fight and war, yet ye have not, because ye ask not.

3 Ye ask, and receive not, because ye ask amiss, that ye may consume *it* upon your lusts.

4 Ye adulterers and adulteresses, know ye not that the friendship of the world is enmity with God? whosoever therefore will be a friend of the world is the enemy of God.

5 Do ye think that the scripture saith in vain, The spirit that dwelleth in us lusteth to envy ?

6 But he giveth more grace. Wherefore he saith, God resisteth the proud, but giveth grace unto the humble.

I do not interpret what the Apostle here saith of wars and fightings, as nationally considered, for it should all along be kept in remembrance, that the Apostle is writing to the Church. And as every believer knoweth well in his own experience, what an holy war, from the moment of regeneration to the day of death, is carried on between the flesh and the spirit, he is here taught from whence to trace the origin, and where alone, in the LORD, to seek strength. Nothing but grace, and the continual renewing of grace, can help the child of GOD, to subdue the flesh, with its affections and lusts. And hence that sweet promise of JESUS to his people. *I will water it every moment.* Isaiah xxvii. 3. And sure enough I am, though in a thousand instances, I see not how it is done, neither can trace the footsteps, or comings of the LORD; yet sure I am, that did not the LORD JESUS by his HOLY SPIRIT continually renew the soul, our spirit would soon languish, and wither, and die. Reader! cherish the thought! *Paul* knew it, and spake confidently of it. *Though our outward man perish,* (saith he,) *yet our inward man is renewed day by day.* 2 Cor. iv. 14. But JESUS carrieth the matter higher than his servant, for he saith, that he will water his vineyard and his Church *every moment.* Not day by day only. Not occasional visits now and then, but momently, that is, unceasingly. So that, even when the Church is at the lowest, and is tempted to exclaim, *my strength and my hope is perished from the* LORD; Lament. iii. 18. it is not so : for JESUS's watering ceaseth not. Yea, when we are causing him to serve with our sins, and wearying him with our iniquities; even then the LORD is blotting *our transgression for his own sake, and will not remember our sins.* Isaiah xliii. 24, 25.

I beg the Reader to notice what is said of adulterers and adulteresses : Not naturally so only, but spiritually. All coldness and departures from the LORD, are adulterous acts towards our lawful right husband. And, therefore, the reproof is given to shew, that friendship with the mammon of this world, is as a wife's treacherously departing from her husband.

I do not think it necessary to swell these pages with a Comment on what is so very plain, in the several verses that follow. It will be enough to observe, how blessedly the several directions are accompanied with the assurance, that the LORD's strength shall be made perfect to his people in their weakness. And I admire the very blessed manner in which the LORD puts the question, and himself answers it. *Do ye think that the scripture saith in vain, that the spirit that dwelleth in us lusteth to envy ?* As if the LORD had said ; Do ye think, that it was not needful in GOD the HOLY GHOST to inform the Church, that, though regenerated, yet, the unrenewed part of every believer, even their body of sin and death, they carry about with them ; still hath the same carnal mind, or spirit, which is enmity against GOD ?

Ought ye not to know it, and to have it always in remembrance? Can you suppose, that such an awful account would be given in the scripture, unless it were necessary; that not only in a state of unrenewed nature, but in God's children when renewed by grace, there is still in that body of sin and death they carry about with them, the same evil imaginations described. Gen. vi. 5. and Rom. viii. 7. Reader! do you not know this, and in the dust confess it before God? I bless my God, I do! And, oh! what sad havoc would the enemy make with those lusts of mine, if God did not give *more grace* to keep them under, than *Satan's* fuel, and my corruptions, to make them burn? Oh! for grace, never to lose sight of this indwelling evil, and also this more grace of my God. And do thou, dearest Lord, as this scripture is not said in vain, grant, that it never may be in vain to my soul. *But he giveth more grace.* Yea, where grace is already given, and the child of God truly regenerated, the Lord will give *more.* And the Lord will give more of that very grace, which shall effectually oppose, and overcome my very lust, be it what it may, to evil. Oh! the sweetness, seasonableness, blessedness of this scripture, which rips open the knowledge of the wound, and gives an effectual balsam, in Christ's blood, to heal. *He giveth more grace.*

7 Submit yourselves therefore to God. Resist the devil, and he will flee from you.

8 Draw nigh to God, and he will draw nigh to you. Cleanse *your* hands, *ye* sinners; and purify *your* hearts, *ye* double minded.

9 Be afflicted, and mourn, and weep: let your laughter be turned to mourning, and *your* joy to heaviness.

10 Humble yourselves in the sight of the Lord, and he shall lift you up.

11 Speak not evil one of another, brethren. He that speaketh evil of *his* brother, and judgeth his brother, speaketh evil of the law, and judgeth the law: but if thou judge the law, thou art not a doer of the law, but a judge.

12 There is one lawgiver, who is able to save and to destroy: who art thou that judgest another?

Though in the first Chapter of this Epistle, verses 2, and 12, I dwelt somewhat long upon the subject of temptation; yet, in addition to what was there said, I know not how to resist the present occasion, of offering, if but a short remark, on the gracious precept, and gracious promise blended with it, of baffling the devil by resisting him; and drawing nigh to God, who is always drawing nigh to his people.

It is very certain, that *Satan* knoweth not who are, or who are not the LORD's people, while in their state of unregeneracy. And, therefore, it is said, that he goeth about *as a roaring lion, seeking whom he may devour:* not whom he *will,* for if he had the will, that would be all; but whom he *may.* 1 Pet. v. 8. Now, in his impudent attacks upon a child of GOD, it is very blessed, when through grace, we are enabled to resist him by faith. Those now in heaven, are said *to have overcome by the blood of the Lamb.* Rev. xii. 11. And certain it is, *Satan* will flee from nothing, but the blood of the cross.

Secondly. The very resisting the devil in the LORD's strength, cannot but ultimately succeed. For the devil always dreads that CHRIST is at hand. When he finds in the child of GOD, the grace of resistance; if he still tempts, he tempts with fear. So that when the precept is, *Submit yourselves therefore to* GOD: This calls in GOD's presence, and protection. And, when it is added, *draw nigh to* GOD, *and he will draw nigh to you:* this secures victory. And *Satan's* devices are then carried on, before his flight, in cowardly fear. He dreads CHRIST's presence, and he fears the consequence.

Once more. It is the disgrace of *Satan* to be overcome, in the triumph of a child of GOD over every single temptation. He feels ashamed, and skulks away. Not as much from our victory, and his disgrace, that the worm *Jacob* should thresh the mountains; but from the ultimate victory, which every successful skirmish on our part, puts him in mind of. And the punishment that may be inflicted upon him for his attempt, even before his final ruin, no doubt works upon him now, as it did in the days of CHRIST's flesh. Hence that question: *What have we to do with thee,* JESUS, *thou* SON *of* GOD? *Art thou come hither to torment us before the time?* Matt. viii. 29. And may we not conclude, that often now, though we know it not, the LORD doth punish him, and rebuke him; as the HOLY GHOST hath given us a beautiful example of in that precious scripture: Zech. iii. 2. From all these considerations, I think, we may, through grace, derive sweet instruction and comfort, that where the LORD's precepts are blended, as in this instance, with the LORD's promise, boldly the child of GOD may go forth, in the name of the LORD, and in the LORD's strength resist the devil's policy. For, as the armies in heaven, overcame by the blood of the LAMB, so the same precious blood is the sure sign of victory now upon earth. They that are with JESUS, both here and there, are *called, and chosen, and faithful.* Rev. xvii. 14.

13 Go to now, ye that say, To-day or to-morrow we will go in to such a city, and continue there a year, and buy and sell, and get gain:

14 Whereas ye know not what shall be on the morrow. For what *is* your life? it is even a vapour, that appeareth for a little time, and then vanisheth away,

15 For that ye *ought* to say, If the Lord will, *we* shall live, and do this, or that.

16 But now ye rejoice in your boastings: all such rejoicing is evil.

17 Therefore to him that knoweth to do good, and doeth *it* not, to him it is sin.

What a beautiful transition the Apostle makes from the subject of the foregoing verses, to what is contained in the opening of this? From the frail tenure of human life, which, in numberless cases, is sometimes crushed, even before the moth, and, in its highest strength, is but as the vapor exhaled from the earth, or the bubble on the water, which are scarce formed before they both dissolve into air, and are instantly lost; the Apostle shews the Church the inconsiderateness and folly of all plans, but such as are founded in divine wisdom, and are looking for divine strength to carry them on. How can any man, who is not the sure proprietor of the present hour, calculate on a day or a year. Reader! bring home the reasoning to your own heart. Know you that there will be a morrow for you? Is it certain your life will be prolonged to that morrow? Nay, if it should, is it certain health will come with it? Will strength also, intellect, ability, purpose, yea, all things concur, in such a way and manner, that the schemes of this day shall be realized on the morrow?

But those words of the HOLY GHOST, by his servant, to a child of GOD, may be spiritually considered, I conceive, with great sweetness. There is a day, a year fast approaching, when the redeemed will enter into that blessed city which hath foundations, whose Builder and Maker is GOD. They are now the citizens of that country; and it is their proper home. There they will indeed continue a year, even an eternal year, for they will go out no more. Rev. vii. 15. and in the truest sense of the words, buy and sell, and get gain. Prov. xxiii. 23. Even now, then, they are supposed, by virtue of their union with CHRIST, and interest in CHRIST, to be on the daily look out for that morrow which shall call them home. They are GOD's property, and consequently GOD's care. And, as in this life, the LORD raiseth for them waters in the wilderness, and rivers in the desert, to give drink to his people, his chosen; Isa. xliii. 20. so in that blessed climate, where none of the inhabitants shall any longer say I am sick, there the LORD will give them living waters, and all tears will be wiped away from all eyes. Isa. xxxiii. 24. Rev. vii. 17. Reader, pause over the subject. GOD's sovereignty in the choice, is the bottom and everlasting foundation of all these mercies. Ephes. i. 4, 5, 6. The SON of GOD's betrothing his Church before all worlds, and the redemption of his Church in the time-state of her being, brings up the vast blessing, and places it on its own proper basis. Ephes. i. 7. And GOD the HOLY GHOST, by regenerating life, and grace, and unction, makes the redeemed suited subjects for glory in the inheritance, among all them that are sanctified. See Commentary, Ephes. i. 3—10. Oh! the blessedness of that morrow, when the whole Church shall enter into the gates of the holy city. They are GOD's chosen, *the first fruits of his increase and holiness to the* LORD. Jer. ii. 3. They are consecrated to his service, to be *kings and priests to* GOD *and the* FATHER: and all their holy employment in this city will be the gain of *durable riches and righteousness.* Rev.

i. 6. Prov. viii. 18. And, as the culminating crown of all, to sum up their unspeakable felicity, the nearness and union into which the whole Church, and every individual of it, as the spouse of CHRIST, will then be brought, is that of an everlasting communion with GOD and the LAMB. This *people have I formed for myself!* Isa. xliii. 21. Reader! is it your language? My soul! is it thine? When will that morrow come, when I shall go to this blessed city! *Haste, haste, my beloved, and until the day break and the shadows flee away, be thou like a roe, or a young hart upon the mountains of division.* Song ii. 17.

REFLECTIONS.

MY soul! while reading this Chapter, and hearing GOD the SPIRIT putting that solemn question to thee, *from whence come wars and fightings* in thy two-fold nature; a spirit regenerated, and a body of flesh virtually all sin: oh! bless that gracious, that sovereign, that bountiful GOD, who, by his quickening and illuminating power, hath opened thine eyes to the view of the awful state in which thou wert born in nature, and the distinguishing mercy manifested to thee in grace; and though still groaning under a body of sin and corruption, bless the LORD for thy redemption in CHRIST, by which thou hast gotten the victory, through our LORD JESUS CHRIST. And, my soul, see! that amidst all the wounds from sin, which, in the present warfare thou art daily sustaining, bless thy GOD and SAVIOR, the issue of the conflict is not doubtful. Thy GOD will give thee grace to resist the devil, and he will flee from thee. Thy GOD will enable thee to draw nigh to him, and he will draw nigh to thee. *Satan* knoweth that he hath but a short time. Let nothing keep thee from the throne of grace. Here all thy strength is found. Look to JESUS, who is both thy wisdom, and righteousness, and sanctification, as well as redemption. *In Him shall all the seed of Israel be justified, and shall glory.* And, do thou look forward with holy joy to the morrow, the day, even the great day of GOD, when JESUS will come to take thee home to his eternal kingdom. Let men of the world, from the world, seek their supreme joy. Yea, let them go from city to city, to traffic in the concerns of this world's good. Be it thy happiness to eye JESUS, even in the necessary things the body is occupied with here below. Soon thou shalt have done with all earthly employments, and the everlasting enjoyment of GOD in CHRIST will be thy portion for evermore.

CHAP. V.

CONTENTS.

The Church is here taught, in the Opening of this Chapter, the shortlived Enjoyments of the Wicked. GOD's faithful Ones are reminded of the Blessedness of Patience; and what precious Advantages arise from Prayer.

GO to now, ye rich men, weep and howl for your miseries that shall come upon *you*.

2 Your riches are corrupted, and your garments are moth-eaten.

3 Your gold and silver is cankered; and the rust of them shall be a witness against you, and shall eat your flesh as it were fire. Ye have heaped treasure together for the last days.

4 Behold, the hire of the labourers who have reaped down your fields, which is of you kept back by fraud, crieth: and the cries of them which have reaped are entered into the ears of the Lord of sabaoth.

5 Ye have lived in pleasure on the earth, and been wanton: ye have nourished your hearts as in a day of slaughter.

6 Ye have condemned *and* killed the just; *and* he doth not resist you.

When the Reader hath duly pondered the many solemn things, which are here said of the ungodly and unregenerate, if the LORD be his teacher, I venture to think that it will strike him, as it doth me, that there can hardly be a passage more tremendously alarming, to shew the folly, as well as sin, of the rich worldling, than what is here said. Nothing can be more clear than the LORD's design in it. The HOLY GHOST is all along writing to the Church. His sole object is the instruction and comfort of the Church. In doing which, the LORD seems in these few verses, but still wholly in the Church's hearing, and for the Church's good; to turn to the unregenerate, and in this rousing apostrophe, to expostulate with them on their extreme folly. The images are finely chosen, being taken from the things which worldly men make their idol. Their contemptible nature is strongly expressed. The cobweb covering, and the canker even of gold, not only testify their folly, but become witnesses against them in the end, in that they could not use them themselves, neither would let others who needed them. But let not the Reader mistake, as if this address was delivered in a way of persuasion to *them*, but wholly for the benefit of the LORD's people. Every part and portion in the word of GOD, is done with an eye to the Church. And whenever the LORD the SPIRIT steppeth aside to represent the final end of the ungodly, ordained of old to this condemnation, it is with the express design, to impress upon the minds of the LORD's redeemed ones, by such awful representations, the nature of that distinguishing mercy vouchsafed them.

7 Be patient therefore, brethren, unto the coming of the Lord. Behold, the husbandman waiteth for the precious fruit of the earth, and hath

long patience for it, until he receive the early and latter rain.

8 Be ye also patient; stablish your hearts: for the coming of the Lord draweth nigh.

9 Grudge not one against another, brethren, lest ye be condemned: behold the judge standeth before the door.

10 Take, my brethren, the prophets, who have spoken in the name of the Lord, for an example of suffering affliction, and of patience.

11 Behold, we count them happy which endure. Ye have heard of the patience of Job, and have seen the end of the Lord; that the Lord is very pitiful, and of tender mercy.

We have within the compass of these verses, some very precious views, for the child of GOD, and especially the exercised child of GOD, to ruminate upon: and, if the Reader will indulge me, and GOD the HOLY GHOST will teach both Writer and Reader, very sure I am, that we shall rise up from the review of them with much spiritual profit.

And, *first*. By the command to the brethren, who are regenerated in CHRIST, to be patient unto the coming of the LORD; the child of GOD is taught to expect exercises. There will be, there must be, many dark and trying seasons. And in those seasons, the best taught children of GOD will be hard put to it, unless faith is always in lively exercise, to trust GOD where we cannot trace GOD. The HOLY GHOST therefore begins this sweet portion, after he had told the Church in the verses going before, the sure ruin of the ungodly; that though their patience should be exercised, yet they should rest in this one grand and unalterable conclusion, *the* LORD *is coming*. And when he comes, all will be fully and clearly explained. Therefore, saith the LORD, patiently wait this time, and be assured of this one thing, the LORD's ways, and the LORD's heart, are towards thee for good in all things. Rom. viii. 28.

Secondly. Having gained this great point, and set it down as a truth perfectly clear and impossible to be questioned, that GOD's dealings with his redeemed in CHRIST, are full of love, and conducted with unerring wisdom; we are next taught, that the best way, and the only way, by which we can rightly interpret the LORD's dealings towards his people, is, to do as the husbandman doth, in waiting for the precious fruit of the earth. What a beautiful and striking similitude the LORD hath chosen to represent this sure harvest by, of the fruits of his everlasting love? What, to the human eye, apparently more unpromising, or more unlikely to bring forth, than when the seed is not only cast into the earth and buried over, but must absolutely rot and die before there can be any product. See John xii. 24. and Commentary. Such then is the harvest of grace. When the LORD hath totally thrown to the ground, and buried over all our designs, and plans, and exertions; yea, even to our prayers, as in the case of *Israel*, no answers have been given, and matters have appeared darker than before: (see Exod. v. throughout,) then most blessed it is, to behold, of a sudden, light rise out of obscurity, and hope against hope come in to our joy and delight? Reader! say, (if you know the Lord,) hath the Lord at any time, when bereaving you of earthly comforts, when withering your gourds, and breaking your cisterns, when stripping you like the oak of its leaves in the winter; you have stood, as in the midst of the forest, desolated and forlorn; hath Jesus, during those seasons of nature's sorrows, refreshed in grace your soul? Hath the Lord given you increasing faith, increasing spiritual strength, hath he blessed you with the more frequent visits of his love, opened to you his covenant, shewn you his secrets, said unto you, *Fear not, I am with thee, I have redeemed thee, I have called thee by thy name, thou art mine?* Surely, here is the fullest testimony to what the Apostle hath said, and encouragement enough to be always on the watch-tower for such manifestations of his grace, in the expectation of the coming of the Lord drawing nigh.

Once more. The Apostle beautifully sums up the argument, in proposing to the Church the example of the Prophets, and particularly in the instance of *Job*, by way of shewing the blessedness of suffering afflictions with patience. *Behold!* (saith he,) *we count them happy which endure.* Yes! The people of God do count the Lord's exercised ones under trial, when found faithful, as eminently distinguished with the divine favor. It is indeed a mark of the Lord's regard for them. They are thereby called to high dignity and honor. *Paul* told the Church of the *Corinthians*, that they were babes in Christ, and could not, from their tender age, bear the strong food of the Gospel. Children, truly and savingly regenerated, they were; but yet only children. 1 Cor. iii. 1, 2. But, when the Lord calls an old veteran in the holy army to sharp and trying conflicts, and blesseth him with strength in the battle, this is an high honor on the saint! And the Apostle saith, *Behold, we count them happy which endure.*

But what is the world's estimate of good? Alas! the very reverse. Ask men of the world, what they conceive a goodly portion? They will make no hesitation to decide, and decide so positively, as though their maxims were undeniable. We count them happy, they will say, which have all this world's good; riches, titles, mansions, and a profusion of all creature comforts. But, who shall cast the lot? Who shall determine with whom the advantage is? Reader! it is already determined, and God himself hath decided. It is hardly possible to read the xlixth Psalm, Job xxi. 13. or the lxxiiird Psalm, where the characters of the prosperous worldling is drawn in his full colors, without trembling. And when from the Word of God, we turn to the contemplation of the world, and behold such awful departures going on, from one generation to another, the child of God cannot but arise up, under all his exercises, how pressing soever to flesh and blood they may be, and say with him of old, *Blessed is the man whom thou chastenest, O* Lord, *and teachest him out of thy law, that thou mayest give him rest from the days of adversity until the pit be digged for the wicked.* Psalm xciv. 12, 13.

12 ¶ But above all things, my brethren, swear not, neither by heaven, neither by the earth, neither by any other oath: but let your yea be yea; and *your* nay nay; lest ye fall into condemnation.

13 ¶ Is any among you afflicted? let him pray. Is any merry? let him sing psalms.

14 Is any sick among you? let him call for the elders of the church; and let them pray over him, anointing him with oil in the name of the Lord:

15 And the prayer of faith shall save the sick, and the Lord shall raise him up; and if he have committed sins they shall be forgiven him.

16 Confess *your* faults one to another, and pray one for another, that ye may be healed. The effectual fervent prayer of a righteous man availeth much.

17 Elias was a man subject to like passions as we are, and he prayed earnestly that it might not rain; and it rained not on the earth by the space of three years and six months.

18 And he prayed again, and the heaven gave rain, and the earth brought forth her fruit.

19 Brethren, if any of you do err from truth, and one convert him;

20 Let him know, that he which converteth a sinner from the error of his way shall save his soul from death, and shall hide a multitude of sins.

I include the whole of these verses under one reading, for shortness' sake. The things here spoken of are too plain to need much observation. Prayer is here held forth in its own strong features. For that prayer which is awakened by grace, cannot fail to be answered in mercy. What the Apostle calls *effectual, fervent* prayer, means, in the original, *inwrought* prayer. And it is inwrought by the Great Author and Inditer of prayer, the HOLY GHOST. Moreover, it is in direct correspondence to the will of GOD, our FATHER. Rom. viii. 26, 27. And no less in perfect harmony with the intercession of the LORD JESUS CHRIST. John xvi. 13, 14, 24. The righteous man here alluded to, can be no other than CHRIST, who is, as *John* saith, our Advocate. 1 John ii. 2. *Elias,* that is, *Elijah,* is spoken of by name, in proof how far the efficacy of inwrought prayer will reach. But, that the answer to his prayers, arose not from any merit in himself, but wholly from being accepted in Christ, is evident from what is said of him, *a man subject to like passions as we are;* that is, born in the *Adam*-nature of the same fallen seed, of whom it is truly said, there is *none that doeth good, no not one.* Rom. iii. 12. See the history of the success of *Elias'* prayer, 1 Kings xvii. 1. and 1 Kings xviii. 41. to the end.

I beg the Reader to attend, with some degree of earnestness, to the two last verses in this Chapter, in order for the right apprehension. By the *sinner* here said to be converted from error, cannot be supposed is meant one that was before unregenerate, for the Apostle calls them *brethren*, and saith to them, if any of *you do err.* And though the Lord is pleased, sometimes in the first awakenings from sin, to use instruments for this purpose, yet, no where is it said, that these instruments convert. This is the Lord's sole work. Creating-work, and renewing-work, are both the Lord's. It should seem to imply no more than this, that if a child of God hath backslidden from the Lord, absented himself from ordinances, neglected the means of grace, brought reproach upon the cause of the Lord Christ, by his behaviour, and, for a while, seemeth to have gone back into the world; and if the Lord, so disposing, sends one of his faithful ones, whether a minister, or any other, after him, and under the Lord's blessing he is brought back to the footsteps of the flock, tell him, saith the Apostle, that he shall save a soul from death, that is, the dead and dying state into which he had fallen, and shall be instrumental in the Lord's hand, *to hide a multitude of sins;* that is, not his sins whom the Lord employs in this service, but the other's, whose sins lay before open and uncovered to every observer's view. That this must be the real sense of the passage, is evident from the plainest truths of God's Holy Word. The saving a soul from death, can belong to none but God. Neither can salvation be found, but in Christ. Acts iv. 12. And the conversion of the heart to God, at the first, and the recovery of the soul in all the after-falls and deadenings of it, belong only to the province of the Holy Ghost. But what a very sweet and gracious encouragement is this scripture to the Church at large, and especially to those who labor in the word and doctrine, to search, and seek out, as Jesus saith he will, and as Jesus certainly doth, by his Holy Spirit, the sheep of Christ's fold, in all places whither they are scattered, in the dark and cloudy day. Precious Lord! do as thou hast said! Ezek. xxxiv. 12.

REFLECTIONS.

In closing up this short, but sweet scripture, let not the Reader overlook the tender care and watchful love of God the Holy Ghost to the Church, in uniformly, from Chapter to Chapter, shewing the striking contrast between his people and the ungodly. While the rich worldling is bid to weep and howl in the awful prospect of miseries before him, the faithful, though poor in this world, but rich in faith, and heirs of the kingdom, are desired to rejoice in their exercises, and in patience to possess their souls, for the coming of the Lord draweth nigh.

But, precious Jesus! who can look to the Prophets, and holy men of old, gone before, for examples of suffering afflictions and patience, without passing through, and beyond the whole cloud of these witnesses, to behold thee, pre-eminent in suffering, as in nature. Oh! thou Lamb of God! thou didst endure, in the days of thy flesh, all that contradiction of sinners against thyself, lest thy people should be weary and faint in their mind. Oh! for grace, to eye thee in all, and to behold thee, as God our Father hath set thee forth, the Lord our righteousness!

And, no less, Almighty God and Father! be it thy Church's glory, to know thee, in thine own everlasting, unchangeable, and unceasing love, fully made known and secured in the person of thy dear Son, and confirmed, and sealed to thy Church by the Holy Ghost. Glory, praise, and power, be to the united source of all our mercies, Father, Son, and Holy Ghost, now and ever.

Farewell James! faithful servant of God, and of the Lord Jesus Christ! The Church of God, while blessing the Almighty Author of all scripture, for this portion also of divine truth, hail thee as the Lord's messenger, in bringing it to the people. Sweetly will all the faithful meditate upon it day by day, until the Lord shall bring them home to realize all the great subjects contained in it, in absolute enjoyment. Oh! for grace, to be always in the exercise of faith upon those rich promises; that we may be patient, have our hearts established, knowing that *the coming of the* Lord *draweth nigh.*

THE FIRST EPISTLE GENERAL

OF

PETER.

GENERAL OBSERVATIONS.

WE enter here upon a most blessed portion of the Inspired Word of God. Oh! what unspeakable mercies doth the Church owe God the Holy Ghost, for such an invaluable treasure! This is indeed so precious a part of the sacred canon of scripture, that in the most daring days of infidelity, none ventured to call its authority in question. But, Reader! do not fail to remark, that the most blessed testimony of God's word is, God's teaching by it. And thousands now upon earth, can set their seal to this Epistle of *Peter*, in having been taught in it by the Lord. And tens of thousands are blessing GOD for the instructions they once received from it, when upon earth, who are now in glory.

The Epistle is not addressed to any particular Church or person, and therefore it is called *General*. It should seem, that though *Peter* was himself a Jew, and once deeply entrenched in *Jewish* prejudices, yet, in his own history, under the LORD's grace to him, he learnt enough, before his departure out of life, to see very clearly, that CHRIST's Church was but ONE. *Peter* well understood this. Song vi. 9. And with joy, being so directed by the HOLY GHOST, sends his Epistle, with his Apostolic benediction, to the strangers scattered abroad.

The *time* when this Epistle was written, is not so perfectly known, as to speak upon it decidedly. Some place it as early as the year of our LORD GOD 44. And some as late as 65. The *place* appears to have been *Babylon*, from whence the Apostle wrote it. Not figuratively, but literally *Babylon*, the chief city of the *Chaldean* empire. All times, and all places, when and where the LORD the SPIRIT is pleased to raise up and send forth his servants, with what a demonstration of the SPIRIT, and of the power, do they come?

But the chief observations, in a general way, that we are concerned to remark in this place, is, the blessed contents of this holy book, in relation to doctrine. And here it must be said, that though short (according to our greediness for more) this blessed Epistle is, yet we have in it all the leading points of our most holy faith. The everlasting love of GOD, our FATHER, in his choice of the Church in CHRIST, before all worlds; the redeeming grace, and love, and mercy of JESUS to his Church; and the regenerating, illuminating, sanctifying love of GOD the HOLY SPIRIT; all, and every part of these foundation-truths, are most blessedly, sweetly, and powerfully set forth, through the whole of this Epistle. I will not in this place anticipate the Reader's expectation, by here entering upon them. My soul is looking forward, with much pleasing delight, of going over the several Chapters, and there to contemplate at large the precious features as they arise before us. The LORD give both Writer and Reader of this *Poor Man's Commentary*, if it be his holy will, a blessed opportunity! Do thou, Almighty Author of thine own most sacred word, *take of the things of* CHRIST, *which thou hast here recorded, and shew to us;* and refresh our souls abundantly with this feast of fat things, that *our hearts may rejoice, and our joy none take from us*. Amen!

CHAPTER I.

CONTENTS.

The Apostle, after opening his Epistle with Salutation, immediately establisheth the fundamental Truth of the Covenant in Christ, *and breaks out into an Hymn of Praise for the Divine Love. He shews, that Redemption by* Christ *is nothing new. He dwells most delightfully on the infinite Preciousness of* Christ's *Blood; and finisheth this first Chapter with an affectionate Exhortation.*

PETER, an apostle of Jesus Christ, to the strangers scattered throughout Pontus, Galatia, Cappadocia, Asia, and Bithynia,

Nothing can be more proper than the Apostle's putting his name and office, and the glorious Person's authority from whom he received his Apostleship, at the opening of this Epistle. This puts an end to all dispute. For when we read the divine truths contained in those writings, the mind is immediately directed to enquire from whom, and by what authority are these things said? Here is at once the answer. It is *Peter,* the Apostle, and especially called to the office of an Apostle by Christ himself.

The persons to whom *Peter* (directed by the Holy Ghost) writes, are the strangers, meaning God's *Israel,* scattered as God's *Israel* are scattered throughout the earth, that they may be gathered. Compare Jer. xxxii. 37—44. with Gen. xlix. 10. with John xi. 52. And these several provinces of proconsular *Asia,* were intended to take in and comprise all the places where the Lord had a people. See Matt. xxiv. 31. Reader! pause and consider. Is not this precious book of God intended for all the strangers by nature to the covenant of promise, who from everlasting were given of the Father to the Son, redeemed by Christ in the time-state of the Church, and through the Spirit are brought nigh by the blood of Christ? Ephes. ii. 11—13.

Do they not prove their interest in it, by the sweet teaching and application of it to their own state and circumstances? If all the children are to be taught of God, and from hence a child of God receives instruction, can any thing be higher, in proof, both that they are children, and herein learn divine teaching? Isa. liv. 13.

2 Elect according to the foreknowledge of God the Father, through sanctification of the spirit, unto obedience and sprinkling of the blood of Jesus Christ: Grace unto you, and peace, be multiplied.

Reader! the oftener I read this precious verse, the more my soul becomes impressed with the sublime truths contained in it. Was there ever a form of words chosen, or can be chosen, to express the plainest and most palpable truths by, than is here used; both to shew and manifest the existence of the three distinct personalities of the God-

HEAD, and their distinct office-characters, as revealed to the Church of GOD in CHRIST? What can more fully prove the joint operation of the HOLY THREE in ONE, by way of defining their distinct personality; and, at the same time, what more fully shew their oneness in all the essential nature and design, and in their merciful tendencies to the Church? Let us briefly consider each.

Elect, according to the foreknowledge of GOD *the* FATHER. This foreknowledge doth not simply mean that divine perfection which comprehends an intimate acquaintance with all things, and which hath relation to all that is past, present, and future; but fore-appointment, choice, election, purpose, will, and pleasure. And therefore hath a special reference to what is uniformly ascribed, throughout the whole scriptures, to the personal act of GOD the FATHER, in the economy of grace. The Apostle *Paul* hath a similar phrase, when speaking with peculiar respect to the personal act of GOD the FATHER, he ascribes the election of the Church of GOD in CHRIST to him. *According* (saith he) *as he hath chosen the Church in him before the foundation of the world.* Ephes. i. 4.

The next act of grace the Apostle takes notice of is in the same direct reference to the Person of GOD the HOLY GHOST: *Through sanctification of the* SPIRIT. Here is evidently included, the gracious work of the HOLY GHOST, under all the branches of his sovereign power, in regeneration; and the whole blessings of spiritual life, arising out of it. And, in this distinct agency of the HOLY GHOST, the Person, and GODHEAD of the LORD the SPIRIT, flowing from the same love and complacency to the Church as the FATHER, are equally and expressly ascribed to Him, as his own free, gracious, and sovereign acts.

The *third* enumeration of grace, is in reference to the LORD JESUS CHRIST, under the two great branches of his love to his Church, namely, his obedience, and his death, which the Apostle names by the words, *unto obedience, and sprinkling of the blood of* JESUS CHRIST. Some have ventured to make the application of this obedience, as if was meant the obedience of CHRIST's people. But not to mention that all the obedience of creatures are but *effects* of grace, and not in any part the *cause* of salvation; how highly unsuitable and improper would it be, to introduce any thing belonging to the creature, in the midst of those high and distinguishing acts of sovereign grace and mercy, which belong only to GOD, and which GOD in his threefold character of Person hath shewn the Church? Surely nothing can be more plain and self-evident, than that the LORD the SPIRIT, by his servant the Apostle, is here declaring to the Church the foundation truth of our holy faith, of the existence of the Three Persons in the GODHEAD; and that by these distinct acts of grace, they are known in the Church: and, that they have mutually entered into this Covenant-engagement with each other, for the accomplishment of those gracious works to the Church. And hence, the benediction which follows, comes from those holy Persons unitedly; which, if the obedience of the creature was admitted between, would render improper, *grace unto you, and peace be multiplied.*

If the Reader will indulge me one moment, to offer a short reflection by the way, as we go, I would say, on this blessed verse of

GOD by the Apostle, (which is an epitome, or compendium of all the precious things of our holy faith;) what a full and compleat provision is here at once made, by and in the Persons of the GODHEAD themselves, for the present, and everlasting security and welfare of the whole Church of GOD? The FATHER's choice, in which there can be no change. The SON's obedience and blood, to which there can be nothing added, and is of the same everlasting efficacy yesterday, and to-day, and for ever. And the HOLY GHOST's regenerating, sanctifying grace, renewing and making holy, and eternally keeping so, by which the chosen in CHRIST are blessed in time, and blessed to all eternity! Oh! the preciousness of this Scripture!

And, what a miserable going off from this everlasting Covenant, which is *ordered in all things and sure*, must that be, which some men are so fond of, but which none of them ever found could make happy; that these grand sources, act but as procuring causes, to bring men into an ability of doing somewhat towards their own salvation; that their obedience, joined to the sprinkling of the blood of CHRIST, may become the united cause of their acceptance. And thus, they make no more of the great and finished salvation of CHRIST, the regeneration of the heart by the HOLY GHOST, and the everlasting love of the FATHER in the choice of the Church, *to be holy, and without blame before him in love;* than that of vamping and brushing up the old nature anew, and sending it forth a second time, at a peradventure, that man's free will may join GOD's grace, and so the first disobedience of man by the fall, be repaired by the after good behavior of the sinner; and CHRIST and he share the merits jointly together, of eternal life and salvation? Reader! what think you of this? Would you adventure your soul upon it? Would you think such a righteousness as this safe to enter eternity with? Would you go forth at the call of GOD into the eternal world with a covering so flimsy? Reader! I know not what your views are: but I bless GOD that *I have not so learned* CHRIST. But in how many hearts such an error reigns, in how many congregations such an error is taught in this awful day, I leave with the LORD. Sufficient be it for me, to bear, thus publicly, my testimony against it.

3 Blessed *be* the God and Father of our Lord Jesus Christ, which according to his abundant mercy hath begotten us again unto a lively hope by the resurrection of Jesus Christ from the dead,

4 To an inheritance incorruptible, and undefiled, and that fadeth not away, reserved in heaven for you,

5 Who are kept by the power of God through faith unto salvation ready to be revealed in the last time.

I beg the Reader to observe, how the mind of the Apostle was carried out, in consequence of what he had just before said. No sooner doth he contemplate the elect of GOD, and the sanctified by the

Spirit, and the justified in the obedience and sprinkling of the blood of Jesus Christ; but he falls a blessing God and the Father, yea, the whole Persons of the Godhead, for having so blessed the Church in Christ with such abundant mercy and grace. The soul of *Peter* could not contain himself, in the view of such unspeakable goodness. His heart, like *Elihu*, wanted vent. Job xxxii. 19. Since God had so blessed the Church, *Peter* called upon every heart to bless God. The same is remarkable of *Paul*, in the opening of his Epistle. Ephesians i. 3.

And, let the Reader further remark, how sweetly the Apostle dwells upon the blessed work of regeneration, by which the child of God is brought into the personal enjoyment of all the privileges, both of election and redemption. *Peter* calls it God's *abundant mercy*. And very sure, it may well be called so. For abounding must be that grace, which, when in the *Adam*-nature of sin our souls lay dead, as to our own view, we were without God, and without hope in the world; then, to be quickened together with Christ, and begotten to this lively hope, and to such an inheritance. What but grace, yea, abundant grace, could have given birth to such mercy?

I will detain the Reader with one observation more, on these verses, respecting the inheritance. Not so much to notice the nature of this inheritance itself, or the properties of it; though these things might be, and indeed, under grace would be both profitable and delightful to meditate upon, being said to be incorruptible, and undefiled, and that fadeth not away; but I pass by these things for the present, the rather to call the Reader to that part of the Apostle's words, wherein he saith, that this inheritance is *reserved in heaven for you, who are kept by the power of* God, *through faith, unto salvation, ready to be repealed in the last time*. There appears to be so much sweetness, so much love and grace manifested by God the Father, to the persons of his people, in this reserving of the inheritance for them, that I do beg the indulgence of a few moments, to state the subject as it strikes me.

And, *first*. Nothing can be more plain and clear, from what is here said by the Apostle, than that He who so graciously elected their persons, as graciously appointed their inheritance. And hence one of those holy men of old, who knew his right in it, as if conscious that the one arose out of the other, blessedly, and thankfully said: *The* Lord *is the portion of mine inheritance, and of my cup; thou maintainest my lot. The lines are fallen unto me in pleasant places; yea, I have a goodly heritage*. Psm. xvi. 5, 6.

Secondly. This inheritance is reserved, and reserved in heaven for you, and you yourself are kept by the power of God through faith, unto salvation; and this is always ready to be revealed, when your turn comes, even if it be in the last time. Reader! behold here, what an accumulation of mercies are heaped up, one upon another, more preciously piled than all the gold of the miser. Here is the security of the inheritance, and the security of the owner; God himself becomes the garrison to defend both. And, whatever ages, or generations the Lord hath appointed to run out, before you, for whom his grace hath designed this mansion, shall come, none shall have it, for it is reserved for *you*. He that chose *you*, at the same time chose *your inheritance* in Christ, yea, Christ himself. And, therefore, as CHRIST saith: *Let no man take your crown!* that is, no man shall. Rev. iii. 11. Oh! the unspeakable blessedness contained in such a view founded in such a will as GOD's election-will, secured in such a purpose as GOD's finished redemption-purpose in CHRIST, and reserved in such an unalienable reservation as the being kept by the power of GOD the SPIRIT's grace, through faith unto salvation.

Reader! oh! beg for grace, rightly to prize your mercies. From whence do they all flow? Peter answers: *Elect according to the foreknowledge of* GOD *the* FATHER. How are they reserved? Peter again replies: They are *reserved in heaven for you, who are kept by the power of* GOD, *through faith, unto salvation.* Who secures them? GOD himself. For it is by the power of GOD both the person and the inheritance are kept. And, it is always to be revealed: for *when* CHRIST *who is our life shall appear, then will the Church,* in every individual of her members, *appear with him in glory.* And what is it but this, which in the present time-state of the Church, hath reserved the LORD's remnant in the earth, *according to the election of grace?* Rom. xi. 5.

6 Wherein ye greatly rejoice, though now for a season, if need be, ye are in heaviness, through manifold temptations.

7 That the trial of your faith, being much more precious than of gold that perisheth, though it be tried with fire, might be found unto praise and honour and glory at the appearing of Jesus Christ:

Wherein ye greatly rejoice; that is, in the sure prospect which ye have of possession, yea, even now, in the actual enjoyment by faith, see Ephes. ii. 6. of this promised inheritance, both by gift, and by purchase. And, though now sometimes hard put to it, by the temptations, and trials of *Satan* and the world, heaviness is induced; yet the consciousness, that the issue is not doubtful, but sure victory over all must be the end, bears the soul up in the strength and grace of CHRIST JESUS.

I beg the Reader not to overlook what the HOLY GHOST saith on this subject, (for it is a blessed testimony,) concerning the trial of faith, in the children of GOD; that it is *more precious* than of gold that perisheth. It is a sweet comparison, and most wisely chosen, to shew the superiority of faith to gold. For though gold, if it be *pure* gold, when put into the hottest fire, will *lose* nothing, and come out the brighter; yet it will *gain* nothing by the process. The same quantity thrown into the furnace, it will be well if it come out; more it cannot. But not so by faith. True faith, the faith of GOD's elect, will be increased tenfold by the trial; and the oftener it is tried, the greater both in quantity and in quality, it will become. Let the Reader attend to this distinction, and learn to bless GOD the HOLY GHOST for so gracious a testimony. And if he be a child of GOD, let him learn moreover, the great grace and condescension of a faithful GOD in CHRIST, in bringing him to such trials. My Brother! be assured of this one most certain truth: The LORD can never try your faith, but he affords you thereby an opportunity, both to try, and to prove his love and faithfulness. *David* knew this so well, that he cried out, under his sharp exercises: *I know, O* LORD, *that thy judgments are right; and that thou in faithfulness hast afflicted me.* Psm. cxix. 75. And you cannot but know, that every skirmish with the foe, the LORD designs for your comfort, and his own glory. Sometimes by enabling you to resist the devil, you are led to see, that he flees from you. Sometimes, when he comes in like a flood, you discover CHRIST's strength made perfect in your weakness; and the LORD the SPIRIT lifts up CHRIST *a standard against him.* Isaiah lix. 19. And even in those fiery darts of his which wound, and when in grappling with the foe, for the time the poor buffeted soul seems to give way, and fall under; even then, the soul, which is strong in the faith, shouts victory in the blood of the Lamb, and cries out, even as he falls: *Rejoice not against me, O mine enemy; when I fall, I shall arise; when I sit in darkness, the* LORD *shall be a light unto me.* Micah v. 7, 8. Oh! it is blessed, it is precious, yea, much more precious than of gold that perisheth, when faith is tried, though with fire. For the child of GOD is an infinite gainer, and the LORD GOD of his tried child will make it ultimately appear in the end, that his Almighty hand was in it, when *it is found unto praise, and honor, and glory, at the appearing of* JESUS CHRIST.

8 Whom having not seen, ye love; in whom, though now ye see *him* not, yet believing, ye rejoice with joy unspeakable and full of glory:

9 Receiving the end of your faith, *even* the salvation of *your* souls.

These are very sweet verses. The persons to whom *Peter* wrote, had never seen CHRIST's face in the flesh; and yet they loved him, believed in him, and rejoiced in him, as their hope of glory. And the Apostle saith, that by virtue of this inwrought faith, they did *now, in the present life,* receive the end of their faith, even the salvation of their souls. The Apostle talks of an absolute, immediate possession. They did, as the HOLY GHOST declares the Old Testament saints did, *by faith obtain a good report;* and proved, that faith is the *substance of things hoped for, the evidence of things not seen.* Heb. xi. 1, 2. They are said to be *receiving* the end of their faith, not as if to *receive* it another day. They are *now*, to all intents and purposes, in *possession.* They realize CHRIST, live upon CHRIST, enjoy CHRIST. All their views of CHRIST, are full of glory. Reader! bring this doctrine home, and it is as much ours *now*, as it was believers' *then,* if so be our faith is of the same operation of the SPIRIT of GOD, as their's. We have never seen CHRIST in the flesh. But we have seen more. CHRIST returned to glory: and GOD the HOLY GHOST, according to CHRIST's most sure promise, come down. And what is the effect? He hath given us to believe the record which GOD hath given of his SON. 1 John v. 10. And, doth not He who gives his people grace to believe the record, give with it the blessed fruits and effects also? Doth not GOD sometimes work in the hearts of his redeemed, a joy unspeakable, and full of glory, in the certainty of that glory, which shall be revealed? It is *unspeakable*, for their souls are sometimes so elevated with it, as for a while to be lifted up above themselves, above sin, sorrow, death, and *Satan*, that, like *Paul*, they hardly know whether in the body or out of it. And it is *full of glory*, for it is glory itself by anticipation. And why should it be thought incredible for the LORD at times to bless New Testament saints, less than He did Old Testament believers? Let those men, who would tempt us to alter scripture, and would teach us to call CHRIST's salvation not finished, abridge these enjoyments in themselves as they may; but let not the faithful in CHRIST JESUS be led away by such error, and fall from their own stedfastness. If the peace of GOD be a peace that *passeth all understanding;* so is the end of faith in believing, *a joy unspeakable and full of glory*. And, if the Almighty *Giver* of faith be, as He calls himself, the *Rewarder* of faith: Heb. xi. 6. here is the present reward as a pledge and earnest of the sure glory that follows; now *receiving* (mark the word, not to be *received*, but now *receiving*) *the end of our faith, even the salvation of our souls.*

10 Of which salvation the prophets have enquired and searched diligently, who prophesied of the grace *that should come* unto you:

11 Searching what, or what manner of time the Spirit of Christ which was in them did signify, when it testified before-hand the sufferings of Christ, and the glory that should follow.

12 Unto whom it was revealed, that not unto themselves, but unto us they did minister the things which are now reported unto you by them that have preached the gospel unto you with the Holy Ghost sent down from heaven; which things the angels desire to look into.

Reader! pray observe, what an honorable testimony the HOLY GHOST here gives to the Prophets, for their diligent search and enquiries after CHRIST and his salvation. And yet still more observe, how, and by what means, they were enabled so to do; namely, by *the* SPIRIT *of* CHRIST *which was in them*. Oh! the preciousness of this testimony of GOD the HOLY GHOST, to the GODHEAD of CHRIST! We can never be sufficiently thankful to the LORD the SPIRIT, for such tokens of his love. By his servant *Peter*, in this most blessed passage, and by a similar one in the third Chapter of this same Epistle, we have a double testimony of CHRIST's personal ministry, in those first ages of the Church. *Here*, it is said, that when the Prophets were searching, and enquiring diligently, concerning the grace that should come unto the Church, in the latter day dispensation; the SPIRIT of CHRIST was in them. And *there*, it is said, Chap. iii. 19, 20, that it was His SPIRIT which went and preached unto the spirits in prison, in the days of *Noah.* From both which passages, nothing can be more plain, than that it was CHRIST, both in the Prophets, and in *Noah*, which wrought in the acts of those ministries. CHRIST'S SPIRIT in the Prophets, and in *Noah.* And as *Stephen*, when full of the HOLY GHOST, explained, in like manner, of the ministry of *Moses.* *This is He* (said *Stephen* speaking of CHRIST) *that was in the Church in the wilderness, with the angel which spoke to him in the Mount Sinai, and with our fathers who received the lively oracles to give unto us.* Acts vii. 38, 55, 56. Reader! in the view of such palpable testimonies to the GODHEAD, and glory of the SON of GOD, are you astonished at what is going on around you, in marking the signs of the times, in the present CHRIST-despising generation? So am not I. By this same Apostle, the HOLY GHOST foretold the Church to expect it. *There shall be false teachers among you, who privily shall bring in damnable heresies, even denying the* LORD *that bought them, and bring upon themselves swift destruction.* 2 Peter ii. 1, &c. And, by another Apostle, the HOLY GHOST hath taught the Church how to explain the cause. *For there are certain men crept in unawares who were before of old ordained to this condemnation.* Mark, that Jude 4. there needs no Comment.

Let the Reader further observe, on this passage of *Peter*, that the SPIRIT of CHRIST by the Prophets, marked out two great volumes in the history of CHRIST, by which his Person and Offices should be known; namely, *his sufferings,* and *the glory that should follow.* On these, in proof, I need not dwell; for the Old Testament in predicting, and the New Testament in recording, their accomplishment, are full in testimony. But I pray the Reader, to notice, with particular attention, what is added, in proof of the LORD's mercy over his Church, that the ministry of those holy men, with all their diligence and earnestness, was not unto themselves, but unto us. Not that they themselves were altogether ignorant of the Person of CHRIST, and of both his sufferings and glory. For all that died in faith, saw, with less or more clear view, the *day of* CHRIST, with *Abraham afar off, rejoiced, and were glad.* But they had a revelation, that to us they ministered, meaning, the accomplishment would be in the fulness of time. And the Gospel is therefore said *to be preached, with the* HOLY GHOST, *sent down from heaven;* meaning, that the LORD the SPIRIT presides over his Church and ministry, and when he is pleased to bless his word to the people, he speaks to them by his inward grace, while their ears are engaged, in attending the outward word, as it is said. Acts x. 44. *While Peter yet spake these words, the* HOLY GHOST *fell on all them which heard the word.* Concerning the desire of Angels for information, and their ministry, I have already dwelt on this subject, Heb. ii. 17. to which I refer.

13 Wherefore gird up the loins of your mind, be sober, and hope to the end for the grace that is to be brought unto you at the revelation of Jesus Christ;

14 As obedient children, not fashioning yourselves according to the former lusts in your ignorance:

15 But as he which hath called you is holy, so be ye holy in all manner of conversation.

16 Because it is written; Be ye holy; for I am holy.

These are sweet exhortations, arising out of what went before. It is, as if the Apostle had said, if Angels are so much alive, as to be for ever prying into those things, which only as servants they have a command to obey, when you, as children and heirs of GOD, and joint heirs with CHRIST, have interest in, and fellowship with, see that you gird about your loins with truth; Ephes. vi. 14. and live upon that inheritance which is CHRIST himself, now by faith, as ere long you will in full fruition. And as all communications from the LORD towards you, are in a way of grace, and for the glory of his grace, and all is from the LORD himself, to himself; see that that life of grace is daily maintained, and kept up, and carried on, by constant communications from him. And, Reader! do observe, how the HOLY GHOST, by his servant, points out the method by which this life is preserved. *As he which hath called you, is holy; so be ye holy in all manner of conversation.* GOD's call is to holiness. And GOD's grace works in us this holiness in CHRIST, and from CHRIST. And hence, when he saith, *be ye holy, for I am holy*; this is not a bare precept, but the communication of grace enabling. He wills his people, into what He hath himself appointed. He worketh in them, both to will, and to do, of his pleasure. His grace is to this express purpose. And it is *to the praise of the glory of his grace,* when this is done. And which proves, that the work is his grace, and not man's labors, or man's merit; for then it could not be in either sense, *to the praise of his grace.* And, as it is on earth in grace; so hereafter in heaven in glory, the final, and full presentation of the Church is to himself, and for himself, to be *to the praise of the glory of his grace, wherein he hath made us accepted in the Beloved!* Oh! the unspeakable riches of GOD in CHRIST! See a similar precept of CHRIST, John xv. 4. and Commentary.

17 And if ye call on the Father, who without respect of persons judgeth according to every man's work, pass the time of your sojourning *here* in fear:

18 Forasmuch as ye know that ye were not redeemed with corruptible things, *as* silver and gold, from your vain conversation *received* by tradition from your fathers;

19 But with the precious blood of Christ, as of a lamb without blemish and without spot.

20 Who verily was fore-ordained before the foundation of the world, but was manifest in these

21 Who by him do believe in God, that raised him up from the dead, and gave him glory: that your faith and hope might be in God.

22 Seeing ye have purified your souls in obeying the truth through the Spirit unto unfeigned love of the brethren, *see that ye* love one another with a pure heart fervently.

23 Being born again, not of corruptible seed, but of incorruptible, by the word of God, which liveth and abideth for ever.

24 For all flesh *is* as grass, and all the glory of man as the flower of grass. The grass withereth, and the flower thereof fadeth away.

25 But the word of the Lord endureth for ever. And this is the word which by the gospel is preached unto you.

I include the whole of what remained in the Chapter after the former observations, having already far exceeded my limits to a *Poor Man's Commentary*. And indeed, what the HOLY GHOST hath here so blessedly set forth, though if followed up to the full, would furnish many volumes, yet may be comprized, in the leading features of it, within a small compass.

We have, *first*, the Church admonished, in their calling on the FATHER to keep in remembrance, in all their approaches to the throne, their safety and security in CHRIST, in whom GOD beholds the Church, and accepts the Church, as freely, fully, and everlastingly justified in CHRIST; and as holy in CHRIST *without blame before him in love*. And though the FATHER, without respect of persons, as they are in themselves, and considered without an eye to CHRIST, judgeth according to every man's work; yet the chosen in CHRIST by the FATHER is a personal thing; and GOD hath respect to his dear SON, and views the persons of his redeemed in Him. Yea, CHRIST himself was fore-ordained for this express end, and set forth by the FATHER, a propitiation, through faith in his blood. Pass, therefore, saith the Apostle, the time of your sojourning here in fear, that is, not in the bondage fear of servants, but the dutiful fear of children. Rom. viii. 15—17.

Secondly. Lose not sight of your oneness and interest in CHRIST, by which ye are not only betrothed to Him for ever, and that before the foundation of the world; but also have been redeemed by him, from the *Adam*-state of sin in which ye were involved by nature, during this time-state of the Church. And as ye know that ye were not redeemed with corruptible things, such as the contemptible idols of carnal men, silver and gold, but with the precious blood of CHRIST, as *of a Lamb without blemish, and without spot*; see to it, that this knowledge, and this conviction, be productive of all the blessed effects, in living upon CHRIST, walking with CHRIST, rejoicing in CHRIST, and making Him what GOD hath made him to the Church, which is his body, *the fulness of Him that filleth all in all.* Reader! mark the very sweet words of GOD the HOLY GHOST on this vast subject, and observe, how very strong the LORD hath worded the faith of them that believe in GOD by Him, *that your faith and hope might be in* GOD. Not that your faith and hope might be in your own improvements. Not in a work wrought *in* you, but *for* you; even centering both faith and hope in GOD. Oh! how sweet, when CHRIST is made in the believer's view as set forth in GOD's; and when received by him, as he is made of GOD, *wisdom, righteousness, sanctification, and redemption, that, according as it is written, he that glorieth let him glory only in the* LORD. 1 Cor. i. 30.

Thirdly. As in all the other parts of our interest in the covenant of grace, so here eminently the Church is taught her blessedness in the new-birth, from the power of GOD the HOLY GHOST, which, in common with the electing-love of the FATHER, and the redeeming-love of the SON, brings the people of GOD into the enjoyment of all their mercies, being born of that incorruptible seed which liveth and abideth for ever. And, hence, amidst all the mutable circumstances of our sinful, fallen, dying nature, which, like grass, is but of momentary continuance; this spiritual birth everlastingly secures the being, and well-being of all CHRIST's redeemed. They are born again, their adoption-character is thereby proved; and they are manifested to be the heirs of GOD, and joint heirs with CHRIST. Oh! the preciousness of these divine truths! Oh! the unspeakable mercy, when GOD hath revealed them to his people by the SPIRIT!

REFLECTIONS.

SURELY we have reason to bless GOD for the dispersion of his people, in that so much grace is manifested, and hath been manifested in their recovery. All which proves the original and eternal election of the Church by GOD the FATHER, the purchase of their redemption by the LORD JESUS CHRIST, and their regeneration and sanctification by the HOLY GHOST. And that sweet promise is confirmed in every instance, of a child of GOD brought back by sovereign grace, *Hear the word of the* LORD, *O ye nations, and declare it in the isles afar off, and say, He that scattered Israel, will gather him, and keep him as a shepherd doth his flock!*

And, Reader! shall we not both join the Apostle's hymn, in the conscious recovery of our poor fallen nature, by the resurrection of CHRIST from the dead, and in the assurance of that inheritance, incorruptible and undefiled, to which all his redeemed are begotten, and which is reserved for them in heaven, who are kept by the power of GOD through faith unto salvation; shall we not bless GOD for his unspeakable gift! And though in the way to our possession of this secured inheritance, there is a *needs-be* to meet with manifold temptations, yet, even these temptations, under divine grace, minister but to greater glory; and every exercise of faith becomes more precious than gold that perisheth!

Precious JESUS! thou art more glorious and excellent than the mountains of prey. And though we see thee not by sight, yet do thy people love thee, the fairest and the loveliest of ten thousand. Thy salvation, the Prophets spake of, guided by thy SPIRIT within them. Thy finished redemption, the HOLY GHOST hath given thy Church grace to believe, in the preaching of the Gospel, in thy presence and power, sent down from heaven. And while angels desire to look into these things, by way of discovery of their wonderful nature and extent, it is the unspeakable happiness of thy people to be taught of GOD, and to believe in GOD, that their faith and hope might be in GOD.

Oh! LORD the SPIRIT! thou who hast given to thy Church this sweet scripture, give to them the knowledge and apprehension of all its blessed contents in their hearts. And, since, by thy sovereign work of regeneration, thy people are born again, and brought into the knowledge and love of GOD in CHRIST, give them also grace to live in the daily enjoyment of their high privileges. May they have such a daily sense of the electing love of GOD, the sanctification of the SPIRIT, and the redeeming, cleansing, and renewing efficacy of the blood of JESUS, as to believing in the sweet communion and fellowship of the whole, as to be found, *unto the praise, and honor, and glory, at the appearing of* JESUS CHRIST.

CHAP. II.

CONTENTS.

This Chapter begins with an Exhortation arising from the former. A blessed Account of CHRIST *is given, both in the Beginning and Close of the Chapter. Very interesting Relations are made of* CHRIST, *to allure the Church to the Love of Him.*

WHEREFORE laying aside all malice, and all guile, and hypocrisies, and envies, and all evil speakings,

2 As newborn babes, desire the sincere milk of the word, that ye may grow thereby:

3 If so be ye have tasted that the Lord *is* gracious.

4 To whom coming, *as unto* a living stone, disallowed indeed of men, but chosen of God, *and* precious,

5 Ye also, as lively stones, are built up a spiritual house, an holy priesthood, to offer up spiritual sacrifices, acceptable to God by Jesus Christ.

This Chapter opens with an exhortation to the Church, from what went before. The new-birth, being confirmed in all its blessed properties, and the spirit being born into that incorruptible life, which liveth and abideth for ever, the people of GOD are here very properly called upon to testify the certainty and reality of these things, and that in a double manifestation. *First*, by laying aside all that evil conversation, and those evil actions, which marked the unregeneracy of their nature, while in that state. And, *Secondly*, in being alive to those holy desires after CHRIST, which are the evident tokens of the new-birth. I admire the beauty, as well as elegance of the Apostle's figure, in considering the new-born child of GOD as a babe in CHRIST. For, in the first awakenings of the spiritual life, every child of GOD, in his attainments, can be considered no higher. And a very blessed testimony it is of the new-birth, when the child of GOD desires the breasts of consolation; hungers and thirsts after CHRIST, and is longing more for the knowledge of JESUS, and communion with JESUS, than the babe of nature testifies its health in cries for its daily food. And, indeed, under the presumption which the Apostle makes, and which is the sure consequence of being born again, the soul hath tasted that the LORD is gracious; this spiritual sense, which belongs only to the regenerate, makes the child of GOD exceedingly anxious to drink deeper into the glorious truths of CHRIST, and his redemption. For the soul hath now felt somewhat of the plague of his own heart, hath had some views of the glories of CHRIST, and the suitableness of JESUS to his wants, as a poor sinner; and thus having known somewhat of his own emptiness, and CHRIST's all-sufficiency, the earnest longing of the soul is for the being satisfied with the breasts of consolation, and *to milk out and be delighted with the abundance of* CHRIST's *glory*. Isa. lxvi. 10, 11.

There is an uncommon degree of beauty in the expression, *to whom coming*. The words imply, not one act, but a constancy of action. It is as if he meant to say, *always* coming; and for this plain reason. All our springs of spiritual life are in CHRIST. And the stream doth not depend more upon the constancy of supply from the fountain, than the new-born child of GOD (yea, and the eldest believer, and, if possible, with increasing need,) doth upon the momentary supplies from CHRIST. Reader! do you know any thing of this in your own attainments? Blessed and happy are you if you do. Very sure I am, that it is a secret but little known in the present day. The greater part of professors, yea, and too many of GOD's dear children also, are calculating the state of grace in which they stand, more by their own feelings, than by what they are receiving from CHRIST's fulness. They live like bees in the winter, in their own hives, upon their own substance, and thereby make to themselves a wintery dispensation, instead of coming out to the sweet light, and life, and everlasting fulness of the Sun of Righteousness. Whereas the HOLY GHOST here teacheth the Church a more excellent way. By always coming to CHRIST, every day, and all the day, under a conscious sense of our own emptiness, and JESUS's all-sufficiency, *we receive out of his fulness grace for grace*. John i. 16. And it is a sweet life. They only know the blessedness of it, who so use CHRIST, as GOD in his rich mercy hath appointed him. For my own part, I love to feel my wants, and poverty, and leanness, that I may carry all to CHRIST, and make an exchange for his fulness, riches, and soul-renewing comforts. And very sure I am, that if I did not feel these things, but were puffed up in my own fleshly mind, the throne of grace would not be often visited by me. Oh! how truly blessed it is, when God the Spirit gives the soul a feeling sense of her poverty; then points to Jesus, who is all fulness, to supply; then leads the soul to Christ, and opens a communication with Christ, for the supply of every want, and the enjoyment of his all-suitableness and all-sufficiency. Oh! the loveliness of the Apostle's words, *to whom coming!*

The figure of a *stone*, and a *living* stone, in allusion to Christ, is uncommonly striking and just. As the first and last in the spiritual building, his Church, Christ is the Rock of Ages. And to intimate both the eternity of his nature, and the source of life to his people, he is called a *living* stone, having life in himself. And I leave the Reader to form his own conclusions, under grace, whether the very expression doth not carry with it the fullest conviction of the Almightiness of his person; for otherwise, the very term *living stone*, would be inadmissible. And I beg the Reader not to overlook the striking contrast between God's esteem of Christ, and man's, by nature. *Disallowed indeed of men, but chosen of God, and precious!* What can be more decisive, in proof of the natural enmity of the human heart by the fall! And what more blessed to a child of God, of having been taken out of the quarry of nature, and being built upon Christ, when become living stones, deriving life from Him, and offering up through Him, and in Him, the spiritual sacrifices of praise for redeeming love, coming up with acceptance before God upon the altar Christ Jesus?

6 Wherefore also it is contained in the scripture, Behold, I lay in Sion a chief corner stone, elect, precious: and he that believeth in him shall not be confounded.

7 Unto you therefore which believe *he is* precious: but unto them which be disobedient, the stone which the builders disallowed, the same is made the head of the corner.

8 And a stone of stumbling, and a rock of offence, *even to them* which stumble at the word, being disobedient; whereunto also they were appointed.

I need not tell the Reader what scripture the Apostle hath gathered this beautiful passage from. *Isaiah* was directed, ages before, to proclaim Christ to the Church under this strong figure. Isa. xxviii. 16. But, indeed, the whole book of God is full of the same glorious truth. See Deut. xxxii. 4. 2 Sam. xxiii. 3. Psm. cxviii. 22, 23. Ephes. ii. 20. But what I particularly beg the Reader to observe is, the beauty and fulness of the similitude. Christ, and his Church, his Zion is founded by Jehovah. It is the Lord, in his three-fold character of Person, which hath founded it. Isa. xiv. 32. Hence Christ, in his union of God and Man in One Person, is the *foundation* on which the whole building rests. He is also the *whole strength*, which unites, and keeps the building together. Believers are said to be rooted and built up in him. Coloss. ii. 7. And he is also the *finisher*, in whom, and by whom all the building, fitly framed together, *groweth to an holy temple in the* LORD. Ephes. ii. 19 to the end. And, if the Reader will pause but for a moment, and consider how very fully this is proved, as it relates to all the points of the spiritual building in CHRIST, he will discover the blessedness of the whole.

First. In CHRIST's Person. All temporal, spiritual, eternal blessings, are centered in CHRIST's Person. Hence his people, in him, are brought into a communion and fellowship by their union with him, into the enjoyment of those things; and, without which, there can be no blessing in either department, in the life that now is, or that which is to come.

Secondly. In CHRIST's offices. His obedience, and death; his law-fulfilling, and law-satisfying sacrifice; his surety-ship, engagements, and sin-atoning offering; his death, resurrection, ascension, and unceasing priesthood; all these, and every other which CHRIST wrought on earth, and is now carrying on in heaven, make him the whole foundation of his Church to rest upon, for all the purposes of time and eternity.

And, *lastly,* to mention no more: In CHRIST's relations to his people, he becomes the first and the last, to include all and every one of the tenderest relationship, which constitute the Father, Husband, Brother, and the Friend; so as to fill all, and perform the part of all, yea, infinitely nearer than all, being the Head of his body the Church, *the fulness that filleth all in all,* to the *members of his body, his flesh, and his bones.*

Reader! pause over the view; and look one moment longer before you quit this beautiful portion of the Word of GOD, and consider the different reception this HOLY ONE finds in GOD the FATHER's esteem, his people, and the world. In GOD the FATHER's esteem, he is declared to be the chief corner stone, elect, precious. Yea, GOD speaks of him as One in whom his soul delighteth! And so great, and holy, and gracious, that *he that believeth on him shall not be confounded.* In his people's esteem, he is so precious and so highly beloved, as to be the altogether lovely, and the fairest among ten thousand. But to the world, a stone of stumbling, and a rock of offence. He is despised and rejected of men. His Person, his offices, his humble birth, his obscure life, his mean death; yea, all that relates to him as the SAVIOR of sinners, renders him an object of scorn. Oh! thou precious LORD of thy people! how is it that I was made to believe in thee, while thousands reject the counsel of GOD against their own souls!

9 But ye *are* a chosen generation, a royal priesthood, an holy nation, a peculiar people; that ye should shew forth the praises of him who hath called you out of darkness into his marvellous light:

10 Which in time past *were* not a people, but *are* now the people of God; which had not ob-

What a blessed and honorable testimony hath God the Holy Ghost here given of the Lord's people. *A chosen generation!* Yes! chosen *in* Christ, before the world began. Ephes. i. 4. Chosen *for* Christ, to be his companion, spouse, and people, on whom he might make his love to shine for ever; in giving all that is communicable from himself here in grace, and hereafter in glory. *A royal priesthood.* Yea, *both kings and priests to* God *and his* Father. Rev. i. 6. Truly ordained by the unction of the Spirit at regeneration. And truly offering up their daily offerings in Christ, through the blood of sprinkling, which gives a blessedness and a savor to their persons and services, being accepted in the Beloved. Eph. i. 6. *An holy nation.* So God called his Church, when he first formed his people into a Church in the Wilderness, and when he declared *that they should be to him a peculiar treasure, unto him above all people.* Exod. xix. 5, 6. And, although they are scattered, and live as *the remnant of Jacob* was said to be, *in the midst of many people*, while unconnected with any: Micah v. 7. yet, altogether they form a numerous body, and are holy in the Lord. Levit. xi. 44. John xvii. 19. *A peculiar people.* Peculiar indeed! Their habits, manners, customs, pursuits, desires, differ wholly from all others, through the grace given them. They are, as *Joshua and his fellows, men wondered at.* Zech. iii. 8. And how should it be otherwise, being called upon by the predestinating love of God the Father, to dwell alone in his purpose, choice, and will, peculiarly chosen to an union with Christ; and specially the objects of the regenerating grace of God the Holy Ghost! And the effects which follow cannot but be the result of such a cause. He that called them from the darkness of the Adam-nature of sin, in that call brought them into the fellowship of Christ, who is himself their light and their life. And, as, while in a state of unregeneracy they were altogether unconscious of the electing love of God the Father, and the union-love, and redemption-love of Jesus Christ, and therefore in this sense might be truly said to be far off as those which had no head, and were not formed into a people; but now, by the renewing of the Holy Ghost, shed upon them abundantly through Jesus Christ, they were brought nigh, and made *heirs according to the hope of eternal life.* Titus iii. 4—7.

11 ¶ Dearly beloved, I beseech *you* as strangers and pilgrims, abstain from fleshly lusts, which war against the soul;

12 Having your conversation honest among the Gentiles: that whereas they speak against you as evil-doers, they may by *your* good works, which they shall behold, glorify God in the day of visitation.

13 Submit yourselves to every ordinance of man for the Lord's sake: whether it be to the king, as supreme;

14 Or unto governors, as unto them that are sent by him for the punishment of evil-doers, and for the praise of them that do well.

15 For so is the will of God, that with well-doing ye may put to silence the ignorance of foolish men;

16 As free, and not using *your* liberty for a cloke of maliciousness, but as the servants of God.

17 Honour all *men.* Love the brotherhood. Fear God. Honour the king.

18 ¶ Servants, *be* subject to *your* masters with all fear; not only to the good and gentle, but also to the froward.

19 For this *is* thankworthy, if a man for conscience toward God endure grief, suffering wrongfully.

20 ¶ For what glory *is it*, if when ye be buffeted for your faults, ye shall take it patiently? but if when ye do well, and suffer *for it*, ye take it patiently, this *is* acceptable with God.

There is somewhat very affectionate and endearing in this request of *Peter.* He calls the Church, *dearly beloved,* to shew the oneness and common interest which the whole mystical body of CHRIST, whether Apostles, or of the lowest of the people, have together. And by *strangers,* he means, strangers and pilgrims upon earth. Such should have their affections in heaven, yea, on CHRIST, carrying all their wishes and purposes, and desires, before them there. They are supposed to know, yea, they cannot but know, that the body of sin and death they bear about with them, while below, hath all its affections opposite to grace. And, under those impressions, to be always upon the watch over the fleshly lusts of the body, which war against the soul. And, above all, to seek the blessed influences of the HOLY GHOST, to keep the heart with all diligence, by whom alone the deeds of the body can be mortified. Rom. viii. 13.

The argument the Apostle adds to this, from the shame the ungodly will take in beholding the honest conversation of the LORD's people, is very striking. Though at present they speak against you, as evil doers, they are conscious, at the same time, that they accuse you falsely. And, therefore, in the day of judgment, those very actions of your's, which, contrary to their own consciences, they now speak against, shall be then their greater condemnation, your greater comfort, and to GOD's glory. What a spur this is, under GOD's grace, to encourage the redeemed of the LORD to an holy life and conversation? The precepts which follow in these verses are too plain to need any comment.

21 For even hereunto were ye called; because Christ also suffered for us, leaving us an example, that ye should follow his steps:

22 Who did no sin, neither was guile found in his mouth.

23 Who, when he was reviled, reviled not again; when he suffered, he threatened not; but committed *himself* to him that judgeth righteously.

24 Who his own self bare our sins in his own body on the tree, that we, being dead to sins, should live unto righteousness: by whose stripes ye were healed.

25 For ye were as sheep going astray; but are now returned unto the Shepherd and Bishop of your souls.

How very blessed is introduced here the person and actions of CHRIST! And, let the Reader observe, how CHRIST's death is first spoken of, as a Surety, before that his meekness is held forth as an example. I mention this the rather, because those wretchedly deluded men, who wish to rob the LORD JESUS of his glory, and, consequently, the Church of her happiness, in talking of CHRIST dying only as a martyr to his religion, and wholly as an example of patience to his people under suffering, bring forth this passage, as, in their view, justifying their argument; whereas, in fact, it is the reverse. For this very portion first mentions CHRIST's *suffering for us;* before that it is added, he becomes *our example,* that we should follow his steps. A plain proof that the *former* is the grand *cause* the HOLY GHOST first insisted on; and the *latter,* but as a sweet *effect* arising out of it. And when the whole volume of testimonies in scripture to this glorious doctrine of atonement is taken into the account, to what a miserable expedient must such men be reduced, who shelter themselves under such a flimsy covering for their unbelief? How fully CHRIST speaks of his giving his life, *a ransom!* Matt. xx. 28. How blessedly Paul also testifies of it. He *gave himself* (saith *Paul*) *an offering and a sacrifice to* GOD, *for a sweet smelling savor.* Ephes. v. 2. *Who gave himself for our sins.* Gal. i. 4. CHRIST *died for our sins, according to the scriptures.* 1 Cor. xv. 3. And this same Apostle, in the next Chapter, saith, that CHRIST *also hath once suffered for sins, the just for the unjust, that he might bring us to* GOD. Observe, it is *for* sins, and the just *for* the unjust. And how could either be, but as a sacrifice for sins, and as in the room and place of the sinner? 1 Peter iii. 18.

I need not tell the Reader, acquainted with his Bible, that the greater part of these verses is a quotation from the prophecy of Isaiah, liii. And who can read the account of either, among the LORD's people, dry-eyed, or unaffected in heart? The Prophet, as though he had been in the hall of *Pilate*, describes the sufferings of Christ as accurately, seven hundred years and upward before the event came to pass, with all the blessed consequences resulting from it. And, here the Apostle goes over the subject again, who was himself an eye-witness of it. 1 Peter v. 1. The close of the Apostle's account is very blessed. He considers the Church as sheep, and Christ the shepherd. He beholds them as having gone astray, like sheep, in the *Adam*-fall of nature, and now brought back by the recovery of grace. And what I beg the Reader not to overlook in this relation is, that they were sheep before they strayed. And they were Christ's sheep, given him by the Father, before he purchased them in redemption, from their *Adam*-wanderings, by his blood, and brought them back by his Spirit. Oh! the preciousness of this to my soul! Yes! through grace, I am now returned to the Great Shepherd and Bishop of Souls! His is a diocese indeed, over which the Lord exercises his Pastoral care, by watching over it night and day, lest any hurt his fold. Isa. xxvii. 3. But where shall we look for any other? Precious Lord Jesus! thou art the same still in heaven! Thou art our High Priest for ever, after the order of *Melchizedec!*

REFLECTIONS.

Blessed Lord God the Holy Ghost! since by regeneration thou bringest the children into their adoption-character in Christ Jesus, give me the daily influences of thy grace, that I may live and act up to the high character of my calling; and laying aside all the old corruptions of the old nature, of malice, and guile, and hypocrisies, and evil-speaking, as one new-born in Christ, may all the longings of my soul be after Jesus. Having tasted his graciousness, excite in me a thirst for unceasing enjoyments of him. And however my Lord becomes a stone of stumbling and a rock of offence to the world, may my soul be building upon him, as Jehovah's chief corner stone, elect and precious in Zion; every thing that is blessed for faith to rest upon, in life and death, in time and to all eternity. And, amidst all my weakness and unworthiness, and the slenderness of my faith, give me grace to attend to what thou hast here said, as a token of faith; *unto you therefore which believe, he is precious.* Surely Christ is more precious to me than thousands of gold and silver. And, therefore, my God saith, this is faith. Lord, *I believe, help thou mine unbelief.*

Precious Jesus! thy people is a chosen generation; God the Father hath chosen them, and made them so. They are from the same source, a royal priesthood, an holy nation, a peculiar people! And will not the same grace which hath so distinguished them, cause them to be distinguished also as lights in the world, among whom they shine in a crooked and perverse generation? That grace must be from thee, for all grace is in thee. Enable them, O Lord, to abstain from fleshly lusts, which war against the soul, and to adorn thy doctrine in all things. And while rejoicing in being delivered from sin, and all its tremendous consequences, by thy blood, may they follow, through the sweet influences of thy Spirit, thy example!

Yes! thou Almighty Shepherd and Bishop of souls, thou hast brought back thy blood-bought sheep to thy fold, and thou wilt keep them thine for ever.

CHAP. III.

CONTENTS.

The greater Part of this Chapter is Exhortation. Some few, but deep Things of Divine Truths, towards the Close of this Chapter, are touched upon.

LIKEWISE, ye wives, *be* in subjection to your own husbands; that, if any obey not the word, they also may without the word be won by the conversation of the wives;

2 While they behold your chaste conversation *coupled* with fear.

3 Whose adorning let it not be that outward *adorning* of plaiting the hair, and of wearing of gold, or of putting on of apparel;

4 But *let it be* the hidden man of the heart, in that which is not corruptible, *even the ornament* of a meek and quiet spirit, which is in the sight of God of great price.

5 For after this manner in the old time the holy women also, who trusted in God, adorned themselves, being in subjection unto their own husbands:

6 Even as Sara obeyed Abraham, calling him Lord: whose daughters ye are, as long as ye do well, and are not afraid with any amazement.

7 Likewise ye husbands, dwell with *them*, according to knowledge, giving honour unto the wife, as unto the weaker vessel, and as being heirs together of the grace of life; that your prayers be not hindered.

8 ¶ Finally, *be ye* all of one mind, having compassion one of another; love as brethren, *be* pitiful, *be* courteous:

9 Not rendering evil for evil, or railing for railing: but contrariwise blessing; knowing that ye are thereunto called, that ye should inherit a blessing.

10 For he that will love life, and see good days, let him refrain his tongue from evil, and his lips that they speak no guile:

11 Let him eschew evil, and do good; let him seek peace, and ensue it.

12 For the eyes of the Lord *are* over the righteous, and his ears *are open* unto their prayers: but the face of the Lord *is* against them that do evil.

13 And who is he that will harm you, if ye be followers of that which *is* good?

14 ¶ But and if ye suffer for righteousness' sake, happy *are ye:* and be not afraid of their terror, neither be troubled;

15 But sanctify the Lord God in your hearts: and *be* ready always to *give* an answer to every man that asketh you a reason of the hope that is in you with meekness and fear:

16 Having a good conscience; that, whereas they speak evil of you, as of evildoers, they may be ashamed that falsely accuse your good conversation in Christ.

17 For *it is* better, if the will of God be so, that ye suffer for well doing, than for evil doing.

It is a blessed and sweet testimony to the purity of the faith, in the lives of the regenerated, when, from Christ formed in the heart as the *cause,* all the gracious consequences flow as the *effect.* And where the hidden man of the heart, as the Apostle calls it, is truly formed; there all the relative and social affections, in the several circumstances of public and domestic life, will be the result. The tree made good by grace, in the renewed life, the fruit will be also good. But without this change of nature, by grace, after all the high-sounding commendations, which, from age to age, human philosophy hath said so much about, in praise of moral virtue; there can be no bottom to work upon.

I admire the Apostle's expression, *the hidden man of the heart;* and which, he saith, *is not corruptible.* And indeed, it is impossible it should. For it ariseth from the quickening, and regenerating work of God the Spirit; and, therefore, liveth and abideth for ever. The properties of it, in the source and spring from whence it flows, are hidden; but the blessed consequences, in the streams, arise above ground, and are seen. *The world knoweth us not,* (said John,) *because it knew him not.* 1 John iii. 1. Who shall say, how the Lord hath access to our spirits, so as to keep alive the grace he hath first imparted at regeneration; to excite and call forth the desires of the soul upon the Person, and work, and offices, and relations of Christ? Who shall number the incomings of grace, or the outgoings of the spirit; in prayer, in praise, in the longings after Christ, or the soul-embraces of Christ? These are transactions of the new born child of God; both in joy and grief, perfectly unknown to the world, and in which the stranger cannot intermeddle. The follower of the Lord Jesus, like Jesus himself, hath bread to eat, which the men of the world know not of; but which are in the daily feastings, of the hidden man of the heart, from the manifesfations of Jesus.

Reader! are you in the habit of these things? Do you know them? Yes! if so be the Spirit of Christ dwell in you. Then you can speak of this hidden man of the heart; and though hidden from the world, yet well known and sweetly enjoyed by you. And you can tell me also, that sometimes, what from the dulness and deadness of your affections, what from sin and Satan, the world, and numberless other thwarting circumstances, this life is hidden for the moment, from yourself. The holy flame, is not extinguished, for all the waters cannot quench it; but the ashes cover it from view. And what a mercy is it, that amidst such rubbish, as the best of men carry about with them, in the mass of sin and death of their bodies; the Lord keeps it, by his grace, still alive. The Holy Ghost sweetly assigns the cause by his servant, the Apostle Paul. *Your life is hid with* Christ *in* God. And hence also, the blessed promise that follows is made secure. *When* Christ *who is your life, shall appear, then shall ye also appear with him in glory.* Coloss. iii. 3. See Commentary also there.

If I pause over those verses, in which the Apostle speaks of the plain attire, and lowly deportment of the holy women, our venerable mothers in *Israel,* it shall only be to remark, with what grace they appear to our imagination from the account. I have often thought, that there is a sanctity in the very garments of those professing godliness, which rebukes the light and frivolous dress of the carnal. The mother of *Sisera,* however unconscious of it, paid a very high respect to the daughters in *Israel,* when, to the everlasting reproach of her own infamous character, she concluded her son (though gone, like *Judas* in after ages to his own place,) had robbed their industry. Judges v. 28 to the end.

18 For Christ hath also once suffered for sins, the just for the unjust, that he might bring us to God, being put to death in the flesh, but quickened by the Spirit:

On the interesting subject of Christ's suffering for sins, when he made his soul an offering for sin, and in which he acted, as the substitute and sponsor for his people, our souls may well dwell for ever. It is a subject to be begun in this life, but never to be finished to all eternity. The HOLY GHOST in this scripture, hath very blessedly explained somewhat of the manner of CHRIST's offering, when he saith, *being put to death in the flesh, but quickened by the* SPIRIT. I say *somewhat of the manner*: but our furthest researches, in the present unripe state of our spiritual apprehensions, can go but a very little way. I shall venture to offer my views of this difficult passage to the Reader. But I only propose them as mine, not to decide, but to enquire. Here, as in all other places of this *Poor Man's Commentary*, where there is supposed to be any obscurity, and the enlightened children of GOD, see through different mediums; I simply offer my views, but I leave the Reader, under the HOLY GHOST's teaching, to form his own.

And *first*. CHRIST *is here said, to be put to death in the flesh, but quickened by the* SPIRIT. Very little doubt can arise from these words, but that by the *flesh* is meant, CHRIST's *human nature*. And it should seem as plain, that as CHRIST alone is here spoken of, by the SPIRIT is meant, his *divine nature*; that is, his GODHEAD. And in confirmation, it should be observed, that CHRIST himself declared this, before his death; when he said to the Jews, *destroy this temple,* meaning the temple of his body; *and I will raise it up in three days.* John ii. 19. And the HOLY GHOST, by *Paul*, taught the Church of the *Romans*, that CHRIST was *declared to be the* SON *of* GOD *with power, according to the* SPIRIT *of holiness, by the resurrection from the dead.* Rom. i. 4. Had CHRIST not been a quickening SPIRIT, and had not his own power and GODHEAD gone forth, in this act of raising himself from the dead, his resurrection would not have declared him to have been the SON of GOD with power. We perfectly well understand, that as the offering up of CHRIST, was through the eternal SPIRIT, and all the persons of the GODHEAD were engaged in their several office-characters, in that high transaction; so we as perfectly understand, that all the Persons of the GODHEAD concurred, and co-operated, in the glorious act of CHRIST's, resurrection. See 1 Cor. vi. 14. John xi. 25. 1 Tim. iii. 16. But in this beautiful scripture now before us, there can be but little doubt, that it is CHRIST personally considered, who is spoken of; being put to death in the flesh, that is, his *human* nature, and quickened by the SPIRIT, that is, his *divine*. It is CHRIST only that is here spoken of.

Secondly. The subject meets us very blessedly again, in another view. The SON of GOD, having taken into union with himself, that holy portion of our nature, (Heb. ii. 16.) which contained in it, the seed of holiness, for every individual member of his mystical body, constituting the Church; and having offered himself an offering for sin by his death on the cross, he not only raised himself from the dead, by his own quickening power, but, at the same time, raised and exalted this holy portion of our nature, his own personal body, to the possession of all divine perfections. By virtue of his eternal power and GODHEAD, he communicated to this human nature he had assumed into union with his divine, a glory surpassing all creation. The scripture expresseth it in those unequalled words; *For in him dwelleth all the fulness of the* GODHEAD *bodily.* Coloss. ii. 9. So that in this mysterious union of Person, GOD and Man, CHRIST hath all the attributes of eternity, independency, sovereignty, and glory. For so it is written. *As the* FATHER *hath life in himself, so hath he given to the* SON *to have life in himself; and hath given him authority to execute judgment also; because he is the* SON *of man,* that is, GOD-Man Mediator. Not as the SON of GOD only; for, as such, nothing could be given him; because he possessed in himself, from all eternity, in common with the FATHER and the HOLY GHOST, all divine perfections. But it is as GOD-Man Mediator, whereby he hath *all power given him in heaven, and in earth.* See John v. 26, 27. and Commentary.

Thirdly. From the two foregoing statements, we next arise to a third, growing out of the former; in the blessedness of which CHRIST's whole body, the Church, is included; namely, that by virtue of this union, of CHRIST's human nature with his divine, JESUS, by his quickening SPIRIT, communicates to all his members in his mystical body, *all things that pertain to life and godliness.* 2 Pet. i. 3. For here lies the blessedness of the Church's union with her LORD. JESUS in his two-fold nature, not only possesseth this personal glory, which is peculiarly his own, and incapable of being possessed by any other, or communicated to any other; but, as Head of his body the Church, he hath a power to communicate all communicable grace here, and glory above, to the several members which constitute his mystical body. He hath, (as he said himself,) *power over all flesh, to give eternal life, to as many as the* FATHER *hath given him.* John xvii. And it is this, which makes JESUS so peculiarly endeared, and blessed to his people. Hence, as a quickening SPIRIT, CHRIST is said to raise our bodies, spiritual bodies, which by creation are natural bodies; and sown as such, when they return to the earth. So that, what was *sown in dishonor, shall be raised in glory.* For as in the first *Adam* of the earth, we have borne *the image of the earthy;* so in the second man, which is the LORD from heaven, and the last *Adam* so called, and who was made a quickening SPIRIT, we shall bear *the image of the heavenly.* 1 Cor. xv. 42—49. And this beautiful scripture, which gives so clear an illustration of the doctrine, is yet further explained, by another part of the sacred writings, where the HOLY GHOST by the same Apostle, in allusion to CHRIST as a quickening SPIRIT, saith, *He shall change our vile body, that it may be fashioned like unto his glorious body, according to the working, whereby he is able, even to subdue all things unto himself.* Philip. iii. 21.

Reader! pause, if but for the moment, to remark, what a world of holy joy and comfort ariseth out of this one view of CHRIST, as a quickening SPIRIT. How often doth the child of GOD feel, and groan under, the workings of sin! And how sweet sometimes the prospect of the grave is, where sleeping in JESUS, we shall lay down all the sorrows and distresses, arising from these workings of sin; yea, and all sin together! But here is a prospect of blessedness, even going beyond that. While we look to JESUS as a quickening SPIRIT, we look through the grave, and beyond it. Dying in union with his Person, we become the blessed dead, concerning whom, *John* heard a voice from heaven, declaring them blessed, because *they die in the* LORD. Rev. xiv. 13. And here JESUS, beheld as a quickening SPIRIT, secures their blessed resurrection, because, they who die in the LORD shall arise and live in the LORD. Hence, both living and dying, they are the LORD's. And the HOLY GHOST gives his gracious testimony to the same, as well as marks the vast change, which shall then take place. *He shall change our vile body, and fashion it like unto his glorious body.* JESUS, who quickened his own body, will quicken yours. It went down to the grave a *natural* body. It shall come up a *spiritual* body. It was sown in *corruption;* it shall be raised in *glory.* It doth not yet appear, saith John, what we shall be, but we know, that when he shall appear, we shall be *like him.* 1 John iii. 2. Like him, Reader! do not overlook this. Those vile bodies of ours, which by reason of sin, are so unlike him *now,* shall be like him *then.* And though we know not now, what we shall be, JESUS both knows now, as he will know then; and loves us now, as he will love us then. Oh! that every truly regenerated child of GOD would have this always in remembrance! What, though the body of sin and death distress you daily, yea, will continue to distress you, with its weaknesses, corruptions, and sins, to the last hour; yet when JESUS calls your spirit home, and leads your body down to the house appointed for all living, it shall then distress no more. How many of the LORD's exercised ones is JESUS daily, hourly, calling home, whose bodies called forth the groan but just before JESUS called home the spirit? Oh! for grace and faith, to be always in lively exercise, under the full assurance, that how unlike soever our bodies are to JESUS at death, we shall be like him in our resurrection. Amidst all that is unlovely, and unloving in our bodies now, they are still the property, and must always be the care of the all lovely, and all loving JESUS. His, is to preserve them through life, to watch over them in death, to quicken them at the great rising day, and to present, both body, soul, and spirit, to himself, FATHER, and SPIRIT, *faultless before the presence of his glory, with exceeding joy.* Jude 24. Let every child of GOD, in the prospect of this unquestionable truth, cry out, with him of old, and say: *As for me, I will behold thy face in righteousness. I shall be satisfied when I awake with thy likeness.* Psm. xvii. 15.

19 ¶ By which also he went and preached unto the spirits in prison;

20 Which sometime were disobedient, when once the long-suffering of God waited in the days of Noah, while the ark was a preparing, wherein few, that is, eight souls were saved by water.

21 The like figure whereunto *even* baptism doth also now save us (not the putting away of the filth of the flesh, but the answer of a good conscience towards God,) by the resurrection of Jesus Christ:

22 Who is gone into heaven, and is on the right hand of God; angels and authorities and powers being made subject unto him.

We have here, in the opening of this scripture, a passage, which hath been a subject, to various Commentators, of much perplexity. Christ by his Spirit, preaching to the spirits in prison, hath excited great enquiry, and, as may be well supposed, various opinions; especially among men, untaught of God. But wherefore should it be thought a thing more incredible that Christ's Spirit, should preach *before* the flood, than by his servants the Prophets *after*? The Holy Ghost assures us, by *Peter*, Chap. i. 11, that it was the Spirit of Christ which, in the Prophets, did signify, both his sufferings and his glory. And why may we not suppose, that it was the same Spirit which spake in *Noah*, when he preached the righteousness of Christ by faith? Heb. xi. 7.

It is really curious to observe, to what lengths, the pride of human wisdom will go, in those who have never learnt of God. It would tire my Reader to *hear*, much less would I wish him to *turn over*, the variety of opinions of the carnal, on this passage of scripture. Some have supposed, that Christ at his death, went into hell, to preach to devils, in order to induce them to repent. Others, that he went there, to liberate the souls of his saints, then there. Some, take the words as figurative, and with a freedom of thought peculiarly their own, make the passage to mean no more, than that of the preaching to the Gentiles. And others have considered the prison here spoken of, as the Ark; and that Christ, during the time *Noah* and his family were shut in, preached the Gospel to them. Reader! what miserable work do all men make of God's word, untaught by God's grace! If the Lord be our Teacher, surely there will be no difficulty, in learning of the Lord. And in this case, the passage before us, will not be attended with any obscurity. Nay, I think we shall discover in it, a beautiful and striking testimony, to *the truth as it is in* Jesus. Let us once more read the scripture, under this impression; and looking at the same time up to the Lord, for grace to teach; see what we can make of it.

And *first*. It is said, Christ by his Spirit *went and preached unto the spirits in prison*. Now, hence we learn, one grand undeniable truth; namely, that Christ by his Spirit, actually was in the Church before his incarnation; that he was engaged for his Church in personal acts, at the time here mentioned, before the flood; and that he exercised his ministry, by preaching in the instance here recorded. Now, how mysterious soever these things may be, (and how should they be otherwise than mysterious, to creatures such as we are,) surely they most decidedly prove, the Godhead of Christ. For, upon what other ground, can such things be said, or supposed to be done? Prov. viii. 22 to the end. John i. 10. Rev. xiii. 8.

Secondly. Those to whom Christ preached are said *to have been sometime disobedient, when once the long suffering of* God *waited in the days of Noah*. Now, this silences at once the foolish notion of those noted just now. Indeed, scripture is the best comment of scripture, and there we learn, from the 6th Chapter of *Genesis*, the truest particulars in relation to this disobedience of men. The old world had corrupted itself, and the Lord in determining the destruction of the ungodly, determined the preservation of the chosen seed, in the person of *Noah*. In the instrumentality of *Noah*, (as in the after Prophets, Chapter i. 11,) the SPIRIT of CHRIST preached. And as the HOLY GHOST bears witness, by reason of CHRIST's SPIRIT preaching in *Noah, he condemned the world, and became heir of the righteousness which is by faith.* Heb. xi. 7. Gen. vi. 3.

Thirdly. I beg the Reader, in as particular a manner as any, to notice how the LORD's distinguishing grace is marked in the person of *Noah,* and by the SPIRIT of CHRIST. *Noah* is the first person, concerning whom we read of grace And it is remarkable also, that the first time we meet with the word *grace,* or *covenant,* in the Bible, it is in relation to this man. Gen. vi. 8 and 18. And do not both refer to CHRIST? For who but JESUS is the *grace,* or *covenant* of his people? 2 Tim. ii. 1. Isaiah xlii. 6. And what was it but grace which prepared the *Ark,* or saved those *eight persons* in it; namely, Noah, and his Wife, and his three Sons, and their wives?

Upon the whole, then, I venture to hope, that this sweet scripture, (for indeed it is a sweet one, when opened to us by the HOLY GHOST,) will comfort both the Writer and Reader of this *Poor Man's Commentary,* when considered abstractedly from human policy, and brought under the standard of divine truth; *not as man's wisdom teacheth, but what the* HOLY GHOST *teacheth; comparing spiritual things with spiritual.* 1 Cor. ii. 13.

I shall not detain the Reader, with a long train of observations, on the close of the Chapter, having already so largely trespassed. But I would just beg to remark, on what the Apostle saith in application of the subject, to the present day of the Church, that baptism is called a like figure to the Ark; for both point to CHRIST, and are made blessed only in CHRIST. *Noah's* faith in CHRIST was what the *Ark* typified; and the baptism of the SPIRIT is what alone renders that ordinance profitable, being the representation of redemption in CHRIST. And the return of JESUS to glory confirms the whole work of the cross being done.

REFLECTIONS.

READER! what a beautiful illustration doth this Chapter afford, of the sweet effects of regeneration? All the relative and social duties arise from the work of grace upon the heart, as fruits from good seed, sown in good ground. And where the hidden man of the heart is found, there will be all the sweet properties of grace, in testimony, that GOD dwelleth in his people, by his HOLY SPIRIT.

Blessed LORD! diffuse the sweet influences of thy love, in the minds of thy redeemed; and in the contemplation of the example of JESUS; grant that there may be more of that SPIRIT of the LORD, reigning and ruling among thy people; so that by sanctifying the LORD GOD in our hearts, we may be always ready to give an answer to every man that asketh a reason, of the hope that is in us, with meekness and fear.

Everlastingly be adored and loved, the sinner's LORD, who died, *the just for the unjust, to bring us to* GOD. LORD! let thy quickening SPIRIT, be unceasingly working in our souls, to keep alive in us thy grace, in endless communication, until thou shalt bring all thy

Church, in body, soul, and spirit, to the everlasting enjoyment of our God in glory. Let there be no prison frame to thy people; but as thou art gone into heaven, and all power thine, for thy redeemed upon earth; let every thought of ours, be subject unto thee here below, as all authorities and powers, are subject unto thee above.

CHAP. IV.

CONTENTS.

This Chapter is full of Exhortations. In proposing to the Church, as an Object of unceasing Love, the Lord Jesus Christ; *the People are tenderly invited to follow the* Lord *in the Regeneration.*

FORASMUCH then as Christ hath suffered for us in the flesh, arm yourselves likewise with the same mind: for he that hath suffered in the flesh hath ceased from sin;

2 That he no longer should live the rest of *his* time in the flesh to the lusts of men, but to the will of God.

3 For the past time of *our* life may suffice us to have wrought the will of the Gentiles, when we walked in lasciviousness, lusts, excess of wine, revellings, banquetings, and abominable idolatries:

4 Wherein they think it strange that ye run not with them to the same excess of riot, speaking evil of *you*:

5 Who shall give account to him that is ready to judge the quick and the dead.

6 For for this cause was the gospel preached also to them that are dead, that they might be judged according to men in the flesh, but live according to God in the spirit.

7 But the end of all things is at hand: be ye therefore sober, and watch unto prayer.

8 And above all things have fervent charity among yourselves; for charity shall cover the multitude of sins.

9 Use hospitality one to another without grudging.

10 As every man hath received the gift, *even so* minister the same one to another, as good stewards of the manifold grace of God.

11 If any man speak, *let him speak* as the oracles of God; if any man minister, *let him do it* as of the ability which God giveth: that God in all things may be glorified through Jesus Christ, to whom be praise and dominion for ever and ever. Amen.

Certainly there are no arguments, in a way of persuasion, equal to those, which are drawn from the view of the love of CHRIST to his Church; and especially as manifested towards the Church in CHRIST's sufferings and death. And when GOD the HOLY GHOST, sweetly blends his grace with his word, the child of GOD, cannot but feel the persuasiveness of it, on his soul. We have in this Chapter, some very blessed directions, of the HOLY GHOST, to this amount. And, Reader! why may we not hope, that He who so affectionately recommends, will as effectually give his blessing; and work in us, both *to will, and to do, of his good pleasure?*

And, perhaps, of all the arguments, within the compass of these verses, there is not one, which comes home to the soul, of the regenerated with more endearedness, than that of CHRIST's having suffered for us in the flesh, that we no longer should live to ourselves, but to him. JESUS having all fulness, emptied himself for his people. And when redemption-work was finished, and he returned to glory, yet will he now not consider himself again filled, until the whole purposes of his sufferings and death be answered. If it could be supposed possible for one of CHRIST's little ones to remain behind, in the ruins of this world, JESUS could not consider himself completely blessed without him. He must have his members by tale and number. The flocks must all pass under the hand of him *that telleth them.* Jerem. xxxiii. 13. Reader! what think you of being armed with the same mind. Can we be content without CHRIST? Will a fulness of the creature, a fulness of ordinances, a full house, a full table, yea heaven itself, and JESUS not there, would these satisfy?

I detain the Reader no longer over these verses, (for they are all too plain to need a Comment,) than just to observe, how blessedly the direction is given, for the ministering to GOD's glory, by all the redeemed, whether private believers, or public preachers, when they are called upon to do it, according to the ability which GOD giveth. And the reason is, because GOD must give in to his people grace, before that they can give out to Him praise. But when the heart is turned in all its chords, with GOD's love, then, and not before, the true melody of the soul will vibrate on every string. The soul wound up to praise, is in perfect harmony with the numberless chaunts of old saints, and finds CHRIST, and enjoys CHRIST in every one. *I will love thee,* he will say, *O* LORD *my strength. I will extol thee my* GOD *and King. I will bless thy Name for ever and ever.* If the Reader would desire hymns to this purpose, the Bible is full of them. Exod. xv. 11. Psm. xviii. Psm. xli. 13. Isaiah xxv. 1. Psm. civ. 33, 34. On the subject of *covering a multitude of sins,* see James v. 20. and Commentary.

12 ¶ Beloved, think it not strange concerning the fiery trial which is to try you, as though some strange thing happened unto you.

13 But rejoice, inasmuch as ye are partakers of Christ's sufferings; that, when his glory shall be revealed, ye may be glad also with exceeding joy.

14 If ye be reproached for the name of Christ, happy *are ye;* for the spirit of glory and of God resteth upon you: on their part he is evil spoken of, but on your part he is glorified.

15 But let none of you suffer as a murderer, or *as* a thief, or *as* an evildoer, or as a busybody in other men's matters.

16 Yet if *any man suffer* as a Christian, let him not be ashamed; but let him glorify God on this behalf.

17 For the time *is come* that judgement must begin at the house of God: and if *it* first *begin* at us, what shall the end *be* of them that obey not the gospel of God?

18 And if the righteous scarcely be saved, where shall the ungodly and the sinner appear?

19 Wherefore let them that suffer according to the will of God commit the keeping of their souls *to him* in well doing, as unto a faithful Creator.

It is probable the Apostle had in view, the ruin of *Jerusalem* when he thus spake; which, according to our LORD's prophecy concerning it, was then drawing nigh, and which was afterwards most awfully accomplished. All that is here said, of their being reproached for CHRIST, and the time being come of judgment, beginning at *Jerusalem,* in the temple, that is, the house of GOD, literally took place. But the directions will, in a greater or lesser degree, suit the Church of CHRIST in all ages. And our holy faith hath the sweetest, and most compleat consolations in JESUS himself, for the support of all his people. I do not think it necessary in this place to go over them again, or to offer any other. But I shall beg to dwell upon one of the Apostle's observations in this paragraph, which, perhaps, may not be so generally understood, but which may be profitable, under-

The Apostle, having stated some of the very trying exercises which he foresaw would take place in the Church, and among the LORD's people, observes, that if such be the chastisements of GOD on his redeemed, which were all to sanctify, and not to expiate; he demands, in a solemn manner, what must be the awful destruction of the despisers of the Gospel, on whom these punishments would fall in a way of judgment, unmingled with mercy? For, saith he, *And if the righteous scarcely be saved, where shall the ungodly and the sinner appear?* It is this passage I would beg the Reader to indulge me with offering a few observations upon.

In the Proverbs of *Solomon*, we find somewhat similar, in a comparative statement, of the godly, and the irreligious; from whence, it is probable, the Apostle might take the expression. *Behold, the righteous shall be recompensed in the earth; much more the wicked and the sinner.* Prov. xi. 31. If both were recompensed according to their deserts, and without an eye to CHRIST, sad would be the best of them. But in our apprehension of these words by the Apostle, we must interpret them by the standard of scripture; *comparing*, as the HOLY GHOST saith, *spiritual things with spiritual.* 1 Cor. ii. 13.

When it is said, *if the righteous scarcely be saved;* by which, if meant the righteous in CHRIST, (and no other can be meant, because salvation is in no other: Acts iv. 12.) it is not intended to say, that any doubt, or fear, can arise, concerning their salvation, as to the certainty of it. For the scripture uniformly asserts, from beginning to end, the glory and security of that everlasting Covenant, which is *ordered in all things and sure.* And *Israel* is said to be *saved in the* LORD *with an everlasting salvation, and shall not be ashamed nor confounded, world without end.* Isaiah xlv. 17. Neither is it intended to convey the least idea, as if the Church of CHRIST, or any individual of the Church, was in so critical a situation, that he doth but just escape, and, as *Job* saith, with *the skin of his teeth.* Job xix. 20. For such is the fulness, greatness, and almightiness of the salvation, as it is in CHRIST, that there is a redundancy of merit in it, which never can be fully recompensed to the Church of JESUS, so as to say, there is no more to receive, and it is now fully paid; no, not to all eternity. And, such is the finished salvation the LORD JESUS hath wrought out, and brought in, and which is to all, and upon all that believe; that neither sin nor *Satan,* neither law nor justice, neither death, hell, nor the grave, neither the world that now is, or that which is to come, can bring a single charge against GOD's elect; for it is CHRIST *that hath died, and it is* GOD *that justifieth, who is he that condemneth?* Rom. viii.

What then did the Apostle mean? Surely he meant to shew the preciousness of the salvation. None but CHRIST could save them. And CHRIST not without blood. Had CHRIST not undertaken it, there was none other. And is it not very properly called the righteous *scarcely* saved; when it be considered, that had JESUS declined it, had JESUS put the cup of trembling from him instead of drinking it to the dregs, had the apprehension of the load of sin, the cataracts of his FATHER's indignation, and the vials of his FATHER's wrath, the fiery darts of *Satan,* and the baseness of his people's ingratitude; had these kept the SON of GOD from his purpose, our souls must have been kept from redemption; and, therefore, the HOLY GHOST graciously reminds us of the preciousness of CHRIST, and his love, in the scarcity of a redemption, which none but himself could accomplish!

Reader! ponder well the subject, and then echo to the question, the trembling question of the Apostle, and which none can answer: *where shall the ungodly and the sinner appear? Oh! hear ye this, all ye that forget GOD; lest he pluck you away, and there be none to deliver you?*

The Chapter closeth very sweetly and blessedly. To commit the keeping of the soul to GOD, in well doing, as unto a faithful Creator, is an act of great faith and grace; and none but the Almighty Author of both, can enable the child of GOD so to do. It not only relates to a dying hour, but every living hour, and especially the trying hour. The Apostle is evidently alluding to the fiery trial, and the time of persecution he had just before spoken of, when judgment would begin at the house of GOD. But it suits all times and seasons; and all cases of the LORD's people. And, I pray the Reader to notice the peculiarity of the title given to the LORD, of *a faithful Creator*, as the ground of sure confidence, for the safe committing the soul into his Almighty hand. *A faithful Creator!* What! is GOD as Creator, called upon to be faithful? Did not man, by transgression, forfeit all the promises made at his original creation? Yes! most certainly he did. But the Apostle is looking to GOD, in the character of a faithful GOD, on the *new creation* in CHRIST JESUS; and here he holds GOD to his faithfulness, in Covenant-promises in CHRIST JESUS. See, Reader! the strength of the argument, on this most sure ground. And it is not in my view, the smallest beauty and blessedness of this scripture, that GOD, in his threefold character of Person, is fully engaged by this glorious name, of *a faithful Creator*, to the fulfilment of all his Covenant-promises. GOD the FATHER justly claims the glory of creation. Isaiah xlii. 5. GOD the SON hath the same glorious work ascribed to him; *for without him was not any thing made that was made.* John i. 3. And GOD the HOLY GHOST was equally engaged in the *old creation*, when JEHOVAH, by the WORD of the LORD, made the heavens, and all the host of them, by the Breath, or SPIRIT of his mouth. Psm. xxxiii. 6. And, in the *new creation*, it is GOD the HOLY GHOST, by regeneration, that quickens the souls of the people, which were before *dead in trespasses and sins*. Ephes. ii. 1. Very blessedly, therefore, both in life and death, in times of comfort, or times of persecution, all the regenerated of the LORD may contemplate this Covenant-GOD; and *commit their souls into him in well-doing, as unto a faithful Creator.*

REFLECTIONS.

BE faithful followers of JESUS! what can arm you for the fight, and holy warfare equal to constant, firm, unshaken views of JESUS, and his unequalled sufferings? And look forward to the sure, and not very distant hour, when you will cease from suffering, and for ever cease from sin! Enough of transgression hath indeed marked our lives while we were in a state of unregeneracy. Oh! that the days to come may be marked with grace, for the end of all things is at hand; and, therefore, may we always be seeking strength from the LORD, to wait on the LORD, and to watch in prayer.

Precious Jesus! do thou prepare all thy redeemed for every fiery trial, and for every conflict. Thy presence will make even the wilderness and the solitary place to blossom as the rose. And, oh! the blessedness of reproach, when it is truly for thy sake. But do thou, Lord, keep all thy little ones from every thing of evil, which might bring reproach on thy blessed cause. Let there be no temptation to dishonesty suffered to prevail over thy people, and still less to cruelty and evil doing. But to all the unjust sufferings of thy redeemed, may we learn to glorify God on this behalf. And, oh! blessed Lord, grant all thy martyrs, like *Stephen*, to die in the full enjoyment of faith, and in and through thee, to commit their souls into thy hands, as *unto a faithful Creator!*

CHAP. V.

CONTENTS.

The Apostle closeth his Epistle with this Chapter: and a blessed Close it is. As an Elder himself, he calleth upon the Elders, to feed Christ's *Flock; and both Elder and Younger to be in the Affection of Brethren.* Peter *speaks very delightfully on the* God *of all Grace, and ends with his Apostolic Blessing.*

THE elders which are among you I exhort, who am also an elder, and a witness of the sufferings of Christ, and also a partaker of the glory that shall be revealed:

2 Feed the flock of God which is among you, taking the oversight *thereof*, not by constraint, but willingly; not for filthy lucre, but of a ready mind;

3 Neither as being lords over *God's* heritage, but being ensamples to the flock.

4 And when the chief Shepherd shall appear, ye shall receive a crown of glory that fadeth not away.

There is somewhat very affecting in the Apostle's account of himself, at the opening of this Chapter, in that he calls himself an Elder, and a Witness of the sufferings of Christ, and also a partaker of the glory that shall be revealed. We feel the expressions the more, because it is impossible but to connect with them our knowledge of what Jesus hath said to *Peter*, signifying what death he should die; and now behold the aged Apostle drawing nigh the time. John xxi. 19. The Reader will not overlook, with what delight the hoary saint mentions his being a witness of Christ's sufferings, and a partaker in all the communicable parts of Christ's glory. And, I mention this the rather, because it is one of the great points of faith,

Men of a yea and nay gospel may, and indeed cannot but be, halting between two opinions. The peradventure life, must be a peradventure death. But not so the truly regenerated and faithful. Our father's names would not have been handed down to us with such honorable testimony, had they so lived, and so died. Instead of being to us *a cloud of witnesses*, they would then have proved as the wife of *Lot, pillars of salt*: Heb. xii. 1. Gen. xix. 28. Reader! do not too hastily pass this by. I say, and the word of God will bear me out in what I say, it is the faith of God's elect, *to know the truth, and the truth to make them free.* John viii. 31, 32. And, wherever God the Holy Ghost hath savingly called any of his children by grace, they are supposed to be justified freely, to have *daily access in the grace wherein they stand, and to rejoice in hope of the glory of* God. Rom. v. 1—5. Hence *Paul* founded his confidence. Philip. i. 6. 2 Tim. iv. 6—8. Hence *John* his. 1 John v. 19, 20. And hence *Peter* his. A witness for Christ, and having a sure hope of being *a partaker of the glory that shall be revealed.*

I hardly think it necessary to remark to the Reader, how much the words of Christ were in the mind of *Peter*, since he useth almost the same words which Jesus did to him, in recommending the most endeared attention to Christ's flock. John xxi. 16, &c. It would form the substance of a distinct volume, to shew what may be supposed to be implied under the expression, of feeding Christ's Church, which is called his flock; and in how many ways it is capable of being performed. Feeding is a comprehensive term, for the whole service of the ministry. To watch over the flock, to know their persons, have an acquaintance with their spiritual state and circumstances, to administer ordinances, to go in and out before the fold, to visit the sick, to comfort those that mourn, to pray *with* the people, and to pray *for* them; and, like Jesus himself, whose glorious example they are supposed to have always in view, to bear as our Great High Priest doth, the whole sheep-fold in the arms of faith and love before the throne, and watch in prayer for kind answers of peace; these are among the daily ordinary employments of the ministry. And, he that knows or considers the arduous and difficult nature of the employment, would rather shrink from the call, than run unsent. To engage in it for filthy lucre sake, must argue the most insensible mind, or the most hardened. And, as to the idea of rank and dignity in temporal distinction from the office; never, surely, could the Apostles of Christ have conceived the possibility of such a thing, who when receiving ordination from their Bishop, were taught to expect nothing but obloquy and reproach from men, for their services; and whose general precept was, when *persecuted in one city, to flee to another.* Matt. x. 23. *Neither* (saith he) *being lords over* God's *heritage.* The Lord's heritage or *portion is his people:* (we read, Deut. xxxii. 9.) *Jacob is the lot of his inheritance.* And a most gracious instance of condescending love it is, in the Lord to consider his Church, his fold, in so endearing a manner. He is, indeed, the Lord of it. But it is a perversion of names, to talk of any other lord over it, among men, whose highest dignity, when found faithful, is to be *servants* to the household of faith, *for* Jesus's sake. 2 Cor. iv. 5.

The crown of glory the Apostle speaks of, which the under pastors in the fold are to receive, when the Chief Shepherd shall appear; must not be considered under the idea of reward. All is of grace, free, rich, unmerited grace. And, indeed, if the Reader carefully observes the Apostle's words he will find, that nothing like a recompence is mentioned. The highest and best servant in the LORD's house, whether Apostles, Prophets, or Evangelists, Pastors, or Teachers, have no claim to reward; yea, from the multitude of errors and neglects which have mingled with their best performances, need pardon for all. And very blessedly JESUS hath taught as much, in one of his beautiful discourses: *Which of you* (said CHRIST) *having a servant plowing, or feeding cattle, will say unto him by and by, when he is come from the field, Go, and sit down to meat? And will not rather say unto him, make ready wherewith I may sup, and gird thyself, and serve me, till I have eaten and drunken; and afterward thou shalt eat and drink. Doth he thank that servant because he did the things that were commanded him? I trow not. So likewise ye, when ye shall have done all these things which are commanded you, say, We are unprofitable servants: we have done that which was our duty to do.* Luke xvii. 7—10. Who that reads this statement of CHRIST with an understanding heart, will evermore talk of rewards from the LORD for services? But, on the other hand, who that reads what the same LORD hath said by his servant the Prophet, of neglect in the office of the ministry, and is conscious of coming under such an awful character, but must tremble for the eventual consequences? See Ezek. xxxiv. throughout.

Great Shepherd of thy blood-bought sheep! What a relief is it to the mind of thy most diligent under-pastors in thy fold, that amidst all the negligence, and wretched services of men, thy flock shall not, in a single instance, be overlooked, or go unfed, of GOD. JESUS himself will feed his flock like a Shepherd! He himself is, and will be their pasture. He saith himself, *Behold I, even I, will both search my sheep, and seek them out!* LAMB of GOD! that art in the midst of the throne, do as thou hast said! Look on all thy fold here below. Surely they are equally dear to thee, every one of them, with those that are above. And, as they are in a wilderness, they need thy care. Shortly the chief Shepherd will appear, and unite the whole in one *beautiful flock.* Jerem. xiii. 20. And they shall *then pass again under the hand of him that telleth them.* Jerem. xxxiii. 13.

5 ¶ Likewise, ye younger, submit yourselves unto the elder. Yea, all *of you* be subject one to another, and be clothed with humility: for God resisteth the proud, and giveth grace to the humble.

6 Humble yourselves therefore under the mighty hand of God, that he may exalt you in due time:

7 Casting all your care upon him; for he careth for you.

8 ¶ Be sober, be vigilant; because your adversary the devil, as a roaring lion, walketh about, seeking whom he may devour.

9 ¶ Whom resist stedfast in the faith, knowing that the same afflictions are accomplished in your brethren that are in the world.

10 But the God of all grace, who hath called us unto his eternal glory by Christ Jesus, after that ye have suffered a while, make you perfect, stablish, strengthen, settle *you*.

11 To him *be* glory and dominion for ever and ever. Amen.

12 By Silvanus, a faithful brother unto you, as I suppose, I have written briefly, exhorting, and testifying that this is the true grace of God wherein ye stand.

13 The *church that is* at Babylon, elected together with *you*, saluteth you; and *so doth* Marcus my son.

14 Greet ye one another with a kiss of charity. Peace *be* with you all that are in Christ Jesus. Amen.

Of all men, *Peter* found most occasion, as an Elder in the Church, and from solemn experience in his own heart, to admonish the whole family of CHRIST against *Satan*. JESUS, his dear LORD and Master, who so graciously forewarned *Peter* of his fall, and so mercifully, at the same time, comforted him with the assurance of his recovery, through his High Priestly office, in praying for the preservation of his faith; very blessedly commanded him, that when he was converted, he should strengthen his brethren. See Luke xxii. 31, 32. And, beyond all doubt, upon numberlesss occasions, from the moment that JESUS turned and looked upon *Peter*, and in that glance of the eye, accompanied with CHRIST's power in his heart, he became a blessed instrument in the LORD's hand for good, in strengthening the LORD's people. And yet still more, as the hoary Apostle was now about to close his Epistle, and shortly after his life with it, he had in view the most lively impressions upon his mind, both of his own disgrace, and the LORD's mercy; and, therefore, is earnest to admonish the Church of the dangers to which they are always exposed in the subtilty of Satan, and that their only security is in the LORD, the GOD of all grace.

But, over and above the Apostle's anxiety on this account, and on this interesting subject, I would humbly ask, do we not see the yet infinitely higher grace and love of GOD the HOLY GHOST on this occasion? Was it not the LORD the SPIRIT that here taught the Church, and from the instance of the fall of so great an Apostle, how to be looking for grace from the GOD of all grace, to resist the fiery darts of *Satan*? I cannot but believe, that this was the tender and gracious design of GOD the HOLY GHOST, to make choice of his servant *Peter*, that in the close of his life, he should leave on record, for the comfort of GOD's Church in the earth, to the very latest period of time, and *Peter's* history might be an illustration of it, that they who are kept are not their own keepers, but they are preserved by *the power of* GOD *through faith unto salvation.* And very blessed is it, to see the watchful eye of GOD the SPIRIT over the Church in this particular, to keep the little ones in the faith against all temptation, and against all danger of finally falling away, while supported by *the* GOD *of all grace, who hath called his people unto eternal glory by* CHRIST JESUS!

I must not trespass. But I do humbly beg the favor of a little further indulgence, to dwell a few moments over this most interesting passage of the Apostle. The Apostle knowing that self-will and presumption, in his own instance, were the sad causes, on his part, which gave *Satan* such an handle over him; before he admonisheth the Church concerning the devil, in going about as a roaring lion, he calls upon them to humble themselves under the Almighty hand of GOD, and to be sober and vigilant. He knew, by woeful cost, what combustibles for explosion are in the human heart, to ignite with the fiery darts of *Satan*; and, therefore, urgeth to the damping of all pride, which, like gunpowder, when moistened, will resist flame. But the Apostle, while enjoining this great wariness of conduct, teacheth them still more, to look to the LORD for security. *Casting all your care upon him,* (saith he,) *for he careth for you.* Here was the grand resource, yea, the only one. All our preparations, humblings, watchings, and the like, unless found in CHRIST, and CHRIST undertakes for us, will stand as nothing against the wiles of *Satan.* Like the *Leviathan* in the mighty waters, *he laughs at the shaking of the* human *spear.* Job xli. 29. The greatest saint, in his own strength, is no more than a feather in the hurricane of the devil's temptations. And, the Apostle hath described him in such a way, in this Chapter, as cannot but carry conviction to every heart taught by sad experience, as *Peter* was, what a formidable foe, and of the most implacable kind, he is. *Your adversary* (saith he) *the devil, as a roaring lion, walketh about, seeking whom he may devour.* Who can read this account, and call to remembrance the awful ravages he made upon the man who so describes him, but must tremble! An adversary indeed, and of the deepest subtilty, unmercifulness, and power. A lion, yea, a roaring lion, whose yells, could we hear them, would alarm more than thunder. I have often thought, what a mercy it is, that to us he is invisible. Surely the very sight of him, would make all the beasts of the forest to shrink with fear, and drive them to their dens, to escape his fury. And yet, Reader! if the LORD JESUS give but grace to his people, the feeblest of his little army can easily overcome him, in the blood of the LAMB.

Let us look at the subject a moment in this point of view. This scripture tells us, that he is walking about, seeking *whom he may devour.* Observe: not whom he *will,* for then it would be all the Lord's people; but whom *he may.* And, therefore, that *may* shall not reach to one of them. He may, for the Lord's greater glory, and the foe's greater disgrace, tempt many of them, yea, all of them into sin: But to devour them, he cannot. *No weapon formed against them shall prosper.* Isaiah liv. 17. And, *no temptation shall take them but what is common to man; and with every temptation, the* Lord *will make a way to escape, that they may be able to bear it.* 1 Cor. x. 13. And that other sweet promise, brings up the rear; *the* God *of peace shall bruise Satan under your feet shortly.* Rom. xvi. 20. Reader! do not lose sight of these things, for they are most precious. And while we resist *Satan,* stedfast in the faith, that faith is supported, yea, given by the Lord. And faith in his blood must crown all. The same afflictions, leading to the same triumphs, are accomplished in our brethren, which are in the world: Yea, *the armies in heaven* overcame in the same way; *by the blood of the Lamb, and by the word of their testimony, and they loved not their lives unto death.* Rev. xii. 11.

But we do not stop here. The Holy Ghost, by the Apostle, adds yet further comforts. As the life of faith is a continual warfare, and God's chosen ones must be tried ones; that precious scripture is given, which is enough to lift the heart of him that through grace feels its sweet influence, above all the exercises and sufferings he may be called upon to endure. *But the* God *of all grace, who hath called us unto his eternal glory by* Christ Jesus, *after that ye have suffered awhile, make you perfect, stablish, strengthen, settle you. To whom be glory and dominion for ever and ever. Amen.* If endless volumes were written upon this blessed scripture, it would remain unexhausted, and vast resources left unexplored. For what indeed can unfold, and lay open the grace and love of Him, who is here, by way of striking distinction, called *the* God *of all grace?*

I do not remember, in all the Bible, a similar expression. God is, indeed, in numberless places, said to be gracious, yea, *very* gracious; and we frequently read of *the grace of* God. But, the God of *all* grace, is peculiar to this Chapter of the Apostle. And, if I might venture to suppose the cause, I should be led to think, that it is here specially marked from its connection with the subject the Holy Ghost is upon. *Peter* had been winnowed by *Satan.* Peter is admonishing the Church, on the danger of this walking-about adversary. And, having in his own instance suffered so much, he knew, that his recovery, and the safety or recovery after failing, of every other, could only be effected by the God of all grace. Graciously, therefore, the Lord will have the Church taught, that, as the Lord's people have such a great foe to contend with; they may remember, they always have a much greater, even an Almighty Friend, God himself, yea, of all grace, to be their safety. And as from sins, and corruptions, and too often listening to the temptations of *Satan,* they have in themselves no claims upon God, to come forth to their deliverance: God will come forth of his free grace, and not from their deserts, to secure them. Hence, there is a double beauty, and a tenfold blessedness, in God's calling himself here *the* God *of all grace,* where sins and sufferings, and trials and temptations, are the subject in hand; and where, like *Peter*, presumption and self-will, and other sins in us, too often lead us in the way of the enemy. Reader! do you enter into the apprehension of the peculiar blessedness of this title of our Covenant-GOD in CHRIST, upon such occasions? Do you see a glory in it, suited to our poor, and often exercised circumstances? Do you yourself know the LORD, as the GOD of grace, yea, the GOD of *all* grace? And have you found, in your own instance, that where *sin hath abounded, grace doth much more abound?* Oh! then, write it down in the daily memorandums of your mind; yea, beg of GOD the HOLY GHOST to impress the precious truth in the fleshly tables of your heart, that the GOD of all grace, who hath called us unto his eternal glory by CHRIST JESUS, after that we have suffered a while, will make us perfect, stablish, strengthen, settle us.

But let us not stop here. It is further said, that this GOD of all grace hath *called* us unto his eternal glory by CHRIST JESUS. Here the LORD the SPIRIT opens before us another, and a brighter view, even of glory, yea, and of *eternal* glory; and that in a way and manner, which must be eternally safe and secure, being *in* CHRIST JESUS. So that every word in this blessed scripture, as we say sometimes of many things coming together, tells. GOD *calls* to it. Yes! *For whom he did predestinate, them he also called; and whom he called, them he also justified; and whom he justified, them he also glorified.* Rom. viii. 29, 30. And it is his grace, his *free* grace, as the GOD of *all* grace, which is the sole cause. For elsewhere, as the HOLY GHOST teacheth, *we are saved, and called with an holy calling, not according to our works,* (for where grace is the sole cause, it cannot be of works, *otherwise grace is no more grace*: Rom. xi. 6.) *but according to his own purpose and grace given us in* CHRIST JESUS, *before the world began.* 2 Tim. i. 9. So that, he that *gives grace, will give glory.* Grace is the earnest of glory. It is the very charter, the patent, sent from heaven. The HOLY GHOST by *Paul*, calls it *the earnest of the* SPIRIT. 2 Cor. v. 4. the *seal of the promised inheritance.* Ephes. i. 13, 14. The child of GOD at regeneration, receives it as the writings and heavenly parchments of his freehold, or what is infinitely more precious, his free grace inheritance. It is in reversion, indeed, and not to be entered upon, until grace is consummated in glory. But it is as sure as though in present possession; for the GOD of all grace hath *called* us unto it. Yea, even now by faith we sometimes enter upon it; and in CHRIST, our forerunner, who is gone before, and hath taken possession of it in our name, we do see ourselves *raised up together, and made to sit together in heavenliness,* (or as we render it, *in heavenly places,*) *in* CHRIST JESUS. Ephes. ii. 4, 5, 6.

And who is it that the GOD of all grace hath called? *Us*, saith the Apostle. Even those to whom *Peter* writes his Epistle, as the title in the first Chapter shews. *Elect, according to the foreknowledge of* GOD *the* FATHER, *through sanctification of the* SPIRIT, *unto obedience, and sprinkling of the blood of* JESUS CHRIST. 1 Peter i. 2. The Epistle is but one, and sent but to one body of persons. And these are they. And to what are we called? *Even to his eternal glory.* Every word here again is big with importance. We are called to *glory.* Not to purchase it, for it is freely given. Not to merit it, for it is of grace. And it is to *eternal* glory. Not a glory that is short and transient, for it is *eternal*. And they that are called *to it*, are prepared *for it*. For CHRIST hath *power over all flesh, for to give eternal life to as many as the* FATHER *hath given him*. John xvii. 2. And *all that the* FATHER *hath given me*, (saith CHRIST,) *shall come unto me*. And *I give unto them eternal life*. And *I will raise them up at the last day*. Reader! compare these scriptures together, and see how the whole is bound. John vi. 37—40. John x. 24—30. Can any thing be more certain, and eternally secure? And observe that little word, *His*. The GOD of all grace hath called us unto *His* eternal glory. Yes! GOD the FATHER hath a glory, in which, it is said, CHRIST shall one day come. He shall come in the glory of his FATHER, with his angels. Matt. xvi. 27. And CHRIST, as CHRIST, hath a glory, personally considered, for so is he called, *the* LORD *of glory*. 1 Cor. ii. 8. And the glory of all the persons of the GODHEAD, the Church of CHRIST is said to have. Rev. xxi. 11. So that in each, and in all the views of it, the expression *His* eternal glory is blessed.

But, what sums up all, and makes it most precious indeed, is, that the whole is in and by CHRIST JESUS. So that GOD, who is the GOD of all grace, and the Giver of all grace, and, in his threefold character of person, FATHER, SON, and HOLY GHOST, is everlastingly dispensing grace, yea, all grace, and all sorts of grace, in pardoning, renewing, justifying, sanctifying, comforting, sealing, yea, all grace; and, in confirmation, hath called us to his eternal glory, hath given all, both our persons, and our blessings, in CHRIST JESUS. He is our Head and Husband, our Redeemer, our Righteousness, our all in all. He it is which gives a gracious acceptation to our persons; and by whom, and in whom we are predestinated into the adoption of children; Ephes. i. 4—6. and are made heirs of GOD, and jointheirs with CHRIST.

And hence, after the short exercises and sufferings of this transitory life are passed, all the blessed consequences which the Apostle speaks of, will follow. The same which calleth us unto eternal glory by CHRIST, will perfect, stablish, strengthen, and settle all his people in CHRIST; yea, CHRIST himself is our perfection, and our perfection is CHRIST. Paul tells the Church, that we are *to come in the unity of the faith, and of the knowledge of the* SON *of* GOD, *unto a perfect man*. Ephes. iv. 13. And who is this but CHRIST? What perfection but in Him? All our completeness is said to be in Him, *in whom dwelleth all the fulness of the* GODHEAD *bodily*. Coloss. ii. 9, 10. So, then, our perfection, our establishment, our strength, our everlasting settlement and home, is CHRIST. And GOD the HOLY GHOST, in causing *Peter*, of all men, to teach the Church these precious truths, seems, in grace, to have intended the confirmation of the whole still more. For, who is Peter? One whom *Satan* desired, above all men, to sift. One whom *Satan* did sift; and whom, but for CHRIST, would have been winnowed in destruction. Who, then, so well suited to tell poor, buffeted, exercised followers of the LORD JESUS these blessed truths?

Reader! ponder well these things, give yourself wholly to them. To the whole Church of GOD, in the view of them, it may be said, *You see your calling, brethren!* Oh! for grace, to join the Apostle's hymn; and, not as I fear we too often do, with lip-service, as so many words of course, at the end of these sweet writings, but with a soul full of feeling, and turned inside-out, in the unableness to contain the running-over sense of such free sovereign grace and mercy; may we exclaim, *To the* GOD *of all grace be glory and dominion for ever and ever. Amen.*

I detain the Reader no longer with observations on the salutations at the close of this Epistle, than just to remark, that it is probable this *Sylvanus,* is the same person as is elsewhere called *Silas, Paul's* companion, who was also, it should seem, known to *Peter,* and of whose faithfulness the Word of GOD bears testimony. The Church at *Babylon,* means the Church of GOD in that place; and *Peter's* mark of election, proves the sense he had of it. In relation to this *Marcus,* whom the Apostle calls his son, whether it was his son in the flesh, is not certain. For, though *Peter* had a wife, we read not of any children. Matt. viii. 14. As an elder in the Church, *Marcus,* if young, might be called his son. The kiss of charity, founded in the peace of CHRIST JESUS, formed an affectionate conclusion to this most blessed and lovely Epistle. May both Writer and Reader of this *Poor Man's Commentary,* find grace, if it be the LORD's will, so to close it, and to put to it also, their Amen!

REFLECTIONS.

BLESSED be GOD, FATHER, SON, and HOLY GHOST, for this precious Epistle, among all the other divine revelations of covenant-love and mercy in JESUS CHRIST! What a review of the most soul-refreshing truths, in looking back over this short, but comprehensive compendium of GOD's holy word, do we behold, concerning the great things of GOD? Surely, the LORD hath been most gracious to the Church, in the gift of this divine treasury. May the Almighty Giver add to it another blessing, and make it for ever profitable to every child of GOD, in every renewed perusal, as long as the Church continues on earth, until brought home to glory.

Dear *Peter,* thou wert an elder indeed, when, as in this Chapter, thou didst exhort the elders. Blessedly called by JESUS, blessedly distinguished by JESUS, among the Apostles; no wonder *Satan* marked thee as an object to vent his hellish malice upon, with the most decided hatred. The LORD be praised for thy recovery from his infernal spoils. The LORD be praised, for having recorded both thy fall and thy restoration. And the LORD be praised for every single instance, where both have been made blessed to the Church, in teaching, by so remarkable an example, the weakness of our poor nature in the greatest of men; and the strength of divine grace, in recovering the LORD's people in the most desperate cases. Oh! how fully doth both prove, that, as the Apostle himself could well certify, that they who are kept, *are kept by the power of* GOD, *through faith, unto salvation.*

Reader! let us not close our meditation on this blessed book of GOD, without taking one view more of the GOD of all grace, in this most precious account of his rich, free, and sovereign mercy. What, but grace, can call to his eternal glory? What, but grace, can prepare the soul of any one individual for the enjoyment of it? And, what, but a God of all grace, can bear up, and bear on, and bear home the tried and buffeted child of God, against the roaring lion *Satan*, and sometimes the more raging lusts of sin, which arise in our fallen nature? Blessed be the God of all grace, who hath called us to his eternal glory by CHRIST JESUS!

THE

SECOND EPISTLE GENERAL

OF

PETER.

GENERAL OBSERVATIONS.

IF there were any real doubts entertained by the Church of God, concerning the authenticity of this divine record of God's Holy Word, the several parts of its own internal evidence, must have carried every objection before it. For the grand testimony, after all, to the truth of God is, God's own testimony, in divine teaching. For this comes home to the heart. God speaketh in the word, and by the word. And when the LORD's word is accompanied by the LORD's power, and the heart is made to receive *the truth, in the love of it*, here is the threefold witness, by which, as the Scripture saith, every word is established.

This Epistle of the Apostle *Peter*, like the former, is not addressed to any one in particular, but to the Church in general; and therefore called, *The General Epistle*. It is to *them that have obtained like precious faith* with the Writer; consequently, the regenerated Church. The Reader should note this in every Epistle.

There are some very blessed and precious points of doctrine, beside the more general, which are insisted upon somewhat more largely in these Chapters. And very blessed they have proved, and must prove, to the people of God, who have read, and are taught by the HOLY GHOST the gracious knowledge and enjoyment of them.

The *time*, in which it was written, is generally supposed to have been about *two years* after the *former*; not above *three* or *four* years before the overthrow of Jerusalem; and but little more than a *year* before the Apostle suffered martyrdom. Reader! let us enter upon its perusal in prayer; and this will encourage us to hope that we shall close it in praise.

CHAPTER I.

CONTENTS.

The Apostle opens his Epistle in a short Salutation of the Church, and immediately enters upon the blessed Subject of Regeneration. He dwells upon the glorious Manifestation made to him in the Mount of Transfiguration; and concludes the Chapter, in declaring of GOD *the* SPIRIT's *speaking by Holy Men of old.*

SIMON Peter, a servant and an apostle of Jesus Christ, to them that have obtained like precious faith with us through the righteousness of God and our Saviour Jesus Christ:

There are two great points to be attended to, in the very opening of this Epistle, and which are contained in this verse; namely, *first,* of the Persons to whom this Epistle is sent; to *them that have obtained like precious faith* with the Apostles. And, *secondly,* the great object of that faith; GOD, *and our* SAVIOR JESUS CHRIST. Of the *former,* nothing can be more plain and evident, than that this faith is the faith of GOD's elect; Titus i. 1. which is the one, and only faith, both of Apostles and Prophets, and the whole Church of GOD; and, consequently, this whole Epistle is directed to no other. And of the *latter,* it is equally plain and evident, that GOD *and our* SAVIOR here spoken of, is CHRIST, the great object of faith; for his righteousness can be the only righteousness for the Church to lean upon, and trust in. And Reader! think what a glorious object of faith, CHRIST is; and what a righteousness for the Church to obtain, through the free gift and sovereign grace of GOD? Oh! be it my portion to go forth, in the Church here below, and when called upon to enter into the eternity above, to cry out with him of old; *I will go in the strength of the* LORD GOD, *I will make mention of thy righteousness, even thine only.* Psm. lxxi. 16.

2 Grace and peace be multiplied unto you through the knowledge of God, and of Jesus our Lord,

3 According as his divine power hath given unto us all things that *pertain* unto life, and godliness, through the knowledge of him that hath called us to glory and virtue;

4 Whereby are given unto us exceeding great and precious promises; that by these ye might be partakers of the divine nature, having escaped the corruption that is in the world through lust.

5 ¶ And beside this, giving all diligence, add to your faith virtue, and to virtue knowledge;

6 And to knowledge temperance; and to temperance patience; and to patience godliness;

7 And to godliness brotherly kindness; and to brotherly kindness charity.

8 For if these things be in you, and abound, they make *you that ye shall* neither *be* barren nor unfruitful in the knowledge of our Lord Jesus Christ.

9 But he that lacketh these things is blind, and cannot see afar off, and hath forgotten that he was purged from his old sins.

I stay not to observe in this place, the very sweet manner with which *Peter*, as well as the rest of the Apostles, address the Church, in their prayers and benedictions, for grace and peace. But having, more or less, called the Reader's attention to this, in every preceding Epistle, it will be the less necessary in this place, to add any further remarks. But I very earnestly intreat the Reader, to attend with me, to what the HOLY GHOST by the Apostle, hath here so blessedly set forth, concerning the work of regeneration. The first call of grace, by GOD the SPIRIT, is here expressly said to make, the highly favored objects of this divine love, *partakers of the divine nature;* and with that, of all things *that pertain unto life and godliness.* Reader! pause over the marvellous account; and when you have pondered it well, mark down in the memorandums of your inmost soul, the several vast blessings, as far as present apprehension can trace them, of what are included in this unspeakable gift of GOD.

It is GOD the HOLY GHOST, by his quickening and regenerating grace, in giving spiritual life, to *the dead in trespasses and sins,* which brings the child of GOD, into the first discovery of GOD the FATHER's electing love; or GOD the SON's betrothing and redeeming grace. For although the everlasting love of GOD the FATHER, had been running in streams of grace from all eternity; yet, as a river under ground, the blessed properties of it were neither known, nor seen, nor regarded, until at regeneration, GOD the HOLY GHOST opened the eye of the child of GOD, to see the original, and eternal purpose of GOD the FATHER, in choosing the Church in CHRIST, before the foundation of the world; and in predestinating the Church in CHRIST, to the adoption of children. Ephes. i. 4, 5. And never till this blessed period, when GOD the HOLY GHOST brought forth the child of GOD, in the new birth of grace, had the poor sinner any apprehensions, either of the Person of CHRIST, or of his betrothing love, or redeeming mercy. But, as the Apostle *Paul* expresseth it, in his Epistle to *Titus; after that, the kindness and love of* GOD *our* SAVIOR *toward men appeared; not by works of righteousness, which we have done, but according to his mercy he saved us, by the washing of regeneration, and renewing of the* HOLY GHOST, *which He shed on us abundantly, through* JESUS CHRIST *our* SAVIOR; *that we, being justified by his grace, should be made heirs, according to the hope of eternal life.* Titus iii. 4—7.

I pray the Reader, not only to pause over the contemplation of this vast mercy; but, day by day, to ponder it again and again, in his walk of faith through life. Oh! the unspeakable grace, when called from darkness to light; and from the power of sin and Satan, unto the living God.

Now I beg the Reader to observe, with me, how sweetly the Holy Ghost, by the Apostle, hath marked the gracious effects, which arise out of regeneration. Before this great work of the new-birth is wrought, there is not a spiritual mercy we can claim; no, nor even know. As it was in the old creation of nature, darkness was upon the face of the deep, before the Spirit of God moved upon the face of the waters, and God said, *let there be light:* Gen. i. 2, 3. so, in the new creation of grace, it is all darkness upon the face of our mind, until that God, that commanded the light to shine out of darkness, *hath shined in our hearts to give the light of the knowledge of the glory of* God, *in the face of* Jesus Christ. 2 Cor. iv. 6. But, when this is accomplished, the new-born soul, is brought into all the privileges of his heirship. Pardon, mercy, and peace, instantly follow. He is justified freely. Christ is then seen, and known, and enjoyed, (at least there is the new birth-title to all,) as made of God to his people, *wisdom, righteousness, sanctification, and redemption.* 1 Cor. i. 30. Hence the Apostle, speaks so blessedly in this Chapter, *to them that have obtained like precious faith;* they are according to his divine power, even God the Spirit, who communicates the blessings from his quickening life, imparted to them, *made partakers of the divine nature, having escaped the corruptions that are in the world, through lust.* And not only so, but they have *all things given to them, that pertain to life and godliness.* And they are *called to glory and virtue.* And there are *given unto them, exceeding great and precious promises.* And hence, all those additions the Apostle speaks of, and which are the natural *effects* and consequences resulting from this one first *cause,* namely, regeneration, must and will appear. The child of God, by this first quickening life, from God the Holy Ghost; and by the daily renewings of God the Holy Ghost, keeping alive the grace he first imparted, will add to his faith, virtue; and to virtue, knowledge; and to knowledge, temperance; and to temperance, patience; and to patience, godliness; and to godliness, brotherly kindness; and to brotherly kindness, charity. But, Reader! remember these are the fruits and effects of justification; and not in the least degree contributing, as a part cause, to our justification. The Apostle saith, that being by regeneration, made partakers of the divine nature, and thereby having escaped the corruption, that is in the world, through lust; we have all things *given* unto us, that pertain to life and godliness. Hence, what is God's *gift,* cannot be brought into any account of man's *merit.* And, therefore, when the Apostle adds, giving all diligence, to add unto faith, virtue, and the like; these are considered, as so many fruits and evidences of our new-birth character. And the consequence will be, that if these things be in the Lord's people, and they abound in them, they themselves, will neither be barren nor unfruitful in the knowledge of our Lord Jesus Christ. Mark the Apostle's expression! Believers shall not be barren, nor unfruitful in the *knowledge* of Christ. He doth not say, that their aboundings will be recommendations to God; much less, so many party causes, in the promoting their salvation. That salvation is all along considered wholly in Christ. And their regeneration, by which they are made partakers of the divine nature, is wholly from God the Spirit. So that all that is here said of virtue, and brotherly kindness, and the like, are spoken of, but as *effects*, arising out of the first glorious *cause*, and only so many precious testimonies of the renewed life. And therefore, the man that lacketh these things, lacketh the sweet tokens of his christian character, and can give no proof of a work of grace in regeneration, having passed in his heart.

I have been the more particular upon this point, than I should otherwise have been, had I not known, that men are apt to make great errors herein. I wished therefore to state, and place these important truths, on their own proper basis. Faith and all graces, are no party cause of salvation. They are *fruits*, and not the *root*, *effects* not *causes*. Salvation is wholly of Christ. Not a work wrought *in* us, but *for* us. And our new-birth, the blessed consequence of having been given by the Father to the Son, before the foundation of the world; redeemed by the Son, in the time-state of our *Adam*-nature from the fall; and therefore quickened by the Holy Ghost, for the everlasting enjoyment of God, in grace here, and glory for ever. All spiritual pride, all pharisaical righteousness, all supposed merit in ourselves, these things are done away, in those precious views of our mercies, and our salvation from end to end, is hereby known and enjoyed as the whole of grace; *not of works, lest any man should boast*. Ephes. ii. 8, 9.

10 Wherefore the rather, brethren, give diligence to make your calling and election sure: for if ye do these things, ye shall never fall;

11 For so an entrance shall be ministered unto you abundantly into the everlasting kingdom of our Lord and Saviour Jesus Christ.

These are very sweet verses. And they contain a most salutary direction. When a child of God can prove his *calling*, he thereby fully proves at the same time, his *election*. For it is an infallible truth of scripture, *For whom he did predestinate, them he also called*. Rom. viii. 30. And every new-born child of God is himself a living witness of being *called*. But having already, very largely dwelt upon both *election* and *calling*, in this *Poor Man's Commentary*. I have only to refer the Reader, to the same. Rom. viii. 30. and 1 Thess. i. 4, with the notes on both.

12 Wherefore I will not be negligent to put you always in remembrance of these things, though ye know *them*, and be established in the present truth.

13 Yea, I think it meet, as long as I am in this tabernacle, to stir you up by putting *you* in remembrance;

14 Knowing that shortly I must put off *this* my tabernacle, even as our Lord Jesus Christ hath shewed me.

15 Moreover I will endeavour that ye may be able after my decease to have these things always in remembrance.

16 For we have not followed cunningly devised fables, when we made known unto you the power and coming of our Lord Jesus Christ, but were eye-witnesses of his majesty.

17 For he received from God the Father honour and glory, when there came such a voice to him from the excellent glory, This is my beloved Son, in whom I am well pleased.

18 And this voice, which came from heaven, we heard, when we were with him in the holy mount.

What a delightful portrait is here drawn of the Apostle? What a firmness of mind, in the prospect of his approaching death? He knew, that he should end his days by martyrdom. See John xxi. 18, 19. But *Peter* knew also, the sure ground upon which he stood. See Chap. iii. 12—14. And every child of GOD by regeneration, is sure of the same. 2 Cor. v. 5. But, what I beg the Reader more particularly to remark, in the Apostle is, the refreshing views he had of the manifestation CHRIST made to him, in the Holy Mount. The glories of CHRIST's Person, which he then saw, and his own personal interest in CHRIST, came with a full tide of remembrance, upon his mind, in the view of his death, and gave him holy triumph. Reader! it is so with all the people of GOD. *Bethel* visits, once made by the LORD, refresh all the after stages of life. *Jacob* when a-dying, remembered this. Gen. xxviii. 11 to the end, with Gen. xlviii. throughout. *Moses* also had his soul refreshed, when he called to mind, his first view of GOD in CHRIST at the bush. Exod. iii. with Deut. xxxiii. 16. But over and above these, let the Reader particularly attend to the evident design of GOD the HOLY GHOST, in thus appointing *Peter*, to leave this blessed testimony, as his dying testimony, for every regenerated child of GOD to be refreshed with. Here are no cunningly devised fables: no arts, no folly of human philosophy. What *Peter* records is the relation of himself and companions, who were eye-witnesses of CHRIST's majesty. Reader! let you and I attend to his relation.

And *first.* What I would beg the Reader to observe, is the Apostle's account of this solemn and glorious scene, in the Mount. He expressly saith, that it was *the power and coming of our* LORD JESUS CHRIST; and that he, and his companions, were *eye witnesses of his majesty.* Hence it will undeniably follow, that it was the *personal* glory of the GOD-Man Mediator, CHRIST JESUS. Not the *essential* glory of JEHOVAH, in his threefold character of Person, FATHER, SON, and HOLY GHOST. *For no man hath seen* GOD *at any time.* John i. 18. But the *Personal* glory of CHRIST, as GOD-Man Mediator. And which the voice that came to CHRIST, from the excellent glory, confirmed. This voice, both proved indeed, CHRIST to be GOD, and no less at the same time, the GOD-Man Mediator. It proved CHRIST's GODHEAD, for GOD cannot find an object of complacency, but in himself. Hence, CHRIST is *One with the* FATHER, *over all,* GOD, *blessed for ever.* Amen. Rom. ix. 5. And it proved CHRIST to be the Mediator; for this account of him, as his beloved SON, corresponded to the LORD's proclamation of Him, by the Prophet, when he called him *his servant,* and *his elect, in whom his soul delighteth.* Isa. xlii. 1. Let the Reader duly ponder these things, in one point together; and then let him attend to another view in this most blessed scene, as GOD the HOLY GHOST hath represented it.

Secondly. Several days before this transfiguration of CHRIST took place, the LORD JESUS prepared the minds of his disciples, to expect some glorious manifestation of himself. These were the LORD's own words: *Verily, I say unto you, that there be some of them that stand here, which shall not taste of death, till they have seen the kingdom of* GOD *come with power.* Mark ix. 1. Luke ix. 27. Now, nothing can be more plain, than that these words of JESUS referred to some striking, though transient views, of the glories of his kingdom; in which he will appear, *when he comes to be glorified in his saints, and admired in all that believe.* 2 Thess. i. 10. JESUS intended it as a glimpse, a fore-view of his personal glory, in the great day of his kingdom. And, that the Apostles considered it the same, is equally evident, in that *Peter* calls it, the *power and coming of our* LORD JESUS CHRIST. Think, Reader, what a sweet pledge and earnest this was to the disciples, of the sure coming of our LORD? And, how blessedly did the Apostles feel it then; and by them, in the record of the HOLY GHOST, how blessedly hath it wrought ever since, and will work, in the fullest confirmation to our faith, on this great point, to endless generations?

Thirdly. Let us, under the light of scripture, consider, what this glory of CHRIST was, which the Apostles saw, and which *Peter* calls being *eye-witnesses of his majesty.* I have before said, it could not be the *essential* glory of the GODHEAD, for GOD is invisible. But, it is most evident, that it was the GODHEAD, shedding some beams of glory, and brightness, in CHRIST's human nature. Not a mere *outward* glory, shining *upon* the person of CHRIST, but the GODHEAD, shining forth from *within.* The glory of his *divine* nature, manifested through the medium of his *human,* and both forming in one glorious person, CHRIST. *Paul,* under the HOLY GHOST, hath blessedly expressed it, when he saith, *In Him dwelleth all the fulness of the* GODHEAD *bodily.* Coloss. ii. 9. Such, *Peter* saw. *James* did not live long enough to give his testimony, being soon cut off, after the return of CHRIST to heaven, and the descent of the HOLY GHOST. Acts xii. 1, 2. *John's* account is in exact correspondence with *Peter's.* The WORD *was made flesh, and dwelt among us, and we beheld his glory; the glory, as of the only begotten of the* FATHER, *full of grace and truth.* John i. 14. And *Paul,* to whom CHRIST spake from heaven, and manifested forth his glory at the time, saith, that *it was above the brightness of the sun,*

Acts xxvi. 13. Indeed, it made him blind for three days. Hence, then, it must follow, that this manifestation of Christ, at this time, in the Mount, was his glorified body; and such as He will appear in at the last day, when *the moon shall be confounded, and the sun ashamed;* that is, both shall blush, and be eclipsed, at the superior glory of Christ, God and Man in one person; *when the* Lord *of Hosts shall reign in Zion, and in Jerusalem, and before his antients, gloriously.* Isaiah xxiv. 23.

Lastly. That I may not trespass. As this manifestation of the personal glory of Christ was evidently designed for the comfort and joy, not only of those highly favored Apostles, to whom the Lord granted this great blessing, but for the consolation of the Church of God, in all ages; so the Lord's bringing from the dead (or from heaven, it is the same thing,) those two men, *Moses* and *Elias,* to be with Jesus at the time, as plainly proved, that when Christ shall come, at the last day, to his kingdom, all his redeemed shall be with him, Christ's personal glory is, and ever must be, personal; that is, perfectly incommunicable in its very nature. But, there is a glory in that upper world, which is communicable from Christ, as Head, to his body, his members; precisely the same as grace in this lower world is communicable, and Jesus is for ever communicating it to them all, according to the measure of the gift of Christ. So, then, this glorious transaction in the Mount, was plainly intended by our Lord, as a foretaste of that glory of Christ's person, in which he shall one day appear, and all his redeemed shall appear with him in glory. Well might the remembrance of it refresh the dying saint, in the opening prospect then before him. And, why not refresh all the faithful, in the sure testimony here given, since God the Holy Ghost hath so graciously caused it to be recorded, as the departing consolation of the Apostle to the Church. Lord! make it very blessedly so to my soul!

If I detain the Reader any longer on this sweet passage, it shall only be to offer one or two thoughts which arise out of it, for our great encouragement and comfort. And the first, and highest of all thoughts, must be, to notice, and always keep in remembrance, the love and grace which Jesus manifested to all his Church, by this act. It was, in effect, saying, that if, before these my servants taste of death, I will give them a glimpse of my personal glory, that in them all my people may have a fore-taste of the blessedness they shall all be brought to hereafter. *Moses* and *Elias,* shall come out of the other world, by way of shewing them, that all gone before of mine, as well as all that are yet to come, are alike interested in it. Precious Lord Jesus! was this the love of thine heart? And is this the manner of men, O Lord God!

Secondly. Let the Church of the faithful here learn, from *Peter,* that we do not follow cunningly devised fables. We know the power, and coming also, of our Lord Jesus Christ! We are now witnesses, *heart-*witnesses of his majesty, and the sovereignty of his grace, and shortly shall be eye-witnesses of his glory. Oh! the blessedness of regeneration, which brings with it the earnest of the Spirit.

Thirdly. Let the Church seek for grace, everlastingly to keep in remembrance this precious testimony of our Christ's own personal glory. It is Christ's person, which is the great object of our faith.

All our high hopes of everlasting happiness and joy are centered in Him. He is our hope, our joy, our confidence. And, if we are witnesses now to the power and coming of his grace, we shall in due time be witnesses of his divine presence, in glory. *Beloved!* saith John, (and every new-born child of GOD may say the same,) *now are we the sons of* GOD. *And it doth not yet appear what we shall be, but we know that when he shall appear, we shall be like him, for we shall see him as he is.* 1 John iii. 2.

19 We have also a more sure word of prophecy; whereunto ye do well that ye take heed as unto a light that shineth in a dark place, until the day dawn, and the day-star arise in your hearts:

20 Knowing this first, that no prophecy of the scripture is of any private interpretation.

21 For the prophecy came not in old time by the will of man; but holy men of God spake *as they were* moved by the Holy Ghost.

It appears to me to be a great beauty in the plan of this scripture. The Apostle had opened the Chapter, in giving glory to the HOLY GHOST, concerning his great work of regeneration. He then adverted to the glory of the SON of GOD, as manifested in the Transfiguration of CHRIST's own personal glory, and his people's interest in him. He next called the Church to the contemplation of GOD the FATHER's testimony to his dear SON. And now, in conclusion, he calls upon the Church once more, to GOD the HOLY GHOST, as the Founder of the Church, and the Almighty Minister in the Church, in the appointment of all the means of grace, by his holy word, his ordinances, and his whole train of prophecy. Reader! what an evidence here is, at once, both of the GODHEAD of the HOLY GHOST, his Person, his Agency, his Almighty Sovereignty, and the divine authority of his Word? Hence we learn, that no prophecy of scripture is of any private interpretation. Oh! with what veneration is the Church called upon to receive the prophecies of GOD. And, while we bless GOD for all that is fulfilled, to be on the look-out, with humble, faithful watching, for all that remains to be fulfilled. Methinks, I would say for myself, whenever I open at any time the scripture prophecies, these are not the words of men, but what they have delivered here, is as they were moved by the HOLY GHOST!

REFLECTIONS.

BLESSED and HOLY LORD GOD Almighty, FATHER, SON, and HOLY GHOST! Praised be our Covenant GOD in CHRIST, for his unspeakable gift. What everlasting love, adoration, and praise, do thy people owe thee, O FATHER of mercies, and GOD of all grace, for having chosen the Church in CHRIST, before the world! And thee, no less, thou glorious SON of GOD, for having taken thy Church into union with thyself, when the LORD possessed thee, in the beginning of his ways, before his works of old; and for redeeming thy Church from the Adam-fall of ruin, in which, in this time-state, she was involved. And thee, with equal love and praise, O thou eternal SPIRIT, for thy gracious act of regeneration, in quickening the Church, in every individual of her members, whereby alone each child of GOD is brought into an apprehension of the FATHER's love, the SON's grace, and the SPIRIT's fellowship. Blessed, for ever blessed be GOD.

And we specially praise thee, dearest JESUS, for thy mercies to all thy Church, in this grace of thine to the Apostles, in the Mount of Transfiguration. It was surely for thy Church, in all ages, as well as for their personal comfort, so glorious a display of thy glory was vouchsafed. GOD, our FATHER, be praised, for the precious testimony then given to thy SON-ship. And GOD the HOLY GHOST, in causing *Peter*, with his dying testimony, to bless the Church once more in the relation. And now, O LORD, may thy Church, and especially in the present awful day, be blessed of our GOD, with grace to receive and treasure up so sweet a record of the glory of our risen and exalted SAVIOR. Oh! LORD, continually make known to all thy members in grace, thy power and coming. Make known to us, in the blessed prophecies of our GOD, and in all the ordinances of his house of prayer, this power and coming of our LORD JESUS CHRIST. Oh! to be heart-witnesses of CHRIST's majesty here on earth, till we come to be eye-witnesses of his majesty in heaven. Amen!

CHAP. II.

CONTENTS.

We have in this Chapter a very awful Account of the latter-day Heresies. But, while the HOLY GHOST *graciously informs the Church of those Seasons, he as graciously teacheth the Church how to discern their Features, and discover them from the Faithful.*

BUT there were false prophets also among the people, even, as there shall be false teachers among you, who privily shall bring in damnable heresies, even denying the Lord that bought them, and bring upon themselves swift destruction.

2 And many shall follow their pernicious ways, by reason of whom the way of truth shall be evil spoken of.

3 And through covetousness shall they with feigned words make merchandise of you: whose judgement now of a long time lingereth not, and their damnation slumbereth not.

4 For if God spared not the angels that sinned, but cast *them* down to hell, and delivered *them*

into chains of darkness, to be reserved unto judgement;

5 And spared not the old world, but saved Noah the eighth *person,* a preacher of righteousness, bringing in the flood upon the world of the ungodly.

6 And turning the cities of Sodom and Gomorrah into ashes, condemned *them* with an overthrow, making *them* an ensample unto those that after should live ungodly:

7 And delivered just Lot, vexed with the filthy conversation of the wicked:

8 (For that righteous man dwelling among them, in seeing and hearing vexed *his* righteous soul from day to day with *their* unlawful deeds.)

Let the Reader begin the Chapter with prayer, for the spirit of discernment. And he will find, as *John* said, that there is a sure way, under GOD, of discovering false prophets. See 1 John iv. 1—6. And let him first remark, that the Apostle is not speaking of the true, and real Church of CHRIST, which is made up only of regenerated believers; but of a mere nominal professing Church, which have been from the first forming of the Church in *Egypt,* all the way through, and will continue to the end. A *mixed multitude* went up out of *Egypt.* Exod. xii. 38. After the descent of the HOLY GHOST, there were the *Ananiah's* and *Sapphira's* in the visible Church. Acts v. 1, 2. And there must be, the Apostle saith, *heresies among you, that they which are approved may be made manifest among you.* 1 Cor. xi. 19. Tares will grow with the wheat. But, as of the Church of old, all were not *Israel* in the promised line, which were of *Israel,* naturally, and nationally considered; so it is now. Rom. ix. 6, 7. Mingling in the same congregation is a perfectly distinct thing from belonging to CHRIST. All men, generally speaking, are born Christians, that are born in Christian countries, and under the meridian of the Gospel. But this doth not constitute a real Christian. Before any man is a real Christian, he must be new-born. Birth by nature, gives no right to grace. Hence, the real Church of CHRIST is only composed of real regenerated believers. All that join the congregation of CHRIST without this qualification, only constitute what may be called a professing Church.

But we must not stop here. The Apostle saith, that in such a Church, there will not only be mere nominal worshippers, but there shall be *false Teachers.* As there were in the old Church, false prophets, in the *Hananiahs,* and the *Amaziahs,* who impudently stood up to minister in the LORD's name, without the LORD's authority, yea, and in defiance to the LORD's truth; (Jerem. xxviii. Amos vii.) so the latter-day dispensation is to be distinguished with *false teachers* among the LORD's people. What an awful consideration! Reader! ponder it well, for the time is come. *False teachers!* not mere hearers, not the mere congregation, but those who stand up to teach. Oh! how earnest ought the people of GOD to be in prayer to the LORD, to keep his Church from such delusions! Oh! LORD! send I pray thee, *Pastors according to thine own heart,* and according to thine own promise, *which shall feed thy flock with understanding and knowledge!* Jerem. iii. 15.

But it is our mercy, that the same LORD who hath forewarned the Church of these awful times of heresy, hath also fore-armed his people with the source of security, for their defence. The persons here spoken of, are said to be *false teachers among the people.* Look at this, as the *first* standard by which to ascertain their real character. They are not to spring out of the heathen. They are not from among the antient enemies of CHRIST, the Jews. But these false teachers are to arise up from among persons professing Christianity. *There shall be false teachers among you.* Secondly: observe, that as those men are not heathen men, which want to establish heresy from without; but men calling themselves, like yourselves, Christians in name, and wish to praise up heresy *within;* so, the leading feature of their teaching GOD hath graciously marked, they *privily shall bring in damnable heresies, even denying the* LORD *that bought them.* There are several points here marked out, which, if duly attended to, will throw a light over the whole passage, and enable the Church, under GOD's teaching, to discover who they are here described. *First.* They are said privily to bring in damnable heresies. Now privily means an artful, sly, insinuating way. Their plan is deep laid, and done with caution. It is privily; that is, done plausibly, so that their real intention, of subverting the truth, is not immediately discerned. Now, it is worthy observation, that such was the method of false teachers which sprung up in the Old Testament Church, in the *Sanballats,* and *Tobias,* and *Geshems.* Nehem. vi. 10, 11, 12. Yea, the Serpent himself began with deceit, in the first lie ever told in the world, which he practised on our Mother. Gen. iii. 4. And our GOD hath warned his people against the insinuation of all false teachers. *O Israel, thy prophets are like the foxes in the deserts!* Ezek. xiii. 4. And the Church, aware of this craftiness, cried out, *take us the foxes, the little foxes that spoil the vines; for our vines have tender grapes.* Song ii. 15. So much for the craft made use of, in the false teachers privily bringing in their heresies.

Secondly. Let us look at the features of those heresies, which GOD the HOLY GHOST saith, those false teachers shall bring in. The LORD calls them *damnable.* And they are proved to be so, for they bring upon themselves *swift destruction.* And the LORD shews wherefore they are so; for the first relation of the heresy is, *even denying the* LORD *that bought them.* There are several subordinate ones mentioned, such as *coveteousness* in making merchandize and profit of the people, and using *feigned words,* soft and insinuating words, as if wishing above all things the good of the people they are endeavoring to ruin; complimenting with feigned words their good sense, in appealing to their reason and understanding, under the name of *rational* christianity and the like. But the grand object of all their aim, and, therefore, the grand discriminating feature by which the HOLY GHOST hath marked them, is their denial of the LORD that bought them; and by which they bring upon themselves swift destruction.

The question is, what is implied in this heresy? And this is best answered by the similar passage, in *Jude* 4. *denying the only* LORD GOD *and our* LORD JESUS CHRIST: that is, not denying the Being, and existence of GOD, and of CHRIST; but denying the scriptural testimony of GOD, in his threefold character of Persons, and as manifested in covenant transactions in JESUS CHRIST. These damnable heresies, which these men privily bring in, (Jude saith they have crept in unawares in this deed,) level all distinctions of personality in the GODHEAD; they deny the GODHEAD of CHRIST, atonement by his blood, the Person, work, and offices of GOD the HOLY GHOST. So that, while affecting to be called Christians, they would rob the SON of GOD of all his glory, in the denial of his GODHEAD; and their own souls, and the souls of all the redeemed of their happiness, in denying the efficacy of his redeeming blood. They reduce the Gospel to a mere system of ethics, mere moral duties, and count the blood of the Covenant an unholy thing, and do despite to the Spirit of grace! Reader! how can it be otherwise, than that such men should bring upon themselves swift destruction, since, if there be no hope of redemption in the blood and righteousness of CHRIST, *where shall the ungodly and the sinner appear?* 1 Pet. iv. 18. Rom. iii. 19.

By the expression of *the* LORD *that bought them*, must not be supposed, as having any allusion to the redemption by CHRIST. Had JESUS indeed bought them with his blood, he would have regenerated them by his SPIRIT. The sheep of CHRIST, marked in his blood as his property, must have been the objects of his care. But by the buying them, simply hath reference to his providences over them. Like *Israel* of old, as a nation, all the children of *Israel* were included in their deliverance from the *Egyptian* bondage; and as such, might be said to be bought out of that bondage, by the LORD's deliverance of them. Deut. iv. 32—34. Hence *Moses*, in allusion to this, saith to *Israel* nationally considered, *Do ye thus requite the* LORD, *O foolish people and unwise? Is not he thy father that hath bought thee? Hath he not made thee and established thee?* Deut. xxxii. 6.

Reader! ponder these things. Look at what is here said, and contemplate the present day; and then say, whether in the present day, which may well be called a CHRIST-despising generation, the features could have been more accurately described? Had this scripture been written but yesterday, it could not have more suited! And, Reader, look again! *Peter* saith of them, that *their judgment now of a long time lingereth not, and their damnation slumbereth not.* And *Jude*, in yet stronger language saith, *that they were before of old ordained to this condemnation.* Jude 4. An awful account, to trace them up to their first, and original stock. What a decided account, indeed, ordained of old to this condemnation! And the Apostle draws a parallel line between those ordained men, and fallen angels. They are all of the same family. As the one was cast down from heaven; so these are cast out of the Church of GOD. As the one is reserved in everlasting chains of darkness; so these are reserved unto the judgment of the great day. As the fallen angels are cast down to hell; so CHRIST-despisers, and the bringers in of damnable heresies, are reserved for the blackness of darkness for ever. Yea, if there be a misery in hell, greater one than another, surely they, that like *Chorazin*, were once exalted to greater Gospel privileges in the ordinances of a Gospel Church, and despised them, shall have it. Reader! do observe one thing. Despisers of GOD's truth, who have had greater privileges than others of GOD's mercy, (as this land evidently affords,) will have greater condemnation. Perhaps no nation ever had the views of divine truth more clearly unfolded, than *Great Britain*. Perhaps no heretics ever came up to those of this country. The greatest reptiles and monsters are found under the tropics. The greatest infidels, where the Sun of Righteousness shines with most glory!

I must not further trespass, but it is a solemn close to this scripture which the HOLY GHOST makes, by way of confirming the sure judgment of CHRIST-despisers; that the destruction of angels, the overthrow of the whole world by the flood, the burning of Sodom and Gomorrah, and infinitely, and above all, as might have been added, the death of CHRIST, for the salvation of his people; these loudly proclaim the LORD's determination to take vengeance on sin.

9 The Lord knoweth how to deliver the godly out of temptations, and to reserve the unjust unto the day of judgement to be punished:

10 But chiefly them that walk after the flesh in the lust of uncleanness, and despise government. Presumptuous *are they*, self-willed, they are not afraid to speak evil of dignities.

11 Whereas angels, which are greater in power and might, bring not railing accusation against them before the Lord.

12 But these, as natural brute beasts, made to be taken and destroyed, speak evil of the things that they understand not; and shall utterly perish in their own corruption:

13 And shall receive the reward of unrighteousness, *as* they that count it pleasure to riot in the day time. Spots *they are* and blemishes, sporting themselves with their own deceivings while they feast with you;

14 Having eyes full of adultery, and that cannot cease from sin; beguiling unstable souls: an heart they have exercised with covetous practices; cursed children:

15 Which have forsaken the right way, and are

gone astray, following the way of Balaam *the son* of Bosor, who loved the wages of unrighteousness;

16 But was rebuked for his iniquity: the dumb ass speaking with man's voice forbad the madness of the prophet.

17 These are wells without water, clouds that are carried with a tempest; to whom the mist of darkness is reserved for ever.

18 For when they speak great swelling *words* of vanity, they allure through the lusts of the flesh, *through much* wantonness, those that were clean escaped from them who live in error.

19 While they promise them liberty, they themselves are the servants of corruption: for of whom a man is overcome, of the same is he brought in bondage.

20 For if after they have escaped the pollutions of the world through the knowledge of the Lord and Saviour Jesus Christ, they are again entangled therein, and overcome, the latter end is worse with them than the beginning.

21 For it had been better for them not to have known the way of righteousness, than, after they have known *it*, to turn from the holy commandment delivered unto them.

22 But it is happened unto them according to the true proverb, The dog *is* turned to his own vomit again; and the sow that was washed to her wallowing in the mire.

I admire this very beautiful, and gracious scripture, introduced in this place, as a blessed relief to the mind, in the midst of the many judgments. Reader! do not overlook it. Amidst all the exercises of the present awful day, do not lose sight of this; *the* Lord *knoweth how to deliver the godly out of temptations.* Here is enough for a child of God to repose in for ever! But the Holy Ghost is engaged in this Chapter in an awful subject, and the Lord pursues it again. I do not think it necessary to dwell particularly upon the several features of character, which the Holy Ghost hath drawn, of ungodly men. They are all of them very strong and expressive.

Balaam is introduced, to shew what convictions of head-knowledge there may be, void of all heart-influence. This monster of iniquity, while convinced in head-knowledge, that the Israel of GOD was blessed of GOD in CHRIST; hired himself out for the sake of gain, to curse them. And, when he found all would not do to accomplish this end, he recommended *Moab* to a plan which he thought would effectually answer. By advising the Moabites to invite the sons of Israel to come to their sacrifices, they laid a trap to catch *Israel* with the beauty of *Moab's* daughters; and this he knew, would lead *Israel* into idolatry, which would do more to the ruin of *Israel* than all the curses of *Balaam*. Compare Numb. xxiii. xxiv. and xxv. with Rev. ii. 12—17.

I shall only detain the Reader with a short observation, on the close of this Chapter, in the three last verses of it. If the Reader will diligently attend to what is here said, he will discover, that the HOLY GHOST, by the Apostle, is speaking all along of mere nominal professors, as distinguished from the LORD's own people. The outward form of godliness had done enough to induce, in mere professors, a wish for an outward garb of godliness. The reputation of being somewhat religious, had an effect to restrain them from the open commission of more daring offences before men. They had set up somewhat of a reform, observed perhaps family prayer, attended ordinances, and now and then the sacrament of the LORD's Supper. But here it ceased. No awakening by grace, no regeneration of the heart, no union with CHRIST. Hence, though they had escaped the open and notorious acts of pollution which were in the world, yet no work of saving grace was ever wrought in the heart; and, therefore, what begins only in nature, can arise no higher, neither will it ever end in grace. The dog, when sick, and vomits up, soon returns and swallows down again what must everlastingly make sick. And the sow, however you may wash her, will not be easy until she return to wallow again in her favorite mud. It is her nature, and nature never ariseth above her own element. The sheep may fall into the mire, but it will never lay there. But the sow is in her native soil when there, neither can any keep her from it. Oh! how sweet is distinguishing grace!

REFLECTIONS.

READER! what an awful thing it must be, in a Church, calling itself Christian, to be under the direction of false teachers! Professing the name of CHRIST, and yet denying his GODHEAD! Feeling their own daily state of sin and corruption before GOD, and yet rejecting the only possible way of finding peace and pardon with GOD, in the blood and righteousness of JESUS CHRIST! *My soul! come not thou into their secret; unto their assembly mine honor be not thou united.* Oh! for grace, in the midst of a crooked and perverse generation, to brave every opposition of men; and faithfully, fully, and unceasingly, to proclaim the LORD our Righteousness.

Precious LORD JESUS! let thy name be as ointment poured forth. And, as thou knowest how to deliver the godly out of temptation; do thou keep them now, O LORD, in these awful seasons, when the HOLY GHOST is admonishing the Church, that false teachers will arise, even among the people. LORD! give us grace, to discern grievous wolves from true shepherds, and those that love the flock from those that live only to fleece them. My soul is relieved in the view, that JESUS knows his sheep, and is known of them. He will keep them in the dark and cloudy day. He will watch over them for good. He will bring them home, and bring them in, to his everlasting kingdom. Precious LORD JESUS! how safe and secure are all thine, kept by thine own power!

CHAP. III.

CONTENTS.

In this Chapter the Apostle closeth his Epistle, and a beautiful Close he maketh of it. He foretells of the last Days being marked with Scoffers. He assureth the Church of the Certainty of the LORD's *coming, and the Suddenness of it; and ends all in giving Glory to* CHRIST.

THIS second epistle, beloved, I now write unto you; in *both* which I stir up your pure minds by way of remembrance:

2 That ye may be mindful of the words which were spoken before by the holy prophets, and of the commandment of us the apostles of the Lord and Saviour:

3 Knowing this first, that there shall come in the last days scoffers, walking after their own lusts,

4 And saying, Where is the promise of his coming? for since the fathers fell asleep, all things continue as *they were* from the beginning of the creation.

5 For this they willingly are ignorant of, that by the word of God the heavens were of old, and the earth standing out of the water and in the water:

6 Whereby the world that then was, being overflowed with water, perished.

7 But the heavens and the earth, which are now, by the same word are kept in store, reserved unto fire against the day of judgment and perdition of ungodly men.

If there were no other authority than what the opening of this Chapter affords, in testimony, that the Apostle *Peter* is the inspired writer of it; this would be enough. For it proves, *first*, that he had written a former Epistle; *secondly*, that it was to the same persons to whom he sent his first, and in both which he calls them *beloved;* and, *thirdly*, he tells them, that the object of both was one and the same, to stir up their minds to remembrance. And his adverting both to the Prophets of the Old Testament, and to himself and his brother Apostles under the New, shews what a beautiful harmony is in both.

Reader! it is worthy your observation, how much the Apostle's mind was directed by the HOLY GHOST, to admonish the Church of the latter-day heresy, and of heretics. Scoffers are very awful characters. And nothing can more pointedly manifest the bitterness of the heart. The scoffing of men is, in human nature, in correspondence to the hissing of the serpent in his. The devil is the author of both. But we have not simply the sneer, but the contemptuous language of the enemy to contend with. *Where is the promise of his coming?* Alluding to what JESUS said before his departure. John xiv. 3. And so blind, and given up to a deluded mind, are such men; that GOD's Covenant with the earth, which he made after the destruction by the flood, and which the LORD frequently alludes to, in confirmation of his Covenant of grace, they pervert to the very reverse of the LORD's intention. Every man upon earth is this day a living testimony of the *former.* Gen. viii. 21, 22. And GOD makes this an argument for the belief of the *latter.* See Jerem. xxxi. 35, 36. with Gen. ix. 11—15.

But what I more particularly desire the Reader to notice, in confirmation of this Covenant in CHRIST, as all along shadowed forth, under every dispensation, and more especially in this of *Noah* is, that the HOLY GHOST, by *Peter*, refers to it in this very scripture. He expressly declares, that this ark, in which *Noah* and his family were saved, represented CHRIST, while the Patriarch and his household represented the Church. And however inattentively regarded by men, and though, according to philosophers, the rainbow may be accounted for on physical principles, yet GOD, from the first, designed it as a token of his Covenant. And every child of GOD ought to regard it as such, upon every renewed occasion, when that beautiful arch is seen by him in the heavens. GOD saith, that he will look upon it, and remember his everlasting Covenant, and so ought all his people. Gen. ix. 11—16. And it is a further inducement for the child of GOD so to do, not only to bear him up against all the sin and folly of scoffers, but to lead his heart on to the contemplation of JESUS, whom that bow represents. The New Testament Church, in, and through, the ministry of the beloved Apostle, is invited to behold that Rainbow which *John* saw round about the throne, meaning CHRIST. Rev. iv. 3. And this representation of JESUS was intended to teach, that as it encircled the throne, so that no dispensations can issue from the throne but what must pass through it, neither can any manifestations of GOD, in all the departments of nature, providence, grace, or glory, come forth, but in, and through CHRIST. Yea, all the views of JEHOVAH, with which he beholds his Church, must be in, and through Him. Reader! what a thought is this to refresh the soul of the regenerated child of GOD, not only against the blasts of ungodly scoffers, but under all the exercises and trials which the faithful meet

8 But, beloved, be not ignorant of this one thing, that one day *is* with the Lord as a thousand years, and a thousand years as one day.

9 The Lord is not slack concerning his promise, as some men count slackness; but is long-suffering to us-ward, not willing that any should perish, but that all should come to repentance.

10 ¶ But the day of the Lord will come as a thief in the night; in the which the heavens shall pass away with a great noise, and the elements shall melt with fervent heat, the earth also and the works that are therein shall be burned up.

<small>How sweetly the Apostle turns from scoffers, in answering them, in order to comfort the faithful. And what a blessed plan hath he adopted in doing it. The comparative statement of a thousand years, and of a day, is chosen by way of manifesting, that in relation to His Being, and existence, who inhabiteth eternity, all calculations of time lose their very meaning. I AM, which is the LORD's distinguishing name, renders past, present, and future to Him, but as one eternal *Now.* And it should not be forgotten by his people, that it is the eternity of his nature, and the unchangeableness of his purpose, counsel, will, and pleasure, which gives being and accomplishment to all his promises in CHRIST. The people of GOD, therefore, have an everlasting bottom to rest upon, in the assurance both of CHRIST's coming, and his coming to perform all his gracious intentions to his Church. And so sudden, as well as sure, will be his coming, that that great day, or night, will be to all the earth as unlooked for, and unexpected, as when the midnight thief breaks into the house while men sleep. Alarm will rouse up the whole of the unregenerate world, and those awful events will take place with them all, which in various scriptures are so described. Matt. xxiv. 27 to the end.</small>

11 ¶ *Seeing* then *that* all these things shall be dissolved, what manner *of persons* ought ye to be in *all* holy conversation and godliness.

12 Looking for and hasting unto the coming of the day of God, wherein the heavens being on fire shall be dissolved, and the elements shall melt with fervent heat?

13 Nevertheless we, according to his promise, look for new heavens and a new earth, wherein dwelleth righteousness.

14 Wherefore, beloved, seeing that ye look for

such things, be diligent that ye may be found of him in peace, without spot, and blameless.

15 And account *that* the long-suffering of our Lord *is* salvation; even as our beloved brother Paul also according to the wisdom given unto him hath written unto you;

16 As also in all *his* epistles, speaking in them of these things; in which are some things hard to be understood, which they that are unlearned and unstable wrest, as *they do* also the other scriptures unto their own destruction.

17 Ye therefore, beloved, seeing ye know *these things* before, beware lest ye also, being led away with the error of the wicked, fall from your own stedfastness.

I beg the Reader not to overlook the tender solicitude of the Apostle, directed by the HOLY GHOST, towards the Church. Like the pillar of cloud in the camp of *Israel*, which became light to GOD's chosen, and darkness to their foes; so here the great day of GOD, which even for a moment, if thought on, damps all the prosperity of sinners, is, and must be, to every justified child of GOD in JESUS CHRIST, a subject of endless and unceasing joy. Reader! I never can say enough to you, (under the presumption that the LORD hath wrought a saving work of grace upon your soul,) on this great point of faith and assurance in the LORD's promise. Depend upon it, *Peter* could never have said, that he was *looking for*, and *hasting unto*, the coming of the day of GOD, had he entertained the least doubt, or been at any uncertainty as to the issue of his own everlasting happiness in that day. The Apostle knew the certainty of the ground on which he stood. He had already passed from death unto life. He had gone under the sentence of GOD's holy law, which he had broken. He had found redemption in the blood of the cross, and stood perfectly, freely, and fully justified in the righteousness of CHRIST, his Head and Surety. Hence, he had long maintained through grace, fellowship, interest, and communion with GOD in CHRIST; and he now only waited for that great day of GOD, when JESUS would confess him before GOD and men, among all his redeemed in glory. Reader! is it so with you? *Peter's* privilege was not singular. All CHRIST's redeemed ones are the same. And every child of GOD who hath been saved, and called with an holy calling, is supposed to be daily, and hourly, living in the faith and enjoyment of it. Yea, the Church is said to be risen with CHRIST, and made *to sit together in heavenly places in* CHRIST. Ephes. ii. 6. And very sure I am, that it is not only among the triumphs of faith, so to live, and so to walk with GOD, in full assurance of hope; but it is a duty they owe to GOD, in giving the credit of believing him as GOD, in accepting and trusting to the record which the LORD hath given of his dear SON. *And this is the record, that he hath given to us eternal life, and this life is in his* SON. *He that hath the* SON *hath life.* And this, as surely in the life that now is, as in that which is to come. 1 John v. 11, 12. John iii. 36. Oh! for grace then, that, like *Peter*, yea, like all the faithful gone before, to be always looking for, and hasting unto, the coming of the day of GOD. And, as the Apostle saith, to be diligent in the use of all the appointed means of grace, that agreeably to our GOD and FATHER's original and eternal purpose, who hath chosen us in CHRIST, we may then be found in CHRIST, having peace in the blood of his cross, and being washed from sin, and robed in Him, we shall be without spot, and blameless.

And, Reader! what a sweet note on *long suffering* the Apostle dwells upon. And what child of GOD, but in his own experience, can, and doth, sing the same. Oh! the long suffering of my GOD, in the long, long years of my unregeneracy! Was not this salvation? And observe also the love of *Peter* to *Paul*. How sweetly hath he here endeared *Paul's* writings to the Church, and how delightfully doth he determine concerning the supposed difficulties in *Paul's* writings. Hard to be understood, he saith. But by whom? Not by any who are taught of GOD. None of those who are come to CHRIST. For JESUS saith, that *every man who hath heard and learned of the* FATHER *cometh to him.* John vi. 45. None of those taught of GOD the SPIRIT. For *John* saith, that the regenerate have *an anointing from the* SPIRIT, *and know all things.* 1 John ii. 27. Who then are these, the unlearned, and unstable, spoken of? Namely, the self-taught, the wise, and learned of this world, from whom divine truths are hidden, and who wrest the word of GOD, yea, all the scriptures to their own destruction. Hence JESUS thanked the FATHER when upon earth. Matt. xi. 25. And all the faithful thank him now.

18 But grow in grace, and *in* the knowledge of our Lord and Saviour Jesus Christ. To him *be* glory both now and for ever. Amen.

Reader! what is it to grow in grace? Grace is an humbling principle. And what then can a growth in it be, but to be increasing in humbleness. If this growth was formed in any attainment of our own, I fear, that instead of an increase of humility, it would make me proud. Moreover, grace is wholly of GOD, and not of men. If I grow in grace, it must be growth in the grace, that is, in CHRIST JESUS. As such it is wholly out of myself. Moreover, the LORD saith, that in the close of our warfare, *we shall remember and be confounded, and never open our mouth any more because of our shame, when I am pacified toward thee for all that thou hast done, saith the* LORD GOD! Ezek. xvi. 63. I humbly conceive, therefore, that to grow in grace, is to grow more and more humble before the LORD, from this growth in grace bringing the LORD's people into a deeper acquaintance with the plague of their own heart. Our first discoveries of ourselves, under grace, bring us but a little way in our exploring of our own corruption. The LORD doth by us, in the early manifestations of his grace, as he did by *Israel* when he brought them out of *Egypt*. It is said, that GOD *led them not through the way of the land of the Philistines, although that was near; for God said, lest peradventure the people repent when they see war, and return to Egypt. But* God *led the people about, through the way of the wilderness of the Red Sea.* Exod. xiii. 17, 18. So it should seem, for the most part, the Lord doth by his redeemed now, in bringing them out of the spiritual Egypt of sin and death. If the Lord were to bring us through the land of the *Philistines,* I mean, in bringing us at once to behold the depths of corruption in our fallen nature, what soul could survive the sight? But by little and little, leading us down, with increasing discoveries, to view the pit of our own corruption; how increasingly precious Christ becomes, in every new insight of our sins, and his mercy. Is not this to grow in grace?

But this, according to my view of this sweet scripture, will appear yet more confirmed, when we connect in our apprehension of it, what the Holy Ghost hath connected with it. But grow in grace, and *in the knowledge of our* Lord *and* Savior Jesus Christ. Surely, if by growing in grace, I grow more and more out of love with myself, I shall, by that grace in Jesus, grow more in love with Jesus. Exactly in the proportion I loath myself for my defilements, shall I love Jesus more for his holiness. As a growth in grace makes me more self-loathing, and self-abhorring, will not my knowledge of my Lord, and his suitableness to me, render Him more desirable? Suppose *Job* were to tell the Church about his growth in grace? When were his highest attainments, but when in the view of Christ, he lay lower in self-abhorrence than he had ever done before, and cried out in dust and ashes! Job xlii. 5, 6. Suppose *Isaiah* were to give in his testimony of his apprehensions of the same subject? When were his thoughts of himself lowest, and of Christ highest? Was it not in that vision, when he cried out, *Woe is me, I am undone; I am a man of unclean lips. Mine eyes have seen the king, the* Lord *of hosts!* Isaiah vi. 5. Let *Daniel,* holy *Daniel,* give his evidence. And when was his growth in grace at the highest pitch, but when he declared *his comeliness was turned into corruption?* Dan. x. 8. When was *Paul's?* Surely, when after more than *twenty years* had passed from his conversion, he summed up his account of himself, in saying, that *in him, that is, in his flesh, dwelt no good thing.* And, under the weight of it, he made that lamentable cry, *O wretched man that I am, who shall deliver me from this body of death.* Rom. vii. 18—24. Reader! let your own heart say, if so be the Lord hath taught your heart, what is a growth in grace, and in the knowledge of our Lord and Savior Jesus Christ, but, like *Paul,* to feel daily more and more the plague of the heart, and therefrom to be more humbled in ourselves; while growing in the knowledge of Christ, and his all-sufficiency, to take increasing joy in him, and, with *Paul,* say, *I thank* God *through* Jesus Christ *our* Lord!

I shall only detain the Reader one moment longer, to observe, that the short but expressive doxology, with which the Apostle closeth his Epistle, I would recommend the Reader not to pass hastily over, and consider it as so many words of course. Certainly, the sacred writers could never intend such things by such praises. To hallow the Lord's name is the first strain of praise in the Lord's prayer. And the cause wherefore the holy men of old so often burst forth, in the midst of their writings, and at the beginning and end of them is, because their souls, being full of GOD's glory, their mouths in speaking, and their pens in writing, could not refrain to set it forth. It should be our desire, as it is our privilege, to do the same. Both these great Apostles, *Peter* and *Paul*, thus unite in praises to GOD and the LAMB. *To Him be glory both now and for ever. Amen.* Ephes. iii. 21.

REFLECTIONS.

GLORY be to GOD, FATHER, SON, and HOLY GHOST, *Israel's* GOD in covenant for ever and ever! What praises thy people have now to offer, and what praises to all eternity, for thy love to the Church, in CHRIST! Praises to the FATHER's love, in his choice of the Church, from everlasting! Praises to the SON's grace, in marrying his Church, and redeeming her from all iniquity to himself, by his blood! And, praises to the HOLY GHOST, for his love in regenerating mercy, and all his watchful care over the Church, from grace to glory!

And, LORD, while we praise thee, in thy distinguishing mercy, in founding the Church in CHRIST, presiding over it as the Almighty Minister, in the appointment of ordinances, and means of grace; and giving the whole scriptures of our GOD, by inspiration, to make thy people wise unto salvation, through faith, which is in CHRIST JESUS, we find renewed cause to praise thee, O thou eternal SPIRIT, for raising up this blessed scripture, by the instrumentality of thy servant *Peter*, to comfort thy Church with those glorious truths herein contained. Yes! most gracious LORD! it was not only meant to refresh the dying Apostle, in bringing to his recollection CHRIST's glory in the Mount; but the record of it was designed, as it hath often proved, still is proving, and will, to the end of time, be proved a blessed testimony to refresh the souls of thousands! LORD! let it frequently refresh my soul also! And, amidst all the scoffers of the present awful day, let thy people be always on their watch-tower, waiting the LORD's coming. And, in the mean time, growing in grace, and in the knowledge of our LORD JESUS CHRIST.

Farewell, *Peter*, while we bless thy LORD, and our LORD, for thy ministry, we find no less cause to bless the LORD for all the improvements in grace we receive, under divine teaching, for all that is recorded in thine history. The Church of GOD, in heaven and earth, have profited by it. And, ere long, will all join together in the same song of glory, praise, and power, to GOD and the LAMB, for evermore. Amen, and Amen.

THE FIRST EPISTLE GENERAL

OF

J O H N.

GENERAL OBSERVATIONS.

ALL antiquity have, with one consent, ascribed this lovely and loving Epistle to *John*, the Apostle and Evangelist, although he hath not put his name to it. There is a great sameness of stile, and manner in it, as well as in the doctrine, to the other writings of the beloved disciple. The *place* from whence written, and the *time* when, are not so generally agreed upon. But, certainly, it must have been towards the close of John's life, for he speaks of *the last time*; by which he meant the destruction of *Jerusalem*, which JESUS foretold, and which took place but a little while (as some think) after *John* wrote this Epistle: though some have dated it before. The term of *General* Epistle, is intended only to intimate, that it was not directed to any individual person or Church.

But the most material point to be regarded on this occasion is, the very plain and clear marks it bears with it of divine inspiration. Here we rest more than satisfied, and find occasion for thanksgiving and joy. One sweet feature runs through the whole of it, in relation to the Church, namely, the Apostle's testimony to the FATHER's love, the SON's grace, and the HOLY GHOST's fellowship. And, as *John* lived to behold the springing up of deadly heresies in the coming of Antichrist, and the denial of the GODHEAD of our LORD, we have reason to bless GOD for lengthening the Apostle's life, to give the evidence which we have in this Epistle upon record, to this glorious fundamental truth of our most holy faith.

I shall not detain the Reader with any further observations, but only beg of him to bend the knee with me in prayer, that the LORD the SPIRIT, who hath graciously given us the scripture, will give us with it the understanding to apprehend it, that *having an unction from the* HOLY ONE, *we may know all things!*

CHAPTER I.

CONTENTS.

The Apostle begins his Epistle with a glorious Account of CHRIST. *And he assigns this Reason of his Writing to the Church, to bring them into Fellowship with his glorious Person, and the* FATHER *in Him. A blessed Testimony is given to the Blood of* CHRIST *cleansing from all Sin.*

THAT which was from the beginning, which we have heard, which we have seen with our eyes, which we have looked upon, and our hands have handled of the Word of life;

2 (For the life was manifested, and we have seen *it*, and bear witness, and shew unto you that eternal life which was with the Father, and was manifested unto us;

3 That which we have seen and heard, declare we unto you, that ye also may have fellowship with us: and truly our fellowship *is* with the Father, and with his Son Jesus Christ.

4 And these things write we unto you, that our joy may be full.

It is impossible to enter upon this Epistle, where so much display of the glories of CHRIST'S person meets us at the door, without being overwhelmed with the contemplation, if so be GOD the HOLY GHOST be our teacher. Reader! pause, before you go a step further. *That which was from the beginning.* Who, or what can GOD the HOLY GHOST be speaking of, but the LORD JESUS CHRIST; who is emphatically THAT, even that HOLY ONE, who is the sum and substance of all revelation; *by whom were all things created, and who is before all things, and by whom all things consist!* Coloss. i. 16, 17. Not THAT, in his divine nature and essence *only.* For then the words added would be unsuitable; *That which was from the beginning.* What beginning? Not eternity. For eternity hath no beginning. But the beginning of GOD'S going forth in his three-fold character of persons, in those great events which concern CHRIST and his Church. Such as John relates in his Gospel. See John i. 1. and Commentary. And *Paul,* Ephes. i. 4. and Commentary.

That these words are so to be accepted is very plain from what follows; for the Apostle adds, which we have *heard* and *seen.* *No man hath seen* GOD *at any time.* But, *the only begotten* SON, *which is in the bosom of the* FATHER, *he hath declared him.* John i. 18. Hence this glorious THAT is CHRIST, the glorious GOD-Man Mediator; and which *John* opens his Epistle with speaking of, in this most blessed and sublime manner. I detain the Reader to observe with me, the peculiar blessedness in which the HOLY GHOST hath influenced the beloved Disciple to speak of his LORD. THAT. Not his name; but in a more striking and descriptive way of blessedness: THAT. It is similar to the phrase used by the Angel sent to *Mary*, when he called CHRIST, THAT HOLY THING! Luke i. 35. As if (and which is in reality the case,) holiness is only in Him. He, and He alone is holy. He, and He only is THAT. Reader! do, I beseech you, ponder it well. It is at all times sweet. It hath been so in all ages of the Church. Multitudes now in glory have felt the sweetness of this expression, THAT. And, in the present CHRIST-despising generation, it becomes eminently so to the true believer in JESUS. See Isaiah xlix. 7.

But we must not stop here. The beloved Apostle having introduced his Epistle in the first word of it, with this glorious *That*, speaks with confidence and delight of his gracious familiarity with his people, in having allowed them to *hear* him, to *see* him, to *look* upon him; and that their hands have *handled* this word of life. Reader! here again, I beseech you, pause over this account. And when you have done it, ask your own heart this single question. Had *John* considered CHRIST simply as a man, (as some who call themselves Christians presume to do, and yet deny his GODHEAD,) would he have thought it necessary to have said, that he and his companions heard CHRIST, and saw him, looked upon him, and touched him? Would there have been any thing surprizing in those acts? But that he who was, and is GOD, should tabernacle among men, and should manifest his GODHEAD in a bodily substance, go in and out before them, and day by day make himself known to them, in all those wonderful transactions, of which *John* and his brethren the Apostles were ear and eye witnesses: these, indeed, were things to record, and which, while recording, their minds were overwhelmed with the contemplation of such astonishing manifestations!

The Apostle hath put the second verse of this wonderful relation, concerning the Person of CHRIST, in a parenthesis. Not as if it might be omitted, for it is too blessed for that purpose; but because his mind seemed to be, for the moment, lost in the marvellous subject, and he left speaking to the Church, to contemplate more immediately the LORD's Person. And how doth he express himself here? Truly, in the same delightful stile as might most fully shew his apprehensions of the GODHEAD of CHRIST, manifested in a body of flesh. *For the life was manifested,* (saith he,) *and we have seen it.* What life? He adds, *that eternal life which was with the* FATHER, *and was manifested to us.* What words can be more full to the purpose, in confirmation of CHRIST's GODHEAD? For who less than the Eternal GOD, can have Eternal life? And what can be more plain, in confirmation, that the SON of GOD became incarnate, than when the Apostle adds, that this eternal life was manifested, and *we* (he saith) *have seen it;* that is, seen GOD in CHRIST. Similar to what the same Apostle said, in the Gospel which bears his name. *For the* WORD *was made flesh, and dwelt among us, and we beheld his glory: the glory as of the only begotten of the* FATHER, *full of grace and truth.* John i. 14.

The Apostle having thus introduced to the Church the glorious Person of CHRIST, GOD-Man Mediator, in this most exalted point of view; he next proceeds to state the motives for which he sends this Epistle to the LORD's people; namely, that the whole body of CHRIST's Church might have partnership with them, in the knowledge and enjoyment of GOD in CHRIST, and the joy, both of Apostles and People, might be full. This, indeed, is the great object and design of all revelation. And, when GOD the HOLY GHOST hath regenerated the souls of CHRIST's people, and through his quickening and illuminating grace, the child of GOD is brought to see the love of GOD the FATHER, in the choice of the Church before the foundation of the world; and the love of GOD the SON, in having taken into union with himself his Church before time, and redeemed her in time for his glory and delight, to all eternity; then, every individual of CHRIST's mystical body, thus renewed, and thus taught of GOD the HOLY GHOST, is brought into this blessed fellowship and communion with the FATHER, and with his SON JESUS CHRIST.

Reader! pause over the glorious truths here made known. Then make the subject personal and practical. Then ask your own heart, what know you, in a real heart-felt knowledge and enjoyment of them? Recollect what JESUS himself said on the subject, to the FATHER. *That he should give eternal life to as many as thou hast given him. And this is life eternal; that they might know thee, the only true* GOD, *and* JESUS CHRIST *whom thou hast sent.* John xvii. 2, 3. Who can contemplate the unspeakable blessedness of this fellowship with the FATHER, and with his SON JESUS CHRIST, but with the most heartfelt joy! By reason of our union with CHRIST, we have communion with GOD in CHRIST. There is an union between CHRIST and the FATHER, in which we have no part. And, though this union of the FATHER and the SON becomes the cause of ours, yet is it perfectly distinct from, and unconnected with it. And JESUS himself sweetly, and blessedly marks this distinction, when he saith: *At that day ye shall know, that I am in my* FATHER, *and you in me, and I in you.* John xiv. 20. But our blessedness is the more, from having all *in* CHRIST, and *from* CHRIST, and *by* CHRIST. For all is softened and humanized, from coming to us in a nature like our own. See John xvii. and 1 John v. 7. and Commentary in both.

And how sweetly JESUS speaks of this fellowship which his people have with him, here in grace, and hereafter in glory, from their oneness with him. Thus JESUS speaks, in relation to the *former. And I have declared unto them thy name, and will declare it; that the love wherewith thou hast loved me, may be in them, and I in them.* John xvii. 26. And in relation to the *latter;* as it is JESUS's delight to give his people *grace,* so it is to give them *glory.* Hence he saith : *To him that overcometh, will I grant to sit with me in my throne; even as I also overcame, and am set with my* FATHER *in his throne.* Rev. iii. 21. In *both* which, let the Reader observe, that our fellowship is with CHRIST, and with GOD in CHRIST. His Church stands eternally safe and secure in him. And from the human nature in the Person of CHRIST united to the GODHEAD, CHRIST stands in union with the FATHER, and we in him; as he himself hath blessedly said :—*That they all may be one, as thou* FATHER *art in me, and I in thee, that they also may be one in us.* Yea, JESUS adds, *that the world may know, that thou hast sent me, and hast loved them as thou hast loved me.* John xvii. 21—23. What words are these? who shall fully explain them; or what heart fully conceive the extent of blessedness in them! See John xvii. and Commentary.

5 ¶ This then is the message which we have heard of him, and declare unto you, That God is light, and in him is no darkness at all.

6 If we say that we have fellowship with him, and walk in darkness, we lie, and do not the truth.

7 But if we walk in the light, as he is in the light, we have fellowship one with another, and the blood of Jesus Christ his Son cleanseth us from all sin.

8 If we say that we have no sin, we deceive ourselves, and the truth is not in us.

9 If we confess our sins, he is faithful and just to forgive us *our* sins, and to cleanse us from all unrighteousness.

10 If we say that we have not sinned, we make him a liar, and his word is not in us.

By the *message* may, I think, be considered the whole sum and substance of the Gospel. For the Apostle having before so blessedly introduced the LORD JESUS CHRIST, next tells the Church the purport of the divine revelation he brought. And, by the general expression of *light*, to which GOD in his threefold character of Person is compared, is meant to say, that every thing of darkness, (which sin, in all its multiform shapes, may well be called,) must, of consequence, be directly opposed to GOD. Hence, here is an infallible mark to know the Church, and every individual of the Church, by. For, if any man remain in the dark, and blind, and ignorant state of nature in which he was born, unconscious of the plague of his own heart, ignorant of CHRIST's Person as GOD-Man, ignorant of his offices, characters, and relations, hath never been regenerated by the HOLY GHOST, and is still in the *Adam*-state, *dead in trespasses and sins;* for such an one to talk of having fellowship and communion with GOD, when he neither knows GOD nor himself; this shews him to be deceiving himself, with saying *peace, peace, when there is no peace!* Reader! pause over the account, for it is truly awful. And what makes it yet more so is, that it is much more general than is supposed. Our LORD hath given us the representation of a whole professing Church of this kind, in that of *Laodicea*. Rev. iii. 14—18. They thought themselves *rich, and increased with goods, and needed nothing,* whereas He, *whose eyes are as a flame of fire, searching the heart, and trying the reins,* discovered, that they were *wretched,* and *miserable,* and *poor,* and *blind,* and *naked.* And that same Almighty LORD only knows, what multitudes there are of the same character in the present hour, mingling up in what are called Gospel Churches, in a pharisaical righteousness of their own! Such I mean, as though they hold the blessed doctrines of God the Father's everlasting love, in having chosen the Church; God the Son's redeeming love, in working out salvation by his blood and righteousness; and God the Spirit's regenerating mercy for an entrance into the kingdom of heaven; yet consider these but only *part means*, or but *procuring causes*, to their best, and (as they call them) *sincere* endeavors. In all such instances it may be truly said, *darkness hath covered the earth, and gross darkness the people.* Isaiah lx. 2. For, for men to profess having fellowship with God, while walking thus in the vanity of their own minds, is the most awful of all self-deceptions!

But what a blessed relief is it, to the soul of a poor self-condemned and self-loathing sinner, to be so graciously taught by God the Spirit, in this divine scripture, that *if walking in the light, as he is in the light;* that is, being enlightened by God the Spirit to see, as God sees, *sin to be exceeding sinful;* to lay low in the dust before God, under the condemnation of our own mind, convinced that in us, *that is, in our flesh, dwelleth no good thing;* to be daily, hourly, coming to Christ, as the Christ of God; and to Him, as a remedy, full and complete, and of God's own providing for sin; this proves the partnership, fellowship, and interest we have, in all that belongs to Christ, and in which all his redeemed have alike fellowship with God, and with one another; and *the blood of* Jesus Christ *his* Son *cleanseth us from all sin.* Reader! pause over these wonderful words, and ponder them well. The blood of Jesus Christ his Son cleanseth from all sin. Not the blood of bulls, or goats, or lambs, or sacrifices upon a thousand altars! Not the ordinances, means of grace, services, sacraments, prayers, tears, reforms, repentance, or the whole world of offerings, commutations, or charities, even though men would give the fruit of their body for the sin of the soul! Not these. For so far are they, any of them, or all of them put together, from recommending to the favor of God, that they are offensive to God, unless themselves are cleansed, and perfumed in that blood of Christ, which hath perfumed all heaven! Oh! the preciousness of this scripture. *The blood of* Jesus Christ *his* Son *cleanseth us from all sin!* Every word is bigger with importance than all the world! The blood of Jesus Christ. Nothing less than Christ's blood, can take away sin. And no blood but the blood of Jesus Christ, God's Son, can take away sin. And none but the Son of God, one with God, and equal with God, can be competent to this vast work. And not only cleanseth from sin, but *all* sin. Original sin, actual sin, natural sin, spiritual sin, universal sin, yea, all sin. And it cleanseth from all sin, by the infinite dignity of his Person who offered it, the infinite preciousness of the blood he shed for it, and the infinite merit, efficacy, and everlasting power of it, in that, in its cleansing, it cleanseth so as to prevent all future defilements. Oh! the glory of this perfect, full, and finished salvation! It is a *peace-speaking blood;* Heb. xii. 24. a soul-cleansing, sweet smelling blood; Ephes. v. 2. a full redeeming blood, for in it *we have redemption of sins according to the riches of his grace.* Ephes. i. 7. And neither the powers of hell, nor the remains of sin in our own nature, can bring any thing to counteract its efficacy, in the souls that have been cleansed by it. And the Church here on earth, which, through the leadings of GOD the HOLY GHOST, are come to the blood of sprinkling, as well as the Church in heaven, have all the same divine cleansing. The company *John* saw around the throne, were samples of the whole Church; *who had washed their robes and made them white in the blood of the* LAMB. Rev. vii. 14. Reader! write down this blessed scripture for hourly use. Yea, beg of GOD the HOLY GHOST to indent it with his living engraving signet, in the tablet of thine heart: *The blood of* JESUS CHRIST *his* SON *cleanseth us from all sin!*

I will not detain the Reader longer than is absolutely necessary, in observations on what follows. But the verses are too important to be hastily passed by. *John,* under the authority of the HOLY GHOST, having told the Church, that *the blood of* CHRIST *cleanseth from all sin;* though he knew the Church is thereby cleansed from all sin, so that its guilt and filth shall no longer condemn; yet, by what he immediately adds, he plainly shews us, that the bodies of the saints are still the subjects of sin; neither will they be ever free from sin, until they drop into the grave, and return to corruption. *If we say* (saith John) *that we have no sin, we deceive ourselves, and the truth is not in us.* Now here is opened to us an interesting subject, which, if duly studied, under GOD the SPIRIT's teaching, explains to every child of GOD the blessedness of being cleansed from all sin in CHRIST; while yet the best of men still groan under the consciousness of indwelling corruption.

When a child of GOD is first awakened from sin, and regenerated by the HOLY GHOST, and under his divine teachings, and quickening influences, he is brought to a sense of his lost estate by nature, and to a heartfelt knowledge of the LORD JESUS CHRIST by grace; he feels a blessedness in what the Apostle here saith, under the authority of the HOLY GHOST, that he hath fellowship with GOD in CHRIST, and that the blood of CHRIST cleanseth from all sin. But, in the midst of this soul-reviving truth, he feels, and groans under the daily workings of sin in his body, which he discovers to be virtually all sin. He would do *good,* but he finds *evil* present with him. He *delights* in the *law of* GOD, after the *inward* man; but he sees another law in his *members* warring against the law of his mind, and bringing him into captivity to the law of sin, which is in his members. The child of GOD ponders these things with the most poignant distress of soul; and, until they are explained to him by GOD the HOLY GHOST himself, he never can discover a full, and satisfying account.

As an humble means in the LORD's hand, I have, in several parts of this *Poor Man's Commentary,* (see particularly 2 Thess. ii. 13.) endeavored, and wholly on scriptural grounds, to shew, that grace, when renewing the *soul,* makes no alteration upon the *body.* The *body* is wholly a mass of flesh and blood, and bones and arteries. It remains, therefore still carnal. All its pursuits, and desires, and affections, and appetites, are suited to its nature, which is daily tending to corruption. So that grace makes no change in this part of our nature, neither was it ever intended. The original sentence at the fall must be executed. *Dust thou art, and unto dust shalt thou return.* Gen. iii. 19. Hence it is to be sown at death a *natural* body, as it was first formed in the *Adam*-nature of our creation; but by virtue of our redemption by CHRIST, it will be raised, at the resurrection, a *spiritual* body. This is to form the triumphs of CHRIST, in raising our *vile* bodies, to be then fashioned like unto his *glorious* body. This is what the Apostle calls *the redemption of our body*, and which they *who have the first fruits of the* SPIRIT, *wait for*. Rom. viii. 23. But in the mean time, a corrupt, sinful body, whose whole tendencies are corrupt, cannot but be in opposition to the renewed part of the child of GOD, who by regeneration is wholly spiritual, being quickened, which was before dead in trespasses and sins. It is no wonder, therefore, that in a constant daily warfare between such opposite principles, the child of GOD should go mourning. How shall it otherwise be, when a man's own body is everlastingly opposing his own soul? *the flesh lusting against the spirit, and the spirit lusting against the flesh; and these are contrary the one to the other: so that ye cannot do the things that ye would.* Gal. v. 17.

Reader! if this subject be well studied, under the teachings of the HOLY GHOST, and in the lessons practically taken from *the plague of a man's own heart;* it would tend to clear up the point upon true scriptural evidence, and, under grace, enable a child of GOD to extract much good from the seeming evil. It would shew him, more and more, his own unworthiness before GOD, hide all pharisaical pride from his eyes, keep open a constant spring of true sorrow for sin, in making him loathe himself in his own sight; and, above all, endear CHRIST in the glories of his Person, blood, and righteousness, as the sole cause of salvation. But if men unauthorized by scripture, untaught of GOD, will presume to be wise above what is written, and contend, that regeneration renews but in part, and that it is a work wrought alike in soul and body; that there is a progressive holiness and sanctification in the whole man; (though if the advocates for this doctrine would honestly confess, what their daily experience cannot but teach them, that they themselves are living witnesses against what they advance;) I say, it is not to be wondered at, that persons of this complexion are always hanging at an uncertainty, as to the condition of their spiritual state before GOD. For they are building up, in their own strength, a supposed holiness of their own, which is like erecting an house upon the mud, where there can be no foundation. And, as their whole life is at the best but a peradventure; at a peradventure they live and die.

I must beg the Reader's attention to another very sweet, and interesting point, which the HOLY GHOST hath here dwelt upon, by his servant *John. If we confess our sins,* (saith *John,) he is faithful and just to forgive us our sins, and to cleanse us from all unrighteousness.* Is GOD's faithfulness and justice concerned to forgive the sins of his people on their confession of them? Yes! for having received an equivalent payment, yea, more than an equivalent, in the death of CHRIST; the faithfulness and justice of GOD are both engaged, in Covenant-engagements, to discharge the Principal Debtor, now the Surety hath made him free. And in the pardon of all CHRIST's redeemed ones, the LORD remembers, and fulfils his everlasting Covenant. Isa. xlix. 9. Zech. ix. 11. And the confession of sins in the pardoned, is not the *cause* of pardon, but the *effect*. This will always follow, where the grace of GOD brings salvation.

Moreover:—It is among the precious testimonies of our enjoying communion with GOD, that we confess our sins before him. He that hath most communion and fellowship with GOD, will be most open and communicative. It is with GOD's friendship in this particular, as it is with man's: the more we love a man, the more we delight to unbosom ourselves to him. So with GOD in CHRIST, the more the LORD hath our confidence, the more we shall find grace to unfold to him, what we feel by reason of sin. Nay, as our sins and transgressions are all against GOD, the more sensibly we shall feel our love to him, the more we shall feel hurt at offending him. And, therefore, none will be so ready to rip open the soul before GOD, as that soul who loves GOD most, and dreads to do any thing so as to be shy before him. And, as we know, that the LORD knows all our secret sins, which are in the light of his countenance, before we can inform him: so we also know, that so gracious is our GOD, that he hath pardoned them before we have confessed them, and before we called for mercy, he hath answered. Isaiah lxv. 24. Oh! what a thought to comfort us. None but GOD's friendship could admit a friendship like ours! His love, not our deservings, becomes the standard of his favor. Hence, our communion with him, is kept up on our part, in confessing our sins. And on his part, in pardoning them in JESUS.

I will not dwell upon the last verse in this Chapter, though I must not wholly pass it by. *If we say that we have not sinned!* Who among the sons of *Adam* will, or can say this? Original sin, actual sin, sins of omission and commission; all sin, and come short of the glory of GOD. To deny this, must argue a state of blindness indeed, which no truly regenerated child of GOD can be in! But I add no more.

REFLECTIONS.

READER! You and I may well enter upon this blessed portion of GOD with prayer. And surely, under divine teaching, we shall end it in praise. Oh! who can contemplate Him whom *John* saw, heard, and handled, even THAT which was from the beginning, but with holy rapture and delight. Oh! that the object for which *John* declared these things, may be in my instance fully answered; and that I may truly have *fellowship with the* FATHER, *and with his* SON JESUS CHRIST!

Blessed GOD and FATHER! grant that light to thy redeemed, which may enable them to walk in thy light; and to know, by heartfelt experience, that *the blood of* JESUS CHRIST *thy* SON *cleanseth us from all sin.* And, LORD! let thy faithfulness and justice, as well as thy mercy and grace, be my everlasting comfort. GOD *can be just, and the Justifier of him that believeth in* JESUS. And GOD, for CHRIST's sake, will cleanse his redeemed *from all unrighteousness.*

CHAP. II.

CONTENTS.

The Apostle is here affectionately addressing the Church. He speaks sweetly of CHRIST, *in his Advocacy, and in his Propitiation. He calls upon little Children, young Men, and Fathers, in speaking to them of the great Subject of Salvation.*

MY little children, these things write I unto you, that ye sin not. And if any man sin, we have an advocate with the Father, Jesus Christ the righteous:

2 And he is the propitiation for our sins: and not for our's only, but also for *the sins of* the whole world.

I cannot sufficiently admire the blessedness of the subject *John* here enters upon; neither the tenderness to the Church, with which he doth it. *Little children!* is a sweet appellation, well suited for the beloved Apostle to use in his now advanced years, and the Church to receive. It is well, when faithful servants of the Lord so exercise their pastoral charge!

But what I would yet more particularly beg the Reader to keep in view, is the subject, with which he opens this Chapter. He warns the Church against sin. But, aware what a body of sin and death the best of men carry about with them, he bids them, under all sin, and all discouragements, to look to Christ. And how blessedly he speaks. *If any man sin.* And who is there of the Lord's people; which sins not? *We have* (saith he) *an Advocate with the* Father, Jesus Christ *the righteous, and he is the propitiation for our sins.* Observe. *We,* that is, the Church have this Advocate. We have not now to look out for an advocate. We have One, yea, an Almighty One. And he is both an Advocate, and a Propitiation; that is, he hath both paid our debt as a Propitiation, and now takes up our persons and our causes, as an Advocate, to see our sins all cancelled, and done away in his blood. And, observe yet further. This Advocate which we have, is with the Father. He who hath set forth Christ, as a Propitiation in his blood. So that God, who hath given Christ, and set forth Christ as a Propitiation, is He, with whom Christ hath to do, as our Advocate. And I pray the Reader yet further to observe. The Apostle doth not say, we have an Advocate with *our* Father: for though he is our Father in Christ Jesus, and very blessed it is to know him as such, in numberless instances and occasions; yet here, Christ is said to be an Advocate with *the* Father. Not only Christ's Father, and *our* Father, but *the* Father. What! is there more in the expression *the* Father, than *our* Father, or Christ's Father? Yes! upon the present occasion for which *John* writes. For let it be observed, that as *John* is holding forth this encouragement to the Church of Christ, that Christ is an Advocate and Propitiation for his people under the infirmities of sin; he is dealing with us as on the footing of God's justice. He considers the Father, therefore, as God, holy and just; and One that *will not clear the guilty.* Exod. xxxiv. 7. Hence he tells the Church, that Christ is with the Father, both as a Propitiation for sin, having fully paid down on the judgment-seat, the compleat price for our redemption; and also while there, (which he ever is,) he is an Advocate, to plead, and see that his Church is accepted, pardoned, justified, sanctified, and glorified, according to the agreement in Covenant-settlements.

Reader! what a blessed subject is here? Oh! what confidence might the faith of it produce, if grace was always in lively exercise, to come with it before GOD? Who would ever feel deadness, fears, doubts, mis-givings, or even heart-straitenings in prayer, if he beheld the throne of grace, the pardon office, the mercy-seat of the LORD, thus encircled with mercy; JESUS, both the Propitiation for sin, and the Advocate for the cause of his people? What shall stop or silence the plea of JESUS CHRIST the *righteous*, with the *righteous* FATHER? This was our LORD's own plea, when upon earth. *O righteous* FATHER! John xvii. 25. And it is his people's plea, taught by him, and offered up in him, now he is in heaven. And there is a great degree of blessedness in it, when rightly considered. For, when we thus plead, we plead upon the right and footing of GOD's justice. When we look up to GOD, simply as we are in ourselves; we can only look up for pardon and grace, as helpless sinners. But, when we look up in the interest of CHRIST, from an union with CHRIST; we then plead on the score of *justice*. And hence, upon this account it was, that *Paul* called the crown, which he knew was laid up for him, a crown of *righteousness;* because it was the just earnings of CHRIST's blood and righteousness. And *Paul* declared, that when it was given to him, it would be by the *righteous* Judge. 2 Tim. iv. 8. Reader! what know you of these things? Are you so looking to the throne? Can you hear the awful threatenings of GOD's holy law against sin; and yet look undismayed, under the consciousness of a broken law, to the LORD's righteous judgment against every single breach of it, because you behold the whole law fulfilled, in the Person of your Almighty Surety, and know your security in Him? If so, then will you enter into a blessed personal enjoyment of this sweet scripture, in stedfastly beholding and resting upon him, who is your Advocate, and with *the* FATHER, JESUS CHRIST the *righteous;* and who is the propitiation for your sins! See Rom. iii. 25. and Commentary.

I only detain the Reader for the moment, to observe how blessedly the Apostle includes the whole Church of CHRIST, as interested alike in this propitiation, when he saith, and not the propitiation for our sins only, the Apostles, and that Church to whom he was immediately writing; but also for the sins of the whole elect world. Blessed comprehensive mercy!

3 ¶ And hereby we do know that we know him, if we keep his commandments.

4 He that saith, I know him, and keepeth not his commandments, is a liar, and the truth is not in him.

5 But whoso keepeth his word, in him verily is the love of God perfected, hereby know we that we are in him.

6 He that saith he abideth in him, ought himself also so to walk even as he walked.

It should seem, that it is Christ that is here spoken of as knowing him, because the Apostle had been speaking of Christ, in the preceding verses, as our Advocate and Propitiation; and as such, the way he saith by which we know Christ, both in his Person, and in those blessed offices, is manifested in keeping his commandments. All which may be gathered from the Gospel, and which relate to his ordinances: and, as *John* dwells so particularly in this whole Epistle on the grace of love, as the fruit, and effect of God's love to the Church in Christ; it is possible, that he might have an eye to what the Lord Jesus had said in the days of his flesh, of a new commandment he gave them, to love one another. See John xiii. 34. But if the Apostle had a more general reference to the commandments of God, they are all comprized in that one comprehensive obedience, which our Lord, in his Commentary, gave the Jews. John vi. 28, 29.

7 Brethren, I write no new commandment unto you, but an old commandment. which ye had from the beginning, the old commandment is the word which ye have heard from the beginning.

8 Again, a new commandment I write unto you, which thing is true in him and in you; because the darkness is past, and the true light now shineth.

9 He that saith he is in the light, and hateth his brother, is in darkness even until now.

10 He that loveth his brother abideth in the light, and there is none occasion of stumbling in him.

11 But he that hateth his brother is in darkness, and walketh in darkness, and knoweth not whither he goeth, because that darkness hath blinded his eyes.

The new commandment and the old commandment the Apostle here speaks of, are well explained on Gospel principles. And the evidences of obedience he sums up in the fruits of obedience, as manifested in brotherly love. Not what the world seems so fond to inculcate, *universal* love, but the special love of *brethren*; and this on Christ's account. Loving them as brethren, and as members of Christ's body.

12 I write unto you, little children, because your sins are forgiven you for his name's sake.

13 I write unto you, fathers, because ye have known him *that is* from the beginning. I write unto you, young men, because ye have overcome the wicked one. I write unto you, little children, because ye have known the Father.

14 I have written unto you, fathers, because ye have known him *that is* from the beginning. I have written unto you, young men, because ye are strong, and the word of God abideth in you, and ye have overcome the wicked one.

Those different ages, in the members of CHRIST's body are distinctly spoken to, not as if their interest and union with CHRIST were not all the same, and the claims upon them the same, to live to CHRIST, and to walk with CHRIST; but, as those different ages furnish out occasion for promoting the LORD's glory in the earth, by their several graces, arising from that different age, brought into exercise. A babe in CHRIST is as truly part of CHRIST as the oldest saint of GOD. The single leaf on a tree, is as truly part of that tree, as the largest and loftiest branch belonging to it. And in both, it is the root gives support and nourishment, and not the leaf or the branch the tree. So is it in relation to CHRIST's body. The weakest, humblest, and most inconsiderable of CHRIST's members, is as much the FATHER's gift, CHRIST's purchase, and the SPIRIT's work of regeneration, as a Prophet or an Apostle. Paul, under the HOLY GHOST, blessedly explains this. Ephes. iv. 4—13. I beg the Reader to notice how sweetly the Apostle speaks to *little children,* and what a comprehensiveness of expression he folds up in one, *Your sins are forgiven you, for his name's sake.* Hence, here is a compleat justification of their persons, though but children, yea, *little* children; for CHRIST's name sake. I would recommend those who would presume to call in question the finished salvation of CHRIST, to consider this declaration of the HOLY GHOST by *John;* and let them shew the Church, if they can, what is wanting to make this compleat? By regeneration, these little children, babes as they are yet in CHRIST, are *made partakers of the divine nature,* and *have all things that pertain to life and godliness;* and, therefore, *they are washed, they are sanctified, they are justified, in the name of the* LORD JESUS, *and by the* SPIRIT *of our* GOD. Compare 2 Pet. i. 3, 4. with 1 Cor. vi. 11. Isaiah lxv. 20.

The fathers *John* writes to are considered as having long known the LORD, and as such, long proved his faithfulness; and, therefore, can well speak of it, to his glory and the Church's comfort. The LORD (if we may so presume to speak,) delights to be known and acknowledged in his faithfulness. Deut. vii. 9. And holy men of old, when a-dying, took pleasure to recount to the by-standers, of GOD's faithfulness and truth. We have beautiful instances to this amount in scripture record. *Jacob,* Gen. xlviii. 15 to the end. *Joseph,* Gen. l. 24. *Moses,* Deut. xxxiii. 26 to the end. *Joshua,* Josh. xxiii. 1—10. And, in more modern times, the Church of GOD hath not wanted testimonies of old saints, when dying out of time, and going into eternity, faithfully recording the righteous acts of the LORD, as a covenant GOD in CHRIST. Indeed, what can be more suitable and proper?

Young men come in for a portion of the Apostle's address, because, by regeneration, they are made strong in the LORD; the devil hath thereby received his deadly wound, and the sweet communications of grace give a withering to the fleshly lusts which war against the soul. But, Reader! do not overlook in all these, that little children, and old men, and young men, yea, every age in the Church of whatever standing, all derive their being, and well-being in grace, not from themselves or their attainments, but from the LORD. *All these worketh that one and the self-same* SPIRIT, *dividing to every man severally as he will.* 1 Cor. xii. 11.

15 Love not the world, neither the things *that are* in the world. If any man love the world, the love of the Father is not in him.

16 For all that *is* in the world, the lust of the flesh, and the lust of the eyes, and the pride of life, is not of the Father, but is of the world.

17 And the world passeth away, and the lust thereof; but he that doeth the will of God abideth for ever.

Very sweet as these verses are, yet, so very plain are they as to need no comment. The Apostle contrasts the world, with all its pursuits and pleasures, to CHRIST; and, within the compass of a few lines, shews how little to be considered, by souls regenerated, and made new creatures in CHRIST, are all that the world hath to propose, in comparison of the *durable riches and righteousness* which is in JESUS; yea, which is JESUS himself. One view of Him fades the whole. Prov. viii. 18—21.

18 ¶ Little children, it is the last time; and as ye have heard that antichrist shall come, even now are there many antichrists: whereby we know that it is the last time.

19 They went out from us, but they were not of us: for if they had been of us, they would *no doubt* have continued with us: but *they went out,* that they might be made manifest that they were not all of us.

20 ¶ But ye have an unction from the Holy One, and ye know all things.

21 I have not written unto you because ye know not the truth: but because ye know it, and that no lie is of the truth;

22 Who is a liar but he that denieth that Jesus is the Christ? he is antichrist that denieth the Father and the Son.

23 Whosoever denieth the Son, the same hath

not the Father: [*but*] *he that acknowledgeth the Son, hath the Father also.*

24 Let that therefore abide in you, which ye have heard from the beginning, if that which ye have heard from the beginning shall remain in you, ye also shall continue in the Son and in the Father.

25 And this is the promise that he hath promised us, *even* eternal life.

26 These *things* have I written unto you concerning them that seduce you.

27 But the anointing which ye have received of him abideth in you, and ye need not that any man teach you: but as the same anointing teacheth you of all things, and is truth, and is no lie; and even as it hath taught you, ye shall abide in him.

28 And now, little children, abide in him; that when he shall appear, we may have confidence, and not be ashamed before him at his coming.

29 If ye know that he is righteousness, ye know that every one that doeth righteousness is born of him.

By the *last time,* whether the Apostle meant the age of the Apostles, he himself being the only survivor, or the destruction of *Jerusalem,* I do not determine; but that it could have no reference to the end of the world is certain, for the period in the Church which was to succeed the Apostolic age was but just begun. Heresies were to arise, according to what GOD the HOLY GHOST had said by *Paul,* and the last time of the Gospel state was not to come before there had been a falling away, and the man of sin revealed. See 2 Thess. ii. 3—10. and 1 Tim. iv. 1. I desire the Reader to be very attentive to these scriptures. If they are taken in one mass of particulars, they evidently amount to this conclusion: GOD the HOLY GHOST, by the ministry of *John,* the last then living Apostle, was summing up the canon of scripture. And GOD the HOLY GHOST, having given every evidence and testimony by the inspired writings of his servants the Apostles, to the truth as it is in JESUS, tells the Church expressly, that heresies shall come, the chief feature of whose character would be to deny the GODHEAD of CHRIST. Heresies now at the close of *John's* life, began to appear, which, under various shapes and forms, soon swarmed in the Church, that is, the *nominal* Church. And this *John* shews, is a plain testimony of being the last time.

He then draws the feature of their character. *They went out from us,* that is, they joined our assemblies, called themselves Christians, and, as far as outward appearances carried them, they seemed to be of the Church of CHRIST. But, *they were not of us.* Never had the tokens of regeneration, and therefore no features of the true sonship in CHRIST. Reader! do not overlook this. There is but one mark, and that is an infallible one, of a real Christian; namely, the new-birth, or regeneration. Where this is, the proof is unquestionable of a child of GOD. Where this is not, the highest flaming profession is what *Jude* calls, *clouds without water.* Jude 12. I beg the Reader to remark with me, the grace of the LORD, in thus giving his children the sure testimony of a believer, in being born of GOD.

And, let not the Reader overlook what makes every thing blessed in knowledge, namely, having the unction of the SPIRIT, by which we know all things. This is an infallible teacher; and the figure is beautiful. The unction of the SPIRIT, gives light to the spiritual eyes, softens the heart, searcheth the understanding, mollifies the corrupt affections, and becometh the oil of joy and gladness, in imparting a knowledge of all things necessary to salvation.

It appears that *John,* the beloved Apostle, lived long enough to see many of the early heresies. And it is our mercy that he did. For, by reason of it, he hath armed the Church, under the HOLY GHOST, against them. If they dared to creep in, with the denial of the GODHEAD of CHRIST, (which, for the most part, is the foundation of all other heresies,) while *John* was yet alive, who lay in the bosom of CHRIST, what might not be expected from the latter-day apostacy?

I admire the remedy which the Apostle, under GOD the HOLY GHOST, proposeth, for the stability of the faith. *Abide in Him.* A close adherence to JESUS, becomes the sure way of comfort in the faith of JESUS. Our safety in CHRIST, indeed, hath nothing to make it so from any act of our's. It is the LORD's holding *us,* and not *our* holding him, which forms the everlasting security of the Church. Nevertheless, our confidence in Him will, more or less, bring comfort, and prevent us from being ashamed before him, at his coming. There is an *abiding* in CHRIST, which means somewhat more than our merely *believing* in CHRIST. A child of GOD, once savingly regenerated, may be said always to abide *in* CHRIST, though he is not always found in a lively exercise of the actings of faith *upon* CHRIST. He is still in the root, but it is winter with him, and there are no marks of life, in buddings, or blossoms, or fruit. It is plain that the Apostle meant somewhat more than merely confessing CHRIST, when he saith, *Little children abide in him, that when he shall appear ye may have confidence before him.* He certainly meant to say, that by abiding in CHRIST, the child of GOD should constantly have CHRIST in view, be always living *upon* him, and living *to* him. He is supposed, by this abiding, to undertake nothing but in CHRIST's strength, and to aim at nothing but CHRIST's glory. And where this abiding in CHRIST is, there will be an increasing desire after him, and an increasing delight in him. So that *when* CHRIST, *who is* thus *the life* of his redeemed *shall appear, we shall appear with him in glory.*

REFLECTIONS.

READER! let us behold, with holy joy, the gracious provision which GOD, who is rich in mercy, hath made for sin, in the person blood, and righteousness of our Lord Jesus Christ. It is God who hath set Christ forth a Propitiation. And it is God who hath sworn him into the office of our Advocate. Blessed therefore with such a Propitiation, and such an Advocate, in One and the same Person, and of God our Father's own providing, with what confidence may we draw nigh the mercy-seat, under all the discouragements and infirmities of our poor fallen nature?

And, dearest Jesus! may not all thy redeemed behold thee, waiting with delight for employment in that high character of thine, our Advocate, for all thy people, since thou hast already acted as their propitiation, and made compleat satisfaction for them in thy blood? Do thou, Lord, then, take up every cause, and plead in thine own infinite merits, and death, for every one of thine, against all the accusations of Satan, the demands of God's law and justice, and all the fears and misgivings of unbelief, and our own guilty consciences! Oh! the blessedness of the assurance, Jesus can and will save to the uttermost all that come to God by him, *seeing he ever liveth to make intercession for them!*

Hail! no less thou Holy and Eternal Spirit! It is from thee cometh that unction, by which thy people know all things. Oh! for grace from God, to believe in God, and to continue *in the* Father, *and in the* Son, *in the full assurance of the promise of eternal life!*

CHAP. III.

CONTENTS.

The Apostle breaks out in the Opening of this Chapter, into a devout Strain of Admiration and Praise, in the Contemplation of the Love of God. *He draws a Line of Discrimination between the Children of* God, *and the Children of the Devil. Some very sweet Proofs are given of the Character of* God's *Children.*

BEHOLD, what manner of love the Father hath bestowed upon us, that we should be called the sons of God, therefore the world knoweth us not, because it knew him not.

Every word is a sermon. Every expression riseth with increasing glory, in this sweet verse. The mind of *John* appears to have been overwhelmed in the contemplation, and he knew not how to express himself, when calling into view the love of God the Father. Behold! saith he, mark the astonishing mercy, both in the love of God, as it is in itself, and the manner of it, as it is shewn to us; that we, poor creatures, born in the *Adam*-nature of sin, should be called *the sons of* God! From everlasting having chosen us, and chosen us in Christ, his dear Son, given us to Jesus, predestinated us to the adoption of children to himself in Jesus, called us by his grace in Jesus, and accepted us in Jesus, and called us sons of God in Jesus! Oh! what love, yea, what manner of love is here?

And the subject is still heightened, from contemplating the discriminating nature of it; *Therefore the world knoweth us not, because it knew him not.* There is nothing which, under grace, tends to bring home the love of God to the soul, in an overwhelming tide of special manifestation, as when that love is marked to our view in the high flood of distinguishing mercy. The election of grace, shewn in our effectual calling, and that at a time when the whole world lieth in wickedness, gives it the full conviction of God's sovereignty. The world looks on. The world hears the account. The world stands in a state of consternation at what is related. But, all the while, the world is as ignorant of the children of the covenant, as they are of the Lord's design in the covenant. Oh! how striking are the words of Jesus to this effect. *Unto you it is given to know the mysteries of the kingdom of heaven; but to them it is not given.* Matt. xii. 11. And hence the Prophet, *Ah! Lord God, they say of me, doth he not speak parables?* Ezek. xx. 49.

2 Beloved, now are we the sons of God, and it doth not yet appear what we shall be; but we know that, when he shall appear, we shall be like him; for we shall see him as he is,

I beg to detain the Reader at this verse also, just to observe a little of the blessedness of it. *Now are we the sons of* God. Yes! For though carrying about with us a body of sin and death, as we do, yet, by regeneration, being quickened in our spiritual part, we are made *partakers of the divine nature, having escaped the corruption that is in the world through lust.* 2 Pet. i. 4. Hence, therefore, we are now, to all intents and purposes, sons of God. But of the glory, yea, that eternal glory, to which we are begotten and called by Christ Jesus, there are no images or similitudes with which we are acquainted here below, by which we can explain it. Nay, *eye hath not seen, nor ear heard, neither hath it entered into the heart of men to conceive,* of the nature or extent of that glory which shall be revealed. But this we know, that amidst all that want of conformity we now have to the person and image of our Lord, there will be then a likeness, *for we shall see him as he is.* See 2 Cor. iii. 18.

Reader! do pause over this most precious Scripture, for it is indeed most precious. When the holiest child of God takes a view of himself, and dissects the anatomy of his own heart, what an humbling prospect is before him? And when he contemplates the life of Him, of whom it is said, *he was holy, harmless, undefiled, separate from sinners, and made higher than the heavens;* what a striking dissimilarity instantly appears between the Head and the body? And when, under these humbling circumstances, the heart goeth forth sometimes, as it must go in distresses at the view, is it possible the child of God will say, as the question ariseth in the heart, that where there is so little conformity, yea, so much opposition, there ever will be a likeness and agreement? Reader! when questions of these, and the like nature, arise in the soul, I know no part of scripture more sweet and consolatory to silence fears, and strengthen faith and hope, than this very blessed verse of our God.

And, indeed, I cannot but suppose, that GOD the HOLY GHOST, plainly, and evidently designed it for the comfort of the LORD's people, in whose soul a saving change hath been wrought by regeneration, for their constant support under such exercises. A few plain observations on this point will set the matter abundantly clear.

And, *first*. When CHRIST betrothed the Church to himself, he saw her in all that loveliness and beauty in which his FATHER presented her to him. For, as *the King's daughter*, she was, (in the mind of JEHOVAH;) *all glorious within*. And *she is said to have been brought to the King in raiment of needle work*. Psm. xlv. 13, 14.

Secondly. When in the after-state in which JESUS saw her in the *Adam*-nature of her fall, as a loving Husband, JESUS could not but love her the same, and, indeed, he came purposely to raise her up. For it is both his delight and his glory, to *sanctify and cleanse her with his blood, that he might present her to himself a glorious Church, not having spot or wrinkle, or any such thing, but to be holy, and without blemish*. Ephes. v. 26, 27.

Thirdly. JESUS knows and considers, in the mean time, all that loathsomeness, by reason of sin, in which she is during the present time-state of her being. He hath redeemed her from the everlasting evil of it by his blood. And, in testimony of it, he hath renewed her spiritual part by his HOLY SPIRIT. And by his own resurrection from the dead, he hath given her an earnest, and pledge, that as he arose, so shall she arise at the last day. For he will change her vile body, that it shall be like to his glorious body. But, during the present state, she shall learn, by the daily workings of sin, in a corrupt and fallen nature, how great the departure of her *Adam*-state hath been, and how great his love is in redeeming her out of it. By both which, the grave shall become welcome, and CHRIST shall be exalted in her view, and more and more endeared every day of her life to her heart.

Fourthly. JESUS watches over his Church for good, and keeps her night and day, lest any hurt her. And how offensive soever she is to herself, by reason of her present unlikeness to her LORD, JESUS still loaths not her person, though he hates her sins. She is part of himself. *And no man ever yet hated his own flesh, but nourisheth it, and cherisheth it, even as* CHRIST *the Church*. Ephes. v. 29. He knows the hour is coming when he will take her home, and neither sin, nor sorrow, nor the leprosy of sin, or uncleanness, shall beset her any more for ever.

Reader! what think you of the love of GOD the HOLY GHOST, in giving this sweet verse to the Church? *First*, to tell the Church, and every individual of the Church, that amidst all that passeth, in the daily course of their warfare, to distress the soul, from the in-workings, and out-breakings of the body of sin, still the adoption character and sonship is not lost? *Beloved! now are we the sons of* GOD! And, *secondly*, notwithstanding the great unlikeness there is, too often at present, by reason of this sinful body of ours, between CHRIST our holy Head, and we his unholy members; yet the time is hastening when this unholiness of ours, will all be done away. *For we know that when he shall appear, we shall be like him, for we shall see him as he is*. These bodies of ours, which at death, are sown in dishonor, will be raised in glory. *I shall behold thy face in righteousness*, (said

one of old, and every regenerated child of God may say the same,)
I shall be satisfied, when I awake with thy likeness! Psm. xvii. 18.

3 ¶ And every man that hath this hope in him purifieth himself, even as he is pure.

The purity here spoken of must be wholly derived. No man can purify himself. Much less make himself pure, as Christ is pure. But the sense is, that being by regeneration quickened into a new and spiritual life, the child of God that hath this hope in him, beholds himself pure, as Christ is pure in Christ's purity. He considers himself accepted before God in the Beloved. And he pleads on this well-grounded and assured hope, for a compleat justification before God, and a compleat sanctification of himself in Christ on this footing. *Being justified,* (saith the Apostle,) *freely by his grace, through the redemption that is in* Christ Jesus. Rom. iii. 24.

4 Whosoever committeth sin transgresseth also the law; for sin is the transgression of the law.

5 And ye know that he was manifested to take away our sins; and in him is no sin.

6 Whosoever abideth in him sinneth not; whosoever sinneth hath not seen him, neither known him.

7 Little children, let no man deceive you: he that doeth righteousness is righteous, even as he is righteous:

8 He that committeth sin is of the devil; for the devil sinneth from the beginning. For this purpose the Son of God was manifested that he might destroy the works of the devil.

9 Whosoever is born of God doth not commit sin; for his seed remaineth in him: and he cannot sin because he is born of God.

10 In this the children of God are manifest, and the children of the devil: whosoever doeth not righteousness is not of God, neither he that loveth not his brother.

11 ¶ For this is the message that ye heard from the beginning, That we should love one another:

12 Not as Cain, *who* was of that wicked one, and slew his brother, and wherefore slew he him? Because his own works were evil, and his brother's righteous.

I include the whole of these verses under one reading, because the whole subject is but one and the same; though several and various observations arise out of it. I will beg the Reader's attention to them in order. And *first* of sin. *Whosoever committeth sin, transgresseth also the law, for sin is the transgression of the law.* As well as I recollect, this is the fullest account we have of sin, in all the Bible. And yet, all we gather from hence concerning it, is, that sin is the transgression of the law; and that transgression is of the devil. It is defined so far, as to understand the malignity of its nature, and the malignity of its origin. Both bad enough you will say, and very dreadful to consider. But neither of these make discoveries what sin itself is. That it is an infinite evil, because committed against an infinite Being; and, because nothing less than an infinite sacrifice, could do away its baleful effects. Here is bounded our knowledge of it. Unless, indeed, we add to it this further discovery, that, in all creatures, its nature is the same. Where sin is found, whether in men or Angels, the damned in hell, or bad men upon earth, sin is sin wherever it is. And this latter view serves to set forth and magnify the distinguishing riches of grace, wheresoever the LORD recovers his people from the evil of it, and blessedly proves that sweet scripture, that as *sin hath reigned unto death,* so it is *grace* alone *that reigneth through righteousness unto eternal life, by* JESUS CHRIST *our* LORD. Rom. v. 21.

Secondly. Though we cannot any further define sin, yet, as the source and origin of it is traced to the devil, it is our mercy to discover from scripture, as here set forth, that the productions of sin, on the different characters in whom it appears, though all brought about by the agency of the devil, is nevertheless induced very differently, in the different characters of the children of the devil, and the children of GOD. In GOD's children, he acts upon them by temptation. In his own children, by the natural tendency of their heart. GOD's children may, and GOD's children will, by the devil's artifice and seduction, fall into sin; but the children of the devil follow sin by the natural bias of their nature. In the one, they are wrought upon by bondage, fears and servitude, *for whosoever committeth sin is the servant of sin,* JESUS *saith.* John viii. 34. GOD's children are the devil's servants and drudges, and wear his livery, and delight in his work, while in a state of unrenewed nature; but they are not his sons, neither is there any relationship between them. Whereas in the *other,* there is an affinity between the serpent and his seed; so that their actions cannot but correspond. Hence, CHRIST said to the *Pharisees; Ye are of your father the devil, and the lusts of your father ye will do.* John viii. 44.

This different feature of character, forms an eternal line of distinction between the two; and is, as this scripture states, a decided manifestation between the children of GOD, and the children of the devil.

Thirdly. But there is another, and, if possible, yet more clear mark of discrimination, to form the different seeds. For, as they are acted upon differently, so their very nature from the first, is different. The seed of CHRIST are said by CHRIST to be *the children of the kingdom.* The seed of the Serpent, by Him also declared to be *the children of the wicked one.* Our LORD himself hath beautifully explained this, in his parable of the Good Seed and the Tares, See Matt. xiii. 36—40. And although the both are born in the

Adam-nature of sin, and involved alike in the ruin of it, yet, by virtue of this relationship to the two distinct heads, the *one* is brought out of the death of sin, by the quickening and regenerating influence of the Holy Spirit; while the *other* remains unquickened, and for ever *dead in trespasses and sins.* Ephes. ii. 1.

Fourthly. Though the scripture hath not explained, (perhaps it is impossible to explain it to our present unripe faculties,) how the seed of Christ is communicated to the *Adam*-nature, by which that nature in the instance of the Church, is *preserved in* Jesus Christ, *and called,* Jude 1. while in the instance of all others, the deadly seed of the serpent, in every generation to the same nature, brings forth the spawn of sin; yet the fact itself, that it is so, is all that we are interested to prove, and know. And God's promises to his people most fully confirm and establish the truth of the *one,* and, both his word and the nature of them, determine the *other*. To the *one*, the Lord saith, *I will pour my* Spirit *upon thy seed, and my blessing upon thine offspring.* Isaiah xliv. 3. see also Isaiah lix. 21. To the *other,* we hear Christ speaking, *Ye serpents, ye generation of vipers, how can ye escape the damnation of hell.* Matt. xxiii. 33.

Fifthly. The everlasting war, which hath been through all time, and must be through all eternity kept up, between the children of the kingdom, and the children of the wicked one, draws a yet further line of discrimination. For the enmity is on this sole account, according to God's sentence at the fall, which he then pronounced on the serpent, and his venomous brood; *I will put enmity between thee and the Woman, and between thy seed and her seed.* Gen. iii. 15. By which seed of Christ is meant all the children given to him, before the foundation of the world, and all as seed, included in the Covenant of Grace. And by the seed of the serpent is meant, all the race of ungodly men, of whom *Cain* as one, is given as an example in this scripture. He is expressly said to be *of that wicked one.* That the seed of the serpent means men, is evident from another consideration, namely, that Angels do not beget Angels. We no where read of the propagation of spirits by spirits. And we know that the whole crew of the rebellious angels, namely, the devil and his angels which are now in hell, were once in heaven. Rev. xii. 9. Jude 6. So that by the children of the devil are meant men, and not angels or spirits!

Lastly, to add no more. What is here said of the seed of Christ, and their inability to commit sin, is wholly in reference to their spiritual nature. For thus the words express it. *Whosoever is born of* God, *doth not commit sin.* The new-birth, or the being born of God, which is the same thing, is wholly spiritual. For the body of flesh remains the same in the *Adam*-nature of a fallen state. And as it is corrupt and sinful, so its daily tendencies are to corruption. At the last day it will arise a glorified body; and though sown in dishonor at death, it will be raised in glory at the resurrection. Whereas the spiritual part of every child of God, when new born in God from the *Adam*-nature, induced by the fall, being dead in trespasses and sins, is quickened to a new and spiritual life. And, as this scripture blessedly saith, *it cannot sin, because it is born of* God, *and his seed remaineth in him.* It is *born not of corruptible seed, but of incorruptible, which liveth and abideth for ever.* 1 Pet. i. 23.

It hath *all things given to it according to his divine power, which pertain to life and godliness.* And it is made a *partaker of the divine nature, having escaped the corruption that is in the world through lust.* 2 Pet. i. 3, 4.

Reader! after those many observations, I must not trespass any longer than just to say, seeing GOD the HOLY GHOST hath here laid the foundation, so deep and so sure in the privileges of GOD's children; let every child of GOD see to it, that they never lose sight of GOD's mercies, and their interest in him. The seed of CHRIST, chosen in CHRIST, preserved in CHRIST, made holy in CHRIST, accepted in CHRIST, are begotten to all blessedness. Well might the Apostle, under the impression, cry out! *Behold! what manner of love the* FATHER *hath bestowed upon us, that we should be called sons of* GOD.

13 Marvel not, my brethren, if the world hate you.

14 We know that we have passed from death unto life, because we love the brethren, he that loveth not *his* brother abideth in death.

15 Whosoever hateth his brother is a murderer: and ye know that no murderer hath eternal life abiding in him.

16 Hereby perceive we the love *of God*, because he laid down his life for us: and we ought to lay down *our* lives for the brethren.

17 But whoso hath this world's good, and seeth his brother have need, and shutteth up his bowels *of compassion* from him, how dwelleth the love of God in him?

18 My little children, let us not love in word, neither in tongue; but in deed, and in truth.

19 And hereby we know that we are of the truth, and shall assure our hearts before him.

20 For if our heart condemn us, God is greater than our heart, and knoweth all things.

21 Beloved, if our heart condemn us not, *then* have we confidence toward God.

22 And whatsoever we ask, we receive of him, because we keep his commandments, and do those things that are pleasing in his sight;

23 And this is his commandment, That we

should believe on the name of his Son Jesus Christ, and love one another, as he gave us commandment,

24 And he that keepeth his commandments dwelleth in him, and he in him. And hereby we know that he abideth in us by the Spirit which he hath given us.

The exhortation of the Apostle, to feel no astonishment at the hatred of the world, follows very suitedly, after what he had been before observing, on the distinguishing love of God in Christ. If the hatred of the world, be solely on account of our attachment to Christ, so far from becoming a subject of marvel, it ought to be a subject of great joy. Jesus saith, *Behold I, and the children whom the* Lord *hath given me, are for signs and for wonders in Israel!* Isaiah viii. 18. As Christ himself was despised, so are his people. And it is blessed to observe, that as the Person of Christ was despised, so were all his offices. Isaiah liii. 2. His preaching. John vii. 12. His miracles. Matt. xii. 24. His conduct. Matt. xi. 19. And his followers, as the off-scouring of the earth. John vii. 48. 2 Cor. vi. 4—10.

I have often thought, that to a child of God under temptations and fears, and doubts and misgivings, this testimony of the new-birth, in the love of the brethren when higher ones are for a time wanting, becomes very refreshing. There may be with some precious souls, seasons, when former views of Christ's Person, and suitableness, and fulness, and all sufficiency, are not so bright and shining as heretofore. But there are no seasons, in the life of a regenerated believer in Christ, when the love of the brethren, as brethren in Christ Jesus, is done away. Try a child of God in the darkest hours, and this remains. And if I love a child of God, because he is a child of God, I must certainly love him, on whose account I feel that love. So that it is a sweet testimony, in the absence of higher tokens, of our love to the Lord Jesus, when we love the brethren for Jesus's sake.

But when we have carried our love to the brethren of the Lord Jesus's, on his account, to the highest possible pitch of affection, how infinitely short the whole falls, compared to what the Apostle, in the following verse, speaks of Christ's love to his people. *Hereby perceive we the love of* God, *because he laid down his life for us.* The name of God is not in the original; but it is very properly supplied. And that it is Christ who is meant by the name is evident, because it was neither the Person of the Father, nor the Holy Ghost; but God the Son who laid down his life for his people. And it is a sweet scripture on another account, for it is proposed as the highest testimony of his love. It is similar to a verse in the next chapter, iv. 10. *Herein is love.* As if this demonstration of love, outweighed every other. It was love unparalleled, both in greatness and condescension, for Christ the Son of God to take upon him our nature, and for God to give us to Christ, and Christ to us; to bless us in all the departments of nature, and of providence, and of grace, and of eternal glory. But all these lessen to the view, when we rise to this highest, and best of all demonstrations of love, JESUS laying down his life for us; and offering himself an offering and a sacrifice to GOD, for a sweet smelling savor. Ephes. v. 2. How our love to the brethren, with all the warmth of affection, sinks in our esteem, when we contemplate this *love of* CHRIST, *which passeth knowledge!* And in those cases, where men profess both a love to CHRIST and his people, who possess from the bounties of a gracious GOD, much of the good things of this life as they are called, (because when rightly used, they minister to good in the LORD's glory,) but yet distribute them not to the necessities of the saints; how is it possible to interpret such a profession, by actions so totally dissimilar? Reader! depend upon it, if such men have real faith, with such unsuitable practice, it is a very weak faith at the best. He can never be said to trust GOD with his soul, who is over anxious in providing for the body. And very sure I am, that he is really lean in spiritual things, who is fattening on temporal things.

I will detain the Reader no longer in this Chapter, than just to observe, that when the Apostle saith, concerning the condemnation of a man's own heart, that if self accusation becomes painful, the consciousness of the greatness of GOD, and his knowledge of our heart, may excite yet more alarming apprehensions. This is the sense in which the passage may be taken. But there is another sense, and which, if well-founded, ministers to the reverse, and in a way of comfort. If our hearts condemn us, what a blessed relief to a soul under heart reproaches, to look off self to CHRIST. There is more in CHRIST to uphold, more to bless, more to justify, than all the sin of the LORD's people to condemn. And, when a child of GOD is born again, (and it is to such *John* is writing,) this life in CHRIST sin cannot destroy, neither can death or Satan reach it. *Your life is hid with* CHRIST *in* GOD. Coloss. iii. 3. And when the Apostle adds, *Beloved, if our hearts condemn us not;* that is, he doth not mean a cold, insensible, unfeeling heart, (for he is all along writing to the regenerate,) but it is that heart, which, while laying low in the dust before GOD, beholds more in CHRIST to save, than sin unpardoned to condemn; *then* (saith he) *have we confidence towards* GOD. Here again, he doth not mean that it is our strength of faith which gives this confidence, but the full and finished salvation of CHRIST, which gives strength to our faith. Reader! you and I shall do well, (if so be the LORD hath wrought a work of grace upon our hearts,) to apprehend rightly, that our foundation for holy triumphs, doth not rest upon our faith, or the exercise of faith, or any other of the graces and gifts of GOD the HOLY GHOST. Not in these, or any of them, or all of them put together, but the sure resting place of the redeemed soul is in the compleatness of CHRIST's finished salvation, and GOD the FATHER's perfect approbation, and acceptance of the Church in it. This is what the HOLY GHOST so blessedly said, by the Apostle, and what every child of GOD, taught of the LORD, knows to be true; *If we believe not, yet he abideth faithful; he cannot deny himself.* 2 Tim. ii. 13.

REFLECTIONS.

Who can contemplate the love of God, as set forth in this Chapter, in adopting sinners into his family, and calling them sons of God, without being overwhelmed in the view. To behold some of the Lord's family, indigent and poor in all the worldly accommodations of this life; and yet by regeneration, to know them kings and priests to God and the Father? They are indeed unnoticed, unregarded, yea, often despised by the great ones of the earth; and yet, considered in Christ it may be said of them; *of whom the world is not worthy!* And though overlooked and disowned now, what will be the consternation of the ungodly at that great day, when they shall behold them in the likeness of Him, in whose image they will arise.

My soul, I charge it upon thee, to mark well the characters so accurately drawn in this scripture, between the children of God, and the children of the devil. Oh! how gracious hath God the Holy Ghost shewn himself, in those striking discriminations of character, that God's little children may not be deceived. Blessed and eternal Spirit! grant to me thy gracious teachings. So shall I learn the precious tokens of Jesus's love, in laying down his life for his people! Give me grace in the view of it, for his sake to be always alive to testify my love to the brethren. Lord keep my poor soul from the errors of the present day, in high professions mixed with low apprehensions of Jesus. Dearest Lord Jesus! cause me to dwell, by faith, in thee; whilst thou art everlastingly abiding in my heart. And let my daily testimony, that I am thine, be always uppermost in my heart, by the sweet teachings of thy Spirit, which thou hast given me.

CHAP. IV.

CONTENTS.

Here are contained Commands to try the Spirits, and Rules given for discovering of them. Some blessed Things are spoken of Christ. *The Chapter concludes with an Account of* God's *Love.*

BELOVED, believe not every spirit, but try the spirits whether they are of God: because many false prophets are gone out into the world.

2 Hereby know ye the Spirit of God: Every spirit that confesseth that Jesus Christ is come in the flesh *is* of God.

3 And every spirit that confesseth not that Jesus Christ is come in the flesh is not of God, and this is that *spirit* of antichrist, whereof ye have heard that it should come, and even now already is it in the world.

4 Ye are of God, little children, and have overcome them: because greater is he that is in you, than he that is in the world.

5 They are of the world; therefore speak they of the world, and the world heareth them.

6 We are of God, he that knoweth God, heareth us: he that is not of God, heareth not us, hereby know we the spirit of truth, and the spirit of error.

This is a very blessed direction of GOD the HOLY GHOST, by *John*. The Reader should recollect, as he reads it, that the LORD the SPIRIT is about to close the sacred canon of scripture. And as the latter-day heresies, of which the SPIRIT had spoken expressly by *Paul*, (1 Tim. iv. 1.) were now beginning to appear in a more daring and open manner in the world, the HOLY GHOST here gives one infallible mark, by which the child of GOD may try all. I pray the Reader to attend to it with that diligence it demands. There never was a day that needed it more. Never more false spirits coming forward with an impudent face, under the pretence of converting the whole earth, while multitudes of them openly deny the GODHEAD of CHRIST, and disown the person and work of GOD the HOLY GHOST.

Let the Reader attend to what GOD the SPIRIT here saith, of the method whereby the Church is to try the truth from error. *Every spirit that confesseth that* JESUS CHRIST *is come in the flesh, is of* GOD. And, on the contrary, *every spirit that confesseth not that* JESUS CHRIST *is come in the flesh, is not of* GOD. Surely, a volume could not have decided the point more plainly. And what is the confession of JESUS CHRIST's being come in the flesh, but the conviction wrought in the soul, by the regenerating power of GOD the HOLY GHOST, that He, who in his divine nature is *One with the* FATHER, *over all* GOD *blessed for ever*, is, in his human nature, One with his Church and people, and in the fulness of time, hath come and tabernacled among them. Which expression corresponds to the whole purport of revelation on this point, and which the same beloved Apostle hath most sweetly declared, in a single verse of the Gospel which bears his name. *The* WORD (saith he) *was made flesh, and dwelt among us, (and we beheld his glory, the glory as of the only begotten of the* FATHER,) *full of grace and truth.* John i. 14.

Reader! when you hear these very plain words of GOD the HOLY GHOST, concerning the person and coming of the SON of GOD, in substance of our flesh, and behold the whole body of scripture, in both Testaments, bearing testimony to the same; perhaps you are astonished how it is, that such men should arise, who deny CHRIST's GODHEAD, and the HOLY GHOST's Person and Ministry! So am not I! The word of GOD, in many parts, informs the Church of such heresies, and especially in the last times. And the same blessed word tells also of the heretics which shall bring them, *who were before of old ordained to this condemnation.* Jude 4. Hence, therefore, 1 am on the look out for them. And if such heresies were not to arise, I should lose a blessed testimony in the Word of GOD, which hath foretold the Church *of them,* and armed the Church *against them.* And if such heretics were not to come forth among us, we should be at a loss to discover what false spirits they are, which the Church hath to expect, and to contend with.

But still perhaps you will say, by what specious arguments do such men support their wretched cause, so as to give even a plausibility to their system of infidelity? The answer is at hand. *The spirit* (which another Apostle elsewhere speaks of, Ephes. ii. 2.) *that now worketh in the children of disobedience,* can, and doth easily furnish them with weapons for the cause. By compliments to human reason, and by flattery to the pride of human learning, they work upon minds like their own, *to deny the* LORD *that bought them;* (2 Pet. ii. 1.) *and bring upon themselves swift destruction.* Hence, by giving *different interpretations* to those scriptures, which speak too plainly against them to the main points of truth, and by charging others with being *interpolations,* and the like; they give a covering to their heresy, and lull infidels, like themselves, asleep, to their eternal ruin.

But, while neither the heresies themselves, nor the heretics which bring them, ought to excite any surprize to the faithful, who are taught to expect *both,* it is, I confess, matter of astonishment with me, that any should be found, of the truly regenerated believers in CHRIST, which can manifest so little regard to the person and glory of the LORD JESUS CHRIST, as to mingle with those who openly contemn both, in the denial of his GODHEAD. This was a peculiarity of conduct reserved for the *nineteenth* century. And, whatever plausible reasons may be held forth for such a junction, certain it is, that it is in direct disobedience to the positive command of the LORD, on the subject of heresy; *I heard another voice from heaven, saying, Come out of her, my people, that ye be not partakers of her sins, and that ye receive not of her plagues.* Rev. xviii. 4.

But, what is the great and infallible security against being led away by the heresies around, and the discovery of the false spirits which come forth to deceive? There is but one, and a sure one it is, which never hath failed, neither can fail, amidst all the present errors of the day, or all that may arise; namely, the regeneration of the heart, or the being born of GOD. Where GOD the SPIRIT hath quickened a sinner, which was before dead in trespasses and sins, this precious child of GOD hath in himself a full testimony to his sonship, in being born of GOD, and a confirmation also, that JESUS CHRIST is come in the flesh, being GOD and Man in One Person, the CHRIST of GOD.

Reader! look into your own heart, and see whether it be not a most firm and unquestionable security against this, and every other error, of either antient or modern heresy or heretics. If so be the LORD the HOLY GHOST hath regenerated you, and the SPIRIT witnesseth with your spirit, that you are born of GOD. For then hath he taught you *the plague of your own heart.* And what artifice of men, or devils, can bear up against this divine teaching, when you yourself also daily feel, and know how that heart is for ever interrupting your spiritual pursuits, and warring against your soul! So, in like manner, when GOD the HOLY GHOST hath taught you *who* CHRIST *is,* and *the efficacy of his blood and righteousness;* when you have felt the *sovereignty of his grace,* the compleatness and fulness of his *finished sal-*

vation; have known the love of GOD, the sweetness and suitableness of his *promises,* and been fed by them from day to day, can an host of heretics persuade you that these precious things are false, and that JESUS CHRIST, the SON of GOD is not come in the flesh? Oh! how gracious hath our GOD been, to provide such blessed securities for his people against all perilous times like the present!

7 ¶ Beloved, let us love one another: for love is of God; and every one that loveth is born of God, and knoweth God.

8 He that loveth not, knoweth not God, for God is love.

9 In this was manifested the love of God toward us, because that God sent his only begotten Son into the world that we might live through him.

10 Herein is love, not that we loved God, but that he loved us, and sent his Son *to be* the propitiation for our sins.

11 Beloved, if God so loved us, we ought also to love one another.

12 No man hath seen God at any time. If we love one another, God dwelleth in us, and his love is perfected in us,

13 Hereby know we that we dwell in him, and he in us, because he hath given us of his Spirit.

14 And we have seen, and do testify that the Father sent the Son *to be* the Saviour of the world.

15 Whosoever shall confess that Jesus is the Son of God, God dwelleth in him, and he in God.

16 And we have known and believed the love that God hath to us. God is love: and he that dwelleth in love dwelleth in God, and God in him.

17 Herein is our love made perfect, that we may have boldness in the day of judgement: because as he is, so are we in this world.

18 There is no fear in love; but perfect love casteth out fear: because fear hath torment; he that feareth is not made perfect in love.

19 We love him, because he first loved us.

20 If a man say, I love God, and hateth his brother, he is a liar: for he that loveth not his brother whom he hath seen, how can he love God whom he hath not seen?

21 And this commandment have we from him, That he who loveth God love his brother also.

I include all these under one reading, that in a *Poor Man's Commentary* I may not trespass. The *two* great points here dwelt upon are, *first*, the love of God to his people. And, *secondly*, our love to him, and to each other, the members of Christ's body the Church, as flowing from it. God's love the *cause*. Our love the *effect*. A word or two I would beg to offer upon each.

And, *first*. God's love to the Church in Christ. In which is included the love of the whole Persons of the Godhead. But as the source is in God, and wholly resulting from himself; it is impossible to trace it but in the effects. What the Apostle here saith, of our ignorance of God, is very highly in proof. *No man hath seen God at any time.* And how then shall he describe the source of God's love? Indeed, it is never attempted to be shewn, but by effects. *In this was manifested the love of God.* In what? *He gave his only begotten Son. Herein is love. Not that we loved him; but that he loved us.* So that the first thing laid down for our contemplation, is the love of God. God *is love.* And, from all eternity, he hath been giving out demonstrations of that love, in the streams and effects of it. Christ is the first edition of that love: and all the subsequent works are *with* him, and *in* him, and *through* him, and *by* him. Our *Adam-fall*, gave occasion for the greater display of that love. But Christ and his Church were one in the womb of God's love, before the Adam-fall, or even the foundation of the earth was laid.

There are *two* verses in scripture, *one* in the Old Testament, and the *other* in the New, which, if read together, will shew more of this love of God in its antiquity and eternity, and in all its bearings through time and eternity, than all the wisdom of men in all ages of the world can come up to in description, if they were to unite together, to furnish volumes for this purpose. The *first* is *Jeremiah* xxxi. 3. *The Lord hath appeared of old unto me, saying, Yea, I have loved thee with an everlasting love; therefore with loving kindness have I drawn thee:* or as the margin renders it, *therefore have I extended loving kindness unto thee.* Here, we have God himself declaring, that his love to the Church hath been from everlasting; that is, as God himself. For his love, as is himself, is from everlasting. No space could have been before either; for in that case, it could not be said to have been from everlasting. So that God himself, and his love to the Church, are expressed by the same words, from everlasting. The *second* verse is in Ephes. ii. 7. *That in the ages to come he might shew the exceeding riches of his grace, in his kindness towards us through Christ Jesus.* Here we have declared, the ultimate object of that love; and which proves, that as it began from everlasting, so it hath ran through, and still continues to run through, the whole time-state of the Church, to everlasting; like rivers, arising out of the ocean, and running back into it again, everlastingly connected, and for ever flowing. By uniting these glorious scriptures in one view, they form a compleat circle, to shew, that GOD's love to the Church in CHRIST from everlasting, hath been one and the same; and his first design, and last execution, is to shew forth that love, or, as it is here called, the *exceeding riches of his grace*, in that glory resulting from that love, into which the Church is to be brought, and continue in everlastingly. Well might the Apostle say: *Herein is love!* for all other, in comparison, is nothing!

Secondly. Our love to GOD in CHRIST, and to the Church on CHRIST's account. It is scarcely necessary to observe, that all that we can call love or affection in us, either to GOD or his people, are but the mere *effects* from him, and his love to us as the *cause*. *We love him,* (saith the Apostle in this very scripture,) *because he first loved us*. Yea, it is not simply because he loved us, that we love him; for this alone would never have made our stoney hearts susceptible of love; but the LORD accomplished it by his quickening grace, shedding abroad that love in our hearts, in taking away the heart of stone, and giving us a heart of flesh. Ezek. xxxvi. 26. It is by His warming our frozen affections, subduing, and absolutely conquering our natural enmity against him, and winning us over with the cords of love, and the bands of a man, that we are brought over to love him who hath first loved us; or we should have remained enemies to GOD, by wicked works, to all eternity. Reader! pause over the wonderful mercy and grace, yea, *the exceeding riches of his grace;* and mark in the whole, in the FATHER's everlasting purpose, counsel, will, and pleasure, the SON's love, in betrothing and redeeming mercy; and the HOLY GHOST's regenerating, renewing favor; how infinitely great must be *the breadth, and length, and depth, and height of that love of* GOD, *which passeth knowledge!*

REFLECTIONS.

WHAT a relief is it to the child of GOD, amidst all the antichrists, and false prophets and teachers, which the latter-day dispensation is to bring forth, that JESUS hath said, though if it were possible, they would deceive the very elect; yet this assurance confirms their safety in JESUS, they shall not. Whither but for this, might a believer be *tossed about, with every wind of doctrine, and the cunning craftiness of men, whereby they lie in wait to deceive?* Blessed GOD the SPIRIT! be thou everlastingly praised, and loved, and adored, for what thou hast taught the Church in this precious Chapter! Here from thee, thy regenerated people learn, that the knowledge of CHRIST being come in the flesh, having proclaimed redemption in his blood, and regenerating the souls of his redeemed, by his holy SPIRIT; becomes an infallible security, against all the awful heresies abounding in this CHRIST-despising generation. LORD! let thy children know, and especially thy little children, that we have overcome the whole enemies of our salvation in our new birth. *Greater is he that is in us, than all that is in the world.* And oh! for the LORD to shed abroad his love in our hearts, that we may love him who hath first loved us. And, do thou grant, gracious GOD, that in thy strength we may have boldness, looking forward to that great day of our GOD, that when he shall appear, who is our life, our portion, our righteousness, and compleat justification; we may have confidence, and not be ashamed before him at his coming. *For as he is, so are we in this world!*

CHAP. V.

CONTENTS.

The Apostle closeth his Epistle with this Chapter. He points out the Victory of the Regenerate. He most blessedly declares, of the three heavenly, and the three earthly Witnesses. And shews, that the Possession of CHRIST, *by Union with him, is eternal Life.*

WHOSOEVER believeth that Jesus is the Christ, is born of God: and every one that loveth him that begat, loveth him also that is begotten of him.

2 By this we know that we love the children of God, when we love God, and keep his commandments.

3 ¶ For this is the love of God, That we keep his commandments: and his commandments are not grievous.

We shall stumble at the very threshold of this Chapter, and have but very imperfect ideas of what the HOLY GHOST intended to teach the Church by this belief, unless we first consider the scriptural grounds of true faith. I have often thought, that if we were to calculate faith upon the standard of creeds, in prayer-books, and the rehearsal of them in the congregations, one after another, as horses in a team; we might suppose that the whole were believers. But, if we were to examine such persons, upon the principles of the doctrines they profess to believe, perhaps not one in a score could be able to give an answer to any enquiry of the hope that is in them.

It is not the mere lip-service of the acknowledgement of GOD, that implies a real belief in the existence of GOD, either in those that take up upon trust the scriptural testimony, that in this Being of GOD, there exists a plurality of persons; do we any more discover in them a knowledge of Him. So it will follow, that there may be a confession of all that those creeds drawn up by men declare; and yet the heart all the while remain perfectly unacquainted with any saving knowledge of GOD in CHRIST. Reader! remember what all the way through I have been observing, that the regeneration of the heart, or being born again, is the only security for the real knowledge of GOD, Until that the child of GOD is regenerated and made a new creature in CHRIST, he hath no real heartfelt knowledge of the LORD. An entrance into CHRIST'S kingdom in grace, as well as an entrance hereafter into CHRIST's kingdom in glory, can be accomplished no other way. *Ye must be born again.* John iii. 7.

The HOLY GHOST by the Apostle opens this Chapter, in shewing the blessed effects which arise out of this new birth. He believeth that JESUS is the SON of GOD. And how is this wrought? *No man (saith the Apostle Paul) can say that JESUS is the* LORD *but by the* HOLY GHOST. 1 Cor. xii. 3. But, when the HOLY GHOST by regeneration hath opened the eyes of the understanding, in the knowledge *of the mystery of* GOD, *and of the* FATHER, *and of* CHRIST; he then sees, that *in* CHRIST *are hid all the treasures of wisdom and knowledge;* and that *in Him dwelleth all the fulness of the* GODHEAD *bodily:* and, like one of old, taught by the same Almighty Teacher, he crieth out to JESUS, *Rabbi! thou art the* SON *of* GOD! *thou art the King of Israel!* Coloss. ii. 2—10. John i. 49. Hence in this belief, arising from regeneration, and the teaching of GOD the HOLY GHOST, the knowledge of JESUS as the CHRIST, that is, the Sent, the Sealed, the Anointed of the FATHER; implies, all the precious and blessed things included in that high administration. I mean, the apprehension, according to scriptural testimony, of the glorious doctrine of the HOLY THREE IN ONE, which bear record in heaven; the union of GOD and Man in the Person of CHRIST; atonement by his blood; justification in his righteousness; the Person, work, and ministry of GOD the HOLY GHOST; together with all those great things connected with a life of grace here, for the Church of GOD, and the assurance of everlasting happiness in, and through CHRIST, in the life to come. Hence, whosoever hath these blessed views concerning CHRIST and his Church, and from the heart led by divine teaching is thus made acquainted with CHRIST, and believeth that JESUS is the CHRIST; this man hath the SPIRIT bearing witness with his spirit, that *he is born of* GOD. Reader! what say you to these things?

The HOLY GHOST is graciously pleased to add, by way of further evidence, that the child of GOD may have a further, collateral testimony, to the assurance of faith wherein he stands; that every one who loveth CHRIST, loveth also the people of CHRIST. And, as the love of the brethren, when that love is formed for CHRIST's sake, becomes another sweet testimony that we love the LORD of those brethren, when we love them because they are his; so, a desire of obedience, and conformity to what JESUS hath enjoined, on his account, will uniformly mark the people of GOD as his, whose they are, and whom they serve in the Gospel of GOD's dear SON. Reader! it is a sweet testimony, when, not from bondage-frames, but from real heartfelt affection, we follow *the commandments and ordinances of the* LORD *blameless.* Luke i. 6.

4 For whatsoever is born of God overcometh the world; and this is the victory that overcometh the world; *even* our faith.

5 Who is he that overcometh the world, but he that believeth that Jesus is the Son of God?

6 This is he that came by water and blood, *even*

Jesus Christ; not by water only, but by water and blood. And it is the Spirit that beareth witness, because the Spirit is truth.

In these verses we here discover where the strength of the Church lies, and in whom alone she finds victory, even in CHRIST. The Apostle expresseth it by the word *our faith*. But by faith, is meant CHRIST, the great object of faith. *Seeing the* SON, our LORD calls it, and *believing on him*. John vi. 40. And this includes all the blessed properties connected with it. He that is born of GOD, seeth himself a needy, lost, and helpless creature. He beholds a glory in CHRIST, and a fulness and suitableness in CHRIST, for salvation. He discovers also, a warrant in GOD the FATHER, to come to CHRIST, as a remedy of GOD's own providing. He feels an hungering and a thirsting for CHRIST, excited by the HOLY GHOST in his soul. And thus he comes to CHRIST, and finds him to be wisdom, righteousness, sanctification, and redemption. 1 Cor. i. 30. This is to overcome the world, and to have a real soul-enjoying faith, in the assured conviction, that JESUS *is the* SON *of* GOD!

I detain the Reader over the words of this verse, where it is said, that JESUS CHRIST came by water and blood; not by water only, but by water and blood. I have already in the Commentary, John iii. 8. very largely spoken to this subject, to which I refer. And in addition, shall only think it necessary to say, that when the coming of CHRIST is thus here so blessedly spoken of, we cannot be at a loss to apprehend, that as by his blood he hath redeemed his Church; so, by his SPIRIT he hath regenerated her; the HOLY GHOST bearing witness, as the SPIRIT of truth, to her adoption-character. To this purport, is the language of the HOLY GHOST, by the Apostle. *After that the kindness and love of* GOD *our* SAVIOR *toward man appeared, not by works of righteousness which we have done, but according to his mercy he saved us, by the washing of regeneration, and renewing of the* HOLY GHOST; *which he shed on us abundantly, through* JESUS CHRIST *our* SAVIOR; *that being justified by his grace, we should be made heirs according to the hope of eternal life*. Titus iii. 4—7.

7 For there are three that bear record in heaven; the Father, the Word, and the Holy Ghost; and these three are one.

We have here a most blessed scripture, and which, from its vast importance, merits our closest attention. And, as there have been enemies to our holy faith, among the CHRIST-despisers, who would wish to wrest it from us; we have the more reason to prize it highly, to bless GOD for it, and to beg of him to write it on the living tablets of our hearts.

The grand point those heavenly witnesses bear their joint testimony to, is that fundamental doctrine of our most holy faith, namely, that JESUS is the SON of GOD. For this glorious truth, which includes in it the certainty both of his divine, and human nature, brings with it, and confirms all the momentous doctrines of the Gospel. This leading principle, being written by GOD the SPIRIT in regeneration on the heart; our lost estate by nature, and our recovery by grace, together with all the glorious events belonging to the Person, offices, character, and relations of the LORD JESUS CHRIST, blessedly follow, in the wonderful subject of redemption. Patriarchs, Prophets, and Apostles, have set to their seal, and a great part of them in blood, to *the truth as it is in* JESUS. And, to confirm all, these HOLY THREE in ONE from heaven, bear witness to the same, that GOD *hath given* to the Church *eternal life, and this life is in his* SON.

I admire the manner of expression, which the HOLY GHOST, by *John,* hath been pleased to adopt, in giving the Church those heavenly witnesses. He saith, the FATHER, the WORD, and the HOLY GHOST. He doth not say, the FATHER, the SON, and the HOLY GHOST: probably, because it is to the Sonship of JESUS the testimony is here given; and, therefore, the same Person is mentioned by another of his names, the Uncreated WORD. And there is a great beauty, as well as strength, in this. The *Pharisees,* the sworn foes of CHRIST, had objected to his bearing witness of himself. And, although the LORD refuted the weakness of their argument, in terms of the plainest, and most unanswerable nature; see John viii. 13—19. yet, when the HOLY GHOST was pleased, by *John,* to give the Church the relation of those heavenly witnesses; he put an end to all such objections, by calling CHRIST the WORD, and not the SON. It is the Sonship of JESUS, as including every other testimony to his Almightiness of character, which the LORD the SPIRIT here had in view; and there is, therefore, a great beauty and propriety in calling JESUS by his wellknown name, the WORD.

I must not, in a work of this kind, gratify my wishes at the expence of the Reader's time and patience, by entering largely into a subject so great and extensive as these precious words would furnish. But I cannot but beg a short indulgence, to amplify my observations on them a little.

And, *first.* Here is said to be Three which bear record in heaven, that is, from heaven, to the Church upon earth, to this glorious truth, concerning the Person of CHRIST: and that these Three are One. Our first object, therefore, is concerned to establish, from scriptural testimony, the oneness and unity of the divine essence, existing as is here fully stated, in a threefold character of Person. A few observations will clearly prove this point. That there can be but One Infinite, and Eternal GOD, is evident, from the very nature of his Attributes and Perfections. For, as an infinite, and eternal Being, he inhabiteth infinity and eternity. Consequently, there can be no other, for he occupies, and fills all space. This alone is enough, in proof of the oneness, and unity of the divine essence. And hence, we find those glorious distinctions of character commanded to be ascribed to him. *Hear, O Israel, the* LORD *our* GOD *is one* LORD. Deut. vi. 4. So again, *Unto thee it was shewed, that thou mightest know, that the* LORD *he is* GOD, *there is none else beside him.* Deut. iv. 35. And in a language infinitely sublime, and, as one might suppose, would distinguish the Almighty Speaker, we find GOD himself thus addressing the Church: *Thus saith the* LORD *the King of Israel, and his Redeemer the* LORD *of hosts: I am the first, and I am the last; and beside me, there is no* GOD.—*Ye are even my witnesses. Is there a* GOD *beside me? Yea, there is no* GOD; *I know not any.* Isaiah xliv. 6—8. Here is enough, without adding more, (though the Bible is full to the same amount, in confirmation of the unity and oneness of the divine essence. God is One. I will not detain the Reader with quoting at large some of the many passages in the Word of God, which prove, that these distinguishing perfections of character, constituting Godhead, are all equally ascribed to the whole three Persons of the Godhead. I shall content myself with referring to them. I only beg the Reader, however, before he proceeds further, that he will turn to those scriptures as I have marked them; for they not only confirm the one leading truth of our holy faith, of the unity and oneness in the divine essence; but establish what is here said: *that there are* Three *which bear record in heaven, the* Father, *the* Word, *and the* Holy Ghost : *and these three are One.* See Isaiah ix. 6. Zech. xiii. Malachi iii. 1. John v. 17, 18. John x. 30. John viii. 51.—and Isaiah xlviii. 16, 17. Isaiah lxiii. 10. with Deut. xxxii. 12. Isaiah vi. 8. with Acts xxviii. 25, 26. and Luke i. 68. Numb. xii. 6. with 2 Peter i. 21. Levit. xxvi. 11, 12. with 2 Cor. vi. 16. and Rev. xxi. 3. 1 Cor. vi. 19. with 1 Cor. iii. 16, &c.

Secondly. The same holy scriptures which are thus express, in proof of the oneness and unity in the divine essence, are equally express, in revealing the existence of three distinct Persons in this One Godhead. Not only in this verse before us, but in a great variety of other places, throughout the Bible. Yea, we have distinct actions described, concerning each glorious Person, in which they are revealed as speaking to the Church in Christ, or to themselves, concerning the Church in Christ, or in glorifying each other. Thus at the creation of man, we find the words, *let us make man in our image, after our likeness:* Gen. i. 26. So again at the Tower of Babel; *let us go down and confound their language:* Gen. xi. 7. So again, at the vision Isaiah saw: *Also I heard the voice of the* Lord *saying, Whom shall I send, and who will go for us?* Isaiah vi. 8. And, to add no more. At the baptism of Christ, there was given the fullest, and most compleat demonstration of this distinction of Person in the Godhead, when the voice from heaven came saying, *This is my beloved* Son *in whom I am well pleased:* the Son of God in our nature at the same time in Jordan; and the Spirit of God *descending like a dove, and lighting upon him.* Matt. iii. 16, 17. See the Commentary on those verses. In proof of the actions and speakings of the Holy Three; see Matt. xvii. 5. John xii. 28. Acts ix. 4, 5. Acts xxii. 17, 18. Acts x. 19, 20. Acts xiii. 2, 4.

Thirdly. We have these heavenly witnesses bearing express testimony to the Sonship of the Lord Jesus, in all the ministry of Jesus. To bring forward proofs on this point, would be little short of going over again the whole records of the four Evangelists. Every eyeless socket Jesus filled and gave sight to, confirmed his Godhead; because this was a compleat act of creation. And all the works which Jesus did in his Father's name, and every devil he cast out of the bodies of men, by the Spirit of God, bore a like testimony to the divinity of his Person. Hence, we may safely conclude, in full assurance to the truth of this precious verse of scripture, that as the Church is *baptized* in the joint names of *the* Father, Son, *and* Holy Ghost ; Matt. xxviii. 19. and the Church is *blessed* in the joint names, of *the grace of* our LORD JESUS CHRIST, *and the love of* GOD, *and the communion of the* HOLY GHOST: 2 Cor. xiii. 14. so, *there are three that bear record in heaven,* to the Sonship of the LORD JESUS, *the* FATHER, *the* WORD, *and the* HOLY GHOST: *and these Three are One!*

And is it wonderful then, that a scripture so full in point of testimony to all the great and leading truths of the Church of GOD in CHRIST, should be nibbled at by the enemies of CHRIST and his GODHEAD? The greater wonder is, (and only to be explained, by ascribing it to the real source of all safety, GOD the HOLY GHOST, the author of it, watching over his own word,) that it had not been struck out of our Bibles, by the daring hand of infidelity. But, as the great enemy of souls, (who beguiles his children by his deceivings,) not unfrequently, betrays himself by his subtilty, so here, by tempting to the charge of calling this verse an *interpolation,* and being introduced by some other hand, and not written by *John,* shews the fallacy of the argument. For let any plain honest man, by way of trial, read the 6th and 8th verses of this Chapter, and leave out, (as those opposers of GOD's truth would tempt us to do,) the 7th verse; and let him say, supposing he had never seen, or heard the 7th verse, whether it would not strike him, that there was somewhat wanting? What connection could there be, between the last word of the *sixth* verse, and the beginning of the *eighth?* The *And,* which begins the *eighth,* is a conjunction copulative. And on the supposition, the *seventh* verse was omitted, what would there be to join? To such a miserable expedient are those men reduced, in order to support their wretched system!

Reader! I shall detain you no longer, than just to put the question to your heart, whether you can join me in praises, and thanksgivings to GOD the HOLY GHOST, for the sweet and precious record of this verse; concerning those heavenly witnesses. Blessed be GOD the SPIRIT do I say, for such a record! And blessed be GOD the SPIRIT, for accompanying it with his seal in my heart to its truth! For what doth it record, when testifying to the SON-ship of JESUS the SON of GOD, but that GOD *hath sent his* SON JESUS *to bless his people, in turning away every one of them from their iniquities.* Acts iii. 23.26.And are there any that would oppose this, and make light of his GODHEAD, his atoning blood and salvation? Yes? And do they call themselves christians after CHRIST? Yes! And is my Reader astonished at this? So am not I. There was a time, when the great enemy of souls professed christianity, when *the man of sin was revealed the son of perdition,* which the HOLY GHOST by *Paul* foretold, and we know it came to pass. 2 Thess. ii. 3—12. And what is there extraordinary in it, when we read, that such a master of subtilty he is, as it is written, *Satan himself is transformed into an angel of light.* 2 Cor. xi. 14, 15. In the awful days in which we live, we are taught to expect such things. But there is this blessed assurance, from GOD our SAVIOR. *Though many shall come* (saith that watchful LORD. See Isaiah xxvii. 3.) *in my name, saying, I am* CHRIST, *and shall deceive many, and though, except the* LORD *had shortened those days, no flesh should be saved,* yet JESUS saith, that *for the elect's sake whom he hath chosen, he hath shortened the days.* Hence, though *false christs, and false prophets rise, and shall shew signs and wonders, to seduce, if it were possible, even the elect;* yet the impossibility of the thing, is at the same time confirmed, in what Jesus saith. Let the Reader consult, in further confirmation of this blessed truth. Mark xiii. 5—27. Luke xviii. 7, and Romans viii. 28 to the end, and Commentary in all.

8 And there are three that bear witness in earth; the spirit, and the water, and the blood; and these three agree in one.

9 ¶ If we receive the witness of men, the witness of God is greater: for this is the witness of God which he hath testified of his Son.

10 He that believeth on the Son of God, hath the witness in himself; he that believeth not God hath made him a liar: because he believeth not the record that God gave of his Son.

11 And this is the record, That God hath given to us eternal life; and this life is in his Son.

12 He that hath the Son hath life; *and* he that hath not the Son of God hath not life.

13 These things have I written unto you that believe on the name of the Son of God: that ye may know that ye have eternal life; and that ye may believe on the name of the Son of God.

The truth to which those witnesses bear testimony, in earth, is the same to which those spoken of before, bear record in heaven; namely, that Jesus Christ is the Son of God, and in whom we have eternal life. And the witnesses themselves, it should seem, are the Spirit when witnessing to our spirits, of our being children of God, the water of regeneration, and the blood of Christ. And these all correspond to the same. I say, it should seem to be these, because it is added, that this is the witness of God, and which the child of God receives, and which he cannot receive but by regeneration. And hence the unregenerate who receive it not, neither accept it, give God the lie, by the rejection of God's record to his Son. And what an awful state are those men in, who by rejecting his Godhead, cannot but reject with it, the eternal life he brings. For who less than an Eternal Being, can have or bring Eternal life!

And here Reader, if you are a child of God, and by regeneration brought forth to the apprehension of Christ's Person, and the eternal life that is *in* him, and *by* him, I beg of you to pause, and for a moment to contemplate the vast mercy. The Apostle *Peter* was so wrapt up in the view, that unable to contain himself, he called God the Almighty Giver of it; *the* God *of all grace!* The God of all grace (said he) *that hath called us unto his eternal glory by* Christ Jesus. 1 Pet. v. 10. And here the beloved Apostle speaks to the same amount, God *hath given eternal life, and this life is in his*

Son! So that it is a free full gift. And it is impossible to be lost, or alienated, or taken away from the child of GOD, regenerated by the HOLY GHOST, being in CHRIST, and that child of GOD made part in CHRIST, by being quickened or made spiritually alive in him. And there are, among numberless, nameless blessings contained in it, and folded up in it, these *two* more especially striking. *First.* He that hath the SON, hath this eternal life begun in him; a glory begun in the soul, and to be enjoyed here by faith. The *other*, is, that at death, this life eternal in CHRIST, opens to the soul in all its glory, and is enjoyed by immediate sight. There are but these *two* ways of enjoying communion with GOD in CHRIST, either in the life that now is, or in that which is to come. And each is suited for the respective places of enjoyment. Allow me to offer a word or two more on each.

First. Eternal life in CHRIST begins to be enjoyed by faith, the moment of regeneration; when we are then said, to be *made partakers of the divine nature,* and *to have all things given to us, that pertain to life and godliness.* 2 Pet. i. 3, 4. Our LORD's authority on this point, is very sweet, and much to be regarded. *Verily, verily, I say unto you, he that heareth my word, and believeth on him that sent me, hath everlasting life, and shall not come into condemnation, but is passed from death unto life.* John v. 24. And speaking of himself, as the resurrection in that sublime discourse, (which is enough to strike every infidel who denies his GODHEAD, dumb, with everlasting silence,) JESUS said; *I am the resurrection and the life, he that believeth in me, though he were dead, yet shall he live.* Now mark! *And whosoever liveth and believeth in me, shall never die.* John xi. 25, 26. Words, as plain as language can express. The regenerated believer *hath* everlasting life. Right and title, in actual possession by faith. The day of our effectual calling, is the day in which we literally and truly enter upon this inheritance. We are passed from death to life. Die, the child of GOD can no more spiritually. Eternal life is begun in his soul. And this is the sure earnest of eternal glory.

Secondly. Whenever the life of faith ends, (which of course must end at death,) the spirits of just men made perfect, immediately enter upon this eternal life of glory. And this is evident from the very nature of the thing. For otherwise, there would be an interruption to this eternal life in CHRIST. And how in this sense, would the words of JESUS be fulfilled. *He that liveth and believeth in me shall never die?* If the soul ceased its communion with GOD in CHRIST, at the death of the body, neither enjoyed it more until the resurrection; the child of GOD, instead of being a gainer by death, would be an infinite loser. Paul could not then have said, *to die is gain.* Neither would his spirit so have longed, to be *absent from the body, that* he might be *present with the* LORD. Very evidently therefore it is, from this view of the subject, if there were no other, that that eternal life, which GOD hath given us in CHRIST, and to which he bears record as in CHRIST, and which, he that hath the SON, hath in CHRIST; is the beginning of glory, by faith here below, and on the departure of the soul, from the body at death, opens in full fruition of sight, in life eternal. Sweet considerations, *both* of faith on earth, and glory in heaven, from that eternal life we have in the SON of GOD! Reader! look to it, (if so be GOD the SPIRIT witnesseth to your spirit by regeneration, that you are a child of GOD,) that you hold fast your faith and confidence; *let no man take your crown.* You are now in the womb of time, as the infant when in the womb of nature; living by the nourishment of faith, on the eternal life in the SON of GOD, as the child on the nourishment in the womb. And often now, so strong those principles of spiritual and eternal life in CHRIST, are communicated to your spirit, by GOD the SPIRIT, that, when, like *Elizabeth,* you hear the salutation of grace in CHRIST, your soul, like the babe in her womb, leapeth for joy. This is the utmost to be enjoyed by faith, before we leave the present state. But no sooner shall the life of faith cease, than the life of sight begins. Then you will come forth from the womb of nature, and enter into the joy of your LORD. And then, that eternal life, here begun in grace, and there consummated in glory, and all in and from CHRIST JESUS, will bring the whole Church to the highest state of felicity, and to the united praise of the HOLY, and undivided Three, which bear record in heaven, and these Three are One.

14 ¶ And this is the confidence that we have in him, that if we ask any thing according to his will, he heareth us:

15 And if we know that he hear us, whatsoever we ask, we know that we have the petitions that we desired of him.

16 If any man see his brother sin a sin *which is* not unto death, he shall ask, and he shall give him life for them that sin not unto death, there is a sin unto death: I do not say that he shall pray for it.

17 All unrighteousness is sin; and there is a sin not unto death.

18 We know that whosoever is born of God sinneth not: but he that is begotten of God keepeth himself, and that wicked one toucheth him not.

19 *And* we know that we are of God, and the whole world lieth in wickedness.

20 And we know that the Son of God is come, and hath given us an understanding, that we may know him that is true, and we are in him that is true, *even* in his son Jesus Christ. This is the true God, and eternal life.

21 Little children, keep yourselves from idols. Amen.

I shall be very brief, in what remains in this Chapter, having already exceeded my limits. Indeed, what follows are but as so many inferences arising out of what had been said. GOD's children, quickened, regenerated, and made partakers in CHRIST of eternal life, may well be supposed to have great interest, from their union with CHRIST, at the court of heaven. Hence they are here told, that from their confidence concerning JESUS, whatsoever they ask, according to his will, (and never can they wish any thing contrary to his will,) he heareth them. It is as if JESUS, threw the reins of government into their hands, agreeably to that scripture. Isaiah xlv. 11. And if the Reader remembers, the conversation of JESUS with his disciples before his departure, at his parting supper, and what followed, he will discover, that JESUS's whole heart is with his people. *Whatsoever, you shall ask the* FATHER *in my name, he will give it you. Hitherto have ye asked nothing in my name, ask and ye shall receive, that your joy may be full.* John xvi. 23, 24.

Let the Reader, as he passeth over the verse respecting the sin of his brother, observe, that this is spoken of a child of GOD. It is a brother in CHRIST. All sin is justly liable to death. *The soul that sinneth, it shall die.* And but for CHRIST, the surety, the whole race of men, both of the Church and out of it, must have died. But by virtue of CHRIST's redemption, the child of GOD, comes not into the condemnation, or even the commission, much less the guilt of the unpardonable sin. But how blessedly doth the Apostle comfort GOD's children, in the assurance, that by regeneration he that is born of GOD, falls not into the danger of it, but keeps himself, that is, *by faith is kept, through the power of* GOD *unto salvation.* So that Satan, though he hates him, and would do him evil, dares not.

I beg the Reader to remark, what the Apostle saith of GOD's children, knowing their sonship and interest in CHRIST, and at the same time, that they know the whole world lieth in wickedness. If there was not another passage in the Bible in proof of distinguishing grace, surely this would act in point, to shew there must be some great predisposing cause, to mark the Church of GOD, from a whole world, that lieth in wickedness.

And let the Reader further observe, the confidence with which *John* speaks of the SON of GOD being come. *John* knew that JESUS CHRIST of *Nazareth* was come; for he had been his disciple and followed him in his ministry. But he must have learnt from an higher teaching than common knowledge, that this JESUS CHRIST of *Nazareth* was the SON of GOD, or he could not have spoken with such confidence. Yes! GOD's *children are all taught of* GOD. Isaiah liv. 13. And sweet is this evidence. Reader! if you are taught of GOD, you have the same evidence as *John* had. He hath made you also sensible of your lost estate by nature. He hath taught you who CHRIST is, and what he is able to perform. He hath made you out of love with yourself, and in love with him. And you are coming up out of the wilderness of this world, leaning upon CHRIST. Is it so with you? Then hath he given you an understanding to know him that is true, and then are you in him that is true, even in GOD's dear SON JESUS CHRIST. And then will you subscribe, with full consent of soul and heart, that JESUS CHRIST is the true GOD, yea, the only visible JEHOVAH; for He, and He alone, is come forth from the divine essence, to make known the

I have often been struck at the concluding verse of this Epistle. *Little children, keep yourselves from idols!* What could *John* mean? Here is his last verse, his last words, his concluding address to the Church. Did he foresee, that in a Church calling itself christian, idols would be put up? Was *John* looking so far on, as to many centuries after, when images and saints, and reliques would be worshipped? Dear Lord, I would say for the *true Church* of Christ, in the present hour, do thou keep thy people, (for no man can keep alive his own soul,) from the awful delusions all around! Men now may dare to call thy Godhead in question, no law of man preventing them. And others may arise, to introduce idols in the land. Precious Jesus watch over thy true Church, purchased so dearly by thy blood; and rendered so precious to thee, by thy Father's gift, and by the regenerating influence of God the Spirit! Methinks I hear my God and Savior say; Yes, *In that day sing ye unto her, A vineyard of red wine! I the* Lord *do keep it; I will water it every moment; lest any hurt it, I will keep it night and day.* Isaiah xxvii. 2, 3. Oh! how safe and sure amidst all idols, which may desolate a nation abhoring Jesus, is the Church of Jesus! *The gates of hell shall not prevail against it.* Isaiah xlix. 7. Matt. xvi. 11.

REFLECTIONS.

Reader! how gracious was it in our God, to give his Church such tokens as are here marked down, in order that every child of God might know, his having been begotten, to the adoption of children in Jesus Christ. Yes! blessed God, we do know whose we are, and to whom we belong, by our being made believers in Christ Jesus. It is sweet, it is blessed, to know him, and to love him, and to delight in him, who came by water and blood, even Jesus Christ!

Glory be to the three heavenly witnesses, for their united testimony to the Son-ship of Jesus Christ! Lord! give all thy redeemed grace, to receive with holy joy, the record God hath given to his dear Son, and that eternal life which is in him. And oh! may every individual member of his mystical body, rejoice in Christ, and live by faith here, until he come to live in glory hereafter on Jesus, and eternal life in him.

Farewell, thou beloved disciple! we thank our God for his love to thee, and his employment of thee, and for all the benefit the Church hath derived under the Holy Ghost, from thee, in thy ministry. Shortly Jesus will come, and take home his Church, and the Lord shall be then seen, surrounded by his saints, with the whole redeemed Church of God, and all the disciples whom Jesus hath loved.

THE SECOND EPISTLE

OF

J O H N.

GENERAL OBSERVATIONS.

IT is highly probable, from the opening of this Epistle, that it was particularly directed to some one Person, and not the Church at large. But still, from the contents of it, designed for general use. The word translated *Lady*, which corresponds to the Hebrew name *Martha*, might be a general name. But, certain it is, that it hath respect to every child of God, for it is connected with the title *Elect*.

Our chief concern is, to know, that the Writer of it was inspired to the service, and that he wrote it under the immediate influence and direction of the Holy Ghost. And this the testimony of the Church bears witness to, in every age, wherever the Lord hath blessed it in instruction to his people.

We have no particular *date* to it, neither of the *place* from whence it was written. But, neither are these things material. It is but short: yet, if the Lord teach in it, and by it, He can render it sweet. Lord! let thy unction be upon it, and it will then send forth the fragrancy of Christ's name, as *the ointment poured forth!*

THE SECOND EPISTLE OF JOHN.

CONTENTS.

The Apostle opens his Epistle, in calling the Person to whom he writes, Elect. He speaks of the Joy he and his Companions, who were Lovers of the Truth, found in the Opinion they had of the Grace the Lord had given her. He speaks of the Antichrist of the Time, and warns her against all such Teachers. He concludes with affectionate Salutations.

THE elder unto the elect lady, and her children, whom I love in the truth; and not I only, but also all they that have known the truth;

2 For the truth's sake which dwelleth in us, and shall be with us for ever.

3 Grace be with you, mercy, *and* peace, from God the Father, and from the Lord Jesus Christ the Son of the Father, in truth and love.

John very properly calls himself an Elder; for, at the time he wrote this Epistle, he could not be less than an hundred years old; if, as some suppose, it was after his return from banishment. But the principal point for the Church of GOD to regard is, the character to whom *John* wrote; namely, one of the Elect of GOD. And I mention this the rather, because it bears a correspondence to all the Apostle's writings, which are uniformly to the Church, and not unto the world. The salutation of grace, mercy, and peace, are sweet tokens of Apostolic writings to the Church.

And I beg the Reader to notice with what confidence *John* speaks to this lady, in consequence of being an elect child of GOD. He saith, he loveth her for the truth's-sake, meaning CHRIST himself, who is the truth. John xiv. 6. And which *John* saith, *dwelleth in us,* (that is, in all the elect,) *and shall abide in us for ever.* Reader! do not overlook this, for it is blessed. The elect lady, as *John* calls her, had in that election all the blessed fruits and effects wrought up in it, as the bud contains all the future blossoms and foliage of the flower. Together with this electing grace, there is the *calling* grace appointed also. *For whom he did predestinate, them he also called.* Rom. viii. 30. And in the season of that call, there is given the *pardoning* grace to all sins. So blessedly speaks the Apostle. *And you being dead in your sins, and the uncircumcision of your flesh, hath he quickened together with him, having forgiven you all trespasses.* Coloss. ii. 13.

And neither doth the blessing stop here. For *justification* immediately follows. *Being justified freely by his grace, through the redemption which is in* CHRIST JESUS. Rom. iii. 24. And both *sanctification* and *glory* bring up the rear, in the sure events involved in the blessed act of GOD's sovereign love, when, from all eternity, the LORD chose the Church in CHRIST JESUS. Ephes. i. 4. 1 Cor. i. 30. 2 Tim. i. 9. Rom. viii. 30, 31.

4 I rejoiced greatly that I found of thy children walking in truth, as we have received a commandment from the Father.

There is somewhat very blessed in this. We find that not only this elect lady, but some of her children, were in grace. And the good old Apostle felt the joy of it. Nothing can be more delightful to a child of GOD, than when he discovers others that are children also. It was under this view the Psalmist speaks, when he said, *Lo! children are an heritage of the* LORD, *and the fruit of the womb is a reward.* Psm. cxxvii. 3. But, it can only be so spoken, when they arise, like olive branches, round the parent's table, blessed with grace. Sad, and wretched, did the Patriarch view his ungodly children, in the

Absaloms, and *Adonijahs*, and the *Ammons* of his loins; when he cried out, *my house is not so with* God; though he took to himself the blessedness of *the everlasting covenant* God had made with him, ordered in all things and sure. 2 Sam. xxiii. 5.

5 And now, I beseech thee, lady, not as though I wrote a new commandment unto thee, but that which we had from the beginning, That we love one another.

6 And this is love, that we walk after his commandments, this is the commandment, That as ye have heard from the beginning, ye should walk in it.

Let the Reader observe, with me, how sweetly a life of grace in Jesus, leads to a life of holiness in Jesus. *As ye have received Christ Jesus the* Lord, *so walk ye in him, rooted and built up in him.* Coloss. ii. 6, 7. It is impossible to be otherwise. Where Christ is, there must be fruitfulness in Christ. Exhortations here are all sweet, and in season. But to exhort the unawakened and unregenerate, is like the rain upon the sands and desarts, which can produce nothing!

7 For many deceivers are entered into the world, who confess not that Jesus Christ is come in the flesh, this is a deceiver and an antichrist.

8 ¶ Look to yourselves that we lose not those things which we have wrought, but that we receive a full reward.

9 Whosoever transgresseth and abideth not in the doctrine of Christ, hath not God. He that abideth in the doctrine of Christ, he hath both the Father and the Son.

10 ¶ If there come any unto you, and bring not this doctrine, receive him not into *your* house, neither bid him God speed.

11 For he that biddeth him God speed, is partaker of his evil deeds.

12 Having many things to write unto you I would not write with paper and ink; but I trust to come unto you, and speak face to face, that our joy may be full.

13 The children of thy elect sister greet thee. Amen.

There is nothing here which can need a comment, the whole being so very plain and obvious. They shew the affectionate mind of the Apostle, in watching over the Church; and they no less teach how very early the heresies sprung up among the people. Very painful must it have been to the hoary Apostle, who had lain in JESUS's bosom, to live long enough to see men arise who dared to deny that JESUS CHRIST had come in the flesh. But, Reader! had *John* lived to our day, or could he have beheld the infidelity which we are vexed with, what judgments would he not teach the Church they might expect to follow? Not the *true* Church, however, for this is everlastingly and eternally safe; but the *professing* Church, who have frittered away all that is truly valuable in the Gospel of CHRIST, and left nothing to it but the mere name of Christian.

The Apostle very sweetly closeth the Epistle with the greetings from one branch of the LORD's chosen family to another!

REFLECTIONS.

THE Elders in the Church of JESUS may learn from this short, but gracious Epistle of *John* the Elder, how to address the Elect, and with what words of comfort and consolation in JESUS, they are to be spoken to. And there is nothing more strengthening to the Church of GOD, than when old Disciples speak to young ones, concerning GOD's purposes in CHRIST, as manifested in his electing, converting, redeeming, establishing grace! It is blessedly said by one of old, *the righteous shall bring forth fruit in his old age, to shew that the* LORD *is upright.* I do not presume to say so much, but I humbly ask, did not the LORD the SPIRIT cause this Epistle to be sent by *John* to one Elect Lady, to be recorded in the Church, and handed down, through the several ages, to the present hour, on purpose to teach old saints, and especially faithful old ministers, how to speak to the elect children of CHRIST, in the several stations and characters as they stand in grace?

Blessed and eternal SPIRIT! be thou praised for this sweet morsel of thy holy scripture! Let it be a savor, in thine Almighty hand, for good. And let thy servant *John's* ministry in it be owned and blessed of the LORD for good to *all* thy people, that though the Apostle be dead, he may be said yet to speak. Praised be GOD, FATHER, SON, and HOLY GHOST, for all blessings in CHRIST. Amen.

THE THIRD EPISTLE OF JOHN.

GENERAL OBSERVATIONS.

HERE is another short, but precious Epistle of the same Writer, under GOD the HOLY GHOST, as the former. And this is also written to a private person, and not publicly to the Church. Who this *Gaius* was, to whom the beloved Apostle sent this Epistle, is not known, though it hath occasioned much conjecture. He calls him *well-beloved.* No doubt, as a child of GOD, he was so; and, on this account, *John* called him so. *Paul* had a companion of this name, which we read of, Acts xix. 29, and Acts xx. 4. But, it is hardly possible that this was the same person to whom *John* writes this Epistle, for there must have been more than thirty years between the date of those times. However, this is not so material. It is enough for us to know, that this *Gaius* was well-beloved of *John;* and, consequently, one of the elect of GOD. And we know also, that GOD the HOLY GHOST directed the Apostle's heart and pen to write it, and hath caused it to be recorded for the Church's benefit. These things are enough, in recommendation.

I beg the Reader to enter, with me, upon the perusal of it in prayer. And very sure I am, if we pray over it, we shall profit under it. May the LORD therefore bless it to our use, and to the whole Church of GOD in CHRIST. Amen.

THE THIRD EPISTLE OF JOHN.

CONTENTS.

After his usual Salutation, the Apostle tells his beloved Gaius of his Desires, both for his temporal and spiritual Prosperity. He commends him for his Kindness to the Brethren. He remarks of the Opposition made to the Church, by a Man called Diotrephes. *He commends another Man of the Name of* Demetrius. *And concludes his Epistle with Greetings from Friends.*

THE elder unto the well-beloved Gaius, whom I love in the truth.

2 Beloved, I wish above all things that thou mayest prosper and be in health, even as thy soul prospereth.

3 For I rejoiced greatly, when the brethren came and testified of the truth that is in thee, even as thou walkest in the truth.

4 I have no greater joy than to hear that my children walk in truth.

5 Beloved, thou doest faithfully whatsoever thou doest to the brethren and to strangers.

6 Which have borne witness of thy charity before the church: whom if thou bring forward on their journey after a godly sort, thou shalt do well:

7 Because that for his name's sake they went forth, taking nothing of the Gentiles.

8 We therefore ought to receive such, that we might be fellow-helpers to the truth.

Next to the health of the soul, the health of the body is the greatest blessing. And, among the promises of GOD in CHRIST, there are many sweet ones in the Word of God, which are in the Covenant, as they relate to the body. See a string of them, Deut. xxviij. 1—14. And when a child of GOD, regenerated by the HOLY GHOST, is brought, by divine teaching, to build every thing upon CHRIST, for time and for eternity, every thing must prosper, for every thing must be a blessing, Rom. viii. 28. In *temporal* things, the child of GOD hath the sanctified use of all. If the goods of this world abound, there is the covenant-love, and the covenant-grace to accompany them; that, like *Gaius*, the man of GOD is enabled by the LORD to do faithfully, whatsoever he doeth, to the brethren of the Church with him, or to the strangers which belong to the other Churches of the saints from abroad. And, while he doth good to all men, he doth it especially to them that are of the household of faith. And, if the LORD exerciseth him with adversity, still grace gives a sanctifying quality to take out all the bitterness of it. So that, *though the fig-tree do not blossom, neither fruit be found in the vine; though the labor of the olive fail, and the fields yield no meat; though the flock be cut off from the fold, and there be no herds in the stall; yet, the child of* GOD *can, and will say, I will rejoice in the* LORD, *I will joy in the* GOD *of my salvation.* Habak. iii. 17, 18.

And, in respect to *spiritual* things, every thing here is blessed. The child of GOD is blessed with the FATHER's love, the SAVIOR's grace, the HOLY GHOST's fellowship. He hath pardon, mercy, peace, in the blood of the cross. He hath continual manifestations of divine love. JESUS comes to bless him, to comfort him, to encourage him, and to make himself known to him otherwise than he doth to the world. Yea, who shall describe the out-pourings of divine love, or the incomings of divine grace, the child of GOD is continually receiving from the LORD, who is blessing him with all spiritual blessings in CHRIST JESUS?

And, in relation to *eternal blessings*, he hath not only the promise of the life that now is, but of that which is to come. Indeed, eternal life is begun in his soul. For he that hath the SON of GOD hath life. He enjoys it now by faith. *For faith is the substance of things hoped for, the evidence of things not seen.* Heb. xi. 1. And faith is the earnest, given by the SPIRIT of glory. So that, as *John* tells the beloved *Gaius*, where the soul prospereth, the body must have the sanctified enjoyment of all things, which grace sanctifies to prosper also.

9 ¶ I wrote unto the church: but Diotrephes, who loveth to have the pre-eminence among them, receiveth us not.

10 Wherefore, if I come, I will remember his deeds which he doeth, prating against us with malicious words: and not content therewith, neither doth he himself receive the brethren, and forbiddeth them that would, and casteth *them* out of the church.

11 Beloved, follow not that which is evil, but that which is good: he that doeth good, is of God; but he that doeth evil, hath not seen God.

12 Demetrius hath good report of all *men*, and of the truth itself: yea, and we *also* bear record; and ye know that our record is true.

13 I had many things to write, but I will not with ink and pen write unto thee:

14 But I trust I shall shortly see thee, and we shall speak face to face. Peace be to thee. Our friends salute thee. Greet the friends by name.

Every thing contained within the bosom of these verses, is fully explained as it stands before us. I only beg the Reader to remark with me, the striking contrast between *Diotrephes* and *Demetrius*. They are known to us only by name. But how different their characters! How opposed while they lived! How differently regarded when they died. How opposite in the esteem of the Church, through all ages! And how everlastingly opposite, if dying as they are here said to have lived, through all the eternal world? Reader! how blessed to have a good report, of all men; yea, and of the truth itself, which is CHRIST. John xiv. 6. Oh! for the whisper of JESUS, in a dying hour, to confirm his grace in the soul, as manifested in a living hour; that both in life and in death the soul be found in him. Isaiah xliii. 1—4.

REFLECTIONS.

WHAT a beautiful view is here afforded, of the beloved Apostle in his Pastoral Office, addressing the faithful *Gaius*, beloved in the LORD. To behold the venerable saint of GOD, amidst all the infirmities of declining years, thus blessing GOD, and blessing the servant of GOD, in his wishes both for spiritual and temporal prosperity.

But while we look at *John*, who justly commands our veneration and our love, let us look infinitely above *John*, and behold *John's* LORD still blessing all his Church; and every *Gaius* of his redeemed family below, with blessings in himself. Precious, precious JESUS! we desire to praise thee for all that is lovely, in the disciple whom JESUS loved; for all that is lovely in *John*, was, and is derived from thee! LORD! hasten on thy blessed purposes, and bring on thy glorious day, when thou wilt come, *to be glorified in thy saints, and to be admired in all that believe!* To thee, LORD, it belongs, to keep thy Church from falling, and to present it faultless before the presence of thy glory with exceeding joy. In the blessed hope of thy appearing, may all thy Church in thee, and through thee, daily ascribe to FATHER, SON, and HOLY GHOST, Israel's GOD in Covenant, endless praises. Amen.

THE GENERAL EPISTLE

OF

JUDE.

GENERAL OBSERVATIONS.

JUDE is particularly spoken of as the brother of *James*, perhaps to distinguish him from *Judas* the Traitor. For otherwise, it was more the custom to speak of the Jews by descent. *Jude* lived the last of all the Apostles, except *John*. And it could not be well less than *thirty* years after CHRIST's ascension, that he wrote this Epistle. He hath evidently followed the Apostle *Peter*, in his Second Epistle, and thereby confirmed the words of GOD, that, *in the mouth of two or three witnesses, every word shall be established.* Deut. xvii. 6. 2 Cor. xii. 1.

The design of GOD the HOLY GHOST, in sending this Epistle generally to the Church, seems very evident from its contents. Heresies had at this time sprung up, and the Church was infested with them. It is our mercy, that *Jude* as well as *John*,

JUDE.

lived to see them. For under God the Holy Ghost, we owe our possession of those blessed Epistles to this cause. And both the origin and support of heresies, we are expressly told, is, that the truth of God may be thereby manifested among us.

I have only to request the Reader, that here, as in all the former books of Divine Inspiration, we may enter upon the study of it with prayer, that we may end it in praise!

THE GENERAL EPISTLE OF JUDE.

CONTENTS.

The Opening of this Epistle is truly sweet. Jude addresseth all he hath to say to the Church. It is to you, Beloved, Jude saith that he writes. He then, through the greater Part of the Chapter, points out the awful State of the Reprobate. But still it is to the Church he speaks of those Things, for their Consolation and Instruction. Towards the End, he points out the Safety and Blessedness of the Church, and concludes in praise.

JUDE, the servant of Jesus Christ, and brother of James, to them that are sanctified by God the Father, and preserved in Jesus Christ, *and* called:

The opening of this Epistle is ponderous and full of glorious truths. The Lord give grace to his Church, to regard what is here said. *Jude* calls himself a servant of Jesus Christ, and he writes his Epistle to the Church of Christ. To whom should the servant of Christ minister, but to the household of his Lord? I beg once more, that this may be well noticed. I have all along, through the blessed Epistles we have passed, in this *Poor Man's Commentary*, particularly pointed this out to the Reader, that it is to the Church, and not to the world, the servants of our God and Savior write. They, who would be supposed to have more mercy than God himself, are willing to overlook, or have not known this distinguishing character, of those holy writings of the Apostles. Let not the Reader. *Jude* writes *to them that are sanctified by* God *the* Father, *and preserved in* Jesus Christ, *and called.*

If the Reader hath not forgotten the Apostle *Peter's* address, in his first Epistle general to the Church, in the opening of it, he will observe a beautiful correspondence to this of *Jude*; and which, as it shews what a oneness of heart those great Apostles had in divine truths, so will it no less prove to him, that both were under the same divine teaching. See 1 Pet. i. 1, 2. There is, indeed, a difference in the wording of those verses, by those Apostles; but the doctrine is the same. And the different expressions, if rightly considered, give a beauty and blessedness, to the grand truths they deliver and confirm. For, when we find the same divine offices and perfections, in one scripture, spoken of one of the Persons of the Godhead in another, ascribed to either of the other Persons of the Godhead, what are these things, but so many collateral testimonies to the leading article of our most holy faith, that *there are Three that bear record in heaven; the* Father, *the* Word, *and the* Holy Ghost; *and these Three are One.* 1 John v. 7.

In this blessed verse *Jude* ascribes to God the Father the sanctification of the Church. *To them that are sanctified by* God *the* Father. And, without all doubt, God the Father hath chosen the Church in Christ before the foundation of the world, that it should be *holy and without blame before him in love.* Ephes. i. 4. Nevertheless, the word translated in this verse *sanctified;* might have been rendered, (as is well known to the learned,) *beloved in and of* God *the* Father; which, in its meaning, more particularly refers to the electing love of God the Father. Similar to the sense of the same word, in relation to Christ, the glorious Head of the Church. *Say ye of Him* (said Jesus to the Jews) *whom* the Father hath *sanctified?* John x. 30. that is, whom the Father hath chosen? And this title of *Elect* and *Chosen,* as applied to Christ, is the greatest and most endeared in all the Bible, if we may judge by the manner of expression, in which God himself useth it. *Behold my servant, whom I uphold; mine* Elect, *in whom my soul delighteth!* Isaiah xlii. 1. Hence by the Church, whom *Jude* here calls *sanctified* by God the Father, is meant, the *chosen* by God the Father, whom *Peter* calls *a chosen generation,* 1 Pet. ii. 9. and whom *Moses,* under the Holy Ghost, stiles *a peculiar treasure to the* Lord *above all people.* Exod. xix. 5. Reader! pause over the view of the Father's everlasting love, in this special act of his, as it relates to the Church. It is from hence we date all our mercies. It is to this source, from the election of grace, and the being given to Christ, and chosen in Christ, that the Church *is kept by the power of* God, *through faith, unto salvation.* Hence, the Apostle to the Church: *We are bound* (said he) *to give thanks alway to* God, *for you, brethren, beloved of the* Lord, *because* God *hath, from the beginning, chosen you to salvation, through sanctification of the* Spirit, *and belief of the truth; whereunto he called you by our Gospel, to the obtaining of the glory of our* Lord Jesus Christ. 2 Thess. ii. 13, 14.

The next point of doctrine we meet with, in this blessed verse, is, *and preserved in* Jesus Christ. Numberless blessed things are included in this comprehensive expression, *preserved in* Jesus Christ. Every degree of preservation is implied, as well *before* our being called to Christ, as *after.* For, as we are chosen in Christ, before the present time-state of our nature, are truly one with Christ, by his betrothing all his people to himself, when receiving them, as the gift of his Father, before the foundation of the world; so, there is a grace-union with Christ; by virtue of it, which all the members of his mystical body have; and whereby they are secretly, though mysteriously to us, preserved in him, and beheld as one with him, before their being in *Adam,* is brought forth in time. And though this preservation in Christ, doth not keep them, (because it was never intended so to do,) from falling, with the whole race of men, in the *Adam*-transgression, (and indeed, thereby, all the blessings of redemption arising out of that transgression, finds opportunity for exercise,) yet, it keeps them from the unpardonable sin, and from the second death; and it keeps them, in all the covenant privileges, made in the antient settlements of eternity, between the Persons of the

JUDE.

GODHEAD. Who shall calculate or write down, in the history of one child of GOD, much less the whole Church, the wonders of this preserving grace, in the ten thousand times ten thousand instances of it? Preserved *in* JESUS CHRIST, before called *to* JESUS CHRIST. Preserved in all the after stages of life, when called by grace, until grace is finished in glory. The Church in every individual member, may, and indeed ought, daily to ponder the melting subject; but we must enter eternity, and look back over the everlasting hills through all the path the LORD hath brought us on our way; before that we shall have a becoming sense, and apprehension, of the unspeakable blessings, contained in these four words, *preserved in* JESUS CHRIST.

And called! Here, though the blessed name of GOD the HOLY GHOST be not added, yet is it implied; because, in the œconomy of redemption, it is his peculiar office to call sinners *from darkness to light, and from the power of sin and Satan to the living* GOD. The same Almighty SPIRIT, which in the *old creation of nature,* moved over the face of the waters, and said *let there be light,* is He, who in the *new creation of grace,* commands the light to shine out of darkness in the heart, *to give the light of the knowledge of the glory of* GOD, *in the face of* JESUS CHRIST. Gen. i. 3. 2 Cor. iv. 6. And there is a beautiful order in all this, that the hand of each glorious Person of the GODHEAD is seen, in this great work of Covenant-love towards the Church. Turn to these scriptures in proof: Rom. viii. 29, 30. Ephes. i. 3—10. Titus iii. 3—7. And so infinitely blessed and important, is this great grace of the HOLY GHOST, in *calling,* that, until it is wrought, no child of GOD can have any apprehension, either of GOD the FATHER's love in *election,* or GOD the SON's grace in *redemption.* It is by *regeneration* that we are made *partakers of the divine nature, having escaped the corruption that is in the world, through lust!* 2 Pet i. 4, 5.

Reader! let us not dismiss the view of those united mercies, before that we have paused a moment longer, to pay the tribute of praise, on our bended knees, to GOD, in his threefold character of Person, for those unspeakable mercies! Blessed for ever be GOD our FATHER, for sanctifying, setting apart, choosing, and electing the Church in CHRIST, before all worlds, that it should be holy and without blame before him in love! Blessed for ever be GOD the SON, for uniting the Church to Himself, in a oneness and union, preserving her before all time, and preserving through all time, his Church as his own, and redeeming her to himself, for his social spouse and companion, to whom he might impart all communicable grace here, and glory for ever. And blessed for ever be GOD the HOLY GHOST, for calling the Church with an holy calling, and by his regenerating grace, quickening her, when dead in trespasses and sins, and bringing her into a new and spiritual life in CHRIST JESUS! Blessed be the HOLY THREE in ONE, for all our mercies in time, and to all eternity. Ephes. i. 3, 4, 5, 6. Hosea ii. 18, 19. John xvii. 2. 2 Tim. i. 9.

2 Mercy unto you, and peace, and love, be multiplied.

I beg to detain the Reader at this verse, to observe to him, that these Apostolic greetings, ought not to be considered, as it is to be feared they too frequently are, so many words of course. They are like so many prayers, as well as benedictions of the Apostles, and cannot be prized by the Church too highly. *Mercy* from the FATHER, *Peace* in and from JESUS CHRIST, and *Love* in and by the HOLY GHOST, very sweetly follow what was said before as the *fruits* and *effects* of those glorious acts, of the HOLY THREE in ONE, in Covenant manifestations. Reader! it will be both your mercy and mine, if we find those daily fruits, in our daily bread, of the everlasting love of JEHOVAH to his Church in CHRIST! GOD, in his Threefold character of Person, is the fountain of all mercy, peace, and love. And sweet, yea, very sweet it is, when GOD the HOLY GHOST makes known these things to our joy; by his revealing them to us with his gracious influences, in *directing our hearts into the love of* GOD, *and into the patient waiting for* CHRIST. 2 Thess. iii. 5. I would pray for those gracious love-tokens of the HOLY GHOST, that I may live in the enjoyment of the *mercy, peace,* and *love* of the whole Persons of the GODHEAD. But while I enjoy the *fruits,* I would pray yet more, to live upon the *Cause.* While I relish the *gift,* I would infinitely more love, and value the *Giver.*

3 Beloved, when I gave all diligence to write unto you of the common salvation, it was needful for me to write unto you, and exhort *you* that ye should earnestly contend for the faith which was once delivered unto the saints.

It hath been thought by some, (and I see no reason to disprove it,) that *Jude,* when he found his mind first directed to write to the Church, intended to have followed the same course as the other Apostles had done, *Paul* and *James;* and to have spoken *of the common salvation.* He had in view, to have dwelt principally upon those subjects which related to the Person, and glory, and offices, of the LORD JESUS CHRIST. But that he found his mind over-ruled by the HOLY GHOST, to state rather to the Church, the things which belonged to the latter-day apostacy; and, in bringing before them the striking difference between GOD's chosen and reprobates, he might exhort them *earnestly to contend for the faith once delivered unto the saints.* Whether this conjecture be right or not, I will not determine; but very certain it is, that the whole burden of this blessed Epistle is directed to this one purpose, in drawing the line, between the faithful and the ungodly. For, from the end of this verse, to the end of the *nineteenth* verse, the Apostle only speaks of the mockers of the last times, who should walk after their own ungodly lusts, and whose characters were of old ordained to this condemnation, being separate from the LORD's own people, *sensual, and having not the* SPIRIT. So that, if we take the Epistle into one view, after the exordium, from this verse to the end, the Apostle treats but of the *two* distinct classes of people; namely, the *Reprobate,* whose features of character he draws at large; and the LORD's *People,* who are *sanctified by* GOD *the* FATHER, *preserved in* JESUS CHRIST, *and called.* To these latter, the Apostle, in a very blessed and affectionate manner addresseth himself, and closeth the Epistle. We will follow the Apostle through both. But, before we go further, I would beg the Reader to consider, with me, what a strength of argument is in this verse, for every child of GOD to regard, what *Jude* saith of this holy, and earnest contention, for *the faith once delivered to the saints.* What that faith is, the New Testament, in the inspired writings of the Evangelists and the Apostles, most plainly, and fully shew. The great and leading doctrines of the Gospel, in the everlasting love of the FATHER, SON, and HOLY GHOST, more or less, are in every page. The Person, glory, bloodshedding, and righteousness of the LORD JESUS CHRIST, with redemption only in his blood, and regeneration only by GOD the HOLY GHOST; these are the bottom, and foundation of all our mercies. To contend for these, and with earnestness, is to contend for the very life of our souls. An indifferency, or coldness to the open profession of these glorious truths in ourselves, or to the denial of them in others, is wounding the Redeemer, in the house of his friends. It is high treason to the Majesty of GOD. It is traiterously admitting the enemy into our citadel. I leave the Reader to his own thoughts, how far the present day is awfully marked with this character; when the general, yea, I had almost said, the universal plan of professors, is to coalesce, and not suffer mere points of doctrine, as they are called, to interrupt the common philanthrophy of the times. What the Apostle *Jude* would have said, had he lived to have seen it, may be easily gathered from his earnest exhortation in this verse! And what GOD the SPIRIT, the Almighty Minister in his Church, always watching over it, shall judge, cannot be difficult to conceive!

4 ¶ For there are certain men crept in unawares, who were before of old ordained to this condemnation; ungodly men, turning the grace of our God into lasciviousness, and denying the only Lord God, and our Lord Jesus Christ.

5 I will therefore put you in remembrance, though ye once knew this, how that the Lord having saved the people out of the land of Egypt, afterward destroyed them that believed not.

6 And the angels which kept not their first estate, but left their own habitation, he hath reserved in everlasting chains under darkness unto the judgement of the great day.

7 Even as Sodom and Gomorrha, and the cities about them in like manner, giving themselves over to fornication, and going after strange flesh, are set forth for an example, suffering the vengeance of eternal fire.

8 Likewise also these *filthy* dreamers defile the

flesh, despise dominion, and speak evil of dignities.

9 Yet Michael the archangel, when contending with the devil he disputed about the body of Moses, durst not bring against him a railing accusation, but said, The Lord rebuke thee,

10 But these speak evil of those things which they know not; but what they know naturally, as brute beasts, in those things they corrupt themselves.

11 Woe unto them! for they have gone in the way of Cain, and ran greedily after the error of Balaam for reward, and perished in the gainsaying of Core.

12 These are spots in your feasts of charity, when they feast with you, feeding themselves without fear; clouds *they are* without water, carried about of winds; trees whose fruit withereth, without fruit twice dead, plucked up by the roots.

13 Raging waves of the sea, foaming out their own shame; wandering stars, to whom is reserved the blackness of darkness for ever.

14 And Enoch also, the seventh from Adam, prophesied of these, saying, Behold, the Lord cometh, with ten thousand of his saints,

15 To execute judgement upon all, and to convince all that are ungodly among them, of all their ungodly deeds which they have ungodly committed, and of all their hard *speeches* which ungodly sinners have spoken against them.

16 These are murmurers, complainers, walking after their own lusts; and their mouth speaketh great swelling *words*, having men's persons in admiration because of advantage.

17 But, beloved, remember ye the words which were spoken before of the apostles of our Lord Jesus Christ.

JUDE. 471

18 How that they told you there should be mockers in the last time, who should walk after their ungodly lusts.

19 These be they who separate themselves, sensual, having not the Spirit.

I include the whole of this awful Portrait, though made up of different characters, under one view, because they all form but one and the same picture; and all come under one and the same condemnation. We shall do well, under GOD the SPIRIT's teaching, to look both at their persons, and their features, and mark them one by one.

First. They are said to have been *certain men*, which had *crept in unawares*. By which we learn, that the Apostle is not speaking of men of the world among the infidels, who totally disown CHRIST; but certain men, which had crept into the *professing* Church; and therefore acknowledged him. *Paul* had foretold of such apostates, Acts xx. 29, 30: and *Peter* had drawn somewhat more fully their characters. 2 Pet. ii. 13. But *Jude* had lived to see some of them, in his day, as actually come into the professing Church; and, consequently, he foresaw swarms would follow. And I admire the expression, *they had crept in unawares.* For, as the faithful in the congregations, in those times, no more than in ours, had the faculty of discerning spirits, or of reading hearts, such false professors had got in, and been found among them: but then they *crept in.* Serpent-like, they had wormed themselves in, by wriggling: and, as *Satan* transformed himself into an angel of light, the more successfully to deceive; so those his ministers, for a while, appeared in form, as the ministers of righteousness, in a pretended love for CHRIST before the people. 2 Cor. xi. 14, 15. Reader! what a mercy is it in all ages of the Church, that the child of GOD, in whose heart a saving work of grace, by regeneration is wrought, hath this grand consolation for himself, amidst all the coverings of men, *the* LORD *knoweth them that are his!* 2 Tim. ii. 19. And it is an additional mercy, when, in proof of this, the child of GOD desires to be tried, and examined, and brought to the test, for the knowledge of himself, and his real character. And, fearing he may be tempted, from self-love, to judge too favorably of himself on this great point of decision, from the judgment of man, he flies to the scrutiny of GOD. *Try me, O* GOD, *and seek the ground of my heart; prove me, and examine my thoughts; look if there be any way of wickedness in me, and lead me in the way everlasting!* Psm. cxxxix. 23, 24. Here is a standard no hypocrite will have recourse to! This is a fire, and which no tinsel of unregenerated men can bear.

Secondly. Those certain men, which, the Apostle saith, had crept in unawares, appear to have been somewhat more than mere professors of the Gospel, among the people. It should seem, from the mention of certain characters, to whom they are compared, that they were the *Korahs* and *Balaams* of their day; *famous in the congregations, men of renown!* See Numb. chapters xvi. and xxii. &c. They blazed like Comets for a while, and like *wandering stars*, as Jude calls them, they soon went out, *to whom is reserved the blackness of darkness for ever.* Hence, those strong expressions, as descriptive of their real character. *Clouds without water, carried about of winds.* No grace of God in their heart. No work of regeneration upon their soul. A noisy profession only of a name to live, while virtually dead before God. Yea, *twice dead;* dead in the original state of nature, in the *Adam*-fall transgression in which they were born, and under the sentence of the *second death,* from having no part in *the first resurrection.* Observe the expression! *Certain men:* and *of old ordained to this condemnation!* Revelation xx. 6.

Thirdly. The Apostle hath drawn the outlines of their profession and practice. *Ungodly men, turning the grace of our* God *into lasciviousness, and denying the only* Lord God, *and our* Lord Jesus Christ. I pray the Reader to observe with me, that here are no charges of immorality. Had their lives been notorious, for any breaches of the moral law, surely it would have been said, Moreover, as they had crept in unawares into the Church, had their conduct been notoriously corrupt, in any flagrant acts of licentiousness, they would soon have been discovered and turned out. But they are called *ungodly men;* by which term, it should seem, that their conduct was directly levelled against the truths of God. And indeed, the Apostle adds: *Turning the grace of* God *into lasciviousness.* By which, I apprehend, they presumed to charge the free grace of God, which bringeth salvation, with leading to lasciviousness; as if that grace countenanced evil; and that glorious plan, of God's own contriving, in pardoning freely, fully, and compleatly, the sinner, on the sole account of Jesus's blood and righteousness, was, (as modern enemies to the free-grace salvation of Jesus have charged the same,) opening the flood-gates of sin. This seems to have been their ungodliness, and for which they are condemned, as ungodly men. And, it yet appears the more probable, because it is added, that their turning the grace of God into lasciviousness, was also accompanied with *denying the only* Lord God, *and our* Lord Jesus Christ. How could they be said to deny the only Lord God, but in denying his free grace? They could not be supposed to deny his Being. They could not, while they made a *profession* in the Church of Christ, either deny the Being of God, or the Being of Christ. But they indeed virtually denied both, if, like certain modern professors of Christianity, they denied the only Lord God, as existing in a threefold character of Person; and denied our Lord Jesus Christ in his Godhead, and in the efficacy of his blood and righteousness. Reader! look at this scripture in every way and direction in which it can be placed, and look for grace from the Almighty Author of inspiration, to have a right understanding of it. And then ask your own heart, what was *Jude* directed by the Holy Ghost to give all diligence to write to the Church of the common salvation, unless to have guarded the minds of the faithful against the creeping in of such certain men as are here described? What faith but the faith of God's elect, in God the Father's everlasting love, and God the Son's compleat, and finished salvation, could the Apostle mean, when he exhorted the Church, *earnestly to contend for the faith once delivered unto the saints?*

Fourthly. The judgments which are here threatened to such characters, bear an exact correspondence to the conduct, as I have described, under the former observation. When the Lord cometh, with ten thousand of his saints; he is said to come, to convince all that are *ungodly among them.* (Mark! here are the same characters as before called *ungodly men*, verse 4.) And he is said to convince them, not only of their *ungodly deeds*, but of all their *hard speeches, which ungodly sinners have spoken against him*. Who is this LORD, that is here said to come, but the LORD JESUS CHRIST? *For the* FATHER *judgeth no man, but hath committed all judgment unto the* SON. And the reason is immediately subjoined. *That all men should honor the* SON, *even as they honor the* FATHER. John v. 22, 23. And all the parts of scripture which describe the day of judgment, speak of CHRIST the SON of GOD, as the Judge in that day. Matt. xxv. 31, 32. Acts x. 42. 2 Thess. i. 7—10. And who is to convince these men of their ungodly deeds, and ungodly speeches, but He, whose eyes are as a flame of fire, and who, as the HOLY GHOST by *Paul* saith, *shall judge the quick and the dead, at his appearing and his kingdom?* 2 Tim. iv. 1. And who is this *Him*, which they are here said to have spoken all their *hard speeches against*, but the LORD JESUS CHRIST? Reader! ponder well the subject. Look at it again and again. Beg for light from above, to shine upon this solemn scripture, and to shine in your heart. Then look at the world, yea, the professing world, as it now is. Hear the hard speeches spoken daily against CHRIST, and by certain men, crept in unawares into the professing Church, and by a misnomer, calling themselves Christians. They deny his GODHEAD, deny the efficacy of his atonement, deny the merit of his blood and righteousness, and would fain reduce him to the level of a mere man, like themselves! Can your imagination conceive any thing more suitable, between the sin and the punishment here foretold to all such characters, than when JESUS shall come in his glory, and all his holy angels with him, and by the overwhelming brightness of his Person, shall convince and confound, into everlasting paleness and horror, those awful men? Reader! do dwell upon the Apostle's words, concerning this tremendous judgment! *To execute judgment upon all, and to convince all*, of their *hard speeches*, which ungodly sinners have spoken against *him*: yea, against *Him!* Mark that!

Fifthly. There is one point more, which gives a satisfying account to the Church of GOD, respecting those men, in explaining the cause, wherefore, though they have crept in unawares into the Church, by profession, they are wholly void of the smallest possession, in respect to vital godliness; namely, they are *sensual, having not the* SPIRIT. Here is the discrimination of character, which, in all ages, ever hath, and to the end of the world, ever must, and will mark the feature, *between the righteous and the wicked; between him that serveth* GOD, *and him that serveth him not*. Malachi iii. 18. Hence, all we read in this Epistle, yea, and all we read in the other parts of GOD's holy word, concerning men who are *sensual, having not the* SPIRIT; that is, who remain in the old *Adam*-nature of sensual corruptions, unawakened, unregenerated, and never quickened into a new and spiritual life by the HOLY GHOST, is in exact correspondence to what might be expected. They *speak evil of those things which they know not; but what they know naturally as brute beasts, in those things they corrupt themselves. They have gone into the way of Cain; they have ran greedily after the error of Balaam, for reward; and perished in the gainsaying of Core. These are spots in your feasts of charity. Their mouth speaketh great swelling words, having men's persons in admiration, because of advantage.* These are different descriptions, like so many shades in the painting; but all belong to one and the same character, of *sensual men, who have not the* SPIRIT: that is, all that are unregenerate. Not that all men while unregenerate, are like *Cain*, the first *Deist* the world ever had. For GOD's children, while in nature, are so. Neither that all unregenerate men hire themselves out, as *Balaam* did, to curse GOD's people, while conscious in his heart, that *Israel* was GOD's people. Neither do all, that with unhallowed hands dare to enter the Priesthood, as *Korah* and his company, uncalled of GOD, perish, as they did, in the moment of their presumption. Neither do all unregenerate men, who mingle in the feasts of GOD's people at his house, or at his table, though spots of defilement at those places bad enough; yet, neither injure the LORD's people, nor benefit themselves. Neither do all unawakened professors bolster up the *Pharisees* they meet with in their places of worship, though too often compliments to men's persons, whom they have in admiration, are paid, it is to be feared, at the expence of GOD's saving truths. These different shades, are differently seen in different men; but they all belong to one family, and have, in this respect, the same family feature; namely, as *Jude* saith, they are all *sensual, having not the* SPIRIT! Reader! pause once more, and ponder these things well. And observe, from the LORD's teaching, as plain and luminous, as though written with a sun beam; that regeneration, or the new-birth, is the only criterion, and standard of character, before GOD. All the flaming professions in the world, all the seeming zeal, in compassing sea and land to make one proselyte; all the high pretensions, of more love than GOD himself, to convert all the earth, and to save whom GOD hath not saved; all the alms-giving, and alms-gathering, for the innumerable societies, to manifest their possessing the milk of human nature; yea, even the martyrdom of the body, where there is no regeneration of the soul; all these, and every other, leave the professor just where nature found him, in the old *Adam*-nature of sin, unrenewed by the HOLY GHOST, unwashed in the blood of CHRIST, unsanctified, and unchosen by the FATHER; and plainly demonstrate, from scripture testimony, that they have no lot or part in the matter. So that, as I have more than once before observed, in this *Poor Man's Commentary*, those five words of the LORD JESUS CHRIST, throw to the ground all pretensions void of spiritual life, and dash the hopes of all hypocrites: *Ye must be born again.* John iii. 7.

Lastly, to add no more. What *Jude* begins with, in this awful account, the Church makes her first and last conclusion, in tracing the whole to its source; namely, the *certain men* the Apostle saith, which *crept in unawares*, under those several specious forms of character, *were before of old ordained to this condemnation*. This testimony to GOD's sovereignty, so hateful to the sensual, *who have not the* SPIRIT, and so precious to the faithful, who know, by distinguishing grace, their *adoption in* CHRIST JESUS; places the whole truths of GOD upon their proper basis; and explains the subject, in all its different bearings, and in all the variety of circumstances, in which, through all ages, the grace of GOD hath appeared. Reader! pause once more. If the LORD hath mercifully brought you into an acquaintance with the plague of your own heart, and if (as cannot then but be the sweet and precious testimony to the truth as it is in JESUS,) your views of GOD's sovereignty, and your acquaintance with

CHRIST, arising out of it, be in your own soul's experience, look with astonishment at the distinguishing mercy, in partaking in *the faith once delivered to the saints*. Every child of GOD, in the present awful day, of a CHRIST-despising generation, is a wonder to himself, as well as to many. He is a living witness for GOD;. and oh! how ought he to esteem it his highest honor, to bear this loudest testimony to his holy Name; that though the day is not unlike the day of *Elijah*, yet GOD hath still reserved to himself thousands, that *have not, and will not bow the knee to the image of Baal. Even so now*, (saith the HOLY GHOST by the Apostle,) *at this present time also, there is a remnant, according to the election of grace.* Rom. xi. 4, 5.

I do not think it necessary to dwell long on these several verses in this Epistle, which might be gratifying, in a way of curiosity, but are not immediately necessary to be known, in a way of salvation. *Jude* reminds the people, concerning the visible Church in Egypt. Though numbers of *Israel* after the flesh, which accompanied the people of GOD on their deliverance from *Pharaoh*, and thereby had all the advantages of a *temporal* salvation; yet, having no part nor lot in the matter, in the *spiritual* salvation by CHRIST, went no further, for their carcases fell in the wilderness. Rom. ix. 6, 7. Heb. iii. 16 to the end. And the angels which kept not their first estate, not being *elect* angels, but left to the mutability of their own will, fell, and in that fall, were everlastingly condemned. The Reader, in the view of this subject, if taught of GOD, will find subject for endless praise. For such is the unavoidable consequence of all created nature, whether in angels or men, that, if not preserved in CHRIST JESUS, must have been subject to fall. No one creature, either angel or man, being in their own nature secured from falling, unless kept by a power superior to their own. That power can only be the GOD-Man CHRIST. Not as GOD only. For then there could be no standing in with GOD. And as man only, there would have been no omnipotency, to have upheld. But as both, GOD and man in one Person, there is a suitability to the glorious deed. And, therefore, both angel and man, in the election of grace, the *former* by dominion, and the *latter* by union, are elect and preserved. Oh! what cause there is, for unceasing thanksgiving and praise, for the remnant, according to the election of grace! And truly, we may say with the Prophet; *except the* LORD *of hosts had left unto us a very small remnant, we should have been as Sodom, and we should have been like unto Gomorrah*, Isaiah i. 9.

I have given my views, in my *Poor Man's Concordance*, concerning the Archangel, and therefore shall not enlarge on the subject in this place. There can be but one Archangel, from the very name. Those who talk of Archangels, or Arks, seem to have forgotten the sense of words. And as we meet with the name Archangel but twice in the whole book of GOD, and both when speaking of the LORD JESUS CHRIST, there can be but little question that it is him which is referred to, and that by way of office. He is called Prince, or Chief, in the prophecy of Daniel, x. 13, 21. I would not presume to be wise above what is written, but, concerning the contention here spoken of, as no part of scripture hath noticed it, I can say nothing of it with certainty. The chiefest feature in it to remark is, the LORD's meekness. See Zech. iii. 1, 2.

Of *Enoch's* prophecy, the Holy Ghost hath given no record. Perhaps it was not written, but oral. But the account here stated, is, perhaps, in correspondence with all the parts of scripture which relate to Christ's coming. By the seventh from *Adam*, is not meant the seventh person, for, doubtless, numbers both of sons and daughters were born to Adam, and his children, before *Enoch* was born. See Gen. v. 4, &c. But, by the seventh from *Adam*, is meant the *seventh* generation, in the line of the Church, and which were *Adam, Sheth, Enosh, Kenan, Mahalaleel, Jered, Enoch*. 1 Chron. i. 1, 2.

20 ¶ But ye, beloved, building up yourselves on your most holy faith, praying in the Holy Ghost.

21 Keep yourselves in the love of God, looking for the mercy of our Lord Jesus Christ unto eternal life.

22 And of some have compassion, making a difference:

23 And others save with fear, pulling *them* out of the fire; hating even the garment spotted by the flesh.

24 Now unto him that is able to keep you from falling, and to present *you* faultless before the presence of his glory with exceeding joy.

25 To the only wise God our Saviour, *be* glory and majesty, dominion and power, both now and ever. Amen.

The Apostle here enters upon the subject of the Church, in pointing out her safety in Christ, amidst all that he had said before of reprobates. And a very sweet close on this subject he makes of his Epistle. By building up in their most holy faith, and praying in the Holy Ghost, and keeping themselves in the love of God, and looking for the mercy of our Lord Jesus Christ unto eternal life, we must not suppose that the Apostle meant as if the Church was her own keeper, or that she could create faith in her heart whenever she pleased. All the parts of scripture teacheth, and every child of God's heart is in full testimony to the same, that they who are kept, are kept by the power of God, unto eternal life. And the Lord himself confirms the sweet assurance, that the Church is *preserved in* Jesus Christ. Yes, he saith to her, *In that day, sing ye to her a vineyard of red wine. I the* Lord *do keep it. I will water it every moment; lest any hurt it, I will keep it night and day.* Isaiah xxvii. 2, 3. 1 Peter i. 5. But, by building up ourselves in our most holy faith, and praying in the Holy Ghost, is meant a continual waiting for the influences of the Spirit, and, under those influences, attending diligently on the several means of grace and ordinances of the Lord, and strengthening each other's hands and hearts in the Lord. And a sense of our daily need *of* Christ, will, through the Spirit's blessing, lead the soul to a daily abiding *in* CHRIST, and acting faith *upon* CHRIST. And, by looking for the mercy of our LORD JESUS CHRIST, unto eternal life, implies a sure, fixed, and certain hope of being interested in all the blessed and glorious events of that great day of GOD. I admire the Apostle's expression, when he calls it *the mercy of our* LORD JESUS CHRIST. For, surely, it can be nothing but mercy, where there is nothing but undeserving. But, though a mercy, it is a *sure* mercy. For a soul, truly regenerated, is truly justified, and truly sanctified in the LORD, and nothing remains doubtful as to the issue of that day. 2 Peter i. 3, 4. 1 Cor. vi. 11. 1 Cor. i. 30. Isaiah xlv. 24, 25. The Apostle *Jude* would not have been taught by the HOLY GHOST to give the Church this confidence, had a question of uncertainty remained. Neither could the Apostles *Paul* or *Peter* have called the very expectation of it *blessed*, had not an assurance of glory in CHRIST been wrapped up in it. Titus ii. 13. 2 Peter iii. 12. Reader! what saith your experience to these things? Doth *your* heart correspond with the Apostle's?

There is somewhat most affectionate and tender in the love of brethren in JESUS. The compassion shewn to wanderers, and backsliders, and those that are tempted and fallen, and those that are ignorant and out of the way, is sweet. We are propelled, by grace, to stretch forth the helping hand, in any way, and every way, to raise up the fallen. And, as we are ignorant who is, and who is not among the LORD's people, while no work of regeneration appears by outward testimony; we wish to save, as from the fire, those who are in the confines of extreme danger. And though we loath their sins as we loath our own garments, which, by wrapping round our bodies of corruption, are spotted and defiled, yet we love their persons, when the LORD leads out our souls in desires after their salvation.

The concluding clause of this beautiful Epistle is very striking. *Now unto Him that is able to keep you from falling, and to present you faultless before the presence of his glory, with exceeding joy; to the only wise* GOD, *our* SAVIOR, *be glory, and majesty, dominion, and power, both now and ever. Amen.* What a long and beautiful sermon might a preacher, taught of GOD the SPIRIT, find in these words! We cannot for a moment hesitate to know whom the Apostle means. He that hath all along preserved his Church, must be the same that keeps her from falling. And it is the special and personal office of CHRIST, to present his Church to himself at the last day. We no where read in scripture, concerning the person of GOD the FATHER, or GOD the HOLY GHOST, presenting the Church before the throne. It is GOD the SON's *personal* office, as Mediator, to bring her home as a bride adorned for her husband, and present her to himself. Hence that beautiful description given to the Church by *Paul.* CHRIST *loved the Church,* saith *Paul, and gave himself for it, that he might sanctify and cleanse it with the washing of water by the word; that he might present it to himself a glorious Church, not having spot or wrinkle, or any such thing, but that it should be holy, and without blemish.* Ephes. v. 25—27. But, in addition to what is here said, it may be remarked, that all along, from one eternity to another, it is CHRIST's charge, and CHRIST's care, yea, and this scripture saith, his exceeding joy, to watch over his Church, which is part of himself, and to keep her from falling, as well as to present her to himself at last, finally and fully prepared by himself, in body, soul, and spirit, for his everlasting spouse and companion, to run the whole round of eternity with him, in his glory for ever.

Let the Reader pause over this subject, for the meditation of it is sweet. The Church, chosen in JESUS CHRIST before the foundation of the world, is, as *Jude* saith, in the opening of this Epistle, preserved in JESUS CHRIST. And, in the close of it, is commended to CHRIST JESUS, to be kept faultless, and at length presented in glory. *Jude* saith, he is able. And no one can doubt his willingness. And if, as he hath represented it himself, it becomes a subject of such delight to him, to bring home one poor lost sheep, which had strayed from his fold, as to induce him to call his friends and neighbours around him, to rejoice with him over this one which was lost; what exceeding joy may we suppose it will be to the LORD JESUS CHRIST, when he shall bring home his whole flock, consisting of millions of people, to and before a congregated world, saved with an everlasting salvation, so as to wander no more. Reader! have you been much accustomed to consider the subject in this view? Do you, in your own instance, know what it is to be preserved *in* CHRIST JESUS, called *to* CHRIST JESUS, kept *by* CHRIST JESUS, and are now living *upon* CHRIST JESUS? If so, you will need nothing from me to shew you the blessedness of it. But you will feel both the sweetness of *Jude's* words, as well as those of *Paul* to the Church, upon the same occasion, when he said, *Now the very* GOD *of peace sanctify you wholly; and I pray* GOD *your whole spirit, and soul, and body, be preserved blameless unto the coming of our* LORD JESUS CHRIST. *Faithful is he that calleth you, who also will do it.* 1 Thess. v. 23, 24.

The doxology must not pass unnoticed, for it is very blessed. *To the only wise* GOD *our* SAVIOR! That this hymn is suited to each, and to all the Persons of the GODHEAD, as being all engaged, and having all co-operated in the salvation of the Church, is very certain, and all regenerated believers in CHRIST will gladly join in so sweet a song. But, that CHRIST is here specially and personally meant, is evident, because he is specially and personally our SAVIOR. Moreover, it is the LORD JESUS, who is particularly spoken of in the preceding verse, with which this is connected. And, as in those two gracious acts of CHRIST, as mentioned before, namely, *keeping the Church from falling*, and *presenting the Church faultless*, at last, *before the presence of his glory, with exceeding joy*, these are CHRIST's special and personal offices; the praise here ascribed appears to be the immediate consequence the Church desires to give him. And there is one circumstance more, which, in my view, renders it particularly proper, namely, that those ascriptions of praise appear to be the Redeemer's personal right.

The Reader will not need that I should tell him, that GOD only *wise*, our SAVIOR, very blessedly suits him, because, when upon earth, he was upbraided by men for ignorance. *How knoweth this man letters*, (say they,) *having never learned.* John vii. 15. JESUS is worthy of all possible *glory*; because, when he came to redeem his people, he emptied himself of all glory, and *took upon him the form of a servant.* Philip. ii. 7. And surely *majesty* was his inherent right, though, when on earth, *he hid not his face from shame and spitting.* Isa. l. 6. *Dominion* belongeth to the LORD, and an eternal monarchy over all, though, while below, *he had not where to lay his head.* Luke ix. 58.

And all *power* is his for ever, *for he hath power over all flesh, to give eternal life to as many as the* FATHER *hath given him.* John xvii. 2. though the insult offered him on the cross was, *he saved others; himself he cannot save.* Mark xv. 31. Glorious Almighty SAVIOR! GOD only wise, thy Church hail thee! Be thou eternally loved, and praised, and adored: thou art worthy to receive all glory, and honor, and power, and might, *for thou wast slain, and hast redeemed us to* GOD, *by thy blood.*

REFLECTIONS.

READER! hath GOD the HOLY GHOST, in his gracious teachings, blest, to your perusal and mine, this precious portion of his sacred Word? Are we that of distinguished people, who are *sanctified by* GOD *the* FATHER, *preserved in* JESUS CHRIST, *and called?* Oh! then, let us both beg another blessing from our bountiful GOD, and ask for grace, that on our bended knees we may cry out with the Apostle, *thanks be unto* GOD *for his unspeakable gift!*

And we desire to praise the Almighty Minister of his Church, even GOD the HOLY GHOST, for the grace he hath shewn, in fore-warning, and fore-arming his people, concerning the last days heresies. Truly, LORD, we live to *see* them. We live *among* them. And thanks to our GOD, for giving his Church such plain features of character, as are here drawn by his servant, and by which, under the LORD's teaching, we cannot fail to *know* them. Oh! what shall thy people say; what praise shall thy people offer, while reading the striking distinction which mark thy redeemed from the world. The *one,* sanctified, preserved, and called; the *other,* ordained of old to this condemnation, *denying the only* LORD GOD, *and our* LORD JESUS CHRIST!

We bless our GOD for the faithfulness of his servant *Jude,* in this scripture. And, while we look to the Eternal SPIRIT with praise for making him faithful, we would honor the instrument, whom GOD so graciously made use of in the work. *Jude, the servant of* JESUS CHRIST, *and brother of James,* we thank thee for thy labor of love. The whole Church, in all ages, have found cause to thank thee for it, from thy time to the present hour. And, oh! LORD the SPIRIT, give grace to thy faithful *now,* to testify their sense of the mercy vouchsafed the Church in this precious Epistle, *by earnestly contending for the faith, once delivered unto the saints.* Oh! keep thy people, LORD, from being led away with the speciousness of the times! Oh! for grace, to own and praise CHRIST, before a CHRIST-despising generation! Oh! for an holy boldness, from the LORD, to stand up for the LORD, and to resist the bait of supposing we can honor GOD's glory, while silently sitting and mingling with those who dishonor his GODHEAD, disown the Person and Work of the SPIRIT, and boldly deny the electing-love of GOD the FATHER. Unto such assemblies, my soul, be not thou united! LORD JESUS! do thou keep all thine from this, and every other evil, until thou shalt bring all thy redeemed home, and *present them faultless before the presence of thy glory with exceeding joy.* Amen.

THE REVELATION OF St. JOHN THE DIVINE.

GENERAL OBSERVATIONS.

I PRAY for grace, to enter upon this sublime and mysterious Book of GOD, while proposing my humble observations upon it, with the most profound reverence and godly fear. And as I approach the mercy-seat, to bend the knee of my soul, before the GOD and FATHER of our LORD JESUS CHRIST, that in meditating on this blessed portion of his holy word, which relates so immediately to the Person of CHRIST and his kingdom, the LORD may give unto me, *the spirit of wisdom, and revelation in the knowledge of Him.*

Indeed, when first I ventured on this *Poor Man's Commentary* of the Bible, I fully intended, if it should please the LORD to guide me through it, and bring me to this Book of the *Revelation,* to have passed over those sacred Chapters, without presuming to offer any observations of mine. I had seen so many erroneous opinions, from great and good men on this part of the word of GOD, and especially in their calculations of the *times,* when the several Prophecies, yet remaining to be fulfilled, would be accomplished, that I judged it rather presumptuous than wise, to touch this part of the inspired records. And I still think, that as those great and good men, (for great and good men they certainly were, in their day and generation,) have all been found in error, in limiting the period when those prophecies would certainly be fulfilled, it can neither be decent nor proper in men taught of GOD to presume to be *wise, above what is written,* and to offer their conjectures concerning what GOD hath not been pleased to discover. The words of JESUS to his disciples after he arose from the dead, in answer to the anxious enquiry they put to him, concerning the *time* of the LORD's restoring the kingdom of *Israel,* appears decided on this point; *It is not for you to know the times, or the seasons which the* FATHER *hath put in his own power.* Acts i. 6, 7. But when I read again and again, what is said in the opening of this precious Book of GOD; *Blessed is he that readeth, and they that hear the words of this prophecy, and keep those things which are written therein;* I dared not be wholly silent. And I thought moreover, that if God the Holy Ghost (whose guidings in this work I had all along implored, and whose grace in instruction in it I hope I can now, with truth, say I have found,) would still graciously condescend to go before, and follow me, the Lord would keep me from treading in, to that part of the sacred ground, which relates to prophecies yet unfulfilled, by attempting to calculate any *time, when* I might presume on their accomplishment, but leave it wholly to the Lord; while, under his teaching, I might humbly offer my observations, on such only, as we have seen come to pass. With these limitations I felt encouraged to prosecute my *Poor Man's Commentary* on this part also of the divine word, deriving advantage, even from the mistakes of those great servants of the Lord, which have gone before, and which in those points act as light-houses at sea, purposely placed there to keep off the mariner, from approaching too near the rocks, and quicksands around them.

And I confess, that under these later views I have taken of the subject, I have felt additional encouragement, to prosecute my feeble labors for the *Poor Man's Commentary*, on this part of the word of God, from the recollection, that now in the present hour, time hath brought forward many things to view in this scripture, and, through the Lord's teaching, more light hath been thrown upon the predictions here given, than in the day when those great and good men lived, whom I allude to, who for years past have been *gathered to their fathers, and have seen corruption.* Many of the prophecies have since been accomplished, and more seem to be now accomplishing in the earth. And, indeed, on the supposition that we, who are now entered some years into the *nineteeth Century*, are they *upon whom the ends of the world are come*, it must behove the people of God to be on the lookout, like the Prophet on the watch-tower, and in prayer and humble waitings on the Lord, expect those manifestations predicted to be accomplished, concerning his Church That the interests of *Zion*, are at the bottom of all God's designs in the earth, and that the putting down of one kingdom, and raising up of another, have no ultimate object, but of bringing on the Lord's purposes, concerning Christ and his Church; is too clear a truth to need the being insisted upon. And fully assured we are, that when all the prophecies which are in this Holy Scripture, yet remaining to be fulfilled, are accomplished, the last sand, in the hour-glass of time, will have run out; and the whole purposes of the Lord concerning this earth, will be compleated. And then, that event takes place, which *John* heard proclaimed by the Angel, *he lifted up his hand to heaven, and sware by him that liveth for ever and ever, that there should be time no longer.* Then, *the mystery of* GOD *shall be finished.* Then, *the seventh Angel* shall sound, and *great voices will be heard in heaven, saying, the kingdoms of this world, are become the kingdoms of our* LORD, *and of his* CHRIST, *and he shall reign for ever and ever.* Chap. x. 5, 6, 7. and Chap. xi. 15.

The great point of error, into which all my predecessors of Commentators, on this blessed Book of GOD, more or less, have fallen, I shall, through grace, wholly avoid. I shall not knowingly, offer a single attempt, in a way of calculation as to the *time* many have supposed, in which the prophecies herein contained, yet remaining to be fulfilled, will be accomplished. Here, I desire to remain, as much as ever, wholly silent. Indeed, it hath always appeared unto me, to have been along the LORD's design, in relation to the prophecies in general, to throw a veil over them, until they are fulfilled. And then, when they have been brought to pass, so compleat an agreement hath discovered itself, between the prediction and the event, that the LORD's people have found cause to stand the more amazed, at their dulness of perception and the LORD's glory. But there is a manifest wisdom of GOD in the obscurity. It tends to the promotion of greater faith. It calls forth greater dependence upon the LORD. And GOD speaks in his word, and by his word to his people, during the suspence of accomplishment, as he did to the Prophet of old; *Go thy way, Daniel, for the words are closed up, and sealed to the time of the end. Thou shalt rest, and stand in thy lot, at the end of the days.* Daniel xii. 8, 9, 13.

I must not indulge myself with any longer Preface, in an humble work like this, on general points. But I must beg to extend these observations a little further, by way of introduction to the sacred Book of the *Revelation,* which we are going to enter upon. It will be proper at the threshold, to pause a moment and consider, both the LORD's gracious design, in his gift of it to the Church, and also to pray over it, as we enter upon it, that this blessing of a Covenant GOD in CHRIST may be made profitable to our souls.

That *John,* the beloved Apostle, was the Writer of it under GOD, and that the place where those revelations were made to him, was *Patmos* in the *Mediterranean* Sea, and where he was banished for the testimony of JESUS CHRIST, about the year of our LORD GOD *ninety-four;* these are truths, so generally allowed and confirmed, as can need nothing additional, by way of proof, to be observed. And the gracious design of GOD the HOLY GHOST, in sealing up the sacred Canon of Scripture, with so divine a portion of his holy word, hardly requires to be remarked to any gracious Reader. This is a subject, which GOD the HOLY GHOST, hath had the unwearied

GENERAL OBSERVATIONS.

thanksgivings of the Church for, in every age, from *John's* days to ours; neither will this precious portion of divine truth, ever cease to call forth the continued praises of the LORD's people, till time shall be no more.

I shall request permission in this place, to give the Reader a brief statement, according to my view of the whole subject, of this Book of GOD, that he may have a general idea of the whole contents. Such a plan will serve, under the HOLY GHOST's teaching, to guide both the Writer and Reader of this *Poor Man's Commentary*, through the several Chapters; and enable him to discover, that there is a beautiful uniformity of order in the whole design, comprehending the several periods of the Church's history, from CHRIST's appearing to John at *Patmos*, until his second coming at judgment. From such a view, we shall proceed through the several Chapters, with a greater clearness of apprehension, of the whole subject; and, through grace, have our minds better prepared, *to hear what the* SPIRIT *saith to the Churches!*

For the better understanding this sublime Book of GOD, let the Reader recollect, that when the SON of GOD appeared to *John*, as the opening of the *first* Chapter declares, the Seven Churches to whom he sent the messages, contained in the *second* and *third* Chapters, were then in being. Of these the LORD speaks, when he calls them *the things which are.* Rev. i. 19. And all that is contained in those two Chapters, refer to them. But the prophetical part of the Revelation, which begins at the *fourth* Chapter, comes under, what CHRIST calls *the things which shall be hereafter.* Rev. i. 19. Hence, from the *fourth* Chapter is commenced, the prophecies of events, which the LORD foretold his servant *John* should be accomplished in his Church. And in the *fifth* Chapter, we have what may be called the instalment of CHRIST into his High Offices, as the Prophet, Priest, and King of his people. With these preliminary views, if we prosecute the Book, through the several Chapters, we shall discover the beautiful order, connection, and harmony of one great whole, from beginning to end.

And let the Reader recollect no less, that at the time when the LORD JESUS manifested himself to his Apostle *John*, to give to him these revelations, to shew unto his Churches, the *Roman* Empire, which was mistress of the world, was then heathen. *Satan* had universal sway, and excepting that handful of the LORD's people, formed here and there into Churches, the earth was full of idols. The *Jews* nationally considered, for their rejection of the LORD of life and glory, had lost their temple, their government, their beloved *Jerusalem*, and were now scattered over various parts of the globe. This was the state of things respecting religion, when the SON of GOD appeared to his servant *John* as here stated; and delivered to him these predictions, which were from age to age, to be progressively accomplished in the Church, from that period to the final consummation of all things. The sum and substance of the whole, is set forth, though in mysterious terms, to intimate that the Church of CHRIST should be opposed by the powers of darkness; during which, *seals* were to be opened, *trumpets* sounded, and *vials* poured out; but, at length, order should arise out of confusion, and light from darkness. The Church of GOD should triumph over all, and the throne of GOD and the LAMB, be discovered as established for ever.

Such was the state of things, when the subject of prophecy begins at the *sixth* Chapter, with the opening of the *seals*. The ministry of the seals, appears to be principally, if not wholly directed, in the preaching of the Gospel against heathenism. And we find from history, that from about *three hundred years* from the period at the opening of the *first* seal, the *Roman* Empire became Christian; that is, made a national profession of christianity. This event took place in the government of the Emperor *Constantine*.

To the ministry of the *seals*, when finished, succeeded that of the *Trumpets*. The time to the Trumpet ministry takes in a much larger compass than that of the Seals; yea, it should seem is not yet finished. For the sounding of the *seventh* Trumpet is, when the mystery of GOD shall be finished. Rev. x. 7. And it should appear very plainly, that the opening of the *twelfth* Chapter, begins with a new subject of prophecy; I say a *new subject of prophecy*, because the former terminates in the preceding Chapter, with the relation of *the day of the* LORD being come, and the *temple of* GOD *being opened in heaven*. Chap. xi. 18, 19. But though a new subject of prophecy, yet not a new subject, as it concerns CHRIST and his kingdom, for this is but one and the same, through the whole book of Revelation, from the first opening of the seals at the *sixth* Chapter, to the account of the paradise of GOD, in the *twenty-second*. All, and every part under the different predictions, is in relation to CHRIST and his Church.

The twelfth Chapter, as it appears to me, opens with the state of the *Roman* Empire, when it became (nationally considered) no longer heathen, but professing christianity. And now, according to this Chapter, persecution began, from the heresies springing up in the Empire, among the Christians themselves. And this subject occupies the following Chapters to the *eighteenth*, where the final destruction of Antichrist is shewn, in the total overthrow of the *two* great branches of those powers, subverting the truths of GOD in the Eastern and Western world. And these events, evidently remain, at present, unfulfilled.

During this period, the ministry of the *Vials* is said to be exercised. These will all be noted in their proper place. In the mean time, it will be sufficient here to observe, that with the pouring out of the last Vial upon the air, which figuratively should seem to intimate the whole kingdom of Satan, (who in this sense is called *the Prince of the power of the air*, Ephes. ii. 2.) the opposition to CHRIST's kingdom ceaseth for ever. Hence the *nineteenth* Chapter opens with the accounts of the triumphs in heaven, over all the enemies of CHRIST and his salvation. The chaining of *Satan* in the bottomless pit follows in the *twentieth;* and the Church of CHRIST coming down from heaven, as a bride adorned for her husband, is related in the *twenty-first* Chapter. And the whole subject is closed up in the *twenty-second*, with the description of the glory of GOD and of the LAMB, in the salvation of the Church, and the destruction of the wicked. These are the general outlines of this most blessed and precious Book of GOD. I will detain the Reader no longer from entering upon it, than only once again to look up for grace, and the light of the HOLY GHOST, to guide both at the entrance, and through all the departments of it to the end. May that Almighty and Infallible Teacher, direct both heart and pen, that nothing of error may be found in those pages, but all be so graciously dictated by Him, that the LORD's glory, and the Church's happiness, may be ministered unto in these feeble services, through JESUS CHRIST. Amen.

CHAPTER I.

CONTENTS.

After a short Preface of what the Apostle is called to, in the Ministry of this Book of Revelation, he addresseth the Seven Churches of Asia, with the Salutation of Grace and Peace. He speaks most blessedly of the Person and Glory of CHRIST, *in his appearing to Him, and relates what passed at this Interview.*

THE Revelation of Jesus Christ, which God gave unto him, to shew unto his servants things which must shortly come to pass; and he sent and signified *it* by his angel unto his servant John:

2 Who bare record of the word of God, and of the testimony of Jesus Christ, and of all things that he saw.

3 Blessed *is* he that readeth, and they that hear the words of this prophecy, and keep those things which are written therein: for the time *is* at hand.

This is most properly assigned to JESUS CHRIST, the revelation herein given to *John*. For as none was found worthy to open the book and to loose the seals, but CHRIST himself as Mediator, so all revelation, primarily and effectually, must be in him and from him. And I beg the Reader by the way, not to overlook in this relation given of CHRIST, how very fully it proclaims, his eternal power and GODHEAD, since none but one that hath fore-knowledge, could foretell future events. And although in this place, CHRIST is here spoken of, as the CHRIST of GOD, the Mediator, yet such powers demonstrate, what all the scriptures, with one voice declare, that CHRIST is both GOD and Man, in this most blessed character. No sooner was CHRIST set as JEHOVAH's King in Zion, than he instantly acts in that high office, and saith, *I will declare the decree.* Compare Rev. v. 6, 8, with Psm. ii. 6, 7.

By the phrase of *things which must shortly come to pass*, can mean no more, than their beginning to be accomplished. For very certain it is, that we are now arrived into the opening of the *nineteenth* Century; and though much hath been fulfilled, much remains yet to be accomplished. But the commencement of the predictions and events then delivered to *John*, were shortly to be accomplished in part, and thus go on from generation to generation, until the whole were finished.

John was specially chosen, to have these sacred things brought before him, and to deliver them to the Church, for he had enjoyed a more than ordinary acquaintance with the Person of his LORD, during his ministry upon earth. And under the HOLY GHOST, had borne a most decided testimony to the LORD JESUS and his office-character, as the Uncreated WORD and the CHRIST of GOD. John i. 14. 1 John i. 1, 2, 3. Reader! do not overlook the blessedness pronounced on reading, hearing, and keeping in remembrance the glorious records, here given to the Person, and Ministry of the LORD JESUS CHRIST. It is a great encouragement to be diligent in our attention, to this most precious book of GOD. Oh! may the HOLY GHOST open its blessed contents to my view, and write them in my heart, that GOD *in all things may be glorified through* JESUS CHRIST.

4 JOHN to the seven Churches which are in Asia: Grace *be* unto you, and peace from him which is, and which was, and which is to come: and from the seven spirits which are before his throne;

5 And from Jesus Christ, *who is* the faithful witness, *and* the first begotten of the dead, and the prince of the kings of the earth. Unto him that loved us, and washed us from our sins in his own blood,

6 And hath made us kings and priests unto God and his Father, to him *be* glory and dominion for

The names of these seven Churches we have enumerated in the eleventh verse. And, awful to relate, they are now all of them in the hands of the Turks, and under the horrible delusion of the infamous doctrine of *Mahomet;* called in this scripture, *the false Prophet!* Chap. xvi. 13. See Reader! how sure are God's judgments! While the Church of Christ must stand for ever, neither can the gates of hell prevail against it, Nations, that is, professing nations, where that Church hath once flourished, as *Ephesus,* may be given up to utter ruin. The house of God standeth sure, but the Candlestick is a moveable article in the house; and may be removed, when the iniquity of a land (as *Sodom* was before its destruction) is full. Oh! who that seriously lays at heart, the deplorable state of our highly favored nation, but finds cause to tremble, lest God should give it up to barrenness, *for the wickedness of them that dwell therein.* Psm. cvii. 34. A Christ-despising generation, in which his Godhead is impudently denied in open day, and now, no law to punish the daring offenders!

I admire the very blessed expressions in the Apostle's salutation. What a degree of elevation, the souls of Prophets and Apostles arrived at, under divine influence, when speaking the praises of Jehovah. And how much they all delighted, to celebrate each Person of the Godhead; and each office-character belonging to each Person of the Godhead, as revealed to the Church in the Covenant of grace? And wherefore should New Testament saints come short of sounding forth, the high praises of the Holy Three in One, who have such increasing causes, in the increasing testimonies of their grace; accumulating, as that grace must daily do, in the swelling tide continually running from age to age through the Church?

I would not insist upon a single point of doctrine, as being confirmed, but upon evidences the most incontestible. But I would humbly ask, are not the sacred Three in One distinctly spoken of in those hallowed words; *from Him which is, and which was, and which is to come?* From *Him,* in allusion, as may be supposed, to the divine Unity, and in which the whole Three Persons are included. *Which is, and which was, and which is to come;* meaning God the Father, Son, and Spirit, in the eternity and unchangeableness of their essence, as God, and in which, each, and all these divine properties, belong to each, and to all. And in their office-character also, which they have most graciously entered into in the Covenant, those distinctions belong to each and to all. For, as their nature and the engagements to each other, respecting the Church, are everlasting; so, to the Church in Christ, it may and must be said of them, *which is, and which was, and which is to come.* Reader! what a sweet thought is it, that our mercies are everlasting and unchangeable; for the Lord Jehovah from whom they come, is everlasting and unchangeable!

But while we thus give equal glory to the Holy Three in One, both as we contemplate each, and fall in their Personal distinctions, and in their united glory, as the One Eternal Jehovah; we have in this scripture also, very blessed views of each, in those distinctions of character, as they stand in relation to the Church. God the Father in his choice of the Church, in his gift of the Church to Christ, and in all his purposes of grace and mercy, flowing from his everlasting love to the Church, both is, and was, and is to come. What GOD the FATHER now is, such he always was, and such he always will be, to his Church in CHRIST. And what GOD the HOLY GHOST, in his everlasting love to the Church now is, such he always was, and such he always will be; and such the SON as GOD, and as GOD-Man Mediator. There can be no change in either.

But there is another blessed view this scripture furnisheth, namely, where GOD the HOLY GHOST, in his office-character, as it concerns the Church, is called *the seven Spirits which are before the throne.* That is not seven persons, for GOD the HOLY GHOST is One in his Person, as are the Person of the FATHER, and of the SON, but it means GOD the SPIRIT, in his sevenfold gifts and graces, diversified to the Church as they are imparted. *Seven* is a perfect number. And by this perfection, this number is specified, as implying a fullness and perfection of all the gifts and blessings, he imparts to the Church in CHRIST. And it is blessed to observe, that as the HOLY GHOST gives his unction, both to the great Head of the Church, and to all his members, and of the same grace, though not in the same degree; (See John iii. 34. with Ephes. iv. 7.) so, when he anointed CHRIST and abode upon him, (See John i. 32.) as was prophecied, the LORD, the HOLY GHOST is said to have done it, in this sevenfold manner. *First.* He is said to have rested upon him. *Secondly.* The SPIRIT of wisdom. *Thirdly.* Understanding. *Fourthly.* The SPIRIT of Counsel. *Fifthly.* Might. *Sixthly.* Knowledge. *Seventhly.* The fear of the LORD. Isaiah xi. 2. Reader! what beauties are in the scripture! What wonders do they unfold!

One word more on this glorious beginning of the book of Revelation. *John* saith also: *And from* JESUS CHRIST, *who is the faithful witness, and the first begotten of the dead, and the Prince of the kings of the earth.* Here it is very plain, that what is said of CHRIST, is said of him in relation to his Person and offices, as GOD-Man Mediator. Not as GOD only, for then, in that sense, he could not be called *the first begotten of the dead.* Neither as man only; for then, he could not be *the faithful witness,* in revealing things of eternity, and testifying to the eternal truths of JEHOVAH, by his SPIRIT, in the hearts and consciences of his people. But, by the union of both, GOD and Man in one Person, he is *the faithful witness* GOD hath given to the people; and the *Amen,* in whom the Church is blessed for ever. Isaiah lv. 4. Rev. iii. 15. Isaiah lxv. 16. In this sweet and gracious point of view, all that is here said of CHRIST, is truly blessed. He is *the first begotten of the dead,* as he is *the first in the beginning of the creation of* GOD. *All things were made by him.* Colos. i. 15, 16, 17. And in resurrection, the first fruits, and the first and sole cause of resurrection, to his members. For though several instances are on scripture record, of the raising of the dead, before CHRIST arose; yet these were all by his power. This JESUS explained and proved, at the resurrection of *Lazarus;* when, having called him forth from the grave, he declared himself to be *the resurrection and the life:* and having said it, gave the specimen of it, by the immediate miracle that followed. John xi. 25, 43. By *the Prince of the kings of the earth,* doth not simply mean, his government of his Church only, but his universal and everlasting monarchy over the whole creation of GOD. *All power is given to me* (JESUS himself said) *in heaven and earth.* So that our JESUS, as GOD-Man Mediator, hath unlimited sovereignty and dominion, over all the departments of nature, providence, grace, and glory. Matt. xxviii. 18. Ephes. i. 20—23. And add to these, there is a special blessing here spoken of, in reference to his Church; and the Apostle breaks out into an hymn of praise, while he mentions it. *Unto him* (saith he) *that hath loved us, and washed us from our sins in his own blood; and hath made us kings and priests unto* GOD *and his* FATHER; *to him be glory and dominion for ever and ever. Amen.* Reader! do observe the blessedness of what is here said, with a special relation to CHRIST's Church. The Apostle had before spoken of CHRIST's unlimited government over all things, but here it is in his relationship to his body the Church. And do observe yet further, the beautiful order of these unspeakable blessings. Unto him that hath loved us, and washed us. Remark, I pray you, that it is his *love* which is the *cause*. And his *washing* us is the *effect*. I never can say enough to you, nor my own heart also, on all the blessed properties of redemption. What would have become of the whole Church, the whole body of CHRIST's members, fallen in the *Adam*-nature of sin and ruin, had not JESUS redeemed them, and washed them in his blood? But, when we have carried this to the highest pitch of our admiration and praise; still the *cause* of all this is to be extolled and delighted in, before the *effect*. Reader! let you and I daily, hourly, minutely, bless the whole GODHEAD, for all our mercies; pardon and peace with all that are connected with this blessedness, in the blood of the cross; but above all these, let us bless GOD for his love! Oh! who shall describe, what heart shall conceive, the love of GOD, and of CHRIST, *which passeth knowledge?*

7 ¶ Behold, he cometh with clouds; and every eye shall see him, and they *also* which pierced him: and all kindreds of the earth shall wail because of him. Even so, Amen.

How beautifully the Apostle breaks off at this verse, from what he had been saying before, to honor, and glorify the SON of GOD. He is indeed still on the same subject; for his whole heart seemed to be on fire, at what he had been meditating, concerning CHRIST's love, in the redemption of his people. But at this verse, he breaks out in a devout rapture of holy joy, as though he beheld CHRIST as immediately appearing to his view. He connects the blessed subject of washing his people with his blood, as now coming in the clouds, to receive them to himself; and, overpowered with the contemplation, he cries out: *Behold he cometh!* Reader! ponder well the several weighty things in this blessed verse. *First.* The certainty of CHRIST's coming. So the Angels, which attended the ascension of CHRIST, assured the Church of the certainty of his descension. Acts i. 11. *Secondly.* The object of his coming. To judge the world in righteousness, and minister judgment to the people. Psm. ix. 8. *Thirdly.* The different effects produced by his coming; every eye shall see him, they also which pierced him, and all kindreds of the earth shall wail because of him; that is, everlasting horror will come upon all his enemies, all the CHRIST-despisers; all of this description, in all kindreds where they are, shall be tremblingly alive, in the anguish of their souls, at his appearing. But his people shall shout aloud with holy joy at his approach, and put their hearty *even so, Amen,* in confirmation of it. Reader! what saith your heart to these things? If you can welcome JESUS, approach now in ordinances; if his Person, blood, and righteousness, be dear to you *now*, surely His coming will be so then! If JESUS saith *I come quickly!* Can you answer, *even so, come* LORD JESUS? Surely our knowledge and love of JESUS *here*, are sweet testimonies of our delight in him, both *here* and *hereafter.*

8 I am Alpha and Omega, the beginning and the ending, saith the Lord, which is, and which was, and which is to come, the Almighty.

What a blessed verse is here! It should seem, that no sooner had the beloved Apostle ended, as in the verse before, his rapturous expressions, in contemplating the Person of his LORD; but JESUS instantly appeared, and delivered himself in these most precious words, as if confirming all that his servant had said of him. *I am Alpha and Omega.* Thrice in this Chapter, here, and again at the 11th and 17th verses, the LORD JESUS takes to himself these characters of distinction. And, to confirm it yet more finally, and fully, in the last Chapter of this book of the Revelation, as if to leave the impression in full force upon the minds of his people through all ages of his Church, he repeats those names, and puts the whole together: *I am Alpha and Omega, the beginning and the end, the first and the last.* Rev. xxii. 13.

Now let us pause, and consider these solemn words as they are. And then say, what can be stronger, in proof of eternity, and all divine perfections? *Alpha* is the first letter in the Greek Alphabet, and *Omega* the last. There is none that comes before, neither any that comes after. Now, these are the distinguishing characters of JEHOVAH. None is before, none after. Hence we find the LORD taking to himself these attributes, as so many standards of character, in confirmation of his GODHEAD. *Is there a* GOD *beside me? yea, there is no* GOD; *I know not any!* And this is said at a time when the LORD had been using the same language as is here used, saying: *I am the first, and I am the last; and beside me there is no* GOD. Let the Reader compare the scriptures, and he must be led to see, that the language is one and the same, and from the same Almighty Speaker. Isaiah xliv. 6—8. See also Isaiah xli. 4. and xlviii. 12.

9 I John, who also am your brother, and companion in tribulation and in the kingdom and patience of Jesus Christ, was in the isle that is called Patmos, for the word of God, and for the testimony of Jesus Christ.

10 I was in the Spirit on the Lord's day, and heard behind me a great voice as of a trumpet.

11 Saying, I am Alpha and Omega, the first

and the last: and, What thou seest write in a book, and send *it* unto the seven churches which are in Asia; unto Ephesus, and unto Smyrna, and unto Pergamos, and unto Thyatira, and unto Sardis, and unto Philadelphia, and unto Laodicea.

12 And I turned to see the voice that spake with me; and being turned, I saw seven golden candlesticks;

13 And in the midst of the seven candlesticks, *one* like unto the Son of man, clothed with a garment down to the foot, and girt about the paps with a golden girdle.

14 His head and *his* hairs *were* white like wool, as white as snow; and his eyes *were* as a flame of fire;

15 And his feet like unto fine brass, as if they burned in a furnace; and his voice as the sound of many waters.

16 And he had in his right hand seven stars; and out of his mouth went a sharp two-edged sword: and his countenance *was* as the sun shineth in his strength.

17 And when I saw him, I fell at his feet as dead: and he laid his right hand upon me, saying unto me, Fear not; I am the first and the last:

18 *I am* he that liveth, and was dead; and behold, I am alive for evermore, Amen; and have the keys of hell and of death.

19 Write the things which thou hast seen, and the things which are, and the things which shall be hereafter,

20 The mystery of the seven stars which thou sawest in my right hand, and the seven golden candlesticks. The seven stars are the angels of the seven churches; and the seven candlesticks which thou sawest are the seven churches.

The Apostle now enters upon his work, to which the Lord had called him, and begins his relation of it, with an account of himself, where he was, how he was engaged, and the time in which those visions began. There is somewhat very interesting in the Apostle's plain, and artless narrative. A brother, and companion in tribulation to the Church, being at that time in banishment, for the truth as it is in JESUS. It was the LORD's day, not the Jewish sabbath; for though *John* was by birth a *Jew*, yet, after the resurrection of JESUS, the followers of CHRIST changed the *seventh* day of the week into the first, in honor of CHRIST, and called it *the* LORD's *day*. Reader! this is a full confirmation of the LORD's approving the change. And it is a blessed recommendation to the honoring the LORD's day, when we find, as in the instance of *John*, on this day the LORD was pleased to make this glorious manifestation of himself to his servant. May not all regenerated believers in JESUS, humbly expect visits, sweet and gracious, from the LORD, on *the* LORD's *day?* Who that reads this account of *John*, in JESUS's mercies towards him on that day of the LORD, but are encouraged to hope, that in honoring those holy seasons, in the congregation of the faithful, we may be also blest, and be in the SPIRIT on the LORD's day?

I do not venture to enter upon a description, beyond what is here given by the HOLY GHOST, concerning the Person and glory of the LORD. It is infinitely sublime, as represented in these words. All attempts to add to it must fail. I shall only beg to call the Reader's attention to some of the many blessed things contained in it; and may the same Almighty SPIRIT, which was then with *John*, be with all his people, to give them a right understanding in all things!

And, *first*. Our grand concern in this, and all other manifestations given of the LORD JESUS CHRIST is, to pray for a proper, and just apprehension of his Person. Faith's object is CHRIST. And, therefore, in order to have a right foundation to our faith, we must first know CHRIST, or our faith in him, will not be correct. We find here, the LORD JESUS taking to himself all divine perfections. The Alpha, and Omega, the first and the last, which is, and which was, and which is to come, the Almighty. We no less hear him declaring himself under the same distinction of attributes, in his Mediator-character; and, in the moment when he had laid his right-hand upon *John*, and when he added, *I am he that liveth, and was dead, and behold I am alive for evermore!* Now, what can more plainly, or more fully confirm all the great and leading truths of our most holy faith, than that CHRIST is GOD; and that, as CHRIST, in our nature, he is come forth, from the invisibility of the GODHEAD, to reveal the will of GOD to his people. If no man hath seen GOD at any time, if no man can see the face of GOD, and live, and if the only begotten SON, who lay in the bosom of the FATHER, hath come forth, and he only, to declare him; can there be a proof wanting, that it is the SON of GOD, who is one with the FATHER, and the HOLY GHOST, in all the divine attributes, which makes all the revelations that are, or can be made, of himself, and FATHER, and SPIRIT, in our nature; and in the moment of such discoveries, manifests his GODHEAD, by assuming all the perfections of the GODHEAD, and thereby proves that blessed scripture, where it is said, that *in Him dwelleth all the fulness of the* GODHEAD *bodily?* Coloss. ii. 9. Reader! what are your apprehensions of the Person of CHRIST? Remember, it is the very bottom, and foundation of every other article of faith. Bear with me, while I venture to say to you one plain truth of scripture. *No man can say that* JESUS *is the* LORD, *but by the* HOLY GHOST. 1 Cor. xii. 3. When *John,* as here stated, saw CHRIST; and when he heard, and received, and recorded the things he had seen; he was in the SPIRIT. Mark that! And it is GOD the SPIRIT now, as much as then, that can alone cause the spirits of men to the belief of this great truth. When the SON of GOD was upon earth, he referred all his proofs of himself to this divine teaching. *The works that I do in my* FATHER'S *name, they bear witness of me.* John x. 25. And as JESUS by the SPIRIT wrought his miracles, every act of this nature, carried the SPIRIT'S testimony with it, to his GODHEAD. And I pray the Reader to observe what I am going to add on this subject. *John,* we are here told, was in the SPIRIT when he gave this testimony to the GODHEAD of CHRIST. And *David,* we are also told, was under the same blessed teaching, when in SPIRIT he called JESUS LORD. It is CHRIST himself which refers to the cxth Psalm in confirmation of it, when in conversation with the Jews he quoted it: *The* LORD *said unto my* LORD; said David. A plain proof of those Persons in the GODHEAD, and which can be explained on no other ground. Reader! let me take the words of our GOD and SAVIOR, and put the question to *your* heart, which He did to the Pharisees: What think *you* of CHRIST? Matt. xxii. 41—46.

Secondly. Next to the right apprehension of CHRIST'S Person, as the great object of faith, is the conviction of all the leading points, which belong to his office, and relations, and character. His full, and finished salvation, is here most compleatly set forth, and set forth under these strong expressions: *Fear not, I am the first and the last. I am he that liveth, and was dead, and behold I am alive for evermore: Amen, and have the keys of hell and of death.* Observe, what immense things are here spoken of by the LORD JESUS, for his redeemed to rest with full assurance upon. And observe, how the LORD JESUS puts one of his glorious names, the *Amen,* the faithful witness, in the very middle of what he saith, by way of stamping, signing, sealing, and delivering this blessed Charter. It becomes like the Patent of heaven. It confirms, and establisheth the Royal Society of his Kings and Priests, whom he hath made in his Kingdom. It is what I call the everlasting Indenture of the Covenant. And faith gives a right of holding, a present fee-simple, in the inheritance by CHRIST, which is *incorruptible and undefiled, and that fadeth not away.* Oh! the blessedness, when He who laid his right hand upon *John,* confirms with equal assurance, by his HOLY SPIRIT, the princely grant in every heart of his people, which is to the same effect; saying, *Fear not!* Precious, and Almighty JESUS! thou hast indeed the key of all authority and power, even the Key of David; *to open, and none can shut; to shut, and none can open.* Isaiah xxii. 22. LORD! do thou open thy word to my soul! and do thou open my heart to thy word. Oh! the blessed assurance! My GOD, my SAVIOR, hath the key of death, the key of hell, the key of heaven. At his girdle they all hang; and none can open either, but by his authority. How secure are all thy redeemed! Precious JESUS! *all power is thine, in heaven and in earth!*

One word more on this blessed Chapter! JESUS commanded *John* to write the things he had seen. And we have reason to bless the LORD, that he both wrote, and by the LORD'S authority, hath sent what he saw, to his Church. And what a delightful instruction the Church gathers from the whole? Jesus holds all his truly ordained ministers, ordained by God the Holy Ghost, in his Almighty hand, as stars; and he is in the midst of his people, as here he appeared in the midst of the golden candlesticks, to bless them with his presence and his grace. From whence we plainly perceive, where the *one* gains all his ability to preach, and the *other* the ability to hear. Hence those sweet words to the *former*: *As the* Father *hath sent me, even so send I you.* John xx. 21. And to the *latter*: *Lo! I am with you alway, even to the end of the world!* Matt. xxviii. 20. Reader! what saith your soul's experience to these things? It is blessed, yea, very blessed, when the *written* word is accompanied with the *engrafted* word; and when the child of God, hearing what the Spirit saith to the Churches, can set to his seal, that God *is true!*

REFLECTIONS.

Blessed! for ever blessed, be God the Father, for the gift of his dear Son Jesus Christ. Blessed! for ever blessed, be God the Son, for this gracious revelation of himself to his servant *John*, to comfort, and instruct the Church. And blessed be God the Holy Ghost, for causing so sweet and precious a record, to be handed down to the Church from generation to generation, of the word of God, and of the testimony of Jesus Christ. Lord! add a blessing to the whole, and give grace to thy people, that *they may hear what the* Spirit *saith unto the Churches.*

May it be the blessedness and felicity of the Lord's redeemed, to find grace and peace, according to the Apostle's benediction, from Him, *which is, and which was, and which is to come.* Yea! may the Church daily find all Covenant blessings, from God the Judge of all, from Jesus the Mediator of the New Covenant, and from the influence of the Holy Ghost, in his sevenfold gifts and graces, which are before the throne. Oh! the unspeakable mercy of God in Christ. He who hath made us Kings and Priests, unto God and the Father, *having loved us, and washed us from our sins, in his blood!*

Precious Emmanuel! thou who didst bless *John* with thy presence, and gavest him those blessed revelations, to deliver unto thy Church, condescend to visit thy people now. Thou art still the Alpha and the Omega. Thou art still all the blessedness of thy Church and people. Lord! visit thy Churches. No *Ephesus, Smyrna, Pergamos, Thyatira, Sardis, Philadelphia,* or *Laodicea,* ever needed thee more, than the professing Churches of this land, where we dwell. Oh! then, come Lord, and take up thine own cause, lest our Churches, like those of Asia, which are now no more, be desolated, and without inhabitants. If Jesus will come forth with his people, if God the Spirit will ordain ministers, and walk up and down in the midst of his people; then will thy servants be as stars in the right hand of Christ, and his people, like the candlesticks, shining bright with the oil of grace, from Jesus walking in and out among them. Oh! for a little revival in the present day, that the Lord may not remove our candlestick out of its place!

CHAP. II.

CONTENTS.

Here begins the LORD's *Message to the seven Churches. This Chapter contains what was commanded to be delivered to four of them; namely,* Ephesus, Smyrna, Pergamos, *and* Thyatira. *And the Chapter closeth with a solemn Admonition, which is repeated to each:* to hear what the SPIRIT saith unto the Churches.

UNTO the angel of the church of Ephesus write: These things saith he that holdeth the seven stars in his right hand, who walketh in the midst of the seven golden candlesticks;

2 I know thy works, and thy labour, and thy patience, and how thou canst not bear them which are evil: and thou hast tried them which say they are apostles, and are not, and hast found them liars:

3 And hast borne, and hast patience, and for my name's sake hast laboured, and hast not fainted.

4 Nevertheless I have *somewhat* against thee, because thou hast left thy first love.

5 Remember therefore from whence thou art fallen, and repent, and do the first works: or else I will come unto thee quickly, and will remove thy candlestick out of his place, except thou repent.

6 But this thou hast, that thou hatest the deeds of the Nicolaitanes, which I also hate.

7 He that hath an ear, let him hear what the Spirit saith unto the churches; To him that overcometh will I give to eat of the tree of life; which is in the midst of the paradise of God.

I beg on our entrance, of viewing these messages of CHRIST to his Churches, to make one or two general observations, as suited to the whole; and which, I request the Reader to keep in remembrance, through all the parts of this book of GOD.

And, *first*. It evidently appears, from several striking circumstances which meet us in the body of those several Epistles, that what our LORD then caused to be delivered by his servant *John* to those Churches, while it had an immediate eye to them, from the particular things the LORD reproved in them; yet was intended as so many messages to the Church of CHRIST, from that period, to the very end of time; different parts corresponding to the different ages. And, indeed, whoever reads with attention the LORD's charges against some of those Churches, will find, that they were not special to that age, or confined to that Church, to whom the LORD sent it; but that the same spots are seen in the LORD's Church even now. As for example. In this first charge to *Ephesus,* the LORD complains, that she had left her *first* love. Not that the Church was totally void of love, but that it was less warm, and fervent, than in the first days of her espousals. Reader! this is but too common now. And wherever it is found, we here learn how painful it is to CHRIST. See how sweetly the LORD took notice of the first love of the Church, at the coming forth out of Egypt; and how highly the LORD prized it. Jerem. ii. 1, 2, 3. So again, to the Church at *Sardis.* *I know thy works, that thou hast a name, that thou livest and art dead.* Chap. iii. 1. Reader! is not this very resembling the present hour, of the professing Church?

Secondly. Some of those Churches to whom *John* was directed to write, could hardly be said at that time, to be formed, but were forming. We have no account, either of the Church of *Sardis* or *Philadelphia,* before the *Second* Century. It doth not follow, indeed, from hence, that they were not in being. However, from the slenderness of those Churches in general, and from the too much sameness in defects, between those spoken of, and the Church of CHRIST in the several ages since, even to the present hour; we have full authority to conclude that the LORD JESUS, *whose eyes are as a flame of fire,* and who looketh through all time, intended these Epistles for the Church, to the latest period of the world.

Thirdly. To render this statement the more probable, it should be observed also, that while the LORD sent these Epistles to those seven Churches, which were in *Asia;* and some of them hardly in being, there were none of a like nature directed by the LORD to the Churches in *Judæa,* and *Corinth,* and *Colosse,* and *Philippi,* or the *Thessalonians.* All which carries a very strong conviction with it, that not those Churches only, and at that period, the LORD JESUS had in view, but to be of perpetual use in his Church, through all the intermediate ages, to the end of time.

Fourthly. As all these seven Churches are now no more, but the LORD hath, as he threatened he would, removed the candlestick out of its place, and the very ground where those highly favored temples once stood, are in the possession of the deluded followers of the false Prophet; and yet those messages sent to them, are with us, it should seem to be a most plain, and self evident conclusion, the LORD intended those Epistles for persons, and not places; and that in them the LORD still speaks to the Church, here represented by the perfect number *seven,* as representing the whole body in the different periods of time.

Having premised these observations, I would now call upon the Reader, to attend to the precious and important subjects, contained in those Epistles, and according to the order, in which they are here placed.

And *first,* of *Ephesus.* Of this city we have an account. Acts xviii. 19. It was a place of great trade and magnificence, but wholly given to Idolatry. Here the LORD directed the steps of his servant the Apostle *Paul*, and caused him to plant a Church in it. And so greatly did the LORD bless and own his labors, that he continued in it two years; so that *all they which dwell in Asia, heard the word of the LORD, both Jews and Greeks.* Acts xix. 10. Here then, as this Church was in being, the message of the LORD JESUS to it, came under that part of CHRIST's command to *John*, in writing *the things which he had seen, and the things which are.* The other parts, either to Churches afterwards to rise, or of prophecies afterwards to be fulfilled, came under that part of CHRIST's command to his servant, to write of *the things which were to be hereafter.* Rev. i. 19.

The LORD begins his charge, with a short but sublime account of himself. *These things, saith he, that holdeth the seven stars in his right-hand, who walketh in the midst of the seven golden Candlesticks.* What a sweet thought to the Church of JESUS in all ages, both as it concerns the Servants of the LORD, whom he dignifies amidst all their unworthiness, with the name of *stars;* and his people, in the midst of whom he here declares himself to walk, as in the midst of *golden Candlesticks.* Reader! do not fail to keep these things always in remembrance! All the Pastors, the HOLY GHOST ordaineth to the Church, however weak in themselves and humble, JESUS calls them stars, and He it is that holdeth them up, and blesseth them, both in their own souls, and to the souls of his people. And all his regenerated people, they are golden in CHRIST's view, being *comely in his comeliness, which he hath put upon them;* and His is the office, to supply them with grace, amidst all their own darkness, that as golden Candlesticks, *they may shine as lights in the world.* Ezek. xvi. 14. Philip. ii. 15.

The LORD next proceeds to tell the Church, how perfectly well acquainted he was, with all that concerned his people. *I know thy works.* And this includes, the compleat knowledge the LORD hath, of all their persons; and of all their thoughts, and words, and actions. Oh! what a sweet testimony, in proof of CHRIST's GODHEAD! But what I particularly beg the Reader to observe, in the LORD's charge to this Church, (yea, and all the Churches in this and the following Chapter, for the same observation suits the whole,) is, that though the LORD had somewhat against all, yet he had much more to speak in the favor of all, from their union with, and interest in him. This is a great point to be kept in view, and always highly proper, for every regenerated child of GOD, to bless GOD for. From what JESUS here saith, in commendation of the Church at *Ephesus*, it is plain that they were in a state of regeneration. And the GOD of all grace, which had called them to his eternal glory, by CHRIST JESUS, in that call, and by that quickening their souls into a state of spiritual life, had thereby given them, an earnest of that glory. 2 Cor. v. 5. Ephes. i. 13, 14.

As this is a point of great importance, I beg indulgence to state it somewhat more particularly. When GOD the HOLY GHOST quickens a sinner, which before was dead in trespasses and sins, by that spiritual life imparted, the child of GOD is truly and everlastingly united to the LORD JESUS. The HOLY GHOST bears this testimony himself, by his servant *Peter*. *According* (saith he) *as his divine power hath given unto us all things that pertain unto life and godliness, through the knowledge of him, that hath called us unto glory and virtue.*

2 Pet. i. 3, 4. Hence, there is now in this awakened and regenerated new creature, an union with CHRIST, and an interest in CHRIST. He is brought out of darkness and the shadow of death, and being justified freely through the grace that is in CHRIST JESUS, he is habitually in a state of favor, and acceptance with GOD. This is his high calling in CHRIST. And this is the general frame and state of his mind. But beside this *habit* of grace, in which the soul is formed by regeneration, there is an *actual* state, for the exercise of grace upon the Person of CHRIST, belonging to the believer, and this will be more or less lively, as the LORD the HOLY GHOST calls forth into action, the graces by regeneration, which he hath planted in the soul. Here it was in a defect of this exercise, the Church of *Ephesus* was discovered by CHRIST. On this ground, the LORD reproved them. They had not left CHRIST, neither lost their joy and confidence in CHRIST. For JESUS tells them, that he knew their labors and patience, and their hatred for his sake of false Apostles, and the deeds of the *Nicolaitanes*. But, though they had not lost *all* love to JESUS, yet they had left their *first* love. Reader! do not overlook this, for it is a great point to be well understood in the Church of CHRIST. The LORD's children when called by grace, are *savingly* called, and their spirit being born of the SPIRIT, can die no more. But there may be a great leanness of soul, and there will be, where spiritual strength is not spiritually received, by a life of faith upon JESUS day by day. Hence JESUS, when describing his Church, as branches in himself, the Vine enjoins an abiding in him, that is, a lively acting of faith upon him. John xv. 5. If the soul desires a perpetual spring and summer season, it must be induced from drawing all life, and nourishment, and fruitfulness from CHRIST. *From me*, saith the LORD, *is thy fruit found.* Hosea xiv. 8. But it will be winter in that soul where, though there is no separation from the root, and therefore the tree still lives, the communication is just to keep alive, and that's all. Oh! how needful to feel our daily want of CHRIST, and as constantly to be in the exercise of faith upon CHRIST.

But perhaps it may be said, that in the exhortation CHRIST gives to this Church of *Ephesus*, (and in like manner to all his Churches, under the same circumstances,) to remember and repent, on pain in the neglect of which, the LORD saith, that he will remove the Candlestick out of his place, there should seem, as if a total separation from the LORD might follow. To which the answer is direct. All the word of GOD, with one voice declares the work of regeneration, is the imparting of spiritual life, which can die no more. The children of GOD in that sovereign act, are expressly said *to be born again, not of corruptible seed, but of incorruptible, which liveth and abideth for ever.* 1 Pet. i. 23. The *Candlestick*, which is a moveable in GOD's house, (as it is in a man's house,) may be removed out of its place; and as it was indeed in the instance of this Church at *Ephesus*, but the house itself is founded upon CHRIST, the rock of ages; against which the gates of hell can never prevail. GOD's children may, and (without his grace keeping them alive, in active fruitfulness, upon CHRIST's Person and righteousness) GOD's children will, continually feel the workings of sin, in a body which is virtually all sin. But it is CHRIST's special office, to keep all his redeemed from finally falling, and *to present them faultless, before the presence of his glory, with exceeding joy.* Jude 24. Oh! then for grace, *to hear what the* SPIRIT *saith unto the Churches.*

8 ¶ And unto the angel of the Church in Smyrna write; These things saith the first and the last, which was dead, and is alive;

9 I know thy works, and tribulation, and poverty, (but thou art rich) and *I know* the blasphemy of them which say they are Jews, and are not, but *are* the synagogue of Satan.

10 Fear none of those things which thou shalt suffer, behold, the devil shall cast *some* of you into prison, that ye may be tried; and ye shall have tribulation ten days: be thou faithful unto death, and I will give thee a crown of life.

11 He that hath an ear, let him hear what the Spirit saith unto the churches; he that overcometh shall not be hurt of the second death.

Smyrna, the second Church to whom the LORD sent his message, appears to have been not much more than forty miles from *Ephesus,* and neither of them, far remote from *Patmos.* The Epistle to this Church comes now to be considered. Here the LORD takes to himself, in opening his message, those distinguishing perfections of character. *These things saith the first and the last, which was dead and is alive.* Probably the LORD JESUS made choice of these, in a more especial manner, in that he was here arming the Church, against a time of persecution; and therefore, in his own glorious Person, they might be found faithful unto death. By the *Jews* here spoken of, is to be understood, with a special eye to the subject, CHRIST's followers in the regeneration. For, as CHRIST himself was a *Jew* after the flesh, those who professed to be his disciples, were in those days generally called *Jews.* Indeed, we read that *the disciples were called Christians first in Antioch.* Acts xi. 26. But it was only in process of time, that the name became universal. Such, however, could only be properly called so, who were regenerated. Let the Reader observe, that CHRIST calls it blasphemy, to take the name without the grace. It is indeed most awful, to find men who are by works, of the synagogue of *Satan,* call themselves Christians!

Let the Reader observe, and observe with thankfulness, how graciously the LORD JESUS limits the power of Satan. *Fear none of these things, which thou shalt suffer!* The devil would have cast them all into hell, if he could. But no! It shall be only some of them, that he shall exercise by captivity, and that not into hell, but only into a prison. And he would have cast them in for ever. But no! It shall only be for *ten days,* that they shall have tribulation. And this, not for *his* triumph, but for the trial of *their* graces. And JESUS, in bidding them *be faithful,* wills them into it. It is, as if the LORD had said ye shall be faithful. For the crown he promised, was not of doubtful issue. Oh! how sure is it, that the overcomers in CHRIST, having part in the *first* resurrection in grace, shall not be hurt by the *second death.* Rev. xx. 6. LORD! give grace and the hearing ear, *to hear what the* SPIRIT *saith unto the Churches!*

12 ¶ And to the angel of the church in Pergamos write; These things saith he which hath the sharp sword with two edges;

13 I know thy works, and where thou dwellest, *even* where Satan's seat *is;* and thou holdest fast my name, and hast not denied my faith, even in those days wherein Antipas *was* my faithful martyr, who was slain among you, where Satan dwelleth.

14 But I have a few things against thee, because thou hast there them that hold the doctrine of Balaam, who taught Balak to cast a stumbling block before the children of Israel, to eat things sacrificed unto idols, and to commit fornication.

15 So hast thou also them that hold the doctrine of the Nicolaitanes, which thing I hate.

16 Repent; or else I will come unto thee quickly, and will fight against them with the sword of my mouth.

17 He that hath an ear, let him hear what the Spirit saith unto the churches; To him that overcometh will I give to eat of the hidden manna, and will give him a white stone, and in the stone a new name written, which no man knoweth saving he that receiveth *it.*

Pergamos, now called by the Turks *Bergamo,* appears to have been about *threescore miles* from *Smyrna.* The features of character which CHRIST here adopts, seem to have been with a design, to intimate that as the Impostor, which in after ages would arise, to oppose the truth of CHRIST, would accomplish his wickedness with the sword, the LORD would only oppose him, with the sword of the SPIRIT; which is the word of GOD. Ephes. vi. 17. And it is worthy the Reader's remark, that in this Epistle, while the LORD is speaking of those in *Pergamos,* who held the doctrine of *Balaam,* and the doctrine of the *Nicolaitanes,* and tells his people, that if they do not repent, that is, drive them out from their Churches, he will fight *them;* not his people, but *them,* and by that sword of his mouth, namely, his holy word;

convince them of their ungodly deeds, and of all their hard speeches, which they had spoken against him. See Jude 16, and Commentary.

Of the doctrine of *the Nicolaitanes*, we cannot speak particularly. But we find great cause to thank GOD the HOLY GHOST, for the light this passage, throws over the history of *Balaam*. We should not have known, as we now do, the full infamy of this wretch, but from this account. If the Reader will read the story in the book of *Numbers*, how this man hired himself out, to curse GOD's people, while GOD compelled him to bless them, he will discover some very sweet and precious things. He will see, how much the seed of the Serpent, as *Balaam* evidently was, may learn by head knowledge, the truths of GOD, while like him, in heart they abominate them. And the Reader will further learn, how the LORD is unceasingly watching over his people for good, when they themselves, are most unconscious of it. *Balak* and *Balaam*, were planning and contriving *Israel's* destruction, by all the mock services of religion; while *Israel* lay unconscious in their tents, either of the hatred of *Moab*, or the policy of *Balaam*. Reader! who shall say how often, in ten thousand instances, such things are going on now, in the present hour! Precious JESUS! as oft as I think of it, how sweet is that scripture to my soul, and the assurance of its being minutely carried on, to my heart. Isaiah xxvii. 2, 3.

I beg the Reader, before he goes further, to read the history of the Church, concerning this transaction, as it is recorded in the Book of Numbers. *Moab* saw *Israel* conquering the nations around. And under an alarm for his own safety, he sent for *Balaam*, a famous Magician from the East, to come and curse *Israel*. The great rewards *Balak* King of *Moab* offered him, soon prompted this man, to hasten to this employment, but he received continued checks from his conscience not to go. We have the account, Numbers xxii. xxiii. xxiv. and xxv. Chapters. But this relation of the LORD, in this Chapter of the Revelation, explains what those Chapters in the book of Numbers, do not acquaint us with. We here find, that it was *Balaam's* advice to *Balak*, to intice *Israel* to get the displeasure of GOD, by first tempting their young men, with lustful desires to *Moab's* daughters; and, then, *Moab's* daughters to tempt *Israel* to their sacrifices. Reader! see what our corrupt passions tempt even GOD's children to commit. And see what a mercy it is, that JESUS watches over his people for good! Well might one of old cry out, and say, *hold thou me up, and I shall be safe!* Psm. cxix. 117. Oh! Sir! how sure a truth it is, that they who are kept, *are kept by the power of* GOD, *through faith unto salvation*. 1 Pet. i. 5.

I do not think it necessary, to the Reader of this *Poor Man's Commentary*, to swell these pages, by leading him into enquiries from Ecclesiastical History concerning *Antipas*. That he was a faithful servant of the LORD is certain, from the honorable testimony the LORD hath given of him, and a Martyr to the cause of CHRIST. I would rather raise up a prayer from his faithfulness, and beg of CHRIST to give to all his redeemed, the hidden bread which is CHRIST himself, and the white stone with the new name, written therein, even *the* LORD *our righteousness;* to testify whose we are, and whom we serve in the Gospel of GOD's dear SON! Oh! for grace *to hear what the* SPIRIT *saith unto the Churches*.

18 ¶ And unto the angel of the Church in Thyatira write; These things saith the Son of God, who hath his eyes like unto a flame of fire, and his feet *are* like fine brass;

19 I know thy works, and charity, and service, and faith, and thy patience, and thy works; and the last *to be* more than the first.

20 Notwithstanding I have a few things against thee, because thou sufferest that woman Jezebel, which calleth herself a prophetess, to teach and to seduce my servants to commit fornication, and to eat things sacrificed unto idols.

21 And I gave her space to repent of her fornication; and she repented not.

22 Behold, I will cast her into a bed, and them that commit adultery with her into great tribulation, except they repent of their deeds.

23 And I will kill her children with death; and all the churches shall know that I am he which searcheth the reins and hearts; and I will give unto every one of you according to your works.

24 But unto you, I say, and unto the rest in Thyatira, as many as have not this doctrine, and which have not known the depths of Satan, as they speak; I will put upon you none other burden,

25 But that which ye have *already* hold fast till I come.

26 And he that overcometh, and keepeth my works unto the end, to him will I give power over the nations;

27 And he shall rule them with a rod of iron; as the vessels of a potter shall they be broken to shivers; even as I received of my Father.

28 And I will give him the morning star.

29 He that hath an ear, let him hear what the Spirit saith unto the churches,

The *fourth* Church noticed in this Chapter, is that of *Thyatira*. When this Church was formed, and by whom, is not said; but it should seem probable, that there was none there at the time Paul first preached at *Philippi*. For ye are told that *Lydia*, a woman of this city was converted to the faith, when at *Philippi*, through the LORD's opening her heart, under the preaching of the word by *Paul*. Acts xvi. 14. In the opening of this Epistle, CHRIST describes the penetrating power of his omniscience, under the similitude of eyes like unto a flame of fire; and his duration and everlasting firmness, in supporting his Church, and going about unceasingly for her welfare, under the figure of feet of fine brass.

JESUS, in all his Epistles, graciously takes notice, of the graces of his people. *Their righteousness is of me saith the* LORD. Isaiah liv. 17. This should not be lost sight of. *He that gives grace, will give glory.* Psm. lxxxiv. 12. And while he noticeth the infirmities of his people, it is blessed to recollect, the LORD's engagements to do them away. We have a beautiful instance of this. Isaiah lvii. 17. The LORD is there speaking of his Church. He declares his wrath. He hides his face. Still the Church goeth on frowardly. Well! what is the issue? Is there no change in the Church? No. Then GOD will accomplish it. The LORD saith, *I have seen his ways and will heal him.* GOD's grace shall not be outdone, by man's frowardness. Grace shall triumph, even over abounding transgression.

Who this *Jezebel* is, is not said. If this Epistle be, as some have thought, a prophecy alluding to a different period of the Church, than when *John* wrote, and referred not *to the things which then were*, but to *the things which the* LORD *said shall be hereafter;* then it is possible, that the whore of *Babylon*, concerning whom so much is said, in the after Chapters of this book, is meant. The features here drawn of a prophetess, and the committing fornication and the like, carry no doubt, a strong resemblance to each other. But where things are doubtful, it is prudent not to decide. It is enough, however, for our present purpose, in making improvements from this Chapter, to behold in the history of this Church of *Thyatira*, some of GOD's dear ones, of whom He, whose eyes are as a flame of fire, bears testimony to their faith, and charity, and patience. And that though living in perilous times, when a *Jezebel* is suffered among them, yet they themselves in a state of grace, and their last days, more than the first. One consolation, however, there is in this prophecy, (if it be a prophecy,) concerning the latter-day dispensation; namely, JESUS will cast her into a wretched state of pining desolation; and all her children the LORD will kill. And all the Churches shall know, to their joy, and the LORD's glory, the final overthrow of this Antichrist. And in the same hour, the destruction of CHRIST's enemies, and of his Church are destroyed, the LORD will give to his people power over them. *The* GOD *of peace will bruise Satan under their feet shortly.* Rom. xvi. 20. Yea, CHRIST who is the morning star, will be *their everlasting light, their* GOD, *their glory.* Isaiah lx. 19. Rev. xxii. 16. Reader! again let you and I look up for grace, *to hear what the* SPIRIT *saith unto the Churches.*

REFLECTIONS.

Hail! thou glorious Lord! thou Almighty Head of thy Church, and people. Blessed be thy Name, for those gracious messages, to thy redeemed. Truly, Lord, amidst all their spots and defilements, we behold thy mercy over them, and thy grace towards them. Thou bearest testimony to their faith and patience, for all that is wrought in them is thy grace and of thee, have they received it. And yet, Jesus graciously beholds it, and speaks of it, as their own. Lord! give thy Churches, under every state, grace, to be looking wholly unto thee, and to know thee, under all these distinguishing characters. It is thine, O Lord, to hold thy ministers, as stars in thy right hand, and to walk in the favorite haunts of thy Churches, as amidst the golden Candlesticks, thy people. Thou art the first and the last in all the designs of Jehovah; and the first and the last, yea, the whole sum and substance of everlasting joy to all thy people! Thou art the bright, and the morning-star, the sure harbinger of everlasting day, and in the souls of thy people, thou arisest when the Day-spring from on high visitest them. Be thou, Lord, my light, my life, my everlasting portion, that amidst all the darkness of the present state of the world, in thy light I may see light, and walk under the light of thy countenance for ever!

CHAP. III.

CONTENTS.

This Chapter contains the remaining Messages of Christ *to the Churches,* Sardis, Philadelphia, *and* Laodicea. Jesus *manifests his Grace in the sweet Promise of coming and supping with his People.*

AND unto the angel of the church in Sardis write: These things saith he that hath the seven Spirits of God, and the seven stars: I know thy works that thou hast a name, that thou livest, and art dead.

2 Be watchful and strengthen the things which remain that are ready to die; for I have not found thy works perfect before God.

3 Remember therefore how thou hast received and heard, and hold fast, and repent, if therefore thou shalt not watch, I will come on thee as a thief, and thou shalt not know what hour I will come upon thee.

4 Thou hast a few names even in Sardis which

have not defiled their garments: and they shall walk with me in white: for they are worthy:

5 He that overcometh, the same shall be clothed in white raiment: and I will not blot out his name out of the book of life, but I will confess his name before my Father, and before his angels.

6 He that hath an ear, let him hear what the Spirit saith unto the churches.

If, as some have supposed, the former Church-state of *Thyatira*, had reference to *Papal Rome*, and the *Jezebel* there spoken of with her fornications, alluded to the Whore of mystical *Babylon;* then it will follow, that the reformation was that period when the scripture was fulfilled, which describes her impoverished state, expressed under the figure of casting her into a bed of sickness, and killing her children. And then from the same circumstances it will follow, that this Epistle to *Sardis*, is directed to the Church of the present hour; and we are in the *Sardis* state. But we have seen, upon many occasions, the calculations of great and studious men, notwithstanding the most plausible appearances, found to be wrong; that I am free to confess, I am not much disposed to give credence to any. So incompetent are we to judge, by the mere appearances of things, that while a few years ago, the Reformed Church of CHRIST in this land, was led from apparent signs, to hope Antichrist in the heresy of *Papal Rome* was dwindling away, we now behold the Beast propped up, with more human power than she hath had for more than *two Centuries* past. And together with her revival, another Antichrist in the denial of CHRIST's GODHEAD, and now, unrestrained by law, is coming forth, with an uncovered brow in our land. So that while those learned and studious men, speak of the present day of the Church being the *Sardis* state, and that this will shortly be succeeded by the *Philadelphian;* when universal love, and universal light and knowledge, will be diffused through the earth; I read those scriptures differently, and rather am inclined to conclude, very awful events will take place in the Church of CHRIST, before those bright periods come on. But with whomsoever the truth is, one thing is certain; what the LORD here saith to the Church of *Sardis*, opens a very blessed subject of improvement at all times, and especially in the present hour. And I humbly conceive, it will be more suited to the object of a *Poor Man's Commentary*, to seek grace from the LORD, to draw improvements for our present use, than enter into enquiries of what may be hereafter, with which we have no concern. What the LORD said to *Daniel*, suits all of *Daniel's* faith; *Go thy way till the end be. Thou shalt stand in thy lot at the end of the days.* Dan. xii. 13.

Sardis was the chief city of *Lydia*, but now it is a mere village. Its distance was not above thirty miles, or thereabouts, from *Thyatira*. So that those places, which were rather in flourishing circumstances at the time the LORD JESUS sent these Epistles to them, have not a vestige remaining, and are all of them awfully under the delusion of the Impostor of the East. Reader! what a precious consideration it is to my soul, in the moment of writing, that amidst all changes of places, or nations, or men, or things, JESUS changeth not. Neither his Person, nor his love to his Church, can admit the smallest alteration; *he is the same yesterday, to-day, and for ever.* Heb. xiii. 8.

How blessedly the LORD JESUS begins his Epistle to this Church. *These things, saith he that hath the seven* SPIRITS *of* GOD, *and the seven stars.* Here the LORD assumes to himself a sovereignty suited to his Almighty character, and which can be said by no other but by Him *in whom dwelleth all the fulness of the* GODHEAD *bodily.* Coloss. ii. 9. By the seven SPIRITS of GOD, as hath been before observed, (see Chap. i.) is meant the HOLY GHOST in his sevenfold gifts and graces. And, therefore, the LORD JESUS, speaking as Mediator, describes his fulness for his body the Church, GOD *giving not the* SPIRIT *by measure unto him.* John iii. 34. And by having the *seven stars* is meant, that JESUS it is which holds his servants whom he hath appointed to minister in his name. Sweet thought to the faithful, under pastors in the LORD's house! Oh! how blessed to be upheld, taught, guided, sent, blessed, and owned by Him!

If we are under the *Sardis* state, it is a very humbling state. JESUS saith, *I know thy works, that thou hast a name, that thou livest, and art dead!* Reader! if the LORD spake of us *nationally*, bad enough as that would be, yet the true Church of CHRIST might find comfort, that amidst the mere *profession* of the Gospel, by those who know nothing of the Gospel but in the name, the LORD's people *possessing* CHRIST would learn rightly to estimate their privileges. But it is the general state of the Church, in Gospel Churches, of whom CHRIST speaks. Numbers there are who take up with a name to live, who never were regenerated, and consequently are still *dead in trespasses and sins.* And others, who, though quickened by the HOLY GHOST into a new and spiritual life, yet are such babes in the life of grace, as to remain in the weakness and imbecility of childhood the greater part of their days.

That the Church, yea, the true Church of *Sardis*, had many of her members in this state is evident, from what the LORD JESUS immediately added, *Be watchful and strengthen the things which remain, that are ready to die.* Now, here we find, that though so weak and languishing that, to all outward appearances, they were ready to die, yet not dead. There is a mighty difference between spiritually dying and spiritual death. The *former* may be, and too often is, the case of GOD's children. The *latter* can only be said of such as are still in the *Adam*-nature of the fall, unquickened by the HOLY GHOST, and, therefore, *dead in trespasses and sins.* Reader! do mark the different features of character. Painful as it is, and reproachful as it is to a child of GOD, whom the LORD hath regenerated, and called by grace to live in the neglect of ordinances, the throne of CHRIST, reading the scriptures, and the various ways which the HOLY GHOST is pleased to appoint, for keeping up communion in the soul; yet death and dying are two very different things. The *latter* may be, and certainly will be restored, through the favor and life-giving principle of Him that quickeneth. The *former* hath no part nor lot in the matter, nor ever will, notwithstanding the most flaming profession, except the LORD the HOLY GHOST quicken. It is only by regeneration, or the new-birth, that the child of GOD enters into CHRIST's sheepfold. But *he that climbeth up some other way, the same is a thief and a robber.* John x. 1, 2.

Reader! do not overlook what the LORD JESUS here saith, in enforcing *watchfulness, to hold fast,* and *to repent,* in every instance of a truly regenerated child of GOD, who by the new-birth hath *received* and *heard.* Oh! how necessary in the present awful day of much profession, must it be in every child of GOD, to give all diligence, as the HOLY GHOST commands, *to make our calling and election sure.* See 2 Pet. i. 10. And what a blessed thing it is, whether the present day of the Church be, or be not, under this *Sardis* state, that JESUS hath graciously added, for to keep up the spirits of his true children, that *even in Sardis he hath a few names,* that is, a few persons, *which have not defiled their garments;* that is, have not polluted the robes of JESUS' righteousness, in patching them up with a pretended righteousness of their own. Oh! how blessedly JESUS speaks of them. They shall walk with me, saith the LORD. Yes! they do walk *with* CHRIST, and by the strength *of* CHRIST. For so the HOLY GHOST gives testimony of them. *In thy name shall they rejoice all the day, and in thy righteousness shall they be exalted.* Psalm lxxxix. 16. And the LORD declares them *worthy.* For they are accepted in the Beloved. Ephes. i. 6.

What JESUS saith of coming as *a thief in the night,* means, the suddenness, and unexpectedness of his coming, at the moment he comes. But this coming to his people, though sudden to all such as are not always on the look-out for his coming, is not meant in a way of judgment, to condemn them, much less to destroy. The LORD saith, he will *correct his children,* when *they forsake his law, and walk not in his judgment: nevertheless his loving kindness he will not utterly take from him, nor suffer his faithfulness to fail.* Psm. lxxxix. 30—37. And in this very Chapter, (verse 10.) *he will keep his people from the hour of temptation which shall come upon all the world.* Reader! what saith your heart's experience to these things? If this be the *Sardis* state, under which you and I this day are; if JESUS gives this account of it; if, amidst the wonderful relations we hear of, and meet with, every day, the compassing sea and land to make proselytes; if they that have such a name to live, are yet dead before GOD; if *some* are totally dead in trespasses and sins, mere professors without life; if *others,* who have been quickened, have need to strengthen the things which remain, which are ready to die; and, if the LORD hath a few, even in *Sardis,* who, by living *to* him, and living wholly *upon* him, the SON of GOD declares to be worthy, and shall walk with him; pause, and ask your own heart, to which class do you belong? Oh! LORD! give the hearing ear, to all thy redeemed, that they may *hear what the* SPIRIT *saith unto the Churches!*

7 ¶ And to the angel of the church in Philadelphia write; These things saith he that is holy, he that is true: he that hath the key of David; he that openeth, and no man shutteth; and shutteth, and no man openeth;

8 I know thy works; behold, I have set before

thee an open door, and no man can shut it: for thou hast a little strength, and hast kept my word, and hast not denied my name.

9 Behold, I will make them of the synagogue of Satan, which say they are Jews, and are not, but do lie; behold, I will make them to come and worship before thy feet, and to know that I have loved thee.

10 Because thou hast kept the word of my patience, I also will keep thee from the hour of temptation, which shall come upon all the world, to try them that dwell upon the earth.

11 Behold, I come quickly: hold that fast which thou hast, that no man take thy crown.

12 Him that overcometh will I make a pillar in the temple of my God, and he shall go no more out: and I will write upon him the name of my God, and the name of the city of my God, *which is* new Jerusalem, which cometh down out of heaven from my God: and *I will write upon him my new name.*

13 He that hath an ear let him hear what the Spirit saith unto the churches.

Philadelphia was another of the cities of this province in *Asia*. It is now in the hand of the Turks. But though it bears by them the name of the *fair* city, yet, if we may credit Travellers, it is wretchedly inhabited. In distance it is nearly *thirty miles* from *Thyatira*. Our LORD begins this Epistle with those distinguishing characters he assumes to himself, and by which he is personally known, throughout the whole scriptures. *These things, saith he that is holy, he that is true. He that hath the key of David. He that openeth, and no man shutteth; and shutteth, and no man openeth.* In whatever point of view we contemplate our LORD, as GOD, one with the FATHER and the HOLY GHOST, or as GOD-Man Mediator, he is only holy, and true. *Such an High Priest became us who is holy, harmless, undefiled, separate from sinners, and made higher than the heavens.* Heb. vii. 26. And what tends to endear this part of our LORD's character the more to his people is, that in this holiness and truth, all his chosen are interested. So GOD the FATHER, at the first, chose the Church, that it should be in him, *holy, and without blame, before him in love.* Ephes. i. 4. So that He, that is, *the true and faithful Witness,* is also the holiness of his people. He is their *sanctification* and *wisdom;* 1 Cor. i. 30. they are sanctified *in* him, and *from* him, and *by* him. Sweet consideration to the faithful in CHRIST JESUS! And by the key of the house of *David*, considering *David* as a type of CHRIST, and the Church CHRIST's house; Heb. iii. 6. it is his office, both to open and shut, and to none beside doth this belong. This was predicted of CHRIST, under the character of *Eliakim*, by one of the Prophets; and CHRIST confirmed it, in the first opening of this vision to *John*. Chap. i. 18. Isaiah xxii. 20 to the end. Reader! pass not away, from this precious scripture, without first bending the knee of adoration, love, and praise, to this Almighty SAVIOR, at whose girdle hang all the keys of government, in all the departments of nature, providence, grace, and glory. He hath the key to open to all appointments, *to give eternal life to as many as the* FATHER *hath given him*, to gather his people, to pardon, to cleanse, to justify, to sanctify, to glorify them. None can open the grave to his saints, but JESUS. And when he opens, to each and every one he saith, as he did to *Jacob, fear not to go down into Egypt, I will go with thee.* Gen. xlvi. 3, 4. None can open heaven but JESUS. None cast into hell but JESUS. Oh! the preciousness of knowing Him, and his Almighty power; and, that that power is everlastingly in exercise, for blessing and protecting his people!

The LORD having made himself known to his Church of *Philadelphia*, by the special, and personal features of his character, next proceeds to inform them of his knowledge of them, of his grace towards them, in setting before them an open door which none can shut, and of his securing them in the hour of temptation which shall come upon all the world; and of his making all their enemies to come and bend before their feet, and to know that JESUS hath loved them.

The *good works* JESUS speaks of, are the graces of the SPIRIT, producing in them faith, and love, and trust in CHRIST. And by an *open door*, it should seem to imply, the freeness the LORD would give, under this time-state of the Church, to the preaching of the pure Gospel. And, indeed, what is said here concerning the Church of *Philadelphia*, carries with it an assurance, of a greater out-pouring of the SPIRIT, and a greater in-gathering of CHRIST's scattered ones, than in any other period of the Gospel, from the first descent of the HOLY GHOST at the day of Pentecost. The coming of the synagogue of *Satan*, in them that say they are *Jews*, and are not; evidently means a great work of conversion by the LORD's grace, upon those that before persecuted the Church of CHRIST. By the synagogue of *Satan*, is intended those of the LORD's children, which, while in the blindness of nature, and dead in trespasses and sins, were in his service, and wore his livery, and did his work; but now, by regenerating grace, were called out of darkness, and translated into the kingdom of GOD's dear SON. But, by coming and worshipping before the Church's feet, doth not mean worshipping the Church, for the Church is no object of worship, but worshipping, *with* the Church, the LORD; and to know, that the whole Church share in the common love of GOD her SAVIOR. So that those converts from *Satan*, will know their joint interest with the Church in CHRIST.

The glorious things here described, of being kept from the hour of temptation, while the whole carnal world is involved in it; of overcoming in, and by CHRIST; being made a pillar in GOD's temple, and having GOD's name, yea, CHRIST's new name, which, as Mediator, by his righteousness and blood-shedding, he hath purchased; the going no more out, and the like; these are allusions, not to the Church in glory above, but to the period of triumph below. For the Lord saith, let *no man take thy crown*. The heavenly crown cannot be supposed as meant, for who in heaven of the ungodly shall be there to take it. But it means the faith of assurance here below. *Hold that fast*, saith Christ, *which thou hast*; meaning your consciousness, that it is yours, in Christ. Faith gives present right, though not present possession. It becomes a reversionary interest, perfectly sure, and perfectly certain, after death. Faith, therefore, looks at it as such, and grasps it, as certain, as the heir of an inheritance, when he shall attain his majority, and is got out of his nonage. Reader! what saith your experience to these things? If the Lord the Spirit hath regenerated you from the *Adam*-nature of the fall, in that new birth; you are begotten to this lively hope by the resurrection of Jesus Christ from the dead to this inheritance *incorruptible and undefiled, and that fadeth not away*. The thing is certain, and the interpretation sure. Oh! the unspeakable mercy! There is no suspense, no doubt, no peradventures. A regenerated child of God, is in no uncertainty, as to the final issue. If Christ and his righteousness be mine now, it will be then, and then for ever!

One word more, as to the period of this *Philadelphian* state. Here I presume not to speak in the least decidedly. In the general observations at the opening of this mysterious Book of God, I have assigned my reasons, why the Lord hath been pleased to keep the time a secret, until the events be accomplished. And the more I ponder the subject, the more I am convinced that these things are hidden from the Church generally speaking; though, as in the instance of *Daniel*, a child of God, here and there, may have secret intimations given him. See Dan. ix. throughout. And, with respect to carnal men, who have presumed to write on the prophecies of Scripture, unenlightened by grace, untaught of God; we have seen what awful business they have made of it. *They run upon the thick bosses of* God's *bucklers*. Job xv. 26. From such men, every one truly taught of God, cannot but turn away. Whether the Church of Christ be under the *Sardis*-state in the present hour, how far that state is advanced, whether this *Philadelphian* is to succeed it, and how near at hand, I am humbly inclined to believe, no man knoweth these things. As to the features of the Church of *Sardis* being suited to the present hour in many particulars, this may safely be allowed, and yet no conclusion therefrom drawn, how much of it is run out, and how much longer it hath to last. And, though the Church of *Sardis* may be said to be more like the present state of Christ's Church in the earth, than any of the former; yet, it should be observed, that there is not one of the foregoing, but what in it may be discovered spots like our own. In a word, I may be singular, and I may be wrong; but, as I solemnly believe, that there never was a period since the emancipation of this kingdom from Popery, in which vital godliness was at a lower ebb than the present, I am inclined to think, that, before the *Philadelphian*-state, as here described, comes on, there will be a sifting time. Amos ix. 8—10. Then, if the Lord so appoint, may succeed the blessed promises that follow, verse 11 to the end; which are in correspondence to the *Philadelphian*-state, as here described. But the *scena ante penultima*, that is, *the scene before the last*, will be perilous. So CHRIST seems to intimate, in closing up the *Sardis*-state. *I will come on thee as a thief; and thou shalt not know what hour I will come upon thee.* Verse 3.

14 ¶ And unto the angel of the church of the Laodiceans write: These things saith the Amen, the faithful and true witness, the beginning of the creation of God;

15 I know thy works that thou art neither cold nor hot; I would thou wert cold or hot.

16 So then because thou art luke-warm, and neither cold nor hot, I will spue thee out of my mouth.

17 Because thou sayest, I am rich, and increased with goods, and have need of nothing; and knowest not that thou art wretched, and miserable, and poor, and blind, and naked:

18 I counsel thee to buy of me gold tried in the fire, that thou mayest be rich: and white raiment, that thou mayest be clothed, and *that* the shame of thy nakedness do not appear; and anoint thine eyes with eye salve, that thou mayest see.

19 As many as I love, I rebuke and chasten: be zealous therefore and repent.

20 ¶ Behold, I stand at the door, and knock: if any man hear my voice, and open the door, I will come in to him, and will sup with him, and he with me.

21 To him that overcometh will I grant to sit with me in my throne, even as I also overcame, and am set down with my Father in his throne.

22 He that hath an ear, let him hear what the Spirit saith unto the churches.

We are here brought acquainted with the LORD's Epistle to the seventh Church, *Laodicea*. We have a certain account of this Church in the Epistle of *Paul* to the *Colossians;* for he thrice makes mention of it. Coloss. ii. 1. and iv. 13, 15. Its situation was in the province of *Asia*. Like all the former, it is occupied at present by the *Turks*. If, as this Epistle is placed last in point of order, it be thereby meant to say, its period will be last, and succeed the Church of *Philadelphia;* we may generally learn from it, that the glorious spiritual reign of CHRIST, during the *Philadelphian*-state, will be succeeded with an awful lukewarm, and lifeless condition, under this *Laodicean;* and afford a striking display of the LORD's grace, and their undeservings.

The LORD opens this Epistle, as he hath all the foregoing, with ushering in his message with the proclamations of his sovereignty and power. He here calls himself *the Amen, the faithful and true witness, the beginning of the creation of* GOD. Now all these are distinguishing names, belonging only to the SON of GOD; as GOD in the first of them, and as GOD-Man Mediator in the two last. The Old Testament scripture, Isaiah lxv. 16. declares, that *whosoever blesseth himself in the earth, shall bless himself in the* Amen; that is, *the* GOD *of truth; and he that sweareth in the earth, shall swear by the* Amen; that is, *the* GOD *of truth.* Every one knows, that is acquainted with the original, that this is the rendering of it. Now, in the great acts of blessing, or appealing for the confirmation of truth, these distinguishing acts belong only to GOD. And hence CHRIST, when calling himself *Amen*, plainly proves his GODHEAD. But *the faithful and true witness,* and *the beginning of the creation of* GOD, are features of character which belong to him, as GOD-Man Mediator. And by both these, he hath demonstrated his twofold nature, most plainly and blessedly. If the Reader will turn to Coloss. i. 15, and following verses, and the *Poor Man's Commentary* thereupon; it will supersede the necessity of my enlarging upon them, in this place.

JESUS having opened his Epistle to the Church of *Laodicea* with the glories of his names and authority, next begins to speak on the subject for which he sent the message to the Church. And, in the description which the LORD hath given of the state of this Church, it is difficult to know which to admire most, the LORD's compassion, or their awful degeneracy. Considered as the last Church which CHRIST would have upon earth, it is truly distressing. Most of the former had spots upon them, but this of *Laodicea* was over-run with a gangrene. And, what made it, if possible, yet more awful, she is represented as speaking peace to herself, as needing nothing; while, in CHRIST's eye, she was every thing the reverse, and drenched in the deepest poverty. Reader! how oft have I seen in sick rooms, and dying chambers, deceptions of this kind, both spiritually and bodily. It is indeed no uncommon thing in life, by reason of this self-deception, for those who have the spots of death upon them, to be talking of a speedy recovery. And, while every looker-on, but themselves, beholds death approaching; the poor unconscious man himself believes it not, till he drops into eternity. And what it is by the body, so is it by the soul! But, oh! how much more horrible! to behold a sinner without a single work of grace upon his soul; no sense of sin, no knowledge of salvation, ignorant of the plague of his own heart, ignorant of the love and grace of GOD, a stranger to the Person, work, righteousness, and blood-shedding of the LORD JESUS CHRIST; and, with respect to the regenerating mercy of GOD the SPIRIT, as it concerns himself, he hath not so much as heard, whether there be any HOLY GHOST! Reader! how readest thou? What think *you* of these things?

It appears from this message to the Church of the *Laodiceans,* that, notwithstanding the great mass of the people, who professed to be apart in the visible Church, were in this awful state; and concerning whom Jesus declared, that *he would spue them out of his mouth;* yet the Lord had a people among them, for whom he sent this Epistle, and to whom he gave counsel, to buy of him gold and white raiment, and eye-salve. There is somewhat very sweet and endearing in this counsel of Jesus, who is *the Wonderful Counsellor,* and *in whom are hid all the treasures of wisdom and knowledge.* Isaiah ix. 6. Coloss. ii. 3. It holds forth to my view, so very interesting an account of the wisdom, grace, and loveliness of Jesus, that I would beg the Reader's indulgence to dwell a moment upon it.

By *gold tried in the fire,* can mean no other than Christ himself. He hath been tried, indeed, in the fire of every exercise, when for his people he bore the sins and sorrows of his redeemed, in his own body, on the tree. As the Church's Surety, he stood exposed to the fire of God's wrath as a burnt-offering; and all the fiery darts of *Satan,* which in the days of his temptation he endured. And, by *white raiment,* we may well conceive, the Lord means that spotless robe of righteousness, which on the cross he wrought out, for the clothing all his people. And by *the eye-salve to anoint the eyes* of his spiritually blind, can mean no other than the unction of the Holy Ghost, by which, in regenerating grace, in the new birth, and in divine teaching, the Church are brought to know all things. 1 John ii. 20, 27. And it is not the smallest beauty of this scripture, in the counsel of Christ, that what Jesus calls to buy of him, means *without money and without price.* It is all a free gift, free grace, free love. And he that counsels his people thus to buy, gives them the disposition how to buy; namely, coming to him to receive, not to give. The precious things Jesus sells are too precious for purchase. *If a man would give all the substance of his house* for this love of God in Christ, it would utterly be contemned. Song viii. 7. Moreover: these incalculably great blessings, have all been purchased before, by Jesus himself, and with no less a price than that of his own blood. So that, as he bought them for his people, so he counsels them to come and buy of him, in this unusual way of buying; not only without money, but without any thing; neither credit, nor promise, nor deserving. Was there ever heard of such a free grace market as this? Reader! Shall you and I take the counsel of this wonderful Counsellor? Shall we seek Him, as our true riches? Accept his white raiment for our only covering before God, for acceptance? And shall we bless him, for the Unction of his Holy Spirit, in anointing our eyes, to behold thereby, our nothingness, and his All-sufficiency? Shall we hesitate to accept the free gift, and the free grace of God in Christ Jesus? Shall we indeed, be so proud, as rather to purchase, than receive free, rather come before God in our rags, than in the robe of Jesus' righteousness? And all this, at a time when we know, and are told, that Jesus is too rich to need any thing of us; and his only motive for selling in the way he doth, is to shew us, that he needs not us, but that our blessedness he hath in view, and will thereby promote his own glory in our happiness?

This verse, of Jesus telling his Church of his love, in rebukes and chastenings, comes in very blessedly after the former; because, whatever exercises the Lord calls his people to, he will enable them to bear up under: and, having given them gold tried in the fire, and white raiment, and eye-salve, meaning himself, with all his graces, and gifts, and righteousness, in the HOLY GHOST; afflictions in the world ought not to be regarded. Indeed, they are so many sweet and precious love-tokens of his favor. James i. 2, 12.

I admire the love-calls of CHRIST; and the method here spoken of, by which JESUS makes them known to his people. It is a sweet verse indeed, of the LORD JESUS, in which, as we commonly say, every word tells. The SON of GOD a Petitioner at the heart of his people. And the account is ushered in, as it well may, with a *behold!* A note of admiration, that JESUS, the LORD of heaven and earth, should thus ask an entrance! Moreover: where is he? He saith, *I stand at the door and knock.* Marvellous condescension! JESUS stands without! He that by right of creation, redemption, marriage, purchase, conquests, grace, might command all gates to open at his approach, is nevertheless an humble suitor, and stands without. Oh! must not every one that hears of such grace, or that is conscious of such unparalleled mercy, be constrained to cry out, with one of old: *Come in, thou blessed of the* LORD; *wherefore standest thou without.* Gen. xxiv. 31.

But, observe not only the Redeemer's posture, but the Redeemer's method, to gain admission. He knocks at the door of our heart. And how is this done? Oh! who shall count over, or sum up, all the love-calls of CHRIST. By his word, by ordinances, by means of grace, by afflictions, wants, sicknesses, sorrows, bereaving providences in our friends, the near prospect, as it should seem, of death to ourselves; the LORD knocks, and knocks again and again, and rings loud peals through all the chambers of our consciences; all which we totally disregard, hear, but turn from: neither can the LORD, by soothing or by threatening, by judgments or by mercies, have the least effect upon our stony hearts, until He himself *put in his hand by the hole of the door,* opened to his own entrance, and *caused our bowels to be moved for him.* So said the Church of old! And so, blessed be GOD, I know. Song v. 2, 3, 4. Reader! what saith your heart to these things? Have you known JESUS at the door? Have you heard his calls? Hath he made *you willing in the day of his power?* Psm. cx. 3.

Let some child of GOD, that knows what supping with JESUS means, describe those words of the Redeemer. For, though I trust I know well what it is; yet, sure I am, angels are not competent to describe it. The HOLY GHOST hath taught the Church to tell the people somewhat of it, in her love songs, when she describes JESUS as her Husband, bringing her into his banqueting house, and his banner over her was love: Song ii. 4. but, oh! how far short all language is, to convey the full meaning of such unequalled joy? Our poor, cold, and lifeless nature, by reason of that body of sin and death we carry about with us, renders us but too often insensible to the visits of JESUS. Often he comes, looks in at the window, shews himself at the lattices of ordinances; and we, alas! sometimes hardly glance at him, before our thoughts run away to other objects. But, very sure I am, if our souls were but more alive to the visits of JESUS, we should find that this promise of JESUS would be often fulfilled, and night by night He would come with such love, and bring of that love with him, which is better than wine to make the feast with, and in such fulness, as to be both our company, our food, our bread, and our wine. Song v. 1.

I must not close our view of this Epistle, before that I have first taken notice of what the LORD JESUS hath said of his throne, and of his FATHER's throne. *To him that overcometh will I grant to sit with me in my throne, even as I also overcame, and am set down with my* FATHER *in his throne.* I pray the Reader to observe the distinction which is here made, in what is said of these thrones. The throne of JEHOVAH, FATHER, SON, and HOLY GHOST, is the throne of the essential GODHEAD. Here, on this throne, none but GOD himself in his threefold character of Person sits. Nothing created can possibly ascend here. But there is another throne, namely, the Mediatorial throne. And this belongs to CHRIST, as GOD-Man. And JESUS, having married our nature, and thereby having brought that nature into union with himself, brings his redeemed into a participation of this throne. Therefore, CHRIST saith, *To him that overcometh,* that is, to every one truly regenerated by the HOLY GHOST, whom GOD my FATHER hath given to me, and whom I have betrothed to myself, and redeemed by my blood and righteousness; having thus overcome sin and Satan, he shall sit with me on my Mediatorial throne, even as I also overcame, and am set down with my FATHER in his throne of GODHEAD.

Reader! Once more, as we close this Chapter, and with it the LORD's Epistles to the Churches, we are reminded of the hearing ear. *He that hath an ear!* LORD, give the hearing ear, and the seeing eye, *that we may hear what the* SPIRIT *saith unto the Churches.*

REFLECTIONS.

BLESSED LORD of thy Churches! Give thy servants grace to praise thee for such love-tokens of thy favor, that in thine infinite condescension thou didst send those gracious messages to thy Churches; and still more, didst cause them to be handed down to us, even to the present hour. LORD! we see enough to be humbled to the dust in all. There are now the same features of character among thy people. Like *Ephesus,* too many of thy dear children have left their first love. Like *Smyrna,* we have the blasphemy among us of those who profess the truth, but are not. Like *Pergamos,* we have men of corrupt minds, who follow doctrines in head-knowledge, but void of heart-influence: and, like *Thyatira,* we have multitudes now in our land, who not only suffer, but follow the doctrine of *Jezebel,* and are running back to the idolatry of false worship. LORD JESUS! do thou purge the land! And amidst the *Sardis* state, if we are in that state, prepare us for the more glorious one that is to follow, under the *Philadelphian;* and bring on the great day of our GOD. LORD! make it a short work among all *Laodicean* spirits, and hasten that blessed period, when JESUS will close up all in glory.

In the mean time, blessed LORD JESUS, be not sparing of the sweet visits of thy love to thy people! Oh! for grace to hear thy voice, at the door of our hearts, and to receive CHRIST to his holy supper, and to be among those that eat bread in thy kingdom. Even so, Amen. The LORD be praised for these sweet Epistles to his Churches.

CHAP. IV.

CONTENTS.

At this Chapter, we enter upon those Prophecies which relate to the Church of God, from the Ascension of Christ, going on through a regular Progression, to the Descension of Christ, at the great Day of God. John is here introduced into the Visions concerning those wonderful Events. He is led to behold the Throne of God, and the glorified Inhabitants of Heaven round the Throne.

AFTER this I looked, and, behold, a door *was* opened in heaven: and the first voice which I heard *was* as it were of a trumpet talking with me; which said, Come up hither, and I will shew thee things which must be hereafter.

2 And immediately I was in the spirit: and behold, a throne was set in heaven, and *one* sat on the throne.

3 And he that sat was to look upon like a jasper and a sardine stone: and *there was* a rainbow round about the throne, in sight like unto an emerald.

Here is the opening of the second vision, with which *John* was favored. This Chapter appears to have been intended, as preparatory to what was to follow; not unlike the first. In the first Chapter, *John* had that glorious vision of the *Person* of his Lord. The next Chapter, Christ's *message* began, to the Churches. So here, *John* hath in this Chapter, a solemn and glorious vision, of the parties concerned in what was to follow; and then, in the succeeding Chapter, the business for which the Apostle was favored with the vision.

There is here in this Chapter, a view of the Lord's Church, with the Lord himself presiding over it. And one of the most solemn representations which can be. *John* begins it with observing, that after he had received from the Lord his messages to the seven Churches, and, perhaps, for ought we know to the contrary, delivered them; *he looked, and behold a door was opened in the heavens.* By which is meant, that his spiritual faculties were called forth into exercise, and, looking up, he saw heaven opened to his view, as though he had beheld through it, this wonderful, and supernatural sight, which he hereafter describes. The first thing after looking up which attracted his attention was the sound of a voice, inviting him to raise his affections above the earth to heaven; and a promise accompanied the invitation, that he that invited him would shew him things which should be hereafter. And immediately *John* found himself, as he had upon the former vision, in the Spirit; meaning, under divine influences. See Chap. i. 10. Reader! pause, and do not fail to observe, how soon the LORD the HOLY GHOST works upon the spirits of the people. No sooner did *John* hear the voice, but immediately he was in the Spirit.

The throne which *John* saw, and upon which One sat, hath been considered, as representing the Unity of the Divine Nature, in his threefold character of Persons. And the Jasper, Sardine, and Emerald stones, are supposed to be the representation of the Threefold nature of the GODHEAD. But it is observable, that though the brilliancy of these stones set forth the splendor of shining glory, yet no Personal appearance was seen. *No man hath seen* GOD *at any time.* John i. 18. In relation to the Rainbow round about the throne, there can be no question to whom this refers, because the Rainbow, from the very first Covenant of grace made with *Noah*, was declared by the LORD himself, to be the token of the everlasting Covenant. There are so many very blessed things connected with this token of the Rainbow, that I beg the Reader's indulgence, to dwell upon the subject somewhat more particularly.

And, *first.* Let it be considered, how is the Rainbow formed? It is the effect from the sun's beams upon the watery clouds. And CHRIST, the Sun of righteousness, forms, by his shining, the whole effects of the Covenant of grace, upon all that is cloudy, in our nature. So that JESUS is the true Rainbow, of which that beautiful arch, formed in the heavens, is but a type or shadow.

Secondly. As the Rainbow in nature, is held forth by the LORD, to be an everlasting memorial of GOD's Covenant with the earth, that GOD will no more destroy the earth by a deluge: so CHRIST, the Rainbow in grace, is GOD's memorial, and man's confidence, that amidst all the deluge of sin, GOD will not destroy his people, for whom JESUS is the Covenant.

Thirdly. As the Rainbow in nature hath been in all ages the token of GOD's Covenant for the earth's safety, when the LORD brings a cloud over the earth, and the bow is seen in the cloud; Gen. ix. 13, 14. so here, the throne of GOD which *John* saw, was encircled with the Bow, to intimate its everlasting abiding, like to the throne itself; being fixed of an everlasting green like an Emerald, to shew its unfading nature, and its never-ceasing efficacy.

Fourthly. That this Rainbow was, and is CHRIST, is evident, for *John* saw CHRIST upon another occasion, as a mighty Angel come down from heaven, *clothed with a rainbow, and his face was as it were the Sun, and his feet as pillars of fire.* Chap. x. 1. So *John* had seen him before. Rev. i. 15, 16. It is the peculiar prerogative of CHRIST, to shine as the sun upon his people, and to lift up the light of his countenance upon them.

Fifthly. John tells the Church in the fifth verse, that out of the throne proceeded *lightnings, and thunderings, and voices.* Perhaps these were meant to shew, the many dispensations of the LORD, both to the Church, and to the world. But whatever dispensations come from the throne, they must all pass through the Rainbow, for the Rainbow was all round the throne, so that nothing could be manifested but through it. And this, very blessedly teacheth the Church, how everlastingly safe all CHRIST's redeemed must be, since nothing can come to pass, but it must pass his hands. And on the other hand, how awful to his enemies, since CHRIST is in all dispensations, and nothing can escape him.

Lastly. While the Rainbow in the heavens shadows CHRIST, and is designed to point to him, for which purpose GOD hangs out the Bow, it doth but half resemble CHRIST, for it only forms an half-circle in the beautiful Arch we behold. But JESUS encircles the whole throne. Neither is it possible for GOD to look any way to his people, but *in* him, and *through* him. Oh! the blessedness to behold the LORD JEHOVAH, by faith upon his throne; and that throne encircled with mercy, in the Person and glory of the LORD JESUS CHRIST.

4 ¶.And round about the throne *were* four and twenty seats: and upon the seats I saw four and twenty elders sitting, clothed in white raiment; and they had on their heads crowns of gold.

5 And out of the throne proceeded lightnings and thunderings and voices; and *there were* seven lamps of fire burning before the throne, which are the seven Spirits of God.

6 ¶ And before the throne *there was* a sea of glass like unto crystal; and in the midst of the throne, and round about the throne, *were* four beasts full of eyes before and behind.

7 And the first beast *was* like a lion, and the second beast like a calf, and the third beast had a face as a man, and the fourth beast *was* like a flying eagle.

8 And the four beasts had each of them six wings about *him;* and *they were* full of eyes within: and they rest not day and night, saying, Holy, holy, holy, Lord God Almighty, which was, and is, and is to come.

9 And when those beasts give glory and honour and thanks to him that sat on the throne, who liveth for ever and ever,

10 ¶ The four and twenty elders fall down before him that sat on the throne, and worship him that liveth for ever and ever, and cast their crowns before the throne, saying,

11 Thou art worthy, O Lord, to receive glory and honour and power: for thou hast created all things, and for thy pleasure they are, and were created.

I would speak with all possible reverence, on a subject so infinitely sublime, as the one contained in this Chapter; and desire, rather to propose all I have to offer, by way of inquiry, than in a single instance to speak decidedly. But I venture to believe, that as at this Chapter, in the second vision John was favored with, the LORD was about to commit to him, certain prophecies, which his Church would have unfolded and accomplished, in the different ages, from that time, to the consummation of all things; the LORD in this Chapter was preparing his servant's mind for that subject, by the solemn representation of what is here delivered. The LORD therefore begins with an account of the throne of GOD, similar to that of Isaiah vi. where all the sanctities of heaven are around. It is the Church in which GOD erects his throne, therefore we find Elders worshipping before the throne, and though the song they sing is not recorded here, yet it is in the next Chapter, ascribing their redemption to CHRIST. Chap. v. 9. Now this could not be the song of Angels, but men. Hence, those Elders are men.

And it is as evident, that this representation is to set forth that Church upon earth; for the sea of glass, like unto crystal, intimated the fountain opened for sin, and uncleanness, and which are needed not in heaven. And the seven lamps, figurative of the sevenfold gifts of GOD the SPIRIT, are specially for the LORD's people in this life. They are no longer required as principles of regeneration, and quickening in the state of perfection above. Not that the HOLY GHOST through all eternity, ceaseth his sweet influences, either to the Person of the glorious Head of his Church, or his members; but then not in a way as here below, of regenerating, illuminating, convincing, and converting mercy.

Concerning the Elders, and the four Beasts, there needs not to speak of them particularly. The HOLY GHOST hath not thought proper to give the Church deeper views, into the mysteries of the kingdom, than is necessary; and to attempt lifting the veil higher, would be both presumptuous and unprofitable. It is enough for us to understand, that they belong to the Church of GOD: more than this, we need not.

But, Reader! here is enough to gratify our best intellectual faculties, and to employ our contemplation for ever, in attending to the Hymn of Heaven, sung by the whole Choir, the Church. Oh! what unknown glories, in the holiness, greatness, and eternity of the whole Persons of the GODHEAD! This thrice repeating of JEHOVAH's holiness, is striking. All GOD's perfections and attributes, are standards of character, distinguishing the LORD from all his creatures. But yet, we never meet with any other prerogative of JEHOVAH, trebled as this is of his holiness. We do not say *faithful, faithful, faithful*, LORD GOD Almighty! I do not presume to explain. But I think it proper to notice it. Oh! for grace, to join the whole body the Church in the same hymn of praise, till we all come before the throne, in one full body of the redeemed, to praise GOD and the LAMB for evermore! Amen.

REFLECTIONS.

READER! Let us seek grace, that, like the beloved Apostle, we may by faith hear the sweet voice, saying, Come up hither, and like him, may be immediately in the Spirit, when we come to visions and revelations of the Lord!

Oh! Lord the Holy Ghost! as it is thy blessed office to glorify the Lord Jesus; do thou for ever glorify him to the view of thy people, that as oft as thou liftest the eye, and the soul to look to the throne; oh! to see the Lord Jesus, as the Rainbow encircling the throne, and, as God the Father's bow, the everlasting token of God's good will to man. Yea, Almighty Father, behold thy Church in *Him*, through *Him*, and by *Him*, as our everlasting security and portion. And let thy Church begin the Hymn, and all thy redeemed Elders and Men, follow in one vast song in the same, to celebrate the wonders of thy grace. And what a song will that be finally in heaven, when all the redeemed from every nation, country, and clime, shall be assembled before thee, to sing to the Lord's glory for evermore?

CHAP. V.

CONTENTS.

The preceding Chapter, having in Vision opened Heaven; this prosecutes the same Subject, in describing what took place, when the Hymn of the Church had celebrated the Lord's *Glory. Here is an Account of a Book with Seven Seals. None was found worthy to open it but the* Lamb. *The Events which followed.*

AND I saw in the right hand of him that sat on the throne a book written within, and on the back side, sealed with seven seals.

2 And I saw a strong angel proclaiming with a loud voice, Who is worthy to open the book, and to loose the seals thereof?

3 And no man in heaven, nor in earth, neither under the earth, was able to open the book, neither to look thereon.

Perhaps there never was a subject, so admirably calculated to call up the attention, as the contents of this Chapter. Let the Reader recollect the state of *John's* mind. He tells us, that he was in the spirit. He relates, that a door was opened to his view in heaven. He describes, as far as he was able, some of the glorious objects which he saw. He heard thunderings and voices, with lightenings proceeding out of the throne of God and the Lamb. And he heard the hymn of adoration, which was offered to the Lord, from the host before the throne. Such were the things related in the foregoing Chapter. The mind of the Apostle must have been wrapt up in the most sublime meditation, at the time when what is related in this Chapter began to take place. And *John* hath given the particulars in this chapter in the most striking manner.

First. He saw a Book in the hand of him that sat on the throne, sealed with seven seals. Its being so closely sealed, seemed to imply the secrecy of it. And there can be no doubt, what the contents were; for the secrecy of it, and the hand of him in whom it was, plainly shews, that it was the decree of GOD, respecting his Church. I think a beautiful light is thrown upon this scripture, in the second Psalm. For no sooner had GOD, as is there represented, set CHRIST upon his throne, as King in *Zion*, than he saith, *I will declare the decree.* Now as none but CHRIST could open the Book, and declare the decree, as this Chapter shews; it must follow, that it is CHRIST which is represented in this scripture, and none other. See Psm. ii. 6, 7.

Secondly. The proclamation made upon this occasion appears to have been done, for the manifestation of the greater glory of CHRIST. All the creation is called upon to know, who is worthy to open the book, and loose the seals thereof. Not simply who was *able*, but who was *worthy*. The inability of Angels is implied, as well as their unworthiness, for a strong Angel made the proclamation, and consequently he knew no Angel, either *able* or *worthy*. Reader! do not overlook, while reading this scripture, what is said of JESUS, that *verily he took not on him the nature of Angels, but he took on him the seed of Abraham.* Heb. ii. 16. What a sweet thought to the soul. All creatures are nothing in a way of procuring salvation. And this blessed vision *John* saw, had evidently this great design, in shewing the total inability of creatures to heighten the glory of CHRIST. Acts iv. 12.

Thirdly. It is evident, from the representation here made, that the opening this Book, and loosing the Seals thereof, implied the whole design of GOD's plan, concerning the Church; and that in the opening and declaring the decree, was connected with it the fulfilling it, and of which, in the discovery of one worthy to this deed, every thing in salvation is contained. Reader! before you proceed, pause over this view. Sweetly hath GOD taught herefrom in heaven, as well as on earth, the personal and peculiar fitness of CHRIST, as the only Mediator, to raise up our nature from the ruins of the fall. None but Him was able. None but him worthy. None but that Almighty GOD-Man, who is made higher than the heavens, could be competent to this office! Oh! how doth it exalt the SON of GOD to our view! Oh! how ought it to endear him to our hearts.

4 And I wept much, because no man was found worthy to open and to read the book, neither to look thereon.

5 And one of the elders saith unto me, Weep not: Behold, the Lion of the tribe of Juda, the Root of David, hath prevailed to open the book, and to loose the seven seals thereof.

The exercises of *John* are sweetly recorded, for the instruction of the Church. He was called up to heaven. But after a short space he is made to weep, yea, to weep much. Thus we see, that even visions of heaven when opened, are not immediate happiness. Sorrow is often before joy. Reader! recollect that this was but a vision. The redeemed when in reality they enter heaven, will weep no more. Rev. vii. 16, 17. But in fact, *John's* mind was thus kept in suspense, for the greater glory which was to follow. JESUS himself was in the moment near at hand, yea, JESUS was soon after to come forward to *John's* view, and take the book and open the seals in his sight, but to heighten both CHRIST's glory, and *John's* joy; the Apostle shall first be exercised with seeming difficulties. It is so for the most part in the path of the LORD's people. Their way to heaven lies through the valley of *Baca*. *They that sow in tears, shall reap in joy.*

The comfort and encouragement, given by one of the Elders to *John*, is very interesting. He not only tells him to dry up his tears, for there was one found worthy to accomplish all his wishes, but he points out his Person, and by the well known name of *Judah* or *Jehudah*, from whom CHRIST, after the flesh, sprang, the identity of his Person was defined. Gen. xlix. 10. I pray the Reader to pause here, in order to mark the special grace of GOD. It was with *John*, as it is often with the Church. When visions of GOD begin, then come exercises. And when exercises abound, GOD's consolations abound. All the difficulty thrown in the way of *John*, was only to heighten CHRIST's glory to the Apostle's view, and to increase the Apostle's joy and confidence in CHRIST. And what it was with *John*, so is it with all the LORD's people. When none can be found worthy in heaven, or in earth, to deliver the soul; oh! how blessed then is CHRIST.

6 And I beheld, and lo, in the midst of the throne, and of the four beasts, and in the midst of the elders, stood a Lamb, as it had been slain, having seven horns, and seven eyes, which are the seven Spirits of God sent forth into all the earth.

7 And he came and took the book out of the right hand of him that sat up on the throne.

Every thing here mentioned is blessed. CHRIST in the midst of the throne. This is gloriously descriptive of his power and GODHEAD. The centre of the throne can only be suited for Him, in whom all fulness dwells. He could not have been seen in the midst of the throne, had he not possessed it. And he could not have possessed it, had he not been in his divine nature and essence, *One with the* FATHER *over all*, GOD *blessed for ever!* So, that here is a most decided evidence of the GODHEAD of CHRIST. *John* saw him as a Lamb, in the midst of the throne.

Secondly. He saw him stand as a Lamb that had been slain; that is, I apprehend, bearing on his glorified body, the marks of our redemption. As if fresh blood appeared upon him. A sweet assurance this, of the perpetual and everlasting efficacy of his sacrifice. He stood as if he had been slain. Reader! never lose sight of this. The merits of CHRIST's blood are as powerful, and will remain so for ever, as in the moment of his death. *For by one offering he hath perfected for ever them that are sanctified.* Heb. x. 14.

Thirdly. By the midst of the throne must be understood, that all power is his, and that he is there to administer all government. For whether we consider this throne as a throne of grace, or a throne of justice, or a throne of glory, JESUS in the midst of it, implies that his is the office of administration to all. Oh! what a thought for all his redeemed ones to keep in view and cherish, and especially when they are told, that JESUS is there for them, and that they are commanded at all times, and upon all occasions, to come boldly to the throne of grace, *to obtain mercy, and find grace to help in time of need.* Heb. iv. 16.

Fourthly. CHRIST is further described in this scripture, as having seven horns and seven eyes, meaning, as seven is a perfect number, that JESUS hath a perfection of power, and a perfection of knowledge; with the one to bear up and strengthen all his redeemed against their enemies, and to destroy them; and with the other, having all knowledge, to have a clear apprehension of all their wants, and to provide for them. Reader! shall not you and I find comfort from this precious view, of the Lamb of GOD which *John* saw in vision? There can be no question of the efficacy of his blood, for he appeared and stood a Lamb, as it had been slain. There can be no question of his carrying on his High Priestly office for his Church; for he stood as advocates stand to plead. There can be no question of his success, in pleading his own merits and blood, for the marks of that blood were still upon him; and he was in the midst of the throne, to shew his triumphs and his own personal glory. There can be no doubt, but that he will bring all his redeemed up to himself in heaven, for he was seen in the midst of the throne, as if to say, he had taken possession of it in their name. Precious LORD JESUS! give me with the eye of faith, unceasingly to behold thee, in this most blessed view, and let my soul be warmed continually, with the conscious assurance, that I have redemption in thy blood. Then shall I centre all my confidence in the LORD, who is in the centre of the throne for his people.

8 And when he had taken the book, the four beasts and four *and* twenty elders fell down before the Lamb, having every one of them harps, and golden vials full of odours, which are the prayers of saints.

9 ¶ And they sung a new song, saying, Thou art worthy to take the book, and to open the seals thereof: for thou wast slain, and hast redeemed us to God by thy blood, out of every kindred and tongue and people and nation;

10 And hast made us unto our God kings and priests: and we shall reign on the earth.

What a delightful view is here of Christ coming and taking the book out of the right hand of him that sat on the throne? None but Christ could do this? He is the only Mediator. Hence the Prophet described him, as coming alone, and of the people *there were none with him.* Isaiah lxiii. 3. And there is a sublime and beautiful account, of this engagement, and undertaking of Christ, by the Prophet, in which God the Father is the speaker. *And their nobles shall be of themselves, and their Governor shall proceed from the midst of them; and I will cause him to draw near, and he shall approach unto me, for who is this that engaged his heart, to approach unto me, saith the* Lord? Jerem. xxx. 21. Hence we blessedly learn, that Christ, as Mediator, engaged his heart to this service, when he took the book of God's decrees, and undertook to perform them. And he hath performed them. And his redeemed are secured in the performance, and are accepted, sanctified, and everlastingly blessed in him!

The wonderful effect which followed, in Christ's taking the book is here shewn. Instantly the song of redemption broke out in heaven; and the words they sung, are handed down to the Church upon earth. It is called a new song, because redemption-work was newly finished, when Christ on the cross declared it so, and returned to glory; and because it is a new song, which can only be truly sung from new hearts, when renewed by the Holy Ghost. And Christ to whom this song is personally addressed, is supposed here as having lately finished redemption-work, and now returned to glory.

I pray the Reader to observe some of the very sweet and leading notes of this song. *First.* That it is Christ's Person, as Redeemer, who is here said to be worthy of praise. And how ought all his redeemed, conscious, by regeneration, of their union with him, and redemption by him, to make him the daily object of their love, and obedience, and praise, as the Church in heaven do?

Secondly. That the song itself is *redemption.* It was for this Christ was slain, and the Church is redeemed to God by his blood. And this is so blessed a subject, that even angels, who have no concern in it themselves, yet join in it, in blessing Christ for it to others. See verse 13.

Thirdly. This redemption-song hath another great property of sweetness in it, namely, in that it is not only redeeming the Church *from* among men, but redeeming *to* God. So that, while redemption is *in* Christ, and *by* Christ, it is *from* God our Father the mercy also originates and returns. *Thou wast slain, and hast redeemed us to* God *by thy blood. From* God as the first cause, and *to* God as the final end!

Fourthly. This redemption-song hath another precious note in it, namely, in that it is personal and particular. For the redeemed in heaven, which are here represented as singing it, declare that Christ is worthy to take the book, and to open the seals thereof, because he was slain, and had redeemed *them* to God by his blood, *out of every kindred and tongue, and people, and nation.* Not *every kindred,* but *out* of every kindred. Hence personal and particular redemption.

Fifthly. Another delightful note swells the song of redemption; for Jesus hath not only redeemed them from among men, but made them *unto our* God (said they) *kings and priests.* Oh! the blessedness and royalty of Christ's kingdom, where all the family are ennobled and consecrated in Jesus.

Lastly. The song ends with the assurance, *and we shall reign on the earth.* Reader! do observe the expression! The triumphs of Christ's kingdom in the latter-day dispensation, upon the earth, according to this song, will be greater than their spirits now have in heaven; for otherwise they would not have noted it with such joy in their song. In the prospect of it, they seem to lose sight of their present state, and pleasingly anticipate their reign with Christ upon earth. And they chaunt it with a firmness of delight and certainty. *And we shall reign on the earth!* Reader! what say you to this song of redemption? Hath God the Holy Ghost, by regeneration, put this new song in *your* mouth, even thanksgiving to our God! Can you sing it *now?* If so, surely when you come to join this heavenly host, you will sing it *then?*

11 And I beheld, and I heard the voice of many angels round about the throne, and the beasts, and the elders: and the number of them was ten thousand times ten thousand, and thousands of thousands;

12 ¶ Saying with a loud voice, Worthy is the Lamb that was slain to receive power and riches and wisdom and strength and honour and glory and blessing.

13 And every creature which is in heaven, and on the earth, and under the earth, and such as are in the sea, and all that are in them, heard I, saying, Blessing and honour and glory and power *be* unto him that sitteth upon the throne, and unto the Lamb for ever and ever.

14 And the four beasts said, Amen, and the four *and* twenty elders fell down, and worshipped him that liveth for ever and ever.

Here we have another goodly company, but different from the former, ascribing a seven-fold praise to the Lamb. These are described as angels round the throne; yea, *John* saith, every creature that was in heaven, and on the earth, and under the earth, and such as are in the sea, all joining together in ascribing glory and praise to the Lamb. In order for the right apprehension of this hymn of adoration, let it be considered, that the elect angels, who, though not redeemed by Christ, and have no union with Christ, yet, being created by Christ, and kept and confirmed in their state of holiness by Christ, worship, and adore, and obey Him. Their multitude is here described, to intimate what a glorious body they are. And all the creatures of God are said to praise Christ, yea, the very enemies of Christ shall bow their knee before Him, and be made to acknowledge his greatness and his glory. The oath of the Lord hath said it, yea, the Lord hath sworn it. *I have sworn by myself,* (the Lord saith,) *the word is gone out of my mouth in righteousness, and shall not return, that unto me every knee shall bow, every tongue shall swear.* Isaiah xlv. 23. These things explain to us the nature of this last hymn, so differently worded from the former. I do not think it necessary to swell these pages, by enlarging on the several particulars here expressed. The harps, and golden vials, are perhaps in allusion to the Temple service, under the old Jewish dispensation. But the musical instruments of the New Testament Church on earth, and of the New Jerusalem Church in heaven, can mean nothing more than the new-strung chords of the renewed spirit in Christ Jesus. To these, the whole Church of God, both in heaven and earth, will give their hearty Amen. Yea, as one of the sweet names of Christ, and as an ordinance in holy worship, all, and every regenerated child of God will bless himself in Christ, the Amen. See Isa. lxv. 16. 1 Cor. xiv. 16.

Oh! thou glorious Lord of the tribe of Judah, precious Jesus, thou art He whom thy brethren shalt praise, for thou wert alone worthy to take the book, and to loose the seals thereof. Truly, Almighty Lord, but for thy undertaking the Church must have wept for ever! But, praised be God our Father, thou hast redeemed us to God by thy blood. And praised be God the Spirit for giving thy Church this precious record, and handing it down to us with such gracious explainings. All heaven was filled with odours to our Jesus's praise. And all earth shall offer their praises to the Lamb! Lord, amidst the ten thousand times ten thousands, and thousands of thousands, let not my poor soul be silent, who oweth all its mercies to God and the Lamb! Feeble, and poor, and unworthy as it is, still, Lord, hear me when I say, Thou art worthy to receive all praise, for thou wast slain, and hast redeemed me to God by thy blood.

CHAP. VI.

CONTENTS.

With this Chapter commenceth the Opening of the Seals. Here are six of them opened in this Chapter, the various Events of which are enumerated in Prophetical Language, and with these the Chapter closeth.

AND I saw when the Lamb opened one of the seals, and I heard, as it were the noise of thunder, one of the four beasts saying, Come and see.

2 And I saw, and behold, a white horse: and he that sat on him had a bow; and a crown was

CH. VI.] REVELATION. 527

given unto him; and he went forth conquering and to conquer,

Let the Reader attend to the various particulars under these different periods of events, classed under the term of *seals;* every one of which becomes interesting. It appears very plain, that the vision of *seals,* of *trumpets,* and of *vials,* hath each its distinct object in prophecy. The two preceding Chapters having introduced to the Church the divine authority of the whole in GOD and the LAMB; and CHRIST having come forward to open the book, and loose the seals thereof, now enters upon the glorious service. And here begins with the prophecy of the *seals.*

For the better apprehension of the subject it may be proper previously to consider, what we may suppose is meant, according to scripture language, of the term *seal.* Two or three striking significations seem to be folded up in the name. *First.* It certainly implies somewhat that is secret; and such, no doubt, are all the ways and works of GOD, in relation to his creatures. All the mysteries of our holy faith necessarily are secret, and, in some points, must everlastingly be so. And the opposition made to the SON of GOD, in the struggles of the kingdom of darkness, yea, the state of CHRIST's Church, in the *Adam-*nature of the fall, and the natural hatred, even of his own people, until recovered by grace, these are secrets indeed, which the LORD only can explain, and therefore none but CHRIST could be found worthy to open and unfold them to his people.

Secondly. There is somewhat wonderfully striking in those seals, considered with an eye to the LORD's people, as distinguished from the world. To gather into one point of view all that is said of *seals,* and *sealing,* as relating to the Church of GOD, would make a large volume. The sacred purposes and decrees of GOD the FATHER, are frequently expressed by this term. His *treasures are said to be sealed.* Deut. xxxii. 34. *His stars are sealed.* Job ix. 7. And *Job* observed, that *his transgressions were sealed up in a bag;* meaning, well-known. Job xiv. 17. In relation to CHRIST, circumcision is said to be *a seal of the righteousness of faith;* Rom. iv. 11. and regeneration is *the seal of the* HOLY GHOST. 2 Cor. v. 5. And the LORD's knowledge of his people is said to be as a *seal,* because *the foundation of* GOD *standeth sure.* 2 Tim. ii. 19.

Thirdly. By *seals,* and opening them, implies so many pledges, that the things spoken of shall be assuredly accomplished. And we, in the present hour, have this additional testimony, that in the fulfilment of one, all the rest are pledged to be confirmed. Time only can bring to pass, according to the decree, what is said. Nevertheless, in the accomplishment of all that is past, we may safely calculate for all that is to come. The same LORD speaks now, that spoke to the Prophet of old: *But thou, O Daniel, shut up the words, and seal the book, even to the time of the end: many shall run to and fro, and knowledge shall be increased.* Dan. xii. 4.

So much in a general way concerning the *seals.* Let us now attend to the effect, which attended the opening of them. *John* saith, that when the Lamb opened one of them, namely, the *first,* he heard as it were the noise of thunder; *one of the four beasts saying, Come and see.* Now here is an invitation, and that most persuasively introduced, to attend to the wonderful events contained in the opening of the *seals*. And what is the Church called upon for to see? Evidently, CHRIST himself, going forth, by the various methods of his grace, to gather his Church out of the heathen world. Hence, he is represented as on a *white horse,* to intimate the spotless purity of himself and his Gospel; and the *bow* shewed the weapons of his warfare, sure and certain in his victory, *conquering and to conquer.* There is nothing doubtful in this war. *As for those that would not that I should reign over them; bring them hither, and slay them before me.* Luke xix. 27.

But, what I would particularly desire the Reader to attend to in this account is, the *time,* in which this prophecy opened, and the state of the world at its opening. Let the Reader recollect what hath before been remarked in the general observations, at the opening of this book of the Revelation, that the *Roman* Empire was at this time Mistress of the World; and that that Empire was *heathen.* The Jews were now dispersed. CHRIST, therefore, goeth forth, in the purity of his Gospel, to gather together in one, *the children of* GOD *which are scattered abroad.* John xi. 52. A *white horse,* was a beautiful representation both of the purity of his Person, and of his doctrine. And the *crown,* as striking an *insignalia* of his sure victory. So spake the royal Prophet; Psm. xlv. 4, 5, 6. And the HOLY GHOST again confirmed it, in reference to CHRIST: Heb. i. 8. And the succeeding ages of the Church had the felicity to see the accomplishment of this part of the prophecy. For the Empire, which, at CHRIST's ascension, was *heathen,* in a period of about three hundred years, became *christian;* that is, *professed* Christianity; and this in the person of *Constantine* the Emperor, who first openly avowed it. So that by this time, the Gospel had run down all the idols of *Rome.*

I would pause, just to remark the slender means the LORD was pleased to adopt, for this purpose. In the few poor fishermen of *Galilee,* and their companions, the first preachers of the Gospel, we find the only instruments made use of, against all the philosophy of this known world; as if the Church should always have in view the LORD himself, on his white horse, and crown. For when is beheld such a disproportion between the instruments and the work accomplished, it is impossible but to recognize the divine hand. Here, most eminently, GOD chose *the foolish things of the world to confound the wise, and the weak things of the world to confound the mighty.* 1 Cor. i. 27. And, let not the Reader forget, while contemplating the subject as it then was accomplished, how sure a pledge it gave, that in like manner, all opposition should give way throughout the world in every age of the Church before the Gospel, in the sure accomplishment of all the remaining prophecies. CHRIST still appears to the eye of faith, on the white horse, with his crown, *conquering and to conquer,* until the *seventh* trumpet be sounded, and that glorious event follow, when *the kingdoms of this world are become the kingdoms of our* LORD, *and of his* CHRIST, *and he shall reign for ever and ever.* Rev. xi. 15.

3 And when he had opened the second seal, I heard the second beast say, Come and see.

CH. VI.] REVELATION. 529

4 And there went out another horse *that was* red; and *power* was given to him that sat thereon to take peace from the earth, and that they should kill one another: and there was given unto him a great sword.

Here we have the immediate effect of the opening of the *second* seal. And let not the Reader overlook, who it is that opened every one of them. None but CHRIST could be found worthy. Oh! precious thought! All power is our LORD's, in heaven, and in earth. He reigns, and rules over all. By a *red* horse, seems to imply blood. And, as power was given to him that sat thereon, to take peace from the earth, and there was given unto him a great sword; the matter seems plain enough, that where CHRIST, on his white horse, in the meekness and mildness of his Gospel-grace, is not received, the judgments of peace are taken away, and blood-shedding shall succeed. And, in the history of the Church, as recorded from the time of CHRIST's return to glory, to about the year of our LORD GOD 140, there were great slaughters took place in the empire. *John*, the beloved Apostle, died, it is supposed, about ten years after writing this Book of the Revelation. And if this book be dated, as is generally done, Anno 94, then it will follow, that *John* died Anno 104. Reader! pause over this seal, just to remark the plan of divine government. CHRIST on his white horse, if not received, hath his judgments on others that follow. All must bend to his sceptre. He hath sworn to it with an oath. Isaiah xlv. 23. How strong the words of the Psalmist. *Kiss the* SON *lest he be angry, and ye perish from the way, when his wrath is kindled but a little. Blessed are all they that put their trust in him.* Psm. ii. 12.

5 And when he had opened the third seal, I heard the third beast say, Come and see. And I beheld, and lo, a black horse: and he that sat on him had a pair of balances in his hand.

6 And I heard a voice in the midst of the four beasts say, A measure of wheat for a penny, and three measures of barley for a penny; and *see* thou hurt not the oil and the wine.

By this *third* horse, which was *black*, and the scanty measure of corn, which *John* heard proclaimed, as the standard price for a penny, meaning a man's daily allowance; (Matt. xx. 2.) is very plainly taught to us, that it implied *famine:* when *all faces gather blackness,* as the Prophet said, *and when the land was desolate.* Joel ii. 3—6. And GOD long before declared, that such should be the case, when punishments followed, one upon the heels of another. *When I have broken the staff of your bread, ten women shall bake your bread in one oven, and they shall deliver you your bread again by weight, and ye shall eat and not be satisfied.* Levit. xxvi. 26. Now

VOL. III. 3 Y

let the Reader pause, and observe how suitably the Lord's judgements follow the rejection of Christ and his Gospel. Jesus is the bread of life. He comes on a *white horse*, to intimate peace, and plenty. Men reject him. Then comes one on a *red* horse, with a sword for war. Whether we are to consider Christ himself on this red horse, I will not determine, or whether his messenger. For the Prophet Zechariah, in his vision, saw Christ on a *red horse, and behind him there were red horses speckled*, that is, bay *and white*. Zech. i. 8. To this judgment succeeds another, namely, *famine*. And how awful doth the Prophet describe the little effect which follow all judgments, where grace is not in the heart? *I have given you cleanness of teeth in all your cities, and want of bread in all your places, yet have ye not returned unto me, saith the* Lord. Amos iv. 6. But, Reader! what a yet more awful judgment is that, when, for the wickedness of a land, the Lord withdraws his Gospel, gives the land up to a perpetual barrenness of God's truths. Such a state the same Prophet describes, if the Reader would see it: Amos viii. 9 to the end. But let God's people rejoice under all scantiness of the bread that perisheth in using, as long as they have the bread of life broken to them by the Lord himself, from day to day. In times of persecution in this land, the old saints of God used to say, that bread and water, with Christ and his Gospel, was delicious fare. And this proved that sweet scripture, and marked the Lord's distinguishing grace over his people, when the Lord God said: *Behold, my servant shall eat, but ye shall be hungry; behold, my servants shall drink, but ye shall be thirsty; behold my servants shall rejoice, but ye shall be ashamed!* I beg the Reader to turn to the scripture itself, for it is a sweet one, and let him read the whole. Isaiah lxv. 13 to the end.

7 And when he had opened the fourth seal, I heard the voice of the fourth beast say, Come, and see.

8 And I looked, and behold, a pale horse; and his name that sat on him was Death, and Hell followed with him, and power was given unto them over the fourth part of the earth, to kill with sword, and with hunger, and with death, and with the beasts of the earth.

Here, at the opening by Christ, of the *fourth* seal, we have the end, for the present, of the ministry of the *Beasts;* and we hear no more of them until the pouring out of the *Vials*, at the *fifteenth* Chapter, verse 7. and then, but one of them. I do not presume to speak decidedly concerning them, but by their kind invitation to *John*, at the opening of each seal, *to come and see*, I am inclined to consider them, as representing ministers in the Church. We find their number *four*, in their place as before, and again towards the close of this Book of God, worshipping. Rev. xix. 4.

This *pale* horse, and death upon him, closeth up the judgments. Indeed, death, as it relates to the present world, is a final close to all. But here was the awfulness of this judgment, *hell followed.* The LORD had said by his servant the Prophet, that he would bring *his four sore judgments upon Jerusalem; the sword, and the famine, and the noisome beast, and the pestilence.* Ezek. xiv. 21. But here, the tremendous addition at the opening of this *fourth seal,* in hell following death, gives the finishing stroke to misery, and sums up all in everlasting woe!

9 And when he had opened the fifth seal, I saw under the altar the souls of them that were slain for the word of God, and for the testimony which they held :

10 And they cried with a loud voice, saying, How long, O Lord, holy and true, dost thou not judge and avenge our blood on them that dwell on the earth ?

11 And white robes were given unto every one of them ; and it was said unto them, that they should rest yet for a little season, until their fellow servants also, and their brethren, that should be killed as they were, should be fulfilled.

The opening of this *fifth* seal by CHRIST, opens with it one of the most interesting subjects our minds, under the influence of grace, can possibly conceive. I shall beg the Reader's indulgence, to be somewhat particular upon it.

And *first :* the cry of those that had been slain for the testimony of JESUS, is beautifully represented, as under the Altar. Now this proves to us, that on the departure of the faithful from this world, they enter among *the spirits of just men made perfect.* They are under the Altar.

Secondly. They are not unacquainted with the circumstances here below, but take part in all that concerns the Church. Hence their cry, for judging, and avenging CHRIST's cause. What an animating thought to the Church of GOD upon earth! Reader! think of the multitude of martyrs, who are looking over the battlements of heaven, beholding the exercises of the LORD's people here below; Surely, with the eye of faith we may behold them! Yea, with the ear of faith hear them calling upon us, to *be faithful unto death, and* GOD *will give us also a crown of glory that fadeth not away!* Be *ye followers of us, who now through faith and patience, inherit the promises.*

Thirdly. While we regard what is here said, of their cry to GOD, for avenging their blood; and the assurance they here received, that all should be fully done, in due season; let us learn, the highest lesson we can learn below, in the assurance, how much more the blood of CHRIST, yea, CHRIST in Person, having carried up his own blood before the throne, must plead for his redeemed, and the destruction of all his enemies. Oh! how safe and sure, how eternally safe and sure, are all the interests of the Church! How unalterably determined, is the everlasting ruin of all the enemies of our GOD, and his CHRIST!

When the Reader hath duly pondered these things, let him attend to the gracious answers the LORD gave to the cry of those souls, and the blessedness shewn them.

First. Their souls were clothed with white robes, yea, every one of them, had his own separate and distinct robe, as each soul hath his separate and distinct mansion. JESUS's garment of salvation, each redeemed soul must appear in. It is his justifying dress. It is his coronation, his wedding robe. By this JESUS owns his Church, in every individual instance of his people. So the LORD had said to *John*, of the few names he had in *Sardis*. And here we find it confirmed. *They shall walk with me in white,* saith the LORD, *for they are worthy.* Rev. iii. 4.

Secondly. The LORD assigns a reason, for suspending the judgements they called for on their murderers. There were other, their fellow servants, to have the crown of martyrdom. And, therefore, until those men, ordained of old to this condemnation, had filled in the measure of their iniquity, and the LORD's people were ripened for glory, they must rest for a little season. Oh! what subjects of endless meditation and delight, arise out of this one view of the LORD's regard to his people. Did the ungodly but know wherefore they are spared, or did the LORD's people but call to mind, in ten thousand instances, the causes of suspension, in all the numberless cases they hear of, or meet with in the world; how would the *one* tremble, and the *other* in patience possess their souls?

Thirdly. Ponder well the LORD's answer, in another point of view, for the suspension of the destruction of their enemies; in that thousands yet unborn, of the LORD's people, were to arise, to whom those enemies were to be persecutors, and whose happiness was to be increased from such evils. What a subject is here unfolded, and which no man can fill in, of the unborn, the uncalled, the unawakened, of the LORD's hidden ones, all of which are given to JESUS, and which also he must bring. Even down to our times, and so on to the end of the world, there are JESUS's lambs of his fold, which must arise and be worried by the wolves, as the LORD told the Jews. *Some of them shall ye kill and crucify, and some of them scourge in your synagogue, and persecute them* from *city to city.* Matt. xxiii. 34. Hence, therefore, they which are gone before must rest under the altar, until that their fellow servants and their brethren be brought home. Yea, it is on their account, that the world itself standeth!

Fourthly. Let not the Reader overlook that beautiful feature in this representation. The souls under the altar in heaven, are *fellow servants and brethren.* So the LORD himself hath here called them; and it is our mercy to know it, and to keep it in remembrance. Neither are they dearer though in heaven, to our glorious Head, than we are, though here below on earth. All alike the FATHER's gift, and the SAVIOR's purchase, and the subjects of GOD the SPIRIT's regenerating grace. Oh! how ought the consciousness of this, to endear JESUS to our hearts! Our LORD will not fully answer, the cries of his redeemed in heaven, though martyrs to his cause, until that he hath secured his redeemed upon earth, and brought them also home to glory. Reader! think of these things, and bless the LORD for such tokens of his love.

12 And I beheld when he had opened the sixth seal, and lo, there was a great earthquake; and the sun became black as sackcloth of hair, and the moon became as blood,

13 And the stars of heaven fell unto the earth, even as a fig tree casteth her untimely figs, when she is shaken of a mighty wind.

14 And the heaven departed as a scrowl, when it is rolled together; and every mountain and island were moved out of their places.

15 And the kings of the earth, and the great men, and the rich men, and the chief captains and the mighty men, and every bondman, and every freeman hid themselves in the dens and in the rocks of the mountains;

16 And said to the mountains and rocks, Fall on us, and hide us from the face of him that sitteth on the throne, and from the wrath of the Lamb;

17 For the great day of his wrath is come: and who shall be able to stand?

Some have thought, that what is here said under the *sixth* seal, hath respect to the final judgment at the great day of GOD. And to be sure, the awful things which are here related, seem, in the first view of the subject, to favor that opinion. But when it be considered, that there is another seal yet remaining to be opened, independently also of what hath not yet been brought forward, of the *Trumpets* and *Vials*, it must at once strike the mind with conviction, that however strong in allusion to the last day, the things here represented may be, it is impossible.

I do not presume upon this, or any other scripture, of doubtful signification, to speak in the least decidedly, but I venture to observe, that as it strikes me, the whole events here represented, in this strong figurative language, was only intended to point out the awful judgments which should take place, under the ministration of the *sixth* seal. According to the general calculation, as to the time of this sixth seal, there had only run out about *three hundred years*, when it was opened. And the Empire now becoming Christian, (that is, in the *profession* of it,) the persecutions which then began against the true Church, though now arising from heresies within, instead of heathenism without, became more dreadful, if possible, than the former. It was somewhat about this period, that arose that heretic *Arius*, denying the GODHEAD of CHRIST; whose baleful influence hath shewed its malignity in every period, from that time to the present. I venture therefore to believe, that what is here said under the several similitudes of an earthquake, the sun becoming black, and the moon as blood, and stars from heaven falling and the like, are intended to set forth the awful event, in a CHRIST-despising doctrine, such as in the present day, the world professing Christianity is remarkable for. And what figures more suited to speak the monstrous baseness and ingratitude in the foul dishonor shewn to the LORD JESUS CHRIST, than, that at the view of which, the sun turns black, and the moon becomes red with blood? And the eventual consequences to the actors of this perfidious treatment of CHRIST, is as finely represented, in that their discovery when too late, of the glory of the LORD JESUS; and as set forth under all the alarms of their guilty souls, in calling to the mountains and the rocks to fall on them, to hide them, if possible, *from the wrath of the Lamb?* According to my view of this scripture, there appears a striking propriety in the whole, and nothing can be more suited to each other, than the guilt and the punishment. But having said thus much, I leave it with the Reader to make his own conclusion, under GOD's teaching.

REFLECTIONS.

METHINKS I would wait in silent humble adoration, while my GOD and SAVIOR opens the seals one by one, to make known to his Church the mysteries of his kingdom. And while I hear the voice of invitation, *Come and see!* oh! for the LORD that calls to give grace also to hear, that I may understand those prophecies of our GOD.

Precious LORD JESUS! Is it not thou that I behold, going forth on the white horse crowned with victory, *conquering, and to conquer?* And do I not hear thee say, and my soul makes her chearful responses to the same; *As for those that will not I should reign over them, bring them hither, and slay them before me!* Yes, LORD, the red horse of blood, and the black horse of famine, and the pale horse of death, with hell in the rear, are suitable to follow in the execution of thy judgments.

I bless my GOD for unfolding to his Church, the precious view of the souls under the Altar, beseeching the LORD, to avenge their blood on their enemies. May I learn many a sweet lesson herefrom! And when at any time, I am impatient under exercises, waiting for answers to prayer, here may I look up and learn, how to explain all seeming difficulties. If JESUS deferred the answer to them, how shall I complain? I here discover, that delay is not denial. There is *a set time to favor Zion*. And learn, O my soul, a sweeter lesson still. *Abel's* blood called for vengeance. The martyrs of my GOD plead to be avenged. But JESUS's blood for mercy. Oh! what a thought, to comfort a poor sinner!

LORD! what an awful account this Chapter closeth with, of those apostates under the *sixth* seal, and every other who deny CHRIST's GODHEAD, and cause even sun, moon, and stars to blush at their foul ingratitude. Surely their judgment is just. For to whom can they look for salvation, while they deny his power who alone can save. Think then my soul of thy safety and happiness, in having Christ for thy portion! Precious Lord Jesus, say to my soul, *fear not, I am thy salvation!*

CHAP. VII.

CONTENTS.

This Chapter opens with an Account of the Sealing of the Servants of God. *The Number sealed! John hath shewn Him an innumerable Multitude, gathered out of all Nations, standing before the Throne. They are described who they are, and how they came there. The Glories of the* Lamb.

AND after these things I saw four angels standing on the four corners of the earth, holding the four winds of the earth, that the wind should not blow on the earth, nor on the sea, nor on any tree.

2 And I saw another angel ascending from the east, having the seal of the living God: and he cried with a loud voice to the four angels to whom it was given to hurt the earth and the sea,

3 ¶ Saying, Hurt not the earth, neither the sea, nor the trees, till we have sealed the servants of our God in their foreheads.

This is a most sweet and interesting Chapter. Between the close of the events of the *sixth* seal, and before the *seventh* seal is opened, the Lord was graciously pleased, to manifest his watchful care over his Church and people, by sealing them. See that blessed scripture, Isaiah xxvii. 3. A new state of things was now to arise. The heathen world, that is, the *Roman Empire,* and called the *world;* Rom. i. 8. Coloss. i. 6. was now under the *sixth* seal become Christian, that is, professing Christianity. A belief in Christ, was now openly avowed. The Emperor himself, professed his faith in Christ. But amidst this national creed, deadly heresies were now arising to afflict the Church. *Arius* had now sprung up with his awful doctrine in denying the Godhead of Christ, though professing his belief in Christ. And under what a variety of different shades hath his heresy, from that hour, to the present appeared, in what is called the *Christian* world? Christian only in name. Reader! pause and adore the Lord for his grace, in causing his Church to be sealed at such a period, as if to say, when errors of a more than ordinary nature are springing up, then the Lord will appear for his people, and have his servants know, how secure they are, for he hath sealed them. And take one thought more with you on the subject. GOD the SPIRIT hath graciously caused this record of the LORD's care over his Church to be handed down through all ages of his Church, as if to say, let this comfort the LORD's people in perilous times, they are also sealed. For as the LORD watched over them *then*, so doth he *now*. And this one record, is in the place of a thousand arguments, to teach the Church these precious truths. Let men or devils rage, at one time more than another, *nevertheless, the foundation of* GOD *standeth sure, having this seal; the* LORD *knoweth them that are his.* 2 Tim. ii. 19. And the sealed servants of the LORD know also whose they are, and to whom they belong. *For after that ye believed,* saith the HOLY GHOST by the Apostle, *ye were sealed with that* HOLY SPIRIT *of promise, which is the earnest of our inheritance.* Ephes. xiii. 14.

By the four Angels which *John* saw, I am not inclined to think any thing particularly is intended from their number. As there are four corners spoken of, and four winds, alluding to the several directions from whence the various winds blow, so it should seem probable, the four in number of Angels, only mean one for each department. But, by the other Angel so called, whom *John* saw ascending from the east, it is evident could mean none, but the LORD JESUS CHRIST; and though here called an Angel, or Messenger of the Covenant, as he is called, Malachi iii. 1. yet the office he is both there and here said to perform, could belong to none but GOD. *Him hath* GOD *the* FATHER *sealed.* John vi. 27. And his office as GOD-Man Mediator, is to seal his people. Indeed, every thing that is here said of him, implies it. His command to the four Angels prove it, being the head of all principality and power, and whom the Angels worship. Col. ii. 10. Heb. i. 6. And his having the seal of the living GOD no less shews it, for who should have the seal or use it, but He who alone was found worthy to open the book, and to loose the seals thereof. Rev. v. 5. He, *who is the brightness of his* FATHER's *glory, and the express image of his Person, and who upholds all things by the word of his power.* Heb. i. 2, 3. And what a volume of the richest blessings, are included in this view of CHRIST sealing his people? I hope the Reader will indulge me, with mentioning a few of the gracious contents.

First. The Person sealing, is the great and leading point to be regarded in this account. And this, as hath before been observed, could be no other than the LORD JESUS CHRIST. And there is a very blessed consideration, connected with this view of CHRIST's sealing his people. It was not to inform him, for all the names of his people are in his book of life. Luke x. 20. Isaiah iv. 3. Philip. iv. 3. Rev. xxi. 27. And his flock must *again pass under his hand.* Jerem. xxxiii. 13. And all he hath received of his FATHER he hath undertaken for. John vi. 37, 38. and John x. 28. But the sealing of his people seems to have been with a special eye to their comfort. It is, as if the LORD had said, behold the love I have for you, I hereby acknowledge you for mine. Isaiah xliii. 1—7.

Secondly. Who they are that are sealed; namely, *the servants of our* GOD. Such, as the LORD by electing grace, chose from all *eternity;* and by sovereign grace, are called in *time.* They were once, when in the *Adam*-nature, servants of sin; but by regenerating grace, are brought into the family of GOD in CHRIST. And because from all eternity they were sons, they received in the fulness of time the call of adoption by the HOLY GHOST, whereby they cry, *Abba* FATHER! Gal. iv. 6. Coloss. i. 12, 13.

Thirdly. This sealing of GOD, not only confirms whose they are, but their high privileges also. Given by the FATHER, betrothed and redeemed by the SON, and regenerated by the HOLY GHOST, they carry about with them, both the *outward* sign of their seal, and the *inward* testimonies in the effect of grace in the heart. For as seals are worn in sight, and rings on the finger, are tokens to bring to remembrance the friend or giver, so, the sealed soul makes manifest, by every suitable and becoming testimony, his love and attachment to JESUS. *I have set the* LORD (said one of old) *always before me. He is on my right hand, I shall not be moved.* Psm. xxvi. 8. And the child of GOD desires, that CHRIST shall have the whole affections of the heart. The LORD JESUS, may be supposed to have all these things, and much more in view, when he called to his Church and said, *Set me as a seal upon thine heart, as a seal upon thine arm, for love is strong as death, jealousy is cruel as the grave, the coals thereof are coals of fire, which have a most vehement flame.* Song viii. 6.

Fourthly. There is somewhat very expressive, in what is said in the place of sealing; namely, in their foreheads, that is, it shall be open and not concealed. The world shall know whose they are. And although the marking here made, was intended as preparatory to very awful times coming on, yet, GOD would have his people known. Their seal shall be in their foreheads. Now, as the *Arian* heresy was then opening, and beginning to shed its baleful influence, and GOD would bring his redeemed out of great tribulation, (as verse the *fourteenth* sheweth,) it should seem to be very plain, that this sealing took place chiefly, if not altogether, to guard against this most awful heresy, which however little thought of by some, and considered as of small moment with others, will be found a much greater apostacy, than the religion of the beast, or the false prophet. The GODHEAD of CHRIST is the whole bottom and foundation of the faith. The man that denies this, may as well relinquish all that belongs beside to Christianity, for there is nothing left worth retaining. And tremendously awful will be the state of all such at the last day. I would say to every one, under this awful delusion, as *Tertullian* did to *Marcion*, whom he called the Murderer of Truth; Spare said he, the only hope of the whole world! But blessed be GOD, the hand of man might sooner snatch the sun of the natural world from its orb, than take JESUS the Sun of Righteousness from the firmament of his scripture, by denying his GODHEAD, neither would the darkness of the former be half so great as the latter.

I need not dwell long on that part of those verses, by way of explaining, which speaks of not hurting *the earth, or the sea, or the trees.* These are well known to be figurative expressions. Winds imply wars. And the earth seas, and trees mean people. And the winds or wars, are said to be held until GOD hath secured his people. Thus, in the days of *Noah,* before the Ark was ready to receive the Church, the fountains of the great deep were not broken up. These waters were restrained, as those winds are said to be held. But, as soon as *Noah* and his family were housed in the Ark, the deluge followed. Gen. vii. 1—16. In like manner by *Lot.* Yea, to shew the LORD's watchful eye over his people, the LORD said to *Lot, haste thee and escape thither, for I cannot do any thing, till thou be come thither.* Gen. xix. 22—25. Reader! depend upon it, the same is now, as much carrying on, as then. GOD's care over his people, cannot for a moment cease. Sweetly the HOLY GHOST saith by *Peter, Casting all your care upon him, for he careth for you!* 1 Pet. v. 7. Yea, the LORD saith by Moses, *he loveth the people, all his saints are in his hand.* Deut. xxxiii. 3. The Church is *engraven on the palms of his hands, her walls are continually before him.* Isaiah xlix. 16. And it must be so. For GOD the FATHER hath given the Church to CHRIST. JESUS hath taken the Church into union with himself. He hath loved her with an everlasting love. He hath given himself for her, he hath died for her, he hath washed her in his blood, and the HOLY GHOST hath sealed her to the day of redemption. One of the Prophets felt the strength of these blessed truths so forcibly, that under the impression he cried out, *the* LORD *is good, a strong hold* (or strength itself) *in the day of trouble, and he knoweth them that trust in him.* Nahum i. 7.

4 ¶ And I heard the number of them which were sealed: *and there were* sealed an hundred *and* forty *and* four thousand of all the tribes of the children of Israel.

5 Of the tribe of Juda *were* sealed twelve thousand. Of the tribe of Reuben *were* sealed twelve thousand. Of the tribe of Gad *were* sealed twelve thousand.

6 Of the tribe of Aser *were* sealed twelve thousand. Of the tribe of Nepthalim *were* sealed twelve thousand. Of the tribe of Manasses *were* sealed twelve thousand.

7 Of the tribe of Simeon *were* sealed twelve thousand. Of the tribe of Levi *were* sealed twelve thousand. Of the tribe of Issachar *were* sealed twelve thousand.

8 Of the tribe of Zabulon *were* sealed twelve thousand. Of the tribe of Joseph *were* sealed twelve thousand. Of the tribe of Benjamin *were* sealed twelve thousand.

I do not presume to speak decidedly on the subject, when I say, in relation to the number *John* saw sealed, that by the hundred and forty and four thousand of all the tribes of Israel, is not meant exactly twelve thousand of a tribe, and no more, and all the tribes the same, but the sense is, that as twelve is what is called a square number, and the square root of it, when multiplied by itself, must for ever produce the same; so the whole is put here in one determinate number, to intimate the LORD's knowing, numbering, and sealing every one. The HOLY GHOST, by his servant the Prophet, had said, ages before the coming of CHRIST, *that though the people of Israel be as the sand of the sea, yet a remnant of them shall return; the consumption decreed shall overflow with righteousness.* Isaiah x. 22. And the LORD the SPIRIT, by his servant the Apostle, was graciously pleased to remind the Church of this declaration of his, and thereby to keep the expectation of its accomplishment alive in the hearts of his people. See Rom. ix. 27, 28. Here, then, once more, *John* is brought to see the servants of the LORD, in the tribes of Israel, sealed, as if to confirm the blessed assurance, that, as the HOLY GHOST was now about to close the sacred volume of scripture, the Church of GOD might have these things in remembrance, looking forward to the last days events in the earth, when the whole should be accomplished.

Reader! ponder well the thought, for it is blessed. We live in a day approaching to the accomplishment of all the great events prophesied concerning the Church. Sweet is that promise, *He that scattered Israel, will gather him, and keep him as a shepherd doth his flock.* Jer. xxxi. 10. There shall be a day, it is said, *when the Deliverer shall come out of Zion, and turn away ungodliness from Jacob.* Rom. xi. 26. And who shall say where, and in what countries is Israel scattered? Who shall say their number, or count them up by their tribes? *By whom shall Jacob arise, for he is small?* JESUS hath blessedly said, and that's enough to comfort the whole Church of GOD concerning it, that *he will gather his elect from the four winds, from the uttermost part of the earth to the uttermost part of heaven.* Mark xiii. 27. If the Reader wishes to have his soul refreshed with a view of some of the sweet promises concerning this glorious event, he will find a multitude of them in the Bible. Isaiah xliii. 5, 6. Isa. liv. 7. Jer. xxxi. 8. Ezek. xi. 17. Micah iv. Zeph. iii. Zech. x. &c.

In going over the names of the several tribes of Israel, here mentioned, I beg the Reader to notice with particular attention, that *Judah*, though not the eldest of *Jacob's* sons, is first mentioned. I do not here again speak decidedly, but I am inclined to think that precedency was given to this tribe, because our LORD sprang out of Judah. Heb. vii. 14. And very blessed was the dying Patriarch's prophecy to this amount. *Judah! thou art he whom thy brethren shall praise; thy hand shall be in the neck of thine enemies; thy father's children shall bow down before thee.* Gen. xlix. 8. It is blessed to eye CHRIST in every thing, and honor given for CHRIST in all things.

And I would make one observation more respecting those tribes of Israel. If the Reader will consult the Old Testament, concerning the twelve tribes of *Israel*, and compare it with the number here, he will find, that though here are indeed *twelve* tribes enumerated, in correspondence to the number of the sons of *Jacob*, yet one of

Jacob's sons is not mentioned, even *Dan;* whose place is supplied with *Manasses,* one of the sons of *Joseph,* though *Joseph* himself, as a tribe, is also in the number. Various have been the opinions of men concerning it, though the HOLY GHOST is silent upon it. Some have thought it was because the tribe of *Dan* apostatized, in the instance of the idols of *Jeroboam.* 1 Kings xii. 26—30. But, I confess, that this opinion doth not satisfy me. We find the *Danites,* in the days of the Judges, setting up a graven image; and at that time the sons of *Manasseh,* even *Jonathan, the son of Gershom, and his sons,* became the priests of this idol. And yet the tribe of *Manasseh* is among the sealed, though *Dan* is not. This, I think, therefore, cannot be the reason. Judges xviii. 30. *Ephraim,* also, is omitted in this sealing. And the same reason is assigned. By the Prophet *Hosea,* the LORD indeed said, *Ephraim is joined to idols; let him alone.* Hosea iv. 17. But, we find, fourscore years after this, (for so much time had run out between the ministry of *Hosea,* and that of *Jeremiah,*) the LORD, by the latter Prophet, said of *Ephraim, Is Ephraim my dear Son? is he a pleasant child? for since I spake against him, I do earnestly remember him still; therefore my bowels are troubled for him; I will surely have mercy upon him, saith the* LORD. Jer. xxxi. 20. I cannot venture, therefore, to conclude, that those are the reasons. But, if the Reader wishes me to go further, and assign a cause. This I dare not. The HOLY GHOST is silent upon it. I presume, therefore, not to speak upon it. *Dan* is omitted. And we learn from it a solemn truth. And it is our duty to have it in remembrance. What the HOLY GHOST hath said, upon another occasion, meets us here, *If* GOD *spared not the natural branches, take heed lest he also spare not thee.* Rom. xi. 21. If the tribe of *Dan* had then none to seal, what a breaking off was here! And if on the great day of GOD, when the *number of the children of Israel shall be as the sand of the sea, and a remnant shall be brought forth, both sons and daughters;* and that great purpose of GOD is seen, he hath declared what a manifestation will then be made of *the remnant, according to the election of grace?* Very blessed to this point, is that most gracious scripture, *Yet, behold, saith the* LORD, *therein shall be left a remnant, that shall be brought forth, both sons and daughters; behold, they shall come forth unto you, and ye shall see their way, and their doings; and ye shall be comforted, concerning the evil that I have brought upon Jerusalem, even concerning all that I have brought upon it. And they shall comfort you, when ye see their ways, and their doings; and ye shall know that I have not done without cause all that I have done, saith the* LORD GOD. Ezek. xiv. 22, 23.

When the Reader hath made his full observations on this part of the sealing of the tribes of *Israel,* I beg to propose another consideration to him, of a very sweet and refreshing kind, as it strikes my view on the subject, namely, how very gracious and timely it was, thus to seal the Church, before those awful days came on, which we know followed in the persecutions of the people; I mean, not only generally so to the Church at large, but specially with an eye to the LORD's people, the Jews.

In order for the better apprehension of the subject, I would have the Reader connect with it what we now know. Many hundred years have run out since that period. The children of GOD were then beginning, but as it were, to be scattered, to what they have been since. The LORD's antient people, the Jews, had not been driven from their beloved *Jerusalem*, comparatively speaking, but a short space, to what was to run out, before they were to be again called home. The great power that was now arising in the *East*, under the false Prophet, was to take into the different branches of that vast empire, multitudes of the dispersed of Israel. And as that power still remains, and so many ages and generations were to expire, during *Israel's* subjugation, what a mercy was it to the Church thus to be taught, in this vision shewn *John;* that notwithstanding all outward appearances, the LORD had marked, and knoweth them that are his. Let the Reader duly observe this, and notice GOD's love to his Church, in the appointment. And then let him go on to another observation.

CHRIST, the angel *John* saw, coming to seal his people, was beheld by him ascending from the *East*. Surely, this ascension from the East, plainly pointed, as with a finger, that the great cause for which the Church, in the tribes of Israel, was now sealed, was in allusion to the affairs of the Church in the *East*. And, as much about this time, under the *sixth* seal, and before the *seventh* should be opened, the false prophet would arise, and extend his vast empire over the *East;* here the Jews would be scattered in abundance, and therefore the LORD's mark should be upon them. Who shall calculate the number of *Israel* to this hour, which have been, and yet remain, from the time of *John's* vision, through a period of seventeen centuries? We are not come down yet, in our progress through this book of prophecy, to the season of the Trumpets; but we may in this place observe, for the better apprehension of the whole, (which the distant age we live in to that of *John's*, gives us the advantage to form our conclusions upon) that, as we are now, in point of time, under the influence of the *sixth* trumpet, we can discover much of what was prophesied under the *sixth seal*. Who shall say, therefore, how many of his sealed ones, from those regions in the vast empire under the false prophet, the LORD hath been gathering home, from age to age, even to the present hour? When we consider that the awful delusion of *Mahometan* imposture extends its baleful influence over the vast empire, in the East, of *Indostan, Persia, Turkey, Morocco*, we may reasonably conclude, that this sealing, which *John* saw in a vision, was meant to comfort the Church with those views. And, Reader, what an amazing bringing back to the Church, from those regions, will it be, when the LORD shall cause the *seventh Trumpet* to be sounded, and when those voices will be heard in the Church, saying, *the kingdoms of this world are become the kingdoms of our* LORD, *and of his* CHRIST, *and he shall reign for ever and ever ?* Rev. xi. 15.

† But, though I have just glanced at these things, we must not altogether anticipate the history in bringing them forward here. They will meet us in their proper place. In the mean time, it is sufficient for the present to observe, that the LORD was pleased to shew his servant *John*, by vision, in the interval between the *sixth* and *seventh* seal, how safe and secure his redeemed of Israel are. The LORD hath sealed them, and owned them as his. And thus *John's* mind must have been very graciously relieved from the awful persecutions

he was called upon to notice, when the seventh seal came to be opened.

9 After this I beheld, and, lo, a great multitude, which no man could number, of all nations, and kindreds, and people, and tongues, stood before the throne, and before the Lamb, clothed with white robes, and palms in their hands;

10 And cried with a loud voice, saying, Salvation to our God which sitteth upon the throne, and unto the Lamb.

11 And all the angels stood round about the throne, and *about* the elders and the four beasts, and fell before the throne on their faces, and worshipped God.

12 Saying, Amen: Blessing, and glory, and wisdom, and thanksgiving, and honour, and power, and might, *be* unto our God for ever and ever. Amen.

If we admire, as that we cannot but admire, and at the same time bless GOD for the gracious manifestation made to *John*, for the Church's consolation, in the foregoing representation of GOD's care over his tribes of Israel, in sealing them; with what thankfulness ought we, of the Gentile Church, to bless GOD for the discovery made here, of the innumerable body of CHRIST's members, gathered out of all the varieties of the earth. Here is evidently the whole Church of CHRIST, beheld by *John* in a vision, even the bride, the LAMB's wife. Such, as will be seen in reality, in that day when the LORD will make up his jewels. And it should seem to have been intended by way of confirmation, through the medium of *John*, to convince the Church, by so plain and palpable a testimony, that both Jew and Gentile form but one and the same Church in CHRIST. They are no more than one. So saith CHRIST, and blessed it is to know it. *My dove, my undefiled, is but one; she is the only one of her mother; she is the choice one of her that bare her.* Song vi. 9. And this seems to have been particularly designed also for the greater joy of the Church, through *John*; because, as *John* had seen CHRIST *seal* Israel, and nothing had then been said, concerning the sealing of the Gentile Church; here his mind should be refreshed immediately upon, with the representation of the whole Church, both Jew and Gentile, when brought home to glory. Instead of *sealing*, which was a most gracious act, before a time of persecution, *John* shall now see the whole Church after all sorrows are over, when *palms of victory*, and *white robes*, shall shew, that their troubles are ended. And, instead of an hundred and forty and four thousand of *Israel* only, he shall behold a multitude of all Israel, Jew and Gentile, which no man could number; to shew, that CHRIST's triumphs shall bear a suitable correspondence to the Almightiness of his Person and offices; *nations*, that is, some of all nations, *shall be blessed in him, and* all nations *shall call him blessed*.

The best service I can render the Reader, in looking together with him over this most precious scripture, will be, I conceive, to gather out some few of the more special and leading particulars of it, and one by one, offer some remarks, as may be supposed, were particularly intended for them.

And, *first*. John observes, that this blessed society he saw consisted of a multitude, which no man could number. Such views give us a most pleasing consideration, that although the Church of Christ, compared to the world of ungodly, is but as the remnant of *Jacob*, in the midst of many people, and therefore called, by Christ himself, *a little flock:* Luke xii. 32. yet, when the whole redeemed of the Lord comes to be gathered into one, they will form an immense body, and such a multitude as no man can number. Paul, speaking of the Church, saith: *ye are come to an innumerable company of Angels*. Heb. xii. 22, 23. And our Lord himself speaks of his mansions in his Father's house, as *being many*. John xiv. 2. But, it is a blessed thought, that though no man could number them, Jesus can. All his flocks must again pass under *the hand of him that telleth them*. Jerem. xxxiii. 13. All the Father hath given him, *shall come to him*. John vi. 37. Jesus hath all their names in *his book of life*. Rev. xxi. 27. And he saith, that as a good Shepherd, *he calleth them all by name*. John x. 3. Sweet thought, to the least, and weakest lamb, in Christ's fold! However unknown, or unnoticed by the flock, the Great Shepherd both knoweth them, calleth them by name, feedeth them, watcheth over them, and will bring them home to his fold. As it was in coming out of *Egypt*, so it will be in bringing in to heaven; not an hoof belonging to God's Israel will the Lord leave behind.

Secondly. This multitude is to be gathered out of all *nations, and kindreds, and people, and tongues*. And consequently, Christ hath a people in all places; otherwise they could not be said to be gathered out. Here opens a most blessed subject to contemplate. And, I very particularly desire the Reader to bear with me, and hear me with patience, upon this very interesting subject. I find cause to bless God, for what he hath here said of the *Gentile* Church in this place, as I no less would bless him, for what he had before said and done, in *sealing* the *Jewish* Church; for I confess, that I am inclined to think, that in both instances, there was a special design of the Lord in it. I beg indulgence to explain myself.

By *sealing* Israel, before their long oppressed state, under the despotism and delusion of the false prophet in the East, took place, we have seen the watchful eye of God over his Church. And by this further manifestation to *John*, concerning the whole Church, both Jew and Gentile, we no less see, how the Lord hath secured the present, and everlasting interests of all his people. But under both we are led to conclude, that both Jew and Gentile were alike to be gathered from the varieties of the earth. What a thought it is, that the seed of Christ should be thus dispersed over the whole world! And what a thought again follows upon the heels of the former, like wave after wave, in the sea; how the Lord's purposes are accomplished. *His thoughts not our thoughts, neither his ways our ways!* I cannot but admire this plan of infinite wisdom the more, because, for all the *eastern* world there is no prophecy in this whole book of the Revelation, except in this part. Surely, one might suppose, in so large a tract of the inhabited globe, some respect would be had, in a book of this kind, to those who peopled the *East;* and especially, as it was in the East that all the glorious transactions, of man's recovery from the fall, by Christ, was accomplished. But without an eye to what is here said, as referring to them, we have none. From the subsequent parts of those prophecies, to the end of the ruin of Antichrist, every thing that is said, refers to the *Western* world. Hence, therefore, this becomes a precious testimony to the recovery, in after days, of the Lord's appearing for his people. This view was evidently designed to shew the Church, that God hath sealed Israel; and that, from hence also, his Gentile Church should arise; and both be fully known to be the Lord's, when the purposes of God were accomplished.

I would beg to add one word more, upon this gathering of Christ's Church from the varieties of the earth; namely, how blessedly it teacheth us of the safety of God's children, wheresoever they are. Jesus hath marked his sheep. And he will assuredly bring them all home to his fold. Let no child of God, therefore, ever despond, from any situation, or exercise of life. *As the day is, the strength shall be.* Thousands now in glory, were once, when upon earth, encompassed, as we are, with difficulties, and exercised with temptations. They who have entered into rest, have triumphed over all. If the poor, tried, tempted, and exercised child of God, here upon earth, could see the multitude now before the throne, and could hear their account of the Lord's grace, concerning them, while here below; how would it animate, and encourage his mind? He would learn, that what he now feels, they once felt; what he encounters, they once endured. These things would help him, through grace, to go on. And, being encompassed with so great a cloud of witnesses, he would lay aside every weight, and the sin which doth so easily beset him, and run with patience the race that is set before him, looking unto Jesus, *the Author, and Finisher of his salvation!* Heb. xii. 1, 2.

Thirdly. There is one feature more of this multitude *John* saw, which is strikingly descriptive. They are said to have been *standing before the throne, and before the Lamb!* Here we plainly discover, that the throne of God is one, and that Jesus is in the midst of the throne. And we no less discover, from what is said of the Church standing before the throne, that this is both the everlasting safety, and the everlasting happiness of the redeemed. It is our distance from this throne of God, which is the sad cause of all our misery. We live below our privileges. We have too little actings of faith upon the Person of Christ Jesus. *Perfect love casteth out fear.* If we love Christ because he first loved us, we shall soon apprehend the blessedness of always living to him, and living upon him. *In his presence is fulness of joy, and at his right hand are pleasures for evermore!*

Fourthly. They are said to *be clothed with white robes, and palms in their hands.* Intimating that they *had* overcome by the blood of the Lamb, and were therefore crowned with the emblems of victory. There is somewhat very interesting in this account. Jesus hath made all his redeemed kings and priests, to God, and the Father; therefore, as such, they stand before him, both in their royal, and priestly garments. But the sweetest view is, that these robes of white, implied both their sanctity in Christ, and their everlasting freedom from all sin. Oh! the unspeakable felicity of such a state of holiness and sanctification, and that for ever in Christ?

Fifthly. Their hymn of praise is beautiful. *Salvation to our God which sitteth upon the throne, and unto the Lamb.* Let the Reader from hence observe, how the Church gives her acknowledgments unitedly to all the Persons of the Godhead, as being the joint Authors of all her mercies in redemption. And, when it be considered, that all the Persons of the Godhead alike concurred in that vast design, the song of tribute becomes sweet, and suitable, in being addressed to the Holy Three in One. God the Father set forth Christ as a propitiation through faith in his blood. God the Son gave himself an offering, and a sacrifice to God, for a sweet swelling savor. And God the Holy Ghost, through whom that offering was made, is the great cause of regeneration, in making the redeemed the happy partakers, by grace, of those unspeakable mercies. Hence the song of salvation to God, that is, Father, Son, and Holy Ghost, as God; and the Lamb, that is, the God-Man Mediator, Christ Jesus.

Sixthly, Though the Angels are said to fall before the throne on their faces, and to have worshipped God, saying *Amen;* yet they sung not of their salvation; for having, through God's grace, kept their first estate, they needed not salvation. But only as participating in the joy of the Church of God, and rejoicing in the glories of the Lord, they enter with an holy ardor of affection, into all that belongs to the Church's welfare, and therefore, put their hearty *Amen* to the heavenly hymn. And the sevenfold praise that follows, is descriptive both of their views of God's glory, and their happiness in it. *Blessings* say they, for God is blessed in himself, and blessed in his Church and people; yea, is their blessedness, and the fountain of all blessedness. And *Glory,* because God is the glory of his people. His glory is in himself, and of himself; and his glory is great, in the salvation by Christ. Psm. xxi. 5. *Wisdom,* is another of his distinguishing attributes, and most eminently displayed in the salvation by Christ. For Christ himself is both *the wisdom of God, and the power of God to salvation.* 1 Cor. i. 24. *Thanksgiving:* most suitably is this added, for if heaven, in the hierarchies of the place, could be supposed possible to be silent in the contemplation of God's love to the Church, in all that relates to it, the very stones of the earth might be supposed to cry out. *Honor* is also brought into the vast account. For as God, he is to be honored; and as God in Christ, to be everlastingly beheld as the sole source of all honor; and the Lord will take to himself honor, in the destruction of all the foes of our salvation. *Power* is eminently displayed in salvation, since nothing but the wisdom of God could have contrived it, and nothing but the power of God accomplished it. And *Might,* to bear up the whole government, in all the departments of nature, providence, grace, and glory. Well might the heavenly host, therefore, catch fire at the Church's song, and join in, with all their powers, to swell the loud Chorus of praises to God and the Lamb. Reader! shall you and I join our feeble notes to the same? Yes! if so be we know that we have redemption through Christ's blood, even the forgiveness of sins according to the riches of his grace.

13 And one of the elders answered, saying unto me, What are these which are arrayed in white robes? and whence came they?

14 And I said unto him, Sir, thou knowest. And he said to me, These are they which came out of great tribulation, and have washed their robes, and made them white in the blood of the Lamb.

15 Therefore are they before the throne of God, and serve him day and night in his temple; and he that sitteth on the throne shall dwell among them.

16 They shall hunger no more, neither thirst any more; neither shall the sun light on them, nor any heat.

17 For the Lamb which is in the midst of the throne shall feed them, and shall lead them unto living fountains of waters: and God shall wipe away all tears from their eyes.

This is as beautiful and interesting a part as any, of the whole vision. We may suppose, that the mind of *John* was wrapt up in the most profound meditation, as he looked on, and heard, and stood, like one amazed, at what he saw. One of the Elders, therefore, interpreting by *John's* looks, that he longed to enter into a perfect apprehension of the whole, put the question to him, which *John* perhaps would himself, had he presumed, have ventured to ask: *What are these things which are arrayed in white robes? and whence came they?* And the Elder, answering his own question, for *John* and the Church's information, is most gracious. And is, if I mistake not, in direct reference to the Church of God in the *East,* particularly at the time now coming on. And, though I do not presume to suppose, yea, I think the contrary, but that the Church in all ages may be referred to; yet, as this vision was given in a very particular manner, for the comfort of the Church *then,* when the *seventh seal* should open, I do conceive, that *those* here mentioned, as coming out of great tribulation, were those gathered more especially from the *Eastern* part of the world, from among the dominions under *Mahometan* delusion, and had a primary respect to them.

And, I will venture to go further, under an humble hope, that I do not err in the relation, and say, that now in the day in which

I am writing these observations, even in the day and year of our LORD GOD April 1, 1816, I do well remember the return of a godly man from the *Turkish* dominions, during the late war, who had formerly been a member of the Church of GOD to which I belong, and having been called into *Egypt*, there found other godly persons, sent upon a similar occasion of war, with himself; and who, having formed meetings together for sacred worship, had the pleasure to find some from among the inhabitants of that city, who came and joined their services. A plain proof, that GOD's people are scattered; and that JESUS hath his people, whom he is calling from the *East* as well as the *West*, and the *North*, and the *South*. And, oh! what a multitude will arise, from all those different corners of the earth, at the last day, when JESUS shall send his angels to call them home! Though they are now separated by distant seas and climes, though diversified by customs and manners; yet CHRIST, the desire of his people in all nations, hath in all nations a people that serve him: and of all these it will be found, that as the FATHER hath given them to his SON, so all shall come to him; and nothing shall separate the members from the glorious Head of his body the Church, *who filleth all in all.*

I must not trespass too largely, but otherwise the subject is as extensive as it is great, and as interesting as it is beautiful. The Elder that put the question to *John*, answered it himself. He gives an account of their persons, their former state, their present felicity, with the source of all their happiness in CHRIST, and the everlasting home of blessedness, to which they are brought, in the service of GOD and the Lamb, for ever. If the Reader will indulge me with a few outlines, I hope the LORD may make them profitable.

First. They are said *to have come out of great tribulation*. Though it may be safely said, that the Church of CHRIST, in all ages, more or less, come out of great tribulation; for CHRIST himself hath made it a mark of Sonship, that in the world his disciples shall have tribulation, while in him they have peace; John xvi. 33. yet those times which followed the sealing, between the *sixth* and *seventh* seals, were eminently marked with persecutions. The history of the Church, which relates to us the dreadful ravages made by the sword of the false prophet and his followers at that time, most plainly prove it. And indeed, what was the sealing of the hundred and forty and four thousand intended for, but as the LORD's token of love to his Church, before the coming on of those persecutions? Reader! mark then, this first feature in the LORD's people. *They have come out of great tribulation*. Every child of GOD knows somewhat of this, if not from the open persecution of the world, yet from *the plague of his own heart*. It is blessed to know the tribulation from this quarter, in order to endear CHRIST. Till we know somewhat of our own wretchedness, we think lightly of his righteousness.

Secondly. They are said *to have washed their robes, and made them white in the blood of the Lamb*. Reader! I pray you, mark well what is here said. They come out of great tribulation. But that was no cause of their acceptance before GOD. They had white robes, and palms in their hands. But the *former* were not made white by their washing, nor the *latter* put into their hands for their victory. No washing of their's, no sacrifice, no blood of bulls, or of goats; no merits, no works of their's, which they had done; not an atom of their's contributed to it: but it was the blood of the Lamb, the blood of JESUS CHRIST, GOD's dear SON, in which their robes were washed; and *therefore*, that is, for that very cause, and that alone, they were before the throne of GOD, and served him in his temple day and night.

And under this particular, I beseech the Reader to remark yet further, that it is their *robes* which they are said to have washed. Not their sins only, but their robes, that is, their very best things. For a man's robes are his best things. And what may we suppose is implied in their best things, but their best prayers, their best deeds, their most holy services, their LORD's day robes, their ordinance robes, their sacramental robes, their holy conversation robes. All need washing. All must be washed and made white, in the blood of the Lamb, or all become offensive before GOD. Nothing but the blood of the Lamb, can make holy before GOD, neither any but the Person and righteousness of the LORD JESUS justify in GOD's sight. It is in Him and Him only, the Church of GOD find access here in grace or hereafter in glory. He hath made us *accepted in the Beloved*. Ephes. i. 6.

Thirdly. Let our next view of this sweet subject be, to contemplate the blessed consequences which follow. Having looked at them in their Persons, *being washed, being sanctified, being justified in the name of the* LORD JESUS, *and by the* SPIRIT *of our* GOD; let us hear the Elders account to *John* of the blessedness of their *station*. 1 Cor. vi. 11. *They are before the throne of* GOD. They have the immediate enjoyment of GOD and the LAMB. *Here* it is in grace. *Above* it is in glory. *Here*, they enjoy that presence by faith. *There*, in sight. *Here*, in part. *There*, in a fulness of joy at GOD's right hand for evermore.

Moreover, they are described in their *service* of GOD before his throne *night and day*. We know not what the blessedness of such services consist in. We must be endowed with the faculties of the redeemed in glory, to speak of their employments. But we can, in some measure, conceive, what glory must continually pour in upon the soul, when no fleshly corruptions, any longer arise to interrupt spiritual pleasure. We can, and do now at times, for a short moment, when grace is in lively exercise, feel ourselves as in the suburbs of heaven, in contemplating GOD and the LAMB. Sweet and precious, though rare and short, those holy seasons are. But what must it be, when the disembodied spirit of a redeemed regenerated child of GOD, shall join the spirits of just men made perfect, and is fully come not by faith, but by sight, to JESUS *the Mediator of the New Covenant, and to* GOD *the judge of all?*

Fourthly. The Elder added another information, by way of heightening to *John's* view the unspeakable blessedness of the redeemed; namely, that *He that sitteth on the throne, shall dwell among them.* GOD's presence among his people, is the superlative degree of all happiness and glory. Even here on earth, it is the sweetner of all blessings. Where JESUS is, there is blessedness. No blessing void of him can be called a blessing. Hence, for the want of CHRIST it is, that so many aching hearts are in fine houses, while on the contrary, where JESUS is, however poor and humble, the LORD brings all blessedness with him. And what then must it be in heaven, where the immediate presence of GOD and the LAMB, forms the very heaven to the soul? When *John* heard a great voice out of heaven, speaking of peculiar blessedness to the Church, it was to say, behold! *the tabernacle of* GOD *is with men, and he will dwell with them, and they shall be his people; and* GOD *himself shall be with them, and be their* GOD! Rev. xxi. 3.

Fifthly. The blessedness of their state is further described, in their being for ever exempt from *hunger and thirst*, and a compleat freedom from *sickness*, or the pressure of the *sun's heat*. They are brought into that happy climate, *where none of the inhabitants shall any longer say I am sick, for the people that dwell therein shall be forgiven their iniquity.* Isaiah xxxiii. 24. It is blessed here upon earth, to have tasted the heavenly manna, even CHRIST's body the bread of life, spiritual hunger is then satisfied with CHRIST. And when the LORD JESUS gives of the water of life freely, this becomes in the spirit, a well of water springing up to everlasting life. The child of GOD which daily feeds upon JESUS, will hunger no more after the empty, unsatisfying husks of this world. But in heaven, what unspeakable felicity must it be, to have CHRIST for our portion, and to live upon him for ever!

Sixthly. There is somewhat peculiarly sweet and endearing in this whole account, in calling the LORD JESUS the LAMB. There can be no doubt, but that the personal glory of the LORD JESUS, is intended by it. The HOLY GHOST delights in holding up to the Church the Person of her LORD. The inherent holiness of CHRIST, and the personal purity of CHRIST, in that pure portion of our nature, taken into union with the GODHEAD; underived as it was from all created power, possesseth in itself an holiness infinitely beyond the holiness of Angels. For though the Angels which are *Elect* Angels, are kept from sinning, yet this is by election. Their nature, without that electing and preserving grace, being in itself necessarily changeable, as all created excellence must be, would be necessarily subject to fall. And that they do not fall, is wholly to be ascribed to election. For those Angels which were not Elect, have fallen. And hence it is said, GOD *putteth no trust in his servants, and even his Angels he chargeth with folly;* that is, with a weakness capable of sinning. Job iv. 18. But CHRIST in that holy portion of human nature, he took into union with himself, is said to be *holy, harmless, undefiled, separate from sinners, and made higher than the heavens;* that is, higher than Angels, being the uncreated WORD. Heb. vii. 26. John i. 1.

It is on this account, if I do not greatly mistake, that the HOLY GHOST so often dwells in this Book on this expression, when speaking of CHRIST in calling him *the Lamb*. And there are numberless beauties in the name, as it concerns the LORD's Church and People. To mention only a few. *First.* It hath a sweet and sacred allusion to GOD the FATHER's decree, when CHRIST in our nature, was set up from everlasting. Hence he is called in this Book, *the* LAMB *slain from the foundation of the world.* Rev. xiii. 8. And hence also in reference to the same, the names of his people are said to be written, in the LAMB's *book of life.* Rev. xxi. 27.

Secondly. Through all the old Testament scripture, when the HOLY GHOST speaks of the LORD JESUS, under the meekness and gentleness of his character, it is as *the Lamb.* Hence by the Prophet, he is said to have been led *as a Lamb to the slaughter, and as a sheep before his shearers is dumb, so he openeth not his mouth.* Isaiah liii. 7. And no less in the New Testament dispensation, GOD the HOLY GHOST, by the mouth of his servant *John* the *Baptist,* calls upon the Church to behold him, under this endearedness of character. *For looking upon* JESUS *as he passed, he said, Behold the* LAMB *of* GOD! *which taketh away the sins of the world.* John i. 29—36.

Thirdly. GOD the HOLY GHOST never loseth sight of the same, by way of holding up to the Church's view, the personal holiness of the LORD, for when JESUS returned to his exalted state, still it is the LAMB. He, who was, and is the LAMB, *slain before the foundation of the world;* was, and is the LAMB *as had been slain,* which John saw, in *the midst of the throne.* Rev. v. 6. And now again in this vision, as *in the midst of the throne, feeding the Church, leading them to living fountains of waters, and wiping away all tears from their eyes.*

Reader! do not too hastily pass away from those views. The subject is too precious, too blessed to be so treated. Methinks I should like to dwell upon it for ever. LORD the SPIRIT! I would say, give me grace to follow the LAMB whithersoever he goeth. Let my soul gaze upon him by faith, and feed on him in spirit, as my passover sacrificed for my sins. That while JESUS feeds my soul, my soul may feast upon his blood and righteousness, and as JESUS hath said, *he that eateth me, shall live by me.* John vi. 57.

One view of CHRIST, as the Lamb in the midst of the throne, is so blessed, so gracious, and so delightful, for the faithful to meditate upon, that I would very earnestly, and very affectionately recommend it to every true follower of the LORD, as an effectual antidote against the poisonous breath of those men, who think lightly of our LORD, in this present CHRIST-despising generation. I mean, in that his being in the midst of the throne, must imply his GODHEAD. What can CHRIST be in the midst of the throne, and yet not GOD? Is there a hardened mind upon earth, so desperately bent to allow the one, and yet deny the other. Oh! how will such men turn into everlasting paleness, and an horrible dread overwhelm them, when they shall see our JESUS in the midst of the throne, where he now is, and the heavens passing away before his presence with a great noise, and the earth and all that is in it, burnt up.

Oh! the blessedness to GOD's people. Your GOD, your JESUS, is in the midst of the throne. And to you it is a throne of grace, where you are sure *to obtain mercy and grace, to help in all time of need.* It is to you a throne of justice also, where the LAMB is in the midst. For he hath satisfied justice, answered all the demands of the law, silenced all the accusations of Satan against his people, and reigns and rules in his throne of righteousness, to see all the merits of his blood, compleatly answered in blessings to his Church and people. And to you it is a throne of glory, for *the* LORD *that gives grace, will give glory;* and it is CHRIST's own glory which is concerned to see, that *the travail of his soul shall be satisfied,* for *in bringing many sons unto glory,* it behoved JESUS, as the Captain of our salvation, to be *made perfect through suffering.* Reader! shall you and I go to this throne, now JESUS is in the midst of it? Every way, and in every direction, it is open to poor sinners, behind and before, for CHRIST the Lamb slain is in the midst of the throne.

And how he feeds his people, here in grace, and there in glory; surely, every regenerated child of GOD cannot but know. Himself is the whole of our food. By faith, at his house, at his table, in ordinances and means of grace, all spiritual partakers truly eat of his flesh, and drink of his blood. And they find, by soul experience, what the LORD hath said, that *his flesh is meat indeed, and his blood drink indeed.* John vi. 55. And wherefore should it be questioned? If animal life is supported day by day, from the sustenance received in the bread which perisheth with using, shall it be thought incredible, that spiritual life is kept up and maintained, in constant supplies of grace and strength, from the bread of life which is JESUS himself, in the continued communications the LORD makes of himself to his people. Precious LAMB of GOD, that art in the midst of the throne! do thou, while giving out glory to thy redeemed above, feed with grace thy Church below. For surely, LORD, they are equally dear to thee, by every tye which can make them so, by thy FATHER's gift, thine own purchase, the conquest of thy SPIRIT over them in regeneration, and their surrender of themselves to thee, as thine, since thou hast made them *willing in the day of thy power!*

REFLECTIONS.

READER! while we look with holy meditation at this vision which John saw, and mark the four Angels holding as they were commanded, the four winds of the earth, from going forth to destruction, until the LORD had done his gracious purpose towards his servants; let us behold our Almighty JESUS ascending from the East, to mark his own against the day of tribulation! And while we see him so gracious to his *Israel,* and while we see him so gracious to his Gentile Church also, to which you and I belong, oh! for grace, to stand impressed with this most certain assurance that He is the same watchful, loving, and all lovely LORD now, as he was then. He is, He must be JESUS CHRIST; *the same yesterday, and to day, and for ever.* Oh! then, depend upon it, that he hath sealed, he doth seal, and he will seal, every individual one of his redeemed.

And, Reader! let you and I behold our JESUS, (if so be, by regeneration you can call him your's,) encircled with his blood bought sons and daughters, now on his throne. Hath JESUS washed their robes, and will he not wash ours? Hath he made them white in his blood, and shall ours remain uncleansed? Hath he loved his Church only in heaven, and doth he not regard his Church upon earth? Did JESUS shew so much attention to his beloved at the time here shewn, and would not suffer the winds or wars to come on, until that he had sealed his redeemed, and will he behold our exercises, our difficulties and tribulations, and look on unmoved? Oh! no, thou dear REDEEMER! thou art still the LAMB, and still in the midst of the throne. All power is thine, in heaven, and in earth. And such is thy love to thy poor ones below, that thou art watching over them night and day, lest any hurt them, and whoso toucheth them, toucheth the apple of thine eye! Oh! how sure, how safe, how blessed are all thine, both in earth and heaven.

Reader! let us seek grace, to eye CHRIST unceasingly, as in the midst of the throne. He hath all divine attributes, all divine blessings, all suited grace, all suited mercy. To Him may all his people come. In Him they find all suited fulness. From Him they receive the every needed grace. And to Him offer all praise and glory. LORD! hasten the hour, when thy whole Church shall be round thy throne, and thou shalt have wiped all tears from off all eyes. Amen.

CHAP. VIII.

CONTENTS.

We have here, the Opening of the seventh Seal. To this succeeds the seven Angels coming forward with their seven Trumpets. An Angel is seen at the Altar of Incense. Four of the Angels in succession sound their Trumpets. Great Plagues follow.

AND when he had opened the seventh seal, there was silence in heaven about the space of half an hour,

2 And I saw the seven angels which stood before God: and to them were given seven trumpets.

I pause at the very entrance on this Chapter, to observe, that the silence which is said to have been in heaven, by the space of half an hour, at the opening of the *seventh seal*, is not to be supposed, (indeed it cannot be supposed,) as if there was any pause in the presence of GOD and the LAMB in heaven. This would not correspond with all the other accounts in scripture, which are given of that blessed place. We are told that the glorious multitude, cease not night nor day, praising GOD and the LAMB. Rev. iv. 8. But it is spoken rather of the Church, which is sometimes, and not unfrequently called heaven, and the heavenly *Jerusalem* coming down from heaven. Heb. xii. 22. Rev. xxi. 2. And the silence of half an hour, seems only to have been a short prelude while the Angels were preparing to sound their trumpets, and the Angel at the altar offered incense.

The period of the history of the Church, which appears to correspond to this vision, according to the best calculations, seems to have been towards the close of the reign of *Constantine*. The Empire was become Christian in *profession*, and, as such, might be said to have peace from Paganism, and this is perhaps represented by silence for half an hour. But this was only a calm, before a tremendous storm. For, as soon as the Angels began to sound their trumpets, the awful persecutions, which arose from intestine wars, and springing out of damnable errors in doctrine, brought on greater evils, than all the opposition from heathens.

3 ¶ And another angel came and stood at the altar, having a golden censer; and there was given unto him much incense, that he should offer *it* with the prayers of all saints upon the golden altar which was before the throne.

4 And the smoke of the incense, *which came with the prayers of the saints,* ascended up before God out of the angel's hand.

5 And the angel took the censer, and filled it with fire of the altar, and cast *it* into the earth: and there were voices, and thunderings, and lightnings, and an earthquake.

There can be no question who this other Angel was, that came and stood at the Altar with his golden Censer. It could be none but CHRIST. The office he here performed of the High Priest, belonged only to CHRIST. He, and he alone it was, whom JEHOVAH had sworn into this office. Psm. cx. 4. And as this vision was subsequent to the LORD JESUS CHRIST having performed all his offices of Redeemer upon earth, and was now returned to heaven, there to priest it also, in the office of an unchanging priesthood; nothing could be more refreshing to the mind of the beloved Apostle than to have this view of his LORD, before the sounding of the trumpets. And as it must have been refreshing to the mind of *John then,* so ought it to be, and, no doubt, as was designed, it hath been in all ages, and is *now,* to have so precious a representation of JESUS, as in this place is given of him, in the carrying on that glorious character. Heb. vii. 21 to the end. I will beg the attention of the Reader to it, for one moment.

And, *first.* It is very blessed to have such a view of CHRIST in the midst of judgments. Let the Reader remember that this was shewn *John* at the first opening of the *seventh seal.* The *seventh seal* became the prelude of the most distressing events on the earth, which began with the sounding of the *first trumpet,* and hath more or less ever since, continued through the long period, of now nearly *fourteen* centuries, and the last woe trumpet is not yet sounded. Let the Reader first ponder these things, and then consider the grace of the LORD JESUS to his servant *John,* at such a time, and to his Church at all times through him.

Secondly. Let the Reader keep in remembrance the glories of CHRIST's Person, and the blessedness of this office of High Priest, which he was here exercising. The Gospel taught the Church, that when CHRIST had made his soul an offering for sin, he should return to his FATHER, and there carry on his everlasting priesthood. And having spent one life upon earth, in dying for his people, he should spend another in heaven, in seeing the merits of his sufferings and death, recompensed in their salvation. And, that in the execution of this purpose, he should *continue a Priest for ever, after the order of Melchizedec.* Here then we see the blessed truth confirmed. Behold Jesus at the Altar with the golden censer of his own merits, and with the much incense of his own blood, perfuming heaven with the fragrancy! Oh! what a sight for every regenerated child of God, everlastingly to keep in view and never to lose sight of! Well may every truly regenerated believer say, how can I fail of being accepted by God and my Father when coming to him in God's own way, and in God's own appointment, under the influence and grace of the Holy Ghost, and in the name, and blood, and incense, and righteousness of the Lord Jesus Christ. *Behold! O God, our shield! and look upon the face of thine Anointed.* Psm. lxxxiv. 9.

Thirdly. This view of Christ at the Altar of Incense, becomes richly blessed to a poor sinner, when he is enabled by faith to connect with it, the pleasure of God the Father, in the whole transaction. While on earth, three times from heaven God proclaimed his love *for* him, and his most perfect approbation *in* him. And, in proof, God raised him from the dead, and set him at his own right hand, gave him, as Mediator Head of the Church, power over all things in heaven and in earth, telling him, that he must reign till he had put all his enemies under his footstool, and committing to him the final judgment of all things, both quick and dead; because he is the Son of man. Oh! what a relief to all heart-straitenings in prayer, when thus a poor sinner, brought acquainted by grace with the plague of his own heart, thus comes to the throne of grace? What will signify his want of enlargement in himself, when he finds his soul through God the Spirit, so widened to take in the love of God the Father, in such a precious gift of his dear Son, and such views of God the Son's glory, grace, fulness, suitableness, and all-sufficiency, to carry on the purposes of his love towards poor sinners.

Fourthly. And what a finishing view to crown the whole, doth such a manifestation of Christ our High Priest, at the Altar of Incense bring with it, when the child of God, through the Holy Ghost's testimony of Jesus, and in Jesus, discovers the heart of God the Father on Christ's account, receiving, accepting, pardoning, adopting, sanctifying, and blessing the whole Church, and every individual of the Church, with his everlasting love, giving them all grace here, and glory hereafter. Reader! have you duly considered these things, and marked their blessedness? It is in Christ the Son of his love, God beholds his people, having *chosen them in him before the foundation of the world;* and now in the time-state of the Church, having *set* Christ *forth a propitiation through faith in his blood.* Rom. iii. 24, 25. It is in Christ their persons and their prayers are accepted. Jesus upon the golden Censer of his own merits and blood, presents both and perfumes both. And as this scripture saith, *the smoke of the incense, come up with the prayers of the saints, ascending up before God out of his Almighty hand.* Jesus it is which opens to fellowship with God, for we can have no fellowship with God without him. *Having boldness to enter into the holiest by the blood of Jesus.* He it was, who first opened the way by his blood, and now ever liveth to keep it open by his intercession. Heb. x. 19—22. And, as here, in and through CHRIST, we have access by one SPIRIT unto the FATHER, so hereafter, all our drawings nigh, will be in and through him. *In hope,* saith one of the Apostles, *of eternal life, which* GOD *that cannot lie, promised before the world began.* And addeth another, *the* GOD *of all grace, who hath called us unto his eternal glory by* CHRIST JESUS! Titus i. 2. 1 Pet. v. 10. Oh! the blessedness of being in CHRIST JESUS.

6 ¶ And, the seven angels which had the seven trumpets prepared themselves to sound.

It will neither be improper nor unprofitable I hope, under the LORD's teaching, if, before we enter upon the several dispensations which seem to be pointed out, under the several *trumpets,* we do by these as we did by the *seals;* first, take a general view of them, before we enter into the particulars of them. We find, that as on opening of the *fifth seal,* cries went up from under the Altar, from the souls of those, whose blood had been shed by persecution; see Chap. vi. 9, 10. So here, before sounding of the first trumpet, JESUS takes up their cause, and now begins to answer their prayers in the judgments, which, with the sounding of the first trumpet, begins to be poured upon the earth.

Concerning the dispensation of the trumpets, there can be no question, but that their very sound is an alarm. Hence, the Angel thrice proclaims, *woe to the inhabitants of the earth,* after *four* of the trumpets had been sounded, by reason of the greater sorrow that was to follow in the earth, under the sounding of the other *three.* And, indeed, it is evident that the ministry of the *seals,* which referred to the time when the Empire was heathen, had nothing so awful in it, as the ministry of the *trumpets.* Opposition from heathenism and idolatry, however in appearance it may seem more directly injurious to the truth than any other, is not in fact so much as what comes from false views of the truth, and the opposition made from those quarters. The man that confesseth CHRIST, but in that confession denies his GODHEAD, is a greater enemy in reality to CHRIST, than he that denies his being, and his religion altogether. I have found more bitter hatred from *Pharisees,* than from all the ungodly and careless, put them altogether. And very sure I am, that all the open enemies to the truth of the Gospel, in those who deny all revelation, are not to be dreaded for persecution, as much as those are, who on the one hand, reduce the Christian doctrine to a mere system of morality, and while professing themselves to be Christians, deny CHRIST's GODHEAD; or on the other, those who though acknowledging his GODHEAD, and in part his atonement, yet make CHRIST only a procuring cause, and insist upon man's own attainments and improvements, as being a part SAVIOR.

The trumpet dispensation, through the whole of that department, intimated a season of greater persecution to the true Church of CHRIST, though the empire became Christian under the countenance of the Emperors, than while it remained under the darkness of idolatry. Hence the trumpets, from the sounding of the first to the last, are gradually opening the steps, by which the persecutions came forward to the overthrow of the empire. God had appointed in the depths of the wisdom of his providence, that those two powers, the *Mahometan* imposture in the *East*, called the *false prophet;* and the folly and iniquity of Popery in the *West*, called the *Beast;* should both come forward much about the same time, and afflict the people of God. Hence, about this period it was, that upon the opening of the *seventh seal*, we find the spreading of *Mahomet's* imposture covering the *East*. *Arabia, Egypt*, and *Assyria*, soon were detached from the empire of *Rome;* and the Impostor *Mahomet* set up his standard in all that vast empire. On the other hand, in the *Western* world, the trumpery of Popery became soon established; and the great enemy of souls, turning Christian, and taking advantage from the errors of *Arian* heresy, soon proselyted the multitudes to the doctrine, which complimented man's goodness, at the expence of God's truth; and both these soon divided the eastern from the western world, and which, more or less, (for their iniquity is not full,) have continued to the present hour, and must continue, according to this blessed book of prophecy, until the time here predicted, for the accomplishment of both is fulfilled. So much I thought it necessary to observe, on the ministry of the trumpets, in general. We will now go on, under the Lord's permission, and under an humble hope of the Lord's teaching, to the consideration of the sounding of each trumpet; beginning with the first, and following them regularly one after another, according to the order in which they are placed.

7 The first angel sounded, and there followed hail and fire mingled with blood, and they were cast upon the earth: and the third part of trees was burnt up, and all green grass was burnt up.

The *first* trumpet sounded, and there followed *hail and fire mingled with blood, and they were cast upon the earth: and the third part of trees was burnt up, and all green grass was burnt up.* I would beg, once for all, to observe, that these are all figurative expressions. The earth, means the place of action, the empire where Christ's Church is. The grass and trees therein are the people. So speaks the Prophet. *The grass withereth, the flower fadeth, surely the people is grass.* Isaiah xl. 7. Hence, by hail and fire mingled with blood, falling on the earth, or rather people, like the plagues of Egypt, Exod. ix. 23—25. is implied, as then, God's judgments.

But the great point is to discover what those judgments were? Various have been the opinions of Commentators. Some supposing that the empire is intended, which, at this time, was divided into great parties. But I confess, that I am inclined to think, that the empire was no more concerned in these judgments, than as it concerned the Church. For, however humiliating it may be to the pride of men, it is *Zion*, and *Zion* only, that is at the bottom of all God's designs, in the earth. The putting down one empire, or the setting up of another, is only to bring about the Lord's purposes, concerning his Church and people. When this grand object is to be accomplished, the Lord makes what instrument he pleaseth, subservient to the work. An emperor, or a beggar, in raising up, or throwing down, when the Church of Christ needs it, is the same.

One thing is certain, that under the æra of the sounding of the *first* trumpet, the heresy of *Arius* received a deadly blow. The shower of *hail* and *fire* mingled with *blood*, might well be said to represent the check which this awful heresy (of the denial of the threefold Persons in the GODHEAD, and the personal glory of CHRIST,) then received. And, well might such a storm be sent from the LORD. For the earth, on which the storm is said to have fallen, meaning the *professing* Church, was full of this awful heresy. A few only of GOD's hidden ones, comparatively speaking, being preserved from the taint of it. And there is somewhat very descriptive of the different parts of this storm, if we consider it in this point of view. For *hail* injures the vines and trees, and especially young plants, in their early budding. And heresies coming down upon a Church, cannot but induce great barrenness among it. *Fire* intimates the contention which is in all *professing* Churches, where a full, and finished salvation is not uniformly maintained. And *blood*, mingled with the *fire*, hath been known to follow the hot, and violent animosities, among men, who hold not *the truth as it is in* JESUS. Reader! do not dismiss your view of the dispensations under the *first* trumpet, until that you have gathered some sweet and precious instruction from it. It must have been a very awful time, when the *Arian* heresy very generally prevailed. As in nature, so in grace, hailstorms, and fire, and blood, are solemn things. What a mercy it was then, that GOD had a seed to serve him? Depend upon it, the same is now. Never, perhaps, a time more awful, than the present. Men mingle up in societies, and smother their views of things, under the specious pretence, that if we preserve brotherly love towards each other, our views of CHRIST, and his great salvation, we may keep to ourselves. Hence that indifferency to divine things, and that zeal about trifles! Hence that smothering our real sentiments, in order to stand well with others. And men fancy they are doing GOD service, in joining the greatest enemies of CHRIST, who deny his GODHEAD, in order to promote, as they call it, the spread of the Gospel through the earth. LORD! preserve me from such delusions!

8 And the second angel sounded, and as it were a great mountain burning with fire was cast into the sea; and the third part of the sea became blood;

9 And the third part of the creatures which were in the sea, and had life, died; and the third part of the ships were destroyed.

As the *earth* represents the people, so the *sea* can mean no other. It is the scene of action, where these great things were to be transacted. Hence the great whore, hereafter spoken of, is said *to sit upon many waters.* Rev. xvii. 1. And so again, that we may not mistake, the angel which gave *John* his intimation, said to him, *the waters which thou sawest where the whore sitteth, are people, and multitudes, and nations, and tongues.* Rev. xvii. 15. So then, what is said under this *second* trumpet, is like the former, it refers to persons. And the casting of a great burning mountain into the sea, and the third part of the creatures in the sea dying, and the destruction of the ships, can have no reference whatever but to persons, on whom the LORD's judgments alight, for their persecution of the Church. Some have thought, and perhaps rightly thought, that as the former punishment, under the *first* trumpet, had reference to the *Arian* heresy, in denying the LORD that bought them; so this of a burning mountain cast into the sea, might have respect to what hath ever accompanied the denial of the GODHEAD of CHRIST, I mean the denial of the Person, GODHEAD, and ministry of the HOLY GHOST. Here also, as in the former judgment, we read of blood. And the history of those times were very bloody. We read of the LORD's people hiding themselves in corners to avoid persecution. But when GOD hides his people, he manifests himself. And, it is very blessed, often now to remark, what gracious and wonderful interpositions, are sometimes shewn, in the salvation of his chosen! That sweet scripture is fulfilled. *The* LORD *knoweth,* (though they know not,) *how to deliver the godly out of temptation;* while he will reserve *the unjust unto the day of judgment, to be punished.* 2 Pet. ii. 9.

10 And the third angel sounded, and there fell a great star from heaven, burning as it were a lamp, and it fell upon the third part of the rivers, and upon the fountains of waters.

11 And the name of the star is called Wormwood: and the third part of the waters became wormwood; and many men died of the waters, because they were made bitter.

Some have thought, that the false prophet is here meant; but if we attend to the features of character given, we shall not be inclined to this opinion. His name of wormwood, meaning the bitter accompaniments, during this time of the *third* trumpet, seems to point out some more special and peculiar exercise, and of longer bitterness than a quick death: such as *Mahomet* used. And moreover, if, as some have thought, that the period of this trumpet, opened very early in the *fifth* century, and ran on to near the close of it; it could not be, in point of time, the false Prophet; for certainly he did not commence his imposture until the year 600, at the earliest. But, might it not be (I ask the question, but do not decide,) that heretic, who first shone like a meteor, in the firmament of the *professing* Church, possessing great human learning, but soon fell into the awful error, of denying original sin; thereby lessening, or rather doing away, the necessity of redemption. The person I mean, is *Pelagius,* who lived about this time, and whose horrible doctrines have spawned to this hour. Surely he might well be called *wormwood;* for bitter indeed must be that error which strikes at the very root of the Gospel, and, where received, becomes like a deadly poison, causing men to rot, and swell, and at length die, inflated with a fancied purity of nature born with them, and man's free will sufficient to keep himself pure.

Reader! I pray you, pause over the consideration of this awful heresy. And think, what a mercy it is, that the LORD hath made such a provision, by the sovereignty of his grace, for preserving his called and regenerated children, from the dreadful delusion. Wormwood indeed, it may well be called, when the very waters of the sanctuary, which should run in healing streams, are thus poisoned by those who dispense them, (unsent as they are, uncalled of GOD,) and which kill the souls of the unawakened, with their bitterness! Now a child of GOD, through the mercy of divine teaching, hath in himself an effectual remedy, to resist the contagion. Should all the devils in hell, or all the men upon earth, attempt to persuade a child of GOD, whom GOD hath convinced of sin, and brought acquainted with the plague of his own heart, that there is no such thing as original sin; his very feelings must everlastingly contradict him. A man taught of GOD, knows better. He is conscious of indwelling, inbred corruption, and inherent unholiness. He feels his corrupt nature for ever disturbing him, even sometimes in moments of solemn worship. He feels what *Paul* felt, and groans under it as the Apostle groaned, that *when he would do good, evil is present with him.* Think then, what a mercy it is, to have the blessedness of divine teaching, as an antidote against the impudent assertions of man. The LORD knows how distressing it is to a child of GOD, to feel these inward workings. But better is it, to groan under a sense of inward workings of evil, so as to make CHRIST dear, and to compel the soul to go to him continually for deliverance; than in a fancied holiness within, which, whoever talks of, no man of the fallen sons of *Adam* ever knew; to make men proud, and to keep *from* CHRIST, instead of leading *to* CHRIST.

Reader! pause a moment longer. And, if the LORD hath been, and is your Teacher, say, how truly blessed it is, both to have learnt from him original sin, and also the remedy of CHRIST's righteousness and blood-shedding, to do the whole evil of it away. Oh! who shall speak, or describe the preciousness of that grace, whereby the child of GOD both feels and knows the bitterness of original sin, which he had *before* conversion, together with the remains of corruption *after* conversion; and the blessedness of CHRIST's daily cleansing the soul from both, and from all sin? Oh! the sweet consolations of the LORD's strength, daily made perfect in creature weakness, to carry the child of GOD on in the life of grace! The child of GOD knows all these things. They are inlaid truths, in his heart. They are brought forward all the day, and every day, in renewed personal, practical knowledge. To dispute, or contend against them, is to be arguing against our very being. Sure I am of all these things, as much as I am of my very existence. And, blessed LORD; while thou shall bring the whole home to my heart, day by day, as thou art graciously doing, neither men nor devils, can be able to make me relinquish thy truth, in compliment to their false reasoning. Oh! for grace in this CHRIST-despising day and generation, *to contend earnestly for the faith once delivered unto the saints.* Jude 3.

12 And the fourth angel sounded, and the third part of the sun was smitten, and the third part of

the moon, and the third part of the stars; so as the third part of them was darkened, and the day shone not for a third part of it, and the night likewise.

The sounding of the *fourth* trumpet, brought forward a new series of calamities upon the empire, and which are figured to us under the images, of smiting the third part of the sun, and the moon, and the stars. It is well-known, how much the Jews dwelt in figurative language. Indeed, it was the most general method made use of, by ancient nations, to convey instruction. Our LORD himself dwelt much in it. Matt. xiii. 34. By the darkening the luminaries of heaven, is very generally meant, lessening the powers, and reducing the glory, of princes and great men of the earth. At this period, which (if correct according to history,) took place about the middle of the *sixth* century, that is, about the year 540, the empire was brought low indeed. The *Roman* Emperors, both when heathens, and afterwards when *professing* christianity, had, for many centuries, shone as suns, among the lesser lights of the nobles, and as stars in the world. But now the LORD, in his providence, was about to cause a revolution of men and things, with an eye to his Church; and, therefore, as here said, the third part is darkened. And they who are conversant with history will know, that toward the close of this century, and before the rise of the false prophets, *Mahomet* and the Whore, at the opening of the succeeding; (who both sprung up nearly together, about the year of our LORD GOD 600;) the empire gave way to new masters.

But it will be much more to our purpose and improvement, to observe, under this *fourth* trumpet, the progress of error which sprung up to trouble the Church. We have noticed, as we have advanced, under the *three* preceding trumpets, (the first of which began after the empire was changed from heathenism to the *profession* of Christianity,) how much more the true Church of GOD suffered from false friends, than from the more open enemies. The faithful in CHRIST JESUS were always prepared, through grace, to oppose the open idolatries around them. But when professors of the Gospel arose in the very Church itself, speaking perverse things, and heresies, of various forms, sprung up among them, here were more bitter exercises. By means of the *Arian* heresy, in the denial of CHRIST'S GODHEAD, and the counterpart of the same deadly evil, in calling in question the Person, GODHEAD, and work of the HOLY GHOST, under the *first* and *second* trumpets; the peace and comfort of the Church had been broken in upon. And, if, (as is very generally believed,) the *Pelagian* heresy arose within the period of the *third* trumpet, denying original sin, and insisting upon man's purity and free-will to keep the whole law of GOD, whereby the necessity of CHRIST'S death, as a sacrifice for sin, became, in such men's views, superseded, and the regeneration of the heart by the HOLY GHOST done away; what a state was the Church of GOD arrived at by this time? Let not the Reader mistake me. The Church of GOD, that is, the true Church of GOD: by which I mean composed only of *regenerated* believers, can ultimately receive no injury. *The foundation of* GOD *standeth sure, having this seal;* the LORD *knoweth them that are his.* 2 Tim. ii. 19. But I am speaking of the *professing* church; the church, as established in the then Empire, as ours is in the present moment. The nation was then, as ours now is, christian in name. And what an awful state was it arrived at under the *fourth* trumpet: if compared to the days of the Apostles, even though in their time the Empire was heathen?

13 And I beheld, and heard an angel flying through the midst of heaven, saying, with a loud voice, Woe, woe, woe, to the inhabiters of the earth, by reason of the other voices of the trumpet of the three angels, which are yet to sound.!

What is said in this verse hath no connexion with the former, neither doth it form a part of the trumpet proclamations. It is not one of the seven Angels who had the seven trumpets, but another angel which *John* beheld flying through the midst of heaven, that is, through the midst of the church. And the design of his embassy seems to have been, to call up the more awakened attention of the Apostle to what was coming on under the remaining dispensations, which were to take place when the other three angels should sound their trumpets. The Angel intimates this, by thrice repeating woe to the inhabitants of the earth, when these awful times came on, which should take place, as they sounded their trumpets. And awful indeed they have been, still are, and must be, until the whole predictions contained in them are accomplished! We, who stand upon the hill of time which hath been trodden over by the generations since then, and before us, in ascending the rising ground of observation, and now look back, and behold in those already accomplished, in the correspondence between the prediction and the event, can and do see enough to lament; and much more to deplore in what yet remains to be fulfilled. And the generation now which looks on, if taught by grace, in viewing the whole that is past, compared with the prophecies here recorded by divine inspiration, may be well assured that every tittle must and will be accomplished.

It doth not fall within the compass of this chapter to enter upon the subject. This would be to anticipate it; and it will more properly meet our attention, as we prosecute the history of the trumpets, in their due time and place. But, before we finish the present chapter, I would take occasion, from what the angel here said, (whom *John* beheld flying through the midst of heaven,) to observe, that as the times of the *three* last trumpets, evidently take in, not only the whole period of centuries, which have already run out, from the moment the fifth trumpet was sounded, to the present hour, but to the very end of time (for the seventh is not yet sounded, neither will, until it ushers in the kingdom of CHRIST, as is related, chap. xi. 14, 15.) it will be our wisdom to consider the subject, with an eye to the LORD, more especially from the great interest in which the Church is included, in the events coming on, as well as our own personal concern. There cannot remain the shadow of a doubt but that we are now under the *sixth* trumpet. It hath been a long sounding trumpet of woe indeed in the Church. Many hundreds of years have passed since it opened; and no man can ascertain how much longer it will continue. It is blessed to consider, that, when ended, all the powers of antichrist will end with it: and that blessed period will come on when *the kingdoms of this world shall become the kingdoms of our* LORD, *and of his* CHRIST: *and he shall reign for ever and ever.* In the mean time it will be our mercy to watch a gracious GOD, as a gracious God is everlastingly watching over his people for good. *I know the thoughts I think towards you,* saith the LORD, *thoughts of peace, and not of evil, to give you an expected end.* Jerem. xxix. 11. *Say ye to the righteous, that it shall be well with him. Woe unto the wicked, it shall be ill with him.* Isaiah iii. 10.

But, Reader! with these things in view, and in the fullest assurance of faith, knowing that they must be so, allow me to say one word in closing up this chapter. We behold here an Angel pronouncing, *woe, woe, woe,* to the inhabiters of the earth, by reason of the other voices of the trumpet of the three Angels which were then remaining to be sounded. Most evidently the last of these trumpets hath not yet sounded. The two great powers which oppose CHRIST's kingdom, both in the East, and in the West, are still in their plenitude. The *latter* did indeed lately seem to be somewhat tottering; but is now more than recovered from his halting. And indeed great changes are to be expected according to scripture prophecy before the total fall. The death of the witnesses which is to take place before that event plainly shews that his termination is not yet. Rev. xi. 8, 9. But what I would in this place beg to remark is, that after the *second* woe trumpet is said to be past, the *third woe* (not the *seventh* trumpet) is said *to come quickly.* And this is said, before the *seventh* Angel is said to sound. See Rev. xi. 14.

From hence it should seem abundantly clear and evident, that under the *sixth* trumpet, or at the close of it, there is to be the *third woe.* And whoever considers the subject attentively, must conclude that so it will be. I am not, in the very nature of things, (unless the judgements indeed are now at the door,) likely to live to see it, going fast as I now am the way of all the earth. But without a spirit of prophecy (for there can need none more than is before us) great commotions, such as the *third woe* intimates, may be supposed likely to take place before those two Anti-christian powers of *Mahometanism* and *Popery* are destroyed. And however some men may please themselves with the hope that the world is evangelizing, the HOLY GHOST speaketh expressly, and speaketh to the reverse: in the *latter times there will be great departures from the faith.* 1 Tim. iv. 1. The LORD prepare his people for what he is preparing for them! Who that considers the real state of vital godliness in the present day but must be concerned for the eventual consequence. If there was ever a period more suited for that solemn question of our LORD's one than another, the present is eminently so: *when the* SON *of Man cometh, shall he find faith in the earth?* Luke xviii. 8.

REFLECTIONS.

MY Soul! behold the grace of thy GOD, when at opening of the seventh seal, and silence took place in the Church, before the new circumstances of sorrow began, JESUS will be seen at the Altar, in his High Priestly Office, with his golden Censer! Was it not to teach the Church, both then, and now, yea, in all ages, that under every *seal* opened, every *trumpet* sounded, every *vial* poured out, He is unceasingly engaged, for all his redeemed ones, and not a moment intermits his care, but is for ever carrying on the whole purposes of his unchangeable priesthood? Oh! what a blessed view was here opened, for the everlasting consolation of the Church. Ye redeemed of the LORD! Ye Priests of my GOD! Ye Ministers of the sanctuary! never cease to shew the Church JESUS in this endearing office, as always engaged for his people. And do ye follow up petition after petition, neither keep silence, nor give him rest, until he hath made his *Jerusalem* a praise in the earth. Oh! the preciousness, from this blessed view of our GOD, that JESUS it is, at the Altar, which offers up in his incense, the prayers of his saints; and both the persons and offerings of his people ascend before GOD out of this Almighty Angel of the Covenant's hands!

LORD! thy Church finds cause to bless thee to this day, that amidst the destructions which have followed those trumpets, JESUS hath yet a seed to serve him, which are *counted to the* LORD *for a generation.* And, though heresies still abound, yea, are, in various instances, increasing in the earth; yet *the* LORD *knoweth them that are his.* Oh! for grace, to be found faithful, and to live above the reproach of men, by living upon the faithfulness of GOD in CHRIST. And then, while all the woe trumpets have been, or now are sounding, and our GOD shall shew wonders above, and signs in the earth, beneath, blood, and fire, and vapour of smoke, JESUS will own them whom he hath sealed; and the world shall know whose they are, and to whom they belong, when that *great and notable day of the* LORD *shall come!*

CHAP. IX.

CONTENTS.

The fifth Angel sounds his Trumpet. Great and fearful Signs follow. The first Woe is past. The sixth Angel succeeds, and soundeth his Trumpet; and very awful Events take place in the Earth.

AND the fifth angel sounded, and I saw a star fall from heaven unto the earth; and to him was given the key of the bottomless pit.

2 ¶ And he opened the bottomless pit; and there arose a smoke out of the pit, as the smoke of a great furnace; and the sun and the air were darkened by reason of the smoke of the pit.

3 And there came out of the smoke locusts upon the earth: and unto them was given power, as the scorpions of the earth have power.

4 And it was commanded them that they should not hurt the grass of the earth, neither any green thing, neither any tree; but only those men which have not the seal of God in their foreheads.

5 And to them it was given that they should not kill them, but that they should be tormented five months: and their torment *was* as the torment of a scorpion when he striketh a man.

6 And in those days shall men seek death, and shall not find it; and shall desire to die, and death shall flee from them.

7 And the shapes of the locusts *were* like unto horses prepared unto battle; and on their heads *were* as it were crowns like gold, and their faces *were* as the faces of men.

8 And they had hair as the hair of women, and their teeth were as *the teeth* of lions.

9 And they had breast-plates, as it were breast-plates of iron; and the sound of their wings *was* as the sound of chariots of many horses running to battle.

10 And they had tails like unto scorpions, and there were stings in their tails: and their power *was* to hurt men five months.

11 And they had a king over them, *which is* the angel of the bottomless pit, whose name in the Hebrew tongue *is* Abaddon, but in the Greek tongue hath *his* name Apollyon.

12 ¶ One woe is past; *and,* behold, there come two woes more hereafter.

The first thing to be noted in this account, by way of ascertaining the sense and meaning of it, is what is said, that to this star was given the key of the bottomless pit, which clearly defines a *person*. For a star, literally considered, could not receive a key. So that here we gain one point towards our discovery. The next light thrown upon the passage is, that he is said to fall from heaven unto the earth, that is, from the Church, frequently called Heaven. Heb. xii. 22. Rev. xxi. 2. Hence, the person alluded to must have been, by profession at least, of the Church, (that is, one who in words acknowledged CHRIST,) before his fall from it. Now, there is no character in all the history of mankind, to whom it can be applied with such propriety as *Mahomet*, the false prophet. This impostor, as appears by his history, for a time professed Christianity. And what he hath said of CHRIST in his *Alcoran*, though most sadly perverted, shews what information he had acquired in headknowledge, concerning the LORD JESUS. Some, however, have thought, that the *Pope of Rome* is here meant. And some have thought, that both *Mahomet* and the *Pope* are alike intended. Certain it is, that both arose much about the same time, at the opening of the *seventh* century, about the year of our LORD GOD 600. But I think, that *Mahomet* is principally, if not altogether intended; because the transactions under the *fifth* and *sixth* trumpets, are chiefly, if not altogether, concerning the *East;* whereas the *Pope's* heresy is in the *West.* I confess, indeed, that the power here said to be exercised by him over the bottomless pit, best corresponds with the Pope, since by his claims respecting purgatory, it should seem to be the most suited to him. But as the imposture of the false prophet, as well as the Pope both sprung from hell, it suits either, or both of them.

There is somewhat very striking in the account here given of opening the bottomless pit, and a smoke arising like the smoke of a furnace, to darken the sun and air. Whether *Mahomet*, or the *Pope*, their counsel is from hell. And the temptations of *Satan*, do not unfrequently darken the bright rays of CHRIST, the sun of righteousness, to his people's view. Not that CHRIST is himself obscured, for He shines for ever the same. But his people, by reason of the clouds, do not always alike see him; just as the clouds in nature, which make sometimes a dark day. Angels above the clouds, in the clear atmosphere of the heavens, look down upon them, and they are not dark. It is only to us, who inhabit the regions below, which live under their influence, that are sensible of their quality.

I beg the Reader to make the same observation respecting these locusts, as was before made of the key of the bottomless pit, that they mean the persons of men: called locusts because of their number, and swarming as do those pernicious insects of the earth, and because of their deadly quality in poisoning. But that men are meant by them is evident, inasmuch as they were prohibited from hurting the grass, or herbage, or trees. It is men they were to hurt, and them only that were unsealed. There is somewhat very blessed in this information, for several reasons, and I pray the Reader not to overlook either.

First. It forms one of the sweetest thoughts, that the LORD had many *then*, and hath many *now*, of his hidden ones, in this *Eastern* part of the world, where the Impostor set up his standard, to oppose CHRIST; for otherwise, this precept, amounting to a prohibition, that they should only hurt those men which had not the seal of GOD in their foreheads, would have been unnecessary. I beg the Reader not to lose sight of this.

And, *secondly.* Let him take another precious thought from this passage, and observe, that GOD had *sealed* his people, though he permitted them, for wise purposes we cannot explain, to live under such governments.

And, *thirdly.* Let him consider, that though now at this time, the awful delusion of this imposture hath continued for more than *twelve hundred years,* and is as great in its horrible tyranny over the consciences and bodies of men as ever; yet they of the Lord's people who are there still, are known *to* Christ, and known *by* Christ; and from time to time, are gathered out, and gathered home to Christ, *to whom the gathering of his people must be.* Gen. xlix. 10.

Some have thought, and I see no reason to reject the observation, that by the *grass* which these locusts were prohibited from hurting, is meant, the humble followers of the Lord, who are low in the earth. And by the *trees* are meant the higher of the Lord's people, who are like the cedars of *Lebanon.* It may be so. But the most blessed thought is, that both, and every other, their safety is in being sealed, secured, and everlastingly blessed, in Christ. *Come not near any on whom is the mark!* Ezek. ix. 6.

I do not mean to speak decidedly, when I say, I humbly presume, of what is said, that it was given to those locusts not to kill them, (that is, the Lord's people,) but that they should be tormented *five months,* is meant, not in relation to their bodies; for, certain it is, the false prophet slaughtered many who refused to abjure Christ; neither to their souls, for their power reached not to this spiritual part; but to the electing grace of God in Christ, on which account they were sealed. And this view of the subject, if I am right, becomes a sweet and precious subject indeed! Was it not this, (I ask the question,) wherein *Satan* was prohibited, in the instance of *Job?* Behold! said God to the enemy, *he is in thine hand, but save his life;* that is, his *person,* according to the margin in Isaiah. Election is personal. Compare Job ii. 6. with Isaiah xliii. 4.

What is said of the figure of the locusts, their shape, and head, and crowns, together with their having a king over them, becomes only a confirmation, that men are all along intended, and not reptiles. And here again, this authority is so much in resemblance both to *Mahomet* and the *Pope,* that it may be truly said, it is impossible to ascertain which it suits most. They are both properly called *Abaddon,* or *Apollyon,* which signifies *a destroyer.* Which hath destroyed most, is beyond all human knowledge to say; the Impostor of the East, or *the son of perdition,* as the Pope is elsewhere called, of the West. 2 Thess. ii. 3. But both, we are told, shall be finally *cast alive into a lake of fire, burning with brimstone.* Rev. xix. 20.

Reader let us pause for a moment, over the solemn subject! What awful events did the *fifth* trumpet dispensation bring, in the permission of *two* such dreadful heresies to arise, one in the East, and the other in the West. Who would have thought, when the empire became christian, though only in the name, and profession of it; that such events would follow? And what a mystery it is, even now, that those antichristian powers should remain down to the present æra, through a period of more than *twelve* hundred years!

One word more, while we are in a world of mysteries. What a time *Satan* hath had, from *Adam's* fall, to the present hour, over the whole earth, yea, God's children also, while uncalled by grace; and what ten thousand sighs, and groans, hath he called forth by his cruelty, from every heart of our nature, from the first of creation, to the end of the time-state, for to that time his empire is to extend?

And doth the Reader ponder these things with amazement, and do they appear to him perfectly unfathomable? Let him then turn his thoughts within, and for a moment study that world of iniquity; I mean his own heart. And, if so be that the LORD hath called my Reader, by his regenerating grace, to a new, and spiritual life in CHRIST JESUS; he will learn more at home, by way of explaining things abroad, than all the books upon earth (excepting the Book of GOD) can teach him on the subject, to all eternity.

In false prophets, and lying deceivers, we behold the word of GOD fulfilled. They were of old *ordained to this condemnation.* Jude 4. In Satan and his devices, we discover the cause of his malice; *the devil is come down upon the earth having great wrath, because he knoweth that he hath but a short time.* Rev. xii. 12. In all these, we discover from GOD's word, both *cause* and *effect.* But, when GOD chooseth the heart of a sinner for his temple, and He who inhabiteth eternity, whose name is HOLY, prefers to abide *there,* which before was occupied by unclean devils; and instead of taking delight in making the heaven for his throne, and the earth for his footstool, sets up his throne in the broken and contrite heart, saying, *here will I dwell, for I have a delight therein?* here is a subject, enough to set all the world a wondering, and can only be explained by the words of GOD himself: *my thoughts are not your thoughts, neither are your ways my ways, saith the* LORD! Isaiah lv. 8.

13 ¶ And the sixth angel sounded, and I heard a voice from the four horns of the golden altar, which is before God.

14 ¶ Saying to the sixth angel which had the trumpet, Loose the four angels which are bound in the great river Euphrates.

15 And the four angels were loosed, which were prepared for an hour, and a day, and a month, and a year, for to slay the third part of men.

16 And the number of the army of the horsemen *were* two hundred thousand thousand: and I heard the number of them.

17 And thus I saw the horses in the vision, and them that sat on them, having breast-plates of fire, and of jacinth, and brimstone: and the heads of the horses *were* as the heads of lions; and out of their mouths issued fire and smoke and brimstone.

18 By these three was the third part of men killed, by the fire, and by the smoke, and by the brimstone, which issued out of their mouths.

19 For their power is in their mouth, and in their tails; for their tails *were* like unto serpents, and had heads, and with them they do hurt.

20 And the rest of the men which were not killed by these plagues yet repented not of the works of their hands, that they should not worship devils, and idols of gold, and silver, and brass, and stone, and of wood: which neither can see, nor hear, nor walk:

21 Neither repented they of their murders, nor of their sorceries, nor of their fornication, nor of their thefts.

Here we have the opening of the dispensation under the *sixth* trumpet ushered in with this solemn preface: *One woe is past; and behold, there come two woes more hereafter!* Reader! let us attend to what is here said, and ponder it well. For most certain it is, the present time-state of the Church is now under it. And when it will finish, and the *two woes* in it be accomplished, who shall say? Great events are involved in it, and which must come to pass before it will end; these things are most certain. It hath already run on to many hundred years; and the *hour*, and *day*, and *month*, and *year* allowed to it, are not yet fulfilled.

One point concerning this *sixth* trumpet, most clearly proves that it refers to the *East;* namely, in that the river *Euphrates* is by name mentioned. And the establishment of the empire of the impostor *Mahomet*, and his successors, over the East, is no less a proof that his is the delusion meant. Indeed, the propagating his imposture by sword, and with the army almost incredible, as here described, is a full confirmation.

I take great pleasure in calling the Reader's attention once more to the sealing of *Israel*, as represented Chapter vii. who occupied those parts, where the impostor's sword was to make great ravages. And, I beg the Reader never to lose sight of it, as often as he calls to mind the vast territories *Mahometanism* and *Paganism* still occupy in the East, and will occupy, until that blessed period shall arrive, when the *Deliverer shall arise out of Zion, to turn away ungodliness from Jacob*. In the mean time, it is a rich and full consolatory thought, the LORD's *sealed* ones are *saved* ones. JESUS hath marked them as his own; and it is his province to gather them out *of all places, whither they are scattered in the cloudy and dark day*. Ezek. xxxiv. 12.

One of the most interesting parts in this whole book of GOD, and which meets us more or less, every where through it, and in all directions, is the presence of CHRIST, giving commands, and guiding the whole events of his Church. This the Prophet *Ezekiel* learnt, in that vision which he saw, and from whence he was enabled, and directed to teach the Church. Ezek. i. 26. And *John*, in like manner, in these visions he here relates, is observing the same thing.

When the sixth Angel sounded, *John* saith, *he heard a voice from the four horns of the golden Altar, which is before* GOD. Several very interesting views arise from hence.

First. It could be no other than CHRIST that *John* heard, for the golden Altar is the propitiatory, or mercy-seat, for intercession. So that, a voice from hence, must have been JESUS speaking. He is the only Mediator, and High Priest. Exod. xxx. 1—10.

Secondly. It is blessed to recollect he is always there. The opening of this trumpet dispensation, opens with this view of him, carrying on the office of his everlasting, unchanging priesthood. Heb. vii. 21—28.

Thirdly. His command to the Angel, to loose the four Angels, proves no less, that he is a Priest upon his throne, and whom all the angels worship and obey. Zech. vi. 12, 13. Heb. i. 3—6. 1 Pet. iii. 22.

Fourthly. The sameness of CHRIST, in his Person, in his Royalty, in his government, and watchful eye over his Church, is sweetly set forth on this occasion, as in the instance before, when he ascended from the East to seal his servants. *There*, the four Angels were commanded by him, to hold the winds till he had sealed them. And *here*, the four Angels, now the LORD had sealed his servants, were to let loose the ravages of the army on the *Euphrates*, for the carrying on the purposes of his government. Reader! what a mercy it is to have such an High Priest, such an Head, and Husband of his Church and People! Whatever events yet remain to be accomplished, under this *sixth* trumpet dispensation, oh! for grace to call to mind JESUS is at the four horns of the golden Altar before GOD! Oh! for faith to hear his gracious voice, as *John* heard, and to have our souls made blessed as *John's* was, in the grace and faith that is in CHRIST JESUS!

The close of this Chapter is very awful. It is said, that amidst all the persecutions which these enemies brought against the Church, and with which also they oppressed the world, the innumerable murders they committed, the sorceries they practised, their fornication and thefts, they felt no sorrow, neither repentance. Reader! this is a sad but true representation of man, in his fallen, unrenewed state, and universally becomes true, not only in the instance of those here spoken of, but of the whole earth. There can be no true repentance, but from the grace of GOD. There can be no grace, but by regeneration. Without the new-birth, the heart remains hardened, *through the deceitfulness of sin;* yea, the spirit is *dead in trespasses and sins.* Hence, amidst all the studied reforms of men, all the fastings, and penance, and alms-giving, and stripes, pilgrimages, and vows, which the world hath set up, not an individual of the human race, from *Adam* downward, ever truly repented, unless a work of sovereign grace by regeneration, is wrought in the heart, to bring the sinner to GOD. Till GOD takes away *the heart of stone, and gives the heart of flesh,* there is no alteration of the old nature. If all the devils now in hell were liberated from their chains, devils they would still remain. And the damned spirits of the dead now there, must be everlastingly the same, since no repentance is given them. Think then, what an unspeakable mercy it must be, in the person and every instance of the LORD's people, when the LORD calls them by his grace, *from the power of darkness, and translates them into the kingdom of his dear* SON! Coloss. i. 12, 13.

I must not close this Chapter, without first observing, that what is here said of worshipping devils, and idols of gold and silver, and of their murders, and sorceries, and the like, seems to be much more suited to the *Western* heresy, than to the *Eastern*. We do not find in the fabled religion of *Mahomet*, and his imposture, any thing like what is here said of the worship of idols, though abounding, as his infamous doctrine doth, of fornications and adulteries, and uncleanness, which the false prophet grants to his followers, yea, making the future paradise, which he holds out to them in another world, to be made up of the fullest gratification of all their sensual lusts. But the worshipping idols, in praying to crucifixes and the images of pretended saints, these things belong to the *Western* heresy under the Pope, and indeed very clearly define that character. She also, no less than *Mahomet*, hath her allowances of fornication, and uncleanness, and murders innumerable in her inquisition through all ages, even to the present hour, and is said to be *drunken with the blood of the saints.* Chap. xvii. 6. And what can it be more properly called than *sorceries,* the exorcisms and pretended holy water, which are used to amuse and deceive the credulous? And what less name than *thefts* can it be called, the immense sums which in all ages have been gathered by the Pope and his priests, in pretending to pray souls out of purgatory, and putting up masses for the dead? These things, which are the notorious traffic of the *Western* heresy, plainly define the character here meant. So, that though the former part in the opening of the *sixth* trumpet began at the river *Euphrates,* in the Turkish dominions, and most evidently alluded to *Mahomet* and his imposture, yet this latter part, as plainly refers to the heresy in the *West,* and points to the Pope, and his imposture. And there can be no impropriety in considering both. For the sixth trumpet includes in its operations, a period of many hundred years, and is not yet finished, neither will indeed, until *in the days of the voice of the seventh Angel, when he shall begin to sound, the mystery of* GOD *shall be finished, as he hath declared to his servants the Prophets.* Chap. x. 7. Reader! pause over the contemplation, as we behold both these horrible delusions, which have been permitted as the scourge of the Church, for so many ages and generations. And while meditating on the subject, look up for grace, and you will find some very sweet and precious instructions arising therefrom, if so be the LORD is your Teacher.

As, *first.* The opposition from hell, to CHRIST and his kingdom, hath been all along permitted for the greater glory of GOD, and the good of his Church. The serpent's head when bruised, to intimate in due appointed time, his total and everlasting destruction, was to be accompanied with the bruising the seed of the Woman in the heel. CHRIST eminently proved this, in his unequalled sufferings. And all his redeemed, from the first martyr *Abel,* down to the present hour, and so on to the end of time, prove the same.

Secondly. The conflict though painful, hath a sure issue. The GOD of peace will bruise *Satan* under the feet of all his redeemed shortly. *Satan,* having by his temptations overcome our nature, and involved the Church, as well as the world, in the ruins of the fall, hath made even CHRIST's mystical members, his lawful captives. *For of whom a man is overcome, of the same is he brought into bondage.* 2 Pet. ii. 19. But the head of those members hath overcome him, and therefore the LORD thus speaks. *Shall the prey be taken from the mighty, or the lawful captive be delivered? But thus saith the* LORD, *even the captives of the mighty shall be taken away, and the prey of the terrible shall be delivered; for I will contend with him that contendeth with thee, and I will save thy children. And I will feed them that oppress thee with their own flesh, and they shall be drunken with their own blood as with sweet wine, and all flesh shall know, that I the* LORD *am thy* SAVIOR, *and thy* REDEEMER, *the mighty one of Jacob.* Isaiah xlix. 24—26.

Thirdly. In the mean time, GOD's sealed ones, are all saved ones. *No weapon formed against them shall prosper.* Their enemies may be permitted to persecute, yea, burn, destroy, or kill the body. And martyrdom is blessed, when it is endured for CHRIST's sake. Prophets, Apostles, and Saints have waded through blood to the kingdom. Yea, JESUS himself, pre-eminent in all things, was in pre-eminent in suffering. But the end is peace. *Fear not little flock, it is your* FATHER's *good pleasure to give you the kingdom.* Luke xii. 32.

Lastly. When the *sixth* trumpet is fully run out, and all the woes to the Church are ended, then comes the Church's everlasting triumph. Then that event will take place, and which all the redeemed shall see, and they whose souls are now under the Altar calling for judgment, shall all rejoice together, when *the devil that deceived the world, and the beast, and false prophet shall be all cast into the lake of fire and brimstone, and shall be tormented day and night for ever and ever.* Rev. xx. 10. Amen!

REFLECTIONS.

READER! behold how the LORD's judgments rise higher and higher, in the scale of punishment! The *four* first trumpets were bringing forward very awful visitations in the earth, but those *two* of the woe trumpets, how far have they already exceeded in affliction! And who shall say what yet remains to be unfolded, before the period of the sixth trumpet is finished! Let you and I pause, as we contemplate the subject. Let us behold and look back over the long space of so many centuries which have run out, since at the voice of the sixth trumpet sounding, the LORD CHRIST gave command, to loose the four angels at the river Euphrates. Contemplate what ravages have been made! what slaughters followed. And yet no reform, no repentance, no one effect of contrition produced, by the chastisement! Let us next look at home. Doth not the question arise, nationally considered, *what then are we better than they!* No, *in no wise.* What, though the worship of images is not by law established, and prayers to images and saints we are not commanded to do, yet, is the LORD JESUS CHRIST more honored than before? Is his GODHEAD, and his blood and righteousness, considered by all ranks of our people, as the very foundation of *the faith once delivered to the saints?* Alas! how greatly the reverse in this CHRIST-despising day and generation! And while like a flood, the awful heresy of denying his GODHEAD is running through the land, and threatens to carry all before it, there are no laws of restraint to stop the pulpit or the press, from saying or doing as their corrupt nature unsubdued by grace may tempt them, against the glorious Person and finished salvation of the LORD OUR RIGHTEOUSNESS. And what may we suppose will follow such daring ungodliness. Surely, if we calculate from what is past, what is probable to follow, before the *sixth* woe trumpet hath finished his period, very desolating consequences may be looked for. The ear of faith may hear that voice which was once heard and again and again repeated; and never more suited than now. *Shall I not visit for these things, saith the* LORD, *shall not my soul be avenged of such a nation as this.*

One sweet thought will comfort the LORD's faithful ones, under all. JESUS is as the helm. All plagues, whether locusts or men, whether fire or sword, have their power from him. The Church of GOD is still the Church of GOD, and every one is sealed by him. Oh! the precious assurance. Here then Reader, every child of GOD may safely say with the Prophet, LORD! *in the way of thy judgments have we waited for thee.*

CHAP. X.

CONTENTS.

John beholds in vision another mighty Angel come from Heaven. He hath a Book in his Hand. At his crying aloud, seven Thunders make their Responses. He swears by him that liveth for ever and ever, that Time should be no longer. John is commanded to take the Book from him, and to eat it.

AND I saw another mighty angel come down from heaven, clothed with a cloud: and a rainbow *was* upon his head, and his face *was* as it were the sun, and his feet as pillars of fire:

2 And he had in his hand a little book open: and he set his right foot upon the sea, and *his* left *foot* on the earth,

3 And cried with a loud voice, as *when* a lion roareth; and when he had cried, seven thunders uttered their voices.

4 And when the seven thunders had uttered their voices, I was about to write: and I heard a voice from heaven saying unto me, Seal up those things which the seven thunders uttered, and write them not.

CH. X.] REVELATION. 573

This is a short but highly interesting Chapter. Between the sounding of the sixth and the seventh trumpet, CHRIST appears to *John* in vision, to prepare his mind for the relation of certain events, yet to be accomplished. And we may suppose both from CHRIST's coming, and coming as a mighty Angel or Messenger of his own dispensation, it is of the highest signification. I beg the Reader to look at what is here said with the utmost attention, and remark, with me, some few of the striking particularities, distinguished both in CHRIST's Person, and the purpose of his coming.

And, *first*. His Person. *John* describes him as a mighty Angel. Mighty indeed, for he is, as the Prophet, ages before his incarnation, spoke of him by the SPIRIT of inspiration; *His name* (said he) *shall be called Wonderful, Counsellor, the Mighty* GOD, *the Everlasting* FATHER, *the Prince of Peace.* Isaiah ix. 6. And who can question these things, when he hears this mighty Angel, as in the next Chapter, declaring that he will give power to his two witnesses to prophecy. Chap. xi. 3. Who hath witnesses but GOD. Isaiah xliii. 10—12. What Angel ever talked of his witnesses? Yea, more than all, who giveth the power to prophecy, but GOD? Must not that man be hoodwinked indeed, that reads this scripture, and yet questions CHRIST's GODHEAD? The whole world, infidels as well as believers, are compelled to acknowledge that CHRIST is the speaker, when he saith, I will give power to my two witnesses, and they shall prophecy. And who can give a spirit of prophecy to the prophets, but the LORD GOD of the prophets; or what shall their prophecies be witnesses of, but of Him, *to whom all the prophets give witness, that through his name whosoever believeth in him, shall receive remission of sins ?* Acts x. 43. Oh! wretched men, deniers of the GODHEAD of my LORD! Well will it be for you, if the LORD *peradventure should give you repentance to the acknowledging of the truth, that ye may be recovered out of the snare of the devil, who are taken captive by him at his will.* 2 Tim. ii. 25, 26. *Kiss the* SON *lest he be angry, and ye perish from the way, when his wrath is kindled but a little. Blessed are all they that put their trust in him.* Psm. ii. 12.

Secondly. This mighty Angel is said to come down from heaven, *clothed with a cloud.* By which I apprehend, that as he came to publish very awful things, such as, that *time should be no longer,* and, as the next Chapter declares, *the slaughter of his two witnesses;* it was intended to shew, how dark and cloudy, for a while, would be the dispensation now about to take place in the Church, at the close of the *sixth* trumpet, and before the opening of the *seventh. Clouds and darkness* are said to be *round about him;* while *righteousness and judgment are the habitation of his throne.* Psm. xcii. 2. Reader! ponder this well. Remember the *sixth* trumpet is still here operating, when CHRIST was thus seen. The witnesses are not slain. Perhaps the most awful times, which ever took place in the Church of GOD, since the foundation of the world will then be. And if so, what are those men dreaming of, who talk of evangelizing the whole earth, whom GOD hath not evangelized, and who run unsent, whether the HOLY GHOST hath forbidden or not, as in the case of the Apostles, when he himself ordained them they were not suffered to preach the word in *Asia* and *Bithynia.* Acts xvi. 6, 7.

Thirdly. Though CHRIST was clothed with a cloud, perhaps, as I before remarked, it meant to intimate awful dispensations were coming on, yet we find the rainbow was still upon his head. Sweet and precious token to all his dear people. The same bow, which at the destruction of the old world, GOD said he would set in the cloud, in token of his everlasting Covenant, is still there, and must be there for ever. JESUS is the whole of it. And all clouds, and all afflictions, which drown *Egypt* in destruction, and everlasting darkness are to the LORD's Israel, messengers of sanctification and safety. Oh! how blessed is it, to behold our JESUS, GOD's rainbow, in every cloud. As GOD cannot look to the Church in any way, or in any direction without looking through the rainbow which encircles the whole throne, so neither to his people, will he look but in and through his dear SON. Reader! keep this all along in view. This mighty Angel, this precious Almighty GOD-Man, the LORD JESUS CHRIST *John* saw, had a rainbow upon his head. So is he now. So will he everlastingly be. He comes as the bow of the Covenant; yea, he is the whole Covenant. And as GOD our FATHER always beholds the Church in, and through him, so do the Church behold GOD our FATHER, always and only in and through Him.

Fourthly. Beside these manifestations of the LORD JESUS CHRIST, we are told, that *his face was as it were the Sun*, while his *feet* were *pillars of fire*. Perhaps to intimate, that while the Church was about to be brought into fiery afflictions, and in which we know from history, numbers of CHRIST's dear members were burnt at the stake for their adherence to him, yet, the LORD's face would shine upon them, with a continued sunshine of love. He would, lift up the light of his countenance upon them, and give them peace. Reader! do you know any thing of the history of your own country? Remember, the reign of this *sixth* trumpet hath been many hundreds of years. Oh! what numbers of the blessed reformers, burnt for CHRIST's sake in the time of persecution in this land, went in chariots of fire to glory, who, from the light of CHRIST's countenance shining upon them, during the time of their martyrdom, declared, that the passage at the stake in the deepest suffering, became like a bed of roses to their spirits! And remember the reign of the *sixth* trumpet is not ended. Yea, the *two witnesses* which are to be slain before it be passed, have not yet been brought forth in the street of spiritual *Sodom* and *Egypt* for slaughter. Rev. xi. 8. When they are, JESUS will be again seen by faith, by them, though clothed with a cloud, and his feet as pillars of fire; yet, with his glorious rainbow upon his head, and his face shining with ten thousand times greater glory, than the sun in love and grace, and with the sweetest countenance of complacency upon them. Oh! the preciousness of JESUS!

But the subject goes on. *John* saith, that this mighty Angel had in his hand *a little book open*. In the former vision of the ministry of the book, which the same glorious Person, was then said to have taken out of the hand of him that sat upon the throne, the book was sealed. And he, and he alone, was found worthy to open it. That had been then opened, and the purport of it appears to have been now in a great part fulfilled, under the ministry of seals and trumpets. But now, before the final accomplishment of the trumpets, JESUS comes to his servant again. And now he tells him, and his

CH. X.] REVELATION. 575

Church through him, that when the sixth trumpet shall have run fully out, and the seventh trumpet comes to be sounded, there shall be time no longer. CHRIST's compleat reign on earth shall begin, and *the kingdoms of this world, shall become the kingdoms of our* LORD *and of his* CHRIST, *and he shall reign for ever and ever.* Rev. xi. 15.

But though this will be the final consummation, and the mystery of GOD concerning his Church upon earth shall then be finished, yet, as great events are to take place, in the world, and in the Church, from that period in which CHRIST thus appeared to his servant *John*, before the whole is closed, the LORD brings in his hand an *open book*, and which *John* is to eat, that is, to receive the contents of it in his mind, and which are to be made known to the Church, by way of comforting the LORD's people, during the long periods yet to expire, before the accomplishment of the whole. So that here opens a new and distinct prophecy, concerning the great things of GOD. And though the subject is one and the same, of this whole Book of the Revelation, yet, from the opening of this Chapter, in which CHRIST appears to prepare his servant's mind for new prophecies on the subject, we may be on the look out, for other plans of divine teaching, besides the ministry of *seals* and *trumpets;* and to learn from the pouring out of *vials*, GOD's further revelations to his Church. The new series of prophecies opens with the beginning of the *twelfth* Chapter. This, and the intermediate one, the eleventh, are designed as preparatory to it.

There is somewhat very sublime, in what is said of CHRIST setting his right foot upon the sea, and his left upon the earth. Probably to intimate his sovereignty over all. For as he came from heaven, where all angels, principalities, and powers are subject unto him, so here, by those acts, he denotes, his Almighty power upon earth, as the Prophet hath described him; *his dominion being an everlasting dominion, and his kingdom from generation to generation. He doeth,* saith the Prophet, *according to his will in the army of heaven, and among the inhabitants of the earth, and none can stay his hand, or say unto him, what doest thou?* Dan. iv. 34, 35.

And what majesty is expressed, under the words of crying with a loud voice, as when a lion roareth. He is called indeed, *the lion of the tribe of Judah*, to intimate the sovereignty in his Israel. And the answer of the seven thunders is very sublime also, as if making responses to their Creator. Some have considered those thunders as figurative of kingdoms, and some have supposed by them is meant, *ministers* of the Gospel, sometimes called *Boanerges*, or sons of thunder. I do not presume to determine upon it. One thing, however, is remarkable, that *John*, when those thunders answered CHRIST's voice, thought himself called upon to write, as if, while thunders echoed to the LORD, well might his servants. But, as all that was now doing, was only preparatory to what *John* would be taught, he was commanded to wait, until better informed what to write of, when the LORD JESUS came to teach him.

5 And the angel which I saw stand upon the sea and upon the earth lifted up his hand to heaven,

6 ¶ And sware by him that liveth for ever and ever, who created heaven, and the things that therein are, and the earth, and the things that therein are, and the sea, and the things which are therein, that there should be time no longer:

7 But in the days of the voice of the seventh angel, when he shall begin to sound, the mystery of God should be finished, as he hath declared to his servants the prophets.

We cannot read what follows, of the LORD JESUS lifting up his hand to heaven, in a way of solemnity, and swearing to the truth of what he was about to deliver, without being struck with the sublimity of the whole. Let the Reader figure to himself CHRIST as GOD-Man, with one foot upon the earth, and the other on the sea, to imply (as hath been before observed) his supreme authority, and then hear him swearing by him that liveth for ever and ever, and created all things, that *there should be time no longer.* Who less than GOD could so determine? And who but GOD could accomplish such a purpose? We read in another scripture, that when GOD *made promise to Abraham, because he could swear by no greater, he sware by himself.* And that this was GOD our SAVIOR who thus swore to *Abraham* is most evident, as may be seen by looking at the account. It was GOD, it is said, that called upon *Abraham* to offer up his son a burnt-offering. And it was the angel of the LORD that called unto *Abraham* out of heaven the second time, and said, *by myself have I sworn, saith the* LORD. See Gen. xxii. 1, 2, 15, 16. And the HOLY GHOST confirms the whole in the scripture before quoted. Heb. vi. 13. Can any thing be more plain than that in the whole transaction it was GOD our SAVIOR who is all along spoken of? And who, indeed, should it be but Him? He is the only visible JEHOVAH through all the scripture. *No man hath seen* GOD *at any time.* In the invisibility of his essence, as GOD, it is impossible to see him. *But one only begotten* SON, *who lay in the bosom of the* FATHER, and from that bosom came forth in our nature, *he hath declared him.* John i. 18. See Heb. vi. 13. and Commentary. Hence, therefore, in this oath, that there should be time no longer, we behold CHRIST acting in his high character of Mediator, and in the name of the whole GODHEAD, confirming by oath, the counsel of his will.

The days of the voice of the seventh angel were to take place before the period CHRIST swore to should come on, when time should be no longer. The mystery of GOD was first to be finished, that is, the mystery of those wonderful events concerning the Church of GOD, in relation to those anti-christian powers which opposed CHRIST, the Eastern and the Western heresy. But not the mysteries of GOD finished, or made known, in relation to that mystery of the Three sacred Persons in the GODHEAD, the mystery of GOD and man in one Person, and the mystery of CHRIST being one with his Church. These things are never to be finished, neither can be in their very nature so explained, as to be no longer mysterious. The meaning evidently is, that the period will come, under the *seventh* trumpet sounding, when the powers of darkness, whose opposition to CHRIST is now so mysterious, shall be finished, *and the kingdoms of this world shall become the kingdoms of our* LORD, *and of his* CHRIST, *and he shall reign for ever and ever.*

8 And the voice which I heard from heaven spake unto me again, and said, Go *and* take the little book which is open in the hand of the angel which standeth upon the sea and upon the earth.

9 ¶ And I went unto the angel, and said unto him, Give me the little book. And he said unto me, Take *it*, and eat it up ; and it shall make thy belly bitter, but it shall be in thy mouth sweet as honey.

10 And I took the little book out of the angel's hand, and ate it up; and it was in my mouth sweet as honey : and as soon as I had eaten it my belly was bitter.

11 And he said unto me, Thou must prophesy again before many peoples, and nations, and tongues, and kings.

This is a very interesting part of this chapter, *John* is ordered to go to CHRIST, and to take out of his hand the open book. Now observe. When CHRIST took the book from the hand of his FATHER, it was *sealed*. He, and He alone, can open to us the decrees of GOD. *I am the way,* saith CHRIST, *and the truth, and the life; no man cometh unto the* FATHER *but by me.* John xiv. 6. Had not CHRIST come forth from GOD, to make known GOD, never should we have known the way to GOD. But when *John*, or any man, takes the book from JESUS, it must be opened to us, or we shall never understand it. Reader! except JESUS gives the book, opened by himself, to those who minister in his name; and except JESUS by his SPIRIT ordains them; ministers, as they call themselves, or as they are called of men, had better never have ran to the service. Popes, bishops, or prelates, not sent of CHRIST, will have a woeful account to give in, the end of the day. *I have not sent these prophets,* (saith the LORD,) *yet they ran; I have not spoken to them, yet they prophesied.* Jerem. xxiii. 21.

What a lovely view is here given of *John!* Immediately, on command, he went to CHRIST. To whom shall the LORD's servants go but to their Master? From whom can they receive their authority, or their instruction, but from Him? Sweetly *Peter*, who knew this, said, LORD! *to whom shall we go, thou hast the words of eternal life!* And what *John* saith of the sweet taste of the book, and the bitter effects afterwards, is fulfilled in all GOD's servants, who minister in his name, as well as in the hearts of those who are ministered unto. When first the word is received, in joy of the HOLY GHOST, with much affliction, by reason of our conscious sense of sin, every thing we hear of CHRIST, and feel of CHRIST, is sweet. But when persecutions come on, and the conflicts of flesh and spirit are at the height, bitter are the seasons of trial. And what it is with the faithful followers of the LORD, in their private life and conversation, such, in an eminent degree, is it with the ministers of CHRIST in their public ministry. Oh! who shall say what soul exercises he goeth through, both for himself and people, while laboring in the word and doctrine; that is, faithful to GOD and to souls? LORD! do thou give to thy servants grace, that in all things they may approve themselves ministers of GOD!

REFLECTIONS.

OH! thou Almighty Angel, whom *John* saw coming down from heaven! Give me, by faith, to behold thee with the delightful rainbow upon thine head, in token of the everlasting Covenant! LORD JESUS! whatever clouds or darkness thy divine dispensations are clothed with, still never will my faith despond, as long as JESUS appears to my view with his rainbow. Though the Church be in the fiery furnace, and clouds and darkness all around, yet while GOD my FATHER is beholding his Church through CHRIST, and in CHRIST, the bow in the cloud; and while JESUS's face towards his people is as the sun in divine grace, and love, and favor, and the Church looking to CHRIST, and in CHRIST, and through CHRIST to GOD, all is well.

Blessed LORD! thou hast sworn, while taking possession of heaven, earth, and sea as thine, that the hour is hastening when time shall be no longer. Oh! then prepare thy Church, prepare thy people for this great day of our GOD! LORD, in thine own time, which is the best time, finish the mystery of GOD, in breaking down all the powers of antichrist, and thereby finish the mystery of iniquity, which now so much opposeth thy pure Gospel.

LORD! give me the same spirit of obedience as thy servant *John*. Make me to eat and digest thy saving truths. Let all be sweet in thee, however bitter in the world, from flesh and blood. Kings, and nations, and tongues, shall hear thy prophecies, and all thy people shall praise thee.

CHAP. XI.

CONTENTS.

John, at the Command of the Angel, measureth the Temple. The LORD speaks of his two Witnesses: their Power. Their Death, Resurrection, and Ascension. The seventh Angel soundeth his Trumpet. The great Events which follow.

AND there was given me a reed like unto a rod: and the angel stood, saying, Rise, and measure the temple of God, and the altar, and them that worship therein.

2 But the court which is without the temple leave out, and measure it not; for it is given unto the Gentiles: and the holy city shall they tread under foot forty *and* two months.

The beloved Apostle is here employed by the LORD, to measure the *temple of* GOD, *and the Altar, and them that worship therein.* This latter clause of the people, throws a light upon the former, and seems to explain, that, by the whole is meant the Church, the true Church of regenerated believers. The word of GOD, in a great variety of places, speaks of GOD's people as a Church founded on CHRIST. GOD the FATHER, ages before CHRIST's incarnation, called upon the Church to *behold that he laid in Zion, for a foundation, a stone, a tried stone, a precious corner stone, a sure foundation.* Isaiah xxviii. 16. And GOD the HOLY GHOST by *Peter* declares, that this was CHRIST, to whom the Church, *coming as unto a living stone, disallowed indeed of men, but chosen of* GOD *and precious,* became as *lively stones,* and were built up *a spiritual house, an holy priesthood to offer up spiritual sacrifices, acceptable to* GOD *by* JESUS CHRIST. 1 Pet. ii. 4, 8. Psm. cxviii. 22. Acts iv. 11, 12. Ephes ii. 19—22. Rev. xxi. 23.

The allusion which is here made, to the original temple at *Jerusalem,* of the Altar and Court without, seems also to have been intended, as typical of CHRIST and his Church. The LORD makes the bodies of his people, his temple. He calls Zion his rest, and declares that he will dwell in it, for he hath a delight in it. 1 Cor. iii. 16, 17. Psm. cxxxii. 13, 14. 2 Cor. vi. 16. By the *Altar* may be intended, CHRIST, our New Testament Altar, High Priest, and Sacrifice. And by *John's* measuring of it, may be implied seeking from the LORD grace, to contemplate the infinite dimensions of his boundless love, *in the breadth, and length, and depth, and height of it, in that love of* CHRIST, *which passeth knowledge.* Ephes. iii. 16. And by the worshippers are meant, the true faithful followers of the LORD; who worship GOD *in spirit, rejoice in* CHRIST JESUS, *and have no confidence in the flesh.* Philip. iii. 3.

I do not conceive, that this measurement of the Church, was intended to imply any thing in this place, similar to what was done under the former visions, when the LORD himself sealed his people before the four Angels, which held the winds, were to execute their orders. But it should seem rather to have been at this time, graciously intended by our LORD, to let *John* understand by his own measurement of it, that JESUS had his Church still, in all its dimensions, that he knew all his members, and watched over them. This, as it strikes me, was the gracious design in our most gracious LORD. The time was now hastening towards the close of the sixth trumpet. And the total overthrow of both the impostures, in the East and in the West, was coming on. But before these things, the LORD's two faithful witnesses were to prophecy in sackcloth. And when they had fulfilled their ministry, they should be slain, and all the other events follow, introductory to the sounding of the *seventh* trumpet. Hence, therefore, the Lord Jesus commands *John*, first to measure the Church and people. Reader! it is a sweet thought, and everlastingly to be cherished with the utmost affection in the mind, that Christ hath a Church in the worst of times. There is even now, a *remnant, according to the election of grace.* Graciously he watches over it. Sweetly Jesus sings to it, which he calls his vineyard of red wine, for even in bloody times, the song must go on. *I the* Lord *do keep it,* Jesus *saith. I will water it every moment. Lest any hurt it, I will keep it night and day.* Isaiah xxvii. 2, 3.

3 ¶ And I will give *power* unto my two witnesses, and they shall prophesy a thousand two hundred *and* threescore days, clothed in sackcloth.

4 These are the two olive trees, and the two candlesticks standing before the God of the earth.

5 And if any man will hurt them, fire proceedeth out of their mouth, and devoureth their enemies: and if any man will hurt them, he must in this manner be killed.

6 ¶ These have power to shut heaven, that it rain not in the days of their prophecy : and have power over waters to turn them to blood, and to smite the earth with all plagues, as often as they will.

We here enter upon one of the most interesting parts of this whole book of prophecy. I venture to call it so, as it concerns the Church in the present hour. For upon the presumption that it could be ascertained, respecting those *two witnesses* of the Lord, and of the accomplishment of the events here spoken of in this Chapter, a key would be given with it, to unlock the greater part, if not the whole cabinet of this portion of God's most holy word. I do not mean, however, from what I have now said, to intimate as though any such discoveries will be made to any man, or to any set of men, as shall lead to the accomplishment of such purposes. Indeed, I have already observed in the preface to this very Book, that it appears to me, to be the general will of God, none of his prophecies (except in special cases) shall be so known, before the predictions come to be fulfilled. Nevertheless, I am inclined to believe, that though this be the will and pleasure of God, on the general subject of prophecy, yet, he hath as graciously been pleased, while keeping from his people the knowledge of the precise time, for the accomplishment of his purposes, to give them certain insights, for marking the progress as they go. And under this view I venture to repeat, that the clearer apprehension we can make, in relation to those *two witnesses* of the Lord through his teaching, the greater apprehension we shall have of those great events, connected with them.

Under these impressions, I request permission from the Reader, to propose an observation or two, before I enter upon the subject, that I may be perfectly understood, while bringing forward what I have to offer on this point. And I beg to do it in the most humble and unassuming manner. This *Poor Man's Commentary* is, as the title intimates, for humble Readers. It is intended more for the Poor in spirit, than for the learned in human wisdom. It aims not to impose my opinion, but rather from fair statings, to invite the Reader, under divine teaching, to form his own. Hence it hath been my study all along, in points not immediately connected with vital truths, to propose, rather than to decide. But in the momentous doctrines, in which the very life of the believer depends, I have indeed, and to the latest moment of my being, through grace, I am resolved to do, *earnestly contend for the faith, once delivered to the saints.*

Here I feel a boldness well warranted of GOD on those solemn doctrines, such, I mean, as the GODHEAD of CHRIST, the Person, GODHEAD, and Ministry of the HOLY GHOST; and the mystery of the THREE in ONE, which bear record in heaven, on those glorious fundamentals of faith, and of all that is dear to the real christian; here I assume a freedom for an unalterable firmness, which will admit of no accommodation. On this ground I contend, and contend earnestly. In this war, I neither give nor take quarter. With such as deny those doctrines, which are dearer to me than life, will I never knowingly mingle. Very sure I am, notwithstanding the accommodating temper of the present day, in the attempt to amalgamate the different creeds, under the specious pretence of promoting GOD's glory, his glory cannot be promoted by such dissimulation; neither can persons of such opposite doctrines, be found together, however meeting here, in the world to come. I enter my protest against such things. I should consider it high treason, to the majesty of my GOD and SAVIOR, to smother my faith in his GODHEAD; and be found with those who openly deny it. On this ground I compliment no man. Under this banner I take my stand. And here I pray to be found faithful, in life and death: in time and to all eternity.

Having said thus much, I beg permission from the Reader, to offer another observation. I enter with great diffidence on the subject concerning those *two witnesses*, inasmuch, as some of the greatest men, since the day of our LORD, that ever lived upon the earth, next to the Apostles, have erred, (as is plainly proved, by the event not corresponding to their prediction,) in calculating the time of their slaughter. Those errors of theirs, arose from misdating the period, of *the thousand, two hundred, and threescore days.* And from hence we learn, that it is impossible to form a clear judgment when it will be, unless the LORD had marked the data from whence the reckoning is to be made. One thing appears certain. Their death is to be under the sixth trumpet. So are the events which are to follow, when the witnesses shall again be re-animated. Hence, therefore, we may safely conclude, that the *thousand, two hundred, and threescore days,* are not yet run out.

From premising these things, I will now beg the Reader to attend with me to what the LORD hath here said, concerning his *two wit-*

nesses, to whom he hath given power to prophesy for this long period. And, I enter upon the subject the rather, with some little confidence, inasmuch as the advance the Church hath made into the *nineteenth* century from the opening of the *sixth* trumpet, favor our observations for more correctness, in forming conclusions from what is past, in humble waitings for what is to come.

The first point, if it were discoverable, would be to ascertain, who these witnesses are? It would form the subject of no small volume, or perhaps of many volumes, even to enumerate the variety of opinions, which have been given, in all ages of the Church, in relation to this one point. But yet, the subject stands just where it did. No man, as yet, hath been able to ascertain the matter; and perhaps will not, until the LORD himself shall explain it, in the accomplishment. I shall just state before the Reader the mere outlines of the different opinions; and leave it with him, under the LORD's grace, to form his own conclusions.

The great difficulty seems to be, in the very opening of the subject, to discover whether those two witnesses are Persons, or Things. They who favor the idea of *Persons*, have talked of many public characters, from *Enoch*, and *Elijah*, down to the very time of the Reformation from Popery. But a great difficulty lies in the way here, of limiting it to any particular persons; as the time of their prophesying, a thousand two hundred and sixty days, which in prophetical language means years, far surpasseth the boundary of human life, to individuals. And, if this be obviated in the supposition of a succession of persons, there doth not seem a reason for confining the number to *two*.

They who conceive the two witnesses to mean not persons, but things, have concluded, that the Two Testaments of Scripture are intended. And, very certain it is, that a considerable degree of probability is on this side of the argument. For they are the highest, the best, and most unanswerable witnesses, for CHRIST. JESUS himself appealed to the Old Testament, in proof of his Messiahship, when he said to the Jews: *Search the Scriptures, for in them ye think ye have eternal life; and they are they which testify of me.* John v. 39. And, with repect to those two witnesses being clothed in sackcloth, there is no objection in this, to the scriptures; for when we consider, that the whole of the prophecy is veiled in figure, it is no distortion of the figure to say, the scriptures are mourning in sackcloth, from the little attention the world pays to them, in their testimony to CHRIST. And there seems a very strong reason to suppose, that the two witnesses are meant for the scriptures, when it is said, that these are the two olive trees, and the two candlesticks, standing before the GOD of the earth. For the Prophet describes the gifts and graces of the SPIRIT, under the figure of olive trees; Zech. iv. 3. and, in this very scripture, JESUS himself told *John*, that the *candlesticks* mean *the Churches*. Rev. i. 20. So then, under this view, the scriptures are represented by the figure of olive trees; and the Churches which receive the witness of the scriptures, are as candlesticks.

But others have thought, that the *two witnesses* more probably intend, the two Churches of CHRIST, the *Jew* and *Gentile*; both which are witnesses in themselves, of the power of his salvation;

and against whom, both the Impostures of the East and West, are alike inveterate.

I am free to confess, that I am wholly uninformed, with which to say the truth is, or whether either. The LORD, in his own time, which is always the best time, will shew. In the mean season, it will be well for the LORD's people to be always on the watch-tower, and to be attentive to the LORD's testimonies concerning himself. If it be the scriptures of GOD which are meant, certain it is, that, as this scripture saith, if any hurt them by blaspheming their testimony, denying their witness, fire doth proceed from their mouth for their destruction: for the word of GOD is *as a fire, and as an hammer, that breaketh the rock in pieces.* Jerem. xxiii. 29. And JESUS saith, *the word which I have spoken, the same shall judge him at the last day.* John xii. 48. And, in relation to what is said, of shutting heaven, and having power over the waters; we only know what we do know of these things, by the word of GOD.

We shall have occasion hereafter, when we meet with the subject again, to consider it somewhat more particularly. In the mean time I shall leave the Reader to his own reflections.

7 And when they shall have finished their testimony, the beast that ascendeth out of the bottomless pit shall make war against them, and shall overcome them, and kill them.

8 And their dead bodies *shall lie* in the street of the great city, which spiritually is called Sodom and Egypt, where also our Lord was crucified.

9 And they of the people and kindreds and tongues and nations shall see their dead bodies three days and a half, and shall not suffer their dead bodies to be put in graves.

10 And they that dwell upon the earth shall rejoice over them, and make merry, and shall send gifts one to another; because these two prophets tormented them that dwelt on the earth.

11 ¶ And after three days and an half the Spirit of life from God entered into them, and they stood upon their feet; and great fear fell upon them which saw them.

12 And they heard a great voice from heaven saying unto them, Come up hither. And they ascended up to heaven in a cloud; and their enemies beheld them.

13 And the same hour was there a great earthquake, and the tenth part of the city fell, and in the earthquake were slain of men seven thousand: and the remnant were affrighted, and gave glory to the God of heaven.

14 ¶ The second woe is past: and behold the third woe cometh quickly.

A vast subject of divine truths is included within the compass of these verses. But I must use shortness. And indeed, the subject itself is so enveloped in mystery, that our greatest searches go but a little way, in the unfolding. When the witnesses shall have finished their testimony, probably meaning, when the elect Church of GOD shall have been fully instructed in the truth as it is in JESUS, and all that are to be gathered from the varieties of the earth, shall have been brought home; those witnesses, whether persons, or things, shall have the last, and most violent persecution raised against them, from the Beast, whose doctrine first came from hell; for it is *after the working of Satan:* 2 Thess. ii. 9. and shall make such open attack upon them, as to overcome them, and slay them. And, such shall be manifested the bitterness against them by their enemies, that their bodies shall lay unburied, in the street of the great city *Rome;* called *Sodom,* from its filth and uncleanness, and *Egypt,* from its tyranny and oppression.

We learn here, that the truth as it is in JESUS, is to undergo a most violent attack, towards the close of all things. The last bite of the Beast, will be the most dreadful. The laying unburied in the street of the city, cannot mean *literally,* for the city itself is *spiritually* considered. So that this is no objection to the *two witnesses* being the two Testaments, on account of their being said to be killed. For the totally suppressing their truths, is virtually silencing them; and therefore may be said to be killing them. And, their being publicly exposed as dead, may well apply to the publicity through the earth, that the Beast had put them to silence, and to contempt.

The triumph of the ungodly, and their sending gifts to one another upon the occasion of the death of the witnesses, are finely expressed, to shew the bitterness of the heart against the ways of GOD. Oh! what delight is it now, with bad men, to behold any thing of supposed evil happening to the godly. *Aha! say they, so would we have it!* And with what joy do the graceless behold the afflictions of the LORD's *Israel!*

The resurrection of the witnesses, is the opening of the subject, to the final overthrow of both the Beast and the False Prophets. Their ascension to heaven in a cloud, is not literally to be accepted in this sense, but rather of their being publicly owned, in the more glorious state of the Church, now hastening to be established, in the thousand years reign of CHRIST upon earth. And the wonderful change, wrought the same hour upon mystical *Babylon,* by the fall of a third part, and the slaughter of seven thousand, are intended to convey, the beginning of the ruin of both antichristian powers, which are now falling, to rise no more. And hence, the subject is brought to the end of the sixth trumpet's dispensation: *the second woe is past, and behold the third woe cometh quickly!*

But while we pause over the relation, what are the particular improvements we gather from it? No man alive can venture to describe the nature of the calamities the Church will then sustain, just at the close of this *sixth* trumpet. Nay, the very method of the LORD's dealing is hid in mystery; and the death and resurrection of the witnesses, more than of the facts themselves, the LORD hath not revealed. That the time is hastening. That the present state of the Church, and of the world, is under the *sixth* trumpet. That in some recent events, we have seen, and do see, a ripening. These are tokens, in a certain measure and degree, that things are hastening towards the accomplishment. But further we cannot advance. Every thing speaks to the Church of GOD now, as the Angel did to *Daniel* of old: *But go thy way, till the end be, for thou shalt rest; and stand in thy lot at the end of thy days.* Daniel xii. 13.

15 ¶ And the seventh angel sounded; and there were great voices in heaven, saying, The kingdoms of this world are become *the kingdoms* of our Lord, and of his Christ; and he shall reign for ever and ever,

16 And the four and twenty elders, which sat before God on their seats, fell upon their faces, and worshipped God,

17 Saying, We give thee thanks, O Lord God Almighty, which art, and wast, and art to come: because thou hast taken to thee thy great power, and hast reigned.

18 And the nations were angry, and thy wrath is come, and the time of the dead, that they should be judged, and that thou shouldest give reward unto thy servants the prophets, and to the saints, and them that fear thy name, small and great; and shouldest destroy them which destroy the earth.

19 And the temple of God was opened in heaven, and there was seen in his temple the ark of his testament: and there were lightnings, and voices, and thunderings, and an earthquake, and great hail.

We are now arrived under this seventh trumpet, at that great period all along intended, when all the antichristian powers shall be totally subdued, and the reign of CHRIST shall take place in the earth. The expectation of this great day of GOD, is in itself enough, properly considered, to bear up the minds of the faithful through all the events yet to be experienced by the Church, under the sixth trumpet, which most evidently is not yet finished. The outward court is not yet given to the *Gentiles*. The two witnesses have not yet finished their testimony. And, from the low estate of the Gospel in the present hour, in relation to vital godliness; very clear it is, that they are still prophesying in sackcloth. Hence, their death hath not taken place. And hence also, their public exposure in the street of the great city, remains to be fulfilled. And from the joy and mirth, all the enemies of vital godliness shall take, in the death of these witnesses, and their gifts they shall send one to another, it is most sure, some great change will take place, before that the sixth trumpet shall have consumed all the purport of his sounding; and the seventh Angel shall usher in his trumpet with joy, to the people of GOD.

Indeed, the overthrow of those antichristian powers, both East an West, which are at present in a flourishing state; and especially the late revival of the western heresy, which for several years past seemed to have been palsied to a great degree; these are no small symptoms, that the slaughter of the witnesses, which evidently must precede the overthrow both of the Mahometan and Papal powers, may be near at hand. The LORD will prepare his people for all events! But it must be a dream indeed, and of the weakest kind, and formed on a baseless fabric, for any man to suppose, that the *seventh* trumpet is coming on, before that the *second* woe is past.

I shall only detain the Reader in this Chapter just to remark, that the whole contents of it, from beginning to end, is to give a brief statement of what may be looked for, under the *sixth* (which is the second woe,) trumpet; and that the *seventh* merely introduceth the time, but doth not enlarge on the blessed events, which will take place under that happy æra. These are brought forward in the after parts of this blessed book of GOD. So vastly important to the mind and pleasure of our adorable LORD JESUS was the object, that his Church should be taught, from age to age, what would arise in the subsequent days, from his return to glory until his coming again to judgment; that he was graciously pleased to shadow forth the outlines of the subject, under a double series of prophecy. Hence the ministry of *seals* and *trumpets*, which we have gone through to the close of this Chapter, have taught the Church the wonderful subject, from the first commencement of the history from CHRIST's Ascension; until his Descension. And in the next Chapter, the LORD begins the subject again, in another series of prophecy, under the ministry of *Vials;* until the LORD sums up all, in his everlasting kingdom of glory. May the LORD bless to his people, the several Chapters we have gone over, and open to us the several yet remaining to be read; that both may minister to his glory, and our furtherance in grace, by JESUS CHRIST!

REFLECTIONS.

BLESSED LORD JESUS! thy Church finds cause to praise thee, for by gracious watching over thy people, and regarding their interests as thine own. Very sweetly didst thou manifest this love of thine, when commending *John* to measure the temple, and the altar, and them that worship therein. Surely, Lord, if *John* was thus taught to know the dimensions of thy Church and people; Jesus meant to say, that he himself knows all that concerns them. The thought of this, is enough, in the worst of times, to comfort thy chosen. True, Lord, thy witnesses are in sackcloth in the present hour. The waters of the sanctuary run low. But *the* Lord *knoweth them that are his*. In the darkest seasons, Jesus hath a seed to serve him, a generation to call him blessed.

Lord! prepare thy Church for the awful time, when thy witnesses shall be slain. Oh! keep thy Church, in every individual instance of her true members, from the accommodating spirit of the present day. Oh! for grace from thee, thou glorious Lord, to bear up against the torrent running through this land, of mingling *with the heathen, and learning their works*. Carry on thy chosen, through all that remains to be accomplished, under the second woe trumpet of thy counsels. And hasten, in thine own time, that blessed soul-reviving sound, which shall call forth great voices in heaven, and the shouts of thy redeemed upon earth. Though both the Writer, and present Reader of this feeble labor, may not be alive to hail thy coming; yet all thy faithful now in grace, do by faith take part in that glory, which shall then be revealed, when *thou shalt come to be glorified in thy saints, and admired in all them that believe*. Amen.

CHAP. XII.

CONTENTS.

This Chapter opens with the History of the Church, from the Beginning. Here is represented by Figure, that Church, brought forth, and immediately persecuted. A Dragon stands ready to devour. She is preserved in the Wilderness. To these follow an Account of War in Heaven, with the Consequences.

AND there appeared a great wonder in heaven; a woman clothed with the sun, and the moon under her feet, and upon her head a crown of twelve stars:

2 And she being with child cried, travailing in birth, and pained to be delivered.

3 And there appeared another wonder in heaven; and behold a great red dragon, having seven heads and ten horns, and seven crowns upon his heads.

4 ¶ And his tail drew the third part of the stars of heaven, and did cast them to the earth: and

the dragon stood before the woman which was ready to be delivered, for to devour her child as soon as it was born.

5 And she brought forth a man child, who was to rule all nations with a rod of iron: and her child was caught up unto God, and *to* his throne.

6 And the woman fled into the wilderness, where she hath a place prepared of God, that they should feed her there a thousand two hundred *and* threescore days.

We cannot hesitate a moment, under divine teaching, to apprehend what was intended from this figurative representation. The prophecy all along relates to the Church. When the SON of GOD first appeared to *John*, to give him the revelation contained in this book, it was not to tell him of things past; but to shew to his servant, *things which should be hereafter.* Rev. i. 1. Hence, therefore, the birth of this man child could not be, as some have thought, to represent the birth of CHRIST, for that had long before taken place; but of the Church. The LORD is here beginning again the same subject as before; only now, the LORD will make a new representation of the same truths, under a different form. He opens, therefore, with representing Zion bringing forth the Church, which is called a great wonder in heaven. And a wonder indeed, which angels desire to look into. Here is a woman represented, as clothed with the sun. *Zion* clothed with CHRIST her Husband, the Sun of Righteousness. Having put on CHRIST, made comely in his comeliness, and shining in his robes of salvation. The moon, which represented the earth, under her feet, to intimate, that now clothed with CHRIST, she had risen above all the dying, perishing things here below, and became wholly engaged with the glories of her LORD. And, to shew her coronation with CHRIST her husband, she hath a coronet of twelve stars upon her head. Perhaps an allusion also to the adorning of the head and heart with the bright light of the teaching of the twelve Apostles.

The fruitfulness of the Church is blessedly set forth, under this figure, of her being with child; for, it is said of Zion, that *as soon as she travailed she brought forth; before her pains came, she was delivered of a man child!* Isaiah lxvi. 7. Reader! what a sweet thought ariseth from hence. The travailing pains of the soul, are sure tokens of soul-deliverance. The womb of grace, like the womb of nature, is sure to bring forth souls unto GOD. For thus graciously speaks the LORD. *Shall I bring to the birth, and not cause to bring forth? Shall I cause to bring forth, and shut the womb, saith thy* GOD? Isaiah lxvi. 9. And, Reader! what saith the LORD concerning the register of *Zion's* children? Yea, what saith the LORD, concerning *Zion's* King, as well as his brethren? *The* LORD *shall count, when he writeth up the people, that this man* (this GOD-MAN) *was born there!* Psalm lxxxvii. 5, 6.

This other wonder, of a great red dragon in heaven, (that is, in the Church, see Chap. xxi. 1, 2, 3.) meaning the devil, and is so called in verse 9. The seven heads, and ten horns, with seven crowns, of this dragon, defines the place, and authority of this beast. And, that we might not err in application, to whom it belongs, we read in the opening of the next Chapter, that the dragon gave his power and his seat to the beast, which arose out of the sea, having seven heads and ten horns, and upon his horns ten crowns, and upon his heads the name of blasphemy. Now, as all this is figurative of kingdoms, so the description can suit none but *Rome*. For that empire is notoriously known to stand upon seven mountains. The differences of the crowns, in one instance being *seven*, and in the other *ten*, perhaps may be, from three other kingdoms being since added to the empire, Rev. xiii. 1, 2.

The tail of this dragon drawing the third part of the stars after him, implies, (what stars always, when figuratively used in scripture mean, principalities and powers,) that this beast had such influence with certain great ones of the earth, to draw them after him to his devilish policy. So that he got into alliance with him the sovereigns of the earth. And this was eminently manifested, when the Roman empire was heathen. And in the after periods, when professing christianity under the emperor *Constantine*, still the influence of the dragon continued. The devil, by turning christian, found that policy more profitable than even heathenism; for he never more artfully carries on his persecutions against true believers, than when he transforms himself *into an angel of light*. Oh! what multitudes hath his tail drawn after him, from that hour to the present, in persuading men to profess the knowledge and faith of CHRIST, while denying his eternal power and GODHEAD?

I beg the Reader to notice what is said of the Church bringing forth *a man child, who was to rule all nations with a rod of iron*. Let not the Reader suppose, that this meant CHRIST; for CHRIST himself is here shewing his servant *John*, by this figure, the bringing forth of the Church, after his return to glory, and during the period of the Roman government while heathen. The ruling all nations, implied the universal dominion of CHRIST's Church, by virtue of her union with her LORD, as set forth: Psm. ii. So CHRIST promised his Church in his Epistle by *John*, to the Church at *Thyatira*. *He that overcometh and keepeth my works unto the end, to him will I give power over the nations; and he shall rule them with a rod of iron.* Rev. ii. 26, 27. And such we know will be the event, when the *seventh* Angel shall sound the *seventh* trumpet; for then *the kingdoms of this world will become the kingdoms of our* LORD, *and of his* CHRIST, *and he shall reign for ever and ever.* Rev. xi. 15. And we, saith the Church, *shall reign on the earth.* Rev. v. 10.

Some have thought, that this man child represented the emperor *Constantine*, and that the devil the dragon, stood to devour him as soon as born. I venture to believe not so. I humbly conceive, that the representation means the Church in general, yea, the whole body of CHRIST's mystical members, whom the devil, in every individual instance, alike hates. The empire, by turning christian under *Constantine*, did not a single atom promote the LORD's glory, or the Church's interest. Yea, from the awful heresies, which soon after began to arise, the devil found occasion to carry on his diabolical purposes with greater advantage: Besides, the representation here made of the Church, clothed with the sun, and the moon under her feet, and crowned with twelve stars, represents a more glorious state of the Church, than ever was, except in the first ages of the Gospel, when after CHRIST's return to glory, and GOD the HOLY GHOST had visibly come down, the whole body of CHRIST's Church, were of one heart, and of one soul. This was the blessed age of the Church, when living upon CHRIST, professing to be saved wholly in his Person, blood, and righteousness, she might be truly said to be clothed with the sun; and from despising the earthly accommodations, and going about with their lives in their hands, the moon, which represented earthly things, might be said to be under their feet; and the words of the Apostles, and doctrines, as stars, crowning their whole lives and conversation. The LORD, therefore, in beginning the subject again, takes it up from this part, and is describing the history of his Church from *John's* time downward, the better perhaps to prepare the Apostle's mind for the events which were hereafter to follow.

The child being caught up, as soon as it was born, unto GOD, and to his throne, cannot be supposed to mean, taking the Church to heaven immediately on the birth; but rather, it is a beautiful confirmation of that blessed doctrine of grace, that at the new-birth of every child of GOD, the LORD's people are made *partakers of the divine nature, and have all things given them that pertain to life and godliness.* GOD undertakes for them. And *the* GOD *of all grace, who hath called them unto his eternal glory by* CHRIST JESUS, *after they have suffered awhile, will perfect, stablish, strengthen, settle them.* 2 Pet. i. 4, 5. 1 Pet. v. 10.

The wilderness, into which the woman, immediately on delivery, is said to have fled, is a further proof of the observation just made. The wilderness is this world, where, under wilderness dispensation, the Church is placed, during her time-state, from grace to glory. And hence the Church, in the Songs is represented, as *coming up out of the wilderness leaning upon* CHRIST *her beloved.* For no sooner is the LORD JESUS CHRIST known by the child of GOD, at the new-birth, or regeneration, than every thing here, becomes a wilderness, out of CHRIST. The LORD's appointing the Church's feeding in the wilderness, hath a reference to that sweet, but secret mercy, by which, even in times of famine, the LORD gives his chosen ones the bread of life, and the hidden manna, which none knoweth, saving him that receiveth. Say, ye hidden ones of my GOD, is it not so now? And will it not be so for ever, till the LORD, who now feeds, in *secret*, will come to make known his people *openly*, Let the Reader observe what is said here, of *the thousand two hundred and threescore days.* Though no man hath ever yet been able to count those days, neither hath any man been as yet informed of GOD, when the date of them commenced, nor when they shall end; yet the Church, as is here said, is to be fed the whole time; while the LORD's servants, his two witnesses, are to prophecy in sackcloth; and as long as the persecution of the Eastern, and Western, and all other heresies, shall remain. Reader! think what a sweet assurance this is! Look at this sixth verse again. In this wilderness, GOD himself hath prepared a table for his Church. And observe, it is said, that they should feed her there the whole period of years. Who are they that are to feed her? Surely God himself in his threefold character of Persons, will feed his people. His servants, the faithful ministers of his word and ordinances, shall feed her : yea, rather than his Church shall want bread, God will feed her from his very enemies' table. Our God saith now, as He said of old, when his Israel was in a strait: *Moab!* saith God, *let mine outcasts dwell with thee, Moab; and be thou a covert to them from the face of the spoiler.* Isaiah xvi. 4. As if the Lord had said, Moab! thou art a bitter foe to my Israel, and thou wouldest gladly sweep them off from the face of the earth : But I will overrule thee, as I did *Balaam*, to *bless* my people, when he would, at thy instance, have *cursed* them. Numb. xxii. 6. Feed my outcasts; for though they are outcasts, they are *my* outcasts: house them, therefore, and take care of them, till I take them home, from all their wilderness straits and difficulties. Reader! do you know any thing of this in your *own* history? Oh! it is sweet, it is precious, so to do. A child of God finds even straits and difficulties blessed, when thereby it affords opportunity for the Lord's display of grace. These things make the wilderness, and the solitary place, and the desert, to rejoice and blossom, as the rose. Isaiah xxxv. 1.

I said just now, that concerning the period of those *twelve hundred and sixty days*, no man hath ever yet been able to count them, neither hath any man as yet been informed of God, when the date of them commenced, or when they shall end. And I beg very humbly of the Reader, to be on his guard against all the proud presumptuous publications of unenlightened carnal men on the subject, who have attempted and do attempt it. If, from the time of *Daniel's* prophecy concerning those days, (see Dan. xii. 11.) to the present hour, our God hath not thought proper to inform one of his redeemed servants, can it be supposed that the secret will be made known to men, who, though professing Christianity, know nothing more of it than in the name? There is somewhat very awful in my view, in the publications of such characters. But while I shudder at their presumption I am much more astonished that any of God's dear children should be led away by them, to place any confidence in their calculations, untaught of God as they most evidently are. The word of God saith, that *the secret of the* Lord *is with them that fear him*. But we never read that the Lord unfolds, what for wise and gracious purposes, he for a time witholds from his people, to make known to his enemies. Very sure I am, that in the general, the Lord doth not lay open his prophecies further, than to deliver his predictions, and it is the province of his redeemed, to be found in humble waitings for their accomplishments. And when any of his own would say as the Prophet did, *O my* Lord, *what shall be the end of these things?* the answer can hardly be expected more gracious, than was given to the man greatly beloved. *Go thy way Daniel, for the words are closed up and sealed till the time of the end.* Dan. xii. 8, 9.

7 ¶ And there was war in heaven : Michael and his angels fought against the dragon; and the dragon fought and his angels.

8 And prevailed not; neither was their place found any more in heaven.

9 And the great dragon was cast out, that old serpent, called the Devil, and Satan, which deceiveth the whole world: he was cast out into the earth, and his angels were cast out with him.

10 And I heard a loud voice saying in heaven, Now is come salvation, and strength, and the kingdom of our God, and the power of his Christ: for the accuser of our brethren is cast down, which accused them before our God day and night.

11 And they overcame him by the blood of the Lamb, and by the word of their testimony; and they loved not their lives unto the death.

12 Therefore rejoice, *ye* heavens, and ye that dwell in them. Woe to the inhabiters of the earth, and of the sea! for the Devil is come down unto you, having great wrath, because he knoweth that he hath but a short time.

Let the Reader keep in remembrance, that, for the most part, when heaven is spoken of in this book of GOD is meant the Church. Indeed, it can hardly be necessary to observe, that when it is said there was war in heaven, it could not be supposed is meant, that blessed place, where GOD dwells, where all is peace, and holiness, and joy. But, the war here mentioned, was, and still is in the Church. *Michael* by whom is meant CHRIST, is opposed by *Satan*, and the conflict must be as is here stated, in the ultimate termination. But during the contest GOD's dear children, though sure of victory, have many an hard skirmish to sustain from day to day, neither doth the faithful soldier in CHRIST's army, unbuckle his armor, until the LORD undresseth him for the grave.

But if we consider what is here said, with an especial eye to the Church, at the period CHRIST had in view, when instructing his servant *John*, and this also, as leading on by a spirit of prophecy, to the great events then to take place in his Church; and from thence to the end of all things, we must call to remembrance, that this was the period of the Church, after CHRIST's return to glory, and under the time of the Empire being heathen, to the time when the Empire professed Christianity, including a space of about three hundred years. And this brings down the history in this Chapter, to the time of the *Arian* heresy.

So wonderful an event, as that of an whole Empire becoming Christian, (that is *professing* Christianity, and, no doubt, though muktitudes under that character were no other than summer flies basking in the sun-shine of prosperity, yet many of GOD's dear children being now no longer terrified with the threats and persecutions of their pagan neighbors, were enabled to boast aloud in the GOD of their salvation,) might well be supposed to celebrate the LORD's glory in the change. Hence, the loud voice *John* in vision heard in heaven, that is in the Church; *Now is come salvation and strength, and the kingdom of our* GOD, *and the power of his* CHRIST. And let the Reader observe no less, how the faithful as with one voice, attributed all their victory to the LORD JESUS CHRIST. So is it now, and so must it be for ever, during the whole time-state of the Church upon earth. No victory, but in and by CHRIST. No washing from sin, but in his blood. No righteousness but his, to justify before GOD!

And well may the Church rejoice, while the devil grows more and more angry, in the consciousness of the shortness of his triumphs over the Church. For what is the whole of his reign, from the fall of *Adam*, to the time of his being cast into hell for ever. What is six thousand years to eternity? It is no more than a single grain of sand, compared to the globe! I have often thought, if a child of GOD could but keep this always in remembrance, every exercise would be as nothing. Day by day lessens all our sorrows. The one of yesterday is gone to be numbered with the years beyond the flood, never more to return. Like boys at school we may cut off the daily notch, which makes the number to the holidays. Shortly, the last will come to be cut off, and then the child of GOD, hears the chariot wheels of JESUS come to take him home to his FATHER's house.

While, on the contrary, I have as often thought, how short-lived, the triumphs or the pleasures of the ungodly! How must the man of earth, I mean the christless sinner, ingulphed like *Korah* and his company in earthly concerns, begrudge every day that passeth. Each night he might say, as the knell of day tolls for its funeral, there's another day gone of my comforts upon earth, and when the last comes, where am I departing? Hence, it is the world dreads to be told of their age, because they dread to die. Reader! with which class are you standing? If new born in CHRIST, (for that is the only real standard of character,) look out, with holy confidence and joy, for the chariot wheels of JESUS! If unawakened, unregenerated, unrenewed in soul, death cannot but be dreadful!

13 And when the dragon saw that he was cast unto the earth, he persecuted the woman which brought forth the man *child*.

14 And to the woman were given two wings of a great eagle, that she might fly into the wilderness, into her place, where she is nourished for a time, and times, and half a time, from the face of the serpent.

15 And the serpent cast out of his mouth water

as a flood after the woman, that he might cause her to be carried away of the flood.

16 And the earth helped the woman, and the earth opened her mouth, and swallowed up the flood which the dragon cast out of his mouth.

17 And the dragon was wrath with the woman, and went to make war with the remnant of her seed, which keep the commandments of God, and have the testimony of Jesus Christ.

At this verse, if I am correct, may be dated the rise of heresy in the *professing* Church, after the Empire became what is called Christian. When the dragon found, that the Emperor and his court acknowledged Christianity, and the idols had tottered and fallen, being cast out of the palace and city, as an *unclean* devil, he thought it best to come in a *clean* devil. Hence, he himself in his angels or messengers professed Christianity. But, by a master-piece of subtilty, he took up the profession of a new faith, and robbed CHRIST of his GODHEAD. To use the words of our LORD, as long as he had been the strong man armed, and the Empire continued sunk in the darkness of paganism and idolatry, his goods and his captives were at peace. But, when the stronger than he came upon him, and overcame him, his armor of idolatry was over. Hence, he saith I will return into my house, (still *his* house, in every instance where there is no change of heart by regeneration,) from whence I came out. And when he is come, he findeth it swept, and garnished of all the idols he had once set up there. But now returning with all the various heresies, the human mind untaught of GOD is capable of receiving, he enters in and dwells there, and *the last state of that man is worse than the first.* Matt. xii. 43—45.

The flight of the Church into the wilderness, from the persecution raised against her in the city, is a striking but just figure of those wilderness exercises, the LORD's people sustain under persecution. To every child of GOD, truly regenerated by the SPIRIT of GOD, and who from that regeneration and teaching of the HOLY GHOST, knows CHRIST in his GODHEAD, and Person, and offices, and character, the present day is a wilderness day, into which the soul is brought. He cannot but find wilderness dispensation, while he hears the blasphemy. Hence, like *David*, his language is, *Rivers of tears run down mine eyes, because they keep not thy laws,* (CHRIST.) Psm. cxix. 136.

The serpent casting out of his mouth water, as a flood after the Church, very plainly means to shew, the flood of heresy, which the devil about this time raised up in the Church. Not the heresy of *Popery* or *Mahometanism*, for neither of those Anti-christian powers were as yet in being. But the flood of heresy was that of *Arius*, who denied the GODHEAD of CHRIST. And another famous, or rather infamous heretic by this time had appeared, *Pelagius*, who denied original sin, and by insisting upon man's purity by nature, and an holiness of will to obey GOD, he totally set aside among all his followers, the necessity of redemption by Christ's blood. There were also the *Nestorian* heresy, and the *Macedonian* at this time, and followed not by a few. The *former* divided the Person of Christ, and the *latter* would admit neither of the Person nor Godhead of the Holy Ghost. These were among the great torrents of schism, with which the Church of Christ was then beset, beside some lesser sweeping streams, to annoy her in the purity of her worship.

By the earth helping the woman, just as an opening made in the earth, comes seasonably to swallow up a flood, is probably meant, that men of no religion, displeased with the cruelties exercised upon the real godly, in those times (of which profane history is full with the account,) put a stop at them, not unfrequently. The providence of God so over-ruled things, that when *the wrath of man*, instigated by the devil, was very great, the Lord made it to praise him, by inducing the very reverse the enemy intended. And when that wrath was more than ministered ultimately to the Lord's glory, *the* Lord *restrained it*. Psm. lxxvi. 10. Oh! how often may the people of God set their seal to this great truth. Very frequently their enemies are led by the Lord, to do the very reverse of what they design, and become the unconscious ministers of producing good, where they intend evil. When the Jews crucified Jesus, what did they design? In Christ's death, what did they accomplish? When hell pursued the Church with error, what was the object? But from those heresies the devil stirred up, God's taught children, through the Lord's teaching, have learnt the greater blessedness and preciousness of the truth. Oh! the depths of divine wisdom! Oh! the unsearchableness of divine love!

REFLECTIONS.

Reader! if the Church appeared as a great wonder in heaven, when beheld clothed with the sun, and the moon under her feet, and on her head a crown of stars, shall not you and I wonder as we behold her also? Oh! what a lovely sight is the Church, the spouse of Jesus! And what a wonder, that the Son of God should choose for himself such an one, when all the Angels of God were at his command! Yea, Reader! what a greater wonder still, if so be you and I are of Christ's members, in this mystical body! A child of God is the wonder of heaven, the wonder of angels! and oh! how much more a wonder to himself, that while meriting hell, he should be preserved for heaven.

And, Reader! let us look also to the other wonder in heaven, and behold this great red dragon. Let us look at him without fear, while looking to, and depending upon Jesus for help. Jesus hath conquered him for us, and in us; and we know, that *the* God *of peace, will bruise Satan under our feet shortly*. Oh! what a world of wonders are we in, that the worm *Jacob* shall thresh the mountains! But, Reader! never lose sight in whose strength it is, we are made strong. The armies of heaven, overcome by the blood of the Lamb. Yes! there can be salvation in no other. No other name under heaven given among men, whereby we must be saved!

Lord Jesus! cause the earth to help the woman, thy Church, now in the flood of heresies, the Serpent hath belched out of his mouth with a view to destroy her, in this present sinful and spiritual adulterous generation. And while hell in such numberless directions, is making war with the true remnant of thy seed, oh! for the Lord to give that seed to see that more is with us, than all that are against us. Remember, precious Jesus, thine own gracious words, and make them particularly sweet and refreshing to thine own, in the present day of rebuke and blasphemy: *My seed* (thou hast said) *shall serve him, it shall be accounted to the* Lord *for a generation. They shall come and shall declare his righteousness, unto a people that shall be born, that he hath done this.*

CHAP. XIII.

CONTENTS.

This Chapter is introduced with an Account of a Beast arising from the Sea, to whom the Dragon gives his Power. Another Beast cometh also at the same Time upon the Earth. This latter causeth the Earth to worship the Image of the former, and to receive his Mark.

AND I stood upon the sand of the sea, and saw a beast rise up out of the sea, having seven heads and ten horns, and upon his horns ten crowns, and upon his heads the name of blasphemy.

2 And the beast which I saw was like unto a leopard, and his feet were as the *feet* of a bear, and his mouth as the mouth of a lion: and the dragon gave him his power, and his seat, and great authority.

3 And I saw one of his heads as it were wounded to death; and his deadly wound was healed: and all the world wondered after the beast.

4 And they worshipped the dragon which gave power unto the beast: and they worshipped the beast, saying, Who *is* like unto the beast? who is able to make war with him?

5 And there was given unto him a mouth speaking great things and blasphemies; and power was given unto him to continue forty *and* two months.

6 And he opened his mouth in blasphemy

against God, to blaspheme his name, and his tabernacle, and them that dwell in heaven.

7 And it was given unto him to make war with the saints, and to overcome them : and power was given him over all kindreds, and tongues, and nations.

8 And all that dwell upon the earth shall worship him, whose names are not written in the book of life of the Lamb slain from the foundation of the world.

9 If any man have an ear, let him hear.

10 He that leadeth into captivity shall go into captivity: He that killeth with the sword, must be killed with the sword. Here is the patience and the faith of the saints.

Here, if I mistake not, begins the first of *Popery* and *Mahometanism*. And, if I am correct, this Chapter, in point of time, corresponds to the *ninth* Chapter of this blessed Book, which opens with the sounding of the *fifth* trumpet. *Four* hundred years or thereabout, had run out while the Empire was *heathen*. One hundred more or thereabout, under the *professing* Church of Christianity, when the heresies of *Arius* and *Pelagius*, had arisen to harass the LORD's people. And now the heresies of Popery and Mahometanism come forward to commence their horrible war, against the true faith *as it is in* JESUS. And these have both extended their powers, the one East, and the other West, (except in a few instances,) to the present hour, and so will continue during the whole of the *sixth* trumpet's dispensation, and that woe is past. By comparing those scriptures together, the Reader will be best enabled through grace, to behold the correspondence in the history, and what is yet more, will therefrom learn also, somewhat of the grace and tenderness of CHRIST, in giving his Church through *John* a beautiful and most interesting duplicate of what they are so highly concerned to know, of those heresies which have distressed the Church, their beginning, progress, and sure destruction. In this Chapter we have only the features of the former.

Under the similitude of a beast rising up out of the sea, *John* is taught of a new power, coming forth to the persecution of the Church. This beast cannot be the Dragon before mentioned, because in the second verse of this Chapter, the Dragon, that is the devil, is said *to give him his power*. Therefore it will follow by an undeniable conclusion, that if the dragon which *John* saw before, in the *twelfth* Chapter, was the devil, and there so expressly said to be, (see Chap. xii. 3. with 9.) and this same dragon in this Chapter, is said to have given his power to this beast, *John* here saw coming up out of the sea, it must follow that this beast, be who or what he may, hath derived all his power and authority from hell. Laying this down as a proof which no one can deny, it will be our next grand concern, who this beast represents, and what he is.

The *first* account given of him, is of *his strength and power*. He is said to have seven heads and ten horns, and upon his horns ten crowns, and blasphemy upon all. That *Rome* is the seat of this beast's empire, there can be no question. Here it was, that all the great transactions of the Church were carried on. In consequence of its extensive empire at the time that these prophecies were given, it was called the world. Rom. i. 7, 8. Moreover, in further confirmation, it is remarkable, that the city itself stood upon seven mountains or hills, and is said to have had, under the jurisdiction of the empire, seven kingdoms. Hence those heads and crowns. Perhaps in the further extent, the ten crowns implied, that three other kingdoms had been added since the Empire ceased to be heathen, and when overrun by two nations which arose after, namely, the *Goths* and *Vandals*.

The *second* feature which this Chapter noticeth of this beast, is, that the dragon, that is the devil, gave him *his power and his seat, and great authority*. Nothing can more strongly define a thing, than what is here done. The devil could give no authority to this beast, but for devilish purposes. And as the last account we had of the devil in the preceding Chapter was, that he was wrath, and went to make war with the remnant of the seed of the Church, and here in this scripture which immediately follows, we find him giving his power, and his seat, and his great authority, to this beast, it must have been as an Antichristian heresy, to afflict and make war with the true Church of God. This statement must also be allowed as correct.

Thirdly. John saw *one of his heads as it were wounded to death, and yet this deadly wound was healed.* Perhaps this alludes to the destruction of the empire, after it became Christian by profession. For it was mouldered away and divided. Therefore, in point of temporal power, *Rome* was lessened, before that this beast came to the government of it. And this might be intended, by the figure of a *deadly wound*. But now by the great power given to the beast by the dragon, this deadly wound was healed, and *all the world wondered after the beast;* namely, that if the great Emperors gone before had not been able to keep their authority, what a wonderful power must this be, upheld by the dragon, to exercise such authority.

Fourthly. Let the Reader duly observe the bottom of this business. The great object of the whole is to worship the dragon. Yes! the beast, be whoever he may, is only made the tool of this whole concern. It is the devil that is to be worshipped, not the beast. Oh! could the fool, whether it be the Pope or any of his Cardinals, that is here meant by the beast, but see what a tool he is made in this trumpery of shew, how would he revolt at the impudence of the dragon upon the occasion.

Fifthly. Observe, that upon the heads of this beast was *the name of blasphemy*. And blasphemy indeed it must be, in the whole of this concern, which begins as we have seen with the devil, in giving his power, and his seat, and his great authority to the beast, and ends, as we read Chapter xix. and 20th verse, in the beast being taken, and with him the false prophet, and both being cast alive into a lake of fire burning with brimstone.

Sixthly. And it is said, that *there was given unto him, a mouth speaking great things and blasphemies.* Yes. This is the bait by which the dragon, the devil, catches the world of the ungodly, both Popes and Prelates, men of titles, and the rich of the earth. When this devil, this dragon tempted *Job,* he stripped him and made him poor. The devil is grown wiser since. He was foiled *then,* for *Job* belonged not to him, and he could not prevail. He useth a more sure plan *now.* He does all by them that are his, as he did by this beast. He gives his *power to him, and his seat, and his authority.* He gives his followers these rattles, which, like children, shall amuse and lull them on. And a mouth speaking great things and blasphemies. But when the *forty and two months are over,* the mask falls *off,* and their eternal destruction is come.

Seventhly. The dragon is not satisfied with the ruin of this beast only, he must have all his followers. Hence, therefore, it is said, that they not only worshipped the dragon which gave power unto the beast, but they worshipped the beast also, saying, *who is like unto the beast? who is able to make war with him?* Hence we see, that the beast himself shall not only commit blasphemy, and open his mouth to blaspheme GOD, but his followers shall even take the words of GOD's children, and which can only be applied to GOD, when they say, as is upon record, *who is a* GOD *like unto thee,* O LORD, *who is like unto thee, glorious in holiness, fearful in praises, doing wonders.* Exod. xv. 11. And these wretched men, shall dare to use similar language in their addresses to the beast; *who is like unto the beast, who can make war with him.*

Eighthly. Awful to relate, and as a close for the present to this awful account, it is added, that *all that dwell upon the earth shall worship him, whose names are not written in the book of life, of the* LAMB *slain from the foundation of the world.* Hence the power of this beast, and the dragon which hath given for a time his power to him, is much more extensive than is generally supposed. There is no preservative, but in the electing grace of GOD. Blessed be GOD! they are secured, whose names are in the Lamb's book of life. Neither beast nor dragon, neither Pope not devil can touch them. But without this, all the world shall wonder after the beast, and all worship him. Reader! ponder well the account; and beg of GOD to give you *a right understanding in all things.*

11 ¶ And I beheld another beast coming up out of the earth; and he had two horns like a lamb, and he spake as a dragon.

12 And he exerciseth all the power of the first beast before him, and causeth the earth, and them which dwell therein, to worship the first beast, whose deadly wound was healed.

13 And he doeth great wonders, so that he

maketh fire come down from heaven on the earth in the sight of men.

14 ¶ And deceiveth them that dwell on the earth by *the means of* those miracles which he had power to do in the sight of the beast : saying to them that dwell on the earth, that they should make an image to the beast, which had the wound by a sword, and did live.

15 ¶ And he had power to give life unto the image of the beast, that the image of the beast should both speak, and cause that as many as would not worship the image of the beast should be killed.

16 And he caused all, both small and great, rich and poor, free and bond, to receive a mark in their right hand, or in their foreheads :

17 And that no man might buy or sell, save he that had the mark, or the name of the beast, or the number of his name.

18 Here is wisdom. Let him that hath understanding count the number of the beast : for it is the number of a man : and his number *is* Six hundred threescore *and* six.

Various have been the opinions of men, on the subject of this other beast. Some have contended, from the term *other* beast, that notwithstanding this agrees with the former in sentiment and in conduct, yet it cannot be the same. And, no doubt, in the first view of the subject, it should seem to be another character. Nevertheless, it hath been as strongly asserted by others, that it is but one and the same, the former intimating a *temporal* power, and the latter an *ecclesiastical* government; and that both must describe, for the characters can belong to no other than the *Pope of Rome*. I leave the Reader, however, to form his own opinion, under the grace of GOD.

It will be our best improvement, in order to a clear apprehension of the subject, to attend to the particular features of character, by which this beast is described.

First. He is spoken of as a lamb with two horns, probably to intimate his affecting the character of religion, and that of CHRIST the Lamb of GOD. If this be, as is generally supposed, the representation of the Pope, in his papal office, there can be no difficulty in explaining what is here said, in reference to that character. For as the Pope, CHRIST's vicar, as he blasphemously calls himself, and head of the Church, *Peter's* successor, and the like, and agreeably to those assumed titles, he utters great swelling words, and speaks as a dragon, this name of lamb, surrounded as he is with his cardinals, bishops, abbots, and priests, is just as suited to him, under this *ecclesiastical* power which the dragon hath given to him, as the other is considered in his *temporal* pomp, as a prince and sovereign. He and his cardinals, both *ecclesiastical* and *temporal* lords. A pretty groupe!

Secondly. His exercising the same power as the beast before him, seems to imply an identity of person, and that it is one and the same, and the place of government is the same, which could not well be, if it were not so. And, as he is said to enforce the worship of the first beast, it should moreover seem to point to those *Anathemas*, bulls, excommunications, and the like, by which the papal authority is known. On this ground, there doth not appear much difficulty of apprehension.

Thirdly, His deception of them that dwell on the earth, by miracles, or rather pretended miracles, is yet an higher proof still. For no power but the Pontiff, ever assumed the character of working miracles, or rather, palming off upon the common people, the tale of lying wonders. This is so striking a feature of Popery, that it belongs to no other. And to read an account of what some Popes have been said to do this way, is one of the most impudent attempts the world ever had palmed off upon them, excepting indeed, the counterpart of the same, in the *Hegira* of *Mahomet.*

Fourthly. And to crown all. The mark of the beast, in the right hand or forehead of the people, is the finishing account of this awful beast. And to what extent, in what numbers, to how many persons the awful delusion hath reached, who shall calculate or say? Most distressing is it to consider, that, from the ignorance of the common people, and the craft of the higher, in the support of a system, that upon principles of human policy, hath been found the best state-contrivance, to keep the lower order in subjection, multitudes have received the mark, and worshipped the beast. Indeed, the prohibition of trade and employment without the mark, is such in popish countries, that the practice is universal. And still, if possible, more awful to relate, concerning those who profess to know better and to be above such foolish notions, it is to be feared that the numbers are not few, who receive the mark in the moment they deride it, the better to carry on the secular, or ecclesiastical purpose of the world! Such are among the awful deceptions of this heresy.

I forbear to offer a single observation on the number of the beast, *six hundred, three score and six.* Much hath been said and written upon it, by carnal men. Few, I believe, of those taught of GOD, have ventured to give their opinion upon it. The HOLY GHOST saith, *here is wisdom. Let him that hath understanding count the number of the beast.* But it would be well to remember that it is him, that *hath understanding,* none beside. And where the LORD giveth not understanding, the wisest will only stumble at the very threshold of enquiry. I retire from it with diffidence. The LORD in his own time will explain. And here I leave the subject.

REFLECTIONS.

In reading this Chapter, well may the child of God cry out with the Apostle, how doth *the mystery of iniquity already work!* What an awful account is here, of him *whose coming is after the working of Satan, with all power and signs, and lying wonders!* And how hath the Lord, for this cause given the ungodly up, and sent them *strong delusions, that they should believe a lie!*

Can the imagination conceive any view of the dark and ignorant state of the human mind, as great in point of self deception, as is here stated? That men should be brought to worship the beast, and with him the devil, to hear his blasphemy, to receive his mark, and to call him by names which belong to none but God. And that this delusion should descend from father to son, in a regular succession, from one age to another; no man being able to deliver his oul and say, *is there not a lie in my right hand?*

Blessed Lord Jesus! be thou adored, and loved, and praised, and delighted, in that thou hast kept thy people, and secured them from the possibility of worshipping the beast, for thou hast marked all their names in thy book of life. Oh! the blessedness of electing, preserving, redeeming, regenerating grace! Lord! do thou keep my soul in the hour, and from the power of temptation that is coming on the earth! Lord! give me to see the sure cause of rejoicing, in that *my name is written in thy book of life.*

CHAP. XIV.

CONTENTS.

We have here a most beautiful View of Christ, *as a Lamb standing on Mount Zion, his Church, and with him a blessed Company of his Redeemed. An Angel is seen flying in the Midst of Heaven. Another is heard, declaring the Fall of* Babylon. *Here is the Harvest of the Earth, and the Vintage, and Wine Press of the Wrath of* God.

AND I looked, and lo, a Lamb stood on the mount Sion, and with him an hundred and forty *and* four thousand, having his Father's name written in their foreheads.

2 And I heard a voice from heaven, as the voice of many waters, and as the voice of a great thunder: and I heard the voice of harpers harping with their harps:

3 And they sung as it were a new song before the throne, and before the four beasts, and the elders: and no man could learn that song but the hundred *and* forty *and* four thousand, which were redeemed from the earth.

4 These are they which were not defiled with women; for they are virgins. These are they which follow the Lamb whithersoever he goeth. These were redeemed from among men, *being* the first fruits unto God and to the Lamb.

5 And in their mouth was found no guile: for they are without fault before the throne of God.

This Chapter opens, with presenting a most interesting view to the Apostle's mind, to relieve him from the awful scenes he had in the preceding Chapter been exercised with. The reign of Antichrist for the long period of twelve hundred and sixty days, or prophetical years, could not fail of having much depressed *John's* spirits. The LORD, therefore, here gives him a most lovely prospect of the Church. He looked, and beheld the same Lamb which had so often been seen by him in those visions, and now saw standing on Mount *Zion*, his Church; and encircled with his sealed ones, having his FATHER's name in their foreheads. There were many sweet mercies included in this view. As *first*, JESUS still appeared to the Apostle, in his personal glory as the Lamb, as if to intimate the everlasting sameness of his Mediator-character, and the everlasting efficacy of his blood and righteousness. No time, no, nor eternity itself, can make any alteration in JESUS, as JESUS. For although, when all the great purposes of CHRIST's mediation in the kingdom of grace shall be accomplished, and the last elect child of GOD is brought home to the LORD, the LORD JESUS it is said, will deliver up the kingdom to GOD the FATHER, that the whole persons of the GODHEAD may be glorified together, in the accomplishment of their Covenant of grace, yet, the Person of CHRIST as GOD-Man, will eternally remain. No period will ever arrive, wherein CHRIST shall cease to be CHRIST; that is, GOD and Man in one Person. JESUS is, and must be the LAMB for ever. Yea, and all the communications of glory, will be to all eternity *in* Him, and *by* Him, and *through* Him. For he is then, at much as now, the *Head of his body the Church, the fullness of Him, which filleth all in all*. Ephes. i. 22, 23. Hence, the very great blessedness here manifested to *John*, and to the Church through *John*, that CHRIST appeared to him, as *the Lamb on Mount Zion*.

Secondly. The place of manifestation was also gracious, and no doubt intended to teach both *John* and the Church, a most sweet and precious lesson. Mount Zion is CHRIST's Church, of whom it is said, *the* LORD *hath chosen Zion, he hath desired it for his habitation. This* (he saith) *is my rest for ever, here will I dwell, for I have desired it.* Psm. cxxxii. 13, 14. Here it is, JESUS plants his Church. Here, the king is held in the galleries of his ordinances. His presence is Zion's glory, her strength, her security. And this was most blessedly shewn, upon the present occasion to *John*, because the long reign of Antichrist, in the beast and dragon, with all their persecutions, that the Church laying open to such foes, might be taught Zion's king was still in her, watching over her night and day, and watering her every moment. Nothing could be more gracious and timely, than this vision of CHRIST, and of the spot where the Lamb stood. It was in exact correspondence to that scripture, *Sing and rejoice, O daughter of Zion, for, lo! I come, and I will dwell in the midst of thee, saith the* LORD. *For I, saith the* LORD, *will be unto her a wall of fire round about, and will be the glory in the midst of her.* Zech. ii. 5—10.

Thirdly. There is also a very striking beauty in this scripture, that the number of an hundred and forty and four thousand are mentioned, being the very same number whom *John* had in a former vision seen, as sealed by CHRIST. (See Chap. vii. 2.) So that here was shewn, that notwithstanding all the long and wearisome persecutions, not one of them was lost. And moreover, the name of their FATHER, beheld by *John* in their foreheads, became as plain a proof, that they had made an open profession before men, whose they were, and to whom they belonged, in direct defiance to them, who had the mark of the beast. Chap. xiii. 16, 17. Oh! how blessed is it, when the LORD gives grace, in the present hour, to his tried ones, that none of the privileges, of buying, or selling the world's traffic, can induce the LORD's people to worship the beast, or to receive his horrible name in their foreheads.

Fourthly. The mercy of this vision, in seeing JESUS with his redeemed, was intended by way of relief at this time, because the opposition of hell, with the two Antichristian powers, of the East, and the West, were to increase to a still greater degree, in proportion as the time hastened on, for their destruction. It is well known of the serpent of the earth, that he never stretches himself so long as when dying. And the serpent of hell, we are told, is come down with great wrath, *because he knoweth that he hath but a short time.* Rev. xii. 12. The last bite of the beast, will be the deepest. How very sweet and gracious was it therefore in the LORD, when about to shew his servant *John* the yet more violent persecutions coming on from the malice of hell and his auxiliaries, to show him here, that CHRIST was in his Church, and every one of his little ones protected by him, and in everlasting safety.

Fifthly. But the mercy shewn *John* in this representation, and to the Church through him, was extended further. For, in addition to what he saw, he heard also a voice from heaven, (that is, from the Church,) as the voice of many waters, and as thunder, intimating the multitude, probably the same multitude as *John* saw, Chap. vii. 9, chaunting aloud the song of redemption; no doubt the same as *John* heard before, the words of which he hath given us. Chap. v. 9. And, I beg the Reader to notice with peculiar regard, that none could learn the song but the redeemed. What can be more decisive in proof of the sovereignty of grace? In the Church upon earth there are none that truly and spiritually join ordinances, participate in their saving grace, in spirit and in understanding, taste and relish divine things, but the people of GOD. For how can a dead body partake of food? How can a sinner dead in trespasses and sins, until quickened into spiritual life, partake of the bread of life? And equally so in the Church of heaven, none could ever sing or learn the song of redemption, unless redeemed from the earth. Some men dream of heaven as if it was a place that in itself must be productive of happiness. And hence they think, that if they can but get there among the croud, they know not how, and I had almost said they care not how; they should be as happy as the rest. Alas! it is not the *place* which constitutes happiness, but the *presence* of the LORD. Where CHRIST is, and in the soul where CHRIST dwells, there is life and joy eternal. But without this saving change wrought on the soul of a sinner by regeneration, heaven, if it were possible to attain it, (and which is impossible by all that are not born again, John iii. 5.) would produce no happiness; but, on the contrary, misery. For the unrenewed man would be for ever wretched, in hearing this song of redemption, without being able to join in a single note of it, to all eternity.

Sixthly. The features of character given to the LORD's army, come in with much sweetness, to close the account of this vision. And this is by no means the smallest part of the beauty of it. Under the figure of chastity, their attachment to CHRIST is shewn. They are said, not *to have defiled themselves with women.* By which, in a general way of expression, is evidently meant to contrast the LORD's followers from the followers of the beast. The kings of the earth, and all the nations, are said to have committed fornication, and to have been made drunken with the wine of the beast. Chap. xviii. 3. But the LORD's redeemed are described by their chastity to CHRIST, and as the followers of the LAMB whithersoever he goeth. Their mouth without guile, and their being without fault before the throne, cannot be supposed to imply any purity in themselves, for in the similar representation *John* saw, they are said to have washed their robes and made them white in the blood of the LAMB. See Chap. vii. 14. But it is CHRIST's righteousness which is the purity of his people, and their robes of salvation in which they appear before the throne, their royal dress. He hath made them kings and priests to GOD and the FATHER; and therefore, this is the sole account wherefore they stand before his throne and serve him in his temple night and day.

Reader! ponder well this sweet and gracious vision. Think how blessedly the LORD termed it. How full and expressive of his love; not only to *John,* but to the Church, both then and now. And remember, that it is always the same. By faith you and I may see the Lamb still on Mount Zion, and all his redeemed surrounding him. And, oh! for grace, to sing the song of redemption now; for surely then, we shall sing it one day with the whole Church in glory!

6 ¶ And I saw another angel fly in the midst of heaven, having the everlasting gospel to preach unto them that dwell on the earth, and to every nation, and kindred, and tongue, and people,

7 Saying with a loud voice, Fear God, and give glory to him; for the hour of his judgement is come: and worship him that made heaven, and earth, and the sea, and the fountains of waters.

We have here a beautiful description of the preaching of the everlasting Gospel. I do not presume to speak decidedly, on any passage in the word of GOD, which may be considered of doubtful signification; much less, on such, as in this book, which are in any degree mysterious. But I would humbly ask, whether, in what is here said, that it is the *everlasting* Gospel, the Angel, is here said to have been seen by *John* flying in the midst of heaven (that is, the Church,) to preach is not intended, the everlasting preaching of it, in all ages of the Church, against all the heresies which arise? The angel here seen, cannot be supposed to be any one individual person, or messenger, but the representative of all faithful ministers. By the Gospel preached, can mean no other than CHRIST himself, who is the sum and substance of all, and the full finished salvation by him, such as was preached by the Apostles, after the descent of the HOLY GHOST. See Acts v. 42. Reader! what a relation is here at once given of the Gospel? What an importance is annexed to it, in that the LORD's people shall have it preached to them, in whatever nation, kindred, tongue, or people, they shall be? So the LORD hath provided; and so will he accomplish his purpose. Oh! how eternally safe and secure are the redeemed of the LORD. Isaiah xxvii. 13.

8 And there followed another angel, saying, Babylon is fallen, is fallen, that great city, because she made all nations drink of the wine of the wrath of her fornication.

Here is the second Embassy, and reaching to a period still further remote, looking indeed into those times, when the heresy of the West, under the Pope, should begin to give way. I do not presume to ascertain the period; but I find some have, and fixed it to about the opening of the *fifteenth* century. The fall of mystical *Babylon,* meaning *Rome,* began much about this time. The LORD raised up certain characters from among her own communion, which began to call her authority in question.

9 And the third angel followed them, saying with a loud voice, If any man worship the beast and his image, and receive *his* mark in his forehead, or in his hand,

10 The same shall drink of the wine of the wrath of God, which is poured out without mixture into the cup of his indignation: and he shall be tormented with fire and brimstone in the presence of the holy angels, and in the presence of the Lamb:

11 And the smoke of their torment ascendeth up for ever and ever: and they have no rest day nor night, who worship the beast and his image, and whosoever receiveth the mark of his name.

12 Here is the patience of the saints: here *are* they that keep the commandments of God, and the faith of Jesus.

Within these verses we have the awful denunciation against those who worship the beast, and receive his mark. And, what I admire particularly in this account is, the striking contrast, between the Lord's people and the ungodly. While the one is under the awful condemnation of everlasting punishment; the other is said to possess the patience of the saints, in waiting on the Lord.

13 And I heard a voice from heaven, saying unto me, Write, Blessed *are* the dead which die in the Lord from henceforth: Yea, saith the Spirit, that they may rest from their labours; and their works do follow them.

I would desire permission to consider this verse by itself, for the blessedness and sweetness of it. I do not say but that it might be supposed to have an immediate reference to that age in which it was written. But I do say, that the general, yea, the universal consolations of it, are such, as to suit all ages of the Church of God. Every where, and upon all occasions, it must be allowed, that the dead are blessed dead, which die in the Lord. And *John*, being commanded by a voice to write it down, evidently shews, that God the Holy Ghost will have the Church to know their blessedness in this particular. A few of the more striking features will prove it.

As *first*. The blessed dead, which die in the Lord, die in union with Christ. They are, in fact, part of himself; members of his body, of his flesh, and of his bones. And, in the sight of God, to all intents and purposes, they are one. For as Christ is the head of his body the Church, where the head is, the members must be; so that though dying out of time, they still live to him in eternity. And this is what the Apostle said: *For whether we live, we live unto the* Lord; *or whether we die, we die unto the* Lord: *whether we live, therefore, or die, we are the* Lord's. Rom. xiv. 8.

Secondly. The dead are blessed, which die in the Lord, *from henceforth:* because, from the moment of their death, and from henceforth, they are got out of the gun-shot of the enemy. No heresy, no powers of darkness, neither men nor devils, can any more annoy them. Oh! the blessedness of being freed from the malice of the world, and from the powers of darkness. *Satan* cannot any more for ever, throw his fiery darts, to distress the child of God. Even if this had been all, it would have been sweet, to have heard the voice from heaven, saying, *Blessed are the dead which die in the* Lord.

Thirdly. They are blessed which die in the Lord, because their own body of sin shall no more distress them. No further sorrows shall arise from the out-breakings of sin, or the indwellings of corruption. No tears shall fall any more from pain. No anguish from heart-distresses. They rest from their labors, and sorrow and sighing are done away.

And, *lastly*, to mention no more. Dying in the Lord, they rest in the Lord, their spirits are with the Lord. Hence they are blessed in the LORD. *Their works follow them.* What works? Not *good* works, for they have none. LORD! saith the Prophet, *thou hast wrought all our works in us!* Isaiah xxvi. 12. Not their *bad* works, for the LORD hath *washed away all their sins in his blood.* 1 John i. 7. What works then are these, which are said to follow the blessed dead? Perhaps their works and labor of love, in seeing the fruit of their prayers answered in the Church's prosperity. The cries of the soul awakened by grace, and therefore the LORD's work in them, answered in mercy, when meeting before the throne the redeemed of the LORD brought home, like themselves, by the grace that is in CHRIST JESUS.

14 And I looked, and behold a white cloud, and upon the cloud *one* sat like unto the Son of man, having on his head a golden crown, and in his hand a sharp sickle.

15 And another angel came out of the temple, crying with a loud voice to him that sat on the cloud, Thrust in thy sickle, and reap: for the time is come for thee to reap; for the harvest of the earth is ripe.

16 And he that sat on the cloud thrust in his sickle on the earth; and the earth was reaped.

17 And another angel came out of the temple, which is in heaven, he also having a sharp sickle.

18 And another angel came out from the altar, which had power over fire: and cried with a loud cry to him that had the sharp sickle, saying, Thrust in thy sharp sickle, and gather the clusters of the vine of the earth; for her grapes are fully ripe.

19 And the angel thrust in his sickle into the earth, and gathered the vine of the earth, and cast *it* into the great wine-press of the wrath of God.

20 ¶ And the wine-press was trodden without the city, and blood came out of the wine-press, even unto the horse bridles, by the space of a thousand *and* six hundred furlongs.

There can be no question who this Person was John saw on the white cloud. His name, Son of Man, defines his Person and character. And indeed, *John*, at the opening of this vision, had so seen him before. See Chapter i. 13. And his is the office to reap the fruits of his redemption. And the other angel that came out of the temple crying to the LORD JESUS, though no other than a ministering servant, is not to be supposed to be *commanding*, but only *calling* to him. Angels are longing for the period of the Redeemer's glory. And these are said, therefore, to be waiting for JESUS to send them into his harvest, to gather souls. Matt. xiii. 36, &c. But the allusions here made, both to reaping, and vintage, are so much one and the same, in reference to CHRIST's gathering his people, that there can need nothing by way of illustration upon the subject. Instead, therefore, of offering any observations upon what is already so very plain as to need none, I shall rather beg the Reader to attend with me to one or two views, both of this reaping and vintage of JESUS, which are the immediate and sure result of his seed time, in grace; and his redemption-work, in shedding his blood, without the city.

In the *first* place, the thrusting in CHRIST's sickle, to the reaping of his harvest, is secured by every assurance of Covenant-faithfulness; because grace given in the seed-time to his people, is an earnest of glory. It is not said, in the scriptures of eternal truth, that the LORD hath called us merely unto grace, but unto eternal glory by CHRIST JESUS. Grace is the earnest of glory. *He will give grace and glory.* 1 Peter v. 10. 2 Cor. v. 4. Psm. lxxxiv. 11.

Secondly. It is not indeed sufficient to say, that grace leads to glory; for grace is glory begun. Grace, like the bud, which contains all the foliage of the future flower, hath in its bosom, all the openings to glory, in CHRIST JESUS. For what comes *from* CHRIST, leads *to* CHRIST. And as by grace, we are made partakers of the divine nature; so the interest we have in CHRIST, must infallibly secure glory from CHRIST. JESUS himself hath said, *because I live, ye shall live also.* John xiv. 19.

Thirdly. CHRIST's harvest is secured, because it is not liable to be blighted by winds, or storms, or drought, or any other adverse circumstances, which arise. The issue is doubtful. He that hath called his people with an holy calling, hath guarded against all possibilities of peradventures. Difficulties are for men, not for GOD. JESUS himself watches over his people, and his harvest; and it is impossible that it shall fail. And the more discouragements which appear to us, the more opportunity is afforded for the manifestation of his grace. JESUS will perfect his strength, in our weakness; and the end will prove, that the whole is his work, as the whole is his glory.

And, *lastly,* to mention no more. What endears the whole process to the child of GOD, and shews that from beginning to end it is all grace, is that (to use the figure of harvest and vintage here adopted,) when to our view all seems blighted, and the whole appears, again and again, in withering circumstances; yet to Him that looks, he sees a blessing in it, when we can see none; and the LORD at length brightens up his own heritage, and makes the whole smile, and blossom, and bring forth abundantly. Reader! it is blessed to feel and know our own nothingness, and CHRIST's all-sufficiency; that in conscious sense, we can bring forth nothing, but as the LORD JESUS disposeth by his grace, we may daily refer all unto Him, and sweetly hear his voice, when he saith: *From me is thy fruit found.* Hosea xiv. 8.

Lamb of God! give me to behold thee with the eye of faith, as John saw thee in vision, encircled with thine holy army, made holy in thy holiness, and sealed with the Father's name written in their foreheads. Oh! the blessedness of being thus acknowledged by the Father, supported by the Son, and sealed with the Holy Ghost.

Lord! do thou still in those awful times, give to thy servants grace to behold thee standing on Mount Zion. Do thou manifest, Lord, thy love to her, in being in her; and thine affections for her, in defending her. Let thy faithful know, and let thine enemies feel, that Jesus is King in Zion, whom God the Father hath set there. Yea! Lord cause every knee to bow before thee, and every tongue to confess, that Jesus Christ *is* Lord *to the glory of* God *the* Father!

Precious Jesus! let thy everlasting Gospel go on, from age to age, to bear down all before it, of the dreadful heresies of the present day, and all that may hereafter arise. Thy harvest must come. Thy vintage shall be sure. Jesus will cause the blood of the wine-press to be productive of its full blessing. *Men shall be blessed in thee.* And thy people out of all nations shall call thee blessed. And, from time to time, the Lord will gather out his redeemed, and fulfil, in every instance, his holy will and pleasure. The voice John once heard, is for ever sounding in the ear of faith; and may the Lord give grace to his people, to receive and believe the record: *Blessed are the dead which die in the* Lord! Yea, the Spirit confirms the certain truth; for they die in Jesus, and are blessed.

CHAP. XV.

CONTENTS.

The Church, having been prepared in the preceding Chapter, by seeing her Safety in Christ, *is in this Chapter taught concerning the Ministry of the seven Angels, with the seven last Plagues. The Song of Moses and the* Lamb. *The seven Angels come forth from the Temple.*

AND I saw another sign in heaven, great and marvellous, seven angels having the seven last plagues; for in them is filled up the wrath of God.

This is a short, but sweet Chapter. It seems in its contents, principally designed to fortify the Church with the assurance of victory, that the Lord's people, in the worst of times, might feel no fear from any outward exercises, being strengthened with inward grace. It opens with a *sign*, which *John* calls, *great and marvellous*. And great and marvellous it always is, when the *worm Jacob* is *made to thresh the mountains*. And great and marvellous also upon another account, when grace is so blessedly shewn to the Church, in the same moment, the wrath of God is poured out on the ungodly. There is nothing so affecting to a child of God, as when, in the time he feels some new token of God's love, is conscious, when receiving it, he merits God's displeasure; and beholds that displeasure poured out on others, no more undeserving than himself. The words, upon such occasions, burst involuntarily from the heart, overwhelmed under a sense of distinguishing grace: Lord! *how is it that thou dost manifest thyself unto me, and not unto the world.* John xiv. 22.

2 And I saw as it were a sea of glass mingled with fire: and them that had gotten the victory over the beast, and over his image, and over his mark, *and* over the number of his name, stand on the sea of glass, having the harps of God.

3 ¶ And they sing the song of Moses the servant of God, and the song of the Lamb, saying, Great and marvellous *are* thy works, Lord God Almighty; just and true *are* thy ways, thou King of saints.

4 Who shall not fear thee, O Lord, and glorify thy name? for *thou* only *art* holy: for all nations shall come and worship before thee; for thy judgements are made manifest.

By a sea of glass, we cannot literally accept the term, for John saith, that he saw, *as it were*, a sea of glass; meaning, most probably, from its shining quality, or, as the sea not unfrequently is, like a mirror. I do not presume to speak decidedly, but as it is said, that this sea of glass appeared as if mingled with fire, and persons standing upon it, and having the harps of God; I confess, that I am inclined to think, the great truths intended to be represented by the whole, is the fountain of Christ's blood; the work of God the Spirit, as *a spirit of judgment and a spirit of burning;* and the love and grace of God the Father, giving to all the redeemed, who are here said to stand upon it, the song of redemption to sing. And I confess that I am the more inclined to this conclusion, from what the blessed victors over the beast are said to sing. The Song of *Moses* and the Lamb. And what is that but redemption? This song *Moses* sung on the banks of the Red Sea, through which *Israel* was brought safe, while *Egypt* was destroyed. And what was this, but as typical of redemption by Christ? Exod. xv. 1—18. And the joining together the servant and the Lord, in my view, as plain as words can make it, shews that redemption by Christ was then intended; and that *Moses* acted but as Christ's servant. Heb. iii, 5, 6.

But, what I yet more particularly request the Reader to observe with me in this place is, the glorious distinction of character given to the Lamb, as descriptive of all Sovereignty and Almightiness. Nothing can be more palpably clear and evident, than that the words of this song are expressly addressed to Christ. King of saints, is one of the special and personal titles of Christ. He is made King in Zion, by the decree of Jehovah. Psm. ii. 6. And as in all the departments of nature, providence, and grace, CHRIST presides; and in creation, as well as redemption, he is the Author; those glorious titles, and ascriptions of praise, are in common with the FATHER and the SPIRIT, his own. And what a blessed decision then is the whole, to his eternal Power and GODHEAD, *who is One with the* FATHER *over all* GOD *blessed for ever. Amen?* Rom. ix. 5.

The subject here included, which the HOLY GHOST hath taught the Church to gather, in this view of the sea of glass, appears to me to be so highly interesting, that while the Church is called upon to behold the faithful standing upon it, singing the triumphal song of redemption, methinks I would ponder it a little as I look on, and beg the Reader to do the same, that we may both together, if it please the LORD, under his divine teaching, take part in it!

When we behold the opposition of hell, to the Church of GOD, uniformly carried on through all ages, from the first of creation to the present hour, and are assured from scripture, that there will be no intermission in this war until the final consummation of all things; when we take into this view of the subject, that the issue hath nothing doubtful, or uncertain in it; and when we consider no less, that the first, and great design with GOD, in his threefold character of Persons, hath been for the ultimate accomplishment of the divine glory, we cannot but be immediately impressed with this conviction: that the whole, from beginning to end, hath been from all eternity so arranged and ordered, that not a single circumstance could be left, but, in relation to men, or things, without an injury to the one vast plan of JEHOVAH. Comparing great things with small, in the curious construction of a machine, every part hath its distinct operation; and every part, however small, contributes as essentially to the whole, as that whole, when taken together. The Prophet's vision, which he saw, had *eyes in the wheels.* Ezek. i. 18. Hence, all in the vast scheme of the LORD's government, in the kingdom of grace, as well as in all the departments of nature, are ultimately ministering to his glory. Even the very *wrath of man shall praise him.* Psm. lxxvi. 10. However differently the views of bad men, however oppositely they intend, the LORD hath so arranged and ordered, that they shall contribute, and become subservient to the LORD's design. So sure is that scripture. *The* LORD *hath made all things for himself; yea, even the wicked for the day of evil.* Prov. xvi. 4.

Though it is impossible, with our present scanty faculties, to go very far into a discovery of this subject, as opened to us in redemption; yet the mere outlines of it do display a somewhat of glory in it, in relation to the LORD's wisdom, and love, and grace to the Church, as cannot fail, under his divine teaching, to give the redeemed child of GOD an unspeakable pleasure in the view. And, while we look on this sea of glass, and by faith hear the song of redemption, it will be blessed to learn the notes of it, and sing it with them.

The *first* view in which it strikes me, is the divine glory manifested to the Church, in her everlasting relationship to her Husband. This is never to be lost sight of, through all the chapters of redemption. CHRIST, as the Head of his body the Church, was so constituted from all eternity. And as his Church was chosen then to be holy, and without blame before GOD in love, from her union with him; so it is plain, GOD's first design, and the accomplishment of his last purpose, in relation to his Church, must be the same. Holiness, and glory, the LORD first intended. Holiness, and glory, the LORD will surely accomplish. Laying this down as a truth perfectly scriptural, and therefore unquestionable; the word of GOD leads us on to observe, what means the LORD hath ordained, and by what powers he will bring it to pass. Ephes. i. 4, 5. Titus i. 2.

Secondly. We view the Church in the time-state, a fallen sinful state, in which she hath lost all her created holiness in *Adam;* and is brought into sin and misery, with all the tremendous consequences, which arise therefrom. Here gives opportunity to the LORD, for the vast purposes of his redemption. And, as in the eternity past, the Church had all her holiness in CHRIST; and as in the eternity to come, all her holiness and glory are in Him; so here, all the blessings of redemption, in her recovery from this time-state of sin and misery, are founded only in Him : pardon, mercy, and peace, are the blessings derived from his cross; and all CHRIST is, as the Redeemer, and all he hath wrought in redemption, is for this express purpose, to gather his Church from sin and misery, and to present her to himself a glorious Church, made so by himself. 1 Cor. i. 30. Ephes. v. 26, 27.

Thirdly. All the opposition of hell, and all the agents of the devil among men, are only accomplishing the very purposes, which shall best minister to the LORD's glory, and the welfare of his people. Their opposition tends to endear CHRIST. And the sorrows they put the LORD's people to, have a blessed tendency, to wean the heart from the earth, and to make CHRIST and heaven more dear. Yea, the very sense of our own sins, and what we feel from the risings of corruption; all have their use, in the promotion of the LORD's glory, and our happiness. There never would have been such sweetness in heaven, as the redeemed will find there, had they never known sin; nor felt the love and grace of CHRIST, in redeeming them from it. It is blessedly said by the HOLY GHOST, that GOD *was willing to make known the riches of his glory, on the vessels of mercy which he had afore prepared unto glory.* Rom. ix. 23. Now, notwithstanding GOD had afore prepared those vessels unto glory, they never could have been *vessels of mercy,* had they not been first *vessels of sin.* Mercy implies favor shewn to the miserable. Glory and holiness, if given, are given from love, and choice. So that redemption gives a new and additional relish to heaven, and our felicity becomes heightened thereby, in that having once known the sorrows of sin and misery, we sing our song of triumph in redemption, as on a sea of glass, mingled with fire.

Fourthly, and above all. By this blessed process, the Church of GOD derives an unspeakable joy, and full of glory, in knowing CHRIST under his double blessed name, both as an Head, and as a Redeemer; and GOD our FATHER hath a double glory of praise and love, from his Church. He hath chosen us in CHRIST *before the foundation of the world.* And he hath accepted us in CHRIST in time, *to the praise of the glory of his grace.* And GOD the HOLY GHOST hath a double glory of praise and love, in having anointed the Church in CHRIST, when the Church was set up in CHRIST before the world, and when regenerating the Church in CHRIST from the

Adam-fall transgression in time, when *dead in trespasses and sins.* And hence the double song of *Moses* and the LAMB. It would have been a glory inconceivably great and blessed, had JEHOVAH, in his threefold character of Person, when making the Church one with CHRIST, have taken the Church at once to heaven with CHRIST, without passing through this world of sin and misery. It would have been a blessedness unspeakable, and full of glory, even if passing through this world without knowing sin, or misery, or any thing of a fallen state. But then, we should have known nothing of the sweet and gracious office-character of the Holy Persons of the GODHEAD, as we now know them. We should have been for ever ignorant of that electing love of GOD the FATHER, in distinguishing, preserving, pardoning grace, and mercy. We should have lost that sweet and precious character of JESUS, as our Goel, our Kinsman Redeemer; neither should we have known GOD the HOLY GHOST, as the Quickener of our spirits, from death and sin, to life, and righteousness in CHRIST. And heaven itself would never have rung, as it now doth, and for ever will, with the sweet sound of redemption, and the beholding CHRIST as our Redeemer. But now, by this vast scheme, of infinite wisdom, love, and power, we discover (little as our discoveries go towards a perfect apprehension of such a mystery) enough to admire, and in that admiration to adore, the wonders of divine love, in the wonders of divine wisdom. Oh! how may every regenerated, redeemed, justified, and sanctified believer, as he looks on this sea of glass by faith, and hears the blessed spirits singing the song of *Moses* and the LAMB, join the chorus of praise, saying, *Great and marvellous are thy works,* LORD GOD *Almighty; just and true are thy ways, thou King of saints!*

5 And after that I looked, and, behold, the temple of the tabernacle of the testimony in heaven was opened:

6 And the seven angels came out of the temple, having the seven plagues, clothed in pure and white linen, and having their breasts girded with golden girdles.

It is not heaven, the place of the blessed in glory, that is here meant; for what is said soon after, verse 8, of being *filled with smoke*, if there were no other cause, would do this away. But it is the Church, which for the most part all along is intended, when heaven is mentioned. From the Church, therefore, *John* beheld the seven angels, or messengers, coming forth, with the seven last plagues. Perhaps these may mean even some very humble ministers of CHRIST, in his Church. Their number *seven*, (which is a perfect number,) is not very probably intended, a certain number of seven, and no more, neither of one particular period; but the perfection of their order, being ordained by GOD the HOLY GHOST, and their perfection in CHRIST. Their dress also being priestly, in white linen, and girt about the breasts with golden girdles, implies their order, being made both *Kings and Priests to* GOD *and the* FATHER. Rev.

i. 6. Reader! do observe what uniformity in all GOD's people. Their robes, are CHRIST's robes. Their ordination is from CHRIST. And, as the worshippers of the beast, and of the dragon, have *their* marks: so the LORD's people have *their's*. Oh! the unspeakable mercy, in these distinctions! *The* LORD *knoweth them that are his!* 2 Tim. ii. 19. And, let not the Reader forget, that this is the security, against the awful day coming on, when all shall worship the beast, except they whose names are in the book of life of *the* LAMB *slain from the foundation of the world.* Rev. xiii. 8. Ezek. ix. 5, 6.

7 ¶ And one of the four beasts gave unto the seven angels seven golden vials full of the wrath of God, who liveth for ever and ever.

8 And the temple was filled with smoke from the glory of God, and from his power, and no man was able to enter into the temple, till the seven plagues of the seven angels were fulfilled.

We have heard nothing of those beasts since the opening of the vision at the *fourth* Chapter, to the *seventh*, excepting once at the *fourteenth;* but now here is one of them coming forward again, to give the seven vials, full of GOD's wrath, to the seven angels. The beasts, and the angels or messengers, are acting as servants on those high occasions; and, as they all are said to come forth from the temple, it plainly shews, that the judgments to be poured from these vials, on the seat of the beast and false prophet, will be from the Church.

I do not think it necessary to enlarge on this part of the prophecy, as what is here said is only by way of preparation to what is to follow, under the ministry of the vials. The temple filled with smoke should seem to refer to what is said of the LORD's house by Isaiah. Chap. vi. 4. It cannot, I think, as some have supposed, refer to the heresies with which the Church was beset; for those heresies are *from without*, whereas the smoke here is *within*. Moreover, it is said, that the temple was filled with smoke, *from the glory of the* LORD; a decided proof, in my view, that the smoke cannot refer to heresies of any kind. But I leave the Reader to his own conclusions upon the subject, under the grace of GOD.

REFLECTIONS.

READER! we were called upon in the last Chapter, to shout with songs of holy joy, in beholding the LAMB, our great and glorious Redeemer, standing with his Church, on Mount Zion, encircled with his army: and here we are called upon again, to shout with the Church, in beholding the people of GOD, who have gotten the victory over the beast, and over his image, and over his mark, standing upon the sea of glass mingled with fire, singing *the song of Moses and the* LAMB! Oh! the felicity, when from a renewed heart, regenerated by grace, we can sing the praises of Him, *who hath called us out of darkness, into his marvellous light!*

And already we contemplate the sure victory over hell, and all the awful heresies abounding, in the view of the angels going forth from the Church of GOD, with their vials of GOD's wrath, to pour out upon them. Every false religion, every idol, and abomination, shall sink under the dreadful plague, to be poured upon them. The man of sin, that mystery of iniquity, which still doth work, shall be destroyed; and that wicked one, both of East, and West, the LORD will consume with the SPIRIT of his mouth, and destroy, with the brightness of his coming. We see the seven angels coming forth from the temple. We behold them armed with the seven golden vials, full of the wrath of GOD. And, by faith, we contemplate the glory of GOD, which shall assuredly follow, when they begin their awful visitation. LORD JESUS! arm thy redeemed with grace, and strengthen them with power, to bear their testimony against the awful abominations of the day. And, oh! for grace to look on, stand still, and see the salvation of our GOD! For yet a little while, and the antichristian heresy of the West, and the false prophet of the East, shall both be no more; and the true Church of CHRIST shall behold them, with the dragon, all cast alive into the lake of fire and brimstone, and shall never again harass and afflict the Church any more. Even so: Amen!

CHAP. XVI.

CONTENTS.

In this Chapter we behold all the Angels, one after another, pouring out their Vials. The awful Consequences which followed are related. The sudden coming of CHRIST is noticed. A Blessedness is pronounced on him that watcheth.

AND I heard a great voice out of the temple saying to the seven angels, Go your ways, and pour out the vials of the wrath of God upon the earth

As in the opening of this Chapter we are called upon to the observation of the ministry of the *Vials*, which contain the last plagues of our GOD, upon the enemies of the faith; I shall beg to do upon this occasion, as I did before the opening of the ministry of the *Seals*, and the ministry of the *Trumpets*, give some short statement, according to my view, of the *Vials themselves*.

And, *first.* I think it will not admit of a question, but that the opening of the vials, took place at that period, be that period fixed by the different calculations of men, at whatever time it may, when, after the Church had been long persecuted, and darkened, under the Pope and his confederates, the pure Gospel of CHRIST, began to hold up its head. There may be, and indeed there is a diversity of opinion, at what period to place this; whether when this kingdom first began to emerge from popery, or at a more remote period, from the present. I have said before, that though I have here and there spoken in round numbers of years, such as the time that *Pagan* Rome continued, after Christ's return to glory; and the probable time, that *Arius* arose, with his awful heresy: yet I do not mean that this *Poor Man's Commentary* shall have any thing to do with calculating times, or seasons, as the probable period, *when* the predictions in this book, remaining to be fulfilled, may be expected to be accomplished. I know that it would much gratify curiosity, for all men by nature love to be supposed, as seeing more into future events than their neighbors. But though this is very natural, yet it is not from grace. I therefore have confined myself to form judgment of the *facts*, and not of the *times*. These will all open in due course, as the Lord hath appointed. I therefore, on this subject, of the ministry of the *vials*, would make this one general observation, namely, that they certainly opened, when the pure Gospel, after the long obscurity under which it had lain in popish legends, and the trumpery of that heresy, began to lift up its head. Then it was, according to my view, when *John* saw that angel flying in the midst of heaven, *having the everlasting Gospel to preach unto them that dwell on the earth; and to every nation, and kindred, and tongue and people.* Rev. xiv. 6.

Secondly. It is important, for the right apprehension of the ministry of the *vials*, to remember, that though they are placed last, in point of order, in this book; yet the opening of the seals were not all finished, neither the sounding of the trumpets all over, before the *first* vial, and indeed several of the succeeding ones, had performed their ministry. This is abundantly evident, for the greater part of the vials have done their office; indeed all have finished excepting the *two* last: yet the seventh trumpet is not yet sounded, neither will it, (as is most probable,) before the *seventh vial* comes to be poured out.

And, *thirdly.* It may be proper to make one *general* observation more, on the subject of those *vials*, before we go on, to look at each of them particularly; and to remark, that the plagues which follow each vial poured out, do not so totally pass away, as that the whole wrath is expended of one, before the next vial which was to succeed, comes to be poured out. Not so. For we behold the consequences of some of the early vials, even operating now; and, therefore, we are not to conclude, that one woe is past, in all those instances, before another comes. The whole ministry of the vials is directed by the Lord, as his last plagues, to bring down the enemies of his salvation; and, therefore, they are so directed by the Lord, as shall best accomplish this purpose. Having thus stated, in a general way and manner, the subject of the ministry of the vials, at large; we will now prosecute the Chapter, and attend to what may be supposed, under each, as particularly intended.

2 And the first went, and poured out his vial upon the earth; and there fell a noisome and grievous sore upon the men which had the mark of the beast, and *upon* them which worshipped his image.

There can be no doubt, but that it was the Lord Jesus Christ, whose voice *John* heard, as mentioned in the former verse, thus sending forth his servants on their employment; or God the Holy Ghost, whose office it is to ordain to the ministry. In either sense, it is blessed. For in either point of view, it must be attended with success. And most blessed was the success of it. For the effects of the pouring out of the first vial was, that a noisome, and grievous sore, fell upon the men which had the mark of the beast, and upon them which worshipped his image.

The Reader will remember that I do not speak decidedly upon any point of doubtful meaning, but I venture to believe that it was the pouring out of this first Vial, which is said to have been poured upon the earth, that is, the empire of the Pope, which produced a change upon the minds of numbers, concerning him and his heresy. For what is a noisome and grievous sore, in a spiritual sense, but a sense of dissatisfaction. And when the eyes of the common people, here called the earth, through grace, were opened to see the folly of bulls, and grants, and licences, and pardons, all for money, what could sour the mind more, than the having been long hood-winked by such iniquity.

3 And the second angel poured out his vial upon the sea; and it became as the blood of a dead *man:* and every living soul died in the sea.

We have here the *second* Angel's ministry, and the effect of the *second* vial poured upon the sea. Perhaps, as the *earth* might mean the home of the Pope, so the *sea* might mean the distant parts, where his influence extended. As the sea opens a turnpike for commerce and trade, by the sea, it is probable might be meant, death to the Pope's interest abroad, as well at at home. For, as those vials poured out, were full of GOD's wrath, so wherever they came, they brought destruction to his heresy. And it is possible, that this vial had respect to the death of the *Pope's* interest in this kingdom. Death I am sure it must be, to all that do receive the image of the beast in future. And death it is, to all that have received it, in all that is past.

4 And the third angel poured out his vial upon the rivers and fountains of waters; and they became blood.

5 And I heard the angel of the waters say, Thou art righteous, O Lord, which art, and wast, and shalt be, because thou hast judged thus.

6 ¶ For they have shed the blood of saints and prophets, and thou hast given them blood to drink: for they are worthy.

7 And I heard another out of the altar say, Even so, Lord God Almighty, true and righteous *are* thy judgements.

The love of money is the root of all evil. And those who have hired themselves out for the sake of gain, (and no other cause could ever influence any man, to write or speak, on the side of such glaring folly as popery,) to send forth pamphlets in justification of the beast or her whelps, may be supposed to be the rivers and fountains of waters here spoken of, on whom the *third* Angel poured out his vial. And the acknowledgments of GOD's justice, at the pouring out of this vial is very sweetly introduced, as well as confirmed by another angel. What can be more awful, than the contemplation of the unnumbered murders, perpetrated under the inquisition, and other engines of that detestable monarchy, which sheltering itself under the title of holiness, hath been productive of more horrid acts of cruelty, than all the paganism of the world.

8 And the fourth angel poured out his vial upon the sun; and power was given unto him to scorch men with fire.

9 And men were scorched with great heat, and blasphemed the name of God, which hath power over these plagues; and they repented not to give him glory.

By the pouring the *fourth* vial upon the sun, some have thought that the *Pope's* power is meant to have been thereby eclipsed. Indeed, as all the vials are directed to the overthrow of Antichrist, in every way, and by every direction, we may suppose this point under every one hath been accomplishing. And the awful effects of blaspheming GOD is, as might be supposed, the sure result of vials of wrath, poured out upon the ungodly.

10 And the fifth angel poured out his vial upon the seat of the beast; and his kingdom was full of darkness; and they gnawed their tongues for pain.

11 And blasphemed the God of heaven because of their pains and their sores, and repented not of their deeds.

As this is the last vial poured out specially upon the beast, so it is worthy the Reader's observation, that it is said to have been poured out upon the seat of the beast, meaning his whole empire. And I leave the Reader to his own thoughts to consider, whether the wonderful events which the last thirty years have brought forward, in humbling the whole papal authority, may not have been what is here said. Certain it is, that the *sixth* vial is not yet poured out. And when it is, the *Turkish* dominions, as the river *Euphrates* proves, will receive its contents. It will be said, perhaps, that the Pope is lately recovered from his palsyed state. To which it may be answered, yes, he is. But when the *seventh* trumpet comes to be sounded, and the *seventh* vial to be poured out, the whole influence both of Pope, Turk, and devil, will fall to rise no more, and all will be summed up, in the everlasting triumphs of CHRIST.

12 And the sixth angel poured out his vial upon the great river Euphrates; and the water thereof was dried up, that the way of the kings of the east might be prepared.

13 And I saw three unclean spirits like frogs *come* out of the mouth of the dragon, and out of the mouth of the beast, and out of the mouth of the false prophet.

14 For they are the spirits of devils, working miracles, *which* go forth unto the kings of the earth and of the whole world, to gather them to the battle of that great day of God Almighty.

15 ¶ Behold, I come as a thief. Blessed *is* he that watcheth, and keepeth his garments, lest he walk naked, and they see his shame.

16 And he gathered them together into a place called in the Hebrew tongue Armageddon.

The pouring out of the *sixth* vial is yet to come. And when it comes, the chief ministry of it, will be upon the kingdom of the false prophet. This blessed event, brings on the total overthrow of that Anti-christian power. The river *Euphrates* implies his whole territory. And what a wonderful effect will it produce? *Isaiah* the prophet evidently alluded to this in one of his Chapters, where he saith; *And the* LORD *shall be known to Egypt, and the Egyptians shall know the* LORD *in that day. And the* LORD *shall smite Egypt, he shall smite and heal it. And they shall return even to the* LORD, *and he shall be entreated of them, and he shall heal them. In that day shall there be an highway out of Egypt to Assyria, and the Assyrians shall come into Egypt, and the Egyptians into Assyria, and the Egyptians shall serve with the Assyrians. In that day shall Israel be the third with Egypt, and with Assyria, even a blessing in the midst of the land, whom the* LORD *of hosts shall bless, saying, blessed be Egypt my people; and Assyria the work of my hands; and Israel mine inheritance.* Isaiah xix. 21—25. Hence, if this scripture be in reference to this event, as I venture to believe it is, and the *sixth* trumpet overthrow, as I believe it will, the false prophet, and totally destroy his empire, the LORD will bring out his chosen ones that are now there, and by the sovereignty of his grace, will cause the Jews to return and the redeemed to be together, and the LORD will open an highway for all his people, both *Jew* and *Gentile,* bond and free, to return to *Zion* with everlasting songs upon their heads, and when all these Anti-christian heresies are destroyed, his redeemed out of all nations shall come and flow together, and CHRIST will prepare his people for his reign upon earth.

And in confirmation of this, let the Reader further observe, that in the close of what is here said, under the *sixth* vial, the LORD JESUS

CHRIST himself is said to come, and to come suddenly. The LORD will strike the last deadly blow to all the powers. And when the unclean spirits, that is, the spirits of devils, are seen coming out of the mouth of these Anti-christian powers, and are gathering to the battle of the great day of GOD, that is, not the day of judgment, for that is not yet, but to this which is before it, and are drawn there to their own ruin, then will CHRIST's power be known, and felt, and acknowledged by all.

The place of battle called *Armageddon*, is only specified by way of confirmation. It seems to have been taken from *Megiddo*, the valley *Ar*, or more properly *Haar*, signifying the mountain of the same place. I think the name is only used, to shew how open and exposed, as an high mountain it shall be.

17 And the seventh angel poured out his vial into the air; and there came a great voice out of the temple of heaven, from the throne, saying, It is done.

18 And there were voices, and thunders, and lightnings; and there was a great earthquake, such as was not since men were upon the earth, so mighty an earthquake, *and* so great.

19 And the great city was divided into three parts, and the cities of the nations fell : and great Babylon came in remembrance before God, to give unto her the cup of the wine of the fierceness of his wrath.

20 And every island fled away, and the mountains were not found.

21 And there fell upon men a great hail out of heaven, *every stone* about the weight of a talent; and men blasphemed God because of the plague of the hail ; for the plague thereof was exceeding great.

Here ends the pouring out of the vials, and a tremendous pouring out it is. It is said to be into the air, meaning the empire of Satan, who is emphatically called, *the prince of the power of the air*. Ephes. ii. 2. But we must include the whole territories of Pope, and Turk, also, because *Satan's* empire is over them, and the air takes in the whole of their empire and *Satan's* together. And as this puts an end to all the struggles, which for so many hundreds of years have been carried on by hell and its auxiliaries, against the kingdoms of our GOD, and of his CHRIST, we may well suppose, that the decision which is final, will be most strikingly glorious. I shall not in this place, anticipate what is said, in allusion to this great day of

CHRIST, in the latter part of this book of prophecy; but if the Reader will read what is delivered on this subject, Chapter xix. from the 11th verse to the end, he will see the best explanation of the transactions of this *sixth* vial.

I beg the Reader, however, that he will not too hastily pass away from this most blessed view of CHRIST, under the *seventh* vial. If voices, thunderings, and lightening bespake the manifestations of the LORD JESUS, and a great voice came forth from the temple, that is the Church, saying, *it is done.* Oh! how ought we to hail the glorious event! JESUS had before been seen standing upon the earth, and upon the sea, and swearing by him that liveth for ever and ever, that in the days *when the mystery of* GOD *shall be finished, there should be time no longer;* and here we behold the confirmation of the same, and CHRIST himself coming to finish it. Chap. x. 1—7.

Oh! the unspeakable joy, when the Church shall see the blood of the saints avenged, the whore and all her cursed crew, which from age to age, have been drunken with the blood of the saints, cast down to rise no more. And hell repaid his numerous temptations, whereby the saints of GOD, through the whole time-state of the Church, have been assaulted with his devilish cruelties. How will that hymn of praise burst forth from ten thousand times ten thousand souls, in unceasing love and thanksgiving to our adorable LORD; *We give thee thanks,* LORD GOD *Almighty, which art, and which was, and art to come, because thou hast taken to thee thy great power, and hast reigned!* Chap. xi. 17.

REFLECTIONS.

Look up, and contemplate the LORD, sending forth from his Church, the seven Angels, and messengers with his seven last plagues, to take vengeance on his enemies, and to deliver his people. Then let the Reader consider, how sure, how everlastingly sure, is the LORD's Church and people. What though for a while the enemy seems to triumph, and the redeemed of the LORD are oppressed by the mighty, yet *the salvation of the righteous is of the* LORD, *who is also their strength in the time of need.*

How awful are these pourings out of the vials of divine wrath? One after another, arising higher and higher in the scale of judgment. But so desperately hardened in sin, are the enemies of our GOD, and of his CHRIST, that though the sinner is scorched with fire and great heat, yet he only blasphemes the name of GOD, and repents not to give the LORD glory.

My soul! learn from hence, to trace all thy mercies to their source. It is GOD's everlasting love, which hath chosen thee in CHRIST, and preserved thee in CHRIST, and accepted thee in CHRIST, before the foundation of the world. Hence, all thy mercies in JESUS, by which the vials of wrath, poured out upon the ungodly cannot come nigh thee. Blessed JESUS! let my soul be on the look out for thy coming, that no midnight hour may surprize me, no blasphemies of men or devils may alarm me. And, when *Babylon* shall come into remembrance before GOD, and our GOD shall give unto her the cup of the wine of the fierceness of his wrath, thy Church may shout aloud in her destruction, and both heaven and earth praise GOD with exceeding joy.

CHAP. XVII.

CONTENTS.

Under the Representation of a Woman, arrayed in purple and scarlet is shewn to John, the Whore of Babylon. Her Character given. The Victory of the Lamb. The Whore's Punishment.

AND there came one of the seven angels which had the seven vials, and talked with me, saying unto me, Come hither; I will shew unto thee the judgement of the great whore that sitteth upon many waters.

2 With whom the kings of the earth have committed fornication, and the inhabitants of the earth have been made drunk with the wine of her fornication.

We cannot well be at a loss to discover, who is here meant, if we call to remembrance, that in scripture language, Persons are spoken of by figures, and places by waters. That this woman is a city, the last verse of this Chapter, in so many words plainly saith, *the woman which thou sawest, is that great city, which reigneth over the kings of the earth.* And what great city but *Rome*, which had so many provinces under her, and in a religious sense, (that is, I mean a mere *nominal* religion,) how many kings and nations have owned the *Pope's* supremacy. So that nothing can be more clearly defined. Add to these, it is a very usual thing, to call states and empires harlots and whores, when becoming profane and ungodly. Thus the LORD complained of Israel; *How is the faithful city become an harlot.* Isaiah i. 21. Waters and rivers are terms used in scripture for states and people; yea, in this very Chapter, the term is explained. *And he saith unto me, the waters which thou sawest where the whore sitteth, are people, and multitudes, and nations, and tongues,* verse 15. Hence, therefore, here are explanations given, as plain as words can make them, in proof that this great whore, is a great city, that hath rule over the kings of the earth, and the many waters she sitteth upon, expresseth her power and authority. So, that *Papal Rome* and none else, can be meant. This is a great point in discovery.

The next account is, that she is said to commit fornication with the kings of the earth, and the inhabitants of the earth; and to have been made drunk with the wine of her fornication. Now when we consider, how many nations profess popery, surely we discover the awful proof of her fornications. And when we call to mind, the blood of the martyrs she has shed, we may well call her thirst after blood drunkenness. We shall see by and by, as we prosecute the Chapter, the number of those kings, that are tributes to the whore. But this in due time.

3 ¶ So he carried me away in the spirit into the wilderness; and I saw a woman sit upon a scarlet coloured beast, full of names of blasphemy, having seven heads and ten horns.

4 And the woman was arrayed in purple and scarlet colour, and decked with gold and precious stones and pearls, having a golden cup in her hand full of abominations and filthiness of her fornication.

5 ¶ And upon her foreheads *was* a name written, MYSTERY, BABYLON THE GREAT, THE MOTHER OF HARLOTS AND ABOMINATIONS OF THE EARTH.

6 And I saw the woman drunken with the blood of the saints, and with the blood of the martyrs of Jesus: and when I saw her I wondered with great admiration.

Let the Reader recollect, that *John* beheld all this in vision, similar to *Ezekiel*, who, while he was at *Chebar*, his mind was led to *Jerusalem*. Ezek. viii. 3. So *John* was in *Patmos*, and he talks of being carried away in the spirit into the wilderness. All the characters here given of this woman, are descriptive of *Rome* and the *Pope*, and impossible to be applied to any other. The scarlet-colored *beast*, implies the regal power. The names full of blasphemy, are those by which the Pope is known. Such as his holiness, who is a sinner, the vicar of CHRIST, and the Head of the Church. His dress decked with gold, and precious stones, and pearls. But more especially the names in his forehead. And if it be true, as is said that the Popes, until the time of *Julius* the Third, always wore the word *mystery* on their forehead, and that he dropped it, when he found this portion of the scripture was applied to him, and his wearing the word considered a confirmation of it, all these circumstances, are unanswerably decisive to whom they belong. And if to these be added, the hierarchy of cardinals, archbishops, monks, and abbots, their traffic in the sale of indulgencies, holy water, penance, and absolutions, and the nefarious trade, carried on under the color of religion, it should seem, that the title of mother of harlots, and abominations of the earth, cannot be withheld for a moment, either from the place of *Rome*, or the person of the Pope. And though *John*, it appears, was astonished at what he beheld, marvelling perhaps, that there should be such characters upon earth, and at the longsuffering and patience of GOD, in bearing with them; yet, such is the awful depravity of human nature, when void of GOD's grace, that nothing of atrocity can be too bad, for the corrupt heart to follow. Reader, such views, shocking as they are, are yet profitable. Oh! how loudly do they preach to us, the blessed doctrine of distinguishing grace; and which is the sole cause, wherefore one man differs from another.

7 And the angel said unto me, Wherefore didst thou marvel? I will tell thee the mystery of the woman, and of the beast that carrieth her, which hath the seven heads and ten horns.

8 The beast that thou sawest was, and is not; and shall ascend out of the bottomless pit, and go into perdition: and they that dwell on the earth shall wonder, whose names were not written in the book of life from the foundation of the world, when they behold the beast that was, and is not, and yet is.

9 ¶ And here *is* the mind which hath wisdom. The seven heads are seven mountains, on which the woman sitteth.

10 And there are seven kings: five are fallen, and one is, *and* the other is not yet come; and when he cometh, he must continue a short space.

11 And the beast that was, and is not, even he is the eighth, and is of the seven, and goeth into perdition.

12 ¶ And the ten horns which thou sawest are ten kings, which have received no kingdom as yet; but receive power as kings one hour with the beast.

13 ¶ These have one mind, and shall give their power and strength unto the beast.

There can be no doubt, but that when the whole of this blessed book of prophecy comes to be unfolded, every minute circumstance concerning it, will appear to the Church, as plain, that we shall only wonder at our dulness of apprehension, in not having discovered it before. But certain it is, that what is here said, is not rendered so perfectly clear at present, as that the whole is level to our thoughts. That the seven kings are those that worship the beast, we can easily conceive, and that both those that receive the mark of the beast, as well as the beast and false prophet, shall finally be cast into the bottomless pit, these are truths we can readily apprehend. But concerning the beast that was, and is not, and yet is, and the eighth that shall arise and go into perdition, together with those other ten kings, who receive power for one hour with the beast, these things have called forth a great variety of opinions, but there are none on which we can lean with a certainty of assurance, that they are correct. I therefore pass them all by, and desire not to be wise above what is written.

In the place therefore of writing upon mere conjecture and supposition, I would beg to offer a short observation which the present moment seems to furnish, and which, if I am correct, may be profitable. I assume for granted, (what I venture to conclude, none but the worshippers of the beast will deny,) that the woman which *John* saw sitting upon the great waters, is Papal Rome, and if so, the late wonderful events very clearly manifest, that the LORD's purposes concerning this heresy, hath undergone a great change within the last *thirty years!* To what a humiliating state was this Anti-christian power brought, before a late change raised her up again. Now, the Prophet *Daniel,* speaks of the scattering of the power *of the holy people, and then all these things shall be finished.* Dan. xii. 7.

And that *Daniel* had one and the same object in view, and *John* and *Daniel* were both taught by the same HOLY SPIRIT is most certain, by comparing Dan. xii. 7. with Rev. xii. 14. Hence, therefore, I am inclined to believe, that the late humbling of this Antichristian power, is only preparatory to a greater extent of power than she hath ever yet had, and as the language she useth in the next Chapter, seems to imply. And, thus, just before her final overthrow, she shall exult in her security, and seem to bid defiance to heaven and earth. *She saith in her heart, I sit as a queen, and am no widow, and shall see no sorrow.* Chap. xviii. 7. This appears to me to be her present language, in consequence of the recent lifting up, after her former depression. I shall rejoice, if it be the LORD's will, and for the LORD's glory, that I am mistaken in my expectation, and that she will not arise higher. But the *scattering of the power of the holy people,* which the Prophet speaks of, hath not in my view taken place, neither are *the two witnesses* slain, neither hath the *sixth* vial been as yet been poured out. All these events appear to me, to be first expected, before that this intoxicated woman will have her plagues *come upon her in one hour;* and her everlasting destruction follow. And here for the present I leave this subject.

14 ¶ These shall make war with the Lamb, and the Lamb shall overcome them : for he is Lord of lords, and King of kings: and they that are with him *are* called, and chosen, and faithful.

15 And he saith unto me, The waters which thou sawest, where the whore sitteth, are peoples, and multitudes, and nations, and tongues.

16 ¶ And the ten horns which thou sawest upon the beast, these shall hate the whore, and shall make her desolate and naked, and shall eat her flesh, and burn her with fire.

17 For God hath put in their hearts to fulfil his will, and to agree, and give their kingdom unto the beast, until the words of God shall be fulfilled.

18 And the woman which thou sawest is that great city, which reigneth over the kings of the earth.

All indeed make war with the Lamb; that is, with the Lamb's followers. Both *Herod* and *Pontius Pilate*, though in themselves no friends to each other, but when CHRIST or his people are in view, all the *Herods*, and all the *Pilates* of the earth, with the Gentiles and the people of all descriptions of carnal men, are joined together. Every thing in the natural mind, unrenewed by grace, is hostile to CHRIST. But, Reader, observe what is said, *the* LAMB *shall overcome them*. Oh! yes! And in Him, and His righteousness, the feeblest of this little army, shall overcome them too.

I cannot refrain from begging my Reader to remark with me, what a blessed and glorious account is given of CHRIST's Person, and what a lively one of his people. For he is LORD of lords, and King of kings. Yes! blessed for ever, thou Almighty GOD, be thou in thine own eternal nature and essence! Thine own eternal distinctions as one in the GODHEAD make these titles thine. And by creation, providence, grace, and glory, thou, in common with the FATHER and the HOLY GHOST, hast, and art all. And how sweet is it to the souls of thy people, that by means of their oneness with thee, in that nature of theirs thou hast taken into union with thyself, they that are with thee, are *called, and chosen, and faithful*. Yes, LORD! by thy calling them with an holy calling, they are proved to have been chosen of GOD, before the foundation of the world. For whom he did predestinate, them he also called. And by their call in grace, they are made faithful in CHRIST JESUS. Oh! the unspeakable blessedness of such distinguishing grace! Reader! what saith your heart's testimony to these things? Can you, and do you, take up the sweet language the HOLY GHOST by the Apostle teacheth the Church. *Who hath saved us, and called us with an holy calling, not according to our works, but according to his own purpose and grace, given us in* CHRIST JESUS *before the world began*. For the Commentary on the 15th and 18th verses, see the 1st and 2nd. 2 Tim. i. 9.

REFLECTIONS.

BLESSED and condescending Teacher of *John!* Thy Church desire to praise thee, O LORD JESUS, for causing thy servant the Apostle to be shewn, and the Church through him also, concerning this great spiritual whore, which sitteth upon many waters, committeth fornication with the kings of the earth, and the inhabitants thereof, and hath been made drunk with the wine of her fornication. Through thy grace, LORD, instructing thy people, we cannot mistake her character. Her purple and scarlet robes, her gold and proud trappings, the blasphemy of her pretended power, and the names she assumes, her whore's forehead and the mystery she hath put there, all mark her out, as the object of horror and detestation, to thy people. And while we behold her drunken with the blood of thy saints, and with the blood of the martyrs of JESUS, we cannot but wonder, with great admiration! Oh! the awful state to which the nature of man is brought down! Oh! the astonishing extent of the long suffering of Almighty GOD.

Dearest LORD JESUS! the souls of thy people are relieved in the pleasing prospect, that shortly thou wilt come and root out of thy kingdom, all things that offend. She, which hath intoxicated herself with the blood of thy saints, shall have her flesh eaten by those who professed to love her. She, who hated the meek and humble followers of the Lamb, shall herself be despised; yea, they shall hate the whore, and make her desolate and naked, shall eat her flesh, and burn her with fire.

Oh! what a relief to my soul is it, to turn from the view of images so horrible, and to contemplate JESUS under his own rightful character, LORD of lords, and King of kings! May every knee bow before thee! And oh! what praises shall I offer to my GOD, that JESUS hath a seed that serve him, a generation that call him blessed; who are *called*, and *chosen*, and *faithful!* LORD! do thou in those awful times, make them and keep them faithful. It is thy sweet province, and sure I am, it is my LORD's delight, *to keep them from falling, and to present them faultless before the presence of his glory with exceeding joy.* To the only wise GOD, our SAVIOR, be glory and majesty, dominion and power, both now and ever. Amen.

CHAP. XVIII.

CONTENTS.

The Fall of Babylon. GOD's People come out from her. The Kings, and great Men, and Merchants, wail for her. The Saints of GOD rejoice over her.

AND after these things I saw another angel come down from heaven, having great power; and the earth was lightened with his glory,

This is a very blessed and refreshing Chapter, in which we arrive at the close of the history, in that part of it, which concerns the destruction of the whore; here called *Babylon.* The date of this Chapter, must be under the *fifth* vial, and, in correspondence also to the *sixth* trumpet, both which we are still under, though, as I before remarked, in the few general observations on the vials, that they are certainly not so distinct in their ministry, as that one hath fully exhausted all which belonged to it, before the succeeding one came to be poured out, for, frequently, through the whole that is already past, we find from their history, one runs into another. See Chapter xvi. Commentary, on verse 1.

The several parts of this Chapter refresh the Church of GOD, with their blessed informations. The long prayed-for time is here come. She that deluged the earth with the blood of the saints, is now brought to her account. The HOLY GHOST describes the different effects wrought upon the minds of men, in the view of her ruin. Those of states and empires, as well as the shipmasters and merchants, who profited by her delusion on the world, lament her downfall, which involves in it their own. While the Church of GOD, in not only that part of it yet upon earth, but the Holy Apostles and Prophets now in heaven, join in the triumphant song. Who this Messenger is, whom *John* saw coming down from the Church, to give the glorious tidings is not said. A very blessed account of his greatness is given, for it is said, that he lightened the earth with his glory, that is, I apprehend, not the glories of his person, but the glory of his intelligence. It could not be CHRIST I should suppose, because CHRIST is the judge of the whore, and He that will come under the *seventh* vial, to punish in Person, the devil, and the beast, and the false prophet together. Chap. xvi. 15—17.

I admire the grace of the LORD towards *John*, and the Church through him, that it seems to have been immediately after the vision the LORD hath favored him with, in the preceding Chapter of the whore's prosperity and pride, that this of her judgment immediately followed. So sweetly doth the LORD time his mercies to his people, that the lifting up their souls with joy, shall speedily succeed their exercises of sorrow.

2 ¶ And he cried mightily with a strong voice, saying, Babylon the great is fallen, is fallen, and is become the habitation of devils, and the hold of every foul spirit, and a cage of every unclean and hateful bird.

3 For all nations have drunk of the wine of the wrath of her fornication, and the kings of the earth have committed fornication with her, and the merchants of the earth are waxed rich through the abundance of her delicacies.

The loud cry is intended to shew, how extensive, as well as glorious, its blissful proclamation is. Perhaps, many of the LORD's hidden ones are supposed to be in *Babylon* at the time. They shall hear it and rejoice. And multitudes beyond *Babylon*, yea, in those islands of ours and other nations, who have been long oppressed under the secret, if not open tyranny of the whore's influence, shall hear it also. And I beg the Reader to observe, with me, how every feature describes this mystical *Babylon*, this *Rome*. It is now discovered at her fall, how like antient *Babylon* in natural *things*, occupied only by reptiles and venomous creatures, so that no traveller can venture near it; mystical *Babylon* hath been in moral and spiritual things the habitation of devils from her damnable doctrines, and the cage of every unclean and hateful bird, from her sinful, loose, and dissolute practices. See a striking account of *antient* Babylon, in proof of the former instance. Isaiah xiii. 19 to the end. See also for a striking account of *mystical* Babylon, in proof of the latter. 2 Thess. ii. 3—12.

Let the Reader observe the strong expressions of joy in the Angel's repeating his words; *Babylon the Great is fallen, is fallen.* Such mercies cannot be too often repeated. For although, through the protecting grace of the LORD, not a single one of the LORD's redeemed family, can the beast, and the whore, or the false prophet, or the devil, draw away, so as finally to perish, (see Rev. xiii. 8.) yet, what persecutions and punishments, yea, temporal death, hath the inquisition of this heresy occasioned, for the many centuries in which the horrible delusion hath prevailed. Oh! who but must rejoice, in the glorious proclamation, and repeat with holy joy, and praises to the GOD of our salvation: *Babylon the Great is fallen, is fallen.*

When it is said, that *all nations have drunk of the wine of the wrath of her fornication,* it must be understood, as meaning those nations only, where her cursed influence and authority hath reached. *Heathens* and *Mahometans* are not included. Their delusion is from hell also, but under a different shape and character. In countries where Christianity was professed, as it was when the empire under *Constantine* became Christian; that is, became *nominally* so, in a mere outward form; there the devil, by a master-piece peculiarly his own, professed to be a Christian also; the more artfully to deceive. And this gave him an opportunity to introduce a variety of sects, which by denying the glorious truths of the Gospel in CHRIST's GODHEAD, and redemption by his blood, might as effectually lull his subjects on to ruin, as among heathens a total ignorance of CHRIST would accomplish the same. Let the Reader mark these things as he observes what is here said, and as he looks into the world, and if the LORD be his teacher, he will discover, that the devil hath his various ways and operations to deceive. But let the Reader still further observe, that his deceptions can go no further, than the LORD hath limited him. *The* LORD *knoweth them that are his.* And of such the LORD saith, *none shall pluck them out of his hands.* His Israel, his Church, his chosen are scattered. But, *He will search and seek them out, from every place where they are scattered, in the cloudy and dark day.* When *Babylon* falls, his redeemed shall be gathered out of her. When the false prophet is destroyed, JESUS will take care of his outcasts, which are now in the midst of that *Moab.* Isaiah xvi. 4. That sweet verse is a volume in point of fulness, and a whole charter in point of security, to all the LORD's people. *He shall send his angels, and shall gather together his elect, from the four winds, from the uttermost part of the earth, to the uttermost part of heaven.* Mark xiii. 27.

4 ¶ And I heard another voice from heaven, saying, Come out of her, my people, that ye be not partakers of her sins, and that ye receive not of her plagues.

5 For her sins have reached unto heaven, and God hath remembered her iniquities.

6 Reward her even as she rewarded you, and double unto her double according to her works: in the cup which she hath filled fill to her double.

I think it more than probable, that this voice which *John* heard, and which he calls another, by way of distinction from the one before, was CHRIST. *John* doth not call him an Angel. And if he had, we know that CHRIST is not unfrequently called the Angel of the Covenant. Malachi iii. 1. But he saith he heard another voice from heaven, from the Church. And it is not unlikely that it was CHRIST, because JESUS dwells in *Zion*. And he delights to make himself known to his people. He loves to call them so. And here the voice saith *my people*. Every thing is endearing, where we can see JESUS, and hear JESUS.

But I must particularly beg the Reader, to attend to the sweet words themselves. *Come out of her, my people*. May we not suppose, that whenever the fall of *Rome* takes place, many of GOD's dear ones, both already called, and some as yet uncalled, will be there. Nay, may there not be many of JESUS's own, which are then unborn in nature, and therefore must be preserved in the loins, or bowels of their natural parents for the future purpose of regeneration! *Destroy it not, there is a blessing in it*! Isaiah lxv. 8. What a subject to the imagination doth this open. And how many of the LORD's hidden ones may be found there in that day, whom that day's judgment shall minister to their conversion? How many of GOD's timid ones, who, though secretly taught of GOD, like *Lot*, are living in the *Sodom* city, grieved as his soul was, *with the filthy conversation of the wicked*; but from various causes there remain? Psm. cxx. 5. 2 Pet. ii. 7. In all these and numberless other cases, that our imagination cannot form the voice to come out from among her, will be heard and obeyed, for the LORD saith as to Lot, *haste thee, escape thither, for I cannot do any thing till thou be come thither*. And as it was then, so will it be in spiritual *Sodom*, and all similar destructions of the ungodly. *It came to pass when* GOD *destroyed the cities of the plain, that* GOD *remembered Abraham, and sent Lot out of the midst of the overthrow, when he overthrew the cities, in the which Lot dwelt*. Gen. xix. 22—29.

The separating from every thing unsuitable to the faith of a child of GOD, is included in what is here said, and the recompensing the evil an ungodly conduct of infidels hath imposed upon the LORD's people, is perfectly consistent with the precept of *not rendering evil for evil, or railing for railing*. For let the Reader observe, this is not an injury of a *private* and *personal* nature. This is the LORD's cause, and of public concern to the Church. As the whore hath burnt and destroyed, robbed and murdered the saints of GOD, for their adherence to CHRIST, so all that love CHRIST, must give no countenance to her heresies. No favor is to be shewn on any account, to the cause of the whore, though to the persons of the ignorant, in the communion of her heresy, tenderness is to be manifested, if *peradventure*, GOD *should give them repentance to the ac-*

knowledging of the truth, to recover them out of the snare of the devil, who are taken captive by him at his will. 2 Tim. ii. 25, 26.

7 How much she hath glorified herself, and lived deliciously, so much torment and sorrow give her: for she saith in her heart, I sit a queen, and am no widow, and shall see no sorrow.

8 Therefore shall her plagues come in one day, death, and mourning, and famine; and she shall be utterly burned with fire: for strong *is* the LORD God who judgeth her.

I beg the Reader to attend to what is here said, for, in my view, it throws a great light upon the events going on in the present day. Let the Reader recollect, or look back to the observations made in the preceding Chapter, after verse the 13th, and connect what is here said with those remarks. And in addition I would desire to say, that when it be considered, the late ascendency the Pontiff hath gained in those dominions, he had for a while, seemingly lost, and the strides which are still making by him and his agents, to get back to his interest certain powers, which once protested against him, and I think he will be somewhat inclined to think with me, if he be not altogether of my opinion, that Popery, before the total overthrow of it, will be more elevated than ever.

Let the Reader consider, and reconsider those two verses. She is said to be living deliciously, and to say in her heart, *I sit a queen, and am no widow, and shall see no sorrow,* when, in the moment, her plagues shall come upon her in one day, death, and mourning, and famine; yea, she shall be utterly burned with fire. If language conveys any thing, here is great prosperity succeeded by great woe. And, what shall prevent the power of the Pope from being greater than it ever hath been. What shall come between the present indifferency in some, and the cordial affection of others, to a more extensive toleration, and by a transition then hardly perceivable, exalting the whore of *Rome* to her former splendor, yea, greater splendor than ever; when the loose doctrines, and looser conduct of the great mass of men, are already so ripe for it.

It is the mercy of the LORD's people, that by his grace, they are kept from all danger. And it is no less their mercy, to have come out from among her. But this scripture explained by present events, leaves in my view no question, but that this Anti-christian heresy will have a lifting up, just before her final overthrow, in possessing again some of her long-lost territories, and be the queen, as she herself saith of them and all her dependencies in the very hour, the LORD pours out her plagues in one day, and death, everlasting mourning, famine, and fire will be her portion.

9 ¶ And the kings of the earth who have committed fornication, and lived deliciously with her, shall bewail her, and lament for her, when they shall see the smoke of her burning.

CH. XVIII.]   REVELATION.   633

10 Standing afar off for the fear of her torment, saying, Alas, alas, that great city Babylon, that mighty city! for in one hour is thy judgement come.

11 ¶ And the merchants of the earth shall weep and mourn over her: for no man buyeth their merchandize any more.

12 The merchandize of gold, and silver, and precious stones, and of pearls, and fine linen, and purple, and silk, and scarlet, and all thyne wood, and all manner vessels of ivory, and all manner vessels of most precious wood, and of brass, and iron, and marble.

13 And cinnamon, and odours, and ointments, and frankincense, and wine, and oil, and fine flour, and wheat, and beasts, and sheep, and horses, and chariots, and slaves, and souls of men.

14 And the fruits that thy soul lusted after are departed from thee, and all things which were dainty and goodly are departed from thee, and thou shalt find them no more at all.

15 The merchants of these things which were made rich by her, shall stand afar off for the fear of her torment, weeping and wailing,

16 And saying, Alas, alas, that great city, that was clothed in fine linen, and purple, and scarlet, and decked with gold, and precious stones, and pearls!

17 For in one hour so great riches is come to nought. And every ship-master, and all the company in ships, and sailors, and as many as trade by sea, stood afar off.

18 And cried when they saw the smoke of her burning, saying, What *city is* like unto this great city!

19 And they cast dust on their heads, and cried, weeping and wailing, saying, Alas! alas, that great

city, wherein were made rich all that had ships in the sea by reason of her costliness: for in one hour is she made desolate.

The oftener I read this funeral lamentation of the mourners, that follow the whore to her burying; the more I am struck with astonishment, at the impudence of her deceptions, and the forbearance of the Lord. To think that such a mummery should have gulled the nations so many hundreds of years is wonderful! And indeed it would be hardly possible to reconcile it with the common sense of mankind, were it not that so many profited by the cheat. Let the Reader take notice of some of the many.

First. The kings of the earth, who have committed fornication, and lived deliciously with her. These are those who have profited by the same tricks, as the whore herself hath played off, to keep the lower order in subjection. For when confession, and penance, and the profits of all the trumpery of forms and ceremonies are done away, they as well as she, will find cause to lament that their juggling is over.

Secondly. The merchants of the earth will mourn also at her downfall. These are not only the common traders at *Rome*, who take advantage of the religion of the place, to impose upon the foreigners which come to their markets, but chiefly is intended, the whore's merchants; namely, the dealers in pardons and indulgencies, who sell licences for sin, and pray people out of purgatory for money. It is said, verse 13, that their merchandize, is *the souls of men.* And this indeed is the chief traffic. All such must follow the funeral procession, for they will for ever shut up shop, when the whore's plagues come; for as it is here said, *no man buyeth her merchandize any more.*

Thirdly. Every ship-master, and all the company in ships, and sailors, and as many as trade by sea, are involved in the calamity: And well they may. For both at home and abroad, by sea and by land, wherever the whore's influence extendeth, and her priests and people find the trade profitable, the loss of it in money matters must be ruinous. So that the whore's downfall brings after it, the total overthrow of the whorish trade.

Fourthly. But one feature deserves to be noticed under all, namely, while they all bewail and lament her, it is said, that *they all stood afar off.* Here is a striking feature. Though sinners herd together in sin, yet in judgment, they wish to separate. No one helpeth his fellow. Like the first transgressor in the garden, they rather accuse than soften each other's crime. They stand afar off. Oh! the awful state of the ungodly.

20 ¶ Rejoice over her, *thou* heaven, and *ye* holy apostles and prophets: for God hath avenged you on her.

I admire this verse. It comes in with a delightful tide of joy, in the midst of the troubled waters. Here there are several sorts of persons called upon to rejoice in her destruction. *First,* the inhabitants of heaven, meaning the Church now in glory, who, when upon earth, felt and groaned under the oppression of the whore. They, who in another Chapter are described as under the altar in heaven crying out for her destruction. Chap. vi. 10.

Secondly. The holy Apostles and Prophets, whose sacred writings the whore hath perverted, to her nefarious trade, in slaying the souls of men.

And, *Thirdly.* All the faithful of the LORD may be considered as included, because, all the living upon earth, cannot but rejoice that her power is gone.

21 And a mighty angel took up a stone like a great millstone, and cast *it* into the sea, saying, Thus with violence shall that great city Babylon be thrown down, and shall be found no more at all.

22 And the voice of harpers, and musicians, and of pipers, and trumpeters, shall be heard no more at all in thee; and no craftsman, of whatsoever craft *he be,* shall be found any more in thee; and the sound of a millstone shall be heard no more at all in thee;

23 And the light of a candle shall shine no more at all in thee; and the voice of the bridegroom and of the bride shall be heard no more at all in thee; for thy merchants were the great men of the earth; for by thy sorceries were all nations deceived.

24 And in her was found the blood of prophets, and of saints, and of all that were slain upon the earth.

The figure of a great millstone cast into the sea, is only to shew the eternal and unalterable nature of the whore's destruction. She is sunk to rise no more. Neither shall the voice of bridegroom or bride, or a single blessing be found any more within her walls for ever!

REFLECTIONS.

BLESSED be the LORD! the destruction of the whore is come! One hour, when the time all along predicted arrives, is enough, and all her traffic in hunting souls, and ruining the world, is done away for ever. Of what avail is all her pomp, and sitting as a queen among the nations!

Precious LORD JESUS! give thy redeemed grace to hear thy love-calls, and to come out from among her! How many of thy dear ones are now hidden where the seat of the beast is! How many more, yet to be called, are found therein! Oh! bring them out, and house them in thy little Zoar, when thou makest the awful overthrow.

Methinks I would hail the Church, whoever lives to see it in the view of the blessed event. The very prospect of it is blessed. With what joy will the redeemed welcome the day. Yea, heaven itself will take part in the felicity of it. The Apostles and Prophets, gone before, will rejoice over her, when GOD hath avenged his people on her. LORD! be thou eternally and everlastingly praised, in the total overthrow of thine enemies, and the salvation of thy people!

CHAP. XIX.

CONTENTS.

This Chapter opens with an Account of the Joy in Heaven, in the View of the LORD's *Triumphs over Antichrist upon Earth. The Church in Heaven celebrates* CHRIST's *Marriage with his Church. A blessed and glorious View of* CHRIST. *The Beast and false Prophet cast alive into a Lake of Fire burning with Brimstone.*

AND after these things I heard a great voice of much people in heaven, saying, Alleluia; Salvation, and glory, and honour, and power, unto the Lord our God:

2 For true and righteous *are* his judgements: for he hath judged the great whore, which did corrupt the earth with her fornication, and hath avenged the blood of his servants at her hand.

3 And again they said, Alleluia. And her smoke rose up for ever and ever.

John's attention seems here to have been called off from the view which he had been so much delighted with, in beholding the total overthrow of mystical *Babylon*, to hear the congratulations of the multitude in heaven, even the Church, who all took part in the triumph. He hears their hymn of praise, and the words of it. He hath recorded it also for the Church. It begins with the blessed word *Alleluia*, and it ends with the same. The Old Testament Church was remarkable for the use of this word. They generally began and ended all their hymns of praise with it. And to say the truth, it is very sweet. *Praise is comely for the righteous.*

But what I would yet more particularly desire the Reader to observe, in this triumphal song of the Church in heaven, is, that in it they recorded the faithfulness of GOD, in the destruction of Antichrist. There is no perfection of GOD, which the LORD all along commends to his people's notice and regard, more than his faithfulness. *Know now,* saith the LORD by *Moses, that the* LORD *thy* GOD, *he is* GOD, *the faithful* GOD! Deut. vii. 9. And as it is to the

LORD's glory, when he confirms that faithfulness by his fulfilment of his promises; so is it to the credit of the LORD's people, when they as readily, and as chearfully acknowledge it.

The Church, in the ruin of the whore, traced her mercies to this one source. GOD had from the first taught, that *no weapon formed against Israel should prosper.* Hence, when *Rome* turned all her weapons upon the Church, to destroy it, and the LORD did as he had said, and threw to the ground the whole power of the *Pope;* here was a lively proof of GOD's faithfulness. And the Church sung it, It is blessed to eye GOD and CHRIST in all things!

I desire the Reader to take notice of the strong language made use of by the Church in heaven, in calling this heresy the *great whore.* And I beg of him no less to regard what is said of the smoke of her furnace, (as if alluding to *Sodom* and *Gomorrah,*) which rose up for ever and ever. These are grand points.

Let me beg the Reader no less to remark also, what is said of GOD's judgments, in his judging the great whore, namely, that they are *true and righteous.* Her daring opposition to GOD's truth, her blasphemies and unjust traffic in selling pardons, which belong only to GOD to bestow, and her arrogating a right of supremacy in divine things, justly call for divine vengeance. Hence, therefore, her everlasting destruction forms a part, in the great system of what is true and righteous, in the LORD to accomplish. And in the same moment, it is a part of GOD's justice to shelter and protect all his faithful ones; it is a righteous thing with GOD to punish his and their enemies, and to repay him that hateth him to his face.

4 And the four and twenty elders and the four beasts fell down and worshipped God that sat on the throne, saying, Amen; Alleluia.

5 And a voice came out of the throne, saying, Praise our God, all ye his servants, and ye that fear him, both small and great.

6 And I heard as it were the voice of a great multitude, and as the voice of many waters, and as the voice of mighty thunderings, saying, Alleluia: for the Lord God omnipotent reigneth.

7 Let us be glad and rejoice, and give honour to him: for the marriage of the Lamb is come, and his wife hath made herself ready.

8 And to her was granted that she should be arrayed in fine linen, clean and white: for the fine linen is the righteousness of saints:

9 And he saith unto me, Write, Blessed *are* they which are called unto the marriage supper of

the Lamb. And he saith unto me, These are the true sayings of God.

10 ¶ And I fell at his feet to worship him. And he said unto me, See *thou do it* not: I am thy fellow-servant, and of thy brethren that have the testimony of Jesus: worship God: for the testimony of Jesus is the spirit of prophecy.

I beg the Reader to notice what is said here of a voice, which came out of the throne, saying, *praise our* GOD *all ye his servants.* Now the right apprehension of this voice will serve to throw a light upon what follows hereafter. That this voice could not be the voice of GOD the FATHER, SON, or SPIRIT, is, I think, very evident, for if it had, the words would not have been, praise *our* GOD, but praise GOD. The word *our* could not upon this occasion have been proper, since it is calling upon others to praise with the voice that called. Moreover, it should seem to have been a voice from among the multitude which sung *Alleluia,* consequently not the voice of GOD. Add to these things, when it is said, for *the* LORD GOD *omnipotent reigneth,* this is plainly said of CHRIST, whose omnipotency hath been now proved in the destruction of the whore, and her total overthrow. And this hymn is but a continuation of the first hymn, at the opening of the chapter, and repeated again and again in those several verses, third and sixth. For whose is salvation but CHRIST? And to whom all along did *John* hear the hymn of salvation, and glory, and honor, and power, ascribed? Was it not to him, (said they,) that *hath loved us, and washed us from our sins in his own blood?* Chap. i. 5. v. 9.

So once more. What are all the ascriptions of honor which are said to be given to *him,* but to the Person of CHRIST, because that his marriage is come, and hence the gladness and rejoicing of his people? The very marriage is with CHRIST, who from everlasting betrothed his Church to himself from the FATHER's gift, and who, when from the time-state in the *Adam-*fall, hath restored her by redemption; he espouseth every individual to himself by regeneration, at their personal call, and here finally brings home his Church to the marriage supper in the Jerusalem church state in heaven. And with respect to the wife making herself ready, the following verse explains what is meant, when it is said, that to her was granted that she should be arrayed in fine linen, meaning, that the LORD, who provided the wedding garment of his righteousness, puts it on. So the Church, by the Prophet, sings: *He hath clothed me with the garments of salvation, he hath covered me with the robe of righteousness, as a bridegroom decketh himself with ornaments, and as a bride adorneth herself with her jewels.* Isaiah lxi. 10.

And, lastly, to add no more, the whole of this account is closed up by the speaker, whoever it was, in those very remarkable words: *And he saith unto me, these are the true sayings of* GOD. Consequently, it could not be GOD or CHRIST, or the HOLY GHOST, but GOD's messenger, as upon many instances before, we find *John* taught by one or another.

Now, from all these united considerations, nothing can be more plain, than that the words of the following verse is from the same speaker, an angel or messenger, and no more. And though *John*, for the time, in the glorious intelligence he had just received, was so transported, as *Cornelius* was in the case of *Peter*, that he fell down to worship him, yet plain enough it is, that this was from the Apostle's state of mind, and nothing else. And that neither *John* took it to be the Person of CHRIST that was speaking to him, is as certain; for otherwise he would not have said, I have the testimony of JESUS, if he had been JESUS himself.

I have been the more particular than, perhaps, ninety-nine in an hundred would have thought necessary; because some few persons, untaught of GOD the HOLY GHOST, and of a stamp disposed to doubt the GODHEAD of CHRIST, have thought this passage rather leans to that opinion. Than which, when attended to, in these striking particulars, nothing can be more foreign. Most evident it is, from beginning to end, that the whole of what we have gone over, hitherto, in this chapter, is an account *John* received from the ministry of a messenger or angel, and a blessed account it is, *to the truth as it is in* JESUS.

11 And I saw heaven opened, and behold a white horse; and he that sat upon him *was* called Faithful and True, and in righteousness he doth judge and make war.

12 His eyes *were* as a flame of fire, and on his head *were* many crowns; and he had a name written, that no man knew but he himself.

13 And he *was* clothed with a vesture dipped in blood: and his name is called, The word of God.

Here indeed we have CHRIST, as is most evident from his double names, *faithful and true*. His perfections also confirm the glories of his person, for *righteousness is the girdle of his loins, and faithfulness the girdle of his reins*. Isaiah xi. 5. I admire what is said of the many crowns of the LORD JESUS. Who indeed can number them. He *hath* the *essential* crown of GODHEAD. He hath the *Personal* crown of the GOD-MAN, which was, and is his native right, by virtue of that special character of his, and independent of any single act, by which he hath endeared himself to his people. He hath the *Mediatorial* crown, both of office and of work, from the infinite merit and dignity of his labors in redemption. And he hath the *rightful* crown put upon his sacred head, by every individual one of his people, for whom he hath wrought out and accomplished salvation. Oh! the blissful sight of beholding the LORD JESUS, thus wearing his many crowns, and especially when the poor sinner espies among the many, the very one which he had put upon CHRIST'S head, when ascribing to him, as is most justly his due, the sole honor of every poor sinner's salvation.

I must beg the Reader to regard with me, the very great blessedness of the name here spoken of, which no man knew but he himself.

I do not presume to speak decidedly upon such a subject. Indeed, what is here said is enough, one should think, to deter any man, and every man, yea, every Angel of Light, from speaking on so mysterious a subject decidedly. For if no man knoweth this name of JESUS written, but he himself, how presumptuous must it be, in any to attempt the discovery. Reader! pause for the moment, and before you go further, ask yourself, whether any higher testimony can be desired, in proof of CHRIST's GODHEAD. If none can know his *name*, who shall know his *Person?* Who shall declare his generation. Oh! how overwhelming is the testimony to a heart taught of GOD. Truly, dearest LORD, I behold a blessedness in thy words, used upon another occasion, which bring a peculiar strength of expression, when applied here upon this. *No man knoweth the* SON, *but the* FATHER; *neither knoweth any man the* FATHER, *save the* SON, *and he to whom the* SON *will reveal him.* Matt. xi. 27.

But we must not stop here. Though no man knoweth his name, but he himself, yet his name is subjoined, and it is called, The WORD of GOD. Reader! I do beseech you, ponder it well. We are accustomed to this name in the scripture. *John,* in the opening of his gospel, calls CHRIST by this very name, the WORD. But we learn here, that though the LORD is called by this name, no man hath, or can have, a full and clear apprehension of it. I am free to confess, that though I have for many a year past felt a satisfaction in my mind, that the peculiarity of the name, the WORD, belonging to the SON of GOD was intended to express, the infinite dignity of his Person; yet, here I rested and concluded, that this implied the whole, as in relation to his Person and dignity. I now behold in it somewhat more. And although this very scripture, which hath been made the means of awakening an increased apprehension in my mind, of its vast importance, while now reading of it, assures me, and in that assurance, satisfies me at the same time, that the full investigation of it baffles all human knowledge, yet I hope I shall never more read it, but with increased and increasing solemnity, and profound reverence of thought. Oh! what infinite sublimity, must there be in the name; The WORD of GOD! How infinitely great must He be, to whom it peculiarly and personally belongs. How inconceivably deep and secret must the very name be, who, when he came forth from the invisibility of JEHOVAH, to make known what revelations of GOD he hath made, and without whose coming, never could any have been known, still came in a name, that none knoweth but he himself? Precious LORD JESUS! thy name is indeed wonderful! Oh! for grace to be everlastingly contemplating what to all eternity can never be fully known, thou hast a name written, that no man knew but thou thyself; and thy name is called, the WORD of GOD.

One word more on this most precious scripture. *And he was clothed with a vesture dipped in blood!* I pray the Reader, to pause over this most interesting account of JESUS, and while he ponders the subject, look up with an eye of faith, and behold the LORD in this garment of redemption. Surely the design must have been most gracious. And it may well become every child of GOD, to search and seek out the cause of such a condescending revelation of himself, in thus appearing to his people.

It is blessed to eye CHRIST in every name, in every relation, in every office, and in every character. And it is doubly blessed, when the child of GOD knows him in all, enjoys him in all, and lives upon him in all. When in the council of peace before all worlds, CHRIST stood up at the call of his FATHER, the Head and Husband of his people, the Church was beheld in him, accepted in him, made holy in him, and one with him to all eternity, for all the purposes, council, will, and pleasure of JEHOVAH, which should hereafter take place, and in all the circumstances which should follow. CHRIST then stood forth as the Head and Husband of his Church, his spouse; *chosen in him, to be holy and without blame before* GOD *in love*. But when in the after time-state of the Church, at the fall of *Adam*, the Church became involved and implicated in that fall'; the Church was then to know her Head and Husband in another endearing character, namely, her Redeemer and SAVIOR. So that from henceforth, redemption became another great and glorious subject, in the view of the Church; and CHRIST came home recommended and endeared to her affection, both as her Head and Husband, and her Redeemer and SAVIOR, the LORD her righteousness. The HOLY GHOST hath blessedly stated *both*, in that glorious scripture by *Paul* to the *Colossians*. *And he is the Head of the body, the Church: who is the beginning, the first-born from the dead; that in all things he might have the pre-eminence. For it pleased the* FATHER, *that in him should all fulness dwell*. Then cometh the second glorious character of the LORD JESUS as Redeemer. *And, having made peace through the blood of his cross, by him to reconcile all things to himself; by him I say, whether they be things in earth, or things in heaven*. Coloss. i. 18, 19, 20. Hence, we have here, the LORD JESUS CHRIST in his double relation to his Church, both as an Head and SAVIOR. *First*, as an Head in union, the beginning, and the first-born from the dead, as the founder of the future world, for which the Church hath from everlasting been designed, and by his resurrection, to which CHRIST hath begotten the Church. And, *secondly*, as a SAVIOR in redemption, having made peace to all the sins of his body the Church, by the blood of his cross, to reconcile all things to himself. Reader! pause over the wonderful subject, and then again and again, look up and behold him, as *John* here beheld him, on his white horse, with his many crowns, (and, oh! if you can behold the crown of your *own* personal salvation, among the number, and in his vesture dipped in blood. Doth not JESUS seem to speak in this apparel. Doth he not seem to say, wherefore do I wear this but to convince my people of the everlasting efficacy of my blood? And do I not still appear in it, to convince them by such a palpable demonstration, that redemption-work is finished, and I am still clothed in my redemption-robes, to tell my poor ones upon earth, this most assured truth, and to encourage them to come to me, under all their sins and sorrows, and temptations, with full assurance of faith. Reader! were not these among the causes for which CHRIST so appeared to *John?* And shall not his Church feel confidence from it, and look to Him as such, whose name is Faithful and True?

14 And the armies *which were* in heaven followed

him upon white horses clothed in fine linen, white and clean.

15 And out of his mouth goeth a sharp sword, that with it he should smite the nations: and he shall rule them with a rod of iron: and he treadeth the wine press of the fierceness and wrath of Almighty God.

16 And he hath on *his* vesture and on his thigh, a name written, KING OF KINGS, AND LORD OF LORDS.

Having looked at CHRIST, in those most glorious and soul-comforting views in which *John* beheld him, he now saw the armies which followed him; and they were also seen on white horses, clothed in fine linen, white and clean. I venture to take for granted, that by the armies which were in heaven, is meant the Church, the LORD's redeemed ones. Their apparel seems to decide this. Not the angels of light. For though elect angels, and preserved by CHRIST in their holiness; yet, as CHRIST is here peculiarly seen, from his vesture dipped in blood, as a Redeemer; it should seem, that his followers were the redeemed. Moreover, they are called *armies;* more, I should conceive, on account of their militant state, than in this place, of their number. For though the word *armies* implies many, and the LORD's hosts are a great multitude, which no man can number; Rev. vii. 9. yet here the LORD himself is seen, as on his horse of battle, in righteousness, judging and making war; and, consequently, those that follow him, of his armies, are in the field of action.

There is somewhat truly interesting and beautiful, in this description of the Church, in her militant state. They are, as their LORD is, beheld on white horses, to intimate their purity and holiness in CHRIST. They are going after him, and with him, to battle; but not to an uncertain warfare, for He is crowned with the many crowns of victory, and they are clothed in white robes, to intimate, that they have already washed them white, in the blood of the LAMB. Moreover, they are going *after* CHRIST, not *before* CHRIST. This scripture saith, they *followed* him. So that every thing is in beautiful correspondence to the leading truths of our most holy faith. All is *of* Him, and *through* Him, and *by* Him. And if *we love Him, it is because he hath first loved us!*

But though we may, as we are called upon so to do, behold those armies in heaven following CHRIST, and for a moment glance them as they pass; yet, the one only object to dwell upon in this lovely view, is JESUS himself! And the further description given of Him in this scripture, must of necessity hide every other object from any thing more than the mere momentary attention. Reader! do observe how blessedly *John* speaks of him, when he saith: *Out of his mouth goeth a sharp sword, that with it he should smite the nations; and he shall rule them with a rod of iron.* It is a grand feature of character in the LORD JESUS, that while coming forth for the salvation of his chosen, he cometh forth also, for the destruction of his, and their enemies. He saith himself, by the spirit of prophecy, ages be*-*fore his coming, while in the prospect of it; *the day of vengeance is in my heart; and the year of my redeemed is come.* Isaiah lxiii. 4. Habak. iii. 13. And it should be particularly remembered, in this scripture we are now upon, that it is for the destruction of the Antichristian powers, the East, and West heresies, as well as the whole works of Satan, and his kingdom, the LORD JESUS is here beheld, as coming forth clothed in armor. The terms used, of *a rod of iron,* and the smiting them with *the sword of his mouth,* are well known in scripture. Psm. ii. 9. And see John xviii. 6. with the note in the Commentary.

The treading the wine-press of the fierceness and wrath of Almighty GOD, hath a double aspect; as it concerns the LORD's redeemed ones, and as it concerns the unregenerate. CHRIST, as his people's Surety, hath trodden *the wine-press alone;* and *of the people there was none with him.* Isaiah lxiii. 3. And who shall describe the weight, and pressure, on the Redeemer's soul, when he made himself an offering for sin, when he bore their sins, and carried their sorrows? But the wine-press of the fierceness and wrath of Almighty GOD hath respect also to the unregenerate; concerning whom the LORD JESUS saith: *For I will tread them in mine anger, and trample them in my fury, and their blood shall be sprinkled upon my garments; and I will stain all my raiment.* Isaiah lxiii. 3. No doubt, the day, the awful day of our GOD, when he comes to take vengeance on his enemies, will be so awfully marked. Those Antichristian powers, both of the East, and West, the devil, and his whole host, yea, all the unregenerate, in every nation and clime, will be trodden by CHRIST, in the wine-press of GOD's vengeance; and when fully ripened in their iniquity, like the vintage of the vineyard, the LORD will *tread them in his anger, and trample them in his fury, stain all his raiment, and bring down their strength to the earth.*

One sweet view more. JESUS hath another name on his vesture, and on his thigh, which all his redeemed cannot but delight to read, and know him by; namely, KING of kings, and LORD of lords. Yes! Reader! the LORD JESUS CHRIST hath this glorious title in common with the FATHER, and the HOLY GHOST; and specially and personally so, as GOD-Man Mediator. There can be nothing more sweet and refreshing to the Church of GOD, than the contemplation of this distinction of character, both as relating to the nature, and essence of the GODHEAD; and as relating to the personal glory, and dignity, of the GOD-Man CHRIST JESUS. I have, in many parts of this humble work, this *Poor Man's Commentary,* dwelt upon both; as the several subjects leading to them, from the several parts of the holy scriptures, have presented them before us. But, as I am now drawing towards the close of the whole sacred volume, I would crave my Reader's indulgence once more, to drop a word or two on *both.* The longer I live, the more I am convinced, of the present awful, CHRIST-despising generation. And what more trembling times are at hand, I know not; but, from the complexion of things now before us, there appears a sad, sad prospect. Before the final overthrow of those antichristian powers, which this book of GOD clearly predicts, and of which, this very Chapter sounds the glorious triumph; we must expect, from those scriptures, as the last struggle of the beast, and the false prophet, and the dragon, the most violent oppositions; yea, the *two witnesses* of our GOD and SAVIOR, are to lie dead, under their violence, in the great city of the whore, which spiritually is called *Sodom*, and *Egypt, three days and half.* Chap. xi. 7, 10. I hope, therefore, one short view more in relation to this glorious title of our glorious GOD, our SAVIOR, both as it belongs to him, as GOD, in common with the FATHER and the HOLY GHOST; and in his own personal, and Mediator-character, as GOD-Man, will neither be considered unnecessary, nor found unprofitable, under the LORD's teaching.

Of the divine unity, of one GOD in essence, the whole scriptures are full. *Hear, O Israel, the* LORD *our* GOD *is One* LORD. Deut. vi. 4. All, and every part of revelation, confirms the glorious truth. There is, there can be but one GOD. For as all the divine attributes and perfections are, in the highest possible extent, illimitable, and immense; so of necessity, the LORD GOD Almighty, fills all space, and is Omnipresent, and of an Eternal ubiquity. So that, the very idea, of another God, is excluded; for this immensity, and this ubiquity, would be broken in upon. A thing impossible.

The scriptures of GOD, which declare this first and leading truth, do no less at the same time declare, the existence of this first, great, and eternal cause, as existing in a threefold character of Persons, known and distinguished by distinct names, as revealed to the Church: FATHER, SON, and HOLY GHOST. They are called the HOLY THREE, which bear record in heaven; the FATHER, the WORD, and the HOLY GHOST: and these THREE are ONE. 1 John v. 7.

And here, before we go further, I would stop the Reader humbly to propose one short and plain question. Supposing that we had never received this testimony from the scriptures, and supposing, for the first time, that you, or I, were made acquainted with the revelation of the Being of GOD; should we not expect to find, that the nature of his Being and existence, when made known, would be in a way of perfect distinction, from all his creatures? I say, should we not be inclined to think, that when any discovery was made to us, concerning the nature, and Being of GOD, we should expect to find him to differ wholly from our own? Here then it is. The testimony of scripture on this grand point is, that the LORD JEHOVAH doth exist, in the eternity of his nature and Being, in a way totally distinct, and distinguished from, all his creatures; and that, in the nature and essence of the GODHEAD, there are three distinct personalities, of equal glory, power, wisdom, and existence; FATHER, SON, and HOLY GHOST. Reader! what a mercy is it, to every child of GOD, in relation to this great truth, that over and above this blessed scripture testimony, he hath a personal knowledge and apprehension of each glorious Person, in the revelations made to himself, in the FATHER's love, the SON's grace, and the HOLY GHOST's fellowship?

But, to return. The holy scriptures, which declare the unity of the divine essence, and the existence of the THREE PERSONS in that Unity, have as graciously condescended, and in a variety of parts in the divine word, to call each of them by the same distinction of character and title, to make known to the Church, their Oneness in Being, in honor, in dignity, worship, power, and, in short, all the glorious prerogatives of GOD. Hence also, in all the departments of nature, providence, grace, and glory, we are taught, that each glorious Person hath taken part, and doth take part; and both in creation, redemption, sanctification, and all that concerns the Church, in the life that now is, or that which is to come; the whole Persons have come forward, and do come forward, to the Church in CHRIST in Him, as the only possible way, or channel of communication; to teach the Church, from whom jointly, and severally, their mercies flow; and to whom again, in and through CHRIST, their endless praises are to be returned, both here and hereafter. I stay not to quote, or even in this place to refer to the numerous scriptures which are express to this purpose in proof. In numberless parts of this work, I have already done it; and I hope, most plain and satisfactory to every one taught of GOD. I am only now bringing forward, once more, the blessed subject itself, before I conclude my *Poor Man's Commentary*.

Here, however, let the godly Reader pause again, and, as he reads his Bible, let him recollect, if he can, the very many sweet and gracious passages, the word of GOD abounds with, in proof of the Personality of the HOLY THREE in ONE. How often do we find them conversing together? Gen. i. 26. Isaiah vi. 8. John xvii. throughout. Isaiah xlix. throughout. John xii. 28. How often speaking of their delight in each other. Prov. viii. 22 to the end. Matt. iii. 17. John xvii. 23, 24. Rev. iii. 21. John v. 19, 20. John xvi. 15. These are precious things, and precious scriptures in the confirmation of them! Let the godly Reader be very cheery of them.

One word more. The several titles, honors, and dignities, by which the HOLY THREE in ONE are known in scripture, in common one with the other, are all so many further confirmations, and of the most blessed nature, to this divine doctrine. How often do we meet with ascriptions of praise, to each, and to all; as to *the blessed, and only Potentate, the King of kings, and* LORD *of lords!* And to *the King eternal, immortal, invisible, the only wise* GOD, is ascribed glory, both to the FATHER, SON, and SPIRIT. 1 Tim. i. 17. 1 Tim. vi. 15, 16. Compare 1 Pet. v. 11. with 2 Pet. iii. 18. and Jude 25. Compare Isaiah vi. 3. with Rev. iv. 8. and Rev. i. 4.

And the same we find personally offered to the Person of CHRIST, as Mediator; not only in this text before us, but in every part of the word of GOD. In this very book of Revelation, to go no further, we have many instances. Rev. v. 9 to the end. Chap. i. 5, 6. Chap. vii. Reader! look at both. Bless GOD the SPIRIT, for his gracious testimonies to the whole, in his word of truth; and pray for his teachings, to make the whole profitable.

17 ¶ And I saw an angel standing in the sun; and he cried with a loud voice, saying to all the fowls that fly in the midst of heaven, Come and gather yourselves together unto the supper of the great God;

18 That ye may eat the flesh of kings, and the flesh of captains, and the flesh of mighty men, and the flesh of horses, and of them that sit on

them, and the flesh of all *men, both* free and bond, both small and great.

It is not easy to conjecture, who is meant by this Angel which *John* saw, standing in the sun. But he could be no other than a servant. For the sun is the emblem of CHRIST. And it could not be said, that CHRIST was standing in himself. I should conceive, that as he was calling to the fowls of heaven to come to the great supper of GOD, it might be even a very humble servant in the ministry; similar to what is said of the servants in the Gospel, sent out to call in the poor, and maimed, and halt, and blind, to the feast of the word of GOD. Luke xiv. 21. But be who it may, one thing is worth regarding. He is said to be standing in the sun. By which we may, without violence to the expression, interpret it, as standing in CHRIST and his righteousness. Mal. iv. 2. Here every Preacher of CHRIST stands. He is open like the sun; and he preacheth CHRIST, and CHRIST only. And his call of invitation to the supper, is not a call to ordinances, but to triumphs. Let the Reader remember, that this which is represented here, is the total overthrow of Pope and Prelate, Mahomet and Devil. Hence, the people of GOD are called upon to rejoice over them. It is called the supper of the great GOD, even JESUS; for these are *his* triumphs. He it was, who was just before seen by *John*, upon his white horse, with his many crowns, and in his vesture dipped in blood, and his armies following him to victory. Hence, therefore, as a mighty Conqueror, the battle being over, he makes a feast, like all Eastern Princes, for his nobles and princes of the provinces; that is, all CHRIST's redeemed family, whom he hath made kings and priests to GOD and the FATHER, and invites them to the supper; and where he displays the riches of his glorious kingdom, and the honor of his excellent majesty, not many days, no, not an hundred and fourscore days, for these would soon expire, but through a whole eternity, where JESUS shall be glorified in his saints, and they made completely blessed in him, for ever and ever. Esther i. 3—5.

Let the Reader not forget, that it forms an interesting part in the whole plan of redemption, when CHRIST brings home his chosen, that he hath also a compleat triumph over his enemies. It is a grand conclusion to the whole. And the Church is so highly interested in it, that one of the Covenant promises, in the charter of grace, runs in these words: *when the wicked are cut off, thou shalt see it.* Psm. xxxvii. 34. Oh! it is a blessed part in redemption, that *Satan* shall not only be brought down, but *bruised by the* GOD *of peace under our feet.* Rom. xvi. 20.

The battle at *Armageddon* will bring forth before the Church, the everlasting triumph of the Church over the whore and the false prophet; and, if any pagan powers, aided by the devil, are brought into this war, to fight against CHRIST; their destruction is sure. And in seeing their utter destruction; this in prophetical language is, to eat the flesh of kings and captains, of mighty men and horses, both bond and free, both small and great.

19 And I saw the beast, and the kings of the earth, and their armies, gathered together to make

war against him that sat on the horse, and against his army.

20 And the beast was taken, and with him the false prophet that wrought miracles before him, with which he deceived them that had received the mark of the beast, and them that worshipped his image: these both were cast alive into a lake of fire burning with brimstone.

21 And the remnant were slain by the sword of him that sat upon the horse, which *sword* proceeded out of his mouth: and all the fowls were filled with their flesh.

What a blessed scripture is here! So then at last the beast is caught, and the false prophet; and ere long the devil will be taken also. The HOLY GHOST had taught the Church to expect this, in relation to the whore. 2 Thess. ii. 8—12. And the Church of GOD will shout aloud, and say, in the language of the Church of old: *So let all thine enemies perish, O* LORD, *but let them that love him be, as the sun, when he goeth forth in his might.* Judges v. 31.

REFLECTIONS.

OH! the raptures, the joy, the unspeakable felicity, which will break out in heaven, when, like *John* in vision, the Church of GOD will hear in reality, that great voice, of much people, saying *Allelujah, salvation, and glory, and honor, and power, unto the* LORD *our* GOD! The imagination of the human mind cannot conceive the triumphs of the Church, when the LORD shall bring home the redeemed of his people; and the LORD shall have avenged the blood of his servants at the hands of the great whore, who, for so many ages and generations, hath corrupted the earth with the multitude of her fornications!

Oh! ye Church of my GOD, ye followers of GOD, and the LAMB! who shall number up your mercies, or speak the endless felicity of your happy state, when safely brought home from all the exercises of sin and sorrow, and are called to the marriage supper of the LAMB! Ye servants of the LORD! see that ye are arrayed with the fine linen, clean and white, even the righteousness of saints, which is JESUS's robe of salvation! See that GOD, who provides it for you, puts it on. No other can gain admission to the table of the LORD, either here in grace, or hereafter in glory! Oh! for the being so clad, that all the redeemed of the LORD may exult in the language of the Church of old, and say: *I will greatly rejoice in the* LORD; *my soul shall be joyful in my* GOD; *for he hath clothed me with the garments of salvation; he hath covered me with the robe of righteousness, as a bridegroom decketh himself with ornaments, and as a bride adorneth herself with her jewels!*

But, oh! for grace, to behold my God and Savior as *John* saw him, riding on his white horse, in his glorious characters of faithful and true, and in righteousness judging, and making war. Lord! give me to see thee, with thy many crowns. And, oh! for that very one, which thou hast enabled me to put upon thy sacred head, when in the day thou madest me willing to be saved in thine own way, and the knee of my heart bowed before thee; and I cried out, Jesus hath redeemed me, and saved me, and washed me from all my sins, in his blood! Lord! let me daily behold thee, in thy vesture dipped in blood! let me daily read, and know thy name, the Word of God. Let me, to the last moment of my life upon earth, till I fall before thy throne in glory, hail thee, my King, and my God; yea, King of kings, and Lord of lords! Oh! the day, the blissful, happy wedding day, when Jesus will take me home, and while the beast, and the false prophet fall to rise no more, but sink in the lake of fire; I shall, through sovereign grace, behold my God and Savior as he is, and dwell with him for ever. Amen.

CHAP. XX.
CONTENTS.

The Overthrow of Satan. The Devil is seized, and bound for a thousand Years. Christ's *Reign with his Saints. Satan for a short Time loosed. The general Judgment. The Devil cast into the Lake of Fire, where the Beast and the False Prophet are. All cast into Hell, whose Names are not found written in the Book of Life.*

AND I saw an angel come down from heaven, having the key of the bottomless pit, and a great chain in his hand.

2 ¶ And he laid hold on the dragon, that old serpent, which is the devil and Satan, and bound him a thousand years.

3 And cast him into the bottomless pit, and shut him up, and sat a seal upon him that he should deceive the nations no more till the thousand years should be fulfilled; and after that he must be loosed a little season,

We have here the judgment of *Satan,* and his being chained for a thousand years. And from that prison, he is not to be loosed, until the thousand years are expired. I pray the Reader to observe the beautiful order of things, in this divine procedure. First, the beast, and the false prophet, were to be cast into hell. That we saw done, in the foregoing Chapter. Next comes *Satan's* imprisonment. And that is accomplished in the opening of this Chapter. But, though here spoken of as done, because in *John's* vision these things were so represented; yet the events have not yet been done. The beast still

CH. XX.]   REVELATION.   649

reigns. The false prophet still exerciseth his delusion. And *Satan* never more artfully deceived, than he doth now, in the present hour. But these prophecies are to be accomplished in their due course. And here they are recorded in their proper order. And a beautiful, and blessed account it is, taken in one grand whole; and enough to warm the affections of GOD's redeemed ones, into an ardent love to the Person of CHRIST, when GOD the HOLY GHOST graciously becomes our Teacher. I beg the Reader's attention to it, in order,

First. Here is an Angel seen by *John,* coming down from heaven, with a key in his hand, and a chain. Now we cannot be at a loss to know who this is; it can be no other than the LORD JESUS CHRIST. For not only must it be Him, and can be no other, because all power is his in heaven and earth, and he hath *the keys of hell and death.* Rev. i. 18.. but because the personal hatred the devil hath to CHRIST, and the opposition *Satan* hath made to CHRIST and his kingdom, renders it peculiarly suitable and proper, that he should have his punishment immediately from CHRIST himself.

Secondly. Here is the power of CHRIST manifested, in seizing the old serpent, and binding him, and casting him into the bottomless pit, and the time limited for his confinement.

Thirdly. Here is also an account of a time of liberation; for the devil when he shall be at liberty for a little season, and when, as it should seem, he shall again deceive the nations, though but shortly.

Now some have thought, that this confinement of *Satan* began, when CHRIST cast out the devil from the bodies of men, in the days of CHRIST's flesh, and of consequence, the term is expired. And in proof of this opinion, they quote those scriptures, where it is said, that for this purpose, *the* SON *of* GOD *was manifested, that he might destroy the works of the devil.* 1 John iii. 8. And CHRIST himself said, that he beheld *Satan, as lightning fall from heaven.* Luke x. 18, 19. But to these things it may be said, that the purpose of CHRIST's coming, will be as fully answered by Satan's destruction, when the time cometh, as to suppose it hath come. And very certain it is, from the days of CHRIST's being upon earth to this hour, there hath never been a period of shortness, much less of a thousand years, in which the devil's influence on the minds of men, hath been restrained. And, moreover, as the imprisonment of the devil, according to the statement in this scripture prophecy, is to follow the burning alive of the beast and the false prophet, and not before these events, and as neither of these events have as yet taken place, it should seem, that there can be but little question, that the time of the devil's overthrow by CHRIST, is not yet arrived.

I shall take occasion in this place, to offer to the Reader, some few, and, I hope, not unprofitable observations, on this interesting subject of the war Satan hath waged with the LORD JESUS CHRIST and his people, and on scriptural authority. And I pray GOD the HOLY GHOST, that, from his divine teachings, I may be kept from advancing any one single point, but what is in perfect conformity to the word of GOD; and the Reader may be preserved from deriving any thing in those observations, but what shall be in strict consistency with GOD's truth, that both the Writer and Reader of this *Poor Man's Commentary* may be taught of GOD, and be mutually blessed by them to the Lord's glory, and to our souls' furtherance in grace, through Jesus Christ our Lord.

In the prosecution of this service, I shall not think it necessary to go over the whole ground of enquiry concerning *Satan*, and the empire, which from the fall of men he hath established, and in cruelty exercised over the souls and bodies of men, more or less, in every individual instance of the children of *Adam*. This would be too extensive a subject. But I shall take the matter up from that part, which, unhappily for mankind, is too well confirmed, and too strongly proved to our sorrow, to be called in question. I mean, that there is this evil, and formidable foe to our nature, which *walketh about as a roaring lion, seeking whom he may devour*. 1 Pet. v. 8.

Our adorable Lord hath so very fully drawn the outlines, both of the Person and kingdom of *Satan*, in his ministry when upon earth, and the Holy Ghost by his servants, both of the Old Testament and the New, have also so very largely set forth, the several horrible features belonging to both, that a reference to those scriptures, will supersede the necessity of advancing a single line, on these plain points. That there is this *Prince of the power of the air*, as he is called by the Holy Ghost, which *worketh in the children of disobedience*, and that the Church, as well as the whole *Adam* race, had their spirits under his government by nature, is a truth not to be controverted. Ephes. ii. 2, 3. But the scripture is in a great measure if not altogether, silent, from whence this malignity of *Satan* to our nature arose, and wherefore this cursed and apostate spirit, hath taken up such a bitter and irreconcileable hatred to man.

Some great and distinguished men among the Lord's people, gathering into one focus, the several lights which here and there the word of God hath thrown forth upon this subject, have conceived that when the whole rays are centered, they do shine with sufficient clearness, to shew, that this malignity of hell first began, when at the fall of those apostate spirits, they took offence at the Son of God, betrothing the nature of man for a spouse for himself, at the call of God the Father, and not marrying the angelic nature. Their high intellectual powers could not stomach this choice. And therefore, rebellion brake out against the counsel and pleasure of the whole Godhead, Father, Son, and Holy Ghost. And, hence the quarrel with the Son of God became personal. *Satan* attempted to set up a kingdom in opposition to Christ's. Hence he began his malignant purposes upon the first man, made in Christ's image, in the garden of *Eden*. And, hence, the war hath continued ever since, and will remain during the whole time-state of the Church, and Satan's enmity to all eternity.

But be this as it may, very sure we are, that such a deadly foe we have, whose captives, both by original and by actual transgression we are, and under whose dominion we must have lain for ever, had not God our Savior conquered him for us, and conquered him in us. And it is only by his victory that we are delivered *from the powers of darkness, and translated into the kingdom of* God's *dear* Son. It is the personal labors of the Son of God, which have accomplished all the purposes included in redemption; and though all the Persons of the Godhead have manifested the interest they take in this contest, yet the whole efficiency in the executive part of the work is in

CHRIST, and by CHRIST. CHRIST, in his own Person, hath subdued *Satan for* his people. And by his HOLY SPIRIT, he subdues him *in* his people. A few leading points on this most interesting of all subjects, will make this matter abundantly clear, and from the warrant and authority of scripture.

I began from that part, where the word of GOD begins; namely, *Satan's* ruining our nature in the instance of the first man in the garden of *Eden.* Here we date the origin of all the sins and sorrows of life. *By the offence of one, judgment came upon all men to condemnation.* So saith the scripture. And so saith common sense. For as in our first father, we all had an inheritance of holiness, had he kept it in which we were all by right interested : So by his loss of it, and the sin involved in that loss, we are, by right of inheritance, included. *Adam* did then, as many a worthless father doth now, by sin, spent his estate, and left his children beggars. But, Reader! by the way, do not fail to observe, that as by original sin, in a birthright of nature we had no hand in, we are all implicated in *Adam's* sin and misery, so is it the mercy of the Church, that by the birthright of grace to all GOD's people, we are all interested, and take part in CHRIST's righteousness and glory, in which we bore no hand. So sweetly saith the same scripture. *For as by one man's obedience many were made sinners; so, by the obedience of one, shall many be made righteous.* Rom. v. 12 to the end. One caution I beg the Reader to take with him, as he makes application of these scriptures, I mean, that he sees the proof of his relationship, in the right of which the whole depends. Prove yourself my brother, by the birth-right of grace; a child of GOD, before you lay claim to the privileges of a child. For, as upon the supposition I had not sprung from the *first* Adam, so called, and none of his blood had ran through my veins, I certainly should not have been implicated either in his sin or his condemnation; so by a parity of reasoning, unless I can prove my relationship to the *second* Adam so called, I can lay no claim for an interest in his righteousness and justification. It is the relationship which makes out the right of both. Now both you and I too sadly prove we are sprung from the earthly *Adam* in nature. Can we as joyfully prove we are born of the heavenly *Adam* by grace? Sure we are, that we are by *generation* of the first man, which is of the earth, earthly. Are we as sure, that by *regeneration* we are of the second man, which is the LORD from heaven. 1 Cor. xv. 47.

It is truly blessed to observe, how graciously the SON of GOD, when coming into our world to destroy the works of the devil, took up both our cause and his own, and as the apostate spirit, dared to attack the LORD of Life and Glory, JESUS not only came to redeem his people from his power, but to destroy him, and root out every evil from his kingdom. The HOLY GHOST, in one sweet verse of scripture, sums up in a comprehensive manner the whole subject. *For as much as the children are partakers of flesh and blood, he also himself likewise took part of the same, that through death he might destroy him that had the power of death, that is, the devil; and deliver them, who, through fear of death, were all their life-time subject to bondage.* Heb. ii. 14, 15.

But it would be the subject of a volume, yea, many volumes, to go over the track of ground which the scriptures furnish, in shewing Christ's personal triumphs and victories over sin and Satan, death, hell, and the grave. What an huge account might be gathered, if only from that branch of the Lord's first open skirmishes with Satan, in his miracles, when dispossessing him from the bodies of men? And then again from the souls of his people?

That Christ was the glorious Person interested in this great event, of the destruction of Satan and his kingdom, is evident, from every consideration. For against Christ as God-Man, and his kingdom as his glory, the devil bent his whole malice. And hence, when Christ wrought his miracles, and especially in those miracles in which he cast out devils, Jesus made an appeal to those works, as so many demonstrations of his kingdom. *If I*, said Jesus, *cast out devils by the* Spirit *of* God, *then the kingdom of* God *is come unto you*. Matt. xii. 28.

The first, and greatest act of Christ's triumph over Satan, was on the cross. Here, most eminently might it be said, that, *through death, he destroyed him that had the power of death*. For the devil is said to have had the power of death, not from his appointing the time of any man's death, or having any power so to do, but because, by his introducing sin, he hath brought death into the world, which God hath appointed, as the unavoidable consequence of sin, and therefore, the devil is very properly said, on this account, to have been *a murderer from the beginning*. John viii. 44. Hence, Christ by his dying for sin, hath removed the cause of death for his people, in the everlasting effects of it. And as by his death and resurrection, he is said to have overcome death and the grave, so in those glorious acts, he here gave the first death-blow to *Satan* and all his cursed empire; and from the cross and the tomb, the first views of the everlasting mansions of the redeemed were then discovered. 2 Timothy i. 10.

The Holy Ghost, by his servants the Prophets and Apostles, hath caused these victories of Christ to be loudly and joyfully celebrated. The Lord Jesus himself, speaking in the language of prophecy, thus delivered the blissful tidings ages before the event was to take place. *I will ransom them from the power of the grave. I will redeem them from death. O death, I will be thy plagues. O grave, I will be thy destruction; repentance shall be hid from mine eyes*. Hosea xiii. 14. And the same is spoken of Christ by the Apostle, after the great triumph had been accomplished. *And you being dead in your sins, and the uncircumcision of your flesh, hath he quickened together with him, having forgiven you all trespasses, blotting out the hand-writing of ordinances that was against us, which was contrary to us, and took it out of the way, nailing it to his cross; and having spoiled principalities and powers* (that is, those whom *Paul* elsewhere calls *the rulers of the darkness of this world;* see Ephes. vi. 11, 12.) *he made a shew of them openly, triumphing over them in it*. Coloss. ii. 13—15. Hence here the Lord Jesus began the first open display of his personal victory over *Satan*. And hence God the Father's gracious acknowledgment of the same, with the blessed consequence which were first delivered by prophecy, and confirmed by the event. *Therefore will I divide him a portion with the great, and he shall divide the spoil with the strong, because he hath poured out his soul unto death, and he was numbered with the transgressors, and he bare the sin of many, and made intercession for the transgressors.* Isaiah liii. 12. And in the prospect of this, just before the Lord Jesus entered the field of battle, he cried out; *Now is the judgment of this world, now shall the prince of this world be cast out.* John xii. 31.

Secondly. After the Son of God had accomplished redemption-work, and was returned to glory, he sent down the Holy Ghost for the carrying on this victory in the hearts of his people. It was not sufficient, in God's view, for Christ *personally* to conquer *Satan*, he shall be conquered by Christ *mystically*, yea, the poorest, the humblest, the feeblest, of the Lord's members, *in that day shall be as David* by his Spirit dwelling in them. Zech. xii. 8.

But while I begin this subject at this point, of Christ first personally triumphing over *Satan* on the cross, let not the Reader misapprehend, as though none of Christ's chosen were enabled by virtue of their union with Christ, to triumph over Satan in the Lord's strength before. This would be to mistake my meaning. Instances we have upon record, of old Testament saints, of *Job* and others, who in the strength of Christ, were borne up against the devil and his temptations, before Christ, at his incarnation, became manifested to destroy the works of the devil. But what I mean to say, and indeed what the word of God declares, is, that Christ in his own person conquered *Satan*, at his death, upon the cross, and Christ in his members conquers *Satan*, when at any time by the influences of His Holy Spirit, he bears them up against his temptations.

Now it is blessed to behold Christ's triumphs over *Satan*, in every individual instance of his members, when, at regeneration, the Lord brings them out of his prison and sets their souls at liberty. Indeed, the Lord Jesus calls this work himself, the proof of his grace in the hearts of his people. For when Jesus sent *Paul* to preach the Gospel, his commission ran in these words, *I have appeared unto thee for this purpose, to make thee a minister and a witness, both of these things which thou hast seen, and of those things in which I will appear unto thee, delivering thee from the people and from the Gentiles, unto whom now I send thee to open their eyes, and to turn them from darkness to light, and from the power of Satan unto God, that they may receive forgiveness of sins and inheritance among them which are sanctified by faith that is in me.* Acts xxvi. 16—18.

And although the enemy, doth rally again and again, and endeavors to draw back to his prison-house the souls of those that was once led captive by him at his will; yet, blessed be God, there is *that*, in every truly regenerated soul, which in Christ's strength keeping them alive, (the Lord himself being their strength,) that enables the child of God to resist the devil stedfastly in the faith. And, if at any time the Lord, to shew them their own nothingness, and his all-sufficiency, permits the enemy, as in the case of *Job*, to come on more furiously, yet the end is, but for the greater glory of God, the greater good of his people, and the greater disgrace of *Satan*. Yea, even in those cases where, for the moment, the child of God falls, and is led away by the enemy, yet, even then like a captive, reluctantly obliged to march, he goeth on sullen and displeased. And when the grace of Christ recovers him, as *Peter* was recovered by one look of Jesus, oh! how godly sorrow springs up in the soul afresh, and he cries out, *rejoice not against me, O mine enemy, when I fall I shall arise, when I sit in darkness the* Lord *shall be a light unto me.* Micah vii. 8, 9.

Thirdly. But the victory of Christ, in his own Person, over Satan, and the triumphs of Christ in his members, during the time-state of the Church, are here followed by the tremendous one, the opening of this Chapter presents to us. The Son of God having thrown down *Pagan* Rome, *Papal* Rome, and the *false Prophet*, here seizeth upon *Satan*, the ringleader of all, and being now about at this period of his Church, to set up a visible kingdom in this world, and before the final day of judgment, he shuts up the devil for a thousand years, that he shall not, during that time, afflict the people of God, either with persecutions or temptations. What events will mark this æra of the Church, and to what extent the blessings of the Lord's people will reach, we have no further account, than that it will be a time of great ingathering to the Lord.

There will be, according to the predictions of scripture concerning it, the more immediate presence of God our Savior in the midst of his people. *Ezekiel* speaking of it, said, that *the name of the city from that day, shall be* Jehovah *Shammah, the* Lord *is there*. Ezek. xlviii. 35. There will be a great pouring in of the Lord's people, gathered out of all nations. In allusion to this day, it should seem, is that scripture. *Thy people shall all be righteous.* Isaiah lx. 21. Not more righteous in themselves, for Christ is the righteousness of his people, but all of them shall be righteous in being brought home by the Spirit to Christ. There will be true spiritual ordinances, and a true spiritual ministry. *Pastors after* God's *heart*, and *watchmen that shall see eye to eye*. And the people *shall have one heart and one way, and serve the* Lord *with one consent*. Jerem. xxxii. 39. Jerem. iii. 15. Isaiah lii. 8.

Fourthly, and finally. The Lord Jesus will bring Satan, with all his hellish crew at the day of judgment, and completely execute his wrath upon him and them, by fixing them in eternal punishment in hell. This is read to us, verse 10. *And the devil that deceived them, was cast into the lake of fire and brimstone, where the beast and the false prophet are, and shall be tormented day and night for ever and ever.* And let all the people say, Amen and Amen.

Reader! pause one moment more over the wonderful subject, and with me, bless God for the graciousness of those discoveries, concerning both the ruin of Anti-christ and the devil, and all his works. How little should we have known of these things, but for our Lord Jesus in these sweet records. How little do we even now meditate upon them, in a way equal to their vast importance. Think how the Church above, have been watching over these events, which have taken place below since their translation. Think how the spirits of just men made perfect in the Patriarchs, and Prophets, and Martyrs, who died in the faith of Christ before the coming of Christ, when they beheld Christ combating with the devil, in the wilderness, and in the garden, and when by his death he overcame death and the devil, and by his blood paid their ransom, which God had trusted him for, and for which they were received into glory.

That those departed have an intimate knowledge of these things is certain, for we find them (Chapter vi. 10.) crying with a loud voice for vengeance on their murderers, when God explained to them the reason, wherefore they were to wait a little season for the accomplishment of their wishes. And, therefore, how must they have looked on and beheld with holy joy, the LORD JESUS casting down the beast and the false prophet alive in the lake of fire, and chaining Satan for a thousand years in the bottomless pit. And, oh! what joy, what shouts of praise will burst forth from the whole army of heaven, when all the accursed crew, shall be finally sent together into everlasting perdition, and their sentence and execution be in the full view of the congregated world of angels and of men.

4 And I saw thrones, and they sat upon them, and judgement was given unto them: and *I saw* the souls of them that were beheaded for the witness of Jesus, and for the word of God, and which had not worshipped the beast, neither his image, neither had received *his* mark upon their foreheads, or in their hands; and they lived and reigned with Christ a thousand years.

5 ¶ But the rest of the dead lived not again until the thousand years were finished. This *is* the first resurrection.

6 ¶ Blessed and holy *is* he that hath part in the first resurrection: on such the second death hath no power, but they shall be priests of God and of Christ, and shall reign with him a thousand years.

The LORD JESUS promised his people by *John*, that they should set with him upon his throne. Chap. iii. 21. And here is the accomplishment. His people are said to be made kings and priests, to GOD and the FATHER. And agreeably to this, we find them in their regal and priestly office. Various have been the opinions of the LORD's people on this reign of CHRIST. Some have considered it spiritually. Others have supposed it is to be taken *literally;* and that CHRIST will reign with his saints upon earth, otherwise say they, wherefore is *Satan* bound up. He needed not a chain to keep him out of heaven. Rev. v. 10. But the HOLY GHOST hath left an obscurity upon it, and therefore I shall offer no observations of mine upon it.

But whether this reign with CHRIST be a spiritual reign, or whether it is to be literally on the earth, what is said of the *rest of the dead,* even the dead sinners, *twice dead* as *Jude calls* them, dead in soul in the original *Adam*-fall-apostacy, and dead in body, gone down to the chambers of the grave, all of this description lived not during the thousand years of CHRIST's reign with his saints, and the thousand years imprisonment of *Satan!* They will remain, as they were found at death, until the general judgment.

In relation to *the first resurrection*, it should seem to be intended, precisely as the words are. For, as many of the bodies of the saints arose, to celebrate CHRIST's resurrection, so it may be supposed, many also shall arise to celebrate his reign with his saints at his *descension*. And very blessed it is, to consider the subject in this view. For when GOD's children have passed the present time-state of the Church, and their spirits have joined the society of the spirits of just men made perfect, they are then brought into clear apprehensions of the LORD's dealings in the great administration of all things. And wherefore may they not be supposed as raised up in their bodies during this thousand years of CHRIST as well as *Enoch* and *Elijah*, who never died at all. GOD hath immense discoveries to make, through a never-ending eternity of himself, in his threefold character of Persons, in, and through CHRIST, to his Church and people. And, there doth not seem a single cause of objection to his raising such, and such of his redeemed ones as he shall please, to begin in the union of soul and body, to enter into the joy of their LORD.

When it is added, that he is *blessed and holy that hath part in the first resurrection,* if it be considered as referring to a resurrection in grace, no doubt, as all the other parts of scripture declare, the second death can have no power upon them, for they are no longer subject to a spiritual death, being *made partakers of the divine nature.* 2 Pet. i. 4, 5. But I confess that I am more inclined to believe, that the blessedness and holiness here spoken of, hath respect to the first resurrection just before taken notice of, and is in my view a confirmation, that at this thousand years' reign of CHRIST, there shall be a resurrection of such, as the LORD hath appointed to meet the LORD at his government. The thought is pleasing, and I see no objection to it. But here, as in every other instance of doubt, I beg to be considered as never speaking at all decidedly.

7 And when the thousand years are expired, Satan shall be loosed out of his prison.

8 ¶ And shall go out to deceive the nations which are in the four quarters of the earth, Gog and Magog, to gather them together to battle: the number of whom *is* as the sand of the sea.

9 And they went up on the breadth of the earth, and compassed the camp of the saints about, and the beloved city: and fire came down from God out of heaven, and devoured them.

10 ¶ And the devil that deceived them was cast into the lake of fire and brimstone, where the beast and the false prophet *are*, and shall be tormented day and night for ever and ever.

The loosing of *Satan*, and the deceiving of *Gog* and *Magog*, and the nations which are in the four quarters of the earth, opens a new face of things. It cannot mean either the Pope, or false Prophet, for they and all their followers, will a long time before this, have been lost in remembrance from the earth. It is our mercy, however, that the whole is of short duration. *A little season*, it is said in verse 3. And then follows the everlasting overthrow, and perdition of the devil.

11 And I saw a great white throne, and him that sat on it, from whose face the earth and the heaven fled away; and there was found no place for them.

12 ¶ And I saw the dead, small and great, stand before God: and the books were opened; and another book was opened, which is *the book* of life: and the dead were judged out of those things which were written in the books, according to their works.

13 And the sea gave up the dead which were in it: and death and hell delivered up the dead which were in them; and they were judged every man according to their works.

14 And death and hell were cast into the lake of fire: this is the second death.

15 And whosoever was not found written in the book of life was cast into the lake of fire.

Here we arrive to that great day of God, so long, so faithfully foretold, and now so solemnly introduced, with every thing that may strike the mind in the contemplation of it. *First*, it begins with the sight of *a great white throne*. It is a *great* throne, for the Lord Jesus, the judge of quick and dead, who sits on it, is the great and only Potentate, King of kings, and Lord of lords. And it is a *white* throne, to intimate, perhaps, the justice and equity of his administration. And, oh! how great and glorious, and holy, and pure must he be that sits on it, before whom, the earth and the heaven fled away; for *the heavens are not clean in his sight*.

John proceeds. *And I saw the dead small and great stand before* God. Reader! think how solemn the moment, how interesting the event, involved in that day's decision! These must be the dead spoken of before, who lived not during the thousand years of Christ's reign, verse 5. Not the dead now or then, *dead in trespasses and sins* only, but the twice dead, dead in soul, and dead in body, and now raised up to judgment. *The books opened*, is spoken of after the manner of men. But the sense is, it should seem, that of the wretched dead, who died out of Christ, who trusted to equity and not grace, those books, meaning God's knowledge and their own consciences, could not fail of bringing them in guilty before God.

Sea, death, and hell giving up their dead, evidently proclaims the side on which those characters all stand. And their being all judged according to their works, most plainly shew the same. The salvation of GOD's people is not noticed in this judgment; and, consequently, the dead in CHRIST, in sea or land, are not here spoken of. For all that are noticed, are those whose names are not written in the Book of Life. This record is the only security, and a blessed and sure one indeed it is of the LORD's people.

I beg the Reader to notice with me, that nothing is said of the trial of the faithful. Indeed their trial hath taken place long before, when passing under the sentence of a broken law, they fled for refuge to the hope that was before them in CHRIST. It is said, indeed, and blessedly said, *we must all appear before the judgment seat of* CHRIST. 2 Cor. v. 10. But this not for trial, but for the LORD's blessing. *There is no condemnation to them that are in* CHRIST JESUS. Romans viii. 1. And if there be no condemnation *now*, there will be no trial *then*. If the law be answered, as it hath been answered by JESUS our surety *here*, nothing can be brought forth to criminate *there*.

Reader! pause over this statement, and look at it every way, and examine whether it be strictly scriptural.

It is a grand, a momentous concern! If a child of GOD be truly and savingly called, is awakened, regenerated, justified in CHRIST JESUS, and made one with CHRIST, can there be any doubt or suspense as to the state in which he will appear before GOD? Will not CHRIST and his salvation be the same in death as they are in life; and will not his acceptance in the Beloved, be as sure in heaven, as it is here on earth. Could *Paul*, could *Peter*, could all the saints of GOD in the Old Testament and the New, talk with so much assurance of everlasting happiness in CHRIST, and by CHRIST, had a doubt remained of their interest *in* CHRIST, and their union *with* CHRIST? I pray the Reader, if his ground work of assurance be not founded on the same bottom, to see to it on what other footing his faith rests. If the prospect of that day of GOD be blessed, and the hope of it a joy unspeakable and full of glory, here is the strength of it in JESUS. And the assurance of our acceptance in CHRIST *now*, must remove the possibility of failure *then*. Sweetly doth the Apostle sing to this note, when he saith, *for whom he called, them he also justified, and whom he justified, them he also glorified. And if so, what shall separate from the love of* CHRIST.

Reader! beg of GOD the SPIRIT to be your Teacher! Bring this subject daily before the LORD. See to it, that nothing satisfieth your mind, until the LORD himself hath given you an answer of peace. And let every day find some portion or other of it, engaged in your soul's desire in *looking for, and hasting unto* this great day of GOD. And, oh! the unspeakable mercy, to be always on the look out for JESUS, without suspense, without doubt, without fear, but in a fulness of joy, having redemption in his blood, waiting his coming, when CHRIST will own you before the congregated world, as his own, *and present you faultless before the presence of his glory with exceeding joy.*

REFLECTIONS.

OH! the unspeakable joy, the Church, both in heaven and earth, must feel, in CHRIST's triumphs over the devil! What a glorious sight, even in contemplation, to behold CHRIST coming down from heaven, and seizing upon the monster, to cast him into the bottomless pit, where hell and horror reigns.

Praises to our All-conquering JESUS, for shutting him up, during his thousand years' reign with his saints, that their joy shall have no interruption. And blessed be his holy Name, that he will raise up his saints and faithful ones, to sit on thrones with him, during this blissful age, of light, and life, and glory. Nothing of sin, nothing of sorrow, shall interrupt this blessed *Millennium*. And JESUS will have the souls of them that were beheaded for the witness of JESUS, and the word of GOD, and that have not worshipped the beast, but hated the whore; to reign with him. Oh! the felicity of beholding JESUS, and the glory of his Person, and the love of his heart, to his redeemed, his people!

They are indeed blessed, and holy, who have part in the first resurrection. GOD the HOLY GHOST hath said it. And, my soul, beg the LORD to seal the everlasting remembrance of it, in thy inmost affections. On such, the second death hath no power!

And while thy Church, O LORD, are rejoicing with holy triumph, over the devil, and the beast, and the false prophet, in beholding them for ever cast into the lake of endless torment; oh! for grace, in a life of faith on the SON of GOD, to be waiting for that great day of the LORD, when JESUS will come to be glorified in his saints, and to be admired in all that believe. Then will JESUS say to all his redeemed: *Come ye blessed of my* FATHER, *inherit the kingdom prepared for you before the foundation of the world.* LORD! shall this be my happy portion? Will JESUS so own me, when he cometh to make up his jewels? Oh! for the LORD to bless my soul now with grace; and sure I am, that then the LORD will give me glory.

CHAP. XXI.

CONTENTS.

John in Vision is led to see the New Jerusalem. *He beholds* CHRIST *upon his Throne. A Description of the Holy City. The* LORD's *Presence, the everlasting Glory of the Place. None can enter into it, but they whose Names are in the Book of Life.*

AND I saw a new heaven and a new earth: for the first heaven and the first earth were passed away; and there was no more sea.

2 And I John saw the holy city, new Jerusalem, coming down from God out of heaven, prepared as a bride adorned for her husband.

3 And I heard a great voice out of heaven, saying, Behold, the tabernacle of God *is* with men, and he will dwell with them, and they shall be

his people, and God himself shall be with them, and be their God.

Whether what is here said hath respect to the Church, during the thousand years' reign of CHRIST with his saints, or whether after the day of general judgment, is not so clearly said, as to determine positively. But the felicity here described, cannot but make every child of GOD to be longing for such a blessed time, when nothing shall any longer interrupt the joy of the LORD's people. *Paul,* when comforting the Church, under the various dissatisfactions arising from every thing here below, points to this blessed time, and sums up the whole account in those precious soul-reviving expressions. *So shall we ever be with the* LORD. *Wherefore, comfort one another with these words!* 1 Thess. iv. 18.

If I might venture to give my present views of the subject, I would say, that both this, and the succeeding Chapter, are more directed to shew the blessedness of the Church in the thousand years' reign of CHRIST and his people, than touching upon that eternal state, which is to follow. The Prophet *Isaiah* was directed by the HOLY GHOST, to tell the Church of the *new heavens, and the new earth, the* LORD *would create;* and all the blessed consequences which should follow. Isaiah lxv. 17 to the end. And, in another of his Chapters the Prophet gives a very similar description of the Church to what *John* saw in vision, as recorded in this Chapter. Compare Isaiah lx. throughout. All which correspond to the Church on earth.

And, when we consider what follows, of the tabernacle of GOD dwelling with men, and being with them; we certainly cannot be said to do violence to the scripture, even if interpreted with an eye to the change wrought by grace in the LORD's people, when called from darkness to light. *Old things are then passed away, and all things are become new.* 2 Cor. v. 17.

But what seems most decidedly to favor the opinion, that it is the Church in CHRIST's reigning with his saints, which *John* saw, and is here described, is because this Church is said to come down from heaven, and descends of course on the earth; which would not have been so expressed, one should think, if the eternal state of the Church in glory, were intended; for that is uniformly spoken of through all the scripture, as being in heaven.

The holy city, which *John* saw coming down from GOD out of heaven, prepared as a bride adorned for her husband, gives a very blessed idea of the felicities in this reign of CHRIST. But it opens also to a subject connected with it, of a very sweet and spiritual nature. I will beg the indulgence of the Reader to touch upon it. I am free to confess, that, however it might be more gratifying to the generality of Readers, to enter upon a description of what is here said, concerning the glories of this New Jerusalem; I do not feel competent to it. Neither do I consider it can be profitable; for if it had, the HOLY GHOST would have done it to our hands. It is sufficient, it should seem, to that blessed SPIRIT, to state the fact; but no further. The LORD means, in all things, to glorify JESUS, and not to gratify curiosity.

But in the sweet and precious subject, in what is here said, of the tabernacle of GOD being with men, and dwelling with them; here we have a discourse, of the most gracious, the most blessed, yea, of the most glorious nature. Allow me to state some few of the many delightful things contained in it.

And, *first*. The tabernacling of the SON of GOD in our nature, I mean, in taking what he did in that holy, pure, and perfect portion of humanity, hath been, and ever must be, a subject of everlasting wonder, love, and praise. But that the SON of GOD should make choice, as he hath done, in every instance, more or less, of his redeemed to come in, and dwell in an heart inhabited before by Satan, and a cage of unclean birds; here the astonishment ariseth yet higher.

Secondly. The design of the LORD in this dispensation is to demonstrate his love, and the exceeding riches of his grace, in these wonderful acts of our GOD. While the heaven, and the heaven of heavens, cannot contain him, and the heavens are not clean in his sight; the LORD chooseth the heart of a sinner for his residence. Now, Reader! observe, among a thousand things in it, which must for ever excite wonder, and shew that his thoughts are not our thoughts, neither his ways our ways; here is one sweet cause for such an act of unequalled grace, as must for ever endear the LORD to the heart of his people; namely, it is the only way, whereby he should shew to us, his peerless mercy. For, supposing GOD. hath first made us holy; yea, supposing he had so ordered, that we had never sinned; but having made us what we might have thought holy tabernacles in his people for his residence, and taken us to heaven at once; we should indeed have had to have loved him for his love; admired him for his wisdom, and praised him for his power; but then we should have lost, yea, never known one sweet and precious attribute of our GOD, namely, his mercy. Whereas the scripture most sweetly, and blessedly teacheth us, that *the* LORD *delighteth in mercy.* Micah vii. 18. And how, or by what means, could the LORD shew forth his delight in the exercise of it, but upon objects of misery? Well, then, if the LORD delighteth in mercy, and the LORD delighteth to be known by those he loves, in the free, and full, and everlasting exercise of mercy, he must find objects to shew it upon. So then, saith the LORD, it shall be. If those I have loved, with an everlasting love, and chosen to be holy and without blame before me in love in my dear SON, fall into sin and misery, I will magnify my free, and sovereign mercy, in bringing them out of it; and this shall be the way, by redemption in his blood, that I will cause my mercy to shine to the utmost. And thus the scripture speaks concerning it. GOD, *who is rich in mercy, for his great love wherewith he hath loved us, even when we were dead in sins, hath quickened us together with* CHRIST. Ephes. ii. 5. *In whom we have redemption through his blood, the forgiveness of sins according to the riches of his grace.* Ephes. i. 7.

Thirdly. But what still tends to heighten the mercy more is, that GOD most evidently manifests all along, that there is nothing in the objects of his love, from first to last, that hath the least concern in this transaction. It is not their misery, that first awakened his love and mercy; for both were in exercise, not only before they had done either good or evil, but even before they had any being. These plans of GOD, were before sin, before sorrow, before the world was formed. The LORD laid his foundation deep and low, to bring about the purposes of his will; and, therefore, in the vast contrivance, the Lord gave scope for the exercise of all these attributes, wisdom, love, and power; and mercy to be brought forth into the fullest display of its riches, when the sin of his people rendered it so necessary. Reader! pause over this view of the subject; for, according to my apprehension of it, nothing can be more sweet, and precious. Your misery, and my misery, by reason of our sins, are not the cause of God's mercy; for neither our deservings, or undeservings, are at all considered as motives with the Lord for the display of his grace: (for if this had been the case, it would cease to be grace.) But God, who is rich is mercy, for his great love wherewith he hath loved us, takes occasion, from our misery, to make known his mercy, yea, and the fulness of it also in his dear Son. He, therefore, displays his grace, the riches of his grace, yea, the exceeding riches of his grace, in such a way, and manner, as shall magnify the glories of his name, in bestowing the aboundings of his mercy, to overwhelm, and do away the aboundings of sin, that *where sin hath abounded, grace shall much more abound; and as sin hath reigned unto death, even so shall grace reign through righteousness unto eternal life, through* Jesus Christ *our* Lord. Rom. v. 20, 21.

Fourthly. One of the sweetest feelings of the soul also, under these gracious workings of grace from the Lord, ariseth out of it; namely, that in the ebbings and flowings of the mind, when visited by those high tides of God's love and mercy, his tabernacling with his people, and his manifestations, that he is at home in his dwelling, is when their emptiness, and brokenness of heart, makes his presence so seasonably great, and refreshing. Our hearts are often like empty walls, and blessed it is to be so. For when we have nothing, and are nothing, yea, worse than nothing, stripped of all, no chair to sit on, not a table to eat upon, nothing, yea, nothing to put upon it, no purse, no scrip, nor money in our purse, with souls sinking, and hearts fainting, and brought down to the very floor of sorrow; then, to behold the Lord coming in, with love in his heart, and a fulness of grace in his hands; and supplying all we need, in himself, and from himself, in his rich bounty: oh! the blessedness of all this? Oh! who would not wish to be emptied of every thing, and all our trumpery furniture tumbled into the street, that Christ may come in, take possession of our whole souls, and be our God, our all, and our portion for ever!

Lastly, to add no more. Our God must be glorified, and our God must have all the glory. In nature, in providence, in grace, in glory, creatures can add nothing, can bring nothing, can offer nothing. Yea, our very praises for Christ, and all the benefits with Christ, can add nothing to God's glory. His glory is *in* himself. His glory is *from* himself, *to* himself. As we brought nothing to our first creation in nature; so neither can we bring any thing to our new creation in grace. *If the tabernacle of* God *is with men, and he will dwell with them;* it is all of pure, free, sovereign love, and grace. And as God declares, that he hath chosen a broken, and a contrite heart, for his throne; certainly it is his own free choice, and for his own glory, that He is thus pleased to make it so. And blessed be the Lord, for such revelations of his will and pleasure; for now I find, that my nothingness, and emptiness, are exactly suited for his fulness, and all-sufficiency. Lord! drive every buyer and seller from thy temple, even my poor soul; and make it thy fee-simple, and inheritance, as it is justly thine both by creation and redemption, thine for ever!

4 And God shall wipe away all tears from their eyes; and there shall be no more death, neither sorrow, nor crying, neither shall there be any more pain: for the former things are passed away.

Reader! let us pause over this verse, for it is a refreshing one. What a happy climate this must be? Contrast it to the present state. Then look to Jesus, who hath purchased for us such vast mercies. Depend upon it, there is more of Jesus, even in the least of our common blessings, than we are aware of. The thorns of this world, are all the inheritance which sin left us. Therefore, whenever a thorn is taken out, whenever any ease or mitigation to sorrow is found, it is Jesus who is the purchaser of those blessings. How little is this thought of by men? I do not mean men of the world, for how shall carnal, unawakened men think of Jesus, who know not themselves? But I am speaking of the Lord's people. And yet, what a double sweetness would this thought, when coming warm to the mind, put into the enjoyment of every blessing? This is the fruit, and effect of Jesus's love. I wish any child of God, that reads this short observation when I am no more, may, through grace, feel his heart led out to the consideration of it. All blessings, all mercies, are the fruits and effects of Jesus's love; and very blessed it is to eye Jesus in them. I make a nice distinction between the most precious blessing, and Jesus himself, the Giver of that blessing. It is blessed, yea, very blessed, to receive the gifts of Jesus as his gifts. But it is a thousand times more blessed, to know, and enjoy Jesus himself, in those gifts, as the love-tokens of his heart, from whence they come. To love him is blessed, but to be beloved by him in infinitely more blessed. *This* is the cause, the *other* is the effect. He it is, it is said, that will wipe away all tears from the eyes of his people. This is blessed. But wherefore he doth it, is more so. Because he loves them; and they are beloved by him. This is the coronet of the whole. This the head of all blessedness.

5 And he that sat upon the throne said, Behold, I make all things new. And he said unto me, Write: for these words are true and faithful.

6 And he said unto me, It is done, I am Alpha and Omega, the beginning and the end. I will give unto him that is athirst of the fountain of the water of life freely,

Though these distinctions of character, belong in common to all the Persons of the Godhead, (Isaiah xliii. 10. Isaiah xliv. 6, 8.) yet I should humbly conceive, that in this place Christ is the Speaker; because in this *Millennium* state of the Church, it is Christ reigning with his saints. And how very delightful are those declarations to his redeemed? Reader! do you know Christ, under these precious characters? Doth Jesus sit upon the throne of your heart? Hath he there made all things new? Hath he taken away the heart of stone, and given you an heart of flesh? Are your desires, your affections, your appetites, become new, and spiritual? Is he indeed, the *Alpha*, and the *Omega*, in your creed? If the Lord hath created your heart anew, sure I am, you must have made him the *Alpha* of this great work; for creating work, you cannot then but know to be his. But do you know him as the *Omega* too; that is, the Finisher, as well as the Beginner of salvation? If creating-work be his, so is renewing-work, confirming-work, strengthening-work, recovering after backslidings, and raising up again after falls. Do you know the Lord Jesus under all? Then do you make him what God the Father had made him, and what he here declares himself to be, the *Alpha* and *Omega*; the beginning and the end. Oh! it is blessed, as we begin, so to go on, upon a free grace bottom. This is a tried way, a sure way, yea, *the good old way*, which, when a child of God walks in it, he finds rest to his soul. But to halve it with Christ, is robbing Christ of his glory, and the soul of happiness. Jerem. vi. 16.

Reader! listen to what Jesus saith, in the close of this scripture. *I will give to him that is athirst, of the fountain of the water of life freely!* What! is there no qualification needed beside? No! if Christ be welcome to the thirsty soul, that soul is welcome to Christ. Observe, it is a *gift*, not a *purchase*. It is bestowed upon the *thirsty*, not the *full*. Could a poor sinner but see this, he would discover, that the only qualification, is a sense of want, and a view of the Lord's goodness to supply. Hence the ignorance of this is the sad cause of all our misery. And Jesus taught this, to the woman of *Samaria*. She was ignorant that Christ was the gift of God. And to that ignorance, the Lord ascribed the cause, wherefore she asked not for living water from Christ. It is blessed to feel our want, blessed to know where alone is the supply of that want, and blessed to see God the Father's gift in the provision, and blessed when God the Spirit leads to Christ, for the mercy. See John iv. 42. and Commentary.

7 He that overcometh shall inherit all things; and I will be his God, and he shall be my son.

8 But the fearful, and unbelieving, and the abominable, and murderers, and whoremongers, and sorcerers, and idolaters, and all liars, shall have their part in the lake which burneth with fire and brimstone: which is the second death.

Our Lord, within the compass of these two verses, hath marked the striking difference between his people, and the ungodly. Oh! who shall describe the properties of grace? What heart hath ever entered into the *Arcana* of the divine counsels? In the mass of Adam-nature here are some, whom the Lord calls his children, his jewels, his chosen; adopting them into his family, acknowledging himself to be their GOD, and they his people. And here are others, whose nature, void of grace, are manifested to be in the fearful state of servile bondsmen to Satan, whose portion is with Satan for ever, in the lake which burneth with fire. *This is the second death;* meaning an everlasting separation from the presence of GOD and the LAMB.—Reader! pause over the solemn view. And, if so be, GOD hath granted you the quickenings of His HOLY SPIRIT, on whom the second death hath no power; look up with me, and cry out, in words similar to the astonished Apostle: LORD! *how is it that thou hast manifested thyself unto us, and not unto the world?* John xiv.

9 And there came unto me one of the seven angels which had the seven vials full of the seven last plagues, and talked with me, saying, Come hither, I will shew thee the bride, the Lamb's wife.

10 And he carried me away in the spirit to a great and high mountain, and shewed me that great city, the holy Jerusalem, descending out of heaven from God,

11 Having the glory of God: and her light *was* like unto a stone most precious, even like a jasper stone, clear as crystal;

Reader! let you and I bless GOD, for this precious discovery, made to *John*, for the Church's joy, of the Bride, the LAMB's Wife. Here is represented, under the similitude of a temple, (Psm. cxliv. 12.) the whole body of CHRIST, the Church; even every individual, which was given to him by the FATHER, and betrothed by him before all worlds, and now, through sovereign grace, are brought home to that glory, which was from all eternity the first in GOD's designs, and now finished, in his final decree, according to his eternal purpose. The invitation the angel gave to *John*, methinks, I would humbly hope, is given to all the companions of *John*; (Rev. i. 9.) and, therefore, by faith, I would accept the invitation: *Come up hither, and behold the* LAMB's *Wife!*

What a sweet thought it is, that when GOD the FATHER first presented the Church to his dear SON, before all worlds; she was then beheld by CHRIST, as she really was, in all that beauty, and glory, in which GOD presented her, and as she stood before him in his divine mind, *holy and without blame before him in love.* Ephes. i. 4. And though, in this time-state of the Church, she is sunk into such sin and misery, that all her features are changed; yet, I say, it is a blessed thought, that she was not so at the first, neither is she to be so at the last, and for ever. And, therefore, GOD's first, and original design, must be accomplished. She shall be before him holy, and without blame in love. This Church then, this King's daughter, (Psm. xlv. 18.) it should be remembered, hath lost nothing of her relationship by sin. A King's daughter she still was, and is, during the whole of this time-state. And a King's daughter, and a King's Wife, she will remain, to all eternity. Sin destroys not this affinity. All the water of the sea, cannot wash away the relationship. In this betrothing, and union, CHRIST received her at the hands of his FATHER; and she became the object of his desire then, and must, and will remain so, to all eternity.

Well but, say you, she hath fallen into foul dishonor, shame, and misery, since. Yes! she hath. But that did not alienate the affections of her Husband from her. For these are his own words to her. *Thou hast played the harlot with many lovers; yet return again unto me, saith the* LORD. Jerem. iii. 1. And, since nothing but his own grace, put into her heart, would bring her back; that grace the LORD hath given her, and made her *willing in the day of his power.* Hence, this state of sin and misery, afforded a blessed opportunity, for the display of his love. And JESUS came into this our world, in quest of her, he died for her, shed his blood for her, and washed her from all her sins in his blood; and, having clothed her with the robe of his own righteousness, she is now more beautiful than ever, and he hath presented her to himself, *a glorious Church, not having spot, or wrinkle, or any such thing, but is holy and without blemish.* Ephes. v. 27.

It is impossible for the imagination to form to itself any thing more blessed, than the contemplation of CHRIST, and his Church, in the manner, and way, the Angel described it to *John*. In the opening of this Chapter, he saw in a vision, the Church coming down from GOD out of heaven, prepared as a bride adorned for her husband; but this view was in one mass. Here the Angel brought *John* to a nearer, and more distinct apprehension. The Church is here said to have had upon her *the glory of* GOD. And *John's* mind seems to have been somewhat in the frame that *Paul's* was, when caught up to *the third heaven*. 2 Cor. xii. 2, &c.

I do not presume to enter into the full extent of what is here meant by the expression of having *the glory of* GOD. But as I am inclined to think, that what is here said of the Church, during the *thousand years'* reign of CHRIST, relates to those, who are said to be blessed and holy, in having part in the *first resurrection*; and of consequence form part of this Church; the glory of GOD is upon them, both in body and soul. It should seem, that this thousand years' reign is intended for some great and special purposes, in relation to the LORD's kingdom. And as such, those who constitute the Kings and Priests of our GOD in that assembly, will be in a state of perfection, as well in body as soul; and, therefore, will be under the continual manifestations of *the glory of* GOD. And, if the *Shechinah* was frequently in the Church in the Wilderness, and *Moses* was admitted into a more familiar manner than others, to behold the glory of the LORD, until the skin of his face shone, from the reflected brightness; it should seem, that no objection can be supposed to arise, for the saints of GOD, in this *Millennium*-state, to be brought under such displays of glory, in the prospect also, of the near approach to the eternal kingdom. But I speak only presumptively.

12 And had a wall great and high, *and* had twelve gates, and at the gates twelve angels, and

names written thereon, which are *the names* of the twelve tribes of the children of Israel:

13 On the east three gates; on the north three gates; on the south three gates; and on the west three gates.

14 And the wall of the city had twelve foundations, and in them the names of the twelve apostles of the Lamb.

15 And he that talked with me had a golden reed to measure the city, and the gates thereof, and the wall thereof.

16 And the city lieth foursquare, and the length is as large as the breadth: and he measured the city with the reed, twelve thousand furlongs. The length and the breadth and the height of it are equal.

17 And he measured the wall thereof, an hundred *and* forty *and* four cubits, *according to* the measure of a man, that is, of the angel.

18 And the building of the wall of it was *of* jasper; and the city *was* pure gold, like unto clear glass.

19 And the foundations of the wall of the city *were* garnished with all manner of precious stones. The first foundation *was* jasper; the second, sapphire; the third, a chalcedony; the fourth, an emerald;

20 The fifth, sardonix; the sixth, sardius; the seventh, crysolite; the eighth, beryl; the ninth, a topaz; the tenth, a chrysoprasus; the eleventh, a jacinth; the twelfth, an amethyst.

21 And the twelve gates *were* twelve pearls; every several gate was of one pearl; and the street of the city *was* pure gold, as it were transparent glass.

22 And I saw no temple therein: for the Lord God Almighty and the Lamb are the temple of it,

23 ¶ And the city had no need of the sun, neither of the moon, to shine in it: for the glory of God did lighten it, and the Lamb *is* the light thereof.

I do not think it necessary, in a work of this kind, to attempt what I freely confess, I am not competent to perform, an analysis of what *John* hath said, of the gates, and precious stones of this building. They may, for ought I know, have an allusion to the gifts and graces of the HOLY SPIRIT, in their different qualities and colors. But of this I am not sure. And, as the HOLY GHOST hath not thought proper to explain, I dare not offer conjectures. In relation to the *walls*, we may venture to speak with more confidence, for CHRIST himself is both the foundation of Zion, and his salvation GOD hath appointed for walls and bulwarks. And CHRIST is the only gate, or way, for an entrance into the Church below, or above. Isaiah xxviii. 16. 1 Pet. ii. 4, 5. Isaiah xxvi. 1. John xiv. 6. But, though I do not venture on an explanation of these several verses, of the building, and precious stones, here mentioned; I would beg to propose a short remark on what is said, of this city needing not the light of sun, or moon, because the glory of GOD doth lighten it, and the LAMB is the light thereof. There is somewhat in it most blessed. The LORD help us, in some measure, suited to our present capacities to understand it.

And, *first*. Though I can form no one idea whatever, in relation to the *essential* glory of GOD, as GOD; yet, I think, we may derive some apprehensions from what scripture hath said, in relation to the glory of the GOD-man CHRIST JESUS. We have several striking accounts of the sight the Elders of Israel and others had of seeing the GOD of Israel, in the Old Testament scripture, to which I might refer; see Exod. xxiv. 10. Isaiah vi. 1—4. But if we come down to New Testament times, we shall find somewhat more suited to our capacities to lean upon. The Apostle's view of CHRIST's Transfiguration in the Mount; *Stephen's* sight of CHRIST before the Jewish Council; or *Paul's* view of the LORD in the road to *Damascus*: These furnish out sufficient subjects for enquiry on this ground.

The Apostle's account of the Transfiguration is, that CHRIST's *face did shine as the sun.* Now the LORD JESUS, when preparing the minds of those men for this glorious sight, some days before it took place, told them, that there were *some standing there, which should not see death, till they had seen the* SON *of Man coming in his kingdom.* Matt. xvii. 1. Mark ix. 1—8. Now I beg the Reader to observe, from CHRIST's words, that the glory which he was then proposing to display before them, was intended by CHRIST to represent somewhat, though imperfectly, of the glory he would appear in, *in his kingdom.* This I think highly important to be kept in view, in our humble enquiry concerning the light the LAMB is, in the New Jerusalem, which supersedes, and renders unnecessary, the light of sun or moon.

Secondly. Both the Apostles *John* and *Peter,* who have given their testimony to this transaction, as well as the Evangelists who have recorded it, tell the Church, that this glory of CHRIST was abundantly great, and overpowering. *John's* account is: *The* WORD *was made flesh and dwelt among us, and we beheld his glory; the glory as of the only begotten of the* FATHER, *full of grace and truth.* John i. 14. And *Peter,* speaking of it, saith: *We have not followed cunningly devised fables, when we made known to you the power and coming of our* LORD JESUS CHRIST, *but were eye-witnesses of his majesty; for he received from* GOD *the* FATHER *honor and glory, when there came such a voice to him from the excellent Glory: This is my beloved* SON, *in whom I am well pleased.* 2 Pet. i. 16. And the Evangelist *Matthew's* account is, that *his face did shine as the sun.* Matt. xvii. 2. *Paul's* statement of the *Damascus* scene is, that it exceeded the sun. *I saw from heaven* (saith he) *a light above the brightness of the sun.* Acts xxvi. 13.

Thirdly. We shall have a yet stronger matter to help us in our discovery, concerning this glory of our LORD JESUS CHRIST, as the glory in which he will appear, (only infinitely increased,) in his kingdom of the New *Jerusalem*-state; if we call into our remembrance what is said of the two men which appeared with him, at the Transfiguration; *Moses* and *Elias.* They are said to have been talking with JESUS. And they are moreover said to have appeared in glory; that is, I venture to apprehend, in their glorified bodies. *Elias* could not have appeared any other way, for he did not pass through the grave to glory. And of the burial-place of *Moses,* no one ever knew. Hence, therefore, it is but a fair conclusion, that they both appeared in their bodies. And somewhat must have told *Peter* who they were; for it seems plain enough, that he knew them. See Luke ix. 30, 31. Is it not, therefore, a probable conclusion, that the LORD JESUS's glory, upon this occasion, was the same, only in a lesser degree, because, had it been more, the three Apostles then in the body, could not have borne it; and, that both *Moses* and *Elias* were, as those saints of GOD shall be, who are to reign with CHRIST, in his thousand years' kingdom?

Fourthly. From these considerations, we shall now, through grace, be enabled to form some conclusions, how glorious will be the human nature of CHRIST, in that kingdom, from the indwelling GODHEAD. Here is the source, and hence, as this is one and the same as the Essential GODHEAD, though dwelling bodily in CHRIST, it may serve to explain to us, wherefore the glory of GOD, and of the LAMB, are both said in this verse, (23,) to lighten the city. It is the glory of GOD, to all intents and purposes, when shining in, and from CHRIST: *For in Him dwelleth all the fulness of the* GODHEAD *bodily.* Coloss. ii. 9. And hence, this glory, which is the source of all light, yea, the light and life of men, must supersede, and render unnecessary, all the luminaries of heaven. How strikingly the Prophet speaks, when describing this day, in reference to CHRIST's glory. *Then the moon shall be confounded, and the sun ashamed, when the* LORD *of hosts shall reign in Mount Zion, and in Jerusalem, and before his antients, gloriously.* Isaiah xxiv. 23.

Reader! think then, of the present greatness, and glory of the LORD JESUS, by what the disciples saw of him in the Mount, and by what he will then appear, when he lightens his kingdom with his own personal glory? This is He, *whom man despiseth!* This is He, *whom the nation abhorreth!* This is He, whose GODHEAD some call in question; and yet, by a perversion of all language, call themselves Christians! Oh! the awful delusion of those, whom the god of this world hath blinded! But recollect, that the glory in which he appeared in the Mount, was but a glimpse, not a full blaze. The poor disciples could not have borne it. *Paul* was made blind three days, only from a transient view of it. And yet, what was that, compared to the glory *Paul* saw, when by vision he was caught up to heaven? The Apostle could not tell, when the vision was over, whether he had been in the body, or out of the body. 2 Cor. xii. 1—4. Blessed, glorious SAVIOR! Oh! for faith to behold thee now, until with open face, without a medium, we come to thy glory, and *are changed into the same image, from glory to glory, even as by the* SPIRIT *of the* LORD! 2 Cor. iii. 18.

24 ¶ And the nations of them which are saved shall walk in the light of it: and the kings of the earth do bring their glory and honour into it.

25 And the gates of it shall not be shut at all by day; for their shall be no night there.

26 And they shall bring the glory and honour of the nations into it.

27 And there shall in no wise enter into it any thing that defileth, neither *whatsoever* worketh abominations, or *maketh* a lie: but they which are written in the Lamb's book of life.

In the close of this Chapter, in these verses, we have the vast distinction drawn, between the saved and the lost. The nations of them saved, meaning CHRIST's Church, gathered out of all nations, are here said *to walk in the light of the* LORD; meaning, that this is their glory; and the kings of the earth, that is, CHRIST's redeemed ones, redeemed from the earth, from among men, and *made Kings and Priests to* GOD, *and the* FATHER, (Rev. i. 6.) bring all their glory of redemption into it. No gates are shut. No prevention of access to GOD, in CHRIST, and by CHRIST, night, or day. An everlasting union, and communion, is now enjoyed by the saints; and they, even the saints of GOD, bring all the revenue of glory, to GOD, and the LAMB, into it.

But, while the redeemed have thus an entrance abundantly administered unto them, into GOD's everlasting kingdom; here is a final clause, which for ever shuts out all that are not written in the LAMB's Book of Life. The defiled, the worker of abomination, and the lover and maker of a lie. And who are the defiled, but the unregenerate, and unwashed, and unrenewed. They who never felt the SPIRIT's work upon the heart, in quickening them from the death of sin. They who work an abomination, by looking for acceptance, in whole, or in part, in their own righteousness, instead of wholly looking for redemption in CHRIST's blood. And they who feed upon ashes, and not the bread of life, whose *deceived heart hath turned them aside, so that they cannot deliver their souls, and say, is there not a lie in my right hand.* Isaiah xliv. 20.

REFLECTIONS.

Reader! behold with an eye of steady faith, the new heaven, and the new earth, wherein righteousness dwelleth! Yea, look again and again, with rapture, at the Church coming down from God out of heaven, as a bride adorned for her husband! Bless God the Father, in the contemplation, for his electing love, in choosing; for his giving love, in giving the Church to his dear Son; and for all the ten thousand manifestations of his love, in predestinating each, and every individual of the mystical body, to the adoption of children, by Jesus Christ to himself, and accepting the whole Church in the Beloved, to the praise of the glory of his grace!

Bless God the Son, for his betrothing his Church before all worlds, watching over her, in all the time-state of her sad adulterous departure from him; redeeming her with his blood, washing her from her sins, clothing her with his righteousness, bringing her home, and presenting her to himself, in the marriage-supper, prepared for her in his kingdom of glory.

Bless God the Spirit for his anointings in the early formation of Christ and his Church as one, before the foundation of the world, for his quickening and regenerating grace in time, and for all his leadings, teachings, comfortings, and renewings, when glorifying the Lord Jesus to the Church's view, and directing the heart into the love of God. Oh! for grace, while contemplating the Church, the Lamb's wife, to behold with yet greater rapture and joy, the Lamb himself, and bless the whole persons of the Godhead, for all their love and mercy to the Church in Him.

And what a state of unspeakable felicity is the Church here brought to, after all the temptations of *Satan*, the deceivings of the heart, and the opposition from the world. Precious Jesus! thou art the *Alpha* and *Omega* of all blessedness. Blessed are all thy gifts and all thy manifestations in wiping away all tears from off all faces, and putting an everlasting end to all sorrow and sin. But blessed yet more art thou for thy love. Do thou, Lord, who art the everlasting light, and the glory of heaven, be the light and glory of thy Church on earth. Lord! shine daily on my soul, until thou shalt bring me home to this blessed city, where neither sun nor moon shall any more be needful, for thou, Lord, wilt be the light of all the poor Gentiles thou hast brought into thy kingdom, *and the glory of thy people Israel.*

CHAP. XXII.

CONTENTS.

God *the* Holy Ghost *in this Chapter finisheth the Subject of all the Prophecies; and with it, the whole Canon of Scripture. The* Lord *gives the Church a further Account of the Holy City. Here is spoken of, the River of Life, and the Tree of Life; and the* Lord's *Promise, of coming quickly. A gracious Invitation at the End, to all the People of* God. *A solemn Caution, not to add to, or take from, the Things written herein.*

AND he shewed me a pure river of water of life, clear as crystal, proceeding out of the throne of God and of the Lamb.

With what a blessed fulness this Chapter opens! *A river of water of life.* Not a stream, not a pool, which might be subject to dry; but a river. And not only a river, but of water of life; giving life wheresoever it shall come. And what can this prefigure, but the everlasting, ever-living, and ever-flowing love of JEHOVAH, in his three-fold character of Persons; FATHER, SON, and HOLY GHOST? And what a thought it is, to refresh the soul of a child of GOD, this river hath been running in love to the Church in CHRIST from all eternity. Yea, there never was a moment in the eternal world, call that moment in the language of eternity by whatever name you may, in which it can be said that GOD began to love the Church. For this would imply a change in GOD. A thing impossible. Hence, if it be asked, when GOD's love to the Church began; it must be said, from the same time GOD began to be; even from all eternity. Reader! pause, and ponder well this love of GOD; and then look at this river so running from out of the throne of GOD and the LAMB!

But though running from all eternity, and to all eternity; yet you and I could trace nothing of it, until by the washing from it, in regeneration, we were quickened into spiritual life to behold its pure and living streams. It ran, hidden from all view, in the secret purposes of GOD, until by rising above ground in the time-state of the Church, it ran down from the first opening of creation, through redemption in CHRIST's blood; and the water of regeneration by the HOLY GHOST, and all the streams, made glad the city of GOD. Ephes. i. 7. Titus iii. 3, 4, 5. Psm. xlvi. 4.

The properties of this river are most blessed. It is said to be *pure.* And, as it flows from GOD, how shall it be otherwise than pure; and how sure to make clean all hearts wheresoever it comes. It is said to be *clear as crystal.* Yes! every thing is clear in divine truths, when GOD is the Teacher. GOD the FATHER gives clear revelations of his SON. Ephes. i. GOD the SON maketh himself known to his people otherwise than he doth to the world. John xiv. And GOD the SPIRIT taketh of the things of CHRIST, and sheweth to the people, when giving testimony in the heart of the child of GOD to the FATHER's revelation of JESUS. Reader! do not fail to observe that this river was seen by *John* proceeding out of the throne of GOD and the LAMB. This proves the existence of THREE Persons in the GODHEAD. For when CHRIST spake of the HOLY GHOST, as being given to the Church, he described him as *rivers of living water.* John vii. 37—39. Here then we see it. This river proceeded from GOD and the LAMB. And let not the Reader overlook the blessed qualities of this river. It is a River, full, pure, clear, yea, the water of life; giving life wheresoever it comes. Blessed be GOD for opening to the Church's view, through *John*, a sight of this river. And, Reader! if a sight of it be blessed; what must an enjoyment of it be? Oh! the blessedness to drink of it, to wash in it, and to have everlasting life from it, in the united mercies of FATHER, SON, and HOLY GHOST.

2 ¶ In the midst of the street of it, and on either side of the river, *was there* the tree of life, which bare twelve *manner of* fruits, *and* yielded

her fruit every month: and the leaves of the tree *were* for the healing of the nations.

There can be no doubt, but that JESUS himself is the Tree of Life. He is in the midst of the street, for he is the Center of every thing that is blessed. He is the middle Person of the GODHEAD in his divine nature. And he is the Mediator between GOD and man in his human nature. And he is in the midst of the street in standing up to mediate in his Church between a living GOD and dying sinners, while his people are unregenerated, and dead in trespasses and sins. He is also on either side of the river, for he is with *the spirits of just men made perfect;* and He is with his redeemed, here below, which have not yet passed the river *Jordan,* the river of death. He is, as his type *Joseph* represented him, *a fruitful bough, even a fruitful bough by a well, whose branches run over the wall.* Gen. xlix. 22.

But, Reader! look at JESUS as the Tree of Life. Yea, let you and I beg of GOD the HOLY GHOST, that we may not only look at him, but that he will lead us now by faith, before the LORD calls us home in reality, to go and sit down in this paradise of GOD, under JESUS, the Tree of Life. JESUS is suited both for shelter and for food. He hath every thing in him, that can answer all our wants. Like some rich tree, in the midst of a desert, so is CHRIST, in the desert of this world, a luxuriant Tree, whose branches shelter us from the heat, or storm, and at the same time will yield us fruit, to refresh us. And he is the Tree of Life, for there is life in no other, and his people have no life but in him. He saith himself, *because I live ye shall live also.* John xiv. 19. And as he first gives life, so he preserves it. He is an Ever-green. Yea, this scripture saith, that he beareth twelve manner of fruits, and yieldeth fruit every month; and even the very leaves have a medicinal healing quality in them. Reader! can your heart be insensible to these things? JESUS is the Tree of Life. He is so, to both Churches. Here on earth, and there in heaven; being on either side the river. He bears twelve manner of fruits, that is, all variety. He hath pardon, mercy, peace, grace, love, strength, comfort, deliverance in temptations, recoveries in backslidings, helps in times of need, preparation for ordinances, and blessings in the use of them. And every month, yea, every day, the LORD brings them forth. And even the very leaves of providence shall have a somewhat in them to heal. Oh! thou dear LORD! give me to sit down, day by day, under thee, as the Tree of Life; and ere long, sure I am, I shall sit down, to rise no more, under all thy wide-spreading branches of all fullness, in thy paradise for ever!

3 And there shall be no more curse: but the throne of God and of the Lamb shall be in it; and his servants shall serve him:

4 And they shall see his face; and his name *shall be* in their foreheads.

5 ¶ And there shall be no night there; and they need no candle, neither light of the sun; for

the Lord God giveth them light: and they shall reign for ever and ever.

The first of these verses becomes a blessed confirmation, that CHRIST hath redeemed his Church from the curse of the law, being made a curse for her. Gal. iii. 13. Here, in this triumphant state of the Church, CHRIST reigning with his saints, nothing can enter to corrupt. No serpent, for the devil, who entered the first paradise of Eden, is at this time, when CHRIST is with his Church, in hell. No beast, nor false prophet, for they are both in the lake of brimstone and fire. Hence there can be no more curse. Oh! the blessedness of this Church of GOD! And, as a further confirmation, GOD's people are sealed. GOD's throne, and the throne of the LAMB, is in it. GOD enlightens it. They see his face. And he sees theirs, and his name is in their foreheads. And it is again repeated, GOD and the LAMB are their light.

6 And he said unto me, These sayings *are* faithful and true: and the Lord God of the holy prophets sent his angel to shew unto his servants the things which must shortly be done.

7 Behold, I come quickly: blessed *is* he that keepeth the sayings of the prophecy of this book.

8 And I John saw these things, and heard *them*. And when I had heard and seen, I fell down to worship before the feet of the angel which shewed me these things.

9 Then saith he unto me, See *thou do it* not: for I am thy fellow-servant, and of thy brethren the prophets, and of them which keep the sayings of this book, worship God.

I beg the Reader to be very particular in observing the different speakers. Here, we have the Person, from whom *John* was now receiving intelligence, concerning the Church, in her happy state, declaring that what he had delivered, were faithful, and true sayings. And he saith, as plain as words can make any thing, that the LORD GOD of the holy Prophets, that is, CHRIST JESUS, had sent his angel, meaning himself, to shew these things unto his servant *John*. But you will say, how is this proved? I answer. In the opening of this book, (and the opening, from beginning to end, is like a letter, but one thing,) the very first verse, like the direction to a letter, runs thus: *The Revelation of* JESUS CHRIST—mark that!—*which* GOD *gave to him to shew unto his servants* (meaning the Church) *things which must shortly come to pass.* Now mark! *And he sent and signified it, by his Angel, unto his servant John.* Now, if ever any thing of plain, common sense, is to be found, it is here. GOD the FATHER gave to his dear SON a revelation, to come forth, and communicate. This JESUS hath done. And he sent, and signified it, by a messenger, or angel, to *John*. So then, this messenger, this angel, was the person, which this LORD GOD of the holy Prophets, JESUS CHRIST, sent to inform *John*. And *John* was so much struck with the account, that in the moment of the exstacy of his mind, he would have worshipped the angel. But the angel suffered him not. And he gave this reason. *I am thy fellow servant;* that is, a fellow servant of GOD, and of the LORD GOD of the Prophets, JESUS CHRIST: worship him!

But perhaps it will be said by some, is there not some little difficulty in this sense, in respect to the words in the seventh verse, *behold I come quickly! blessed is he that keepeth the sayings of the prophecy of this book*. To which I answer, No! Nay, so far from it, they are rather a confirmation. The Angel reminds *John* of what had passed at the opening of the interview, between JESUS and *John*, as related in the first Chapter, verses 1—3. JESUS had before said, *behold I come quickly*, Chap. iii. 11 Therefore, the Angel repeats those words, to remind *John* of what CHRIST had said. And also to remind him, of what *John* had himself said, concerning blessedness, to those who kept the sayings of the prophecy of this book. Chap. i. 3. Hence, therefore, it is as plain as words can make it, that this Angel now conversing with *John*, was a fellow servant with *John* and not CHRIST; and therefore, he could be no object of worship.

10 And he saith unto me, Seal not the sayings of the prophecy of this book; for the time is at hand.

11 He that is unjust, let him be unjust still: and he which is filthy, let him be filthy still: and he that is righteous, let him be righteous still: and he that is holy, let him be holy still.

Here I conceive CHRIST himself becomes the speaker. And, indeed, at this verse, opens, in some measure, a new subject. We hear no more now to the end of the Chapter, of the Church of CHRIST in the *Millennium*-state. But now here is a charge given by CHRIST, that this book of prophecy shall be an open book, and not sealed. As if the LORD would have all the Church acquainted with it, from generation to generation.

And I pray the Reader to observe in further confirmation, that this decision of CHRIST, of the filthy and unjust, and on the other hand of the righteous and holy, continuing for ever unaltered, proves the Almightiness of the speaker, in this final sentence, (for who but the LORD himself could so decide?) and confirms, that this thousand years reign of CHRIST having began, admitted of no alteration. The subject is solemn, but it is most awfully true. The miserable in eternity, if they were relieved from their misery, cannot be altered from their nature, which is the cause of their misery, and therefore, continuing unchanged in nature, they must continue unchanged in pain. So sure, so certain, is that saying of the LORD by *Abra-*

ham, between the two worlds, between the two natures, the two seeds of CHRIST, and the serpent, there is a great gulph fixed. Luke xvi. 25, 26. There can be no passing from one to another. Neither if there were, would this soften the evil. All the principles in nature, fire and water, heat and cold, life and death, are not more opposed than CHRIST and *Belial;* the children of the evil one; and the children of the kingdom!

12 And, behold, I come quickly; and my reward *is* with me, to give every man according as his work shall be.

13 I am Alpha and Omega, the beginning and the end, the first and the last.

If we needed any additional testimony in proof of the GODHEAD of CHRIST here we have it very blessedly. In the old Testament scripture, we find the LORD, more than once informing the Church, of his coming to their comfort. Thus for example, he saith by the Prophet. *Behold! the* LORD GOD *will come with strong hand, and his arm shall rule for him, behold his reward is with him, and his work before him.* Isaiah xl. 10. And again, *Behold! the* LORD *hath proclaimed unto the end of the world, say ye to the daughter of Zion, behold thy salvation cometh, behold his reward is with him, and his work before him!* Isaiah lxii. 11. And here we find similar language, as also more than once, in this blessed book of GOD. Chap. iii. 11—20. And when we add to these testimonies, that it is CHRIST that is to be the judge both of quick and dead, that *the* FATHER *judgeth no man, but hath committed all judgment unto the* SON; what higher testimonies can we have that it is the SON of GOD all the way through, who, *in our* nature was, and is the visible JEHOVAH, and that He, and He only, is the LORD administrator, in all the departments of divine government. Acts x. 42. John v. 22.

14 Blessed *are* they that do his commandments, that they may have right to the tree of life, and may enter in through the gates into the city.

15 For without *are* dogs, and sorcerers, and whoremongers, and murderers, and idolaters, and whosoever loveth and maketh a lie.

The blessedness pronounced on the LORD's people and the misery on the ungodly, are strongly marked in these verses. Doing the commandments of GOD, as a right to the Tree of Life, is a comprehensive way of speaking, which includes in it an union with CHRIST, and a communion in all that belongs to CHRIST. When CHRIST was preaching in the days of his flesh, and had just mentioned of the sealing of the FATHER, the Jews put the question to him, *what shall we do, that we might work the works of* GOD? To which JESUS made this remarkable answer! *This is the work of* GOD, *that ye believe on him whom he hath sent.* John vi. 27—29. A belief in CHRIST, when that belief is inwrought by the HOLY

Ghost in the soul, will be followed with all the blessed effects, and fruits of obeying Christ's commandments. But, where there is no work of God the Spirit in the soul, there can be no obedience to the commandments in the heart. Hence it is said, that *without are dogs and sorcerers, and persons of all uncleanness,* having never been renewed.

It is a sweet testimony of an union *with* Christ, when we derive all grace for obedience, *from* Christ. Jesus imparts every thing suited to his members; and for this plain reason, because He is the head of all fullness. So that when Christ gives out of his fullness, while the advantage is theirs, the glory is His. When a child of God is first quickened, is it not Christ's Spirit quickening? When a child of God is led on in the way of grace, is it not Christ's grace, made sufficient for him, and the Lord's strength made perfect in his people's weakness. And what a fullness of glory for this communication, from the fullness of his grace, will be accumulated in that day, for Jesus's everlasting crown of Mediator majesty; when Christ shall have the full ascription of glory, from the whole body of his members, and they are all come to this perfect man, Christ Jesus, *according to the measure of the stature of the fulness of* Christ! Ephes. iv. 13.

16 I Jesus have sent mine angel to testify unto you these things in the churches. I am the root and the offspring of David, *and* the bright and morning star.

As we are here drawing nigh to a close, the Lord Jesus doth here again as he did at the beginning, take to himself his own sovereign power and Godhead, and saith, *I* Jesus *have sent mine Angel.* And who but God sends Angels? Oh! how sweet are these accumulated testimonies of Christ's Godhead, to the people of God. How overwhelming to Christ's enemies? But Jesus adds another. He calls himself *the root and the offspring of David.* A circumstance impossible, upon any principle of common sense, but as God and Man, (as Christ indeed is,) in one Person. For, as God, he is the root of *David* and of all things. And, as man, he is the offspring of *David,* after the flesh. 2 Tim. ii. 8. But suppose for a moment, his Godhead was not, how could he have been the root of *David.* Take away his manhood, and how could he be the seed of *David.* Oh! blessed testimony, as Jesus himself stated it to the Pharisees of old. Matt. xxii. 42 to the end, compared with Psm. cx. 1. Romans i. 4. 2 Tim. ii. 8. Beautiful is the similitude the Lord makes of himself to the Morning Star. For, as the root of David, in the old Testament-dispensation, and long before he arose in his incarnation as the Sun of Righteousness, he shone bright and glorious like a star of the first magnitude, and as the sure pledge of day in the firmament of the scriptures, both by David and the other Prophets. And to this hour he continues in his morning risings, as the *day dawn,* and *day star* in the hearts of his people. So that this is a sweet figure in the morning planet of our Jesus, when in the wintry days, he ariseth as the sure harbinger of the Sun of Righteousness, which will follow.

17 And the Spirit and the bride say, Come. And let him that heareth say, Come. And let him that is athirst come. And whosoever will, let him take the water of life freely.

I do not wish to be considered as speaking decidedly upon the subject, but as it strikes me, this is GOD the HOLY GHOST making a response to CHRIST, and the Church following the same, and the looker on, and him that heareth, catching the sound from the same words, as JESUS had so graciously uttered them; and echoing the invitation. When JESUS saith, *Behold I come quickly*, the HOLY GHOST saith, *Even so, come*, LORD JESUS, and the whole Church the Bride, being quickened and regenerated, are longing for his coming. And the *hearer* of the promise, is included in the same, he longeth for it. Yea, the thirsty, and whosoever will, whomsoever the LORD hath put a *thirst* for CHRIST in the heart, and a *willingness* in the soul to receive JESUS, all join in the fervent cry. The water of life is a river, open, free, full, and everlastingly running. All shall be welcome to take their fill from it, if CHRIST by his grace, be welcomed in their hearts to fill them.

I cannot allow myself to pass away from this most gracious verse, before that I have called upon the Reader to observe with me, a certain interesting point concerning it, which may not perhaps before have arrested his notice. But it is worthy our closest remark, that in the last *public* sermon the LORD JESUS ever preached, and which was at the Jewish passover, he closed all he had to say, in words similar to those with which the HOLY GHOST hath closed the canon of scripture. *In the last day, that great day of the feast,* JESUS *stood and cried, saying, If any man thirst, let him come unto me and drink.* John vii. 37. And here we find the HOLY GHOST sealing up the last of his blessed scriptures, in words to the same effect. So that here is CHRIST at one time, and the HOLY GHOST at another, both engaged in the same thing. So earnest is CHRIST, when on earth, and when in heaven, as well as the SPIRIT, that his Church shall hear his voice, and be on the look-out for his coming.

18 For I testify unto every man that heareth the words of the prophecy of this book. If any man shall add unto these things, God shall add unto him the plagues that are written in this book:

19 And if any man shall take away from the words of the book of this prophecy, God shall take away his part out of the book of life, and out of the holy city, and *from* the things which are written in this book:

Here is a solemn testimony, and of CHRIST himself, the faithful and true witness, and delivered in the most decisive manner possible, that the adding to, or taking from the words of the prophecy contained in this book, shall bring on the utter ruin, and everlasting misery of any and every one so offending. And the reason is very obvious. CHRIST is GOD's witness, and his own. He hath delivered the whole truths necessary to salvation. He hath confirmed it in all ages, by Prophets and Apostles, by miracles and signs, and, above all, by his death, resurrection, and return to glory, and by the sending down the gifts of the HOLY GHOST. And in the hearts of his people he hath given yet further confirmation, by the regenerating and quickening influence of GOD the SPIRIT. So that, attested by such evidences, for any man to call those words of CHRIST in question, to prevent or mutilate, to gainsay or resist, cannot but bring down the just judgment of GOD. LORD! give grace to thy people, to receive with meekness thy engrafted word, and to esteem it more than their necessary food.

20 He which testifieth these things, saith, Surely, I come quickly; Amen. Even so, come, Lord Jesus.

This is a most gracious repetition of JESUS's promise to his Church. It ought to be often in our thoughts. The LORD was then at the door of departure. He looks back once more. Before he takes a farewell, he sets his seal to his testimony, and, in his very last words, puts a *surely* to his often before repeated promise, and saith, *surely I come quickly!* And GOD the HOLY GHOST by *John*, in the name of the Church, makes answer to his gracious promise, and saith, *even so come* LORD JESUS! Oh! precious LORD! is it not as if to say, though I leave off speaking publickly to the Church; I do not leave you in private. My heart, my affections are with you. I will come again, and take you to myself, that, where I am, there you may be also. Surely *I come quickly! Even so, come* LORD JESUS!

21 The grace of our Lord Jesus Christ *be* with you all. Amen.

John closeth all with the sweet apostolical benediction. *The grace of our* LORD JESUS CHRIST *be with you all Amen.* Reader! this is among the greatest of all blessings, the grace of our LORD JESUS CHRIST, including, as it doth, the FATHER's love, and the SPIRIT's fellowship. All grace can only be *in* CHRIST. And all grace only *from* CHRIST. And all the actings of our faith upon grace, from the grace given us *by* CHRIST. Oh! then, for the LORD, to give out largely, fully, daily, and momently to his people grace, that *of his fullness we may all receive, and grace for grace.* Once more, may the LORD both say it and confirm it, *the grace of our* LORD JESUS CHRIST *be with you all, Amen.*

REFLECTIONS.

BLESSING, and honor, and glory, and power, be unto him that sitteth upon the throne, and unto the LAMB for ever and ever. LORD! upon the bended knee of thanksgiving and praise, let all thy Church praise thee, for this among all thy other unnumbered mercies, that thou hast given to thy servant *John*, this precious portion of thy sacred word, to shew unto thy Church things which must shortly come to pass. Blessed be the LORD for the accomplishment of such parts, as have been already fulfilled, and of others that are now fulfilling in the earth. And do thou, LORD, give thy servants grace, to wait in full exercise of faith and hope, the accomplishment of all that remains to be fulfilled. And since thou hast caused it to be left upon record for the encouragement of the faithful, saying, *blessed is he that readeth, and they that hear the words of this prophecy, and keep those things which are written therein.* Rev. i. 3. LORD! I beseech thee, let these blessings be my portion, that I may both read, and hear, and keep those glorious truths, by thy grace in my heart.

Let the blessed prospect of this reign of CHRIST in his Church, comfort and encourage all thy people. And while here below, let the souls of thy redeemed both drink and be satisfied with the streams of *that river, which make glad the city of* GOD. Oh! for grace, to sit down oft by faith, till the LORD shall take my soul home to sit down for ever in full enjoyment, under *the Tree of Life*. Precious LORD JESUS! be thou my *Alpha* and *Omega, the beginning and the end* of all my spiritual joys. Thou that art *the root and offspring of David,* and *the bright and morning star;* be thou my all in all, in life, in death, in time, and to all eternity. Blessed be the FATHER, SON, and HOLY GHOST, for all the fulness of blessings, and JESUS, and all his fulness in blessings, both for the life of grace that now is, and for that life of glory which is to come.

And be thou thanked with all the love and affection of a brother, faithful *John!* for thy tenderness to the Church in JESUS, and for all thy ministry and labor of love. We regard the servant while we bless the Master. And blessed be our GOD and SAVIOR, for calling thee to the ministry, highly honored Apostle of our GOD! When JESUS shall come to be glorified in his saints, and admired in all that believe, how will JESUS our GOD and SAVIOR shine in all the fulness of the GODHEAD bodily, encircled with all his Apostles and Prophets, and Martyrs, and the redeemed out of all nations, and kindreds, and tongues, *who have washed their robes, and made them white in the blood of the* LAMB. Oh! for the poorest and unworthiest of all the LORD's redeemed ones, to be found in the throng, and to join the hymn of salvation and praise, with all the Church of GOD for evermore.

And now, Reader, in folding up the whole of my *Poor Man's Commentary,* while I lay low in the dust before GOD, under a conscious sense of unworthiness, and my continued short comings, I desire to set up a renewed *Ebenezer* to the praise of his grace, who hath hitherto helped me, and borne with me, all the way through, in the many years since first I entered upon it, to the hour of writing with my pen the last line of it. The more I contemplate the subject, the more I stand amazed at the LORD's goodness, and my undeservings.

I know not whether, after all my endeavours and earnest desires to exalt the adorable name of JESUS, I have succeeded so far, as that the Reader may perceive, that this is the sole object I have all along had in view. To speak of Him as He really is, I know is impossible. Neither men nor angels are competent to this service.

For, of Him it must be said, without any strain of language, THERE IS NO END OF HIS GREATNESS. But, I have only labored so far and in the best manner I have been able, to hold up, and hold forth, the LORD JESUS CHRIST as GOD's CHRIST, and as the sole perfection of all his people. Oh! that the LORD by his grace, may so seal Him in my heart!

And now, Reader, farewell! I hope the LORD hath pardoned, and will pardon all the errors of this *Poor Man's Commentary*, and that you will pardon them also. And having said this, *I commend you to* GOD, *and to the word of his grace, which is able to build his whole family up, and to give them an inheritance among all them which are sanctified.* Amen. To the one only GOD, FATHER, SON, and HOLY GHOST, be endless praises. Amen, and Amen.

PLYMOUTH, CHARLES VICARAGE,
  April 13, 1816,

Once more made memorable in being my
 birth day, counting Sixty-three years
  of the LORD's grace, and my sins.

Printed by W. Stratford, Crown-Court, Temple-Bar.

ERRATA.

The Reader is desired to pardon the following errors of the Press, amidst others of a less nature, which escaped the Printer's observation:

VOL. II.

Page 33,	line 2,	from the bottom, in the note, *the holy*, should be *thy holy*.
145,	line 4,	in the note, *prayer*, should be *praise*.
284,	line 7,	*knew*, should be *know*.
403,	line 29,	*divine lusts*, should be *divers lusts*.
567,	line 19,	*assimulating*, should be *assimilating*.
653,	lines 31, 32,	*yet untaught*, should be *yea unthought*.
673,	lines 11, 12,	*us the adoption*, should be *unto the adoption*.

VOL. III.

Page 6,	verse 22,	the first *wot*, should be *what*.
9,	line 19,	*no man's faith*, should be *one man's faith*.
14,	line 4,	from the bottom, *weariness*, should be *wariness*.
41,	line 1,	after Coloss. ii. 9. put *Secondly*.
94,	line 14,	last word *second*, leave out.
171,	line 18,	*repeatedly*, should be *reputedly*.
232,	line 2,	*tabulated*, should be *tribulated*.
——,	—— 17,	*warning*, should be *warming*.
242,	line 16	from the bottom, *intentially*, should be *intentionally*.
326,	line 3,	in the reflections, *yet* should be *yes*.
389,	line 10	from the bottom, *heavenliness*, should be *heavenlies*.
446,	line 12	from the bottom, *either*, should be *neither*.
487,	line 6	from the bottom, *fall*, should be *all*.
526,		after the 19th line, put in REFLECTIONS.
609,	line 22	from the bottom, for *The issue is doubtful*, read, *The issue is not doubtful*.
610,		at the top of the page put REFLECTIONS.
612,	line 24,	after the word *left*, add *out*.

Other Related Titles

In addition to *The Poor Man's New Testament* in three volumes that you now possess, Solid Ground Christian Books is delighted to announce our intention to publish the following by summer 2004:

Hawker's *Poor Man's Old Testament Commentary* in six wonderful volumes. This set contains more than 4,200 pages of exposition and reflection by the man who loved Christ and delighted to make Him known to others. The volumes are as follows:

> Volume One: Genesis - Numbers
> Volume Two: Deuteronomy - 2 Samuel
> Volume Three: 1st Kings - Esther
> Volume Four: Job - Psalms
> Volume Five: Proverbs - Lamentations
> Volume Six: Ezekiel - Malachi

Hawker's *Poor Man's Morning and Evening Portions* which is a daily devotional work of more than 900 pages. In the words of Pastor Don Fortner:

> "Robert Hawker's **Poor Man's Daily Portions** is, in my opinion, the very best book of daily devotional readings I have yet read. My wife and I have used it for many years, always with great profit to our souls. Why is it such a blessing? It is full of Christ and full of grace. Every reading leaves the reader looking to, resting in, and rejoicing in our all-glorious Savior.

Hawker's *Concordance and Dictionary to the Sacred Scriptures both of the Old and New Testament* is a large one volume work that was written to assist the people of God in searching the Word of God for themselves. This volume has been long unavailable.

Solid Ground Christian Books
2090 Columbiana Rd, Suite 2000
Birmingham AL 35266
(205) 443-0311
sgcb@charter.net
http://solid-ground-books.com

CPSIA information can be obtained at www.ICGtesting.com
Printed in the USA
BVOW011233020113

308919BV00004B/17/A